Y0-ARC-890

THE SOCIETY FOR OLD TESTAMENT STUDY

BOOK LIST

1986

Printed for the Society

The Society for Old Testament Study

BOOK LIST
1986

Printed for the Society

ISBN 0 905495 05 5

PRINTED BY W. S. MANEY AND SON LTD HUDSON ROAD LEEDS LS9 7DL

Contents

One copy of the *Book List* is supplied free to all members of the Society.

Copies of the *Book List* for 1986 may also be obtained from M. E. J. Richardson, Esq., Department of Middle Eastern Studies, University of Manchester, Manchester M13 9PL, England. The price of these is £6.00 or $12.00 post free for a single copy. Payment should be made by cheque in sterling or U.S. dollars payable to the Society for Old Testament Study, or direct to Post Office Giro Account No. 50 450 4002.

Back copies of some issues of the *Book List* are also available from Mr M. E. J. Richardson. Orders for back issues or multiple copies should not be accompanied by payment; an invoice will be sent.

Review copies of books for the *Book List* should be sent to the Editor:

Dr A. Graeme Auld
New College, Mound Place
Edinburgh EH1 2LX
Scotland

PREFACE

My two immediate predecessors as Editor of the *Book List* both served for seven years, and when I took over it was my intention, if the Society wished it, to serve for the same period. Various circumstances, however, led me to decide to step down one year short of that period, and this is the last *Book List* to appear under my Editorship. I am very pleased that Dr Graeme Auld was willing to take over as Editor, and I wish him every success in the task that lies in front of him.

The Editor of the *Book List* could not do his job without a good deal of help from a great many people. I have particularly valued the contact I have had with scholars overseas in consequence of being Editor of the *Book List*, and I would like to thank them all for the help and advice they have given me. Those who this year have given information or provided reviews include Professor B. Albrektson, Professor M. Bič, Dr C. Conroy, Dr F. García Martínez, Dr K. Jeppesen, Professor G. L. Prato, Dr K. K. Sacon, and Professor A. S. van der Woude. Thanks are also due to those in this country outside the Society who have provided reviews, including not least several of my colleagues at King's College London. This year Professor J. R. Baines, Professor S. G. Hall and Dr G. M. Jantzen have all kindly provided reviews. If the *Book List* can make any claim to comprehensive coverage, it is only because the Editor has been constantly helped by information provided by reviewers concerning books that he might well otherwise have missed. Many reviewers have contributed in this way, but particular thanks are due to Professor W. G. Lambert, Mr A. R. Millard and Dr S. C. Reif. At the practical level I have benefited from the advice, encouragement and help given by my immediate colleagues, Professor R. E. Clements and Mr R. J. Coggins (and, at an earlier stage, Professor P. R. Ackroyd); these, as well as Mrs S. M. Black, Secretary in the Department of Biblical Studies at King's College London, all deserve my thanks. The *Book List* itself has benefited enormously over the years from the care and attention it has received from our printers, and I would like to thank Mr A. S. Maney and his staff for all they have done. Finally, I would like to thank the many publishers throughout the world who have provided books for review for their friendly co-operation.

It is appropriate here to refer to two new scholarly ventures. In Denmark a new periodical entitled *Scandinavian Journal of the Old Testament* (SJOT) has been launched. The Editors are Dr K. Jeppesen and Dr N. P. Lemche, and their address is Department of Old Testament Studies, University of Aarhus, DK 8000 Aarhus C, Denmark. The first issue includes articles, on a wide range of Old Testament and intertestamental topics, by J. Strange, H.-A. Mink, K. A. Tångberg, H. J. Lehmann, H. J. L. Jensen, K. J. Cathcart and K. Jeppesen, F. H. Cryer, and K. Hognesius. The periodical is published by Universitetsforlaget, Aarhus Universitet, DK 8000 Aarhus C, Denmark, and costs approximately £11.00 per year for two issues. It is a pleasure to welcome the appearance of this new periodical, and the Society would like to wish it much success.

Those who are concerned with Aramaic studies will no doubt have already heard of the project for a *Comprehensive Aramaic Lexicon*, to be edited by Professors J. A. Fitzmyer, D. R. Hillers and S. A. Kaufman. The importance of this project does not need to be stated here. Two Newsletters have been issued, and those who have not received these, and would like to do so, are invited to write to The Editors, CAL, Dept of Near Eastern Studies, The Johns Hopkins University, Baltimore, MD 21218, USA.

Every effort has been made to provide the prices of the books included in the *Book List*, but it should be borne in mind that postal charges often have to be added to the prices given here.

The following abbreviations and symbols are employed as in earlier issues:

B.L. = *Book List*
Eleven Years = *Eleven Years of Bible Bibliography* (1957)
Decade = *A Decade of Bible Bibliography* (1967)
Bible Bibliog. = *Bible Bibliography 1967–1973: Old Testament* (1974)

On behalf of the Society I would like to thank the British Academy for making a grant towards the publication costs of this issue of the *Book List*.

KING'S COLLEGE LONDON MICHAEL A. KNIBB

1. GENERAL

ANGELINI, M. G., and others: *Testimonium Christi: Scritti in onore di Jacques Dupont*. 1985. Pp. lxiv, 494. (Paideia Editrice, Brescia. Price: Lire 60,000)

This distinguished Belgian Benedictine scholar has been honoured by *Festschriften* in both French and Italian; this is the latter. His achievement has been in the New Testament field, though the bibliography of his works in this volume shows that he has often concerned himself with the roots of Christianity and with early Christian exegesis of the Old Testament. Of the twenty-three Italian essays in his honour, only two directly concern interpretation of the Hebrew or Greek Old Testament: A. Bonora on 'Amos as Defender of Law and Justice', and a study by G. Scarpat on Wisd. Sol. 2:16, 2:24 and 4:19. A few other contributions discuss New Testament themes in relation to contemporary Judaism. For the rest, the value of this volume is especially for the New Testament scholar. R. P. R. MURRAY

ASSMANN, J., ASSMANN, A., and HARDMEIER, C. (eds.): *Schrift und Gedächtnis: Beiträge zur Archäologie der literarischen Kommunikation*. 1983. Pp. 284. (Wilhelm Fink Verlag, Munich. Price: DM. 48.00. ISBN 3 7705 2132 3)

This volume presents seventeen lectures, prefaced by the citation of Plato's *Phaidros*, 274c–278b on the (de)merits of writing versus memory, and summed up by a concluding essay (A. and J. Assmann). The range covered in considering the functions and interrelations of the use of writing and of oral tradition in cultures is vast: all the way from Ancient Egypt and the Odyssey via rabbinic writings, medieval usage, African traditions, reduction to writing of current North-Pakistani dialects, to written/unwritten music (Isidore of Seville to the Beatles and 'Rock'). Reading the whole is a liberal education in itself. For busy Old Testament scholars, the most germane chapters are those by W. Raible (hermeneutic as a function of written transmission), by W. Schenkel and J. Assmann on beginnings in Ancient Egypt (the latter being a little too theoretical), and the summation by A. and J. Assmann; K. Ehlich's theoretical chapter deserves mention. The work is in no way a systematic treatment of its theme; the range of essays is very disparate in coverage of topics. Nor is any one issue covered in sufficient depth and detail to serve as a work of reference. The work is interesting, but not fundamental.

K. A. KITCHEN

BARR, J.: *Why the World was Created in 4004 B.C.: Archbishop Ussher and Biblical Chronology* (Reprinted from the Bulletin of the John Rylands University Library of Manchester, 67/2). 1985. Pp. 575–608. (The John Rylands University Library of Manchester. Price: £2.50)

Although only a small portion of Ussher's chronology dealt directly with the Bible, 'to him it was clear that the Bible was intended, as far as it went, as a completely accurate chronological guide' (p. 590). Ussher was not an intellectual giant like Scaliger and others on whose foundations he built, but his system was meticulous and ingenious, if at times credulous. This credulousness of course lay in his view of the Bible, though his attitude fitted well into contemporary assumptions: 'In Ussher's time biblical chronology was hovering on the brink between the older and the modern world' (p. 599). The next half-century would see the biblical foundations of his system questioned and undermined. A brief appendix deals with the Old Testament chronological data.

L. L. GRABBE

BERGERHOF, K., DIETRICH, M., and LORETZ, O. (eds.), *Ugarit-Forschungen: Internationales Jahrbuch für Altertumskunde Syrien-Palästinas*, Vol. 16 (1984). 1985. Pp. iv, 394. (Neukirchener Verlag, Neukirchen-Vluyn. Price: DM. 130.00; sub. price: DM. 118.00. ISBN 3 7887 1201 5. Butzon & Bercker, Kevelaer. ISBN 3 7666 9395 6)

L. Kutler defends the theory that the Hebrew word *mar* sometimes means 'strong' in the Old Testment, and J. de Savignac discusses the meaning of *ṣāpôn*. These are the only articles in this volume concerned primarily with the Old Testament. As usual, there are book reviews (some relevant to the Old Testament) and indexes.

J. A. EMERTON

BEST, T. F. (ed.): *Hearing and Speaking the Word: Selections from the Works of James Muilenburg* (Scholars Press Homage Series, 7). 1984. Pp. xvi, 448. (Scholars Press, Chico, California. Price: $26.95; discount price: $17.95. ISBN 0 89130 665 X)

This, the third volume published in honour of James Muilenburg (for the others, see *B.L.* 1963, p. 10 (*Decade*, p. 404); 1976, p. 15), contains three appreciations of him (by T. F. Best, F. Buechner, and B. W. Anderson) and of his work as scholar, and twenty-eight studies by Muilenburg, chosen to illustrate the diversity of his interests and competence and the eloquence and lucidity of his style. Eleven are on criticism and exegesis, three on Old Testament history and theology, four on scholarship and interpretation, six on archaeology; two are meditations; and finally the introduction to Muilenburg's dissertation on the Epistle of Barnabas and the Didache, and his report of the Luther and Zwingli Quatercentenary Conference at Marburg. The bibliography compiled by R. L. Hicks for the 1962 *Festschrift* is reprinted and supplemented by two further lists, by I. J. Ball and T. F. Best. Of the many fine things in the volume it must suffice to mention 'Form Criticism and Beyond', 'The Form and Structure of the Covenantal Formulations', 'The Intercession of the Covenant Mediator (Exodus 33:1a, 12–17)', 'A Study in Hebrew Rhetoric', 'The Linguistic and Rhetorical usages of the Particle *ki* in the Old Testament', and 'The Terminology of Adversity in Jeremiah'. The volume (which includes a photographic portrait) is a fine tribute to the memory of a revered scholar and teacher.

G. W. ANDERSON

BLANK, S. H. (ed.): *Hebrew Union College Annual*. Vol. LV. 1984. Pp. x, 336. (Hebrew Union College — Jewish Institute of Religion, Cincinnati. Price: $20.00. ISSN 0360 9049)

Three articles on this volume will be of particular interest to readers of the *Book List,* all falling within the same broad area. A. I. Baumgarten explains the similarity between Josephus's and Hippolytus's accounts of the Pharisees as due neither to the use of a common source nor to Hippolytus's direct dependence on Josephus. The presence of an apparently positive evaluation of Pharisaic tradition, found only in Hippolytus, leads him to suggest that the latter was dependent on a pro-Pharisaic revision of Jseophus, a suggestion which calls for further detailed analysis. S. J. D. Cohen takes issue with the interpretation of Yavneh as a prototype of the Council of Nicea issuing in a single orthodoxy and the extinction of all other 'sects'. He gives a very lucid presentation of the evidence relevant to the relationship between the Pharisees and the Rabbis, arguing for the diversity of rabbinic Judaism, within which the acrimony of pre-70 C.E. was lost because of the loss of the temple, which had been the focus of previous conflicting interpretations. In an article translated from Hebrew P. H. Peli examines a tradition in the name of R. Eleazar b. R. Zadok concerning 'the havurot that were in Jerusalem'; the tradition invites some comparison with the 'collegia' of Graeco-Roman society and leads to an investigation of mutual benefit as a motive in Jewish sources for doing good.

J. M. LIEU

BOGGIO, G., and others: *Gesù e la sua morte* (Atti della XXVII Settimana Biblica, Associazione Biblica Italiana). 1984. Pp. 408. (Paideia Editrice, Brescia. Price: Lire 35,000)

As might be expected from the title, most of the twenty contributions to this volume will be of only indirect relevance to the concerns of the *Book List*. There are, however, seven essays on Old Testament or Judaic topics. Five of them are exegetical, concerned with the understanding of death in various Old Testament books or passages, as suggesting categories which may help towards illuminating the significance of the death of Jesus. Thus A. Bonora writes on anguish and abandonment in the face of death as seen in the enigmatic Ps. 88, while E. Franco, leaving aside the identity of the Suffering Servant, discusses the religious meaning of his death in Isa. 53. Similarly G. Boggio and M. Perani examine the reaction to death in the books of Jeremiah and Job respectively. Somewhat less familiar ground is traversed by A. Sisti's interesting essay on the violent death of the righteous man in the Wisdom of Solomon. In the area of Judaism, the title of N. Pavoncello's contribution, 'L'esegesi rabbinica del cap. 53 di Isaia', is perhaps somewhat misleading: it is concerned not so much with the frequently discussed views of Jewish commentators on this chapter, but rather with the rabbinic understanding of the expiatory value of suffering and death. Finally, one of the most stimulating chapters is that of R. di Segni on the death of Jesus as seen in the 'Toledoth Jeshu', which whets the appetite for the author's promised edition of these obscure texts. The contributions listed vary in value but all of them have something worthwhile to contribute to the particular theme with which they are concerned.

J. R. PORTER

BOTTERWECK, G. J., RINGGREN, H., and FABRY, H.-J. (eds.): *Theologisches Wörterbuch zum Alten Testament*. Band V. Lfg. 1–2 (Spalte 1–256). 1984. Lfg. 3–4 (Spalte 257–512). 1985. (Kohlhammer, Stuttgart. Price: DM. 56.00 (Lfg. 1–2); DM. 62.00 (Lfg. 3–4). ISBN 3 17 008629 4 and 3 17 008884 X)

Fascicle 1–2, which contains thirty-seven complete articles, begins with that on *mārad* and ends with the first part of that on *nādaḥ*. The words treated most fully are *nābīʾ* (H.-P. Müller, twenty-three columns), *mōšeh* (H. Cazelles, eighteen), *nāgīd* (G. F. Hasel, seventeen), *nābāl* (J. Marböck, fifteen), *mišpāṭ* (B. Johnson, fourteen), *ngd* (F. García-López, thirteen), and *māšaḥ* I with *māšīaḥ* (K. Seybold, twelve). There is a full discussion of the rare word *marzēaḥ* by Fabry. In the article on *maśśāʾ* (Müller) the possibility of a geographical meaning in Prov. 30:1; 31:1 (most recently accepted by Plöger in his commentary) is not mentioned. The article on Moses is only the fourth so far entirely devoted to a single individual, the others being Abraham, David and Gog (!). The article on *māšāl* (under *māšal* I, by K.-M. Beyse) is rather short (four columns) in view of the size of the literature on the subject. On *mišpāḥāh* (H.-J. Zobel) there is, surprisingly, no reference to N. K.

Gottwald's *The Tribes of Yahweh* (1979). The theological content of the article on *māṭaq* with *māṭōq* and other cognates is very small.

Fascicle 3–4, which ends with the first part of the article on *naʿar* (H. F. Fuhs), contains thirty-four complete articles, of which those on *nāḥal* with *naḥᵃlāh* (E. Lipiński) and *nḥm* (H. Simian-Yofre), each with eighteen columns, and on *nādar* with *neder* (O. Kaiser) and *nissāh* and cognates (F. J. Helfmeyer), each with fourteen, receive the fullest treatment. The selection of words according to their theological or religious importance continues to be erratic: for example, there are articles on *nāmēr* (M. J. Mulder) and *nūd* (Ringgren), and eleven columns on *nᵉḥōšet* (Fabry), but none on *nkḥ* and its cognate *nākōaḥ*. The choice of proper names for inclusion also remains difficult to account for: there is no treatment of Noah. The policy of listing some words alphabetically, but others under their root without sufficient cross-references, is confusing and will make it impossible to use the work satisfactorily without recourse to the comprehensive index which will presumably be eventually provided at the end of the final volume. Another difficulty is caused for users by the fairly frequent practice of grouping together in a single article words whose only relationship is a semantic one: thus in this fascicle *ʾētān* is treated under *naḥal* (L. A. Snijders), but there is no cross-reference under *ʾētān* in Band I; in a similar fashion, eight different kinds of snake are listed under *nāḥāš*. The article on *nāsak* and cognates (C. Dohmen) would have been improved by a fuller treatment of the relationship between this verb and *sūk* II. J. Lundbom's name is misspelt in the fascicle index on the front cover. Despite these shortcomings, the general quality of the articles remains high.

R. N. WHYBRAY

CAPPELØRN, N. J.: *Bibelsyn*. 1985. (G. E. C. Gad, Copenhagen. Price: D.Kr. 150.00. ISBN 87 12 11069 8)

After a short, but fine introduction to Luther's view of the Bible and how he used it, written by S. Kjeldgaard-Pedersen, this book offers a presentation of seven different approaches to the Bible. In each case the presentation is made by an adherent of the view in question, followed by a critical response written by another person, and finally an answer from the first one. The sections are on different levels because the range of people involved is too broad. In some cases the opponents simply do not speak the same language and consequently fail to understand each other. That is the case in the chapters about narrative and structuralist approaches. In other cases the essays are more concerned with the history of ideas than with exegesis, e.g. the parts about existential interpretation and feminist theology. Nonetheless, this volume offers a readable introduction to modern discussion about the Bible, addressed to the lay reader. From a scholarly point of view the chapters of most interest are those on conservative exegesis and the historical-critical view.

K. JEPPESEN

CAQUOT, A., LÉGASSE, S., and TARDIEU, M. (eds.): *Mélanges bibliques et orientaux en l'honneur de M. Mathias Delcor* (Alter Orient und Altes Testament, 215). 1985. Pp. x, 488. (Neukirchener Verlag, Neukirchen-Vluyn. Price: DM. 174.00; sub. price: DM. 158.00. ISBN 3 7887 0799 2. Butzon & Bercker, Kevelaer. ISBN 3 7666 9393 X)

Forty-one contributions are included, eleven English, nineteen French, eight German, three Spanish. There is a brief preface, a bibliography of Delcor's writings, and indexes of words, principal texts and topics — unusual in such volumes, but very welcome.

Pentateuch: Gen. 1:1–10 (A. A. Di Lella), illuminating if at times perhaps contrived: Exod. 14–15 (A. Soggin); Exod. 34 (H. Cazelles), good critical discussion; MT divisions (F. Langlamet); Sarah and Abimelech in a near-eastern context (M. Weinfeld); the promise of the land (J. Scharbert); the prophets and P (W. H. Schmidt), rather generalized but inviting further discussion. Prophets: Isa. 6 and Baʿal's throne (J. C. Greenfield); Isa. 9:1–6 (B. Renaud), a good study of poetic form: Isa. 25:6 (R. Martin-Achard); Jer. 10 (W. McKane); Jer. 17 and the sabbath as a late text (J. Briend); Ezek. 16:4, a hapax (A. Saenz-Badillos), well argued; Hab. 3 as vision description (G. Fohrer); the shepherds in Zech. 11 (A. Caquot). Three studies are devoted to the Song of Songs: a good discussion of its canonical place (D. Barthélemy); one on mainly recent Catholic interpretation (H. Haag); questions of unity in 2:8–17 (R. E. Murphy). Two are on *shibboleth* in Judg. 12:6 (J. A. Emerton and A. Lemaire), particularly dealing with philology. Ps. 51 and the walls of Jerusalem (R. J. Tournay) explores links with the exile, and there are notes on Pss. 68, 133, and 137 (J. P. M. van der Ploeg), this last as reflecting on exile. The writing on the wall in Dan. 5 is discussed in relation to Akkadian (P. Grelot). Text criticism and the ancient Hebrew alphabet are discussed by S. Talmon; problems of syntax by Y. Thorion. Feminine aspects of deity (E. Jacob) and concepts of heaven (B. Lang) move usefully into theological areas. The remaining articles move beyond the Hebrew Bible. Edomite names are considered against ancient Arabic prosopography (W. Kornfeld). Ugaritic is represented by a discussion of faith and piety (J. L. Cunchillos) and of formulas in Hebrew and Ugaritic compared (G. Del Olmo Lete). Wisd. 11:16 (M. Gilbert) raises ethical questions. Qumran: the 'messiahs' of Aaron and Israel (W. H. Brownlee); Judas the Maccabee as the 'wicked priest' (F. García Martínez); the 'prophet like Moses' (F. Dexinger) also includes Samaritan thought. Quotations from the Palestinian Targum (A. Díez Macho); ancient rabbinic texts (J. Neusner); and a short discussion of Philonic exposition (V. Nikiprowetzky) extended into the broader post-biblical area. More technically in ancient near eastern studies are the articles on Phoenician inscriptions (M. G. Amadasi-Guzzo), Akkadian texts (M. Dietrich/O. Loretz), the Tell Fekherye bilingual (P.-E. Dion), and on a prayer formula in the Coptic 'Pistis Sophia' (M. Tardieu).

There is great variety here, and much stimulating discussion; at times rather much space is devoted to reviewing earlier work. P. R. ACKROYD

CAZELLES, H., and FEUILLET, A. (eds.): *Supplément au Dictionnaire de la Bible*. Vol. x. Fasc. 58 (*Routes — Sacerdoce*). 1984. Cols. 1021–1244, with several maps and one plate. (Letouzey & Ané, Paris. Price: Fr. 205.00)

This fascicle contains two major articles and parts of two others. That on sacral kingship is divided into three sections: on the Old Testament (Cazelles), on ruler-cults in the Graeco-Roman world (C. Saulnier), and on the Roman Empire, the emperor-cult and the New Testament (É. Cothenet). The title of the Old Testament section — 'sacral kingship and desacralisation of the state in the Old Testament' — indicates its main emphasis. The article on Sabbath (J. Briend) treats the problems fully and with due caution, and this is also true of that on priesthood (*Sacerdoce*, J. Auneau), incomplete but already seventy-five columns long. M. Du Buit, in a long article on roads in biblical times begun in the previous fascicle, treats the subject thoroughly with the aid of eleven local maps in the text and a colour plate of the whole region. There are also shorter articles on the book of Ruth (H. Haag, ten columns), *sabaot* (Cazelles) and the god Sabazios (J. É. Ménard), and a brief note on the Persian festival of the *Sakaea* (*Les Sacées*) and its possible relevance to the book of Esther. The bibliographical articles are on

H. H.Rowley (Cazelles, with a list of Rowley's works taken from Eissfeldt's list in his *Kleine Schriften* V), Saadia (G. Vajda), and Pierre Sabatier (1682–1742, pioneer of *Vetus Latina* studies (P.-M. Bogaert). Finally there is a brief archaeological article on Khirbet Ruheibeh (Briend).

R. N. WHYBRAY

CAZELLES, H., and FEUILLET, A. (eds.): *Supplément au Dictionnaire de la Bible*. Vol. x. Fasc. 59 (*Sacerdoce-Sadducéens*). 1985. Cols. 1245–1544. (Letouzey & Ané, Paris. Price: Fr. 269.00)

This fascicle, which completes volume x, comprises the last part of *Sacerdoce* and three other articles. The article on *Sacerdoce* is divided between J. Auneau on the ancient Near East and the Old Testament and P.-M. Beaude on the New Testament 'background' (Judaism from 200 B.C.) and the New Testament itself. This article covers a vast field, including a survey of priesthood in every known part of the ancient Near East, the biblical terminology of priesthood, a historical review of the Old Testament material, a sketch of the history of the Jewish priesthood from 200 B.C. to A.D.70, and a discussion of a wide variety of biblical and non-biblical Jewish texts from that period. It will be an excellent starting-point for students of this extremely thorny subject. The article on *Sacré* (*et Sainteté*), shared by Cazelles and C.-B. Costecalde (together with P. Grelot on the New Testament), consists mainly of detailed studies of the root *qdš*, followed by a short sketch of the development of the notions of the sacral and of holiness in the Old Testament. In view of the need to minimize overlap with other articles, L. Sabourin on *Sacrifice* concentrates, in his treatment of the Old Testament, on particular aspects of the subject: theories and classification, comparative terminology, and LXX terminology. Particular attention is paid to the expiatory function of blood (Lev. 17:11, 14) and to notions of sacrifice at Qumran. The volume ends with an article by M. Simon on the Sadducees.

R. N. WHYBRAY

CLEMENTS, R. E.: *Jacob's Ladder and Jacob's Well: An Inaugural Lecture delivered on October 18, 1984*. 1984. Pp. 16. (King's College London.)

Taking Jacob's Well (the reasonably assured location of a Gospel narrative) and Jacob's ladder (an element in a visionary experience) as representing respectively the historical-critical and the imaginative and poetic approaches to the 'truth' of the Bible, Professor Clements skilfully links a brief account of the achievement of Samuel Davidson (after whom his Chair is named) in the battle for critical freedom in biblical study with a sketch of the socio-anthropological and literary approaches to the Bible which have been adopted in some quarters in recent years. In his plea for the exercise of both the critical and the imaginative faculties in biblical study Professor Clements maintains an admirable balance.

G. W. ANDERSON

COGAN, M. (ed.): *Beer-Sheva II: Studies by the Department of Bible and Ancient Near East, Ben-Gurion University of the Negev. Presented to Shmuel Abramsky on his Retirement*. 1985. Pp. vi, 44 (English), 188 (Hebrew), including some plates and figures. (Magnes Press, Jerusalem. Price: $25.00. ISSN 0334 225)

The first volume of *Beer-Sheva* — the series is not to be confused with the reports on the excavations at Tell es-Sebaʿ (cf. p. 31) — was published in

1973 but not noted in the *Book List*. This volume contains a bibliography of the honorand's writings and sixteen articles, of which fourteen are in modern Hebrew (with English summaries of varying degrees of informativeness) and the other two are in English. The following (all in Hebrew) will be of particular interest for Old Testament studies: N. Aloni, 'The "Dedication" of the Aleppo Codex'; M. Gruber, 'Feminine Similes Applied to God in Deutero-Isaiah'; Y. Zakovitch, 'Foreshadowing in Biblical Narrative'; M. Paran, 'Two Types of "Laying Hands Upon" in the Priestly Source'; J. D. Safren, 'Ahuzzath and the Pact of Beer-Sheba'; Y. Komlosh, 'The Exegetical Method in Targum to Joel'; T. Rudin-O'Brasky, 'The Appendixes to the Book of Judges (Judges 17–21)'; A. Rofé, 'The Covenant in the Land of Moab (Deut. 28: 69–30:20)'. Also included are a short essay by B. Mazar on 'YHWH Came Out from Sinai', which appeared in English in 1981, and several archaeological articles.

G. I. DAVIES

COLLINS, A. Y. (ed.): *Feminist Perspectives on Biblical Scholarship* (Society of Biblical Literature, Centennial Publications: Biblical Scholarship in North America, 10). 1985. Pp. viii, 144. (Scholars Press, Chico, California. Price: $13.95 (discount price: $9.50); ISBN 0 89130 774 5. Paperback price: $9.50 (discount price: $6.25); ISBN 0 89130 773 7)

As part of the SBL's Centennial Publications, this volume is dedicated to one discipline (feminist hermeneutics) within the overall concerns of 'Biblical Scholarship in North America', a parochialism that cannot be ignored in what follows. A Centenary is an appropriate moment both for reviewing the past and for projecting a map for the future: the oft-told tale of the nineteenth-century forbears of American feminist hermeneutics makes for stirring reading as presented by C. de Swarte Gifford in the first essay of the collection, yet those who look for the stimulus of a map of the future will be disappointed and perturbed. A few signposts are offered by B. Brooten in a careful discussion of the use of method in historical reconstruction with reference to early Christian women, but the remaining essays continue a methodological debate, often descending into poorly disguised apologetic or polemic, which pays scant respect to the reader's own critical judgement. Of these E. Schlüssler Fiorenza presents the case against the 'objectivity' of historical criticism most clearly, while C. Osiek pleads for the validity of a variety of feminist hermeneutical approaches. Others, notably T. Drorah Setel in a general discussion of methodology, and E. Fuchs in two contributions which particularly refer to the Old Testament, are less tolerant of those who fail to see the patriarchalism inherent both in historical criticism and in the total perspective of the Bible. That none of the essays focuses specifically on the New Testament, while three relate to the Old Testament, reflects the greater creativity of feminist approaches in Old Testament study; unfortunately the three essays included here are vitiated by 'uncritical' presuppositions and dogmatic assertions. Adopting a semeiotic approach, N. Furmann explores the theme of garments in the Jacob cycle in order to argue that the possibilities of action and meaning are weighted against women in the narrative, reflecting the narrator's own 'pro-male' stance. It is an analysis which fails to convince: adopting the author's own analogy, if we are to speak of the warp and woof of the fabric of the text, there must be genuine continuity in the threads, signalled by a continuity of vocabulary and terminology. Where this is missing, the patterns will be but the constructions of our own minds, and we can hardly expect anyone else to admire their beauty. E. Fuchs explores first the literary characterization of mothers in the Bible and secondly the theme of deceit by women. Her analyses of the 'annunciation scenes' are sensitive and revealing, a sensitivity that is lost in her refusal to recognize exceptions to the essential patriarchalism of the biblical ideology. With this as a map, readers who have learned much from feminist readings of the Bible will fear for a future of continuing navel-gazing combined with aggression against those who choose other paths. In her introduction A. Y. Collins suggests that those women scholars who declined Elizabeth Cady Stanton's invitation to work on *The Woman's Bible* may have done so 'because they had been socialised to value objectivity more than commitment'. Those who recognize a tension but not a contradiction between the two will find therein a judgement which ill accords with the celebration of the past and hopes for the next hundred years of the SBL.

J. M. LIEU

EMERTON, J. A. (ed.): *Congress Volume: Salamanca 1983* (Supplements to Vetus Testamentum, 36). 1985. Pp. viii, 307. (Brill, Leiden. Price: Fl. 120.00; sub. price: Fl. 104.00. ISBN 90 04 07281 0)

The twenty-one contributions (eleven in English, five each in French and German) are preceded by the address given by the President, L. Alonso Schökel, in memory of D. J. McCarthy who died at the Congress. The President's own contribution: 'Of Methods and Models', handles problems of communication, and the tendency to exclusivity of method in contemporary discussion. For the rest, considerable variety of approach is observable. J. Rogerson offers a useful critical survey of sociological styles of study. A contrast between a modern literary approach to a text (C. Conroy: 1 Kings 1:41–53) and a political and historical (T. Ishida: 1 Kings 1–2) was followed by a joint discussion. Another literary study, of 1 Sam. 1 by R. Polzin, considers levels of speech in relation to the nature and function of a text. A more theological appraisal of literary method applied to Gen. 50: 15–21 is by W. Brueggemann. A less secure use of numerical reckoning in relation to divine speeches in the Pentateuch is offered by C. J. Labuschagne, following up his earlier studies. Sonority and word-play, sometimes rather too fanciful, are applied to proper names in foreign-nation oracles by A. Strus. Precise study of specific texts shows the nature of universalistic thought in Isa. 19:16–25 (L. Monsengwo Pasinya): the abrogation of a divinely given law in Isa. 56:1–7 (H. Donner); the possible exilic background to a group of lamentation-prayer elements in prose texts (T. Veijola). S. C. Reif examines the precise meaning of *ns*ʾ *ʿyn*, and in doing this sheds light on other uses of the verb. G. P. Braulik's examination particularly of *nuaḥ* in deuteronomic material makes interesting discoveries, though whether different levels can be thus detected seems less clear. H.-P. Müller considers Eblaite verbal usage in relation to Hebrew. Questions on the nature and development of exegesis are raised in F. Dreyfus's examination of the concept of divine condescension in Christian, Jewish, and biblical interpretation; in J. Lust's study of the varieties of messianic elements in the LXX (especially for Ezek. 21:30–32); in P. S. Alexander's careful examination of comment in the targumim; in Y.-M. Duval's discussion of actualization in Jerome's exegesis of the prophets; and in Uriel Simon's study of Ibn Ezra and his handling of Isa. 40–66. The contemporary exegetical concerns of the Third World are brought out both by J. S. Croatto and by E. Gerstenberger. There are no indexes.

P. R. ACKROYD

FERNÁNDEZ MARCOS, N., TREBOLLE BARRERA, J., and FERNÁNDEZ VALLINA, J. (eds.): *Simposio Bíblico Español* (*Salamanca, 1982*). 1984. Pp. 772. (Editorial de la Universidad Complutense, Madrid. Price: Ptas. 3,000. ISBN: 94 7491 143 5)

This volume comprises the papers presented at the National Biblical Symposium held in Salamanca in September 1982. Its scope was limited to Old Testament and Early Jewish studies, as a kind of stocktaking before the IOSOT Congress met in the same university in 1983. This distinguished collection amply demonstrates how biblical and Jewish studies are flourishing in Spain today, as is impressively summed up in the closing discourse by Cardinal Enrique y Tarancón, at that time still Archbishop of Madrid. The forty-three papers are all in Spanish, but each is followed by a short summary in English. They are arranged in nine sections, as follows: (I) *Archaeology and the Bible*, with studies on the classification of Upper Palaeolithic in Palestine (J. González Echegaray); 'Neolithization' in Palestine (A. Fernández-Tresguerres Velasco); the plan of Iron Age I houses in Tell Medeineh, Jordan (E. Olávarri Goicoechea); Roman pottery and the geography of Palestine in the New Testament (F. Díez Fernández).

(II) *Ancient Near East and the Bible*: Cuneiform texts in the Museo Arqueologico Nacional (an edition of three texts, with photographs and transcription, by J. García Recio); Ebla and the Bible, philology and exegesis (E. Zurro Rodríguez); Ugaritic antecedents of biblical literary forms (G. del Olmo Lete); Everyday expressions of faith and piety in the greetings in Ugaritic letters (J. L. Cunchillos Ylarri — these two contributions are of notable value); The epigraphic and literary context of Ezra and Daniel (J. Teixidor), which illuminates the Persian concepts of empire and freedom of worship.

(III) *The Hebrew Text*: The Samaritan Hebrew: State of the question (L. F. Girón Blanc); Variants in the Dead Sea manuscripts relating to the *textus receptus* of the Minor Prophets (L. Vegas Montaner); Masora and Exegesis (E. Fernández Tejero); The text of the 'Model Manuscripts' according to the *'Or Torah* of Menahem de Lonzano (M. T. Ortega Monasterio).

(IV) *The Greek Text*: Recension and translation of 2 Kings 17:7–23 (J. C. Trebolle Barrera); The Septuagint and the finds in the Desert of Judah (N. Fernández Marcos); Papyrus 967 as a pre-hexaplar witness to Ezekiel (M. V. Sportorno y Díaz Caro); The 'targumim' and the version of Symmachus (J. González Luis).

(V) *Books of the Old Testament:* On the vocabulary of 'blessing' in the Pentateuch (J. Guillén Torralba); Exegetical studies of Deut. 18:9–22 (F. García López) and Isa. 42:1b (H. Simian-Yofre); Jeremiah and the Nations (J. M. Asurmendi Ruiz); 'Developed Macarisms: a Type of Wisdom Poem' (J. R. Busto Saiz).

(VI) *Themes of the Old Testament:* 'Point of View in Linguistic Correspondences' (L. Alonso Schökel — a contribution to semantics, with special reference to *śmḥ, bwš* and *ṣrh*); The 'two incompatible Yahwehs', or two opposed biblical anthropologies (J. Alonso Díaz — on the often conflicting ethical and cultic concepts of God); Poetic insertions in Old Testament narrative (S. Muñoz Iglesias): The Canon of the Old Testament: history, hermeneutics, theology (J. M. Sánchez Caro).

(VII) *The Targum*: Targumic versions of Gen. 3:22–24 (M. Perez Fernandez); Elements common to the Targum to the Prophets and the Palestinian Targum (J. Ribera i Florit); Targum and contemporary exegesis: some problems of method (J. Fernández Vallina — hermeneutical reflexions apropos of the Targum on Job): Targumic traditions in Syriac Baruch (D. Muñoz León); The 'Midrash about the gifts' and its relation to the

Palestinian Targum (A. Rodríguez Carmona — the gifts are those granted to Israel for the merits of Miriam, Moses, and Aaron).

(VIII) *Intertestamental Literature*: The 'Watchers' in intertestamental literature (L. Díez Merino); The Temple Scroll and sectarian halakah (F. García Martínez); Joseph and Aseneth and the New Testament (A. Piñero Sáenz); Christological *deras* on Psalm 110 in the New Testament (A. del Agua Pérez); Jewish eschatological ideas in the Coptic Apocalypse of Elijah (G. Aranda); Slavery in the time of Jesus and its antecedents (C. Alonso Fontela).

(IX) *Hispano-Jewish Exegesis*: The biblical hermeneutics of Dunaš ben Labraṭ (A. Sáenz -Badillos); The Introductions of Questions of don Isaac Abrabanel (G.Ruiz); Jewish *converso* Hebraists in the University of Salamanca in the fifteenth–sixteenth centuries (C. Carrete Parrondo); Presence of the Bible in the history of the Jewish *conversos* in sixteenth-century Spain (M. D. Esteva de Llolat).

This mere list of titles, with rare added comments, cannot do more than hint at the riches to be found in this volume.

R. P. R. Murray

Hartman, L. (ed.): *Svensk exegetisk årsbok*, 50. 1985. Pp. 182. (CWK Gleerup, Malmö. Price: Sw.Kr.102.00. ISBN 91 40 05115 3)

Four articles in this issue are of direct interest to the *Alttestamentler*. W. McKane poses the question: 'Is there a Place for Theology in the Exegesis of the Hebrew Bible?' Tracing a path which leads from the LXX through Origen, Jerome, Herbert of Bosham, and Adam of St Victor to Richard Simon, he argues that the exegete must use, and confine himself to, rigorous critical methods to ascertain the plain meaning of the Hebrew text. By this standard, Weiser's commentary on Jeremiah is found wanting. R. Sollamo contributes (in Swedish) a detailed examination of the formula 'before the LORD/God' in the Old Testament (where the background is predominantly cultic), the LXX (where the renderings vary little), and the New Testament (where the phrase gives emphasis, adds an ethical element, or refers to worship in heaven). G. André discusses (in Swedish, with brief English summary) whether the woman about whom warnings are given in Prov. 1–9 is a 'strange' woman or another man's wife. Numerous parallels are adduced to elucidate the meaning. It is concluded that only in 6:26, 29 is 'another man's wife' the appropriate rendering. H. Ringgren examines (in Swedish, with brief English summary) Luther's interpretations of the Psalms in various works from 1513 till 1545. He shows how Luther moves from a concern with the precise meaning of the text to the application of it to contemporary events and to Christian theology. There are five articles on New Testament subjects (B. Olsson on Luther's attempt to understand Revelation; P. Stuhlmacher on 'the Law' in Romans; H. Riesenfeld on the reference to the Spirit in Rom. 1:4; B. Gerhardsson on the historical problem of the rise of Christianity; and O. Christofferson on the authentic background to Rom. 8:18 ff.). There are some twenty reviews, including a review article by Å. V. Ström of the Proceedings of the International Colloquium on Apocalypticism (Uppsala, 1979; cf. *B.L.* 1984, pp. 128–29).

G. W. Anderson

Holtz, B. (ed.): *Back to the Sources: Reading the Classic Jewish Texts*. 1984. Pp. 448, including some illustrations. (Summit Books, New York. Distributed in Great Britain by Jewish Chronicle Publications, London. Price: £15.00. ISBN 0 671 45467 6)

This well-planned and attractively presented introduction to eight major areas of Jewish literature is the work of a group of American scholars who are committed Jews, but whose intellectual approach represents a modern application of the principles of the *Wissenschaft des Judentums*. The essays are an admirable combination of the popular and the scientific and, although clearly intended for the edification of the Jewish layman, will also be found useful by both scholars in related fields and those beginning college courses in Jewish studies. Each contribution provides a generally sound introduction to the structure and intent of a particular kind of Jewish literature together with a number of examples, and a guide to further studies that includes a detailed bibliography. Interpretation of the Hebrew Bible is well covered in the articles on biblical narratives, biblical law and midrash, and adequately treated in those devoted to biblical poetry and mediaeval commentaries. There is also a thoughtful preface on reading Jewish texts, and the remaining essays deal with talmudic, philosophical, kabbalistic, ḥasidic, and liturgical literature.

S. C. Reif

Jervell, J., and Kapelrud, A. S. (eds.): *Studia Theologica: Scandinavian Journal of Theology*. Vol. 39, No. 1. 1985. Pp. 1–72. (Universitetsforlaget, Oslo. Sub. price for vol. 39: N.Kr.150.00; $25.00. ISSN 0039 338X)

T. N. D. Mettinger, 'Fighting the Powers of Chaos and Hell — Towards the Biblical Portrait of God' (pp. 21–38), discusses the interrelationship of the concept of God as king with the themes of creation-battle. Zion-battle, Exodus-battle, battle of the Day of the Lord, and the ways in which such ideas were both developed and re-interpreted: a stimulating and wide-ranging study. N. Wyatt, '"Araunah the Jebusite" and the Throne of David' (pp. 39–53), builds on earlier discussions of this theme to develop interesting ideas about the Davidic take-over of royal ideas and status, with the opening up of possibilities concerning the status of Uriah and Bathsheba. The wider problems of kingship and the acceptance of a new ruler and dynasty could provide a fuller warrant for such a suggestive approach. The other two articles in this issue are concerned with New Testament (the book of Revelation) and Christian concepts of freedom.

P. R. Ackroyd

Junge, F. (ed.): *Studien zu Sprache und Religion Ägyptens zu Ehren von Wolfhart Westendorf überreicht von seinen Freunden und Schülern*. 2 vols. 1: *Sprache*. 2: *Religion*. 1984. Pp. 672, with 16 plates; 673–1144, with 45 plates. (Redaktion der Göttinger Miszellen, Prinzenstrasse 21, D–3400 Göttingen. Price: DM. 92.00 and 75.00)

These two volumes contain seventy-six articles on a rather wider range of topics than is indicated by the title, and a bibliography of the dedicatee. Almost all are narrowly Egyptological, and the *Festschrift* is more likely to be useful to Old Testament scholars for comparative purposes than for any distinct contribution to their field.

The strongest section is on Egyptian syntax and morphology, part of the recent revival of interest in the Egyptian language. A. Loprieno writes on aspect and diathesis in Egyptian and Semitic, an article of particular value for the earliest stages of Egyptian. W. Schenkel and A. Shisha-Halevy discuss nominal sentences in Egyptian and Coptic respectively, while H. Satzinger writes an 'Attribut und Relativsatz'. H. J. Polotsky contributes 'Randbemerkungen' to Schenkel's theory of the origin of the Egyptian suffix conjugation in verbal nouns.

F. Junge produces the first-ever article on Egyptian 'linguistics', a valuable attempt to relate metalinguistic vocabulary and such things as naming practices, wordplay, and cryptography, to general attitudes to language. D. B. Redford studies the Egyptian word for 'annals' (forthcoming book). G. Fecht makes an interesting new interpretation of the battle scene in the Story of Sinuhe, while I. Grumach-Shirun discusses part of its opening plot.

In the second volume, *Religion*, J. Assmann contributes an important article on *maat* as linking generations in moral obligation and solidarity: virtue — conformity to *maat* — creates reputation and respect by posterity. J. F. Borghouts analyses two unusual Middle Kingdom mythological texts. A. R. Schulman studies new evidence for the Canaanite god Reshep from Zagazig (Bubastis). R. Hari studies Amarna religion in relation to polytheism, an interesting discussion that neglects other studies. L. Kákosy discusses whether the Egyptians thought the sun was spherical or lentoid and concludes that in rather esoteric knowledge it was a sphere. Of biblical interest, A. Böhlig discusses Aramaic elements in the Nag Hammadi Gnostic corpus, concluding that some Jewish influence, both in Hebrew and in Aramaic, is present, and that the stage of Aramaic in question is J. A. Fitzmyer's Middle/Late Aramaic. Böhlig discounts the hypothesis of Syriac originals for the corpus.

J. R. BAINES

KNIGHT, D. A., and TUCKER, G. M. (eds.): *The Hebrew Bible and its Modern Interpreters* (Society of Biblical Literature, Centennial Publications: The Bible and its Modern Interpreters, 1). 1985. Pp. xxviii, 516, including 2 maps. (Fortress Press, Philadelphia. Price: $29.95. ISBN 0 8006 0721 X. Scholars Press, Chico, California. ISBN 0 89130 671 4)

Fifteen essayists, including the editors, sketch and assess study of the Hebrew Bible since 1945. The first seven contributions treat history (J. M. Miller), archaeology (W. G. Dever), the ancient Near East (J. J. M. Roberts), criticism, both older and newer (R. Knierim and R. C. Culley), religion (P. D. Miller), and theology (G. W. Coats). The next seven focus on sections of the Bible: the Pentateuch (Knight), the historical books (P. R. Ackroyd), the Prophets (Tucker), wisdom (J. L. Crenshaw), lyrics (E. H. Gerstenberger), legends (S. Niditch), and apocalyptic (P. D. Hanson). An essay by W. Harrelson on 'The Hebrew Bible and Modern Culture' completes the review.Mostly modestly written this is a strong collection of often exciting surveys. A paperback edition should quickly rival the stronger one-author 'Introductions' for initiated students. At the beginning of its second century, the Society of Biblical Literature is clearly in good heart!

A. G. AULD

KORT, A., and MORSCHAUSER, S. (eds.): *Biblical and Related Studies Presented to Samuel Iwry*. 1985. Pp. xviii, 274, including some figures. (Eisenbrauns, Winona Lake, Indiana. Price: $25.00. ISBN 0 931464 23 4)

The high number of contributors has meant that many of the twenty-nine essays are rather short. They will be listed in groups by topic. Grammar: T. O. Lambdin re-appraises Philippi's Law, and S. Rosenblatt gives examples of biblical grammar in the Tosefta. Versions: L. G. Running compares the versions of Jer. 18. Lexicography: H. Goedicke explains Gen. 2: 21–22 using Egyptian; J. C. Greenfield clarifies *tĕkūnā* in Nah. 2: 10; M. Held discusses difficult *mîṣ* (Prov. 30:33), *ḥîdâ* and *ḥûd*; G. Krotkoff looks at some Neo-Aramaic terms. History and archaeology: M. Aberbach gives the background to early links between Parthia and Judaea; R. G. Boling examines the list of levitical towns (Josh. 21); and J. Milgrom explains 2 Chron. 29:21–24 using archaeological finds. Poetry and literature: A. Berlin describes features of Ps. 145; J. S. Cooper would see the Joseph stories as literature, not history; D. N. Freedman studies prose particles in parts of the Pentateuch; A. Hurvitz compares 1 Sam. 2 with Ps. 113; and W. L. Moran finds Rib-Hadda of Byblos a kind of Job. Exegesis: both J. J. M. Roberts and A. Rofé study Isaiah; C. A. Moore reports on Esther studies; and H. B. Huffmon explains Gen. 4:7. Religion: J. M. Baumgarten describes the tithes of 11QT; C. H. Gordon finds a Nuzu parallel to the first commandment; M. Haran contrasts temple with synagogue; and G. Mendenhall studies social bonding in religious systems. Other studies are on Lachish Letter 3 (F. M. Cross), EA 8 (B. M. Gittlen), Aqhat (D. R. Hillers), the New Jewish Version (H. M. Orlinsky), E. Renan (L. Smolar), and Resheph (Y. Yadin). W. G. E. Watson

Lagrange, M. J.: *Père Lagrange: Personal Reflections and Memoirs*. With a Foreword by P. Benoit. Translated by H. Wansbrough. 1985. Pp. vi, 249. (Paulist Press, Mahwah, New Jersey. Price: $9.95. ISBN 0 8091 2678 8)

The contents of this fascinating volume fall into two unequal parts. The first, containing Lagrange's personal recollections from the years 1889–1913, tells of the establishment and development of the *École Biblique*, the founding and early years of the *Revue Biblique*, the increasing theological tensions within the Roman Catholic Church, leading to the modernist crisis. The second part contains more personal recollections of Lagrange's early life and education. The historical importance of the first part is obvious. It also reflects Lagrange's scholarly and theological integrity, his unswerving loyalty to truth and to the Church. Both there and in the narrative and reflections in the second part, one gets the impression of a character of great charm and modesty. G. W. Anderson

Lang, B., in conjunction with Kaiser, O., Simotas, P., and Vögtle, A. (eds.): *Internationale Zeitschriftenschau für Bibelwissenschaft und Grenzgebiete*. Vol. 31 (1984/85). 1985. Pp. xiv, 498. (Patmos Verlag, Düsseldorf. Price: DM. 158.00. ISSN 0074 9745)

The adjustments made to the arrangement of the entries in this invaluable annual review of articles and books are now firmly established, and the character of this issue is unchanged from that of the previous year; see the comments in *B.L.* 1984, p. 19; 1985, p. 16. In an introductory note Professor Lang pays a much-deserved tribute to Eleonore Beck, who for thirty-four years has played a major part in the production of *IZBG*. M. A. Knibb

Martin-Achard, R.: *Permanence de l'Ancien Testament: Recherches d'exégèse et de théologie* (Cahiers de la Revue de Théologie et de Philosophie, 11). 1984. Pp. xii, 398. (Revue de Théologie et de Philosophie, Lausanne. Price: Sw.Fr. 40.00. ISSN 0250 6971)

As a tribute to the work of Professor Martin-Achard on his retirement, this collection of twenty-seven of his studies has been issued. There is a short introductory essay on his contributions to scholarship and to the wider field of theology and a bibliography of his writings in which those included in this volume are marked with an asterisk so that their provenance is given. The studies are grouped under: (1) Old Testament theology; (2) the covenant theme; (3) theological themes (*lieux*); (4) exegesis; (5) essays, including two sermons. There is thus a very representative collection, providing a good conspectus of contributions to points of detail (so especially in section 4) and assessments of work in particular fields (a number of studies are reviews of groups of writings relevant to a single topic). The range is wide, and the reader is offered a clear insight into the mind of the author. The collection stands most usefully alongside his well-known larger works.

P. R. Ackroyd

Mayes, A. D. H. (ed.): *Proceedings of the Irish Biblical Association*. Vol. 8. 1984. Pp. iv, 125. (Irish Biblical Association Publications, Trinity College, Dublin. Price: £7.00.)

There is much good matter in this volume. M. Maher writes on the moral problems raised by the manner of Jacob's acquisition of the birthright and on attempts (mainly Jewish) to justify the actions of the principals in the story, K. E. Zappone examines the standpoint of the interpreter, *en route* to a feminist hermeneutic of Scripture, M. McNamara discusses several recent Targum editions (Madrid edition of the Palestinian Targum to the Pentateuch, M. L. Klein's edition of the Fragment-Targums, and A. van der Heide's edition of Targum Lamentations), and K. J. Cathcart considers the language of the Ebla texts and concludes that it is classifiable neither as Canaanite nor as West Semitic, but shares some features with Old Akkadian. M. McNamara returns with a paper on early Irish Bible exegesis, and P. S. Alexander writes on the rabbinic hermeneutical rules, their limitations as far as the definition of midrash is concerned, and the need for modern scholars to devise more rigorous methods of analysis and a more satisfactory terminology.

R. P. Gordon

Mikasa, H. I. H. Prince Takahito (ed.): *Monarchies and Socio-Religious Traditions in the Ancient Near East* (*Papers read at the 31st International Congress of Human Sciences in Asia and North Africa*) (Bulletin of the Middle Eastern Culture Center in Japan, 1). 1984. Pp. viii, 83, with 25 plates and 1 map. (Otto Harrassowitz, Wiesbaden. Price: DM. 58.00. ISBN 3 447 02510 7)

Three of the ten papers from the erstwhile International Congress of Orientalists are significant for the Old Testament. L. M. Muntingh determines the concept of kingship in Syria and Palestine using royal archives of the period (spanning 2400 to 587 B.C.), including those of Ebla. Z. Weisman describes 'The Prophetic Pattern of Anointing Kings in Ancient Israel', updating his earlier paper in *Biblica* 1976. D. T. Tsumura re-examines the Krt Epic which, he argues, has childlessness as its main theme. Also important are L. Cagni's report on studies of Mesopotamia in the Achaemenid period, particularly for its re-evaluation of Cyrus's tolerance; Y. Ikeda's survey of the Neo-Hittites and Aramaeans in the region around Til-Barsip; and D. J. Wiseman's description of palace and temple gardens in Assyria and Babylon. K. Myśliwiec and J. Leclant deal with Egyptian topics. These papers are welcome for bringing new or unnoticed aspects of kingship to our attention, though depth is occasionally sacrificed for detail.

W. G. E. Watson

MÜLLER, G. (ed.): *Theologische Realenzyklopädie* (TRE). Band XIII (*Gesellschaft/Gesellschaft und Christentum VI — Gottesbeweise*). 1984. Pp. 804, including numerous illustrations. (De Gruyter Berlin. Price: DM. 320.00. ISBN 3 11 008581 X)

The main articles of especial interest to readers of the *Book List* in this volume are those on *Gesetz* (K. Koch on the Old Testament, Y. Amir on Judaism), *Glaube* (K. Haacker on the Old and New Testaments, E. Bammel on the intertestamental period and rabbinic Judaism), *Gnade* (H. Graf Reventlow on the Old Testament, R. Goldenberg on Judaism), and *Gott* (G. Lanczkowski on the religio-historical background, W. H. Schmidt on the Old Testament, C. Thoma on Judaism). Haacker considers the problem of the terminology of faith in the Old Testament and includes sections on Isaiah, the 'faith of Abraham', faith in the Moses tradition, Second Isaiah, personal piety and Hab. 2:4. Reventlow, faced with similar terminological problems, discusses in particular *ḥēn, ḥesed* and *rāṣōn*. Schmidt deals with the early period and the main characteristics of the Old Testament concept of God, and then treats the 'God of the prophets' and experience of God in wisdom and the Psalms separately. There are also short articles on Gesenius (J. Hahn), Gibeon (G. Wanke) and Gilgal (E. Otto), and sections on the Old Testament and Judaism in the articles on *Gewohnheit/Gewohnheitsrecht* (E. S. Gerstenberger on the Old Testament, H. G. Perelmuter on Judaism), *Glaubenserkenntnis(se)* (Gerstenberger on the Old Testament, A. Finkel on Judaism), the Golden Rule (H.-P. Mathys on Judaism) and *Gottesbeweise* (N. Samuelson on Judaism, including a short section on the Old Testament, especially Second Isaiah). An index of biblical references, a general index, a list of contributors, a list of contents and an index of illustrations complete the volume.

R. N. WHYBRAY

MÜLLER, H.-P. (ed.): *Bibel und Alter Orient: Altorientalische Beiträge zum Alten Testament von Wolfram von Soden* (Beiheft zur Zeitschrift für die alttestamentliche Wissenschaft, 162). 1985. Pp. xii, 224. (De Gruyter, Berlin. Price: DM. 96.00. IBSN 3 11 010091 6)

Von Soden has been one of the most prolific Assyriologists over the last half-century, and his Akkadian grammar, *Handwörterbuch* and *Syllabar* are standard works. In addition he has been putting out a regular stream of articles on all kinds of topics, and twenty-seven of these which bear on the Old Testament have been reprinted here (with occasional slight corrections). Even some one-page notes on particular words are included. They are enormously varied in topic, and are all extremely learned. The author is a philologist in the old German tradition of Friedrich Delitzsch and Heinrich Zimmern, and like them he combines extremely methodical and reliable work with occasional lapses of judgement in more general matters. However, he is always worth reading, and this gathering of materials widely scattered will make more readily available these *opera minora*.

W. G. LAMBERT

MURAOKA, T. (ed.): *Abr-Nahrain XXIII (1984–1985)*. 1985. Pp. viii, 128, including many figures; 15 plates. (Brill, Leiden. Price: Fl. 64.00. ISBN 90 04 06405 2)

A great variety of fields is covered by this issue of *Abr-Nahrain*. We begin with an exciting (though badly edited) sketch by J. Bowman, 'Solomon and Jesus' (pp. 1–13), of the importance of Solomon and the demonic in the background of many of the sayings and stories of the New Testament, especially in Q. Excellent, despite an unnecessary swipe at Islam. V. A. Clark publishes 'New Safaitic Inscriptions from Sakaka and Azraq' (pp. 14–21), while Y. Ikeda tackles the subject of 'Assyrian Kings and the Mediterranean Sea: The Twelfth to Ninth Centuries B.C.' (pp. 22–31), with special reference to the capture of dolphins. An article by R. G. Jenkins on 'Codex Q and the Hexaplaric Recension' (pp. 32–38) is followed by a second preliminary report on the el-Qitar excavations: 'El-Qitar: Second Season of Excavations, 1983–84' (pp. 39–72) by T. L. McClellan. The late W. Culican contributed to the earlier report (*B.L.* 1985, pp. 18–19). Evidence presented here suggests destruction of the Bronze Age city in the fifteenth–fourteenth century B.C. Several studies follow which deal with finds associated with the Australian expedition to Syria: 'Syriac Inscriptions from the Middle Euphrates' by G. W. Clarke (pp. 73–82), 'Two Syriac Inscriptions from the Middle Euphrates' by T. Muraoka (pp. 83–89), 'A Decorated Christian Tomb-Chamber near Joussef Pasha' by G. W. Clarke (pp. 90–95), 'A Funerary Stele in the District of Membij' by the same author (pp. 96–101), and 'Two Cylinder Seals from el-Qitar' by A. G. Sagona (pp. 102–03) (one is clearly of Mitannian style). Finally, D. Sahas gives a useful survey of 'John of Damascus on Islam' (pp. 104–18). Book reviews and photographic plates complete the volume.

J. F. HEALEY

NORTH, R. (ed.): *Elenchus Bibliographicus Biblicus* of *Biblica*. Vol. 63 (1982). 1985. Pp. 842. (Biblical Institute Press, Rome. Price: Lire 100,000; $65.00. ISSN 0392 7423)

The *Elenchus* continues to provide a mass of bibliographical information relating to biblical studies that is unsurpassed in its extent by any comparable publication. The present issue contains over thirteen thousand entries arranged according to the new pattern established by Professor North. The listing of reviews remains one of the very helpful features of this work.

M. A. KNIBB

PÁKOZDY, L. M.: *JHVH 'šr JHVH* (I.1); *Multi lampades, una lux* (I.2). Válogattot tanulmányok az általános és bibliai vallástörtenet köréből. (Selected studies from the common and biblical history of religion). 1984; 1985. Pp. 171; 187. (Ráday Kollégium, Budapest.)

Both volumes were published on the occasion of the seventy-fifth birthday of Professor Pákozdy. They comprise twenty of his studies and lectures originally published in different journals and now photo-mechanically reproduced. The first volume contains thirteen contributions dealing with questions concerning the Old Testament. With one exception they are written in Hungarian and cover such topics as How to interpret the message of the old covenant; How to preach on Old Testament texts; The use of the divine name in the stories of Balaam; The historiography of the court and popular tales in Israel; Away with the priests! (Mal. 2). — The discussion of whether the proper name of David was Elhanan, is the only one in German (I.1, pp. 137–39; cf. *ZAW* 68 (1956) pp. 257–59). It is based on the identification of *davidum* (from the texts of Mari) with a 'leader', and on the supposition that this title later became the name of the partisan-leader David-Elhanan. — Another question that occupied Pákozdy very much for more than thirty years was the explanation of the name JHVH in Exod. 3:14. In spite of his protests the committee for the new Hungarian Bible translation accepted in 1953 the form 'I am who I am'. In vain he presented to the Hungarian Biblical Council a defence of the meaning 'I shall be who I shall be', with an eschatological aim (reprinted here in I. 1, pp. 117–26). He also published it at the time for a larger audience in *Judaica* XI.4 (1.XII.1955). — To his public lecture on 'Questions concerning the Ancient Israelite Epic poem' (I. 1, pp. 21–33) he appended an English summary (p. 34), but the whole text can be read in German in the *Acta Antiqua Academiae Scientiarum Hungaricae* 23 (1975). — His polemical article with Arpád Szabó about the relation between the biblical narrative of Gen. 3 and a similar tale from the island of Ceram on the west of New Guinea (I.1, pp. 99–109) is completed by a German summary (pp. 109–10). — In the second volume three contributions are dedicated to Qumran problems: Qumran and the Church; The Qumran economy; and A Decade of Qumran research. The last four articles are of an ecclesiological character: The Good Shepherd in John 10; Who is the founder of the Church — Jesus or Peter?; The *ecclesia visibilis* and the continuity of the Church; From exegesis to preaching.

M. Bič

Phy, A. S. (ed.): *The Bible and Popular Culture in America* (Society of Biblical Literature, Centennial Publications: The Bible in American Culture, 2). 1985. Pp. xii, 248. (Scholars Press, Chico, California. Price: $15.95; discount price: $10.50. ISBN 0 89130 640 4. Fortress Press, Philadelphia. ISBN 0 8006 0735 X)

Johnson, J. T. (ed.): *The Bible in American Law, Politics, and Political Rhetoric* (Society of Biblical Literature, Centennial Publications: The Bible in American Culture, 4). 1985. Pp. viii, 204. (Scholars Press, Chico, California. Price: $15.95; discount price: $10.50. ISBN 0 89130 652 8. Fortress Press, Philadelphia. ISBN 0 8006 0614 0)

The Bible has been a pervasive influence on popular culture in the American Southern states, the 'Bible belt'. But this Southern outlook with its strongly conservative biblicism is no longer limited to that region but has its enclaves in other parts of the United States, as Phy points out in the introductory essay of the volume he has edited. The contributors are all from the South or teach there. Subjects include humour, fiction, country music, the 'electronic church' (radio and television evangelistic preachers), selling 'the Good Book', and the Bible as literature for American children.

The volume edited by Johnson is divided into two parts. The first gives a historical perspective, with essays on the transplantation of the Reformation view of the Bible to the New World, the Bible at the time of the American Revolution, and its use in nineteenth-century political life. The second section is thematic, with essays on the influence of biblical religion on constitutional law, views of economic problems, political realism in the nuclear age (focusing especially on Reinhold Niebuhr), and the concept of community. (For volume 3 in this series see *B.L.* 1985, p. 81.)

L. L. Grabbe

Revista Bíblica Brasileira, 1/3 and 1/4. 1984. Pp. 73–104; 105–44. (Centro Communitário Cristo Redentor, Fortaleza. Price: $5.00 per annum)

These two issues complete the first year of the new quarterly reviewed in *B.L.* 1985, p. 21. In 1/3, Fr C. M. de Tillesse explores the idea of Covenant as liberation in the Old Testament (including the book of Daniel). In 1/4 he continues the theme into New Testament eschatology. The final issue also contains a meditation on Roublev's Icon of the Blessed Trinity (which forms the cover picture of each issue), a table of biblical citations, and subject and author indexes embracing all four issues.

J. M. Dines

ROFÉ, A., and ZAKOVITCH, Y. (eds.): *Isac Leo Seeligmann Volume: Essays on the Bible and the Ancient World*. 3 volumes. 1983. Pp. x, 572 (vols. 1–2, Hebrew Section); viii, 346 (vol. 3, Non-Hebrew Section). (E. Rubinstein, Jerusalem.)

Planned and written in the mid-1970s as a *Festschrift* for I. L. Seeligmann, this work has sadly become a memorial volume instead because of the considerable delay in its publication. Indeed, despite an official publication date of 1983, it did not in fact appear until 1985.

The two Hebrew volumes include a photograph of Seeligmann, an appreciation of him as a scholar and teacher by Rofé, and a bibliography of his writings. These were not at all numerous (though of high quality), but the thirty-nine articles which make up the remainder of these two volumes attest the very deep influence which Seeligmann exercised as a colleague and especially as a teacher in the Hebrew University of Jerusalem. Not all these articles by any means are restricted to the Old Testament; alongside the expected forays into the post-biblical and mediaeval fields, there are several which deal exclusively with Greek or Roman topics. It is not possible even to summarize here the diverse group of articles devoted to many aspects of Old Testament study, but some readers of the *Book List* may be glad to learn that a number have already appeared elsewhere (either in translation or revised form) in European languages, e.g. N. Na'aman on the inheritance of the sons of Simeon (*ZDPV* 96 (1980), pp. 136–52), S. Japhet on the historical reliability of Chronicles in biblical research (*JSOT* 33 (1985), pp. 83–107), and E. Tov on the rabbinic traditions concerning the alterations inserted into the Greek Pentateuch (*JSJ* 15 (1984), pp. 65–89).

In the non-Hebrew volume there are twenty-two articles in English, French, and German; again, a few have already appeared elsewhere, whilst the majority are recognizable as spin-offs from, or contributions to, their authors' longer-term projects. Many concentrate on particular texts: E. Lipiński (wisdom elements in Gen. 3, Num. 22:22–35, Gen. 4:1–16 and 1 Kings 3:16–27), H. Ringgren (the Deir ʿAlla inscription), T. Willi (Gen. 4:1–16), R. Rendtorff (Gen. 28:10–22), J. Milgrom (Deut. 16:18), F. Langlamet (2 Sam. 19:32–41), B. O. Long (1 Kings 22:1–38), R. E. Clements (2 Kings 20:12–19 points to a date for the composition of the Deuteronomic History in the reign of Zedekiah), R. J. Tournay (Ezek. 21:13–22), A. S. van der Woude (Jonah 1:16 and 4:5–9), I. Willi-Plein (*nḥm* in Job 42:6), H. G. M. Williamson (1 Chron. 17 and its echoes later in the work), and R. Hanhart (the LXX of Isa. 9:1–7). The remaining articles discuss the relationship between the Old Testament presentation of Israel's history and that reconstructed by modern scholars (J. A. Soggin), the knowledge of God in ancient near eastern and Old Testament historiography (S. Herrmann), 'Anticipatory Titles in Hebrew Narrative' (B. S. Childs), a positive approach to Pentateuchal source criticism in the light of other ancient near eastern literature (J. H. Tigay), the name 'Nabal' (J. J. Stamm), the distinguishing of fact from fiction in prophetic narratives (G. Fohrer), a comparison of the presentation of history in Ezekiel and Daniel (W. Zimmerli), the structure of the book of Esther (M. V. Fox), and observations on the methods used by the translators of the Greek Pentateuch (I. Soisalon-Soininen).

H. G. M. WILLIAMSON

RÖLLIG, W. (ed.): *XXII. Deutscher Orientalistentag vom 21. bis 25. März 1983 in Tübingen. Ausgewählte Vorträge* (Zeitschrift der Deutschen Morgenländischen Gesellschaft, Supplement, 6). 1985. Pp. 444; 23 figures, 62 plates. (Franz Steiner Verlag, Wiesbaden. Price: DM. 220.00. ISBN 3 515 04253 9)

The German Oriental Society's 1983 Congress was not directly concerned with Old Testament studies. Of the seventy papers gathered only a few are immediately relevant. A. Lemaire considers the writing materials available in ancient Israel, attested both by texts and by actual discoveries. Papyrus was probably normal for books of all sorts, but leather may have been used also (although the evidence that leather was chosen for records meant to endure is weaker than Lemaire supposed). In a résumé K. Beyer summarizes additions to be made to his *Althebräischen Grammatik* (1969; *B.L.* 1970, pp. 81–82; *Bible Bibliog.*, pp. 271–72). Grammarians may also note G. Steiner's examination of the circumstantial clause in Akkadian, and F. Junge's investigation of the stages of ancient Egyptian language and their appearance in different types of text. K. Aartun discusses Ugaritic *inr*, concluding it means 'watch-dog', derived from a widespread root *'rn* or *n'r*. In 'Some Problems in Early Aramean History' R. Zadok sketches current knowledge down to 720 B.C., attempts to define which persons and states were Aramean, and promises a monographic study. The status of Safaitic tribal groups and their religion occupy E. Knauf, who decides they were polyheists, like their neighbours, not henotheists. More recent aspects of Semitic, and much on the Far East supply the bulk of the volume.

A. R. MILLARD

Seisho-gaku Ronshū 18 and 19 (The Japanese Biblical Institute Annual). 1984 and 1985. Pp. 163 and 139. (Yamamoto-shoten, Tokyo. Price: ¥3,000 each)

No. 18 contains Y. Suzuki's 'Eschatological Negation in Hosea with special reference to the Jacob tradition in Hos. 12' and M. Sekine's 'Justification and Sanctification — from the viewpoint of the intellectual-historical study of biblical theology'. The former is a detailed study of Hos. 12, which makes use of the author's textual, literary, structural, and theological methodology, and includes a full survey of previous studies of the text. Suzuki finds in Hosea's text a carefully worked-out literary composition, which conveys YHWH's total rejection of Israel in history.

No. 19 contains T. Ishida's article on Solomon's succession. For European readers his main thesis may be studied in two other recent articles of his, which appeared in *Studies in the Period of David and Solomon* (see *B.L.* 1984, p. 16) and in *Supplements to Vetus Testamentum* 36 (see above, p. 14). An application of the method of the structural analysis of folk-tales to the book of Tobit is attempted in T. Saito's article, 'The Structure of Folk-tales in the Book of Tobit'.

K. K. SACON

Seisho to Oriento Sekai (The Bible and the Ancient Near Eastern World, edited by the Institute for the History of Religion). 1985. P. 302. (Yamamoto-shoten, Tokyo. Price: ¥4,800)

This collection of essays is dedicated to the late Professor K. Ōhata, the founder of the Institute for the History of Religion, by his students. Part One consists of four essays on ancient Israelite religion. H. Yoshida discusses the religio-historical background of the right of asylum and the laws of asylum in the Old Testament. H. Sadakata considers the interpretation of Exod. 3:13–15. T. Odashima discusses the interrelationship between prophecy and metrical form, taking Jer. 2:5–9 as an example. A. Tsukimoto points out Shamanistic elements in Israelite prophecy.

Part Two consists of two essays on Judaism. Y. Ichikawa deals with the Pharisees' attitude toward sacrifice at the temple, and K. Ishikawa with the diaspora as a normative condition.

Part Three contains three essays on archaeology and the religion of the ancient Near East. H. Ogawa writes on 'The discovery of "self" in Neolithic Anatolia', K. Watanabe on 'The three seals of the god Ashur in the vassal-treaties of Esarhaddon', and K. Gotoh on 'A small temple at Tel Zeror'.

K. K. SACON

TÖKEI, F. (ed.): *Acta Orientalia Academiae Scientiarum Hungaricae*, XXXVIII. Fasc. 1–2 (pp. 1–262, including some plates); fasc. 3 (pp. 263–459, including some plates). 1984. (Akadémiai Kiadó, Budapest. Price: $44.00 per volume. ISSN 0001 6446)

The only article relevant to Old Testament study is the publication with plates by the late A. Scheiber of fragments from the Taylor-Schechter (Genizah) Collection in the Cambridge University Library of the commentary on Leviticus by Daniel el-Qumisi, a ninth-century Karaite writer.

J. A. EMERTON

VAWTER, B. (ed.): *Old Testament Abstracts*. Vol. 8. Nos. 1–3 (February, June, October 1985). Pp. 350. (The Catholic Biblical Association, The Catholic University of America, Washington, DC. Price per annum: $11.00; single issues: $4.00. ISSN 0364 8591)

The character and scope of this invaluable bibliographical tool are unchanged from previous years. The present volume contains 917 abstracts of articles and 120 book notices.

M. A. KNIBB

VINCENT, J. M.: *Forschung und Verkündigung: Vermischte theologische Schriften und Predigten*. 1985. Pp. vi, 93. (Privately published, Bochum.)

This privately printed volume of shorter studies by Dr J. M. Vincent, who served as *Assistent* to Professor H. Graf Reventlow during 1969–73 and 1980–85 contains a number of contributions of interest to Old Testament scholars. The first essay discusses the relationship between Eduard Reuss of Strasbourg and George Büchner and prints two letters from Büchner to Reuss. Nineteenth-century scholarship also appears as a primary subject in a discussion of the Song of Songs during that century. Besides three sermons from the author there is also a survey of studies of the Decalogue from 1981 to 1985 and a detailed exegetical study of Micah's prophecy against Zion (Mic. 3:12).

The author's previous research on the prophecies of Isa. 40–55 has made a significant contribution to Old Testament studies and these shorter essays will deserve serious attention.

R. E. CLEMENTS

WESTERMANN, C.: *Kyūyaku Seisho*. Translated by M. Tokita. 1985. Pp. 110. (Yorudan-sha, Tokyo. Price: ¥1,300)

This is a Japanese translation of the section 'Altes Testament' in *Arbeitsbuch Religion und Theologie* (1976), edited by the author. The translator has appended a short postscript about the author.

K. K. SACON

2. ARCHAEOLOGY AND EPIGRAPHY

Biblical Archaeology Today: Proceedings of the International Congress on Biblical Archaeology, Jerusalem, April 1984. 1985. Pp. xvi, 534, including some figures, photographs, and maps. (Israel Exploration Society, Jerusalem; Israel Academy of Sciences and Humanities; with ASOR. Price: $30.00. ISBN 965 221 004 8)

The papers, responses, and discussions at the Congress are set out under the sections in which they were organized. I. Biblical Archaeology Today (F. M. Cross, B. Mazar, Y. Yadin), offers reflections on aspects of a subject whose definition still involves controversy. II. Archaeology, History and Bible, offers a series of approaches to the Israelite Settlement (D. N. Freedman, N. K. Gottwald, S. Herrmann, M. Kochavi, A. Mazar): it is clear that there are still assumptions being made which need to be more fully articulated within so complex an area. III. Stratigraphy, Chronology, Terminology (S. Gitin, R. Amiran, W. G. Dever, M. Dothan, D. Ussishkin), offers different aspects of the chronological and terminological problems. Among the respondents, the comments of R. Moorey are particularly helpful. IV. Israel's Neighbours, looks at the Philistines (T. Dothan); Phoenicians (J. D. Muhly); Egypt and Israel (D. B. Redford)—some valuable comments; Ammon, Moab, and Edom (J. A. Sauer) — unfortunately omitting his full bibliography. V. Cuneiform archives, offers reflections on the Mari material (A. Malamat); Ugarit (H. Cazelles); Amarna (D. O. Edzard); Assyriology (H. Tadmor). VI. Hebrew and Aramaic Epigraphy, has Writing in Israel (A. R. Millard, with a useful response by A. Demsky); Balaam at Deir ʿAlla (A. Lemaire; B. Levine more on the historical context; and a very full response by E. Puech) — the problem of the language remains; Aramaic-Akkadian archives from Gozan-Harran (E. Lipiński) — mainly business documents. VII. Dead Sea Scrolls, covers purity and exclusion (L. H. Schiffman); Halakhic material (J. M. Baumgarten; E. Qimron with J. Strugnell); relationships to New Testament themes (H. Stegemann; D. Flusser). VIII. Biblical Jerusalem (P. J. King, A. D. Tushingham, Y. Shiloh, B. Mazar, N. Avigad), covers both the history of excavation and discussion of recent work. A special session was devoted to Sumerian studies (T. Jacobsen on 'the Temple'; S. N. Kramer on 'mythology'). The closing session had C. H. Gordon surveying Ugaritic Research, and E. E. Urbach in some broader reflections on the study of the past. There is much here beyond the main papers, in responses which are often papers in their own right—only a few have been mentioned—and in the reported discussions. Apart from a list of abbreviations, there is no indexing; in a volume of this kind, this is a serious deficiency.

P. R. Ackroyd

Blaiklock, E. M., and Harrison, R. K. (eds.): *The New International Dictionary of Biblical Archaeology*. 1983. Pp. xxx, 485, including numerous figures, with 28 colour photographs and 23 maps. (Regency Reference Library, from Zondervan, Grand Rapids, Michigan. Price:. $24.95. ISBN 0 310 21250 2)

The word 'international' in the title of a study of the Bible has now become an assurance of a stance acceptable to conservatives, and so it is here. The main thrust of this work is to illustrate how 'archaeology has demonstrated the historical and geographical reliability of the Bible'. There are twenty contributors, with the two editors much the most prolific. Articles for the most part refer to sites, but there is generous treatment of the kind of *realia* that would normally be discussed in a Bible dictionary. The illustrations are clear, and the cross-referencing system helpful, the maps on the whole somewhat less so. The quality of individual articles varies enormously. Some, though they might be thought too technical for a volume of this kind, will deserve the attention of all scholars concerned with the subject under discussion, particularly for their full and detailed bibliographies. In particular a number of studies by E. Yamauchi on very varied topics (e.g. Cyrus, Kassites, cultic prostitution, Solomon, Susa, Urartu) give especially full coverage. Elsewhere the treatment is usually much briefer, and often much more tendentious (cities of the plain) or oddly dismissive (Dead Sea Scrolls, Nag Hammadi). In short, something of a curate's egg: parts are to be warmly recommended, others are frankly disappointing.

R. J. COGGINS

BROWNRIGG, R.: *Come, see the place: A Pilgrim Guide to the Holy Land*. 1985. Pp. xiv, 269, including figures and maps. (Hodder & Stoughton, London. Price: £2.95. ISBN 0 340 37164 1)

This is a handbook for the Christian visitor to Palestine who wishes to be reasonably informed about what may be seen, and guided in an approach which will inform and enlarge religious understanding. If, inevitably, many questions are simplified, there is no lack of good information. Very properly, the reader is given some sketch of post-biblical history, though this could usefully have been extended to give rather more about the period from the Crusades to the present day. Judaism and Islam are given some space, though the concentration is on Christian aspects. It does not, of course, have the detail of the new four-volume guide by O. Keel and others (*B.L.* 1984, p. 38; 1985, p. 37); nor does it go as deeply as the short guide by J. M. Miller (*B.L.* 1984, p. 33). But it is much better than many of the popular works which skate over the difficulties or show no awareness of them.

P. R. ACKROYD

BUCHANAN, B.: *Catalogue of Ancient Near Eastern Seals in the Ashmolean Museum*. Vol. II: *The Prehistoric Stamp Seals*. Edited by P. R. S. Moorey. 1984. Pp. xx, 43; 16 plates. (Oxford University Press. Price: £20.00. ISBN 0 19 813403 7)

Unlike cylinder seals, stamp seals from the ancient Near East have been little studied. The author, who published the cylinders of the Ashmolean collection, died before he could complete the volume on stamp seals, and P. R. S. Moorey has undertaken to complete and publish at least some of the material. This part, dealing only with the prehistoric, reflects the best current knowledge on the subject, but is the least pertinent for Old Testament scholars. The majority, showing only patterns of lines or animals, are not easily interpreted to throw light on the civilizations which produced them. The next volume scheduled for publication is to deal with the first millennium stamp seals, and this will have much greater relevance to the Old Testament.

W. G. LAMBERT

GIVEON, R.: *Egyptian Scarabs from Western Asia from the Collections of the British Museum* (Orbis Biblicus et Orientalis, Series Archaeologica, 3). 1985. Pp. 202, including 457 figures. (Universitätsverlag, Freiburg. Price: Sw.Fr. 64.00. ISBN 3 7278 0332 0. Vandenhoeck & Ruprecht, Göttingen. ISBN 3 525 53653 4)

The scarabs published in this book belong to the Western Asiatic Department in the British Museum (as distinct from the Egyptian Department) because they all derive from the Near East, often from specific sites and excavations, and were not found in Egypt. In his introduction Giveon sketches the nature, roles, and history of scarabs: an Egyptian amulet based on the dung-beetle (emblem of life's renewal). Such trinkets served as amulets, sometimes as seals (when, as often, they were inscribed or decorated on their flat bases). Ranging from the early Middle Kingdom (*ca.* 2100 B.C.) to the Late Period, the majority published here are either of Hyksos date or from the New Kingdom (i.e. from the Canaanite Middle and Late Bronze ages, *ca.* 1700–1100 B.C.).

The Catalogue proper goes by sites, from south to north (T. Fara S., T. Ajjul, Gezer, Byblos, etc., up to Carchemish), then eastward (T. Halaf, Kuyunjik, and Ur), ending with minor find-spots and unlocated. Opposite the description of each piece are drawings of the base, side, and top, and a photograph of the base (or of a cast of it). Bibliography and indexes complete a neat, easy-to-use reference work. A good number of pieces have been earlier published in excavators' reports; many others are newly published here. Middle-Kingdom statuary found in Canaan (p. 16 and n. 34) may have been brought thither in Hyksos times (cf. Helck, *Ugarit-Forschungen* 8 (1976), 101–15). The reading of most pieces is reliable. However, No. 21 (p. 28) is probably Usimare (Ramesses II) beloved of Ptah and Thoth, not Sethos II; Nos. 40, 41 (p. 122) are probably not Intef V, but just 'lucky' signs, despite Giveon; and No. 19 (p. 144) is certainly not Padiusir, but Padiese — cf. the envoy to Canaan and Philistia, Padiese, known long since (Steindorff, *Journ. Eg. Archaeol.* 25 (1939), 30 ff.).

K. A. KITCHEN

HADIDI, A. (ed.): *Studies in the History and Archaeology of Jordan*. Volume II. 1985. P. 358; numerous figures, plates, and maps. (Department of Antiquities, Amman, Jordan; Routledge & Kegan Paul, London. Price: £40.00. ISBN 0 7102 0734 4)

The volume presents forty-one papers given at the Second International Conference on the History and Archaeology of Jordan, held in Amman in 1983. It matches the first volume (see below) in style, and includes a brief introduction by Dr Hadidi, reports of speeches, and an index. Its primary theme is 'Jordanian Environment: Geographical and Historical'; its range is wide, but with much that will be of interest to users of the *Book List*.

There are discussions relating to the nature of environmental influence on human life: D. Baly, pp. 19–24, comments usefully to correct simplified views, and in particular 'The desert is monotheistic' (also alluded to by H. Chadwick, pp. 175–77, in a more general discussion of the great religions and the environment). Particular areas — the Jordan valley (W. van Zeist, pp. 199–204, on past and present, and R. North, pp. 205–15, entertainingly on the earlier cartography of the area); the Wadi Araba (T. Raikes, pp. 95–101); the Azraq basin (A. Garrard and others, pp. 109–15, J. B. Nelson, pp. 39–44, and D. D. Gilbertson and others, pp. 347–52); the Hesban region and its food production (L. Geraty and Ø. LaBianca, pp. 323–30) — are investigated from various angles. Valuable analysis of earthquake records and evidence suggests scope for a fuller survey including the period before 31 B.C. (Z. El-Isa, pp. 229–35). The importance of qualified handling of biblical evidence is drawn out by K.-H. Bernhardt, pp. 179–82, and the theme is also touched on by Baly: it is proper to see it stressed that what is said in the Old Testament about the areas east of the Jordan appears in a 'western' Palestinian context. The importance of the recovery of older photographs and the development of good archives for evidence of sites and buildings since altered or lost is shown by C. Gavin (pp. 279–85).

Much of the volume handles very early material, or covers the later periods, particularly Byzantine and Islamic. The articles are in English except for four in French; in two instances, the Arabic text is printed alongside an English text or summary. Another useful and stimulating collection.

(Volume I, reviewed in *B.L.* 1984, p. 31, is also distributed now by Routledge & Kegan Paul. Price: £35.00. ISBN 0 7102 0735 2.)

P. R. ACKROYD

HARRIS, R. L., and SCHONFIELD, J. (eds.): *Bulletin of the Anglo-Israel Archaeological Society: News and Meetings of the Society 1983–84*. 1984. Pp. 49, including some plates and maps. (Anglo-Israel Archaeological Society, London. Subscription: £7.00 per annum for non-members. ISSN 0266 2442)

After an Editorial, accounts of the Biblical Archaeology Congress held in Jerusalem in 1984 (see p. 27), and of the activities of students whom the Society enabled to visit Israel, lectures given to the Society are summarized. Reports of lectures on chalcolithic sties in the Negev (T. Levy) and on a late Roman pottery (F. Vitto) are accompanied by several relevant to Old Testament studies. C. Vita-Finzi spoke of geological changes in historical times, Y. Shiloh of his excavations in the City of David (1981–83), and S. Gibson of agricultural terraces, presses, and other signs of farming activity around Jerusalem in biblical times. R. Giveon presented results of excavations at a site near Megiddo occupied from Chalocolithic to Roman times, probably Geva of Egyptian records. He also gave a lecture on evidence for the Exodus, arguing that the Israelites were a group of the Shasu people, the Shasu appearing on Egyptian monuments circumcised and wearing tasselled kilts. Making such summaries available in advance of fuller publication is useful. R. D. Barnett closes the issue with a brief obituary of Y. Yadin.

A. R. MILLARD

HERRMANN, C.: *Formen für Ägyptische Fayencen: Katalog der Sammlung des Biblischen Instituts der Universität Freiburg Schweiz und einer Privatsammlung* (Orbis Biblicus et Orientalis, 60). 1985. Pp. xxx, 167, including numerous figures; 29 plates. (Universitätsverlag, Freiburg. Price: Sw.Fr. 68.00. ISBN 3 7278 0325 8. Vandenhoeck & Ruprecht, Göttingen. ISBN 3 525 53683 6)

This work publishes nearly fourteen-hundred examples of small baked clay moulds used for producing faience amulets, beads, ring-bezels, and pieces for inlays. Three-quarters of these are in the collection of Freiburg University's Biblical Institute, the remainder being in Herrmann's own collection. It seems likely that most of these pieces come from the Qantir district in the Egyptian East Delta, the site of Pi-Ramesse (Raamses of Exod. 1:11), dating to the nineteenth/twentieth dynasties (thirteenth/twelfth centuries B.C.). Of royal names mentioned, Herrmann cites Ramesses V as the latest. However, the name-form without the element 'Mery-Amun' is the proper nomen of Ramesses X (Amenhirkhopshef III), not of Ramesses V (Amenhirkhopshef I), which would extend the date down two decades to *ca.* 1100 B.C. The subject matter of the moulds includes figures of gods, of wild and domesticated animals, birds, plant life, hieroglyphs, and a few royal names. For clarity, Herrmann made the published drawings from modern impressions ('Positiven') taken from the series of ancient moulds (his 'Model' or 'Form'); both appear in the plates. This is the fullest series to be published; it illustrates the range of small trinkets favoured by Egyptians in the late second millennium B.C. in the general period of the Hebrew sojourn and exodus.

K. A. KITCHEN

HERZOG, Z., with BRANDFON, F. R., and RAINEY, A. F.: *Beer-Sheba II: The Early Iron Age Settlements* (Tel Aviv University, Publications of the Institute of Archaeology, 7). 1984. Pp. xvi, 134, including 42 figures; 16 plates. (Institute of Archaeology, Tel Aviv University, and Ramot Publishing Company, Tel Aviv. Price: $25.00)

Colleagues of the late Yohanan Aharoni continue the publication of the discoveries they made under his direction (see *B.L.* 1976, p. 20), following his concepts very closely. This is especially obvious in Z. Herzog's chapter on the cultural background and A. F. Rainey's on the historical-geography of the Negeb. Both accept Mazar's hypothesis about the patriarchal stories and Aharoni's linking of them with the earliest Iron Age buildings and well at Tel Beer-Sheba, bringing other arguments, sometimes circular, in attempts to support them. Of more lasting value are the detailed reports on stratigraphy and architecture, by Herzog, and on pottery by Brandfon, the latter giving extensive references to parallels and a chart of comparative stratigraphy. Shorter reports deal with faunal remains, flora, flints, one and a half scarabs, and small Iron Age sites up to twenty miles to the west. The fortified town of Stratum V obliterated much of Strata IX–VI, and the exact stratigraphy is crucial (it is never substantiated by drawn sections). Nomads' silos mark the initial stage, then a series of small houses, basically of the four-room type, a gateway in Stratum VII implying an enclosed settlement. The mediocre remains are tantalizing; they reveal a struggling community on the edge of the desert, pasturing flocks of small and large cattle, but not growing grain, if the pollen evidence can be trusted. The discovery of iron tools deserves note (two sickles, a chisel, a hoe, and a knife, none adequately described). This publication is welcome and an encouraging sign that this important site will be adequately documented in due course.

A. R. MILLARD

HOPPE, L. J.: *What Are They Saying about Biblical Archaeology*? 1984. Pp. 107, including some figures. (Paulist Press, Ramsey, New Jersey. Price: $4.95. ISBN 0 8091 2613 3)

This is a lightweight book with the aim of introducing the general reader to what biblical archaeologists are doing and saying. Chapters 1, 2, and 7 deal with theoretical points: the use and abuse of biblical archaeology, what an excavation project entails, and the future of biblical archaeology. Chapters 3 to 6 describe excavation projects at Ebla, Jerusalem, Caparnaum, and Nabratein by way of illustration of problems, methods of excavation and accomplishments. The bibliography is quite good, with useful comment on some of the cited works. The map of major archaeological sites in Syria does not show Mardikh (Ebla), and, apart from the plan of the synagogue at Caparnaum and the pediment stone at Nabratein, the figures could have been omitted without loss to the text.

J. R. DUCKWORTH

KEEL, O., and SCHROER, S.: *Studien zu den Stempelsiegeln aus Palästina/Israel*. Band I (Orbis Biblicus et Orientalis, 67). 1985. Pp. 115, including 97 figures. (Universitätsverlag, Freiburg. Price: Sw.Fr. 29.00. ISBN 3 7278 0336 3. Vandenhoeck & Ruprecht, Göttingen. ISBN 3 525 53690 9)

The author continues his work on art from the Old Testament world with a project to catalogue and study stamp seals from Palestinian excavations. This, the first volume of studies arising from that project, consists of two articles. The first, of thirty-seven pages and by Keel, usefully surveys the various categories of artefacts with depictions from Palestinian excavations and answers some criticisms of previous works of his, in some cases adding new material. Schroer, who is working under Keel, in fifty-seven pages studies Middle Bronze IIB scarabs from Palestine for figures wearing garments with very thick edges and compares them with Syrian depictions of the same on especially cylinder seals and as bronze figurines. This is a useful collection of data, a few being hitherto unpublished, and most are presented in competent drawings. The current opinion that the figure so dressed is a ruler is accepted without serious discussion. The project is questionable in that the objects chosen for study cannot be separated from Syrian art (as is abundantly demonstrated here), so that to be successful this must become a study of Syrian art of the period. If competently achieved, one may hope that light on the Old Testament will be thereby engendered.

W. G. LAMBERT

MAHMOUD, A.: *Neo-Assyrian Sculptures from Šaddikanni* (*Tell Ajaja*) (Assur, 4/2). 1983. Pp. 4; 4 plates. (Undena Publications, Malibu, California. Price: $2.50. ISBN 0 89003 147 9)

This report describes briefly and illustrates a winged human-headed bull and a stone relief of a winged bull before a stylized tree which guarded a gateway built by an Assyrian governor at his seat on the middle Habur late in the ninth century B.C. Continuing excavations at this important site, first investigated by Layard, as Arban, may reveal more about the state of a governor at that time, and about a strategic town in eastern Syria.

A. R. MILLARD

MAZAR, B., and YADIN, Y. (eds.): *Eretz-Israel: Archaeological, Historical, and Geographical Studies*. Vol. 18: *Nahman Avigad Volume*. 1985. Pp. x, 80 (English), xvi, 434 (Hebrew); 88 plates, numerous figures. (Israel Exploration Society with the Institute of Archaeology, the Hebrew University, Jerusalem. Price: $60.00)

Sixty-five scholars honour Avigad, mostly writing in Hebrew. Ten discuss aspects of Jerusalem; among them B. Isaac presents a Greek inscription recording the donation of a pavement, apparently for Herod's Temple, A. Demsky proposes a new reading in the 'trumpeters' inscription, H. Geva and Z. U. Ma'oz discuss the 'First Wall' and the Hasmonean and Herodian town plan. Y. Shiloh's report on fifty-one Hebrew bullae from the 1982 City of David excavations is notable; one seal may have belonged to Gemariah son of Shaphan named in Jer. 36. Thirteen papers headed Epigraphy include first publications of a pre-exilic ostracon from Horvat Uzza in the Negev listing personal and place names (I. Beit-Arieh) and of an early fifth-century B.C. Phoenician ostracon from Akko (M. Dothan). The late Y. Yadin reassessed the Lachish Letters as drafts of messages sent to Jerusalem, and A. Lemaire has presented seven newly found seals. Analysis of seal impressions on jars bearing the *lmlk* stamps has led Y. Garfinkel to posit an administrative hierarchy in Judah. Additionally there are studies of 'The Pronoun *She* in Biblical Hebrew in the Light of Ancient Epigraphy', in which B. A. Levine finds more importance in Phoenician and Punic parallels than in Aramaic influence, of catch-lines in ancient books (M. Haran), of the land as the key to the covenant (H. M. Orlinsky), and of the demotic papyrus containing a poem in Aramaic, which M. Weinfeld argues is the pagan forerunner of Ps. 20:2–6. The most notable epigraphic essay is F. M. Cross's edition of the first papyrus from Wadi Daliyeh, a slave-sale of 335 B.C. Related to this is E. M. Myers's study of the post-exilic seals Avigad edited, and their contribution to our knowledge of officialdom in Persian times. Archaeological topics are varied; of the twenty-seven essays note R. Hachlili and R. Merhav's investigation of the *menorah*, concluding that the form described in Exodus is post-exilic, A. Mazar's account of excavations at Tell Batash (Timnah), and I. Finkelstein's re-interpretation of the Negev 'fortresses' as built by nomads in the process of settlement. These and all the other essays make this an important volume for biblical scholars and archaeologists alike.

A. R. MILLARD

SHILOH, Y.: *Excavations at the City of David.* I: *1978–1982: Interim Report of the First Five Seasons*. (Qedem, Monographs of the Institute of Archaeology, The Hebrew University of Jerusalem, 19). 1984. Pp. xii, 72 (English), including 34 figures, 40 (Hebrew); 41 plates (Israel Exploration Society, Jerusalem. Price: $24.00. ISSN 0333 5844)

The interim report on the first five seasons of Professor Shiloh's excavations on the south-eastern hill of Jerusalem has appeared with commendable promptness. Text and notes in English are given at the front, plans and photographs in the middle, and the original Hebrew version of the same notes and text at the back. First the discoveries made in each area are described separately; then a synthesis indicates the results for each of twenty-one strata dating from the Chalcolithic period to medieval times. The emphasis is chiefly on stratigraphy and there is little detailed information (though there are some photographs) on the pottery and other small finds. Much new light is shed on Jerusalem in the Hellenistic and early Roman periods, but the most interesting features from the biblical period are an enormous stepped stone structure, which Shiloh dates convincingly to the tenth century B.C. and regards as a retaining wall, perhaps for a citadel on the summit of the hill, a cache of fifty-one clay bullae from the early sixth century, one of which is inscribed *lgmryhw* [*b*]*n špn* (cf. Jer. 36:10, etc.), and the clearance of 'Warren's Shaft', which Shiloh perhaps too hastily dates to the Israelite period. This is a clear and informative publication which will help to satisfy other scholars' appetites until the definitive reports begin to appear.

G. I. DAVIES

SMELIK, K. A. D.: *Behouden schrift: historische documenten uit het oude Israël*. 1984. Pp. 175, with 21 figures. (Ten Have, Baarn. Price Fl. 22.50. ISBN 90 259 4180 X)

The seventy or so texts and fragments selected for translation in this elegant paperback date from between 1000 and 500 B.C. and were found in present day Israel and Jordan. After an introductory chapter on writing, the texts, which can only loosely be termed 'historical', are grouped chiefly according to place of origin. First, the Gezer Calendar, the oldest Hebrew inscription. Moabite texts come next, then Hebrew inscriptions from Jerusalem, including the Siloam plaque, followed by texts from Transjordan (Ammonite and Deir ʿAlla inscriptions), from Yavneh-yam, Arad and Lachish. Seals, stamps, and weights are included as are the fragments from Khirbet el-Qom, Kuntillet ʿAjrud, etc. Relevance for the Old Testament is highlighted throughout with the use of lengthy quotations. The illustrations (mainly of the inscriptions), maps, and plans are clear, while the bibliography is up to date and very helpful. (Note: for new readings in Lachish Ostracon 3 see now F. M. Cross in *Biblical and Related Studies Presented to Samuel Iwry*, pp. 41–47 (above, pp. 18–19).)

W. G. E. WATSON

SUDER, R. W.: *Hebrew Inscriptions: A Classified Bibliography*. 1984. Pp. 170, including numerous illustrations. (Associated University Presses, London. Price: £29.50. ISBN 0 941664 01 5)

The laudable concept is 'to collect basic bibliographic resources on the publication, classification, and analysis of each inscription' and arrange them according to the categories developed during the past hundred years. Indeed, the work is claimed to 'represent a comprehensive collection of material from the early nineteenth century until 1982'. After General Works, Hebrew inscriptions are treated by provenance; seals have their own section (3) and are listed by site or, where that is unknown, by owners' names. Ammonite and Moabite texts are treated similarly, and section 7 covers the alphabet's origins. Any bibliography attains some value by its collection and ordering of references. Sadly, the value of this one is reduced by its arrangement, inconsistencies, and omissions. Much more useful would be a listing of *all* seals by their owners' names, for example. Inscriptions found in Jerusalem by K. M. Kenyon and published by J. Prignaud in *Revue Biblique* 77 and the Kenyon Volume are omitted, as are the ostracon from Tell Masos (given in Lemaire's *Inscriptions Hebräiques*. I: *Les Ostraca*, known to Suder) and the important statue from Amman that has often been reproduced. A far more detailed and accurate work of this sort would be of real help to the study of Hebrew; this, regrettably, gives little aid.

A. R. MILLARD

WENKE, R. J., and others: *Archaeological Investigations at El-Hibeh 1980: Preliminary Report* (American Research Center in Egypt, Reports, 9). 1984. Pp. xii, 141; 25 figures, 12 plates. (Undena Publications, Malibu, California. ISBN 0 89003 155 X. Paperback edition: ISBN 0 89003 154 1)

This is a preliminary report of five weeks spent on the ancient site at El-Hibeh in northern Middle Egypt, mapping its topography, collecting surface pottery, etc., re-examining the temple site, and digging two test sequences to obtain a stratigraphic time-sequence. This report has been issued in the absence of opportunity to continue fieldwork. While the full range of occupation runs from *ca*. 1070 B.C. (twenty-first dynasty) to Byzantine times, no clear, detailed correlation of successive historical epochs with the stratigraphy obtained is given. The temple has long been near totally destroyed, and no results are given of work on it; it was built by Shishak, who vanquished Rehoboam. Of greater value are the sections on faunal and plant remains and textiles; the initial and final 'theoretical' studies seem out of place in this valiant attempt to maximize results from very limited data. Most plates are clear except for some items reduced to black blots on pls. III–VI; the inscribed brick in pl. XB is upside down.

K. A. KITCHEN

WRIGHT, G. R. H.: *Ancient Building in South Syria and Palestine* (Handbuch der Orientalistik, VII, 1, ii: B, Lfg. 3, 1 and 2. Vol. 1: *Text*; Vol. 2: *Illustrations*. 1985. Pp. xxiv, 539; xvi, 367 illustrations. (Brill, Leiden. Price: Fl. 420.00; sub. price: Fl. 380.00. ISBN 90 04 07091 5 and 90 04 07170 9)

The publication of this handbook is a major landmark in the study of the archaeology of the Levant, for it is the first comprehensive treatment of its subject to appear. There are chapters on the geographical and historical background, the broad outlines of the history of building as illustrated by excavations, and foreign connections; but the heart of the book and its most valuable feature is a chaper entitled 'Elements of Building', which occupies over three-hundred and fifty pages. Here are collected together examples of different types of building and building technique from a multitude of excavation reports, so that it is possible (with the help of the full commentary and the equally rich volume of plans) to see quickly what is now known (or thought — Wright is careful to point out uncertainties or disagreements) about almost any aspect of the architecture of Palestine from the Mesolithic period to the end of Persian rule. Any book of this kind is bound soon, in a certain sense, to become out of date because of the continuing process of discovery, but sufficient material is now available for this volume to remain an invaluable work of reference and point of departure for archaeologists, biblical scholars, and their students for many years to come.

G. I. Davies

3. HISTORY AND GEOGRAPHY

Aḥituv, S.: *Canaanite Toponyms in Ancient Egyptian Documents*. 1984. Pp. xx, 214; 12 plates, 13 text-figures, 5 maps. (Magnes Press, Jerusalem; Brill, Leiden. Price: $28.00. ISBN 965 223 565 4)

This convenient, compact book falls into two parts. In the first, Aḥituv lists the principal ancient Egyptian sources that mention place-names in Western Palestine, including data extending into Transjordan, Phoenicia, and Lebanon/Syria. These sources comprise essentially the great topographical lists of such names inscribed as symbols of victory and far-flung dominion by the imperial pharaohs of the New Kingdom, plus Shoshenq I (Shishak), along with the Middle-Kingdom 'execration-texts' of the early second millennium B.C., which also list places and groups in western and eastern Palestine and beyond. Less extensive sources include royal and private inscriptions and some administrative and literary documents. A cross-section of such sources features in the plates and figures. The bibliographical notes in this section are kept brief, but are not always sufficient.

The second, main half of the book is a gazetteer of such Levantine place-names (in European alphabetic order) from these Egyptian sources. In each case there is given the hieroglyphic spelling (in very poor hieroglyphs), Hebrew form, and source-reference, followed wherever possible by a succinct discussion or note on the possible identification(s), geographical and linguistic, of each toponym, with some notes to previous discussions. Aḥituv has many new suggestions that differ from his predecessors in this very tricky field. Some may well prove convincing; in other cases less so; and his refusal (p. 189) to accept the perfectly good example of Dibon in Moab is perverse, because the archaeological data are defective, but the philology and 'context' impeccable. The maps at the end include many locations mentioned in the book and are pleasingly clear — but the hints at relief are too scrappy to have any value. The main drawback to this kind of book is that a real study of these names still requires one to go back to the sources themselves, to study context, etc. An Egyptian index of the Egyptian toponyms (in transliteration) should have been included.

K. A. Kitchen

ALON, G.: *The Jews in their Land in the Talmudic Age (70–640 C.E.)*. Translated and edited by G. Levi. Vol. 2. 1984. Pp. xviii, 323–801. (Magnes Press, Jerusalem. Price: $30.00. ISBN 965 223 468 0)

This volume completes the English translation of Alon's *Toledot*. Alon was arguably one of the greatest of modern Jewish historians of antiquity. He was noted for his erudition and his independent judgement. The general reader will find here much material, particularly on the Amoraic period, not readily available elsewhere. For an assessment of Alon and his work see the review of volume 1 in *B.L.* 1981, p. 35.

P. S. ALEXANDER

BALCER, J. M.: *Sparda by the Bitter Sea: Imperial Interaction in Western Anatolia* (Brown Judaic Studies, 52). 1984. Pp. xviii, 597, including 23 figures, 5 maps, and 2 plates. (Scholars Press, Chico, California. Price: $39.95 (discount price: $29.95); ISBN 0 89130 657 9. Paperback price: $29.95 (discount price: $19.95); ISBN 0 89130 818 0)

Sparda or Sfarda (Sardis) was the name given by the Persians to the satrapy formed out of the conquered kingdom of Lydia. This monograph presents a careful study of the political, social, and economic history of the territory under the Lydians from 700 B.C. and then under the Persians from 547 to 447 B.C., the last date being that of the Peace of Callias. While this history has conventionally been studied from the Greek viewpoint, here an Asian viewpoint is adopted. There are indirect references to Jews in the Persian Empire (none, however, to the exiles of Sepharad mentioned in Obad. 20). It is accepted that a Judaean faction plotted to place Zerubbabel on his ancestral throne about 520 B.C.; this is perceived as fitting into a pattern of similar provincial revolts at the beginning of the reign of Darius I. The account of Darius's rise to power is particularly convincing. So valuable a contribution to our understanding of a century of Persian rule in Western Asia supplies a context for Jewish history during that period.

F. F. BRUCE

CATE, R. L.: *These Sought a Country: A History of Israel in Old Testament Times*. 1985. Pp. 413. (Broadman Press, Nashville, Tennessee. Price: $9.95. ISBN 0 8054 1232 8)

This is a clearly structured outline history of Israel from Abraham to Alexander, written from an avowedly Christian standpoint; it seems to be addressed mainly to a conservative readership, so that what to a critical viewpoint occasionally appears as special pleading may be a way of indicating to the un- (or anti-)critical that history cannot simply be read off the pages of the Bible. An introductory chapter discusses the issues raised in studying Israel's history, and a conclusion spells out some of the messages learnt. In between come seven identically structured sections, each outlining the sources of our knowledge of the period, the main problems to be considered, and the international background; then the relevant historical outline is sketched, and some conclusions drawn as to the lasting significance of the period being discussed. This could be a useful first serious introduction to the study of the history of ancient Israel.

R. J. COGGINS

DEXINGER, F., OESCH, J. M., and SAUER, G. (eds.): *Jordanien: Auf den Spuren alter Kulturen*. 1985. Pp. 191, including 110 illustrations in colour and 1 map. (Tyrolia-Verlag, Innsbruck. Price: Sch. 480.00. ISBN 3 7022 1565 4)

A beautifully produced and illustrated book which its editors direct to those who do not sufficiently appreciate the many archaeological, historical, and artistic treasures of the Hashemite kingdom. It is thus in some measure a guidebook: one for reading before or after a visit. It has popular appeal, but it also provides in the sections of text written by its twenty-one contributors (two from Jordan, the rest from Austria), clear accounts of the main areas and places, concentrating on the trans-Jordanian part of the kingdom. It covers all periods from the pre-historic to the Islamic and mediaeval, with some look at the contemporary scene. Its particular merit is that it provides comments on many matters of concern to the biblical scholar from a non-biblical viewpoint, making judicious use of the biblical text, but with an independent slant which enriches the understanding. Guidance on further reading is offered both at the end of each section and in a list at the end of the book. A chronological table, map and index are included.

P. R. ACKROYD

FRIEDMAN, E.: *El-Muhraqa: Here Elijah Raised his Altar*. Edited by F. Foresti. 1985. Pp. 48, including 2 illustrations. (Distributed by Edizioni de Teresianum, Rome. Price: Lire 3,000.)

The author's main purpose is to defend the authenticity of the tradition which identifies *el-muhraqa*, at the south-eastern extremity of Mount Carmel, with the scene of Elijah's contest with the prophets of Baal (cf. *Ephemerides Carmeliticae* 22 (1971)). Brief notes on the site's geographical surroundings and the modern Carmelite presence there are also included.

G. I. DAVIES

GALBIATI, E. R., and ALETTI, A.: *Atlante storico della Bibbia e dell'Antico Oriente: Dalla preistoria alla caduta di Gerusalemme nell'anno 70 d.C.* (Enciclopedie per Tutti, 7.) 1983. Pp. 256, including 73 map pages and one chart in colour. (Editrice Massimo, Milan. Price: Lire 80,000. ISBN 88 7030 711 5)

Introductory material covers (a) biblical books, languages, and problems of transliteration of names (pp. 7–10); (b) history (pp. 11–23), distinguishing what can and cannot be shown in an atlas (Gen. 1–11, Tobit, Judith, and Esther are excluded); problems in the remainder of the material, including non-biblical texts only for the monarchical period; and a discussion of 'salvation history'; (c) a description of the physical geography, with map and sectional chart (pp. 24–26); (d) archaeology, summarizing periods and the development of the discipline, and including a list of major sites, with some of them and some major near eastern sites briefly discussed (pp. 27–40). Numerous indexes conclude the volume. So far, so good.

The main part (pp. 41–224) consists of the maps (many divided up), each introduced with some statement of what they represent, with biblical references and comment on religious significance. Most of this is very traditional. As in some other such atlases, detailed movements of individuals, groups and armies are drawn with coloured lines and arrows. Esther being excluded, it is odd to find the journeys of Elimelech, Naomi, and Ruth mapped, as well as those of Lot, Abraham, and the angels. (Did the angels go only by road?) The result is an often misleading impression of geographical and historical knowledge, matched by what appears to be a virtual ignoring of the problems of identification — map 57/2 allows two identifications of Emmaus. This is evidently an atlas intended for general use, in a popular series, it can hardly be taken as a serious study of the problems of biblical geography and history. Perhaps we may hope it will *not* be translated.

P. R. ACKROYD

GERSCHEVITCH, I. (ed.): *The Cambridge History of Iran*. Vol. 2: *The Median and Achaemenian Periods*. 1985. Pp. xviii, 946, with 48 plates, some figures and maps. (Cambridge University Press. Price: £55.00. ISBN 0 521 20091 1)

The opening chapters of this volume deal with background: Elam and Media (I. M. Diakonoff), Anshan (J. Hansman), the Scyths (T. Sulimirski), all providing comprehensive reviews indicating the many problems of interpretation of the limited evidence. Users of the *Book List* will welcome those chapters which deal more directly with areas impinging on Old Testament studies: J. M. Cook on the rise of the Achaemenids, now overtaken by his 1983 volume *The Persian Empire* (not noted in the *Book List*); Max Mallowan on Cyrus the Great, rather idealistic; the religion of the period by M. Schwartz (compare Mary Boyce in *CHJ* 1: see *B.L.* 1985, p. 34); Aramaic by J. C. Greenfield (overlapping a related chapter in *CHJ* 1). Wider background is provided for Jewish life in Babylonia (A. L. Oppenheim) and in Egypt (E. Bresciani). The remaining chapters move further from the Old Testament, but it is nonetheless important to recognize both the background they provide and the many indications that historical problems exist for other parts of the empire similar to those for Palestine. The Greek aspect appears in a chapter on Persia and the Greeks (A. R. Burn) and one on Alexander (E. Badian); the Behistun relief (Ann Farkas), Persepolis (R. T. Hallock), Pasargadae (D. Stronach), and others dealing with further aspects of archaeology, numismatics and chronology make up an impressive volume which shows signs — not least in the number of contributors now deceased — of having been a long time in production.

P. R. ACKROYD

JAGERSMA, H.: *A History of Israel from Alexander the Great to Bar Kochba*. Translated by J. Bowden. 1985. Pp. xiv, 224, including 4 maps. (SCM Press, London. Price: £9.50. ISBN 0 334 02049 2)

This is a translation of *Geschiedenis van Israël van Alexander de Grote tot Bar Kochba*, published in 1985 by J. H. Kok of Kampen (Price: Fl. 39.90; ISBN 90 242 2816 6). It forms a continuation of the author's earlier *Geschiedenis van Israël in het Oudtestamentische Tijdvak*; see *B.L.* 1981, p. 39; 1983, p. 35 (the English translation). It is marked by the same characteristics as its predecessor: a concise style; a proper recognition of the limits of our knowledge and of the many uncertainties involved in attempting to reconstruct the history of the period; abundant references in the endnotes both to ancient sources and to modern secondary literature. There is no separate bibliography, but the volume includes chronological tables, indexes, and four maps (the one of the Roman empire being of very limited use). On the whole the account is reliable, and this volume could form a useful textbook for students. But there are some weak sections, e.g. those on 'apocalyptic' and on 'the Hasidaeans', and there are some surprising statements. Thus, e.g., it is surprising to read (p. 59): 'According to II Macc. 14.6 Alcimus joined forces with the Maccabees'; or to see 'CD' explained as meaning 'Covenant of Damascus' (p. 78); or to find Pilate (and his predecessors) still referred to as 'procurator' (p. 117). Further, the translation contains oddities and mistakes, e.g. on p. 11: 'In 331 B.C. Darius was killed at Gaugamela, which lay in the plain of Arbela east of the Tigris. The following year Darius was killed by one of his satraps.' In its English form at least this work cannot be recommended without considerable reservation.

M. A. KNIBB

KASHER, A.: *The Jews in Hellenistic and Roman Egypt: The Struggle for Equal Rights* (Texte und Studien zum antiken Judentum, 7). 1985. Pp. xviii, 424. (Mohr, Tübingen. Price: DM. 148.00. ISBN 3 16 144829 4)

This long and learned volume is really two books rolled into one; and it is the parts designed as subordinate which are often the more interesting and are likely to be the more widely used. The one element, originating in a Hebrew thesis, is a complex new solution to the thorny problems about Jewish claims to citizenship in Greek cities (down to Trajan). Kasher argues that when the Alexandrian Jews (or those of Cyrene, Antioch, or Caesarea Maritima) sought *politeia*, they always meant rights in and for their own quasi-autonomous civic entity rather than participation through equal citizenship of the wider community. There are parallels in the treatment of other ethnic, non-Greek groups. This is a line to which both E. M. Smallwood in her history of the Jews under Roman rule and S. Applebaum in his chapters in *Compendia Rerum Iudaicarum ad Novum Testamentum* have tended, but to pursue it to Kasher's extremes requires special pleading, which is indeed not absent here. His fervour has at the same time led him to study in an exhaustive and most illuminating way the evidence for important background issues. Thus there is a remarkable chapter on Jewish life in the Egyptian *chora* (with sensible maps) and a very valuable section on Jews as Roman citizens (including freedmen). It may not always be easy for the reader concerned with some of the more general matters to find his way amidst the dense discussion to all that concerns him. The summary of conclusions is clear but brief. The volume's fine appearance makes it pleasant to use, in spite of the uncertain quality of the translation's English idiom and of the proof-reading.

T. RAJAK

KAUFMANN, Y.: *The Biblical Account of the Conquest of Canaan*. Translated by M. Dagut. With a preface to the reissue by M. Greenberg. 1985 (1953). Pp. 147, including 7 maps. (Magnes Press, Jerusalem. Price: $15.00. ISBN 965 223 556 3)

The Hebrew version of this book was not noted in the *Book List*; the English, with a title different from that of the current reissue, has already been reviewed (*B.L.* 1954, p. 23 (*Eleven Years*, p. 560); *B.L.* 1958, pp. 27–28 (*Decade*, pp. 103–04)). Moshe Greenberg's new preface supplies some interesting background to Kaufmann's involvement with the books of Joshua and Judges, and is not uncritical of the author's use of Joshua as a reliable historical account of the conquest and settlement. However, in his endorsement of Bright's judgement that the book is 'a healthy corrective and a refreshing contrast to overmuch nihilism', Greenberg is too generous with a work which, while understandably innocent of more recent sociological study, is less acceptably devoid of reference to the archaeological data and dismissive of the traditio-historical approaches of Alt and Noth.

A. D. H. MAYES

KNAUF, E. A.: *Ismael: Untersuchungen zur Geschichte Palästinas und Nordarabiens im 1. Jahrtausend v. Chr.* (Abhandlungen des Deutschen Palästinavereins). 1985. Pp. x, 133, including 1 map. (Otto Harrassowitz, Wiesbaden. Price: DM. 52.00. ISBN 3 447 02348 1)

This thesis starts from the unproven equation Ismael = Šumu'il, an Arabian location mentioned in seventh-century B.C. Assyrian texts. A history is reconstructed from sparse and fragmentary sources, the Old Testament,

Assyrian royal inscriptions, North Arabian epigraphy, and later historical references which seem to fit in with presumed P or later P^g (538–522 B.C.) sources of Gen. 16; 21:8–21 and with 1 Chron. 5:18–22, the subject of detailed and heavily documented study. It is argued that the Ishmaelites were not south Palestinian nomads who worshipped a god El roi at a cult-centre Lahai Roi but were a proto-beduin confederation centred on Duma. Hagar is equated (doubtfully) with an Arabian oasis Agarum, and Nebaiot(*nbyt*) shown to be neither historically nor philologically confirmed as the Nabataeans. The latter is the standpoint already in Ephʿal's history of the Arabs in the ninth–fifth centuries (see *B.L.* 1983, p. 34).

D. J. Wiseman

Matthiae, K., and Thiel, W.: *Biblische Zeittafeln: Geschichtliche Abrisse, chronologische Übersichten, Überblickstafeln und Landkarten zur alt- und neutestamentlichen Zeit*. 1985. Einführungsheft, pp. 87; 6 chronologische Übersichten, 20 Überblickstafeln, 10 Landkarten. (Neukirchener Verlag, Neukirchen-Vluyn. Price: DM. 34.00. ISBN 3 7887 0795 X)

The chronological synopses and the maps of this composite work summarize the political history and geography of Israel and the surrounding ancient Near East from the mid-second millennium B.C. to A.D. 150. The *chronologische Übersichten* present side by side in clearly contrasting colours the dynastic histories of Egypt, Palestine, Syria, Mesopotamia, Greece, and Macedonia, and Rome (the chronology mainly follows Jepsen, *Von Sinuhe bis Nebukadnezar*, Berlin, 1979). Accompanying these are twenty annotated charts and genealogies presenting, e.g., 'Der Stammbaum Sauls', 'Der Beamtenstab Davids und Salomos', 'Die Hohenpriester in der persischen und ptolemäischen Zeit'. These charts are potentially the most useful part of the work, providing the starting point for seminars (e.g., on the Solomonic administration, or the post-exilic high-priestly succession). The *Einführungsheft* gives a potted history of Israel and Judah, their several imperial masters, and the Parthians and Nabataeans. The whole is presented with maximum clarity and minimum fuss.

J. R. Bartlett

May, H. G., Hunt, G. N. S., and Hamilton, R. W.: *Oxford Bible Atlas*. 3rd edition, revised by J. Day. 1985 (1984). Pp. 144, with 92 illustrations and 25 maps. (Oxford University Press. Price: £8.50; ISBN 0 19 143452 3. Paperback price: £4.95; ISBN 0 19 143451 5)

This new edition of the *Oxford Bible Atlas* was originally published in 1984 and was reviewed in *B.L.* 1985, p. 40. The need for a reprint within only a year is an indication of its value and usefulness.

M. A. Knibb

Niemann, H. M.: *Die Daniten: Studien zur Geschichte eines altisraelitischen Stammes* (Forschungen zur Religion und Literatur des Alten und Neuen Testaments, 135). 1985. Pp. 348. (Vandenhoeck & Ruprecht, Göttingen. Price: DM. 84.00. ISBN 3 525 53808 1)

The general history of the tribe of Dan may be fairly familiar. The particular merit of this book is that it fills out that history in all possible detail with a meticulous study of both the available Danite traditions and the results of archaeological investigation of Tel Dan. Taking those traditions in an order which establishes itself as a reflection of the chronological order of major events in the life of the tribe, the author treats first Judg. 1:34–35, followed by

Judg. 5:17; 17–18; 13–16; and the tribal sayings of Gen. 49 and Deut. 33. From this the following reconstruction emerges: the Danites, an independent group possibly deriving from the southern part of east Jordan, attempted to infiltrate the plain of Aijalon but were pushed back into the mountain territory. A major part of them migrated to the north, where they are presupposed at the time of Deborah's battle against Sisera, to be dated between 1160 and 1130 B.C. The Samson traditions derive from a time later than Judg. 1:34–35 and the migration of Judg. 17–18, since they presuppose a Danite family living in the area which the Danites had previously been unable to penetrate (Judg. 13:25). Such Danite remnants were, however, in time absorbed by neighbouring Israelite tribes and the main history of the tribe was followed through in the north, where the city which they captured became a significant religious centre and border fortification in the monarchic period. This illuminating and thorough study successfully integrates traditio-historical and archaeological study into a comprehensive synthesis which makes a considerable contribution to our understanding of early Israelite history. A. D. H. MAYES

PACOMIO, L., and VANETTI, P.: *Piccolo Atlante Biblico: Storia, geografia, archaeologia della Bibbia*. 1985. Pp. 64, with numerous maps, illustrations, diagrams, and an index to the maps on the end papers. (Edizione Piemme, Casale Monferrato. Price: Lire 15,000)

A book of coloured pictures, maps, and chronological charts, with introductory discussions to various periods up to A.D. 135, and some comments on the problems of the biblical text. It offers a simplified presentation, which shows little awareness of the major historical and geographical problems: there is, for example, no discussion of identification, and the period of the exile is shown as a blank between the monarchy and the restoration. It appears to be expensive at the price. P. R. ACKROYD

ROGERSON, J.: *The New Atlas of the Bible*. 1985. Pp. 237, including numerous illustrations and maps. (Macdonald, London: Price: £14.95. ISBN 0 356 10706 X)

This atlas aims 'to illumine the geographical setting of the biblical narratives' (a precise phrase). Part I briefly describes the biblical literature; Part II gives a traditional 'Outline of Biblical History' from Abraham to Paul, with a short, colourful appendix 'The Bible in Art'. Rogerson reaches his theme with Part III, 'The Bible and Geography', where he retells the biblical narratives in the light of his topographical analysis of eleven major regions of ancient Israel. This is a revamped George Adam Smith, with superb illustrations and without the scholarly detail, based on Rogerson's own experience of walking the land with his students. Some details should be noted: p. 29, Anim lacks its location; p. 37, Gerasa appears twice, once in Samaria; p. 114 places Ezion-Geber at T. el-Kheleifeh, but the photograph on p. 124 is puzzling; p. 138, Capernaum is wrongly located (cf. p. 129); p. 146, the Ataroth of Num. 32 is not in Samaria; p. 181 names the Nicanor or Beautiful Gate, but compare the plan on p. 182; p. 192, for Aeon read Aenon; p. 197, the plan of T. es-Sultan shows only the MB glacis retaining walls, not the MB walls; pp. 202–03, Teman is a region, not a city. One serious limitation is the unnecessarily miniscule print used on the maps. However, this atlas will certainly stimulate its readers to some understanding of Rogerson's conclusion, 'In the Bible, geography shades into theology'. (German, French, and Dutch editions of this atlas are also available, viz. *Land der Bibel* (Christian

Verlag, Munich. ISBN 3 88472 106 2); *Nouvelle Atlas de la Bible* (Brepols, Turnhout. ISBN 2 503 52010 3); *Atlas van de Bijbel* (Elsevier, Amsterdam and Brussels. ISBN 90 10 05554 X).)

J. R. BARTLETT

THIEL, W.: *Die soziale Entwicklung Israels in vorstaatlicher Zeit*. 2., durchgesehene und ergänzte Auflage. 1985. Pp. 192. (Neukirchener Verlag, Neukirchen-Vluyn. Price: DM. 32.00. ISBN 3 7887 1221 X)

The first edition of this thorough study was published in 1980 and reviewed in *B.L.* 1982, pp. 32–33. In this second edition the text has been reproduced unchanged, but Thiel has added a nine-page bibliographical supplement, mostly of recent publications, and a one-page list of corrigenda.

M. A. KNIBB

4. TEXT AND VERSIONS

AUFRECHT, W. E.: *A Bibliography of the Deir ʿAlla Plaster Texts* (Newsletter for Targumic and Cognate Studies, Supplement 2). 1985. Pp. 7. (Department of Near Eastern Studies, University of Toronto. Price: $2.00. ISSN 0704 59005)

Over forty items dealing with the Deir ʿAlla material, or which are considered to be relevant in a more general way, are listed.

R. P. GORDON

BUSTO SAIZ, J. R.: *La Traducción de Simaco en el Libro de los Salmos* (Textos y Estudios 'Cardenal Cisneros', 22). 1985. Pp. xxvi, 756. (Instituto 'Arias Montano', Consejo Superior de Investigaciones Científicas, Madrid. Price: Ptas. 3,500. ISBN 84 00 04334 0)

This is an unchanged reprint of a doctoral dissertation published originally in 1978. It contains three parts, of which the first (running to some three hundred and fifty pages) contains a minutely detailed study of the translation technique of the fragments of Symmachus for the Psalter; the fragments themselves are re-edited in the second part, while the third provides Greek-Hebrew and Hebrew-Greek indexes for this material.

S. P. BROCK

CIMOSA, M.: *Il vocabulario di preghiera nel Pentateuco greca dei LXX* (Quaderni di Salesianum, 10). 1985. Pp. 86. (Libreria Ateneo Salesiano, Rome. Price: Lire 10,000. ISBN 88 213 0117 6)

The four main chapters of this study are devoted to: *euchesthai* and compounds, *deisthai, proskunein*, and other verbs used in the context of prayer. Relevant passages are discussed individually, and both the Greek and the Hebrew terms are also considered in their wider context.

S. P. BROCK

CLARKE, E. G.: *Targum Pseudo-Jonathan of the Pentateuch: Text and Concordance*. 1984. Pp. xx (English), 701 (Aramaic). (Ktav, Hoboken, New Jersey. Price: $150.00. ISBN 0 88125 015 5)

The British Museum manuscript Add.27031 containing the Pseudo-Jonathan Targum was published by M. Ginsburger in 1903 and by D. Rieder in 1972. The edition under review is not just another edition and is not an end in itself. Its *raison d'être* lies in the fact that the Concordance, which forms a substantial part of the work, could not have been compiled without first producing a text in machine-readable form. For the preparation of the text every effort has been made to present a faithful copy of the manuscript and to correct it where necessary. The full text of the manuscript is given, with chapter and verse numbers inserted for easy location. The lemmata have been omitted, and an apparatus (which would largely record orthographic variants) has been thought unnecessary. In the Concordance the number of lexical entries has been reduced by clustering under a single entry the various forms of each lexeme, and care has been taken to prevent the computer from identifying homographs incorrectly. This work is likely to prove an invaluable tool in the hands of scholars who seek to throw new light on the textual history of Pseudo-Jonathan. Of course, a work of this kind could not have been done by one man, and the volume is the result of a team effort. Professor Clarke has been fortunate to have had dedicated assistance and advice from W. E. Aufrecht, J. C. Hurd, and F. Spitzer. An English translation has already been prepared and should appear before long.

P. WERNBERG-MØLLER

CLARKE, E. G. (ed.): *Newsletter for Targumic and Cognate Studies*. 11:2. 1984. Pp. 8. 12:1. 1985. Pp. 13. (Department of Near Eastern Studies, University of Toronto. Sub. price: $5.00 per volume. ISSN 0704 59005)

As in previous numbers, entries are divided between Targumic and Aramaic studies. No. 11:2 is dedicated to the memory of Alejandro Díez Macho. No. 12:1 includes summaries of ten journal articles written in Arabic. The *Newsletter* continues to be a useful source of information for those working in the Targumic and Aramaic fields.

R. P. GORDON

DÍEZ MERINO, L.: *Targum de Job: Edición Príncipe del Ms. Villa-Amil n.5 de Alfonso de Zamora* (Bibliotheca Hispana Biblica, 8). 1984. Pp. 389. *Targum de Proverbios: Edición Príncipe del Ms. Villa-Amil n.5 de Alfonso de Zamora* (Bibliotheca Hispana Biblica, 11). 1984. Pp. 314. (Consejo Superior de Investigaciones Científicas, Madrid. Price: Ptas. 3,000 and 2,000. ISBN 84 00 05742 2 and 84 00 05804 6)

The first work of a series in which the author hopes to publish the *editio princeps* of the whole of the Aramaic version and Latin translation of the Prophets and the Hagiographa prepared by Alfonso de Zamora, and originally meant for the Complutensian Polyglot, appeared in 1982 (*B.L.* 1985, p. 45). The volumes on Job (MS. Villa-Amil no. 5, fols. 19a–50a) and Proverbs (fols. 128b–154b), like the one on Psalms, apart from the Aramaic text and Alfonso's Latin translation, contain a number of important detailed surveys and articles on various targumic topics (history of targumic research in the relevant areas, editions, manuscripts (including, in the case of Job, the Qumran targum), the place of these targums within targumic literatures generally, comparison with the Massoretic text and the ancient versions, translation techniques, linguistic features, haggadic themes, characteristic traits, description of Alfonso's Latin translation and comparison with the Antwerp and London Polyglot). These volumes constitute an important contribution to targumic studies, not only by the publication of the texts and the detailed and critical articles on them, but also by focusing attention on the specifically Spanish tradition of targumic literature.

P. WERNBERG-MØLLER

DUTHIE, A. S.: *Bible Translations and How to Choose between Them*. 1985. Pp. 127. (Paternoster Press, Exeter. Price: £3.50. ISBN 0 85364 400 4)

A series of articles originally written for the magazine *Harvester* has here been gathered into book form. Reference is made (not always in very clear form) to forty-four complete translations of the Bible into English (plus sixty-seven of the New Testament only), and the characteristic problems facing translators are set out, with some sensible comments on the structure of different languages, the issues raised by word-for-word and meaning-for-meaning rendering, the problems involved when particular confessional standpoints obtrude, and so on. Bravely an order of merit is attempted, in which top place for the general reader is shared by the *Good News Bible* and the *New Jerusalem Bible*. The author is a lecturer in linguistics, and, while he is not concerned with original scholarship here, his little book has a quality of informed common sense which would make it useful reading for those concerned with translating the Bible or teaching others to do so.

R. J. COGGINS

FERNÁNDEZ MARCOS, N. (ed.): *La Septuaginta en la Investigación Contemporánea* (*V Congreso de la IOSCS*) (Textos y Estudios 'Cardenal Cisneros', 34). 1985. Pp. 285. (Instituto 'Arias Montano', Consejo Superior de Investigaciones Científicas, Madrid. Price: Ptas. 3,500. ISBN 84 00 05938 7)

This collection of eighteen papers (all in English) is divided into four sections. I, Use of the versions in textual criticism (covers LXX, Peshitta, Armenian, Coptic, and Old Latin); II, Translation technique in the LXX (this includes valuable contributions by I. Soisalon-Soininen, R. Sollamo and A. Aejmelaeus); III, Studies on method, and on particular books; IV, Current projects (opening with a paper by E. Tov on the computer-assisted alignment of Greek-Hebrew equivalents, and closing with a survey, by the editor, on Septuagint research in Spain). Although it was not to be expected that all aspects of current interests in the Septuagint could be covered, this volume nevertheless offers a fairly representative coverage.

S. P. BROCK

FERNÁNDEZ TEJERO, E. (ed.): *Estudios Masoreticos (V Congreso de la IOMS) Dedicados a Harry M. Orlinsky* (Textos y Estudios 'Cardenal Cisneros', 33). 1983. Pp. 250, with 5 photographs. (Consejo Superior de Investigaciones Científicas, Madrid. Price: Ptas. 2,500. ISBN 84 00 05553 5)

This volume contains the papers read at the Fifth Congress of IOMS in 1983, as well as the text of short addresses by E. Fernández Tejero, A. Dotan, H. M. Orlinsky, L. Alonso Schökel and S. Morag. H. M. Orlinsky and M. Weinberg write on a problem in the Masorah at Amos 2:1; E. J. Revell analyses *nesiga* in construct nouns and verb forms of the Masoretic text; J. Gutmann traces the origin and development of Masoretic decoration in Bible manuscripts; A. Dotan describes the omission of gemination conditioned by phonological circumstances in B19a (the Leningrad Codex); E. Fernández Tejero reports on her own and Dr Ortega Monasterio's journey to Cairo to study the Cairo Codex of the Prophets, and their feelings of excitement and sadness about this matter; P. Rivière and M. Serfaty examine the use of the *paseq* in the biblical prose books and present comparative tables showing the considerable variations in manuscripts and printed editions as regards its use; Y. Yannai discusses a problem in the Hebrew text of 2 Kings 4:8–37; S. Morag reconstructs the main phases in the history of the biblical text and vocalization in Yemen in the period of transition from the old tradition to the tiberian; L. Díez Merino presents a detailed account of the rich marginal targumic masorah of MS. Vat. Ebr. 448, which in his opinion contains the best text of the Onkelos Targum; N. Allony (who sadly died in May 1983, the year of the Conference) writes on Ibn Balʿam's (Arabic) preface to the medieval grammatical work *Horayat Hakkore* (Instruction to the Reader), a work on masoretic grammar and accents; and E. Fernández Tejero and M. T. Ortega Monasterio present and compare in detail the masoretic notes to Joel in the Aleppo Codex, the Cairo Codex and B19a, the Leningrad Codex.

P. Wernberg-Møller

Freedman, D. N., and Mathews, K. A., with contributions by Hanson, R. S.: *The Paleo-Hebrew Leviticus Scroll* (*11QpaleoLev*). 1985. Pp. xii, 135, including 19 plates, with 1 folded plate. (American Schools of Oriental Research. Distributed by Eisenbrauns, Winona Lake, Indiana. Price: $19.95. ISBN 0 89757 007 3)

This volume, the official publication of the 11QpaleoLev materials of the Rockefeller collection in Jerusalem, completes the publication of the Qumran Cave 11 material. Apart from a continuous section comprising parts of Lev. 22–27, there are several small fragments including, in an appendix, one in the possession of Georges Roux of France — all reproduced here by high contrast photography which is the work of R. Schlosser, photographer of the Huntington Library. K. A. Mathews's doctoral dissertation on the Leviticus fragments served as a working basis. Chapter 1 deals with the history of the find and describes the material in detail. In chapter 2 R. S. Hanson analyses the script from the palaeographical point of view and dates the scroll to around 100 B.C.E. Chapter 3 contains a transcription of the text in Hebrew square script, with a text-critical apparatus. Chapter 4 (the longest in the book) concentrates on orthography and aims at placing the spellings of 11QpaleoLev within the development of orthographic practices in the last half of the first millennium B.C.E., as reflected in the spelling systems of the Qumran material as a whole; and the conclusion is reached that 11QpaleoLev reflects the orthography chosen by the rabbis for the standardized text of the Pentateuch. The volume concludes with a bibliography.

P. Wernberg-Møller

Grossfeld, B.: *Concordance of the First Targum to the Book of Esther* (Society of Biblical Literature, Aramaic Studies, 5). 1984. Pp. xii, 174. (Scholars Press, Chico, California. Price: $11.25; discount price $7.50. ISBN 0 89130 635 8)

For the text of Paris Hebrew 110 (Bibliothèque Nationale) upon which this computerized concordance is based see *B.L.* 1984, p. 45 (*The First Targum to Esther*). The concordance is divided into four parts: Roots, Proper Names, Particles, and Greek Loan Words. The Introduction contains a description of the computer programme used in the preparation of the concordance.

P. W. Coxon

Miles, J. R.: *Retroversion and Text Criticism: The Predictability of Syntax in an Ancient Translation from Greek to Ethiopic* (Society of Biblical Literature: Septuagint and Cognate Studies Series, 17). 1985. Pp. xii, 212. (Scholars Press, Chico, California. Price: $16.50 (discount price: $10.95); ISBN 0 89130 878 4. Paperback price: $10.95 (discount price: $7.50); ISBN 0 89130 879 2)

This is an original approach to the study of translation technique. Miles is concerned with the process of transferral from Greek syntax to Geʿez syntax. As a control he takes Esther 1–8, and his chapter 1 describes the process of transferral there as exactly as possible; chapter 2 outlines the findings in tabular form. Chapter 3 next tests the findings by seeking to predict, on the basis of the charts in chapter 2, the Geʿez syntax of Esther 9, using the Greek as a starting point. In chapter 4 the reverse test, seeking to predict the Greek syntax, is made for Esther 10. In the final chapter the two approaches, of chapter 3 and chapter 4, are then applied to 3 Ezra 3 and 4 Baruch 1 respectively. The interest of this methodology for anyone who attempts to make retroversions from a daughter translation to a parent text will be obvious. The Ethiopic is given in transcription (following Lambdin's system).

S. P. Brock

Pisano, S.: *Additions or Omissions in the Books of Samuel: The Significant Pluses and Minuses in the Massoretic, LXX and Qumran Texts* (Orbis Biblicus et Orentalis, 57). 1984. Pp. xiv, 295. (Universitätsverlag, Freiburg. Price: Sw.Fr. 78.00. ISBN 3 7278 0315 0. Vandenhoeck & Ruprecht, Göttingen. ISBN 3 525 53679 8)

Attitudes towards the text-critical value of LXX Samuel are liable to dramatic shifts. Pisano submits sixty-nine passages to a detailed analysis, and argues that in the vast majority of cases the reading in MT represents a form of text closer to the original than does either 4QSam[a] or the LXX. While the full discussions are welcome, some readers may find that the conclusions which Pisano draws are not always convincing. Even if Pisano were always right, the editorial changes he identifies in LXX should definitely not be attributed to the translator, but to some stage in the prehistory of the Septuagint's Hebrew *Vorlage*. The prominence given to the Lucianic ('Antiochian') text in passages outside the so-called *kaige* sections seems undue.

S. P. Brock

Roberts, C. H., and Skeat, T. C.: *The Birth of the Codex*. 1985 (1983). Pp. x, 78; 6 plates. (Oxford University Press, for the British Academy, London. Price: £14.00. ISBN 0 19 726024 1)

This is a reprint of a book published in 1983, but not then noticed in the *Book List*. It provides an authoritative study of the transition from roll to codex format in ancient book production: in particular the authors are concerned with the intriguing fact that the nascent Christian community evidently preferred the codex to the roll (then the norm) from a very early date. The book is a greatly expanded and updated form of a masterly article by Roberts in the *Proceedings of the British Academy* 40 (1954), pp. 169–204 (some interesting paragraphs, mainly on fourth-century testimonia to the codex form, have, however, been dropped). The study is now arranged in short chapters. Two hypotheses for the Christian adoption of the codex are tentatively offered (Roberts originally put forward one), and there is a separate chapter on 'the Christian codex and the canon of Scripture'.

S. P. BROCK

Vetus Latina. Die Reste der altlateinischen Bibel, nach Petrus Sabatier neu gesammelt und herausgegeben von der Erzabtei Beuron. 11/1: *Sapientia Salomonis*. Herausgegeben von Walter Thiele. 7. Lieferung: Sap 13, 1–18, 18. 1984. Pp. 481–560. (Verlag Herder. Freiburg im Breisgau. Price: DM. 65.00; sub. price: DM. 57.00. ISBN 3 451 00486 0).

This seventh fascicle brings this very meticulous edition of the Wisdom of Solomon nearer to completion; for previous fascicles see most recently *B.L.* 1984, p. 47. One further fascicle, now in preparation, will be the final stage in a volume of the finest scholarship.

J. BARR

WAHL, O.: *Der Proverbien- und Kohelet-Text der Sacra Parallela* (Forschung zur Bibel, 51). 1985. Pp. 175. (Echter Verlag, Würzburg. Price: DM 39.00. ISBN 3 429 00936 7)

The Sacra Parallela is an important early Byzantine florilegium of biblical and patristic texts, attributed to John of Damascus. The extant manuscripts (one of which has fine illuminations, recently studied by K. Weitzmann) no longer preserve the original form of the florilegium. Wahl here provides the textual evidence for the excerpts from Proverbs and Ecclesiastes, prefaced by a short introduction. The format follows that of his earlier monographs on the florilegium's quotations from the Prophets (1965) and Ben Sira (1974), the former of which was noticed in *B.L.* 1968, p. 20 (*Bible Bibliog.*, p. 74). Those interested in the textual transmission of the LXX will be grateful for this painstaking assembling of materials.

S. P. BROCK

WONNEBERGER, R.: *Leitfaden zur Biblia Hebraica Stuttgartensia*. 1984. Pp. vi, 136. (Vandenhoeck & Ruprecht, Göttingen. Price: DM 14.80. ISBN 3 525 52180 4)

WONNEBERGER, R: *Understanding BHS: A Manual for the Users of Biblia Hebraica Stuttgartensia* (Subsidia Biblica, 8). Translated by D. R. Daniels. 1984. Pp. xii, 100. (Biblical Institute Press, Rome. Price: Lire 11,000. ISBN 88 7653 559 4)

The preparations for these two monographs have gone through various stages, and the English edition is not an exact translation of its German counterpart. Although the two volumes largely overlap as far as contents are concerned, they differ in layout, and the German edition is somewhat longer. Through an analysis of the 'language' of the apparatus in BHS according to modern linguistic procedures (speech-act theory and linguistic structuralism especially) the author seeks to clarify the function of the text-critical expressions used there. His purpose is partly to help the student of the Hebrew Bible use BHS properly, and partly, through the grouping of the *sigla* in a hierarchical system of five main categories according to functions, to expose the weaknesses of the apparatus in BHS (its subjective value judgements, ambiguities, inconsistencies, etc.) and thus to provide a firm foundation for the future development of apparatus 'language' in critical editions of texts in general. However, in spite of its shortcomings, the 'immense value' of BHS is recognized. These monographs are full of shrewd observations and trenchant, constructive criticism. Dr Wonneberger rightly complains about the lack in BHS both of adequate information about the *sigla* used and of over-all planning, and about its inability to reflect truly the more or less accepted state of text-critical research when it was published.

P. WERNBERG-MØLLER

ZIEGLER, J.: *Beiträge zum griechischen Iob* (Mitteilungen des Septuaginta-Unternehmens (MSU), XVIII: Abhandlungen der Akademie der Wissenschaften in Göttingen, Phil.-Hist. Klasse, III, 147). 1985. Pp. 112. (Vandenhoeck & Ruprecht, Göttingen. Price: DM. 68.00. ISBN 3 525 82430 0)

Whereas other recent contributions to this series have dealt primarily with the textual history of the LXX book in question, Ziegler's monograph consists of a collection of detailed studies which concern readings of the 'Three' (well indexed) and various scholia in the LXX manuscripts of Job (the most interesting of which concerns the nature of Job's affliction). Anyone with a special interest in the 'Three', in particular, would do well to consult this monograph. For Ziegler's edition of LXX Job, see *B.L.* 1983, p. 44.

S. P. BROCK

5. EXEGESIS AND MODERN TRANSLATIONS

ALONSO SCHÖKEL, L., and VÍLCHEZ LÍNDEZ, J.: *Sapienciales*. I: *Proverbios* (Nueva Biblia Española: Comentario teológico y literario). 1984. Pp. 603. (Ediciones Cristiandad, Madrid. Price: Ptas. 2,300. ISBN 84 7057 358 6)

This is the third part to appear of the major commentary series to accompany the NBE. It follows those on the Prophets, in two volumes (*B.L.* 1981, pp. 50–51), and on Job (*B.L.* 1984, pp. 48–49). Now, with another collaborator, Professor Alonso Schökel has built on his previous work in *Los Libros Sagrados* to provide, first, an introduction to wisdom literature (for this volume is prior to Job in the plan of the series) and then his own commentary on the book of Proverbs. The general introduction (pp. 17–92) has two parts and a bibliography. First Professor Alonso Schökel offers his own characterization of the wisdom tradition, showing a preference in many contexts for the strikingly low-key word *Sensatez* (good sense) rather than the familiar yet more solemn *Sabiduría*. Then J. Vílchez contributes a history of research on Old Testment wisdom literature, finally suggesting that the location of wisdom needs to be revised so as to integrate it more in the tradition of divine revelation.

The commentary on Proverbs (pp. 94–536) contains its own introduction: first a chapter of usual introductory character with a bibliography (Vílchez) and then 'The Form of Proverbs: a Comparative Study' by Alonso Schökel. The comparative material is all Spanish, reasonably enough; but one wishes we could enjoy his insights on a wider field, as is surveyed in *The Wisdom of Many: Essays on the Proverb*, ed. W. Mieder and A. Dundes (Garland, New York, 1981). In the following section, on stylistic procedures, the author shows his characteristic mastery.

The main commentary, entirely by Professor Alonso Schökel, follows from p. 153. Each section, in the NBE version, is followed by stylistic analysis and theological commentary, always sensitive to the relationships of expression in the Bible or elsewhere. Other scholars are rarely referred to, and the pages are splendidly uninfested by footnotes. The flexible renderings of the wisdom vocabulary are particularly striking. If there is a neglected dimension it is, perhaps, shown in a lack of interest in some textual problems, e.g. in Prov. 30:1–6. Finally there is an impressive set of Indexes prepared by A. Pinto, starting with an 'Ideological Index' inspired by the *Diccionario Ideologico* of Casares.

R. P. R. MURRAY

ANDREW, M. E.: *Responsibility and Restoration: The Course of the Book of Ezekiel*. 1985. Pp. vi, 255. (University of Otago Press, Dunedin, New Zealand. Price: $NZ 30.00. ISBN 0 908569 32 7)

This is essentially a concise theological commentary on the book of Ezekiel, designed to be read straight through and to encourage study of this prophetic book. It is well acquainted with major recent critical studies of Ezekiel, but is intended to mediate between this critical work and the pastor, or teacher, to whom the book is unfamiliar. It adopts a positive critical approach, following rather closely the lines adopted by W. Zimmerli of an Ezekiel School which has served to edit and shape the original prophecies. It concentrates the main points of its exegesis on the major theological questions raised by the text, and it sets these in the context of Ezekiel's prophetic ministry. The study will prove valuable for teachers and pastors and should promote an interest in the several larger commentaries on Ezekiel that are currently available.

R. E. CLEMENTS

BALDWIN, J. G.: *Esther: An Introduction and Commentary* (Tyndale Old Testament Commentaries). 1984. Pp. 126. (Inter-Varsity Press, Leicester. ISBN 0 85111 639 6. Paperback price: £2.95; ISBN 0 85111 840 2)

This fine verse-by-verse commentary, with a substantial introduction, is directed to the non-specialist reader, but has something of value to the scholar also on every page. Among its distinctive characteristics: illuminations from Persian culture (mostly artifactual, and not all by any means from Herodotus), thoughtful juxtapositions of the text with other Old Testament passages (such intertextuality being much more than a matter of using the concordance), altertness (on a small scale) to feminist and materialist dimensions in the text, concern for a literary reading (including some nicely written pages in the introduction), a definitely Christian perspective (just occasionally obtrusive), some elaborate excursuses (on fasting, vengeance, portions, and 'Esther and Jewry'), the first two animated by an apologetic and moralizing tendency. Is the book historical? The story-teller transports us to 'a fabulous oriental world' (p. 55), but the accuracy of many details is confirmed by our expanding knowledge (p. 23); many features of the plot seem improbable, but there is nothing intrinsically impossible or improbable in the central incident (p. 24). The author concludes, not unreasonably, that the evidence is ambiguous. The reader must not suppose, one imagines, that the use of the past tense to recount what is going on in the narrative (e.g. 'Mordecai's obstinacy was calculated to provoke a reaction') implies a presumption of historicity. All that is missing from this ample and skilful study is hermeneutic of suspicion.

D. J. A. CLINES

BEEK, M. A.: *Prediker/Hooglied* (De Prediking van het Oude Testament). 1984. Pp. 231. (Callenbach, Nijkerk. Price: Fl. 65.50; sub. price: Fl. 59.00. ISBN 90 266 0737 7)

In the best traditions of Dutch scholarship Dr Beek has provided a sympathetic and thoughtful exposition of Ecclesiastes and the Song of Songs, with close attention to Hebrew grammar and philology and the near eastern background. He sees both books as essentially life-affirming. The Song of Songs is a collection of poems with unifying strophes, proclaiming the God-given beauty of human affection. Qohelet is seen not as an atheist, nor a sceptic, but as a person of his time (third century B.C.), rebellious yes, but sensitive to the feelings of ordinary people and valuing human companionship as a divine gift. Dr Beek asserts strongly that these books greatly enrich the corpus of scripture. Perhaps one's only regret is that, apart from the work of Loader on Ecclesiastes, Dr Beek has not utilized some of the more recent literature-orientated publications on these two books.

J. W. ROGERSON

BÉLANGER, R.: *Grégoire le Grand: Commentaire sur le Cantique des Cantiques* (Sources chrétiennes, 314). 1984. Pp. 150. (Éditions du Cerf, Paris. Price: Fr. 90.00. ISBN 2 204 02227 6)

A thorough edition with French opposite Latin, Introduction and notes. Gregory's text is sorted from mediaeval confusion with other commentaries. Commentary ceases at Song of Songs 1:8, but is manifestly Origenist: the Bride is the Church, but also the Soul destined for spiritual union with God.

S. G. HALL

BUBER, M., and ROSENZWEIG, F.: *Bücher der Kündung* (Die Schrift verdeutscht, 3). 8. Auflage der neubearbeiteten Ausgabe von 1958. 1985. Pp. 782. (Lambert Schneider, Heidelberg. Price: DM. 46.00)

This is a further reprint of Buber's translation of the Latter Prophets, described by an earlier reviewer as 'a treasure'. See the review of the seventh edition in *B.L.* 1979, pp. 51–52, and also *B.L.* 1983, p. 46.

M. A. KNIBB

CATTANI, L.: *Rashi di Troyes: Commento alla Genesi*. Prefazione di P. De Benedetti ("Ascolta, Israele!" Commenti alle Scritture delle tradizioni ebraica e cristiana, 1). 1985. Pp. xxxiv, 445. (Marietti, Casale Monferrato. Price: Lire 40,000. ISBN 88 211 8450 1)

Cattani's translation of Rashi's commentary on Genesis is aimed not only at students of rabbinics, but also at a more general readership. It is clear, literal, and equipped with a helpful apparatus of references to biblical and rabbinic sources and occasional explanatory notes. He has also provided a concise introduction to Rashi and his exegesis together with a judicious bibliography, a glossary, indexes of biblical references and French glosses, and a list of rabbis with their dates. An interesting preface by Paolo De Benedetti completes this handsomely-produced volume, which gets a promising new series off to a splendid start. Origen's commentary on Romans is promised next.

N. R. M. DE LANGE

CRAIGIE, P. C.: *The Twelve Prophets*. Volume 2: *Micah, Nahum, Habakkuk, Zephaniah, Haggai, Zechariah and Malachi* (The Daily Study Bible: Old Testament). 1985. Pp. x, 249. (Saint Andrew Press, Edinburgh; Westminster Press, Philadelphia. Price: £3.95. ISBN 0 7152 0538 2)

The first volume of this commentary was reviewed in *B.L.* 1985, p. 54. This volume covers the remainder of the Twelve Prophets, including some of the most obscure passages in the prophetic literature. In general the exposition is clear and attractive, with sensitive reference to modern experience and, where appropriate, to the Christian significance of particular passages. An imaginary Scottish parallel illuminates for English readers the series of puns on place-names in Mic. 1:10–16. On literary questions an essentially conservative position is adopted, e.g. most of Micah is ascribed to the prophet, serious doubt attaching only to 4:1–5 and 7:8–20, and the possibility is canvassed that Zech. 9–14 may come from a later period in the prophet's life. The emphasis is very much on the final form of the books, and natural divisions are not always followed: e.g. Zech. 6:9–14 is attached to 6:1–8; while chapters 7 and 8 are treated as separate units!

A. GELSTON

Da Gud skabte: Første Mosebog 1 til Anden Mosebog 15. And *Tolvprofetbogen*. Det gamle Testamente i ny oversættelse. 1985. Pp. 156 and 185. (Det danske Bibelselskab, Copenhagen. Price: D.Kr. 83.15 and 84.00. ISBN 87 7523 232 4 and 87 7523 234 0)

The Danish Bible Society has this year released two trial translations of parts of the Old Testament, the third and fourth in a series (for an earlier volume see *B.L.* 1983, pp. 49–50). The first one, called 'When God Created' is a translation of Gen. 1–Exod. 15; it was made by a group of Old Testament scholars connected with the Department of Biblical Studies at the University of Copenhagen. The other translation, the Book of the Twelve Minor Prophets, was made by another group based at the University of Aarhus. The style of the translations is the same as the earlier trial translations, a concise Danish of the 1980s. At the end of each book there are lists of deviations from the massoretic consonantal text.

K. JEPPESEN

EDLER, R.: *Das Kerygma des Propheten Zefanja* (Freiburger Theologische Studien, 126). 1984. Pp. xii, 275. (Verlag Herder, Freiburg im Breisgau. Price: DM.38.00. ISBN 3 451 20087 2)

This *Inauguraldissertation* is a lucid and painstaking study of the book of Zephaniah in order to elicit the prophet's message, and will be indispensable for future work on Zephaniah. A translation and a brief summary of textual criticism are followed by a chapter on the historical background, in which Zephaniah's ministry is dated in the minority of Josiah. The greater part of the work consists of a study of the text itself. First, portions, ranging from two or three verses to a few words, which are considered not to derive from Zephaniah, are discussed, and here inevitably not all the author's judgements will command universal assent. Then the 'authentic' passages are examined in detail in a thematic order rather than that of the canonical text. A final chapter summarizes the themes of Zephaniah's message. Unfortunately there are a number of inaccuracies in the Hebrew words quoted, especially in the vocalization.

A. GELSTON

GIBSON, J. C. L.: *Job* (The Daily Study Bible: Old Testament). 1985. Pp. x, 284. (Saint Andrew Press, Edinburgh; Westminster Press, Philadelphia. Price: £3.95. ISBN 0 7152 0536 6)

'Job is a real sufferer', says the author at the outset and warns against toning down or spiritualizing or sentimentalizing the book and its language. Dr Gibson's interpretation is the fruit of more than two decades' teaching, and one is grateful for his tentative and yet powerful conclusions. The style is as vigorous as the book of Job demands. You feel that the author stands 'under' rather than 'over' the book, though he is fully aware of scholarly disputes concerning the text and modern approaches to ambiguity in hermeneutics. For example, on 19:23–29 Gibson immediately confronts his reader with the perplexing options of redemption and the vision of God either before or after death, and engages his attention to the Christian tradition of Resurrection on the one hand, and the non-Christological and non-Handelian criticism of the famous passage on the other. Gibson steers a middle course in which God does champion Job's cause, and the bodiless shade becomes aware of the moral presence. Throughout this excellent book, ideal for non-professionals, he avoids a one-dimensional boredom of explanation so that theophany and theodicy are freed from mere abstractions. Elihu is not permitted to confuse the scene with second-rate argumentation. In the end Job is brought to his knees, 'not in reluctant, but in willing, surrender'. This is a grand contribution to the never-ending stream of Job commentaries.

U. E. SIMON

GUTBROD, K.: *Das Buch vom Lande Gottes: Josua und Richter* (Die Botschaft des Alten Testaments, 10). 4., neu bearbeitete Auflage. 1985. Pp. 319. (Calwer Verlag, Stuttgart, Price: DM. 28.00. ISBN 3 7668 0774 9)

This revised edition (for an earlier review see *B.L.* 1952, pp. 32–33; *Eleven Years*, pp. 403–404) offers an up-to-date and thoughtful introduction to, and exposition of, Joshua and Judges. The critical approach to the origin of the books is accepted, but no attempt is made to provide more than the minimum by way of reference to the critical literature, and no bibliography of further reading is appended. This is a book with a well-executed but limited purpose, from which the reader is not to be distracted: to elicit the message of Joshua, understood as the conclusion to the Pentateuch, giving the realization of the promise to the patriarchs; and that of Judges, understood as the introduction to the history of Israel under the monarchy culminating in its destruction.

A. D. H. MAYES

HABEL, N. C.: *The Book of Job: A Commentary* (Old Testament Library). 1985. Pp. 586. (SCM Press, London, Price: £20.00. ISBN 0 334 02103 0)

This well-written and well-produced limp-backed volume is an important addition to the commentaries on Job, making a distinctive contribution from the angle of literary analysis and appreciation. The Introduction of some fifty pages establishes this perspective, making clear the idiom and concepts of the literary approach and showing how it bears upon our understanding of the book's form and message. The Commentary then proceeds through the units of text, in each case offering first translation, then textual notes, then comment on literary features, then a verse-by-verse analysis of the sense. The approach to problems of text and translation is conservative and restrained. The literary comments deal with surface structure or pattern, framing techniques, envelope constructions, chiasm, adaptation of traditional forms, word-play, irony, subtle echoes from one speaker to another, imagery, and the pervasive legal metaphor.

Although dislocation in the third cycle of speeches is admitted, the book is otherwise treated as a literary whole, a rich paradoxical totality. It is not a question of poetic dialogue inserted into a given prose frame, but of a traditional story retold with massive dialogue as a feature of the plot. The Elihu episode has its part here, being intended by the great poet as an ironic anticlimax. Job's response to God (42:6) is translated in the tradition of Maimonides: 'I retract and repent of dust and ashes' — he withdraws his case against God and leaves off his lamentation.

J. H. Eaton

Hentschel, G.: *1 Könige* (Die Neue Echter Bibel). 1984. Pp. 142. *2 Könige* (Die Neue Echter Bibel). 1985. Pp. 131. (Echter Verlag, Würzburg. Price: DM 28.00 each; sub. price: DM 24.00 each. ISBN 3 429 00904 9 and 3 429 00948 0)

In accordance with the general format of this series the commentary in these two volumes on the books of Kings is based on the *Einheitsübersetzung*, which is printed in full in the upper portion of each page, with an occasional brief textual note when a variant has been accepted. A short introduction of some dozen pages gives a clear indication of Hentschel's approach to these most important historical sources. His analysis of the content leads him to three redactors, one a historian (DtrH), a second being responsible for insertions showing an interest in prophets (DtrP), and a third called a nomistic redactor (DtrN). He thus subscribes broadly to the view current in the works of Smend, Dietrich, and Veijola. The sources used by the redactors were: the Solomonic source behind 1 Kings 1–11, the chronicles of the Kings of Israel and Judah and prophetical narratives. There is also a brief discussion of the problem of chronology, where, like other German commentaries, there is a preference for Jepsen's schema. Comments on shorter sections and individual verses, although necessarily brief, are adequate and provide the reader with clear and concise guidance on how to interpret the text. In working his way through the text, the author refers not simply to the contribution of the redactors, but also to the historical background of the events described and to some of the problems associated with them, to points of archaeological interest and the identification of sites, and to general points that have to be borne in mind in seeking a theological understanding of the text. These are helpful commentaries.

G. H. Jones

Japhet, S., and Salters, R. B.: *The Commentary of R. Samuel ben Meir Rashbam on Qoheleth* (Publications of the Perry Foundation for Biblical Research in the Hebrew University of Jerusalem). 1985. Pp. 256, including 17 plates. (Magnes Press, Jerusalem; Brill, Leiden. Price: $28.00. ISBN 965 223 517 2)

Rashbam's Commentary on Qoheleth has not been as well known and used as might have been expected. As Professor Japhet points out in her excellent Introduction, only H. L. Ginsberg among modern scholars seems to take any real notice of it. One reason for its neglect is the measure of doubt which has sometimes been expressed as to the Commentary's authenticity; but Japhet's careful and detailed arguments should now finally dispel any lingering hesitations about our accepting this work as being from the Rashbam's pen.

The Commentary is extant only in a single manuscript, Hamburg Cod. 32, which was published by A Jellinek in 1855. Japhet and Salters present a facsimile of this manuscript (pp. 219–35). Jellinek's edition proved unsatisfactory: not only were there several printing errors, but in many places Jellinek had altered the text without giving any indication to the reader that he had done so. The present editors have printed the text of the manuscript with only a minimum number of changes, and they carefully indicate what these alterations are and where they occur. Thus their edition introduces the division of the manuscript into chapters and verses corresponding to those of the Hebrew text of Qoheleth; prints the scriptural lemmata in larger type; reproduces a text free of the scribal errors noted in the manuscript itself, relegating notice of the corresponding scribal activity to footnotes; and makes necessary emendations to the text, noting the original manuscript reading in the apparatus. The inclusion of a facsimile of the manuscript affords an easy means of checking the edition against the original.

The language of the Commentary is, in places, very difficult, and the translators have coped well in their efforts to render the sometimes convoluted and often repetitive prose into readable English. The remarks in the Introduction about Rashbam's exegetical formulas and techniques are very much to the point, and Japhet and Salters have managed to encapsulate a lot of valuable information about Jewish mediaeval exegesis in a short space. There is a small, but carefully selected bibliography (pp. 242–44). There are a few typographical errors, including 'madmess' for 'madness', and the inscrutable form 'vjna', both on p. 65.

C. T. R. Hayward

Knight, G. A. F.: *The New Israel: A Commentary on the Book of Isaiah 56–66* (International Theological Commentary). 1985. Pp. xviii, 126. (Eerdmans, Grand Rapids, Michigan. ISBN 0 8028 0021 1. Handsel Press, Edinburgh. Price: £4.75; ISBN 0 905312 46 5)

This is a sequel to the commentary on Isa. 40–55 in the same series (see *B.L.* 1985, p. 59). Chapters 56–66 are here taken to be the work of one of the first of the Babylonian exiles to return to Jerusalem and to have been completed, possibly with the assistance of 'disciples', before 525 B.C. The work represents a point of view opposed to that of the 'priestly group' among the immigrants. More emphasis is placed on theological interpretation than on accuracy of exposition: for example, it is not true to say (p. 71) that 'the name Bozrah means "vintager"'; and on the following page the statement that the verb *ṣāʿāh* (63:1) means 'march' as well as 'stoop', which is then made the basis of an extended comment on the nature of God, is based on a failure to realize that 'march' here (in the RSV) is a translation not of the Hebrew text but of a common emendation of the text from *ṣʿh* to *ṣʿd*.

R. N. Whybray

Van Leeuwen, C.: *Amos* (De Prediking van het Oude Testament). 1985. Pp. 420. (Callenbach, Nijkerk. Price: Fl. 99.50; sub. price Fl. 89.50. ISBN 90 266 0738 5)

This volume is a contribution to the series of theological commentaries on the Old Testament edited by A. S. van der Woude, C. van Leeuwen and the late A. van Selms. The theological exposition is laid on a sound critical foundation. The text and exegesis of each section is analysed (the Hebrew words being given in transliteration) before its general argument is opened up. There are no exciting novelties here, but the scholarship is up to date. Amos, it is held, was no pioneer in his insistence on social ethics: his God was the God of Moses and the Torah, whose covenant with Israel called from the beginning for justice, mercy and humility. Van Leeuwen sees no reason to deny the notes of hope to Amos; he was a preacher at the eleventh hour, no doubt, but until midnight hope remains.

F. F. BRUCE

LINDSEY, F. D.: *The Servant Songs: A Study in Isaiah*. 1985. Pp. xii, 170. (Moody Press, Chicago. Price: $7.95. ISBN 0 8024 4093 2)

Written on the basis of the assumptions of 'the inspiration and inerrancy of Scripture, the unity of the sixty-six chapters of Isaiah, and the reality of predictive prophecy' (p. xi), this is an extremely competent defence of the christological interpretation of the 'Servant Songs' (defined as Isa. 42:1–9; 49:1–13; 50:4–11; 52:13–53:12). The author possesses a detailed knowledge of the history of interpretation and of recent work. The tone is scholarly rather than polemical: 'critical' studies are not rejected out of hand but engaged with in serious dialogue, and, in many cases, referred to with approval on particular points of interpretation.

R. N. WHYBRAY

MCCONVILLE, J. G.: *Ezra, Nehemiah and Esther* (The Daily Study Bible: Old Testament). 1985. Pp. xii, 199. (Saint Andrew Press, Edinburgh; Westminster Press, Philadelphia. Price: £3.50. ISBN 0 7152 0532 3)

This is a very successful addition to a highly regarded series. Particularly noteworthy is the amount of information and exegesis contained without effort in a paragraph-by-paragraph commentary. The lay readership for which the series is designed is well served by the non-technicality and the quality of the writing, which is lively but never condescending. Reflective or devotional comments are relatively sparse, but well-informed and thoughtful, and comment is usually sharply distinguished from reporting. Moral and theological problems raised by the text are sensitively handled, but some readers may feel a little sceptical of the view that is apparently taken here, that everything done by the principal characters of these books seems to have been fundamentally right and all for the best. Nehemiah was, indeed, courageous, godly, and wise (pp. 78–79), or so he would have us believe, but would Scripture be any less instructive if he was haughty, insensitive, and self-centred as well?

D. J. A. CLINES

MAARSINGH, B.: *Ezechiël*. Deel I (De Prediking van het Oude Testament). 1985. Pp. 235. (Callenbach, Nijkerk. Price: Fl. 75.00; sub. price: Fl. 69.00. ISBN 90 266 0741 5)

This first part of a new commentary in a well-established series covers fifteen chapters of Ezekiel. It is to be completed in two further parts. It is inevitably rather unsatisfactory to have a division which cuts across the obvious sections of the book; normally we should expect a first volume to cover 1–24. In some degree therefore a judgement on the commentary awaits the appearance of part two in which the remainder of the first section of the book will be discussed.

The pattern of commentary is already familiar. Introductory matter is minimal, noting in particular what then becomes clear in the commentary, that much reference is made to the ancient versions and their handling of Ezekiel; and indeed considerabale reference is made to the most ancient commentary traditions. The bibliography — selective but supplemented by the mainly bibliographical notes — shows that the author has used all the main recent works on Ezekiel; but it is good that the commentary itself is written essentially with the main look at the text rather than at what everyone else has said. The result is a fairly cautious but clear exposition, characterized both by sensible comments on the text and by reasonable homiletic notes to individual passages.

P. R. Ackroyd

Mortari, L.: *Il Salterio della Tradizione: Versione del Salterio greco dei LXX*. 1983. Pp. 333. (Piero Gribaudi, Turin. Price: Lire 25,000)

This Italian translation of the LXX Psalter (here justifiably treated as a religious document in its own right) is based on the Sixtine text, reprinted in the Bagster/Zondervan edition of the LXX (*B.L.* 1975, pp. 38–39), whose verse division and numbering are also adopted; the text thus differs in many details from that of liturgical Psalters printed in Greece. Ps. 151 is included, but of the Odes only the three New Testament ones are given. Interpretative notes are provided for select passages. The introduction is well informed and contains sections on Christ and the Psalms, the Adversary, LXX in general, LXX Psalter, LXX and the Gospel, and the present translation. In the fairly full bibliography mention might have been made of two English translations of the LXX Psalter, by Lazarus Moore (Madras, 1966, 1971), and by the Holy Transfiguration Monastery (Boston, 1974). A companion volume, *I Padri commentano il Salterio della Tradizione*, by J.-C. Nesmy and others, is announced.

S. P. Brock

Nakazawa, K.: *Kū no Kū — Chi no Haiboku* (Vanity of Vanities — Defeat of Wisdom). 1985. Pp. 230 (Yamamoto-shoten, Tokyo. Price: ¥3,600)

This exposition of the book of Ecclesiastes, given originally in the form of a series of lectures in 1979–1981, focuses upon the frustration of Qoheleth in his search for wisdom. The author works out his theme with the aid of his own translation and includes many discussions of alternative renderings and of key words and phrases.

K. K. Sacon

Partain, J., and Deutsch, R.: *A Guide to Isaiah 1–39* (TEF Study Guide, 21). 1986. Pp. x, 262. (SPCK, London. Price: £5.95. ISBN 0 281 04182 2)

This is a basic commentary to Isaiah 1–39, offering a brief critical introduction to the text and concentrating mainly on a clear explanation and amplification of the material. The primary work on Isa. 1–12 was undertaken by J. Partain, and the commentary on the remaining chapters, with some revision of the earlier part, by R. Deutsch. In keeping with the aim of the series as a whole it is aimed at the needs of the younger churches, particularly those of Asia and Africa. On the assumption that it will be read by many students and pastors for whom English is a second language there is a general concern to put the meaning of the text in plain language. Detailed textual criticism and references to secondary literature are avoided, while a good deal of attention is placed on the basic religious ideas. It is skilfully done by teachers who have clearly had much experience of working with the kind of readership that they address, and it fulfils its intended purpose very well.

R. E. Clements

Payne, D. F.: *Deuteronomy* (The Daily Study Bible: Old Testament). 1985. Pp. xiv, 197, including 2 maps. (Saint Andrew Press, Edinburgh; Westminster Press, Philadelphia. Price: £4.95. ISBN 0 7152 0531 5)

Payne avoids getting embroiled in a discussion of the date of Deuteronomy by affirming its Mosaic authority rather than necessarily his authorship, and by suggesting that although its message is in many ways timeless it may have had its greatest historical impact at the end of the period of Babylonian exile. His commentary then proceeds in the manner established for this series (cf. *B.L.* 1982, p. 44) and succeeds well in explaining the laws against their Israelite background while at the same time managing to outline their contribution to a Christian consideration of a wide range of contemporary issues. This is a valuable addition to the series.

H. G. M. Williamson

Petersen, D. L.: *Haggai and Zechariah 1–8: A Commentary* (Old Testament Library). 1985. Pp. 320. (SCM Press, London. Price: £12.50. ISBN 0 334 02041 7)

A substantial commentary in English on these two prophets has long been overdue. This one is welcome not only because it fills this gap, but because it comes from one who has already contributed to the study of this period with his book *Late Israelite Prophecy* (*B.L.* 1979, p. 87). Its attention to past and contemporary scholarly discussion is a little less than full, but it is marked by some interesting and provocative individual insights. The book of Haggai is not so much a collection of prophecies in the style of pre-exilic prophetic books as an historical narrative interested in events of the settlement period and the parts played in those events by Haggai, Joshua, and Zerubbabel. That is why individual prophetic speeches are not as fully recorded as in the other prophetic books. The picture presented in Ezra 5–6 of Haggai and Zechariah as prime movers in the rebuilding of the temple is mistaken as far as Zechariah is concerned. He saw Yahweh as no longer being localized in a temple and was concerned to provide a theological rationale for the post-exilic reconstruction which was consciously corrective of much in Ezek. 40–48. The lack of any indexes whatever seriously reduces the usefulness of this book.

R. A. Mason

Rendtorff, R.: *Leviticus* (Biblischer Kommentar — Altes Testament, iii, Lfg.1). 1985. Pp. 1–80. [Neukirchener Verlag, Neukirchen-Vluyn. Price: DM. 18.50; sub. price: DM. 15.40. ISBN 3 7887 0786 0)

This first fascicle of Rendtorff's eagerly awaited commentary on Leviticus covers the first chapter of the book. It follows the regular format of the Biblischer Kommentar series. After an Introduction to Lev. 1–7 as a whole, there follow a translation of the opening seventeen verses and a detailed verse-by-verse exegesis with extensive bibliographies, together with a long excursus on the 'laying on of the hand' and another substantial one on the word *'isheh*. Within a brief review it is hardly possible to give the author's views the consideration they deserve, but attention may be called particularly to the Introduction, where Rendtorff sets out his general approach to Leviticus. He rejects any idea of a separate 'P' document: 'P' is only to be understood as the final redactional stage of the entire Pentateuch. Hence he abandons any attempt to divide up the text of Leviticus into chronologically distinct compositional stages, such as P^g, P^s, P^o, etc. 'The understanding of the biblical text in its existing form', he writes, 'is the prior duty of exegesis'. All this is in marked, not to say refreshing, contrast with the approach of previous scholars such as Noth and Elliger, though it has been more characteristic of recent English work on Leviticus. Refreshing too is the author's willingness to revise some of his own earlier opinions and his caution over reaching conclusions where the evidence, as is so often the case, is indecisive. Two other characteristics of this commentary may be noted. First,

Rendtorff's examination of difficult terms in Leviticus always centres on their usage within the priestly material and the Old Testament generally, and his discussions here provide one of the most valuable and stimulating features of his work. Secondly, he pays close attention to post-Biblical Jewish material and shows how often this illuminates some of the problems of sacrificial terminology and practice in Leviticus. It hardly needs saying that Rendtorff's work, with its many original insights, promises to be of major importance for the increasing interest among scholars in the Old Testament sacrificial cultus. Many questions which the present fascicle raises will no doubt find their elucidation in future instalments.

J. R. Porter

Rogerson, J. W., and McKay, J. W.: *Shihen II: 73–150*. Translated by T. Murakami. 1984. Pp. 314. (Shinkyō-Shuppan-sha, Tokyo. Price: ¥3.500)

This is a Japanese translation of the second half of the original three volumes of the Cambridge Bible Commentary on the N.E.B.: *Psalms 1–50, 51–100, 101–150* (1977); see *B.L.* 1978, pp. 55–56; also *B.L.* 1985, p. 64, for the first part of the translation.

K. K. Sacon

Schreiner J.: *Jeremia II: 25, 15–52, 34* (Die Neue Echter Bibel). 1984. Pp. 149–282 (Echter Verlag, Würzburg. Price: DM 28.00; sub. price: DM 24.00. ISBN 3 429 00909 X)

The objectives of this commentary were described in connection with the first volume (1:1–25:14), and some indication of its critical stance was also indicated (cf. *B.L.* 1982, p. 51). The second volume completes the work: it is a neat combination of translation and concise commentary, attractively produced.

W. McKane

Smith, R. L.: *Micah-Malachi* (Word Biblical Commentary, 32). 1984. Pp. xviii, 358. (Word Books, Waco, Texas. Price: $22.95. ISBN 0 8499 0231 2)

The pattern of the Word Biblical Commentary Series is now firmly established and well known. An Introduction to each prophetic book discusses the person of the prophet, his time and historical setting, followed by attention to questions of authorship, structure, date, text, and the 'message' of the book. The books are then dealt with section by section, with translation followed by textual notes and discussion of form, structure, and the meaning of the contents.

This is a most welcome addition to the series and to the all too scanty material in English on many of these books. It is likely to be a standard work for some time to come. Very full bibliographies are given and detailed attention to recent scholarly discussion of issues. When Dr Smith advances his own views, they are often enlightening and always worthy of serious consideration. Indeed, if one were to voice a criticism, it would be that less deference to 'authorities' and more of the writer's own opinions would have been welcome.

R. A. Mason

De Vries, S. J: *1 Kings* (Word Biblical Commentary, 12). 1985. Pp. lxiv, 286. (Word Books, Waco, Texas. Price: $22.95. ISBN 0 8499 0211 8)

The aims and format of the Word Biblical Commentary series have been previously noted (cf. *B.L.* 1985, pp. 53–54). In his full Introduction Professor de Vries sets out his main line of approach, which is critical of the search for deeper layers of tradition advocated by Smend, Dietrich, and Veijola, who, in his opinion, have gone much too far. Although admitting that there was more than a single stage of redaction, de Vries wishes to engage in a form- and tradition-critical methodology that concentrates on the original structure, setting and intention of individual units in order to perceive the authentic word of God. He is thus content to refer simply to Dtr, which is defined as a deuteronomistic school that produced the deuteronomistic redaction in the exilic period, and to late post-deuteronomistic glosses. Whilst in sympathy with the author's search for elemental oral and written units, the present reviewer is less convinced by his treatment of the Ahijah prophecy in 1 Kings 11:29–39, for instance, than by the analysis proposed by Dietrich and accepted by Würthwein. However, this commentary can on several counts be commended: there are in the Introduction valuable sections on sacred history as theological testimony and on the text of Kings; the translation and textual notes are based on a painstaking comparison and judicious use of the variants; the historical and archaeological explanations are reliable, although perhaps brief; the 'explanation' of the text is done competently and with restraint, and the author has been wise enough to omit this section when nothing new or deserving special comment arises from the text.

G. H. JONES

WEISER, A.: *Eremiya-sho* 1–25 shō. Translated by A. Tsukimoto. 1985. Pp. 536. (ATD-NTD Seisho Chūkai Kankō-kai, Tokyo. Price: ¥5,300)

This is a Japanese translation of the first twenty-five chapters of *Das Buch Jeremia* (ATD) from the seventh edition of 1976; see *B.L.* 1970, p. 37 (*Bible Bibliog.*, p. 227) for a note on the sixth edition, the latest to be reviewed in the *Book List*. In a postscript the translator discusses the significance of the book in the light of recent developments in the study of Jeremiah.

K. K. SACON

VAN DER WOUDE, A. S.: *Zacharia* (De Prediking van het Oude Testament). 1984. Pp. 325. (Callenbach, Nijkerk. Price: Fl. 75.00; sub. price: Fl. 68.00. ISBN 90 266 0740 7)

With this volume the author completes and complements the commentary on Haggai and Malachi with which the Zechariah material so closely belongs (see *B.L.* 1983, p. 57). It also, I assume, completes his contribution to the Book of the Twelve in this well-known series (see Micah, *B.L.* 1977, p. 54; Jonah/Nahum and Habakkuk/Zephaniah, *B.L.* 1979, p. 65). It is appropriate to congratulate him on work of a consistently high standard, in which so many contributions are made to the understanding of individual passages and to the prophetic books as literary units.

Here, as we should expect, the commentary is divided into the two main sections: 1–8 and 9–14. Each is provided with a short introduction; in the latter case, where so many different views have been argued, there is a useful critical overview of the alternatives. For Zech. 1–8, the assessment of the differing emphases of Zechariah and Haggai is well brought out. There is a particularly useful discussion of 8:9–13 which provides some, inevitably problematic, clues to the evolution of the Zechariah (and Haggai) tradition.

Clarity of discussion, valuable references in the notes, excellent bibliography and indexes make this a fine climax to this part of the series. (Only Joel and Obadiah are still to come.)

P. R. ACKROYD

ZUCKER, M. (ed.): *Saadya's Commentary on Genesis*. 1984. Pp. xix (English), 69, 487 (Hebrew). (Jewish Theological Seminary of America, New York. Price: $20.00. ISBN 0 87334 023 X)

It is regrettable how few of the major Jewish works of the geonic period survived into the late mediaeval and modern periods and therefore particularly welcome when a text such as this can be reconstructed from Cairo Genizah fragments, other manuscripts, and quotations by later writers. The acknowledged expert here reproduces the Judaeo-Arabic text of Saadya's introductions and his commentary on the first half of Genesis together with a useful Hebrew translation, detailed annotations, and appendixes containing other work by Saadya and Samuel ben Ḥofni. Zucker's Hebrew introduction, summarized in English, deals with the Gaon's attitude to earlier rabbinic exegesis, the relationship of his commentary to his philosophy, his polemics against Karaism, the effect on later commentaries, and the parallels with qur'anic interpretation. A significant gap has been filled, and publication is promised of the remaining sections of the commentary that have come to light, namely, those on Exodus and Leviticus. More accurate citation of the classmarks given in the indexes would have permitted the easier identification of the manuscript fragments.

S. C. REIF

6. LITERARY CRITICISM AND INTRODUCTION

(including History of Interpretation, Canon, and Special Studies)

AMSLER, S.: *Les Actes des prophètes* (Essais bibliques, 9). 1985. Pp. 94. (Labor et Fides, Geneva. Price: Sw.Fr. 16.00. ISBN 2 8309 0040 5)

Expanding on his chapter in the 1980 Westermann *Festschrift* (*B.L.* 1981, pp. 7–8), Amsler examines in some detail thirty-one prophetic actions and points up the relevance of such a study to a Christian readership. The actions are found to share a number of characteristics: they were always paradoxical, shocking even, in nature; they were intended to provoke reaction on the part of spectators and are enshrined in narratives which seek to achieve the same effect with readers; they provided an analogue for the imminent actions of YHWH or for the effects on men of his actions, and in some measure, though not in a magical sense, they helped to shape these coming events; the accounts of the actions are normally accompanied by oracles — the oracles explain the actions, while the actions render one alert and receptive to the oracles; finally, each action was unique to a particular prophet, for if prophets had repeated the actions of their predecessors, they would have detracted from their surprise value. Amsler expresses himself clearly and usually takes cognisance of other viewpoints; his short book will serve the general reader well.

B. P. ROBINSON

ARCHER, G. L., JR: *A Survey of Old Testament Introduction*. Revised Edition. 1985 (1974). Pp. 537. (Moody Press, Chicago. Price: $15.95. ISBN 0 8024 8447 6)

Archer's *Survey* has been a vade-mecum of conservative students of the Old Testament ever since its first publication in 1964 (though not previously noticed in the *Book List*). Now the second, 1974, edition has been reissued in paperback, but little has in fact been changed since the work's first appearance. After an introductory chapter on Inspiration, the first third of the book is 'General Introduction' (text and canon, and, in great detail, the critical study of the Pentateuch, and why it is in error); the remainder is 'Special Introduction' dealing with each book in turn. The decisive criteria are authorship, date, and historicity, and so it is not surprising that Genesis, Isaiah, and Daniel receive two chapters each. A rigidly conservative line is followed throughout, with no deviation permitted. (It is striking, for example, to find E. J. Young criticized for his failure to accept the Solomonic authorship of Ecclesiastes.) The type of liberal scholarship which is regarded as the enemy to be repelled (and no less harsh expression would be appropriate) is that of an earlier generation; even when it was first published it must already have had an old-fashioned air. In sum, there is a great learning here, coupled with total confidence that God's will and word can be discerned down to the smallest detail; some will derive great comfort from such a presentation, others will be repelled.

R. J. Coggins

Bastiaens, J., Beuken W., and Postma, F.: *Trito-Isaiah: An Exhaustive Concordance of Isa. 56–66, especially with reference to Deutero-Isaiah. An Example of Computer-Assisted Research* (Applicatio, 4). 1984. Pp. 148. (VU Boekhandel/Uitgeverij, Amsterdam. Price: Fl. 37.50. ISBN 90 6256 185 3)

This computer-generated concordance, a sequel to the study of Deutero-Isaiah by E. Talstra and others (*B.L.* 1982, p. 74), includes listings of the inseparable prepositions, conjunction, article and interrogative. The listing of each item (properly 'lexeme') gives its total frequency, and, as the context of each occurrence, a phrase of two or more words. The fount is not ideal (*t*ʿ looks like *ḥṣ*); there are no marks for *Sin* and *Shin*, and no vowels. While homographs have separate lists, identification is sometimes difficult (e.g. *ʾl* is *ʾel*, *ʾl* I is *ʿal*). The frequency, in either section, of every lexeme found in either Deutero- or Trito-Isaiah is given on pp. 123–47. Overall counts follow (p. 148). The introduction is at times obscure (in relation to what are the 'unica' (p. 14) unique?) and some of the results claimed (e.g. that divine glory is seen at Isa. 40:6 and Trito-Isaiah, but heard or declared everywhere else in Deutero-Isaiah) were attainable through traditional concordances. Not the least interest of the book is that it exemplifies the listings of features and combinations that can be extracted from the underlying database.

M. P. Weitzman

Beckwith, R.: *The Old Testament Canon of the New Testament Church and its Background in Early Judaism*. 1985. Pp. xiv, 528. (SPCK, London. Price: £35.00. ISBN 0 281 04155 5)

The subject of the Old Testament Canon of the early Church is one which, for some years now, has been crying out for a scholarly and up-to-date treatment. It is not just that new evidence has come to light since Ryle wrote his book on the Canon; it is, according to Beckwith, that 'most of the existing literature suffers from serious faults of method. Far better use could have been made of the older evidence if it had been more adequately assembled and more accurately analysed.' The author of this book has not only answered the aforementioned need, but has done so in a comprehensive manner.

Between a short Introduction and shorter Conclusion there are substantial chapters, entitled: The Witnesses to the Canon, The Fact of the Canon, The Titles of the Canon, The Structure of the Canon, The Order of the Canonical Books, The Number of the Canonical Books, The Identity of the Canonical Books: Books Included as Canonical and Books Excluded as

Uncanonical. In addition there are five appendixes: The scrolls from the Cairo Genizah and the Meaning of the Term 'Fifths', The Order of the Prophets and Hagiographa in the Jewish Tradition, The High Priests of the First Temple in Scripture and Tradition, The Four Greek Versions of Ecclesiastes in Origen's Hexapla, The Canon in the Early Ethiopian Church.

The twenty-five years spent in producing this book have been well spent, for it must surely become a standard textbook on the subject for the foreseeable future. Its comprehensiveness is marred only by the fact that it lacks a Bibliography.

R. B. SALTERS

BERLIN, A.: *The Dynamics of Biblical Parallelism*. 1985. Pp. xii, 179. (Indiana University Press, Bloomington, Indiana. Price: $27.50. ISBN 0 253 31850 5)

Here is 'a fresh approach to parallelism as a whole' (p. 2), not just further sub-classification, and it marks a significant advance in our understanding of parallelism in Hebrew poetry. The author adopts Roman Jakobson's broad approach to parallelism, defined by her as the 'phenomenon of combining elements which are in some way linguistically equivalent' (p. 29). This means that parallelism is not confined to the level of the couplet but extended to the whole of a poem. Dr Berlin then examines four aspects of parallelism: grammatical, lexical, semantic, and phonological. Besides guiding us through the complexities of recent debate, with perceptive evaluation of the contributions made by T. Collins, M. O'Connor, J. Kugel, and others, she provides illuminating discussion of word-pairs and 'sound-pairs'. A final chapter shows how different aspects of parallelism interact. Notes, bibliography, and indexes are provided. In a concise way the author explains linguistic principles at work in Hebrew verse very clearly with the use of well-chosen and deftly analysed examples.

W. G. E. WATSON

BEYERLIN, W.: *Weisheitlich-kultische Heilsordnung: Studien zum 15. Psalm* (Biblisch-Theologische Studien, 9). 1985. Pp. 116. (Neukirchener Verlag, Neukirchen-Vluyn. Price: DM 19.80; sub. price: DM 17.80. ISBN 3 7887 0785 2)

The author here adds to his succession of books devoted each to one psalm (see *B.L.* 1979, p. 68; 1980, p. 62; 1981, p. 67; 1984, p. 65). Psalm 15 is examined methodically from every critical angle and eventually envisaged as a post-exilic composition. Its use is located in festal gatherings in the outer court of the temple, possibly before a gate to the inner court. The psalm is found to combine the salvation expressed in the sacral institution of temple worship with the teachings of the wisdom tradition. This brisk and detailed study will be valued, though it would be unwise to underestimate concern for the ethics of daily life in festal institutions from remotest times.

J. H. EATON

BLANCHET, R., BONVIN, B., CLERC, D., GALLAY, R.-M., MÜLLER, D., ROULET, P., and WISSER, L.: *Jérémie: Un prophète en temps de crise. Dossier pour l'animation biblique* (Essais bibliques, 10). 1985. Pp. 180, including some illustrations. (Labor et Fides, Geneva. Price: Sw.Fr. 18.00. ISBN 2 8309 0042 1)

Done by a group of scholars, the aim of this work is to bring the prophet Jeremiah to life and to demonstrate the contemporary relevance of the book which bears his name. It is concerned also to lay out particular topics and to indicate how they should be organized and presented for group discussion.

There is an emphasis on the sense of alienation by which Jeremiah was seized, the loneliness he endured, and the doubts which rose insistently in his mind. His intellectual and moral courage, and the confused and sorrowful times in which he lived, are thought to combine to make him an especially effective exemplar for those who endure the struggles of the soul and march through the night of doubt and sorrow in our own troubled times.

An account of the principal characteristics of Old Testament prophecy and of the 'writing prophets' is followed by a sketch of Jeremiah in the context of his times, an age when Judah was beset with political trials and dangers. A conspectus of the book of Jeremiah and some consideration of its composition and literary genres is followed by a selection of themes: Jeremiah's vocation as gathered from the call narrative and its continuation in 1:4–19, the relation between knowledge of God and the doing of what is just, the use of acted parable by the prophet Jeremiah, and true and false prophets. Finally, some thought is given to how a transfer is to be effected from a consideration of a true prophet of the past, and the historical framework in which he lived and worked, to a discovery of what it entails to live prophetically in the present as a member of a prophetic community — the Christian Church.

W. McKane

Blum, E.: *Die Komposition der Vätergeschichte* (Wissenschaftliche Monographien zum Alten und Neuen Testament, 57). 1984. Pp. xii, 564. (Neukirchener Verlag, Neukirchen-Vluyn. Price: DM. 98.00; sub. price: DM. 89.00. ISBN 3 7887 0713 5)

In this meticulous traditio-historical analysis of one of Rendtorff's 'larger units' in the Pentateuch (see *B.L.* 1978, p. 76) Blum provides an opportunity to test the thesis that these developed separately before their eventual combination by a deuteronomistic editor. He finds four successive stages in this separate development of the patriarchal narratives: the Jacob and Abraham narratives each developed by itself in two main stages, and they were then combined in two successive 'editions', later-monarchical and exilic. Alt's 'god of the fathers' hypothesis which led Noth and others to look for the origins of the patriarchal stories in a hazy 'nomadic' period is rejected: the earliest material is no older than the United Monarchy. That this material did develop in the way proposed here is certainly possible; but the method necessarily involves building a series of hypotheses one upon the other so that a single weak argument may destroy the whole edifice. Blum is justified, however, in pointing out that until similar work has been done on the other 'larger units' of the Pentateuch it will not be possible to test the hypothesis fully. Meanwhile this is a most thorough piece of work, with valuable discussions of many controversial questions, e.g. on the use of the 'divine names' as a criterion for source analysis.

R. N. Whybray

Boadt, L.: *Reading the Old Testament: An Introduction*. 1984. Pp. 569, including some maps and illustrations. (Paulist Press, Mahwah, New Jersey. Price: $6.95. ISBN 0 8091 2531 1)

An excellent student's introduction to the study of the Old Testament, with useful maps and line-drawings (all black and white). Boadt presents consensus views on critical questions. Introductory chapters on geographical, historical, and archaeological background and on pentateuchal criticism lead into a broadly chronological presentation, with excursions into 'Daily Life in Ancient Israel', 'Canaanite Religion and Culture', and 'Israelite Worship and Prayer'. There are brief concluding sections on the canon, and on Old Testament theology. The clear charts and diagrams will help to make this a useful teaching aid, for much the same readers as B. W. Anderson's *The Living World of the Old Testament*.

J. BARTON

BORI, P. C., and PESCE, M. (eds.): *Annali di Storia dell' Esegesi*, 1/1984. 1984. Pp. 312. (Edizioni Dehoniane, Bologna. Price: Lire 18,000)

This volume contains the Proceedings of the Research Seminar on Jewish and early Christian exegesis held at Idice di San Lazzaro (Bologna) in October 1983. Of the thirteen papers (all in Italian), at least ten fall within the scope of the *Book List*. M. Simonetti surveys patristic exegesis of Isaiah in the fourth and fifth centuries. Two papers deal with the recovery of individual commentaries on the Psalms from patristic catenae: M. A. Rossi on Cyril of Alexandria and G. M. Vian on Athanasius. M. Pesce analyses Paul's use of scripture in the light of Jewish exegesis. C. Gianotto considers 'The Figure of Melchizedek in Jewish, Christian and Gnostic tradition (2nd–3rd centuries C.E.)' (cf. below, pp. 120–21), and L. Rosso 'The Fortune of Enoch in Ancient Judaism: Values and Problems'. P. C. Bori and G. C. Gaeta study 'The Ethiopian Wife and the Prophetic Primacy of Moses (Num. 12)', and C. Colafemmina the prophetesses Debora and Hulda, both essays surveying both Jewish and Christian sources. This volume contains material of real value, and it is to be hoped that it will have successors.

R. P. R. MURRAY

BOST, H.: *Babel: Du texte au symbole* (Le Monde de la Bible). 1985. P. 268. (Labor et Fides, Geneva. Price: Sw.Fr. 35.00. ISBN 2 8309 0035 9)

The author brings to this work a thorough analysis of the text and demonstrates that the nine verses of the Genesis narrative demand an understanding of the historical and cultural context. His exegesis rests upon the Mesopotamian roots without succumbing to merely archaeological research. Bost investigates the highly complex relationship between three themes: the confusion of languages, the dispersion of the human race, and the construction of the tower of Babel. He reflects upon well-known and speculative views, from Gunkel to Westermann and beyond. Literary and form criticism are applied to a thorough analysis of each verse. Special chapters are devoted to the affinity of the Hebrew tradition and the Babylonian perspective, the ziggurat and the epic of Enmerkar.

Part II deals with the after-life of Babel, the developing symbolism in midrashim and legends, and the Hellenistic syncretism. Dante opens the medieval chapter of interpretation, and the problem of language itself becomes central in modern utopias and ideologies. Barth among many contemporaries prepares us for the rich ambiguities of the hermeneutical process. Bost discerns a polyphonic dialectic which reaches out to Kafka as well as to psychoanalytic insights. He ends on a Christian note of 'Word-*kenosis*'. I enjoyed the combination of technical expertise and readable modernity.

U. E. SIMON

BRENNER, A.: *The Israelite Woman: Social Role and Literary Type in Biblical Narrative* (The Biblical Seminar, 2). 1985. Pp. 144. (JSOT Press, Sheffield. Price: £5.95. ISBN 0 905774 83 3)

This book has two concerns: (1) it explores the role of women in ancient Israel in the socio-political sphere outside their traditional domestic function, ranging from queens to prostitutes; and (2) it examines literary paradigms of female types and behaviour. The author chooses to draw her evidence from Old Testament narrative rather than from law on the grounds that it is difficult to distinguish in the latter between the ideal and the actual. It is her intention that male attitudes reflected in the material should not be *a priori* defined as biased or hostile. In her conclusions, however, they emerge as such. The position of women in ancient Israel, she concludes, compares unfavourably with some aspects of Mesopotamian, Egyptian, and Canaanite societies. A number of interesting observations are made, but one senses that a broader selection of material might have led her to modify some of her conclusions. Is it, for example, fair to conclude, mainly on the evidence of Hos. 2–3, that 'women are viewed as chief practitioners of fertility cults by Hosea'?

G. I. EMMERSON

BRUEGGEMANN, W.: *David's Truth in Israel's Imagination and Memory*. 1985. Pp. 128. (Fortress Press, Philadelphia. Price: $5.95. ISBN 0 8006 1865 3)

In four main chapters (originally delivered as lectures) Brueggemann expounds the differing portrayals of David which he finds in the various literary components of Samuel, a few Psalms, and Chronicles. He acknowledges particular interest in developing the insights gained from literary appreciation and sociological analysis. Thus, the 'truth' of his title does not refer to 'facticity, not what happened, but what is claimed, what is asserted here about reality' (p. 14). Like much of Brueggemann's work, this short book is at once infuriating and enthralling — infuriating because of its undigested jargon, one-sided statements and occasional downright errors (cf. p. 105), and enthralling because it is so often suggestive of fresh angles of approach to familiar material. Thus while the book is clearly aimed at the intelligent general reader, there are also buried here approaches to interpretation which deserve the attention of specialists.

H.G. M. WILLIAMSON

CARNITI, C.: *Il Salmo 68: Studio letterario* (Biblioteca di Scienze Religiose, 68). 1985. Pp. 121. (Libreria Ateneo Salesiano, Rome. Price: Lire 15,000. ISBN 88 213 0113 3)

This is substantially a doctoral thesis done at the Biblicum in Rome under the late Dennis McCarthy and defended in January 1984. The writer has accepted the challenge to defend the unity and coherence of Psalm 68, of which so many have despaired. Her method eschews questions of form- or redaction-criticism, to concentrate on the consonantal text in its given form; in this she traces a structure, neither on 'structuralist' lines nor by rules of logic, but by following the patterns of key images and statements about God and his people. These reveal their own 'logic' and 'a development of thought which proceeds more by intuition than by reasoning' (p. 22). The writer offers her own translation, fully annotated, and then a detailed analysis in five sections. The case is well argued with both insight and literary sensitivity. The work concludes with an excursus on 'The Presence of God in Heaven and on Earth'.

R. P. R. MURRAY

COATS, G. W. (ed.): *Saga, Legend, Tale, Novella, Fable: Narrative Forms in Old Testament Literature* (JSOT Supplement Series, 35). 1985. Pp. 159. (JSOT Press, Sheffield. Price: £14.50; ISBN 0 905774 84 1. Paperback price: £6.50; ISBN 0 905774 85 X)

The five categories of the title have a chapter devoted to each, followed by a further chapter illustrating each category. The editor introduces the collection with a study of the importance of genres for exegesis and contributes about one-third of the book. R. Neff's study of saga is complemented by the editor's piece on the Moses narratives as heroic saga. A very useful chapter on legend by R. M. Hals has as a supplement a 1973 essay on Balaam by Coats. Coats provides the chapter on tale and offers a further chapter illustrating the use of tale by considering the three stories in Genesis which deal with the threat to the host caused by the patriarchs' manipulations of their wives. L. Humphreys analyses novella and contributes a further chapter on the story of Esther and Mordecai as an example of an early Jewish novella. A. Vater Solomon's treatment of fable is supplemented by her chapter on Jehoash's fable of the thistle and the cedar. The volume is deceptively lightweight in appearance, but contains a most useful collection of articles and some good studies of specific biblical texts. Perhaps too much Coats — but otherwise a most worthwhile contribution to the growing literature on narrative forms in the Bible.

R. P. Carroll

Collins, J. J.: *Daniel, with an Introduction to Apocalyptic Literature* (The Forms of the Old Testament Literature, 20). 1984. Pp. xii, 120. (Eerdmans, Grand Rapids, Michigan. Price: $14.95. ISBN 0 8028 0020 3. Distributed in Great Britain by Paternoster Press, Exeter. Price: £12.95)

This work conforms to the established pattern of the series. It begins with a discussion of basic apocalyptic genres, their social setting, and intention, with a brief note on related genres. A second section deals with the form, setting, and intention of the book of Daniel as a whole, while the longest part discusses in greater detail the genre, setting, and intention of each individual unit within the book. In the manner of the series a most useful glossary of form-critical terms is supplied. Very full bibliographies enhance the value of the work, especially relevant here since the controversies over the exact nature and definition of 'apocalyptic' continue without apparent resolution.

No one could wish for a clearer or more authoritative guide to such a study than Professor Collins. Is the reviewer alone, however, in feeling a slight sense of unease about a series which concentrates only on Form Criticism? It gives the impression of being an exercise in descriptive labelling. It is very useful to have labels in supermarkets so that we can tell the meat from the fish counter. But this is useful only as a step towards eating the food. Form Criticism is a useful handmaid who, with the other servants, can minister to our understanding of the meaning of the text. When she poses as the mistress of the house, it seems rather an empty place. Fortunately Professor Collins has elsewhere greatly helped our understanding of the Book of Daniel.

R. A. Mason

Conrad, E. W.: *Fear Not Warrior: A Study of 'al tîrā' Pericopes in the Hebrew Scriptures* (Brown Judaic Studies, 75). 1985. Pp. viii, 185. (Scholars Press, Chico, California. Price: $30.95 (discount price: $25.95); ISBN 0 89130 864 4. Paperback price: $25.95 (discount price $20.95); ISBN 0 89130 865 2)

This argues that the formula 'fear not' is primarily associated with the genre of the War Oracle, the pre-battle address of comfort to the warrior.

One of Conrad's aims is to provide an alternative to Begrich's hypothesis of a Priestly Oracle of Salvation in Deutero-Isaiah. According to Conrad these passages follow the particular form of the War Oracle addressed to a king, with the community in place of the king.

Conrad's thesis seems well established on the whole since he examines a range of contexts. Where he is to be faulted, however, is in a breach of his own stated intentions: 'The study does not attempt to get behind the text to focus on social institutions . . . It is concerned rather with the rhetorical features of the text itself' (p. 1). Yet he attempts to force all his 'fear not' passages into the war setting. Thus, he argues that Jeremiah and Elijah are 'prophetic warriors' even though the language of war ('orders', 'battle', 'ammunition') mainly occurs not in the texts but in Conrad's own discussion of them. A similar problem is found with his treatment of passages dealing with the temple and the patriarchs. Could not the 'fear not' formula have taken on the rhetorical function of response to *any* opposition or obstacle, thus losing particular association with the War Oracle (assuming this was its origin)? Nevertheless, this is an important book and should provoke wide discussion.

L. L. GRABBE

DAVIES, P. R. *Daniel* (Old Testament Guides, 4). 1985. Pp. 133. (JSOT Press, Sheffield. Price £2.95. ISBN 1 85075 002 5)

The fifth in the new series *Old Testament Guides*, this short volume fully lives up to the guidelines set by the editors, especially in the lucid manner in which the author presents his survey of important critical issues and assesses the advances made in the study of Daniel in recently scholarly work. Short sections deal with its history and language, and these are followed by excellent excursuses on literary genre (the story cycle, the vision series). Major themes of the book are discussed (the God of Daniel, the Jewish hero, the gentile King, the 'son of man' and the 'holy ones'), and an attempt is made to identify the book's authors with the 'wise' of chapters 11 and 12 who lived in the period preceding the Maccabean rebellion and added to a group of stories about an exilic hero a series of visions attributed to him. Appended to each section is a select bibliography. The book of Daniel is well served by a number of good commentaries in English, French, and German. This volume marks a useful supplement to them in its discussion of the book's major problems.

P. W. COXON

DREYER, H. J., and GLUCK, J. J. (eds.): *Semitics*. Vol. 9 (Miscellanea, 47). 1984. Pp. viii, 164. (University of South Africa, Pretoria. Price: R.5.90. ISBN 0 86981 312 9)

Of these mostly technical and somewhat forbidding papers the most original as well as exegetically rewarding is Lars Lode's 'Postverbal Word Order in Biblical Hebrew' (pp. 113–64), establishing the standard sentence patterns in Genesis and classifying the meanings of deviations from the patterns. S. F. Grober on 'The Hospitable Lotus' explores the varying metaphoric values of the lotus in the Song of Songs, though it is doubtful that he proves the unity of the book thereby. M. M. Dick studies the syntactic patterns of Obadiah according to the principles of M. O'Connor, T. Collins, and A. Cooper, concluding that only an eclectic and composite application of their theories is adequate to the text. J. A. Durlesser argues from a close rhetorical study of Ps. 1 and Jer. 17:5–8 that the two are literarily independent; some questionable claims about sound repetitions are made. A curious, interesting, but ultimately unconvincing paper by Y. Gamzu on 'The Semitic and Hellenic Types of Narrative' applies E. Auerbach's famous distinction to two modern Jewish poetic reworkings of Gen. 22 and the return of Odysseus. D. Grossberg points to the fact that the lifespans of the patriarchs are 7×5^2, 5×6^2, 3×7^2, and $5^2 + 6^2 + 7^2$, but less authoritatively argues both that these mathematical relationships were intended by the narrator and that they have meanings.

D. J. A. CLINES

EATON, J. H.: *Job* (Old Testament Guides, 5). 1985. Pp. xii, 70. (JSOT Press, Sheffield. Price £2.95. ISBN 0 905774 97 3)

To summarize the contents, structure, style, and linguistic and theological problems of Job in a study guide of under seventy pages is no mean task, but Eaton has fulfilled it with distinction. In this book the reader may well be confronted by the enormous complexities of Job without losing heart. It is the ideal introduction for beginners at school and/or university. Clarity and elegance of presentation aid the wanderer in the maze. Eaton does not minimize the difficulties and underlines the divergence of modern critical approaches by giving a useful list for further reading. It is interesting to note that he is not seduced by the more extravagant hypotheses, such as the agnostic-atheistic interpretations, nor by the quasi-orthodox defence of Elihu as a worthy disputant. Even the Epilogue is saved from derision. Job's uniqueness is not impaired by comparisons with the treatment of suffering in non-biblical cultures — 'each work must be appreciated as a whole and in its own context'. For Eaton the prevailing of the truth and not life after death provide the answer to Job.

U. E. SIMON

EVANS, G. R.: *The Language and Logic of the Bible: The Road to Reformation*. 1985. Pp. xxiv, 192. (Cambridge University Press. Price: £22.50. ISBN 0 521 30548 9)

Gillian Evans's sequel to *The Language and Logic of the Bible: The Earlier Middle Ages* (*B.L.* 1985, p. 77) is a vast sweep from Alexander of Hales to Bellarmine, including Aquinas, Wyclif and the chief Reformers among others. It concentrates on linguistic and logical treatment of the Bible: epistemological status, rhetorical background, application of text to logical problems, methods of resolving scripture's own contradictions. Within its limits the book is erudite, sound, and lucid; it is also original. Evans concludes that creative developments in such as Augustine, Wyclif, and Luther come from apprehending an inner biblical logic missed by piecemeal treatment, and that continuity in exegesis remains more significant than novelty. A corrective to modern arrogance, and meat for exegetes who wonder what they are for.

S. G. HALL

FISHBANE, M.: *Biblical Interpretation in Ancient Israel*. 1985. Pp. xviii, 613. (Oxford University Press. Price: £35.00. ISBN 0 19 826325 2)

Fishbane's study of the emergence within the Old Testament of an extensive pattern of methods and techniques of exegesis, often referred to as 'inner-biblical' exegesis, must certainly be acclaimed as a major scholarly achievement. The phenomenon has frequently been recognized and often treated in piecemeal fashion, but not in the thorough and comprehensive way that is demonstrated here. His study necessarily touches upon a wide range of basic disciplines: text criticism, legal history, literary redaction, as well as the wider realm of theological and religious interpretation. The notion that the text somewhow stands apart from interpretation, which is then a level of meaning conferred upon it, is firmly challenged by Fishbane's showing how the biblical text incorporates within itself a vital history of interpretation. In view of the importance of the subject it is perhaps surprising that we have had to wait until now for a work on this scale dealing with it.

Fishbane begins with text criticism itself and draws attention to the work of earlier scholars, but particularly A. Geiger in the nineteenth century, in demonstrating that the Hebrew text–transmission implies an ongoing and developing pattern of hermeneutical understanding. What the text means has been the subject of a continuing process of revision, development, and comment, since the context in which this text has had to be understood has itself been in a process of constant change. Fishbane then proceeds to explore this phenomenon in four main areas. These concern the scribes themselves who must be postulated as the agents of the transmission and preservation of the text, the legal interpreters who sought to establish the application of its rulings to a changing social context, and a broader homiletical (Aggadic) type of exegesis. The fourth part deals with mantological exegesis by which the author refers to the interpretation of dreams, visions, and omens. This section is noticeably shorter than the others, which means that the prophetic literature is given rather less attention than the legal and historical parts of the canon.

Fishbane says much about the work of scribes in antiquity in general, although he notes that relatively little information has been preserved for us about the particular sphere of the early Hebrew writings. We are compelled to piece together a picture from the analogies of practice elsewhere. Basic to the tracing of a pattern of such interpretation is the necessity to distinguish between the *traditum*, which forms the original deposit, and the *traditio*, by which it was preserved and made meaningful to subsequent generations.

Since it has always been a matter of fundamental importance to Jewish thinking that there exists a demonstrable continuity of understanding between the Hebrew biblical tradition and the manner of its interpretation in later Jewish foundation documents, especially the Mishnah and Talmud, it is clear that Fishbane's study has a direct bearing on the understanding of this. At the same time he pays considerable attention to the ways in which early Christian writings also show themselves to be heirs of this ongoing tradition of inner-biblical exegesis. Coming at a time when the issues of hermeneutics and theological significance are being forced into ever closer relationship to each other, it is evident that what Fishbane has to say touches upon many points of interest to all aspects of biblical study. It will be a long time before the work is superseded, and its careful inductive manner, attention to demonstrable evidence in the text itself, and copious references to secondary material make it an invaluable work of reference. It represents a vital prolegomenon to other areas of literary introduction.

R. E. Clements

Fraade, S. D.: *Enosh and his Generation: Pre-Israelite Hero and History in Postbiblical Interpretation* (Society of Biblical Literature, Monograph Series, 30). 1984. Pp. xvi, 301. (Scholars Press, Chico, California. Price: $29.75 (discount price: $19.95); ISBN 0 89130 724 9. Paperback price: $19.95 (discount price: $13.50); ISBN 0 89130 725 7)

This excellent volume (based on a 1980 University of Pennsylvania Ph.D. thesis) supplies a first-class survey and assessment of the exegetical history of Gen. 4:26. The evidence falls into two main classes. The pre-rabbinic Jewish sources, the Samaritan and Mandaean traditions and, in a suitably modified version, early Christianity interpret the verse and the figure of Enosh in a positive light. By contrast, rabbinic Bible interpretation is negative and discovers in Gen. 4:26 the origin of idolatry, classifying Enosh and his contemporaries as representatives of one of the especially wicked generations of mankind. Professor Fraade's conclusions are based on a careful (philological and literary) analysis. The volume demonstrates the rich potentialities of a comparative historical study of ancient Jewish (and Christian) Bible exegesis.

G. VERMES

GALBIATI, E., and PIAZZA, A.: *Pagine difficili della Bibbia* (*Antico Testamento*) (Sorgenti di Vita, 1). 5th edition. 1985. Pp. 446. (Massimo, Milan. Price: Lire 25,000. ISBN 88 7030 700 X)

This aid to Bible study for Italian readers first appeared in 1951 (*B.L.* 1954, p. 35; *Eleven Years*, p. 572), and reached its fourth edition in 1966. In the preface to this fully revised edition the authors (now respectively Prefect of the Ambrosian Library, Milan, and Bishop of Albenga) explain how the book has remained in demand and still meets a need. it has been brought up to date for readers in the 1980s: the further reading list shows how Bible study has been revolutionized in Italy in the last twenty years. The original task was to counter the near-fundamentalism which dominated the Italian seminaries. Vatican II initiated a vast Biblical revival in Italy, as elsewhere, but a number of theological anxieties affecting the understanding of the Bible still trouble many clergy and laity. Over a third of this book concerns the early chapters of Genesis, discussing literary genres and how the doctrines of *creatio ex nihilo* and original sin relate to exegesis. Much of the rest also concerns literary genres and the biblical modes of narrative, dealing with the anxiety about the sense in which the Bible can be said to be true. (This is, of course, a question which worries others besides Italian Catholics, and it might well find more of a place in unversity syllabuses.)

R. P. R. MURRAY

GARSIEL, M.: *The First Book of Samuel: A Literary Study of Comparative Structures, Analogies and Parallels*. 1985. Pp. 169. (Revivim Publishing House, Ramat Gan, Israel; distributed by Robinson Bookstore, 31 Nachlat-Benjamin, Tel Aviv, Israel. Price: $14.00)

This is a welcome translation into English of a book published in Hebrew in 1983 and reviewed in *B.L.* 1984, p. 67. Garsiel regards 'the author of Samuel as a conscious literary artist working upon older materials, and as being in consequence truly an author and not merely an editor' (p. 77). This he endeavours to demonstrate by studying the thematic, phraseological, and verbal parallels between different incidents both within 1 Samuel and beyond. An introduction discusses the value of this method in relation to others in current scholarly use. Five main chapters then follow, dealing in turn with 'The Narratives about Samuel the Leader', 'Rule by Judges and the "Custom of the King"', 'The Young Saul in Comparison with other Leaders', 'The Portrayal of Saul's Degeneration and Fall', and 'Saul versus David'. There is a bibliography, but unfortunately no index of biblical references, though one is necessary for a work like this in which passages are not always discussed at the points where readers might expect to find them. There is much that is suggestive here, especially where the analysis remains within the context of 1 Samuel. Some of the verbal parallels sought beyond its pages, however, appear far more speculative.

H. G. M. WILLIAMSON

Gnuse, R. K.: *The Dream Theophany of Samuel: Its Structure in Relation to Ancient Near Eastern Dreams and its Theological Significance.* 1984. Pp. xiv, 264. (University Press of America, Lanham, Maryland. Price: $28.75; ISBN 0 8191 3716 2. Paperback price: $14.50; ISBN 0 8191 3717 0)

Only the second half of this work is concerned with Samuel. The first half is devoted to surveys of references to dreams in ancient near eastern literature and in the Old Testament; this material provides a useful equivalent in English to the standard work on the subject by Ehrlich. Then 1 Samuel 3 is analysed in detail and taken to be, not a call narrative, but an auditory message dream of a common ancient near eastern literary type; it is not to be regarded as a reliable historical source of knowledge about Samuel, but is a part of a deuteronomistic interpretation of the people's past traceable in 1 Sam. 1–3. Brief final chapters assess the Samuel traditions in general and draw together the main conclusions of the study. The book stems from a Vanderbilt Ph.D. thesis, and traces of its origin are all too apparent (more than seven hundred footnotes; every scholarly cul-de-sac remarked upon), but it is a useful survey of a wide range of significant material.

R. J. Coggins

Gottwald, N. K.: *The Hebrew Bible: A Socio-Literary Introduction.* 1985. Pp. xxx, 702, including many maps, tables, and charts. (Fortress Press, Philadelphia. Price: $34.95; ISBN 0 8006 0853 4. Paperback price: $19.95; ISBN 0 8006 1853 X)

Norman Gottwald wrote an excellent introduction to Old Testament study, *A Light to the Nations*, as long ago as 1959 (*B.L.* 1960, pp. 26–27; *Decade*, pp. 206–07). Since then much has changed in biblical scholarship, and so this is an entirely new book, though it follows the broad historical focus of the earlier work. Different approaches to the Hebrew Bible (confessional, historical-critical, literary, and social science based) are set out, its physical setting described and its literary development outlined. Then the main texts are discussed within their appropriate historical context. Understanding is facilitated by numerous tables and charts, and more than sixty pages of English bibliography are appended. Throughout Gottwald states his own position clearly, not least in chapter headings such as 'Monarchy: Israel's Counterrevolutionary Establishment', but he gives full recognition to alternative views (e.g. on pre-monarchic Israel) and a fair presentation of those areas where controversy currently rages (e.g. source-criticism of the Pentateuch). His method works better for the historically related material, but overall this new presentation may be most warmly commended for its breadth and sympathy of coverage: the only hesitation comes from the fact that so substantial a work may seem rather daunting for the students for whom it is clearly intended.

R. J. Coggins

Graffy, A.: *A Prophet Confronts his People: The Disputation Speech in the Prophets* (Analecta Biblica, 104). 1984. Pp. xii, 148. (Biblical Institute Press, Rome. Price: Lire 34,000; $17.00. ISBN 88 7653 104 1)

One of the features of the speeches of the prophet Ezekiel is the frequency with which he reports what the people are saying and proceeds to refute their opinion. This device, which is certainly not limited to Ezekiel, has been given the name 'disputation speech', but according to Graffy it is used too loosely 'for other kinds of speech besides the clearly recognisable sequence of quotation of the people and refutation of their words'. The author begins with a critical survey of the way the disputation speech has been presented in genre study, concluding that unless there is a strict quotation-refutation pattern in a text, the genre is absent; and he proceeds to take this as his criterion throughout the study. He examines the elements of the genre and then considers its setting in the life of ancient Israel. Times of crisis promoted the shape of the disputation speech as the prophet confronted his people directly with a view to correcting their mistaken views. Finally, it is proposed that the New Testament too contains some examples of the genre in the preaching of Jesus.

There is no doubt that the author has produced a thought-provoking study that will make scholars consider whether or not they have been careless in their investigations of these matters. Some scholars, however, will wonder why some passages are not included for discussion. The fact that the sharp pattern — introduction: quotation: refutation — is absent does not mean that their function in context is different. Furthermore, should the presence of *hôy* at the beginning of an otherwise conforming speech disqualify that speech for inclusion in the disputation category?

R. B. SALTERS

HIRSCH, D. H., and ASCHKENASY, N. (eds.): *Biblical Patterns in Modern Literature* (Brown Judaic Studies, 77). 1984. P. viii, 243. (Scholars Press, Chico, California. Price: $21.95 (discount price: $17.95); ISBN 0 89130 813 X. Paperback price: $17.95 (discount price: $14.95); ISBN 0 89130 814 8)

The essays gathered here were originally presented to the 1982 conference of the Institute for Literary Research of Bar Ilan University: on biblical substructures and tragic form in Hardy and Agnon (N. Aschkenasy); the biblical ground of Bialik's poetry (H. Barzel); Abishag in the Bible and some modern accounts (M. Baumgarten); Chaucer and the Bible (L. Besserman); the tradition and style of biblical wisdom literature (M. Bloomfield); Job in a Y. H. Brenner novel (M. Brinker); literalism and typology in the American imagination (E. M. Burdick); 'motifs bibliques' in Camus (L. Cohn); the 'American Daniel' in Hawthorne (S. Deykin Baris); biblical imitation in *Joseph Andrews* (H. Fisch); the Song of Songs and the juxtaposition of holy and sexual in seventeenth-century England (N. Flinker); conflicting (logocentric and empirical) tendencies in Western culture (N. Frye); the creation of Eve in Proust (J. Hassine); the Song of Songs and two Henry James novels (D. H. Hirsch); the reassertion of biblical views in European romanticism (W. Z. Hirst); Genesis and the reversal of sexual knowledge in Shakespearean and more recent sex comedies (Z. Jagendorf); translating biblical rhythm (H. Meschonnic); a García Marquez novel as Genesis rewritten (M. Morello-Frosch); the myth of Eden and modern urban consciousness (E. Sicher). A stimulating collection.

D. M. GUNN

KEEL, O.: *Deine Blicke sind Tauben: Zur Metaphorik des Hohen Liedes* (Stuttgarter Bibelstudien, 114/115). 1984. Pp. 208, including 123 line-drawings. (Verlag Katholisches Bibelwerk, Stuttgart. Price: DM. 34.80. ISBN 3 460 04141 2)

The Song of Songs excels in the free use of similes, personifications, allusions, euphemisms, and figures of speech which may be loosely called metaphors. The author addresses himself to every significant *tertium comparationis* of this abundant picture language and begins his study with nine principles of interpretation. These love-poems of longing derive from stereotypes common to the ancient Near East, but Palestine is the natural and cultural centre of this erotic symbolism. Traces of polytheism are unmistakable. Most important of all, not the forms of, but the power associated with, physical properties must control our understanding: nose= snorting, indignation, annoyance; eye= not round circle, but shining in radiance, etc.

The major part of this very successful and thorough analysis, which really amounts to a commentary, applies the principles critically to the intriguing comparisons, such as the towers, the lions, dawn, full moon, sun, and, very fully, the doves and the lotus flowers. Throughout Keel keeps his conversation alive with former and contemporary scholars and experts, expressing agreement and disagreement with a nice lightness of touch. His argumentation is illustrated with line-drawings and occasionally the text is enlivened with poetic parallels from German lyricism. For the author there can be no doubt that these fragments of love poetry require no allegorizing to make them acceptable to the biblical tradition of the affirmation of life. If mysticism employs the metaphors, let the 'donkey' be remembered who carries them. On page 24 read Baudelaire for Matisse! U. E. Simon

Kikawada, I. M., and Quinn, A.: *Before Abraham Was: The Unity of Genesis 1–11*. 1985. Pp. 144. (Abingdon Press, Nashville, Tennessee. Price: $9.95. ISBN 0 687 02602 4)

Genesis 1–11 are here treated as a paradigm of the literary unity of the Pentateuch. The level of argument is scholarly rather than polemical: the case for the documentary analysis of these chapters is presented fairly, but is rejected as failing to take into account the even more impressive evidence of a coherent fivefold structure adapted by a literary artist from a familiar near eastern literary tradition. This pattern is then traced in the Pentateuch as a whole, and also in other biblical narrative texts. An epilogue, rather loosely connected with the main thesis, argues that the assumption of single authorship can rescue biblical texts from the stigma of moral backwardness: the book of Judges is read as the work of an author as horrified by some of the events which he relates as a modern reader might be. This is a stimulating and wide-ranging book; but its theses need a much more solid treatment if they are to be accepted as more than a mere *tour de force*. R. N. Whybray

Krašovec, J.: *Antithetic Structure in Biblical Hebrew Poetry* (Supplements to Vetus Testamentum, 35). 1984. Pp. xiv, 143. (Brill, Leiden. Price: Fl. 52.00. ISBN 90 04 07244 6)

This monograph is a useful introduction to an almost neglected topic. In the opening section the author sets out some definitions of antithesis and outlines his own approach. Most of the book is taken up with discussion of examples in 'epic' literature (i.e. Judg. 5), the psalms (Ps. 73 and others) and a few excerpts from Jeremiah, Ezekiel, and Job. Final observations and conclusions complete the work, and there is a list of passages where antithesis occurs (pp. 124–27). There are many misprints. The author is weakest when using ancient near eastern material but otherwise stimulating. W. G. E. Watson

Kronholm, T.: *Den verksamme Guden: Ett bidrag till Predikarens verklighetsuppfattning, speciellt hans teologi* (Religio: Skrifter utgivna av Teologiska Institutionen i Lund, 4). 1982. Pp. 62. (Teologiska Institutionen, Lund. Price: Sw.Kr. 25.00. ISSN 0280 5723)

This booklet, the Swedish title of which means 'The Active God', begins with a useful survey of introductory problems: the language of Ecclesiastes, the literary structure of the book, its date, its relation to extra-biblical texts, etc. The main part consists of an attempt — in my view not quite successful — to show that the Preacher's scepticism is not his last word, only the dark background of a deep belief in God's ceaseless and merciful activity in the world. The references to literature on Ecclesiastes are very full, though with a number of uncommon and unexplained abbreviations.

B. ALBREKTSON

KUTSCH, E.: *Die chronologischen Daten des Ezechielbuches* (Orbis Biblicus et Orientalis, 62). 1985. Pp. 82. (Universitätsverlag, Freiburg. Price: Sw.Fr. 18.00; ISBN 3 7278 0327 4. Vandenhoeck & Ruprecht, Göttingen. ISBN 3 525 53685 2)

As its title implies, Professor Kutsch's study is an attempt to clear up the questions concerning the precise definition of the dates given in the book of Ezekiel. In a clearly set out examination he argues that the first Babylonian capture of Jerusalem took place on 2 Adar 598/7 (= 16 March 597), which was also reckoned as 'the first year of exile'. The second capture of Jerusalem then occurred on the ninth day of the fourth month 587/6 (= 29 July 587). The years of Nebuchadnezzar's reign are set one year too high in 2 Kings 25:8 (= Jer. 52: 12), and Zedekiah was installed as king in Jerusalem on 1 Nisan 597 (= 13 April 597). All the dates in the book of Ezekiel are then in line with this numbering, save for Ezek. 24:1 (and also 2 Kings 25:7). It is then possible to dispense with the frequently proposed conjectures over Ezek. 32:1 and 33:21 and only becomes necessary to adopt an emendation in respect of Ezek. 26:1, where originally the numbering must have referred to the twelfth year. The reference to the ninth year in Ezek. 24 is reckoned according to the regnal year of Zedekiah, and the thirtieth year of Ezek. 1:1 refers to the era of 'exile'. Altogether a careful and convincing reconstruction.

R. E. CLEMENTS

LIPTZIN, S.: *Biblical Themes in World Literature*. 1985. Pp. viii, 316. (Ktav, Hoboken, New Jersey. Price: $20.00. ISBN 0 88125 063 5)

In this thoroughly unpretentious text the author does a signal service for the study of the Old Testament by displaying a selection of the vast range of effects the biblical narratives have had upon 'world' (that is to say, European) literature. Liptzin was formerly professor of Germanic and Slavic Languages at the City University of New York, and his familiarity with these literatures makes his work more rounded than many similar studies restricted to the Anglo-American literary tradition. In most of his twenty-eight chapters he focuses upon Old Testament personages, not just those with obviously complex characterization in the biblical narratives, like Moses, Samson, David, and Job, but also upon lesser figures like Hagar, Asenath, Rahab, and Abishag that have also appealed to the literary imagination. Despite the vast range of literatures of which the author has control, the pace is unhurried, and he always has time to describe the plot of Byron's *Cain* or D. H. Lawrence's *David*, and many other works. It is a highly readable book, not at all a catalogue. It goes without saying that to consider what creative writers of various cultures have done with the biblical narratives often yields fresh insights for professional biblical scholars, and, no less importantly, situates their own work within a broader humanistic enterprise as well as developing their own personal culture. In a commendatory afterword, Elie Wiesel rightly remarks that such a study leads not only to a better knowledge of the biblical characters but to a deeper self-knowledge as well.

D. J. A. CLINES

LOHFINK, N. (ed.): *Das Deuteronomium: Entstehung, Gestalt und Botschaft* (Bibliotheca Ephemeridum Theologicarum Lovaniensium, LXVIII). 1985. Pp. xii, 382. (Leuven University Press; Uitgeverij Peeters, Leuven. Price: B.Fr. 2,000. ISBN 90 6186 171 3)

This volume collects twenty-eight of the papers (some of them revised and expanded) delivered at the thirty-third Colloquium Biblicum at Louvain in August 1983. The first three deal with aspects of the history of research: M. J. Paul writes on some influences on de Wette, J. Lust on A. Van Hoonacker's position regarding Deuteronomy (a bibliography of Van Hoonacker's writings is also appended in commemoration of the fiftieth anniversary of his death), and Lohfink himself reviews recent studies of 2 Kings 22–23. The remaining essays cover the widest possible spectrum of Deuteronomy studies. Many choose to focus on particular passages: L. Laberge and D. L. Christensen (the LXX and structure of Deut. 1–11 respectively), J. van Goudoever (1:3), L. Perlitt (defending traditional critical scholarship in debate with new literary methods on the basis of Deut. 1–3), C. Brekelmans (Deut. 5), J. Vermeylen (an intricate four-stage redactional study of Deut. 5–11), C. T. Begg (Deut. 9:21 depends upon Exod. 32:20, which has important implications favouring conventional source criticism), G. Braulik (the laws of Deut. 12–26 are based on the order of laws in the Decalogue), S. A. Kaufman (Deut. 15 and the date of P), F. García López (17:14–20), C. Locher (22:13–21), M. Anbar (27:2–8 and Josh. 8:30–32), A. Rofé (28:69–30:20 and the antiquity of the covenant concept), P.-M. Bogaert (32:43), J. Luyten (32:1–43), H.-J. Fabry (Josh. 4:21 ff.), and G. Vanoni (2 Kings 23:25–25:30 is stylistically different from Dtr). The remaining studies cover oral and written law (S. Amsler), law and theology (J. Halbe), the northern roots of Deuteronomy (M. Weinfeld), the social setting of the law (H. Cazelles), Jerusalem in the Deuteronomic History (L. J. Hoppe), divine speech (C. J. Labuschagne), the Gibeonites (A. D. H. Mayes), and the career of Jeremiah in the light of Deut. 31:10–13 (W. L. Holladay). In conclusion, one thing is certain: we are still as far from agreement as ever about even so fundamental a matter as the appropriate methods to use in the study of Deuteronomy.

H. G. M. WILLIAMSON

MCCONVILLE, J. G.: *Law and Theology in Deuteronomy* (JSOT Supplement Series, 33). 1984. Pp. x, 214. (JSOT Press, Sheffield. Price: £18.50; ISBN 0 905774 78 7. Paperback price: £8.95; ISBN 0 905774 79 5)

The author argues that the distinctive theology of Deuteronomy is reflected in its laws, and that the loose and inexact manner in which the laws are formulated is related to Deuteronomy's 'readiness to paint a partial picture of the ritual pertaining to any aspect of the cult in order to further its overriding theological and hortatory concerns' (p. 154). It is argued that it is the failure to recognize this characteristic of the book that has led to the 'error' of regarding discrepancies between it and other law-codes in the Pentateuch as evidence for the historical development of Israelite religion. It is concluded that there is no need to posit any other setting for the book than that which the book itself claims — the eve of the settlement. It is also maintained that the book is a substantial unity. Many readers will ask, however, whether the differences between Deuteronomy and, for example, P are explained away rather than explained here, and whether sufficient consideration has been given to the possibility that reasons other than those here advanced account for Deuteronomy's evident lack of interest in ritual and sacral traditions which contrasts so strikingly with the Priestly Code. Thus, for example, the question what sort of society is presupposed by the particular nature and emphasis of Deuteronomy as compared with other law-codes such as P is not raised.

E. W. NICHOLSON

MCKENZIE, S. L.: *The Chronicler's Use of the Deuteronomistic History* (Harvard Semitic Monographs, 33). 1985. Pp. viii, 219. (Scholars Press, Atlanta, Georgia. Price: $16.50; discount price: $10.95. ISBN 0 89130 828 8)

Despite the apparent implications of the title, this interesting dissertation is mainly concerned with the Deuteronomistic History rather than the Chronicler. Following his supervisor, F. M. Cross, McKenzie accepts the theory of a double redaction of the History, and attempts to find reliable criteria for identifying the second edition (Dtr 2). In pursuit of the suggestion that the Chronicler's use of Samuel-Kings might help, a detailed textual analysis of that use is offered, examining omissions, additions, and parallels. This careful discussion will prove useful even if McKenzie's own conclusions are not accepted. His two main proposals are in fact not easily compatible with each other: on the one hand he shows that the Chronicler's *Vorlage* of Samuel differed from that of Kings (which might imply a developed stage in textual tradition); on the other hand he maintains that the Chronicler had before him the first rather than the second edition of the Deuteronomistic History (which suggests a very early stage in the development).

R. J. COGGINS

MAYES, A. D. H.: *Judges* (Old Testament Guides, 3). 1985. Pp. 98. (JSOT Press, Sheffield. Price: £2.95. ISBN 0 905774 58 2)

Three chapters give surveys of the literary composition of Judges, the social and cultural background, and the relation of the book to historical reconstruction of the Judges period. Each is done with great assurance and expertise, but so full and condensed that the new student will have to work hard to master it. The composition theory, based on Noth's continuous Deuteronomic history and using Richter's theory of a short *Retterbuch* as the original core, inevitably leads to much complexity and is presented a little too confidently. The other two chapters have great value as summary discussions of such issues as the amphictyony theory, Israel as a 'segmentary' society, charismatic leadership, the minor judges, and the problems of dating events. At the beginning we are told that Israelite history writing is concerned with 'making the past meaningful for the present', but a certain lack of concentration on theological perspectives is the one weakness of an excellent contribution to the series. The classified bibliographies are well chosen and comprehensive.

B. LINDARS

MILLER, W. T.: *Mysterious Encounters at Mamre and Jabbok* (Brown Judaic Studies, 50). 1984. Pp. viii, 243. (Scholars Press, Chico, California. Price: $24.95 (discount price: $18.25); ISBN 0 89130 816 4. Paperback price: $18.25 (discount price: $13.50); ISBN 0 89130 817 2)

The author takes two well-known passages (Gen. 18:1–16 and 32:23–33) and examines the history of their interpretation in the light of J. A. Sanders's two hermeneutical modes, 'constitutive' and 'prophetic'. Even if one is not convinced of the value of this undertaking, one can appreciate a good deal of what Miller has done. Taking each passage separately (it is never actually explained why these two passages are chosen), the author begins by tracing the early Jewish hermeneutic in the ancient versions and the targums. This is followed by a study of early Christian and Alexandrian Jewish interpretation. As a result, the early interpretations, as reflected in versions and commentators, Jewish and Christian, are laid bare, and we get a glimpse of exegesis in the pre-critical period. One might have wished for more passages treated in this way, and it may be that this work will renew interest in the field.

R. B. Salters

Neher, A.: *L'Essenza del Profetismo*. Traduzione di E. Piattelli. Presentazione di R. Fabris (Radici, 4). 1984. Pp. xvi, 290. (Editrice Marietti, Casale Monferrato. Price: Lire 28,000. ISBN 88 211 8333 5)

This interpretation of the prophets from a Jewish standpoint first appeared in 1955 (see *B.L.* 1956, p. 50 (*Eleven Years*, p. 757); *B.L.* 1973, p. 41 (*Bible Bibliog.*, p. 463)). This Italian translation by E. Piattelli was made from the third edition of 1983, which has not been noted in the *Book List*, but which is unchanged except for a new preface of a few pages. This work is an appropriate addition to the Italian series *Radici*, which sets out to cater for Jewish-Christian dialogue, and already contains Buber's *Moses* (*B.L.* 1985, pp. 73–74). An introduction by R. Fabris sets the work in the context of Jewish-Christian dialogue.

A. Gelston

Nielsen, K.: *For et træ er der håb: Om træet som metafor i Jes 1–39* (Bibel og historie, 8). 1985. Pp. 411. (G. E. C. Gad, Copenhagen. Price: D.Kr. 180.00. ISBN 87 12 07122 6)

The title is a quotation from the book of Job: 'For there is hope for a tree' (14:7). The Job text continues: 'if it be cut down, that it will sprout again, and that its shoots will not cease'; this idea, according to the author, lies behind the use of tree imagery in Isa. 1–39. Trees are used in metaphors which bridge the gap between prophecies of doom and prophecies of hope. The function of the tree metaphor is *informative*, being a theological interpretation of the political situation, and *performative*, engaging the audience in a specific view of life. These are useful metaphors because they are able to produce a new understanding of the original message. The first part of the book deals with the history of research and the methods used (pp. 15–90), and the second consists of analyses (91–335). Trees are used in two different kinds of metaphors, one of cutting (Isa. 10:33–11:9, 10; 14:4b–20; 37: 22b–32; 6:12–13; 2:12–17; 4:2–6; 32:15–20), another of burning (9:7–20; 10:16–19; 1:29–31). The investigation of these texts forms the major part of the book; not all the analyses are successful, but as a whole they are a useful contribution to Isaiah research. A special section is devoted to the Song of the Vineyard (Isa. 5:1–7; cf. 27:2–6), and this is the most interesting and cogent part of the monograph. The book will be of interest to readers with a literary approach to the Bible as well as for those who are concerned with more traditional exegetical questions.

K. Jeppesen

OHLER, A.: *Studying the Old Testament: From Tradition to Canon*. Translated by D. Cairns. 1985. Pp. x, 388. (T. & T. Clark, Edinburgh. Price: £17.50. ISBN 0 567 09335 2)

This is the English translation of Ohler's two-volume work, *Gattungen im AT: ein biblisches Arbeitsbuch*, published in 1972, 1973 (see *B.L.* 1974, p. 56). It is essentially an introduction to the Old Testament, but not of the conventional *Einleitung/Einführung* type. Five substantial chapters cover the whole range of biblical material in terms of the peculiarities of Hebrew thought and language (1), narrative and poetic categories (2), prophets, teachers of wisdom, and theologians (3), the composite works of the Pentateuch, the Deuteronomistic History and Chronicles (4), and the question of the unity of the Old Testament (5). Each section begins with the exposition of a piece of text, and from this Ohler develops her treatment of the particular forms of literature under consideration. It is quite a dense book with a wealth of exegesis undergirding a fine presentation of the many issues involved in introducing the intelligent student to the study of the Hebrew Bible. The time gap between the original book and its English translation gives some of its views (e.g. patriarchs, covenant, Jeremiah, etc.) an old- fashioned look, but the earnest seeker after knowledge will not find them obtrusive. I would commend this book to the bright student of independent means or the lecturer tired of the fixed-form Old Testament introductions.

R. P. CARROLL

RADDAY, Y. T., and LEVI, Y.: *An Analytical Linguistic Key-Word-In-Context Concordance to the Book of Exodus* (The Computer Bible, 28). 1985. Pp. 407. (Biblical Research Associates, Wooster, Ohio. Price: $45.00. ISBN 0 935106 23 5)

This volume follows the format of Radday's previous computer-generated concordances (*B.L.* 1978, p. 75 (Judges); 1980, p. 73 (Genesis, Five Scrolls)). Part I gives listings for whole words only; thus all occurrences listed of *l*- are combinations with pronomial suffixes. No vowels appear, but stars indicate words containing *Sin*. Morphological analysis (including a syllable count) in numerical code accompanies every entry. This distinguishes homographs (e.g. adverb *ʾl* and preposition *ʾl*), except those representing the same part of speech; thus the lists for *ʾammāh* and *ʾāmāh* have identical headings. Part II lists the occurrences of every verb. Word frequencies appear in Part III only (under heading *šk* (i.e. 'frequency')), where the words stand not in alphabetical order but in descending order of frequency. (Different conjugations of one root count as separate lexemes.) The final page tabulates how many words occur once, twice, and so on, in Exodus. Significantly, the commonest nouns (excluding names) are 'son', 'people' (*ʿam*) and 'land', against 'son', 'land' and 'father' in Genesis.

M. P. WEITZMAN

RADDAY, Y. T., SHORE, H., and others: *Genesis: An Authorship Study in Computer-Assisted Statistical Linguistics* (Analecta Biblica, 103). 1985. Pp. xx, 263. (Biblical Institute Press, Rome. Price: Lire 35,000; $20.00. ISBN 88 7654 103 3)

As criteria for an objective comparison of the Genesis material conventionally assigned to J, E, and P, the frequencies of fifty-four allegedly content-free features — such as construct nouns or hiphʿil verbs — were selected. Numerous statistical tests (pp. 32–122; pp. 32–51 are by D. Wickmann), and representations of the data in tree or map form (pp. 122–90), by computer, distinguished J and E from P but not from each other. The authors, on no statistical ground, attribute the singular position of P to its different content. Another tripartite division of Genesis, into narrative (N), human speech (H) and divine speech (D), was similarly investigated: H and D distinguished themselves from N but not from each other. Now human and divine speech in fact differ in style, as a thoughtful contribution by C. Rabin explains (pp. 218–24). One may infer that the indistinguishability of J and E attests not (as Radday and Shore contend) their identical origin but the insensitivity of the analysis, 'unassailably objective' though it be. This section includes a table (pp. 65–72) showing how the frequencies of some thirty features (such as *w–*) vary in different segments from the average for all Genesis. A further tripartite division, into chapters 1–11, 12–36, and 37–50, was also studied, and linguistic differences detected between the three divisions.

A different approach, by M. A. Pollatschek and Radday (pp. 191–214), rested on the numbers of words occurring once, twice, thrice . . . in a given segment. It distinguished, N, H, and D clearly — and P, J, and E almost equally clearly. Pollatschek and Radday argue that as divided authorship can hardly be supposed for NHD, it should not be supposed for PJE. Greater justice is done to the statistical findings by Rabin's suggestion that narrative, human speech, and divine speech each had its own norms, upon which each source superimposed its own distinctive usages. A novel alternative is proposed in S. Talmon's summing-up (pp. 225–35): a single narrator 'practically quoted' human and divine utterances from pre-existing materials.

The technicalities and special pleading should not obscure the linguistic differences which Radday and Shore's analysis (pp. 52–190) detected between P and JE. Their concluding claim of 'massive evidence that Genesis is a unity' (p. 190) is a massive *non-sequitur*.

M. P. Weitzman

Ravasi, G.: *I Salmi*. 1985. Pp. 246. (Editrice Àncora, Milan. Price: Lire 12,000. ISBN 88 7610 111 X)

This excellent introductory account of the Psalms assumes a considerable familiarity on the part of the reader with the content of the Bible as a whole, but no technical theological knowledge. After six pages of general introduction, the book is divided into seven sections on form-critical lines: hymns, laments, psalms of confidence, thanksgiving psalms, royal psalms, psalms of instruction (subdivided into historical and wisdom psalms), and liturgies. In each section there is a brief introduction on the characteristics of the form and an indication of other psalms belonging to this category, followed by a brief commentary on a few representative psalms, some thirty-three psalms being treated in all. The liturgical and devotional use of the psalms in a Christian context is in mind throughout, and the book will be of value to all who are engaged in this activity without the benefit of theological training. (The author has also written a full-scale commentary on the Psalms: see *B.L.* 1983, p. 52; 1985, p. 64.)

A. Gelston

Rendtorff, R.: *The Old Testament: An Introduction*. Translated by J. Bowden. 1985. Pp. xii, 308. (SCM Press, London. Price: £12.50. ISBN 0 334 02089 1)

For a description of this important Introduction see *B.L.* 1984, p. 78. The English translation on the whole reads well. The useful system of marginal cross-references has been retained, and English editions of German publications, where available, have been given in the bibliographies instead of the original German editions. This book provides a valuable working-tool for students (and scholars), and it is excellent that it has now been made available in English.

M. A. Knibb

Rofé, A.: *Reflections on the Question of the Composition of the Books of the Law and the Prophets* (in Hebrew). 1985. Pp. vi, 148. (Academon Press, Jerusalem. Price: $6.00.)

The eight articles reprinted here (one in English, the remainder in modern Hebrew, without English summaries) reflect Rofé's commitment to a 'literary-historical' criticism of the Bible which is more inclined to a traditio-historical approach than, for example, to the once standard documentary theory of Pentateuchal origins. His foreword hints at the deep-seated resistance to the latter which still exists in Israel and the difficulties encountered by critical scholars there. The essays (which were first published between 1966 and 1985) include one on the Pentateuch (on Gen. 24), five on passages in the Former Prophets (Josh. 20; Josh. 24:28–33 in LXX; Judg. 2:6–3:6; 1 Sam. 10:27 according to 4QSam[a] (in English); 2 Sam. 24 and 1 Kings 18–19), and two on issues in the Latter Prophets (the separate existence of Trito-Isaiah and the Deuteronomistic contribution to the book of Jeremiah). The conclusions reached are sometimes unusual, but they deserve attention because they are founded on a careful study of the text.

G. I. Davies

Rüterswörden, U.: *Die Beamten der israelitischen Königszeit: Eine Studie zu śr und vergleichbaren Begriffen* (Beiträge zur Wissenschaft vom Alten und Neuen Testament, 117). 1985. Pp. viii, 169. (Kohlhammer, Stuttgart. Price: DM. 44.00. ISBN 3 17 008819 X)

This study of the Hebrew root *śr* and related words, with particular interest in the period of the monarchy, was originally presented as a dissertation to the University of Bochum. Many different aspects of the root's usage are explored: the occasions on which it overlaps with *ʿbd*, with which it is not identical; its usage in military circles; its occurrence without a *nomen rectum* to refer to a military leader; its use in ethnic and geographical designations; etymology; synonyms; the various officials listed among the *śārîm*; an examination of other titles which are not directly linked and whose bearers did not belong to the *śārîm*. The author manages to locate all the occurrences of the root somewhere under these various headings and to give them some attention. Throughout his study he takes extra-biblical evidence into consideration; this is especially evident in his section on the Joseph narrative, in his treatment of the root *rb*, and in his scattered references to Hebrew seals, ostraca, and inscriptions. Although the format of a dissertation, with its many divisions and sub-divisions, still dominates the present version of the work, it is a useful and informative piece of research.

G. H. Jones

Steck, O. H.: *Bereitete Heimkehr: Jesaja 35 als redaktionelle Brücke zwischen dem Ersten and dem Zweiten Jesaja* (Stuttgarter Bibelstudien, 121). 1985. Pp. 117. (Verlag Katholisches Bibelwerk, Stuttgart. ISBN 3 460 04211 7)

Increasingly attention in the book of Isaiah has been drawn to the questions relating to the overall redaction of the book. Among these the most prominent has been that concerning the connection of chapters 40 ff. with 1–39. As its title indicates the present study is devoted to Isa. 35 which is regarded as having been specifically composed to facilitate the joining together of 'First' with 'Second' Isaiah. At this stage the former probably comprised most of Isa. 1–34 and the latter chapters 40–62. A closely related redactional stratum of material is further to be seen in Isa. 11:11–16, 27:12–13 and 62:10–12. It should probably be dated in the later Persian era and must be seen, not as a series of independent units, but as part of the continuing process of re-interpretation of prophecy which motivated this type of editorial work.

The study is certainly an important one and is symptomatic of a markedly changed approach to the problems of this prophetic book. Gone are the days of a simple threefold division made up of materials which were treated as more or less self-contained and independent. Steck makes some interesting and positive suggestions and offers some fresh light on the long and complex process by which the book of Isaiah took shape.

R. E. CLEMENTS

VAN DER WAL, A., and TALSTRA, E.: *Amos: Concordance and Lexical Surveys* (Applicatio, 2). 1984. Pp. 135. (VU Boekhandel/Uitgeverij, Amsterdam. Price: Fl. 29.50. ISBN 90 6256 264 7)

This work is due to the same research group as the study by Bastiaens and others of Trito-Isaiah and follows the same format (see above, p. 61). One notes from the frequencies that conjunctive *waw* accounts for almost exactly 11.2% of the text (measured in lexemes) in each of Deutero-Isaiah, Trito-Isaiah, and Amos. On pp. 107–19 it can be seen how often each lexeme appears in each of the six units into which van der Wal divided Amos in *JSOT* 26, pp. 107–13. This reveals, for example, that *ṭōb* and *raʿ* are confined to the unit 5:7–6:12. The lexemes common and exclusive to various pairs and triplets of units are listed on pp. 134–35. It is instructive to compare the frequencies in A. Even-Shoshan's concordance (*B.L.* 1979, p. 16; 1981, p. 14); for example, the average number of occurrences of *lōʾ* per page of the Letteris text is 3.7 over the whole Old Testament, but 8.8 in Deutero-Isaiah, 6.3 in Trito-Isaiah, and 7.9 in Amos.

M. P. WEITZMAN

WATSON, W. G. E.: *Classical Hebrew Poetry: A Guide to its Techniques* (JSOT Supplement Series, 26). 1984. Pp. xx, 457. (JSOT Press, Sheffield. Price: £25.00; ISBN 0 905774 57 4. Paperback price: £12.50; ISBN 1 85075 048 3)

The main aim of this book is 'to provide a working tool for lecturers and students who need a reference book in a rapidly expanding field', and it 'is intended principally for readers with a good working knowledge of classical Hebrew' (p. ix), although many Accadian and Ugaritic examples are also given. After lists of abbreviations and *Festschriften* and an introduction, there are chapters on poetic texts in other Semitic languages, the method to be used in analysing Hebrew poetry, the Hebrew poet in action, metre ('only an accentual (stress-based) theory can account for Hebrew metre', p. 103), parallelism, stanza and strophe, verse-patterns, sound, imagery, poetic devices, and secondary techniques. Each chapter has many examples and bibliographical references, and the last chapter is devoted to 'worked examples' before the closing comments. Full indexes are provided. The book is clearly written and, as is plain from the list of contents, comprehensive in character, and it is good that alternative theories (e.g. of metre) are considered in a number of places. Watson does not, however, always point out that some of the theories that he accepts (e.g. that there was a vocative *lamedh* in Hebrew) and some of the translations that he offers are open to question (e.g. 'fatherless' for *'ebyônîm* in Job 29:16 (p. 243); 'you should govern' for *tinḥal* in Ps. 82:8 (p. 293); 'my bones' for *'ăṣāmênû* in Ps. 141:7 (p. 319); 'for himself' for *lānû* in Ps. 47:5 (p. 371)). On the other hand, the statement on p. 29 that Hebrew had a phrase *dm 'sym* is certainly a slip of the pen. Watson's judgement is usually as balanced as it is well informed. He is to be commended for preparing a highly successful and useful handbook.

J. A. EMERTON

WEINFELD, M.: *Deuteronomy and the Deuteronomic School.* 1983 (1972). Pp. xviii, 467. (Clarendon Press, Oxford. Price: £27.50. ISBN 0 19 826626 X)

Much has happened in the study of Deuteronomy and the Deuteronomic corpus as well as in related topics such as the covenant since this book was first published (see *B.L.* 1973, p. 46; *Bible Bibliog.* p. 468). It may be asked, for example, whether the Deuteronomic 'school' was quite so monolithic in its outlook and theology as Weinfeld seems to suggest, and whether more allowance should now be made for important shifts and developments in the course of its activity. Whether Deuteronomy is as dependent upon the form, structure, and terminology of ancient near eastern treaties as the book argues needs also to be re-examined. But there is much that remains of value, for example, its extensive treatment of 'demythologization' and 'secularization' in Deuteronomy. This reprint of it is to be welcomed.

E. W. NICHOLSON

WEIPPERT, H., SEYBOLD, K., WEIPPERT, M.: *Beiträge zur Prophetischen Bildsprache in Israel und Assyrien* (Orbis Biblicus et Orientalis, 64). 1985. Pp. x, 93. (Universitätsverlag, Freiburg. Price: Sw.Fr. 22.00. ISBN 3 7278 0329 0. Vandenhoeck & Ruprecht, Göttingen. ISBN 3 525 53687 9)

These three valuable studies originated independently of Westermann's monograph (*B.L.* 1985, p. 99), in connection with a Symposium at Freiburg in 1984. Helga Weippert surveys Amos's similes and metaphors, paying special attention to animal imagery, and drawing on the pictorial legacy of the ancient Near East to illustrate and interpret some of the material. She concludes that a high proportion reflects the prophet's experience as a Judaean countryman. Klaus Seybold draws attention to the satirical tone of Zephaniah's similes and metaphors. Caricature takes the place of accusation in judgement-oracles. His use of this characteristic as a criterion to distinguish Zephaniah's words from those of the traditionists is more debatable. Manfred Weippert examines seventh-century Assyrian prophecies. Although mostly addressed to the king they use homely images, such as the goddess as a nursing-mother to the king. Some have parallels in the Old Testament, e.g. the hostile insects in Isa. 7:18 and the protective bird in Isa. 31:5.

A. GELSTON

WILSON, G. H.: *The Editing of the Hebrew Psalter* (Society of Biblical Literature, Dissertation Series, 76). 1985. Pp. xiv, 278. (Scholars Press, Chico, California. Price: $17.25 (discount price: $11.50); ISBN 0 89130 766 4. Paperback price: $11.50 (discount price: $7.75); ISBN 0 89130 728 1)

This interesting and important study sets the discussion of the Psalter first in the context of Mesopotamian hymnic literature, suggesting cautiously the degree to which that material is relevant to the biblical sphere. In two substantial chapters devoted to the Qumran Psalms manuscripts, there is careful and critical discussion of the different views taken of these in relation to the Hebrew Psalter; the texts are analysed and the indications of alternative and viable forms of psalm collections are drawn out. Two concluding chapters discuss evidence of editorial work on the Hebrew Psalter, considering the significance of superscriptions and their absence, the divisions into books, and the thematic grouping of psalms. Tables throughout and three appendixes help to set out the evidence with completeness and clarity. If, particularly in the final chapter, the discussion is inevitably more subjective, the conduct of the argument is throughout lucid and well-presented. The author has made out a very good case for a purposeful construction of the Psalter, and has contributed substantially to a difficult area in a manner which invites a closer look at the Psalter as a whole and not just at individual psalms and psalm-groups. Notes, Bibliography, and Indexes add to the usefulness of the volume.

P. R. Ackroyd

Van Der Woude, A. S.: *Profeet en Establishment: Een verklaring van het boek Micha* (Serie Exegetische Studies, 1). 1985. Pp. 126. (J. H. Kok, Kampen. Price: Fl.19.90. ISBN 90 242 2785 2)

Closely built upon the author's important commentary of 1976 (see *B.L.* 1977, p. 54), this short general presentation of the book of Micah is directed to the non-technical, general reader. It incorporates concise exegesis of much of the text, and pays special attention to the political, social and religious situation of the prophet's time. The opening sections sketch what may be said about the prophet and his life-context, the period to which he belonged, the making and nature of the book, and the social and religious establishment against which his message was directed. The latter sections offer the exegesis of the chosen texts, and a discussion of Israel's messianic hope, linked to particular passages in the book. A final section discusses chapters 6–7, described as 'Deutero-Micah', a northern element combined with the Micah material. As would be expected, van der Woude offers much illuminating comment, often controversial, but always worth attention. Such a series, it may be hoped, will provide what is so often needed: the transmission of technical discussion in acceptable form to a wider audience.

P. R. Ackroyd

Zenger, E.: *Israel am Sinai: Analysen und Interpretationen zu Exodus 17–34*. 2. Auflage. 1985. Pp. 200, including 8 illustrations. (Akademische Bibliothek, Altenberge. Price: DM. 24.80. ISBN 3 88733 030 7)

Zenger is one of those actively engaged on Pentateuchal research who continue to believe in J and E in something like their traditional form. Not that his mind has stood still: the analysis of the Sinai-pericope offered here (pp. 130–55) differs somewhat from his earlier conclusions in *Die Sinaitheophanie* (1971). Other detailed chapters treat the structure of Exodus in its present form (the central Sinai section begins at Exod. 17:1 (cf. 17:6)), the literary analysis and interpretation of Exod. 17:1–7 and 8–16, the traditions of Yahweh as the 'God from Sinai' and the 'God at Sinai' (only the former is early), and the theology of the pre-exilic strata J, E, and Je (i.e. R^{JE}, which introduced, in Ex. 34, the idea of legislation at Sinai). A brief introduction and conclusion relate the teaching of Exodus to modern liberation theology. In this second edition — the first (1982) was not noted in the *Book List* — some misprints are corrected and two small changes made in the treatment of the J material (pp. 157, 162–63).

G. I. Davies

7. LAW, RELIGION, AND THEOLOGY

CHILDS, B. S.: *Old Testament Theology in a Canonical Context*. 1985. Pp. xvi, 255. (SCM Press, London. Price: £10.00. ISBN 0 334 02230 4)

Since the issue of canonical criticism as a fresh basis for an approach to the study of the Old Testament was raised by Professor Childs more than a decade ago, it has received extensive discussion. Much of the argument has revolved around the question of an appropriate basis for a theological evaluation of the literature, rather than with more narrowly conceived literary issues of sources, form or structure in the various writings. There is a certain logical appropriateness therefore in the presentation by Professor Childs of an Old Testament theology with questions concerning the canon as a central feature. In the outcome two broad impressions may be put forward. The first of these is that this further volume will be much valued as a rich and wide-ranging contribution to the problems concerning what the Christian church should do about Old Testament theology. The second, more negative, comment is that, when viewed critically, it is not at all clear that canon criticism does fulfil its promise of offering a way through many of the difficulties that have been felt. It represents a further dimension of reference, which is at times useful, but essentially the basic problems about the nature of an Old Testament theology remain what they were, and are neither advanced nor hindered by the literary and historical questions relating to the canon.

Having made these broad points, it must also be said that all who are concerned about what to do with the Old Testament in the study of theology will find a great deal that is stimulating, fresh, and interesting in this book. It is in scope no more than a sketch of how the subject might be treated, but it raises most of the central issues with useful guides to other literature. Childs sees Old Testament theology as a distinctively Christian discipline, although one of its purposes will be to explore with Judaism a common interest in the interpretation of the Hebrew Bible. It must also keep itself apart from simply re-evaluating what the New Testament does with the Old.

Overall the structure of the presentation is clear and successful, without claiming to represent the only form that an Old Testament theology should take. It is built around the ideas of revelation and response with the theme of the revelation of the divine law coming in the central position. This leads to some awkward tensions, as for example the treatment of ritual and purity laws in chapter eight, whereas the cultus, which is viewed more as Israel's response, does not come until chapter fourteen. Some of the chapters are surprisingly brief, often doing little more than alluding to more extended development of the issues in the larger volumes on the subject. The major purpose appears to be to offer a critique of a number of basic positions that have tended to become central in much recent discussion. There is a greater degree of sensitivity to the way in which Jewish scholarship approaches several of the themes than has generally been shown by Christian Old Testament theologies.

Looked at as a summary guide to the major religious themes of the Old Testament there are some unexpected emphases. The themes of election, covenant, and the nationhood of Israel are left in the background, whereas the human dimension of individual existence within the parameters of a given set of moral and social conditions occupies the foreground. It is a volume that is full of interest and insight, but for all the expectation aroused by its title, it endeavours to reconstruct a distinctive theological basis underlying the Old Testament, without too great an emphasis upon the ways in which the finished canon has actually been used in Christian tradition.

R. E. CLEMENTS

DOHMEN, C.: *Das Bilderverbot: Seine Entstehung und seine Entwicklung im Alten Testament* (Bonner Biblische Beiträge, 62). 1985. Pp. 311. (Peter Hanstein, Königstein/Ts. and Bonn. Price: DM 84.00. ISBN 3 7756 1076 6)

This dissertation submitted to the Catholic Theological Faculty in Bonn traces the development in Old Testament religion of the prohibition of cultic depictions of the deity. The author holds that being 'nomadic' in origin, the religion of Israel was from the outset cultically pictureless. The earliest form of Exod. 20:23, written in the pre-monarchic period when the Israelites were becoming urbanized, sought to safeguard the 'nomadic' heritage. In the early monarchy the ark, the cherubim, and the Bethel bull-cult were not regarded as heterodox. However, growing prophetic opposition to worship of other gods led to a prohibition of cultic representations of the deity, and the actions of Manasseh were probably the cause of the prohibition in the earliest deuteronomic version of the Decalogue. This basic outline does not do justice to the detailed examinations of Exod. 20:23; 32:1–35; 34:17; Lev. 19:4; 26:1; Deut. 4:16–18, 23, 25; 5:8; and 27:15. Also, there are discussions of the meaning and use of *pesel* and *massekah*, and the 'image of God', and an examination of *nun-paragogicum* as a possible redactional indicator. Altogether this is a very informative book.

J. W. ROGERSON

DOLL, P.: *Menschenschöpfung und Weltschöpfung in der alttestamentlichen Weisheit* (Stuttgarter Bibelstudien, 117). 1985. Pp. 88. (Verlag Katholisches Bibelwerk, Stuttgart. Price: DM. 21.80. ISBN 3 460 04171 4)

After observing that the notions of the creation of mankind and of the world are never found together in Proverbs, the former occurring only in chapters 10–29 and the latter only in chapters 1–9, the author traces their development especially in the wisdom literature down to Ecclesiasticus and the Wisdom of Solomon. The sayings in Prov. 10–29 were originally 'Volksweisheit'; and those which refer to God as creator, especially 14:31; 17:5; 22:2; 29:13, arose from specific pre-exilic situations and may be compared with the teaching of Amos. The creation passages in Prov. 1–9 and Job 28, on the other hand, are theological reflections with a quite different origin. In the deutero-canonical literature the two themes are combined, and are used to support such themes as predestination and a 'scientific' view of the universe. Some statements need a rather fuller justification, and occasionally too much depends on problematic interpretations of particular texts; but this is an interesting attempt to deal with aspects of a subject which have previously passed unnoticed.

R. N. WHYBRAY

FOHRER, G.: *Fede e Vita nel Giudaismo* (Studi Biblici, 69). Translated by V. Gatti. 1984. Pp. 226. (Paideia Editrice, Brescia. Price: Lire 15,000)

This is the Italian translation of Fohrer's *Glaube und Leben im Judentum* (1979: *B.L.* 1980, p 87). A note added to the Introduction says that a few corrections by the author have been incorporated.

R. P. R. MURRAY

FOHRER, G.: *Storia della Religione Israelitica* (Biblioteca di Cultura religiosa, 45). Translated by C.M. Santandrea. 1985. Pp. 485. (Paideia Editrice, Brescia. Price: Lire 40,000)

Fohrer's *Geschichte der israelitischen Religion* appeared in 1969 (*B.L.* 1970, p. 63; *Bible Bibliog.*, p. 253) and the English version in 1973

(*B.L.* 1974, p. 67). With this Italian version the publishers have served the author well for the fourth time.

R. P. R. MURRAY

FRANCH, J. A. (ed.): *El Mito ante la Antropología y la Historia* (Colección Monografias, 72). 1984. Pp. x, 194. (Centro de Investigaciones Sociológicas, Madrid. ISBN 84 7476 082 8)

This volume consists of seven papers given at a seminar of the Universidad International Menendez Pelayo at Santander in July 1982. Although the first two chapters on the history of the study of myth in the nineteenth and twentieth centuries respectively are worth the attention of Old Testament scholars, only one of the essays will be of direct concern to them: this is the contribution by Luis Alonso Schökel on Mythical and Symbolic Language in the Old Testament. It is largely based on a discussion of two passages, Isa. 26:19 and Ezek. 37: 1–10, from which the author shows how the original concepts of myth turn into symbolic language in Old Testament prophecy and poetry, leading on in turn to the symbolic reading of the Old Testament in the Church. The treatment is interesting, but the essay as a whole is somewhat superficial and rambling: those familiar with the writings of Austin Farrer and S. H. Hooke will find Alonso Schökel's approach much better represented there.

J. R. PORTER

GARCÍA TRAPIELLO, J.: *Il problema morale nell'Antico Testamento* (Sorgenti di vita, 17). Translated by R. Sorgia. 1983. Pp. 214. (Editrice Massimo, Milan. Price: Lire 10,000. ISBN 88 7030 706 9)

Translated, with some revision of the notes and bibliography, from the Spanish (1977: but not noticed in the *Book List*), the present work discusses the theological problems raised by those elements in the Old Testament that have been perceived as ethically imperfect by later readers, both Jewish and Christian. The author begins with a synthesis of the positive ethical values characteristic of the Old Testament. Then he surveys the main classes of ethically problematic passages and illustrates with interesting quotations the history of attempts to solve the problem by allegorical and apologetical means. Finally he offers his own principles of solution that take into account historical development, cultural conditioning, and literary genres. This useful work is not aimed at specialists (who might wish to query an occasional detail) but at all readers interested in deepening their understanding of the ethical challenge presented by the Old Testament.

C. CONROY

GERSTENBERGER, E. S., and SCHRAGE, W.: *Kurushimi*. Translated by H. Yoshida and H. Udono. 1985. Pp. 393. (Yorudan-sha, Tokyo. Price: ¥3,200)

This is a Japanese translation of *Leiden* (1977); see *B.L.* 1978, p. 90; 1982, p. 82. A note about the authors and a discussion of the theme have been added by H. Yoshida.

K. K. SACON.

GNUSE, R.: *You shall not Steal: Community and Property in the Biblical Tradition*. 1985. Pp. x, 162 (Orbis Books, Maryknoll, New York. Price: $9.95. ISBN 0 88344 799 1)

This is an important study of the intention of the Eighth Commandment which, it is maintained, has too often been misunderstood as primarily laying down the inviolability of private property, a view which has not been without its influence on Western civilization. The author examines the biblical evidence in great detail and argues cogently that the real intention of the commandment is to widen the understanding of theft to include above all the denial to the individual, however humble, of the right to possess what is needful for a worthwhile existence. The commandment thus reflects the belief that Israel's God sought to create a community of equals. This is illustrated from the legal sections of the Old Testament, especially Deuteronomy, from the prophetic oracles and elsewhere. The Deuteronomists were perhaps too idealistic, but they did preserve the ideal as an inspiration for the future. What was both a losing and ever-renewed struggle against materialism (originally Canaanite civilization) is sketched in Israel's history, in Judaism, in early Christianity, in patristic literature and on through history, and we are left with the challenge to us today to actualize the biblical message in life and especially in interior attitude. The author avoids too facile applications of biblical pronouncements to present-day situations but leaves one in no doubt of their essential relevance.

N. W. Porteous

Gnuse, R.: *The Authority of the Bible: Theories of Inspiration, Revelation and the Canon of Scripture*. 1985. Pp. vi, 153. (Paulist Press, Mahwah, New Jersey. Price: $6.95. ISBN 0 8091 2692 3)

Gnuse's aim is to present a simple account of current views of biblical authority for students and interested readers. He classifies the theories under five main heads: inspiration (in four types, strict verbal, limited verbal, non-textual, and social), salvation history, existential, Christocentric, and 'models of limitation' (leaving the canon open and limiting its authority). In each section he sets out the theory, often with reference to particular scholars, and then assesses its strengths and weaknesses. Two further chapters consider the historical origin of the canon and recent ecumenical discussions of biblical authority. The whole is well set out and clearly expressed, and there is a useful bibliography. Gnuse succeeds admirably in his limited aim.

C. S. Rodd

Grimm, W.: *Die Heimkehr der Jakobskinder (Jes. 43, 1–7): Bedeutungen eines Prophetenwortes für die Biblische Theologie* (Europäische Hochschulschriften, xxiii/251). 1985. Pp. viii, 103. (Peter Lang, Bern, Frankfurt am Main and New York. Price: Sw.Fr. 25.00. ISBN 3 8204 8270 9)

The author, whose earlier work *Die Verkündigung Jesu und Deuterojesaja* (second edition, 1981) was not noted in the *Book List*, here responds to what he describes as a contemporary insistent demand for a 'biblical theology' with an exegesis of Isa. 43:1–7. On the purely Old Testament level he has made a useful contribution to the understanding of this passage, showing how Deutero-Isaiah took up traditional Old Testament themes in formulating his message to the exiles. His principal purpose, however, is to link the passage to the teaching and passion of Jesus and to New Testament theology generally. Here he illustrates the difficulty of constructing a biblical theology by succumbing to the temptation of pressing his case too far.

R. N. Whybray

Hanson, P. D.: *L'Écriture une et diverse: Interprétation théologigue* (Lectio Divina, 122). Translated by J.-P. Bagot. 1985. Pp. 178. (Éditions du Cerf, Paris, Price: Fr. 126.00. ISBN 2 204 02408 2)

This is a translation of *The Diversity of Scripture* (1982); see *B.L.* 1983, pp. 86–87. It differs from the original only in the omission of the Series

Foreword and of the Indexes of Scripture references, authors and subjects. The translator does not attempt to mitigate the infelicities of Hanson's prose style.

B. P. ROBINSON

HAYES, J. H., and PRUSSNER, F. C.: *Old Testament Theology: Its History and Development*. 1985. Pp. xii, 290. (SCM Press, London. Price £15.00. ISBN 0 334 02231 2)

According to the preface this is a revised and expanded version of part one of Prussner's 1952 Chicago dissertation. It is not absolutely clear whether Hayes is responsible for post-1952 additions, or only for revisions following Prussner's death in 1978. Either way, the result is a very effective and useful book. It traces the dawn of Old Testament theology from the reformation through Protestant scholasticism to the rise of historical criticism in the eighteenth century, and the progress of Old Testament theology through the nineteenth and twentieth centuries. There are many brief summaries of the work of individual scholars, and an attempt is made to place them in their wider theological and philosophical context. In spite of the vast amount of ground covered, the treatment is not shallow, and the documentation and orientation are valuable. This is a very welcome book.

J. W. ROGERSON

HEISTER, M.-S.: *Frauen in der biblischen Glaubensgeschichte*. 1984. Pp. 226. (Vandenhoeck & Ruprecht. Göttingen. Price: DM. 32.00. ISBN 3 525 60362 2)

Maria-Sybilla Heister has offered a wide-ranging review of the roles of women and the attitudes to women in the Bible which is all the more powerful for being understated. The seven chapters handle women in the patriarchal narratives; woman's position in the historical period of biblical Israel; woman in the sacral realm of biblical Israel; woman in prophetic preaching; woman in the Song of Solomon; humanity as man and woman in the creation texts — and the reinterpretation of these texts in early Judaism and Paul: and the role of women in the Gospels. Heister is able to document many retreats in the biblical texts after brave starts in accepting the equality and leadership of women. An English translation of this detailed and readable volume would be welcome.

A. G. AULD

HYERS, C.: *The Meaning of Creation: Genesis and Modern Science*. 1984. Pp. x, 203. (John Knox Press, Atlanta. Price: $11.95. ISBN 0 8042 0125 0)

The attempt is here made to hold the middle ground between fundamentalist creationism and those who regard science as having disproved Genesis. Hyers has some valuable comments to make on the different characteristics of scientific and religious language, and on the belittling effect of literalism when applied to the text of Genesis. (Whether his eirenic approach will in fact persuade those who 'know' that Genesis is either literally true or utter nonsense is another matter.) The latter part of the book explores other issues relating to creation, notably the different worlds envisaged by the two creation accounts, the conventional dates of J and P being accepted; and a final chapter outlines a theology of creation as 'controlled accident'. Overall this is an interesting contribution to a topic of much present-day interest.

R. J. COGGINS

JOHNSON, B.: *Rättfärdigheten i Bibeln*. 1985. Pp. 135. (Gothia, Gothenburg. Price: Sw.Kr. 90.00. ISBN 91 7728 194 2)

Dr Johnson begins his study with a consideration of the modern idea of righteousness, examining the relevant terms in the Scandinavian languages and in English, German, and French. He then turns to Greek and indicates the shift of meaning (resulting from Hebrew influence) to be found in the LXX, and describes briefly how the idea was understood and expressed in the languages of Israel's neighbours. This leads to a survey of the idea in the Old Testament, the Qumran texts, the New Testament, and Judaism. The longest section of the book discusses 'righteousness' in the Old Testament in relation to words expressing similar and opposite meanings. Emphasis is laid on the salvific rather than the legal understanding of 'righteousness' and on its close relationship to the covenant. This is an extremely valuable study, closely argued and well documented. An English summary is appended (pp. 119–22).

G. W. ANDERSON

KAISER, O.: *Der Mensch unter dem Schicksal: Studien zur Geschichte, Theologie und Gegenwartsbedeutung der Weisheit* (Beiheft zur Zeitschrift für die alttestamentliche Wissenschaft, 161). 1985. Pp. x, 292. (De Gruyter, Berlin. Price: DM. 98.00. ISBN 3 11 010095 9)

The new editor of ZAW and BZAW here presents a collection of sixteen essays of which only two are published for the first time. Only eleven of them are concerned with the Old Testament; the remainder deal with aspects of Greek thought and literature or with more general theological and philosophical themes. There is a strong emphasis on the kinship between Greek and Hebrew ideas. The wisdom books of the Old Testament and Apocrypha receive the most attention, but there are also articles on the prophets and on the book of Jonah. Each essay contributes in its own way to the general theme stated in the title of the book. There is, inevitably, a fair amount of repetition, especially in the four essays wholly or partly concerned with the teaching of Qohelet; but the collection as a whole gives a good indication of Kaiser's interpretation of a major aspect of Old Testament theology. Written over a period of some twenty years, these essays are intended to be preliminary studies for a forthcoming Theology of the Old Testament, which will evidently be characterized by an emphasis on the Old Testament writers as thinkers whose relevance to the problems of the modern world is no less than that of Greek philosophy.

R. N. WHYBRAY

KAISER, W. C., JR: *The Uses of the Old Testament in the New*. 1985. Pp. xvi, 270. (Moody Press, Chicago. Price: $13.95. ISBN 0 8024 9085 9)

The book is aimed at vindicating Kaiser's conviction that all Old Testament quotations which bear on Christian faith are correctly understood and applied by the New Testament writers. Scholars who claim that the ideas and techniques of Qumran and rabbinic exegesis can elucidate the New Testament are mistaken, and indeed tend to undermine the truth of Scripture. Selected passages of various types are studied. In every case it is asserted that the passage has one sense only (even typology, as in 1 Cor. 10:1–12, does not transgress this), and the passage is handled according to the intention of the original author. This bold proposition rests on the argument put forward by Kaiser in his *Toward an Old Testament Theology* (see *B.L.* 1980, p. 91) that God's promise is the fundamental category of biblical thought, first made known to Eve. Particular prophecies apply to the prophet's own situation, but were uttered with awareness of the promise, and may contain details which apply only in the fulfilment in Christ. There is thus a concept of serial fulfilments, culminating in the Last Day. Kaiser thinks that his argument helps to overcome the long-standing difference between dispensational and covenantal theologians. Critical scholars are unlikely to be impressed. Difficulties are often glossed over, and there are strained arguments and special pleading, besides the all-pervading dogmatism of the author.

B. Lindars

Kleinknecht, K. T.: *Der leidende Gerechtfertigte: Die alttestamentlich-jüdische Tradition vom 'leidenden Gerechten' und ihre Rezeption bei Paulus* (Wissenschaftliche Untersuchungen zum Neuen Testament, 2. Reihe, 13). 1984. Pp. x, 422. (Mohr, Tübingen. Price: DM. 68.00. ISBN 3 16 144867 7)

This book is not, in fact, yet another instance of the deplorable genre of monographs placing a superficial review of Old Testament/Jewish literature at the service of New Testament exegesis (frequently Paul, and usually Romans). Kleinknecht is explicitly wary of the pitfalls of this genre and offers a 'traditio-historical' method inspired by Gese. In line with this approach to the theme of the righteous sufferer, the author, fully aware of the dangers, proposes a 'tradition' from as early as the pre-exilic period, largely on the basis of individual lament psalms and some prophetic texts. In the postexilic period the predominance of wisdom-inspired treatments and eschatological solutions within this 'tradition' is pointed out. To its credit, at least half of this book deals with an extensive range of non-New Testament material, but inevitably other scholars, primarily German, are leaned upon heavily. Indeed, the range of his material suggests a much more complex picture than he attempts to draw, while its variety calls into doubt the validity of the concepts of 'tradition' and 'tradition history' when applied here. A sequence of texts, even when some of them are exegeses of earlier texts, does not necessarily form a tradition. To make the mistake of thinking so is not Kleinknecht's alone, of course; it is a common misconception. But it does seem fatal to the thesis attempted here.

P. R. Davies

Lang, B. (ed.): *Anthropological Approaches to the Old Testament* (Issues in Religion and Theology, 8). 1985. Pp. xii, 175. (Fortress Press, Philadelphia. ISBN 0 8006 1771 1. SPCK, London. Price: £3.50. ISBN 0 281 04172 5)

The book follows the regular pattern of this series, consisting of a number of articles, or extracts from books, illustrating the bearing of anthropological studies on the Old Testament. Here there are ten of these. Two of them represent a comparatively early period, the 1954 essay by F. Steiner and that of 1955 by J. Schapera, both of which use African kinship systems to elucidate the relations between Jacob and Joseph in Gen. 47–48 and the sin of Cain respectively. There follow J. W. Rogerson's well-known critique of the concept of corporate personality, T. W. Overholt's interesting comparison of Jeremiah with a prophetic figure from North American Indians, and B. Lang's chapter, from his book noticed in *B.L.* 1984, pp. 97–98, on peasant poverty in Israel with particular reference to Amos. Mary Douglas's seminal discussion of the 'Abominations of Leviticus' leads on to examples of the newer approaches of structural anthropology as represented by Leach's paper on the Logic of Sacrifice. Criticisms and refinements of the views of these authors are offered in two contributions by M. P. Carroll on Leviticus and on Genesis, and a final essay on Sacrifice in Leviticus by D. Davies, while building on Douglas's investigation, calls attention, from the standpoint of biblical scholarship, to some aspects which she has insufficiently appreciated. Some of the contributions in this volume will be familiar to Old Testament scholars, but others much less so, and it is valuable to have them all collected together to show the importance and fruitfulness of the increasing dialogue between anthropologists and Old Testament specialists. Whether this book, as the publishers claim, 'provides the complete material needed for a course on anthropology and the Old Testament', is another matter. Here one may feel a certain disappointment with the editor's introduction, for it only partly lives up to its title, 'Anthropology as a New Model for Biblical Studies'. For while it is informative about the older ethnographical approach, it does little to elucidate the concepts and methods of structuralist anthropology which have proved so important, but often so bemusing, in the most recent study of the Old Testment.

J. R. PORTER

LEVENSON, J. D.: *Sinai and Zion: An Entry into the Jewish Bible* (New Voices in Biblical Studies). 1985. Pp. xii, 227. (Winston Press, Minneapolis. Distributed by Geoffrey Chapman, London. Price: £14.95. ISBN 0 86683 961 5)

This is a stimulating and well written account of Old Testament religion with special reference to the two great mountain traditions. The writer is free from the anti-critical assumptions of so many Jewish scholars, and he makes full use of Gentile scholarship; but his theology is unequivocally Jewish. Non-Jewish readers will, however, find in it much to admire and ponder.

The two traditions are seen as having different emphases but being complementary. The Sinai tradition uses the language of history (which is not to say, by any means, that all that is narrated actually occurred; even the existence of Moses is uncertain). It speaks of a God who intervenes to speak to a chosen group of people and to make demands on them. Basic to this tradition, and not a secondary insertion in it, is the concept of the covenant, which was borrowed from Israel's neighbours. YHWH is represented as a loving but unpredictable and jealous suzerain who will brook no rivals.

Whereas the Sinai tradition emphasizes the precariousness of life, the Zion tradition offers security and stability. It deals not in the particularities of historical, or pseudo-historical, events, but in symbol and myth. Zion is the cosmic mountain, an impregnable stronghold, the earthly counterpart of the heavenly abode (Levenson finds here a two-tier view of reality verging on philosophical idealism). Zion is not only a piece of real estate, it is the garden of Eden, the navel of the earth, the gate of heaven. Levenson's interpretations are supported here by detailed exegesis of specific texts.

The traditions are not to be considered alternative options, the Sinai tradition being the preserve of the North, the Zion that of the South. Rather, the co-existence of the two traditions in a state of creative tension is attested in Judah from at least the time of Micah. Further, the Davidic covenant often subsumed Sinaitic features, and after 586 the Sinai tradition came to speak more immediately to Jews than did the Zion tradition.

In a work of this sort, controversial statements are inevitably made. They are, however, always supported by competent argumentation, and the author calls in aid the work of reputable scholars. A constant concern is to point up a continuity between Old Testament religion and Judaism today. Levenson argues, for example, that Christians have been selective in their approach to the Old Testament, setting the Sinaitic law aside while making much of the Davidic tradition; Jews on the other hand are more true to the Old Testament in that they show allegiance to both mountain traditions. In his life of prayer, sabbath observance and fulfilment of the commandments the Jew lives in a covenant bond with God that respects the insights of both traditions.

B. P. ROBINSON

LEVIN, C.: *Die Verheissung des neuen Bundes in ihrem theologiegeschichtlichen Zusammenhang ausgelegt* (Forschungen zur Religion und Literatur des Alten und Neuen Testaments, 137). 1985. Pp. 303. (Vandenhoeck & Ruprecht, Göttingen. Price: DM. 74.00. ISBN 3 525 53811 1)

It is argued that the earliest oracles of salvation in Jeremiah are 29:5–7* and 32:15b and that these alone may be from the prophet himself. Shortly after the catastrophe of 587 B.C. 16:14–15aα and a nucleus of the sayings in 31:27–34 (without reference to a 'new covenant') were incorporated into the book. The notion of a covenant between God and Israel was developed during the latter part of the exilic period, and 31:27–34 received its present form subsequently in the early fifth century B.C. The book goes on to discuss the subsequent history of the covenant promises in the Old Testament, the 'law in the heart' in 31:33a, and 'The New Covenant and the New Testament'. Whilst there is much that is of interest in this book, it may be asked whether the literary and redactional analysis of such passages as 31: 27–34 is not over-refined and whether, for example, the view that the 'new covenant' passage was not an original unity is valid. It must be questioned also whether the notion of a covenant between God and Israel emerged as late as the date here proposed.

E. W. NICHOLSON

LOHFINK, N.: *Unsere grossen Wörter: Das Alte Testament zu Themen dieser Jahre*. 3. Auflage. 1985. Pp. 254. (Neukirchener Verlag, Neukirchen-Vluyn. Price: DM 24.80. ISBN 3 7887 0768 2. Verlag Herder, Freiburg im Breisgau. ISBN 3 451 20359 6)

A third, and now paperback, edition of a very good book already noted in *B.L.* 1978, pp. 96–97; *B.L.* 1983, p. 90. The only significant updating is in the back-cover photograph of the author.

A. G. AULD

MCCOMISKEY, T. E.: *The Covenants of Promise: A Theology of the Old Testament Covenants*. 1985. Pp. 259. (Baker Book House, Grand Rapids, Michigan. Price: $10.95; ISBN 0 8010 6200 4. Paperback price: $10.95; ISBN 0 8010 6183 0)

It is argued that 'the people of God, from the time of Abraham on, are under two covenantal administrations: the promise-oath and the particular administrative covenant in force at the time. Thus, a bicovenantal structure governs the disposition of the inheritance for God's people' (pp. 172–73). In each 'era' an 'administrative covenant' accompanies a promise covenant. Thus circumcision was a *bĕrît* which operated in conjunction with the promise *bĕrît* sworn to Abraham; the law is called a *bĕrît*, but Moses refers as well to the *bĕrît* sworn to Abraham, Isaac, and Jacob; the new covenant is called a *bĕrît*, but both Jeremiah and the writer of Hebrews acknowledge the continuing force of the promise *bĕrît* and *horkos* (oath). The presuppositions and the arguments are thoroughly conservative throughout this book.

E. W. NICHOLSON

NIDITCH, S.: *Chaos to Cosmos: Studies in Biblical Patterns of Creation* (Scholars Press Studies in the Humanities, 6). 1985. Pp. x, 114. (Scholars Press, Chico, California. Price: $13.95 (discount price: $11.95); ISBN 0 89130 762 1. Paperback price: $9.25 (discount price: $7.95); ISBN 0 89130 763 X)

Some of the ways in which the Hebrew myths of chaos, creation, and cosmos have been influential are here explored, with literary and anthropological interests foremost. Five creation themes are discerned in Gen. 1–11 and illustrated from other creation myths from varied sources, all of which display the same 'chaos to order' pattern. The latter part of the book explores the similarities and differences between Gen. 1–11 taken as a whole and other biblical examples of the search for paradise. This is a study which succeeds in looking at familiar material in a fresh way, and should serve admirably for its intended purpose, as introduction to a College liberal studies programme.

R. J. COGGINS

OEMING, M.: *Gesamtbiblische Theologien der Gegenwart: Das Verhältnis von AT und NT in der hermeneutischen Diskussion seit Gerhard von Rad*. 1985. Pp. 266. (Kohlhammer, Stuttgart, Price: DM. 69.00. ISBN 3 17 008860 2)

The problems of biblical hermeneutics and of the construction of a biblical theology are currently being brought into an increasingly close relationship. It seems that a theology must be seen as a distinctive hermeneutical way of approaching and using the text of the Bible, and at the same time all assumptions of interpretation about its literature require some evaluation concerning its religious nature. It has been one of the great stimuli of the work of the late Professor Gerhard von Rad to have drawn together these theological and hermeneutical approaches to the Hebrew Bible and to have studied them more closely in relationship to each other. Oeming's dissertation, which was presented at the University of Bonn, begins with the traditio-historical presentation of an Old Testament theology by von Rad and criticizes this in the light of the philosophical hermeneutics of H. G. Gadamer. Much attention is given to the nature of language and to the idea of a theological exegesis, which for von Rad focused on such themes as promise, typology, and saving-history. This critique provides a framework to a wider examination of a number of pertinent issues concerning the relationship of the Old Testament to the New. Oeming regards this very rightly as a major issue with which any biblical theology must deal, and one which involves a number of basic hermeneutical assumptions. Much of the remainder of the work is then taken up with the work of those scholars who have tried to build upon some of the insights and suggestions of von Rad. So the works of H. Gese, P. Stuhlmacher, A. H. J. Gunneweg and B. S. Childs all come under critical review.

The author's goal is to draw out from these different approaches to the exegete's task what he finds to be the most constructive and helpful features. He regards a significant tension to be evident between the demands of a strictly lexical-historical approach and that of a theological evaluative one. Much of the value of the study lies in its ability to single out major from minor questions and its concern to clarify and criticize the assumptions which underlie the works of scholars from very different backgrounds. There is much to think about, and, aside from some very pertinent assessments of work already done, some suggestive ideas for future investigation.

R. E. CLEMENTS

PRINSLOO, W. S.: *The Theology of the Book of Joel* (Beiheft zur Zeitschrift für die Alttestamentliche Wissenschaft, 163). 1985. Pp. viii, 136. (De Gruyter, Berlin. Price: DM. 74.00. ISBN 3 11 010301 X)

The introduction to Dr Prinsloo's study of the book of Joel begins with a brief sketch of some questions concerning Old Testament theology, although this touches only marginally on the main aspects of the exegesis in the body of the text and appears to imply no more than that the book of Joel is concerned with the nature and activity of the God of Israel. The main part of the work consists of a critical examination and exegesis of Joel and is necessarily very much engaged with the most recent commentary work of H. W. Wolff and L. C. Allen.

The study is essentially a commentary in itself and prints out the Hebrew text in transliteration, offering careful text criticism, but, regrettably, no separate English translation. This lack, when coupled with the use of transliteration, makes the study rather cumbersome to work through, although most readers will have a normal Hebrew text to hand. Prinsloo is critical of Wolff's attempt to demonstrate a near symmetrical structure in the units of which the book is composed and to argue for the overall unity of the book on the basis of this. He offers an interesting, and rather modified, picture of his own of the overall structure. As to the unity of Joel, Prinsloo notes the many arguments against this, but insists that we are in any case primarily concerned with the final form of the text. He dates the work in the post-exilic period, regarding it as an eschatological work occasioned by the experience of a locust plague. There is a good study of the importance of Joel 4:4–8 (pp. 106–10), with its reference to Greeks, as a basis for the overall dating of the text. The study is carefully done, but is rather dogmatically inclined to press the case for a unified book. One might also have wished, in view of the title, for a more critical approach to the complex questions about the nature of Jewish eschatology and the possibility of a progressive build up of a text which cannot be precluded simply on the evidence of symmetrical, or chiastic, structures.

R. E. Clements

Radmacher, E. D., and Preus, R. D. (eds.): *Hermeneutics, Inerrancy, and the Bible: Papers from ICBI Summit II*. 1984. Pp. xiv, 921. (Acadamie Books, from Zondervan, Grand Rapids, Michigan. Price: $16.95. ISBN 0 310 37081 7)

ICBI is the International Council on Biblical Inerrancy, and this volume consists of sixteen papers read at their second summit meeting, each followed by two responses. Important issues, such as genre criticism, language, author's intention, and philosophical presuppositions affecting hermeneutics, are discussed and the notes provide evidence of wide reading, not limited to conservative literature. I was left with a nagging question: if, as the participants affirm, the meaning in each biblical text is 'single, definite and fixed' and applies to all cultural contexts, and the Holy Spirit alone enables believers to apply the scriptures to their lives, to what purpose are these nine hundred pages of argument?

C. S. Rodd

Reventlow, H. Graf: *Problems of Old Testament Theology in the Twentieth Century*. Translated by J. Bowden. 1985. Pp. xiv, 194. (SCM Press, London. Price: £6.95. ISBN 0 334 02232 0)

The original German edition of this volume was published in 1982 and reviewed in *B.L.* 1983, pp. 93–94. It is here excellently translated and should enjoy a wide popularity. It is primarily a survey of the discipline of Old Testament theology with a very full bibliographical coverage of primary and secondary material. It is built around the major themes that have tended to dominate the discussion of the subject: salvation history, the problem of the 'centre' of the ideological world of the Old Testament and the relationship of Old Testament ideas to their environment. It concludes with outline treatments of the themes of creation, myth, and wisdom. Each section is furnished with a good critique of the methods and aims of the major scholarly figures involved. It is a highly serviceable guide for students and teachers alike so that, together with its companion volume on biblical theology by the same author (*B.L.* 1984, p. 102), it presents a valuable groundwork to major areas of scholarship.

R. E. CLEMENTS

ROGERSON, J. W.: *Antropologia e Antico Testamento* ("Dabar": Studi biblici e giudaistici, 2). Introduzione di C. Grottanelli. Traduzione di C. Benetazzo. 1984. Pp. xx, 128. (Editrice Marietti, Casale Monferrato. Price: Lire 16,000. ISBN 88 211 6763 1)

This is an Italian translation of the book published in 1978 and favourably reviewed in *B.L.* 1980, pp. 97–98. What is new is Grottanelli's Introduction which takes the form of an extended and, on occasion, critical, review of Rogerson's work. Not only does Grottanelli call attention to some discussions which have appeared since the first publication, but he also makes interesting suggestions for further study of various topics with which Rogerson deals. The whole Introduction is worth reading as evidence of the lively interest in social anthropology, and its bearing on the Old Testament, which has developed in Italy during recent years.

J. R. PORTER

SAKENFELD, K. D.: *Faithfulness in Action: Loyalty in Biblical Perspective* (Overtures to Biblical Theology, 16). 1985. Pp. xviii, 158. (Fortress Press, Philadelphia. Price: $8.95. ISBN 0 8006 1540 9)

Katherine Sakenfeld describes this work as an 'expansion of selected theological themes' from her earlier *The Meaning of Hesed in the Hebrew Bible* (*B.L.* 1979, p. 89). As in the earlier study, she begins with *ḥesed* in the narratives. From this human basis she moves to consider 'God's Covenant Loyalty' (Mosaic and Davidic), 'God's Loyalty to Members of the Covenant Community', and 'Loyalty: The Calling of the People of God'. In the last chapter she glances briefly at the New Testament and then discusses the place of loyalty in a number of present-day situations. This valuable study will not only be of interest to students of the Old Testament, but because of its emphasis upon loyalty in human relationships will guide those concerned with Christian Ethics to a better understanding of ways in which the Old Testament can be used in ethical discussion and decision making.

C. S. RODD

SCHMIDT, W. H.: *Rekishi ni okeru Kyūyaku-Seisho no Shinkō*. Translated by T. Yamaga. 1985. Pp. 574 and 66 pages of indexes and bibliography. (Shinchi-Shobō, Tokyo. Price: ¥7,800)

This is a Japanese translation of the fourth enlarged edition of *Alttestamentliche Glaube in seiner Geschichte* (1982); see *B.L.* 1984, pp. 102–03 for the English edition. There is a portrait of the author, and the translator has added a bibliography which includes both works by the author and many Japanese books and articles.

K. K. SACON

SICRE, J. L.: *"Con los pobres de la tierra": La justicia social en los profetas de Israel*. 1984. Pp. 506. (Ediciones Cristiandad, Madrid. Price: Ptas. 2,100. ISBN 84 7057 364 0)

This is both a substantial and an interesting and unusual work. The genesis of the book was a course of lectures on the struggle for justice in the

Israelite prophets delivered by the author at the Pontifical Biblical Institute in Rome in 1979–80. But Sicre tells us that he had for some years been increasingly involved with the problem of justice in society, sharpened by a visit to El Salvador in 1976, and evidence of his personal concern is to be found throughout this volume. On the other hand, Sicre has already made substantial contributions to the study of Old Testament prophecy (see *B.L.* 1981, pp. 50–51), and the present work amply displays his learning and expertise in this area. There are two introductory chapters, one on the concern for justice in the ancient Near East, presenting a useful collection of texts, and a second on the socio-economic development of Israel down to the eighth century, which brings together a good deal of material not easily available elsewhere. In the main part of the book, the prophetic message on the theme of social justice is surveyed in eight chapters, dealing in turn with the major figures from Amos to Malachi. In each case, an opening section discusses the personality and historical setting of the prophet, then follow translations of the relevant biblical passages, accompanied by detailed philological, literary, and critical comments, while a final section draws all the material together to give an overall picture of each prophet's ideas. Here there is evidence of wide reading, and Sicre shows that he is thoroughly at home with the modern exegetical studies of individual prophets, while giving his own fresh interpretations in many cases. A final, and briefer, part first lists the author's conclusions about the prophetic teaching as a whole on society and the injustice within it under various headings and then poses three questions for our own day which, perhaps inevitably, are more suggestive than conclusive. There is a thirteen-page bibliography and indexes of authors cited, biblical passages, Hebrew words, and main topics. Much interest has recently been paid on the continent to the question of the relevance of the Old Testament to modern social problems, and Sicre's work is a valuable contribution to the continuing discussion. Its wide and sound scholarship in particular will recommend it highly to those concerned with the study of the prophets generally, as well as to those specially interested in the theme with which it deals.

J. R. Porter

Smart, N., Clayton, J., Katz, S., and Sherry, P. (eds.): *Nineteenth Century Religious Thought in the West.* Vol. iii. 1985. Pp. x, 342. (Cambridge University Press. Price: £30.00. ISBN 0 521 30114 9)

Five of the nine essays in this volume will particularly interest Old Testament scholars, those by John Kent on Religion and Science, N. Rotenstreich on Jewish Thought, R. E. Clements on the study of the Old Testament, Edmund Leach on British and French anthropological interpretations of religion, and Roland Robinson on Max Weber. Each contribution is well documented and has a bibliographical essay.

Inevitably, those contributors whose subject matter is limited in scope are able to write at greater depth, and generally, with greater interest. Robinson on Weber is able to contrast him with Hegel, Marx, and Troeltsch in a valuable contribution in view of Weber's continuing importance in Old Testament studies. Leach's contribution is characteristically idiosyncratic, but with illuminating discussions of Robertson Smith and Evans-Pritchard. Kent concentrates on the controversies of the second half of the nineteenth century, Rotenstreich on monotheism and on the relation between tradition, revelation, and history, while Clements traces the path from the late eighteenth century to Wellhausen.

J. W. Rogerson

TOLBERT, M. A. (ed.): *The Bible and Feminist Hermeneutics* (Semeia, 28). 1983. Pp. iv, 126. (Scholars Press, Chico, California. Price: $9.95; discount price: $6.95. ISSN 0095 571X)

The seven essays in this volume relate to the fundamental question, 'Is the Bible to be an ally or an adversary in the struggle for human rights, equality and dignity?' 'Tradition and Convention in the Book of Judith' (T. Craven) explores the theme of continuity and change, drawing a comparison with the stories of Esther and Ruth. The unconventional behaviour of these women in male dominated societies both conserved and challenged tradition. A sensitive study of Exod. 1:8–2:10 (J. C. Exum) makes the case for reassessing traditional assumptions about women's role in the biblical story. She notes the inherent irony: 'without Moses there would be no story, but without the initiative of these women there would be no Moses.' In their refusal to co-operate with oppression the liberation of Israel from Egypt begins. Four essays deal with New Testament subjects. In the final stimulating essay the editor discusses the profoundly paradoxical nature of feminist hermeneutics, 'using the Bible as liberator to defeat the Bible as patriarchal authority.' In asking how one deals with a biblical text 'so completely saturated in an unacceptable perspective' she draws an interesting comparison with Bultmann's demythologizing.

G. I. EMMERSON

VAWTER, B.: *Job and Jonah: Questioning the Hidden God*. 1983. Pp. vi, 126. (Paulist Press, Ramsey, New Jersey. Price: $4.95. ISBN 0 8091 2524 2)

Several recent ventures in Old Testament theology have been concerned with the theme of the hiddenness of God and particularly his (real or imagined) capriciousness. Here Job and Jonah are regarded as roughly contemporary products of the early post-exilic period, each showing the limitations of orthodox piety as found in the wisdom movement and in prophecy. Each book is making the point that God's ways are often hidden, obscured from shallow conventional belief. This is a lively and entertaining study, laced with interesting literary cross-references and thought-provoking *obiter dicta*, which warns of the disservice we do to the Bible by reducing biblical faith to a comfortable orthodoxy.

R. J. COGGINS

VIRGULIN, S.: *Profeti e Sapienti: uomini dello Spirito*. 1985. Pp. 182. (Edizioni Borla, Rome. Price: Lire 15,000. ISBN 88 263 0678 8)

For those who read Italian, this will prove a very useful book on its particular level. It deals with the significance for spirituality of the prophets, psalmists, and wisdom writers, the last category including Sirach and the Wisdom of Solomon, as occurring in the Roman Catholic canon. Thus it is another example of the movement for biblical renewal in the Roman church, with its concern that spirituality be deeply rooted in Scripture. Hence the writer deals only incidentally with literary and critical questions and concentrates firmly on the religious message of the books, each of which, following an introduction to each category setting out the major themes, is expounded individually. The treatment reflects the generally accepted 'middle-of-the-road' critical position, but it is based on wide reading, as the useful bibliographies to each section indicate. The whole is clearly and comprehensively written. Old Testament specialists will not find anything new in it, but it will provide a valuable introduction to many of the great religious themes of the Old Testament for a wide range of readers, especially if they follow up in their Bibles the references which the author so abundantly furnishes.

J. R. PORTER

WESTERMANN, C.: *Théologie de l'Ancien Testament* (Le Monde de la Bible). Translated by L. Jeanneret. 1985. Pp. 327. (Labor et Fides, Geneva. Price: Sw.Fr. 48.00. ISBN 2 8309 0026 X)

This is a French translation of *Theologie des Alten Testaments in Grundzügen*, which was received warmly in *B.L.* 1980, p. 101; an English translation was noted in *B.L.* 1983, p. 97. A bibliographical supplement for this French edition has been prepared by T. Roemer, and the jacket contains a good introduction by R. Martin-Achard.

A. G. AULD

WILLIAMS, T.: *Form and Vitality in the World and God: A Christian Perspective*. 1985. Pp. xii, 356. (Clarendon Press, Oxford. Price: £22.50. ISBN 0 19 826671 5)

The student of the theology of the Old Testament must welcome a rare work which considers the story of Israel, Judaism, and the phenomenon of Jesus from the point of view of an acknowledged philosophical distinction. The summary here given of the Old Testament and of Judaism in the intertestamental period, as illustrating the polarity of form and vitality, is undeniably well done. Even those who will question this or that conclusion will admit that this is a fair presentation of what contemporary scholars are saying. The method adopted is legitimate, and has the effect of re-establishing the relevance of the Old Testament to the world at large, as well as providing a principle for a synoptic view of what is otherwise so easily separated into mutually unintelligible bits. Can the theologian of the Old Testament confine himself to his own discipline? This suggestive and challenging work suggests that he must be ready to take risks and, like Dr Williams, ask the world's questions if he is to communicate beyond his own charmed circle.

D. R. JONES

8. THE LIFE AND THOUGHT OF THE SURROUNDING PEOPLES

ARCHI, A.: *Testi Amministrativi: Assegnazioni di Tessuti* (*Archivio L. 2769*) (Archivi reali di Ebla, Testi, 1). 1985. Pp. xvi, 322; 55 plates. (Missione Archeologica Italiana in Siria dell'Università degli Studi di Roma "La Sapienza". Distributed by Herder Editrice e Libreria, Rome. Price: Lire 75,000)

BIGA, M. G., and MILANO, L.: *Testi Amministrativi: Assegnazioni di Tessuti* (*Archivio L. 2769*) (Archivi reali di Ebla, Testi, 4). 1984. Pp. xvi, 333; 51 plates. (Missione Archeologica Italiana in Siria dell'Università degli Studi di Roma "La Sapienza". Distributed by Herder Editrice e Libreria, Rome. Price: Lire 75,000)

EDZARD, D. O.: *Hymnen, Beschwörungen und Verwandtes* (*aus dem Archiv L. 2769*) (Archivi reali di Ebla, Testi, 5). 1984. Pp. 63; 59 plates. (Missione Archeologica Italiana in Siria dell'Università degli Studi di Roma "La Sapienza". Distributed by Herder Editrice e Libreria, Rome. Price: Lire 30,000)

For earlier volumes of this series see *B.L.* 1985, p. 115. Nos. 1 and 4 continue the publication of the administrative archives, these two being devoted to documents about cloth and garments. They are competently done and include photographs of the tablets, transliterations, notes and exhaustive indexes of names and words. Slow but sure progress is being made in understanding the documents and the language. Volume 5 gives all the literary texts so far identified (all there are, it is hoped), a total of twenty-six tablets, in both hand copies and photographs. Save for the incantations, which have already been edited elsewhere, the texts are transliterated, but no translations are attempted, though notes offer occasional guidance on meaning. They are all very difficult, though some are Sumerian and some are Semitic. Most, if not all, were certainly composed in Mesopotamia, not Syria. Some of the incantations have a possible claim to Syrian origin, but this is not certain. The difficulties may be illustrated by the fact that since publication it has turned out that one of these 'literary' texts is in fact a list of Sumerian words in phonetic orthography, and one of the Semitic texts turns out to be a translation of a Sumerian text previously known from a Sumerian site. While this material is full of interest, it is clear that it does not have the relevance to the Old Testament of the Ugaritic literary corpus.

W. G. LAMBERT

ASHER-GRÈVE, J. M.: *Frauen in altsumerischer Zeit* (Bibliotheca Mesopotamica, 18). 1985. Pp. xxii, 223; 6 tables, 32 plates. (Undena Publications, Malibu, California. Price: $55.00; ISBN 0 89003 161 4. Paperback price: $45.00; ISBN 0 89003 162 2)

This is a little-changed 1979 Ph.D. thesis of the University of Basel, and a brave attempt at a very difficult subject. The period covered is *ca*. 3200–2300 B.C., and the area is southern Mesopotamia with attention to evidence from surrounding countries. For the earlier part of this period there is virtually no usable written material, and though there is for the later part, it is not especially informative on many aspects of the status of women in society. Since the author is more an art historian than a philologist, the study begins always from depictions of (or presumably of) women. The collection of material is very useful, if not quite complete, and presents some previously unpublished objects. The arguments are well informed over the whole range of material bearing on the problems, but the author is not adept at presenting a case systematically. Even when one may accept the conclusions, one feels that alternatives should have been seen and presented before a particular interpretation is adopted.

W. G. LAMBERT

ASSMANN, J.: *Ägypten — Theologie und Frommigkeit einer frühen Hochkultur* (Urban-Taschenbücher, 366). 1984. Pp. 287. (Kohlhammer, Stuttgart. Price: DM 24.00. ISBN 3 17 008371 6)

In nine chapters Professor Assmann sets out his own very individual, but very stimulating and valuable view of several aspects of ancient Egyptian religion. In the first, introductory chapter, he reviews the scope of 'religion', and divides his topic into 'implicit theology', covering the actual practice of the cult, cosmology and mythology, in which the emphasis falls on maintaining relations with the gods; and 'explicit theology', historically conditioned relations with 'God' (as distinct from the gods), theodicy, the nature of God and the gods. 'Implicit' takes up chapters 2 to 6. Here are reviewed the role of local temples and city-gods, their economic role, and the significance of cult-statues; then the role of cosmology, of language (word-play, etc.), and of myths, with a summing up. Chapters 7–9 cover 'explicit theology': the emergence of theodicy in the Middle Kingdom (after upheavals) which prepared the way for the great changes in the New Kingdom. Then there arose very clearly the concept of deity behind the familiar gods, leading to a 'new solar theology' which concentrated on the visible phenomena of the sun, discarding the traditional mythological imagery; from this sprang the peculiar monotheism of Akhenaten (on which Assmann is very enlightening), but more important, the elaborate pantheism of the following Ramesside period that formed much of the basis of Egyptian religion down to Hellenistic/ Roman times. The main drawback of this little book is its author's continued habit of inventing his own terminology for religious phenomena; this does not make for reasy reading.

K. A. KITCHEN

BAINES, J.: *Fecundity Figures: Egyptian Personification and the Iconology of a Genre*. 1985. Pp. viii, 446, including 199 figures. (Aris & Phillips, Warminster. Price: £32.00. ISBN 0 85668 087 7. Bolchazy-Carducci, Chicago, Illinois. ISBN 0 86516 122 4)

The central subject of this very solid volume is a particular and characteristic type of figure to be found on ancient Egyptian temple-walls (at the base) and in various other religious contexts. This is the commonly portly male figure with heavy breasts and stomach — a figure who personified affluence and material prosperity. In Egyptological writings such figures are often referred to as 'Niles' or 'Nile-gods' — wrongly, as Baines correctly remarks. Rather, they represent the Nile-*flood* or Inundation, but not in the role of a major deity. Hence he offers the far superior term 'fecundity figures'. These figures are especially prominent in two religious/artistic contexts: leading (later, forming) series of offering-bearers, bringing the products of various provinces of Egypt to the king, or in his name to the gods; or in an antithetic pair, binding the heraldic lotus and papryus plants of Upper and Lower Egypt around the hieroglyphic symbol for 'union' (*sma*), signifying the uniting of the 'Two Lands' of Egypt — commonly on the sides of thrones on royal statuary, and on actual furnishings. The innumerable variations in form and usage across the span of almost three millennia (from the Pyramid Age to the Roman epoch) are studied by Baines in close detail.

But the first part of his study is devoted to the question of the definition of the kinds of personification to be found in pharaonic Egypt and their roles and relationships. It is this section of the book that perhaps comes closest to the interests of Old Testament scholars, rather than the main consideration of the fecundity representations themselves. Compared with the very simple and limited use of personification in, e.g., Proverbs, one finds relatively more varied and more sophisticated forms and use of personification in Egypt from at least the mid-third millennium B.C. onward — the product not of intellectuals, but of basically an agricultural/pastoral culture and community that lived close to nature.

K. A. KITCHEN

BEINLICH, H.: *Die "Osirisreliquien": Zum Motiv der Körpergliederung in der altägyptischen Religion* (Ägyptologische Abhandlungen, 42). 1984. Pp. 329. (Otto Harrassowitz, Wiesbaden. Price: DM. 148.00. ISBN 3 447 02498 4)

In Egyptian mythology the god Osiris was slain by his brother Seth who later hacked his body to pieces, scattering the fragments throughout Egypt. Osiris's widow Isis recovered the fragments, arranging for tomb-shrines in each province where she had found a fragment; the reassembled body was embalmed by Anubis. But over a century ago, the discovery in temples of the Graeco-Roman period of major texts linking various portions of the god's body with different provinces led quickly to the belief among Egyptologists that these portions had become revered as local holy relics of Osiris, much like the medieval veneration of relics of saints in Christendom. This scholarly hypothesis became almost universally accepted as fact. However, in the present work, and for the first time, Beinlich has collected in reliable translation (and in hieroglyphs, for one large, ill-edited series of texts) all the major inscriptions that bear on the topic—with the result that the century-old hypothesis of a reliquary cult of Osiris is shown to be a phantom. What the texts do state is that Egypt was identified with the body of Osiris, and each province with a member of his body. In the great processional texts each province figuratively brings its particular portion for Osiris, to reunite his entire body. This concept and composition Beinlich is able (on factual criteria) to date well before the Graeco-Roman period, to the seventh century B.C., in the context of the effective reunification of Egypt by the twenty-sixth Dynasty, after the Assyrian withdrawal and the prior centuries of real political fragmentation. Links between specific provinces and bodily portions of Osiris rest upon word-play and graphic devices typical of Egyptian religious thought. On the full evidence presented, Beinlich's work is entirely convincing; it well illustrates (1) that modern theories however long-lived and widely held remain fallible, not sacrosanct; and (2) the need to go back to original sources, accurately and in full.

K. A. KITCHEN

CURTIS, A.: *Ugarit* (*Ras Shamra*) (Cities of the Biblical World). 1985. Pp. 125, including 25 plates and 5 figures. (Lutterworth Press, Cambridge. Price: £6.95. ISBN 0 7188 2457 1)

The discovery of ancient Ugarit and of its language are first described in brief. Then comes an outline of the city's history from the Neolithic period to its sack in 1200 B.C., with emphasis on the last two centuries when Ugarit flourished. This overlaps the following portrayal of everyday life in Ugarit. After an outline of the principal myths and legends comes the longest section, on the religion of Ugarit. The last chapter points out the value of Ugaritic for understanding the Old Testament. This very basic introduction has helpful suggestions for further reading. (For other volumes in this series see *B.L.* 1983, pp. 26, 30, 107.)

W. G. E. WATSON

DAUM, W.: *Ursemitische Religion*. 1985. Pp. 223, with some figures. (Kohlhammer, Stuttgart. Price: DM. 89.00. ISBN 3 17 008589 1)

Written in a lively style without footnotes (for a non-specialist audience?), Daum's book is based on three sources of information: folk-tales and fairy-tales, folk customs, and religious rites described in texts. The tales and customs are principally those of south-west Arabia (especially Yemen). These are described on the basis of an earlier publication by Daum, and from them the author reconstructs an original Semitic rain-myth and related offerings-ritual, which are argued to lie behind the basic rites of Islam and Judaism. Other ancient Semitic religious traditions (Canaanite, Mesopotamian) are discussed in less detail. In relation to Judaism, however, there are detailed discussions of Passover, Tabernacles and circumcision. Conclusions include the following: the climatic conditions implicit in the myth suggest a non-Arabian origin for the Semites; the Passover is not a nomadic pastoral festival and the unleavened bread should be regarded on comparative grounds as integral to the rite, not a distinct Canaanite element added later. This is a rich and challenging book, though there is a tendency to force everything into the single mould of the rain-myth. Thus Ugaritic El becomes a water-god identifiable with Yam and in conflict with Baal. The folk-tales undoubtedly have much to offer, but they should not be regarded as an infallible guide to everything. One wonders about the author's axiomatic 'Nichts in unseren Märchen ist zufällig' (p. 162).

J. F. HEALEY

DIETRICH, M., KÜMMEL, H. M., LORETZ, O., and OTTEN, H.: *Rechts- und Wirtschaftsurkunden/Historisch-chronologische Texte: Historisch-chronologische Texte II* (Texte aus der Umwelt des Alten Testaments, I/5). 1985. Pp. 451–520. (Gerd Mohn, Gütersloh. Price: DM 54.00; sub. price: DM 46.00. ISBN 3 579 00064 0)

For previous fascicles see last *B.L.* 1985, p. 117. This one contains annotated translations of selected Hittite royal documents of historical content, and of Syro-Palestinian cuneiform documents of the second millennium, from Ugarit, Alalakh, Kamid el-Loz and Amarna. Most of this material is not in *ANET* and is useful to illuminate the cultural background of the Old Testament. The scholarly standard is high, but constrictions of space made problems of choice impossible. Who will benefit from five out of some three hundred and fifty Amarna letters?

W. G. LAMBERT

CONRAD, D., DELSMAN, W. C., KAPLONY-HECKEL, U., KAUSEN, E., MÜLLER, H.-P., and MÜLLER, W. W.: *Rechts- und Wirtschaftsurkunden/Historisch-chronologische Texte: Historisch-chronologishe Texte III* (Texte aus der Umwelt des Alten Testaments, I/6). 1985. Pp. 521–671. (Gerd Mohn, Gütersloh. Price: DM. 118.00; sub. price: DM. 98.00. ISBN 3 579 00065 9)

This completes the first volume of this work (see above and *B.L.* 1985, p. 117 for previous fascicles), and a title page and table of contents (fifteen pages) has been issued for those wanting to bind up the fascicles issued in stiff cloth. Kaplony-Heckel translates Egyptian historical texts selected as relevant to the Old Testament, some of which are not readily available reliably translated elsewhere. Five Lachish ostraca and the Moabite stone are rendered respectively by Conrad and H.-P. Müller. The latter also treats the Kilamuwa and Azitawadda inscriptions. The major relevant Aramaic inscriptions are done by Delsman, while W. W. Müller presents a group of Old South Arabic and early North Arabic inscriptions. As before, the work is up-to-date, competent, and well presented. Three pages of additions and corrections to the previous fascicles (pp. 669–71) should not be overlooked. The next volume with religious texts can be expected in quick succession.

W. G. LAMBERT

HACKETT, J. A.: *The Balaam Text from Deir 'Allā* (Harvard Semitic Monographs, 31). 1984. Pp. xii, 147, including script charts. (Scholars Press, Chico, California. Price: $11.95 (discount price: $7.50); ISBN 0 89130 723 0)

This monograph contains the text and translation of, and a commentary on, the Deir 'Allā inscription concerned with the prophet Balaam. It is a useful supplement to the *editio princeps* (Hoftijzer and van der Kooij, *Aramaic Texts from Deir 'Alla*, 1976; *B.L.* 1978, p. 29), but the actual inscription is not reproduced in photographic or copy form. After discussion of script and presentation of text and translation there is an interesting excursus on the *šaddayīn*-deities in the text (for which cf. Deut. 32:17; Ps. 106:37: *šdym*, normally related to *šēd*, 'demon'). A description of the grammar follows and, most importantly, a detailed consideration of the identification of the language of the inscription. The evidence on this is not decisively clear, but the author rejects the often accepted Aramaic classification of the dialect (despite phonological indications, masc. plur. in *–yn*, etc.) in favour of a South Canaanite classification (Moabite has the masc. plur. *–n*, N–prefix conjugation also in Canaanite, etc.). A glossary and script charts are appended.

J. F. HEALEY

HARI, R.: *New Kingdom Amarna Period: The Great Hymn to Aten* (Iconography of Religions, XVI/6). 1985. Pp. x, 28; 43 plates. (Brill, Leiden. Price: Fl. 64.00. ISBN 90 04 07031 1)

This fascicle in the section of the *Iconography of Religions* devoted to Egypt provides an outline of the episode of rather specialised worship of the sun-disc instituted by the pharaoh Amenophis IV who called himself Akhenaten (mid-fourteenth century B.C.). The excellent high-quality plates give a fair cross-section of the range of religious representations during this period. Hari begins by offering large excerpts from the famous hymn to the Aten (sun-disc), points out the lack of any real theological document from Amarna, and makes needless reference to the misleadingly superficial views of Freud on Moses (as an 'Egyptian'), Psalm 104 and supposed monotheistic origins. More usefully he outlines the religious/political background and origins of Atenism, then comments on the didactic names of the Aten, Akhenaten's break with the old religion, the cult celebrated in the temples of Aten, the omission of the old, elaborate Egyptian views on the afterlife, and eventual erasure of the name of Amun on the monuments, the lack of impact of Atenism on ordinary Egyptians, the end of the epoch, demolition of its monuments, and defamation of Akhenaten by the Ramesside kings. As he admits, Atenism left a very slender inheritance; here, a reference to recent works by Assmann would have helped.

Besides the Freudian nonsense, other small slips occur: p. 3, there is no evidence for foreign origins of Atenism (or for Queen-mother Tiyi); p. 6, Amun's high priests never became kings — but military generals obtained both the priesthood and kingship, which is rather different. The plates are very good, but some captions have strayed or are wrong. In the text Rames, Rameses and Ramosis are all bad forms for the one name Ramose; various doubtful suggestions are stated too positively, e.g. that Amenophis III and his queen Tiyi actually lived apart at Amarna and Malqata (W. Thebes) respectively. (For other fascicles in this series see in this issue, pp. 106, 108, 122; also *B.L.* 1978, pp. 105–06; 1982, p. 94.)

K. A. KITCHEN

HOFFMEIER, J. K.: Sacred *in the Vocabulary of Ancient Egypt: The Term* DSR *with special reference to Dynasties I–XX* (Orbis Biblicus et Orientalis, 59). 1985. Pp. xvi, 281, including 24 figures. (Universitätsverlag, Freiburg. Price: Sw.Fr. 78.00. ISBN 3 7278 0324 X. Vandenhoeck & Ruprecht, Göttingen. ISBN 3 525 53682 8)

This monograph is a word-study of a widely-attested Egyptian term to be found in texts spanning three thousand years of ancient Egyptian history. The period covered here runs from the beginning to *ca.* 1100 B.C., with some reference to later occurrences. Beginning with the logogram of arms brandishing a particular type of baton, Hoffmeier shows that this word began with the sense of waving a stick, leading on to steering (with an oar) and warding off opposition, clearing the way in both secular and ritual (processional) contexts, passing on to the concept of separation (cf. Hebrew *bādal*) between entities (*e.g.* heaven and earth), and therewith into the fully religious field of meaning, of being 'separate', set apart, segregated, hence sacred, holy, applying to deities, kings, images, places, etc. The whole development can be seen to have taken place already in the third millennium B.C.; later periods continue the range of usages for many centuries and add further detail. A comprehensive range of data is reviewed; various suggestions for further, unrelated meanings of *d*sr (e.g., 'splendid', 'raised up') are eliminated as erroneous, clarifying not a few difficult contexts. An unpretentious, careful study, which Old Testament scholars should find useful in studying Hebrew terms for 'holy', 'separate' and the like.

K. A. KITCHEN

HUTTER, M.: *Altorientalische Vorstellungen von der Unterwelt: Literar- und religionsgeschichtliche Überlegungen zu "Nergal und Ereškigal"* (Orbis Biblicus et Orientalis, 63). 1985. Pp. viii, 187. (Universitätsverlag, Freiburg. Price: Sw.Fr. 48.00; ISBN 3 7278 0328 2. Vandenhoeck & Ruprecht, Göttingen. ISBN 3 525 53686 0)

This is not a technical work of Assyriology, but a highly readable study of the literary features of the Nergal and Ereškigal myth and its religious significance. The two principal versions of the text (from Amarna and Sultantepe) are presented in translation with philological notes. The two versions are analysed in detail from a structural point of view: the Sultantepe version has divisions marked in the text. Different emphases in the two are explained on the basis that the Amarna text is earlier, written down (in northern Syria?) before the story reached canonical form (*ca.* 1000 B.C.). As to content, the main theme of 'how Nergal came to be the husband of Ereškigal and god of the underworld' is explored in full, as are the various motifs of the texts and the other deities involved. Similarities with other texts describing descents into the underworld are demonstrated (e.g. the descent of Ugaritic Baal). The Sultantepe version may be pro-Ereškigal propaganda in support of her cult, though the author finds a wider, religio-philosophical message: death is the unavoidable fate of man.

J. F. HEALEY

JACOB-ROST, L., and MARZAHN, J.: *Assyrische Königsinschriften auf Ziegeln aus Assur* (Vorderasiatische Schriftdenkmäler der Staatlichen Museen zu Berlin, Neue Folge, 7). 1985. Pp. 14 and 50 plates in line. (Akademie-Verlag, Berlin. Price: M. 48.00)

This is a fascicle of hitherto unpublished brick inscriptions of Assyrian kings, now in the Berlin Museum. They are given in cuneiform hand-copies only, and are thus only of use to cuneiform scholars. However, this is well done basic material from which in due course editions and translations of Assyrian royal inscriptions will be supplemented and corrected, and then the material will be generally accessible to Old Testament scholars.

W. G. LAMBERT

KINNIER WILSON, J. V.: *The Legend of Etana: A New Edition*. 1985. Pp. x, 150, with 32 plates. (Aris & Phillips, Warminster. Price: £17.50. ISBN 0 85668 258 6)

This edition of a very fragmented, and not well-known, Babylonian legend is to be welcomed. It gives a full presentation with reconstruction, translation, notes and the cuneiform text in transliteration and hand-copy. Many of its themes relate to those of interest to Old Testament studies, for it is a human story involving kingship and succession, childlessness, a search for the 'plant of life', repeated flights on eagle's wings to the gates of heaven, dreams, prayers to several deities for help and a remarkable deliverance when falling to earth. Hostility between prolific, and speaking, eagle and serpent and the seemingly tragic end with the assassination of Etana by his son are also involved. Variation in the text between the earliest and latest versions is also instructive. Only further textual discoveries can prove or deny the reconstructions proposed here in an edition which far updates those, such as in *ANET*, hitherto available to the non-specialist reader for comparative purposes.

D. J. WISEMAN

KUPPER, J.-R.: *Archives royales de Mari*. XXII: *Documents administratifs de la salle 135 du Palais de Mari.* 2 vols. 1983. Pp. viii, 1–303; 304–618, 5 plates. (Éditions Recherche sur les Civilisations, A.D.P.F., Paris. Price: Fr. 93.00. ISBN 2 86538 058 0)

BARDET, G., JOANNÈS, F., LAFONT, B., SOUBEYRAN, D., and VILLARD, P.: *Archives royales de Mari*. XXIII: *Archives administratives de Mari* I. 1984. Pp. x, 651. (Éditions Recherche sur les Civilisations, A.D.P.F., Paris. Price: Fr. 110.00. ISBN 2 86538 074 2)

TALON, P.: *Achives royales de Mari*. XXIV: *Textes administratifs des salles "Y et Z" du Palais de Mari*. Vol. I: Texte. Vol. II: Planches. 1985. Pp. vi, 299; xiv, 144 plates. (Éditions Recherche sur les civilisations, A.D.P.F., Paris. Price Fr. 161.00. ISBN 2 86538 099 8)

In these volumes Francophone Assyriologists continue to edit the vast archives of documents from the palace destroyed in the mid-eighteenth century B.C. Almost thirteen hundred cuneiform tablets are published in these volumes, giving a further view of the extent and detail of clerical activity in a city which combined both urban and nomadic folk, the majority of Amorite stock. While most of the texts list amounts of wine, metal, cattle, cloth and garments, brought into or issued from the palace, there are also numerous records concerning the movement and condition of personnel. Long lists of named individuals note that some are missing, and some dead (vol. XXII). One group of tablets reports on the disposition of some Yaminites sent on expedition to Babylon, listing them by towns, noting some in settlements (vol. XXIII). Others deal with the liberation of captives and their distribution according to their skills (vol.XXIII). The detailed accounts of gold used for decorating a throne, and for other purposes, with their precision in minute amounts, and notes of losses in refining (vol. XXII), are additional examples of the realities which lie behind ancient annals and other records in which kings boast of their gifts to the gods. Volume XXIII celebrates the fiftieth anniversary of the discovery of Mari, and all these volumes are issued under the direction of D. Charpin and J.–M. Durand, who thus bring an impressive renewal to the work begun by the late André Parrot and Georges Dossin. Only such sometimes tedious presentations as these make possible informative syntheses like that by Stephanie Dalley (*B.L.* 1985, p. 118) and produce incidental information about Palestinian cities of the time (there is a possible mention of Hazor in vol. XXIV, no. 75).

A. R. MILLARD

LALOUETTE, C.: *Textes sacrés et textes profanes de l'ancienne Égypte*. I: *Des Pharaons et des hommes: Traductions et commentaires* (Connaissance de l'Orient. Collection UNESCO d'œuvres représentatives, Série Égypte Ancienne). Préface de P. Grimal. 1984. Pp. 345. (Gallimard, Paris. Price: Fr. 135.00. ISBN 2 07 070142 5)

This work contains a wide-ranging set of translations into French of a good cross-section of ancient Egyptian texts from the time of the pyramids to the Hellenistic age. The first half is centred on the pharaoh: his divine origination, roles as mediator between people and gods and conqueror, and his posthumous destiny. The second half focusses on other Egyptians, high and low: high officials' autobiographical inscriptions, literary compositions on life's vicissitudes, wisdom-writings and funerary spells. This considerable variety of texts includes famous historical works such as the dream-stelae of Tuthmosis IV and Tanutamun, Tuthmosis III's Battle of Megiddo and Ramesses II's Battle of Qadesh and Hittite treaty; the celebrated stela of Pi(ankh)y's conquest of Egypt from Nubia, and Merenptah's 'Israel stela'. Wisdom includes Ptahhotep, Khety for Merikare, Amenemhat I, Satire on the Trades, Aniy, Petosiris and the Eloquent Peasant. The birth-legend of pharaoh (Westcar and Hatshepsut versions), hymns to kings, banquet-songs, a dream-interpretation text, and samples from the Pyramid and Coffin Texts and the Book of the Dead round out the series. The translations are straightforward and reliable (one might at times query some details); the seventy pages of notes stay on a simple, general level, aiming at elucidating Egyptian allusions for the non-specialist. The issue of further translations in this series appears to be intended; the result of such an undertaking will be to make available to readers of French a considerable body of texts of use for ancient studies, and of some value for Old Testament background.

K. A. KITCHEN

LÉVÊQUE, J.: *Sagesses de l'Égypte Ancienne* (Cahiers Évangile: Supplément au Cahier Évangile, 46). 1983. Pp. 98. (Éditions du Cerf, Paris. Price: Fr. 34.00. ISSN 0222 9714)

In this neat little booklet, part of a series on documents illustrative of the world of the Bible, the editor has drawn on reputable Egyptological sources to present French translations of or from fifteen ancient Egyptian instructional 'wisdom' works of the same type as Proverbs; eight are given complete, of the other seven, extracts of varying length. The translations are preceded by a brief introduction pointing out how such texts in part reflect the culture that produced them, and in part share the same universally human concerns to be found in such texts in other cultures. 'Inserts' at various points include a table of the principal such texts from Egypt in historical sequence; a note on the evolution of social concept, not of literary form; a note on the non- monotheistic value of the term 'god' in these texts; notes on Egyptian concepts of 'spirit' and *maat*; an inadequate note on 'genre littéraire' in these texts and in Proverbs; a note on Ben-Sira's high view of the learned scribes; and simple notes on Egyptian scripts. The rather brief bibliography indicates the core of the compiler's sources; curiously, for a work issued in 1983, there is nothing after 1977 (the very important work of 1979 edited by Hornung and Keel (*B.L.* 1981, p. 106) is omitted, among others). In the introduction to Amenemope (p. 53) the Cairo ostracon is wrongly ascribed to the nineteenth Dynasty instead of to the twenty-first (as Černý had in fact suggested). The twelfth century would be a better date than *ca*. 1400 for this work. Rather more is now available of 'Man to his Son', Hordjedef, the 'Loyalist' instruction and probably of Amennakht than is indicated in this booklet. Nevertheless it remains an attractive and simple presentation of a series of texts important for biblical background.

K. A. KITCHEN

VAN LOON, M. N.: *Anatolia in the Second Millennium B.C.* (Iconography of Religions, xv/12), 1985. Pp. x, 47; 46 plates (Brill, Leiden. Price: Fl. 76.00. ISBN 90 04 07105 0)

This clear, well documented and illustrated essay shows how Anatolian religion and iconography amalgamated Mesopotamian genealogy and hierarchy of gods and their clear-cut cosmic division of labour with Syria's colourful mythology full of adventure stories and explanations of natural phenomena, and with Anatolia's own reverence for geographic features. The former two elements predominated until the late second millennium when an Olympus- type pantheon and characteristic iconography emerged. This provides useful background for later North Syrian and thus 'Canaanite' religious developments. (For other fascicles in this series see in this issue pp. 103, 108, 122; also *B.L.* 1978, pp. 105–06; 1982, p. 94.) D. J. WISEMAN

Mari. Annales de Recherches Interdisciplinaires. Tome 1. 1982. Pp. 189, numerous figures, 8 plates. Tome 2. 1983. Pp. 221, including numerous figures and 6 plates. Tome 3. 1984. Pp. 284, numerous figures. Tome 4. 1985. Pp. 625, numerous figures. (Éditions Recherche sur les Civilisations, A.D.P.F., Paris. Prices: Fr. 100.00, 128.00, 172.00, 399.00. ISBN 2 86538 047 5, 052 1, 084 X, 134 3)

With the retirement and deaths of André Parrot and Georges Dossin, the original archaeologist and epigrapher respectively of Mari, a new set-up has emerged: Jean Margueron as archaeologist and Jean-Marie Durand as epigrapher, aided by Dominique Beyer and Dominique Charpin in the two fields, and guided by an expert committee. This publication of the new team is in fact a journal (abbreviation: *M.A.R.I.*), and it has achieved a huge amount in the first four years of its existence. Old finds have been subjected to a fresh scrutiny, and many unpublished things have been made available. Some of the articles are highly technical, of little immediate interest to Old Testament scholars not also near eastern archaeologists or cuneiform scholars, but there are also articles of direct interest: J. M. Sasson on 'An apocalyptic vision from Mari?' (1, 151 ff.), and many in Tome 4, which gives the papers of a colloquium summing up the present state of Mari studies in all aspects: note W. G. Lambert, 'The Pantheon of Mari' (pp. 525–39); P. Bordreuil, 'Ashtart de Mari et les dieux d'Ougarit' (pp. 545–47); and A. Lemaire, 'Mari, la Bible et le monde nord-ouest sémitique' (pp. 549–58). Save for nomadism, virtually every major aspect of Mari has been substantially shaken up and advanced in these volumes so that they are an essential supplement to previous and currently appearing volumes of excavations and texts. W. G. LAMBERT

METZGER, M.: *Königsthron und Gottesthron: Thronformen und Throndarstellungen in Ägypten und im Vorderen Orient im dritten und zweiten Jahrtausend vor Christus und deren Bedeutung für das Verständnis von Aussagen über den Thron im Alten Testament* (Alter Orient und Altes Testament, 15). 2 volumes. 1985. Vol. 1 (Text): pp. x, 391, including 526 figures; vol. 2 (catalogue and plates): pp. viii, 272; 130 plates. Neukirchener Verlag, Neukirchen-Vluyn. Price: DM. 218.00; sub. price: DM. 198.00. ISBN 3 7887 0724 0. Butzon & Bercker, Kevelaer. ISBN 3 7666 9327 1)

This thesis, completed in 1968 but updated to 1971, amasses examples of stools, chairs and armchairs from Egyptian, Mesopotamian and Syrian objects, mostly reliefs and seal impressions. All are meticulously classified, though whether (throne) podium, platform or pedestal is not always clear from the earliest examples. Form, decoration or relief is described with emphasis on the Egyptian decorations as the most numerous. Thrones that are certainly identifiable are few, and for Mesopotamia there is inevitably some indetermination as to the occupant of the seat, whether god, king or high official. The analysis is by historical periods within Egypt. Mesopotamia, Syro-Palestine and Anatolia. The emphasis is on sphinxes, lions and mixed creatures standing beside the throne. Throughout there is little reference to textual data in this discussion of the art form.

Part II discusses Solomon's throne, said to be of Egyptian form on a high podium of Mesopotamian (ziggurat) style, with pairs of lions flanking the steps. This is compared with the throne of Idrimi. Similar influences and mixed style are attributed to the concept of Yahweh's throne *yôšeb hakk^{e}rûbîm*. Whereas the sphinx-throne, the lion-dragon and winged creatures are argued to be interrelated with the cherubim, the first is said to have taken over Egyptian elements and to have become the king's throne later in the second millennium. Metzger considers the sphinx as a guardian figure nowhere attested as supporting a deity. In Egypt it represents pharaoh, whereas in Syro-Phoenicia it is the weather-god. The cherubim combine the function of all throne-related creatures and, in the Old Testament, are exclusively associated with Yahweh. The ark is not taken to be a throne or pedestal (Jer. 3: 16–17 being interpreted as a later redactional reinterpretation), and the winged creatures represent the clouds of heaven above which Yahweh was enthroned. While all will not be convinced by the interpretations, the detailed data will help everyone engaged in similar studies.

D. J. WISEMAN

MYŚLIWIEC, K.: *Eighteenth Dynasty before the Amarna Period* (Iconography of Religions, XVI/5). 1985. Pp. xii, 39; 48 plates. (Brill, Leiden. Price: Fl. 68.00. ISBN 90 04 07028 1)

This work is part of a whole series that aims to illustrate the visual repertoire of specific religions through the course of history — in this case, Egypt, *ca.* 1550–1400 B.C. Within thirty pages the author gives an introductory sketch of Egyptian history of the period, then proceeds to give a fair (if rather generalised) account of the main known religious phenomena: layout, function and decoration of temples, especially of the subject-matter on their walls. This covers representations of rituals, daily or special, royal ceremonial (coronation, jubilees), and royal victory in a theological framework. He then passes on to two major Theban festivals, funerary rites (including those of burial), and finally funerary compositions (e.g. the Book of the Dead). As the author himself rightly makes clear, the main evidence at this time derives almost entirely from Thebes and Nubia in the south, as very little is sufficiently recovered from elsewhere — hence the 'Theban' flavour of this work.

Sometimes the generalisations are a little too hasty; thus Thebes ceased to be the political/administrative capital under Tuthmosis III and probably from Tuthmosis I. And the front pylon of a temple (as the last part to be built) was most unlikely to name a temple's founder, except in the case of personal funerary temples of individual kings. Some slips in English may confuse the unwary. Almost throughout (e.g. pp. 6, 9, 19, 20, 21) 'barge' is wrongly used for 'portable boat-shrine' as carried on the shoulders of the priests. It is the great river-boat that normally is termed a barge, on account of its great size. On p. 25 'lecturer' should be 'lector(priest)'. The illustrations are of high quality. (For other fascicles in this series see in this issue pp. 103, 106, 122; also *B.L.* 1978, pp. 105–06; 1982, p. 94.)

K. A. KITCHEN

OCKINGA, B.: *Die Gottebenbildlichkeit im alten Ägypten und im alten Testament* (Ägypten und Altes Testament, 7). 1984. Pp. 175. (Distributed by Otto Harrassowitz, Wiesbaden. Price: DM 65.00. ISBN 3 447 02513 1)

The author offers here a study of the ancient Egyptian words for 'image', examining each of seven different terms, and carefully and very clearly setting out the particular nuance and emphasis of each, on explicit textual evidence. In each case he devotes a particular section to usage of the term with reference to the king as 'image' of deity. These terms fall into two main groups. The first four terms have in common (for the king) the role of the god's representative upon earth, his 'image' in that sense. The king is the (general) likeness, the (visible) image, of deity; the image of the sun-god, and the 'mouthpiece' of deity. Three terms comprise the second group. Here we have terms more widely applicable to men at large, not just the king. But as relating king to deity, these terms reduce him to being merely similar to deity in his role and nature, not fully the 'image of God'. Studied through time, one may see the progressive weakening of the theological standing of the pharaohs, during the third and second millennia B.C., from son of the god (having his nature) to mere 'mouthpiece', a trend reflected in the terms studied here. Finally, Ockinga reviews the possibility of links between the concept of men in God's image in the Old Testament and the Egyptian usages and concepts he has just elucidated. There are clear distinctions and contrasts insofar as in Egypt only the king stands in God's image, not other men, as in the Old Testament. However, he would see the possibility of some significant parallels between Egyptian royal ideology and Gen. 1:26–27, and some similarity of distinction between the Hebrew word-pair *ṣelem/dĕmūt* and the Egyptian pair *tut/khenti*. And in Egypt one may note the intelligent consciousness of mankind like the gods, distinguishing them from the beasts (Aniy), which comes close to biblical distinctions. A clear and useful study.

K. A. KITCHEN

ROUAULT, O.: *Terqa Final Reports*. No. 1: *L'Archive de Puzurum* (Bibliotheca Mesopotamica, 16). 1984. Pp. xxii, 92, including numerous figures; 20 plates. (Undena Publications, Malibu, California. Price: $29.50; ISBN 0 89003 103 7. Paperback price: $19.50; ISBN 0 89003 102 9)

In 1977 and 1978 fourteen cuneiform texts and many fragments were recovered from one room of a house. They lay smashed amidst a variety of objects, thrown out, the excavator explains in his introduction, as rubbish (see *Terqa Preliminary Reports* No. 10; *B.L.* 1981, p. 26). Six of the texts record purchases of property by Puzurum, a man who figures in other texts also. The dating on some deeds, by years of the kings of Khana, suggests the collection belongs to the latter part of the eighteenth century B.C., after Hammurabi had destroyed Mari, and covers three generations. Two texts, found elsewhere at the same time, are presented, one of mathematical tables, the other a votive bead. More documents were found in later seasons, some connected with Puzurum, others from a temple and a school. Publication of all these and a re-edition of those found earlier this century will enlarge knowledge of this society through its personal names, many of them 'Amorite', its history as revealed in the date-lines, and expressions such as 'to eat' an oath, and the frequent use of 'remission' (*andurārum*). Meanwhile here is a clear presentation with photographs, hand-copies, transliteration and translation, and an index of names, which can be easily used by any scholar.

A. R. MILLARD

SAGGS, H. W. F.: *The Might that was Assyria*. 1984. Pp. xii, 340. (Sidgwick and Jackson, London. Price: £16.95. ISBN 0 283 98961 0)

The world is gradually realizing that the Assyrians were not just Babylonians who spoke with a northern accent and did a lot more raping and pillaging than their southern neighbours. But to find an up-to-date and reliable account of their history and culture in English has been impossible. Saggs is one of the few scholars in the world who could give us a well written book full of the results of his personal research in this field. His *The Greatness that was Babylon* (*B.L.* 1964, pp. 69–70; *Decade*, pp. 537–38) has served us so well for so long, and this account of an ancient people he clearly admires, and of their country he clearly loves, has been an inspiration to read. As soon as it was published, it was picked for Book Club promotion, and it should certainly find a place on the school library shelf as well as in the private study of the Old Testament scholar.

M. E. J. RICHARDSON

TEIXIDOR, J.: *Un port romain du désert: Palmyre* (Semitica, 34). 1984. Pp. 127; 8 plates. (Librairie d'Amérique et d'Orient Adrien-Maisonneuve, Paris. Price: Fr. 140.00. ISBN 2 7200 1030 8)

Teixidor's earlier monograph, *The Pantheon of Palmyra*, was noticed in *B.L.* 1981, p. 111. In the present work his primary concern is with the commercial life of Palmyra. Part I, entitled 'La ville caravanière', includes valuable sections on routes, while Part II is concerned with the famous 'tariff', or municipal tax law promulgated by the city council in A.D. 137. An appendix gives a translation of the Palmyrene text of the tax law (an English translation of the Greek, by J. R. Matthews, is now available in *Journal of Roman Studies* 1984).

S. P. BROCK

9. APOCRYPHA AND POST-BIBLICAL STUDIES

DEL AGUA, A.: *El método midrásico y la exégesis del Nuevo Testamento* (Biblioteca Midrásica, 4). 1985. Pp. 337. (Institución San Jerónimo para la Investigación Bíblica, Valencia. Price: Ptas. 1,500. ISBN 84 86067 11 1)

This beautifully produced book, a study conducted under the supervision of the late Professor A. Díez Macho, investigates the midrashic use of the Old Testament in the New according to three patterns: promise-fulfilment, insertion-substitution, and opposition. The author presents the midrashic method as a kind of complement of the classical methods of exegesis. The bulk of his work is formed by an analysis of New Testament texts according to this method, but the first part of the book deals with the midrashic method in early Judaism, including not only the rabbinic literature, but the targumic and Qumran literature as well. The book has a comprehensive bibliography and is well indexed.

F. GARCÍA MARTÍNEZ

AVERY-PECK, A. J.: *Mishnah's Division of Agriculture: A History and Theology of Seder Zeraim* (Brown Judaic Studies, 79), 1985. Pp. xxxii, 441. (Scholars Press, Chico, California, Price: $39.25 (discount price: $32.25); ISBN 0 89130 888 1. Paperback price: $32.25 (discount price: $25.95); ISBN 0 89130 889 X)

Each tractate of the Mishnah Order *Zeraim* (except *Berakhoth*) is individually analyzed, and laws from the period before A.D. 70, from the time of the Yavnean authorities (A.D. 70–140), and from the period of the Ushan masters (A.D. 140–200) are separately and systematically set out in the context of their historical development. Professor Avery-Peck is in substantial agreement with the other scholars who have most recently studied the tractates of this Order and have published their findings in *Brown Judaic Studies* (see, e.g., *B.L.* 1980, pp. 124–25; 1982; pp. 106, 115; 1983, pp. 108, 113; 1984, pp. 133–34; 1985, pp. 126–27). His work is a most timely and useful addition to the series, not least because it brings into a convenient and comprehensive synthesis the major results of research into this Order of the Mishnah initiated by Jacob Neusner and his pupils. Avery-Peck agrees with Neusner that most of the anonymous material in the tractates is to be dated in the Ushan period. The authorities before 70, he argues, supplied very little on which later rabbis chose to build. The foundations of the Order were laid by Yavneans, who expected the re-building of the Temple: their outlook was conditioned by their view of holiness and sanctification as God-given norms to which Israel must conform (almost mechanically) to restore the universe to its original order. Ushans, faced with the aftermath of Bar-Kokhba's revolt and the prospect of the Temple never being rebuilt, reacted against this Yavnean theology and shifted emphasis onto the *intention* of the lay Israelite as he carried out the requirements of the law. The Ushan view, which effectively determined the over-all meaning of the Order in its final form, was that what the individual Israelite declared holy was indeed consecrated, and it was his intention and perception which imposed God's order — still paramount despite the catastrophes of 70 and 132 — on an otherwise chaotic and disordered world.

C. T. R. HAYWARD

BARTLETT, J. R.: *Jews in the Hellenistic World: Josephus, Aristeas, the Sybilline Oracles, Eupolemus* (Cambridge Commentaries on Writings of the Jewish and Christian World 200 BC to AD 200, Volume 1, Part 1). 1985. Pp. x, 209, including 7 maps. (Cambridge University Press. Price: £25.00; ISBN 0 521 24246 0. Paperback price: £8.95; ISBN 0 521 28551 8)

This volume belongs to a new series alongside the Cambridge Bible commentaries, which fills the gap between the Old Testament and the New; for other volumes in the series see below, pp. 124–25; also *B.L.* 1985, pp. 134, 149. A fresh English translation is given of important sections of the Letter of Aristeas, the Sybilline Oracles, Eupolemus (as quoted by Eusebius) and Josephus: well over half the book is devoted to Josephus. Before each excerpt come any necessary comments on date and general literary questions like authorship. Full notes follow the excerpts and include detailed discussion of political history, geography, liturgical practice, etc. Particularly useful to general readers will be the information on Josephus, information sometimes difficult to obtain in a popular style. Bartlett writes an introduction of ten pages describing the Jews in the hellenistic world, tracing the process of hellenisation and putting the authors in historical perspective. It is useful to have the intertestamental period made available to non-specialists in such a readable and informative way.

J. G. SNAITH

BEN-CHORIN, S.: *Narrative Theologie des Judentums anhand er Pessach-Haggada: Jerusalemer Vorlesungen*. 1985. Pp. 165. (Mohr, Tübingen. Price: DM. 28.00. ISBN 3 16 744913 6)

The author is well-known for his outstanding mediation of Judaism and rabbinical traditions to Christian readers. The present work is the fifth volume in a series of a most readable Theologia Judaica (for previous volumes see

B.L. 1980, pp. 80, 109–10; 1982, pp. 99–100; 1984, p. 121). It not only presents and interprets the Haggada of the Passover from within Judaism, but also examines and stresses New Testament parallels, if only to insist on the Eucharistic institution as a Passover. Ben-Chorin is not uncritical of the growth of some Jewish and Christian traditions. His commentary abounds in good sense and felicitous references to Goethe, Heine and even Shakespeare. It is a rich feast fed by Old Testament texts.

U. E. SIMON

BERCHMAN, R. M.: *From Philo to Origen: Middle Platonism in Transition* (Brown Judaic Studies, 69). 1984. Pp. x, 359. (Scholars Press, Chico, California. Price: $29.95 (discount price: $25.95); ISBN 0 89130 750 8. Paperback price: $25.95 (discount price: $17.95); ISBN 0 89130 815 6)

The focus of this study is the place of Jewish and Christian Platonism within the wider Hellenistic context in the first three centuries A.D. It demonstrates the author's contention that proper understanding of the major writers of this period requires awareness of the questions they were tackling, who they were arguing with, and the assumptions they shared even with their opponents. It is insufficient to read them only to decide on their orthodoxy or heresy, or even just as a stage in theological progress.

The book divides into three sections. The first discusses the Middle Platonic conception of reality, and the difficulties which this posed for them in their theory construction. Two ways of dealing with these difficulties were proposed: one by Antiochus of Ascalon and the other by Eudorus of Alexandria. Philo, Clement, and Origen can be read as various efforts at harmonization of these methods. The second section of the book discusses epistemology. The central problem for Jewish and Christian thinkers was to give an account of their scriptures, given the shared Middle Platonist assumption that revelation is the first principle of all discursive knowledge. From this flows the third section, which shows how the scriptures were used in conjunction with the rules of dialectic in order to deduce from them systems of first principles. Berchman concludes with an extended illustration of this from Origen's *Periarchôn*.

G. M. JANTZEN

BIETENHARD, H.: *Der tannaitische Midrasch Sifre Deuteronomium.* Mit einem Beitrag von H. Ljungman (Judaica et Christiana, 8). 1985. Pp. x, 943. (Peter Lang, Bern, Frankfurt am Main and New York. Price: Sw.Fr. 222.00. ISBN 3 261 03311 8)

This series of books entitled *Judaica et Christiana* already includes two volumes by Professor Bietenhard in which he offers us a translation of Midrash Tanhuma as edited by Buber (see *B.L.* 1982, p. 100; *B.L.* 1983, p. 104). The present work keeps much the same format as the previous books: a translation of the text which is fairly literal, with notes, at times extensive, by way of comment on language and text. The first seventy-seven pages of the translation are the work of Henrik Ljungman, which he published in 1964. Thereafter, Bietenhard offers us his own rendering of the Sifre as edited by Louis Finkelstein. The notes and commentary are particularly valuable; the lack of an introduction to the text, however, is noticeable. It is understandable that Bietenhard was reluctant to make a long book even longer, and his most impressive commentary goes some way to supplying the lack of an introduction; but even a short discussion of the date, provenance, language, manuscript tradition, and relationship of the document to other rabbinic sources would have been useful. Nonetheless, this translation is a worthy addition to an already well-established series.

C. T. R. HAYWARD

BLACK, M., in consultation with VANDERKAM, J. C.: *The Book of Enoch or 1 Enoch: A New English Edition with Commentary and Textual Notes*. With an Appendix on the 'Astronomical' Chapters (72–82) by O. Neugebauer (Studia in Veteris Testamenti Pseudepigrapha, 7). 1985. Pp. xvi, 467. (Brill, Leiden. Price: Fl. 180.00. ISBN 90 04 07100 8)

The stated objective of this work is 'the recovery of the original Enoch, so far as that can be reasonably deduced'. Black has revised, 'in the light of the new evidence', the English translation of Ethiopic Enoch made by R. H. Charles (1912) from a critical text, and provided an extensive textual commentary and notes.

Black's 'translation' is not a translation of one Ethiopic manuscript, or of a critical Ethiopic text, but of a reconstruction in which the Ethiopic variants most suggestive of Greek are selected and retroverted, and then translated into English with notice taken of Aramaic and Hebrew possibilities; methodologically, this is unsatisfactory. In addition, in the retroversion into Greek unjustifiable assumptions have been made about what the 'normal' Ethiopic sentence should look like, and over-reliance has been placed on MS Ṭana 9.

Detailed evaluation must await fuller reviews; meanwhile, the volume should only be used by those competent in Ethiopic, and other students of Enoch should be referred to M. A. Knibb's text and translation (1978), or to H. F. D. Sparks (ed.), *The Apocryphal Old Testament* (1984).

R. W. COWLEY

BROOKE, G. J.: *Exegesis at Qumran: 4QFlorilegium in its Jewish Context* (JSOT Supplement Series, 29). 1985. Pp. xii, 390. (JSOT Press, Sheffield. Price: £18.50; ISBN 0 905774 76 0. Paperback price: £8.95; ISBN 0 905774 77 9)

A major concern of this exhaustive study of 4QFlorilegium is to show that recognition of the use in 4QFlor, and in Qumran literature generally, of exegetical techniques familiar from the later rabbinic writings is essential for a proper understanding of the Qumran texts. In the first chapter the author uses examples drawn from Philo and the targums in support of the view that rabbinic techniques such as *nôṭārîqôn* and *gĕzērâ šāwâ* were used in the pre-tannaitic period, even though the formulation of the rabbinic *middôt* themselves belongs to a later period. In chapter 2, occupying the major part of the book, the author first attempts to establish the text of 4QFlor, drawing attention in his supporting commentary to the exegetical techniques that are used. Further sections of this chapter are devoted to the structure and literary form of 4QFlor, to its theology, and to a traditio-historical study covering CD 3:12b–8:20; Acts 13:33–37; Hebr. 1:5; Acts 15:16; 2 Cor. 6:14–7:1. Brooke argues that 4QFlor is best described as a midrash, albeit of a distinctive kind ('Qumran Midrash'). He further argues that the first two parts of what survives of this document (1:1–13; 1:14–2:6(?)) do form a unity, despite some differences stemming from the lack of the word *pēsher* in 1:1–13. He suggests that the main biblical texts that form the basis of 4QFlor (from 2 Sam. 7; Ps. 1; Ps. 2) are held together by their common concern (as coronation texts) and by virtue of being used in a common liturgical setting, and he concludes: 'might it not be suggested that 4QFlor is a midrash on texts that have their setting at Qumran as part of the liturgy of the Feast of Tabernacles?' In the last chapter of the book he discusses, by way of example, the use of exegetical techniques in a range of other Qumran writings (11QtgJob; 1QpHab; 1QM 10:1–8; 1QS 2:2–4; CD 7:13b–8:1a; 4QTest; 11QMelch).

This is a careful and interesting study which deserves serious attention, although its origin as a dissertation (completed under W. H. Brownlee at Claremont) is, despite extensive revision, still apparent.

M. A. Knibb

Camponovo, O.: *Königtum, Königsherrschaft und Reich Gottes in den frühjudischen Schriften* (Orbis Biblicus et Orientalis, 58). 1984. Pp. xiv, 492. (Universitätsverlag, Freiburg. Price: Sw.Fr. 98.00; ISBN 3 7278 0316 9. Vandenhoeck und Ruprecht, Göttingen. ISBN 3 525 53680 1)

This is a useful collection and discussion of passages from a wide range of early Jewish writings — with the exception of Philo, Josephus, the rabbinic writings and the New Testament, but including the LXX and the targums. It is a revised version of a dissertation presented by a Swiss scholar to the University of Freiburg in 1983. The author has an impressive grasp of the secondary literature and of the critical problems the various writings raise, but his discussions of individual passages are usually quite brief. The results which finally emerge will not surprise biblical scholars.

G. N. Stanton

Cazeaux, J.: *L'Épée du Logos et le Soleil de Midi* (Collection de la Maison de l'Orient Méditerranéen, 13/2). 1983. Pp. 184. (Maison de l'Orient, Lyon. Price: Fr. 120.00. ISBN 2 903264 03 1)

In a rather less ambitious and technically detailed study than an earlier one (see *B.L.* 1984, p. 122) the author again discovers in Philo's exposition elements of structure which do not impose themselves on a straightforward reading of the text. Almost always the structure is that of a more or less clearly discernible chiasmus. The treatises studied on this occasion are *De Cherubim* and *De Abrahamo*. Cazeaux detects a recurrent feature which he calls 'redondance': the Pentateuch 'donne à son lecteur assez de répétitions entre les passages, ou assez de ressemblance interne entre deux récits d'apparence étrangère, pour que l'esprit les superpose, les comprenne l'un par l'autre' (p. 92). By exploiting this feature Philo aimed to 'reflect the unity of the truth of Scripture' in what Cazeaux calls 'un rabbinisme classique' (p. 120). In explicating Philo's technique in this respect the author displays an impressive familiarity with the Philonic corpus so as to 'interpret Philo by Philo' in writing of an elegance matching that of the texts explored. One's only hesitation lies in the suspicion that Philo is in fact less ordered and subtle in his disposition of material than Cazeaux's study — which is partly commentary and rather more extended paraphrase — tries to demonstrate.

C. J. A. Hickling

Charlesworth, J. H. (ed.): *The Old Testament Pseudepigrapha*. Vol. 2: *Expansions of the "Old Testament" and Legends, Wisdom and Philosophical Literature, Prayers, Psalms, and Odes, Fragments of Lost Judeo-Hellenistic Works*. 1985. Pp. l, 1006. (Doubleday & Company, Garden City, New York. Price: $40.00; ISBN 0 385 18813 7. Darton, Longman and Todd, London. Price: £30.00; ISBN 0 232 51627 8)

Volume i of this major undertaking was reviewed in *B.L.* 1984, pp. 122–24. As the subtitle indicates, this second volume covers four different types of literature; the last section is given as a supplement, since the writings included were not originally pseudepigraphic. Excluding the Supplement, there are twenty-five texts, ranging in date from the seventh/sixth century B.C. (Aramaic Aḥiqar) to the fourth century A.D.; some of these survive only in very fragmentary form (Jannes and Jambres, Eldad and Modad, Prayer of Joseph). A few texts appear here for the first time in an English translation (e.g. Syriac Sentences of Menander)

The presentation follows the patterns of volume I. There are thirty-two different contributors (six from this side of the Atlantic). The quality of the contributions is on the whole high; several are very good (that by C. Burchard, on Joseph and Aseneth, is outstanding). These two volumes with their extensive (albeit rather amorphous) collection of texts will no doubt rapidly become a standard work of reference. Scholars will want to turn to it especially for some of the less familiar documents, many of which have been excellently served (a few, however, need to be approached with caution). An index of just over eighty-five pages enhances the value of the collection.

S. P. Brock

Charlesworth, J. H.: *The Discovery of a Dead Sea Scroll (4QTherapeia): Its Importance in the History of Medicine and Jesus Research* (ICASALS Publication, 85–1). 1985. Pp. vi, 41, including 3 plates. (Texas Tech University, Lubbock, Texas. Price: $6.00)

Under the somewhat unexpected sponsorship of the International Center for Arid and Semi-Arid Land Studies of Texas Tech University, Professor Charlesworth has issued the text of a lecture containing general considerations on ancient Jewish and non-Jewish medicine apropos of 4QTherapeia. This (probably) medical fragment was first printed by J. M. Allegro in *The Dead Sea Scrolls and the Christian Myth* (1979), pp. 235–40 (cf. *B.L.* 1980, pp. 108–09). The translation of the document included in Charlesworth's pamphlet is without philological justification and essentially follows Allegro's. The principal value of the lecture lies in raising the question of the relationship between ancient Jewish medicine and Essenism (and the New Testament). The author announces a fuller annotated study to appear as an appendix to H. C. Kee's forthcoming work on medicine, miracle and magic. Two corrections are offered in view of this publication. (1) 4QTherapeia (dated by Charlesworth to the first century A.D.) cannot be 'at least fourteen centuries' older than the earliest manuscript of *Sepher Asaph*, since Bodl. 2138 is assigned to the twelfth or early thirteenth century; cf. Elinor Lieber, *Dumbarton Oaks Papers* 38 (1984), p. 238. (2) The word rendered as 'exorcist' in 4QPrNab is *gzr*, not *shbq*. Neither is the latter, an Aramaic verb, 'the Qal active participle of *shbq*, that is *shōbhēq*'.

G. Vermes

Charlesworth, J. H.: *The Old Testament Pseudepigrapha and the New Testament: Prolegomena for the Study of Christian Origins* (Society for New Testament Studies, Monograph Series, 54). 1985. Pp. xxiv, 213. (Cambridge University Press. Price: £19.50. ISBN 0 521 30190 4)

Here are the reflections of the editor of *The Old Testament Pseudepigrapha*, prompted by the proofreading of its first volume. Chapter 1 is a shrewd, if overly concise, account of past achievement and future challenge in Pseudepigrapha research. Chapter 2 argues that the Pseudepigrapha give the lie to any concept of 'normative' or 'sectarian' Early Judaism, but also suggests that the all-pervasive cosmic and eschatological concerns of the Pseudepigrapha characterize such Early Judaism. Chapter 3, again too briefly, offers some methodological suggestions for comparing the New Testament and the Pseudepigrapha, and sketches a few predictable examples.

Then, from p. 94 to the end, is an Appendix giving the proceedings of the SNTS Pseudepigrapha seminars from 1976 to 1983. A good deal of ground is certainly covered in this book, analysis and synthesis are nicely balanced, and nearly every New Testament scholar would learn much from the contents. But the volume, though stimulating and informative, is much more modest than the title, length or price suggest.

P. R. Davies

Chiesa, B., and Lockwood, W.: *Ya'qūb al-Qirqisānī on Jewish Sects and Christianity: A Translation of 'Kitāb al-anwār', Book I.* With two Introductory Essays (Judentum und Umwelt, 10). 1984. Pp. 200. (Peter Lang, Bern, Frankfurt am Main and New York. Price: Sw.Fr. 47.00. ISBN 3 8204 8061 7)

Qirqisani's account of the various Jewish sects (including the Samaritans and Christians), written in the early tenth century, has long been recognised as an important historical source. The Arabic text was edited with an introduction and notes in Russian in 1894, and an English translation of this text was published by Leon Nemoy in 1930. Nemoy subsequently published a much improved text in his edition of the complete *Kitab al-anwar*, and he included some extracts in his *Karaite Anthology*. The present volume contains an English translation by Wilfred Lockwood, Librarian and Director of the Chester Beatty Library in Dublin, of Harkavy's introduction and Nemoy's text, together with a preface and introduction in Italian by Bruno Chiesa, Professor of Hebrew in Venice. It is thus something of a pot-pourri, and it must be said that it is not an easy book to handle. The reader has to contend not only with two languages (as well as a good deal of Arabic and Hebrew, and some French and German, in the notes), but with a text reproduced from typescript in a particularly cramped and inelegant format, and with three sets of endnotes, without the benefit of running heads to help him find his way around. All these faults could have been more or less easily avoided (at a price, no doubt), and the effort would have been worthwhile, because there is a wealth of valuable information here, which would interest not only specialists but a wider readership besides, including students of the text and interpretation of the Hebrew Bible. Inevitably in a work of this complexity there are some minor slips and omissions (it is surprising to find no mention of S. J. Isser, *The Dositheans*, reviewed in *B.L.* 1977, p. 104), but overall the authors are to be congratulated on a thorough and meticulous work of scholarship.

N. R. M. De Lange

Cohen, M. S.: *The Shi'ur Qomah: Texts and Recensions* (Texte und Studien zum Antiken Judentum, 9). 1985. Pp. x, 240. (Mohr, Tübingen. Price: DM. 88.00. ISBN 3 16 134907 X)

Shi'ur Qomah is a collection of mystical traditions, emanating from the circles of the *ba'alei ha-merkavah*, concerned with the names and dimensions of the body of God. 'The daily recitation of the text was intended by its author', claims Cohen, 'as a sort of mystic meditation that, by virtue of the mystery and sanctity of its detail, would enable the pious to ascend . . . to heaven, and to gaze on the godhead.' Following his earlier study of 1983, Cohen now offers the complete Hebrew text of the traditions. His theories about the interrelationship of the various recensions (especially his view that BL 10675 = Gaster 187 is the *Urtext* of Shi'ur Qomah) will be strongly contested, but whether or not he is right does not affect the value of his edition, because he has scrupulously given in full the texts of all the recensions. Only those who have worked on this material can fully appreciate the immense labour which has gone into Cohen's work. This is by far the richest edition of any part of Hekhalot literature ever produced, and it is a real service to scholarship. Cohen adds some notes to the texts, as well as translations (taken over from the 1983 study). Translating the Hekhalot treatises is a nightmare, and Cohen, on the whole, has done an accurate, workmanlike job. However, some of his renderings are very infelicitous, and fail dismally to convey the strange and powerful beauty of the original.

P. S. ALEXANDER

COLLINS, J. J.: *The Apocalyptic Imagination: An Introduction to the Jewish Matrix of Christianity*. 1984. Pp. viii, 280. (The Crossroad Publishing Company, New York. ISBN 0 8245 0623 5)

John Collins draws together in this volume the results of his earlier studies to provide an excellent introduction to the Jewish apocalyptic literature. In the first chapter he provides a good discussion of the problems of definition which follows the lines of his contributions to *Apocalypse: The Morphology of a Genre* (Semeia, 14: see *B.L.* 1981, p. 115). He offers *inter alia* helpful comments on the distinctions between the genre apocalypse, apocalyptic eschatology, and apocalypticism, but it still seems doubtful to the reviewer whether it really is helpful to speak of 'apocalypticism'. The following chapters deal with the individual apocalypses: the early Enoch literature, Daniel, the Similitudes of Enoch, apocalyptic literature from the period after A.D. 70 (4 Ezra, 2 Baruch, the Apocalypse of Abraham), and apocalyptic literature from the diaspora (2 Enoch, 3 Baruch, the Testament of Abraham). There are also chapters on related genres (the Sibylline Oracles, testaments); on Qumran as an 'apocalyptic community', even though, as Collins states, 'there is no clear example of an actual apocalypse that was composed at Qumran'; and a brief section on Jubilees on the basis that, although a borderline case, 'the *Rahmengattung* or generic framework of Jubilees is an apocalypse'. In an Epilogue Collins discusses the importance of Jewish apocalypticism in relation to early Christianity. The book includes a full bibliography and subject and author indexes.

Collins makes many helpful and perceptive comments about the apocalypses, particularly about the circles in which they were composed, the kind of language they use, and the purposes they were intended to serve. There are inevitably some statements which one would wish to question, perhaps particularly in the chapter on Qumran. But this book as a whole may be warmly recommended as an up-to-date and reliable account of the Jewish apocalyptic literature.

M. A. KNIBB

DEAN-OTTING, M.: *Heavenly Journeys: A Study of the Motif in Hellenistic Jewish Literature* (Judentum und Umwelt, 8). 1984. Pp. xvi, 323. (Peter Lang, Bern, Frankfurt am Main, and New York. Price: Sw. Fr. 68.00. ISBN 3 8204 7433 1)

Dean-Otting examines the motif of journeys to heaven through seven texts. A larger amount of attention is paid to 1 Enoch, 3 Baruch, and the Testaments of Levi and of Abraham as being extant in 'original Greek translations'. Secondary translations are treated more briefly: 4 Ezra, the Apocalypse of Abraham and 2 Ezra. Dean-Otting's work is most thorough with detailed bibliographies of ancient and modern literature, copious notes, and indexes of Near-Eastern and classical texts (including Greek magical papyri), the Bible, the pseudepigrapha and the rabbinic literature. Each text is studied individually, and a collective picture of the motif emerges which is seen to make important contributions to apocalyptic literature and thought, but a contribution distinctly different from that of other ancient literature. A brief survey covers similar texts from the ancient Near East, Philo and classical antiquity. Amid the detail significant discoveries are made: for example, esoteric doctrines and polemics hidden in 3 Baruch. A thorough and careful study.

J. G. Snaith

Díez Macho, A.: *Apócrifos del Antiguo Testamento*. Vol. 1: *Introducción General*. 1984. Pp. 414. (Ediciones Cristiandad, Madrid. Price: Ptas. 1,750. ISBN 84 7057 361 6)

The last work of Professor Díez Macho, posthumously published, provides the General Introduction for the series *Apócrifos del Antiguo Testamento* (see *B.L.* 1985, pp. 129–30). The first part of the work discusses the main problems of this kind of literature, such as apocalyptic genre, origin, date, sociological background, mythical language, etc. The second part analyzes one by one all the works included in the collection, and the third presents systematically some major theological topics: God, angels and demons, dualism and eschatology (both the second and the third part were revised by M. Pérez Fernández). In order to avoid duplication with the introductions to the other volumes, Díez Macho concentrated his attention on the theological aspects of each apocryphon, a feature that distinguishes this introduction from other similar works and makes it worthwhile reading even for specialists. There is a detailed general index, but no bibliography.

F. García Martínez

Dommershausen, W.: *1 Makkabäer. 2 Makkabäer* (Die Neue Echter Bibel). 1985. Pp. 188. (Echter Verlag, Würzburg. Price: DM. 34.00; sub. price: DM. 29.00. ISBN 3 429 00955 3)

The latest addition follows the usual format of this series: brief introduction, short bibliography, and then commentary printed below the *Einheitsübersetzung* on which it is based. A brief chronological table is appended, but there are no indexes. Most of the views expressed are well-established: 1 Maccabees is a translation from Hebrew, dating from around 100 B.C., and is a historical tale told for propaganda purposes; 2 Maccabees was composed in Greek, around 30 B.C., with a much more Hellenistic form. The commentary avoids direct reference to the work of other scholars, though it is clearly aware of recent discussions. Its particular strength may be the way in which parallels with, and allusions to, earlier Old Testament material are noted.

R. J. Coggins

Engel, H.: *Die Susanna-Erzählung: Einleitung, Übersetzung und Kommentar zum Septuaginta-Text und zur Theodotion-Bearbeitung* (Orbis Biblicus et Orientalis, 61). 1985. Pp. 205, with an 11–page appendix. (Universitätsverlag, Freiburg. Price: Sw.Fr. 54.00. ISBN 3 7278 0326 6. Vandenhoeck & Ruprecht, Göttingen. ISBN 3 525 53684 4)

This book examines two Greek versions of the book of Susannah: the Septuagint and Theodotion. A long introduction discusses text and canonical status in Judaism and Christianity together with the history of exegesis to modern times. The relation of Theodotion's translation to the LXX is then discussed together with LXX redactions. The LXX text is printed opposite a German translation and followed by a commentary of nearly fifty pages. The

Theodotion text is given similar treatment. The theological emphasis of the LXX is then outlined and is shown to be heightened in Theodotion. There follow a large, detailed bibliography and fully adequate indexes. That this volume is written to be a useful working tool is shown by the inclusion of the Greek text and the German translation of both versions in parallel pages detachable in a pocket at the back. Such a thoughtful addition makes it easy for students to use and is very welcome.

J. G. SNAITH

FIENSY, D. A.: *Prayers Alleged to be Jewish: An Examination of the Constitutiones Apostolorum* (Brown Judaic Studies, 65). 1985. Pp. xii, 249. (Scholars Press, Chico, California. Price: $29.95 (discount price: $21.95); ISBN 0 89130 795 8. Paperback price: $21.95 (discount price: $17.25); ISBN 0 89130 796 6)

Fiensy examines claims of Kohler that AC 7.33–38 is a version of the Seven Benedictions of the synagogue, and the more extensive claims of Bousset and Goodenough to find Jewish liturgical material in AC. He identifies (as they never did) the editorial method, and finds Kohler right and the others wrong. He shows that the prayers were probably borrowed by Christians in Syria from synagogue practice some time in the third Christian century, and then embodied in the Constitutions by an author who would not have borrowed them direct. Texts are fully set out and the relevant parts of AC translated and annotated. A very useful study, very well done.

S. G. HALL

FOSSUM, J. E.: *The Name of God and the Angel of the Lord: Samaritan and Jewish Concepts of Intermediation and the Origin of Gnosticism* (Wissenschaftliche Untersuchungen zum Neuen Testament, 36). 1985. Pp. xiv, 378. (Mohr, Tübingen. Price: DM. 128.00. ISBN 3 16 144789 1)

The main concern of this work, originally an Utrecht dissertation under G. Quispel, is indicated by the sub-title: to explore the vexed problem of Gnostic origins. Basically the thesis is that the role of the demiurge, often seen as a difficulty in the proposed Jewish background of Gnosticism, can be illustrated by Samaritan usage. To this end an outline of early Samaritan history and literary survivals is offered, with particular emphasis on Dositheanism. The main body of the book is then given over to discussing a great variety of texts, Jewish and Samaritan, Christian and Gnostic, relating to the name of God and the divine angel. A very full bibliography is provided, but the reference index is unfortunately limited to the Bible and Apocrypha. There is great learning here, which will make the book a valuable source of reference, but a more precise traditio-historical method in the use of so diverse a range of texts would have been welcome. At times unidiomatic English and rather frequent printing errors make the book less easy to use than it might have been.

R. J. COGGINS

FOX, B. D. (ed.): *Tradition, Transition and Transmission. Jubilee Volume in Honor of Dr. I. O. Lehman*. 1983. Pp. viii, 139. (Cincinnati. Available from the editor at Temple Emanuel, Woollahra, Sydney, Australia.)

This privately-printed and inexpensively-produced paperback contains ten brief essays in honour of a German-Jewish scholar closely associated with Reform Judaism who is best known for the important responsibilities he enjoyed as a curator of Hebraica at the Bodleian Library and later at the Hebrew Union College Library in Cincinnati. There are articles of Jewish communal interest by and about Reform rabbis, as well as contributions about Jewish philosophy and Christian versions of the Kabbala, and an interesting account by E. I. J. Rosenthal of how Leopold Zunz and Abraham Geiger enjoyed a warm friendship in spite of their differences about the traditional practices of Judaism. Of more direct interest to *Book List* readers will be B. S. J. Isserlin's note on archaeological evidence from the ancient Near East to match Plato's description of Atlantis and, perhaps, P. J. Haas's analysis of the mishnaic text *Ma'aser Sheni* 2: 1–4.

S. C. REIF

FUKS, L., and FUKS-MANSFELD, R. G.: *Hebrew Typography in the Northern Netherlands 1585–1815: Historical Evaluation and Descriptive Bibliography*. Part 1. 1984. Pp. viii, 232; 10 plates. (Brill, Leiden. Price: Fl. 70.00. ISBN 90 04 07056 7)

The authors are to be commended on producing an important new work of reference with excellent indexes. Their introduction traces briefly the history of Hebrew printing and bibliography and provides helpful facts about their general characteristics. In the body of the work full bibliographical details are given of 278 Hebrew books of considerable variety printed in Leiden, Franeker and Amsterdam, and the systematic catalogues thus produced are interspersed with interesting and readable information about the professional lives and social background of the various printers, culled from a number of sources, among them local Dutch archives. Particularly noteworthy are the co-operation of Jews and non-Jews in printing ventures, the significant role of Dutch Christian Hebraists in promoting the publication of Hebrew Bibles and grammars and translations of Jewish religious texts, and the attention given to such figures as Plantin, Radaeus, Broughton and Menasseh ben Israel. It is pity that a few minor errors in English and some less than satisfactory plates have escaped the sub-editorial eye.

S. C. REIF

GIANOTTO, C.: *Melchisedek e la sua tipologia: Tradizioni giudaiche, cristiane e gnostiche* (*sec. II a.C. — sec. III d.C*) (Associazione Biblica Italiana, Supplementi alla Rivista Biblica, 12). 1984. Pp. 311. (Paideia Editrice, Brescia. Price: Lire 40,000)

The slender data of the Old Testament about Melchizedek gave rise to exegetical developments of wide diversity in which polemic, especially between Christians and Jews, played a part. The interests of the author of this painstaking and judicious doctoral thesis centre on the use of Gen. 14 and Ps. 110 in Second Temple Judaism and Gnosticism, and these two chapters form nearly half the book. Gianotto thinks it likely that both the Hasmoneans and the Samaritans invoked the Melchizedek passages in support of their claims, respectively, to the priesthood and to the authenticity of the Gerizim sanctuary, while the silence of Jubilees about Melchizedek indicates its authors' hostility to both claims. Melchizedek's elevation to celestial status is studied both in 11QMelch and in 4Q'Amram^{b}; it arose, Gianotto thinks, from the abruptness of this figure's appearance in Gen. 14 (p. 84). It became, in turn, the starting-point for several identifications of Melchizedek in later Judaism, gnosticism and heterodox Christianity, Shem, Michael, the Son of God and the Holy Spirit being the most notable. The gnostic texts, which include Jeu and Pistis Sophia as well as N.H.C. IX, have here been closely studied, and the findings correlated with the relevant accounts of Christian heresiarchs so as to offer some tentative connections. Shorter chapters show how first- to third-century Christian writers, beginning with the author of the Epistle to the Hebrews (to which a chapter is devoted) used Melchizedek to controvert circumcision and the Law: neither Abraham nor his royal host was circumcised or law-observant. To this polemic the Jews probably replied in ways which can be traced in the rabbinic references to the Melchizedek texts. This whole rich essay in history of interpretation is introduced by a full report on the *status quaestionis* about Gen. 14 and Ps. 110 themselves. Only at a relatively late period, Gianotto believes (p. 31), could the diverse traditions in the former have been 'assembled and fused' into a single narrative, while the latter belongs to the period of the divided monarchy: it supports the institution of kingship by underlining its cultic functions in the face of the growing pretensions of the priests (pp. 40–41). (See also the review of the volume edited by Bori and Pesce, above p. 64.)

C. J. A. HICKLING

GOLDSTEIN, J. A.: *II Maccabees: A New Translation with Introduction and Commentary* (The Anchor Bible, 41A). 1983. Pp. xxiv, 595. (Doubleday & Company, Garden City, New York. Price: $18.00. ISBN 0 385 04864 5)

Like its companion volume on 1 Maccabees (1976; see *B.L.* 1978, p. 119), this is a personal interpretation and is not intended to provide a catalogue of other views. Goldstein does indeed engage with other scholars when he feels it necessary, and many of his discussions provide a model of comprehensive detail. Nevertheless, to become aware of important alternative views which should be considered, readers will not always find much help here.

Goldstein's thinking is still in process, as evidenced by many corrections to earlier opinions expressed even in his commentary on 1 Maccabees. He is certainly not to be criticized for continuing to develop his ideas, but it would have helped to bring the corrections to his first volume all together in one place. As it is, they are inconveniently scattered throughout the introduction, notes, and commentary. There is a good deal of repetition, which may actually be helpful for occasional consultation, despite the tedium for one who reads straight through the volume. However, the editing of this extra bulk (which would probably come to at least twenty-five per cent) would have made room for greater reference to other opinions and perhaps even for occasional further discussion on some points; in addition, Goldstein at times refers to future volumes on Daniel and other projected studies for the development of certain points. Few are likely to agree in detail with Goldstein's reconstruction, but he is never less than stimulating and at times brilliant. The volume is a worthy tribute to his mentor, E. J. Bickerman.

L. L. GRABBE

GREENSPAHN, F. E., HILGERT, E., MACK, B. L. (eds): *Nourished with Peace: Studies in Hellenistic Judaism in Memory of Samuel Sandmel* (Scholars Press Homage Series, 9). 1984. Pp. xvi, 237. (Scholars Press, Chico, California. Price: $23.95; discount price: $15.95. ISBN 0 89130 740 0)

In a combined effort, Hebrew Union College, Cincinnati, the Center for Judaic Studies, Denver, the Divinity School of Chicago and the Philo Institute have erected a worthy memorial to the much-loved and greatly-lamented Samuel Sandmel, a specialist in Hellenistic Judaism and the New Testament, and an ecumenist of international renown. The volume includes, in addition to moving personal testimonies and an exchange of letters between Sandmel and the late V. Nikiprowetzky, seven essays on Philo (by Y. Amir, G. Delling, R. D. Hecht, B. L. Mack, V. Nikiprowetzky, J. R. Royse, D. R. Schwartz and A. Terian); one paper on Josephus (by L. H. Feldman); another on Seleucid chronology (by B. Z. Wacholder); and a full bibliography of Samuel Sandmel.

G. Vermes

Groner, T.: *The Legal Methodology of Hai Gaon* (Brown Judaic Studies, 66). 1985. Pp. xviii, 209. (Scholars Press, Chico, California. Price: $24.95 (discount price: $19.95); ISBN 0 89130 748 6. Paperback price: $19.95 (discount price: $15.95); ISBN 0 89130 841 5)

Rav Hai Gaon (939–1038) is an important figure in the history of Jewish law, being one of the initiators of the genre of 'responsa literature' which was to become one of the most important sources of Jewish law. The present study provides an introduction to the life and literary activity of Hai Gaon, discusses the view he took of the authoritative sources of Jewish law (Tradition and Practice, and the Babylonian Talmud), and analyses the methodology employed in the responsa. From this it is clear that Hai Gaon's primary source of reference was the Babylonian Talmud. The Bible itself was viewed through the eyes of the Talmud.

B. S. Jackson

Gutmann, J.: *The Jewish Sanctuary* (Iconography of Religion, xxiii/1) 1983. Pp. xii, 34; 48 plates. (Brill, Leiden. Price: Fl. 60.00. ISBN 90 04 06893 7)

Of the twenty-four sections of this series covering worldwide religious traditions past and present, those dealing with Islam, Judaism and Christianity (xxii–xxiv), and with Mesopotamia and Egypt (xv–xvi), are the ones likely to be of most interest to Old Testament scholars; for other fascicles in the series see in this issue pp. 103, 106, 108; also *B.L.* 1978, pp. 105–06; 1982, p. 94 (xxiii/3, I. Shachar's *The Jewish Year*, 1975, was apparently missed). In this fascicle a professor of art history at Wayne State University provides a bibliography, an introduction, and individual descriptions of seventy-three items mainly from the Rubens and Jewish Museum collections in London and the Skirball Museum in Los Angeles, together with photographs, some of them apparently reproduced from other publications, not original negatives. The topics include the customs and ornamentation associated with the pentateuchal scrolls and where they are housed, scribal practices, prayer-shawls and phylacteries, synagogue furniture and symbols such as *menorah* and *magen david*. Although few items here pre-date the fifteenth century, Gutmann traces their earlier background and use through many centuries in east and west and assesses the degree of dependence on biblical precedents.

S. C. Reif

Hengel, M.: *Rabbinische Legende und frühpharisäische Geschichte: Schimeon B. Schetach und die achtzig Hexen von Askalon* (Abhandlungen der Heidelberger Akademie der Wissenschaften, Phil.-hist. Klasse, 1984/2). 1984. Pp. 62. (Carl Winter Universitätsverlag, Heidelberg. Price: DM 42.00. ISBN 3 533 03557 3)

Professor Hengel begins his analysis of the famous story of Simeon b. Shetach's execution of the eighty witches of Ashkelon with a critical analysis of the tradition in its various forms, setting these in their probable historical order of development. He then examines the primary motifs and personalities involved: the mode of execution (was it hanging or crucifixion?); Simeon himself and 'his times'; Ashkelon; and the eighty witches. Building on his celebrated discussion of crucifixion and hanging as death penalties in pre-70 Judaism, and on Neusner's form-critical analysis of the Simeon traditions, Hengel turns his attention to Ashkelon as the last remaining pagan city in Hasmonaean, Herodian and Roman Judaea, and to a discussion of women and witchcraft in this period. He concludes that the story of Simeon's execution of witches in Ashkelon is *in itself* unhistorical, but then goes on to enquire into the historical origins of the material.

He argues that the story presents us with a kind of code which, when deciphered, refers us to the time of Queen Alexandra Salome and the Pharisees' return to power. Their execution of their opponents is enciphered in the story about Simeon: Ashkelon stands for the 'pagan' city of Jerusalem under Sadducee control, and the 'witches' for the opponents of the Pharisees, denigrated as 'women' in a kind of defamatory manner attested elsewhere in classical antiquity. Hengel compares such rabbinic 'encoding' of historical events with the cryptic allusions to persons, places, and happenings recorded in the Qumran Scrolls and in other literature of that period. His final comments about method offer particularly illuminating insights into some of the implications of this stimulating monograph, and suggestions for further developments of the approach which he has adopted.

C. T. R. HAYWARD

HOLLANDER, H. W., and DE JONGE, M.: *The Testaments of the Twelve Patriarchs: A Commentary* (Studia in Veteris Testamenti Pseudepigrapha, 8). 1985. Pp. xxiv, 469. (Brill, Leiden, Price: Fl. 156.00. ISBN 90 04 07560 7)

This full-scale commentary on the Testaments of the Twelve Patriarchs — the only other approaching it in scale is the one by Charles — brings to a successful conclusion work undertaken by Professor de Jonge and his collaborators that stretches back over more than three decades. For those familiar with this work, which began with de Jonge's thesis (*B.L.* 1954, p. 88 (*Eleven Years*, p. 625); 1977, p. 105), and was continued by the *editio minima* (see *B.L.* 1973, pp. 59–60 (*Bible Bibliog.*, pp. 481–82) for the second edition), the volume entitled *Studies on the Testaments of the Twelve Patriarchs* (*B.L.* 1977, p. 105), the Critical Edition of the text (*B.L.* 1979, pp. 132–33), as well as by Hollander's study of Joseph in the Testaments (*B.L.* 1982, p. 107) — to mention only the most important publications, the present volume will contain few surprises. It represents a sustained attempt to interpret the Testaments as they are, and the authors are very sceptical indeed about the possibility of reaching any certain conclusions about previous stages in the formation of the present book. The approach is quite deliberately synchronic, not diachronic.

The Introduction of some eighty-five pages begins with a brief discussion of previous work and an indication of the stance of the authors; but there is no detailed *Forschungsbericht*, and indeed no Bibliography, and reference is made to other publications (of their own and of others) for information of this kind. It is in line with this approach that throughout the work the authors do not as a rule take issue with the views of other scholars, although they have clearly taken account of them. The authors deal in the Introduction very clearly and succinctly with the text, related Hebrew and Aramaic material, and the literary form and structure of the Testaments, and are able to do so because they have already covered these matters very thoroughly in previous publications. The sections of the Introduction dealing with the contents (ethics, beliefs about God and Beliar, expectations concerning the future) are particularly valuable; in them the authors provide a systematic treatment of all the relevant materials in the Testaments. The last two sections of the Introduction deal with the question of the way the Testaments functioned as a Christian document and the question of provenance. Significant parallels in attitudes towards Israel and the law are noted with Justin, Irenaeus and Tertullian. The conclusion reached is that 'the Testaments received (more or less) their present form some time during the second half of the second century in Christian circles. We have no means of telling where these circles are to be located.'

In the commentary proper each testament is provided with an introduction. The translation, which is divided into convenient sections, is based on the text in the Critical Edition, each section being followed by text-critical notes, an analysis of the structure, and detailed exegetical notes which include a mass of helpful references to relevant parallels in a wide range of Jewish, Christian and Classical writings. Translations of the Hebrew Testament of Naphtali, Midrash Wayissa'u and the Aramaic and Greek Levi fragments are given in three appendixes, the last the work of J. C. Greenfield and M. E. Stone. There are no indexes: for Greek words we are referred to the index of the Critical Edition, and for the rest to the detailed Table of Contents. This omission seems a pity.

The debate as to whether the Testaments are a Jewish document adopted to Christian use or a Christian composition will no doubt continue, but it seems somewhat sterile. The authors are surely right in their view that it is very difficult to speak with certainty about any supposed earlier stages in the composition of the Testaments. Whether this is accepted or not, there can be no question that they have produced a work of real scholarship which cannot be ignored by those who write about the Testaments in the future.

M. A. KNIBB

HÜBNER, H.: *Wörterbuch zur Sapientia Salomonis mit dem Text der Göttinger Septuaginta* (J. Ziegler). 1985. Pp. 40, 24*. (Vandenhoeck and Ruprecht, Göttingen. Price: DM. 18.00. ISBN 3 525 52181 0)

As the usual Greek-German dictionaries are inadequate for the Wisdom of Solomon and Liddell and Scott's Lexicon is so expensive, Hübner has produced this volume as a useful working tool for students. Ziegler's Greek text (*B.L.* 1963, p. 21 (*Decade*, p. 415)) is printed in full. Helpful comments are given on difficult Greek words and expressions wih occasional references to Semitic or Greek backgrounds; existing translations are sometimes compared with brief notes where necessary. Vocabulary not in Langenscheidt's dictionary is given together with vocabulary of dubious meaning, and the whole is arranged under chapter and verse, not alphabetically. Comments and translations are selective: verses with no difficult words are omitted, but all unusual words and expressions receive brief comment. More discussion of usages in classical Greek philosophy would have been useful, but this volume should succeed in making the study of the Wisdom of Solomon more widespread.

J. G. SNAITH

DE JONGE, M. (ed.): *Outside the Old Testament* (Cambridge Commentaries on Writings of the Jewish and Christian World 200 BC to AD 200, 4). 1985. Pp. xvi, 263. (Cambridge University Press. Price: £32.50; ISBN 0 521 24249 5. Paperback price: £11.95; ISBN 0 521 28554 2)

Extracts from twelve of the Pseudepigrapha with brief introductions and bibliography. Each of the contributors has already done a translation of the entire writing in question for another project. The extracts themselves are of sufficient length to allow the student to gain a reasonable impression of the works that are included; helpful notes are also provided for each extract. While one might disagree about the inclusion or exclusion of a particular work or extract, that would be to quibble. The book is a useful tool for its intended purpose, to introduce students to some of the major 'intertestamental' Jewish writings, and is to be heartily recommended. (For other volumes in this series see above, p. 111; also *B.L.* 1985, pp. 134, 149.)

L. L. GRABBE

JÓNSSON, J.: *Humour and Irony in the New Testament. Illuminated by Parallels in Talmud and Midrash* (Beihefte der Zeitschrift für Religions- und Geistesgeschichte, 28). 1985. Pp. 315. (Brill, Leiden. Price: Fl. 80.00. ISBN 90 04 07500 3)

This is a reprint of a book first published in 1965 (not noted in the *Book List*), which seeks to be a contribution to the study of the relationship between religion and humour. Although primarily focussing on the New Testament, introductory chapters examine the essence of humour and its place in religion and then explore from this perspective Graeco-Roman sources, the Old Testament and, at greater length, Talmud and Midrash. Parallels, particularly but not exclusively from Talmud and Midrash, are also used in the examination of the New Testament material. The author does not analyse the techniques of humour but is concerned to demonstrate the use of anecdotes which would have raised a smile, as well as of irony, for educational purposes, usually in exploring relationships between people and with God. He argues that this use of humour in the New Testament, although differently expressed in the Johannine literature, in Paul and in the Jesus tradition of the Synoptics, owes much to the influence of the use of such techniques by the Rabbis. Largely dependent on Anthologies for the rabbinic stories, the book frequently reads like a catalogue and is cumbersome, lacking that lightness of touch which would convey a living humour; nonetheless, it will provoke a more 'visual' reading of the material, presenting the participants to our imaginations as people as quick to smile at others or themselves as are we.

J. M. LIEU

LIGHTSTONE, J. N.: *The Commerce of the Sacred: Mediation of the Divine among Jews in the Graeco-Roman Diaspora* (Brown Judaic Studies, 59). 1984. Pp. xvi, 217. (Scholars Press, Chico, California. Price: $18.75; discount price: $12.50. ISBN 0 89130 664 1)

Lightstone's major premise is that there is a good deal of mileage to be got out of an anthropological approach to ancient Judaism. More specifically, he discerns a fundamental contrast between the world-view implicit in the structure of the temple cult and that of the Graeco-Roman diaspora (characterized as a 'decentralized "shamanistic" mediation of the sacred'). The student who is prepared to wrestle with turgid, excessively self-conscious prose and sloppy grammar, large-scale repetitions and carelessly typewritten text will find some stimulating perceptions which challenge many of the received views of Judaism in the Graeco-Roman world. Readers of this *Book List* may be interested not only in Lightstone's development of his comparison between biblical and post-biblical attitudes, but also in his investigation of the various roles played by the scriptures in diaspora Judaism, and notably the function of the sacred scrolls as effectively holy relics which transform the synagogue into a holy place. In his preface Lightstone states: 'I cannot claim to have contributed fresh evidence relevant to better understanding of

Hellenistic Judaism . . . This study, nevertheless, does in my view shed further light on the data in question, by strength of asking dfferent (*sic*) questions.' There is some substance in his claim, but his work would have been vastly improved by ruthless copy editing and careful proofreading.

N. R. M. de Lange

Luttikhuizen, G. P.: *The Revelation of Elchasai* (Texte und Studien zum Antiken Judentum, 8). 1985. Pp. xii, 252. (Mohr, Tübingen. Price: DM. 98.00. ISBN 3 16 144935 5)

In Hippolytus, Origen (quoted by Eusebius), Epiphanius, the Cologne Mani Codex and the *Fihrist* of al-Nadim reference is made to a religious teacher called Elchasai (Elxai, Alchasaios). Scholars have long puzzled over the question of just who this Elchasai was, and whether or not the various groups which appealed to his authority should be identified. Luttikhuizen's solution to the problem is as follows. During Trajan's Parthian war of 114–117 C.E. a Jew in northern Mesopotamia composed an Aramaic apocalypse proclaiming the imminence of the *eschaton*, and explaining what men must do if they were to escape condemnation on the day of judgement. This apocalypse was supposedly revealed by a gigantic angel who was called *hyl(') ksy(')* — 'Hidden Power'. It was this title which, in Greek corruption, gave rise to the name Elchasai. From Hippolytus and Origen we can infer that a Greek version of the Apocalypse of Elchasai was accepted as authoritative by a Judeo-Christian sect which proselytized among the churches of Rome and Palestine in the period 220–250 C.E. These are the 'Elkesaites' properly so called. Epiphanius's 'Elkeseans/Sampseans', and the baptists referred to in the Mani Codex, are two quite different groups, with different teachings: they did not know of the Apocalypse of Elchasai, though they may have had a vague tradition of Elchasai as the name of a respected teacher. There is bound to be speculation in handling material as abstruse and confused as this. Luttikhuizen, however, proceeds carefully, with a full display of the evidence. His learned monograph is a model of clarity and good judgement. He has succeeded in adding to the sum of our knowledge about late Jewish apocalyptic, and about Jewish literary activity outside the land of Israel in the early second century C.E.

P. S. Alexander

Maier, J.: *The Temple Scroll: An Introduction, Translation and Commentary* (JSOT Supplement Series, 34). 1985. Pp. xii, 147. (JSOT Press, Sheffield. Price: £18.50; ISBN 1 85075 003 3. Paperback price: £8.95; ISBN 1 85075 004 1)

This is an English translation of *Die Tempelrolle vom Toten Meer*, which was published in 1978 and reviewed in *B.L.* 1980, p. 120. It provides, like the German original, a concise introduction, including a detailed and very useful analysis of the contents of the Temple Scroll (pp. 1–19), a translation of the scroll (pp. 20–57), and explanatory notes (pp. 58–136). The translation has been revised, and the notes have been considerably expanded, to take account of the scholarly literature on this document that has appeared since the German edition. The notes include references to the English translation of Yadin's edition of the scroll (see below, pp. 138–39), and there is a bibliography, a new feature in comparison with the German original. This English version of Maier's work, which in effect amounts to a completely new edition, is not without flaws; but, despite this, it is good to have such a useful volume available in English.

M. A. Knibb

MILLER, S. S.: *Studies in the History and Traditions of Sepphoris* (Studies in Judaism in Late Antiquity, XXXVII). 1984. Pp. xii, 160. (Brill, Leiden. Price: Fl. 60.00. ISBN 90 04 06926 7)

In a revised version of his New York University Ph.D. thesis Professor Miller offers a careful, philologically based, analysis of rabbinic traditions relating to Ṣippori — Sepphoris. The main topics examined are the *castra*, both Jewish and Gentile, of the city, and its *'arkhē* or *'arkhē,* archives or (according to Schürer) government. There follows a section discussing individual priests like Joseph ben Elem (or, perhaps better, 'Illem) who temporarily replaced the High Priest, Matthias ben Theophilus in 4 B.C., and priestly groups, in particular the *mishmar* of Yeda'yah associated with Sepphoris in Amoraic times. Miller's useful literary prolegomena will have to be combined with A. Büchler's important pioneering researches published earlier in this century, as well as with Josephus's accounts and the findings of archaeology, in order to produce a full study of the history of one of the most important Galilean cities.

G. VERMES

NEHER, A.: *Kotoba no Hoshū*. Translated by T. Nishimura. 1985. Pp. 338. (Sōbun-sha, Tokyo. Price: ¥5,000)

This is a Japanese translation of *L'exil de la parole* (1970); see *B.L.* 1972, p. 73 (*Bible Bibliog.*, p. 417). In a postscript the translator discusses the significance of the book and the author's more recent works.

K. K. SACON

NEUSNER, J.: *A History of the Mishnaic Law of Appointed Times*. Part 5: *The Mishnaic System of appointed Times* (Studies in Judaism in Late Antiquity, XXXIV/5). 1983. Pp. xxvi, 254. (Brill, Leiden. Price: Fl. 108.00. ISBN 90 04 06929 1)

This volume concludes the Mishnah and Tosefta order *Mo'ed* and presents Professor Neusner's ideas concerning the system of appointed times (for the previous volumes see *B.L.* 1982, p. 112; 1984, pp. 131–32). His approach to mishnaic law differs from the traditional study of the development of Halakhah (from the Bible to the Talmud and beyond) in that he concentrates exclusively on the Mishnah as a historico-literary unit. That is to say, it is envisaged as possessing an autonomous meaning and a structure deliberately devised which need to be investigated for their own sake. The history of the mishnaic law is an internal history, limited to an analysis of the contribution only of the Tannaim, i.e. the pre-70 masters, the Yavnean teachers (70–135) and those from Usha (140–170), reaching the redactional stage under Judah ha-Nasi at around 200. Neusner's stance is logical and valid, but it does not exclude — indeed it postulates — further enquiries, both progressive and retrogressive, to enable the student fully to grasp what is peculiar to the Mishnah in historical perspective.

G. VERMES

NEUSNER, J.: *A History of the Mishnaic Law of Damages*. Part 3: *Baba Batra, Sanhedrin, Makkot. Translation and Explanation* (Studies in Judaism in Late Antiquity, XXXV/3). 1984. Pp. xxxii, 293. (Brill, Leiden. Price: Fl. 148.00. ISBN 90 04 07137 7)

Neusner's comprehensive study of the development of the Mishnaic law of *Neziqin* (cf. *B.L.* 1985, p. 135) continues with the translation and form-analytical explanation of the tractates Baba Batra, Sanhedrin and Makkot.

The evaluation of the 'system' will be presented in the final volume dealing with this *Seder*. The translation is based on the text published by H. Albeck and does not refer even to significant manuscript variants. There are occasional doubtful renderings such as 'There are many domains (*r*[e]*shuyyoth*) in heaven' and further, 'What business is it of ours to convict this man of a capital crime (*Mah laḥūv lanū b*[e]*damō shellazeh*)' (Sanh. 4:5). Perhaps a list of corrigenda will be appended to the final volume of *Damages*?

G. VERMES

NEUSNER, J.: *The Talmud of Babylonia: An American Translation*. I: *Tractate Berakhot* (Brown Judaic Studies, 78). 1984. Pp. viii, 435. (Scholars Press, Chico, California. Price $34.95 (discount price: $29.95); ISBN 0 89130 808 3. Paperback price: $29.95 (discount price: $17.95); ISBN 0 89130 809 1)

NEUSNER, J.: *The Talmud of Babylonia: An American Translation*. VI; *Tractate Sukkah* (Brown Judaic Studies, 74). 1984. Pp. viii, 285. (Scholars Press, Chico, California. Price $33.75 ($22.50); ISBN 0 89130 786 9. Paperback price: $22.50 ($15.95); ISBN 0 89130 788 5)

NEUSNER, J.: *The Talmud of Babylonia: An American Translation*. XXIIIA: *Tractate Sanhedrin, Chapters 1—3* (Brown Judaic Studies, 81). 1984. Pp. viii, 208. (Scholars Press, Chico, California. Price: $24.95 ($18.50); ISBN 0 89130 799 0. Paperback price: $18.50 ($12.95); ISBN 0 89130 800 8)

NEUSNER, J.: *The Talmud of Babylonia: An American Translation*. XXIIIB: *Tractate Sanhedrin, Chapters 4–8* (Brown Judaic Studies, 84). 1984. Pp. viii, 259. (Scholars Press, Chico, California. Price: $27.95 ($21.75); ISBN 0 89130 801 6. Paperback price: $21.75 ($14.95); ISBN 0 89130 802 4)

NEUSNER, J.: *The Talmud of Babylonia: An American Translation*. XXIIIC: *Tractate Sanhedrin, Chapters 9–11* (Brown Judaic Studies, 87). 1985. Pp. viii, 237. (Scholars Press, Chico, California. Price: $29.95 ($23.00); ISBN 0 89130 803 2. Paperback price: $23.00 ($17.25); ISBN 0 89130 804 0)

The commencement of the project to which these volumes belong was signified in *B.L.* 1985, p. 136. In the first volume the hope was expressed that the entire project would be completed by 1994, with Professor Neusner committing himself to the translation of five of the tractates. With these volumes his personal contribution is completed, before the first of the volumes emanating from his colleagues has appeared. Each of the volumes carries the same Preface (explaining the character of the project as a whole), together with an Introduction to the particular tractate translated in it. These Introductions provide translations of the principal biblical texts with which the tractate is concerned (for Sukkah and Sanhedrin), and outline the contents and arrangement of the tractate. There are indexes, mainly to names. For biblical passages the reader will need to revert to the indexes to the Soncino translation.

B. S. JACKSON

NEUSNER, J.: *Genesis Rabbah: The Judaic Commentary to the Book of Genesis. A New American Translation*. Vol. I: *Parashiyyot One through Thirty-Three on Genesis 1:1 to 8:14* (Brown Judaic Studies, 104). 1985. Pp. xvi, 360. (Scholars Press, Atlanta, Georgia. Price: $35.75 (discount price: $26.75); ISBN 0 89130 931 4. Paperback price: $26.75 (discount price: $21.75); ISBN 0 89130 932 2).

NEUSNER, J.: *Genesis Rabbah: The Judaic Commentary to the Book of Genesis. A New American Translation* Vol. II: *Parashiyyot Thirty-Four through Sixty- Seven on Genesis 8:15 to 28: 9* (Brown Judaic Studies, 105). 1985. Pp. xvi, 430. (Scholars Press, Atlanta, Georgia. Price: $34.95 ($29.95); ISBN 0 89130 933 0. Paperback price: $29.95 ($24.95); ISBN 0 89130 934 9).

NEUSNER, J.: *Genesis Rabbah: The Judaic Commentary to the Book of Genesis. A New American Translation.* Vol. III: *Parashiyyot Sixty-Eight through One Hundred on Genesis 28:10 to 50:26* (Brown Judaic Studies, 106). 1985. Pp. xvi, 398. (Scholars Press, Atlanta, Georgia. Price: $33.95 ($28.55); ISBN 0 89130 935 7. Paperback price: $28.55 ($23.55); ISBN 0 89130 936 5)

Professor Neusner here provides a new translation of *Bereshit Rabbah*, following the text and commentary of Theodor and Albeck, and acknowledging a generous debt to the translation by H. Freedman in the Soncino edition. He aims for 'a more colloquial and American English' than Freedman, while at the same time systematically dividing the text into its minimal sense-units, in a manner which will be familiar to the users of Professor Neusner's earlier works. Unlike his earlier practice, however, he has included in these translation volumes a succinct commentary on the discursive characteristics of the various passages, emphasising the themes stressed by the compilers of the documents, as seen from their selection of material and the manner of their organisation of it. In these volumes the author does not concern himself with the prior literary history of the components which make up the text, now taking a rather more sceptical view of the possibility of answering such questions than he has done in some earlier works. He also defends his lack of attention to conventional philological questions (p. xiv) in a manner which will not commend itself to all his readers: he is satisfied that we understand the basic sense of the text as well as we are likely to; further attention to philological questions is not likely to advance the kind of discursive analysis and interpretative questions with which he is interested. Such a position can, perhaps, be defended, but only if put in relative rather than absolute terms. The reading which Professor Neusner here proposes, and which he announces as the theme of major interpretative works to come, focuses upon the 'recurrent points of polemic' which emerge from what is said, and the manner in which it is presented. These are identified in terms of the new religio-political situation with which the compilers of the document, around 400 A.D., were faced: viz., the conversion of the Roman Empire to Christianity. This prompted renewed attention to the salvific history of Israel, as derived from a (non-fundamentalist) reading of Genesis. Neusner contrasts the concern of this text with that of the Mishnah: 'Genesis Rabbah presents a deeply religious view of Israel's historical and salvific life, in much the same way that the Mishnah provides a profoundly philosophical view of Israel's everyday and sanctified existence' (p. ix). We may thus expect in forthcoming works a new and stimulating contribution to the history of Israel's ideas. The manner of presentation of the present translation will, as the author anticipates, serve a useful didactic objective, in facilitating reference to the smallest discursive units, and pointing to issues deserving of classroom discussion.

B. S. JACKSON

NEUSNER, J.: *Our Sages, God, and Israel: An Anthology of the Talmud of the Land of Israel.* 1984. Pp. xxx, 181. (Rossel Books, Chappaqua, New York. Price: $19.95. ISBN 0 940646 18 8)

The sub-title of this volume indicates its character and its relationship to Professor Neusner's work in translating and interpreting the *Yerushalmi*. Here, he selects passages from the translation (ones whose meanings, he claims, are not problematic), arranging them in chapters on Death; Israel's Condition; God's Condition; God and Israel: The Common Condition; Our Sages: Humanity 'In our Image, After Our Likeness'; Our Sages: Humanity at Its Most Human; Our Sages in Society; Our Sages and Israel; Our Sages, God, and Torah; Our Sages, God, and Israel. Each passage is prefaced by a short paragraph introducing the issue to which it is addressed. Professor Neusner seeks in this way to make accessible to a wide audience (going beyond scholars and students) those messages of the *Yerushalmi* which he considers most apposite to present-day concerns. An Introduction summarises the literary history and the context of the document. The main theme is the role of the sage in the world-view presented by the *Yerushalmi*: 'The classic issues of Jewish existence undergo a complete revision and restatement in the encounter with the figure of the sage: the human being in God's image and likeness' (p. xxviii). In this collection the author largely avoids passages whose prime concern is the exegesis of the Mishnah. Nor is biblical exegesis a prominent theme. Nevertheless, the source index includes biblical passages, and the attitude of the sages to the Bible is a theme examined through the extracts in the chapter on Our Sages, God, and Torah.

B. S. JACKSON

NEUSNER, J.: *From Mishnah to Scripture: The Problem of the Unattributed Saying* (Brown Judaic Studies, 67). 1984. Pp. viii, 126. (Scholars Press, Chico, California. Price: $20.95 (discount price: $13.95); ISBN 0 89130 759 1. Paperback price: $13.95 (discount price: $11.95); ISBN 0 89130 749 4)

While much of the Mishnah records the opinions of named authorities, a proportion of its sayings are unattributed. What is the significance for the history of the Mishnah, of this anonymous material? Does it, perhaps, form the bedrock of the Mishnah and go back to its pre-history? Or is it a redactional layer imposed by the final framers of the Mishnah? This is the problem which Neusner considers in this well-argued study, based on his monumental *History of the Mishnaic Law of Purities*. He concludes: (1) Unattributed sayings make up only a small proportion of the Mishnah and Tosefta (around ten per cent). (2) Apart from *Zabim*, ideas presented in unattributed sayings cannot be differentiated from those in the named ones. (3) Only rarely do we find ideas or facts taken for granted in unattributed sayings that stand at the logical beginning of the principles and propositions of a given tractate. (4) As a group unattributed ideas do not form a bridge back to Scripture: they are not the missing link between the Written and the Oral Torah. For the companion work, *In Search of Talmudic Biography*, see below.

P. S. ALEXANDER

NEUSNER, J.: *In Search of Talmudic Biography: The Problem of the Attributed Saying* (Brown Judaic Studies, 70). 1984. Pp. viii, 139. (Scholars Press, Chico, California. Price: $19.95 (discount price; $14.95); ISBN 0 89130 752 4. Paperback price: $14.95 (discount price: $9.95); ISBN 0 89130 758 3)

This forms the matching half to Neusner's *From Mishnah to Scripture*, which deals with the problem of the unattributed saying (see above). Much of the material in the present volume has been quarried from Neusner's *Eliezer ben Hyrcanus: The Tradition and the Man*. Neusner intends to produce a series of digests of his weightier tomes, in order to make his ideas more readily accessible to students. This is a worthwhile project. The sheer size of his major works is daunting to the undergraduate. A little essay such as this offers an excellent introduction to his methods.

P. S. ALEXANDER

NEUSNER, J.: *The Peripatetic Saying: The Problem of the Thrice-Told Tale in Talmudic Literature* (Brown Judaic Studies, 89). 1985. Pp. viii, 199. (Scholars Press, Chico, California. Price: $18.95 (discount price: $15.95); ISBN 0 89130 830 X. Paperback price: $15.95 (discount price: $10.75); ISBN 0 89130 831 8)

The relationship between the various 'canonic' texts of early Rabbinic Judaism (Mishnah, Tosefta, Yerushalmi, Bavli, Sifra and so on) is a vexed question, which can only be solved by studying the material they hold in common — the peripatetic sayings (to use Neusner's shorthand). Neusner asks: 'What does it mean when a saying moves from one document in the canon to yet another in the same canon? And how are we to interpret shifts and changes in versions of a tale as it is told over and over again in its journeys from one piece of writing to the next?' In answering these questions he argues that we must avoid the common *ad hoc*, piecemeal approach exemplified by Halperin's *Merkabah and Rabbinic Literature*. In opposition to this 'incremental history' he expounds his own 'documentary-historical theory', in which due regard is given to the *general* tendencies of the various documents. This profound analysis of a major issue in the study of early Judaism will interest anyone who has ever seriously wrestled with a synoptic problem.

P. S. ALEXANDER

NEUSNER, J.: *Formative Judaism: Religious, Historical and Literary Studies*. Fourth Series: *Problems of Classification and Composition* (Brown Judaic Studies, 76). 1984. Pp. 214. (Scholars Press, Chico, California. Price: $24.95 (discount price: $16.95); ISBN 0 89130 782 6. Paperback price: $16.95 (discount price: $13.95); ISBN 0 89130 783 4)

The diverse essays collected in this volume fall into two broad categories: problems of classification and problems of composition. Under the former Neusner considers such topics as: Is Judaism a scriptural religion? Does midrash fall into the category of folklore? Is Philo rabbinic or is the Mishnah Hellenistic? Under the latter he addresses himself largely to the question of how the Bavli was put together, and offers detailed case-studies of Berakhot 2a–9b, 30b–33a, 34a–b, and Arakhin 2a–5b. Neusner, as always, is scintillating and provocative. There is much to be learned from a perusal of this book.

P. S. ALEXANDER

NEUSNER, J.: *The Pharisees: Rabbinic Perspectives* (Studies in Ancient Judaism, 1). 1985. Pp. x, 316. (Ktav, Hoboken, New Jersey. Price: $19.95. ISBN 0 88125 067 8)

When *The Rabbinic Traditions about the Pharisees before 70* first appeared in 1971 it was welcomed as 'epoch-making' because of its application of form-critical and redaction-critical methods to those traditions (*B.L.* 1973, p. 61 (Bible Bibliog., p. 483)). Since then no discussion of that material or of the Pharisees has been able to ignore Neusner's methodology or his conclusions. The present volume is intended to make these available for students in less than a third of the original length. To illustrate the texts the Introduction (ch. 1) and analyses of texts concerning the Chains of Pharisaic

Tradition (ch. 2) and Gamaliel (ch. 11) are reproduced from Vol. I (=pp. 1–7, 11–23, 341–76); and the Introduction to the Houses of Hillel and Shammai (ch. 14) with the analysis of Zeraim from the discussion of Mishnah-Tosefta (ch. 16i) from Vol. 2 (=pp. 1–5, 41–120). In presenting the conclusions, the introductory and concluding sections of the analyses of Units of Tradition and of Verifications (ch. 17, 18iii-v, 19i, ix–xi, 20i, vi-viii), together with the discussion of the History of Traditions (ch. 21), are taken from Vol. 3 (= pp. 1–4, 64–106, 140–185, 223–300). The pages have been reproduced as originally printed but have been renumbered; however, cross-references in the text have not been changed with the result that they can only be pursued by reference to the original work even where the relevant pages are included in the present volume. This could have been avoided if the original volume and page numbering as given above had been retained alongside the new. Perhaps most to be regretted is the absence of any introductory essay by the author or another scholar commenting on the significance of the original study and summarising the debate it provoked; similarly there is no bibliography to bring that discussion up to date. Such additions would have considerably enhanced the value of this book; nevertheless many 'students' will welcome access to such a classic study in so convenient a form.

J. M. Lieu

Newton, M.: *The Concept of Purity at Qumran and in the Letters of Paul* (Society for New Testament Studies, Monograph Series, 53). 1985. Pp. x, 171. (Cambridge University Press. Price: £19.50. ISBN 0 521 26583 5)

Newton appears to have adopted an important agenda in addressing the question of purity in pre-70 C.E. Judaism, and in citing the influence upon his work of Douglas and Neusner. But the premise that 'both the early Christians and those at Qumran claimed to represent the Temple' which he uses to justify his comparison of Paul and Qumran is only the first of a number of unexamined assumptions made about Qumran in the forty-three pages of treatment it receives. Newton may be right that for Paul 'getting in' to the church is a question of righteousness, while 'staying in' (note the terminology of E. P. Sanders) is a question of purity; one can read Paul in so many ways. But we learn nothing about Qumran; ignorance of the important differences between CD and 1QS on the question of the community, of the problem of Josephus's account of the Essenes and the Temple, and of the issue of the Temple Scroll itself (which Newton hardly uses at all) make this essay of no use as a comparison — as if Paul and Qumran were comparable in any case; they are quite different entities in most respects.

P. R. Davies

Novak, D.: *Halakhah in a Theological Dimension* (Brown Judaic Studies, 68). 1985. Pp. xii, 174. (Scholars Press, Chico, California. Price: $19.75 (discount price: $16.25); ISBN 0 89130 757 5. Paperback price: $16.25 (discount price: $10.45); ISBN 0 89130 829 6)

This is a collection of nine essays which continue and develop the halakhic and theological discussions initiated by the author in his book *Law and Theology in Judaism* (see *B.L.* 1976, p. 96). Most of the essays have been published elsewhere. These include: 'Can Halakhah be both Authoritative and Changing?'; 'The Conflict between Halakhah and Ethics: The Case of *Mamzerut*'; 'Annulment in lieu of Divorce in Jewish Law'; 'Divorce and Conversion: Is a Traditional-Liberal Modus Vivendi Possible?'; 'Women in the Rabbinate?'; 'Alcohol and Drug Abuse in the Perspective of Jewish Tradition'; and 'Jewish and Contemporary Bioethics'. Two essays appear in print for the first time, namely 'The Threat of Nuclear War: Jewish Perspectives'; and 'The Logic of the Covenant: An Essay in Systematic Jewish Theology'.

The vast range of the topics under discussion is bewildering; and it is disconcerting to find, for example, an essay on the threat of nuclear war cheek by jowl with a carefully argued plea for Traditional and Liberal Jews to arrive at a halakhic consensus on the rules of divorce and conversion. At times it is not easy to perceive what might give coherence to the collection of papers. The essays themselves are generally of high quality and clearly express the writer's deep learning and often brilliant originality. They are read with profit as individual discrete papers. But if there is an underlying unity, it may be discerned, perhaps, in Novak's insistence that the Aggadah must not be ignored in the discussion of halakhic problems. Here his final essay on the logic of the covenant is instructive in its attempt to show how the Aggadah and Halakhah interact with one another; and here, to some extent at least, he begins to come to grips with criticism of his earlier work, that it 'could cover just about anything in Judaism' (see p. ix).

C. T. R. Hayward

Penna, R.: *L'Ambiente Storico-Culturale delle Origini Cristiane. Una documentazione ragionata* (La Bibbia nella Storia, 7). 1984. Pp. 320; 1 map. (Edizioni Dehoniane, Bologna. Price: Lire 18,000)

An anthology of contemporary source-materials for Christian origins, each extract accompanied by brief comment on its content and significance. The texts in Part 1 illustrate the cultural environment, Jewish and Greco-Roman, and are subdivided into convenient if not entirely systematic categories like 'Qumran', 'Non-apocalyptic Palestinian Apocrypha', 'Aretalogy', or 'Emperor cult'. Part 2 illustrates the three general genres of New Testament literature (biography/historiography, epistolography and apocalyptic), and Part 3 comprises those texts directly attesting the early Christian movement (e.g. Pliny, Talmud) or historical characters named in the New Testament (e.g. Pilate's inscription at Caesarea Maritima, the *Testimonium Flavianum*). There is something of a counterpart in English in F. G. Downing's *Strangely Familiar*, which penetrates much further beneath the surface of the New Testament cultural environment; but this book offers a more mainstream selection of materials and thus a more helpful and, because of its scope, flexible teaching resource.

P. R. Davies

Porton, G. G.: *Understanding Rabbinic Midrash: Texts and Commentary* (Library of Judaic Learning, 5). 1985. Pp. xxiv, 232. (Ktav, Hoboken, New Jersey. Paperback price: $11.95. ISBN 0 88125 056 2)

This anthology of midrashic texts in English translation is primarily intended for those interested in early rabbinic interpretation of the Hebrew Bible but daunted by its language and method. The passages, from Sifra, Mekhilta, Sifre on Numbers and Deuteronomy, Genesis Rabbah and Leviticus Rabbah, are prefaced by brief details of the teachers encountered, the standard commentaries, the nature of the midrashic *genre* and the characteristics of each midrash selected, and each chapter of translation is followed by a chapter of 'comments' and one of 'conclusions'. These latter chapters constitute amplifications and summaries of the texts, with some suggested explanations of their exegesis, rather than novel and technical research for the specialist. Where historical background is noted, Porton takes matters no further than his teacher, Jacob Neusner, and while the translations adequately convey the sense of the original, there are enough questionable renderings to warrant a note of caution about their uncritical use. (A hardback edition (ISBN 0 88125 055 4) is also available.)

S. C. REIF

ROWLAND, C.: *Christian Origins: An Account of the Setting and Character of the most Important Messianic Sect of Judaism.* 1985. Pp. xx, 428. (SPCK, London. Price: £12.50. ISBN 0 281 04110 5)

To encompass the Jewish background, the ministry and teaching of Jesus, Paul and the emergence of Christianity as a religion, in some three hundred pages of text is no mean feat, and many a student seeking an introduction to the origins of Christianity will be grateful to Christopher Rowland for it. The author's view of Christianity reflected in the subtitle means that *Book List* readers will want to pursue the argument to the end of the book, although of most obvious interest will be the Introduction and the discussion of 'Jewish Life and Thought at the Beginning of the Christian Era' (pp. 1–108). Here they will find little that has not been described more fully and with more attention to scholarly debate elsewhere — for it is not Rowland's aim to introduce readers to that debate so much as to a unitary view of the material. He is at his most stimulating in discussion of apocalyptic and of the tension between utopianism and pragmatism, as well as in his use of Christian evidence to fill out the picture of a diversified Judaism; elsewhere he is disappointing — Torah receives surprisingly short shrift, while 'Jewish groups' only go beyond Josephus's account in the inclusion of Scribes and of Christianity, with little mention of the majority of the people. It is religious thought rather than life that predominates, despite the author's avowed interest in socio-economic approaches to the study of the period. The value of the section is not as an introduction to the Judaism of the period so much as providing a coherent and credible context for Christianity, but in so doing the reasons and stages by which Christianity became a separate religion remain rather more obscure.

J. M. LIEU

RUBINKIEWICZ, R.: *Die Eschatologie von Henoch 9–11 und das Neue Testament* (Österreichische Biblische Studien, 6). Translated by H. Ulrich. 1984. Pp. viii, 175. (Österreichisches Katholisches Bibelwerk, Klosterneuburg. Price: Sch. 188.00. ISBN 3 85396 069 3)

This is a German translation of a Polish *Habilationsschrift* which was accepted in 1981 by the Theological Faculty of the Catholic University of Lublin. Its purpose is to examine the extent to which the eschatology of 1 En. 9–11 is reflected in passages of the New Testament, and it is divided into three roughly-equal parts. In the first Rubinkiewicz deals with the text of 1 En. 9–11 and with introductory matters relating to this passage; he argues *inter alia* that these chapters, though building on chapters 6–8, represent an independent document which was written at the end of the fourth or the beginning of the third century B.C. in support of Ezra's reform. In the second section Rubinkiewicz discusses the eschatology of 1 En. 9–11 under the three headings, Evil and its Causes, the Day of Judgement, and the Reign of God; he also discusses the kind of response (purification of the land from foreign cults, abandonment of mixed marriages, etc.) implicitly demanded of those for whom these chapters of 1 Enoch were originally written. Rubinkiewicz bases much of his argument on an examination of the Old Testament background of the material and of particular expressions used in the text, and this section contains a good deal of detailed exegesis. Amongst various points made by Rubinkiewicz reference may be made to his view that the story of the sin of Shemihazah and his companions reflects a concern with the worship of foreign gods, and to his view that 1 En. 10:16 is a messianic text in which the messiah is envisaged as a new Abraham. In the third part Rubinkiewicz first discusses a number of specific New Testament passages which appear to quote from, or allude to, 1 En. 9–11 and then considers in more general terms the relationship between the eschatological perspective of 1 En. 9–11 and that of the New Testament. There is a bibliography, but no index.

Rubinkiewicz makes a number of interesting points, but not all will be convinced by his views, and it may be wondered whether at times in his detailed exegesis he attempts to build too much on too slender a foundation. There are a fair number of misprints of various kinds, and there are some weaknesses in the presentation of the textual material. M. A. KNIBB

SAYLER, G. B.: *Have the Promises Failed? A Literary Analysis of 2 Baruch* (Society of Biblical Literature, Dissertation Series, 72). 1984. Pp. viii, 171. (Scholars Press, Chico, California. Price: $15.75 (discount price: $10.50); ISBN 0 89130 651 X. Paperback price: $10.50 (discount price: $6.95); ISBN 0 89130 781 8)

The author of this dissertation, a pupil of G. W. E. Nickelsburg, argues that the key to the understanding of 2 Baruch is the recognition that it was composed in response to the events of A.D. 70 as a story — 'a story in which Baruch and then his community move from grief to consolation'. (She acknowledges that the catalyst for her approach was the article by E. Breech on 4 Ezra.) The main part of her dissertation consists of an analysis of the literary structure of 2 Baruch (chapter 2) and an examination of the primary issues identified by the literary analysis (chapter 3). In the former she argues that the story is organized in seven blocks of material (1–5; 6–20; 21–30; 31–43; 44–52; 53–76; 77 – the Epistle of Baruch (78–87) is in her view secondary), and she suggests that the analysis of the way in which the story has been carefully put together reveals the literary unity of 2 Baruch. In the latter she discusses the material relevant to the two issues that she believes to be primary in 2 Baruch: 'the vindication of God as just and powerful in the wake of the destruction; and the survival of the faithful Jewish community in the aftermath of the destruction.' These chapters are preceded by a brief introduction (including a history of research) and are followed by a discussion of the historical situation reflected in 2 Baruch in the attempt to see what can be said about the real world of the author (chapter 4), and by a comparison of 2 Baruch with a number of related documents — Pseudo-Philo, 4 Ezra, the Apocalypse of Abraham, the Paraleipomena of Jeremiah, and the Gospel of Matthew (chapter 5). *Inter alia* she favours a Palestinian provenance for 2 Baruch, but does not believe it possible to date the book precisely. She does not attempt to resolve the question of the literary relationship of 2 Baruch and 4 Ezra, but she does contrast what she perceives as the practical, pastoral thrust of the former with the much more speculative approach of the latter.

This dissertation represents a laudable attempt to examine 2 Baruch in its own right (and not as an inferior version of 4 Ezra), and it contains some useful observations. But it is not clear that the emphasis on treating 2 Baruch as a story adds significantly to our understanding of the book, and there are a number of statements and views that are open to question, including not least those concerning the literary structure of 2 Baruch. It is, for example, by no means certain that chapters 78–87 are secondary, but if they are not, Sayler's analysis of the sevenfold structure that seems to underline 2 Baruch is called into question. The dissertation contains some repetition and could have been shortened.

M. A. KNIBB

SCHIFFMAN, L. H.: *Who was a Jew? Rabbinic and Halakhic Perspectives on the Jewish-Christian Schism*. 1985. Pp. xii, 131. (Ktav, Hoboken, New Jersey. Price: $14.95; ISBN 0 88125 053 8. Paperback price: $8.95; ISBN 088125 054 6)

This slim book (some seventy pages of text and twenty-five of endnotes) is an expanded version of a contribution to the volume *Aspects of Judaism in the Greco-Roman Period*, edited by E. P. Sanders and others (see *B.L.* 1982, p. 116). The author has collected together the various tannaitic texts that deal with questions of Jewish identity, and studied them in the context of the early development of the Christian Church, viewed from a traditional perspective. He relies heavily on older authorities such as Travers Herford, and refrains for the most part from engaging with more recent scholarly reassessments of the historical evidence. Nor is he concerned with Christian arguments about the nature of the true Israel. His focus is firmly on legal definitions: Christians of Jewish birth were Jews while gentile converts to Christianity were not. Consequently the 'schism' was not a rift within the body of Israel, but the takeover by outsiders of a Jewish movement. 'It was the *halakhah* and its definition of Jewish identity which saved the Jewish people and its heritage from extinction as a result of the newly emerging Christian ideology.'

N. R. M. DE LANGE

SCHÜRER, E.: *Historia del pueblo judío en tiempos de Jesús 175 a.C. — 135 d.C.* Edición dirigida y revisada por G. VERMES. F. MILLAR/M. BLACK. Con la colaboración de P. VERMES. Tomo I: *Fuentes y Marco Histórico*. 1985. Pp. 792. Tomo II: *Instituciones Polīticas y Religiosas*. 1985. Pp. 798. (Ediciones Cristiandad, Madrid. Price: Ptas. 8,500. ISBN 84 7057 366 7; 84 7057 367 5)

This is a beautifully done Spanish translation of the 'new Schürer' (see *B.L.* 1974, p. 91; 1980, pp. 125–26). The translators (J. Cosgaya/A. Piñero, vol. 1; J. Valiente Malla, vol. 2) have corrected some of the misprints of the English edition and supplemented the bibliographies with the latest relevant works in Spanish.

F. GARCÍA MARTÍNEZ

SCHWARZ, G.: *"Und Jesus sprach": Untersuchungen zur aramäischen Urgestalt der Worte Jesu* (Beiträge zur Wissenschaft vom Alten und Neuen Testament, 118). 1985. Pp. x, 362. (Kohlhammer, Stuttgart. Price: DM. 68.00. ISBN 3 17 008826 2)

The first part of this book starts with the thesis that, after a century of work on the subject, it is certain that Jesus usually spoke Aramaic. Schwarz examines the Semitic words in the Gospels (taking a conservative view of the authenticity of the attribution to Jesus of the relevant sayings, though not always of the exact wording). His discussion is generally well informed and sensible. When he considers *ephphatha*, however, he fails to bring out one of the main points of the argument of Isaac Rabinowitz (whose name he spells wrongly) that the word is Hebrew; moreover, though Rabinowitz has not succeeded in proving that the word cannot be Aramaic, he has at least shown that it may be Hebrew. Schwarz then discusses some further passages where, he believes, there are Aramaisms, or retroversion into Aramaic reveals mistranslation in the Greek or explains variants. He concludes that this part of the book has confirmed his thesis about the language of Jesus. The second part develops the argument that much of the teaching of Jesus was poetic in form. The third seeks to get behind the Greek to the Aramaic original of a number of the sayings of Jesus and to obtain a better understanding of them. The three appendixes, respectively, refute the argument of S. T. Lachs for the Hebrew original of some passages in the New Testament, suggest an Aramaic original for Luke 2:14, and discuss the official language of the church in the first century A.D. with special reference to an Aramaic list of canonical Old Testament books. There are a bibliography, a list of possible Aramaic equivalents of many Greek words in the New Testament (Schwarz gives the sources of the Aramaic words cited — a help when one is dealing with different Aramaic dialects), and an index of biblical and other ancient references. Not all Schwarz's arguments in this book are convincing, but he has made a helpful contribution to the subject. This work underlines the need for a New Testament scholar to have a good knowledge of Aramaic.

J. A. EMERTON

Starý zákon: překlad s výkladem: Apokryfy (The Old Testament: translation with commentary. The Apocrypha). 1985. Pp. 480. (Kalich, Prague. Price: Kčs 64)

The Apocrypha-volume forms a complement to the commentary series noticed in *B.L.* 1985, p. 66, and in previous issues. It is the first new Czech translation of these non-canonical books to be undertaken by Protestant scholars since the sixteenth century, and it was produced in cooperation with representatives from other Churches. The Introduction includes a long discussion about the growth of the canon and its different forms, and about the use of the Apocrypha in different Churches. Then, in the first part of the book, follow all the Apocrypha accepted by the Neovulgata as 'deutero-canonical' books and in the second part the remaining scriptures regarded in the Bibles of Orthodox Churches as 'non-canonical' books. The Apocrypha were translated from the Greek text of Rahlfs, but for Ecclesiasticus and Psalm 151 use was also made of the Hebrew text; 4 Ezra was translated from the Latin text compared with the Old Slavonic version. The edition forms in its 'Roman Catholic' part a preparation for the Czech Bible translation intended for the Roman Catholic Church to be printed in 1986.

M. BIČ

UHLIG, S.: *Das äthiopische Henochbuch* (Jüdische Schriften aus hellenistisch-römisher Zeit, v/6). 1984. Pp. 461–780. (Gerd Mohn, Gütersloh. Price: DM. 198.00. ISBN 3 579 03956 3)

For previous fascicles in this series see most recently *B.L.* 1985, p. 127. This fascicle, appropriately dedicated to Ernst Hammerschmidt, Bertold Spuler and Edward Ullendorff, provides a translation of the Ethiopic text of Enoch together with detailed notes and an introduction. The translation is based primarily on Eth I, but takes proper account of the evidence of Eth II and of the Greek and Aramaic versions. The notes, apart from numerous references, are inevitably taken up to a considerable extent with textual matters, but exegetical issues are not ignored. The fairly short introduction deals well with the textual history (although one or two points seem doubtful or unclear), but is perhaps less satisfactory when discussing such topics as the circles in which Enoch was composed, Enoch as an apocalypse, etc. However, some of these matters are further discussed in the separate introductions which are provided for each of the five sections of the book (Uhlig makes the break between the fourth and the fifth section at the end of chapter 91). There is a useful bibliography, and the fascicle also contains name and reference indexes. This learned work forms a valuable addition to the series. The author's incidental comments on Enoch in its Ethiopian context form only one of many points of interest.

M. A. KNIBB

WERNER, E.: *The Sacred Bridge: The Interdependence of Liturgy and Music in Synagogue and Church during the first Millennium*. Volume 2. 1984. Pp. xviii, 271. (Ktav Publishing House, New York. Price: $29.50. ISBN 0 88125 052 X)

Werner supplements his 1959 volume with a collection of further ingenious and scholarly essays tracing parallels and links between Judaism and Christianity at all periods. He has important things to say on music in Hellenistic Palestine, Essene and early Christian musicology, psalmody and psalm-calendars, *Kedusha* and *Sanctus*, and more. Unfortunately the 'technical and personal difficulties' which delayed the book make it fail in one specified purpose, 'to bring the studies of the basic problem up to date.' Some items are unchanged from periodical publications to which no specific reference is given. On Melito the two critical editions and direct comment on this material (first published in *HUCA* 27, 1966) go unnoticed. 'Most recently' invariably refers to works between 1956 and 1964; indeed I find nothing after 1965 in the documentation except Werner's own work. Despite flaws and anachronistic compilation, it remains a useful and interesting book. It is also irenic; it would be more so if the author perceived that most Christians see the *Improperia* as divine reproach to themselves, not as an anti-Jewish tract.

S. G. HALL

VAN DER WOUDE, A. S. (ed.): *Bijbels Handboek*. Deel IIB: *Tussen Oude en Nieuwe Testament*. 1983. Pp. vi, 319 including 48 illustrations. (Kok, Kampen. Price: Fl. 55.00. ISBN 90 242 1361 4)

Volumes I and IIA dealing respectively with the world of the Bible and the Old Testament were reviewed in *B.L.* 1984, p. 27. Volume IIB covers the history and religion of Palestinian Judaism from Alexander the Great to 63 B.C. (A. S. van der Woude), the Hellenistic World including its philosophy, culture and religion (G. J. D. Aalders), intertestamental Jewish literature including the Apocrypha, Pseudepigrapha, Dead Sea Scrolls, Philo, Josephus and early rabbinic literature (J. T. Nelis), the use of the Old Testament as scripture up to and including the New Testament (J. L. Koole), and biblical exegesis in the first century A.D. including Qumran, rabbinical Judaism and the New Testament (M. J. Mulder). Perhaps as befits a reference work intended for general use, the treatment stays well within the mainstream of scholarly opinion, and not very much literature post-about 1978 is referred to — probably an indication of the original deadlines set to the authors. The Temple Scroll, for example, is only very briefly described. However, the volume continues the high standards of its predecessors and is handsomely produced.

J. W. ROGERSON

YADIN, Y.: *The Temple Scoll.* Vol. 1: *Introduction*. 1983. Pp. xxiv, 419. Vol. 2: *Text and Commentary*. 1983. Pp. xii, 486. Vol. 3: *Plates and Text*. 1977. Pp. vii (English), ix (Hebrew); 82 plates (65 with the text on the facing page). Vol. 3A: *Supplementary Plates*. 1977. Pp. iv (English), iv (Hebrew); 40* plates. (The Israel Exploration Society, The Institute of Archaeology of the Hebrew University of Jerusalem, and The Shrine of the Book, Jerusalem. Distributed by the Israel Exploration Society. Price: $240.00 (plus $30.00 postage))

This is the English edition of Yadin's *Megillat ha-Miqdash*, which was published at the end of 1977 (a brief reference to the Hebrew edition was made in *B.L.* 1980, p. 120). The delay in the preparation of the English edition enabled Yadin to take some account of the responses of scholars to the Hebrew edition, and so this work is more than a straight translation; but the differences between the two editions are not all that great. Volume 1 provides a brief account of the acquisition of the scroll, and a full discussion of its physical condition, orthography, language, etc.; but the bulk of this volume is taken up with a systematic presentation of Yadin's by now well-known views concerning the contents of the scroll. New in this volume is a section headed Addenda et Corrigenda (pp. 405–19), in which Yadin discusses, with reference to the individual chapters and sections of the volume, the views and comments of other scholars. The text, a translation and a detailed commentary are given in volume 2. Here Yadin has accepted into his text a number of readings suggested by other scholars and has given others as alternatives; an index of these corrected and alternative readings is provided on a loose sheet. This volume also includes at the end a reconstructed text and translation, a concordance, and a reference-index. Volume 3 (plates and transcription) and volume 3A (supplementary plates, including fragments of the text from other manuscripts) are the same as in the Hebrew edition and, indeed, bear the date 1977.

Yadin regarded the Temple Scroll as a sectarian document, and this view had important implications for his understanding of various aspects of this work. It does, however, seem open to question whether it really is a sectarian writing, and there is perhaps more to be said for the view that the scroll embodies older traditions which were taken over by the Qumran sect — a possibility which Yadin himself also considered.

The translation into English reads well, and it is excellent that such an important work has been made available in a form that will be more widely accessible to scholars.

M. A. KNIBB

YADIN, Y.: *The Temple Scroll: The Hidden Law of the Dead Sea Sect.* Edited by M. Pearlman. 1985. Pp. 261, including numerous illustrations and 24 colour plates. (Weidenfeld and Nicolson, London. Price: £14.95. ISBN 0 297 78411 0)

This book, which was completed by Professor Yadin shortly before his death in 1984, is essentially a popular presentation of the material in volume 1 of the work reviewed above. It provides a blow-by-blow account of the acquisition of the Temple Scroll (here there is much greater detail than in the edition); a description of the scroll; a discussion of its contents under the four headings: the Festivals, the Temple, Purity, and Statutes of the King; and a concluding discussion of the date and status of the scroll and of its wider significance for Qumran and New Testament studies. There are numerous illustrations, including twenty-four colour plates that are partly relevant to the Temple Scroll, and partly to Qumran studies in general. There is a short bibliography, to which more thought might perhaps have been given, and a subject-index. This book will no doubt serve the general reader well, but scholars who wish to be informed about Yadin's views on the Temple Scroll will want to use the work reviewed above.

M. A. KNIBB

10. PHILOLOGY AND GRAMMAR

CARREZ, M.: *Les Langues de la Bible: Du papyrus aux bibles imprimées* (Dossiers pour l'animation biblique). 1983. Pp. 111, including many illustrations. (Le Centurion, Paris. Price: Fr. 65.00. ISBN 2 227 35106 3)

Aimed roughly at the adult-education level, this paperback covers much ground fairly well. It begins from the Semitic words in the New Testament and gives an informative sketch of the history and features of each of the three biblical languages. There is a good introduction to New Testament text-criticism, in which the author is obviously at home. On the Old Testament side the coverage is adequate, though some details are misleading (there is no Ugaritic wisdom literature and the Gezer Calendar is not an example of a clay tablet). There are many excellent illustrations, though two are printed upside down, a common error with esoteric scripts! A little learning on the biblical languages may be a bit difficult to use, but it is unlikely to be dangerous and it might encourage people to further study.

J. F. HEALEY

FRONZAROLI, P. (ed.): *Studies on the Language of Ebla* (Quaderni di Semitistica, 13). 1984. Pp. viii, 281. (Istituto di Linguistica e di Lingue Orientali, Università di Firenze. Distributed by Herder Editrice e Libreria, Rome. Price: Lire 32,600)

The colloquium papers offered here are very varied in scope, material, and interest. Those discussing the general features and relationships of 'Eblaite' are premature: much more spade work is needed on details before such generalizations can be valid. As relevant to the linguistic background of Hebrew, the treatment of prepositions by H. Limet, the discovery of a preposition *min*(*u*) 'from' by J. Krecher, the presentation of the Semitic numerals by V. Brugnatelli, and the glossary of 'Eblaite' words so far established, by P. Fronzaroli, must be mentioned. The last paper, by O. Loretz, surveys the *ḫapiru* problem so far as it concerns the Hebrews, and deals with allegedly relevant material from Ebla.

W. G. LAMBERT

HOFTIJZER, J.: *The Function and Use of the Imperfect Forms with Nun Paragogicum in Classical Hebrew* (Studia Semitica Neerlandica, 21). 1985. Pp. viii, 144. (Van Gorcum, Assen. Price: Fl. 25.00)

The three forms of the Hebrew imperfect with a final *-n*, 2nd fem. sing., 3rd masc. plur. and 2nd masc. plur., are examined here. They are classified in a whole variety of ways by context, which can be grammatical, syntactical, prose or poetry, and by 'document' (JE, D, P, etc.), as well as by other categories. From this array of sub-types the author draws suitably sober conclusions, but throughout makes no comparison with other Semitic languages or even with later stages of Hebrew. An index of the passages discussed is provided.

W. G. E. WATSON

MITCHEL, L. A.: *A Student's Vocabulary for Biblical Hebrew and Aramaic*. 1984. Pp. xxiv, 88. (Academie Books, from Zondervan, Grand Rapids, Michigan. Price: $5.95. ISBN 0 310 45461 1)

This clearly printed work lists Hebrew and Aramaic words by frequency in a manner that has some advantage of simplicity, arrangement by root or theme being disregarded. Words, with meaning and transliterations, are listed alphabetically in compact groups according to frequency. Thus for Hebrew we have words occurring (1) over 500 times (2) 500–200 times (3) 199–100 times (4) 99–50 times (5) 49–10 times. For the 648 biblical Aramaic words the distinction becomes finer: (1) over 50 times (2) 50–20 times (3) 19–13 times (4) 12–10 times (5) 9–8 times (6) 7 times — and so on down to the inevitably large group of 236 words occurring once. In separate Hebrew and Aramaic indexes all the words are arranged alphabetically and a reference is given to locate them in their lists. While some no doubt will find the lists useful, others may reflect that these frequencies would not correspond to those in the texts likely to be studied, and that, beyond the words listed in any elementary course, vocabulary is best assimilated in context.

J. H. EATON

MURAOKA, T.: *Emphatic Words and Structures in Biblical Hebrew*. 1985. Pp. xviii, 206. (Magnes Press, Jerusalem; Brill, Leiden. Price: $28.00. ISBN 965 223 554 7)

By publishing his thesis, submitted in Jerusalem more than sixteen years ago, Muraoka has served his Hebraic colleagues well. The thesis was available as a mimeographed typescript and has been the best discussion of the subject. But the author was a student before Dahood completed his commentary on Psalms, before McKane on Proverbs, Andersen on the verbless clause, Aartun on particles, and other similar works, which take up the questions raised by Muraoka but do not quote his work. This carefully-produced book has brought the thesis up to date. It is hard to think that any serious biblical commentary in the next few years will be able to avoid making frequent reference to this book.

M. E. J. RICHARDSON

NAVEH, J., and SHAKED, S.: *Amulets and Magic Bowls: Aramaic Incantations of Late Antiquity*. 1985. Pp. 293; 40 plates. (Magnes Press, Jerusalem; Brill, Leiden. Price: $28.00. ISBN 965 223 531 8)

The excellent quality of this text-edition of fifteen amulets, fourteen incantation bowls, and eight magical texts from the Cairo Genizah is immediately apparent. The book contains good photographs of all texts, as well as autograph copies of the amulets, an informative introduction, complete glossaries, and philological notes which span the breadth of Aramaic magical texts. Furthermore, many readings of previously published texts have been corrected, with duplicate passages among published magic bowl texts identified; in some cases, a critical apparatus of variants between duplicate passages might have been justifiable.

The importance of the new finds published here lies in the textual parallels between amulets from Palestine and Babylonian magic bowls (Amulet 15 and Bowl 12a), which are particularly significant because magic bowl traditions are usually reflected in the Babylonian rather than the Jerusalem Talmud. Moreover, the dating of excavated Palestinian amulets in this corpus to the fifth–sixth centuries A.D. probably reflects a similar date for the Babylonian magic bowls, which are usually considered (on uncertain evidence) to be sixth–seventh centuries A.D.

Old Testament scholars will find the indexes useful in tracing the use of biblical verses in ancient magical texts.

M. J. GELLER

SAPORETTI, C.: *The Middle Assyrian Laws (Sign Index, Frequency Tabulations and Word Index)* (Cybernetica Mesopotamica: Graphemic Categorization, 2). 1984. Pp. vi, 118. (Undena Publications, Malibu, California. Price $12.00. ISBN 0 89003 120 7)

Computer aided analysis has produced a series of tables showing the ways Assyrian scribes used 194 different cuneiform signs to write a particular body of texts in the twelfth century B.C. When promised analyses of other contemporary documents are published, any peculiarities of one text-type will appear. If the project is extended to other areas and eras, it may allow a more accurate delineation of scribal relationships and point to the flow of cultural influences. Meanwhile, the present fascicle, dull as it may appear, is useful for Assyriologists, not least in its complete concordance of the vocabulary, and by charting every spelling it illustrates the amount of inconsistency the scribes accepted, a matter of some interest for study of the biblical text.

A. R. MILLARD

SEGERT, S.: *A Basic Grammar of the Ugaritic Language with Selected Texts and Glossary*. 1984. Pp. xxvi, 213. (University of California Press, Berkeley, California. Price: £37.95. ISBN 0 520 03999 8)

The first Ugaritic grammar that Segert published was acclaimed as concise, clear, and affordable. Unfortunately it was generally inaccessible to English readers, for it was a translation from an original German typescript into Russian, and the USSR stocks were quickly exhausted. The need for a new grammar in English has long been recognized; Gordon's indispensable vade mecum is regrettably cumbersome to use, and the Driver/Gibson editions of the texts are very weak on grammatical annotations. Segert's *Basic Grammar* is contained in Parts 2–7 of this book (rather less than one hundred pages). There is an unevenness in the morphological and syntactical sections which, in view of the nature of the material, would have been difficult to avoid. But the beginner is bound to ask 'How basic is basic Ugaritic grammar?' While professional Semitists enjoy working in the Ugaritic field to reconstruct the phonetic spectrum and deconstruct the etymological architecture, the first priority of the Ugaritic teacher is to show how Ugaritic as we have it distinguishes basic features like gender, number, tense, and mood. These facts are tucked away amidst a wealth of extra information which will be needed only at the secondary level of study. Furthermore, there is often a sad lack of illustrative quotations in the grammar. This could have been remedied in the Chrestomathy (Part 8, itself almost as long as Parts 2–7), where some texts are provided with model philological commentaries. However, these notes have only occasional cross-references to Parts 2–7. A grammar need not contain a chrestomathy, and if on this occasion the two tasks had been separated completely, we should have had a grammar certainly more concise, probably more clear, and theoretically more affordable.

M. E. J. RICHARDSON

THOMPSON, S.: *The Apocalypse and Semitic Syntax* (Society for New Testament Studies, Monograph Series, 52). 1985. Pp. x, 155. (Cambridge University Press. Price: £17.50. ISBN 0 521 26031 0)

It is generally accepted that the strange Greek of the Apocalypse is due to the influence of Semitic syntax, Hebrew rather than Aramaic. This monograph confirms this conclusion, emphasizing that the Hebrew is biblical Hebrew. The author pays special attention to the influence of the Hebrew verb; he finds that even the *waw* consecutive construction has left its mark on the syntax of the Apocalypse. Biblical Hebrew influence is also detected in the construction of noun clauses and subordinate clauses. It is suggested that 'the necessity of expressing sacred themes in a gentile tongue was rendered less distasteful so long as it preserved the tenses and other essential syntactical features of the sacred language'.

F. F. BRUCE

VLEEMING, S. P., and WESSELIUS, J. W.: *Studies in Papyrus Amherst 63: Essays on the Aramaic Texts in Aramaic/Demotic. Papyrus Amherst 63*, Vol. 1. 1985. Pp. 113, including 5 plates. (Juda Palache Instituut, Amsterdam. Price: Fl. 35.00. ISBN 90 71396 01 0)

In 1949 R. A. Bowman issued an initial study of this papyrus of twenty-three columns, aided by the demoticist C. F. Nims (JNES, 3). Since Bowman's death in 1979, Nims and R. C. Steiner have been studying the text in the USA (it is in the Pierpont Morgan Library), independently of the two Dutch scholars. In this monograph Vleeming and Wesselius offer several short studes, often differing sharply from the interpretations of the Americans. Among the essays are 'Papyrus Amherst 63 and the Bible' and 'The lamed-imperfect in Papyrus Amherst 63'. Most valuable is the preliminary edition of various sections of text. One is a long story of relations between king Ashurbanipal of Assyria and his brother, Shamash-shum-ukin, king of Babylon, given in translation only. (It is notable that other stories of the same sort were current in Egypt in demotic papyri of similar, Ptolemaic date.) Four compositions are hymns, three described as 'Israelite'. The first is thought from similarities of phrasing to be based upon Ps. 20:2–6, 8. However, all four hymns served polytheistic worshippers of YHW, Adonay, Baal and other deities, and one may wonder whether the comparable phrases in the first are sufficient to prove dependence, or not. Certain linguistic features are closer to Hebrew and Ugaritic than to Aramaic, indicating that the poems are translations. Clearly Papyrus Amherst 63 is an important document for biblical studies, linguistically, culturally, and for the history of Judaism. Who were the authors of the compositions, why was it written? These questions provoke speculation. However, there is much uncertainty yet about the interpretation, both of the script, for demotic is not as easy to read as Egyptian, and the ambiguities are multiplied in this adaptation to write Aramaic; and of the language that appears to result, Aramaic, with other elements. The problems are illustrated by the divine name which is thought to be read YHW, but could be read *'lhyn*! Further studies from competent Egyptologists and Semitists will be awaited eagerly, and, in due course, a full edition. Meanwhile, it is premature to build theories about the origins of Ps. 20 or other bibical hymns on the basis of this papyrus.

A. R. MILLARD

WEINBERG, W.: *The History of Hebrew Plene Spelling*. 1985. Pp. x, 190. (Hebrew Union College Press, Cincinnati. Distributed by Ktav, Hoboken, New Jersey. Price: $15.00. ISBN 0 87820 205 6)

The Academy of the Hebrew Language and the Department of Education and Culture of the State of Israel have been attempting for a long time to create an official standard orthography for Modern Hebrew. The task has proved an enormously complex one, and Professor Weinberg has devoted some years to the study of the problem. The bulk of the present volume was published in articles in HUCA, vols XLVI–L (1975–80). Although the author traces briefly the history of *plene* spelling back to Canaanite and Hebrew inscriptions dating back to early biblical times, and also surveys the scribal practices in biblical manuscripts, there is little of interest to the biblical scholar in this volume, to which an additional chapter on developments since 1977 has been added.

P. WERNBERG-MØLLER

ZORELL, F., and others: *Lexicon Hebraicum Veteris Testamenti*. 1984. Pp. 1*–16*, 913–1005. (Biblical Institute Press, Rome. Price: Lire 40,000; $28.50. ISBN 88 7653 557 8)

The ninth fascicle of this work, which completed the Hebrew part of the lexicon, was reviewed in *B.L.* 1955, p. 75 (*Eleven Years*, p. 708). The original plan to include an Aramaic section was abandoned, and the words *et Aramaicum* were deleted from the title, after the publication of a dictionary of Biblical Aramaic by E. Vogt in 1971 (*B.L.* 1972, p. 79; *Bible Bibliog.*, p. 423). This new fascicle brings the whole Hebrew lexicon to its conclusion. The prefatory pages to the whole volume contain a preface written in 1976 by L. Semkowski (1891–1977), who completed the lexicon after Zorell's death, a preface written in 1940 by Zorell himself (1863–1944), a note by P. Boccacio, who is the editor of this final fascicle, and lists of sigla and abbreviations. There follows a Latin–Hebrew index, with introductory comments by Boccacio, who stresses that the reader should always refer back from the index to the lexicon itself. Finally, there is a list of corrigenda to the lexicon.

J. A. EMERTON

Books Received too Late for Notice in 1986

The books in the following list will be reviewed in the *Book List* for 1987.

ANATI, E.: *L'Arte Rupestre del Negev e del Sinai*. 1979. (Jaca Book, Milan.)

ANATI, E.: *Har Karkom: Montagna Sacra nel Deserto dell'Esodo*. 1984. (Jaca Book, Milan. ISBN 88 16 40135 4)

BEALE, G. K.: *The Use of Daniel in Jewish Apocalyptic Literature and in the Revelation of St. John*. 1984. (University Press of America, Lanham, Maryland. ISBN 0 8191 4290 5 (hardback), 0 8191 4291 3 (paperback))

BEAUCAMP, E.: *Israël en prière: Des Psaumes au Notre Père*. 1985. (Éditions du Cerf, Paris. ISBN 2 204 02265 9, ISSN 0588 2257)

BEAUCHAMP, P.: *L'Uno e l'Altro Testamento: Saggio di Lettura*. (Translation of *L'Un et l'autre Testament: Essai de lecture*, 1976). 1985. (Paideia Editrice, Brescia.)

BOTTERWECK, G. J., RINGGREN, H., and FABRY, H.-J. (eds): *Theologisches Wörterbuch zum Alten Testament*. Band v. Lfg. 5–6 (cols 513–768). 1986. (Kohlhammer, Stuttgart. ISBN 3 17 009075 5)

BROWN, R. E.: *Biblical Exegesis and Church Doctrine*. 1985. (Paulist Press, Mahwah, New Jersey. ISBN 0 8091 0368 0 (hardback), 0 8091 2750 4 (paperback))

BRUEGGEMANN, W.: *The Message of the Psalms: A Theological Commentary* (Augsburg Old Testament Studies). 1984. (Augsburg Publishing House, Minneapolis. ISBN 0 8066 2120 6 (paperback))

BUBER, M.: *Le Fede dei Propheti* (Radici, 5). 1985. (Editrice Marietti, Casale Monferrato. ISBN 88 211 6765 8)

Bulletin of the Anglo–Israel Archaeological Society, 1984–85. 1985. (Anglo–Israel Archaeological Society, London.)

BUTLER,, J. T., CONRAD, E. W., and OLLENBURGER, B. C. (eds): *Understanding the Word: Essays in Honor of Bernhard W. Anderson* (JSOT Supplement Series, 37). 1985. (JSOT Press, Sheffield. ISBN 0 905774 88 4)

CADUFF, G. A.: *Antike Sintflutsagen* (Hypomnemata, Untersuchungen zur Antike und zu ihrem Nachleben, 82). 1986. (Vandenhoeck & Ruprecht, Göttingen. ISBN 3 525 25180 7)

CAGNI, L. (ed.): *Il Bilinguismo a Ebla: Atti del convegno internazionale (Napoli, 19–22 aprile 1982)* (Istituto Universitario Orientale Napoli, Dipartimento di Studi Asiatici, Series Minor, 22). 1984. (Distributed by Herder Editrice e Libreria, Rome.)

CASTEL, F.: *The History of Israel and Judah in Old Testament Times*. (Translation of *L'Histoire d'Israel et de Juda*, 1983). 1985. (Paulist Press, Mahwah, New Jersey. ISBN 0 8091 2701 6)

CLEMENTS, R. E.: *The Prayers of the Bible*. 1986. (SCM Press, London. ISBN 0 334 02268 1)

COGGINS, R. J., and RE'EMI, S. P.: *Israel among the Nations: A Commentary on the Books Nahum, Obadiah, Esther* (International Theological Commentary). 1986. (Handsel Press, Edinburgh. ISBN 0 905312 52 X. Eerdmans, Grand Rapids, Michigan. ISBN 0 8028 0048 3)

CORTESE, E.: *Da Mose a Esdra: I libri storici dell'Antico Israele*. 1985. (Edizioni Dehoniane, Bologna.)

Davidson, R.: *Jeremiah* (Volume 2) *and Lamentations* (The Daily Study Bible: Old Testament). 1986. (Saint Andrew Press, Edinburgh. ISBN 0 7152 0529 3. Westminster Press, Philadelphia.)

Donner, H.: *Geschichte des Volkes Israel und seiner Nachbarn in Grundzügen*. Teil 2: *Von der Königszeit bis zu Alexander dem Grossen* (Grundrisse zum Alten Testament. Das Alte Testament Deutsch: Ergänzungsreihe, 4/2). 1986. (Vandenhoeck & Ruprecht, Göttingen. ISBN 3 525 51666 5)

Doron, P.: *Interpretation of Difficult Passages in Rashi*. Part 1: *Genesis and Exodus* (in Hebrew). 1985. (Ktav, Hoboken, New Jersey. ISBN 0 88125 081 3)

Dumortier, J., and Liefooghe, A.: *Jean Chrysostome: Commentaire sur Isaïe* (Sources Chrétiennes, 304). 1983. (Éditions du Cerf, Paris. ISBN 2 204 02070 2. ISSN 0750 1978)

Finnestad, R. B.: *Image of the World and Symbol of the Creator* (Studies in Oriental Religions, 10). 1985. (Otto Harrassowitz, Wiesbaden. ISSN 0340 6792)

Gager, J. G.: *The Origins of Anti-Semitism: Attitudes toward Judaism in Pagan and Christian Antiquity*. 1983. (Oxford University Press, New York. ISBN 0 19 503316 7)

Goulder, M. D.: *The Song of Fourteen Songs* (JSOT Supplement Series, 36). 1986. (JSOT Press, Sheffield. ISBN 0 905774 86 8 (hardback), 0 905774 87 6 (paperback))

Greenlee, J. H.: *Scribes, Scrolls, and Scripture: A Student's Guide to New Testament Textual Criticism*. 1985. (Eerdmans, Grand Rapids, Michigan. ISBN 0 8028 0082 3. Distributed by the Paternoster Press, Exeter.)

Guinot, J.-N.: *Théodoret de Cyr: Commentaire sur Isaïe*. Tome III (Sections 14–20) (Sources Chrétiennes, 315). 1984. (Éditions du Cerf, Paris. ISBN 2 204 02262 4. ISSN 0750 1978)

Heider, G. C.: *The Cult of Molek: A Reassessment* (JSOT Supplement Series, 43). 1986. (JSOT Press, Sheffield. ISBN 1 85075 018 1 (hardback), 1 85075 019 X (paperback))

Jacq, C.: *Egyptian Magic*. 1985. (Aris & Phillips, Warminster. ISBN 0 85668 299 3. Bolchazy Carducci Publishers, Chicago. ISBN 0 86516 118 6)

Jervell, J., and Kapelrud, A. S. (eds.): *Studia Theologica: Scandinavian Journal of Theology*. Vol. 39, No. 2. 1985. (Universitetsforlaget, Oslo. ISSN 0039 338X)

Lancellotti, A.: *I Salmi*. 1984. (Edizioni Paoline, Rome. ISBN 88 215 0687 8)

Lang, B.: *Wisdom and the Book of Proverbs: An Israelite Goddess Redefined*. 1986. (Pilgrim Press, New York. ISBN 0 8298 0568 0)

Langevin, P.-É.: *Bibliographie Biblique (1930–1983)*. 1985. (Les Presses de l'Université Laval, Québec. ISBN 2 7637 7060 6)

Lategan, B. C., and Vorster, W. S.: *Text and Reality: Aspects of Reference in Biblical Texts* (Semeia Studies). 1985. (Fortress Press, Philadelphia. ISBN 0 8006 1514 X. Scholars Press, Atlanta, Georgia. ISBN 0 89130 823 7)

McKane, W.: *Jeremiah*. Vol. 1: *Introduction and Chapters 1–25* (International Critical Commentary). 1986. (T. & T. Clark, Edinburgh. ISBN 0 567 05042 4)

Maier, J., and Schäfer, P.: *Piccola Enciclopedia dell'Ebraismo*. (Translation of *Kleines Lexikon des Judentums*, 1981). 1985. (Casa Editrice Marietti, Casale Monferrato. ISBN 88 211 8329 7)

Marks, J. H.: *Visions of one World: Legacy of Alexander*. 1985. (Four Quarters Publishing Co., Guilford, Connecticut. ISBN 0 931500 10 9 (hardback), 0 931500 09 5 (paperback))

Martin, G. T.: *Scarabs, Cylinders and Other Ancient Egyptian Seals: A Checklist of Publications*. 1985. (Aris & Phillips, Warminster. ISBN 0 85668 317 5)

Mazar, A.: *Excavations at Tell Qasile*. Part 2 (Qedem, Monographs of the Institute of Archaeology, The Hebrew University, Jerusalem, 20). 1985. (Israel Exploration Society, Jerusalem. ISSN 0333 5844)

Moraldi, L.: *L'Aldila dell'Uomo*. 1985. (Arnoldo Mondadori Editore, Milan.

Mottu, H.: *Les 'Confessions' de Jérémie: Une protestation contre la souffrance* (Le Monde de la Bible). 1985. (Labor et Fides, Geneva. ISBN 2 8309 0061 8)

Müller, G. (ed.): *Theologische Realenzyklopädie* (TRE). Band xiv (*Gottesdienst–Heimat*). 1985. (De Gruyter, Berlin. ISBN 3 11 008583 6)

Nadav, M., and Weiser, R.: *Selected Manuscripts and Prints: An Exhibition from the Treasures of the Jewish National and University Library*. 1985. (HaMakor Press, Jerusalem.)

Neusner, J.: *A History of the Mishnaic Law of Damages*. Part 4: *Shebuot, Eduyot, Abodah Zarah, Abot, Horayot. Translation and Explanation* (Studies in Judaism in Late Antiquity, xxxv/4). 1985. (Brill, Leiden. ISBN 90 04 07269 1)

Neusner, J.: *Genesis and Judaism: The Perspective of Genesis Rabbah: An Analytical Anthology* (Brown Judaic Studies, 108). 1985. (Scholars Press, Atlanta, Georgia. ISBN 0 89130 940 3 (hardback), 0 89130 941 1 (paperback))

Patrick, D.: *Old Testament Law*. 1986. (SCM Press, London. ISBN 0 334 02228 2)

Petuchowski, J. J.: *Come I Nostri Maestri Spiegano la Scrittura*. (Translation of *Wie unsere Meister die Schrift erklären*, 1982). 1984. (Editrice Morcelliana, Brescia.)

Von Rad, G.: *Scritti sul Vecchio Testamento*. (Translation of essays from *Gesammelte Studien zum Alten Testament*, 1958 and 1973). 1984. (Jaca Book, Milan. ISBN 88 16 35074 1)

Ravasi, G.: *Cantico dei Cantici*. 1985. (Edizioni Paoline, Milan. ISBN 88 215 0951 6)

Richards, L. O.: *Expository Dictionary of Bible Words*. 1985. (Zondervan Publishing House, Grand Rapids, Michigan. ISBN 0 310 39000 1)

Rouillard, H.: *La Péricope de Balaam (Nombres 22–24): La Prose et les 'Oracles'* (Études Bibliques, n.s., 4). 1985. (J. Gabalda, Paris. ISBN 2 85021 015 3, ISSN 0760 3541)

Russell, D. S.: *From Early Judaism to Early Church*. 1986. (SCM Press, London. ISBN 0 334 00496 9)

DI SANTE, C.: *La Preghiera di Israele: Alle Origini della liturgia cristiana*. 1985. (Casa Editrice Marietti, Casale Monferrato. ISBN 88 211 8334 3)

SAVOCA, G.: *I Profeti di Israele: Voce del Dio Vivente* (Radici, 6). 1985. (Edizioni Dehoniane, Bologna.)

SAWYER, J. F. A.: *Isaiah*. Volume 2 (The Daily Study Bible: Old Testament). 1986. (Saint Andrew Press, Edinburgh. ISBN 0 7152 0528 5. Westminster Press, Philadelphia.)

SCHIMANOWSKI, G.: *Weisheit und Messias: die jüdische Voraussetzungen der urchristlichen Präexistenzchristologie* (Wissenschaftliche Untersuchungen zum Neuen Testament, 2. Reihe, 17). 1985. (Mohr, Tübingen. ISBN 3 16 144997 5, ISSN 0340 9570)

SCHNABEL, E. J.: *Law and Wisdom from Ben Sira to Paul: A Tradition-Historical Enquiry into the Relation of Law, Wisdom and Ethics* (Wissenschaftliche Untersuchungen zum Neuen Testament, 2. Reihe, 16). 1985. (Mohr, Tübingen. ISBN 3 16 144896 0, ISSN 0340 9570)

SEEBASS, H.: *Il Dio di tutta la Bibbia: Teologia biblica per l'orientamento alle fede* (Studi Biblici, 72). (Translation of *Der Gott der ganzen Bibel*, 1982). 1985. (Paideia Editrice, Brescia.)

VAN SELMS, A.: *Job: A Practical Commentary* (Text and Interpretation). 1985. (Eerdmans, Grand Rapids, Michigan. ISBN 0 8028 0101 3)

SODERLUND, S.: *The Greek Text of Jeremiah: A Revised Hypothesis* (JSOT Supplement Series, 47). 1985. (JSOT Press, Sheffield. ISBN 1 85075 028 9 (hardback), 1 85075 029 7 (paperback))

STOW, K. R.: *'The 1007 Anonymous' and Papal Sovereignty: Jewish Perceptions of the Papacy and Papal Policy in the High Middle Ages* (Hebrew Union College Annual, Supplements, 4, 1984). 1986. (Ktav, Hoboken, New Jersey. ISBN 0 87820 603 5)

TERRIEN, S.: *Till the Heart Sings: A Biblical Theology of Manhood and Womanhood*. 1985. (Fortress Press, Philadelphia. ISBN 0 8006 0752 X)

THOMPSON, H. O. (ed.): *The Answers Lie Below: Essays in Honor of Lawrence Edward Toombs*. 1984. (University Press of America, Lanham, Maryland. ISBN 0 8191 3745 6 (hardback), 0 8191 3746 4 (paperback))

TIGAY, A. H. (ed.): *Empirical Models for Biblical Criticism*. 1985. (University of Pennsylvania Press, Philadelphia. ISBN 0 8122 7976 X)

TÖKEI, F. (ed.): *Acta Orientalia Academiae Scientiarum Hungaricae*, XXXIX. Fasc. 1. 1985. (Akadémiai Kiadó, Budapest. ISSN 0001 6446)

VAN DER TOORN, K.: *Sin and Sanction in Israel and Mesopotamia: A Comparative Study* (Studia Semitica Neerlandica, 22). 1985. (Van Gorcum, Assen. ISBN 90 232 2166 4)

TSUKIMOTO, A.: *Untersuchungen zur Totenpflege* (kipsum) *im alten Mesopotamien* (Alter Orient and Altes Testament, 216). 1985. (Neukirchener Verlag, Neukirchen-Vluyn. ISBN 3 7887 1200 7. Butzon und Bercker, Kevelaer. ISBN 3 7666 9394 8)

Übersetzung des Talmud Yerushalmi, herausgegeben von M. Hengel, H. P. Rüger, P. Schäfer. Band I/6: *Terumot-Priesterhebe*, übersetzt von G. A. Wewers. 1985. (Mohr, Tübingen. ISBN 3 16 144987 8)

ULLENDORFF, E.: *A Tigrinya Chrestomathy* (Äthiopistische Forschungen, 19). 1985. (Franz Steiner Verlag, Stuttgart. ISBN 3 515 04314 4)

Vetus Latina. Die Rest der altlateinischen Bibel, nach Petrus Sabatier neu gesammelt und herausgegeben von der Erzabtei Beuron. 11/1: *Sapientia Salomonics*. Heraus-gegeben von Walter Thiele. 8.Lieferung: Sap.18, 18 bis Schluss; Nachträge, Register. 1985. (Herder, Freiburg im Breisgau. ISBN 3 451 00487 9)

WEISS, J.: *Studies in Eastern European Jewish Mysticism*. Edited by D. Goldstein. 1985. (Oxford University Press/Littman Library, Oxford. ISBN 0 19 710034 1)

WISEMAN, D. J.: *Nebuchadrezzar and Babylon* (The Schweich Lectures, 1983). 1985. (Oxford University Press for the British Academy, London. ISBN 0 19 726040 3)

Index of Authors

(N.B. — Names occurring more than once in the same review or on the same page are listed on their first occurrence only.)

The Society for Old Testament Study is a British Society for Old Testament scholars. Candidates for membership, which is not confined to British subjects, must be nominated by two members of the Society. Residents of the British Isles are normally admitted to ordinary membership and non-residents to associate membership. All correspondence concerning domestic affairs of the Society should be sent to:

Dr A. H. W. Curtis
Faculty of Theology
University of Manchester
Manchester M13 9PL
England

ISBN 0 905495 05 5

THE SOCIETY FOR OLD TESTAMENT STUDY

BOOK LIST

1987

Printed for the Society

The Society for Old Testament Study

BOOK LIST
1987

Printed for the Society

ISBN 0 905495 06 3

PRINTED BY W. S. MANEY AND SON LTD HUDSON ROAD LEEDS LS9 7DL

Contents

One copy of the *Book List* is supplied free to all members of the Society.

Copies of the *Book List* for 1987 may also be obtained from M. E. J. Richardson, Esq., Department of Near Eastern Studies, University of Manchester, Manchester M13 9PL, England. The price of these is £6.00 or $12.00 post free for a single copy. Payment should be made by cheque in sterling or U.S. dollars payable to the Society for Old Testament Study, or direct to Post Office Giro Account No. 50 450 4002.

Copies of the *Book List* for 1966, 1968–1977 inclusive, and 1979–1986 are also available from Mr M. E. J. Richardson. Orders for back issues or multiple copies should not be accompanied by payment; an invoice will be sent.

Review copies of books for the *Book List* should be sent to the Editor:

Dr A. Graeme Auld
New College, Mound Place
Edinburgh EH1 2LX,
Scotland

PREFACE

The daunting task of learning the annual processes by which this volume comes to be has been considerably eased by the ready support of all my predecessors, our printers, the company of reviewers, departmental and faculty colleagues, and friendly contacts in many publishers.

Particular thanks are due to Michael Knibb who has been a patient and careful instructor. The Society is delighted that London University has recognized his academic contribution with a personal chair. Then Mr A. S. Maney, young Mr Maney to Professor G. W. Anderson, whose detailed knowledge of more than four decades of the *Book List* is as close as any, has with his colleagues given careful support to the new editor. Closer to home, Dr J. C. L. Gibson, my head of department, has given ready encouragement. He also should be congratulated for completing on schedule the editorship of the *Daily Study Bible: Old Testament*; while not designed for the academic market, the series has attracted not a little critical praise. Miss M. Rankin has provided much secretarial support. And Dr A. P. Hayman has joined the ranks not just of reviewers, but of those marvellous colleagues prepared to do extra late in the year.

It has been a great pleasure that the members of Professor Knibb's international support-group have willingly agreed to continue their invaluable supply of both intelligence and reviews. I have enjoyed friendly contact with Professor B. Albrektson, Professor M. Bič, Professor H. Cazelles, Dr F. García Martínez, Dr K. Jeppesen, Professor G. L. Prato, Dr K. K. Sacon, and Professor A. S. van der Woude. Last, but far from least, I owe a considerable debt to several colleagues at home without whose recommendations and supply of books which had not yet come to my hand this present volume would have been much slimmer. These include Dr R. P. Carroll, Dr R. J. Coggins, Dr P. R. Davies, Mr A. R. Millard, Dr S. C. Reif, Dr W. G. E. Watson, and Professor R. N. Whybray.

A third Newsletter has been issued in connection with the Comprehensive Aramaic Lexicon; it too is available from The Editors, CAL, Dept of Near Eastern Studies, The Johns Hopkins University, Baltimore, MD 21218, USA.

The end of the heading of the review of the Lehman Jubilee volume (*B.L.* 1986, p. 119) has been found misleading by some readers. This book is available in several bookshops.

The following abbreviations and symbols are employed as in earlier issues:

B.L.	= *Book List*
Eleven Years	= *Eleven Years of Bible Bibliography* (1957)
Decade	= *A Decade of Bible Bibliography* (1967)
Bible Bibliog.	= *Bible Bibliography 1967–1973: Old Testament* (1974)

On behalf of the Society I have pleasure in thanking the British Academy for making a grant towards the publication costs of this issue of the *Book List*.

NEW COLLEGE EDINBURGH A. GRAEME AULD

1. GENERAL

BÄTZ, K., and MACK, R.: *Sachtexte zur Bibel: Hilfen zum Verstehen und Erzählen*. 1985. Pp. 120. (Verlag Ernst Kaufmann, Lahr. Price: DM 22.00. ISBN 3 7806 0487 6. Kösel Verlag, München. ISBN 3 466 36130 3)

BÄTZ, K., and MACK, R., with illustrations by H. Witzig and F. Testa: *Sachbilder zur Bibel.* 2nd edition, 1984. Pp. 31 (illustrative material), 24 (commentary). (Verlag Ernst Kaufmann, Lahr. Price: DM 22.00. ISBN 3 7806 0463 9. Kösel Verlag, München. ISBN 3 466 36129 X)

These two attractively produced volumes form a matching pair, aimed at providing teachers of religion and their pupils with aids to greater understanding of the biblical world. The volume of texts surveys archaeological and historical problems, and then deals with daily life, legal matters, and cultic and religious texts. The last sections deal with the Judaism of the 'inter-testamental' period and the life of Jews in the Roman Empire. There are extensive extracts from relevant texts, both biblical and extra-biblical (the latter could have been more clearly identified), and 67 illustrations, mostly line-drawings. This is complemented by the Volume of *Sachbilder*, which takes the form of a folder with maps, charts and drawings on one side and a brief accompanying text on the other. The whole is reminiscent of the 'companion volume' to the Cambridge Bible Commentary, *Old Testament Illustrations*, by C. M. Jones (*B.L.* 1972, p. 23; *Bible Bibliog.*, p. 369), but is on a more lavish scale and is of course more up to date.

R. J. COGGINS

BERGERHOF, K., DIETRICH, M., and LORETZ, O. (eds.): *Ugarit-Forschungen: Internationales Jahrbuch für die Altertumskunde Syrien–Palästinas*. Vol. 17 (1985 — the title page says 1986, but a slip inside corrects the error). 1986. Pp. iv, 443. (Neukirchener Verlag, Neukirchen–Vluyn. ISBN 3 7887 1242 2. Butzon & Bercker, Kevelaer. ISBN 3 7666 9460 X. Price: DM 143.00; sub. price: DM 130.00)

Y. Avishur compares the list of a son's duties in Aqht with Ezekiel 8. J. L. Boyd examines the roots *ndr* and *nzr*. Dietrich and Loretz discuss Hebrew *'mr* ('lamb') and *pḥd*, and also Hebrew *spr* and *'prt*, in relation to Accadian and Ugaritic, and Ugaritic *'db* and *'ḏb* and Hebrew *'zb*; and the latter also discusses Pss. 49, 131:2b, and the late P. C. Craigie's use of Ugaritic in his commentary on Psalms 1–50. R. M. Good writes on Ugaritic and Hebrew *nht*, S. Layton on the Hebrew expression 'to set the face', H. Niehr on the root *'šr*, and W. von Soden on Hebrew *nāṭar*, while J. P. van der Westhuizen uses Hebrew *dmm* and *dlp* to elucidate a Ugaritic passage. J. Sanmartín Ascanso discusses the Israelite settlement in Canaan, V. Sasson the Deir 'Alla text, N. Wyatt J. Day's book *God's Conflict with the Dragon and the Sea*, and R. Zadok the non-Hebrew names of Israelites before the Hellenistic period. Other articles are also relevant, if less directly, to Old Testament study. As usual, there are extensive indexes.

J. A. EMERTON

BIČ, M.: *Ze světa Starého zákona I* (From the world of the Old Testament I). 1986. Pp. 365 with 29 maps and illustrations. (Kalich, Prague. Price: Kčs 65)

This is the first volume of an extensive work intended as a compendium or encyclopedia to the Old Testament. It contains five sections, each of five chapters: I. The Ancient Orient (1. Egypt, 2. Babylonia and Assyria, 3. Syropalestine, 4. Iran, 5. The invasion of the West). II. Palestine (6. The natural conditions, 7. The population in earlier periods, 8. Archaeological findings, 9. Israel, 10. The culture of Israel). III. On the paths of God (11. The comings and guests, 12. The delivered slaves, 13. The whole earth is mine, 14. The divided house, 15. The new opportunity). IV. Man — a creation of God (16. In the purpose of God, 17. In the family, 18. Natives and foreigners, 19. Lords and slaves, 20. Life and death). V. God and his work (21. The names of God, 22. The work of God, 23. Revelation, 24. Covenant, 25. The last things).

The second volume, already prepared for printing, also contains five sections: VI. The cult, VIII. The oldest written documents, VIII. The Book of books, IX. The post-canonical literature, X. The Old Testament in the church, but it will be printed only in 1988. This compendium is not only the only one in Czech, but in fact in any slavic language.

M. Bič

Blank, S. H. (ed.): *Hebrew Union College Annual.* Vol. lvi. 1985. Pp. 269 (English), 44 (Hebrew). (Hebrew Union College–Jewish Institute of Religion, Cincinnati. Price: $20.00. ISSN 360 9049)

Biblical scholars and Hebraists will be particularly interested in six of the thirteen essays in this latest issue. J. G. Gammie examines the angelology and demonology in the Septuagint of the book of Job and indicates where these concepts differ from those in the MT. The book of Jubilees receives the attention of J. Schwartz and B. Z. Wacholder, the former finding reflections of contemporary events in the variations between Jacob's 'return to Bethel' in Gen. 35:1–16 and Jubilees 31–32, and the latter discussing the date of the eschaton in Jub. 49:22–50:5 and CD 1:1–10 and 16:2–3. The linguistic interest is served by the articles of J. Naveh on a Jewish Aramaic tombstone epitaph found at Zoar and recording a death 386 years after the destruction of the second temple and by W. Weinberg's observations on the pronunciation of Hebrew recorded in rabbinic sources. M. Haran continues earlier research with a detailed study of the preparation of Hebrew Bible scrolls by Jewish communities from Qumran to the Middle Ages. The remaining essays cover rabbinic, historical, philosophical, liturgical, and modern Hebrew themes.

S. C. Reif

Botterweck, G. J. and Ringgren, H. (eds.): *Theological Dictionary of the Old Testament.* Vol. v (*hmr–YHWH*). Translated by D. E. Green. 1986. Pp. xxi, 521. (Eerdmans, Grand Rapids, Michigan. Price: $27.50. ISBN 0 8028 2329 7; for the whole set 0 8028 2338 6)

This volume appears six years after the previous one and is a translation of Band iii, Lfg. 1–4 of the *Theologisches Wörterbuch zum Alten Testament*, published 1977–80, of which a later part is reviewed immediately below. (For fuller information on the translation project see *B.L.* 1976, p. 8; 1979, p. 9; 1980, p. 12; 1982, p. 8) The translation has been done very competently by the translator of vol. iv. For this volume the system of transliterations of Hebrew letters and vowel-points has been revised and greatly improved in various respects, the chief improvements being the abandonment of v, ch, ts and sh as alternatives for w, ḥ, ṣ and š and the substitution of ḇ for bh (and similarly with the other b^{e}gadk^{e}path letters). (Unfortunately in the Table of Transliterations the line has been accidentally omitted under ḏ). As in previous volumes, there is no index of English key words corresponding to that of German key words in the original, and the index of biblical passages is also omitted. However, the project is a worthwhile one, and it is to be hoped that the succeeding volumes will appear more rapidly.

R. N. Whybray

Botterweck, G. J., Ringgren, H., and Fabry, H.-J. (eds.): *Theologisches Wörterbuch zum Alten Testament*. Band v. Lfg. 5–6 (Spalte 513–768). Lfg. 7–8 (Spalte 769–1024). 1986. (Kohlhammer, Stuttgart. Price: DM 62.00 for each double fascicle. ISBN 3 17 009075 5 and 3 17 009284 7)

Fascicle 5–6 begins with the final part of *naʿar* and ends with the first part of *sᵉdōm*, and contains thirty-four complete articles. The selection of words for their supposed religious or theological significance is necessarily a somewhat subjective matter, and as in earlier parts of the work there are some surprising choices (e.g. *nāpaḥ*). No words which might possibly be thought appropriate for inclusion seem to have been omitted, except possibly *nōqēd*, which has been held by some scholars to be a cultic technical term and so perhaps deserves a brief notice. The fullest treatments are accorded to *nātan* and its cognates (E. Lipiński and Fabry) and *nepeš* (H. Seebass), with twenty columns each, followed by *nāśā'* (D. N. Freedman, B. E. Willoughby, and Fabry, sixteen columns — but *nāśī'* (H. Niehr) is treated in a separate article of ten columns), *naʿar* (H. F. Fuhs, twelve columns, *nṣb/yṣb* (J. Reindl) and *nāqam* (Lipiński), each with eleven. (*maṣṣēbāh* has already been treated in a separate article.) Other substantial articles include *nāpal* (with *nēpel* and *nᵉpīlīm*, Seebass), *nāqāh* (with *nāqī'* and *niqqāyōn*, G. Warmuth), *nēr* (with *nīr*, D. Kellermann) and *sbb* (F. García López). Fascicle 7–8 contains thirty-three complete articles and concludes with the first part of what promises to be a long article on *ʿābar* (Fuhs). There is one very long article on *ʿābad* and cognates (Ringgren, U. Rüterswörden and H. Simian-Yofre, thirty-one columns). Sinai (P. Maiberger and C. Dohmen), *sākak* and cognates (T. Kronholm) and *sēper* (Dohmen, F.-L. Hossfeld and H. Reuter) also receive lengthy treatment. Sinai is one of the very few proper names to be included in the work. *sāpar* (with *mispār*, J. Conrad), *sōpēr* (Niehr) and *sēper* are treated in separate articles. The article on *sūp* includes a section on *yam sūp* by M. Ottosson. Under *sāmak* (D. P. Wright, J. Milgrom) there is included, with some hesitation, *śᵉmīkāh* (Judg. 4:18). A cross-reference indicates that *sūk* has already been dealt with under *nāsak*. The inclusion of **seren* (K.-D. Schunck) as a significant religious term is justified only if Noth's interpretation of *sarnē nᵉḥōšet* in 1 Kings 7:30 is accepted.

R. N. Whybray

Briend, J. and Cothenet, E.: *Supplément au Dictionnaire de la Bible*. Vol. xi. Fasc. 60 (*Safaïtique–Saint Esprit*). 1986. Cols. 1–256. (Letouzey & Ané, Paris. Price: Fr. 218.00)

With this new volume J. Briend and E. Cothenet assume the joint editorship of the *SDB*, although H. Cazelles and A. Feuillet continue to be associated with it as 'directeurs honoraires'. This fascicle contains three major articles, on the wisdom tradition ('courant de sagesse') in the Old Testament, on the *Wisdom of Solomon* and on the Holy Spirit (the last of these being divided into two parts, of which the New Testament part will be completed in the next fascicle). There are also two short articles, on the Safaitic language and texts (J. Ryckmans) and on Tell es-Sa'idiyeh (J. B. Pritchard). The wide-ranging and admirable article on the wisdom tradition by the late A. Vanel pays particular attention to theological issues inherited by Israel from its Near Eastern background, and shows how the questions of the limits of human wisdom and of its relationship to the wisdom of God lay behind much of the religious thought of the Old Testament. M. Gilbert on the *Wisdom of Solomon* provides a full-scale introduction to the book: text, literary structure, genre, unity, date (the reign of Augustus), Hellenistic influence and theology. The article 'Saint Esprit: Ancien Testament et judaïsme' (Cazelles, R. Kuntzmann, Gilbert, Cothenet and J.-E. Ménard) discusses the terminology (*rūaḥ*, *pneuma*) and then traces the concept of the Spirit (of God) through the books of the Old Testament, the *Wisdom of Solomon* and the literature of Qumran, with a final section on 'spirit' in Hellenism and the Gnostic literature. As always the contributors are well-known masters of their subjects, and the very full bibliography continues to be one of the work's outstanding features.

R. N. WHYBRAY

BROMILEY, G. W. (ed.): *The International Standard Bible Encyclopedia.* Vol. 3: K–P. Revised Edition. 1986. Pp. xx, 1060; numerous illustrations, including 70 in colour. (Eerdmans, Grand Rapids, Michigan. Price: $37.50. ISBN 0 8028 8163 7)

This third volume of the revised *International Standard Bible Encyclopedia* has been edited according to the principles described in the review of volume 1 (*B.L.* 1981, pp. 10–11), while the editorial team is the same as that for volume 2 (*B.L.* 1983, p. 9), viz. Bromiley, E. F. Harrison (New Testament), R. K. Harrison (Old Testament), W. S. LaSor (Biblical Geography and Archaeology), L. T. Geraty (Consulting Editor for Archaeology), and E. W. Smith, Jr (Project Editor). Like its two predecessors this volume is very much of a mixed bag. There is much helpful information about persons and places mentioned in the Bible and Apocrypha, and while some of the longer articles are quite poor (e.g. in this volume on the books of Maccabees), others provide useful introductions to the topics with which they deal. But the concern, which periodically manifests itself, to defend conservative positions severely restricts the overall value of this work.

M. A. KNIBB

BUTLER, J. T., CONRAD, E. W., and OLLENBURGER, B. C. (eds.): *Understanding the Word: Essays in Honor of Bernard W. Anderson* (JSOT Supplement Series 37). 1985. Pp. 389. (JSOT Press, Sheffield. Price: £18.50 ($28.50); sub. price: £13.95 ($21.50). ISBN 0 905774 88 4)

This festschrift for one of the outstanding American biblical scholars of recent decades consists of eighteen essays and a list of his writings. They are held together by an approach to the Bible as *The Word* and therefore reflect a very characteristically American focus on the documents of ancient Judaism and Christianity. But in spite of such a theologically circumscribed approach there is a great amount of solid exegetical and hermeneutical material in this book. It consists of W. Brueggemann, 'Imagination as a Mode of Fidelity'; B. C. Ollenburger, 'Biblical Theology: Situating the Discipline'; R. E. Murphy, 'The Song of Songs: Critical Biblical Scholarship vis-à-vis Exegetical Traditions'; H. C. White, 'Reuben and Judah: Duplicates or Complements?'; E. W. Conrad, 'The Community as King in Second Isaiah'; G. W. Coats, 'Lot: A Foil in the Abraham Saga'; K. D. Sakenfeld, 'Theological and Redactional Problems in Numbers 20.2–13'; J. J. M. Roberts, 'Amos 6.1–7'; M. L. Newman, 'Rahab and the Conquest'; P. D. Hanson, 'Conflict in Ancient Israel and Its Resolution'; C. Westermann, 'The Old Testament's Understanding of History in Relation to that of the Enlightenment'; P. Trible, 'The Other Woman: A Literary and Theological Study of the Hagar Narratives'; W. Zimmerli, 'The "Land" in the Pre-exilic and Early Post-exilic Prophets'; D. L. Migliore, 'Barth and Bloch on Job: A Conflict of Interpretations'; D. P. Niles, 'The Word of God and the People of Asia'; J. P. Sampley, 'Romans and Galatians: Comparison and Contrast'; H. C. Kee, 'Messiah and the People of God'; J. C. Beker, 'Paul's Letter to the Romans as a Model for Biblical Theology: Some Preliminary Observations'. An excellent collection, full of good things, and most fitting as a festschrift for Bernhard Anderson.

R. P. CARROLL

HARRINGTON, W. (ed.): *Proceedings of the Irish Biblical Association.* Vol. 9. 1985. Pp. iii, 138. (Irish Biblical Association Publications, Dublin. Price: IR £7.00)

Most of the articles in this volume are potentially of interest to students of the Old Testament. W. Riley writes on biblical narrative as traditional narrative in which community values are transmitted (with some effacement of 'original author' and 'original meaning'), C. McCarthy discusses the Davidic genealogy in the book of Ruth and the 'enriched dimension' of the Ruth story, K. Jeppesen sees the *maśśā' bābel* in Isaiah 13–14 as intended to associate the destruction of Babylon with the message of Isaiah, and D. O'Connor writes on Job 38–41 and its rejection of myth in the understanding of theodicy. Other studies of interest and profit are by C. T. R. Hayward, on Jewish traditions in Jerome's commentary on Jeremiah and in the Targum to Jeremiah, and by T. Finan, on the innocent sufferer as seen in Greek literature, and especially the *Iliad*.

R. P. GORDON

HARTMAN, L. (ed.): *Svensk exegetisk årsbok*, 51–52 (1986–87). 1986. Pp. 237, portrait. (C. W. K. Gleerup, Malmö. Price: Sw.Kr. 73.00. ISBN 91 40 05115 3)

This double issue is a *Festschrift* for the distinguished professor of New Testament at Lund, Birger Gerhardsson, on his sixtieth birthday. Of the twenty-four contributions three are on Old Testament subjects. B. Albrektson offers a perceptive discussion of the relationship between translation and interpretation, with reference to the work of J. Barr and the Swedish philosopher G. Hermerén. Under the title 'Who reckoned righteousness to whom?', B. Johnson writes on Gen. 15:6, reconsidering M. Oehming's view that Abraham is the subject of 'reckoned', which on syntactical and other grounds he rejects (English). T. Mettinger argues that though the designation of Yahweh as King is rare in Isa. 40–55, its occurrence at a decisive point (52:7) expresses a theme (Yahweh's victory over chaos) which pervades the entire prophecy (English). H. Räisänen writes on Islamic exposition of the Koran and Christian biblical exegesis. The remaining essays are on New Testament subjects. P. Block writes on theories of the origin of Christianity; P. Borgen re-examines the eucharistic tradition in 1 Cor. 10f.; H. C. Cavallin compares John 11:25 with Mark 12:18–27 and parallels and Pauline texts concerning the resurrection of the dead; L.-M. Dewailly considers possible occurrences of hendiadys in the New Testament; G. Forkman shows how the Fourth Gospel depicts changes in human character; B. Frid submits a brief note on *plēn* in Roman Times (English); L. Hartman discusses the meaning of *sōmatikōs* in Col. 2:9; D. Hellholm writes on a textgrammatical construction in Matthew and B. Holmberg on nuances of reciprocity in *allēlōn*; H. Hyldahl discusses a phrase in 1 Cor. 11:25 and Luke 22:20 (Danish); R. Kieffer considers Jewish purification rites and Christian baptism; E. Larsson re-examines the 'we'-passages in Acts; E. Lövestam relates Acts 20:18–35 to farewell speeches in the Old Testament; H. Moxnes writes on meals and the new community in Luke (English); M. Müller examines Matthew's understanding of the Messiahship of Jesus (Norwegian); B. Olsson considers 'mission' according to Luke, John, and 1 Peter; H. Riesenfeld discusses, with reference to the submissions of the Oxford scientists Humphreys and Waddington, the date of Jesus's death; H. Sahlin contributes a study of Matt. 5:39–42; H. Simonsen appraises M. Müller's study of the Son of Man (Danish); and S. Westerholm writes on Gal. 5:14, 'fulfilling the whole law of God' (English). Unless otherwise indicated, the articles are in Swedish.

G. W. ANDERSON

HERRMANN, S.: *Gesammelte Studien zur Geschichte und Theologie des Alten Testaments* (Theologische Bücherei, 75). 1986. Pp. 236. (Chr. Kaiser Verlag, München. Price: DM 48.00. ISBN 3 459 01618 3)

The studies collected here include some of the author's well-known articles: 'Mose', 'Der alttestamentliche Gottesname', 'Das Werden Israels', 'Autonome Entwicklungen in den Königreichen Israel und Juda', 'Die konstruktive Restauration'; together with other less well known or less accessible papers: 'Geschichtsbild und Gotteserkenntnis', 'Die Naturlehre des Schöpfungsberichtes', 'Das "apodiktische Recht"', 'Die Königsnovelle in Ägypten und in Israel', and 'Prophetie und Wirklichkeit in der Epoche des babylonischen Exils'. In two hitherto unpublished essays, which were originally contributions to the *Biblischer Kommentar* project, the author, in a detailed discussion of the work of Kutsch, maintains the appropriateness of the translation 'Bund' for *b^{e}rit* ('"Bund" eine Fehlübersetzung von "*b^{e}rit*"?'), and questions the determinative role which Wolff in his commentary on Jonah assigned to the categories of satire, irony and the grotesque ('Hans Walter Wolffs Verständnis des Buches Jona'). A further collection of essays, on Israelite prophecy and the history of religion, is promised.

A. D. H. MAYES

JAPHET, S. (ed.): *Studies in Bible 1986: Scripta Hierosolymitana: Publications of the Hebrew University, Jerusalem*. Vol. XXXI. 1986. Pp. viii, 437. (Magnes Press, Jerusalem. Price: $30.00. ISSN 0080 8369)

This volume marks two events, the sixtieth anniversary in 1984/5 of the founding of the Hebrew University of Jerusalem and the convening of the Twelfth Congress of the International Organization for the Study of the Old Testament in Jerusalem in the summer of 1986. There are seventeen contributions all from members of the Department of Bible, all of whose members are represented. M. Greenberg writes on 'More Reflections on Biblical Criminal Law'; M. Haran on 'Midrashic and Literal Exegesis and the Critical Method in Biblical Research'; A. Hurvitz on 'The Term *liškôth šārîm* (Ezek. 40:44) and its Place in the Cultic Terminology of the Temple', arguing that it is indicative of the exilic period; S. Japhet (the editor) on 'The Relationship between the Legal Corpora in the Pentateuch in Light of Manumission Laws', challenging the customary chronological order of Deuteronomy and the Holiness Code; S. Kamin on 'Rashbam's Conception of the Creation in Light of the Intellectual Currents of his Time'; S. Kogut 'On the Meaning and Syntactical Status of *hinnēh* in Biblical Hebrew', finding vital clues in *Ma'aśéh Efod*; S. E. Loewenstamm on the phrase *nah^{a}lath ha-Elōhîm*, discussing the tensions between the biblical concept of God as the God of all nations and Israel as his special 'inheritance' and the relation of the term to people and land; S. M. Paul on the phrase '*massā melek sārîm* — Hosea 8:8– 10 and Ancient Near Eastern Royal Epithets', *massā* here meaning more 'tribute' than 'burden'; A. Rofé on 'The History of the Cities of Refuge in Biblical Law'; B. J. Schwartz on 'A Literary Study of the Slave-girl Pericope — Leviticus 19:20–22'; A. Shinan and Y. Zakovitch on 'Midrash on Scripture and Midrash within Scripture', arguing as several have done in recent years that there is real continuity between the two in chronology as well as method; S. Talmon on 'Emendation of Biblical Texts on the Basis of Ugaritic Parallels'; Z. Talshir on 'Linguistic Development and the Evaluation of Translation Technique in the Septuagint'; E. Tov on 'The Growth of the Book of Joshua in the Light of the Evidence of the LXX Translation'; M. Weinfeld on 'The Day of the Lord: Aspirations for the Kingdom of God in the Bible and Jewish Liturgy'; M. Weiss on 'The Contribution of Literary Theory to Biblical Research — Illustrated by the Problem of She'ar Yashub', in this case the method of 'total interpretation' shows the name to convey a threat; and R. Westbrook on 'The Prohibition on Restoration of Marriage in Deuteronomy 24:1–4'. For all their variety of treatment and theme these articles together afford an interesting, and perhaps unique, insight to contemporary Jewish study of the Old Testament. It will be an especial pleasure for those who enjoyed the hospitality of the Department at the Congress in Jerusalem.

R. A. MASON

JERVELL, J. and KAPELRUD, A. S. (ed): *Studia Theologica: Scandinavian Journal of Theology*. Vol. 39, no. 2. 1985. Pp. 73–169. Vol. 40, no. 1. 1986. Pp. 1–79. (Universitetsforlaget, Oslo. Sub. price: vol. 39: N.Kr. 150.00; $25.00; vol. 40: N.Kr. 165; $27.00. ISSN 0039 338 X)

For the first issue of vol. 39, see *B.L.* 1986, p. 17. The second contains B. Olsson, 'A Decade of Text-Linguistic Analyses of Biblical Texts at Uppsala' (pp. 107–26), surveying various studies, and in particular explaining and discussing the value of the approaches by the author himself (on John), by D. Hellholm (on Hermas), and by B. Wiklander (on Isa. 2–4: see *B.L.* 1985, p. 99). If the terminology in these and related works, alluded to and listed, is not always entirely clear, the awareness of the problems of interpreting texts makes this a useful discussion. J. T. Willis, 'An Important Passage for Determining the Historical Setting of a Prophetic Oracle — Isaiah 1.7–8' (pp. 151–69), offers a careful analysis of text and versions, argues strongly for the MT, and considers historical setting and subsequent use: a clear discussion, related to the author's other prophetic studies. The first issue of vol. 40 offers K. Nielsen, 'Is 6:1–8:18* as Dramatic Writing' (pp. 1–16), a sensitive handling of the text, arguing for the section as presenting Isaiah's message with his own interpretation of it: the discussion does, however, reveal the problems of the relation of structural analysis to the determining of the unit to be considered, since the break at 8:18 is hypothetical. It is strange that there is no mention of H. Kimura, *Isa. 6:1–9:6. A Theatrical Section of the Book of Isaiah* (1981. See *B.L.* 1983, p. 69). T. Fornberg, 'Textual Criticism and Canon. Some Problems' (pp. 45–53) considers the witness in different text-forms to levels of interpretation; relating this to the question 'Which text is inspired?' he attempts to define a broader view of inspiration. Included in vol. 39, no. 2, are articles on Hebrews 13:16 and on Third World Theologies. Vol. 40, no. 1 also contains a very technical discussion of a psychological aspect of the question of hermeneutics, and one on baptism as initiation in Acts.

P. R. ACKROYD

KRAFT, R. A., and NICKELSBURG, G. W. E. (eds.): *Early Judaism and its Modern Interpreters* (The Bible and its Modern Interpreters, 2). 1986. Pp. xviii, 494. (Fortress Press, Philadelphia, Pennsylvania. ISBN 0 8006 0722 8. Price: $24.95. Scholars Press, Atlanta, Georgia. ISBN 0 89130 669 2)

Following the pattern set by its companion volume on the Hebrew Bible (see *B.L.* 1986, p. 18), this collection of essays 'documents the major developments in the study of "early Judaism" (ca. 330 B.C.E. to ca. 138 C.E.) from about the mid-40s' (Preface, p. xi). In Part One (Early Judaism in its Historical Settings) Shaye Cohen deals with 'The Political and Social History of the Jews in Graeco-Roman Antiquity', Gary Porton with 'Diversity in Postbiblical Judaism', James Purvis with 'The Samaritans and Judaism', and John Gager with 'Judaism as Seen by Outsiders'. In Part Two (Recent Discoveries) we have Jerome Murphy-O'Connor on 'The Judean Desert',

Sebastian Brock on 'Other Manuscript Discoveries', Eric Myers and Thomas Krabel on 'Archaeology, Iconography, and Nonliterary Written Remains' and Yaakov Meshorer on 'Jewish Numismatics'. In Part Three a wide range (though not all) of Jewish literature from this period is surveyed. Emanuel Tov writes on the LXX, Daniel Harrington on 'The Bible Rewritten (Narratives)' and Maurya Morgan on 'The Bible Explained (Prophecies), Anitra Kolenkow and John Collins on the Testamentary Literature, Robert Doran on 'Narrative Literature', Harold Attridge on 'Jewish Historiography', John Collins again on 'Apocalyptic Literature', Burton Mack and Roland Murphy on 'Wisdom Literature', James Charlesworth on 'Jewish Hymns, Odes and Prayers', and finally Anthony Saldarini on 'Reconstructions of Rabbinic Judaism'. The overall impression one gains from this volume is how immensely diversified and, perhaps also, fragmented this field of study has become. It will be of great value for those of us who are struggling to keep a grip on such a rapidly expanding subject. A. P. HAYMAN

KUTSCH, E.: *Kleine Schriften zum Alten Testament: zum 65 Geburtstag herausgegeben von L. Schmidt und K. Eberlein* (Beiheft zur Zeitschrift für die alttestamentliche Wissenschaft 168.) 1986. Pp. ix, 392. (De Gruyter, Berlin. Price: DM 152.00. ISBN 3 11 010368 8)

Twenty shorter studies and essays by Professor Ernst Kutsch of Erlangen are presented here in celebration of the author's sixty-fifth birthday. All but two of them have appeared in print earlier and are left unchanged from their original presentation. The collection is divided into three sections, the first of which deals with questions of chronology and of Israel's cultic calendar. The question of the precise year of Jerusalem's downfall (586 or 587) heads the first, followed by a study of the combining of the festivals of Passover and Unleavened Bread, the dating of the autumn festival celebration in Exod. 23:16 and the nature of the sabbath. There is also a study of rites of ritual mourning and self-deprecation.

The nine essays on historical and prophetic issues are each built around the exegesis of a specific passage: Judg. 6:11–24; 2 Sam. 2:4 and 5:3; 2 Sam. 7; Isa. 1:18–20; 44:1–5, 52:13–53:12; Jer. 9:22–3; Jer. 47:1–7 and Jl. 1–2. Each serves excellently to combine a detailed exegesis of the text with attention to wider theological issues.

In the third section, which deals with specific themes of Old Testament theology, the same combination of exegetical method with theological exposition is to be found. The first of these, entitled 'Menschliche Weisung — Gesetz Gottes', is concerned with the development of the concept of *tora* in the Old Testament. This is followed by a study of the Paradise narrative of Gen. 2–3 and two studies relating to the book of Job. The first tackles the theme of the Righteous Sufferer and the second considers the relationship between Job 31 and the divine speeches in Job 38ff. There is a further essay on the nature and meaning of suffering in the perspective of the Old Testament and an examination of Luther's translation of Psalm 118:21 and Psalm 18:36. At the end of the collection there is a bibliography of the writings of Ernst Kutsch. Altogether this forms a most stimulating and admirable study with a wide range of interest. R. E. CLEMENTS

LANG, B., in conjunction with KAISER, O., SIMOTAS, P., and VÖGTLE, A. (eds.): *Internationale Zeitschriftenschau für Bibelwissenschaft und Grenzgebiete*. Vol. 32 (1985). 1986. Pp. xiv, 447. (Patmos Verlag, Düsseldorf. Price: DM 168.00. ISSN 0074 9745)

There are summaries of almost 3,000 books, articles, and reviews in this invaluable 'review of biblical studies'. Dr Lang's Preface notes the beginning of 'a new effort to review only those articles and books that are of scholarly interest', and a revision of the classification system: separating secular and religious institutions from biblical theology and history.

A. G. AULD

LANGEVIN, P.-É.: *Bibliographie Biblique (1930–1983)*. Tome III. 1985. Pp. liv, 1902. (Les Presses de l'Université Laval, Québec. Distributed through Editions ESKA, Paris. Price: Fr. 1125.00. ISBN 2 7637 7060 6)

The two earlier volumes of this monumental tool were warmly received in *B.L.* 1974, p. 11 and 1978, p. 20. This third and still larger volume both updates and again extends the coverage offered in its predecessors. In addition to the 120 journals already covered in Tome II, 43 more have been reviewed as far back as 1930 where relevant. The closing tables in five languages present the works listed in all three volumes under more than 2,000 topical headings. At well over £100, this fine volume cannot be afforded by all serious scholars; but they should ensure that it is available in the libraries they use.

A. G. AULD

LEWICKI, T. (ed.): *Folia Orientalia.* Vol. XXIII (1985–1986). 1986. Pp. 374. (Polska Akademia Nauk–Oddzial W Krakowie, Komisja Orientalistyczna, Wroclaw. Price: ZL 430.00. ISSN 0015 5675)

The *Folia Orientalia* (not previously reviewed in the Book List) is an annual, Polish publication which contains articles and book reviews in English, French and German on a wide variety of topics appertaining to Oriental Studies. To the readers of the Book List the following articles are of interest: on the literary structure of Ps. 103 (P. Auffret); the Palmyra Tariff (E. Lipiński); the Exodus as a revitalization movement (T. D. Profitt); Egyptian Scarabs in Poznan (J. Śliwa); Dead Sea Scrolls research in Poland (S. Medala); and a Polish Dead Sea Scrolls bibliography, arranged according to subjects (Z. J. Kapera).

P. WERNBERG-MØLLER

MAIER, J., and SCHÄFER, P.: *Piccola Enciclopedia dell'Ebraismo*, traduzione di Daniela Leoni. 1985. Pp. xiv, cols. 679. (Marietti, Casale Monferrato. Price: Lire 45,000. ISBN 88 211 8329 7)

The German original of this handy one-volume encyclopedia was reviewed in *B.L.* 1982, p. 109. It has been discreetly revised for an Italian readership by the translator, Daniela Leoni, with help from Amos Luzzatto. The revisions mainly concern Italian history, but biblical studies make their appearance, for example in the entries 'Cassuto, U.', 'Castelli, D.', 'Giudeo-Italiano', and 'Immanuel Romano'. In general, however, the volume still leans rather heavily towards Germany, and there is an abundance of entries whose connexion with Judaism is tenuous (Christian writers, popes, antisemites, hebraists). It is a pity that 42 columns are wasted at the end on a list of headwords, which does not even distinguish between articles and cross-references. But there is a great wealth here, not only of information but also of stimulating insights; the biblical entries range from staple fare such as 'Bibbia', 'Critica biblica', 'Interpretazione' to suggestive short items on such topics as 'Carne' and 'Scala del cielo'.

N. R. M. DE LANGE

MARTIN, J. D., and DAVIES, P. R. (eds.): *A Word in Season: Essays in Honour of William McKane* (JSOT Supplement Series 42). 1986. Pp. xi, 266. (JSOT Press, Sheffield. Price: £25.00 ($37.50); sub. price: £18.00 ($27.50). ISBN 1 85075 016 5; 1 85075 047 5 Pbk)

To celebrate his sixty-fifth birthday a number of Willie McKane's colleagues, friends and former students have contributed eleven essays towards a festschrift which includes a bibliography of McKane's work (compiled by R. B. Salters). E. W. Nicholson writes on 'Israelite Religion in the Pre-Exilic Period: A Debate Renewed'; P. R. Davies meditates on 'Sons of Cain'; J. F. A. Sawyer considers '"Blessed be My People Egypt" (Isaiah 19:25): The Context and Meaning of a Remarkable Passage'; R. B. Salters examines 'Lamentations 1:3: Light from the History of Exegesis'; P. W. Coxon analyses 'The Great Tree of Daniel 4'; and W. Johnstone surveys 'Guilt and Atonement: The Theme of 1 and 2 Chronicles'. The second-half of the book is devoted to post-biblical studies and consists of J. D. Martin, 'Ben Sira — A Child of his Time'; J. C. Vanderkam, 'The Prophetic-Sapiental Origins of Apocalyptic Thought'; B. Paradise, 'Food for Thought: The Septuagint Translation of Genesis 1:11–12'; D. R. G. Beattie, 'Towards Dating the Targum of Ruth'; and J. G. Fraser, 'A Prelude to the Samaritan Pentateuch Texts of the Paris Polyglot Bible'. Individually and collectively the essays are stimulating and have much to offer the learned reader. Curiously no contributor has attempted an essay on the subject of Jeremiah, hence it must be deduced that the doyen of British Jeremiah studies would appear to have no disciples in this field! In welcoming this fine collection of essays for McKane's sixty-fifth birthday I would wish him good health and long life — long enough to finish his ICC on Jeremiah.

R. P. CARROLL

MÜLLER, G. (ed.): *Theologische Realenzyklopädie* (TRE). Band XIV (*Gottesdienst–Heimat*). 1985. Pp. 804, 16 Plates, 3 maps. (De Gruyter, Berlin. Price: DM 320.00. ISBN 3 11 008583 6)

The following articles and parts of articles in this volume are of particular importance for Old Testament and related studies: *Gottesdienst* (B.-J. Diebner on the Old Testament), *Haggada* (H. Bietenhard; there will also be a separate article on Midrash), *Halacha* (L. Jacobs), *Hebräisch* (D. Michel on the Old Testament, F. Werner on post-biblical Hebrew), *Heil und Erlösung* (A. Schenker on the Old Testament), *Heilige Stätten* (D. Kellermann on the Old Testament) and *Heiligkeit* (D. Kellermann on the Old Testament). There are articles on Habakkuk (E. Otto), Haggai (H. W. Wolff) and the Holiness Code (H. D. Preuss), and biographical articles on H. Graetz (M. Graetz), K. H. Graf (J. Hahn), Gressmann (R. Wonneberger), Gunkel (R. Wonneberger) and Harnack (F. W. Kantzenbach). Biblical cities are represented by articles on Hazor (V. Fritz), and Hebron (P. Welten). Other articles containing some matter relevant to Old Testament and Judaic studies include those on the Greek of the New Testament (F. Rehkopf), Greek religion (W. Burkert), *Handauflegung* (A. T. Hanson), *Haus* (F. Werner, K.-H. Bieritz, C. Kähler), *Heidentum* (H.-W. Gensichen, J. Sievers), *Heilige/Heiligenverehrung* (G. Larsson), *Heiliges Land* (R. L. Wilken), and *Heiligung* (J. Riches). G. Lanczkowski has contributed sections on the religio-historical background to many of the above-named articles. Finally, the article on *Graphik* (C. Rietschel) is illustrated with twenty-five reproductions of works of art from the fifteenth century to Chagall, including a number of Old Testament scenes.

R. N. WHYBRAY

MÜLLER, G. (ed.): *Theologische Realenzyklopädie* (TRE). Band XV (*Heinrich II — Ibsen*). 1986. Pp. 808, including 8 plates and 1 map. (De Gruyter, Berlin. Price: DM 320.00. ISBN 3 11 008585 2)

This volume contains articles on three Old Testament books: Job (J. Ebach), Hosea (J. Jeremias) and the Song of Songs. The last of these comprises a section on the literary characteristics of the Song (H. Graf Reventlow) followed by extended accounts of the history of its interpretation both Jewish (P. Kuhn) and Christian (U. Köpf and J. M. Vincent). Two articles on general theological topics contain sections of interest to readers of the *Book List*: those on the lordship and kingdom of God (E. Zenger, L. Jacobs) and on hermeneutics (L. Schmidt). That on Hellenism, however, is almost entirely devoted to New Testament matters (H. D. Betz). There are articles on Hezekiah (S. Herrmann), Herod (G. Baumbach), Hillel and his school (together with Shammai — R. Goldenberg), Jerome (P. Nautin), Hengstenberg (J. Mehlhausen) and Herder (E. Herms). The Enoch literature is dealt with by P. Sacchi and the Hittite religion by J. Ebach. General users of the encyclopedia will be surprised to learn that Henry VIII (of England) was the son of Henry IV (p. 9).

R. N. WHYBRAY

MURAOKA, T. (ed.): *Abr-Nahrain* XXIV (1986). 1986. Pp. vii, 207, incl. many figs., 6 plates. (Brill, Leiden. Price: Fl. 94.00. ISBN 90 04 08285 9)

This volume is dedicated to Professor John Bowman and is a worthy tribute. P. S. Alexander provides an admirably clear, indeed programmatic, discussion of 'The Textual Tradition of Targum Lamentations' (pp. 1–26). The Yemenite and western recensions should be presented in a synoptic edition and the editions of Sperber and Levine are severely criticized. S. Billigheimer reviews 'The Concept of Love in Jewish Religious Philosophy' (pp. 27–50), ranging down to the modern era, and in a follow-up to earlier articles B. E. Colless provides a brief note on 'The Nestorian Province of Samarqand' (pp. 51–57). There follows A. H. Johns's discussion of 'Solomon and the Queen of Sheba: Fakhr al-Dīn al-Rāzī's Treatment of the Qur'anic Telling of the Story' (pp. 58–82), a reminder of the continued life of biblical lore in Qoranic exegesis. T. L. McClellan continues the series of reports on the Melbourne excavations at Tell el-Qitar in Syria: 'El-Qitar: Third Season of Excavations, 1984–85' (pp. 83–106). This is mainly concerned with Early Bronze Age remains, while A. G. Sagona describes 'An Early Bronze Age IV Tomb at El-Qitar, Syria' (pp. 107–19). Professor Muraoka himself deals in detail with 'Hosea V in the Septuagint Version' (pp. 120–38). A. Murtonen's 'On Structural Growth in Languages' (pp. 139–54) starts, somewhat surprisingly, from his own collection of material of an Australian aboriginal language called Pintupi. He argues that there *are* structurally primitive languages and that some phenomena in Semitic can be explained as remains of a primitive structure. This leads to an interesting challenge to received wisdom, which largely assumes, for example, that Proto-Semitic had many complexities which have been simplified in the gradual formation of the attested languages. J. F. A. Sawyer's 'Cain and Hephaestus' (pp. 155–66) does not seem to mention Hephaestus, though it does find possible relics of metalworking traditions in Genesis 4. M. E. Stone's discussion of 'Categorization and Classification of the Apocrypha and Pseudepigrapha' (pp. 167–77) raises some fundamental questions on terminology and presuppositions in this field, while A. Tal publishes 'The Samaritan Targumic Version of "The Blessing of Moses" (Dt 33) according to an Unpublished Fragment' (pp. 178–95). Finally A. Vööbus reports on the 'Discovery of an Unknown Syrian Author: Theodōṭē of Amid' (pp. 196–201). Reviews complete the volume.

J. F. HEALEY

NADAV, M., and WEISER, R.: *Selected Manuscripts and Prints: An Exhibition from the Treasures of the Jewish National and University Library*. 1985. Pp. 36 (English), 92 (Hebrew), including many illustrations and colour plates. (Jewish National and University Library, Jerusalem. Price: $20.00)

Having collected its printed and manuscript treasures since 1892, the institution that today functions as Israel's national library and as the library of the Hebrew University of Jerusalem and of the Jewish people worldwide takes pride in having the largest number of Hebrew manuscripts and of printed Jewish books as well as important archives, maps and items of special scientific, artistic, and musical interest. As part of the sixtieth anniversary celebrations of the Hebrew University an exhibition of sixty items was mounted in the summer of 1985 and the present catalogue provides detailed descriptions in Hebrew and English of these exhibits, together with many plates, twelve of them splendidly reproduced in colour. Included among the biblical texts are the tenth-century Damascus Codex, a thirteenth-century Samaritan pentateuch, a thirteenth-century Vulgate, and printed editions by Bomberg, Soncino, and Koberger. Also described are autographs and other manuscripts of Maimonides, the Worms Maḥzor, Genizah fragments, other Bibles and prayer-books, and some later *varia*.

S. C. Reif

North, R. (ed.): *Elenchus Bibliographicus Biblicus of Biblica.* Vol. 64 (1983). 1986. Pp. 874. (Biblical Institute Press, Rome. Price: Lire 120,000; $85.00. ISSN 0392 7423)

The *Book List* is always happy to salute such an impressively large annual compendium of bibliographical assistance. This user not only appreciates its comprehensiveness but also enjoys the often devastating aptness of its choice of a single phrase from an article or review to sum up its critique.

A. G. Auld

Von Rad, G.: *Scritti sul Vecchio Testamento.* 1984. Pp. 248. (Editoriale Jaca Book, Milan. Price: Lire 13,000. ISBN 88 16 35074 1)

A translation of nine essays drawn from both the 1958 *Gesammelte Studien zum alten Testament* and the 1973 *Gesammelte Studien zum alten Testament II* (for which see *B.L.* 1960, p. 6f and 1974, p. 12f. respectively).

P. R. Davies

Revista Bíblica Brasileira. Ano 3, 1–4. 1986. Pp. 1–36; 37–76; 77–100; 101–24. (Nova Jerusalém, Fortaleza CE. Brazil. Price: $15.00 p.a.)

See *B.L.* 1985, p. 21; *B.L.* 1986, p. 23. The four issues for 1986 have continued with a New Testament theme ('Gospel'). The writing, as before, has all been done by Padre de Tillesse himself. A new and valuable pedagogical feature is a section of book and journal reviews (including a descriptive appreciation of the *Book List* and its history, 3/1, p. 32), indicative of the author's wide interests and his ability to make an international contribution to the all-important area of Biblical study in contemporary Brazil.

J. M. Dines

Richards, L. O.: *Expository Dictionary of Bible Words.* 1985. Pp. xv, 720. (Zondervan Publishing House, Grand Rapids, Michigan. Price: $19.95. ISBN 0 310 39000 1)

This book is meant primarily for the non-specialist and depends for what is of excellence on the linguistic ability of the writer. Most Bible Word Books reflect the theological stance of their authors and this is very much the case here — with the author writing particularly for those of a conservative evangelical persuasion, who would appreciate the homiletical — as opposed to exegetical — style of a large proportion of the articles. Many of them reflect current debates on theological and practical issues and point to the American scene rather than to the general. One might have wished for less to be read into the scriptures.

Despite its shortcomings, the book can be recommended for the non-linguistic layman who desires to know something of the Hebrew and Greek background to the words of the English Bible. Such would find the copious indices a help. It is a pity, however, that the book confines itself to the NIV and the new American version of the AV, but this fact probably indicates the clientele for whom the book is designed.

R. J. HAMMER

Seisho-gaku Ronshū 20 (The Japanese Biblical Institute Annual). 1985. Pp. 131. (Yamamoto-shoten, Tokyo. Price: ¥3,000)

Of three articles, two are related to the Old Testament field. T. Koizumi discusses 'Towards the historico-scientific reconstruction of the ancient history of Israel' (pp. 5–49), criticizing scholars' unconscious confusion of faith and historical science. 'Judicial Administration of the royal state in the deuteronomic reformation' is discussed by Y. Suzuki (pp. 50–94). Based upon his form-critical analysis with serious attention to the second person singular formulation of the individual laws of the judicial administration in which the 'elders' have some role, such as Deut. 25:5–10; 21:18–21; 22:13–21, he asserts the exstence of certain juristic state officials and a higher court of justice at the time of Josiah's reformation. Codification of the Deuteronomic law under the guidance of the state is positively suggested.

K. K. SACON

SIMON, U. (ed.): *Studies in Bible and Exegesis, Vol. 2: Presented to Yehuda Elitzur*. 1986. Pp. 282. (Bar-Ilan University Press, Ramat-Gan. Price: $19.00, plus postage and packing. ISBN 965 226 062 2)

A felicitous citation from Genesis 49:8 heads the preface to this collection of Hebrew essays, all connected in some way or other with biblical themes. After a tribute to Yehuda Elitzur as teacher and scholar and a bibliography of his writings, A. Levi-Feldblum writes on the prohibition of usury in Lev. 25:35–8, H. Fisch on Numbers 11, U. Simon on the birth of Samuel (55 closely argued pages), M. Ben-Yashar on the last kings of Judah, S. Vargo on Micah 7:8–10, G. H. Cohen on name-giving in Ruth, R. Kasher on patterns in miracle-working, and I. Finkelstein on 'The Israelite Settlement—The Sociological School in the light of Archaeological Evidence'. The remaining articles are devoted primarily to medieval subjects (Y. Ratzaby, M. Perez, M. Cohen on the 'Masoretic Text' and medieval textual tradition, and A. Saltman).

N. R. M. DE LANGE

TALMON, SH.: *King, Cult and Calendar in Ancient Israel: Collected Studies*. 1986. Pp. 244. (Magnes Press, Jerusalem. Price: $22.00. ISBN 965 223 651 9)

This is a collection of essays by Talmon published over a span of thirty years. The earliest of them, 'The Rule of the King — 1 Sam. 8:4–22' sets Samuel's words in the actual historical context of Saul's reign, thus displaying a certain literalism in treatment of the biblical text which characterizes much Jewish scholarship and reads somewhat strangely to others. Yet this may here be as much a mark of its time of composition (1956) for, by the latest of the essays, 'The Emergence of Jewish Sectarianism in the Early Second Temple Period', Weber is criticized because he 'did not sufficiently take into account that crucial gap between the historical actualities and their recordings which are coloured by the recorder's existential situation' (p. 175). This essay, indeed, affords a valuable critique of Weber's sociological reconstruction of post-exilic Jewish life. Other essays deal with 'Kingship and the Ideology of the State', 'Judges 18:21' which, it is argued, is not 'anti-judges' since *melek* here is synonymous with *šōpēṭ* and the words merely refer to a period when there was no judge to lead Israel, 'The Judean *'am haa'reṣ*', the 'Gezer Calendar', 'the Cult and Calendar Reform of Jeroboam I', 'Biblical Vision of the Future Ideal Age', and 'Types of Messianic Expectation at the Turn of the Era'.

A number of these articles were published in sources now difficult of access and some were previously not available to the English reader. The appearance of this book is therefore welcome and is powerful testimony to the breadth of interest and depth of scholarship of its author.

R. A. MASON

THOMPSON, H. D. (ed.): *The Answers Lie Below: Essays in honor of Lawrence Edmund Toombs*. 1984. Pp. xxv, 401, including 35 illustrations. (University Press of America, Lanham, Maryland. Price: $30.75. ISBN 0 8191 3745 6)

The twenty essays in this *Festschrift* are appropriately divided between archaeology (nine essays), the Bible (ten essays) and theology (one essay), for Toombs's range of scholarship was wide. The volume, which is reproduced from typescript, also includes a photograph of Toombs, a biographical sketch and a list of publications. The following contributions are likely to be of the greatest interest to Old Testament scholars: 'Village Subsistence: Iron Age Ai and Raddana' (J. A. Callaway); 'The Boundary between Ephraim and Manasseh' (E. F. Campbell: compare N. Naaman's study (below, p. 34), pp. 145–66); 'The Wadi el-Hasa Archaeological Survey' (B. MacDonald); 'Madaba — An Iron Age Tomb' (H. D. Thompson); 'The List of Seven Peoples in Canaan: A Fresh Analysis' (K. G. O'Connell); 'Wisdom and Humanism' (J. Priest); 'The Original Position of Job 28' (C. C. Settlemire); and 'Literary-Graphic Representation of Babylonian Deities in the Sixth Century B.C.' (Prescott W. Williams). There are also four articles on archaeological methods, which are a fitting tribute to one who had been director of the new excavations at Tell el-Hesi, where Flinders Petrie introduced stratigraphical excavation to Palestine.

G. I. DAVIES

THOMPSON, J. A.: *Handbook of Life in Bible Times*. 1986. Pp. 384, including numerous illustrations. (Inter-Varsity Press, Leicester. Price: £14.95. ISBN 0 85110 633 1)

This encyclopedic work aims to cover archaeology, everyday life and the background to individual biblical texts. It is arranged in sections as follows: Introduction (geography and archaeology), People at home (towns, houses, customs, clothes), Food and drink (water-supply, agriculture, cooking), Industry and commerce (measures, trade, government), Culture and health (writing, music, medicine), Warfare and Religion (non-Israelite, Israelite, Christian). There are excellent photographs, drawings and maps, as well as indexes. Biblical references are printed in the margins. This is a useful work of reference, suited especially to study-groups and to school libraries.

J. F. HEALEY

Tökei, F. (ed.): *Acta Orientalia Academiae Scientiarum Hungaricae*, xxxix, fasc. 1 (pp. 1–176), fasc. 2–3 (pp. 177–408). 1985. (Akadémiai Kiadó, Budapest. HU ISSN 0001 6446)

Apart from book reviews, there is nothing directly on the Old Testament in this volume, but an obituary of Alexander Scheiber is of interest to Hebrew scholars.

J. A. Emerton

Townsley, D. and Bjork, R.: *Scripture Index to the New International Dictionary of New Testament Theology*. 1985. Pp. 320. (Zondervan, Grand Rapids, Michigan. Price: $8.95. ISBN 0 310 44501 9)

The three volumes of the dictionary itself were favourably reviewed in the *Book List* when they first appeared (1976, p. 10; 1977, p. 9; and 1980, pp. 12f). Where relevant its articles always discuss the Old Testament usage of a New Testament word (mainly as found in LXX and other versions, but with MT compared). This citation index allows ready access to these discussions. Old Testament references are found on pp. 11–133; New Testament on pp. 134–263. The citations of 'selected extrabiblical literature' include Old Testament Apocryphal and Pseudepigraphical Literature (pp. 265–90); Qumran Writings (pp. 290–99); Jewish Hellenistic Writers (pp. 300–10); Early Christian Literature (pp. 310–13); and Rabbinic Writings (pp. 313–17).

A. G. Auld

Vawter, B. (ed.): *Old Testament Abstracts*. Vol. 9, nos. 1–2 (February, June 1986). Pp. 1–114, 115–234. (The Catholic Biblical Association, The Catholic University of America, Washington DC. Price per annum: $14.00; single issues: $5.00. ISSN 0364 8591)

This most useful bibliographical tool continues to provide wide coverage of periodicals and, to a lesser extent, of books that are concerned with the Old Testament and related disciplines.

M. A. Knibb

Van Der Woude, A. S. (ed.): *The World of the Bible. Bible Handbook, Volume 1*. 1986. Pp. xii, 400. (Eerdmans, Grand Rapids, Michigan. Price: $34.95. Distributed by Paternoster Press, Exeter. Price: £31.00. ISBN 0 8028 2405 6)

This background book, translated from the Dutch by S. Woudstra, stands out in its class. Avoiding loose generalizations, it presents clearly ordered, detailed information, supported by good bibliographies and index. J. H. Negenman (Old Testament) and B. Van Elderen (New Testament) write on geography. H. J. Franken contributes a polemical chapter on archaeological method and interpretation which, with C. H. J. de Geus's chapter on the development of Palestinian archaeology, should be required reading for all students. J. C. de Moor, J. Hoftijzer, and G. Mussies write on systems of writing and languages; E. Tov and J. S. Sibinga present the textual witnesses and textual history of the Old and New Testaments. The climax comes with K. R. Veenhof's magisterial survey of the history of the ancient near east to Alexander the Great — a book in its own right (pp. 203–327, double-columned), and a *tour de force*. This is followed with M. A. Beek's briefer but well pointed history to the second-century A.D., and K. Roubos's 'Biblical institutions'. The illustrations, some in colour, are well-chosen and well-annotated, and not restricted to the old favourites. The only weak point is the mapwork, limited to the end-papers. I read this book with growing respect. The editor, an honorary member of the Society, must be congratulated.

J. R. Bartlett

2. ARCHAEOLOGY AND EPIGRAPHY

ALBRIGHT, W. F.: *Paresutina no Kōkogaku*. Translated by E. Totoki and M. Tomura. 1986. Pp. 291 and a ten-page index with a map, 63 figures and 32 pictures. (Nihon Kirisuto Kyōdan Shuppan-kyoku, Tokyo. Price: ¥4,200)

This is a Japanese translation of *The Archaeology of Palestine*, 4th edition. An essay entitled 'Dr Albright, my teacher' is written as a preface by Y. H. Sacon.

K. K. SACON

ALI AL KHALIFA, SH. H., and RICE, M. (eds.): *Bahrain through the Ages: The Archaeology*. 1986. Pp. 526, 168 illustrations. (KPI Kegan Paul, London. Price: £25.00. ISBN 0 7103 0112 X)

These forty-eight papers, originally read to the 1983 archaeology conference in Bahrain, give a comprehensive review of the present state of our knowledge of the archaeology and history of the region from prehistoric to Hellenistic times. They inevitably concentrate on the relation of ancient Bahrain (Dilmun) as an entrepôt between Mesopotamia and the Indus Valley (G. Weisgerber, J. P. Joshi) and on the trading seals (T. C. Mitchell, P. Kjaerum) which mark it. Early textual references to Dilmun (H. J. Nissen) and possible Amorite (mar.tu) influences are covered (J. Zarins). Major sites discussed include the mass cemeteries (K. Frifelt, C. C. Lamberg-Karlovsky), the Barbar temple (H. H. Andersen, P. Mortensen and B. Doe), and the long enduring occupation of Qal'at al-Bahrain (F. Højlund). Evidence from the Iron Age and textual references from L. Assyria (P. Lombard, D. Oates) form the only link with Old Testament times but are sufficient to show a continuous sea-trade through the Gulf contemporary with that known elsewhere for the Gulf of Aqabah and the Re(e)d Sea. There are some useful articles on archaeological method and conservation. With this fine volume the archaeology of Bahrain, and with it the whole Gulf, has come of age.

D. J. WISEMAN

ANATI, E.: *L'Arte Rupestre del Negev e del Sinai*. 1979. Pp. 140, including illustrations and 62 pp. of colour plates. (Jaca Book, Milan. Price: Lire 28,000)

This illustrated work on the rock art of the Negev and Sinai is the first title in a series entitled 'Le orme dell'uomo' (of which Anati is general editor). After two preliminary chapters on the history of the discoveries (from 1856 on) and on style and chronology, successive chapters deal with Style I (the art of the hunters), Style II (the beginnings of domestication), Style III (realistic and dynamic figures), Style IV (the expansion of pastoralism) and the later styles, which reflect the drastic changes in the human environment, way of life, and social and economic structure which took place from the closing centuries B.C. onward. Much of the material has been made accessible to the scholarly world only quite recently, and its scientific study has scarcely begun. When it is satisfactorily interpreted it will greatly enrich our knowledge of the early culture of the areas covered.

F. F. BRUCE

AVIGAD, N.: *Hebrew Bullae from the Time of Jeremiah, Remnants of a Burnt Archive*. 1986. Pp. 139, many photographs. (Israel Exploration Society, Jerusalem. Price: $20.00. ISBN 965 221 006 4)

A group of clay bullae were found somewhere in Judah over ten years ago. Avigad publishes 225 of them, now mostly in the Israel Museum and one private collection. They bear imprints of 211 small stamp seals, three pictorial, the rest bearing early Hebrew names. Palaeography points to a date about 600 B.C. Avigad supports this by identifying 'Berechyahu son of Neriyahu the scribe' on one and 'Yerahme'el the king's son' on another with Jeremiah's secretary and an official named in Jer. 36. Most seals bear names of owners and their fathers, five have grandfathers' names also. Nine names are new to Hebrew onomastics, notably *'šrḥy* and *'šryḥt*, apparently built with Asherah's male counterpart. Others offer variations of known names, e.g. *gʿly*, *yhw'ḥ*. Some impressions show one man owned several seals, one six, another four. One man's patronym is spelt both *'lsmk* and *'lysmk*, demonstrating again freedom in use of the vowel letter. Avigad discusses how many papyrus documents these bullae once sealed and what sort of archive they represent, concluding there was probably one seal per deed, and that they belonged to a public archive outside Jerusalem. This is an expert presentation of importatant evidence for knowledge of Judean society and administration, epigraphy, and name-giving.

A. R. MILLARD

BETZ, H. D.: *The Greek Magical Papyri in Translation: Including the Demotic Spells*, Vol. 1: *Text*. 1986. Pp. lviii, 339. (University of Chicago Press, London. Price: £33.95. ISBN 0 226 04444 0)

The burning described in Acts of the magical books at Ephesus was not an isolated case of magic being suppressed in the Greco-Roman world, and it has been tempting to ignore Classical magic ever since. In fact, this renders papyrological survivals all the more important, and this was appreciated in 1973–74, when Albert Henrichs re-edited and completed the volumes of Papyri Graecae Magicae which Karl Preisendanz had produced for Teubner in 1928–31. Now New Testament scholars are carrying the beacon: this volume and its projected sequels are to be part of a *Corpus Hellenisticum Novi Testamenti*. Preisendanz has been much amplified, with demotic material and much more Greek, and though one is referred to the original publication for the Greek text, the explanatory notes attach throughout also to the Greek. This was a sensible and economical policy. In the same way, the forthcoming indexes will cover both original and translation. The present volume will no doubt be most heartily welcomed in New Testament circles when the projected collection of parallels with early Christian literature is available; but it deserves careful attention already now.

T. RAJAK

BIENKOWSKI, P.: *Jericho in the Late Bronze Age*. 1986. Pp. xii, 240 (including 50 pp. of graphs, plans and plates). (Aris & Phillips, Warminster, Wiltshire. Price: £22.00. ISBN 0 85668 320 5)

The claims once made for a close correlation between archaeological evidence from Jericho and the story of its capture in Joshua 6 were decisively undermined by the abandonment (except for a few scholars) of a fifteenth-century date for the Exodus and by the results of Kathleen Kenyon's excavations, which showed that the walls associated with Joshua by J. Garstang were a millennium older than he thought. But other finds made by Garstang, some of them unpublished, do belong to the Late Bronze Age (LBA) and Bienkowski here presents a fresh analysis of them in the context of the other excavations at the site and more recent archaeological research: he uses, for example, microscopic examination and X-ray analysis to distinguish 'ware groups' among the pottery, and is able to document a decline in quality during the LBA, which he correlates in a useful concluding chapter with wider indications of economic and cultural regression at this time. His date for the end of LBA occupation at Jericho (*c.* 1275 B.C.) is a little later than those proposed by Kenyon, but the evidence (even allowing for erosion) is that the settlement was small, restricted to the area of the 'Middle Building' in the south-eastern part of the tell, and that it was not destroyed by fire, so that the biblical account is at best a greatly exaggerated version of its capture, if it is historical at all.

G. I. DAVIES

CARENA, O.: *Il Resto di Israele: Studio storico-comparativo delle iscrizioni reali assire e dei testi profetici sul tema del resto* (Associazione Biblica Italiana, Supplementi alla Rivista Biblica, 13). 1985. Pp. 108 (Edizioni Dehoniane, Bologna. Price: Lire 12,000. ISBN 88 10 30201 X)

The notion of a 'remnant' was not confined to Israel as the author shows by setting out over ninety passages from Assyrian royal inscriptions which also use various terms for the same concept. According to C., in Israel the idea of a remnant existed before the exile and its negative aspects, evident from Assyrian documents, were inverted by prophets such as Amos, Isaiah and Micah as part of their message of hope.

The bibliography, long as it is, does not make up for the lack of explanatory notes to the Assyrian texts quoted, though the formal analysis in chapter 2 is helpful. For example, unless one knows that *sittu* is a variant spelling of *šittu* ('remnant') the constant switch between the two is disconcerting. Also, difficulties in the passages from the Babylonian Epic of Erra, quoted on page 44, are ignored. In the main, though, the presentation of neglected material and the freshness of approach are both very welcome.

W. G. E. WATSON

DAVIES, G. I.: *Megiddo* (Cities of the Biblical World). 1986. Pp. xii, 116. (Lutterworth, Cambridge. Price: £6.95. ISBN 0 7188 2586 1)

The author has done a great service in producing this archaeological history of Megiddo in such a clear way from the vast and complicated array of literature about this site. A chapter each is devoted to identifying the site and its geographical setting, and recounting the various archaeological excavations that have taken place there. The following four chapters deal with its history from Neolithic times to the Persian period and after as illustrated from the archaeological discoveries. And there is an interesting account of the attack of Tuthmoses III. The illustrative line drawings are excellent, as is the quality of photographic reproduction. There is ample reference for further reading at the end of each chapter, and an appendix describes the main features to be seen, numbered on an accompanying photograph, for visitors to the site.

J. R. DUCKWORTH

HARRIS, R. L., and SCHONFIELD, J. (eds.): *Bulletin of the Anglo-Israel Archaeological Society: News and Meetings of the Society 1984–5*. 1985. Pp. 89. (Anglo-Israel Archaeological Society, London. Price: £7.00. ISSN 0266 2442)

This *Bulletin* commemorates Yigael Yadin with four addresses about his activities (D. Astor, R. Barnett, J. Kane, G. Vermes). There follow summaries of lectures on new discoveries at minor sites in Jerusalem (D. Bahat), on seven seasons at Tell Batash, Timnah, revealing heavy Late Bronze Age, Philistine, and Iron Age occupation (G. Kuhn), on work at Dor (E. Stern), at Acco (M. Dothan), and at Lachish, where traces of the Assyrian siege were found (D. Ussishkin). R. Gonen read two papers, one differentiating Late Bronze Age pit burials from cave burials (perhaps Canaanite and Amorite respectively), the other commenting on often ludicrous attempts to identify the 'Ten Lost Tribes'. (Note that Halah is not difficult to identify, as asserted; it is Assyrian Halahhu, N.E. of Nineveh, see ICC *Kings*.) Headed 'Current Research' is a preliminary note by J. Gunnenweg and I. Perlman concluding through neutron activation analysis that 'Herodian' lamps from Avdat, Meiron and Jerusalem were all made in Jerusalem. There are also reports from four grantees, and obituaries of Lord Segal and Miss Olga Tufnell. The increase in size from 49 pages (see *B.L.* 1986, p. 30) reflects the Society's health.

A. R. MILLARD

HERZOG, Z.: *Das Stadttor in Israel und in den Nachbarländern*. Translated by M. Fischer. 1986. Pp. x, 176, with 116 figures. (Verlag Philipp von Zabern, Mainz. Price: DM 148.00. ISBN 3 8053 0572 9)

The appearance of this German translation of Herzog's doctoral dissertation (originally published in Hebrew in 1976) is to be greatly welcomed. It provides a detailed account and discussion of the city-gates found in Palestine (the 'Israel' of the title is intended as a geographical term but even when recognized as such it is misleading), Syria and Anatolia from the Chalcolithic, Bronze, and Iron Ages. The development of different forms of gate is traced with special attention to the functions, military and civil, which they served, and a concluding chapter summarizes these functions with references to literary as well as archaeological evidence. For the German edition references to the recent discoveries at Acco and Dan have been added, and there are some other minor changes, but the detailed defence of Y. Aharoni's views about the Israelite gates at Megiddo has regrettably not been modified to take account of subsequent publications by D. Ussishkin and Y. Shiloh. The provision of a comprehensive series of plans is the more useful for their being incorporated into the text at appropriate places, rather than being collected at the end as in the original edition.

G. I. DAVIES

LEVINE, L. I., and NETZER, E.: *Excavations at Caesarea Maritima: 1975, 1976, 1979 — Final Report* (Qedem, Monographs of the Institute of Archaeology, Hebrew University of Jerusalem, 21). 1986. Pp. xi, 206. (Israel Exploration Society, Jerusalem. Price: $24.00. ISSN 0333 5844)

This fine-looking volume is essentially a report of fairly recent excavations, conducted over four seasons, in two principal zones of the ancient city of Caesarea, but it contains also a general conspectus of the earlier excavation record (with some bibliographical guidance) and one of the city's history, as it may be interpreted now from the various sources. The latter cannot, of course, be a substitute for the important full-length works now available, including one by Lee Levine himself (1975); and it has little connection with the main reports. That part of the Byzantine city which lies in the North of Crusader Caesarea was the primary target of the digs; but the Crusader city wall was also surveyed, and, of most interest in this context, a promontory to the South (near the theatre), revealed in 1976, revealed rooms, mosaic flooring and vaults in addition to a previously-known pool; these the authors propose to have been a promontory palace built by Herod and later the 'procurator's praetorium'. A second major focus for the city is suggested, complementing the area of harbour and temple. The new site is given a separate chapter, though its coins are analysed together with the rest. The whole report, though 'final', is described as limited in certain directions by 'time and budget'.

T. RAJAK

MAZAR, A.: *Excavations at Tell Qasile.* Part 2 (Qedem, Monographs of the Institute of Archaeology, The Hebrew University, Jerusalem, 20). 1985. Pp. x, 257, with 58 figs and 99 photos. (Israel Exploration Society, Jerusalem. Price: $24.00. ISSN 0333 5844)

The second part of this report (for the first see *B.L.* 1982, p. 25) presents the pottery and other small finds from the 1971–74 excavations, together with general conclusions and reports on laboratory studies. As in the previous volume detailed discussion is restricted to the Iron Age strata and very largely to Strata XII–X (*c.*1150–1000 B.C.), to which the important Philistine temples belong. The pottery sequence at Tell Qasile is important for the chronology of Philistine pottery and at significant points Mazar's conclusions differ from those of the magisterial work of T. Dothan. The site, which lies on the northern outskirts of Tel Aviv, was founded as a port town as Philistine hegemony extended northwards and Strata XI–X illustrate well the flourishing culture of the Philistines in the eleventh century, when they began to pose a major threat to the Israelite tribes in the hill country.

G. I. DAVIES

MILDENBURG, L.: *The Coinage of the Bar Kokhba War* (Typos: Monographien zur antiken Numismatik, VI). 1984. Pp. 396 and 44 plates. (Verlag Sauerländer, Aarau, Schweiz. Price: Sw.Fr. 230. ISBN 3 7941 2634 3)

This elegant and wide-ranging publication was conceived in 1940; since then, large numbers of Bar Kokhba coins have emerged from hoards (though few by systematic excavation) and the author's dedication has followed and registered them through dealers to many collections, largely private. Most significant to scholarship is that the new corpus comes with a proposed complete die-sequence for the coinage, a task which was particularly demanding because all the Bar Kokhba coins (in contrast to those of the First Revolt) were overstruck on other, non-Jewish issues, and comprised an irregular as well as a regular issue. There are also chapters reassessing the history of the revolt, in which the hard evidence of the coins and also the documents is made to triumph over the brief and 'subjective' literary sources, whose limitations are stressed. The numismatic methodology and data are set out with unusual completeness. An interesting section compares from all angles the coin issues of the two revolts, though one cannot accept the description of the slogans in the first case as 'fact' and in the second as 'propaganda' and it is misleading not to mention the First Revolt inscriptions saying 'freedom of Zion' and 'of the redemption of Zion'.

T. RAJAK

MILLARD, A. R.: *Treasures from Bible Times.* 1985. Pp. 189, including numerous illustrations. (Lion Publishing, Tring. Price: £9.95. ISBN 0 85648 587 X)

This splendidly produced work contains a long series of short discussions of up to about four pages, covering the whole of Near Eastern archaeology from Ur and Ebla to Qumran and Masada. The photographs are magnificent and the text is always clear, giving a reliable account of the many different subjects in this field which are of interest to readers of the Bible. It will be particularly useful in the school context and for Bible-study groups. If there are any criticisms, they might be that the author seems a little bit over-defensive on some points (for example on Qumran) and that the format of short items on many topics results in an episodic style and a lack of continuity. This last fault is, however, compensated for by the ease with which one can read individual sections.

J. F. HEALEY

PARDEE, D.: *Les textes hippiatriques* (Ras Shamra II). 1985. Pp. 77, including photographs. (Éditions Recherche sur les Civilisations, A.D.P.F., Paris. Price: Fr. 82.00. ISBN 2 86538 125 2)

This is a definitive re-edition of the four Ugaritic hippiatric texts based upon re-examination of the tablets themselves. There are many new readings as a result. Apart from copies and photographs, the author provides a transliteration and a vocalized reconstruction, as well as detailed information on the divergences between his own and earlier readings. The detailed discussions of lexical items will be of interest to Old Testament scholars. Plant-names and maladies of horses play a prominent role here, though Pardee is reticent in the identification of plants. As he notes in a preface, another monograph on the same subject has recently appeared and should be read in conjunction with the present work: Ch. Cohen and D. Sivan, *The Ugaritic Hippiatric Texts: A Critical Edition*, New Haven, 1983.

J. F. HEALEY

PRITCHARD, J. B.: *Tell es-Saʿidiyeh: Excavations on the Tell, 1964–1966.* (University Museum Monograph 60). 1985. Pp. xvi, 88; 189 figures. (The University Museum, University of Pennsylvania, Philadelphia. Price: $60.00. ISBN 0 934718 60 1)

Pritchard reports on his excavations of the summit (Areas 23, 31, 32) and staircase (Area 14) of Tell es-Saʿidiyeh (identified by Albright as Zaphon, by Glueck as Zarethan). (The report on the LB–IA cemetery of Area 17 was published in 1980, but not reviewed in *B.L.*) Material from the sounding reaching Stratum VIII is still unpublished, and Pritchard begins with Stratum VII (*c.* 825–790 B.C.), with its mud-brick city wall and houses. It was abandoned; Stratum VI (*c.* 790–750 B.C.) used its wall. Stratum V (*c.* 750–730 B.C.) had a new layout, with back-to-back pillared terrace houses; it was destroyed by fire. Stratum IV (*c.* 730–600 B.C.) used the area solely for storage silos and bins. A major feature from strata VII to V was the covered stairway from the summit to the water supply. The pottery from strata VII to IV shows clear links with Samaria, Hazor, Megiddo, and Tell el-Farʿah (N), but only occasional links with Phoenicia or the rest of Transjordan. Pritchard cannot demonstrate stratigraphical links between strata VII–IV and III–I (which lie in Area 31); III, II, and I provide important evidence for the Persian, Hellenistic, and early Roman periods. This is an admirably clear and readable report, though a major disaster has confounded the correspondence of drawings and descriptions on Figure 18 (with resultant reference errors on pages 73 and 77 and possibly elsewhere), and inscription no. 1 (p. 86) reads *šmn* (see Fig. 175a–d), not *šmm*.

J. R. BARTLETT

RAST, W. E. (ed.): *Preliminary Reports of ASOR-Sponsored Excavations 1980–1984* (BASOR Supplement No. 24). 1986. Pp. 164, with 138 illustrations. (Eisenbrauns, Winona Lake, Indiana, for the American Schools of Oriental Research. Price: $20.00. ISBN 0 89757 324 2)

Of the reports included here those on the 1983 season at Sardis and the 1984 season at ʿAin Għazāl are, for all their intrinsic interest, far removed from the main concerns of Old Testament scholars, and a third (on Caesarea Maritima 1980) can reasonably be described as marginal to the subject. The other three describe projects of great potential importance for Old Testament study. The continuation of work at Pella of the Decapolis in 1982 and 1983 is described by R. H. Smith and A. W. McNicoll, who argue for practically continuous occupation at the site from the Middle Bronze Age to the Islamic period, on the basis of extensive excavations over a number of years. Both the remaining reports relate to new initiatives of established regional projects, involving the excavation of tells with a similarly long history of occupation. E. D. Oren, M. A. Morrison and I. Gilead report on the first two seasons (1982 and 1983) at Tel Haror (perhaps the site of Gerar) within the context of the 'Land of Gerar' project, and L. T. Geraty and other members of the 'Madaba Plains' project summarize the results of their work in 1984 at Tell el-ʿUmeiri (south of Amman), which included evidence of changing systems of food production and the discovery of a seal inscribed *lmlkm'wr ʿbd bʿlyšʿ*, 'belonging to Milkom-Ur, minister of Baalyasha': the latter is perhaps the Ammonite king mentioned in Jeremiah 40:14.

G. I. DAVIES

SEKIYA, S.: *Zōho-Kaitei Zusetsu Kyūyaku-Seisho no Kōkogaku* (An illustrated Old Testament Archaeology. The 2nd Revised and Supplemented Edition). 1986. Pp. 139, numerous illustrations (13 in colour), maps, plans, figures, charts, and chronological tables. (Yorudan-sha, Tokyo. Price: ¥5,400)

This is a useful handbook to Old Testament archaeology arranged from the Patriarchal Age to the Second Jewish War. A short historical sketch to the present day is appended in the last chapter. An eleven-page supplementation is given on Mt Ararat, the roads Abraham may have passed and Machpelah, the Exodus road and Tell el-Amarna, and Tell Dan.

K. K. SACON

TUSHINGHAM, A. D.: *Excavations in Jerusalem 1961–1967*. Vol. I. 1986. Pp. 528 (including 81 pp. of figures and 92 pp. with 185 plates) together with 37 folded sheets of plans, sections, and elevations. (Royal Ontario Museum, Toronto. Price: CAN$145.00. Distributed by Brill, Leiden. Price: Fl. 340.00. ISBN 0 88854 317 4)

This is the first of several eagerly awaited volumes publishing the results of the fieldwork led by K. M. Kenyon for the British School of Archaeology in Jerusalem in several areas in and close to the Old City of Jerusalem. It deals with two of the most readily separable sites: principally the Armenian Garden within the SW corner of the Old City, but also the much disputed wall 450 m north of the present northern wall. Dr Tushingham and the Royal Ontario Museum became important contributors to the project in 1962. His evidence from the Armenian Garden (pp. 1–177) relates to periods from the Iron Age to the Ottoman. Of most concern to readers of the *Book List* are the argument that the area was used for quarrying, and was outside the city in all periods of the royal Judaean era; and the demonstration that its first continuous occupation was as part of a palace built by Herod the Great and restored probably by Herod Agrippa. After lying ruined for some 500 years following A.D. 70, the area was developed by ecclesiastical foundations. Tushingham is careful to correlate his work with the evidence of subsequent Israeli excavations in sites to north, south, and east. Such discussion is a feature also of E. W. Hamrick's argument (pp. 213–32) that the northern wall was a barrier wall. The other separate sections, by J. Y. Hayes on 'Hellenistic to Byzantine Fine Wares' (pp. 179–94), and R. B. Y. Scott on 'Weights from the 1961–1967 Excavations', both deal comprehensively with material from all the Kenyon sites. The many separately folded sheets boxed with the large paperback volume may prove a headache to librarians; however, many non-specialist readers will join their more technical colleagues in appreciating the clarity with which daunting material is explained.

A. G. AULD

YADIN, Y., and GEVA, S.: *Investigations at Beth Shean: The Early Iron Age Strata* (Qedem, Monographs of the Institute of Archaeology, Hebrew University of Jerusalem, 23). 1986. Pp. xv, 95, with 39 figs and plans, and 90 photos. (Israel Exploration Society, Jerusalem. Price: $24.00. ISSN 0333 5844)

In 1983 Yigael Yadin conducted his last excavation in a carefully selected area on the summit of the ancient mound of Beth-shean, hoping thereby to cast new light on the history of the Judges period. Only a small area was excavated, and Yadin died before he could fully integrate what he found into existing archaeological and historical knowledge. Four strata, covering the twelfth to the tenth centuries B.C., were identified, the main new discovery being a period (Stratum 3) late in the twelfth century when this area of the mound at least ceased to be built up and was occupied by pits and boundary-walls. As in the excavations of the inter-war period, no Philistine pottery was found. In the report Geva (who is to be congratulated on its speedy appearance) gives a detailed account of the stratigraphy of the excavated area and the pottery associated with each stratum. Much must remain uncertain until a wider area can be excavated, but the possibility of correlations with Hazor Stratum XII and Megiddo Stratum VIB promises eventually to fulfil Yadin's hopes of important new insights into early Israelite history.

G. I. DAVIES

YASSINE, K.: *Tell el Mazar I: Cemetery A*. 1984. Pp. xxv, 195; 69 figures. (The University of Jordan, Amman; distributed by the author, P.O. Box 410403, Amman. Price: $30.00 plus $2.00 shipping and handling)

In 1977–79 Yassine excavated an Iron IIc fifth-century B.C. cemetery at Tell el Mazar, about 3 km north-north-west of Tell Deir ʿAlla. Yassine describes individually 85 burials, mainly oriented east–west. The males appeared to be buried in extended position, often with weapons beside them, and the females in crouched position, with ornaments and cosmetic goods. However, Yassine's view of sex-differentiated burials is not wholly supported by the physical evidence from the skeletons presented in chapter 6 by Dr A. Disi and his colleagues from the Department of Biology at Jordan University. The pottery (mainly the smaller types) showed 'striking' comparison with vessels from Amman, Sahab, and Meqabalein; this should be compared with Pritchard's conclusions from the slightly earlier material at Tell es-Saʿidiyeh (see this *B.L.* p. 27). A large number of metal artefacts were found, including bronze bowls of Syrian tradition, and iron weapons. There are five stamps seals (two inscribed with names), one cylinder seal, and eight scarabs. Though sadly full of misprints and minor errors, this is an important contribution to our limited knowledge of the Jordan valley in the Persian period.

J. R. BARTLETT

3. HISTORY AND GEOGRAPHY

AHLSTRÖM, G. W.: *Who Were the Israelites?* 1986. Pp. x, 134, and 3 figures. (Eisenbrauns, Winona Lake, Indiana. Price: $12.50. ISBN 0 931464 24 2)

Ahlström's introductory chapter to this new investigation of the origin and history of the name 'Israel' embraces the facts of geography and the state of the question. Then, after chapters on 'Population Groups and Theories' and 'Some Evidence from Archaeology', he expounds in chapter 4 his first conclusion: that 'Israel', as indeed 'Judah' which it included, was originally a territorial name. 'The Role of the Sea: Mythological Historiography' argues both that Exod. 15 and Judg. 5 are later than often claimed, and that their categories are not those of empirical history. The longest chapter then reviews 'The Peoples of the Territory Israel' in the closing centuries of the second millenium B.C.E. Chapters 7 and 8 expound two shifts in meaning, firstly 'Israel: A National Name' from the time of Saul, then 'Israel: An Ideological Term'. Only the latter remained applicable to Judah after Solomon's death. This is a valuable rescrutiny of much well-nigh intractable material.

A. G. AULD

CASTEL, F.: *The History of Israel and Judah in Old Testament Times.* 1985. Pp. vii, 267. (Paulist Press, Mahwah, New Jersey. Price: $8.95. ISBN 0 8091 2701 6)

This work was originally published in 1983 as *L'Histoire d'Israel et de Juda* (not noted in *B.L.*, and not seen); the modification of the original title for the translation is curious, since much the longest and most detailed chapter is devoted to the Roman occupation. It is essentially a straightforward outline history, accepting a moderate critical position, and intended for leaders of bible study groups and the like. The text is interspersed with frequent maps and line-drawings, and with extracts from both the biblical text and from relevant non-biblical material. The overall impression is a favourable one, the types of problems encountered being clearly set out; in places the detailed study is not always so encouraging, as there are a number of factual errors, especially in the later period, and some very odd misprints. The translation is clear, but the value of the footnotes and bibliography will be limited, since they are largely confined to works written in French. Despite these reservations, this will be a useful addition to the histories available at a non-technical level.

R. J. COGGINS

DONNER, H.: *Geschichte des Volkes Israel und seiner Nachbarn in Grundzügen.* Teil 2: *Von der Königszeit bis zu Alexander dem Grossen* (Grundrisse zum Alten Testament. Das Alte Testament Deutsch: Ergänzungsreihe, 4/2). 1986. Pp. viii, 233–511, including 4 maps. (Vandenhoeck & Ruprecht, Göttingen. Price: DM 36.80. ISBN 3 525 51666 5)

This second volume of Donner's excellent study (for a review of the first see *B.L.* 1985, p. 35) brings the history of Israel from the division of the kingdom (or, rather, the refusal to renew the personal union of Israel and Judah) up to Alexander the Great. A concluding twenty-five-page supplement traces the outline of the later history up to Bar Kochba.

The clarity and balance of the first volume feature also here, and there is a persuasive cogency of presentation, making full and effective use of both biblical and non-biblical sources, which reinforces what are often quite traditional views. On the question of Assyrian influence on religion in Judah, Donner points out the ambiguous nature of the account of the altar at Damascus, and the deuteronomistic nature of the account of Hezekiah's reform, and argues that it was only in the seventh century, especially under Manasseh, that Assyrian forms gained entry into the Jerusalem temple. Josiah's reform involved their expulsion, and to that extent was concerned with the purity of Israel's worship; the reform's concern with cultic unity, however, was religious in nature and arose from the demands of the book (an earlier form of Deuteronomy) found in the temple. This is altogether a worthwhile and useful addition to existing accounts of Israel's history.

A. D. H. MAYES

DOWLEY, T.: *High above the Holy Land.* 1986. Pp. 64. (Hodder & Stoughton, London. Price: £9.95. ISBN 0 340 39088 3)

This book consists of twenty-eight high-quality aerial photographs of places mostly with a Christian interest, but including some of the more famous archaeological sites, and general views of the country, illustrating the main features: the Jordan, Samaria, the Dead Sea, Hermon, and Galilee. Each double-page plate has an inset giving a close-up of some detail of the main view, or a relevant human feature. There are accompanying maps identifying the location of the view in many cases, and some line drawings by way of illustration. The accompanying descriptive text, by F. F. Bruce, is usually prefaced by a relevant scripture passage. All in all this is a well-produced book of its kind.

J. R. DUCKWORTH

FRICK, F. S.: *The Formation of the State in Ancient Israel* (The Social World of Biblical Antiquity Series, 4). 1985. Pp. 219. (Almond, JSOT Press, Sheffield. Price: £18.50 (£9.50 paper). ISBN 0 907459 51 X (0 907459 52 8 paper))

Opting for an understanding of history as evolutionary process, rather than as the story of deliberate human actions, the author seeks to unravel something of the enormous complexity of interactions involved in the evolution of the Israelite social system. Having given a critical overview of some general evolutionary processes which have been proposed, the author focuses on the specific question of how and why states were formed and reviews attempts to explain the emergence of the Israelite state. The inadequacy of these has led to the formulation of alternative models which adopt one of three approaches: the conflict approach, the integrative, or the synthetic. The last, being a truly systemic approach which views the state as the output of any one or more of a number of factors without any single prime mover, has been used in three versions. The first two are systemic multilineal models of cultural evolution distinguished by the role assigned to agriculture. The agricultural version is the one particularly appropriate to Israel. It sets forth different evolutionary trajectories relating to varieties in agricultural risk, diversity and productivity, as well as the size and character of the environment. As far as Israel is concerned it is a matter of development from an egalitarian society to a chiefdom to a state, an evolution which is documented more thoroughly as the book proceeds. The third variation of the synthetic model is the catastrophe theory of Renfrew which, in a form highly appropriate for ancient Israel, deals with sudden changes and discontinuities in socio-cultural systems as the product of gradual and continuous changes in the control variables within that system.

The author goes on to describe the nature of early Israel as a segmentary lineage system and then as a chiefdom. The first stage can only be sketched since there is little evidence for it apart from ethnographic analogies, while the second may be described in more detail on the basis of archaeological and literary study. The changes which led from the one to the other, the chiefdom being characterized by the ability, through a social ranking system, to retard the fissioning tendencies of a segmentary society, are seen as inseparable from, though not determined by, techno-environmental factors. The remainder of the book then considers agriculture, and especially the agriculture of the central highlands, from this perspective.

This is a densely written and important study which greatly enriches our understanding of the processes involved in the evolution of early Israel.

A. D. H. MAYES

GARBINI, J.: *Storia e Ideologia nell'Israele Antico* (Biblioteca di storia e storiografia dei tempi biblici, 3). 1986. Pp. 254. (Paideia Editrice, Brescia. Price: Lire 30,000)

This book is an anti-history of Israel, written with a simplicity which belies the complexity of the problem. The basic theory is that the Old Testament story of Israel is written so long after the events. It betrays its ignorance time after time, often displaying clear signs of exilic or postexilic composition. Given the paucity of material remains for the pre-exilic period, there is no way to verify (or totally falsify) most of the record; so a history cannot be written, and we must be content to deal with a religious text inspired by ideological concerns. After an opening chapter reviewing the treatment of Israel's history in scholarly literature, we are given a series of raids on historical epochs — the Davidic 'empire' (dismissed as an 'improbability'), the monarchical period (riddled with implausibilities and unsupported by external evidence), the origin of Yahwism, Abraham, Moses, the twelve tribes, and so on. The often oversimplified arguments will not all survive the thousands of qualifications which the biblical scholar will easily produce; but the basic thesis is one which is finding increasing support in the discipline.

P. R. DAVIES

HOPKINS, D. C.: *The highlands of Canaan: Agricultural life in the early Iron Age* (The Social World of Biblical Antiquity Series, 3). 1985. Pp. 326, including 3 maps. (Almond, JSOT Press, Sheffield, in association with The American Schools of Oriental Research. Price: £20.00, paperback £10.50. ISBN 0 907459 38 2 and 0 907459 39 0 (paperback))

Hopkins studies the interaction of environment and population in the central highlands of Canaan during the transition from LB to IA to shed light on the emergence of Israel. He begins by examining the geomorphology (emphasizing the environmental diversity), the climate (which 'varied around a mean closely resembling present conditions' (p. 107)), the vegetation and soils (attributing the severe degradation to human, not climatic activity), and the population and their settlement patterns (with useful discussion of housing, settlement density, and reasons for siting). Chapters 7–9 turn to agricultural practice: water conservation by terracing and irrigation; soil conservation by fallowing and rotation; the agricultural calendar and patterns of land use. These practices are seen as responses to the varied environmental challenges and opportunities, as the settlers tried to reduce the risks of agricultural failure and raise and feed an adequate labour force. And 'since social relations are the best insurance against subsistence failure', agricultural needs influenced the development of the social structure (p. 261) and formed the matrix for part of Israel's literature (p. 273). Hopkins dispels some myths (e.g., that Israel's emergence depended primarily on the introduction of iron, or the use of plastered cisterns, or the practice of forest clearance) and demonstrates that historians of early Israel must take more seriously the complex environmental realities. But a livelier prose style would have helped greatly.

J. R. BARTLETT

LEMCHE, N. P.: *Early Israel. Anthropological and Historical Studies on the Israelite Society Before the Monarchy* (Supplements to Vetus Testamentum, 37). 1985. Pp. xv, 496 + 1–16 (Danish abstract). Brill, Leiden. Price: Fl. 168.00. ISBN 90 04 07853 3)

Contrary to what might be inferred from the subtitle, this is a well organized monograph, not a collection of separate studies. Armed with a mass of well chosen anthropological and archaeological data, Lemche discusses recent and current theories of the origin and social structure of early Israel. He dismisses views that the early Israelites were nomads or that they were immigrants into or conquerors of Palestine. On the other hand he finds no evidence to support the theory of an internal revolt within Canaanite society. He thinks it probable that the earliest Israelites were people who moved, as individuals or in small groups, from the Canaanite cities which were in a state of economic decline, into the country, where they were enabled to make a living in previously uncultivable regions through the development of new methods of agriculture. This is a well worked-out hypothesis, though like some other hypotheses which it seeks to replace it does not offer a satisfactory explanation for the prominence of the Exodus and Settlement themes in the Pentateuch.

R. N. WHYBRAY

MAZAR, B.: *The Early Biblical Period: Historical Essays*. 1986. Pp. ix, 266. (Israel Exploration Society, Jerusalem. Price: $24.00 ($18.00 for IES members). ISBN 965 221 005 6)

This collection of Mazar's writings, marking the occasion of his eightieth birthday, comprises revised versions of studies published over the last forty years (the dates and places of original publication are not always provided). The essays are: 'The Middle Bronze Age in Canaan', 'The Early Israelite Settlement in the Hill Country', 'The Historical Background of the Book of Genesis', 'The Philistines and the Rise of Israel and Tyre', 'The Military Elite of King David', 'The Cities of the Territory of Dan', 'Geshur and Maachah', 'King David's Scribe and the High Officialdom of the United Monarchy of Israel', 'Pharaoh Shishak's Campaign to the Land of Israel', 'The Aramean Empire and its Relations with Israel', 'The Historical Background of the Samaria Ostraca', 'Lebo-Hamath and the Northern Border of Canaan', 'Beth-she'arim', 'Gaba and Harosheth of the Gentiles', 'The Phoenicians in the Levant', 'The Phoenician Inscriptions from Byblos and the Evolution of the Phoenician–Hebrew Alphabet'. The essays throughout reflect all that is best of particularly Israeli scholarship; at times, as, for example, with the treatment of the Israelite settlement, one might wish for more in the way of theoretical reflection on the issues involved, but the range of disciplines brought to bear here on historical problems, archaeology, epigraphy, historical geography, and textual study, has provided a mine of information for assimilation.

A. D. H. MAYES

MILLER, J. M., and HAYES, J. H.: *A History of Ancient Israel and Judah*. 1986. Pp. 523. (SCM Press, London. Price: £17.50. ISBN 0 334 02042 5)

This attractively produced volume is billed as the first major attempt to write a history of Israel in English — English translations of works by continental scholars do not of course, count — since John Bright's *History* appeared in 1959 (Eng. edn. 1960). It is replete with illustrations, charts, maps, and framed excerpts from relevant extra-biblical sources; it has no footnotes; and in a further bid to help the non-specialist reader terms like Pentateuch, Hexateuch and Deuteronomistic History are discarded in favour of the instantly recognizable 'Genesis–II Kings'. The story-line of the Old Testament from Creation to the end of the Persian period is followed, but the authors decline to engage in historical reconstruction until they arrive in the late pre-monarchical period. Their second chapter ('The Question of Origins') is strong on the problems confronting the would-be historian of the pre-judges period and is an excellent example of that particular genre. The pity is that some readers may conclude not only that Genesis–Judges is no-history, but also that it is nothing else of any value. This is, to be sure, a familiar problem wherever these books are judged by the sole canon of historicity. In their treatment of the monarchical period the authors eschew adherence to a single chronology on the ground that, though systems can be devised, there are too many uncertainties to warrant such. This does not, however, deter them from some lightweight speculation early on about schematic chronology in the Old Testament (pp. 58f.). What is the general reader meant to deduce, for example, from the observation that by 'counting forward with the biblical figures and taking into account chronological data that would have been available to later Jews, one arrives at the conclusion that the year 4000 after creation was approximately the date of the rededication of the Temple in 164 B.C.E. following the Maccabean rebellion' (p. 59)? Is this approximate correspondence almost significant? And are we to think that the rededication was arranged in accordance with some Mesopotomian-type *dārum* principle rather than the political exigencies of the mid-second century B.C.? Chronological agnosticism is also compatible, apparently, with a commitment to Greek data where the Greek and Hebrew traditions differ. For the rest, the authors deserve much credit for a fresh and engaging account of Israelite history. Their expectation that in some quarters their treatment will be regarded as 'overly gullible' in its respectful approach to the Old Testament material is surely unlikely to be fulfilled.

R. P. GORDON

NA'AMAN, N.: *Borders and districts in biblical historiography* (Jerusalem Biblical Studies, 4). 1986. Pp. 275. (Simor, Jerusalem. Price: $24.00. ISBN 965 242 005 0)

Na'aman studies the boundaries of Israel and its tribes, beginning with the relationship between the tribal inheritances and the borders of Canaan. Josh. 13–19 is an historiographic composition, based ultimately on David's census records, but written not for administrative purposes but to symbolize Israel's twelve-tribe unity and legitimise David's conquests, which are described in Judges 1's list of unconquered Canaanite cities. Chapter 3 investigates Marom/Maron (= Tel Qarnei Hittin) and the Zebulun/Naphtali border, resolving a topographical problem by taking Rimmon (*rmwn*, Josh. 19:13) as metathesis for Maron/Marom (*mrwn*). Chapter 4 examines the Ephraim/Manasseh border, and by relocating the land of Hepher prepares the way for the revision of Solomon's first and third administrative districts (1 Kings 4) in chapter 5 (compare map 6 with Aharoni's *Land of the Bible*[2] map 23). Chapter 6 is a welcome new look at the Levitic cities, undermining much scholarly fantasy; chapter 7 neatly explores Egyptian and Israelite perceptions of Sinai. Na'aman requires of the reader close attention to text and map — but as in all such studies the reader needs to know exactly which map the author is using. Na'aman's major concern is to show how the geographical lists were used by the biblical historiographers and how they relate to the administration of the united kingdom, and here Na'aman offers a useful corrective to those who view all lists as straightforward records, and, overall, an original contribution to Israel's historical geography.

J. R. BARTLETT

SILVER, M.: *Economic Structures of the Ancient Near East.* 1985. Pp. 211. (Croom Helm, London. Price: £22.50. ISBN 0 7099 3370 3)

The author, a professor of economics in the City University of New York, has already put Old Testament scholars in his debt with his 1983 study of Israel's political economy, *Prophets and Markets* (not noted in the *Book*

List). The latter, presupposing that changes in the economy may cause significant changes in the cultural and religious superstructure, which changes have a 'feedback' effect on the economy, argued that the new affluence of Israelite society in the eighth century led to demands for social justice, and that the prophets who, as educated members of the establishment, promoted reforms along these lines, were responsible for the resulting decline in Israel's economic and political strength. An appendix to that book on 'Markets and Entrepreneurs in the Ancient Near East' provided a preview of the more comprehensive study which is now offered.

The present study begins by examining the role of temples as commercial centres which protected and facilitated trade, promoted professional standards, facilitated monopolistic practices, and in general reduced transaction costs, so serving economic growth. The prevalence of family ties in business was also a reaction to high transaction costs, in that opportunistic behaviour within the firm was thereby diminished and trade secrets were protected. A part of this same strategy was the employment of women in managerial positions, and the use of slaves whose activities could be controlled. Having examined the evidence for private industrial enterprise, as opposed to temple or state monopoly, and for long distance trade, by road and water, with its effects in terms of costs, the study goes on to refute in detail the view that markets, as regulators of supply and demand, with prices of goods determined on that basis, were not to be found in the Ancient Near East. Price variations, resulting from seasonal, political and other factors, point to the existence of true markets rather than a state economy organized on the principle of redistribution. Both textual and archaeological evidence point to long periods of free market activity interspersed with periods of state economic regulation. This is a thoroughly documented study, which should serve as an indispensable resource for future study in a field with which students of Israelite history and religion will wish to become more familiar.

A. D. H. MAYES

WISEMAN, D. J.: *Nebuchadrezzar and Babylon* (The Schweich Lectures, 1983). 1985. Pp. xii, 142 including 14 figs, 9 plates. (Oxford University Press for the British Academy, Oxford. Price: £17.00. ISBN 0 19 726040 3)

Though not comprehensive, a great deal of material has been gathered and pressed into this book, which deals with Nebuchadnezzar II of Babylon. The first chapter covers the man and his achievements, the second deals with Babylon as his city, and the third brings together generally related material which did not find a place in the first two. Though the actual lectures were an abbreviated version of this text, the book reads like lectures: there is rarely any critical discussion of sources, but conclusions are presented briefly, with reference to appropriate bibliography. This is unfortunate since many biblical scholars will be unable to make independent evaluation of much of the material drawn upon, and some of the conclusions are controversial. Thus on page 45 two generally rejected interpretations of E.KI, a writing of the name of Babylon, are noted, while on page 91f. J. Brinkman's judicious comments on this writing are misrepresented as referring to a Sumerian myth. Daniel is treated as a primary source from the first page, only on page 109 are the doubts of many scholars mentioned. Further, the book teems with small errors of all kinds, and while one might blame the printer for 'Medean', who is responsible for 'Philistinian' and 'Edomic'?

W. G. LAMBERT

4. TEXT AND VERSIONS

Barthélemy, D.: *Critique textuelle de l'Ancien Testament.* 2: *Isaïe, Jérémie, Lamentations* (Orbis Biblicus et Orientalis, 50/2). 1986. Pp. xviii, *71, 1013. (Éditions Universitaires, Fribourg. Price: Sw.Fr. 300.00; Sub. price: Sw.Fr. 270.00. ISBN 2 8271 0322 2. Vandenhoeck & Ruprecht, Göttingen. ISBN 3 525 53692 5)

The first volume of this weighty and expensive series was noticed in *B.L.* 1984, pp. 43–44; for a more detailed and critical discussion see the writer's review in *Journal of Theological Studies*, 37, 1986, pp. 445–50. The procedure has been slightly altered (p. *1) in response to criticisms, but the result seems to have been to make the work even longer: over a thousand pages for a selection of examples from two major books and one short one! The editor's intense interest in the *history* of Bible versions is reflected in the lengthy introduction as well as throughout the comments. But, the more one sees of it, the more one feels that there is something perverse in the entire design of this work, with its stifling accumulation of names of past exegetes, its level of scholarship which will be far too profound for the practical Bible translators who are supposed to be guided by it, its bizarre practice whereby the committee 'votes' for the degree of probability to be ascribed to a form of text, and its acceptance of far-fetched exegetical speculations to justify the MT.

J. Barr

Clarke, E. G. (ed.): *Newsletter for Targumic and Cognate Studies.* 13. 1986. Pp. 12. (Department of Near Eastern Studies, University of Toronto. ISSN 0704 59005)

As well as published articles and books in the fields of Targumic and cognate studies (this latter including much useful information on non-Targumic Aramaic texts), the editor has included the titles of the seventeen papers on Targum read during the 1985–86 session by members of the research group on Targumim convened by Professor M. H. Goshen-Gottstein at the Institute for Advanced Studies of the Hebrew University in Jerusalem.

R. P. Gordon

Estin, C.: *Les Psautiers de Jérome à la lumière des traductions juives antérieures* (Collectanea Biblica Latina, 15). 1984. Pp. 238. (San Girolamo, Rome; distributed by Brepols, Turnhout. Price: B.Fr. 2,950)

This reworking of a thesis done under J. Fontaine centres on a detailed and accurate study of Jerome's use of the antecedent Greek versions as presented in Origen's *Hexapla.* After chapters surveying the texts before Jerome and his successive versions of the Psalms, and summarizing Jerome's quantitative dependence on the various Greek versions, the texts for detailed study are presented. These correspond to the Ambrosian palimpsest fragments of the Hexapla on the Psalms published by G. Mercati (Rome, 1958): these cover parts of Psalms (LXX) 17, 27–31, 34, 35, 45 and 88. The corresponding witness of Jerome's versions is given in columns, the underlying Hebrew and various Greek renderings being given word by word in an apparatus below, with textual notes on all the evidence. The following chapters study 'Jerome's criteria for choosing between the Greek versions' and 'stylistic aspects of Jerome's work'. Two appendices survey the evidence of Jerome's letters and textual variants. This is the most careful study yet of Jerome's principles and methods as a translator, though it is done on a very restricted base, determined by the texts surviving in Ambr. pal. 1098. Jerome appears on the one hand as firmly attached to the LXX-based liturgical tradition, but on the other as often arbitrarily eclectic.

R. P. R. MURRAY

GREENLEE, J. H.: *Scribes, Scrolls and Scripture: A Student's Guide to New Testament Textual Criticism*. 1985. Pp. viii, 102. (Eerdmans, Grand Rapids, and Paternoster Press, Exeter. Price: £6.95. ISBN 0 8028 0082 3)

This is a simple and mainly reliable account of the textual criticism of the New Testament, intended for conservative and fundamentalist Christians who are alarmed at the very thought that KJV might not be totally accurate and trustworthy. The author himself displays the tension that arises, when he says, after regretfully dismissing the *pericope de adultera* from the text of the Fourth Gospel, 'It is nevertheless clear that it cannot be called a part of the inspired gospel record'. He has yet to learn about canonical criticism. The name of Griesbach is never mentioned, and there are no suggestions for further reading.

B. LINDARS

HARL, M.: *La Genèse* (La Bible d'Alexandrie, 1: Traduction du texte grec de la Septante, introduction et notes). 1986. Pp. 336. (Éditions du Cerf, Paris. Price: Fr. 145.00. ISBN 2 204 02591 7)

This volume is the first of a series which is intended to encompass the whole of the Greek Bible, the remaining books of the Pentateuch being planned to appear within the next four or five years. It consists of a French translation of the Septuagint text, preceded by an introduction and accompanied by notes. The introduction is in three parts: the first considers the title, the divisions of the text (including the divisions of the Hebrew), and the early Jewish and Christian traditions of interpretation; the second part looks at the Greek vocabulary: God, covenant, man, religion, and everyday life; the third part is concerned with Greek style. The notes, which occupy somewhat more space than the text, are of three sorts: philological (explaining the precise meaning of the Greek), comparative (comparing the Greek and the Hebrew), and exegetical (referring to the Jewish and Christian interpretations based on the Greek text). The volume concludes with four useful and ingenious indexes: discrepancies between LXX and MT in the matter of proper names; Greek words studied in the introduction and notes; themes (a French–Greek glossary); and passages which are important either because the Greek is notably different from the Hebrew or because they give rise to important patristic interpretations.

The massive project of which this volume represents the first-fruits could hardly be undertaken (nowadays) by one person. In fact it is the work of a team, originally formed by Madame Harl herself in 1981 and directed by her since — or rather several teams, since the work has snowballed, and in addition to the metropolitan team in Paris there are now 'regional' groups in Aix en Provence, Lyons, and Grenoble. The present reviewer must declare an interest: he has often been privileged to sit in on the deliberations of the Paris team, which bring together specialists on patristic Greek, Hebrew, and cognate disciplines such as archaeology or iconography, with research students and occasional visitors; and he can testify to the meticulous attention to detail which often leads to an hour being spent on the translation and annotation of a single verse or two. This is a splendid initiative: it is far more than a translation of a translation; it is a work of high intelligence and sensibility, which will bring a text which is one of the foundation stones of Christianity within the reach of anyone who can read French, and also has a good deal to say to those who know Greek.

N. R. M. DE LANGE

KOHLENBERGER, J. R. III: *The NIV Interlinear Hebrew–English Old Testament*. Vol. 4: *Isaiah–Malachi*. 1985. Pp. xiii, 591. (Zondervan, Grand Rapids, Michigan. Price: $24.95. ISBN 0 310 38880 5)

This is the fourth and final volume of the work which was described in *B.L.* 1982, p. 36; 1983, p. 42. A brief Introduction reiterates the purpose of this tool and gives salutary advice and warnings. The work is chiefly meant for those who are 'beginning Hebrew students as well as those reviving their language skills or improving their reading pace and translation skills'. The type-setting of these handsome volumes is a great achievement. The interlinear literal word-by-word renderings, backed up by the column of NIV on each page, will generally be found helpful, though there are problems. In Jonah 1:5–6, for example, 'from on her' should be 'from on them', while 'how to-you sleeping' should be 'what to-you sleeper'. This aid will give courage to many to use the Hebrew Bible.

J. H. EATON

LEVIN, I.: *The Quedlinburg Itala. The Oldest Illustrated Biblical Manuscript* (Litterae Textuales: A Series on Manuscripts and their Texts). 1985. Pp. 128, including 8 colour plates and 58 half-tone illustrations. (Brill, Leiden. Price: Fl. 96.00. ISBN 90 04 07093 1)

This beautifully produced (though only paperback) volume, measuring 35 × 29 cm, is the fruit of doctoral studies in New York, research in Rome and a fellowship at Dumbarton Oaks. The subtitle reveals the importance of the subject. This uncial codex of a pre-Vulgate text of (at least) Samuel–Kings was preserved in Quedlinburg (near Magdeburg), but sadly the extant fragments of this unique manuscript are limited to five folios, including six sides of text and four of illustrations, grouped in fours on three pages and a pair on the fourth. The codex was destroyed by a seventeenth-century bookbinder who used it as binding material for civic records. Part of the pigment of each surviving painted page adheres to the boards to which the leaves were glued. This makes reconstruction of the pictures difficult but not impossible. Dr Levin provides excellent colour photographs of the painted pages and of their imprints on boards, and reconstructs the subjects in clear line drawings. The successive chapters examine the script (the extant fragments are from 1 Sam. 9 and 15, 2 Sam. 2–3 and 1 Kings 5–6), the still decipherable cursive instructions to the artist, and above all the vivid illustrations to the extant passages: their style, technique, indications of tradition and imperial imagery, their likely origin (Rome) and probable date (second quarter of the fifth century). All the argumentation is abundantly supported by good illustration of comparative material. This is a major contribution to the subject of early bible illustration, which will surely remain definitive.

R. P. R. MURRAY

MCCARTER, P. K., JR.: *Textual Criticism: Recovering the Text of the Hebrew Bible*. 1986. Pp. 94. (Fortress Press, Philadelphia. Price: $4.95. ISBN 0 8006 0471 7)

After a refreshing survey (Chapter 1) of the logical principles of textual criticism, the causes of corruption are carefully analysed (Chapter 2). The examples are well chosen, if sometimes dogmatically treated (e.g. the words found in LXX and Samar, but not in MT at Lev. 15:3 are declared original, without regard to their possibly being an expansion imitating V. 25). The last chapter offers criteria for choice between rival readings surviving either in Hebrew or in an ancient translation. No example and little discussion, however, appears of the treatment — whether by emendation or through comparative philology — of the many places where no satisfactory reading seems extant. The author instead teaches emendation by peppering his own text with mistakes (e.g. *h'yrym* for 'the cities', 'errors of the scribes' for *tiqqūnē sōpĕrīm*, and the ascription to Pesh. at 1 Sam. 14:41 of a text longer than MT and resembling LXX). One appendix briefly characterizes what he considers the main witnesses in each biblical book. Texts preserved in Hebrew, and LXX, receive good coverage throughout; too little is said of the other ancient translations, at one point (p. 68) dubbed versions of MT. Another appendix gives publication details up to 1985 of Dead Sea copies. There is also a glossary of text-critical terms.

M. P. WEITZMAN

PEREZ CASTRO, F. (ed.): *El Codice de Profetas de El Cairo.* IV: *Isaias* (Textos y Estudios 'Cardenal Cisneros', 36). 1986. Pp. 227. (Instituto 'Arias Montano', Consejo Superior de Investigaciones Cientificas, Madrid. Price: Ptas. 2,800. ISBN 84 00 06174 8)

This part of the Cairo Codex, containing the book of Isaiah, has been prepared for publication by Carmen Munoz Abad, Emilia Fernandez Tejero, Maria Teresa Ortega Monasterio, and Maria Josefa Azcarraga Servert. The volume follows the pattern of the preceding volumes, see *B.L.* 1985, p. 46 and *B.L.* 1983, pp. 42f.

P. WERNBERG-MØLLER

(*Peshitta*): *The Old Testament in Syriac According to the Peshitta Version*, edited on behalf of the International Organization for the Study of the Old Testament by the Peshitta Institute, Leiden. Part III, fasc. 3: *Ezekiel*, prepared by M. J. Mulder. 1985. Pp. xxxvi, 113. (Brill, Leiden. Price: Fl. 82.00. ISBN 90 04 07314 0)

The Introduction to this fascicle is among the most informative, both in reminding us about the principles governing the edition (on which see *B.L.* 1977, p. 38 and 1978, p. 44), and in describing the manuscripts. These are considered in seven groups (which, however, do not constitute families except in one case): (A) five manuscripts of the sixth to the eighth centuries, including the Ambrosian 7a1, chosen as the basic text for the whole edition, and the Paris 8a1, judged to contain the best text; (B) four palimpsest fragments from the fifth to the seventh centuries; (C) a family consisting of the Laurentian 9a1 and four copies; (D) five manuscripts containing the Prophetic Books (ninth to twelfth centuries); (E) the 'Buchanan Bible'; (F) Lectionaries, six Western and two Eastern (ninth to eleventh centuries), and finally (G) twenth-three manuscripts later than the twelfth century, some of which have been collated in full, others only in part; these are not cited in the second apparatus but their data are filed in the Peshitta Institute. The printing of the text appears to be of the usual excellent standard.

R. P. R. MURRAY

SODERLUND, S.: *The Greek Text of Jeremiah: A Revised Hypothesis* (JSOT Supplement Series, 47). 1985. Pp. xi, 304. (JSOT Press, Sheffield. Price: £18.50. ISBN 1 85075 028 9)

This book is taken up with inner-Septuagintal textual problems in the book of Jeremiah and also with relations between the Hebrew and Greek texts of that book. It offers a detailed consideration of Jeremiah xxix, involving Greek manuscripts, patristic citations and daughter versions of the Septuagint. In another chapter there is a critical essay on J. Ziegler's edition of the Septuagint of Jeremiah, notable for the mastery which Soderlund has

achieved over this complicated piece of work. His critique will be a great help to any who intend to come to grips with Ziegler's edition in connection with a more comprehensive study of the book of Jeremiah.

A chapter is devoted to an appraisal of Emanuel Tov's preference for a hypothesis of revision over one of a plurality of translators in order to explain disparate phenomena in the Greek text of Jeremiah, and a final chapter consists of a criticism of J. G. Janzen's book. Although Soderlund is more cautious than Janzen and less inclined to assume that a Hebrew *Vorlage* is, for the most part, reflected in the earliest Greek text that can be recovered, he is, nevertheless, travelling the same road as Janzen is so far as he is not disposed to explain the shorter Greek text as an abridgement unrelated to a Hebrew text.

The reviewer examined the thesis from which the book derives and was very impressed by it. The book, however, does not contain a single, interlocking, cumulative argument and tends rather to break up into cognate but independent critical essays, each of which has its own conclusion. The value of the book would be enhanced if it were supplied with an index of the passages of the book of Jeremiah or other biblical passages which are discussed in it and this would be a straightforward task. It would encourage scholars whose primary interest is in the Massoretic text to use Soderlund as a work of reference. It would also perhaps advance his concern that every passage should be treated on its merits and that the explanatory power of a hypothesis should not be claimed too hastily.

W. McKane

Strothmann, W., assisted by Johannes, K., and Zumpe, M.: *Konkordanz zur syrischen Bibel: Die Propheten.* (Göttinger Orientforschungen, Series 1, vol. 25). 1984. Pp. xxviii, 2679 (4 vols). (Otto Harrassowitz, Wiesbaden. Price: DM 380.00)

This work, covering the prophetic books (including Daniel), continues the projected Göttingen concordance to the Peshitta of the Old Testament. Earlier volumes covered Qohelet (ed. Strothmann, 1973) and Psalms (ed. N. Sprenger, 1976; *B.L.* 1979, p. 49). Under every entry title, the different forms are carefully broken down into separate lists by gender, number and so on. Even prepositions are listed, albeit only those with pronomial suffixes. Names throughout the Old Testament will appear in a future volume, and are excluded here. Upon spot checks, the listings seem complete, except for many entries under the noun *brā.* Hebrew equivalents are not given. The arrangement of entries, though planned to follow Brockelmann's Lexicon, is sometimes odd (e.g. adjective *gawāyā* stands among forms of noun *gawā*). Curiously, despite the progress of the Leiden critical edition, this concordance rests on the Walton and Urmia prints. (Thus references in Ezek. 21 are five verses behind MT.) It is nevertheless very useful, given the rarity of variants that concern vocabulary.

M. P. Weitzman

Syrén, R.: *The Blessings in the Targums. A Study on the Targumic Interpretations of Genesis 49 and Deuteronomy 33* (Acta Academiae Aboensis, Ser. A, vol. 64, nr 1). 1986. Pp. 259. (Åbo Akademi, Åbo. Price: FIM. 85.00. ISBN 951 649 223 1)

A thorough and well-documented examination of the several Pentateuchal Targums to two chapters which, because of their poetical nature, tempted the ancient Targumists to disclose their hand to an uncommon degree. Syrén distinguishes between 'translation' and 'addition' and examines them separately. The section on 'translation' is followed by a comparison with other ancient versions of the chapters. Theological and historical elements

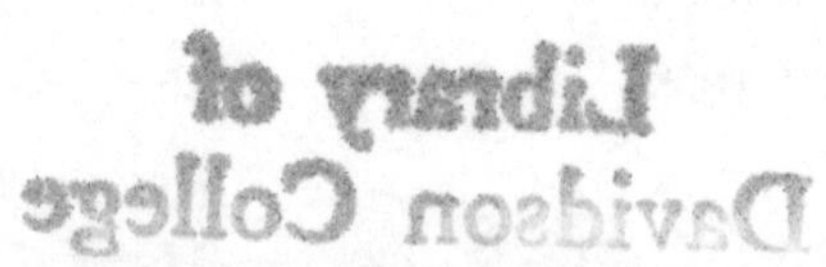

figure prominently in Section II ('The Additions'), as do parallel expositions in other Jewish and Christian sources. This section also includes under 'Passages which may reflect actual conditions' observations on toponymy, liturgical life-setting, etc. The third main section discusses the relationship between Targum Onqelos and the Palestinian Targums, concluding that Onqelos is substantially dependent upon some sort of Palestinian Targum tradition. Syrén, however, does not regard the extant Palestinian Targums to Genesis 49 and Deuteronomy 33 as representing the earliest form of the Targum, if only because the influence of other Targum passages is evident in these chapters. In this connection, it would have been interesting to have Syrén's considered comments on P. Grelot's theory about Targum Isaiah 63:1–6 and the Palestinian Targums to Genesis 49:11f. Many other questions are, however, discussed ably throughout, including that of the relationship of the Peshitta in particular to the Pentateuchal Targums, the relative dating of literal and non-literal Targum, and the significance of individual verses in Targum — for example, Pseudo-Jonathan to Deuteronomy 33:11, which Syrén is happy to date to the time of John Hyrcanus I. The book is adequately indexed, but the incidence of misprints is high.

R. P. GORDON

TRAFTON, J. L.: *The Syriac Version of the Psalms of Solomon: A Critical Evaluation*. (Septuagint and Cognate Studies, 11). 1985. Pp. xvi, 276. (Scholars Press, Atlanta, Georgia. Price: $22.95. ISBN 0 89130 910 1. Paperback price: $15.95. ISBN 0 89130 911 X)

This monograph adopts as a working hypothesis the general opinion that the Psalms of Solomon, which are extant only in Syriac and Greek, were originally written in Hebrew. It is concerned to evaluate the Syriac version as a witness to the original text, and is the first full-scale investigation of the Syriac version *in toto* with the purpose of determining the language from which it was translated. The conclusions reached are that the Syriac version was made at least primarily directly from the Hebrew original, though a Greek manuscript may have been consulted for two passages in Psalm 13, that the Greek version is overall a slightly more reliable witness to the original text than the Syriac, but that in at least forty readings the Syriac is to be preferred to the Greek. The writer has substantiated his main thesis that the Syriac version is a significant textual witness for the Psalms of Solomon.

A. GELSTON

Vetus Latina. Die Reste der altlateinischen Bibel, nach Petrus Sabatier neu gesammelt und herausgegeben von der Erzabtei Beuron. 11/1: *Sapientia Salomonis*. Herausgegeben von Walter Thiele. 8. Lieferung: Sap 18, 18 bis Schluss; Nachträge, Register. 1985. Pp. 561–98 and 1–8. (Verlag Herder: Freiburg im Breisgau. Price: DM 39.00; sub. price: DM 34.50. ISBN 3 451 00487 9)

The first fascicle of this major edition appeared in 1977 (see *B.L.* 1980, p. 48); since then portions have been published regularly, and this one brings the text of Wisdom to an end. The scrupulous scholarship of the whole is reinforced by the six pages of additions and corrections; the *Register* enables the reader to see at a glance the coverage of the individual manuscripts and the places at which patristic sources have cited the book. The edition has deserved the highest praise throughout.

J. BARR

5. EXEGESIS AND MODERN TRANSLATIONS

AITKEN, K. T.: *Proverbs* (The Daily Study Bible: Old Testament). 1986. Pp. x, 264. (Saint Andrew Press, Edinburgh; Westminster Press, Philadelphia. Price: £4.25. ISBN 0 7152 0533 1)

A wide-ranging, readable presentation of the book of Proverbs which takes trouble to link material in the book with similar proverbial material elsewhere in the Old Testament, notably the historical books, but sometimes in the New Testament. In the first nine chapters the Hebrew order of verses is followed, but from chapter 10 verses are arranged, completely out of sequence to form blocks treating similar topics — to help the popular reader: such topics include types of character (the simple, the scoffer, the righteous, etc.), wisdom in various settings (home and community, market, lawcourt, etc.) — some proverbs not included under headings are treated at the end. A full (and essential!) index enables the reader to find any particular verse in this confusing arrangement. This arrangement sadly breaks up, for example, the block of proverbs similar to the Egyptian Proverbs of Amenemope in 22:17–24:22; however, it does facilitate thematic discussion on specific issues for the general reader, for whom the series is intended.

J. G. SNAITH

AULD, A. G.: *Kings*. (The Daily Study Bible: Old Testament). 1986. Pp. ix, 259. (Saint Andrew Press, Edinburgh; Westminster Press, Philadelphia. Price: £4.25. ISBN 0 7152 0523 4)

One of the latest additions to the Daily Study Bible, written by Dr Graeme Auld, covers the two books of Kings, including a printing of the RSV text, in some two hundred and fifty pages. Because of this it was inevitable that the author's exegetical comments had to be cut short, but they never give the impression of being too general and superficial. It is obvious that Dr Auld has made himself fully conversant with the great number of literary, historical, and exegetical questions that arise in connection with those two books. But one of the strengths of his work is that the author has not been trapped in complicated treatments of detail; his exposition of the text is direct, clear, and succinct.

Of course one would wish a fuller treatment of many subjects, such as the reasons for not accepting the general view about the Succession Narrative. Again because of the rather provocative practice of placing two alternative interpretations in the form of a question (cf. on 1 Kings 1:4), the author's own view at times eludes us. Furthermore, the movement from the Old Testament itself to a Christian interpretation is at times sudden and jerky, e.g. the comment on fulfilment on p. 19. These observations, however, are not criticisms of the author, but emphasize that, because of the almost impossible task of having to expound the meaning of the two books for the ancient Hebrews and at the same time indicating what they mean for twentieth-century Christians within the restricted space allotted to him, such short-cuts could not be avoided. Dr Auld has tackled the task valiantly, has produced a readable commentary and has competently fulfilled the aims of the Daily Bible Study series.

G. H. JONES

BEAUCAMP, E.: *Israël en prière. Des Psaumes au Notre Père* (Lire la Bible, 69). 1985. Pp. 263. (Éditions du Cerf, Paris. Price: Fr. 84.00. ISBN 2 204 02265 9)

The chapters in this book are arranged in the order of the petitions of the Lord's Prayer, and Beaucamp considers the relation to it of the Old Testament psalms. He notes the background of the psalms in the religions of the ancient Near East and their place in the faith of Israel, and also seeks to bring out their significance for the Christian reader. The book ends with a study of Psalms 22 and 119.

J. A. EMERTON

BIBELKOMMISSIONEN (trans.): *Bibeln. Tillägg till Gamla testamentet. De apokrypha eller deuterokanoniska skrifterna.* 1986. Pp. 530, 2 maps. (Liber Allmänna Förlaget, Bibelkommissionens utgåva, Stockholm. Price: Sw.Kr. 170.00. ISBN 91 38 09373 1; ISSN 0375 250 X)

This volume contains the new Swedish translation of the Apocrypha in its entirety (cf. *B.L.* 1985, p. 49). In the main title the neutral term 'tillägg' ('addition', 'supplement') is deliberately used, the terms 'Apocrypha' and 'Deuterocanonical Writings' being relegated to the subtitle. The books are arranged in accordance with their literary character: narrative (Tobit, Judith, and Esther, of which the entire Greek text is translated), historical (1 and 2 Maccabees), Wisdom (of Solomon and of Jesus Sirach), additions to the prophetic books (Baruch, the Letter of Jeremiah, additions to Daniel), and the Prayer of Manasseh. Careful critical scrutiny has been devoted to the text on which the translation is based. Whereas the 1921 Swedish translation of Tobit was made from the shorter Greek text, the longer text is the basis of the present rendering. Sirach has been translated from the Greek text, variants being recorded in one appendix and selected passages from the Hebrew text in another. There are brief introductions to the Apocrypha as a whole and to the several books, short explanatory footnotes to the translation, an appendix containing longer but concise notes on persons, places, and special terms, and some useful tables, an index to the sections of the books, and twenty pages of text-critical notes. Thus this splendid volume contains not only an excellent new translation but also materials for a miniature handbook to the Apocrypha.

G. W. ANDERSON

BOICE, J. M.: *The Minor Prophets: an expositional commentary.* Vol. 2: *Micah-Malachi.* 1986. Pp. 281. (Zondervan, Grand Rapids, Michigan. Price: $14.95. ISBN 0 310 21580 3)

Writing for the general Christian public as an aid to devotion the author enlivens his material with numerous anecdotes and lengthy digressions, and ranges widely over both Old Testament and New Testament by way of illustration, undoubtedly reflecting his preaching style. The content is generally sound, and there are lively sketches of historical background. As a popular way of approaching the prophets for devotional purposes it is readable and informative. Those who are not offended by its fundamentalist presuppositions will find it deeply challenging.

G. I. EMMERSON

BRAULIK, G.: *Deuteronomium 1–16,17.* (Die Neue Echter Bibel, 15. Lfg.). 1986. Pp. 120. (Echter Verlag, Würzburg. Price: DM 28.00; sub. price: DM 24.00. ISBN 3 429 00997 9)

'It is a particular concern of this commentary to expound the value as a guide in affairs of the church and the community which Deuteronomy has enjoyed even to our own times' (p. 17). The book whose present value is thus stressed is seen as having as its original core the cultic decalogue of Exodus 34:10–26 and the ethical decalogue of Deuteronomy 5:6–21. These were commented on and elaborated, the cultic decalogue was reformulated in terms of centralization following Hezekiah's reforms, and an early form of the book was the basis of Josiah's reform. The similarities between Deuteronomy and vassal treaties owe their existence to the covenant theology which was formulated in Judah to oppose the might of Assyria. After the exile the traditions were reinterpreted in terms of a new covenant theology which stressed not the obedience of Israel but the grace of God in response to the faith of the Patriarchs. The exilic and post-exilic situations led to an expansion of the legislative material of chapters 19–25. Among the earliest examples of the *Wirkungsgeschichte* of Deuteronomy is the Temple Scroll, which may originate from the fourth or third centuries. As is usual in this series, the text of the *Einheitsübersetzung* is given at the top of each page with commentary beneath.

J. W. ROGERSON

BRUCE, F. F.: *The International Bible Commentary with the New International Version*. 1986. Pp. xv, 1629. (Zondervan Publishing House, Grand Rapids, Michigan. Price: $24.95. ISBN 0 551 01291 9)

This volume is a revision of the earlier 1979 edition of the work (reviewed in the *B.L.* 1981, p. 55), largely demanded by the substitution of the New International Version of the Bible for the Revised Standard Version as the basic text commented upon. One supposes that the change was dictated largely by the American market, where the more conservative look upon the RSV with suspicion, but are happy with a version which comes from the 'evangelical stable'. Professor Bruce has taken over the general direction through the death of its earlier general editor, G. C. D. Howley, and, as one would expect, he has ensured an updating of bibliographies and the correction of errors on the earlier edition. It is certainly reasonably priced and can be recommended.

J. J. HAMMER

BRUEGGEMANN, W.: *The Message of the Psalms. A Theological Commentary* (Augsburg Old Testament Studies). 1984. Pp. 206. (Augsburg Publishing House, Minneapolis. Price: $10.95. ISBN 0 8066 2120 6, paperback)

This is not a commentary on the entire Psalter. The royal psalms, the songs of Zion, and the historical psalms are omitted as not being of prime importance for the general aim of the work, which is theological and pastoral. Critical methods in the study of the Psalms (as in the work of Gunkel, Mowinckel, and Westermann) are presupposed rather than expounded, and account is taken of sociological and rhetorical analysis. The psalms treated are arranged in three groups, expressing the themes orientation (joy in the goodness of God, creation, law), disorientation (the anguish of alienation, suffering, and death), and new orientation (hymns of thanksgiving). These themes are linked to Jewish suffering followed by hope and new life, and the crucifixion of Jesus followed by resurrection. This is all worked out in detail in the interpretation of individual psalms, always in close application to the experience of the believer and worshipper. A brief concluding chapter relates the Psalms to theodicy. This thought-provoking book requires and repays close study.

G. W. ANDERSON

BRUEGGEMANN, W.: *Sōseiki*. Translated by T. Mukai. 1986. Pp. 642. (Nihon Kirisuto Kyōdan Shuppan-kyoku, Tokyo. Price: ¥6,200)

This is a Japanese translation of *Genesis* (Interpretation: A Biblical Commentary for Teaching and Preaching) (1982; *B.L.* 1985, p. 50). A bibliography of the book in Japanese and a postscript are appended by the translator.

K. K. SACON

CARROLL, R. P.: *Jeremiah: A Commentary* (Old Testament Library). 1986. Pp. 847. (SCM Press, London. Price: £20.00. ISBN 0 334 02093 X)

This massive commentary represents the detailed application to the book of Jeremiah of the approach explained in Dr Carroll's earlier book, *From Chaos to Covenant. Uses of Prophecy in the Book of Jeremiah* (1981; *B.L.* 1982, p. 58). Central to it is the thesis that Jeremiah is not a biography of the prophet, incorporating his recorded utterances in prose and verse, but an anthology of material, only a small amount of which consists of the genuine (poetic) utterances of the prophet himself. The editors, who belong to 'deuteronomic' circles of the exilic and post-exilic period, have used Jeremiah's poems together with a great many later narratives and sermons to create a work which conformed to the idea of a 'prophetic' book current in their day. Despite its length, the commentary is not intended as an exhaustive guide to all the critical problems of the book (though there are few on which light is not shed) but represents a consistent reading of the text from this redaction-critical point of view. Especially interesting is the respect accorded to the Greek version, which Carroll regards as an earlier edition than the present Hebrew book and which he accordingly comments on in detail. His work is refreshingly free from the neutral style one associates with large commentaries, so that even in passages of detailed exegesis one has the sense that the author is addressing the reader directly. This makes it possible to read through the commentary, rather than merely consulting it, in a way which is seldom the case with a work of this length. Scholars who see the book of Jeremiah differently from Dr Carroll will naturally find much to disagree with, but will nevertheless recognize here a stimulating work which no one who seeks to understand the prophetic books of the Bible can afford to overlook. The bibliography is extensive, but does not attempt to be exhaustive: it lists the works which were used, rather than all the works that were consulted, in writing the commentary. In every way this is one man's reading of Jeremiah, rather than a 'definitive' commentary for all time: and none the worse for that.

J. BARTON

COGGINS, R. J., and RE'EMI, S. P.: *Israel among the Nations: A Commentary on the Books Nahum, Obadiah, Esther* (International Theological Commentary). 1985. Pp. x, 140. (Handsel Press, Edinburgh. Price: £4.95. ISBN 0 905312 52 X. Eerdmans, Grand Rapids, Michigan. ISBN O 8028 0048 3)

The aim and nature of this series of commentaries have been indicated in *B.L.* 1985, pp. 48 and 56f. The title of the present volume explains the grouping of these particular Books in a single commentary, though one might have expected Jonah and Ruth to be included in the same category. These Books are not the most readily susceptible of theological interpretation, but the commentators (Coggins on Nahum and Obadiah, Re'emi on Esther) have handled a difficult assignment well. Both show a judicious caution in handling modern scholarly theories. The cream of the theological exposition is to be found in the introductions, which in the case of Obadiah and Esther are nearly half as long as the commentaries. The reviewer is left wondering how meaningful to the intended readership are the discussions of textual variants in Nahum and Obadiah or the allusions to the Additions in the LXX of Esther.

A. GELSTON

CRAIGIE, P. C.: *Ezekieru-sho.* Translated by K. Tomoeda. 1986. Pp. 494. (Shinkyō Shuppan-sha, Tokyo. Price: ¥2,900)

This is a Japanese translation of *Ezekiel* (The Daily Study Bible: Old Testament) (1983; *B.L.* 1984, p. 51).

K. K. SACON

DAVIDSON, R.: *Ecclesiastes and the Song of Solomon* (The Daily Study Bible: Old Testament). 1986. Pp. viii, 162. (Saint Andrew Press, Edinburgh; Westminster Press, Philadelphia. Price: £4.25. ISBN 0 7152 0537 4)

This commentary follows the same general form as other volumes in this series: the language is pleasantly non-technical and readable. The pages are not littered with footnotes or references, but it is plain that the author has done his homework well. Anyone knowing scholarly literature on these books can recognize knowledge of them appearing at the right moments. References in the portion on *Ecclesiastes* to topics like job-satisfaction and Watergate show that the commentary keeps topical, relating well to contemporary life. *Ecclesiastes* is shown to be particularly thought-provoking in just the way its author intended. On the *Song of Solomon* different interpretations are sketched briefly in the Introduction, and lightly picked up in the commentary; but links between human love and the mystical self-giving love of God are explained in four pages of 'Retrospect' at the end — adroitly done. A stimulating study in readable language.

J. G. SNAITH

DAVIDSON, R.: *Jeremiah*, Volume 2, *and Lamentations* (The Daily Study Bible: Old Testament). 1986. Pp. ix, 214. (Saint Andrew Press, Edinburgh; Westminster Press, Philadelphia, Pennsylvania. Price: £4.25. ISBN 0 7152 0529 3)

An attractively written devotional commentary on Jeremiah 21–52 and Lamentations, based on a careful critical exegesis of the text. (For the companion volume, see *B.L.* 1984, p. 51.) The reader who wants to use these two Old Testament texts in Christian reflection will be well served by Professor Davidson's lively and challenging presentation.

J. BARTON

DAVIDSON, R.: *Sōseiki.* Translated by Y. Ohno. 1986. Pp. 394. (Shinkyō Shuppan-sha, Tokyo. Price: ¥4,200)

This is a Japanese translation of the Cambridge Bible Commentary on the N.E.B.: *Genesis 1–11* (1973); see *B.L.* 1974, pp. 31–32) and *Genesis 12–50* (1979); see *B.L.* 1980, pp. 50–51).

K. K. SACON

DELITZSCH, F.: *Salomonisches Spruchbuch* (Die Theologische Verlagsgemeinschaft). 1985. Pp. 556. (Brunnen Verlag, Giessen and Basel. Price: DM 78.00. ISBN 3 7655 9205 6)

This reprint of Franz Delitzsch's commentary on Proverbs, originally published in 1873 but still extremely valuable to serious students especially for its discussions of philological matters, will be generally welcomed.

R. N. WHYBRAY

GORDON, R. P.: *1 and 2 Samuel. A Commentary*. 1986. Pp. 375. (Paternoster Press, Exeter. Price: £12.95. ISBN 0 85364 420 9)

The publication elsewhere of his introduction (see *B.L.* 1985, p. 80f.) permits a relatively brief introduction, including sections on the history of its problems and on the text — both done with marvellous clarity and economy — and a section on the figure of David. The commentary itself is also highly informed by the secondary literature. Thanks to the use of footnotes these references do not clog the comment itself; on the other hand views tend to get noted rather than discussed. The current interest in character and plot within these books is well accommodated alongside linguistic and historical observations. Finally, the unusual *readability* of the commentary is guaranteed both by the unpredictability of the comments and the occasional flash of wit, e.g. 'the depressingly fecund Peninnah' (p. 72) and David behaving like 'some taciturn cowboy hero' (p. 183).

P. R. DAVIES

GOULDER, M. D.: *The Song of Fourteen Songs* (JSOT Supplement Series, 36). 1987. Pp. viii, 94. (JSOT Press, Sheffield. Price: £12.00 ($18.00). ISBN 0 905774 86 8. Paperback price: £4.95 ($7.50). ISBN 0 905774 8 87 6)

The author expounds the Song as a semi-continuous sequence of fourteen scenes moving in progression from the arrival of a princess at Solomon's court to her proclamation by the king as his favourite wife. Disregarding previous approaches to the book (the anthology view, most ably presented by G. Gerleman, is pronounced a counsel of despair) he argues that the fourteen poems are connected and chart the progress of the courtship and marriage of a young Arabian princess to the king. To achieve this, royal terminology is effectively accepted on its face value and is teased out of the range of literary disguises and travesties (king, gardener, shepherd, shepherdess etc.) commonly recognized by scholars. A bold attempt is made to render the original into English verse using loose hexameters and some traditional lyric meters. The result is a contrived and stilted translation which does not add up to a fluent version (e.g. 'Stare at me not though darkened I be, that the sun has beheld me; Hot with me too were my mother's sons and made me a worker Out in the vineyards at home . . .' in 1:6). The comments focus attention on the 'straightforwardly erotic' surface meaning of the Song. Many of these are highly idiosyncratic and forced (see e.g. the exegesis of 4:13). Suggestive sexual symbolism is a recognized feature in the Song but it is difficult to escape the impression that a plethora of erotic allusions has been read into the details of the imagery at the expense of their cumulative effect in generating the atmosphere of pastoral idyll (see e.g. the comments on 1:4, 3:4, 4:5ff., 6:2ff., 7:3ff., 10, 8:1ff.). Curiously the coy view that the Song celebrates only the delights of marital love (physical consummation takes place after the wedding in 5:1) leads to the unlikely situation in Song Three (2:8–17) in which the girl bids her lover to her bed 'not of course to sleep with her, for they are not yet married' (p. 3)!

In the Discussion at the end of the monograph a number of topics are raised including the book's structure, date of composition (fourth to third centuries B.C.), implied doctrine (to win acceptance for foreign marriages) and life-setting (the interesting idea is floated that the poem came into existence in the context of Pentecostal worship under the influence of biblical passages like Gen. 37ff. and Hosea 13).

P. W. COXON

GRAY, J.: *Joshua, Judges, and Ruth* (New Century Bible Commetary). 1986. Pp. xiii, 427. (Eerdmans, Grand Rapids, Michigan. ISBN 0 8028 0018 1. Marshall, Morgan & Scott, London. Price:£11.95. ISBN 0 551 01215 3)

The first edition of this work was published in 1967 (*B.L.* 1968, pp. 23f.). This second edition has been extensively revised, particularly so in the case of Joshua and Judges. The most notable addition to the 'General Introduction to Joshua and Judges' is a section on 'The Historical Value of Joshua and Judges' which takes account of recent views on early Israel as originating in a core group of militant worshippers of Yahweh which then incorporated local disaffected and underprivileged groups of Canaanites. Critical problems arising in the study of Joshua and Judges are also freshly discussed in the light of recent contributions, and the commentary on both books is revised and adjusted where necessary. Much the same conclusions as were argued in the first edition's treatment of Ruth are retained, but they are freshly discussed and argued to take account of contributions since 1967. A new section on the text of Ruth has also been added. Unfortunately the energy and industry which Dr Gray has devoted to this revised edition are not matched by its production — the binding is such that with little use pages begin to come adrift.

E. W. NICHOLSON

GROSS, H.: *Ijob* (Die Neue Echter Bibel, 13. Lfg.). 1986. Pp. 152. (Echter Verlag, Würzburg. Price: DM 34.00; subscription price: DM 29.00. ISBN 3 429 00998 7)

This commentary on Job will be valued for its beautifully clear layout, convenience, and conciseness. A brief introduction outlines the main issues and gives a useful bibliography (not quite up to date). The commentary is printed clearly in two columns on each page beneath the translation (which is the *Einheitsübersetzung*). Stages of growth are recognized in the book's formation, the last being the addition of Elihu's speeches. But the emphasis is on the whole, which, Gross thinks, may indeed have been redacted by the author himself, and which cannot be reduced without damage. Elihu's speeches retard the action and make all the clearer the point that the problem is beyond man's explanation. It is left to God to give the answer in the revelation of his wise but inscrutable care of all his creatures.

J. H. EATON

GROSS, H., and SCHREINER, J.: *Klagelieder, Baruch* (Die Neue Echter Bibel, 14. Lieferung). 1986. Pp. 89. (Echter Verlag, Würzburg. Price: DM 24.00; sub. price: DM 19.80. ISBN 3 429 00999 5)

The general nature and aims of the Neue Echter Bibel have been discussed in earlier issues of the *Book List* (e.g. 1982, p. 51). The two contributors to this volume approach their task differently. H. Gross mentions briefly and without names various approaches to the authorship, composition, and purpose of Lamentations, leaving many issues open. For him, the variety of forms (including individual and communal lament) and breadth of influences (prophetic, Wisdom and Deuteronomistic traditions) show how the people of God, in the darkest hour of their history, drew on all their resources to interpret the disaster in terms of faith.

Schreiner, on the other hand, summarizes mainly his own views on Baruch, stating that the main sections were originally independent and from different periods: 1:15–2:35 with its dependence on the prayer in Dan. 9 is from the Maccabaean period; the Wisdom section 3:9–4:4 is contemporaneous with Ben Sirach; then 4:5–5:9, with its parallels to Pss. Sol., is to be dated not before the first century B.C.E. The quite independent 'Letter of Jeremiah' belongs to the beginning of the Hellenistic era and was directed to the Jews in Babylon. Baruch shows how parallels were drawn from the lessons which had to be learned from the Exile for the readers of a later time. The book stands in the prophetic succession, but its ascription to Baruch shows that it belongs to the era of written exegesis of earlier prophecy.

Both writers, within the narrow confines of space the series permits, work wonders in putting biblical scholarship at the service of the worship, liturgy and devotion of the Church.

R. A. MASON

HOLLADAY, W. L.: *Jeremiah 1: A Commentary on the Book of the Prophet Jeremiah Chapters 1–25* (Hermeneia). 1986. Pp. xxii, 682. (Fortress Press, Philadelphia. Price: $44.95. ISBN 0 8006 6017 X. SCM Press, London. Price: £41.00. ISBN 0 334 00778 X)

The first volume of Holladay's large-scale commentary on Jeremiah in the Hermeneia series appeared soon after McKane's ICC and Carroll's OTL and thus three major commentaries on Jeremiah have entered the arena of Jeremiah studies (granted that two are only the job half-done!) in the same year! The Hermeneia housestyle is well known by now and Holladay provides a highly detailed presentation of the text in terms of bibliography, his own translation of the Hebrew, notes on that text, preliminary observations (occasional), structure, form, setting, interpretation, and aim. This style often leads to overlap and repetition, so perhaps the commentary could have been shorter than it is. There are also many footnotes (few pages lack footnotes) and these often attempt to provide encyclopedic information on aspects of the text. With the double column presentation typical of Hermeneia this is a large volume and will constitute, on its completion, a massive commentary on the book of Jeremiah. The bibliography is not intended to be comprehensive, but, along with the footnotes, is formidably adequate. The physical aspects of the commentary are very pleasing and the reader does not have to have three hands to read it with ease opened out on table or desk.

Holladay's approach to Jeremiah and his work on the text over four decades now are too well known for there to be any surprises in this volume. At the moment he is of the opinion that the poetry and prose (by and large) of the book come from the prophet Jeremiah (born in 627 and beginning his ministry in 615). The oft-remarked similarity of the prose to deuteronomistic terminology and ideas he attributes to counterproclamations of Jeremiah's made at the septennial readings of Deuteronomy (cf. Deut. 31:9–13) which, in characteristically Holladay fashion, he confidently dates to the autumns of 615, 608, 601, 594, 587! The evidence in the Bible for this is nil, but it is an interesting proposal and it clearly allows Holladay to read the book of Jeremiah with a confidence that many exegetes will find staggeringly audacious (and perhaps not a little cavalier?). The brevity of the introduction to the commentary (ten pages on 'A Chronology of Jeremiah's Career') is accounted for by Holladay's decision to leave the arguments for his reconstruction of the chronology until the second volume. In a commentary of this size it may be wise to leave the general introduction until the end of the exegetical work, but a few *arguments* at the outset of the work might have been equally wise.

In spite of the rather conventional reading of the text this commentary contains a wealth of detailed exegesis of the Hebrew text (often quite technical in its range and scope) and a thorough discussion of the secondary literature on Jeremiah. There is of course the by now inevitable Holladay techniques of rearranging the text, decoding it, and confident assigning of historical-social settings for specific pericopés which assume a far greater knowledge about the text than a commentator has the right to assume. It is all very much 'the life and times of Jeremiah the prophet' approach to the text—*c'est magnifique, mais elle n'est pas l'exégèse*! The second volume may redress this imblance in presentation of contemporary discussions about the interpretation of the book of Jeremiah, but until then this volume may be recommended as a magnificent account of Holladay's *present* thinking on the subject of the book's meaning.

R. P. CARROLL

HOLM-NIELSEN, S.: *Tolvprofetbogen fortolket*. 1985. Pp. 288. (Det danske Bibelselskab, Copenhagen. Price: D.Kr. 165.00. ISBN 87 7523 236 7)

In a Danish series of popular Bible commentaries (see *B.L.* 1985, p. 63) a good and readable book on the Minor Prophets has been published. After a general introduction to the Book of the twelve Prophets the author deals with the books in chronological order. The commentary is divided in three parts each of which has a short introduction to the historical, political, sociological, and religious problems of the period. The first section is about 'the prophets of the last days of Northern Israel', Amos, Hosea, and Micah. Then follow 'the prophets of the last days of Southern Israel', Zephaniah, Nahum, Habakkuk, and with some reservations Joel and Obadiah. In the third section, 'the prophets after the exile', the books of Haggai, Zechariah (in two parts, chapters 1–8 and 9–14), Malachi, and Jonah are interpreted. In front of the commentaries pericope for pericope is an introduction to each prophet in which the thread from the general introduction is taken up, followed by a few words about the special problematics of the book and the prophet, and ending in a review of the content. In connection to the introductions a short, but illustrative review of recent learned discussion is presented.

K. JEPPESEN

HOUTMAN, C.: *Exodus*. Deel I: *Exodus 1:1–7:13* (*Commentar op het Oude Testament*). 1986. Pp. 504. (J. H. Kok, Kampen. Price: Fl. 99.00. ISBN 90 242 0922 6)

A commentary that devotes 500 pages to the first seven chapters of Exodus promises to be a major work. Readers will not be disappointed. Part of the length is due to the fact that pages 24–168 review all the important Hebrew words to be found in Exodus, including proper names, and the exposition of the text proper begins at page 218. Houtman assumes the position outlined in his *Inleiding in de Pentateuch* (*B.L.* 1981, p. 72) that in its final form Exodus is part of a work comprising Genesis to 2 Kings and dating from the exile. The commentary is an elucidation of the literature within its setting, and Houtman argues that it is not the task of the commentator to try to reconstruct the history of Israel. The documentary theory is not mentioned until page 217, and then only briefly. It plays no role in the exegesis, and Exodus 6:2ff., for example, is taken to be a continuation of the dialogue in chapter 3. The commentary is rich in detailed philological, literary, and thematic comment, and is extensively documented. One looks forward to the subsequent volume(s).

J. W. ROGERSON

KEEL, O.: *Das Hohelied* (Zürcher Bibelkommentare: Altes Testament, 18). 1986. Pp. 268. (Theologische Verlag, Zürich. Price: Sw.Fr. 33.50. ISBN 3 290 14739 8)

Keel's extensive work on Ancient Near Eastern iconography and his recent study of figurative language in the Song of Songs, itself described as a work 'which really amounts to a commentary' (*B.L.* 1986, p. 73, on *Deine Blicke sind Tauben*) admirably fit him as a commentator on the biblical text. His introduction proposes a northern, probably late pre-exilic origin for the poems, which are love poetry without any specific formal or cultic setting. The figurative language in which the poems are so rich probably originates in cultural usage, and this can be appreciated the more readily through visual illustrations, of which the book contains no fewer than 168, many of striking originality. The attractively written commentary lays emphasis upon the positive value that is given to sexual love as a part of the beauty of the created order.

R. J. COGGINS

KEIL, C. F.: *Die zwölf kleinen Propheten* (Die Theologische Verlagsgemeinschaft). 1985. Pp. viii, 718. (Brunnen Verlag, Giessen and Basel. Price: DM 88.00. ISBN 3 7655 9204 8)

This is a reprint of the third edition (1888) of Keil's commentary on the Minor Prophets, published posthumously in Leipzig with an appreciatory foreword by Franz Delitzsch. Keil's defence of conservative views in this as in his other works may no longer be acceptable to most modern scholars, but there is still valuable material here which deserves the attention of serious students both of the prophetical books themselves and of the history of exegesis.

R. N. WHYBRAY

KORENHOF-SCHARFFENORTH, M. with MAHN, K. and REICHLE, E. (eds.): *'Aus den Brunnen schöpfen . . .'. Geschichten aus der Hebräischen Bibel und dem Neuen Testament. Von Frauen erzählt und ausgelegt.* 1986. Pp. 120. (Neukirchener Verlag, Neukirchen-Vluyn. Price: DM 19.20. ISBN 3 7887 0790 9)

In ten short chapters stories relating to women in the Hebrew Bible (Tamar, Rachel in Jer. 31, Leah and Rachel, Hannah and Peninnah, Abigail and the nameless woman of Judg. 9) and in the New Testament (the poor widow, the woman who was a sinner, Martha in John 11, Mary and Martha) are retold in a variety of modern literary forms, by five German biblical teachers (Korenhof-Scharffenorth and Reichle, together with I. Böhm, F. Rupprecht and J.-U. Schwarz). (The last chapter is a 'pseudo-Pauline' epistle presenting the insights of 1 Cor. 11 in terms appropriate for the contemporary church situation.) Some bring out genuine exegetical insights which are neglected at our loss; others, though they move a long way from the biblical basis, still show something of the power of these stories to produce new patterns of reflection. Each chapter has an 'afterword' referring to relevant scholarly discussion, and a bibliography. The 'wells' of the title are the place where women traditionally have met and preserved the community's self-understanding. Altogether an interesting and challenging collection.

R. J. COGGINS

LANCELLOTTI, A.: *I Salmi. Versione, Introduzione, Note* (Parole di Dio: Nuovissima Versione della Bibbia dai testi originali, 18c). 1984. Pp. 999. (Edizioni Paoline, Rome. Price: Lire 25,000. ISBN 88 215 0687 8)

This forms part of a new Italian edition of the bible which has been appearing in fascicles for some years. The author has also contributed the volumes on Matthew and the Apocalypse. The fascicles of *Psalms* began to appear in 1977; this is the first one-volume edition of the whole. The Italian translation has been highly praised: its vocabulary is clear and modern, though it keeps close to Hebrew idiom. It is vigorously rhythmical without aiming at the regularity of 'Gelineau' psalmody. There is a 63-page General Introduction, another introduction of 8–12 pages to each of the five books, and a short one to each psalm. Beneath the text are very brief textual notes, mostly on divergences from the MT (especially following the LXX), and then commentary, suitable for an educated but not technical readership. The lines of interpretation are perhaps closest to Kraus; this reviewer would have liked to see more sensitivity to the implications of poetic structure. But this is a fine volume in a fine series.

R. P. R. MURRAY

LOADER J. A.: *Ecclesiastes: A Practical Commentary* (Text and Interpretation). Translated by J. Vriend. 1986. Pp. vii, 136 (Wm. B. Eerdmans, Grand Rapids, Michigan; distributed by Paternoster, Exeter. Price: $6.95, £6.20. ISBN 0 8028 0102 1)

This new series of paperback Commentaries (Texts and Interpretation), translated from a recent Dutch series *Tekst en Toelichting* edited by A. S. van der Woude, aims to furnish the pastor and layman with clear and concise explanations of every book in the Bible. Each commentary begins with an introduction dealing with such questions as the origin of the book, its author, etc., and then tackles the text section by section.

Professor Loader, whose careful search on Ecclesiastes is known to us from his 1979 BZAW monograph (*B.L.* 1980, p. 71), exhibits the same care and lucidity in this volume. He packs a great deal into a short space, yet the reader does not feel he is being bombarded or swamped by technical language. It is bound to succeed in the constituency for which it is intended.

R. B. SALTERS

MCKANE, W.: *A Critical and Exegetical Commentary on Jeremiah*. Volume 1: *Introduction and Commentary on Jeremiah I–XXV* (The International Critical Commentary). 1986. Pp. cxxii, 658. (T. & T. Clark, Edinburgh. Price: £24.95. ISBN 0 567 05042 4)

With the publication of McKane's first volume of his commentary on Jeremiah the revamped ICC series has filled a notorious gap in the old series. In this volume McKane provides a thorough introduction to the textual and compositional aspects of Jer. 1–25 and offers his own distinctive account of the development of the text. The commentary is a philological scrutiny of the Hebrew text, the ancient versions of Jeremiah, and the history of its interpretation. These are its outstanding strengths and will guarantee its importance to Jeremiah studies. In these matters it will have few rivals. At times ponderous, even turgid, it is quintessential McKane: slow, thorough, and painstaking in its dissection of the text, the versions, and the major Jewish and Christian commentaries on Jeremiah. If at times it tells the readers far more than they wanted to know and if often the individual trees are so scrutinized that the wood itself disappears, these are faults consonant with the ICC format. Overall judgement of how it deals with the *meaning* of the book of Jeremiah must be suspended until the appearance of the second volume.

McKane's distinctive contribution to the interpretation and understanding of the book of Jeremiah, especially the problems of its composition, is his thesis of a 'rolling corpus' as the origin of the text. The corpus of the text is built up by small pieces of pre-existing texts triggering exegesis or commentary, so that the MT is to be understood as commentaries on the elements of the Jeremianic corpus. In this corpus poetry has generated poetry and prose and prose has generated prose. Over a long period, piecemeal, exegetical expansions and untidy, desultory aggregation of material have produced Jer. 1–25 and this is *not* held together by a comprehensive framework of literary arrangement. The processes behind this accumulation of discrete pieces are both dark and irrecoverable and 'there is more of accident, arbitrariness and fortuitous twists and turns than has been generally allowed for' (pp. xlix f.). This notion of a 'rolling corpus' strikes me as the best account so far of the formation of the book of Jeremiah because it allows for the sheer untidiness of the text and does not play sophisticated games with the text (of the kind indulged in by Holladay and the rhetorical form critics of American biblical scholarship).

A general review of the literature on the study of Jeremiah is postponed until the second volume, but throughout the commentary on the text McKane scrutinizes virtually every significant study on the text. His commentary is therefore a close reading of the Hebrew text and a comprehensive treatment of the secondary literature. He takes a conventional view of the prophet Jeremiah as the main source of the poetry in the book (admitted as a basic assumption), but distances Jeremiah from the prose material and is reticent about labelling the prose as deuteronomic-deuteronomistic. He is rightly dubious about attaching specific pieces of text to external historical events, but does regard many of the individual laments as coming from Jeremiah himself. His few comments on the theology of the text (pp. xcvii ff.) are sane and excellent. The detailed exegesis of the text and its secondary literature analysis is beyond the scope of this notice, but McKane is never less than diligent in his scrutiny of the text and always responsible in his handling of the issues raised for interpretation by it. With many of his interpretations of individual texts I would not argue and I often found myself in full agreement with his judgements about the weight that should be given to the general interpretation of a section (surprisingly so perhaps!). The twenty-page bibliography is devoted to works cited in the commentary and a further bibliography will appear in the second volume. This is not always an easy to read commentary (the initial section devoted to the LXX text is formidably technical for the first part of a commentary), but it is always a conscientious work and will provide a fundamental basis for serious work on the text of Jeremiah for the next century or so of biblical studies.

R. P. CARROLL

OSWALT, J. N.: *The Book of Isaiah: Chapters 1–39* (The New International Commentary on the Old Testament). 1986. Pp. xiii, 746. (Eerdmans, Grand Rapids, Michigan. Price: $29.95. ISBN 0 8028 2368 8)

In conformity with the NICOT pattern already familiar to readers of the *Book List*, Oswalt offers and defends his own translation before detailed exposition of each section of this first major portion of Isaiah. The secondary literature is widely and fairly cited, and the commentary sensitive and readable. And yet from the beginning of the lengthy introduction (pp. 1–76) the book is a puzzle, with the 'text' (that the Book of Isaiah is a literary unity from the eighth century, and that 'the original transmitters of the book intended it to be understood as a unit whose meaning was to be found solely by reference to the life and teachings of the prophet Isaiah') in tension with various 'sub-texts' (for example, that each of its three main sections — 1–39, 40–55, 56–66 — has to be understood against a different historical background). Oswalt is candid that the prophets' main burden was the concerns of their own times, and that the extent of Isaiah's message about the far future is quite untypical. His answer is that 'questions are raised in the first part of this rare book that require the issue of the Exile to be addressed in advance' (p. 27). He commends Childs's canonical criticism of the book — at least as the best of a bad critical job. Many readers will put down this book wiser — and sadder.

A. G. AULD

RAVASI, G.: *Cantico dei Cantici.* 1985. Pp. 237. (Edizioni Paolini, Milan. Price: Lire 18,000. ISBN 88 215 0951 6)

This commentary on the Song of Songs by a scholar who manages to write competently and with originality 'popular' commentaries is concerned equally with the poetry of the Hebrew text and with its parallels and influence elsewhere, especially in medieval and modern European literature. The first part, an introduction entitled 'When God speaks the language of lovers' briefly traces literal, allegorical and symbolic ways of opening this 'lock with many keys'; the second part, the commentary proper, concentrates largely on aesthetic aspects, though with a good deal of reference to other biblical books, as if to insist on the rightness of the Song to be in the canon. The third part, called 'The Thousand Songs' traces 'the song' in its many forms from ancient Mesopotamia, Arabia, through the Talmud and Ibn Ezra to Mokher Sefarim and Chagall, then through music from Schütz to Honegger. The appeal of the book is perhaps less to students of the Bible than to laypeople with an interest equally in the Bible and in literature generally; the erudite author knows, *inter alia*, of a 1859 translation of the Song into the dialect of Lancashire as spoken in Bolton (p. 37f.) and a parody of 1 Cor. 13 by George Orwell (p. 221).

P. R. DAVIES

RIDDERBOS, J.: *Isaiah* (Bible Student's Commentary). Translated by J. Vriend. 1985. Pp. vii, 580. (Zondervan Publishing House, Grand Rapids, Michigan. Price: $24.95. ISBN 0 310 45270 8)

This is a further volume in a series which, when completed, will provide an English translation of the Dutch conservative series of commentaries, the *Korte Verklaring der Heilige Schrift*, adapted to conform to the accompanying text of the NIV. The general character of the series has been indicated in reviews of earlier volumes in *B.L.* 1982, p. 40; 1983, p. 48; 1984, p. 57. This is the first of the volumes on the prophetical books to appear in English. Most of the Introduction is devoted to a detailed discussion of authorship in which the editor tries to reconcile his commitment to the 'truthfulness' of Scripture with his recognition of the difficulties attending the attribution of the whole book to the eighth-century prophet, and will be somewhat tedious reading for those for whom this is not a live issue. Within the limitations of his basic standpoint Ridderbos has expounded the text adequately for the lay reader, but there is little sign that Isaiah studies since 1950–51, the date of the original publication of the book in Dutch, have been drawn upon.

R. N. WHYBRAY

RUSSELL, D. S.: *Danieru-sho*. Translated by R. Makino. 1986. Pp. 381. (Shinkyō Shuppan-sha, Tokyo. Price: ¥2,400)

This is a Japanese translation of *Daniel* (The Daily Study Bible: Old Testament, 1981) (see *B.L.* 1982, p. 50).

K. K. SACON

SACON, K. K.: *Toki wo Ikiru* (To Live Through Time). 1986. Pp. 246 (Yorudan-sha, Tokyo. Price: ¥1,800)

This is the third book of the author's series, the Old Testament Speaks to the World of Today (see *B.L.* 1976, p. 41 and *B.L.* 1981, p. 61). Forty exegetical studies of selected Old Testament passages, eleven of which are taken from Jeremiah, attempt to shed light on the ailing world, from a self-conscious methodological standpoint of searching after the biblical meaning as a person who shares the contemporary agony.

K. K. SACON

Samuelsbøgerne og Kongebøgerne, and *Hezekiels bog*. Det gamle Testamente i ny oversættelse. 1985. Pp. 304 and 139. (Det danske Bibelselskab, Copenhagen. Price: D.Kr. 60.00 and 84.00. ISBN 87 7523 248 0 and 87 7523 203 0)

The Danish Bible Society has published two more volumes in the series of trial translations of the Old Testament (see *B.L.* 1983, pp. 49–50, and 1986,

p. 51). The Books of Samuel and Kings are translated by a group of scholars from the department of Biblical Studies at the University of Copenhagen, and edited by H. Gottlieb and S. Holm-Nielsen, while the Book of Ezekiel has been translated in Aarhus, except for chs. 40–48, which are done by J. Strange, Copenhagen. Ezekiel is edited by S. Nielsen and K. Jeppesen. Lists at the end of each volume indicate where the Danish translation deviates from the massoretic consonantal text.

K. JEPPESEN

SAWYER, J. F. A.: *Isaiah*. Volume 2 (The Daily Study Bible: Old Testament). 1986. Pp. x, 225 (Saint Andrew Press, Edinburgh; Westminster Press, Philadelphia. Price: £4.25. ISBN 0 7152 0528 5)

This volume completes the study of the book of Isaiah in this popular series and follows the pattern established in volume 1 (*B.L.* 1985, p. 65). The aim is consciously seen to present a thematic approach, rather than to reiterate conventional literary and historical conclusions about the text, and to link the book of Isaiah with a large range of issues. There are many fresh suggestions about familiar passages and some interesting attempts at a serious endeavour to read the book of this prophet as a single whole. The discussion is broken up into shorter daily portions in accordance with the plan of the series.

R. E. CLEMENTS

VAN SELMS, A.: *Job: A Practical Commentary* (Text and Interpretation). 1985. Pp. vii, 160. (Wm. B. Eerdmans, Grand Rapids, Michigan; distributed by Paternoster, Exeter. Price: $8.95; £8.95. ISBN 0 8028 0101 3)

Translated from a Dutch series, this is *not* the commentary by van Selms on Job reviewed in *B.L.* 1983, p. 54; 1985, p. 65. It is a practical, non-technical exposition by a very capable and experienced scholar. It has a very distinctive method of exposition, which makes it compelling reading. Apart from a short orientation for each new section, the commentary is in the form of a paraphrase of the speeches, keeping the first person and using enough freedom and expansion to cover all the points the commentator wishes to make. The accusations of Eliphaz in chapter 22, for example, are handled thus: 'From the judgment that has befallen you, we can infer only one thing: God has a long list of sins — too long to enumerate — to charge you with. Just let me mention a few things that rich people tend to do; perhaps you will recognize something of your own conduct here and there. Someone comes to make a small loan from you and you demand a pledge . . .'. Full marks for imagination!

J. H. EATON

STUDIUM BIBLICUM FRANCISCANUM: *Minsūki* (Numbers). 1986. Pp. vi, 245, 2 maps. *Yoeru-sho, Amosu-sho, Obadeya-sho, Yona-sho, Mika-sho, Nahomu-sho, Habakuku-sho* (Joel, Amos, Obadiah, Jona, Micah, Nahum, and Habakkuk). 1986. Pp. vi, 342, a map. *Yobu-ki* (Job). Pp. vi, 327. (Chūō Shuppan-sha, Tokyo. Price: ¥2,800, 3,500, and 3,500)

These three volumes are now added to the series of the twelve books so far published (cf. *B.L.* 1985, p. 66). They follow the same format: an introduction, a translation from the Hebrew text into Japanese as well as explanatory notes and comments. A text-critical note is added in each volume.

K. K. SACON

WEISER, A.: *Shihen Chū. 42–89 hen.* Translated by Y. Shioya. 1985. Pp. 337. (ATD–NTD Seisho Chūkai Kankō-kai, Tokyo. Price: ¥3,600)

This is a Japanese translation of Psalms 42–89 of *Die Psalmen* from its eighth edition (1979).

K. K. SACON

WESTERMANN, C.: *Am Anfang: 1. Mose (Genesis)* (Kleine Biblische Bibliothek). 1986. Pp. x, 1–260; vi, 261–497. (Neukirchener Verlag, Neukirchen–Vluyn. Price: DM 48.00. ISBN 3 7887 0759 3)

The well-established *Biblischer Kommentar* series is universally acclaimed for its detailed coverage of all aspects of the texts being studied, but often this attention to detail has led to an end-product of rather daunting scope. The publishers have therefore decided to produce much smaller versions of some of the full-scale commentaries. Wildberger's *Isaiah 1–39* has been so treated (see *B.L.* 1985, pp. 67f.); now Westermann's great commentary on Genesis is reduced in scope to appear in two compact paperback volumes. (For the original, see *B.L.* 1975, p. 53 for the first fascicle, *B.L.* 1983, p. 55 for the completed work.) Omitted from the larger volumes are the philological details, the discussion of religio-historical background, full bibliographies, and the accounts of earlier scholarship. Much of the detailed comment on individual verses has also gone. Most of the remainder is to be found here, though often in somewhat abbreviated form. The general structure of the three-volume original is thus preserved in a way which should help to increase its availability. Despite all the omissions this is still a substantial work of scholarship.

R. J. COGGINS

WESTERMANN, C.: *Genesis 12–36. A Commentary*. Translated by J. J. Scullion. 1986. Pp. 604. (SPCK, London. Price: £40.00. ISBN 0 281 04187 3. 1985. Augsburg Publishing House, Minneapolis)

For notices of the German original of this commentary in the *Biblischer Kommentar* series, see most recently *B.L.* 1983, pp. 55–56. The previous volume of the translation, containing Gen. 1–11, was noticed in *B.L.* 1985, p. 67. The translator cannot be praised too highly for his accurate, lucid, and idiomatic translation, as well as for the impressive despatch with which he has now completed the whole of the commentary. Westermann's work now becomes the most substantive commentary on Genesis in English, always stimulating, refreshingly independent, unmistakably Germanic.

D. J. A. CLINES

WILLIAMSON, H. G. M.: *Ezra, Nehemiah* (Word Biblical Commentary, 16). 1985. Pp. lii, 417. (Word Books, Waco, Texas. Price: $22.95. ISBN 0 8499 0215 0)

Well-prepared by his study of *Israel in the Books of Chronicles* (see *B.L.* 1978, p. 82) and his commentary on *1 and 2 Chronicles* (see *B.L.* 1984, p. 61), the author has now contributed an impressive companion commentary. His familiar negative conclusion that the Books of Ezra and Nehemiah were not the work of the Chronicler is given new force. Yet more interesting are his positive, if modestly expressed, proposals for the three main stages in the composition of these books: (1) the writing of the Ezra and Nehemiah 'memoirs' and other primary sources 'all more or less contemporary with the events they relate' (p. xxxv); (2) their combination to form the bulk of Ezra 7–Neh. 13; and (3) the addition around 300 B.C.E. of the introductory Ezra

1–6. The notes that follow each section of W.'s translation economically offer clear advice on issues of text, grammar, and idiom; and the commentary proper presses through treatment of detail to its proper goal: discussion of meaning. Any who dislike the author's conclusions will have to wrestle carefully with his arguments. This reader looks forward to his next book.

A. G. AULD

WOLFF, H. W.: *Dodekapropheten 6. Haggai* (Biblischer Kommentar, Altes Testament XIV/6). 1986. Pp. ix, 100. Neukirchener Verlag, Neukirchen–Vluyn. Price: DM 42.00; sub. price: DM 38.00. ISBN 3 7887 1244 9)

This distinguished commentary, dedicated to the Regents and Faculty of Saint Olaf College, USA, follows the general lines of the series and of Wolff's earlier commentaries on the Minor Prophets. However, Wolff is concerned to defend Haggai as much more than a 'minor' prophet. A true prophet — not, despite his overwhelming concern for the Temple, a 'cult prophet' — he was a man whose feet were firmly placed on the ground; and as such he was one of the dominating figures of the post-exilic community, the main instigator of the rebuilding of the Jerusalem Temple, and so responsible for inaugurating a new era in Jewish history. Unlike Joshua and Zerubbabel he was probably a native of Judah. The book was composed in three main stages. The kernel consists of the oracles of Haggai himself (1:4–11; 2:15–19; 2:3–9; 2:14; 2:21b–23) which were subsequently assembled, probably by a pupil, into a collection and provided with explanatory material (1:12b–13; 2:11–13; 1:2). Finally an editor (Haggai's 'chronicler') added further introductory material (1:1–3; 1:15a; 1:15b–2:2; 2:10; 2:20–21a). This editor also removed 2:15–19 from its original position after 1:15a in order to stress the notion that it was only after Zerubbabel's rejection of the attempt by Samaritans to join in the building of the Temple that the divine blessing was restored to the community. The divine promise and appointment of Zerubbabel at the end of the book (2:20–23), which strike a universal note, are an integral part of Haggai's message, which should be interpreted in their light.

R. N. WHYBRAY

6. LITERARY CRITICISM AND INTRODUCTION

AULD, A. G.: *Amos* (Old Testament Guides). 1986. Pp. 89. (JSOT Press, Sheffield. Price: £2.95 ($3.95). ISBN 1 85075 005 X)

This is an excellent addition to this useful series, which examines major issues in the study of individual books of the Old Testament and provides annotated bibliographies of works accessible to students. Dr Auld examines Amos's visionary experience, his relationship to other kinds of prophets, and attempts to place him on the map of Israel's institutions. He then approaches Amos afresh by examining the oracles on the nations, the literary structure of the book, and Amos's social and religious critique of Israel, before summarizing the message of the prophet as a whole. The reader will gain a clear picture both of the teaching of Amos and of current scholarly opinion about his book.

J. BARTON

BARTON, J.: *Oracles of God: Perceptions of Ancient Prophecy in Israel after the Exile.* 1986. Pp. xii, 324. (Darton, Longman and Todd, London. Price: £12.95. ISBN 0 232 51666 9)

The author of the very fine *Reading the Old Testament* (*B.L.* 1985, p. 71) has now written an excellent book on the interpretation of biblical prophecy in early Jewish and Christian circles. As is now to be expected of Barton, this is a highly readable book, lucid, intelligent, humorous, and rational. It discusses a very wide range of extra-biblical literature, especially Philo and Josephus, and will become an indispensable textbook for the student working in the field of Jewish and Christian beginnings. Barton's aims are to register and classify conceptions of prophecy that occur in the New Testament period and to try to draw some new maps of this terrain. He is successful in his aims and provides a very thorough discussion of many matters relating to prophecy and also to the canon of scripture. What is so good about his book is his refusal to accept the conventional readings of the texts without scrutinizing these texts himself and offering new, and in my opinion more accurate, readings. Thus he treats the term 'canon' as something which obscures rather than clarifies and prefers to work with the far vaguer concept of 'scripture'. Much of what he says on this matter is salutary and in conflict with Childs on canon (and, I am sure, with Beckwith's recent large-scale volume). A prophet in the period of Barton's scrutiny is 'an idealized hero around whom hagiographical legends are likely to cluster' (p. 99) and thus there is an abyss between the modern approach to and understanding of prophecy and those of the ancient Jewish and Christian communities. Barton classifies the ancient understanding of biblical prophecy into four types of information provided by readings of the prophets: (1) halakah; (2) predictions of divine intervention in history of a decisive kind (i.e. the eschatological reading of prophecy); (3) prognostications of future events which reveal the shape and consistency of the divine plan for human history; (4) the revelation of secret truths of a speculative and mystical nature. Each type is clarified and discussed in a chapter devoted to its classification and there is a wealth of judicious exegesis underlying each analysis. In his conclusion Barton ventures to suggest that applying the term 'prophet' to the figures often thought of as prophets may be misleading and favours Heaton's term 'laymen' for them. I could not agree more! An excellent book.

R. P. CARROLL

BEAUCHAMP, P.: *L'Uno e l'Altro Testamento: Saggio di Lettura*. 1985. Pp. 366. (Paideia Editrice, Brescia. Price: Lire 30,000)

An Itaian translation of the French original, noticed in *B.L.* 1978, p. 60. For the Italian edition the author adds some further thoughts (pp. 7–10), in which he associates his work with recent developments such as those seen in R. Meynet, J. A. Sanders, and Northrop Frye.

J. BARR

BERG, H. K.: *Biblische Texte verfremdet*. I: *Grundsätze–Methoden–Arbeitsmöglichkeiten*. 1986. Pp. 136. (Calwer Verlag, Stuttgart. ISBN 3 7668 0808 7. Kösel Verlag, München. Price: DM 19.80. ISBN 3 466 36366 7)

The oddness of the title in this book lies in the author's concern to apply to biblical teaching and learning the principle enunciated by the dramatist Berthold Brecht that a familiar idea, or text, needs to become unfamiliar and strange if its truth is to be fully perceived. This volume, as the first in a series, explains and illustrates the method with a view to using it in religious education. The plan is carried through with considerable insight and humour so that the illustrations given from the Bible attain their end very effectively. The author argues that the roots of such a technique of *Verfremdung* lie in the Bible itself and clearly anyone concerned with teaching the Bible in Religious Education will value the many suggestions set out here. That there is a risk of falsifying the biblical intention the author admits, but against this must be set the great freshness and stimulus which his approach offers. There is a range of helpful quotations from contemporary authors and much of the material in this volume is drawn from the Old Testament, especially the Psalter.

R. E. Clements

Bjørndalen, A. J.: *Untersuchungen zur allegorischen Rede der Propheten Amos und Jesaja* (Beihefte zur Zeitschrift für die alttestamentliche Wissenschaft, 165). 1986. Pp. xi, 398. (De Gruyter, Berlin. Price: DM 168.00. ISBN 3 11 010105 X)

A complex study, of which the first 132 pages are devoted to discussing the definition of allegory for the purposes of this work — 'a chain of metaphors related to one another in a specific manner' (p. 1), to consideration of the nature of metaphor, specifically in relation to the concept of God, and to 'metaphoric allegory'. There follow detailed analysis and discussion of Amos 2:9 and 5:2; Isa. 1:2; 1:5–6; 8:14–15; 9:13; 9:17–20; and, most fully, 5:1–7. The basis for the approach is the work of A. J. B. N. Reichling, critically assessed and modified. In the discussion of the texts, space is devoted to questions of genuineness, and, on that basis, to the contention that allegory was present in the biblical writings long before Greek influence was felt. The very limited amount of material considered relevant and the particular definition of allegory — however legitimate that may be thought — do leave the impression, as so often with such analyses, that a different definition or a different choice of texts, could have produced other results. This is not to deny that the critical discussion of the texts and their interpretation clarifies many issues; it may, perhaps, assume the possibility of a precision which the material does not necessarily admit. A substantial bibliography and indexes are provided.

P. R. Ackroyd

Bullock, C. H.: *An Introduction to the Old Testament Prophetic Books*. 1986. Pp. 391. (Moody Press, Chicago. Price: $19.95. ISBN 0 8024 4142 4)

An earlier work of the author was reviewed in *B.L.* 1981, p. 67 and the present book follows a similar pattern. After a general introduction, each book of the latter prophets of the Hebrew canon is discussed in its presumed historical order, with the addition of Daniel and Lamentations. Each chapter considers such issues as the date and historical setting of the particular prophet, the contents and structure of the book and its religious message. The previous reviewer noted that Bullock's standpoint is conservative, something even more marked in this succeeding volume. Thus the book of Isaiah is the deposit of a single author, 'Daniel' is dated in the sixth century B.C., the book of Jonah was written long before the Babylonian exile and recounts the career of the prophet of 2 Kings 14:25, and so on. In the same way, the existing books consist very largely of the genuine words of the prophets to whom they are ascribed. Nevertheless, Bullock always argues his case moderately, he is aware of other opinions — the excellent and up-to-date bibliography covers some thirty-four pages — and summarizes them clearly and fairly. So the book certinly fulfils the requirements of an Introduction and those coming to the study of the prophets will find it a comprehensive and well presented guide, even where they may dissent from the author's own views.

J. R. Porter

Camp, C. V.: *Wisdom and the Feminine in the Book of Proverbs* (Bible and Literature Series, 11). 1985. Pp. 352. (The Almond Press, Sheffield. Price: £25.00 ($37.50). ISBN 0 907459 43 9. Paperback price: £10.95 ($15.95). ISBN 0 907459 42 0)

Camp first surveys authors who have linked Proverbs with other documents from the Ancient Near East (Albright, Boström, Bauer-Kayatz,

Ringgren), and studies special forms like self-predication (cf. Bauer-Kayatz), the instruction form (cf. Whybray, McKane and Bauer-Kayatz) and the History of Religions approach (Mack, von Rad, Habel, Lang).

She then examines female wisdom as a literary figure, a metaphor arising from women's social role in society. Such roles are treated in detail: manager of a household, counsellor, harlot and adulteress, the 'wise woman', sexually aggressive women (including Ruth!) and feminine roles in sexual and covenant love. Literary and theological problems in the whole proverb collection are then treated with wisdom's 're-contextualization' after the exile. Personification is examined as a stylistic device, and wisdom is seen as a religious symbol in the special social conditions after the exile. An interesting study with much food for thought, usefully integrating literary and socio-historical interests.

J. G. SNAITH

CAMPBELL, A. F.: *Of Prophets and Kings: A Late Ninth-Century Document (1 Samuel 1–2 Kings 10)* (The Catholic Biblical Quarterly Monograph Series 17). 1986. Pp. vii, 240. (The Catholic Biblical Association of America, The Catholic University of America, Washington D.C. Price: $7.50. ISBN 0 915170 16 7)

This is a closely argued attempt to establish the existence of a pre-deuteronomistic prophetic record now taken up into Samuel and Kings. Implications of the theory are described in relation to the beginning of the story of the rise of David, to the expansion of the prophetic record to bring the history up to the end of the northern kingdom, and to an independent southern text dealing with the history of the southern kingdom; but the writer's chief contribution is the theory of a tightly structured prophetic narrative describing prophetic interventions, in the designation and rejection of kings, organized around five major figures: Saul, David, Jeroboam, Ahab, and Jehu. It originated among the disciples of Elisha and had the purpose of setting the commissioning of Jehu in the context of prophetic tradition. As the first literary presentation of Israel's history in Canaan, it prepared the ground for the deuteronomistic history.

This is a thorough study, and not least of its significant arguments is the criticism of Dietrich's proposals for a prophetic stage of redaction of the deuteronomistic history. It is admitted, however, that the text of the prophetic record is identified not by characteristic language and style but by prophetic concerns and interests, and that its origins lie in a group rather than a person; the extent to which these points might indicate a cycle of prophetic stories which only with deuteronomistic editing became part of a narrative, rather than a pre-deuteronomistic prophetic narrative, must be the subject of further discussion.

A. D. H. MAYES

CORTESE, E.: *Da Mosè a Esdra: I libri storici dell'Antico Israele.* 1985. Pp. 319. (Edizioni Dehoniane, Bologna. Price: Lire 18,000)

The author is of the opinion that Israel was already a nation by the time of David when the first history of Israel (the Yahwist account) came to be written. With this in mind he takes the reader through the historical books of the Old Testament, grouped into three sets: the Tetrateuch, the Deuteronomistic work and the Chronicler's account. Two synoptic tables are provided (for the J and P documents in Genesis and for the parallel accounts in Sam.–Kings and Chronicles). As the bibliography shows C. is strongly influenced by works in German and in general is well informed. However, since there is virtually no reference to comparative ancient Near Eastern material (for example, the chronological table pp. 244–47 names no foreign rulers) the impression given is that Israel developed in self-contained isolation. In the main the emphasis is on literary and theological aspects. Within these limitations a very readable introduction.

W. G. E. WATSON

DEURLOO, K. A., *et al.* (eds.): *Amsterdamse Cahiers voor exegese en Bijbelse theologie 6*. 1985. Pp. 198. (J. H. Kok, Kampen. Price: Fl. 30.50. ISBN 90 242 0677 4)

Dutch interest in biblical translation and dislike of the *Groot Nieuws Bijbel* are particularly evident in this collection, four articles, by F. H. Breukelman, K. A. Deurloo and Aleida van Daalen, Hanna Blok, and L. van den Bogaard being devoted to these topics. The most interesting are by Blok on the different functions of the forty-five geographical names in Amos, and by van den Bogaard, who compares the *Groot Nieuws Bijbel* rendering of passages from Amos with the equivalent versions in English, French, German, and Spanish, raising the question posed by Buber and Rosenzweig as to whether content can be translated while disregarding the form of the original. Another article on Amos by A. J. O. van der Wal argues that 3:1–2 conclude chapters 1 and 2, while articles on the books of Kings by K. A. D. Smelik and J. van Dorp discuss the composition of 1 Kings 16 to 2 Kings 15, and the narrative of the death of Ahab. K. A. Deurloo examines Genesis 4:25–26, P. W. van der Horst describes the exegesis of the Jewish–Hellenistic writers Demetrius, Artapanus, and Eupolemus, R. Zuurmond gives a brief history of the interpretation of Habakkuk 2:4 to A.D. 135, and B. P. M. Hemelsoet expounds the significance of the mountain in the Sermon on the Mount in the light of Old Testament references to mountains.

J. W. ROGERSON

DEURLOO, K. A., and HOOGEWOUD, F. J. (eds.): *Te Beginnen bij de letter Beth. Opstellen over het Bijbels Hebreeuws en de Hebreeuwse Bijbel voor Dr Aleida van Daalen*. 1985. Pp. 205. (J. H. Kok, Kampen. Price: Fl. 36.00. ISBN 90 242 0923 4)

Dr Liet van Daalen, who taught Hebrew at Amsterdam University from 1948 to 1985 is honoured by twenty-two mostly short articles dealing mainly with the teaching of Hebrew, modern translations of the Old Testament, and some recent developments in Old Testament study. If many of the contributions are brief sketches rather than detailed articles, this does not mean that the volume is lightweight, even if its contents are unusual. It is certainly very interesting. For example, we learn that as recently as 1970 Hebrew was taught in more than 90 grammar schools in Holland and that although it is no longer an official optional subject, there is still a positive demand for it in schools. The most substantial and scholarly articles are by K. A. D. Smelik, who gives a literary reading of the Mesha Inscription, T. Witvliet, who considers sympathetically the Old Testament work of the Brazilian-based Carlos Mesters, and J. Aalders, G. van Ginneken and E. Pot, who contribute to feminist interpretation of the Bible a powerful apology for the importance of Rebecca. It is clear from many tributes in the essays that Dr van Daalen has been an inspiring teacher of Hebrew and that she has made an important contribution to Old Testament study in Holland, not least through her involvement in the translation 'een vertaling om voor to lezen'.

J. W. ROGERSON

DUMORTIER, J., and LIEFOOGHE, A.: *Jean Chrysostome: Commentaire sur Isaïe* (Sources Chrétiennes, 304). 1983. Pp. 103. (Éditions du Cerf, Paris. Price: Fr. 331.00. ISBN 2 204 02070 2)

J. Dumortier was responsible for the introduction (pp. 9–34), for editing the Greek text, and for the footnotes, and the late A. Liefooghe prepared the French translation. The commentary extends from Isaiah 1:1 to 8:10. The book ends with an appendix on the Armenian version, and indexes of biblical references, proper names, and a list of contents.

J. A. EMERTON

EATON, J. H.: *Kingship and the Psalms* (second edition). 1986. Pp. xiii, 246. (JSOT Press, Sheffield. Price: £6.95 ($9.95). ISBN 0 905774 89 2)

Since its publication in 1976 (see *B.L.* 1977, p. 61) *Kingship and the Psalms* has established its place in scholarly literature on both subjects; on a re-reading one can see why. The arguments for extending Gunkel's original list of ten 'Royal' Psalms are still persuasive (though not, to me, irresistible), and the study of the thirty-one Psalms with clearly royal content plus the twenty-three arguably containing the same, leading to the survey of royal rites in the Ancient Near East and the comprehensive treatment of the idea of the Kingly Office remain both attractive and instructive. To this new edition Mr Eaton has added an appendix discussing some of the related material that has appeared during the past decade, and this updating enhances the book's usefulness.

E. B. MELLOR

FOHRER, G.: *Vom Werden und Verstehen des Alten Testaments* (Gütersloher Taschenbücher Siebenstern, 1414). 1986. Pp. 269. (Gerd Mohn, Gütersloh. Price: DM 19.80. ISBN 3 579 01414 5)

This is a semi-popular and straightforward introduction to the books of the Old Testament in the order of the Hebrew canon, with an initial account of canon and text. Fohrer takes as his starting point the completed, canonical text and works back to the sources and underlying traditions. This has the somewhat curious effect of treating the pentateuchal sources in the order P, D, E, J, and N, and dealing in turn with Third, Second and First Isaiah, and Trito-Zechariah, Deutero-Zechariah and Zechariah. Alternative theories are mentioned, with some small discussion, but essentially this is a presentation of Fohrer's own conclusions. No bibliographies are given, and in the preface the few footnotes are designated 'examples' of the literature.

C. S. RODD

FOKKELMAN, J. P.: *Narrative Art and Poetry in the Books of Samuel. A full interpretation based on stylistic and structural analyses.* Vol. II: *The Crossing Fates. I Sam. 13–31 & II Sam. 1.* (Studia Semitica Neerlandica, 23). 1986. Pp. x, 796. (Van Gorcum, Assen. Price: Fl. 115.00. ISBN 90 232 2175 3)

Fokkelman's work on Samuel, of which this is the second volume, must be acknowledged to be a unique work within contemporary biblical scholarship (vol. 1 was reviewed in *B.L.* 1982, p. 60).

Its uniqueness lies not in its length or detail, but in the range of considerations Fokkelman believes are relevant for the interpretation of the text (from individual sounds to the structure of the total work). Prescinding entirely from genetic questions, he examines the texture of the final form of the text as a unity in the service of a 'full interpretation'. That means, not a processing of every element of the text through the twelve levels of signification he analyses for any biblical writing, but a reporting on those results that appear most interesting. The work could have been much longer.

Because the method and the style of execution are individual to the author, and because he not unjustifiably refrains for the most part from interacting with other commentators out of 'fatigue at the wrong questions put in such abundance and the never-ending speculation concerning the origination and background of the text' (p. 694), the reader, who is a different person, is excited, exasperated, illuminated, and bored by turns. Everyone should take the measure of Fokkelman's achievement by at least sampling his work on a text familiar to them. One's frank disbelief at the weight so often laid upon small details of the text that are claimed to have a structural function, and one's suspicion that the text is being divinized into an object immeasurably more significant at every point than any human author could possibly have intended should not obscure for the reader the subtlety and penetration of Fokkelman's vigorous exposition.

D. J. A. CLINES

GITAY, Y.: *Prophecy and Persuasion. A Study of Isaiah 40–48* (Forum Theologiae Linguisticae, 14). 1981. Pp. xii, 242. (Linguistica Biblica, Bonn. Price: DM 25.00. ISBN 3 87797 024 9)

Recognizing that the need to persuade his audience of the genuineness and authority of his message was a particularly pressing one in the case of the exilic prophet 'Deutero–Isaiah', the author of this monograph applies to these chapters the principles and rules laid down in the 'classical rhetorical theory' of Aristotle, Quintilian and other classical writers, and reaches the conclusion that they comprise ten major 'rhetorical units'. Research into the literature of the pre-classical world has hitherto laboured under the difficulty that, in the absence of any specific treatises on the subject, the data available for study have necessarily been restricted to the internal evidence provided by the texts themselves. On the principle that the classical rhetorical treatises can be regarded as codifications of earlier widespread practices of the art of persuasion, Gitay's attempt to use these treatises as a basis for the elucidation of an earlier 'rhetorical' text is of considerable interest to the biblical scholar; and further exploration of this approach could well prove fruitful. The method, however, clearly needs further refinement; and not all readers will be convinced that the division of the text and the structural scheme proposed here for Isa. 40–48 is the only plausible one.

R. N. WHYBRAY

GONÇALVES, F. J.: *L'Expédition de Sennachérib en Palestine dans la Littérature Hébraïque Ancienne* (Études Bibliques, n.s., no. 7). 1986. Pp. xi, 578 (J. Gabalda et Cie., Paris; distributed by Uitgeverij Peeters, Leuven. Price: Fr. 620.00; B.Fr. 3,800. ISBN 2 85021 021 8)

A work of almost six hundred pages on the problems relating to the biblical record of Sennacherib's campaign against Hezekiah in response to the latter's rebellion in 705–701 B.C. may at first appear to be unduly long. However, the subject covers not simply a major historical event but also touches upon some of the most central features of Isaiah's prophecies and their interpretation. The care and detail with which the author looks at the questions amply repay the reader. Furthermore recent discussions of these issues, which include special attention by B. S. Childs (1967) and the reviewer (1980), have certainly not resolved all the questions that have arisen.

The first part of the study by Gonçalves covers the historical details concerning the impact of Assyrian intervention in the Syro-Palestinian sphere and the nature of the imperial control that was imposed. The importance of this for the fall of the Northern Kingdom and for Hezekiah's Reform are fully examined. The second part looks in detail at the preaching of the prophet Isaiah in relation to the revolt against Assyria by Hezekiah, seeing a clear condemnation of this. Egypt is denounced as a useless ally in Isa. 30:1–5; 31:1, 3 and Judah in Isa. 30:15–17; 22:8b–11. Yahweh is alone to be regarded as the Protector of Judah and Jerusalem. By refusing this trust the people have rejected their God, who has turned to become their enemy.

Part three of the study examines the non-Isaianic prophecies in Isa. 1–35 which relate to Sennacherib's campaign. In this Gonçalves follows, with some modifications, the position advocated by Hermann Barth that a major reinterpretation and redaction of Isaiah's prophecies was made in Josiah's time. This then relates closely to the fourth part of the study which looks at the narratives of 2 Kgs. 18–19 and 2 Chron. 32. In this Gonçalves stresses the marked divergencies between the B^1 and B^2 accounts which look back upon the events of 701 B.C. The B^2 account is seen as an exilic composition particularly concerned to maintain a rigidly monotheistic understanding of Jerusalem's survival from Sennacherib's threat, but its collapse before the armies of Babylon. This is a sumptuous study, with the fullest bibliography available to date, and a careful and balanced approach. I very much hope that it will at last lay the ghost of the attempts to invent a second (hypothetical) campaign on the part of Sennacherib as a way of understanding the complexity of the biblical narratives themselves and their relationship to the preaching of Isaiah. Altogether this is a first class study. R. E. CLEMENTS

GRADWOHL, R.: *Bibelauslegungen aus jüdischen Quellen*. Bd. 1: *Die alttestamentlichen Predigtexte des 3. Jahrgangs*. 1986. Pp. 253. (Calwer Verlag, Stuttgart. Price: DM 34.00. ISBN 3 7668 0800 1)

This book is the fruit of Christian–Jewish dialogue. The first of four volumes, it contains a selection of Jewish exegesis on eighteen Old Testament passages appointed for preaching in the third year of the German Evangelical cycle. Eight passages are from the Torah, eight from the latter prophets, and one each from 1 Kings and Lamentations. In each case the German text is followed by a section on its context, a section on leading words in the Hebrew text, a section on the history of its exegesis, and an indication of its relevance to the modern situation. An introductory chapter of sixteen pages sketches an outline of the history of Jewish exegesis from Mishnaic times to the present day. This work is to be commended as it will encourage preachers to study the Old Testament with awareness of Jewish exegesis, a selection of which it provides in a handy form. A. GELSTON

GREEN, J. B.: *How to Read Prophecy*. 1986. Pp. 154. (Inter-Varsity Press, Leicester. Price: £4.50. ISBN 0 85110 760 5)

This is to be recommended as a sound and practical guide to Bible study in general, and to prophets and apocalyptic in particular. The author writes skilfully: the book is always simple, but never superficial. The importance for sound interpretation of literary genre, historical setting, and context is stressed, and there is a helpful discussion of symbolism. The author urges on his readers that these books were written 'not to provide raw material for end-time speculation . . . but to fulfil a redemptive and ethical purpose.' Written to some extent with fundamentalist readers in mind, this work has the merit, particularly in the not insubstantial footnotes, of encouraging study of books in the mainstream of biblical scholarship. Another commendable feature is its glossary of technical terms. G. I. EMMERSON

Guinot, J.-N.: *Théodoret de Cyr: Commentaire sur Isaïe.* Tome iii (Sections 14–20) (Sources Chrétiennes, 315). 1984. Pp. 479. (Éditions du Cerf, Paris. Price: Fr. 380.00. ISBN 2 204 02262 4)

After lists of abbreviated references to books and of sigla, this work offers the Greek text, with a French translation and some comments in footnotes, of the commentary (from Isaiah 44:23 to the end) by this influential Antiochene exegete of the fifth century. There are indexes of biblical references, subjects, and Greek words, and chronological tables of the Old Testament period. This is primarily a book for patristic scholars.

J. A. Emerton

Haag, H.: *Der Gottesknecht bei Deuterojesaja* (Erträge der Forschung, 233). 1985. Pp. xliii, 204. (Wissenschaftliche Buchgesellschaft, Darmstadt. Price: DM 44.50. ISBN 3 534 09045 4)

This is the most comprehensive survey of the literature on the 'Servant Songs' of Deutero–Isaiah to appear for many years, and will be of immense value to all serious students of the subject. After a bibliography of some six hundred books and articles on the 'Songs' published since 1892, the volume comprises six parts which review in turn the earlier bibliographical literature, works on the history of interpretation, studies of critical problems (the number and extent of the 'Songs', language, style, text, authorship, literary, tradition- and redaction-criticism, *Gattung*), the interpretation of the 'Songs' both before and since Duhm's commentary of 1892 up to the present time, studies of individual passages, and 'theology'. There is inevitably a certain amount of overlap, but the arrangement of the material is competent and easy to follow. The final section on 'theology' might profitably have been expanded even at the expense of further overlap. This is an indispensable work.

R. N. Whybray

Hartberger, B.: *'An den Wassern von Babylon . . .': Psalm 137 auf dem Hintergrund von Jeremia 51, der biblischen Edom-Traditionen und babylonischer Originalquellen* (Bonner Biblische Beiträge, Bd. 63). 1986. Pp. ix, 305. (Verlag Peter Hanstein, Frankfurt am Main. Price: DM 78.00. ISBN 3 7756 1078 2)

The sub-title indicates the contents of this careful and detailed study. Slightly more than half of the main text is devoted to Jer. 51 and slightly less than an eighth directly to Ps. 137. Some of the philological conclusions will not convince all readers, but the strength of the work lies in its attention to textual, philological, and historical questions, and appropriate use is made of Babylonian source material. In general the Masoretic Text is found to be the best witness, though the LXX is carefully evaluated. Hartberger concludes that Ps. 137 is closely related to the situation of the Jewish exiles in the capital city of Babylon. Local colouring is found in the references to the canals, the poplars and the mountain-rock out of which the walls and paved roads were constructed. A general conclusion drawing together the results of the study would have helped to clarify its presentation.

A. Gelston

Im, T.-S.: *Das Davidbild in den Chronikbüchern* (Europäische Hochschulschriften xxiii, Vol. 263). Pp. 197. (Peter Lang, Frankfurt am Main, Bern, New York. Price: Sw.Fr. 45.00. ISBN 3 8204 8900 2)

This Bonn dissertation by a South Korean scholar both benefits from and contributes to the recent revival of interest in the work of the Chronicler. Its basic concern is to set out the Chronicler's presentation of David as an idealized portrayal of 'theocratic messiansism'. Detailed analysis of 1 Chronicles shows how adaptation of earlier material, especially the re-shaping of 1 and 2 Samuel, has contributed to this picture. Separate chapters deal with the genealogies and with David as the ideal ruler of Israel, as the model of true worship, the founder of the favoured dynasty, successful warrior, and preparer of the temple site. All of these themes are held to be reflected in the messianic aspirations of the Chronicler's own community — a conclusion with which not all will agree though it is strongly argued here. In any case this is a clearly presented study of the Chronicler's exegetical methods.

R. J. Coggins

Imbach, J.: *Die Bibel Lesen und Verstehen. Eine Hinführung.* 1986. Pp. 194. (Kösel, München. Price: DM 24.80. ISBN 3 466 20282 5)

The writer aims, in non-technical language, to introduce to those who are non-plussed by the strangeness and incredibility of much in the Bible, approaches which have become familiar in Faculties of Theology but not yet in the pews. A foreword stresses that the Bible deals not with literal truth but aims to lead the reader to God and that its writings must be studied in their original historical and cultural context. The chapters deal with 'Revelation and Holy Scripture', 'The Search for the Original Text', 'The Truth of the Bible', 'Literary Forms and Types', 'From the Jesus of History to History with Jesus', 'What the Bible Says About God', and 'The Bible as a Source of Power for Living'. A brief guide to further reading and a glossary of terms used in biblical studies add to the usefulness of the book.

When so few of the results of scholarly study of the Bible have filtered through to inform and delight the minds of the people in the pews, all well-informed and executed attempts to mediate them (of which this small book is certainly one) are welcome.

R. A. Mason

Jeppesen, K., and Cryer, F. H. (eds.): *Tekster og tolkninger — ti studier i Det gamle Testamente.* 1986. Pp. 175. (Anis, Aarhus. Price: D.Kr. 118.00. ISBN 87 7457 045 5)

'Texts and Interpretations' is a collection of studies written by ten scholars connected to the department of Old Testament Studies, the University of Aarhus. The book is well suited to demonstrate what is going on in Old Testament research, and each article is based on the author's sympathetc insight in his or her topic. N. P. Lemche writes about Deut. 26:5–9 and K. Nielsen about Isa. 8:5–8; both of them discuss items which they have treated more scrupulously in recent books. H. Gottlieb deals with Isa. 7:14 analysing carefully the Hebrew texts, translations in antiquity, and tendencies in modern translations. On the basis of Isa. 2:2–5 B. Otzen writes about Jerusalem and the Zion ideology especially in the period of the first temple and after its destruction. Two articles are about the transmission of history in the Old Testament, in both cases related to the deuteronomistic tradition. F. Cryer deals with the traditions and the redaction history in connection with the introduction of kingship, 1 Sam. 7–12, and E. Kragelund Holt writes about deuteronomistic theology, starting in Jer. 37–44. B. Rosendal tackles with zest one of the collections in the Proverbs (22:17–24:33) and relates it to the casuistic and apodictic commandments and prohibitions in the book of Covenant. K. Jeppesen deals with the suffering servant of Isa. 53 in the interpretation of the Old Testament, Judaism, the New Testament, the church fathers, ending up with the place of the text in the service of Good

Friday. H. Aa. Mink's article is on marriage and divorce in the Old Testament, the Dead Sea scrolls, and rabbinic literature, related to the pericope on divorce in Mark 10. The two last mentioned articles demonstrate how ridiculous that 'theology' is, which likes to think that the Old Testament is inferior in a theological context. Last but not least to be mentioned is the opening, and in a way most interesting contribution: H. J. Lundager Jensen's analysis of what he calls the Babel myth, the story about the tower of Babylon, Gen. 11, a structural analysis of a text in its context as he calls his article in the subtitle. All contributions contain a short survey of the most important recent literature.

S. HOLM-NIELSEN

JOBLING, D.: *The Sense of Biblical Narrative*. II: *Structural Analyses in the Hebrew Bible*. (JSOT Supplements, 39). 1986. Pp. 153. (JSOT Press, Sheffield. Price: £12.50 ($18.50); ISBN 1 85075 010 6. Paperback price: £5.95 ($8.95); ISBN 85075 011 4)

This is a sequel to the book with the same title reviewed in *B.L.* 1979, p. 80, now re-printed as Volume I. As the author himself notes, the application of structural methods to the study of the Biblical text has become more widespread and familiar since the date of his earlier work, although readers may still find it useful to refer to the index of technical terms which he provided there. Like the first volume, the present book consists of three studies of different sections of the Old Testament. These are preceded by an interesting Introduction in which Jobling indicates how his thoughts and methodology have developed in the intervening years. He finds his work taking two new directions in particular. First, a concern with what is called 'deconstruction', which may perhaps be defined as an awareness of how Biblical texts sometimes leave unresolved or indeterminate the issues with which they wrestle and, secondly, an interest in finding the relevance of structuralist methodology for liberation and feminist theologies in their approach to the Bible.

The first chapter indicates the significance of 'deconstruction' in its title, 'Myth and its Limits in Gen. 2:4b–3:24'. Jobling finds tensions in these chapters between a dominant 'fall' presentation and an alternative model of 'a man to till the earth', which really undermines it, and between a predominantly patriarchal outlook and a more positive attitude towards woman, ending with a critique of P. Trible's feminist interpretation. Similarly, the second chapter, juxtaposing Judg. 6–9 and 1 Sam. 1–12, to illuminate Deuteronomic political theory, argues for an essentially indeterminate Deuteronomistic presentation of kingship — it shows monarchy as both good and bad. This may not seem a very startling conclusion but it is the fresh approach to it here which is of interest. The third study is the most wide ranging and challenging, touching on some of the issues of liberation theology. Starting here from Gottwald's *The Tribes of Yahweh*, the author isolates three different ideological understandings of the place of Transjordan in Israel within the Old Testament. Unlike some structuralists, Jobling is always profoundly concerned with exegesis: he writes clearly, his work is well arranged and there is no over-parading of technical terms, so that his views can be assimilated even by a reader not too familiar with the technicalities of structuralism. There are points of detail that could be questioned and sometimes too much may be being read into particular passages. But the whole is most stimulating and often throws a refreshingly new light on the subjects discussed. Anyone concerned with the Old Testament should take serious account of this book.

J. R. PORTER

KOHATA, F.: *Jahwist und Priesterschrift in Exodus 3–14* (Beiheft zur Zeitschrift für die alttestamentliche Wissenschaft, 166). 1986. Pp. xii, 372. (De Gruyter, Berlin. Price: DM 94.00. ISBN 3 11 010649 3)

This is a detailed investigation of the relation between P and the older sources of the Pentateuch (JE) with special reference to Exodus 3–14. An introductory chapter briefly defends the traditional view that P was originally an independent source, and surveys the different explanations that have been offered of its relationship to JE. There follow chapters on the call of Moses, the plagues and miracles wrought in Egypt, the Passover narrative, and the narrative of the miracle at the sea. It is found that the author of P knew JE but that the relationship of what he wrote to the older sources is by no means uniform. In places he seems to have used it directly for his own narration but in other places was dependent upon a tradition underlying JE, whilst in still other places he was dependent upon a tradition evidently different from that reflected in JE. This will prove to be one of the more significant studies devoted to P in recent years.

E. W. NICHOLSON

LANG, B.: *Wisdom and the Book of Proverbs: an Israelite Goddess redefined.* 1986. Pp. xii, 192. (The Pilgrim Press, New York. Price: $10.95. ISBN 0 8298 0568 0)

Ther is such a throng of ideas in this book that one is reduced to a kind of bewilderment. It is exciting and learned and should be read, but to read it is as exhausting an experience as going round a large art gallery, and one wishes that Professor Lang's inventiveness was less fertile and that he would settle down to the more leisurely consideration of fewer ideas.

The main argument is that the Wisdom who appears in Prov. 1:20–33, 8:1–36 and 9:1–6,11–18 is a goddess and that the original context of the portrayal is polytheistic. She is a daughter of the Creator God El; perhaps Athirat is her mother, or else, like Athena, the daughter of Zeus, she was born without the assistance of a mother. She has a special relationship to kings (8:15), and to the scribal profession which has royal connections (8:16). Hence she is the goddess of scribal learning or of 'wisdom' with a more general content, and her devotees are encouraged to form an erotic attachment to her (8:17). Whereas Lady Wisdom is accorded the status of a goddess and receives a mythological interpretation, Lady Folly in chapter 9 is described as a work of fiction and is explained as a paradigm of a prostitute. There is an interest in history of exegesis which takes off with a consideration of the figure of Wisdom in Sirach and Wisdom of Solomon and which engages with more far-reaching developments in the last section of the book.

There are many matters which could be taken up, but one must suffice. Not all the alleged substitutions of 'Yahweh' for an original 'El' or 'Elohim' serve the same end: there are those whose aim is to establish a polytheistic context, where 'Elohim' is translated 'gods' (1:29; 8:35; 9:10), and those where 'El' or 'Elohim' is held to be a reference to a Creator God other than Yahweh (Gen. 2:7; 14:22; Prov. 8:22). Nor are the cases of Gen. 2:7 and 14:22 identical to that postulated for Prov. 8:22: the argument in respect of the Genesis passages is that by the insertion of 'Yahweh' Elohim and El Elyon respectively have been identified with Yahweh (cf. Gen. 14:19). At Prov. 8:22, it is alleged, 'El' or 'Elohim' has been deleted and replaced by 'Yahweh'.

W. MCKANE

LUST, J. (ed.): *Ezekiel and his Book: Textual and Literary Criticism and their Interrelation* (Bibliotheca Ephemeridum Theologicarum Lovaniensium, LXXIV). 1986. Pp. 391. (Leuven University Press; Uitgeverij Peeters, Leuven. Price: B.Fr. 2700. ISBN 90 6186 213 2)

The fruit of the 1985 Ezekiel colloquium at Louvain is garnered here in 31 papers (15 in English, 10 in German, 6 in French). There is a useful group on the textual criticism of the book, chiefly focused on LXX, but including also a report introducing the Leiden Peshitta volume (Mulder) and a presentation of fragments from Qumram (Lust); Jewish influence on English and Dutch translations is also discussed (Verdegaal). Approaches redactional, rhetorical, semiotic etc. are well represented in the central group of papers. Several of these relate to a single passage (e.g. Ez. 15 by Simian-Yofre), while others cover a wider field, such as the chronology of redaction in chs. 1–24 (Clements). The final group concerns aspects of the book's thought, such as individual responsibility (Joyce) and the significance of the cult (Monloubou); comparisons of the symbolic acts with street-theatre and of Ezekiel's valley of bones with Zoroastrian funeral grounds (Lang) make stimulating reading. Altogether, this collection makes a valuable contribution to study of the text and interpretation of Ezekiel.

J. H. EATON

MACK, B. L.: *Wisdom and the Hebrew Epic: Ben Sira's Hymn in Praise of the Fathers*. 1986. Pp. xiii, 263. (University of Chicago Press, Chicago. Price: $21.25. ISBN 0 226 50049 7)

Hengel's work has noticeably increased publications on Ecclesiasticus and its author. Here several sections of Ben Sira's book are examined: the hymn in praise of the fathers (chapters 44–51), the description of the learned sage (39:1–11) and the hymn to the creator (42:15–43:35). Mack claims Ben Sira created a 'mythic charter' for Judaism of the second temple period. He detects several background influences, including Egyptian mythology and Greek historiographic and encomiastic literatures. To these are added distinctively Jewish ideas of glory and greatness. The poem, a kind of midrash, is examined both synchronically and diachronically, with some use of structuralism; liturgical and didactic modes of speech are seen to be combined. Hellenistic influence lies especially in the use of early pre-exilic history as epic (whence Ezra's omission?) and in the educational technique used. There is a useful bibliography and index of passages, but regrettably no index of authors cited.

J. G. SNAITH

MARCUS, D.: *Jephthah and his Vow*. 1986. Pp. 77. (Texas Tech Press, Lubbock, Texas. Price: $25.00. ISBN 0 89672 136 1. Paperback price: $15.00. ISBN 0 89672 135 1)

Paying full attention to the long tradition of interpretation of the story of Jephthah, this brief monograph summarizes the case for and against the view that Judges 11 has in mind the sacrifice of the daughter. Its aim seems to be to rehabilitate the interpretation, stemming from the Kimhi family, that the eventual fate of Jephthah's daughter was to be consecrated to a life of perpetual virginity. 'My conclusion is that while I personally favor a non-sacrificial fate for Jephthah's daughter, the evidence is so ambiguous that it must be admitted that both conclusions are possible.' (p. 50) Taking his lead from the rabbis, Marcus argues that the theme of the story is Jephthah's rash vow, and hence the fate of his daughter could be left deliberately ambiguous. He bring no new arguments to the debate, and I was not convinced.

A. P. HAYMAN

MILLER, P. D. JR.: *Interpreting the Psalms*. 1986. Pp. x, 164. (Fortress Press, Philadelphia. Price: $10.95. ISBN 0 8006 1896 3)

The author has set himself the task of presenting, in summary form, the findings and concerns of scholarly research, and at the same time suggesting expository ideas relevant to today's faith community. The overall aim seems to be accessibility combined with integrity; the envisaged readership is church members, teachers, and preachers, though this could also be an excellent introduction for undergraduates. Part One is sequential, but its chapters (on current issues in interpretation, history and content, poetry, and the interpretation of laments and hymns) can also be read as independent units. Part Two gives what few books of this kind attempt — an expository analysis of ten Psalms, covering a 'spread' of literary forms and spiritual themes. Apart from some technical language in the chapter on poetry, it seems to me that the aim is fulfilled, and that readers, whether or not coming new to the Psalms, will be encouraged to find out more.

Scholarship and devotion are sometimes uneasy partners, but here they go well together.

E. B. Mellor

Miscall, P. D.: *I Samuel. A Literary Reading* (Indiana Studies in Biblical Literature). 1986. Pp. xxv, 198. (Indiana University Press, Bloomington. Price: $32.50; Paperback price: $9.95. ISBN 0 253 34247 3)

Not exactly a commentary, this book treats blocks of chapters at a time, giving a detailed, literary reading of I Samuel — literary in the modern sense, as Miscall deliberately challenges many presuppositions of historical criticism and ignores questions of correcting the Hebrew text on the basis of Septuagint and Qumran readings. Hebrew quoted is sometimes inaccurate (cf. 'establish — *qum*' rather than the hiphil). Holy war is treated only as 'a textual issue' [*sic*] without any attempt at historical description. The author confidently blazes his new trail, but is over-emphatic in use of the first person singular, which the reviewer finds tedious. Those seeking historical or linguistic commentary (cf. S. R. Driver's work) will be disappointed; those wishing to see the new literary criticism worked out in one of the historical books will find Miscall's work rewarding, but they must understand technical terms like 'metonymic dispersion', 'specific lures' and 'deconstruction'.

J. G. Snaith

Mottu, H.: *Les 'Confessions' de Jérémie: Une protestation contre la souffrance* (Le monde de la Bible). 1985. Pp. 205. (Labor et Fides, Genève. Price: Sw.Fr. 27.00. ISBN 2 8309 0061 8)

This study of the complaints in the book of Jeremiah (8:18–23; 11:18–12:6; 15:18–21; 17:5–18; 18:18–23; 20:7–18; 45:1–5; also 1:4–19; 31:31–34) treats them as utterances of the prophet Jeremiah as representative of the corporate self of the community. Thus the poems are more kerygmatic than biographical and represent an outcry against the suffering of the poor at the hands of the rich, oppressive elements in society. The approach to the text follows very much that of Volz, Holladay, Ittmann and Gunneweg (with special reference to Bonhoeffer's understanding of Jer. 45), but combines this reading of the text with modern approaches to hermeneutics and political theology. At times Mottu's argument is not easy to follow because of the hermeneutical framework he employs to jump from text to modern analysis (e.g. from Isa. 53:4–6 to Max Scheler in ten pages via Calvin, Kierkegaard and Nietzsche plus a consideration of Jer. 31:31–34 is a dizzying performance!) and becuase of his tendency to line up modern monopoly capitalism with the wicked of the Hebrew Bible! There is some profoundly tendentious argument going on in this book which sits uneasily with the brilliance of its rhetorical writing about the text of Jeremiah and its sensitive understanding of the poems as protest against suffering. As homiletics this is a very interesting book, but it lacks a certain sharpness when reading the biblical text. Mottu has, I think, missed a good opportunity to provide a dialectical account of the laments in Jeremiah as the cry of outrage against suffering *in contrast to* the poems there which indict the *whole* community as wicked and oppressive (e.g. 5:1–6,20–25; 6:9–11; 9:2–8). But it is a lovely read and thoroughly recommendable for stimulating argument and reflection on the text.

R. P. CARROLL

NARÉ, L.: *Proverbes salomoniens et proverbes mossi: Étude comparative à partir d'une nouvelle analyse de Pr 25–29* (Publications universitaires européennes: Sér. 23, Théologie, Vol. 283). 1986. Pp. xiii, 461. (Lang, Frankfurt am Main, Bern, New York. Price: Sw.Fr. 76.00. ISBN 3 8204 8968 1)

The Mossi people are the largest element in the West African state of Upper Volta. In their oral culture proverbs are ideally suited for transmitting the rich inheritance of wisdom, and are in daily use in conversation, law-courts, education, recitals, and songs. Abbe Laurent Naré here offers a careful comparison of this material, in form and content, with sections of Proverbs (10–22, and more especially 25–29). Well over half the discussion, however, analyses the biblical material. The following sections of comparison reveal some formal and many thematic resemblances between the Hebrew and Mossi sayings. The most notable similarity is the view of God, for the Mossi proverbs express a traditional monotheism — God as unique, common to all peoples, sovereign, invisible, omnipresent, immortal, creator of all, omniscient, omnipotent, just judge. For this reviewer's needs, this learned book would have offered less about Proverbs, more about the Mossi, and the print would have been three times as large.

J. H. EATON

NEWSOME, J. D., JR. (ed.): *A Synoptic Harmony of Samuel, Kings, and Chronicles; with related passages from Psalms, Isaiah, Jeremiah, and Ezra.* 1986. Pp. 275. (Baker Book House, Grand Rapids, Michigan. Price: $16.95. ISBN 0 8010 6744 8)

This work achieves its aim of providing English readers with a synoptic view of related Old Testament texts similar to several English synopses of the Gospels. The translation is basically that of the RSV adjusted where it would otherwise obscure similarities or differences in the underlying Hebrew texts. The ordering of the 176 sections is mostly that of 1 Sam. 31–2 Kgs. 25; however, space is made after 2 Sam. 6:19a for the comparison of Pss. 96; 105f. with 1 Chron. 16:4–42. Other Psalms and portions of Isaiah and Jeremiah are included where appropriate. The final section compares the opening verses of Ezra with the end of Chronicles. Indexes provide ready access to all the biblical texts printed. Some acknowledgement of text-critical issues, at least the often very different LXX version of Samuel–Kings, would have further increased the value without adding undue complexity.

A. G. AULD

VON NORDHEIM, E.: *Die Lehre der Alten.* II: *Das Testament als Literaturgattung im alten Testament und im alten vorderen Orient* (Arbeiten zur Literatur und Geschichte des hellenistischen Judentums, 18). 1985. Pp. vi, 164. (Brill, Leiden. Price: Fl. 60.00. ISBN 90 04 07313 2)

The first part of this work, which was noticed in *B.L.* 1981, pp. 123–24, was devoted to the testaments that are to be found in the pseudepigrapha, and particularly to the Testaments of the Twelve Patriarchs. In this second part the author extends his form-critical analysis backwards and examines the testaments in the Apocrypha (1 Macc. 2:49–70; Tobit 4; 14:3–11) and in the Old Testament itself (1 Kings 2:1–2, 5–10; Gen. 49 + 50:12–13; Deut. 31:2, 5–6a, 7–8, 14–15, 23 + 32:48–52 + 34:1–8; Josh. 23 + 24:29–30). He also compares the testament form with the *Bundesformular* and examines a number of Mesopotamian and Egyptian wisdom writings to see whether any relationship exists between them and the Israelite testaments.

The author's conclusions are for the most part reasonable: the testament represents a specialized form of wisdom teaching, and, despite apparent similarities, the testament form is not dependent on the *Bundesformular*; no relationship can be discerned with Mesopotamian wisdom writings, but there is a definite similarity with such Egyptian works as the Teaching of Ptahhotep, and it is conceivable that the impulse for the development of the testament form in Israel came from Egyptian wisdom teaching. However, not all the detailed points made by von Nordheim will carry conviction, as, for example, his views with regard to Gen. 49–50. Von Nordheim argues that it was only the addition of 49:29–33; 50:12–13 to 49:1a, 2–28a that gave this material — at a relatively late stage in the formation of this complex text — the form of a testament; in his view it possesses the least qualifications to be classed as such and cannot therefore be regarded as standing at the beginning of the development of the testament form. Whether the details of his literary analysis are right or not, von Nordheim here seems to ignore the influence which Gen. (48)49–50 undoubtedly exericised on later testamentary material. Further von Nordheim's view of the completely subordinate character of references to the past and prophecies of the future in testaments in comparison with ethical teaching — expressed here in such statements as '"Rückblick auf die Vergangenheit" und "Zukunftsansage" fungieren letzen Endes als indirekte Mahnung' (p. 79) — remains unconvincing. The two volumes of this work form the revised version of a 1973 Munich dissertation, and this no doubt accounts for the fact that in places the treatment of the Old Testament material seems slightly dated. There is no index. M. A. Knibb

Noth, M.: *Mōse Gosho Denshō-shi.* Translated by T. Yamaga. 1986. Pp. 456 and 13 pages indices. (Nihon Kirisuto Kyōdan Shuppan-kyoku, Tokyo. Price: ¥5,200)

This is a Japanese translation of *Überlieferungsgeschichte des Pentateuchs* (1948) (see *B.L.* 1950, p. 45; *Eleven Years*, p. 262). A very compact survey of recent studies of the subject after Noth and a detailed biographical note are appended by the translator. K. K. Sacon

Olson, D. T.: *The Death of the Old and the Birth of the New: The Framework of the Book of Numbers and the Pentateuch* (Brown Judaic Studies 71). 1985. Pp. viii, 253. (Scholars Press, Chico, California. Price: $29.95. ISBN 0 89130 885 7. Paperback price: $22.95. ISBN 0 89130 886 5)

It is argued that the census lists in Numbers 1 and 26 provide the unifying literary and theological framework of the book, and that the structure which this gives to the book may be summarized as 'the death of the old and the birth of the new'. The 'old generation' who experienced the exodus and the revelation at Sinai is condemned to die in the wilderness (Numbers 1–25); the 'new generation', signalled by the new census in Numbers 26, 'stands on the edge of the promised land and recalls the warnings and promises of the past as it looks forward to its own destiny (Numbers 26–36)'. This unifying framework and theme is further indicated by a number of formal and thematic indicators throughout the book, and is found to be consistent with the redactional structure of the Pentateuch as a whole. In a final section Olson draws out the implications of this unifying theme of the book for the interpretation of selected portions within Numbers (the spy story in chapters 13–14, the Balaam cycle of stories in Numbers 22–24, and selected legal passages) and for the function of Numbers within the broader context of the Pentateuch.

E. W. NICHOLSON

OVERHOLT, T. W.: *Prophecy in Cross-Cultural Perspective: A Sourcebook for Biblical Researchers* (SBL Sources for Biblical Study, 17). 1986. Pp. x, 368. (Scholars Press, Atlanta, Georgia. Price: $26.95; members price: $19.95. ISBN 0 89130 901 2)

The heart of this anthology is its lengthy second chapter (pp. 21–308) reproducing texts from many anthropologists on prophet-like figures, mostly from the Americas but also from the Arctic, Africa, India, and the Pacific. The opening chapter raises methodological questions; the third treats 'The Sociology of Storytelling and the Transmission of the Intermediary's Words'; while a short final chapter returns to method in handling 'Anthropological Materials and the Old Testament'. The many texts are a convenient resource; and Overholt's questions supply a handy frame.

A. G. AULD

PARKER, T. H. L.: *Calvin's Old Testament Commentaries*. 1986. Pp. 239. (T. & T. Clark, Edinburgh. Price: £14.95. ISBN 0 567 09365 4)

Among Calvin's voluminous expository works on the Old Testament, only those on the Pentateuch, Psalms, and Isaiah were written as commentaries. The others were delivered as lectures and sermons. With the sermons Dr Parker, whose authority as a student of Calvin is unequalled in England at least, has already dealt in *The Oracles of God* (1947). Most of the present volume is devoted to the lectures. These were delivered systematically in Latin, from 1550 to 1564, without notes (the lecturer allowed himself the use of a Hebrew Bible as he lectured), and taken down stenographically. But they were the product of careful study: Calvin knew what he was going to say before he mounted the dais.

Dr Parker does not here enter into questions about Calvin's Old Testament text or the sources of the historical and geographical information with which he explains it; he discusses rather his principles of interpretation, with special reference to his views on the relation between the Testaments. Calvin had little time for the allegorical method; when he himself (occasionally) interpreted the text figuratively or applied its message to persons and tendencies of his own day, he preferred to call his method *anagoge*, and held that it was demanded by the letter of scripture.

F. F. BRUCE

PATRICK, D.: *Old Testament Law*. 1986. Pp. 278. (SCM Press, London. Price: £8.50. ISBN 0 334 02228 2)

This is the first British edition of the volume whose 1985 American edition was fully reviewed in *B.L.* 1985, p. 89.

A. G. AULD

PECKHAM, B.: *The Composition of the Deuteronomistic History* (Harvard Semitic Monographs, 35). 1985. Pp. xii, 155. (Scholars Press, Atlanta. Price: $13.95. ISBN 0 89130 909 8)

In seventy-three pages of text, twenty of notes and forty-five of tabulations the author propounds a new and comprehensive theory of the composition not only of what is usually known as the Deuteronomistic History but of the Pentateuch as well. For him, the 'Deuteronomistic History' means the whole of Genesis to 2 Kings, virtually in its present form. This historian used as his sources J, Dtr[1] (material now found in Deuteronomy to 2 Kings 18), P and E, each of which was a distinct work and apparently composed in that order. His work was later supplemented by the addition of the legislative material in Leviticus (Ps). The book reads like a preliminary sketch for a substantial monograph not yet written. It is hardly possible to make a critical judgement of it in its present condensed form, as it makes very little attempt to deal with the immense problems raised by its remarkable proposals.

R. N. WHYBRAY

PETUCHOWSKI, J. J.: *Come i nostri maestri spiegano la Scrittura.* 1984. Pp. 149. (Morcelliana, Brescia. Price: Lire 9000)

Translated by G. Scandiani from a book originally published in 1982 under the title *Wie unsere Meister die Schrift erklären* (not noted in *B.L.*), this is a modest but clear and helpful presentation of a number of extracts from the medieval Hebrew commentaries, selected to illustrate not only their quality and variety, but also their development, and their potential interest for the Christian reader, to whom the work is primarily addressed.

N. R. M. DE LANGE

POLAN, G. J.: *In the Ways of Justice Toward Salvation: A Rhetorical Analysis of Isaiah 56–59* (American University Studies, Series VII, vol. 13). 1986. Pp. xiv, 360. (Peter Lang, New York, Bern, Frankfurt am Main. Price: Sw.Fr. 92.00. ISBN 0 8204 0280 X; ISSN 0740 0446)

On the basis of rhetorical criticism, Polan defends the coherence of Isaiah 56–59 as a literary section and its division into the following units: 56:1–8; 56:9–57:21, 58:1–14; and 59:1–20. These units are then each subjected to careful analysis by way of a close reading, in which such devices as chiasmus, inclusion, distant parallelism and repetition feature prominently. In addition, each unit is found to display some particular device which distinguishes it from the others. A concluding chapter summarizes the findings, discusses the thematic structure of the section as a whole and briefly sketches its leading theological motifs. Little attention is paid to textual problems (which one might have supposed would be important), to secondary literature before 1950, to the development and historical setting of this section, or (except very occasionally) to the evident links between these chapters and the rest of Isaiah. Polan acknowledges some of these limitations and justifies them as lying beyond the scope of what his method can achieve. It is difficult to avoid the conclusion that sometimes too much is being built on too little, though how much will depend upon each reader's prejudices. This is nevertheless a helpful contribution to the exegesis of these chapters and some of its insights should now be integrated into the wider context of the book.

H. G. M. WILLIAMSON

RENDSBURG, G. A.: *The Redaction of Genesis.* 1986. Pp. xii, 129. (Eisenbrauns, Winona Lake, Indiana. Price: $12.50. ISBN 0 931464 25 0)

The author claims that 'this book demonstrate[s] conclusively that the stories of Genesis are aligned not in an ad hoc or haphazard manner, rather along well-conceived and deliberate lines' (p. 99). He does so on the basis of alleged examples of chiasmus and 'theme-words'. According to him, Genesis is the work, not of one author, but of four compilers, who were responsible for different parts, or perhaps of one compiler who edited the whole. Although such redaction 'does not a priori militate against the conclusions of the JEDP Theory' (p. 101), Rendsburg believes that his conclusions 'render it untenable' (p. 104). Reasons are advanced for dating the work during the United Monarchy, but recent arguments for a much later date are not considered. Rendsburg expounds his theories with admirable clarity and conviction, but not all readers will find his arguments compelling. It is not merely that there are examples of lack of symmetrical order for which he has to find explanations. More seriously, many of the alleged examples of chiasmus or 'theme-words' will not appear as significant to others as they do to Rendsburg; e.g. '*b[e]nî 'atōnô*, "son of his she-ass", in 49:11, brings to mind *'ônān*, "Onan", . . . in 38:4, 38:6, 38:9' (p. 84), the common verb '*yābō'*, "he came", in 49:10, suggests *wayyābō'*, "he comes", in 38:18' (p. 85). Nor does he work out fully an explanation of the process of compiling. Although he writes of 'compilers', the detailed correspondences that he postulates suggest rather wholesale rewriting of the sources. If so, how does he account for the presence of the differences in the material and the inconsistencies, etc., that led to the Documentary Hypothesis? Still, Rendsburg performs a useful service to scholarship by stimulating others to reconsider old theories and to look again at the evidence.

J. A. EMERTON

RESENHÖFFT, W.: *Die Genesis im Wortlaut ihrer drei Quellenschriften* (European University Studies, XXIII/27), boxed with *Beiträge zur abschliessende Genesis-Analyse der Ausgabe von Wilhem Resenhöfft*. 1974, 1984. Pp. 200, 30. (Peter Lang, Frankfurt am Main, Bern, New York. Price: Sw.Fr. 41.70. ISBN 3 261 01028 2)

Various *Book List* reviewers have remained unimpressed by both the main work reissued here and its successor studies (see *B.L.* 1975, p. 69; 1980, p. 75; 1982, p. 70; 1984, p. 79). The author did not live to see this final thirty-page supplement published.

A. G. AULD

ROBERTSON, D.: *Bungaku toshite-no Seisho*. Translated by S. Arai. 1986. Pp. 204. (Kyobunkwan, Tokyo. Price: ¥1,800)

This is a Japanese translation of *The Old Testament and the Literary Critic* (1977) (see *B.L.* 1978, p. 76).

K. K. SACON

ROBINSON, B. P.: *Israel's Mysterious God: An Analysis of Some Old Testament Narratives*. 1986. Pp. xii, 94. (Grevatt & Grevatt, Newcastle upon Tyne. Price: £7.45 (U.K.), £8.45 (overseas). ISBN 0 947722 01 7)

A number of Old Testament passages are examined, each of which the author finds to a greater or less extent illustrates some aspect of the 'mystery' of God's nature which puts him beyond human calculation and definition. The passages dealt with are the stories of Joseph, Saul and Elijah and the Books of Joshua, Ruth, Job, Ecclesiastes and Jonah. The work is aimed at the general reader and makes use of traditional literary and historical critical methods as well as more recent approaches which concentrate on the final form of the text.

The material is well and informatively handled, the style clear and the argument persuasive. Perhaps, since no section has concluding observations, a general conclusion to the book linking the individual studies and drawing out the main themes of the book would have given greater unity to the whole.

But it is a welcome addition to the *Book List* both for its subject and its method of treatment.

R. A. MASON

ROUILLARD, H.: *La Péricope de Balaam (Nombres 22–24). La Prose et les "Oracles"* (Études Bibliques, Nouvelle série no. 4). 1985. Pp. 526. (J. Gabalda et Cie, Paris. Price: Fr. 400.00. ISBN 2 85021 015 3)

An introduction tracing the history of research into the Balaam pericope is followed by ten chapters which investigate the relation of the poetic oracles to their prose setting. It is argued that the oracles were not originally independent compositions but were composed along with their narrative framework. This narrative framework was composed in four main stages over a period of a century or so beginning *ca.* 650 B.C.: a first author composed 22:2–21 and 22:36–23:26; a second author added the story of Balaam's donkey in 22:22–35; a third author added 23:27–24:26, and a fourth contributed 24:7–19. Two late additions (24:20–22 and 24:23–24) were made in the post-exilic period. The traditional analysis of the chapters into J and E is thus rejected. The final chapter (Chapter XI) discusses the setting of the pericope in the book of Numbers as a whole. The work also includes a discussion of the relation of the biblical material concerning Balaam to the Deir Alla inscription. Detailed responses to this work will need to ask whether the different stages which it posits for the growth of the pericope can be sustained or are based upon a rather over-refined analysis. Its implications for the currently much debated question of the nature and extent of J and E in the composition of the Pentateuch are similarly controversial. It contains many good insights, and all future discussions of this pericope will derive much from it. It suffers, however, from being far too long. Avoidance of a certain amount of repetition and a curtailment of some unnecessarily detailed discussions could have reduced its length substantially and made it altogether more readable than it is.

E. W. NICHOLSON

SAEBØ, M.: *Fortolkning til Salomos Ordspråk, Forkynneren, Høysangen, Klagesangene* (Bibelverket). 1986. Pp. 351. (Luther Forlag, Lunde Forlag, Oslo. Price: N.Kr. 285.00. ISBN 82 531 6059 3)

The series to which this commentary on Proverbs, Ecclesiastes, Canticles, and Lamentations belongs is intended for 'believing and thinking Bible readers'. Special attention and greater space are given to Proverbs and Ecclesiastes (particularly the former) because of their importance for Old Testament Theology and Wisdom teaching. The introduction to Proverbs deals with the Wisdom tradition in Israel and the ancient Near East, the Wisdom literary style, the character of Wisdom teaching in Proverbs, and the various collections contained in the book. An epilogue to the commentary offers a rationale for the arrangement of these sections. Similarly, an overall structure is suggested for Ecclesiastes; and there is a useful discussion of the book's challenges to traditional Wisdom teaching. Saebø rejects the allegorical–metaphorical and cultic–mythological interpretations of Canticles, holding that it is a collection of wedding songs with unity of style, theme, and *Sitz im Leben.* He offers an interesting defence of its canonical status. Lamentations is presented as the book which, more effectively than almost any other part of the Old Testament, expresses the religious and theological shock caused by the catastrophe of 587. The treatment is brief, but here, as throughout the volume, critical judgements and theological interpretation are presented with balance and clarity. Professor Saebø is to be congratulated on a volume which should serve the purpose of the series admirably.

G. W. ANDERSON

SAVOCA, G.: *I Profeti di Israele: voce del Dio Vivente.* (La Bibbia nella Storia, 3). Pp. 224. (Edizioni Dehoniane, Bologna. Price: Lire 15,000)

This is a serious account for the non-specialist Christian reader, and to be commended for its combination of scholarship and readability. The Israelite prophets are first set against a wider cultural background, with a brief survey of the prophetic phenomenon in the Ancient Near East. There follows an outline of Israelite prophecy before the eighth century, but nearly four fifths of the book is devoted to an account of the classical Old Testament prophets, in each case the presentation being historical and biographical where possible, with the prophetic sayings reviewed in chronological order. A paragraph each is devoted to Baruch and Daniel. An overall summary and evaluation concludes the book. Attention is sometimes drawn to differences of opinion among scholars, but at other times particular positions are stated without any indication that there are alternatives (e.g. in the identification of Immanuel or the treatment of the Servant Songs).

A. GELSTON

SCHMID, H.: *Die Gestalt des Mose* (Erträge der Forschung, 237). 1986. Pp. x, 144. (Wissenschaftliche Buchgesellschaft, Darmstadt. Price: DM 36.00; sub. price: DM 24.00. ISBN 3 534 09620 7)

In five chapters Schmid surveys developments in critical study of the Pentateuch and of the role of Moses in particular since *c.*1960. The first, and much the longest, is mainly concerned with the crisis through which Pentateuchal criticism has passed since 1970. (The sub-title of the book is *Probleme alttestamentlicher Forschung unter Berücksichtigung der Pentateuchkrise.*) It provides an admirably clear and fair survey of a complex field. Briefer discussions follow of references to Moses outside the Pentateuch; of the various titles and roles ascribed to him; of those figures associated with him; and of the figure of Moses in canonical, traditio-historical and historical contexts. There is a full bibliography and a scriptural index. It is an indication of the complexity of discussion in this area that the publishers have decided to produce another volume so soon after the appearance in the same series of W. H. Schmidt: *Exodus, Sinai und Mose* (see *B.L.* 1984, pp. 80–81); the two books should in fact complement one another very usefully.

R. J. COGGINS

SCHWEIZER, H.: *Biblische Texte Verstehen: Arbeitsbuch zur Hermeneutik und Methodik der Bibelinterpretation.* 1986. Pp. 199 (Kohlhammer, Stuttgart. Price: DM 34.00. ISBN 3 17 009392 4)

Most readers may find this work heavy going, at least on an initial survey, although it is designed as a basic textbook into modern hermeneutical methodology. Its specific concern is with the fundamentals of semantic theory when used in application to the biblical text. Its aim is therefore to show the kind of bridge that is established between language, and its embodiment in an ancient text, and the contemporary world. In particular it seeks to recognize the context of Church life and faith experience in which the biblical text is read. A significant number of Old Testament passages are used by way of example, among them such complex passages as Hos. 1 and Ps. 48:13–15. The author shows that something more is required in interpreting a religious text than simply to attempt to reconstruct the original author's intention and that a complex interaction of language, ideas, and meaning is involved. There are excellent bibliographies and diagrams appended to each section and the work as a whole can be regarded as an introduction to the field of semantic theory and hermeneutics as developed in a philosophical direction by H. G. Gadamer and P. Ricoeur.

The subject itself is not an easy one, especially for those who are new to it, and this work has come from a writer who has specialized in teaching the value of a knowledge of these contemporary disciplines for the field of religious education.

R. E. CLEMENTS

SEYBOLD, K.: *Die Psalmen: eine Einführung* (Urban Taschenbücher, Bd. 382). 1986. Pp. 215. (Kohlhammer, Stuttgart. Price: DM 24.00. ISBN 3 17 009424 6)

In eleven relatively short chapters this handbook covers the entire range of subjects which are appropriate in an introduction to the Psalter: its transmission and origin; structure and style; ancient music and musical instruments; psalm types and titles; religious and theological content; the Psalmists' conceptions of life and death, the 'I' and the 'we'; the understanding of the cosmos and of chaos, and the use of mythical elements; ancient Near Eastern psalmody; the influence of the Psalter from ancient times to the present day, including some reference to modern German translations; and a sketch of the history of psalm interpretation. There are forty illustrations in the text and adequate references to literature. In comprehensiveness, compression, and clarity a remarkable achievement.

G. W. ANDERSON

STERNBERG, M.: *The Poetics of Biblical Narrative: Ideological Literature and the Drama of Reading* (Indiana Literary Biblical Series edited by R. M. Polzin). 1985. Pp. xiv, 580. (Indiana University Press, Bloomington. Price: $57.50. ISBN 0 253 34521 9)

An immensely dense but wonderfully enjoyable book on the strategies of reading the narratives of the Bible. Sternberg offers an exhaustive account of the narrator's art in the Bible without whoring after fashionable modern literary ideologies. In a highly polemical fashion he argues against much recent discussion of the Bible as a literary work whilst providing a splendid set of his own close readings of specific narratives which embodies a persuasive account of the literary and ideological nature of the Bible. Moving on from Erich Auerbach's justifiably famous and seminal essay 'Odysseus' Scar', he demonstrates the highly complex and ambiguous narrative style used by the biblical writers and constructs a poetics which refuses to disambiguate the text yet does justice to it. The close readings are brilliant, illuminating the text and making this reviewer laugh *with* the text at times and at other times recognize the impenetrable enigmas, opacities, ambiguities beyond the close readings. All the well-known features of standard literary analysis are here (e.g. narration, point of view, ambiguity, surface and depth, prolepsis, pattern, repetition, persuasion, rhetoric, poetics, etc.) but allied to a sophisticated understanding of biblical literary ideology as, what Sternberg calls, 'foolproof composition' (i..e. though difficult to read and easy to underread, overread, even misread, it is virtually impossible to counterread). Narratives from Genesis (Jacob and his brothers), Judges (Sisera, Eglon), Samuel (David and Uriah), and much else besides, are given close readings which make this book a marvellous volume which, price part, every biblical scholar must read.

R. P. CARROLL

TIGAY, J. H. (ed.): *Empirical Models for Biblical Criticism*. 1985. Pp. xv, 307. (University of Pennsylvania Press, Philadelphia. Price: $37.50. ISBN 0 8122 7976 X)

The cumulative weight of the several studies in this volume will be welcomed by those scholars who, like this reader, have been pursuing a similar path. Tigay contributes three chapters in addition to an Introduction and Summary and Conclusions: 'The Evolution of the Pentateuchal Narratives in the Light of the Evolution of the *Gilgamesh Epic*'; 'Conflation as a Redactional Technique'; and 'The Stylistic Criterion of Source Criticism in the Light of Ancient Near Eastern and Postbiblical Literature'. E. Tov writes on 'The Composition of 1 Samuel 16–18 in the Light of the Septuagint Version'; and 'The Literary History of the Book of Jeremiah in the Light of its Textual History'. There are single contributions from A. Rofe, 'Joshua 20: Historico-Literary Criticism Illustrated'; Y. Zakovitch, 'Assimilation in Biblical Narratives'; and M. Cogan, 'The Chronicler's Use of Chronology as Illuminated by Neo-Assyrian Royal Inscriptions'. No one should claim again the absurdity of compositional techniques deduced by last century's biblical critics lacking parallel in the biblical world. A paperback edition at a considerably lesser price would be a useful pedagogic tool.

A. G. AULD

WATSON, W. G. E.: *Classical Hebrew Poetry: A Guide to its Techniques* (JSOT Supplement Series, 26). 1984, 1986. Pp. xx, 460. (JSOT Press, Sheffield. Price: £12.50 ($18.95). ISBN 1 85075 048 3)

That a long and technical book welcomed as recently as *B.L.* 1986, pp. 81f. has required such an early paperback reprint is sufficient pointer to its reputation. Dr Watson has increased its usefulness by adding a bibliographical supplement of more than 100 titles.

A. G. AULD

ZIEGLER, J.: *Iob 14, 4–5a, als wichtigster Schriftbeweis für die These "Neminem sine sorde et sine peccato esse" (Cyprian, test 3, 54) bei den lateinischen christlichen Schriftstellern* (Bayerische Akademie der Wissenschaften, Phil.-Hist. Klasse, Sitzungsberichte, Jahrgang 1985.3). 1985. Pp. 43. (Verlag der Bayerischen Akademie der Wissenschaften and C. H. Beck, Munich. Price: DM 12.00. ISBN 3 7696 1536 0. ISSN 0342 5991)

Job 14:4–5a, which is at least partly glossed or paraphrased by LXX, Vulgate, and Targum, is the text most often cited from Job by both Greek and Latin church fathers. The author has used the dossier in the Vetus Latina Institut, Beuron. After briefly summarizing the early Greek evidence, he presents the Latin citations exhaustively to the twelfth century under the aspects of literary form and theological content, showing how the text was firmly believed to teach the Christian doctrine of original sin.

R. P. R. MURRAY

7. LAW, RELIGION, AND THEOLOGY

ALONSO SCHÖKEL, L.: *La Palabra Inspirada: La Biblia a la luz de la ciencia del lenguaje*. 1986. Pp. 409. (Ediciones Christiandad, Madrid. Price: Pts 1,300. ISBN 84 7057 393 4)

This is the third Spanish edition of a work originally published through the Biblical Institute in Rome in 1964. The author (who is primarily an Old Testament scholar) was much influenced in his studies by Cardinal Bea, when the latter was Professor in the Biblical Institute, but he brings to his work an additional interest in modern literary and poetical criticism.

The present edition has been brought up to date, so far as bibliographies are concerned, but the general structure and argument are unchanged from the first edition. Growing interest in Biblical studies within the Roman Catholic Church has necessitated the re-issue of the book, and it speaks in the main to a Roman Catholic readership, being concerned particularly to place the scriptures in their churchly context. The interest of the volumes lies less in the exegesis of the text than in the methodology of its transmission and communication.

R. J. HAMMER

BROWN, R. E.: *Biblical Exegesis and Church Doctrine*. 1985. Pp. 171. (Paulist Press, Mahwah, New Jersey. Price: $8.95. ISBN 0 8091 0368 0)

This is a polemical book comprising a series of essays commending a centrist position in Catholic scholarship between liberal biblical exegesis and ultra-conservative theology. Most users of the *Book List* may share this reader's surprise at finding so little on the Old Testament in a work which begins 'by insisting that people take seriously that Jesus was a Palestinian Jew', and whose essay on 'The preaching described in the Book of Acts' affirms the importance of telling the Old Testament story.

A. G. AULD

BRUEGGEMANN, W.: *Hopeful Imagination: Prophetic Voices in Exile*. 1986. Pp. x, 146. (Fortress Press, Philadelphia. Price: $7.95. ISBN 0 8006 1925 0)

This is a book for the preacher, particularly in the context of the American churches. It originated in two series of lectures to Pastors' Conferences, and stresses the contemporary relevance of the biblical material. Apart from brief introductory and concluding chapters the main body of the book consists of three pairs of studies on the prophets of the exilic age. In each case the first study is a general assessment of the prophet's response to the exilic crisis, while the second is a more detailed examination of a sample passage (Jeremiah 30:12–17, Ezekiel 36:22–32 and Isaiah 54). Readers will vary in their perception of the parallel between Israel in exile and Western capitalism and consumer materialism. There is a danger of eisegesis in this approach, but this work will have achieved much if it stimulates preachers to engage in study of the text and to wrestle with its essential message.

A. GELSTON

BUBER, M.: *La fede dei profeti* (Radici, 5). 1985. Pp. xliii, 240. (Casa Editrice Marietti, Casale Monferrato. Price: Lire 26,000. ISBN 88 211 6765 8)

A translation of *Der Glaube der Propheten* from *Werke* II: *Schriften zur Bibel* (Verlag Lambert Schneider, Heidelberg — Kösel Verlag, Munich, 1964, pp. 231–484) by Andrea Poma who also contributed the introduction and brief bibliography. After a short biography the introduction is devoted to an account of Buber's approach to the bible, including his emphasis on such aspects as its oral origins and appropriate techniques for translating Hebrew. With due allowance for its date this is a refreshing book to read.

W. G. E. WATSON

CLEMENTS, R. E.: *The Prayers of the Bible*. 1986. Pp. 295. (SCM Press, London. Price: £7.95. ISBN 0 334 02268 1)

Words addressed to God are an important source of information about the religious beliefs of communities, as well as serving as models for the use and encouragement of others. It is thus good to see these brief studies of twenty-five prayers, of which seventeen are from the Old Testament. An introductory chapter defines the varieties of prayer and the importance of the subject in the Bible. The studies themselves mostly avoid critical matters (e.g. 1 Kings 8:22–53 is treated as Solomon's prayer) and concentrate upon the religious importance of the prayers. This is done with frankness and with sensitivity to wider theological concerns, and the book would provide excellent material for lay study groups or for courses of instruction on prayer, as well as being a guide to the spirituality of the Old Testament.

J. W. ROGERSON

CLEMENTS, R. E.: *In Spirit and in Truth: Insights from Biblical Prayers*. 1985. Pp. 295. (John Knox Press, Atlanta, Georgia. Price: $9.95. ISBN 0 8042 0071 8)

This is the American edition of the volume reviewed immediately above under the title *The Prayers of the Bible*.

A. G. AULD

CRÜSEMANN, F.: *Wie Gott die Welt regiert: Bibelauslegungen (Kaiser Traktate, 90)*. 1986. Pp. 80. (Chr. Kaiser Verlag, Munich. Price: DM 10.00. ISBN 3 459 01640 X)

The book consists of four studies for the general reader based on Col. 1:15–23, Gen. 8:20–9:17, Lev. 25:1–13 and the Decalogue. An attempt is made to relate the issues of God's 'Lordship' raised by these passages to the problems and tensions of the modern world. A firm mastery of the biblical texts allied to the writer's strong conviction as to their relevance to the present, marks every step of the argument. Inevitably such exegesis bears an occasional whiff of the subjective but it stands in a noble tradition of re-interpretation and re-application of the biblical material to later situations, a tradition which has its roots in the Bible itself.

R. A. MASON

EBACH, J.: *Ursprung und Ziel: Erinnerte Zukunft und erhoffte Vergangenheit*. 1986. Pp. 176. (Neukirchener Verlag, Neukirchen-Vluyn. Price: DM. 34.00. ISBN 3 7887 1209 0)

A stylish collection of essays in which a dialogue is established between various parts of the Old Testament and themes in the writings of Walter Benjamin, Karl Kraus, and Theodor Adorno, mostly (as the riddling subtitle suggests) concerned with the nature and origin of mankind and its eschatological hopes. The early chapters of Genesis, the book of Job, the story of the manna, and some prophetic texts are the principal Old Testament passages discussed, together with Plato's *Symposium* and Virgil's Fourth Eclogue, and there is much use of rabbinic material. The author shows how distinctive is the biblical understanding of human nature, human hopes and the human lot by comparison both with classical antiquity and with modern 'establishment' morality, while seeing the true heirs of the biblical approach in some modern political theology. There is a particularly interesting chapter on work and rest in the Old Testament, with some sharp criticisms of the use of biblical material in the Papal encyclical *Laborem exercens* (1981). This is a difficult book, from a philosophical tradition alien to most British readers, but full of original insights, and with much to contribute to biblical theology and hermeneutics.

J. BARTON

EPSZTEIN, L.: *Social Justice in the Ancient Near East and the People of the Bible.* Translated by J. Bowden. 1986. Pp. xii, 178. (SCM Press, London. Price: £7.95. ISBN 0 334 02334 3)

This is a translation of the French original reviewed in *B.L.* 1984, p. 91.

J. R. PORTER

GOTTFRIEDSEN, C.: *Die Fruchtbarkeit von Israels Land: zur Differenz der Theologie in den beiden Landesteilen.* Europäische Hochschulschriften: Reihe 23, Theologie; Bd. 267. 1985. Pp. 213. (Peter Lang, Frankfurt am Main, Bern, New York. Price: Sw.Fr. 47.00. ISBN 3 8204 8736 0)

As its sub-title indicates, the purpose of this thesis is to examine the theme of the fruitfulness of the land and its relationship to Yahweh, which the author sees as being understood very differently in Israel and Judah respectively. The first section discusses the topic in northern prophecy, surveying Elijah, Elisha, Hosea, and the early period of Jeremiah's ministry which the author considers to be influenced by northern prophetic concepts. Next comes an extended examination of the Yahwistic corpus as representative of southern traditions and a shorter survey of the Elohist source. A further chapter deals with the occurrence of the theme in *Stammessprüche* and in hymns and psalms from north and south respectively. Next follows a key chapter comparing the northern and southern understandings of the fruitfulness of the land. Finally, there comes a section on Deuteronomy, which the author sees as combining northern and southern traditions, and a rather sketchy survey of the theme in exilic and post-exilic material. The arrangement of the book could have been made better and easier to follow: it would have helped if all the evidence from the north and from the south had been dealt with in separate blocks before the comparison between them was attempted.

As the author sees it, the issue is how nomadic Israel viewed its situation in a new agricultural environment. Briefly, in the north the aim was to assert Yahweh over against Baal as the giver of the soil's products: he can give but equally take away and his activity in nature is of the same character as in history. By contrast, in the south, Yahweh is much more clearly the lord of the regular round of the seasons and his bringing Israel into a fertile land is to be understood by the concept of 'blessing'. As the author puts it, for the south the key verbs are 'grow' and 'flourish', for the north 'give' and 'take away'. However, within the two areas there are markedly different emphases representing the outlook of different circles. Thus, the Elisha circle, the Rechabites and, it would seem, the Elohist do not associate Yahweh with nature and agricultural life in any real way, while, in the south, Pss. 65 and 72 view the deity very much as a 'nature god' and were probably not originally Yahwistic at all. Many of the conclusions rest on assumptions about the date and provenance of various texts and, indeed, about the early history and background of Israel, with which not everyone might concur. Nevertheless, the work displays a range of interesting suggestions and insights and makes a valuable contribution to the study of an important aspect of the Old Testament.

J. R. PORTER

GOWAN, D. E.: *Eschatology in the Old Testament.* 1986. Pp. x, 150. (Fortress Press, Philadelphia. Price: $9.95. ISBN 0 8006 1906 4)

Gowan attempts to provide an up-to-date comprehensive introduction to eschatology in the Old Testament, aimed at the educated layman rather than the scholar. Emphasizing traditions rather than teachings of individual authors, he focuses on the final canonical form of the literature but also tries to give the diachronic development of the various traditions. He argues that Zion plays a prominent role in most of the Old Testament eschatological traditions and uses it as the focal point of his study, sub-dividing it as follows: Peace in Zion — the transformation of human society; People of Zion — transformation of the person; Highest of all the Hills — transformation of nature. Each section gives not only the Old Testament views but also contains a synopsis of the 'post-Old Testament' development and a look at the contemporary hermeneutical implications.

Gowan's treatment is generally clear and common-sensical. However, he hovers uneasily between the 'canonical' approach and a fully diachronic one: he fails to be properly diachronic by concentrating on the canonical Old Testament material when in fact some of his 'post-Old Testament' material is as early as certain of the Old Testament passages he considers. Further, he fails to be fully canonical in that he does not take appropriate account of Daniel. Surely, this most eschatological section of the Old Testament deserves to be treated as more than an appendix, which is the way G. has handled it. Gowan has given us a very useful overview but fails to provide the 'recent, comprehensive introduction' that would have been most welcome.

L. L. Grabbe

Gowan, D. E.: *Eschatology in the Old Testament*. 1987. pp. xi, 150. (T. & T. Clark, Edinburgh. Price: £11.95. ISBN 0 567 09453 7)

This is the British imprint of the work whose original American edition is reviewed immediately above.

A. G. Auld

Green, A. (ed.): *Jewish Spirituality from the Bible through the Middle Ages* (World Spirituality: An Encyclopedic History of the Religious Quest, 13). 1986. Pp. xxv, 450. (Routledge & Kegan Paul, London. Price: £39.50. ISBN 0 7102 0926 6)

This book is designed as part of a twenty-five volume collection, and as one of a pair on Judaism (the other covers the period 'from the sixteenth-century revival to the present'). It is itself divided chronologically into three sections, and the articles most directly relevant to this *Book List* are found in the first, 'Foundations: The Biblical Age' (the others are entitled 'Emergence: The Rabbinic Age' and 'Reflections: The Medieval Age'): D. Sperling, 'Israel's Religion in the Ancient Near East', attempts to set the scene by considering what was distinctive in Israelite religion; J. D. Levenson looks at the function and symbolism of the Jerusalem temple, M. Fishbane at prophecy, J. Rosenberg at scripture, and J. L. Kugel at the Psalms. It is hard to gauge the readership at which these essays are aimed: certainly not the general public. The style is American Academic (muddy and selfconscious); technical terms and allusions abound, and there are the inevitable endnotes, demanding a command of several languages.

Postbiblical Judaism is treated less systematically but on the whole in a more accessible style, and several of the contributions have a bearing on the biblical tradition. M. Himmelfarb has a short but clear and well-focused study of visionary tours of heaven in the apocalyptic literature. D. Winston, in a thoughtful essay on Philo, considers briefly the antecedents of his Logos theology and the character of his use of scripture. Two articles, by R. Goldenberg and D. C. Matt, discuss attitudes to law. And there is an excellent account of medieval allegory by F. Talmage. Remarkably, there is no attempt to get to grips with the central topic of prayer and worship in postbiblical Judaism, or with the place of spirituality in ordinary Jewish life: indeed by contrast with the brief but fairly comprehensive treatment of biblical religion, later Judaism is represented to a disconcertingly large extent by peripheral or ephemeral phenomena. In other words, the book lacks balance, and a sense of its own direction. This impression is reinforced by a scattering of unattributed translations from the sources and of intriguing illustrations with not a word to explain why they are there, or how they relate to the text.

N. R. M. DE LANGE

HEIDER, G. C.: *The Cult of Molek: A Reassessment* (JSOT Supplement Series, 43). 1986. Pp. xvii, 446. (JSOT Press, Sheffield. Price: £22.50 (sub. £16.50). ISBN 1 85075 018 1. Paperback price: £10.50 (sub. £7.95). ISBN 1 85075 019 X)

In the first ninety pages the author surveys studies on Molek from the seventeenth century to the present with special attention to O. Eissfeldt's contribution. Next he presents written evidence on this deity from the ancient Near East (Syria, Mesopotamia, Phoenicia, etc.). Chapter three is devoted to archaeological evidence for cultic child sacrifice and in chapter four the pertinent Old Testament passages are examined. A short concluding chapter is followed by appendices listing personal names with the component *ma-lik* (from Ebla) and *mlk* (from Mari and Ras Shamra). There is no index. The long bibliography does not include W. G. Lambert on Nergal (*Bibliotheca Orientalis* 30 [1973] pp. 355–63) or E. Lipiński on Melqart (*Actes de la XVIIe Rencontre Assyriologique Internationale*, Ham-Sur-Heure, 1970, pp. 30–58) both of significance. On the other hand, an unpublished dissertation by P. Mosca is used extensively. Heider provides strong indications that Molek was an ancient underworld deity but he does not then ask why fire in particular was used in his cult. In all a sober and comprehensive account.

W. G. E. WATSON

HOYLES, J. A.: *Punishment in the Bible*. 1986. Pp. xi, 148. (Epworth Press, London. Price: £5.95. ISBN 0 7162 0425 8)

This book comes out of the writer's long experience as a prison chaplain, and has the practical purpose of bringing biblical insights to bear on the present treatment of offenders. Its content is thus somewhat broader than the title suggests. The Old Testament material, less than a third of the whole, is considered under three heads: Punishment as Vengeance, the Concept of Justice, and Punishment and Reconciliation. The author finds the chief Old Testament contribution to the present debate to lie in the interaction of individual accountability and the corporate responsibility of society. He pleads ultimately for therapy not punishment as the goal of penal reform, based, for the Christian, on the theology of the cross. This is not a book for the specialist.

G. I. EMMERSON

JOHNSON, C. B.: *The Psychology of Biblical Interpretation*. 1983. Pp. 119. (Zondervan, Grand Rapids, Michigan. Price: $5.95. ISBN 0 310 33281 8)

This book very much reflects the American scene for which it was written. The Fundamentalists in the USA have given the impression that there is an inevitability and rectitude about their particular interpretation. The present writer, who comes from a conservative evangelical background, draws upon his psychological know-how (for he is a psychologist rather than a Biblical scholar) to argue for pluralism in interpretation. He indicates that the text as such does not provide us with a single interpretation, but allows for a plurality of interpretations which are influenced by the variegated patterns of experience and tradition.

R. J. HAMMER

KIPPENBERG, H. G.: *Kodai Yudaya Shakai-shi.* Translated by Y. Okuizumi and K. Konno. 1986. Pp. 283 and 19 pages of index and bibliography. (Kyōbunkwan, Tokyo. Price: ¥3,800)

This is a Japanese translation of *Religion und Klassenbildung im antiken Judäa*, 2. erweiterte Auflage (1982) (see *B.L.* 1983, p. 89).

K. K. SACON

KLOOS, C.: *Yhwh's Combat with the Sea: A Canaanite Tradition in the Religion of Ancient Israel.* 1986. Pp. 243. (Brill, Leiden. Fl. 84.00. ISBN 90 04 08096 1)

There has been much discussion on the problem of Yahweh's relation with Baal and El. This is an important contribution to the debate, based on an examination of two primary texts. Ps. 29 is first treated. Arguments that it presupposes the cult of El are rejected, and it is concluded that the imagery of the psalm is based on the Ugaritic myth of Baal's conflict with the sea. A cosmogonic meaning for the Ugaritic myth is rejected, and consequently no such meaning is recognized in this or other Old Testament versions of the sea-battle. It is concluded (p. 124) the Yahweh functioned at one time as an Israelite Baal.

Exodus 15 is then dealt with. This is argued to be another account of the primary Ugaritic myth. A cosmogonic meaning is again rejected and any amalgamation of Egypt and the sea discounted, as is a cosmological significance for *yam sūp*. A shrewd analysis is offered of the relation between myth and history, and it is determined that 'mythology was transformed into national history' in the Reed Sea story (p. 190), which is thus to be classified as a charter myth (p. 206). The argument is so tightly developed that at times it is hard not to feel that there must be *some* objections to this reasoning! But a comprehensive and balanced treatment of recent work is offered, with original discussion of much of the key vocabulary (particularly *bq*ᶜ, *hsb*, *mbwl*, *qp*', *thwm*). While the theological debate will continue, this study will have an important place in it.

N. WYATT

KOCH, D.-A.: *Die Schrift als Zeuge des Evangeliums* (Beiträge zur historischen Theologie, 69). 1986. Pp. xii, 406. (Mohr, Tübingen. Price: DM 198.00. ISBN 3 16 144990 8)

This is a well researched and substantial dissertation presented at the University of Mainz on the subject of Paul's use of the Old Testament scriptures. Out of five main exegetical chapters it is the first which will be of most direct interest to Old Testament scholars in which the author examines the specific quotations to be found in Paul's epistles. In this he draws attention to the surprising lack of citations from, and allusions to, the books of Jeremiah, Ezekiel and Daniel. A careful examination is given of the implied *Vorlage* of the Pauline quotations and their particular position within the history of the Septuagint text tradition. Special note is made of the evidence provided by the Pauline usage for the substitution of the title KYRIOS for the Tetragrammaton in the Old Testament.

The main thesis of the book ranges extensively beyond these more formal textual issues and demonstrates that Paul consistently regarded the Old Testament scriptures as possessing a contemporary relevance for the Christian community. These scriptures were assumed to declare the message of the Gospel, although often in a hidden and analogical way. The two issues which drew forth from Paul the most strongly defensive use of scriptural quotations are those concerning the idea of the righteousness of God as a saving work and the plan to incorporate Gentiles along with Jews in the purpose of the divine election.

As a major study in a prominent area of the early Christian use and adoption of the Old Testament this is clearly a work of outstanding importance.

R. E. CLEMENTS

LATEGAN, B. C., and VORSTER, W. S.: *Text and Reality: Aspects of Reference in Biblical Texts* (Semeia Studies). 1985. Pp. 123. (Fortress Press, Philadelphia. Price: $14.95. ISBN 0 8006 1514 X. Scholars Press, Atlanta. ISBN 0 89130 823 7)

Do biblical narratives 'refer' only within the 'world of the text' or do they say something about a real world existing outside the text? Two South African scholars struggle with this problem, bringing in all the fashionable world of structuralism, reception analysis and the like. Each offers two essays, Vorster more favouring the 'narrative world' and Lategan wanting some contact with external reality. The central interest lies in the New Testament but the latter part of the volume has much to say about Nathan's parable spoken to David.

J. BARR

L'HEUREUX, C. E.: *Life Journey and the Old Testament: An Experiential Approach to the Bible and Personal Transformation*. 1986. Pp. ix, 171. (Paulist Press, Mahwah, New Jersey. Price: $8.95. ISBN 0 8091 2828 4)

The Introduction to this volume, directed not just to those in the field of religious education but also to academic colleagues 'too exclusively oriented to purely intellectual matters', describes the author's own transformation in the midst of a traditional career teaching Old Testament after contact with the Jungian psychological category of individuation. 'David's story', especially the conflict with Absalom, stories of response to divine call, episodes of faith and trust in the Bible, and 'Dis-ease and Healing in the Psalms' are the stuff of the four main chapters. A substantial appendix (pp. 145–70) discusses 'Historical Criticism and Beyond'.

A. G. AULD

LINDARS, B.: *Good Tidings to Zion: Interpreting Deutero-Isaiah Today*. 1986. Pp. 25. (John Rylands University Library of Manchester, Manchester. Price: £1.50). Reprinted from *Bulletin of the John Rylands University Library of Manchester*, vol. 68, no. 2 (Spring, 1986)

In this rewarding lecture, Barnabas Lindars first reviews some of the most recent work on the formation of the Book of Isaiah, stressing the developing consensus that both chapters 1–39 and 40–55 have been subject to a complex process of alteration, expansion, and, especially, adaptation in the light of the developing circumstances of the people of Israel. The dynamic process of *updating* was applied more to the material of chapters 1–39 in order to affirm its continuing relevance than to chapters 40–55 which always lay in the future for every new generation of editors; but these chapters too underwent an equally dynamic process of *reinterpretation* that continued long after the finalization of the text. The second part of the lecture examines how particular reinterpretations of Deutero-Isaianic material about the Servant of Yahweh and the theme of universalism can encourage us to regard the Biblical text as containing multiple levels of meaning.

D. J. A. Clines

Locher, C.: *Die Ehre einer Frau in Israel: exegetische und rechtsvergleichende Studien zu Deuteronomium 22, 13–21* (Orbis Biblicus et Orientalis 70). 1986. Pp. xviii, 464. (Universitätsverlag, Freiburg. Price: Sw.Fr. 111.00. ISBN 3 7278 0356 8. Vandenhoeck & Ruprecht, Göttingen. ISBN 3 525 53697 6)

This major study is concerned with the interpretation of Deut. 22:13–21 against the background of Mesopotamian legal texts. After a detailed and comprehensive treatment of the textual, literary, stylistic, and formal characteristics of the passage, the author turns to a comparison of the law with the extra-biblical parallels. The latter are in three groups, dealing with, firstly, the virginity of a young girl on the point of marriage, secondly, divorce, and, thirdly, false accusation and false witness at law. The study is an exhaustive one, which, even though making little reference to the present general deuteronomic context of the law, aims to create a more general ancient oriental legal context within which that law is to be understood. It is also a fruitful study,with extensive critical reviews of, and positive contributions to, the discussion of major issues. The deuteronomic law is argued to have originated in the record of a legal decision (vv. 13–19) which, through the addition of vv. 20–21, was transformed into a casuistic law. The law is concerned with the virginity of the bride, the Hebrew term (and its Akkadian cognate) meaning 'virgin' in legal texts with the more general sense of 'young girl' being appropriate elsewhere. The law reflects a widespread concern and custom, even though its deuteronomic formulation is unique. This is a significant contribution to issues of legal, historical, and anthropological interest, as well as to the question of the origin and development of a deuteronomic law.

A. D. H. Mayes

Mathys, H.-P.: *Liebe deinen Nächsten wie dich selbst: Untersuchungen zum alttestamentlichen Gebot der Nächstenliebe (Lev. 19, 18)* (Orbis Biblicus et Orientalis, 71). 1986. Pp. xii, 201. (Universitätsverlag Freiburg, Schweiz. Price: Sw.Fr. 56.00. ISBN 3 7278 0357 6. Vandenhoeck & Ruprecht, Göttingen)

All too frequently the understanding of the meaning and significance of the well-known commandment in Leviticus 19:18 is coloured by its still more famous usage by Jesus in the New Testament. On the other hand, where this is not so, exegesis of it too often tends to limit itself to an understanding of it within a narrow context of ancient Israelite society. This stimulating monograph — the most thorough study of this topic known to this reviewer — dispels any illusion that the meaning of Leviticus 19:18 is clear and in no need of more than a brief treatment. The first chapter, concentrating on *'hb l[e]* and *kamôka*, defends the traditional but often contested translation 'thou shalt love thy neighbour as thyself', and the second follows this up with a detailed discussion of the words *'hb, re[a]'* (and related terms), *ger*, *kamôka* in Leviticus 19:18, 34. Chapter III examines the commandment in its immediate context in Leviticus 19 and in the Holiness Code as a whole (with a valuable discussion of the Holiness Code as a 'programme' of renewal in the exilic/post-exilic period). A fourth chapter ('Die historische Verortung des Liebesgebotes') discusses the function of the commandment at various stages in the history of Israelite society as well as in the Qumran writings and in the early church. The fifth and final chapter examines the commandment in relation to other commandments in the Pentateuch, notably the command to love God in Deuteronomy 6:5, and ends with a discussion of its significance for the study of Old Testament ethics.

E. W. NICHOLSON

MOLTMANN-WENDEL, E., SCHÖNHERR, A., and TRAITLER, R. (eds.): *Seid fruchtbar und wehrt Euch: Frauentexte zum Kirchentag* (Kaiser Traktate, 93). 1986. Pp. 84. (Chr. Kaiser Verlag, München. Price: DM 10.00. ISBN 3 459 01643 4)

'Be fruitful and *fortify*' is the title-giving and longest chapter of an attractive series of papers, meditations and poems prepared by women theologians from both German states, Switzerland, and the USA for a 1985 German church conference. Most relate to different aspects of the Noah-chapters in Gen. 6–9; 'blessing', images and names for God, and a sermon on Ps. 24 are also included. High-point is the dialogue between Mrs Noah, one of the daughters in law, and Noah.

A. G. AULD

MOON, C. H. S.: *A Korean Minjung Theology — An Old Testament Perspective*. 1985. Pp. x, 83. (Orbis Books, Maryknoll, New York. Price: $7.95. ISBN 0 88344 250 7)

Minjung in Korean means 'the people' or 'the masses', and *minjung* theology is liberation theology in a Korean setting. The author, an Old Testament professor at the Presbyterian Theological Seminary in Seoul, sees in Israel's history as interpreted by Mendenhall an analogy with the present situation in Korea which offers hope to an oppressed people.

R. N. WHYBRAY

NICHOLSON, E. W.: *God and His People. Covenant and Theology in the Old Testament*. 1986. Pp. xii, 244. (Oxford University Press, Oxford. Price: £22.50. ISBN 0 19 826684 7)

The subject of covenant in the Old Testament has passed through a number of significant stages in recent years. The dramatic surge of interest in the subject occasioned by Martin Noth's theory of an Israelite amphictyony, and the understanding of this as a tribal federation, followed by the extensively employed arguments for the influence of ancient Near-eastern vassal treaty forms upon the Old Testament, each made a contribution. These were followed in turn by the distinctive linguistic-analytical approach of E. Kutsch and a more critical, but highly theological, rejoinder to all of these in the work of L. Perlitt. Professor Nicholson's work is an excellent survey of the whole debate beginning with a historical survey of the subject since the critical work of J. Wellhausen and drawing special attention to the importance of M. Weber's sociological concern with divine covenants as a social institution. Before the Second World War this brought about a significant shift away from preoccupation with treatment of covenant as a purely theological idea and a fuller recognition of its role as a social institution.

Five key texts concerning the pre-Deuteronomic origins of the notion of Israel's divine covenant are examined in part two. Especially important among these are those in Hosea, linking it with the prophetic movement of the eighth century B.C. Overall, however, it was the Deuteronomic movement a century or more later which developed a fully elaborated theology of covenant, as Perlitt has demonstrated. This is a most valuable book for the amount of ground that it covers and for the eminently sound and balanced perspective that it brings to a subject that has suffered more than one kind of distortion during the past three decades.

R. E. CLEMENTS

PALMER, B. (ed.): *Medicine and the Bible*. 1986. Pp. 272. (Paternoster Press, Exeter, for the Christian Medical Fellowship. Price: £7.95. ISBN 0 85364 423 3)

All but two of the contributors to this volume are medical doctors. The first four chapters deal with medical matters in the Bible. D. J. Wiseman and C. J. Hemer set out details of diseases and medical practice in the ancient Near East (including the Old Testament) and the New Testament world. A. S. Darling examines the 'Levitical Code' and concludes that, while some requirements may have promoted hygiene and health, the code was given primarily to ensure ceremonial holiness. S. G. Browne's article on leprosy in the Bible summarizes his earlier publications. The remaining chapters discuss ethical questions (abortion, homosexuality, issues of conscience facing a doctor), demon possession, and spiritual healing. The overall approach is conservative.

C. S. RODD

REVENTLOW, H. GRAF: *Gebet im Alten Testament*. 1986. Pp. 334. (Kohlhammer, Stuttgart. Price: DM 36.00. ISBN 3 17 009238 3)

Professor Reventlow has produced a thorough and comprehensive study of prayer in the Old Testament. The main part of the work, which divides into seven chapters and has the general title of 'The Forms of Old Testament Prayers', gives an analysis of short prayers in ancient prose, hymns of praise, supplication, thanksgiving, intercession, artistic forms of prayer in later times and redactional work on Psalms. The field of study is an important one, and the author has combined his analysis of biblical material with short paragraphs set within the text, but with a narrower spacing, which cite other discussions of the subject. The work is, therefore, a handbook to guide its readers to a full and detailed study of the subject-matter; it is an excellent guide that is boldly attempted and competently achieved.

Professor Reventlow's analysis is set in the context of present-day discussion; this is done in an introductory section, which stands as a valuable study in itself and extends to over 70 pages. The discussion outlined extends from Thomas Aquinas to Dorothee Sölle and the author surveys the attitude towards prayer among the adherents of different philosophical and theological trends until he reaches the contemporary interest in the subject. It is in response to these discussions that the author has undertaken his analysis of the Old Testament material. But because of the nature of the Old Testament material itself and the type of analysis it demands, it has not been possible to build many bridges between the main part of the study and the survey in the introduction.

Like other writings by Professor Reventlow, this study is a major work on the subject; its readers will be greatly enriched by working gradually and carefully through it.

G. H. JONES

REVENTLOW, H. GRAF: *Problems of Biblical Theology in the Twentieth Century*. 1986. Pp. xvii, 188. (SCM Press, London. Price: £7.95. ISBN 0 334 02277 0)

This volume is the translation by John Bowden from the original German which was published in 1983 and was reviewed *B.L.* 1984, p. 102. This English edition is a corrected and enlarged version and will make a useful book accessible to a wider circle. In view of the overwhelming mass of bibliographical material here presented, it might prove useful to the reader to direct attention to p. 12 where reference is made to the essays by von Rad, Noth, and Zimmerli (translated in *Essays on Old Testament Interpretation*, edited by Westermann, SCM Press, 1963) which heralded von Rad's *Old Testament Theology*. The section on the work of van Ruler, Miskotte, and Marquardt and the link with the Barthian theology (p. 54 ff.) is important for the understanding of the relation between Christianity and Judaism. In this connexion two fascinating books have been overlooked, viz. Lev. Gillet, *Communion in the Messiah* and O. S. Rankin, *Jewish Religious Polemic*. Full reference is given to the current debate about the Canon (v. esp. Brevard Childs and Reventlow himself) with its bearing on the question of the possibility and nature of a Biblical theology. Perhaps more could have been done in the translation to loosen up the tighly-packed style of the German original.

N. W. Porteous

Di Sante, C.: *La Preghiera di Israele: Alle origini della liturgia cristiana* (Radici, 6). 1985. Pp. xiv, 242. (Casa Editice Marietti, Casale Monferrato. Price: Lire 20,000. ISBN 88 211 8334 3)

This book succeeds in its aim to inform its Christian readership of its own Jewish liturgical roots. A brief description is given of the main sources: Mishnah, Talmud, and Siddur. A detailed account follows of the *Shema'*, *Tefillah*, and Reading of the Torah, with the accompanying benedictions, prefaced by an introduction to the *berakah* form. Among individual, family and synagogue prayers the meal blessings and Sabbath and Passover ceremonies are of special interest. The annual festivals and fasts are briefly described. Where appropriate, reference is given to Old Testament origins and background; but while awareness is shown of the complexity of the origins of Passover and Unleavened Bread, Purim is said simply to be linked to a historical event related in Esther. The book is thus essentially descriptive rather than critical. On page 172 one of the mid-week Torah readings is assigned to Tuesday instead of Monday (as correctly on p. 115).

A. Gelston

Schedl, C.: *Zur Theologie des Alten Testaments: der göttliche Sprachvorgang in Schöpfung und Geschichte*. 1986. Pp. 248. (Herder, Wien. Price: ÖS 275.00/DM 38.00. ISBN 3 210 24828 1)

The late Professor Schedl was convinced that insight into holy writings could be obtained by a complicated numerological system which he described as 'logotechnic'. He has applied his method to the New Testament and the Quran, and here it is proposed as the key to Old Testament theology. Each chapter of the book contains complicated numerological calculations, the exact relevance of which to the sometimes interesting observations on the biblical texts being discussed is not wholly clear. There are helpful comments on the early stories in Genesis and the descriptions in Genesis and Exodus of a divine covenant, but too much of the book is devoted to speculations about the meaning of the precise number of words and letters in particular texts for a wholly coherent picture to emerge. Unhappily the author was killed in a traffic accident shortly before the publication of this book.

R. J. Coggins

SCHMIDT, W. H.: *The Faith of the Old Testament.* 1986. Pp. x, 302. (Basil Blackwell, Oxford. Price: £7.95. ISBN 0 631 15305 5)

This is the first paperback edition of the volume deservedly well-reviewed in *B.L.* 1984, p. 102, and now available at little over half the original price.

A. G. AULD

SEEBASS, H.: *Il Dio di tutta la Bibbia. Teologia biblica per l'orientamento alla fede* (Studi Biblici, 72). Translated by G. Fantoma. 1985. Pp. 293. (Paideia Editrice, Brescia. Price: Lire 20,000)

This is the Italian translation of Seebass's *Der Gott der ganzen Bibel* (1982; *B.L.* 1983, p. 95). The rendering and presentation appear as excellent as is usual in this series.

R. P. R. MURRAY

SMEND, R.: *Die Mitte des Alten Testaments: Gesammelte Studien, Bd. 1* (Beiträge zur evangelischen Theologie, Bd. 99). 1986. Pp. 246. (Chr. Kaiser Verlag, München. DM 38.00. ISBN 3 459 01658 2)

The author tells us that the impetus to publish this work came from requests to republish his Article, 'Die Mitte des Alten Testaments', published in 1970. This gave him the incentive to publish with it a number of other Articles, all similarly related in one way or another to some aspect of Old Testament Theology. It is particularly fitting that it should be accompanied by his Article, published in 1963, on 'Die Bundesformel', because, for Smend, the 'heart' of the Old Testament is the concept, 'I will be your God and you shall be my people'. This is seen as central, however, not in any static, fixed sense, but rather as a basic principle which could develop and be modified in many ways as Israel's history and religious experiences unfolded. It is surprising how well much of Smend's earlier writing on 'Covenant' has stood up to the changed climate of more recent scholarship, which is more than can be said of some other writing on the subject at that time. Other Articles among the twelve published here include studies of 'Das Nein des Amos', 'Theologie im Alten Testament', '"Das Ende ist gekommen". Ein Amoswort in der Priesterschrift', 'Elemente alltestamentlichen Geschichtsdenkens', 'Der Ort des Staates im Alten Testament', 'Essen und Trinken — ein Stück Weltlichkeit des Alten Testaments', and 'Nachkritische Schriftauslegung'. It is good to have these Articles, published over more than twenty years in a number of places, brought together, and most encouraging to see that this is labelled 'Gesammelte Studien, *Bd. 1*.

R. A. MASON

SPREAFICO, A.: *Esodo: Memoria e promessa: Interpretazioni profetiche* (Supplementi alla Rivista Biblica, 14). 1985. Pp. 176. (Edizioni Dehoniane, Bologna. Price: Lire 25,000. ISBN 88 10 30202 8)

The literary pattern of the Exodus as historical event, as the exile (Anti-Exodus) and as the promised return (New Exodus) is here traced in pre-exilic prophecy (Hosea, Jeremiah, Ezekiel, Micah, and Amos). 'Literary pattern' is defined as a combination of paradigmatic and syntagmatic elements. These are isolated for the Exodus theme in the five books and set out in well over sixty tables, though occasionally the accompanying explanation is several pages away. The Exodus theme emerges as more important than previously realized.

In the main the author is concise and clear, though it would have been better if the section on Hosea 2 had come later on in the book since it is such a variation of the pattern described. Most of the Hebrew passages are translated and a mini-vocabulary in the form of a one-page insert is also provided. The author has accumulated a wealth of data and so opened the way for further study of a significant topic.

W. G. E. WATSON

STÄHLI, H.-P.: *Solare Elemente im Jahweglauben des Alten Testaments* (Orbis Biblicus et Orientalis, 66). 1985. Pp. ix, 60. (Universitätsverlag, Freiburg, Schweiz. Price: Sw.Fr. 19.00. ISBN 3 7278 0335 5. Vandenhoeck & Ruprecht, Göttingen. ISBN 3 525 53689 5)

Beginning with the personification of the sun and the portrayal of him with chariots and horses in a mosaic discovered at the sixth-century A.D. synagogue of Beth-Alpha, Professor Stähli introduces his investigation into the possible presence of a solar cult in the Old Testament. After giving in the following section a brief summary of the different views taken over the years, ranging from the rather cautious judgement that no direct evidence is available because of enthusiastic purging of non-Yahwistic elements from the Old Testament to the bolder assertion that Israel did have a solar mythology and religion, the author launches his own examination of the evidence. The natural starting-point is with pre-Israelite Canaanite religion, and particular attention is attached to names such as Beth-shemesh and to the east–west orientation of the Jerusalem temple. Passages suggesting the subordination of the sun to Yahweh are then examined, and also particular Old Testament phrases denoting that the sun is 'life'. Other passages receiving detailed attention are those connecting the sun with Yahweh and then considering Yahweh as the sun. Before drawing his own affirmative conclusions Professor Stähli considers the criticisms that have been made of attempts to establish the presence of solar elements in the faith of the Old Testament.

Although this book does not tread new ground, it contains a concise and useful treatment of the available material. The argument has been presented clearly and attractively, as would befit a work that originated as an invited lecture at the University of Neuchâtel.

G. H. JONES

TERRIEN, S.: *Till the Heart sings: a Biblical Theology of Manhood and Womanhood*. 1985. Pp. x, 260. (Fortress Press, Philadelphia. Price: $24.95. ISBN 0 8006 0752 X)

The attempt is here made to counter the charge that the Bible supports male domination, by sketching a biblical theology which portrays woman as the crown of creation. The Old Testament section concentrates on Gen. 1–3 and the Song of Songs, together with the wisdom literature, Proverbs 8:22–31 being given special attention as 'the pivot of Scripture'. The liberalism inherent in material of this kind was, however, thwarted by the Jerusalem priesthood of the later period, for whom circumcision was the sign of membership of the covenant community. The latter part of the book is devoted to the New Testament and the developing Christian church, in which the legacy of Paul (himself at times guilty of 'theological immaturity') was largely dissipated. This is a splendid piece of polemic, thought-provoking and challenging, with some vigorous thrusts against fundamentalists of different kinds. It can hardly be regarded as a definitive portrayal of the biblical view of sexuality. Always the nagging doubt remains (and it is not removed by references to 'canonical dynamics'): if it is legitimate to select biblical material in support of an attractive cause, on what ground can its selective use on behalf of other, less welcome, views be rejected?

R. J. COGGINS

De Tillesse, C. M.: *Nova Jerusalém. Eclesiologia.* Livro Primeiro: *Reino de Deus.* Primeira Parte: *Estudo Bíblico.* 1986. Pp. 171. (Editora Nova Jerusalém, Fortaleza, CE, Brazil: Price: Cz. $40,00)

This is the first part of an undertaking by the author of the *Revista Bíblica Brasileira* to produce what he hopes will prove to be a radically new account of the origin and nature of the Church. He develops themes first treated in the *Revista* to show that the theology of liberation is rooted firmly in the Old Testament (p. 157). As in the earlier articles, his direct and lucid prose incorporates and makes accessible to his Brazilian readership some of the more significant of recent European and American scholarly work in Biblical Studies. Relevant to readers of the *Book List* will be the first two chapters (it is not clear where chapter 2 begins, but presumably on p. 49) on 'Historical and Social Aspects' (i.e. of the Kingdom of God as presented in the Bible), and 'The First Covenant'. The work is to be completed with two further volumes on 'The Birth of the Church at the Last Supper' and 'The Holy Spirit in the Church'. The present volume carries a foreword by Cardinal A. Lorscheider of Fortaleza.

J. M. Dines

Van Til, H. J.: *The Fourth Day.* 1986. Pp. xii, 286. (Eerdmans, Grand Rapids, Michigan; distributed by Paternoster, Exeter. Price: £8.85. ISBN 0 8028 0178 1)

The debate between creationism and evolution would seem to most in Britain to be little more than a 'storm in a Victorian teacup', but it is a living issue in the U.S.A., largely due to the agitation of Fundamentalist groups who desire creationism to be taught as a scientific theory. The writer addresses himself to such a situation. He writes as a distinguished scientist, but also as a convinced Christian who belongs to a conservative Calvinist Church. Writing very convincingly, he seeks to indicate that there can be no contradiction between a theology which sees in the scriptures an emphasis on God as creator and his own convictions about the validity of scientific research and discovery. Rather than preclude it, the very acceptance of God as creator becomes the basis for the scientific inquiry. The writer is convinced of the authority of scripture and is conservative in his approach, but his bibliographies display a broader interest. The attempt to integrate scripture and science is less successful than the separate treatment of each, which precedes the attempt.

R. J. Hammer

Vermeylen, J.: *Le Dieu de la Promesse et le Dieu de l'Alliance: le dialogue des grandes institutions théologiques de l'Ancient Testament* (Lectio Divina 126). 1986. Pp. 375. (Éditions du Cerf, Paris. Price: Fr. 186.00. ISBN 2 204 02594 1; ISSN 0750 1919)

This is an attractive and readable guide to the theological themes of the Old Testament, intended for 'un large public cultivé'. The author presents a historical account of the faith of Israel, divided into four periods: the pre-exilic period (beginning with David — he doubts whether anything useful can be said of the faith of 'pre-historic' Israel); the Exile; the Persian period; and the Hellenistic age. In each he sees Israelite faith as a tension between the static, sacral, establishment view of reality and the prophetic, ethical, risk-taking religious approach of which the classical prophets are the paradigm case. The scheme works better for the first two periods than the last two, but it has many merits, and the author is careful to stress that *both* types of religion are needed for a durable faith. The work surveys a remarkably large number of Old Testament texts in an accessible way, becoming technical only when his own theories of 'relectures' necessitate very fine distinctions between different redactional levels in, for example, the 'deuteronomistic' corpus or the book of Isaiah. This would be an excellent book for a student beginning Old Testament studies and wanting an overall theological orientation.

J. BARTON

VISCHER, W.: *L'Écriture et la Parole.* (Essais Bibliques No. 12). 1985. Pp. 208 (Labor et Fides, Geneva. Price: Sw.Fr. 25.00. ISBN 2 8309 0055 3)

The French Protestant scholar W. Vischer was born in 1895 and this collection of studies and addresses by him is intended as a celebration for his ninetieth year. As a scholar who sought to establish a bridge between dogmatic theology in the Reformed tradition and critical Old Testament exegesis Vischer came to popular attention through the publication in 1934 of the work which was later translated into English as *The Witness of the Old Testament to Christ* (1949; see *B.L.* 1950, p. 69; *Eleven Years*, p. 286). Volume 2 appeared in 1942 but remained untranslated into English. Vischer taught for a period in Germany until ejected from his post in 1934 when he returned to his native France. A close friend and follower of Karl Barth he worked strenuously to establish a firm role for the Old Testament in Christian theology and for a positive and constructive recognition of the importance of the Jewish people for Christian faith. Seven shorter exegetical studies are published here, three of them on prophetic themes (Isaiah 6–9, Jeremiah, and Deutero-Isaiah), one on the Song of Songs and the remainder illustrating the author's interest in the relationship between Old and New Testaments. Scholars who have hitherto known only the rather over-strained attempts at a form of Christological exegesis of the Old Testament exemplified in the author's major work will greatly welcome this fuller picture of a remarkable Christian figure. He sought to combine the qualities of theologian, pastor, and educationalist in a remarkable way.

R. E. CLEMENTS

WOLFF, H. W.: *Old Testament and Christian Preaching*. 1986. Pp. 110. (Fortress Press, Philadelphia. Price: $8.95. ISBN 0 8006 1905 6)

The contents of this book have appeared in German at various dates and in various contexts. There are ten sermons on Old Testament texts, a brief discussion of the place of the Old Testament in preaching and of the mutual relationship of the Old and New Testaments, and a summary statement concerning the premises, necessity, and principles of typological interpretation. The sermons are forceful, lively, based on perceptive exegesis, and effectively related to the contemporary situation. The author's views on typology are presented with admirable clarity. The translation (by Margaret Kohl) is excellent.

G. W. ANDERSON

8. THE LIFE AND THOUGHTS OF THE SURROUNDING PEOPLES

CADUFF, G. A.: *Antike Sintflutsagen* (Hypomnemata. Untersuchungen zur Antike und zu ihrem Nachleben, 82). 1986. Pp. 308. (Vandenhoeck & Ruprecht, Göttingen. Price: DM 68.00. ISBN 3 252 25180 7)

As is to be expected from the series of which it forms part, this book is primarily concerned with the interpretation of flood stories in Greek and Latin literature, in which the central figure is Deukalion, whose similarity, if not identity, with Noah was frequently noted by Philo and later Christian writers. In the first part, the relevant texts are given in German translation. They are analysed in the second part, where Caduff concludes that the Deukalion saga represents a fusion of a tribal legend of the Leleges group with ancient Near Eastern flood traditions in the course of the seventh century B.C. Hence, in the third section, which is concerned with interpretation, he is led to compare and contrast the Deukalion and related material with the Hebrew, Sumerian, and Accadian flood stories, in the course of discussions of such themes as theodicy, the sacrifice on a mountain, flood stories as ritual aetiologies and the flood hero's journey to the other world. Hence it is this part which is most likely to interest readers of the *Book List*. For Genesis, the author relies heavily on Westermann's commentary and, for the Mesopotamian evidence, on the standard works of Lambert-Millard, ANET, Heidel, Beyerlin, and Labat. Thus specialists in these areas will learn little new and the ways in which the author sometimes interprets these texts to buttress his own interpretations of the flood legend raise considerable doubts. He is careful to note the differences, as well as the resemblances, between the ancient Near Eastern stories and the Greek and Latin traditions, and also the differences between themselves in the former area. But is it really the case that in all the ancient Near Eastern versions — including presumably the Old Testament — the deity responsible for sending the flood finally appears not as the almighty but as 'der Übertölpelte und Unterlegene'? or that the flood hero's journey in his vessel indicates that he is to be understood as a *pharmakos*? However, the author's very thorough tracing of the antecedents and development of the Graeco-Roman flood stories makes out a strong case for a real connection with their Mesopotamian counterparts and in this respect represents a solid achievement.

J. R. PORTER

DIETRICH, M., HECKER, K., HOFTIJZER, J., KAMMERZELL, F., LORETZ, O., MÜLLER, W. W., RÖMER, W. H. PH., and STERNBERG, H.: *Religiöse Texte. Deutungen der Zukunft in Briefen, Orakeln und Omina* (Texte aus der Umwelt des Alten Testaments, II/1). 1986. Pp. 157. (Gerd Mohn, Gütersloh. Price: DM 118.00; sub. price: DM 98.00. ISBN 3 579 00066 7)

This continuation of the new German '*ANET*' (see *B.L.* 1986, p. 102 for the first volume) presents ancient Near Eastern texts (in whole or excerpt) dealing with mantic dreams, oracles, predictions, omens, and other techniques claiming to provide knowledge of the future: Sumerian by Römer, Babylonian and Assyrian by Hecker (but Mari letters by Dietrich), Ugaritic omens by Dietrich and Loretz, Egyptian material by Kammerzell and Sternberg, the Deir ʿAlla inscription by Hoftijzer, South Arabic inscriptions (all Sabaean in fact) by Müller. Only a small number of those given here also appear in *ANET* or similar works. As before, the translations are reliable, suitably introduced and provided with bibliographies and notes. The Deir ʿAlla inscription is of course the most directly related to the Old Testament and it has been allowed much more comment than the other texts. But the whole fascicle gives a fair picture of its topic throughout the Near East.

W. G. LAMBERT

FAHR, H.: *Herodot und Altes Testament* (Europäische Hochschulschriften: Reihe 23, Theologie; Bd. 266). 1985. Pp. 140. (Peter Lang, Frankfurt am Main, Bern, New York. Price: Sw.Fr. 30.00. ISBN 3 8204 8524 4. ISSN 0721 3409)

This monograph comprises two essays: one on 'Cambyses: Guilt and Destiny in Herodotus' and one on 'Cyrus: A Royal Saviour for Jews and

Greeks'. Cambyses does not figure in the Old Testament, but along with him Fahr treats another example of *hybris* from Herodotus — Xerxes, who presents an unimpressive image in the story of Esther. Cyrus, on the other hand, is portrayed very positively both in Herodotus and in the Old Testament — especially in DtIs. In DtIs he is Yahweh's anointed agent for the restoration of Israel; in Herodotus he is the agent of heaven in liberating the Greek cities of Asia Minor from the domination of Croesus. Herodotus and the Old Testament writers of the same general period reveal a theological understanding of history; this comparative study is interesting, if rather lacking in depth.

F. F. BRUCE

FINNESTAD, R. B.: *Image of the World and Symbol of the Creator: On the Cosmological and Iconological Values of the Temple of Edfu* (Studies in Oriental Religions, 10). 1985. Pp. x, 174, and 9 plates. (Harrassowitz, Wiesbaden. Price: DM 44.00. ISBN 3 447 02504 2)

The sub-title is a truer guide to this book's contents than is the bland, meaningless main title. The starting-point is an Egyptian text in the Temple of Horus at Edfu (Ptolemaic period) which presents a local myth of creation — the waters, a reed-float on which a divine falcon alights, the earth that then holds it firm, forming Edfu (town and landscape) and its temple of the falcon-god. The rest of the volume seeks to expound this text (with over-use of the turgid jargon of 'history of religion') and the significance of the temple as (at once) image of the local cosmos (Edfu) and itself a deity-impregnated 'icon' receiving due honour, as well as a place of practised cult.

K. A. KITCHEN

FISCHER-ELFERT, H.-W.: *Literarische Ostraka der Ramessidenzeit in Übersetzung* (Kleine Ägyptische Texte, ed. W. Helck). 1986. Pp. x, 93. (Harrassowitz, Wiesbaden. Price: DM. 36.00. ISBN 3 447 02611 1)

Mainly jottings on slips of limestone and pottery from Western Thebes of the late second millennium B.C. Egyptian ostraca often contain short literary compositions complete, besides many excerpts from longer works. The major publications (Černý-Gardiner; Posener) simply offer hieroglyphic transcriptions. This convenient little book offers a dozen quite well-preserved short texts in copy and translation with notes, making them generally accessible. Section I offers the short wisdom-instruction of Hori, and a short interjection. Section II has five hymns, including a splendid hymn to the Nile-flood. Section III has one text of funerary import. None has been fully translated in print before. A useful source-book within its limits.

K. A. KITCHEN

FRONZAROLI, P. (ed.): *Studi Yemeniti*, 1 (Quaderni di Semitistica, 14). 1985. Pp. vi, 200, with 2 folding maps, 34 pp. of plates and 13 pp. of Arabic summaries. (Istituto di Linguistica e di Lingue Orientali, Università di Firenze, Florence; distributed by Herder, Rome. Price: Lire 46,000)

The results of several recent Italian missions to Yemen are collected here. S. Mazzoni reports on the surface survey, A. Avanzini on historical questions and new-found inscriptions, L. Bettini on the spoken Arabic of the al-Baraddūn region, and G. Canova on traditions and folklore concerning the Banū Hilāl. There are English summaries of these four articles on pp. 187–96. Professor Fronzaroli as editor contributes a preface on the general scope of the investigations.

J. BARR

GUBEL, E., and LIPIŃSKI, E. (eds.): *Phoenicia and its Neighbours* (Studia Phoenicia III). 1985. Pp. 240, including illustrations. (Uitgeverij Peeters, Leuven. Price: B.Fr. 1,800. ISBN 90 6831 029 1)

These are the papers from a symposium held in Brussels in 1983. After an introduction by D. Homès-Fredericq (pp. 5–11), H. Limet discusses 'Les relations entre Mari et la côte méditerranéenne sous le règne de Zimri-Lim' (pp. 13–20) and M. Trokay 'Montures de sceaux-cylindres cassites et ornementations de pendentifs chypriotes' (pp. 21–44). P. Swiggers in 'Byblos dans les lettres d'el Amarna' (pp. 45–58) deals with historical problems, while J. Servais's contribution, 'Architectures funéraires mycénienne et ougaritique: un parallèle à éviter' (pp. 59–67), emphasizes the differences between the two tomb-building traditions. R. Echt provides a study of 'Les ivoires figurés de Kamid el-Loz et l'art phénicien du IIe millénaire' (pp. 69–83). Of more direct relevance to the Old Testament, specifically to the problem of Molek, is an article by J. B. Hennessy on a 'Thirteenth Century B.C. Temple of Human Sacrifice at Amman' (pp. 85–104), dealing with an important piece of new evidence. J. B. Meyer's 'Zur Herkunft der etruskischen Lebermodelle' (pp. 105–20) will be of less interest, though the next two contributions are important: G. Bunnens, 'Le luxe phénicien d'après les inscriptions royales assyriennes' (pp. 121–33), questioning the usual view of Phoenician luxury goods, and G. Kestemont, 'Les phéniciens en Syrie du nord' (pp. 135–61), reconstructing the expansion of Phoenician commercial colonies and influence beyond the Phoenician homeland. There follows a series of art-historical notes: E. Warmenbol, 'La statuette égyptisante de Sfiré' (pp. 163–80); E. Gubel, 'Phoenician Lioness Heads from Nimrud' (pp. 181–202); F. Vandenabeele, 'L'influence phénicienne sur la coroplasthie chypriote' (pp. 203–11). Returning to the Old Testament, we have E. Lipiński, 'Products and Brokers of Tyre according to Ezekiel 27' (pp. 213–20), while of considerable importance for Phoenician religion are P. Bordreuil, 'Le dieu Echmoun dans la région d'Amrit' (pp. 221–30), and C. Tzavellas-Bonnet, 'Melqart, Bès et l'Héraclès dactyle de Crète' (pp. 231–40).

J. F. HEALEY

HERRMANN, G.: *Ivories from Room SW 37 Fort Shalmaneser* (Ivories from Nimrud, Fasc. IV). 1986. Part 1: pp. 288, 33 drawings, 1 colour plate. Part 2: 422 pp. of plates. (British School of Archaeology in Iraq, London. Price: £100.00. ISBN 0 903472 10 4)

Nimrud (ancient Calah) has yielded more carved ivories than any other ancient near eastern site. The 1,500 pieces catalogued here lay in a storeroom, smashed when Median and Babylonian looters tore the gold foil from the richly decorated furniture. The pictures offer much ancient craftsmanship to admire, and the catalogue describes each piece precisely. Introductory chapters discuss the styles of carving, allocating groups to different 'schools' or 'workshops', located in Syria–Phoenicia. A large group of 'Egyptianizing' ivories, some bearing hieroglyphs as decorative or magical signs, is discussed in detail by K. A. Kitchen (chapter 4). The dominant Phoenician style shows many links with the ivories found at Samaria. This link is strengthened by the inclusion of a Hebrew inscription (Gibson, *TSSI* I, 19, 20) as well as numerous other West Semitic words and fitters' marks (studied briefly by the reviewer, chapter 5). It can plausibly be maintained that the furniture kept in Room SW 37 of Fort Shalmaneser included pieces taken by Sargon from the Israelite palace and mansions in Samaria, so enriching any reconstruction of the luxury Israelite nobles enjoyed. This is a major contribution to the study of a particularly attractive ancient form of art.

A. R. MILLARD

JACQ, C.: *Egyptian Magic*. 1985. Introduction by A. R. David. Pp. xiv, 162, frontispiece, 46 figures. (Aris & Phillips, Warminster. Price: £5.95. ISBN 0 85668 299 3. Bolchazy-Carducci, Chicago. ISBN 0 86516 118 6)

This book is not a detailed, analytical treatise on ancient Egyptian magic, but is its author's very personal and 'atmospheric' presentation of that art as if 'from within', as if he believed in the farrago of ancient spells — an approach that will not appeal to all. The ten main chapters deal with the social range of magic, credentials, and powers of magicians, apparatus, deities as patrons of magic, conflicts, magic and medicine including love and childbirth, animals, and Coptic magic. The approach is original but tends to be obsessive; and much fuller documentation is desirable. The headings to the Notes (pp. 158–61) have strayed: for Introduction, read Chapter 1; for Chapter 1, read Chapter 2, and so in turn correct the numbers of the other chapter-heads. There is a tendency to over-interpret data; in fig. 2, Isis merely presents or supports the king before Osiris — no hint occurs that she 'pours fluid' on to his neck, while the supposed 'incense burner' is in fact a libation-vessel as in fig. 20 (correctly described as the king pouring water — but its identification as 'polarised energy' requires justification). Lack of care and rigour is at times apparent: fig. 1 illustrates heart amulets, not heart-scarabs (for which, see fig. 14); p. 13, Khaemwaset was priest of Ptah not Re. On pp. 88–91, it is not made clear that the narratives cited are tales about the reigns mentioned, not documents from those reigns.

K. A. KITCHEN

KREBERNIK, M.: *Die Beschwörungen aus Fara und Ebla*. (Texte und Studien zur Orientalistik, 2). 1984. Pp. xvi, 385, including 5 plates in line. (George Olms, Hildesheim, Zürich, New York. Price: DM 48.00. ISBN 3 487 07479 6)

Fara is a Sumerian site in southern Iraq, Ebla of course in Syria. From both, cuneiform tablets of mid-third-millennium date inscribed with incantations have been found, and they are edited together here because the Fara incantations, all Sumerian, are occasionally duplicated in the Ebla tablets. The latter also contain some in a Semitic language (called 'Eblaite' by many), and since these are the only genuine literary documents from Ebla with any claim to be of Syrian origin, they are part of the intellectual ancestry of Canaanite religion. Number twenty-six in the sequence of this book names six gods, of which five are known from administrative records of the Ebla palace. All this material is extremely difficult and the very competent author mostly comments on the texts, only occasionally being able to translate a phrase or sentence.

W. G. LAMBERT

LÜSCHER, B. (ed.): *Totenbuch Spruch 1, nach Quellen des Neuen Reiches* (Kleine Ägyptische Texte, ed. W. Helck). 1986. Pp. ix, 73. (Harrassowitz, Wiesbaden. Price: DM 32.00. ISBN 3 447 02646 4)

Ancient Egypt's so-called *Book of the Dead* was a long series of spells to benefit the dead magically in the afterlife; it remains an important Egyptian source for religious concepts. Besides examples on coffins, stelae, tombs, etc., its spells fill innumerable funerary papyri. A full re-edition from all second and first millennium sources would be a colossal undertaking; hence, scholars still make shift with the century-old editions by Naville and Budge. This little book offers a practical solution. In parallel columns, it presents the hieroglyphic text of Spell 1 from 20 good MSS, including the ancestral Coffin Text; brief text-critical notes are included at the end. If followed by further such editions of other spells, this work (and successive parts) will be an immense boon to Egyptologists — only to Old Testament scholars, if they read ancient Egyptian; otherwise, they must rely on the excellent translations by Allen, Barguet, and Faulkner.

K. A. KITCHEN

MARTIN, G. T.: *Scarabs, Cylinders and other Ancient Egyptian Seals: a Checklist of Publications*. 1985. Pp. viii, 61. (Aris & Phillips, Warminster. Price: £7.95. ISBN 0 85668 317 5)

Scarab-beetle shaped seals and other seal-stones of Egyptian inspiration, or of other origin bearing Egyptian script or decoration, have been found in Egypt and the Levant in considerable quantity. This slim, neatly-produced work is exactly what its title states: a full list of publications of such seals (excluding archaeological site-reports). Almost 700 items are given in alphabetical order of authors, editors, etc.; very little can have been missed. On page 35, under no. 336, read 'Alalakh' for 'Alaleth'.

K. A. KITCHEN

MORALDI, L.: *L'Aldilà dell'Uomo nelle Civiltà Babilonese, Egizia, Greca, Latina, Ebraica, Cristiana e Musulmana*. 1985. Pp. 265. (Arnoldo Mondadori Editore, Milan. Price: Lire 16,500. ISBN 0026286 5)

This work of *haute vulgarisation*, by a scholar teaching in the University of Pavia, surveys beliefs about the afterlife in a number of early religions and cultures. When he comes to the Hebrews, he finds little positive in the canonical Hebrew Bible, in which Ecclesiastes says 'the last word' on the subject; postbiblical writings, and in particular 1 Enoch and 4 Ezra, are more fruitful. Similarly in the classical world he is specially interested in the Orphic and mystery contributions to the outlook on life beyond death, and in Christianity he strikes a rich vein in the gnostic literature: he prints in full an Italian translation of the Apocalypse of Paul (a late fourth-century attempt to describe what Paul saw in the third heaven, things, according to 2 Cor. 12:4, 'which man may not utter'). In Islamic literature special attention is paid to the late *Kitāb al-miʿrāj*, which exhibits Zoroastrian influences.

F. F. BRUCE

SPRONK, K.: *Beatific Afterlife in Ancient Israel and in the Ancient Near East* (AOAT, 219). 1986. Pp. ix, 398. (Verlag Butzon und Bercker, Kevelaer. ISBN 3 7666 9454 5. Neukirchener Verlag, Neukirchen–Vluyn. Price: DM 129.50; sub. price: DM 117.00. ISBN 3 7887 1114 0)

The main emphasis of this study, originally a thesis, is on the traditions of Ugarit and Israel, although space is also given to other ancient near eastern traditions (of Asia Minor, Greece, Mesopotamia, Persia, and Egypt). Archaeological evidence is not neglected but texts, especially literary texts are to the fore. Besides relevant passages in Ugaritic, Old Testament texts scrutinized include Gen. 6:1–4; Isa. 14, 26, 52–53; Ezek. 37; Pss. 16, 49, 73, 103; Job 19, and Dan. 12. The introductory historical survey begins with inner-Hebrew interpretation and takes us right up to recent debate. According to Spronk, belief in a happy hereafter can be traced back to Canaanite (practically equated with Ugaritic) tradition and persisted beyond the Old Testament period. Spronk has covered the ground well but some of his interpretations are open to question.

W. G. E. WATSON

VAN DER TOORN, K.: *Sin and Sanction in Israel and Mesopotamia: a comparative study* (Studia Semitica Neerlandica, vol. XXII). 1985. Pp. viii, 252. (Van Gorcum, Essen. Price: Fl. 45.00. ISBN 90 232 2166 4)

The author moves from a study of Israelite and Babylonian penitential prayers to investigate the underlying ideas. After an introduction, he considers rules for conduct under the heading Ethics and Etiquette. Included here are rules of purity and dietary observances, which, like other observances, are seen to be somewhat comparable in the two cultures. Sanctions involved in oaths and curses are the major topic of Chapter 3, their perceived effects, the Wrath of the Gods, of Chapter 4. Here the problem of the individual and his sufferings is to the fore, illnesses, 'leprosy', among them, childlessness and poverty. Perception of these as 'suffering' rather than simply pain or nuisance is culturally conditioned. Chapter 5 discusses briefly the secret sin. Having stressed many similarities, the author tries to find the social basis of these behaviour patterns in an 'aristocracy' in each society. He accounts for the demise of Babylonian and the continuance of Israelite ideas in the unity of faith and practice the latter demands. A long appendix presents some fragmentary Babylonian prayers in transliteration and translation, with hand-copies of several manuscripts. This is an informative and well-documented comparison, with many provocative observations, and several points which will not command general assent. One question remains unanswered: Would a parallel exercise yield similar results for Egypt, the Hittites, or ancient Greece? What distinguished Israel from her neighbours now asks for renewed study.

A. R. MILLARD

TSUKIMOTO, A.: *Untersuchungen zur Totenpflege 'kispum' im alten Mesopotamien* (AOAT, 216). 1985. Pp. ix, 260. (Neukirchener Verlag, Neukirchen-Vluyn. Price: DM 115.00. ISBN 3 7887 1200 7; Butzon and Bercker, Kevelaer. ISBN 3 7666 9394 8)

The care of the dead in Babylonia is the subject of a variety of texts, and the publication of over seventy found at Mari concerning the *kispum* has given a greater understanding of the ideas and activities involved. After a careful analysis of all texts mentioning *kispum* and of others concerning ghosts and burial, this Tübingen thesis sets out conclusions which are relevant for Old Testament studies and will deserve attention by archaeologists and anthropologists as well, especially where they deal with the burials of illiterate societies. Care for the dead stressed the solidarity of the family and the authority of its head. In politics it could have propaganda value, asserting legitimacy. Attention to the rites could also counter illness and demons, who might cease to afflict the living if they were given the care proper to the dead. Only the unburied and unattended dead presented a threat. The cult involved offerings of food and water, but this was not a shared meal as many have claimed. At Mari the provisions for the living king's meal were not connected with the *kispum*. Mentioning the names of the dead was an element in the rite, an element found outside Mesopotamia (e.g. at Ugarit), and, with others falling outside this investigation, worthy of further study.

A. R. MILLARD

9. APOCRYPHA AND POST-BIBLICAL STUDIES

BAMMEL, E. *Judaica: Kleine Schriften I* (Wissenschaftliche Untersuchungen zum Neuen Testament, 37). 1986. Pp. vi, 331. (Mohr, Tübingen. Price: DM 148.00. ISBN 3 16 144971 1)

This collection of the author's articles spans thirty-five years, and comprises forty items, written either in German or in English. Fifteen articles on Jewish history are mostly concerned with conditions under Roman domination, illuminating points of detail in the period. A small section on Qumran is concerned with problems relating to the identification of the sect and the relation between Zadokites and Sadducees. Another short section on Rabbinica takes up particular sayings of the rabbis which have seized the author's interest, ending with a fascinating study, not previously published, of the great array of persons with whom Jesus is compared in Jewish sources. This paves the way for the longest section, consisting of sixteen articles on Jewish and Christian dialogue. Many of these relate to Bammel's special study of the *Toledoth Jeshu* and references to Jesus in other Jewish literature, in which he traces the issues at stake in these polemical writings, and shows how they often have roots which can be discerned in the New Testament itself. Another unpublished article demonstrates that the Jew referred to by Celsus represents the views of Jews who opposed Christianity in the time of the Apostolic Fathers. The collection contains two other unpublished pieces. All the articles are notable for the use of detail, often from rare and inaccessible sources, but it must be said that they are often hard going, whether in German or English.

B. LINDARS

BASNIZKI, L.: *Der Jüdische Kalender. Entstehung und Aufbau.* 1986. Pp. 69. (Athenäum Jüdischer Verlag, Frankfurt. Price: DM 19.80. ISBN 3 7610 0387 0)

This charming little book, the work of a professional Jewish mathematician who taught in German schools between the two world wars, was originally published by J. Kaufmann in Frankfurt in 1938 and was primarily intended to guide Jewish schools and communities in matters concerning the Jewish calendar, as well as to encourage more general scientific interests. The lunisolar nature of the Jewish calendar is theoretically explained and practically demonstrated, with diagrams, calculations, and illustrations to clarify the details of the varying lengths of months, the adjustments made to accommodate feasts and fasts, and the manner in which the lunar and solar systems are made to tally every nineteen years ('*Vom Mond wird unsre Zeit regiert, Doch nach der Sonne korrigiert*' — p. 38). The original beneficiaries have of course now disappeared and Professor Basnizki (1885–1957) had to emigrate to Brazil but academic Jewish studies in contemporary Germany will appreciate this new edition, updated by Werner Glaser at the family's request and supported by the Heidelberg municipality.

S. C. REIF

BEALE, G. K.: *The Use of Daniel in Jewish Apocalyptic Literature and in the Revelation of St. John.* 1984. Pp. xiv, 349. (University Press of America, Lanham, Maryland. Price: $24.75. ISBN 0 8191 4290 5)

As a visionary work concerned with the meaning of current events Daniel had a profound influence on subsequent apocalyptic writing. In this Cambridge Ph.D. thesis Beale plots out the extent to which it is used in Qumran, the Pseudepigrapha and Revelation, paying particular attention to the implied methods of exegesis and the purposes for which it is employed. Because of their relevance to current events Dan. 2, 7, 11, and 12 are most frequently referred to. Often they provide the controlling scheme, as in 1QS 3–4, where the writer was especially indebted to Dan. 11–12. In the heavily biblical 1QM 1 over fifty per cent of the quotations are from Daniel. It is shown that the basic frame is provided by Dan. 12:1–3, and references to Dan. 11 are subordinate to this. It is at this point that Beale discovers an 'ironic typology', whereby the writer 'saw the final assault of the end-time enemy as an antithetic type of his own deafeat.' Further Daniel allusions in the other literature surveyed show that this kind of 'polemic irony' is a recurring feature in the composition of eschatological scenes. It also occurs in Revelation in passages where there is allusion to Daniel. In these passages Daniel is again the controlling factor, though many other eschatological references are brought into play. Daniel was especially important for the author of Revelation, because he was aware of close parallels of situation between the loyal Jews in Daniel and the Christians for whom he was writing. Though some may feel that Beale is too optimistic in tracing the direct influence of Daniel, this is an impressively argued thesis which may well stimulate further studies of scriptural influence. Beale's work is notably free from the wild and speculative claims of Old Testament background so often made in contemporary study of the New Testament. B. LINDARS

BICKERMAN, E.: *Studies in Jewish and Christian History*. Part 3 (Arbeiten zur Geschichte des Antiken Judentums und des Urchristentums, Band IX). 1986. Pp. xvi, 392. (Brill, Leiden. Price: Fl. 220.00. ISBN 90 04 04395 0, 90 04 07480 5)

The appearance of the third volume of Bickerman's *opera minora* (for the first two see *B.L.* 1977, p. 8; *B.L.* 1981, p. 9) was delayed by his death in 1981. In addition to eighteen pieces by him (five of them long review articles) it includes a photograph of Bickerman and a brief biography of him by Morton Smith. Most of the articles deal with topics more closely related to the New Testament than the Old, but there are three on Old Testament themes which were published in Bickerman's last years, too late to be included in one of the earlier volumes. One of these, 'Nebuchadnezzar and Jerusalem', deals with the Assyrian and Babylonian ideology of war, especially its religious aspects. A second, 'The Generation of Ezra and Nehemiah', uses the Murashu archive to argue that the Babylonian Jewish community underwent a religious reform in the early fifth century; and the third, 'En marge de la Bible', contains two studies of Achaemenid chronology. There are ample indexes of subjects and references. Bickerman was a scholar of remarkable gifts and the studies in these volumes exhibit them to the full, for all their author's disparaging reference to them as done for 'fun', as a diversion from his primary concern with classical history. G. I. DAVIES

BIETENHARD, H.: *Der Tosefta-Traktat Sota: Hebräischer Text mit kritischem Apparat, Übersetzung, Kommentar* (Judaica et Christiana, 9). 1986. Pp. 332. (Peter Lang, Bern, Frankfurt am Main, New York. Price: Sw.Fr. 58.00. ISBN 3 261 04041 6)

In this follow-up to his edition of Sota for the 'Giessener Mischna' (1956), Bietenhard takes as his base text the Erfurt MS, and systematically records in the apparatus variants from the Vienna MS and Alfasi. (This vital information has to be gleaned, by the way, from an obscure footnote on page 274. There is no discussion of the text-witnesses, or justification of this editorial procedure!) The notes, which are substantial, take the form of discrete glosses appended to the translation, and cover diverse matters: problems of language, Biblical references, halakhah, archaeological, and historical points. Little attempt is made to analyse the argument of the work as a whole, or of the individual chapters. The brief introduction is taken up largely with a discussion of the relationship of Mishnah Sota to Tosefta Sota. The translation is on the whole careful and competent, and extensive indices are supplied listing the Sages, the Greek and Latin loanwords, and the Biblical verses to be found in the text. This volume may serve a purpose as an introduction to a Tosefta tractate for non-specialists, but it will be disappointing to the *cognoscenti*: it makes little reference to, or use of, non-German scholarship: Lieberman seems to be ignored; Neusner is mentioned once (the reference being to his *Life of Yohanan ben Zakkai*); Schürer is cited from the 4th German edition.

P. S. ALEXANDER

BORGEN, P. (ed.): *The Many and the One: Essays on Religion in the Graeco-Roman World Presented to H. Ludin Jansen* (Relieff, No. 15). 1985. Pp. 265. (Tapir Publishers, Trondheim. Price: N.Kr. 120.00. ISBN 82 519 0670 9. ISSN 0333 029 X)

The octogenerian Jansen is probably best known to Old Testament scholars for his study, *Die Henochgestalt*. This *Festschrift* reprints Jansen's essays on psalmody in late Judaism (translated from the 1937 Norwegian article), consecration in *T. Levi*, marriage rites in Tobit, itinerant Jewish preachers in the Hellenistic period, plus several essays on the New Testament and on Greek literature and religion. There are also four essays by colleagues: on Manichaeism, Socrates' daemon, Augustinian poetry, and Paul's epistle to the Galatians.

L. L. GRABBE

BURGMANN, H.: *Zwei Lösbare Qumrânprobleme: Die Person des* Lügenmannes, *Die Interkalation im Kalendar*. 1986. Pp. 299. (Peter Lang, Frankfurt am Main, Bern, New York. Price: Sw.Fr. 65.00. ISBN 3 8204 8368 3)

This volume consists of xerographic reproductions of ten articles published in journals between 1971 and 1981. Seven of these (including one on the 'Teacher of Righteousness') are gathered as Burgmann's answer to the first 'solvable problem', the solution being that the 'Liar' of the Qumran literature is the Maccabean Simon; the remaining three produce a solution to the problem of intercalation of the 364-day calendar based on data in the book of Daniel. This is a convenient assembly of Burgmann's researches on Qumran. On the 364-day lunisolar, its practicality has indeed been questioned on the slim objection that there is no evidence of how it was intercalated. However, several theoretical possibilities exist beside Burgmann's, all simpler than the system described in rabbinic sources for intercalating the lunar calendar. All this assumes, of course, that we have a consistently described calendar at Qumran, and meanwhile we await Milik's publication of a Qumran fragment apparently reconciling the 364-day and lunar calendars. On the identity of the 'Liar', doubt must remain whether it is really sober to assume that cryptically-phrased midrashim can deliver historical identifications in the way Burgmann (and most others) assume. It remains to be shown that the writers of the *pesharim* (let alone moderns) knew the identity of the 'Liar' or whether he was the same person as the 'Spouter of Lies', 'Man of Scoffing' or even the 'Wicked Priest'. *This* problem is likely to remain insoluble.

P. R. DAVIES

COHEN, J. M.: *Horizons of Jewish Prayer*. 1986. Pp. 368. (The United Synagogue, Woburn House, London WC1H 0EZ. Price: £7.50 paperback. ISBN 0 907104 08 8. Also available in hardback)

Although primarily designed as a popular presentation intended to edify members of the Jewish community, Cohen's book is rich in information relating to the history, theology and practice of Jewish prayer and, furnished as it is with notes, bibliography and index, will be found useful by students of Judaism from the second temple period until today. As an orthodox rabbi, as well as an established academic, the author combines traditional rabbinic teachings with the findings of modern scholarship and intersperses historical surveys with interesting speculations, contemporary religious comment and halakhic guidance. Not surprisingly, his critical treatment of the Old Testament is, to say the least, somewhat restrained but the scientific strength of the volume increases as it moves into the talmudic period and, despite some minor inaccuracies, there are sound insights into developments in medieval and modern times.

S. C. Reif

Derrett, J. D. M.: *Studies in the New Testament*, Vol. iv: *Midrash, the Composition of the Gospels, and Discipline*. 1986. Pp. x, 244. (Brill, Leiden. Price: Fl. 112.00. ISBN 90 04 07478 3)

Eighteen articles are here reprinted, all published between 1979 and 1984. They are concerned with specific points in the New Testament, but the Old Testament is frequently invoked to help to elucidate them. Midrash in the title refers to New Testament passages held by Derrett to be evolved out of Old Testament material. This use of the term, frequent among New Testament scholars, is inaccurate, and should be avoided. There is rich use of Derrett's encyclopedic knowledge, including references to Jewish law. The only article not concerned with the New Testament is a fresh examination of *beḥuqey hagoyim* in CD 9.1. It is suggested that this refers to courts operated by Jews for resident aliens on the basis of the Noachic laws.

B. Lindars

Doron, P.: *Interpretation of Difficult Passages in Rashi*. Part 1: *Genesis and Exodus* (Hebrew). 1985. Pp. 277 and 4 pp. of English summary. (Ktav, Hoboken, New Jersey. Price: $20.00. ISBN 0 88125 081 3)

Essential requirements for the student of the medieval Jewish commentaries are to understand the problem that they are addressing and not to lose sight of the fact that one is seeking an explanation of their comments rather than attempting one's own interpretation of the verse. A traditional rabbinic scholar here introduces Rashi's commentary with a summary of thirteen basic, recurrent principles that underlie it and that include his exegetical use of the literal and homiletical senses, the talmudic–midrashic and targumic sources, the syntactical structure and the literary context. Interestingly, Doron's analysis is not without its parallels to the more scientifically based work recently published by Sarah Kamin, *Rashi's Exegetical Categorization* (see p. 108 below). In the body of the book scores of Rashi's comments are explained in an educationally sound fashion and with the assistance of many earlier super-commentaries and the text of the first edition of 1474. Altogether, a helpful introduction to the texts for those who read modern rabbinic Hebrew.

S. C. Reif

Eilberg-Schwartz, H.: *The Human Will in Judaism: The Mishnah's Philosophy of Intention* (Brown Judaic Studies, 103). 1986. Pp. xiv, 250. (Scholars Press, Atlanta, Georgia. Price: $31.95; members price: $26.95. ISBN 0 89130 938 1)

Eilberg-Schwartz argues that in the Mishnah, in contrast to the Bible, intention is of fundamental importance in determining the status of an action: only if an action contrary to the law was intended does it constitute transgression, because only in this case does the act repudiate divine authority, or negate the divine will. In the Mishnah, however, the idea of intention is invoked only in cultic or religious contexts i.e. (to use traditional categories) in *misvot bein adam le-maqom*, not in *misvot bein adam le-adam*. In the religious domain human intention plays a role in the classification of objects. Where the category into which an object falls is uncertain, the sages will consider the intention of its user as a pertinent factor. In the Mishnah's view man, like God, has the power to affect the structure of reality by an act of will: e.g., his intention will determine whether an object is classified as food or as waste. This correlation between the divine and the human will is part of what is meant by saying that man is in the image of God. Man is able so to act because God has made man his agent. Eilberg-Schwartz shows that there are strong affinities between the concerns of the P-source of the Pentateuch and the Mishnah: both reflect the typical interest of intellectuals (as described by Weber) in systematization. However, the Mishnah's notions of intention are significantly absent from P (and, indeed, from 11QTemple as well). Following a Durkheimian model Eilberg-Schwartz argues that this difference indicates that P and the Mishnah emanated from two groups of different social composition — the former from the hereditary, priestly class, which was supported by tithes, the latter from a non-hereditary guild of scholars, a meritocracy which supported itself through a variety of occupations. This study, which began as a doctoral dissertation under the supervision of Jacob Neusner, exemplifies two of the basic axioms of the 'Brown School', viz that (1) the Mishnah embodies a coherent system; and (2) that it is the foundation document of Rabbinic Judaism (hence the connection between the title and subtitle of the work). Intention is one of the most complex problems both of philosophy and law, and it might seem an ambitious topic for a dissertation. Though Eilberg-Schwartz tends to overstate his case, and his analysis does not always plumb the depths, he has unquestionably made a valuable contribution to an important and difficult subject.

P. S. ALEXANDER

EISENMAN, R. H.: *James the Just in the Habakkuk Pesher* (Studia Post-Biblica, 35). 1986. Pp. x, 110. (Brill, Leiden. Price: Fl. 42.00. ISBN 90 04 07587 9)

Eisenman here takes further the thesis propounded in his *Maccabees, Zadokites, Christians and Qumran* (1983): the 'Righteous Teacher' (*Moreh ha-Ẓedeq*) of Pesher Habakkuk is James the Just (= *Ya'aqov ha-Ẓaddiq*) and the community envisaged by the document is the so-called 'Jerusalen Church' of which James was the head; Paul is the 'Man of Lying (*'ish ha-kazav*) who flouted the Law in the midst of the whole congregation' (1QpHab v, 11–12) = 'the Pourer out of Lying (*maṭṭif ha-kazav*) who led many astray' (1QpHab x, 9); the 'Wicked Priest', the opponent of the Righteous Teacher in Pesher Habakkuk, is the high priest Ananus who, according to tradition, was responsible for the death of James the Just. The greater part of the book is taken up with a detailed exegesis of Pesher Habakkuk in the light of these identifications. Eisenman's arguments in defence of his idiosyncratic position are not easy to follow. He shows acute (and sometimes justified) scepticism of the more orthodox academic views; yet at the same time he accepts with remarkable credulity much of the patristic evidence on James the Just. Symptomatic is his comment on the tradition found in Epiphanius and others that James 'wore the mitre of the High Priest': 'One should be chary of dismissing vivid details such as these without carefully considering them' (p. 4). He does not subject to proper critical analysis the patristic sources on James, and shows little sensitivity to the conventions of hagiography. The only real impediment to his identifications, he avers, lies in the standard interpretation of the archaeology of Qumran (see p. 75). He recapitulates here his arguments (set out more fully in *Maccabees*) against De Vaux's reading of the archaeological data. In keeping with other proponents of a very late dating for the Qumran community he is rather dismissive of the trained archaeologist's interpretation of archaeological evidence. His innuendo that opponents of his views may be motivated by 'ideological' or 'psychological' considerations (see p. 75) is not acceptable in the context of academic debate. It is also a double-edged argument. Is Eisenman himself unaffected by 'ideological' or 'psychological' considerations in propounding such unusual theories? Despite some useful insights in the detailed analysis of Pesher Habakkuk, this monograph is too idiosyncratic to contribute much to Qumran research and is likely to remain something of a curiosity.

P. S. ALEXANDER

FUJITA, N. S.: *A Crack in the Jar: What ancient Jewish documents tell us about the New Testament.* 1986. Pp. viii, 308. (Paulist Press, Mahwah, New Jersey. Price: $9.95. ISBN 0 8091 2745 8)

Intended, as the title implies, to catch a wide readership, this is a serious attempt to explain the significance of the documentary finds in the Judaean wilderness not only for the New Testament, but for the wider study of Judaism and Christian origins in the intertestamental period. Besides the Dead Sea Scrolls from Qumran, Fujita describes the finds from Masada, Naḥal Ḥever, etc., and also the older documents from Wadi-ed-Daliyeh and the Christian documents from Khirbet Mird. Particular attention is given to the problems posed by the Temple Scroll. The chapters that follow systematically relate the finds to ancient Jewish history (the Samaritan sect, the Qumran community, the first and second Jewish revolts), to the study of the Old Testament, to the rise of Christianity, and to mysticism at Qumran and in Rabbinic, Christian, and Gnostic literature. Though the information given is inevitably selective, the book succeeds in conveying a broad spectrum of the religious sects and movements of the time, and the final chapter, introducing Merkabah and Hekaloth literature, references to speculations on 'two powers in heaven', and the relation of all this to the beginnings of Gnosticism, will be new to many non-specialist readers. Usually Fujita presents his material with suitable caution. Unfortunately this deserts him when dealing with the New Testament. Enthusiasm for possible links between Qumran and Christian origins leads him to assert that 'John the Baptizer must have played an important role in the interlinkage between the two groups,' and other even more speculative views are expressed. As he tends to tone them down later without retracting them, the reader is likely to be rather confused. Otherwise this is an excellent work of popularization, and very well informed. There are several illustrations and plans in the text.

B. LINDARS

GAGER, G. J.: *The Origins of Anti-Semitism: Attitudes towards Judaism in Pagan and Christian Antiquity.* 1983. Pp. viii, 312. (Oxford University Press, New York. Price: £21.50. ISBN 0 19 503316 7)

Gager provides a broad, fascinating and well-informed argument contesting many of the views of Rosemary Reuther and her predecessors. Judaism provoked profound internal divisions within both Christians and pagans alike, but the pro-Jewish voices have largely been lost from the record, which was written by the anti-Judaistic winners. Paul is not to be regarded as the source of Christian anti-Judaism. For him, Christ was the fulfilment of God's promise to redeem the gentiles, but did not represent an abrogation of God's covenant with Israel, nor the replacement of Jews by Christians as the chosen people of God. This well-written book should appeal to lay discussion groups as well as a scholarly audience.

B. S. Jackson

Goldman, B.: *The Sacred Portal: A Primary Symbol in Ancient Judaic Art* (Brown Classics in Judaica). 1986, reprint of 1966 edition. Pp. 215, and 30 pp. of photographs. (University Press of America, Lanham, Maryland. Price: $15.75. ISBN 0 8191 5269 2)

Goldman's book is essentially a commentary on the Beth Alpha synagogue mosaic and its symbolism. It is an interesting essay, wide-ranging and richly documented. The purpose of reprinting it twenty years after its first appearance is a puzzle. It is not old or important enough to have achieved monumental status, but it now wears a distinctly dated air, in view of the large amount of subsequent work on Byzantine synagogues in Palestine and their iconography. (On Beth Alpha in particular it is worth mentioning the new interpretation by L. Dequeker, 'Le zodiaque de la synagogue de Beth Alpha et le Midrash', in *Bijdragen, tijdschrift voor filosofie en theologie*, 47 (1986), pp. 2–30.) Reprinting earlier work is an easy option; what would be more useful now is a comprehensive survey of all the interpretations that have been offered of these enigmatic mosaics.

N. R. M. de Lange

Hagner, D. A.: *The Jewish Reclamation of Jesus: An Analysis and Critique of the Modern Jewish Study of Jesus*. 1984. Pp. 341. (Zondervan, Grand Rapids, Michigan. Price: $9.95. ISBN 0 310 33431 4)

The author has made a special study of the Jewish reclamation (*Heimholung*) of Jesus in our day, a process which will be complete, in Harry A. Wolfson's words, when readers can 'pass on from Talmudic and Midrashic selections to those of the Gospels without being conscious of any difference'. He finds, however, that in this process less than adequate justice is done to the evidence of the Gospels: only a very careful selection of Gospel passages would leave readers conscious of no difference between them and the rabbinical literature. He writes in a sympathetic and eirenic spirit (he acknowledges the encouragement given him at the outset of this study by the late Samuel Sandmel), but maintains that no advantage accrues to dialogue between Jews and Christians by the papering over of cracks which still divide the Jewish and Christian assessments of Jesus.

F. F. Bruce

Van Henten, J. W., De Jonge, H. J., Van Rooden, P. T., and Wesselius, J. W. (eds.): *Tradition and Re-Interpretation in Jewish and Early Christian Literature. Essays in Honour of Jürgen C. H. Lebram* (Studia Post-Biblica, 36). 1966. Pp. viii, 313. (Brill, Leiden. Price: Fl. 168.00. ISBN 90 04 07752 9)

Like many *Festschriften*, the title belies the contents. Twenty-three brief articles (German and English; one Dutch with English summary) deal with subjects as diverse as Egyptian Aramaic ostraca and sixteenth–eighteenth-century interpretations of the Apocalypse. Items of interest to *Alttestamentler* are those by M. J. Mulder on Jachin and Boaz (sites of rituals in early Israel), B. Hartmann on Ps. 141:5d–7 (indications of Canaanite and Babylonian cult traditions; Persian or Hellenistic period, possibly from Babylon), H. Gese on Hosea 12:3–14 as a literary unity (against general opinion). W. A. M. Beuken on the use by Trito–Isaiah of earlier Isaianic materials, illustrated in detail from 56:9–57:13, A. S. van der Woude on Malachi 2:10–16 (protests against maltreatment of Jewish wives because of foreign wives; divorce is not at issue), A. van der Kooij on the Old Greek of Daniel 11, and P. B. Dirksen on Peshitta MSS of Judges. There are also very interesting articles on the Two Messiahs in the *Testaments of the Twelve Patriarchs* (M. de Jonge), the dating of *IV Maccabees* (J. W. van Henten), the (apparently poorly-attested) Jewish revolt against Gallus (P. Schäfer).

P. R. Davies

Höffken, P.: *Elemente kommunikativer Didaktik in frühjüdischer und rabbinischer Literatur* (Religionspädagogik in der Blauen Eule, 1). 1986. Pp. 536. (Verlag die Blaue Eule, Essen. Price: DM 56.00. ISBN 3 89206 113 0)

The consideration of a number of Jewish texts, biblical and post-biblical, in the light of various modern educational theories has produced an interesting study, originally presented as an *Habilitationsschrift* in the Faculty of Education of the University of Bonn. After introductory sections dealing with the important place of education in Judaism and with previous work in the field, the main parts of the book deal with characteristic types of educational device: 'antitheses', which include parables, symbolic actions, and the like; 'heroes and anti-heroes', in particular the use in Judaism of stock examples drawn mainly from the biblical tradition; and the varied use of narratives in a didactic context. There is a full bibliography, but the lack of an index of references severely limits the immediate usefulness of the book; this is a pity, for there are many interesting insights which enable the reader to gain fresh perceptions of the distinctive characteristics of early Judaism.

R. J. Coggins

Kamin, S.: *Rashi's Exegetical Categorisation in Respect to the Distinction Between Peshat and Derash* (Hebrew). 1986. Pp. 297. (Magnes Press, Jerusalem. Price: $20.00. ISBN 965 223 628 4)

Of the few Old Testament scholars who have paid attention to Rashi's exegesis, most would assume (at least since Zunz 1822) that the medieval commentator had not only a clear idea of what *peshat* and *derash* were, but had a preference for the former. It is Rashi's frequent use of the phrase *peshuto shel miqra* which suggests this point of view, and it is a view which seems to be confirmed by his famous avowal at Genesis 3:8 when, in the context of midrashic explanation, Rashi states that he is only concerned with *peshuto shel miqra* and with such Agadoth as explain the words of scripture in a manner fitting to them. That may have been Rashi's intention but, as Joseph Kara discovered, it is not so easy, in these matters, to adopt such a singleminded approach. But against this one should note that most of Rashi's interpretations are based on Rabbinic writings which, by their very nature, pertain to the *derash* approach. The answer to the problem therefore lies surely in asking the question of Rashi's view of *peshat* and *derash*; and it is interesting to note in this regard that Rashi hardly used these terms and certainly never defined them.

There are five chapters in this book. Dr Kamin begins by examining the phrases *peshiteh deqara* and *peshuto shel miqra*. She then discusses a number of passages in Rashi's commentaries where the problem raises its head, albeit in an ambiguous manner; and follows this with a careful look at the root *drš* and the term *peshuto* first in isolation, and then in the commentaries. Finally, she examines the meaning and scope of the final part of Rashi's dictum '. . . such Agadoth as explain the words of scripture in a manner fitting to them'.

We are indebted to Dr Kamin not only for the research which she shares with us here, but also for the clear and systematic presentation.

R. B. SALTERS

KÜCHLER, M.: *Schweigen, Schmuck und Schleier: Drei neutestamentliche Vorschriften zur Verdrängung der Frauen auf dem Hintergrund einer frauenfeindlichen Exegese des Alten Testaments im antiken Judentum* (Novum Testamentum et Orbis Antiquus, 1). 1986. Pp. xxii, 539. (Universitätsverlag, Freiburg. Price: Sw.Fr. 98.00. ISBN 3 7278 0362 2. Vandenhoeck & Ruprecht, Göttingen. Price: DM 142.00. ISBN 3 525 53900 2)

Küchler seeks to elucidate certain New Testament passages about the subservience of women (esp. 1 Tim. 2:8–15 and 1 Cor. 11:3–16) in the light of their Old Testament exegesis and early Jewish interpretative traditions. The Old Testament passages examined are primarily found in Genesis, especially Gen. 2–6. Although these New Testament passages appeal to the Old Testament, Küchler argues that they in fact disregard the intention of the Old Testament writers but instead depend on early Jewish exegeses which are hostile to women. The Jewish interpretative traditions show two tendencies: (1) to emphasize the erotic content of the Old Testament narratives; (2) to demonize these same accounts by making beautiful women the cause of the presence and spread of evil in the world (especially found in the Enochic tradition of the sin of angels with women), emphasizing two aspects of this: (a) makeup to enhance beauty and (b) knowledge of the hidden arts. Whatever New Testament scholars may say about K.'s conclusions, his detailed study certainly establishes the existence of the afore-mentioned tendencies in Jewish literature. Where one has reservations is with regard to his sharp distinction between 'the Old Testament' and 'early Judaism'. If for example Gen. 6:1–4 is a fragment of a myth about women and heavenly beings as is currently thought, can one treat the Enochic tradition as only an exegesis of the Old Testament passage?

L. L. GRABBE

LEEMHUIS, F., KLIJN, A. F. J., and VAN GELDER, G. H. J.: *The Arabic Text of the Apocalypse of Baruch. Edited and translated with a parallel translation of the Syriac Text.* 1986. Pp. viii, 154. (Brill, Leiden. Price: Fl. 76.00. ISBN 90 04 07608 5)

The identification in 1974 of an Arabic translation of the Apocalypse of Baruch has provided a means of checking the one existing manuscript of the Syriac version of the Apocalypse proper (chapter 1–77). In the book here reviewed, the Arabic text is printed together with translations of the Arabic and Syriac versions side by side. For the Epistle (chapter 78–87) the Syriac text of the final Epistle of the Milan Manuscript is printed alongside the Arabic version. The Introduction contains a list of nearly fifty passages in which emendations to the Syriac suggested by modern editors may be confirmed by the Arabic version, and the book ends with notes on the text and translation of the Arabic and Syriac versions.

J. W. ROGERSON

LEVY, B. B.: *Targum Neophyti 1, A Textual Study* (Studies in Judaism). Vol. I: *Introduction, Genesis, Exodus*. 1986. Pp. x, 450. (University Press of America, Lanham, New York, London. Price: $36.50. ISBN 0 8191 5464 4. Paperback price: $21.75. ISBN 0 8191 5465 2)

Levy's aim is to clarify, by means of a painstaking, verse-by-verse analysis of the Targum against the original Hebrew, the complex literary process by which Targum Neophyti 1 (= N) reached its final, composite form. He uncovers the various strata largely by establishing the standard elements and translation procedures of N, and noting deviations from the norm. Much light is thrown on the translation-techniques of N, and at numerous points Levy is able to improve on the transcriptions, or supplements, proposed by Díez Macho in the *editio princeps*. The date of N — as of all the Targumim — is a notoriously complex question. Observing the especially close parallels between N and the Tannaitic midrashim (Mekhilta deR. Ishmael, Mekhilta deRashbi, Sifra, Sifrei and Midrash Tannaim to Deuteronomy), Levy argues that much of the midrashic content of N was introduced into the text in the late Tannaitic or Amoraic periods. He even finds evidence that 'the translator(s) of N had before them written midrashic texts' (p. 78f.). In his doctoral dissertation (New York University 1974), scheduled to appear in a revised form as a supplement to the *Textual Study*, Levy suggested that N's Aramaic is 'relatively late' in character. As to date he concludes: 'While N may be assumed to contain some older ideas, the bulk of it dates well past the first century, and in its final form it appears to be from the Talmudic era' (p. 79). The commentary is full of acute and interesting observations (note, e.g. the suggestion that there are a few poetic passages in N). There is nothing comparable to it available. It will be an essential tool for anyone who wants to make discriminating use of the Targum. (See also pp. 122–23 below.)

P. S. ALEXANDER

LYALL, F.: *Slaves, Citizens, Sons: Legal Metaphors in the Epistles*. 1984. Pp. 288. (Zondervan, Grand Rapids, Michigan. Price: $9.95. ISBN 0 310 45191 4)

The thesis of this book written by a lawyer from a conservative theological standpoint is that (1) the legal metaphors of the New Testament epistles are better understood when their legal background is identified; (2) with the exception of redemption, this is more likely to have been Roman rather than Jewish or Greek law. Topics discussed include the slave and freedman; aliens and citizens; adoption; inheritance; the family; fiduciary trusts; mercantile images and redemption. A number of appendices serve to supplement the author's argument.

A. PHILLIPS

MARKS, J. H.: *Visions of one world: legacy of Alexander*. 1985. Pp. 257. (Four Quarters Publishing Company, Guilford, Connecticut. Price: $15.95. ISBN 0 931500 10. Paperback price: $9.95. ISBN 0 931500 09 5)

Marks's theme is the influence of Alexander's 'ecumenical vision' on the history of the millennium that followed him. The Macedonians, Romans, and Byzantines were heirs to Alexander's attempt to integrate the near eastern and Mediterranean worlds, while the Sasanian and Islamic empires, also heirs, demonstrated the final impossibility. Marks capably distinguishes the wood from the trees and gives a clear survey (e.g., of the complex Diadochoi period), emphasizing the political and military rather than the social and cultural history (except for a useful chapter on aspects of Hellenistic culture). Each chapter ends with sensibly limited suggestions for further reading. Apart from some unfortunate misprints and the sadly inadequate maps (the reader needs a good classical atlas), this is a stimulating guide for students of Hellenistic Judaism and early Christianity.

J. R. BARTLETT

NEUSNER, J.: *Ancient Judaism and Modern Category Formation: 'Judaism', 'Midrash', 'Messianism', and Canon in the Past Quarter-Century* (Studies in Judaism). 1986. Pp. xiv, 123. (University Press of America, Lanham, Maryland. Price: $22.50; ISBN 0 8191 5395 8. Paperback price: $9.75; ISBN 08191 55396 6)

This is the first book in a new series, edited by Neusner, entitled *Studies in Judaism.* It consists mostly of a re-shaping of material which Neusner has published elsewhere. He states that his purpose is to demonstrate that the categories normally used by scholars to describe the religion of the Jewish people (Juda*ism*, midrash, messianism) 'violate the inner composition of the data they are employed to classify . . . They generate constructions that distort the data subject to categorization' (p. xi). Neusner denies that there is any such entity as 'Judaism'; rather, scholars can only describe 'Judaisms'. The Judaism he wishes to discuss is that for which the generative category can only be 'Torah' — by which he means the rabbinic canon of writings. The book constitutes a defence of Neusner's current methodology in his series of studies on the individual documents of the rabbinic canon. It perpetuates his polemic against Geza Vermes on how to compare midrashim, and against Ephraim Urbach and E. P. Sanders on how to describe rabbinic Judaism. The implications for the present in the battle between American 'Judaisms' and Israeli Orthodoxy are always lurking beneath the surface.

A. P. HAYMAN

NEUSNER, J.: *Comparative Midrash: The Plan and Program of Genesis Rabbah and Leviticus Rabbah* (Brown Judaic Studies, 111). 1986. Pp. xiii, 211. (Scholars Press, Atlanta, Georgia. Price: $28.95 (discount price: $22.95). ISBN 0 89130 940 3)

Having completed his analysis of rabbinic literature on a document by document basis, insisting always that we must know each document in its individuality before making claims about 'rabbinic literature', Neusner here turns to problems of comparison, using as a basis his recently completed studies of Genesis and Leviticus Rabbah. The Introduction deals at length with the theory of comparison (though not engaging with contemporary literary theory). The literary structures of Genesis Rabbah are then examined, and those of Leviticus Rabbah, analysed in earlier work, are reviewed. Next comes comparison. The two documents show the same formal and redactional characteristics. This justifies comparison of their theological programmes, which again display close similarity: 'The message is that when Israel obeys the will of their father in heaven, no nation can rule over them, and, when they do not, then the least of nations governs them. The thesis is that because of God's rule Israel should take heart; Israel can overcome its sorry condition in this time, in this world.' An Appendix provides a highly critical account of the theories of comparative midrash of Renée Bloch and Geza Vermes; such work ignores the documentary context of the traditions it compares. This is a serious and pioneering attempt to introduce new methodological perspectives into the study of rabbinic literature. But, not for the first time as regards Neusner's work, one has to ask whether *inclusio unius est exclusio alterius*.

B. S. JACKSON

NEUSNER, J.: *Genesis and Judaism. The Perspective of Genesis Rabbah: An Analytical Anthology* (Brown Judaic Studies, 108). 1985. Pp. xiv, 208. (Scholars Press, Atlanta, Georgia. Price: $28.95; discount price $22.95. ISBN 0 89130 940 3)

Having completed his three-volume commentary on Genesis Rabbah (*B.L.* 1986, pp. 128f.), Neusner here presents an anthology taken from his earlier work, designed to show, by way of example, 'how Judaic Sages brought their questions to Scripture and also listened to Scripture's answers'. Genesis, for the early rabbinic sages, gave meaning to the claim that man was made in God's image. In so doing, they reveal multiple layers of meaning in the text, rejecting the modern fundamentalism that looks only for the 'original' meaning ('the one determined by a long-dead context of obscure and unimaginative philology'). The dominant method of scriptural understanding is 'the power to hear Scripture's harmonic music, to perceive each of its distinct melodic lines, all at once, all together, and all in deep union of ultimate meaning'. The stories of Genesis, commencing with the Creation, provide messages about the meaning of the story to come, that of the children of Israel. The fifteen chapters of the book, organized in four thematic parts, range over theological issues (e.g. the doctrine of merits, the encounter with God, the Temple, and the celebration of Creation), narrative topics (Abraham, Isaac, Jacob, the Matriarchs), and the historical context informing rabbinic interpretation (e.g. relations with Rome, expectations of redemption). All Neusner's didactic skills are deployed in this book, designed to introduce a new audience into early rabbinic interpretation of the Bible.

B. S. Jackson

Neusner, J.: *A History of the Mishnaic Law of Damages.* Part 4: *Shebuot, Eduyot, Abodah Zarah, Abot, Horayot. Translation and Explanation* (Studies in Judaism in Late Antiquity xxxv/4). 1985. pp. xxxi, 275. (Brill, Leiden. Price: Fl. 148.00. ISBN 90 04 06853 8; 90 04 07269 1)

Following the principles and rules adopted for the series, and applied to the previous volumes of *Damages* (cf. *B.L.* 1985, p. 135; 1986, pp. 127–28), Professor Neusner presents here the last five Mishnah and, where appropriate, Tosefta tractates of this *Seder*. Two of these, however, *Eduyot* and *Abot*, reveal themselves as misfits as far as the thesis of the general project is concerned, namely 'that Mishnah constitutes its own best commentary, and that Mishnah's commentary is effected through its formal traits'. To quote the author: 'Neither tractate presents a fertile field for the demonstration of the stated thesis or the opposite.' Nevertheless, he concludes: 'Proof of the correctness of my exegetical thesis, therefore, derives from those points at which the thesis is irrelevant and from the simple fact that, where the thesis fails, there — in the contrast — we see its power' (p. ix).

G. Vermes

Neusner, J.: *A History of the Mishnaic Law of Damages.* Part 5: *The Mishnaic System of Damages* (Studies in Judaism in Late Antiquity xxxv/5). 1986. pp. xxxi, 228. (Brill, Leiden. Price: Fl. 104.00. ISBN 90 04 06853 8; 90 04 07270 5)

In the concluding volume of *Neziqin*, Professor Neusner describes his understanding of the 'system' underlying the fourth *Seder* of the Mishnah; outlines the formation of the eight tractates; and advances his views on 'the unfolding' of the law of damages between 70 and 170, but essentially in the post-Bar Kokhba period. His own summary of his findings is as follows: 'The character and interests of the division of Damages present compelling, indeed probative evidence of the larger programme of the philosophers of Mishnah. Their intention is to create nothing less than a full-scale Israelite government, subject to the administration of sages. This government is fully supplied with a constitution and by-laws (Sanhedrin, Makkot). It makes provision for a court-system and procedures (Shebuot, Sanhedrin, Makkot), as well as a full set of laws governing civil society (Baba Qamma, Baba Mesia, Baba Batra) and criminal justice (Sanhedrin, Makkot). This government, moreover, mediates between its own community and the outside world ("pagans"). Through its system of laws it expresses its judgement of the others and at the same time defines, protects, and defends its own society and social frontiers (Abodah Zarah). It even makes provision for procedures to expiate its errors (Horayot). The (the non-existent) Israelite government imagined by the second-century philosophers centres upon the (then non-existent) Temple . . . Mishnah is above all an act of imagination in defiance of reality' (pp. 173–74).

With this volume, Professor Neusner's mammoth contribution to his Mishnah project (five Orders out of six and no less than forty-three tomes) has come to an end. 'It is not possible' — he confesses in the last paragraph of the Preface — 'to put into words my feelings as I write these concluding words to my final volume of my history of the law of the Mishnah. I began the work. I finished the work. Thank God' (p. xv).

G. VERMES

NEUSNER, J.: *Judaism in the Matrix of Christianity*. 1986. Pp. xix, 148. (Fortress Press, Philadelphia. Price: $12.95. ISBN 0 8006 1897 1)

Neusner's essential thesis in this book is that as we move from the second to the fifth centuries C.E. some things in rabbinic Judaism remained the same — 'doctrines governing fundamental categories of Israel's social life to which the triumph of Christianity made no material difference.' (p. 24). But other things did change — 'those components of the sages' worldview that now stood in direct confrontation with counterparts on the Christian side' (p. 24). In separate chapters he treats those that did not change (the doctrine of the emotions and the structure of sanctification) and those that did (the doctrine of Rome, the Messiah, Torah and methods of biblical exegesis). The book is a hymn to the vitality of a rabbinic Judaism which, in contrast to Christianity, when 'Islam gained its victory' in the Middle East and North Africa 'retained the loyalty and conviction of the people of the Torah' (p. xii). We have here the simplest and most straightforward summary of the results of Neusner's recent work on the Yerushalmi and the Palestinian midrashim. The book should be on the reading lists of all courses dealing with Judaism in Late Antiquity.

A. P. HAYMAN

NEUSNER, J.: *Judaism and Scripture: The Evidence of Leviticus Rabbah* (Chicago Studies in the History of Judaism). 1986. Pp. xxii, 641. (University of Chicago Press, Chicago and London. Price: £42.50. ISBN 0 226 57614 0)

The bulk of this book consists of a new translation of *Leviticus Rabbah* in the format and the style used for Neusner's translation of *Genesis Rabbah* (see *B.L.* 1986, pp. 128f.). The author translates the base text presented in Margulies's edition, which is an emended and corrected version of a tenth-century manuscript now in the British Museum. This belongs to only one of three recensions in which *Lev.R.* has been transmitted, not to speak of the substantial amount of the text preserved in the Genizah fragments. Margulies despairs of restoring the 'original text' of *Lev.R.* (see his edition, vol. 5, p. xxxif.). As usual, Neusner sidesteps this issue, though he is aware of the problem. For a recent critique of his methodology in this respect with reference to *Gen.R.* see Peter Schäfer, 'Research into Rabbinic Literature', *JJS*, XXXVII (1986), 146ff.

Neusner's translation is much more intelligible than the older Soncino version and it certainly makes the argument easier to follow. Errors in the translation are rare. However, there are frequent mistakes in cross references, both in his own internal reference system and in biblical references which sometimes follow EVV and sometimes the Hebrew. A more serious drawback is that Neusner does not relate his judgements on the original form of a text to the manuscript evidence, even when such evidence would support his opinion (e.g., Parashah I:3. 7), let alone when it undermines his conclusion (e.g., I:4.5F — what Neusner regards as the original conclusion of I:4 is, in fact, omitted by the Genizah fragment).

In a lengthy introduction (130 pages), Neusner places *Lev.R.* in its context within the emerging rabbinic canon of writings. He sees it as a radical departure from the texts produced in the 200 years after the Mishnah (*Tosefta*, *Sifra*, and the two *Sifres*). Unlike these earlier texts its authors 'make no pretense at all at undertaking a verse-by-verse or even phrase-by-phrase exegesis of their chosen text. Rather, they selected a large topic and, using the chosen verse, worked out the sense and implications — the inner logic, the structure, the governing principle — of that topic' (p. 13). Neusner argues forcefully, and I think convincingly, that *Lev.R.* is not a miscellany — 'a scrapbook', but a carefully constructed statement about Israel and its salvation in the crisis caused for Judaism by the consolidation of the Christian Empire *c.* 400 C.E. With the initial proviso about the state of the manuscript evidence, this book marks a major advance in understanding the haggadic midrashim.

A. P. HAYMAN

NEUSNER, J.: *The Religious Study of Judaism: Description, Analysis, and Interpretation.* Vol. 1. (Studies in Judaism). 1986. Pp. xvi, 172. (University Press of America, Lanham, Maryland. Price: $23.50. ISBN 0 8191 5393 1. Paperback price: $11.75. ISBN 08191 5394 X)

Completed three weeks later than *Ancient Judaism and Modern Category Formation*, this book goes over the same ground. It also updates and revises papers which Neusner has published earlier. He explains his method of working in his Acknowledgements:

> Over the years I work and rework essays of mine, in the beginning through successive drafts, later in shorter and longer versions of the same study, each with its intended audience and for its distinct purpose. In this book, some are old and completely rewritten, others are new.

Your reviewer recognized material he had not seen before, in some form or other, in chapter 1 (Parsing the Rabbinic Canon: Explaining a Fresh Approach), chapter 2 (Defining a New Category: The Virtues of the Inner Life in Formative Judaism) — a remarkably penetrating essay, and chapter 8 (The Theological Enemies of Religious Studies) — a sustained polemic against the position of Religious Studies in the American universities which would be equally applicable in the UK. Chapter 1 summarizes in nine pages where Neusner's studies have brought him to date and points to where he will go in the future. If the following is anything to go by, the future looks promising:

> '. . . while people commonly maintain that Christianity in the first century was born in the matrix of Judaism, in fact, Judaism in its most enduring form in the fourth century was born in the womb of Christianity. (p. 11)

For those without the time to tackle Neusner's larger publications, these essays will provide rewarding reading.

A. P. HAYMAN

NEUSNER, J.: *The Religious Study of Judaism: Description, Analysis, Interpretation. The Centrality of Context.* Vol. 2. (Studies in Judaism). 1986. Pp. xiii, 215. (University Press of America, Lanham, Maryland. Price: $24.50. ISBN 0 8191 5450 4. Paperback price: $12.75. ISBN 0 8191 5451 2)

These essays 'serve to illustrate the larger issue of the definition and role of context in the study of religion, its text and its ideas' (p. x). As the author tells us in his Preface, chapter 1 (Description and Category-Formation) 'reworks ideas in the Preface and Chapter Two of my *Ancient Judaism and Modern Category Formation*'. Chapter 2 is an attempt 'to introduce Judaism to beginning students of religion' (p. 29). Chapter 3 (Description and the Category of History: Another Exercise) is a survey of the development of Judaism (in interaction with Christianity) in the first four centuries C.E. Chapter 4 is a revision of the preface to Neusner's translation of *Sifre*. Chapter 5 is a revision of the introduction to Neusner's translation of *Genesis Rabbah* (see *B.L.* 1986, pp. 128f.). Chapter 6 is another of Neusner's exercises in tracing the development of an idea (in this case, Israel's attitude to Rome) through the principal documents of rabbinic Judaism. In this paper he completely disowns one he published on a similar topic one year earlier ('*To See Ourselves as Others See Us*', edited by J. Neusner (1985), pp. 373–96). Chapter 7 is a hatchet job on Michael Walzer, *Exodus and Revolution* (1985) and Aaron Wildavsky, *The Nursing Father: Moses as Political Leader* (1984). Again, this book will be of use to those with no time to read the larger works from which these essays are mostly drawn.

A. P. HAYMAN

NEUSNER, J.: *The Tosefta: Its Structure and its Sources* (Brown Judaic Studies, 112). 1986. Pp. xi, 250. (Scholars Press, Atlanta, Georgia. Price: $39.95; members price: $29.95. ISBN 1 55540 049 3)

In this monograph, addressed to the problem of the relationship between the Tosefta and the Mishnah, Neusner challenges the traditional view that the Tosefta consists of *baraitot* 'left over' after the editing of the Mishnah. This is only partially true: the relationship between the two documents is much more complex. The matter of the Tosefta can be classified into three broad categories: (A) commentary on the Mishnah, which takes the form of verbatim quotation + interwoven glosses and supplements; (B) rulings which at first sight appear to be autonomous of the Mishnah, but which, on closer inspection, prove to be responding to, and amplifying, statements in the Mishnah; (C) rulings which are genuinely independent of the Mishnah, and bear no relationship to its text. In the redaction of the Tosefta the material belonging to each of these categories tends to be kept together within a chapter, and is usually arranged with category A first, B next and C last. The Tosefta, Neusner concludes, is, on the whole, post-Mishnaic, and emanated from the same circle of Sages as the Mishnah. Indeed, it can be seen as the earliest stage of commentating on the Mishnah, a forerunner of the *gemarot* of the Bavli and Yerushalmi. However, since there are some notable materials in the Mishnah about which the Tosefta appears ignorant, and a few instances where the Tosefta is arguably prior to the Mishnah, the Tosefta probably reached conclusion *before* the final redaction of the Mishnah as we now have it. This study reprints the sections on the relationship between Mishnah and Tosefta scattered through Neusner's 22 volume *History of the Mishnaic Law of Purities (1974–77)*. It covers, therefore, only the Order of *Tohorot*. However, since that constitutes about 18% of the whole Tosefta, it offers a substantial basis for generalizing. Whether or not one agrees with Neusner that he has 'finally solved the problem of the Tosefta's structure and sources' (pp. x–xi), this is undoubtedly one of the most important analyses of the problem to appear in recent years.

P. S. ALEXANDER

PRAAG, H. VAN: *Damit die Erde Blüht: Das Phänomen Israel* (Judentum Heute). 1986. Pp. 128. (Scriba Verlag, Köln. Price: DM 16.80. ISBN 3 921232 37 6)

This work, which has appeared in Dutch as *Het verschijnsel Israel*, is in the series *Judentum Heute*. The author, who has written a number of books, is

Rektor der Internationalen Universität Lugano, and is concerned to contribute to the on-going Christian-Jewish dialogue. He does this by looking for aspects of Christianity and Judaism which are related, in spite of traditional views one of the other, and by criticizing some features of both faiths which are not of the essence of true religion but which keep adherents sceptical of one another. The book seems to be directed at the thinking layman rather than the scholar, and members of the society, though finding it interesting, need not be detained by it.

R. B. SALTERS

REEG, G.: *Die Geschichte von den Zehn Märtyrern: Synoptische Edition mit Übersetzung und Einleitung* (Texte und Studien zum Antiken Judentum, 10). 1985. Pp. vi, 107, and pp. 109* of Hebrew text. (Mohr, Tübingen. Price: DM 258.00. ISBN 3 16 144783 2)

The well-known story of the martyrdom of ten rabbis by the Romans at the time of the Bar Kochba revolt is found, in differing forms, in a number of sources. This painstaking parallel edition of the various texts (only a few of which date back as far as the fourteenth/fifteenth century) follows the excellent model of P. Schäfer's synopsis of the Hekhalot literature. It is therefore of interest not only from the point of view of its contents, but also for its method, which has implications for the edition of any 'text' which has no clear, fixed form. The approach is carefully explained in the introduction, as is the use of the computer in the preparation of the edition.

N. R. M. DE LANGE

RONAI, A., and WAHLE, H.: *Das Evangelium — ein jüdisches Buch?: Eine Einführung in die jüdischen Wurzeln des Neuen Testaments* (Herderbücherei 1298). 1986. Pp. 190. (Herder, Freiburg im Breisgau. Price: DM. 9.90. ISBN 3 451 08298 5)

The joint effort of an orthodox Jew and a Roman Catholic nun, this booklet is intended to provide an elementary introduction to the Jewishness of Jesus and of the New Testament for Christians with no prior historical or theological education. The major topics (Jesus's childhood, baptism, teaching, attitude to Jews and Gentiles; the last Supper; and the separation of the Church from Judaism) are all presented first from a Jewish, then from a Christian point of view. There is no scholarly pretence and a truly irenic spirit characterizes the whole enterprise.

G. VERMES

ROTH, N.: *Maimonides. Essays and Texts: 850th Anniversary*. 1985. Pp. 169. (The Hispanic Seminary of Medieval Studies, Madison. Price: $10.00. ISBN 0 942260 59 7)

Having delivered a number of papers at conferences commemorating the 850th anniversary of Maimonides's birth, the author was reluctant to subject them to the delays normally associated with the conventional channels of publication, preferring to publish them more hastily in this way in a revised form, together with other work of his, including a review of I. Twersky's *Introduction to the Code of Maimonides* (New Haven, 1980), six new translations of Maimonidean texts and some bibliographical guidance. Since the main themes relate to the place of Maimonides in medieval cultural history, especially in Spain, and to specific aspects of his philosophy, they are of little relevance to Old Testament scholarship, but there is a brief treatment of Maimonides on Hebrew language and poetry that may attract the attention of Hebraists. Those whose wider interests include Maimonides should be aware of the highly individual nature of some of the views ('Maimonides was never a rabbi') and the polemical style in which many of them are expressed.

S. C. REIF

RUSSELL, D. S.: *From Early Judaism to Early Church*. 1986. Pp. 150. (SCM Press, London. Price: £4.50. ISBN 0 334 00496 9)

The author writes here for the non-specialist, addressing the same readership and covering the same period as in his earlier volume, *Between the Testaments* (1960; *B.L.* 1961, pp. 61f.; *Decade*, pp. 304f.), to which this is intended as a supplement. Inevitably there is some overlap in content, though subjects treated there are dealt with briefly here. The new material consists of a brief section on Judaism and Jesus, and chapters on Biblical Interpretation in Early Judaism and the New Testament, The Development and Meaning of Torah, Prayer and Mediation, and Demonology and the Problem of Evil. Footnotes have been avoided. The bibliography is updated, doubled in length, and includes more reference to primary sources. It deserves to be widely used alongside its companion volume.

G. I. EMMERSON

SCHIMANOWSKI, G.: *Weisheit und Messias: Die jüdischen Voraussetzungen der urchristlichen Präexistenzchristologie* (Wissenschaftliche Untersuchungen zum Neuen Testament, 2. Reihe, 17). 1985. Pp. xiii, 410. (Mohr, Tübingen. Price: DM 78.00. ISBN 3 16 144997 5)

As the sub-title indicates, this monograph aims at uncovering the Jewish roots of the New Testament presentation of the pre-existent Christ. Of the two terms in the main title, Wisdom, 'the beginning of Yahweh's ways', is, of course, well attested in the Hebrew Bible; the other, Messiah, belongs in its special sense to post-biblical Judaism. The author's treatment of the Wisdom concept in the Hebrew Bible and in the Hellenistic tradition (LXX, etc.) is therefore directly relevant to his main purpose; his study of the pre-existent Messiah in post-biblical Judaism (the Ethiopic Enoch, the Targums, rabbinic literature in general) deals more with parallel developments. If this be borne in mind, the work will prove to have great value as it traces the growth of the idea of pre-existence in Jewish thought, quite apart from its provision of a background to the development of the idea in primitive Christianity.

F. F. BRUCE

SCHMIDT, F., *Le Testament grec d'Abraham. Introduction, édition critique des deux recensions grecques, traduction* (Texte und Studien zum Antiken Judentum, 11). 1986. Pp. ix, 199. (Mohr, Tübingen. Price: DM 98.00. ISBN 3 16 144949 5)

Francis Schmidt began his doctoral thesis on the *Greek Testament of Abraham* in 1971 under the direction of M. Philonenko, and this critical edition and translation of the text is the fruit of fifteen years sustained and painstaking study of a complex and important document. In his Introduction, Schmidt gives detailed descriptions of the extant MSS and clearly states the principles which he has followed in presenting the text: the long and short recensions of the *Testament* are edited and discussed separately. We are given a fine account of the ancient versions (Slavonic, Roumanian, Coptic, Arabic, and Ethiopic) and the previous translations of the text. There is excellent scholarship here, which increases one's regret that Schmidt says nothing about the date and provenance of the original *Testament*: even a few general remarks on these subjects would have been welcome. The text of the short recension according to the two families represented in the manuscript tradition is given first. Rather than printing a composite text, Schmidt chooses an eleventh-century Italo-Greek MS Milan Ambrosian Greek 405 (G 63) f. 164r–171r to represent the first family of the short recension: all significant variant readings of the other MSS in the family are faithfully recorded in the apparatus. The translation is set on the page opposite to the text, and is generally accurate, reliable, and readable. Schmidt takes MS B as representative of the second family of this recension: no translation is given, but variant readings of the other manuscripts are supplied in the apparatus. Omissions from MS B are supplied from MS F.

The long recension survives in three families of MSS which represent a long, short, and very short text. Schmidt argues for the originality of the long text, and presents it in printing MS A, which M. R. James used for his edition and translation of the Testament in 1892: again, all MS variants are given in the apparatus. A final index of Greek words, which is effectively a concordance to both recensions, usefully concludes this valuable edition.

C. T. R. HAYWARD

SCHNABEL, E. J.: *Law and Wisdom from Ben Sira to Paul: a Tradition Historical Enquiry into the Relation of Law, Wisdom and Ethics* (Wissenschaftliche Untersuchungen zum Neuen Testament: 2. Reihe, 16). 1985. Pp. xvi, 428. (Mohr, Tübingen. Price: DM 84.00. ISBN 3 16 144896 0)

Scholars frequently note the correlation of law and wisdom in Ben Sira's work and in Pauline thought separately, but few have brought the two together or seen development of this link in the inter-testamental period. Schnabel traces the history of these concepts not only in Ben Sira and Paul, but through the whole period in between, with separate sections on the Wisdom of Solomon, Baruch and the Apocalypse of Baruch, the Letter of Aristeas, the third Sybilline oracle and the fourth books of Ezra and Maccabees — with detailed attention to the Dead Sea Scrolls. Studies treating so many varied texts need to be meticulous in detail, and Schnabel shows such meticulous diligence in notes and bibliography as well as in exact references to particular passages. This book will be a mine of information for anyone studying the period covered by the title, whether studying Jewish or Christian works: bibliography and indexes of subjects, authors and passages cited are commendably full.

J. G. SNAITH

SCHÜRER, E.: *The History of the Jewish People in the Age of Jesus Christ (175 B.C.–A.D. 135)*. A New English Version revised and edited by G. Vermes, F. Millar and M. Goodman. Volume III. 1. 1986. Pp. xxii, 704. (T. & T. Clark, Edinburgh. Price: £25.00. ISBN 0 567 02244 7)

The first two volumes of the new Schürer were noticed in *B.L.* 1974, p. 91; 1980, pp. 125–26. With the appearance of the first part of the final volume, where 'modernization reaches a climax' (p. v), the publication of the revision of this classic work is brought almost to completion. Section 31, for which Fergus Millar took primary responsibility, provides a masterly survey of the literary, archaeological and epigraphic evidence for the diaspora and examines the internal organization and life of the diaspora communities. The remainder of the work (sections 32–34) provides an introduction to the literature of the intertestamental period, but here, instead of the old distinction between Palestinian and Hellenistic Judaism, a distinction solely on the basis of language has been introduced. Section 32, which was revised by Geza Vermes, is concerned with works composed in Hebrew or Aramaic and includes a chapter on the Qumran sectarian literature. Section 33A, revised by Martin Goodman, is devoted to Jewish writings composed in Greek. Sections 33B (on Jewish writings of which the original language is uncertain) and 34 (on Philo) will appear in the second part of this volume together with the much-needed indexes. The present part includes a valuable and interesting chapter by Philip Alexander on Jewish incantations and books of magic.

One may still wonder, particularly on reading the present volume which contains so much new material, whether the decision to revise an old work, albeit a classic, rather than to prepare a totally new one was correct. But granted that this decision was right, one can only congratulate the editors on what they have done. For the wealth of information it contains, its balanced views, and its very full and up-to-date bibliographies, this work will remain indispensable to scholars for many years.

M. A. KNIBB

SEGAL, A. F.: *Rebecca's Children: Judaism and Christianity in the Roman World*. 1986. Pp. xii, 207. (Harvard University Press, Cambridge, Mass. and London. Price: £16.95. ISBN 0 674 75075 6)

This is a survey of the development of Judaism and Christianity during the Roman period and is primarily intended for the general reader. The book is clear, balanced, and shows itself well abreast of current scholarship. The one frustrating aspect to the specialist reader is that he will find many statements to query with regard to interpretation or nuance; in most cases Segal undoubtedly has good reasons for his particular view, but one would like to see it justified in more detail. The frequency of queries is by no means due to deficient scholarship on Segal's part but to the many disputed points of interpretation for the history of this period. Although Segal does indicate differences of opinion, the breadth of coverage makes detailed discussion impossible in the text. However, one way of overcoming this problem would have been to devote his notes to the finer points of the debate and to explain reasons for a particular interpretation. As it is, the notes are infrequent and brief, usually giving fairly basic secondary sources. In his preface, Segal refers to the 'controversial ideas' in the book: they are controversial only when compared with certain standard handbooks which are out of date and often extremely conservative. For those abreast of current scholarship, S. appears decidedly middle of the road. Highly recommended for students.

L. L. GRABBE

STENHOUSE, P.: *The KITĀB AL-TARĪKH of ABŪ'L-FATḤ translated into English with Notes* (University of Sydney Studies in Judaica, No. 1). 1985. Pp. xxxvi, 249, and Pp. lxxvii of notes. (Mandelbaum Trust, University of Sydney. Price: A$ 43.50., plus A$ 5.00 postage and packing. ISBN 0 949269 75 1)

Abū'l Fatḥ's fourteenth-century *Chronicle* has never been translated in its entirety into a modern western language. Now Stenhouse has followed up his edition of the Arabic text with this literal but perfectly readable translation. The *Chronicle* is divided into chapters for ease of reference; there are more than 1,000 notes, mostly dealing with lexicographical points but also drawing attention to historical and other details. Specific points in the translation will require assessment by the select company of Samaritan Arabists; for the rest it is helpful to have available a manageable version of this work, often referred to as an important contribution to Samaritan self-understanding, but rarely accessible in practice. R. J. Coggins

Stow, K. R.: *'The 1007 Anonymous' and Papal Sovereignty: Jewish Perceptions of the Papacy and Papal Policy in the High Middle Ages*. 1986. Pp. 89. (Ktav Publishing House, Hoboken, New Jersey. Price: $18.75. ISBN 0 87820 603 5)

This book will be of great interest to those engaged in medieval studies, but it should also interest students of Judaism generally.

Although a great deal has been written about papal attitudes to the Jews in the Middle Ages, very little has been said about Jewish attitudes to the popes. The author of this book seeks to redress the balance by giving us an insight into Jewish thinking of these times.

The author concentrates primarily on two documents: the thirteenth-century *Milhemet Misvah* of Meir b. Simeon of Narbonne, and the brief but intriguing narrative known simply as 'The Terrible Event of 1007' whose author is unknown. Stow admits that he is being selective here, as indeed he must be, but he is careful not to exclude reference to other discussions of the period. In fact, before addressing himself to these texts, he provides a background in two chapters — 1. Old and New Views: An Introduction. 2. The Growth of Papal Policy.

The main section of this work is the third chapter: Jewish Perceptions of Papal Policy. The Author begins briefly with *Milhemet Misvah*. A mature and sophisticated approach to the thirteenth-century world emerges here. The papacy may work to Jewish advantage, yet it is neither sufficiently powerful nor secure to guarantee its constant reliability. Nor is any individual pope a friend. The popes grant and protect what the canons permit and no more. But better the canons you know than the whim of a king you don't know. Stow then takes a hard look at the '1007 Anonymous'. Long considered legitimate, this document is found to belong to the thirteenth century, informing Jews of that period (by means of a tale of one, Jacob b. Yekutiel) of their position *vis à vis* the papacy, and assuring them of papal protection under the law, the author remaining anonymous probably because of the fear of some king. The position taken by Stow is a sound one and makes a real contribution to the history of the period (in the realm of Judaism and Jewish–Christian relations).

R. B. Salters

Tubach, J.: *Im Schatten des Sonnengottes: der Sonnenkult in Edessa, Harran und Hatra am Vorabend des christlichen Mission*. 1986. Pp. xviii, 546, and 12 plates. (Otto Harrassowitz, Wiesbaden. Price: DM 198.00. ISBN 3 447 02435 6)

By carefully combining the testimonies of classical western and eastern sources this book provides a completely new look at these three important religious centres. Their importance for establishing the later development of ancient Mesopotamian religion as a seedbed for Christian evangelists and a harvest field for Islam is well known (cf. recently Altheim und Stiehl, Drijvers, Segal, to whom the writer regularly refers). By narrowing his field to Sun worship he has been able to treat each site separately in exhaustive detail, and include reasoned arguments of interest, to art historians, theologians and epigraphists alike. The plates are clearly presented and indispensable — it is a pity that there are not more — and new translations of Aramaic inscriptions concisely annotated. I know of two theses in this area of study, both by Iraqi scholars, which have been presented at British Universities. Tubach mentions one of them (J. K. Ibrahim, London, 1981) but not the other (Adil H. H. al-Jadir, Cardiff, 1984). But we may conclude that this field of study continues to be appreciated where it all began as well as in Europe.

M. E. J. Richardson

Übersetzung des Talmud Yerushalmi, herausgegeben von M. Hengel, H. P. Rüger, P. Schäfer. Band I/6: Terumot–Priesterhebe, übersetzt von G. A. Wewers. 1985. Pp. xi, 240. (Mohr, Tübingen. Price: DM 122.00. ISBN 3 16 144987 8)

Terumah is the portion of produce set aside for the priests. It is a prominent term in the Mishnah (from the very first sentence on); the rules associated with it rest in the main on Num. xviii:8ff. This judiciously annotated translation follows the excellent pattern set in earlier volumes (see *B.L.* 1985, p. 147). The next tractate, *Peah*, is already announced, but the sad news of Wewers's early death presumably means that this magnificent series of pioneering translations will be cut short—unless another translator can be found with his remarkable combination of skills.

N. R. M. de Lange

Watson, F. B.: *Paul, Judaism and the Gentiles. A Sociological Approach* (Society for New Testament Studies, Monograph Series, 56). 1986. Pp. xii, 246. (Cambridge University Press. Price: £22.50. ISBN 0 521 32573 0)

This lucid and elegant study rejects the traditional picture of Paul as a champion of the doctrine of 'sola gratia' in the face of a Judaism which took its stand on human achievement and good works. Such a Lutheran view, argues Watson (with E. P. Sanders), misrepresents both Paul and Judaism. Watson's Paul was a man who recognized that Judaism, like the Christian gospel, was based on both grace and good works. His campaign was against those Judaizers, among them the authorities of the Jerusalem church, who saw the church as a reform movement within Judaism. Early on in his preaching ministry experience had taught Paul to abandon this view, and the position that in his letters he wished to propagate was that the church is a sect clearly differentiated from the Jewish community. Paul's theology should be viewed as a historically conditioned ideology which he deployed in the interests of justifying the separation from Judaism. Light, Watson, argues, is shed on what Paul was really doing — something 'sociological', in a very broad sense — by an examination of parallels between the literature produced by Paul, the Johannine church, and Qumran: in each case we find a sectarian group justifying its secession from the parent body by the use of a rhetoric compounded of denunciation, antithetical language, and a reinterpretation of the inheritance in such a way as to claim it as the exclusive possession of the secessionists. Evidence for Watson's thesis about Paul's sectarian view of the church is drawn from a study of his letters: Galatians and Philippians are examined fairly briefly, and half the book is devoted to a careful and illuminating analysis of Romans, which is interpreted not as a systematic dogmatic treatise but, more sociologically, as an attempt to persuade a Jewish Christian congregation in Rome to sever links with the synagogue and to join in fellowship and worship with the Roman gentile congregation that it had hitherto shunned.

There is a whiff of reductionism about this book, but the thesis is very cogently argued and I am persuaded that there is a fair amount of substance in it. A fascinating book, which students of Christian origins will have to take very seriously.

B. P. Robinson

Weiss, J.: *Studies in Eastern European Jewish Mysticism*. 1985. Pp. viii, 272. (Oxford University Press/Littman Library, Oxford. Price: £18.00. ISBN 0 19 710034 1)

Although the subject of these essays, eighteenth-century Hasidism, seems *a priori* to offer only limited appeal to *Book List* readers, nevertheless acquaintance with this fairly recent resurgence of charismatic Judaism may shed valuable light on a certain type of popular religion which flourished in Old Testament times and in the inter-Testamental age. Eight out of the sixteen papers included in this volume have never been published, and a further three appear here for the first time in English. They form an impressive collection and convey the authoritative views of one of the leading experts on Hasidism, whose tragic death in 1969 dealt a grievous blow to scholarly research into East-European Jewish mysticism.

G. VERMES

10. PHILOLOGY AND GRAMMAR

ARMSTRONG, T. A., BUSBY, D. L., and CARR, C. F.: *A Reader's Hebrew–English Lexicon of the Old Testament.* Vol. III: *Isaiah-Malachi.* 1986. Pp. viii, 220. (Zondervan, Regency Reference Library, Grand Rapids, Michigan. Price: $14.95. ISBN 0 310 37010 8)

This is part of a proposed four volume work designed as an aid to rapid reading of the Hebrew text, particularly for students and clergy. Words occurring fifty times or less in the Old Testament are listed by chapter and verse, with a note of their frequency. Other words are listed in alphabetical order in an appendix. Each entry refers to the appropriate page in *BDB*, thus giving quick access to the information provided there. A defect noted in the review of vol. II (*B.L.* 1983) has been rectified, and difficult forms are included under chapter and verse even when their root appears in the appendix. The usefulness of the volume is therefore much increased. I note a missprint in the Hebrew script on page 154, in the vocalization on page 170, and a strange example of incorrect information on page 149. It should, however, prove a helpful tool for those for whom it is designed.

G. I. EMMERSON

BEYER, K.: *The Aramaic Language: Its Distribution and Subdivisions.* 1986. Pp. 61. Translated by J. F. Healey. (Vandenhoeck and Ruprecht, Göttingen. Price: DM 25.00. ISBN 3 525 53571 6)

This volume contains a translation of the first chapter, 'Die Verbreitung und Gliederung', of K. Beyer's book, *Die aramäischen Texte vom toten Meer samt den Inschriften aus Palästina, dem Testament Levis aus der Kairoer Genisa, der Fastenrolle und den alten talmudischen Zitaten* (Vandenhoeck and Ruprecht, Göttingen, 1984), pp. 23–76. E. Ullendorf reviewed this monumental work in in *B.L.* 1985, p. 150. Deservedly the panoramic survey of Aramaic dialectology from first millennium Old Aramaic to contemporary Modern Aramaic has been made available for non-German reading students and stands well on its own, although a translation of Beyer's important second chapter which comprises a diachronic account of Aramaic phonology is a desideratum. The translation is excellent and the footnotes which have been brought up to date contain a store of historical and bibliographical information.

P. W. COXON

CAGNI, L. (ed.): *Il Bilinguismo a Ebla: Atti del convegno internazionale (Napoli, 19–22 aprile 1982)* (Istituto Universitario Orientale, Dipartimento di Studi Asiatici, Series Minor 22). 1984. Pp. xix, 487. (Istituto Universitario Orientale, Naples. Distributed by Herder Editrice e Libreria, Rome. Price: Lire 50,000)

Twenty-one papers from the Naples conference are published here, with a posthumous article of M. Dahood appended. The theme, bilingualism at

Ebla, is highly technical, covering Sumerian and its relationship to the Semitic language (or languages?) known from the Ebla archive. Great learning is displayed in many of the contributions and important advances are made, but much is not directly relevant to the Old Testament. Hebraists interested in Semitic grammar should refer to the articles of H.-P. Müller (the verbal system), K. Hecker (word forms expanded by two *t*'s), B. Kienast (same as Hecker), F. Vattioni (evidence for Aramaic?), and F. A. Pennacchietti (genitive constructions). M. Dahood, 'Hebrew hapax legomena in Eblaite', treats Eblaite as he has previously Ugaritic. The abundant originality needs much sifting.

W. G. LAMBERT

GOLOMB, D. M.: *A Grammar of Targum Neofiti* (Harvard Semitic Monographs, 34). 1985. Pp. viii, 253. (Scholars Press, Chico, California. Price: $16.75. ISBN 0 89130 891 1)

Based on a Ph.D. thesis which was confined to Genesis, this work sets out to produce a synchronic model of the language of the whole of Targum Neofiti. The author eschews confusion between the spoken and literary forms of the language, between oral translation and written Targum, and between evidence found in Mishna and that in Gemara. He argues that Targum Neofiti is not a simple translation but an interpretative commentary. It is a coherent body of literature and, if interpolations and medieval copyist phenomena are excluded, its language is reasonably consistent. After a short chapter on orthography the book offers a systematic record of the accidence of Neofiti, comprehensive except for a section on numerals. A final chapter on syntax is more selective, covering compound verbal forms (auxiliary use of *hwh*), expression of the direct object, use of the predicate adjective and expression of the genitive relation. (See also pp. 109–10 above.)

A. GELSTON

NICCACCI, A.: *Sintassi del verbo ebraico nella prosa biblica classica* (Studium Biblicum Franciscanum, Analecta N. 23). 1986. Pp. 127. (Franciscan Printing Press, Jerusalem. Price: $5.00)

These notes on the syntax of the Hebrew verb derive directly from teaching experience and indirectly from W. Schneider's *Grammatik des biblischen Hebräisch* (see *B.L.* 1976, p. 106 and *B.L.* 1980, p. 134). Like Schneider, Niccacci has applied the text linguistics of H. Weinrich to classical Hebrew. This means that N. describes the different verbal forms (*wayyiqtol*, *qatal*, etc.) not as isolated grammatical abstracts or even as parts of a sentence but in terms of longer stretches of text. The author begins by setting out key oppositions (nominal/verbal clauses; narrative/discourse; narrative/comment; foreground/background; new information versus old, etc.) which he then applies to Hebrew syntax. He shows, for instance, that when a chain of identical verbal forms is broken the reason can be determined. For example, the interruption by *w*^{e} + interposed word(s) + *qatal* of a *wayyiqtol* sequence serves as comment on the event narrated. One of his conclusions is that the basic verbal forms in Hebrew prose are not *yiqtol* and *qatal* but *wayyiqtol* and *qatal*. He also discusses emphasis, introductory particles and other topics including syntax in poetry. There are indices. A clear, concise handbook well illustrated by examples.

W. G. E. WATSON

NORIN, S. I. L.: *Sein Name allein ist hoch. Das Jhw-haltige Suffix althebräischer Personennamen untersucht mit besonderer Berücksichtigung der alttestamentlichen Redaktionsgeschichte* (Coniectanea Biblica, Old Testament Series 24). 1986. Pp. 227. (Gleerup, Malmö. ISBN 91 40 05113 7)

Following an earlier brief study of Hebrew theophoric personal names with prefixed *yhwh*-elements (*VT* 29 (1979), pp. 87–97), Norin here studies in detail the suffixed forms. His purpose is to account for the mixture of variant forms (*-jhw*, *-jh*, and *-jw*), and also to enquire whether their distribution sheds light on the redaction-history of the Deuteronomistic History, the Book of Jeremiah and the 'Chronicler's History'. Both the extra-biblical and biblical material point to a chronological development, with the *-jhw* form predominating from the seventh century B.C. and the *-jh* form after the Exile; but geographical provenance and theological motives also played a major role. The study has brought to light many fascinating facets of the phenomena. As a contribution to the study of redaction-history it also deserves serious consideration, although in view of the complex nature of the factors involved it may be questioned whether some of the data here presented might not be interpreted differently and made to support alternative redactional theories.

R. N. WHYBRAY

RIBICHINI, S., and XELLA, P.: *La terminologia dei tessili nei testi di Ugarit* (Collezione di Studi Fenici, 20). 1985. Pp. 102. (Consiglio Nazionale delle Ricerche, Roma.

A study of seventy-eight lexical terms relating to textiles in Ugaritic forms the core of this work. The materials used, the workers involved and their products are described in the short introduction. In the appendix several Ugaritic passages concerned with the supply and manufacture of textiles are transliterated and translated. The indices provided include a list of Hebrew terms discussed. In fact, there are always remarks in the text on whether or not particular words are relevant to the Old Testament. Although some of the terms remain obscure, this survey gives us a valuable glimpse of everyday life in the kingdom of Ugarit in the Bronze Age.

W. G. E. WATSON

RICHTER, W.: *Untersuchungen zur Valenz althebräischer Verben, 1. 'RK* (Arbeiten zu Text und Sprache im Alten Testament, 23. Band). 1985. Pp. x, 180. (Eos Verlag, St Ottilien. Price: DM 30.00. ISBN 3 88096 523 4)

This study is concerned with the classification of the parts and constructions of sentences in the Hebrew Bible, especially with regard to the contribution of verbs to sentence structure. For this purpose the verb *'RK* is chosen and all its occurrences are subjected to a thorough syntactical analysis. After an introduction of 25 pages, most of the book consists of this treatment of *'RK* and in appearance resembles a book of algebra. It is a study which those conversant with structural linguistics will want to have. Applied to all Hebrew verbs, the treatment would eventually lead to new kinds of syntactical concordances and lexicons.

J. H. EATON

SILVERMAN, M. H.: *Religious Values in the Jewish Proper Names at Elephantine* (Alter Orient und Altes Testament, Bd. 217). 1985. Pp. xxii, 311. (Neukirchener Verlag, Neukirchen-Vluyn. Price: DM 148.00. ISBN 3 7887 1223 6. Butzon & Bercker, Kevelaer. ISBN 3 7666 9423 5)

This book has been in the making (by way of a 1967 dissertation) since 1963. It is nevertheless curious that Grelot's work (1972) arrived in time for inclusion only in the footnotes and that Kornfeld's monograph (1978) could not be consulted at all (let alone the Aramaic texts from North Saqqâra, published in 1983). However, it is unlikely that they would have caused Silverman to change his presentation in any significant way. There are two aspects to the book. On the one hand we have a very detailed collection and discussion (grammatical, lexical etc.) of all the personal names from Elephantine, with particular attention to those of west-semitic origin. Moreover, Silverman attempts carefully to date each text on whatever grounds are available, and this leads him into the second and more controversial aspect of his work — an attempt to discern a religious trend in what he sees as a development in the style of Jewish names. Briefly, the Elephantine community at first reflects the heritage of Judah at the time of the exile but then develops in a way which prefigures later Egyptian Hellenistic Judaism. There is much use of statistics here in an area where there are so many unknown factors that we really cannot be sure what influenced parents in the choice of names for their children. Moreover, the data base for some of the statistical tables is perilously narrow. However, Silverman is well aware of these and other dangers. He carefully justifies each step of the argument and he does not hide (though he may underestimate) the enormous assumptions which he sometimes has to make. But these comments should not detract from the value of the great wealth of material which he has so painstakingly assembled and arranged.

H. G. M. Williamson

Sperber, D.: *A Dictionary of Greek and Latin Legal Terms in Rabbinic Literature.* 1984. Pp. 226. (Bar-Ilan University Press, Ramat Gan. Price: $32.50. ISBN 965 226 050 9)

This is a pilot project, the first in a series of small specialized etymological dictionaries dealing with specific topics. There are well over three thousand Greek and Latin loanwords in rabbinic literature and this dictionary contains less than two hundred words culled from rabbinic texts of the first five or six centuries of the common era (the Roman and early Byzantine period). The work is intended as a help to scholars working in a variety of fields, philological, historical, and cultural. Some words of disputed origin are not included. Special attention is paid to morphological and dialectal phenomena and their relationship to Greek dialectology as attested in epigraphic and papyrological sources. The author expresses the hope that a larger dictionary will appear which will supercede the magnificent work of Samuel Kraus, *Griechische und Lateinische Lehnwörter im Talmud, Midrash und Targum* (1899).

P. Wernberg-Møller

Stähli, H.-P., and Chiesa, B.: *Corso di Ebraico Biblico.* Vol. 1: *Grammatica Ebraica*, translated by B. Chiesa from H.-P. Stähli, *Hebräisch–Kurzgrammatik*, 1984. Vol. 2: *Esercizi, Crestomazia e Glossario.* 1986. Pp. xvi, 109 (Vol. 1), 191 (Vol. 2) (Paideia Editrice, Brescia. Price: Lire 24,000 (2 vol. set))

Volume 1 of this set comprises grammar and syntax, and is a translation of Stähli's short Hebrew grammar (reviewed in *B.L.* 1985, pp. 156–57). Some changes have been made and a brief bibliography, by R. Contini, of works in Italian has been inserted. The second volume (exercises, selection of texts and glossary) is not a translation but was compiled by Chiesa to complement the grammar. Since vol. 1 is laid out as a reference grammar (with some account of diachronic elements) and since the exercises of vol. 2 accompany each section of the grammar, the whole work can be used as a refresher course by students who have done one year of Hebrew. The choice of texts for translation is wide and there are extensive notes. Some thought has gone into the 1,600-word glossary and in general the printing, Hebrew script included, is clear.

W. G. E. WATSON

ULLENDORFF, E.: *A Tigrinya (Təgrəñña) Chrestomathy* (Äthiopistische Forschungen, 19). 1985. Pp. 242; 1 plate. (Franz Steiner Verlag, Stuttgart. Price: DM 86.00. ISBN 3 515 04314 4)

This work forms in many respects a companion volume to the author's *An Amharic Chrestomathy* (1965; revised edition: 1978; not noticed in the *Book List*). It provides an introduction to the study of Tigrinya and a description of the language, grammatical tables, a selection of texts, a very valuable Tigrinya-English glossary, and a select bibliography. Documents written in Tigrinya date from comparatively recent times, and the texts reproduced here are representative of the fairly limited range of Tigrinya literature. They include the first chapter of Ruth, extracts from books, official documents, newspaper articles, and also letters written to the author during his period of service in Eritrea. The texts have for the most part been photographically reproduced from the original sources, but there are occasional annotations and corrections in the margin. This book, which has been written with the author's characteristic mastery and erudition, is not of direct concern to Old Testament scholars, but it is important to all those concerned with the Semitic languages in their wider context.

M. A. KNIBB

ZUBER, B.: *Das Tempussystem des biblischen Hebräisch. Eine Untersuchung am Text* (Beihefte zur ZAW, 164). 1986. Pp. xii, 198, 18 detached tables in end-pocket. (De Gruyter, Berlin. Price: DM 84.00. ISBN 3 11 010402 4)

An unusual and eccentric work, which rejects the common aspectual theory of the Hebrew verb system and proposes a solution in terms of an opposition between *indicatival* and *modal-futuric* (e.g. p. 12). The strength of the argument lies in the numerous cases where the current handbook views fail to fit the facts. A peculiarity of the approach is the degree to which the author depends upon the tenses used by the LXX and Vulgate as evidence relevant to his theory. Special studies are undertaken into the role of common particles like *kī* or *gam*, and into tenses in the Qumran documents. The reader has to master a completely new terminology. The reader cannot avoid the feeling that a veritable minefield of snags and traps lies under the surface of the argument.

J. BARR

Books Received too Late for Notice in 1987

The books in the following list will be reviewed in the *Book List* for 1988.

ABITZ, F.: *Ramses III. in den Gräbern seiner Söhne* (Orbis Biblicus et Orientalis, 72). 1986. (Universitätsverlag, Freiburg, Vandenhoeck & Ruprecht, Göttingen. ISBN 3 7278 0369 X, 3 525 53701 8)

ACHTEMEIER, E.: *Nahum — Malachi* (Interpretation: a Bible Commentary for Teaching and Preaching). 1986. (John Knox Press, Atlanta, Georgia. ISBN 0 8042 3129 X)

AEJMELAEUS, A.: *The Traditional Prayer in the Psalms* and SCHMIDT, L.: *Literarische Studien zur Josephsgeschichte* (BZAW 167). 1986. (De Gruyter, Berlin. ISBN 3 11 010480 6)

ALBERTI, A. and POMPONIO, F.: *Pre-Sargonic and Sargonic Texts from Ur edited in UET 2, Supplement* (Studia Pohl, Series Major 13). 1986. (Biblical Institute Press, Rome. ISBN 88 7653 585 3)

ALONSO SCHÖKEL, L.: *Hermeneutica de la Palabra* I: Hermeneutica biblica (Academia Christiana 37). 1986. (Ediciones Cristiandad, Madrid. ISBN 84 7057 401 5)

ANDERSEN, F. I. and FORBES, A. D.: *Spelling in the Hebrew Bible* (Biblica et Orientalia, 41). 1986. (Biblical Institute Press, Rome. ISBN 88 7653 342 7)

AUGUSTIN, M. and KEGLER, J.: *Bibelkunde des Alten Testaments: ein Arbeitsbuch*. 1987. (Gerd Mohn, Gütersloh. ISBN 3 579 00079 9)

BALDWIN, J. G.: *The Message of Genesis 12–50: From Abraham to Joseph* (The Bible Speaks Today). 1986. (Inter-Varsity Press, Leicester. ISBN 0 85110 759 1)

BARGUET, P.: *Les Textes des Sarcophages Égyptiens du Moyen Empire* (Littératures Anciennes du Proche-Orient, 12). 1986. (Éditions du Cerf, Paris. ISBN 2 204 02332 9, ISSN 0459 5831)

BARKER, K. L. (ed.): *The Making of a Contemporary Translation: The purpose and method of the New International Version*. 1987. Hodder and Stoughton, London, for the International Bible Society. ISBN 0 340 40263 6)

BARSOTTI, D.: *Meditazione sul Libro di Guiditta* (Collana Bibbia e Liturgia 29). 1985. (Queriniana, Brescia)

BARTHÉLEMY, D., GOODING, D. W., LUST, J. and TOV, E.: *The Story of David and Goliath: Textual and Literary Criticism — Papers of a Joint Research Venture* (Orbis Biblicus et Orientalis, 73). 1986. (Éditions Universitaires, Fribourg, Vandenhoeck & Ruprecht, Gottingen. ISBN 3 7278 0372 X, 3 525 53702 6)

BECKER, J.: 1 *Chronik* (Die Neue Echter Bibel: Kommentar zum Alten Testament mit der Einheitsübersetzung, Lfg 18). 1986. (Echter Verlag, Würzburg. ISBN 3 429 01038 1)

BLANQUART, F. (ed.): *Le Création dans l'Orient Ancien* (Congrès de l'ACFEB, Lille (1985). Lectio Divina 127). 1987. (Éditions du Cerf, Paris. ISBN 2 204 02595 X, ISSN 0750 1919)

BOCKMUEHL, K.: *Books: God's Tools in the History of Salvation* (Regent College Monographs, 1). 1986. (Regent College, Vancouver and Helmers & Howard, Colorado Springs. ISBN 0 88865 414 6)

BODENMANN, R.: *Naissance d'une Exégèse: Daniel dans l'Eglise ancienne des trois premiers siècles* (Beiträge zur Geschichte der Biblischen Exegese, 28). 1986. (Mohr, Tübingen. ISBN 3 16 145143 0)

BOTTERWECK, G. J., RINGGREN, H., and FABRY, H.-J. (eds): *Theologisches Wörterbuch zum Alten Testament*. Band V. Lfg. 9–10 (Cols 1025–1208, Index and Title Pages for Vol. v). 1986. (Kohlhammer, Stuttgart. ISBN 3 17 009465 3)

CENTRE: INFORMATIQUE ET BIBLE (ed.): *Bible and Computer: The Text — Proceedings of the First International Colloquium* (Louvain-la-Neuve (Belgique) 2–3–4 septembre 1985) (Travaux de Linguistique Quantitative, 37). 1986. (Champion–Slatkine, Paris–Genève. ISBN 2 05 100769 1, ISSN 0773 3968)

CLAUSS, M.: Geschichte Israels: *Von der Frühzeit bis zur Zerstörung Jerusalems (587 v.Chr.)*. 1986. (Verlag C. H. Beck, München. ISBN 3 406 31175 X)

COGGINS, R. J.: *Haggai, Zechariah, Malachi* (Old Testament Guides). 1987. (Sheffield Academic Press. ISBN 1 85075 025 4)

COHEN, D.: *La Phrase Nominale et l'Évolution du Système Verbal en Sémitique: Études de syntaxe historique* (Collection Linguistique publiée par la Societé de Linguistique de Paris, LXXII). 1984. (Éditions Peeters, Leuven–Paris. ISBN 2 8017 0000 0)

COX, C. E.: *Hexaplaric Materials Preserved in the Armenian Version* (Septuagint and Cognate Studies, 21). 1986. (Scholars Press, Atlanta, Georgia. ISBN 1 55540 028 0, 1 55540 029 9 (pbk))

CURTO, S. and MONTEVECCHI, O.: *Egitto e Società Antica* (Atti del Convegno Torino 8/9 VI–23/24 XI 1984). 1985. (Vita e Pensiero, Milano. ISBN 88 343 3003 X)

DURAND, J.-M. and Kupper, J.-R. (eds): *Miscellanea Babylonica: Mélanges offerts à Maurice Birot*. 1985. (Éditions Recherche sur les Civilisations, A.D.P.F., Paris. ISBN 2 86538 147 3)

EBERLEIN, K.: *Gott der Schöpfer — Israels Gott: Eine exegetisch-hermeneutische Studie zur theologischen Funktion alttestamentlicher Schöpfungsaussagen* (Beiträge zur Erforschung des Alten Testaments und des Antiken Judentums). 1986. (Peter Lang, Bern, Frankfurt am Main, New York. ISBN 3 8204 8921 5, ISSN 0722 0790)

EGGER, R.: *Josephus Flavius und die Samaritaner: Eine terminologischer Untersuchung zur Identitätsklarung der Samaritaner* (Novum Testamentum et Orbis Antiquus, 4). 1986. (Universitätsverlag, Freiburg, Vandenhoeck & Ruprecht, Göttingen. ISBN 3 7278 0373 8, 3 525 53903 7)

ELIADE, M. (Editor in Chief): *The Encyclopedia of Religion*. 1987. (Macmillan, New York, Collier Macmillan, London. ISBN 0 02 909480 1 (set))

FERGUSON, D. S.: *Biblical Hermeneutics: An Introduction*. 1987. (SCM Press, London. ISBN 0 334 01906 0)

FOX, E.: *Now These Are The Names: A new English Rendition of the Book of Exodus — translated with Commentary and Notes*. 1986. (Schocken Books, New York. ISBN 0 8052 4020 9)

GALBIATI, E. (ed.): *Dizionario Enciclopedico della Bibbia e del Mondo Biblico*. 1986. (Massimo, Milano. ISBN 88 7030 719 0)

GARCÍA MARTÍNEZ, F., DE GEUS, C. H. J. and KLIJN, A. F. J. (eds): *Profeten en profetische gestalten* (Essays in honour of A. S. van der Woude). 1985. (J. H. Kok, Kampen, G. F. Callenbach, Nijkerk. ISBN 90242 4036 0)

DE GENNARO, G.: *L'Antico Testamento Interpretato dal Nuovo: Il Messia* (Studio Biblico Teologico Aquilano). 1985. (Edizioni Dehoniane, Napoli)

GIBERT, P.: *Bible, Mythes et Récits de Commencement* (Parole de Dieu). 1986. (Éditions du Seuil, Paris. ISBN 2 02 009379 0)

GIVEON, R., KERTESZ, T.: *Egyptian Scarabs and Seals from Acco* (From the Collection of the Israel Department of Antiquities and Museums). 1986. (Universitätsverlag, Freiburg. ISBN 3 7278 0371 1)

GONEN, R.: *Biblical Holy Places: an illustrated guide*. 1987. (A. & C. Black, London. ISBN 0 7136 2872 3)

HAAG, E. and HOSSFELD, F.-L. (eds): *Freude an der Weisung des Herrn:*

Beiträge zur Theologie der Psalmen – Festgabe zum 70. Geburtstag von Heinrich Gross (Stuttgarter Biblische Beiträge, 13). 1986. (Verlag Katholisches Bibelwerk, Stuttgart. ISBN 3 460 00131 3)

HADIDI, A. (ed.): *Studies in the History and Archaeology of Jordan* II. 1985. (Department of Antiquities, Amman, Routledge & Kegan Paul, London. ISBN 0 7102 0734 4)

HART, G.: *A Dictionary of Egyptian Gods and Goddesses*. 1986. (Routledge & Kegan Paul, London. ISBN 0 7102 0167 2)

HAYTER, M.: *The New Eve in Christ: The Use and Abuse of the Bible in the Debate about Women in the Church*. 1987. (SPCK, London. ISBN 0 281 04262 4)

HECKER, K. and SOMMERFELD, W. (eds): *Keilschriftliche Literaturen: Ausgewählte Vorträge der XXXII. Rencontre Assyriologique Internationale* (Berliner Beiträge zum Vorderen Orient, Bd. 6). 1986. (Dietrich Reimer Verlag, Berlin. ISBN 3 496 00879 2)

HOGLUND, K. G., HUWILER, E. F., GLASS, J. T. and LEE, R. W. (eds): *The Listening Heart: Essays in Wisdom and the Psalms in honor of Roland E. Murphy* (JSOT Supplement Series, 58). 1987. (Sheffield Academic Press. ISBN 1 85075 085 8)

HORN, J.: *Studien zu den Märtyrern des Nördlichen Oberägypten I: Märtyrerverehrung und Märtyrerlegende im Werk des Schenute — Beiträge zur ältesten Ägyptischen Märtyrerüberlieferung* (Göttinger Orientforschungen: Reihe Ägypten; Bd. 15). 1986. (Otto Harrassowitz, Wiesbaden. ISBN 3 447 02576 X, ISSN 0340 6342)

JEPPESEN, K. and LEMCHE, N. P. (eds.) *Scandinavian Journal of the Old Testament*, Vol. 1. 1987. (Aarhus University Press. ISBN 87 7288 082 1, ISSN 0901 8328)

JOÜON, P.: *Ruth: Commentaire philologique et exégétique* (Deuxième édition anastatique corrigée) (Subsidia Biblica, 9). 1986. (Biblical Institute Press, Rome. ISBN 88 7653 586 1)

KILIAN, R.: *Jesaja 1–12* (Die Neue Echter Bibel: Kommentar zum Alten Testament mit der Einheitsübersetzung, Lfg. 17). 1986. (Echter Verlag, Würzburg. ISBN 3 429 01041 1)

KITCHEN, K. A.: *The Third Intermediate Period in Egypt (1100–650 BC)* (2nd ed. with supplement). 1986. (Aris & Phillips, Warminster, Wiltshire. ISBN 0 85668 298 5)

KOCH, K.: *Daniel (1, 1–21)* (Biblischer Kommentar: Altes Testament, Bd. XXII, 1). 1986. (Neukirchener Verlag, Neukirchen-Vluyn. ISBN 3 7887 0788 7)

KUGEL, J. L. and GREER, R. A.: *Early Biblical Interpretation* (Library of Early Christianity, vol. 3). 1986. (Westminster Press, Philadelphia. ISBN 0 664 21907 1)

LARCHER, C.: *Le Livre de la Sagesse ou La Sagesse de Salomon* III (XI, 1–XIX, 22 (Études Bibliques, n.s. 5). 1985. (J. Gabalda, Paris. ISBN 85021 016 1, ISSN 0760 3541)

LOPRIENO, A.: *Das Verbalsystem im Ägyptischen und im Semitischen: zur Grundlegung einer Aspekttheorie* (Göttinger Orientforschungen: Reihe 4, Ägypten; Bd. 17). 1986. (Otto Harrassowitz, Wiesbaden. ISBN 3 447 02583 2, ISSN 0340 6342)

MCCARTHY, D. J.: *Institution and Narrative: Collected Essays* (Analecta Biblica, 108). 1985. (Biblical Institute Press, Rome. ISBN 88 7653 108 4)

MCCOMISKEY, T. E.: *The Covenants of Promise: A Theology of the Old Testament Covenants*. 1985. (Inter-Varsity Press, Nottingham. ISBN 0 85110 773 7)

MCGOVERN, P. E.: *Late Bronze Palestinian Pendants: Innovation in a Cosmopolitan Age* (JSOT/ASOR Monograph Series, 1). 1985. (JSOT Press for the American Schools of Oriental Research. ISBN 0 905774 90 6)

McGregor, L. J.: *The Greek Text of Ezekiel: An Examination of its Homogeneity* (Septuagint and Cognate Studies, 18). 1985. (Scholars Press, Atlanta, Georgia. ISBN 0 89130 902 0, 0 89130 903 9 (pbk))

MacQueen, J. G.: *The Hittites and their Contemporaries in Asia Minor* (revised and enlarged edition) (Ancient Peoples and Places, 83). 1986. (Thames and Hudson, London. ISBN 0 500 02108 2)

Magall, M.: *Archäologie und Bibel: Wissenschaftliche Wege zur Welt des Alten Testaments.* 1986. (DuMont Buchverlag, Köln. ISBN 3 7701 1644 5)

Martin-Achard, R.: *La Loi, Don de Dieu: Aux Sources de l'Ancien Testament.* 1987. (Éditions du Moulin, Aubonne (CH))

Mayer, G.: *Die jüdischer Frau in der hellenistisch-römischen Antike.* (Kohlhammer, Stuttgart. ISBN 3 17 009391 6)

Meynet, R.: *Initiation á la Rhétorique Biblique: Qui est donc le plus grand?* Tome 1: Texte; Tome 2: Planches ("Initiations"). 1982. (Éditions du Cerf, Paris. ISBN 2 204 01868 6)

Muñoz Leon, A. (ed.): *Salvacion en la Palabra: Targum–Derash–Berith* (En Memoria del profesor Alejandro Diez Macho). 1986. (Ediciones Cristiandad, Madrid. ISBN 84 7057 390 X)

Neef, H.-D.: *Die Heilstraditionen Israels in der Verkündigung des Propheten Hosea* (BZAW, 169). 1987). (De Gruyter, Berlin. ISBN 3 11 01093 1)

Neri, U.: *Genesi* (Biblia: I libri della Bibbia interpretati dalla grande Tradizione, AT, 1). 1986. (Gribaudi Editore, Torino)

Neusner, J.: *Israel and Iran in Talmudic Times: A Political History* (Studies in Judaism). 1986. (University Press of America, Lanham, Maryland. ISBN 0 8191 5729 5, 0 8191 5730 9 (pbk))

Neusner, J.: *Israel's Politics in Sasanian Iran: Jewish Self-Government in Talmudic Times* (Studies in Judaism). 1986. (University Press of America, Lanham, Maryland. ISBN 0 8191 5725 2, 0 8191 5726 0 (pbk))

Niehr, H.: *Herrschen und Richten: Die Wurzel špt im Alten Orient und im Alten Testament* (Forschung zur Bibel, 54). 1986. (Echter Verlag, Würzburg. ISBN 3 429 01012 8)

North, R. (ed.): *Elenchus Bibliographicus Biblicus of Biblica.* Vol. 65 (1984). 1987. (Biblical Institute Press, Rome. ISBN ISSN 0392 7423)

Olofsson, S.: *Guds Ord och Människors Språk: En bok om bibelöversättning.* 1986. (EFS förlaget, Uppsala. ISBN 91 7080 721 3)

Oost, R.: *Omstreden Bijbeluitleg: Aspecten en achtergronden van de hermeneutische discussie rondom de exegese van het Oude Testament in Nederland — Een bijdrage tot gesprek.* 1986. (J. H. Kok, Kampen. ISBN 90 242 5486 8)

Orrieux, C.: *Les Papyrus de Zenon: L'horizon d'un grec en Égypte au IIIe siècle avant J.C.* 1983. (Macula, Paris. ISBN 2 86589 008 2)

Pettinato, G.: *Ebla: Nuovi orizzonti della storia.* 1986. (Rusconi, Milano. ISBN 88, 18 12036 0)

Pettinato, G.: *Semiramide.* 1985. (Rusconi, Milano. ISBN 88 18 18003 7)

Pomponio, F., Ribichini, S. and Xella, P.: *Studi Epigrafici e Linguistici sul Vicino Oriente antico.* Vol. 3. 1986. (Essedue Edizioni, Verona)

de Pury, A.: *Le Chant de la Création: L'homme et l'univers selon le récit de Genèse 1* (Cahiers Bibliques, 1). 1986. (Éditions du Moulin, Aubonne (CH))

Sarna, N. M.: *Exploring Exodus: The Heritage of Biblical Israel.* 1986. (Schocken Books, New York. ISBN 0 8052 3982 0)

Scharbert, J.: *Genesis 12–50* (Die Neue Echter Bibel: Kommentar zum Alten Testament mit der Einheitsübersetzung). 1986. (Echter Verlag, Würzburg. ISBN 3 429 01035 7)

Schmitt, J. J.: *Isaiah and his Interpreters.* 1986. (Paulist Press, Mahwah, New Jersey. ISBN 0 8091 2826 8)

Schriftwerke, Die: verdeutscht von Martin Buber— mit einer Beilage: *Martin Buber: Zur Verdeutschung des letzten Bandes der Schrift*. 1986. (Verlag Lambert Schneider, Heidelberg. ISBN 3 7953 0183 1)

SICRE, J. L.: *Los Profetas de Israel y su Mensaje: Antologia de textos* (Academia Christiana, 35). 1986. (Ediciones Cristiandad, Madrid. ISBN 84 7057 394 2)

SIRAT, C., CAUDERLIER, P., DUKAN, M. and FRIEDMAN, M. A.: *La 'Ketouba' de Cologne: un contrat de marriage juif à Antinoopolis* (Abhandlungen der Rheinisch-Westfälischen Akademie der Wissenschaften: Papyrologica Coloniensia, XII). 1986. (Westdeutscher Verlag, Wiesbaden. ISBN 3 531 09921 3, ISSN 0078 9410)

SKA, J. L.: *Le Passage de la Mer: Étude de la construction, du style et de la symbolique d'Ex 14, 1–31* (Analecta Biblica, 109). 1986. (Biblical Institute Press, Rome. ISBN 88 7653 109 2)

STULMAN, L.: *The Other Text of Jeremiah: A reconstruction of the Hebrew Text Underlying the Greek Version of the Prose Sections of Jeremiah with English Translation*. 1985. (University Press of America, Lanham, Maryland. ISBN 0 8191 4989 6)

TESCAROLI, L.: *I Salmi nella Tradizione Ebraica: nuova traduzione dal testo masoretico*. 1985. (Città Nuova, Roma. ISBN 88 311 4907 5)

THOMPSON, B. P.: *Scripture: Meaning and Method — Essays presented to Anthony Tyrrell Hanson*. 1987. (Hull University Press. ISBN 0 85958 460 7)

TURGMAN, V.: *De L'Autorité de Moïse — Ex 15, 22–27*. 1987. (KO'AMAR, Eilsbrunn)

Übersetzung des Talmud Yerushalmi, herausgegeben von M. Hengel, H. P. Rüger, P. Schäfer. Band 1/2; *Pea-Ackerecke,* übersetzt von G. A. Wewers. 1986. (Mohr, Tübingen. ISBN 3 16 745068 1)

VANSTIPHOUT, H. L. J., JONGELING, K., LEEMHUIS, F., and REININK, G. J. (eds): *Scripta Signa Vocis: Studies about Scripts, Scriptures, Scribes and Languages in the Near East, presented to J. H. Hospers*. 1986. (Egbert Forsten, Gröningen. ISBN 90 6980 008 X)

VAWTER, B. (ed.): *Old Testament Abstracts*, Vol. 9/3. 1986. (The Catholic Biblical Association, The Catholic University of America, Washington, D.C. ISBN ISSN 0364 8591)

Vetus Latina. Die Rest der altlateinischen Bibel, nach Petrus Sabatier neu gesammelt und herausgegeben von der Erzabtei Beuron. 12: *Esaias*. Herausgegeben von R. Gryson. 1. Lieferung: Is. 1, 1–22. 1987. (Herder, Freiburg im Breisgau. ISBN 3 451 00439 9)

VIEWEGER, D.: *Die Spezifik der Berufungsberichte Jeremias und Ezechiels im Umfeld ähnlicher Einheiten des Alten Testaments* (Beiträge zur Erforschung des Alten Testaments und des Antiken Judentums, 6). 1986. (Peter Lang, Bern, Frankfurt am Main, New York. ISBN 3 8204 8948 7, ISSN 0722 0790)

VOGT, E.: *Der Aufstand Hiskias und die Belagerung Jerusalems 701 v. Chr.* (Analecta Biblica, 106). 1986. (Biblical Institute Press, Rome. ISBN 88 7653 106 X)

WEBER-MÖCKL, A.: *'Das Recht des Königs, der über euch herrschen soll': Studien zu 1 Sam 8, 11ff. in der Literatur der frühen Neuzeit* (Historische Forschungen, 27). 1986. (Duncker & Humblot, Berlin. ISBN 3 428 05963 8)

WEINFELD, M.: *The Organizational Pattern and the Penal Code of the Qumran Sect* (Novum Testamentum et Orbis Antiqua, 2). 1986. (Universitätsverlag, Freiburg, Vandenhoeck & Ruprecht, Göttingen. ISBN 3 7278 0363 0, 3 525 53901 0)

WESTERMANN, C.: *Genesis 37–50: A Commentary*. 1987. (SPCK, London. ISBN 0 281 04277 2)

WEVERS, J. W., with the assistance of QUAST, U. (eds.): *Septuaginta, Vetus Testamentun Graecum Auctoritate Academiae Scientiarum Gottingensis editum.* Vol. II, 2: *Leviticus.* 1986. (Vandenhoeck & Ruprecht, Göttingen. ISBN 3 525 53444 2)

WHIGHAM PRICE, A.: *The Ladies of Castlebray: A story of nineteenth-century travel and research.* 1985. (Alan Sutton, Gloucester. ISBN 0 86299 228 1)

WHYBRAY, R. N.: *The Making of the Pentateuch: A Methodological Study* (JSOT Supplement Series, 53). 1987. (Sheffield Academic Press. ISBN 1 85075 064 5, 1 85075 063 7 (pbk))

WILLIAMSON, H. G. M.: *Ezra and Nehemiah* (Old Testament Guides). 1987. (Sheffield Academic Press. ISBN 1 85075 065 3)

VAN DER WOUDE, A. S. (ed.): *Crises and Perspectives.* (Papers read at the joint British–Dutch Old Testament Conference held at Cambridge, U.K., 1985.) (Oudtestamentische Studiën, XXIV). 1986. (Brill, Leiden. ISBN 90 04 07873 8, ISSN 0169 9555)

XELLA, P. (ed.): *Archeologia dell'Inferno: L'Aldilà nel mondo antico vicinoorientale e classico.* 1987. (Essedue Edizioni, Verona. ISBN 88 85697 15 1)

XELLA, P.: *Gli Antenati di Dio: Divinità e miti della tradizione di Canaan.* 1982. (Essedue Edizioni, Verona)

XELLA, P.: *La Terra di Baal (Ugarit e la sua civiltà)* (Biblioteca di Archeologia). 1984. (Armando Curcio, Roma)

Index of Authors

(N.B. — Names occurring more than once in the same review or on the same page are listed on their first occurrence only.)

The Society for Old Testament Study is a British Society for Old Testament scholars. Candidates for membership, which is not confined to British subjects, must be nominated by two members of the Society. Residents of the British Isles are normally admitted to ordinary membership and non-residents to associate membership. All correspondence concerning domestic affairs of the Society should be sent to:

Dr A. H. W. Curtis
Faculty of Theology
University of Manchester
Manchester M13 9PL
England

The Society for Old Testament Study is a British Society for Old Testament scholars. Candidates for membership, which is not confined to British subjects, must be nominated by two members of the Society. Residents of the British Isles are normally admitted to ordinary membership and non-residents to associate membership. All correspondence concerning domestic affairs of the Society should be sent to:

Dr A. H. W. Curtis
Faculty of Theology
University of Manchester
Manchester M13 9PL
England

ISBN 0 905495 06 3

THE SOCIETY FOR
OLD TESTAMENT
STUDY

BOOK LIST
1988

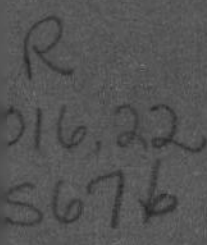

Printed for the Society

The Society for Old Testament Study

BOOK LIST
1988

Printed for the Society

ISBN 0 905495 07 1

PRINTED BY W. S. MANEY AND SON LTD HUDSON ROAD LEEDS LS9 7DL

Contents

One copy of the *Book List* is supplied free to all members of the Society.

Copies of the *Book List* for 1988 may also be obtained from M. E. J. Richardson, Esq., Department of Middle Eastern Studies, University of Manchester, Manchester M13 9PL, England. Back numbers of the *Book List* are also available from Mr Richardson. Orders should not be accompanied by payment; an invoice will be sent. The price of these is £6.00 plus postage or $16.00, for a single copy. Payment should be made by cheque in sterling or U.S. dollars payable to the Society for Old Testament Study, or direct to Post Office Giro Account No. 50 450 4002.

Review copies of books for the *Book List* should be sent to the Editor:

Dr A. Graeme Auld
New College, Mound Place
Edinburgh EH1 2LX,
Scotland

PREFACE

In presenting this *Book List*, it is a pleasant duty for me to record my appreciation of the efforts made towards its accurate and attractive production by our printers, Messrs W. S. Maney and Son. I have again enjoyed the friendly advice of scholars abroad. Professor B. Albrektson, Professor M. Bič, Professor H. Cazelles, Dr F. García Martínez, Dr K. Jeppesen, Professor G. L. Prato, Dr K. K. Sacon, and Professor A. S. van der Woude have either drawn my attention to books or supplied reviews or both. And this has been no less true of many colleagues within these islands who do much more for the Society *Book List* than (simply?) respond to requests to review. While thanking all who have reviewed, I would like to record my appreciation of the further help of Professor P. R. Ackroyd, Dr R. P. Carroll, Dr R. J. Coggins, Professor K. A. Kitchen, Professor M. A. Knibb, Mr A. R. Millard, Dr S. C. Reif, Dr W. G. E. Watson, and Professor R. N. Whybray.

The following abbreviations and symbols are employed as in earlier issues:

B.L. = *Book List*
Eleven Years = *Eleven Years of Bible Bibliography (1957)*
Decade = *A Decade of Bible Bibliography* (1967)
Bible Bibliog. = *Bible Bibliography 1967–1973: Old Testament* (1974)

On Behalf of the Society I have pleasure in thanking the British Academy for making a grant towards the publication costs of this issue of the *Book List*.

NEW COLLEGE EDINBURGH — A. GRAEME AULD

1. GENERAL

VON ALLMEN, J.-J. (ed.): *Biblický slovník* (Czech translation of the *Vocabulaire biblique*, published by Delachaux et Niestlé, Switzerland 1954, 3rd edition 1964, under the leadership of Jan Mířejovský). 1987. Pp. 360 (Kalich, Praha. Price Kčs 45.00)

The translation of this *Vocabulaire*, prepared by J.-J. von Allmen and a group of his co-operators in the years 1945–53, was translated into the Czech language by a group of young theologians of the Evangelical church of Czech Brethren from 1975, as there is a living interest for the study of the Bible among the people and such a work was lacking. The book will be a great help for many, who are searching for the exact meaning of any important biblical term. The *Vocabulaire* offers at least 300 of the most important terms and names in the Bible. The delay in the translating is explainable by the necessity to control all the references with the Czech Bible and by the death of two translators.

M. BIČ

BERGERHOF, K., DIETRICH, M., and LORETZ, O. (eds.): *Ugarit-Forschungen: Internationales Jahrbuch für die Altertumskunde Syrien–Palästinas*. Vol. 18 (1986). 1987. Pp. v, 483. (Neukirchener, Neukirchen-Vluyn. ISBN 3 7887 1249 X. Butzon & Bercker, Kevelaer. ISBN 3 7666 0553 3. ISSN 0342 2356

Eleven of the articles in this volume, which begins with an obituary to P. C. Craigie, are directly relevant to the Old Testament. Loretz offers a colometric study of Ps. 19:2–7 and contests alleged affinities to Ugaritic texts. He and Dietrich also reject attempts to explain *bṣqlnw* in 2 Kings 4:42 with the help of Ugaritic *bṣql*, but accept the identification of Ugaritic *ʿrgz* with Hebrew *ʾgwz*, 'nut, nut tree'. In addition, they argue that *ʿl* can mean 'from' in Ugaritic as well as in Hebrew. C. H. Gordon finds 'Ḥaby, possessor of horns and tail', not only in Ugaritic, but also at Ebla and in Isa. 26:20 and Hab. 3:4. M. I. Gruber argues that the Hebrew *qᵉdēšâ* 'was a prostitute with no cultic function', whereas the Accadian *qadištu* had a cultic function but was not a prostitute. M. C. A. Korpel and J. C. de Moor discuss 'The fundamentals of Ugaritic and Hebrew poetry'. I. Kottsieper maintains that *yēʿāṣēb* and *yissākēn* in Eccles. 10:9 mean 'will cut himself'. T. Podella discusses a rite of mourning in the Mediterranean world. S. Segert examines the Aramaic poems in Demotic script in Papyrus Amherst 63, including an Aramaic paraphrase of Ps. 20. W. von Soden writes on Hebrew *hitʿārēb* and *sanwērîm*. D. T. Tsumura considers 'Literary insertion, AxB pattern, in Hebrew and Ugaritic'. N. Wyatt finds traces of kingship myth in Isa. 14, Ezek. 28, Gen. 2–3, and the story of Moses. W. Zwickel argues that the lavers in Solomon's temple were connected with the cult of Asherah. The usual indexes are at the end of the volume.

J. A. EMERTON

BLANK, S. G. (ed.): *Hebrew Union College Annual*. Vol. LVII. 1986. Pp. 212 (English), 86 (Hebrew). (Hebrew Union College–Jewish Institute of Religion, Cincinnati. Price $20.00. ISSN 0360 9049)

There is an atmosphere of scholarly iconoclasm in this issue. S. A. Kaufman argues, against the palaeographers, that the inscribed Aramaic text found in 1979 in the ancient Sikanu in Syria, taken with other evidence, demonstrates the existence of a number of such traditions and necessitates greater caution in dating inscriptions and developments in the history of the alphabet. Epigraphic and philological considerations have led R. Ratner and

B. Zuckerman to question the reading 'a kid in milk' of KTU 1.23 and to express doubt about the supposed parallel with passages such as Exodus 23:19. Proposed Semitic etymologies for the name 'Essene' are rejected by J. Kampen who prefers to find the origin in the Greek title of the cultic functionaries of Artemis at Ephesus, first applied to the Jewish sect by Nicolaus of Damascus. M. Hengel's assumption of an extensive degree of penetration of Palestinian Jewish society and culture by Hellenism is challenged by L. H. Feldman while R. Kasher (in Hebrew) indicates the shortcomings of MS Neofiti 1 as an accurate copy, given the manner in which its transmitters and copyists have altered the Palestinian material on which it was originally based. There are also four articles on topics in medieval and modern Hebrew literature.

S. C. Reif

Bockmuehl, K.: *Books. God's Tools in the History of Salvation* (Regent College Monographs 1). 1986. Pp. 39. (Regent College, Vancouver and Helmers and Howard, Colorado Springs. ISBN 0 88865 414 6)

Examples of the influence of books in religious (Luther, Calvin, pietism and Methodism) as well as secular history (social reform and communism) show how they have led to renewal, education, mission and faith. This is a general encouragement and powerful plea to use literature to make the Bible and its message more widely known. This laudable aim accords with that of this *B.L.* but this monograph has no real direct relation, or reference, to Old Testament studies.

D. J. Wiseman

Botterweck, G. J., Ringgren, G., and Fabry, H.-J. (eds.): *Theologisches Wörterbuch zum Alten Testament.* Band v. Lfg. 9–10 (Spalte 1025–1208, pp. [605–31]. i–xiv), with cloth binder. 1986. (Kohlhammer, Stuttgart. Price: DM 92.80. ISBN 3 17 009465 3)

This double fascicle completes vol. v of the work and is provided with the usual indices etc. It contains the last part of the article on *ʿābar* (H. F. Fuhs and twenty complete articles. Of these, those on *ʿwd* (with *ʿēd*, *ʿēdūt* and *teʿūdāh*, H. Simian-Yofre and Ringgren), *ʿābar*, *ʿibrī* (D. N. Freedman and B. E. Willoughby), *ʿāwōn* (K. Koch), *ʿōlām* (H. D. Preuss) and *ʿēdāh* (Levy — no initials are given, and his name is omitted from the list of contributors! —, J. Milgrom, Ringgren and Fabry) are the longest, but there are also important discussions of *ʿēden* (B. Kedar-Kopfstein), *ʿāwel/ʿawlāh* (J. Schreiner) and *ʿad* (i.e., 'perpetuity', E. Haag). Since other ethical terms have been included, *ʿwt* (Pi. 'make crooked') should perhaps have been given a place here. Some other items, such as *ʿagālāh*, *ʿēder*, *ʿwp* and *ʿwl* (*ʿōlēl*), which have limited theological significance, might, on the other hand, have been omitted. But the quality of the contributions remains high.

R. N. Whybray

Botterwerck, G. J., Ringgren, H., and Fabry, H.-J., (eds.): *Theologisches Wörterbuch zum Alten Testament.* Band vi. Lfg. 1–2 (pp. xvii–xxxi, Spalte 1–224). 1987. Kohlhammer, Stuttgart. Price: DM 74.00. ISBN 3 17 009626 5)

This volume has been provided with a revised list of abbreviations which is intended eventually to be placed at the end of the completed volume but has for convenience been printed here at the beginning of this fascicle. The fascicle begins with *ʿzz* (S. Wagner) and ends with the first part of *ʿēmeq* (K.-M. Beyse), It contains thirty-one complete articles. The longest items are those on *ʿālāh* and cognates (H. G. Fuhs), *ʿelyōn* (H.-J. Zobel), *ʿōlāh* (D. Kellermann), *ʿayin* ('eye') (F. J. Stendebach), *ʿîr* (E. Otto) and *ʿam* (E. Lipiński). All words and roots of theological significance in this alphabetical range appear to have been treated. On the other hand, it may be questioned whether *ʿāleh*, 'leaf' (Beyse) has great theological significance, and whether *ʿāmad* (Ringgren) deserves ten columns. It is also not clear that *ʿāmīt* (misspelled *ʿāmīn* in the Table of Contents) is really a theological term. The article on *ʿayin*, 'eye' (*ʿayin*, 'spring' has a separate entry, by J. Schreiner) seems excessively long at eighteen columns. That on *ʿîr* (also eighteen columns) contains much sociological and political information about cities in the ancient Near East and Israel which, though hardly theological, is of considerable interest.

R. N. WHYBRAY

BRIEND, J., and COTHENET, E.: *Supplément au Dictionnaire de la Bible*. Vol. XI. Fasc. 61 (*Saint Esprit-Salut*). 1987. Cols. 257–512. (Letouzey & Ané, Paris. Price: Fr. 224. 00 (subscr). ISBN 2 7063 0161 9 (series); 2 7063 0116 3 (vol. XI))

This fascicle begins with the concluding part of the long article on the Holy Spirit (some 270 columns), an article of interest both to Old Testament and New Testament specialists and to readers concerned with the relationship between the theologies of the Old Testament and early Judaism and those of the New Testament (H. Cazelles, R. Kuntzmann, M. Gilbert, E. Cothenet, J. E. Ménard, J. Guillet, J. P. Lémonon, A. Vanhoye, J. Cantinat). This is followed by an article of some thirty columns on the Holy Sepulchre. The remainder of the fascicle comprises an article of fifty-five columns on Solomon, a brief note on Zelophehad (A. Lemaire), and the first part of an extensive article on salvation (salut). The article on Solomon comprises sections on Solomon in the Books of Kings (J. Briend), Chronicles (P. Abadie), the Psalms, the wisdom books, the LXX, Judaism and the New Testament (J. Brière). The section on Kings is a thorough treatment of the historical, literary and theological problems involved; that on the wisdom books brings out in an illuminating way the diversity of attitudes towards Solomon reflected in this literature. The incomplete fragment of the article on salvation deals with that concept as reflected in ancient Egypt (D. Meeks) and Mesopotamia (A. Bouchard).

R. N. WHYBRAY

CAZELLES, H.: *Autour de L'Exode (Études)* (Sources Bibliques). 1987. Pp. 438. (Gabalda, Paris. Price: Fr. 542.00. ISBN 2 85021 024 2)

It is a pleasurable convenience to have access in a single volume to twenty-six varied studies 'about Exodus' by a master of the art. A few were not previously published. The many have not only been collected from diverse publications, but also revised and their bibliographies updated for this volume (even one of them published as recently as 1987). They are presented in five groups: four preliminary data (Pentateuch as Torah, God of Abraham, Hebrews, and 2nd millenium B.C. populations in Palestine); seven studies related to decalogue, torah and law, covenant, and *mishpat*; three on toponymy; ten on texts, both on individual verses (3:14; 19:6; 32:4; 34:21) and on larger redactional and stylistic issues; and finally two appendices, on 'The theological figure of Moses in biblical tradition' and 'Aspirations to justice in the prebiblical world: the divine response according to the biblical revelation'. Many co-workers will not find such scholarship overpriced at close to £55.00; it should certainly find a place in libraries.

A. G. AULD

CENTRE: INFORMATIQUE ET BIBLE (ed.): *Bible and Computer: The Text—Proceedings of the First International Colloquium (Louvain-la-Neuve (Belgique) 2–3–4 Septembre 1985)*. 1986. Pp. 454. (Champion–Slatkine, Paris–Genève. Price: BFr. 2,200.00. ISBN 2 05 100769 1, ISSN 0773 3698)

Eighteen months after it was established, the *Association Internationale Bible et Informatique* held its first colloquium and the proceedings (some only as abstracts) have been made available in this volume. Like it or not, the computer is an important tool in academic research today and we are now in a position to assess what has been achieved and to determine what the future holds in store, though the present rate of progress is such that already some aspects of the book seem dated, for example, the description of the 'mouse' (p. 121).

Topics range from the introductory (e.g. Y. Chiaramella's 'Computer science and text') to the technical (e.g. proposals for printing Hebrew and Greek using machine code; the application of statistics to text-grammar). As there are nearly forty contributions, several of which relate to the versions and the New Testament, it is preferable not to list them all. E. Tov's concluding address, 'A new generation of Biblical Research', is a lucid and well-informed account of the problems we will inevitably have to face. These include access to existing databases, the actual use and application of databases, and how to convince scholars of the positive gains from using computers while remaining aware of their limitations. Also important are E. Talstra on encoding a database of biblical Hebrew texts and W. T. Claassen on semi-automatic morphological analysis.

For those of use who wish to know at which centres scholars are working on projects involving computers and the bible, and how far they have progressed, this is the book to consult. The English of some contributions is poor and the print is sometimes quite small. A bibliography for 1981–85 is provided (pp. 311–21).

W. G. E. WATSON

CHARLESWORTH, J. H. (ed.): *Journal for the Study of the Pseudepigrapha*. Issue 1. 1987. Pp. 127. (JSOT Press, Sheffield. Price: £10.50 ($19.50) for individuals; £30.00 ($50.00) for institutions. ISSN 0951 8207)

The Journal for the Study of the Pseudepigraphia and Related Literature has been launched to provide a forum for the work of scholars in this rapidly growing field, and to enable the Pseudepigrapha to stand in their own right, rather than as mere adjuncts to the Christian Bible. Incredibly, as the back cover observes, the discipline has no journal of its own. The new arrival is therefore a welcome addition to the Sheffield family of journals, and we wish it every success. It will appear three times a year, in English.

Articles will cover the whole field of early Judaism and early Christianity, including the Apocrypha, Josephus, Qumran, Philo, and major developments in research on both individual documents and themes. The first issue comprises: I. M. Gafni, 'Pre-Histories of Jerusalem in Hellenistic, Jewish and Christian Literature'; J. C. VanderKam, 'Hanukkah: Its Timing and Significance According to 1&2 Maccabees'; F. I. Andersen, 'Pseudepigraphical Studies in Bulgaria'; B. Zickerman, 'The Date of 11Q Targum Job: A Paleographic Consideration of its Vorlage'; R. J. H. Shutt, 'Josephus in Latin: A Retroversion into Greek and an English Translation'; R. K. Fenn, 'Sociology and Social History: A Preface to a Sociology of the New Testament'. The Book Review Editor is Professor J. C. VanderKam, Box 8103, North Carolina State University, Raleigh, NC 27695–8103, USA, who would be pleased to hear from scholars who wish to review books. Prospective articles should be addressed to Professor J. H. Charlesworth, Princeton Theological Seminary, CN 821, Princeton, NJ 08542, USA.

M. BARKER

CONRAD, E. W., and NEWING, E. G.: *Perspectives on Languages and Text: Essays and Poems in Honour of Francis I. Andersen's sixtieth birthday, July 28, 1985*. 1987. Pp. xxviii, 443. (Eisenbrauns, Winona Lake, Indiana. Price: $32.50. ISBN 0 931464 26 9)

For a versatile scholar, a diverse collection! Apart from appreciations of the man, poems by him and others, curriculum vitae with list of publications, there are thirty-one essays grouped in five sections: Semitics, Statistics and Linguistics, Hebrew Bible, Greek Bible, Religion. There is surely something for everyone. I began with 'The Mesopotamian Counterparts of the Biblical Nephilim' (A. Draffkorn Kilmer), staggered through 'A Theory of Language Organisation Based on Hjelmslev's Function Oriented Theory of Language' (B. Kerr), relaxed with 'The Australian Aborigines and the Old Testament' (H. C. Spykerboer). Soon I was led into the New Testament with '"Walking" as a Metaphor of the Christian Life: the Origins of a Significant Pauline Usage' (R. Banks), and then on to 'The Buddha in the West, 1800–1860' (P. C. Almond). Then, turning back, I was much instructed by a piece by M. O'Connor on the single, double and treble pseudo-sorites in Hebrew verse. And so it went on — an impressive volume and a worthy tribute.

J. H. EATON

DEURLOO, K. A., HEMELSOET, B. P. M., HOOGEWOUD, F. J., SMELIK, K. A. D., and ZUURMOND, R (eds.): *Amsterdamse cahiers voor exegese en Bijbelse theologie*, 7. 1986. Pp. 147. (Kok, Kampen. Price: Fl. 24.90. ISBN 90 242 0862 9)

Ten of the twelve essays relate to the Old Testament and its background. K. A. Deurloo and R. Zuurmond, in a joint article, argue that the pointing *b*[e] of *b*[e]*reshit* in Genesis 1:1 is a deliberate alteration of an original *ba* in order to exclude the possibility that God created the world by means of (instrumental *ba*) *reshit*. 'Breath of God' is the preferred translation of *ruah* [e]*lohim*. K. A. Deurloo expounds the 'image of God' in the light of the theme of *tol*[e]*dot* in Genesis, understood as the inauguration of Israel. T. Meijknecht compares Genesis 2–4 with Ezekiel 28, 31 and 36, concluding that the narrative was written in Babylon during the exile. J. Dubbink considers the apparent doublet of the entry to the ark (Genesis 7:7–9 and 13–16a) and sees it as functioning in the whole story to stress God's initiative and graciousness. Noah is seen as a second Adam. J. Wagenaar considers the use of motifs drawn from mythology in Exodus 15, Isaiah 51 and Habakkuk 3. Whether it helps to label these uses as 'prophetic mythology' is, however, to be doubted. J. van Dorp treats the revolution against Athaliah in 2 Kings 11. Although the material has much in common with the Jehu cycle, it reflects a Judean view of kingship. B. Hemelsoet discusses the function of 'The Lord our Righteousness' in Jeremiah 23:5–6 and 33:14–16 and in the LXX. A colometric printing out of Psalm 23 enables R. Oost to contrast two 'metaphoric' sections (vv. 1–3, 4) with two 'situational' sections (vv. 5, 6) while a similar setting out of the Yavne Yam Ostracon by K. A. D. Smelik leads to the conclusion that the Ostracon was written for the wronged worker by a professional scribe with considerable literary and advocational skill. M. Rozelaar proposes that *raqqah* means 'throat'. This useful volume is marred by numerous mistakes in the Hebrew type in the first four essays.

J. W. ROGERSON

Eliade, M. (Editor in Chief): *The Encyclopedia of Religion,* Vol. 14 (Spells — Towers). 1987. Pp. vi, 584. (Macmillan, New York, Collier Macmillan, London. Price: $850.00 (set). ISBN 0 02 909850 5, 0 02 909480 1 (set))

Unhappily the distinguished chief editor (d. 1986) was unable to witness the publication of his monument to contemporary study of religion. Of obvious concern to *B.L.* readers in the volume made available for review are the articles on Spinoza (B. Winston), Synagogue (M. A. Cohen on 'History and Tradition'; J. Gutman on 'Architectural Aspects'), Talmud (R. Goldenberg), Ten Commandments (W. Harrelson), and Torah (E. E. Urbach). Biblical material is handled within R. M. Green's study of Theodicy. And the relevance of entries on Spirit Possession, Structuralism, Study of Religion, Syncretism, and Theology needs no exposition. That the sub-article on Mediterranean Temples can move from Egypt to the Aegean with a mention of only Tell Taayanat within the Levant may serve to keep us humble.

A. G. Auld

Evans, C. A., and Stinespring, W. F. (eds.): *Early Jewish and Christian Exegesis: Studies in Memory of William Hugh Brownlee.* (Scholars Press Homage Series). 1987, Pp. xxii, 281. Scholars Press, Atlanta, Georgia. Price: $44.95 (members price: $29.95). ISBN 1 55540 108 2)

This volume honours William Brownlee whose unexpected death in 1983 did not provide the time to produce a Festschrift. The sixteen essays are prefaced by a Foreword from J. M. Robinson, and In Memoriam from W. F. Stinespring, both of which give portraits of William Brownlee, the man and the scholar, and record his contribution to Qumran Studies. The essays are in three sections: The Function of Scripture in the Old Testament, comprising R. P. Knierim, 'Customs, Judges and Legislators in Ancient Israel'; C. Mabee, 'Judicial Instrumentality in the Ahimelech Story'; E. A. Martens, 'Narrative Parallelism and Message in Jeremiah 34–38'; L. L. Grabbe, '"The End of the Desolation of Jerusalem": From Jeremiah's 70 Years to Daniel's 70 Weeks of Years'; K. H. Richards, 'The Old Testament and Its Inheritors'. The second section, 'The Function of Scripture in Inter-Testamental Literature', comprises G. J. Brooke, 'The Biblical Texts in the Qumran Commentaries: Scribal Errors or Exegetical Variants?', J. C. Trever, 'The Qumran Teacher — Another Candidate?' W. S. LaSor, 'Interpretation and Infallibility: Lessons from the Dead Sea Scrolls'; J. H. Charlesworth, 'The Pseudepigrapha as Biblical Exegesis'. The third section, 'The Function of Scripture in the New Testament', comprises W. Klassen, 'Jesus and the Messianic War'; J. A. Sanders, 'A New Testament Hermeneutic Fabric: Psalm 118 in the Entrance Narrative'; J. T. Sanders, 'The Prophetic Use of Scriptures in Luke–Acts'; J. R. Butts, 'The Voyage of Discipleship: Narrative, Chreia and Call Story'; C. A. Evans, 'Obduracy and the Lord's Servant: Some Observations on the Use of the Old Testament in the Fourth Gospel'; E. E. Ellis, 'Traditions in the Pastoral Epistles'.

M. Barker

Friedman, R. E., Williamson, H. G. M. (eds.): *The Future of Biblical Studies: The Hebrew Scriptures* (Semeia Studies). 1987. Pp. ix, 207. (Scholars Press, Atlanta, Georgia. Price: $20.95 (members price: $13.95); ISBN 1 555 40097 3. Paperback price: $13.95 (members price: $9.95); ISBN 1 555 40098 1)

The title of this symposium is misleading: the eight essays are more a critique of past scholarship and a statement of the present situation than a programme for the future. The contents are as follows: R. A. Oden surveys the place of biblical studies within the history of European thought, while J. D. Levenson, with minor forays into the New Testament, shows how an implicit anti-Semitism has shaped much Old Testament scholarship, as had a dubious application of Christian dogmatic presuppositions. A. Cooper writes on the need for a more mature literary critical approach to the problem of hermeneutics, and R. E. Friedman pleads for an intelligent application or source critical principles to biblical exegesis. B. Halpern considers the problems faced by the historian of ancient Palestine in using the Bible as source-material and the positions of biblical scholarshiup as the key to interpretation. J. A. Hackett writes on the impact and implications of feminist approaches to biblical studies, T. Ishida discusses the status of Adonijah's claim to the throne, and H. G. M. Williamson concludes with some observations on the historical problems of the books of Ezra and Nehemiah. There are some stimulating discussions in this book, which are particularly useful for the literary, critical, and historical aspects of biblical studies, and some refreshing elements of humour. Its achievement may be described as a timely stocktaking and a survey of past pitfalls rather than a concerted programme for the future, which is addressed only briefly from time to time in the body of the book, and in Williamson's final *envoi*.

N. WYATT

FUKS, L. and FUKS-MANSFELD, R. G.: *Hebrew Typography in the Northern Netherlands 1585–1815: Historical Evaluation and Descriptive Bibliography*. Part 2. 1987. Pp. viii, 233–505 and 16 plates. (Brill, Leiden. Price: Fl. 120.00. ISBN 90 04 08154 2)

The first part of this study was published in 1984 and welcomed in the *Book List* as 'an important new work of reference with excellent indexes' (*B.L.* 1986, p. 120). In the second part the authors continue to provide both background information about the personal and commercial vicissitudes of the printers as well as technical bibliography about their publications, thus completing both a readable history and a reliable catalogue. Another ten Amsterdam printers are treated, including Uri Phoebus b. Aaron Witmund Halevi, Joseph and Immanuel Athias and David de Castro Tartas, and the total number of entries, in which Hebrew Bibles obviously appear in considerable number, is taken up to 639 and the beginning of the eighteenth century. The indexes cover Hebrew and English names and titles, subjects, financiers, compositors, correctors, approbations and laudatory poems and the plates reproduce parts of the printed texts.

S. C. REIF

GALBIATI, E. (ed.): *Dizionario Enciclopedico della Bibbia e del mondo biblico*. 1986. Pp. xi, 851. (Massimo, Milano. Price: Lire 56,000 ISBN 88 7030 7190 0)

L. H. Grollenberg's *Encyclopaedia of the Bible* and W. Corswant's *Dictionnaire d'archéologie biblique* were combined and then completely revised, expanded and updated to form the present volume. Listed alphabetically are not only items that occur in the bible (Old Testament and New Testament) such as 'Leviathan', 'shekel' and the like but also material which belongs more to introductory textbooks 'schools', 'translations of the bible', etc.) and to theology ('conscience', 'resurrection'). There are a number of illustrations, including black and white photographs, but some of the maps are minute. Appendices list peoples mentioned in the bible, the books of the bible, weights and measures, etc., but there is no bibliography. Note that pp. 826 and 827 should be interchanged. In spite of its evident bias towards the New Testament this is an acceptable reference book for the general reader.

W. G. E. Watson

Henry, A.: *Biblia Pauperum: A Facsimile and Edition.* 1987. Pp. x, 178. (Scolar Press, Gower House, Aldershot, Hampshire. Price: £42.00. ISBN 0 85967 542 4)

Dr Henry believes her volume to include the only uncoloured facsimile of a forty-page blockbook Biblia Pauperum in print; it is made up mostly from a printed copy in Dresden, dating to *c.* 1460. Her edition includes a transcription, English translation, commentary, and notes, with the illustrations considered as an integral part of the overall meaning, stylistically and formally as well as iconographically. Dr Henry's impressive blend of scholarship and sensitivity to the subtleties of both text and pictorial design guides the reader through the complexities of medieval thought. She is at pains to dispel any idea of it being a book for the 'simple poor', as its title might suggest. It is an illustrated book of Typology, the biblical system encompassing Old and New Testaments that sees 'all time and history as part of God's patterned plan', which was central to the thinking of the Church Fathers and continued undiminished into the medieval period. Dr Henry likens the book both to an icon and to musical chords, and she delights in peeling back the layers for the reader. Indeed, she not only suggests that its original purpose may have been as an aid to Lenten meditation but recommends it to the modern reader for a similar purpose.

S. J. Auld

Hoglund, K. G., Huwiler, E. G., Glass, J. T. and Lee, R. W. (eds.): *The Listening Heart: Essays in Wisdom and Psalms in honour of Roland E. Murphy* (JSOT Supplement Series 58). 1987. Pp. xiii, 351. (Sheffield Academic Press. Price: £22.50 ($32.50). ISBN 1 85075 085 8)

Former and current students of Roland Murphy here honour him on his retirement from the Divinity School of Duke University. The best-known of the contributors, J. Crenshaw, provides a short account of Murphy's work in the wisdom field, centring on appraisal of the concept of 'order'; he helpfully differentiates his own position in appended notes. Fifteen essays follow, some six relating to the Psalms, the rest chiefly to wisdom literature. The large proportion contributed by current doctoral candidates conveys a good impression of a younger generation of research and will be useful to all working in these areas. T. Cartledge writes interestingly on the sudden transition to praise in the laments, B. Roberts Gaventa compares the Wisdom of Solomon and St Paul, J. Glass seeks out the theme of Ps. 19, B. Geller Nathanson studies women in Jewish and Roman antiquity, and F. Wilson constructively criticizes the theory of a Yahwistic redaction of Proverbs. The general quality of thought and expression is indeed a tribute to the honoured teacher.

J. H. Eaton

Jeppesen, K., and Lemche, N. P. (eds.): *Scandinavian Journal of the Old Testament.* Vols 1 and 2. 1987. Pp. ii, 149 and 157. (Aarhus University Press. ISBN 87 7288 082 1 and 87 7288 084 8; ISSN 0901 8328)

The prospect of this new journal was reported in the editorial of *B.L.* 1986. It is a pleasant task now to report on the two numbers for 1987. In their brief introduction, the editors eschew nostalgia for abandoned Nordic positions, and feel unable to describe a contemporary common Scandinavian point of view. Their main purpose is to offer a platform for Nordic colleagues to address international audiences; but they will accept contributions from abroad, especially in reaction to articles in *SJOT*. Detailed instructions for contributors are provided in No. 1, pp. 129–46. A list of the contents of these first numbers will help readers expect the range of fare to be offered: J. Strange, 'The Transition from the Bronze Age to the Iron Age in the Eastern Mediterranean and the Emergence of the Israelite State'; H.-A. Mink, 'The Use of Scripture in the Temple Scroll and the Status of the Scroll as Law'; K. A. Tångberg. 'Die Bewertung des ungeborenen Lebens im alten Israel und im alten Orient'; H. J. Lehmann, 'The Syriac Translation of the Old Testament — as Evidenced around the Middle of the Fourth Century (in Eusebius of Emesa)'; E. K. Holt, '*dʿtʾlhym* und *ḥsd* im Buche Hosea'; H. J. L. Jensen, 'Die Frauen der Patriarchen und der Raub der Sabinerinnen. Eine Bemerkung zur Entstehung der Völker und der Struktur der Identität'; K. J. Cathcart and K. Jeppessen, 'More Suggestions on Mic 6,14'; F. H. Cryer, 'The 360-Day Calendar Year and Early Judaic Sectarianism'; K. Hognesius, 'A Note on 1 Chr. 23'; F. H. Cryer, 'To the One of Fictive Music: OT Chronology and History'; H. J. L. Jensen, 'Über den Ursprung der Kultur und der Völker. Eine transformationskritische Analyse von Komplementarität und Verlauf in der jahwistischen Urgeschichte'; A. Laato, 'Hezekiah and the Assyrian Crisis in 701 B.C.'; S. Holm-Nielsen, 'Die Verteidigung für die Gerechtigkeit Gottes'; H. M. Barstad, 'On the So-called Babylonian Literary Influence on Second Isaiah'; K. A. Tångberg, 'Eblaite. An Introduction to the State of Research on the Cuneiform Tablets'; H. Gottlieb, 'Das kultische Leiden des Königs. Zu den Klageliedern 3,1'; and N. P. Lemche, 'Rachel and Lea. Or: On the Survival of Outdated Paradigms in the Study of the Origin or Israel, I'. Brief summaries of the articles conclude each number. We wish this attractive new project every success.

A. G. AULD

JERVELL, J., and KAPELRUD, A. S. (eds.): *Studia Theologica*: Scandinavian Journal of Theology. Vol. 40. no. 2. 1986. Pp. 81–156. Vol. 41, no. 1. 1987. Pp. 1–82 (Norwegian University Press (Universitetsforlaget), Oslo. Sub. price: N.Kr. 180.00 ($30.00). ISSN 0039 338 X)

The first issue of Volume 40 was reviewed in *B.L.* 1987, p. 13. The present issue contains one Old Testament article: Magne Sæbø, 'Sigmund Mowinckel and His Relation to the Literary Critical School', originally delivered for the centenary of Mowinckel's birth, at the S.B.L. meeting in Strasbourg in August 1984. Careful consideration is given to Mowinckel's relationship to literary criticism, treating his work in two periods, divided at 1944/45, showing his relationship to traditio-historical method and his continuing concern, alongside his primary work on the cult, with the problems of a historical study of the Old Testament. It is a useful study, though some of the renderings of Mowinckel could be turned into more acceptable English. Two articles are on New Testament topics: one, on Johannine questions, is the first Mowinckel lecture in 1986 by H. Koester; the other, on Paul, by T. Callan. The remaining article is on third world theologies.

The first issue of Volume 41 contains three articles, none on Old Testament topics. E. Lövestam writes on 'Paul's address at Miletus' (Acts 20: 18–35). pp. 1–10; H. Sahlin on 'Adam-Christologie im Neuen Testament', pp. 11–32, touching on some Old Testament questions; B. D. Larsen, 'Le ministère dans l'église. À propos d'un document oecuménique', pp. 33–82.

P. R. ACKROYD

Kirisutokyo Gaku (Christian Studies). New Series, 27 and 28. 1985, 1986. Pp. 160, 120. (Japanese.) (St Paul's (Rikkyo) University, Tokyo. ISSN 0387 6810)

In number 27 I. Koshiishi offers a new 'Historical Consideration of the Formation of the Landnahme'. In number 28 P. B. Kobayashi argues that the fifth vision in Amos (9:1–4) is closely associated with the doxology which follows and is the work of a redactor rather than of Amos himself. This number also contains a critical aricle by Y. Udo on Noth's *Überlieferungsgeschichte des Pentateuch*, recently translated into Japanese.

R. N. WHYBRAY

KOHLENBERGER, J. R. III: *Words about the Word: A guide to choosing and using your Bible* (Regency Reference Library). 1987. Pp. 218. (Zondervan, Grand Rapids, Michigan. Price: $9.95. ISBN 0 310 39361 2)

This is a remarkably comprehensive survey of the many modern English translations of the Bible and of the basic aids to Bible study which are available. The first two chapters deal with Canon and text respectively. The author then discusses the characteristics which make a translation good and the merits of different kinds of translation, drawing attention particularly to the difference between formal and dynamic equivalence. There follows a survey and appraisal of many English versions, with guidance on choosing those which are most useful for different age groups and readers from different religious backgrounds. Study Bibles are next listed, described, and evaluated in considerable detail. Guidance is also given on differing formats and bindings and on acquiring a core library of reference books. The entire presentation is admirably clear and is enriched by many useful charts. Two appendices summarize much of the guidance given in the book and provide lists of Bible distributors, mainly in North America. In discussing the qualities of a good translation the author rightly emphasizes accuracy; but when (p. 113) he says 'the only way you can determine the accuracy of a version to your own satisfaction is to read that version in comparison with others', he forgets the importance of the original text.

G. W. ANDERSON

LANG, B. (ed.): *Internationale Zeitschriftenschau für Bibelwissenschaft und Grenzgebiete,* Band XXXIII 1985/86. 1987. Pp. xv, 528. (Patmos, Düsseldorf. Price: DM 158.00. ISSN 0074 9745)

This volume of the annual 'review of biblical studies' is about one-eighth larger than its predecessor, and is priced at DM. 10.00 less — a double enhancement of an already valuable asset. In its warm reviews of *B.L.* 1985 and 1986, it queries the seeming 'British peculiarity' of abbreviating authors' first names, notes the occasional personal bias betrayed by reviewers, and congratulates the outgoing editor.

A. G. AULD

LEIBOWITZ, J. O. (ed.): *Proceedings of the Second International Symposium on Medicine in Bible and Talmud* (Jerusalem, December 18–20, 1984. *Koroth*, vol. 9, no. 1–2). 1985. Pp. 264. (The Israel Institute of Medical History, Jerusalem.)

This special issue of *Koroth*, a journal devoted to the history of medicine and science, consists of four main lectures and twenty-seven papers, some very brief, and is mainly concerned with medicine in the Talmud. Of the contributions directly related to the Bible, perhaps the most stimulating are

L. Hogan's discussion of the LXX reading at Gen 20: 4b, though the differences between the Hebrew and Greek of Sirach 38: 15 are more complicated than he seems to realize, and the paper by M. Kichelmacher and I. Magli, providing an anthropological interpretation of ritual impurity in the Bible. Some of the problems connected with *ṣarā'th* are considered in the context of the illnesses of Naaman (D. A. Bennahum), Miriam (E. Davis) and Hezekiah (F. Rosner). I. Papayannopoulos, with others, writes on Baldness in the Old Testament and on Tobit's blindness. Some considerations worthy of attention by Old Testament students are to be found in the papers on Medical *topoi* in the Bible (G. Roth). Toxicology and the Bible (R. Schoental), Alcohol and drunkenness (G. Weindling) and Anthropological aspects of the child in Luke's gospel (J. N. Neumann), but those on Matriarchal fertility and adoption (S. H. Blondheim) and Anointing with oil (A. Ohry) do not say a great deal. It is clear from this collection that the Old Testament is a much less fruitful field for the history of medicine than is the Talmud but the approach of the contributors here to the former is not without its interest for Biblical scholars.

J. R. PORTER

LÜDEMANN, G., SCHRÖDER, M.: *Die Religionsgeschichtliche Schule in Göttingen: Eine Dokumentation*. 1987. Pp. 148, incl. 80 illustrations. (Vandenhoeck & Ruprecht, Göttingen. Price: DM 19.80. ISBN 3 525 53582 1)

More than a handsome catalogue to an exhibition mounted in Göttingen in August 1987 during the forty-second meeting of the Studiorum Novi Testamenti Societas, this richly illustrated volume will make fascinating reading for all interested in the work of Bornemann, Bousset, Eichhorn, Gunkel, Hackmann, Heitmüller, Otto, Rahlfs, Troeltsch, Weiss, and Wrede. Faces, *curricula vitae*, examination reports, title pages, and correspondence are all sampled of this most influential group of scholars whose *Habilitationsschriften* were presented in Göttingen around the year 1890. Their study together and their emerging contribution are sketched in a series of essays.

A. G. AULD

MARKS, J. H., and GOOD, R. M. (eds.): *Love and Death in the Ancient Near East: Essays in Honor of Marvin H. Pope*. 1987. Pp. 258. (Four Quarters, Guildford, Connecticut. Price: $27.50 plus $5.00 postage and handling. ISBN 0 931500 06 0)

Of the thirty-five contributions to this Festschift, twenty-two deal wholly or partly with Old Testament matters, the remainder covering the whole range of Near Eastern studies. M. J. Dahood elucidates some biblical problems with the help of Eblaite material, M. Goshen-Gottstein writes on Abraham, and D. R. Hillers on the imagery of dust. S. A. Kaufman demonstrates structural similarities between the decalogue and Near Eastern law-codes, R. E. Murphy writes on the Song of Songs, J. van Seters on the elements the court history of David shares with other ancient literatures, and D. N. Freedman on the death of Ab(i)ner. T. Frymer-Kensky discusses plant-metaphors in the Bible and in Near Eastern texts, R. M. Good offers a convincing explanation of the problematic *ᶜānâ* in Exod. 32:18, and M. Greenberg and J. C. Greenfield comment respectively on Ezek. 16 and Deut. 32:24. R. L. Hicks offers further disussion on the Song of Songs, while S. Segert considers Prov. 2:21–22, and D. C. Snell contributes notes on both books. J. H. Tigay discusses Ps. 8:4–5, P. D. Hanson aspects of the symolism in Zechariah, and T. W. Mann aspects of the narrative in Num. 16:1–20:13. N. H. Richardson analyses Ps. 106, J. M. Sasson the mandrake narrative in

Gen. 30:14–24, R. R. Wilson Ezek. 28 and J. Goldin appropriately ends the biblical contributions with discussion of the death of Moses and its interpretation.

The editors evidently invited contributors to be guided by the themes in the title (cf. Song 8:6!), and at times the constraint this must have imposed shows. However, the opportunity this afforded to have two motifs studied from a number of different perspectives and in different but related fields has thrown up some interesting and at times original discussion, which is not often an achievement of Festschrifts. It is a pity that a delay in publication means that work completed by 1981 has been delayed for six years, with no opportunity offered (see Preface) for up-dating contributions, since in some instances they have been partly overtaken by events. The usefulness of the work as a whole for research is made unnecessarily onerous by the omission of any indices, and it is a pity that editors do not now insist on a standard means of reference to the Ugaritic texts (*KTU* being the most logical choice). These criticisms apart, the book is a contribution to the comparative study of ancient Near Eastern culture worthy of the pioneering work of its dedicatee.

N. WYATT

MAYES, A. D. H (ed.): *Proceedings of the Irish Biblical Association*. Vol. 10. 1986. Pp. 110. (Irish Biblical Association Publications, Dublin. Price: IR £7.00 ($7.00))

This volume honours Fr Wilfrid Harrington, a founder editor of the *Proceedings*. The eight contributions represent a wide spectrum of biblical scholarship: J. Neusner, 'What do we do when we study the Bible?'; A. D. H. Mayes, 'The Gibeonites as a Historical and Theological Problem in the Old Testament'; C. K. Barrett, 'St John: Social Historian'; J. H. Charlesworth, 'The Background and Foreground of Christian Origins'; B. C. McGing, 'The Governorship of Pontius Pilate: Messiahs and Sources'; D. Brearley, 'The Irish Influence in the Expositio Iohannis iuxta Hieronimum in Angers BM 275'; J. Rogerson, 'Anthropology in the Old Testament'; K. J. Cathcart, 'Legal Terminology in Habakkuk'. In an excellent collection of pieces my favourite is Jacob Neusner's contribution which showed him at his acerbic best, warning biblical scholars that they were concerned with everything about the Bible except religion, and questioning the value of the results. 'What we have is the net result of a long period of academic self absorption, people meeting only with one another (then not very often) to discuss their own navels. And that, I submit accurately portrays the present state of biblical studies: what people study when they study the Bible' (p. 3). This is certainly not true of the scholar to whom the volume is dedicated!

M. BARKER

MOMIGLIANO, A.: *Pagine ebraiche*, a cura di Silvia Berti (Saggi 703). 1987. Pp. xxxi, 254. (Giulio Einaudi, Milan. Price: Lire 26,000 ISBN 88 06 59927 5)

Arnaldo Momigliano is best known as for his work on Greco-Roman history and on historiography. However, as S. Berti justly remarks in her interesting introduction, the study of Jewish history and culture was an essential element in his work. She has earned the gratitude of all those interested in this aspect of his writings by collecting together in this volume twenty-three items otherwise accessible only with difficulty, scattered in the volumes of his wonderfully rich *Contributi alla storia degli studi classici e del mondo antico* and elsewhere. Several of them have been translated into

Italian from English or German: an English edition of the whole collection would be desirable. The essays range in date from 1931 to 1968, and in subject-matter from ancient history to modern scholarship. Of particular interest to readers of this *Book List* are those on the relationship of biblical to classical studies, on Jews and Greeks, on Daniel and the Greek theory of the succession of empires, on 2 Maccabees, on apocalypse and exodus in Jewish tradition. Of less direct concern are those on 'prophecy and historiography' (thoughts on the Sibylline Oracles delivered on receiving an honoury degree at Marburg in 1986), on Max Weber's definition of Judaism as a Pariah-religion, and a number of studies on Josephus. A moving preface by Momigliano testifying to his Jewish background and upbringing was written in hospital in Chicago in July 1987; his death in London the following month is a great loss to the world of true scholarship and marks in some sense the end of an era.

N. R. M. DE LANGE

MÜLLER, G. (ed.): *Theologische Realenzyklopädie* (TRE). Band XVI (*Idealismus — Jesus Christus IV*). 1987. Pp. 795, including 8 Plates and 7 maps and plans. (De Gruyter, Berlin. Price: DM 360.00. ISBN 3 11 011159 4)

This volume contains several major articles on Old Testament subjects. In that on Israel R. Albertz discusses the name, the social forms and the political and religious meanings of Israel in the Old Testament period, while C. Thoma deals with 'Israel' in early Judaism, H. Hübner with the New Testament usage, and W. Kickel with the modern use of the term. H. Seebass on the Yahwist considers that 'source' to be the 'most unstable of the source-critical hypotheses of the Pentateuch', but proceeds to give a useful account of it. S. Herrmann's article on Jeremiah and the Book of Jeremiah gives a full account of the course of Jeremiah studies with a very full bibliography, while O. Kaiser's article on Isaiah and the Book of Isaiah is a magisterial contribution by a major commentator on that book. The article on Jerusalem is arranged historically (P. Welten on the history of archaeological excavation and on the Old Testament period, with three plans, J. K. Elliott on the New Testament, L. M. Barth on Judaism, J. Wilkinson on the Early Church, F. Heyer on the Middle Ages to the present day).

There are shorter articles on biblical personalities: Isaac (Albertz, M. Brocke — the latter mainly on the Aqedah), Jacob and the Blessing of Jacob (H.-J. Zobel, G. Larsson), Jehu (K.-H Bernhardt) and both Jeroboams (V. Fritz). Three articles on Jewish writers — Isaac Abravanel and Judah Halevi (H. G. von Mutius) and Isaac Luria (K. Hruby) — and four on Christian exegeses — Isidore of Seville (R. J. H. Collins), James of Edessa (H. J. W. Drijvers), Jacob of Sarug (W. Hage) and Jan van Ruysbroeck (P. Verdeyen) — provide information on the history of exegesis. There are also brief articles on Yahweh (mainly on the origin of the name, M. Rose), Jericho (Bernhardt) and the *Sefer Yezira* (R. Goetschel), and an extensive treatment of Iranian religions by G. Lanczkowski. The volume ends with the first part of what will be an immense article on Jesus Christ, to be continued in Band XVII, which does not, however, deal in detail with the Jewish background but refers the reader to an article on the Messiah to appear in a forthcoming volume.

R. N. WHYBRAY

MUÑOZ LEÓN, D. (ed.): *Salvación en la Palabra. Targum — Derash — Berith.* En memoria del profesor Alejandro Díez Macho. 1986. Pp. 848. (Ediciones Cristiandad, Madrid. Price: Ptas 6,225. ISBN 84 7057 390 X)

This is a worthy memorial to A. Díez Macho (1916–84), probably best known internationally for his discovery and edition of Targum Neofiti, but a scholar of extraordinary depth and range, and one of the main architects of the present strength of Iberian biblical studies, especially in his own speciality of targum. Besides the usual biographical notes and bibliography, the contributions (mainly in Spanish, but fourteen in English, seven in French and one each in Italian and German) are grouped in six sections as follows: (1) *Hebrew and Greek Bible.* Subjects covered include: the Sabbath (J. Alonso Díaz); Baruch 4:9–19 (L. Alonso Schökel); the Aleppo Manuscript (D. Barthélemy); the midrash on Exodus in Wis. Sol. (J. Busto Saiz); *Hokmah* in Isaiah (G. Cañellas); God's 'smile' in the Bible (G. R. Castellino); the transition from prophetic time to apocalyptic time (M. Delcor); motifs in four cosmic legends in Genesis (J. Guillén Torralba); the biblical manuscripts from Kaifeng (I. Lehman); 'What is a land flowing with milk and honey?' (E. Levine); the death of Moses in *Sifre Deut.* (T. Martínez Saiz); conceptions of insipiration in Philo (A. Piñero Sáenz), and articles on Hebrew textual traditions by A. Pedro Navarro, E. J. Revell and J. Trebolle Barrera. Section (2), *'The Biblical Environment'*, contains two articles of Ugaritic interest (J. L. Cunchillos Ilarri, G. del Olmo Lete) and one on Mari (J. García Recio).

Appropriately, Section (3), *Targum*, contains contributions of great distinction: 'D' Ex 22,4 à Is 6,13 par les targums' (H. Cazelles); the epithets of Noah (E. G. Clarke); a list of Grecisms and Latinisms in Tg. Neof. 1 (L. Díez Merino); methodology of Tg. Jonathan, esp. on Isai 1 (P. Doron); comparative targum study (M. H. Goshen-Gottstein); 'An ancient treaty ritual and its targumic echo' (J. C. Greenfield); the dispute of the trees in Tg. 2 of Esther 7:10 (P. Grelot); 'Targumic Toseftot from the Cairo Geniza' (M. L. Klein); implicit use of *'al tiqre* in the Qumran Job targum (R. le Déaut); relative use of *d-* and *dy* in Tg. Pal. (E. Martínez Borobio); 'On Englishing the Targums' (M. McNamara); the Peshitta of Ezekial in relation to MT, LXX and Tg. (M. J. Mulder); Targum and midrash on Gen 1:262–27, 2:7 and 3:7–21 (M. Pérez Fernández); Prophetism according to Tg. Jonathan and Tg. Pal (J. Ribera); Moses' death according to Tg. Dt 34:5 (A. Rodriguez Carmona); parallelistic structures in Tg. Neof.: Dt 32:1–43 (S. Segert), and an unedited fragment of the Samaritan Tg. (A. Tal).

Section (4), *Pseudepigrapha and Qumran*, contains reflexions on the virginal conception of Jesus à propos of a Coptic fragment on Enoch (G. Aranda Pérez); the Jewish dietary laws in Ep. Arist. 143–69 (N. Fernández Marcos); the 'new Jerusalem' and the future temple in the Qumran MSS (F. García Martínez). Section (5), *New Testament*, contains seven items, which go beyond our scope. Section (6), *Mediaeval Spanish Judaism*, presents eight essays which, besides their intrinsic scholarly merits and interest, illustrate how this late flowering of Jewish studies in Spain can be said to show an aspect of ecumenical reconciliation.

R. P. R. MURRAY

MURAOKA, T. (ed.): *Abr-Nahrain* xxv (1987), 1987. Pp. vii, 170, incl. figs.; 10 plates. (Brill, Leiden. Price: Fl. 65.00 ($32.50). ISBN 90 04 08427 4)

Abr-Nahrain reaches the milestone of its 25th volume with the 1987 issue: the journal is now well established. In this issue of the Melbourne-produced annual J. Bowman writes on 'Jonah and Jesus' (pp. 1–12), following up his earlier essay on 'Solomon and Jesus' (1985). His concern is with the Jonah tradition in the background to the New Testament and the emergence of this in synoptic Q. G. Bunnens in 'A Slave for Alalakh Looked for in Ugarit (RS 4.449)' (pp. 13–18) gives a philological and historical interpretation of a 15th-century B.C. Ras Shamra Akkadian text dealing with enslavement for debt. Similar provisions are found in Alalakh tablets. G. W. Clarke and P. J. Connor ('Inscriptions, Symbols and Graffiti near Joussef Pasha' (pp. 19–39)) discuss in detail and provide copies and photogaphs of a series of short inscriptions in Greek letters from near El-Qitar in Syria. The main ones are associated with tombs and date to the fifth/sixth centuies A.D. B. E. Colless in 'The *Letter to the Hebrews* and the *Song of the Pearl*' (pp. 40–55) gives a translation of the *Song of the Pearl* and interprets it as a Christian allegory drawing on *Hebrews*. It is not, according to the author, gnostic, as others have supposed. T. Harviainen discusses 'Pseudo-Pausal Forms of Passive Stems in Palestinian Punctuations and the Position of Stress in Hebrew' (pp. 56–67), concluding that the examples cited are not to be regarded as evidence of widespread penultimate stress in Hebrew. T. Muraoka and Z. Shavitsky present the first part (' to *y*) of a word-list, 'Abraham Ibn Ezra's Biblical Hebrew Lexicon. The Five Megilloth: I' (pp. 68–91). This reconstructs Ibn Ezra's mental dictionary on the basis of extant writings. The final article is a long and highly specialized one by S. Powels on 'Relations between Samaritan and Arabic Astronomical Calculations' (pp. 92–142). Reviews complete the volume.

J. F. HEALEY

MYERS, A. C. (revision ed.): *The Eerdmans Bible Dictionary*. Associate eds: J. W. Simpson Jr, P. A. Frank, T. P. Jenney, R. W. Vunderink. 1987. Pp. x, 1094. (Eerdmans, Grand Rapids, Michigan. Price: $29.95. ISBN 0 8028 2402 1)

This is a translation of the *Bijbelse Encyclopedie*, first published in 1950 (*Eleven Years*, p. 299), edited by F. W. Grosheide assisted by W. H. Gispen (Old Testament; archaeology), F. J. Bruijel (botany; zoology); and A. van Deursen (geography; archaeology; daily life). The *Encyclopedie* reappeared in 1975 in two volumes, thoroughly revised by W. H. Gispen, B. J. Oosterhoff, H. N. Ridderbos, W. C. van Unnik and P. Visser. This edition contained additional articles on biblical theology, and some new entries were inserted from the 1959 edition co-edited by Grosheide) of *Christelijke Encyclopedie*. The one-volume 3rd edition incorporated only minor corrections. For the English edition, in one volume, a significant number of articles have been revised, and a number of new ones added. The object of this further revision has been partly to update the work (e.g. on matters archaeological) and partly to make what had originally been a specifically Evangelical enterprise representative of a broader spread of opinion and to do justice to 'the breadth of American biblical scholarship, including insights from critical analysis of literary, historical, and sociological issues'. The contributors include Jews and Roman Catholics as well as Protestants from various traditions, and the bibliographies attached to major articles are calculated to reflect a variety of viewpoints. The standpoint of the English version may be described as enlightened conservatism. Typical perhaps is the Daniel entry, where we read that the book is a composite work created 'by an author-compiler towards the extreme end of the Old Testament period', and consisting, in ch. 1–6, of 'midrash based on historical fact' and, in 7–12, of 'apocalyptic prophecy [which] makes known God's will in timeless terms that have value for every age'. Not unnaturally, some contributors are more open to critical approaches than others: thus the treatment of Gen. 1–2 s.v. 'Creation' leaves decisions to the reader, whereas the Abraham article, although noting the views of Van Seters and Thompson and listing their books in the bibliography, does not hesitate to lay out before us a biographical account of the patriarch's life. The entries for Isaac and Jacob have even fewer nuances. Apart from such eruptions of *partis pris*, the main weakness of the Dictionary is that even in this latest revision it still shows much more interest in history, geography and natural science than it does in literary matters. 'Midrash' gets fewer words than 'Jehudijah', 'Javan' or 'mildew'; and articles on David, Saul (who oddly does not rate a bibliography) and Samson pay little or no attention to the literary features of the stories. (Among New Testament topics, the entry on the Fourth Gospel is very dated; Paul is said, s.v. 'Celibacy', to 'condone' celibacy [but more accurately, s.v. 'Sex', to 'endorse' it]; despite the ecumenical spread of contributors the 'Mary' entry contains a schoolboy howler on the Immaculate Conception; and there is no entry about the Western Text.) Despite such defects this Dictionary is calculated to prove a valuable reference work; I hope it sells well enough to receive a further broadening revision.

B. P. Robinson

Neusner, J., Levine, B. A., and Frerichs, E. S. (eds.): *Judaic Perspectives on Ancient Israel.* 1987. Pp. xviii, 318. (Fortress, Philadelphia. Price: $34.95. ISBN 0 8006 0832 1)

No mere sketch of contents can do justice to the flair and enthusiasm that characterize this volume dedicated to H. L. Ginsberg. A Preface by Neusner and Introduction by Frerichs precede fourteen essays in five sections by mostly American Jewish scholars. Exegesis is represented by Levine on 'The Epilogue to the Holiness Code. A Priestly Statement on the Destiny of Israel', which includes a critique of A. Hurvitz on the relation of P and Ezekiel; by M. I. Gruber, whose brief but extensively annotated text on 'Women in the Cult According to the Priestly Code' draws attention to P's non-sexist language; by J. Milgrom, whose paper on 'The Structures of Numbers: Chapters 11-12 and 13–14 and Their Redaction' touches on ch. 16 also, and is too modestly styled 'Preliminary Gropings'; and by S. A. Kaufmann on 'Rhetoric, Redaction, and Message in Jeremiah': this analyses Jer. 3:1–4:2 as a chiastic structure centred on 3:12–13, and suggests that Jeremiah and Deutero–Isaiah were the true prophetic founders of Judaism. Religion and History are powerfully represented by an exciting account of 'The Development of Israelite Monotheism ', in which B. Halpern reviews a wide range of evidence under the title '"Brisker Pipes than Poetry"'; and by A. Rofé's extended treatment of 'The Battle of David and Goliath: Folklore, Theology, Eschatology': against J. Lust and E. Tov (see below p. 44) with whom he often makes common cause, Rofé argues that LXX represents a novel blend of harmonization and abridgment — however, the primary text (MT) is late Persian, reflecting messianic expectation, with the only-twice-named Goliath an originally anonymous figure of late biblical paradigmatic fiction.

Literature is well-served by S. A. Geller's '"Where is Wisdom?" A Literary Study of Job 28 in Its Settings'; by R. Alter's 'Structures of Intensification in Biblical Poetry' (said to be reprinted from *The Art of Biblical Narrative*, 1981, but in fact from *The Art of Biblical Poetry*, 1985, reviewed below on p. 69); and by R. E. Friedman on 'The Hiding of the Face: An Essay on the Literary Unity of Biblical Narrative'. Under Traditions of Scholarship , E. L. Greenstein offers 'A Reading of Esther', a book which belongs not to the chronological structures of the 'Old Testament' but to the carnival mock seriousness of Purim; while F. F. Greenspahn presents fine examples of the contribution of medieval scholars from the Arab milieu. Two shorter and one longer essay on Theology ensure that the debate will go on: L. H. Silberman considers 'The Question of Job's Generation. *She'elat Doro Shel "Iyob"*: Buber's Job' — a work written when the 'final solution' was 'but a cloud the size of a man's hand on the horizon of history'; H. Yavin asks how far 'Modern "Doxologies" in Biblical Research' prove that our scholarship, despite methodologies sanctioned by the arts and sciences, is still the quest for religious faith; and J. D. Levenson explains 'Why Jews Are Not Interested in Biblical Theology', quoting with approval M. Goshen-Gottstein whose rather different approach to the contribution of Jewish Biblical Theology concludes the volume for F. M. Cross reviewed on p. 110.

A. G. Auld

North, R. (ed.): *Elenchus Bibliographicus Biblicus* of *Biblica.* Vol. 65 (1984). 1987. Pp. 872. (Biblical Institute Press, Rome. Price: $85.00. ISSN 0392 7423)

An opening note on 'Some innovations' informs us how the *Elenchus*, while discussing an on-line computer service, is also moving to shorten the two-year delay caused by its mass and editing-procedures. We salute each improvement to this multi-faceted tool. Editors and librarians alike will sympathize with the comments on the alphabetization of surnames beginning with a prefix, with more readers prepared to look for Von Rad under V– than ready to give up on von Harnack under H–.

A. G. Auld

Proceedings of the Ninth World Congress of Jewish Studies, Jerusalem, August 4–12, 1985. Division A: *The Period of the Bible.* 1986. Pp. v, 246; iv, 144 (Hebrew). (World Union of Jewish Studies, distributed by Magnes Press, Jerusalem. Price: $20.00. ISSN 0333 9068)

This volume presents a photographic reproduction of those lectures delivered within Division A of the 1985 Congress whose texts were made available to David Assaf on behalf of the organizers. They are: R. Giveon, 'New Material Concerning Canaanite Gods in Egypt'; H. J. Katzenstein, 'Some Reflections Concerning El-Amarna 296'; M. Anbar, 'The Kings of the Bini-Yamina Tribes in the Mari Texts'; G. J. Wenham, 'Sanctuary Symbolism in the Garden of Eden Story'; F. Polak, 'Literary Study and "Higher Criticism" according to the Tale of David's Beginning'; S. Segert, 'Symmetric and Asymmetric Verses in Hebrew Biblical Poetry'; F. Landy, 'Gilead and the Fatal Word'; D. N. Freedman, 'Deliberate Deviation from an Established Pattern of Repetition in Hebrew Poetry as a Rhetorical Device'; A. Reichert, 'The Song of Moses (Dt. 32) and the Quest for Early Deuteronomic Psalmody'; D. L. Christensen, 'The Numeruswechsel in Deuteronomy 12'; B. O. Long, 'Framing Repetitions in Biblical Historiography'; C. T. Begg, '*berit* in Ezekiel'; A. H. J. Gunneweg, 'Habakkuk and the Problem of the Suffering Just'; J. Magonet, 'The Structure of Isaiah 6'; M. Sæbø, 'From Collection to Book — A New Approach to the History of Tradition and Redaction of the Book of Proverbs'; A. Cooper, 'Structure, Midrash and Meaning: The Case of Psalm 23'; J. Milgrom, 'The Priestly Impurity System'; W. Rehfeld, 'Deuteronomic Time'; J. Ribera, 'The Image of the Prophet in the Light of the Targum Jonathan and Jewish Literature in the Post-Biblical Period'; D. Muñoz Leon, 'Memra in the Targum to Isaiah'; M. Wilcox, 'The Aramaic Targum to Psalms'; D. R. G. Beattie, 'Ancient Elements in the Targum to Ruth'; E. L. Greenstein, 'The Role of Theory in Biblical Criticism'; W. O. McCready, 'The Dead Sea Scrolls Response to Change: Traditionalists or Reformers?'; L. H. Schiffman, 'Liturgical Texts from Qumran Cave IV'; E.-M. Laperrousaz, 'Quelques remarques archéologiques concernant la chronologie des occupations esséniennes de Qoumrân'; N. G. Cohen, 'Philo's Tefillin'; J. G. Gammie, 'The Hellenization of Jewish Wisdom in the Letter of Aristeas'; M. Mach, 'Are there Jewish Elements in the "Protoevangerlium Jacobi"?'; G. E. Howard, 'Shem-Tob's Hebrew Matthew'; L. H. Feldman, 'Josephus' Version of Samson'; L. Archer, 'The "Evil Woman" in Apocryphal and Pseudepigraphical Writings'.

And in Hebrew: I. Singer, 'The Settlement of the Sea Peoples in the Shores of Canaan'; S. Iwry, 'A New Look at the Biblical Flood Story and its

Meaning in the Context of Genesis 1–11'; Z. Ben-Barak, 'The Case of Naboth in the Light of Documents from Mesopotamia — A New Perspective': I. Gottlieb, 'Aspects of First-Person Narrative in the Bible'; Y. Zakovitch, 'Rationalization of Miracle Motifs in Biblical Narrative'; Z. Weisman, 'The Interrelationship between J and E in the Jacob Narratives — Re-examined'; Sh. Gelander, 'David and his God in the Eyes of the Royal Historiographer'; S. Zalewski, 'Rehoboam and his Advisers (1 Kings 12)'; Y. Elitzur, 'Melkizedek between Genesis 14 and Psalm 110'; B.-Z. Lurie, 'The Problem of Chronology in Judges 1'; Y. Amit, 'The End of the Book of Judges'; Sh. Vargon, 'The Social Background of Reproach Prophecies from the Latter Half of the 8th Century'; H. M. I. Gevaryahu, '"The End of Prophecy" — A Religious, Literary and Historical Problem'; N. Shupak, 'The "Sitz im Leben" of the Biblical and Egyptian Wisdom Literature'; M. Tsevat, 'Should we develop a Jewish Theology of the Bible?'; A. Shinan, 'Pseudo-Jonathan Targum — Its Nature and Date'; M. Perez, 'Transposition of Words (Hypallage) in the Commentary of R. Abraham ibn-Ezra'; A. Kloner, 'ABCDerian Inscriptions in Jewish Rock Cut Tombs'; H. N. Rosel, 'The Military Conquest of Palestine according to the Book of Joshua'; J.-G. Kahn, 'The Concept of "Physis" in the Philosophy of Philo'.

A. G. AULD

Revista Bíblica Brasileira, Ano 4/1–2, 1987. Pp. 1–48; 49–80. (Nova Jerusalém, Fortaleza, Ce. Brazil. Price: US$15.00 p.a.)

The first two numbers of this year's *RBB* pave the way for a systematic study of the Old Testament. This should be excellent for those encountering the Old Testament for the first time. A brief introduction (1–11) outlines the different Canons and makes a preferential option for that of the Hebrew Bible as an interpretative tool. The detailed study begins with an introduction to the Davidic narratives in Samuel and Kings, as containing the oldest historical writing in the Old Testament. This is followed by a presentation of the main themes, and an interesting analysis of two possible literary strands, identified as 'apologetic' and 'satirical' (49–71). The book review sections are greatly expanded, and there is an exegetical study of Dt. 8:1–6 by Sr Maria Celina Nogueira, who works directly from the Hebrew text (28–32). Both these last items will extend the appeal of *RBB* to a variety of readerships. The journal in fact continues to grow in scope and authority, so it is to be hoped that the editor's appeal for increased circulation (3–5) will meet with success. Articles are invited for publication, and the editor would also be glad to receive copies of other journals, on an exchange system with the *RBB*.

J. M. DINES

TAYLOR, J.: *As it was written: An Introduction to the Bible*. 1987. Pp. iv, 164. (Paulist Press, New York/Mahwah, New Jersey. Price: $7.95. ISBN 0 8091 2843 8)

Since Vatican II the Roman Church has been concerned to encourage systematic reading and study of the scriptures. Dr Taylor is currently teaching in a New Zealand Seminary, and has written this book at an extremely elementary level for lay Catholics who accept the Church's magisterium and are ready to begin their study of the Bible. Each chapter incorporates questions for further discussion and consideration. It is difficult to see, however, how the more extended bibliography can be used, when there are no indications of the academic level of the books listed.

R. J. HAMMER

THOMPSON, B. P.: *Scripture: Meaning and Method – Essays presented to Anthony Tyrrell Hanson.* 1987. Pp. xviii, 245. (Hull University Press, Hull. Price: £19.50. ISBN 0 85958 460 7)

A *Festschrift* is in many respects a dual-purpose volume, celebrating the work and many-sided interests of the scholar to whom it is dedicated and, at the same time, seeking to present something fresh for scholars to consider. This volume fulfils both aims remarkably well and honours the work of Professor A. T. Hanson who has frequently, and strongly, argued for the enduring influence of the Old Testament upon Christian tradition. The major part of the book is taken up with fourteen essays, divided betweeen meaning and method in the study of Holy Scripture. Several of them deal with connections between the Old and New Testaments. It is those dealing with 'method' which have the most direct bearing upon the Old Testament and Early Judaism.

L. L. Grabbe presents a sharp critique of Fundamentalist approaches to biblical interpretation with special reference to the Book of Daniel. I. Ellis compares the exegetical writings of F. D. Maurice with a number of recent attempts to develop a synchronic approach to biblical interpretation. He finds in Maurice a remarkable anticipation of several of their features. R. N. Whybray submits the whole attempt to develop an Old Testament theology to a very critical scrutiny in a revised version of his Presidential Address to the SOTS. Fr Barnabas Lindars examines the use of themes from the Joseph and Asenath story in the Christian Eucharist, and J. W. McKay traces a number of similarities between the Old Testament prophetic movement and present-day Charismatic movements in the Christian Church. A more detailed literary examination concludes the volume in the shape of an essay by J. L. North on the influence of Pindar on Philo of Alexandria. Altogether this makes an interesting volume in honour of a scholar who has maintained a deep interest in the field of Old Testament Research.

R. E. CLEMENTS

TÖKEI, F. (ed.): *Acta Orientalia Academiae Scientiarum Hungaricae*, XL Fasc. 1 (pp. 1–216); fasc. 2–3 (pp. 217–368). 1986. (Akadémiai Kiadó, Budapest. ISSN 0001 6446)

These fascicles contain nothing on the Old Testament.

J. A. EMERTON

VANSTIPHOUT, H. L. J., JONGELING, K., LEEMHUIS, F., and REININK, G. J. (eds.): *Scripta Signa Vocis: Studies about Scripts, Scriptures, Scribes and Languages in the Near East presented to J. H. Hospers.* 1986. Pp. 331. (Egbert Forsten, Groningen. Price: Fl. 65.00. ISBN 90 6980 008 X)

As a Festschrift presented to J. H. Hospers on his sixty-fifth birthday this volume reflects the latter's wide interests. Most of the articles are of interest to students of the Bible and the north-west semitic languages, such as those by C. J. Labuchagne (composition techniques in Deuteronomy), M. E. Vogelzang and W. J. van Bekkum (meaning and symbolism of clothing in Ancient Near Eastern texts), C. H. J. de Geus (lamps in ancient Israelite tombs), J. F. Sawyer (biblical semantics), A. Schoors (*ki* in Koheleth), B. Jongeling (*l* in 1 Sam. 16:7), A. S. van der Woude (bilingualism in Daniel), J. W. Wevers (the Greek version of Exodus), J. Hoftijzer (two problems in the third Lachish letter), K. Jongeling (*K* and variants in Punic), H. J. W. Drijvers (Peshitta of Solomon's Wisdom), C. Molenberg (the story of 'Habakkuk's dinner' in Syriac Literature), A. Klugkist (origin of the Mandaic script), F. Leemhuis (the Tell Fekherye inscription), K. Aartun (the origin and meaning of the name AQHT), J. van Dijk (ᶜAnat, Seth and the seed of Prēᶜ), E. Lipinski (Ugaritic and biblical scribes), H. L. J. Vanstiphout (cuneiform writing and literature), H. te Velde (scribes and literacy in the ancient Near East).

There are also a few articles of less direct interest to students of the Bible and the North-west Semitic languags on *al Tawḥīdī* (G. J. van Gelder), Akkadian and Sumerian (G. Haayer), a seventh-century Syriac homily (G. J. Reinink), the Yezīdīs of Northern Iraq (W. H. Ph. Römer), a recently discovered South-Arabian inscription (J. Ryckmans), two Akkadian auxiliary verbs (K. R. Veenhof), an eighteenth-century Hebrew ode (G. Vos), and the Cushitic article (A. Zaborski).

P. Wernberg-Møller

Vawter, B. (ed.): *Old Testament Abstracts*. Vol. 9, no. 3 (October 1986). McCreesh, T. . (ed.): *Old Testament Abstracts*. vol. 10, no. 1 (February 1987). Pp. 235–383; 1–98. (The Catholic Biblical Association, The Catholic University of America, Washington DC. Price per annum: £14.00; single issues: $5.00. ISSN 0364 8591)

Old Testament Abstracts is firmly established as one of the important bibliographical tools available to Old Testament scholars. That this has come about is due in very large measure to Bruce Vawter, who was not only involved in the initial planning for OTA, but also served as its first editor and himself undertook much of the work of abstracting and reviewing. All Old Testament scholars will have learnt with sadness of his death at the end of 1986. (The first issue of *OTA* for 1987 contains an obituary of him by J. Jensen.) Those who use this *List* will wish both to pay tribute to the work of Bruce Vawter, and to offer encouragement to the new General Editor, Thomas P. McCreesh.

M. A. Knibb

Whigham Price, A.: *The Ladies of Castlebrae: a story of nineteenth-century travel and research*. 1985. Pp. xiv, 242. (Alan Sutton, Gloucester. Price: £10.95. ISBN 0 86299 228 1)

A fascinating account of the unglamorous twins, Maggie and Agnes Smith, born in Ayrshire in 1843, raised by their wealthy solicitor father and rendered independent by his death in 1866, who travelled two years later via Constantinople and Cairo to the Nile Cataract and Jerusalem. Their formal training in Greek began ten years later. After each in turn had been married for a very few years in their forties, the widowed Mrs Gibson and Mrs Lewis settled to a life of more than thirty years of scholarship in Cambridge, where they entertained the famous, provided the land for Westminster College's move from London, and focused their own research on Syriac, Arabic, and Greek MSS from St Catherine's in Sinai to whose library they made two successful expeditions. Honoured by seven doctorates in all, their example should encourage all 'mature students'!

A. G. Auld

Wigoder, G. (ed.): *Illustrated Dictionary and Concordance of the Bible*. 1987. Pp. 1,070. (Macmillan, New York and London. Price: £90.00. ISBN 0 02 916380 3)

A notable team of editors, Sh. M. Paul (Old Testament), B. T. Viviano (New Testament), and E. Stern (Biblical Archaeology), presided over by Professor Wigoder, has led an able team of Israeli and American scholars in the production of a handsome and visually satisfying volume. As dictionary, it includes about 3,500 items defining biblical proper names, based on the text of the New King James Version. Interspersed are other sorts of article: gazelle and tamarisk are treated within comprehensive listings of animals and plants; each biblical book and group of books is separately introduced, including those from the Apocrypha; topics like afterlife find a place despite the absence of the word from the biblical text. The book's inner margins list all occurrences of an item, so providing the concordance. The generous outer margins carry a wealth of apt illustration: seals bearing names, details of places. Qumran fragments of books — with larger photographic features within the text of perhaps half the pages. While space is not wasted, there is an absence of clutter. The scholarship is uncontroversial: discreet silence is often preferred to honest doubt. And '. . . a concatenous pattern whose sequential ordering is determined by the mnemonic device of catchwords, phrases and ideas common to the two oracles contiguous to one another' is a rare example of language itself requiring a dictionary.

A. G. AULD

WIND, J. P.(ed.): *The Bible and the University: The Messianic Vision of William Rainey Harper* (SBL Centennial Publications). 1987. Pp. viii, 190. (Scholars Press, Atlanta, Georgia. Price: $18.95 (member price: $13.95); paperback price: $13.95 (member price: $9.95). ISBN 1 55540 129 5; 1 55540 130 9 (pbk))

Harper's achievement as scholar, teacher, religious leader, and University President are here impressively presented against a background of varied developments during 'the last moments when Americans were able to believe, without second thoughts, that their nation could be the messianic deliverer of the world'. These developments were the changing pattern of American society from village to metropolitan ways of life, the changing pattern of education at various levels, and the impact of critical scholarship on biblical study. It is admitted that Harper was not a seminal scholar, but that his distinctiveness lay in his ability to 'blend and reconcile' views often felt to be incompatible, and further that in some important ways he anticipated later developments in biblical study, particularly regarding the relationship of revelation to history. His impact on the work of Seminary, Sunday School, and College is described and assessed. Particular attention is given to his influence as President of the University of Chicago and his version of the 'messianic role' of the University in a democracy, later critical evaluations (and caricatures) of which are summarised and commented on. The value of this illuminating study is enhanced by the admirable documentation.

G. W. ANDERSON

WOLFF, H. W.: *Studien zur Prophetie — Probleme und Erträge. Mit einer Werkbibliographie* (Theologische Bücherei, 76). 1987. Pp. 195. (Chr. Kaiser, Munich. Price: Dm 36.00. ISBN 3 459 01683 3)

Nine of the ten essays in this volume have appeared before; the tenth, dealing with literary-historical study of Haggai, is hitherto unpublished. The essays cover a wide range. Some are general: 'Prophecy from the Eighth through the Fifth Century' (the original German text, of which a translation appeared in *Interpretation* 1978); 'The prophetic experience of God'; 'The actual message of the classical prophets' (*Zimmerli Festschrift*, 1977); 'Prophet and Institution' (in *Charisma und Institution*, ed. T. Rendtorff, 1985) 'Conception of the End and the crisis of direction' (*Krauss Festschrift*, 1983), all touching on the major issues in recent study of the prophets. Special studies: 'Micah's understanding of his vocation' (Göttingen Congress); a careful study of right and wrong interpretations of Joel 4:9–12, Isa. 2:2–5, Micah 4:1–5; Obadiah as a cult-prophet acting as interpreter; humour in Jonah.

These are not all easy of access; so it is particularly useful to have these studies by a scholar who looks broadly as well as in detail (cf. his BK commentaries on the Minor Prophets, still not completed) at the prophetic books and messages.

P. R. Ackroyd

Van Der Woude, A. S. (ed.): *Crises and Perspectives: Studies in Ancient Near Eastern Polytheism, Biblical Theology, Palestinian Archaeology and Intertestamental Literature* (Papers read at the joint British–Dutch Old Testament Conference held at Cambridge, U.K., 1985: Oudtestamentische Studiën XXIV). 1986. Pp. 149, (Brill, Leiden. Price: Fl. 88.00; sub. price: Fl. 68.00. ISBN 90 04 07873 8; ISSN 0169 9555)

These papers represent the permanent record of what was an excellent Summer Meeting of SOTS in Fitzwilliam College, Cambridge in July 1985. They are wide-ranging in their concerns and learned in their execution and reflect well on the SOTS presidency of Professor R. E. Clements. J. C. de Moor contributes a fascinating study of 'The Crisis of Polytheism in Late Bronze Ugaritic'; N. Poulssen's 'Time and Place in Genesis v' is a charming, allusive reflection on Genesis v, especially v. 29; G. I. Davies offers a thorough analysis of the complexities of archaeological contributions to the study of the Hebrew Bible in his 'Megiddo in the Period of the Judges'; E. W. Nicholson gives a typically lucid account of the history of thought on biblical covenant in 'Covenant in a Century of Study since Wellhausen'; K. A. D. Smelik's 'Distortion of Old Testament Prophecy: The Purpose of Isaiah xxxvi and xxxvii' is an absorbing consideration of the complexities involved in the relation between the Isaiah text, its parallel occurrence in Kings, and Jer. xxxvii; L. Dequeker provides an interesting but complicated treatment of '1 Chronicles xxiv and the Royal Priesthood of the Hasmoneans'; J. D. Martin develops some earlier thoughts on Ben Sira's messianism in his 'Ben Sira's Hymn to the Fathers: A Messianic Perspective'; and T. Rajak concludes the volume with her very useful analysis of 'The Sense of History in Jewish Intertestamental Writing'. Altogether there is some very good but heavy scholarship represented in this volume, with some excellent collections of footnoted secondary literature (especially Davies, Smelik, and Rajak).

R. P. Carroll

2. ARCHAEOLOGY AND EPIGRAPHY

Albenda, P.: *The Palace of Sargon, King of Assyria: Monumental Wall Reliefs at Dur-Sharrukin, from original drawings made at the time of their discovery in 1843–1844 by Botta and Flandin* (Synthèse, 22). 1986. Pp. 280 (inc. 3 maps), 153 plates, 97 figures. (Editions Recherche sur les Civilizations, ADPF, Paris. Price: Fr. 352.00. ISBN 2 86538 152 8; ISSN 0291 1663)

Sargon II of Assyria, the father of Sennacherib mentioned in Isaiah 20:1, broke with tradition by building himself a new palace in what was planned to be a totally new town, Dur-Sharrukin, the modern Khorsabad. Its remains (mistaken for Nineveh!) were the object of the first French excavation in the Near East, under P. E. Botta. A large number of stone wall reliefs in varying states or preservation were uncovered, but only a small number eventually reached Western museums. Some rapidly disintegrated in the air. Drawings were made on the spot, some by Botta, more by his artist E. Flandin, which were published from engravings in their massive five-volume work *Monument de Ninive* (Paris, 1849–50, reprint Osnabrück, 1972). In 1980 the original drawings were discovered in Paris and these are published here in photographic reproduction as the closest one can get to what Botta uncovered. In addition photographs are provided of as many of the originals as survive and could be reached. The text surveys all the excavations at the site, explains the architectural settings of the various reliefs, and offers a commentary on them, while C. B. F. Walker edits the few captions. Detailed catalogues of drawings and existing reliefs supply necessary information. Save for these catalogues, the text is also given in French translation by A. Caubet. This is a careful scholarly work of lasting value, though the commentaries avoid matters of religion, mythology and history. One scene (pl. 98) shows a siege of Ekron not referred to in the king's surviving inscriptions.

W. G. LAMBERT

ASSMANN, J., BURKARD, G., and DAVIES, V. (eds.): *Problems and Priorities in Egyptian Archaeology*. 1987. Pp. 311, 32 plates. (KPI Ltd, London and New York. Price: £40.00. ISBN 0 7103 0190 1)

In 1985, the Ägyptologisches Institut at Heidelberg University celebrated its seventy-fifth anniversary by holding an international colloquium on needs and methodology in field-work in Egypt. This volume gathers up the papers then presented. The Heidelberg Institute is currently much engaged with the recording and publication of private (decorated) tomb-chapels in Western Thebes. Thus, four of the sixteen papers touched on the study and publication of such chapels. Two more deal with epigraphy on standing monuments, especially temples. Five tackle questions of excavation and evaluation of artefacts. Others deal with socio-economic issues on an archaeological basis. The whole is prefaced by a short history of the Institute. Valuable to Egyptologists rather than for Old Testament scholars.

K. A. KITCHEN

BORDREUIL, P.: *Catalogue des Sceaux Ouest-Sémitiques Inscrits de la Bibliothèque Nationale, du Musée du Louvre et du Musée biblique de Bible et Terre Sainte*. 1986. Pp. x, 133. (Bibliothèque Nationale, Paris. Price: Fr. 220.00. ISBN 2 7177 1750 1)

The three Paris collections hold 140 seals inscribed in Phoenician (39), Hebrew (20–7 unpublished), Moabite (9), Ammonite (16), and Aramaic (56). Many are well-known, including the Hebrew seal of *'byw 'bd 'zyw*, the master believed to be the king of Judah. Without a royal title such an attribution remains uncertain, and so cannot act as a firm key for dating the engraving. Distinctive names are exceptions, and that applies to perhaps the most important seal published here, no. 86, *lnrš' 'bd 'trsmk*, where the master can hardly be other than the king of Arpad of *c.* 780 B.C., father of Mati-el of the Sefire treaties. This is one of 35 seals formerly owned by Henri Seyrig, almost all notable pieces. Valuable for palaeography and language, the seals also offer varied iconographic contributions, notably the fire- offering scene (*ātaš–zāhr*) on an Achaemenid cylinder (no. 136). Bordreuil gives clear descriptions and brief comments of each seal, with bibliographies and comparisons, providing rich material for further research. His definitive catalogue advances the study of ancient Levantine glyptic, an instructive aspect of the Old Testament's cultural world.

A. R. MILLARD

Collon, D.: *First Impressions: Cylinder Seals in the Ancient Near East.* 1987. Pp. 208, including 966 illustrations. (British Museum Publications, London. Price: £25.00. ISBN 0 7141 1121 X)

Seals of ancient Western Asia are important for the history of art and as evidence of legal practice as attesting or protecting rights. Since the materials and designs vary according to period and place they serve also to illuminate their archaeological context and the chronology. This excellent book by the leading British scholar in this particular and technical field of study is both a reliable introduction and comprehensive reference work to the whole subject. It should replace Frankfort's standard work on the subject (1939).

The scope is wide, from Proto-historic to Hellenistic times throughout the Middle East, and covers seal designs and history (part I); their use in society (II); and the subjects and themes represented (III). The miniscule art depicts aspects of daily life, and beliefs and practices including deities and demons, temples and altars, sacrifice and banquets, myths and legends; and illustrates many matters from dress to music and dancing and warfare. It offers a source too often overlooked as little represented in this region outside Egyptian tomb paintings and the glimpses afforded by Assyrian palace wall-reliefs.

Syria/Palestine is included; but since stamp seals are touched upon but briefly the reader interested only in the Old Testament needs to remember that these were used concurrently with the cylinder form throughout much of the area and time, though after the ninth–eighth centuries B.C. they predominate (cf. Gen 41:41–42; Jb. 38:14). A companion volume at this same standard which would include these and the inscribed Hebrew stamps would be most useful.

D. J. Wiseman

Hadidi, A. (ed.): *Studies in the history and archaeology of Jordan,* II. 1985. Pp. 358. (Department of Antiquities, Amman, and Routledge & Kegan Paul, London, Boston, Melbourne and Henley. Price: £38.00. ISBN 0 7102 0734 4)

Here are forty-three papers given at an Amman conference (1983) on 'Jordanian environment: geographical and historical'. Its major concern was environmental archaeology: climate, vegetation, ecology, geomorphology, hydrology, natural resources, seismology, agriculture, erosion, urbanization all came within its scope. D. Baly in an introductory essay discusses environment as process. Among the following essays, D. O. Henry and G. O. Rollefson make important contributions on the Late Pleistocene environment in southern Jordan, as does D. Kirkbride on the Pre-Pottery Neolithic environment of Petra. J. R. Harlan reconstructs the EB environment of Moab. K. H. Bernhardt presents the biblical evidence for natural conditions and resources in east Jordan, and E. Will describes the Hellenistic and Roman urbanization of Jordan. L. Geraty and Ø. LaBianca discuss 'food-procuring strategies' in the Hesban region. H. Chadwick considers the relation of the great religions to the environment. Other studies relate to the Nabataean, Byzantine and subsequent periods, or to technical and scientific matters. While *Book List* readers will note the importance of these environmental studies for their own historical concerns, HRH Crown Prince Hassan, in his preface, underlined their value for modern environmental planning. This is a welcome and exciting successor to volume I (*B.L.* 1984, p. 31).

J. R. Bartlett

HARRIS, R. L., and SCHONFIELD, J. (eds.): *Bulletin of the Anglo-Israel Archaeological Society: News and Meetings of the Society 1985–6*. 1986. Pp. 79. (Anglo-Israel Archaeological Society, London. Price: £8.00. ISSN 0266 2442)

Summaries of six lectures occupy pages 16–55 of this issue. E. Braun, whose visit to Britain the Society financed, gives an account of important excavations revealing Neolithic and Early Bronze Age houses at Yiftahel, Y. Shiloh outlines results of his work in the City of David, and G. Barkay surveys ideas about the extent of Iron Age Jerusalem in the light of recent discoveries, rather harshly criticizing the late Dame Kathleen Kenyon. Rediscovery of Jerusalem in the nineteenth century was part of Y.Ben-Arieh's lecture, and reconstruction of the Byzantine Cardo the subject of E. N. Krendel's. D. Barag presents arguments to show that the *menorah* gained prime importance as a Jewish symbol only after A.D. 70, eventually embracing Messianic connotations. S. Gibson's research report describes the excavation of a small Byzantine 'monastery' near Jerusalem, and D. Stacey a cemetery south of Jericho containing Middle Bronze Age tombs. D. Barag also provides an obituary of Dr R. D. Barnett. D. Jacobson's research report, pp. 56–68, presents evidence that Herodium was less a fortress than a luxurious defensible residence of Hellenistic style, hence a 'chateau'. With this paper the Society's *Bulletin* steps beyond summaries of lectures to the initial publication of original research. If it continues in this way its value will grow, and it will become essential to libraries concerned with the biblical world.

A. R. MILLARD

KENYON, K. M.: *The Bible and Recent Archaeology* (revised edition by P. R. S. Moorey). 1987. Pp. 192. (British Museum Publications, London. Price: £9.95. ISBN 0 7141 1681 5)

Roger Moorey has completely re-written Kathleen Kenyon's summary 105-page account of biblical, principally Palestinian archaeology, concentrating on work done since the 1978 publication. Major changes concern the Patriarchs and the Conquest. For the former Moorey follows T. L. Thompson's dictum, 'Archaeological materials should not be dated or evaluated on the basis of written texts which are independent of these materials', allowing a few traditions survived from before 1200 B.C. The dictum is not operated for later periods. 'Canaan in the Bronze Age' is a clear account of important discoveries, including the archives of Ugarit and proto-alphabetic texts from Palestine, closing with the Israel Stele and the recent proposal that damaged reliefs from Karnak reflect Merneptah's campaign in Canaan. Two chapters discuss the end of that era, one the Egyptian and Philistine roles, the other the Israelite, stressing the problems of identification inherent in the term Israelite, and the difficulties archaeology creates for understanding Joshua–Judges. The biblical texts for David and Solomon are evaluated through familiar discoveries, the Temple, gateways, city walls and 'stables' succinctly assessed as signs of central control. Jerusalem, both the Kenyon and Shiloh excavations, Lachish, Arad, and the Negev enigmas for Kuntilet Ajrud and Horvat Qitmit give material evidence for Judean culture, Hazor and Dan principally for Israel, with a glance at Transjordanian sites. Welcome is Chapter 8, 'From the Exile to Herod the Great', covering the end of Judah, the Persian period, which recent finds illustrate, including a fine incense burner from Jordan, and Hellenistic times, with coverage of Qumran. Finally, Moorey tells of Herod's buildings as now known, and brings up to date the discussion of the Holy Sepulchre's site. Although perhaps overestimating the contribution of archaeology to interpreting the Bible in its earlier part, this is a clear and authoritative survey of the current situation.

A. R. MILLARD

McGOVERN, P. E.: *Late Bronze Palestinian Pendants: Innovation in a Cosmopolitan Age* (JSOT/ASOR Monograph Series 1). 1985. Pp. xx, 184. (JSOT Press for the American Schools of Oriental Research, Sheffield. Price: £30.00 ($45.00). ISBN 0 905774 90 6)

While Late Bronze Age towns in Palestine generally display a decline from the heights of Middle Bronze Age culture, their ruins have yielded much more jewellery, in particular pendants. At the start of the Late Bronze Age golden pendants with Syrian associations are found, then in Late bronze IB Egyptian styles became more common, moulded in faience. This type increased in Late Bronze IIA and was very popular in Late Bronze IIB, when echoes of Amarna fashions appear. This class is more common in the lowlands than in the hills, where local types hold sway. P. McGovern has catalogued and analysed 359 examples, arranging them in six classes by shape, and examining their provenances. He has had access to many unpublished specimens, notably from Beth-Shan, and gives information on comparable pieces from Syria and elsewhere. Such a study faces the problems of accident in preservation and discovery, problems McGovern has noticed but which need emphasis in the statistical presentation of the final chapter. Egyptian style pendants, he claims, attest Egyptian presence, but this is doubtful unless they are well distributed in company with other signs of Egyptian occupation. Many pendants are found in shrines where they may have adorned statues as necklaces, others found in houses adorned individuals and may be seen as amulets. This is a workmanlike assessment of some of the raw material for reconstructing Canaanite religious practices.

A. R. MILLARD

MAGALL, M.: *Archäologie und Bibel: Wissenschaftliche Wege zur Welt des Alten Testaments*. 1986. Pp. 240. (DuMont Buchverlag, Köln. Price: DM 28.00. ISBN 3 7701 1644 5)

Her crisp style allows the author to deal with a lot of material in a helpful presentation of how archaeology has come to inform our view of the biblical world. She begins with a brief review of the history of archaeology in the Holy Land. The opening chapter reviews extra-biblical witnesses to relevant facts and myths up to the period of Darius. The next nine chapters handle patriarchs, conquest, rise of monarchy, united monarchy, northern Israel, Judah, return from exile, Herod, and tangible remains of the time of Jesus — all in pleasingly critical fashion. There follows a brief guide for first-time visitors to twenty-one of the sites mentioned in the main text, a chronological table, and a list of the museums (including smaller kibbutz museums) with archaeological finds. The many black-and-white illustrations are well-chosen, if not always well produced; the eight central colour pages are excellent.

A. G. AULD

NEGEV, A.: *The Late Hellenistic and Early Roman Pottery of Nabatean Oboda; Final Report.* (Qedem, Monographs of the Institute of Archaeology, The Hebrew University of Jerusalem, 22). 1986. Pp. xxii, 144. (Israel Exploration Society, Jerusalem. Price: $24.00. ISSN 0333 5844)

This complete catalogue, covering both Nabatean and non-Nabatean ware, both pots and artefacts, records the results of excavations conducted at

Oboda (Avdat) by the author during 1958–61. The enormous quantities of Nabatean ware yielded by the site, much of it from a large dump which had also contained numerous coins, made possible a chronology for the ware. This has since been revised, notably in the light of a smaller quantity of better stratified material from Mampsis, excavated by the author from 1965 on. There is no identifiable Nabatean pottery from earlier than the first century B.C.; and, at the other end, it is not clear how far the painted pottery industry at Oboda survived the Arab attacks of between A.D. 50 and 73. In an excessively brief introduction, the author gives some indication of the problems of relating the history of the Oboda manufacture (a workshop was discovered in 1981) to the wider picture of the development of Nabatean pottery and of the vicissitudes of the Nabatean people. The catalogue itself is illustrated with copious excellent drawings and photographs of small pottery fragments and these suggest the difficulties involved in settling the classification of types and designs. They also convey an impression of the refinement and richness of the painted ware at its height.

T. RAJAK

ORRIEUX, C.: *Les Papyrus de Zenon: L'horizon d'un grec en Égypte au IIIe siècle avant J.C.* 1983. Pp. 161. (Macula, Paris. Price: Fr. 80.00. ISBN 2 86589 008 2)

The papyrological archive of Zenon, agent of Ptolemy Philadelphus's finance minister in the middle years of the second century B.C., have received a dispersed publication and a large scholarly literature. Although only about 40 out of some 1,200 documents concern Palestine, where Zenon spent a year on behalf of his master, these are of immense importance as virtually the only sound evidence for the region during its century of Ptolemaic rule. A few other documents concern Egyptian Jews in the Fayum. An accessible conspectus of the dossier would therefore be of interest to the *B.L.*'s readers. But this exercise in 'haute vulgarisation' is so Gallic in style and so sketchy in contents as to be of little use for the purpose. There is a brief presentation of that remarkable Jewish correspondent Tobiah the Ammonite, but the allusion to the lineage, which stretches back at least to the time of Zechariah, is unhelpful, its significance never emerging. The famous pagan formula in one of his letters prompts a sentence about Jewish Hellenization, after which we are swept on to other territory.

T. RAJAK

PARPOLA, S.: *The Correspondence of Sargon II, Part I: Letters from Assyria and the West* (State Archives of Assyria, Vol. I). 1987. Pp. xxvi, 262, 40 figs., and 1 folded map. (Helsinki University Press. Price: FIM 180.00; £24.95. ISBN 951 570 003 5)

The Neo-Assyrian Text Corpus project provides the first of four volumes with 265 of the *c.* 1300 letters assigned to Sargon of Assyria over ten years *c.* 715 B.C. They were mostly sent to or from governors and high officials and are a rich, sometimes neglected, source for recovering the everyday life of the time. The texts are given in transliteration with a clear English translation (with a few quaint exceptions), full indexes and related illustrations. The Introduction discusses letter-writing and the postal system which held this 'Empire of communications' together.

Most of the letters are intelligence reports referring to events in Phrygia, Urartu and the Cimmerians by the crown-prince Sennacherib. Others concern unrest among the restless Arabs partly controlled by an embargo of iron to them (179); the resistance of the men of Samaria to corn-taxes imposed (200) or the reaction to the Assyrian yoke (183). Army operations, including supplies of horses, charioteers and depots; the movement of foreign delegates, tribute, prisoners and deportees show the importance placed on all this by the Assyrian administration system. As would be expected there is emphasis too on the selection and transportation of timber, bull-colossi, and stone for building Sargon's new palace at Dūr-Šarrukēn (Khorsabad) (see above, p. 28). Details of repairs to temples, of the cult, rituals, festivals, and even of the weather, as of individuals seeking refuge in a temple (236) and care for widows of fallen soldiers (21) will be welcomed by those looking fo material to compare with the Old Testament. This initial volume portends a valuable series.

D. J. WISEMAN

PEARLMAN, M.: *Seisho no Hakkutsu Monogatari.* Translated by K. Onodera. 1987. Pp. 318 + 8 pp. index. (Yamamoto Shoten, Tokyo. Price: ¥4,800)

This is a Japanese translation of *Digging up the Bible* (1980) (see *B.L.* 1981, p. 32). The translator appended a list of reference books in Japanese.

K. K. SACON

SUSSMAN, A., and GREENBERG, R. (eds.): *Excavations and Surveys in Israel 1986* (Volume 5, English Edition of *Hadashot Arkheologiyot*, nos. 88–89, edited by I. Pommerantz). 1986. Pp. vii, 127, with 2 maps and numerous plans, photographs and drawings. (Israel Department of Antiquities and Museums, Jerusalem (available from Eisenbrauns, P.O.B.275, Winona Lake, Indiana 46590). Price: $10.00. ISSN 0334 1607)

Excavations and Surveys is the English version of the official annual bulletin of the Israel Department of Antiquities. The current issue, which includes some photographs for the first time in addition to the invaluable plans and drawings, contains nearly a hundred reports on excavations and surveys, mainly carried out in 1986, as well as ten briefer items. The full range of archaeological periods are covered. Reports relating to the biblical period include those on the important excavations at Ashkelon, Tel Batash (Timnah) and Dor, and finds of particular interest from Tel Miqne/Ekron (extensive evidence of the oil industry of the seventh century B.C.), Mount Ebal (further data on the 'cult place' of the Judges period) and Jerusalem (an inner gate of the city of the late Israelite monarchy near the southern approach to the temple). This is by far the fullest and best guide to current excavation in Israel and the occupied territories.

G. I. DAVIES

TEIXIDOR, J.: *Bulletin d'Epigraphie sémitique (1964–1980).* (Bibliothèque archéologique et historique, tome CXXVII). 1986. Pp. 513. P. Geuthner, Paris. Price: Fr. 280.00. ISBN 2 7053 0335 9)

J. Teixidor and the editors of *Syria* served Semitists well by publishing an annual survey of newly published West Semitic inscriptions and comments on studies of others from 1967 to 1979. Now Teixidor's perceptive comments and helpful bibliographic notes are reproduced in a single volume, with the original annual indices and a final index of all texts from *Corpus Inscriptionum Semiticarum* I and II discussed, and all those from H. Donner and W. Röllig's handbook. There is also a consolidated list of provenances. The author has taken the opportunity to add twenty-six pages of Addenda and Corrigenda. Among numerous pertinent observations, the most notable is the further evidence that the Arslan Tash amulets are not ancient (pp. 471 f.). This is a volume which all scholars and libraries concerned with West Semitic texts and inscriptions, including Hebrew, will have to acquire and consult.

A. R. MILLARD

La Voie Royale. 9000 ans d'Art au Royaume de Jordanie. Exposition, Musée de Luxembourg, 26 Novembre 1986–25 Janvier 1987. 1986. Pp. 304, black and white, and colour photographs. (Association française d'Action artistique, Paris)

This volume commemorates the first major exhibition of antiquities from Jordan in Europe. Objects from Amman were joined by some from Paris collections, and Jordanian and French scholars collaborated in describing them. After an introductory essay for each major period stands a selection of typical artefacts. There are familiar pieces: the Shihan stele, the Moabite stone (translated by A. Lemaire), and the Ammonite statuary (eight pieces, each illustrated, five in colour), items from Petra. Recent discoveries are also displayed, several previously unpublished, including the Pre-Pottery Neolithic B figures from Ain Ghazal which show how the fragments from Jericho once appeared, ivory carved plaques from Middle Bronze Age Pella, a remarkable Tell el-Yehudieh ware puzzle-jug topped with a woman's head, cylinder seals, Achaemenid metal-work from the Umm Udheinah tomb, and Hellenistic, Roman, and Byzantine material from Qweilbeh (painted tombs), Khirbet es-Samra (mosaics), etc. Ammon, Moab, and Edom occupy fifty pages, the pottery and glyptic showing overall similarities with the Palestinian, but revealing local variations. The absence of any example of Edomite painted ware is disappointing. All the Iron Age seals are drawn from Paris collections and figure in Bordreuil's catalogue (see p. 29), except for Palty the *mazkir*'s fine one. This catalogue makes a well-illustrated introductory handbook to the archaeology of Jordan.

A. R. MILLARD

YON, M. (ed.): *Le centre de la ville (Ras Shamra-Ougarit III): 38*–44* campagnes (1978–1984),* (Éditions Recherche sur les Civilisations, mémoire no. 72). 1987. Pp. 374. (ADPF, Paris. Price: Fr. 357.00. ISBN 2 86538 169 2)

This important volume contains detailed studies arising out of recent campaigns at Ras Shamra under the direction of Marguerite Yon. The speed of publication is admirable, though there is no pretence that this is the last word on the material here published. The area being excavated reflects, perhaps, the changing perspectives of Near Eastern archaeology — it is an area of residential character of the Late Bronze period and is important because of the information it provides on the everyday life of the city which produced in the same period such fine works of art and literature. The contributions are on the following topics: the organization of the habitat (of a series of residential buildings), water facilities, two new tombs under the houses, olive oil production facilities in one building, and a 'local' religious building. There are also specialized reports on groups of finds: bone and ivory objects, terracottas objects, glassware, rhytons, bronze tools and weights. Of the few points of biblical interest one is a discussion of the presence of the hippopotamus in the Levant in the second and first millenia B.C. (reference being made to Job 40:15–24). The excavation of the area continued in 1986 and some of this later evidence has been taken into account in final editing.

J. F. HEALEY

3. HISTORY AND GEOGRAPHY

BOROWSKI, O.: *Agriculture in Ancient Israel: The Evidence from Archaeology and the Bible.* 1987. Pp. xxii, 215. (Eisenbrauns, Winona Lake, Indiana. Price: $20.00. ISBN 0 931464 27 7)

Borowski divides his work into four parts. In the first he considers the place of agriculture, then describes results of recent archaeological attention to ancient environments, especially the land-shaping techniques of terracing and run-off farming, drawing on work by L. E. Stager. These important matters deserve fuller treatment with more diagrams. Land Tenure (private, royal, priestly) and the Calendar complete Part I. Part II covers field work and grain production (ploughing, harvesting and storing); Part III, the plants and fruits grown; and Part IV, soil fertility, pests and diseases. In these sections the biblical texts, linguistic identifications and archaeological and palaeobotanical evidence are brought together, the linguistic side being a little light. It would be revealing to tabulate the relation between written reports of plants and the occurrence of physical remains which the author mentions. There is a well illustrated presentation of recent advances in knowledge about oil presses (pp. 119ff), and description of wine production. These are gaps, e.g. on *boṭnîm* reference is lacking to M. Stol's work (see *B.L.* 1981, pp. 110f), and to modern discussion of mixtures (Lev. 19:19; Dt. 22:9); and some of the exegesis is dubious — do Dt. 32:14 and Ps. 73:6 imply animal remains were used as fertilizers? However, it is convenient to have the information collected and arranged clearly.

A. R. MILLARD

CLAUSS, M.: *Geschichte Israels: Von der Frühzeit bis zur Zerstörung Jerusalems (587 v. Chr.).* 1986. Pp. 238. (Verlag C. H. Beck, München. Price: DM 32.00. ISBN 3 406 31175 X)

The framework of this account follows a generally familiar pattern: a discussion of the geographical setting and the sources available followed by a description of the early semi-nomadic origins of the Hebrews, the complex process of settlement, the rise of the monarchy and its history until the exile. Within this framework, however, the author has included much that reflects recent interest in the nature of Israelite society: the contribution of archaeology to our understanding of the nature and size of the family; the life style and religion of semi-nomadic Hebrews and the effect of settlement on economic and social organization and on religion; the basic equality of life in pre-state Israel because of the absence of a central authority which might guarantee private property and its use as a base for exerting political power; the rise of the monarchy (under David rather than Saul, who is reckoned among the deliverers) and the development of the royal bureaucracy, army, economy and trade. This is a clear and concise account, unencumbered with notes, though provided with a topical bibliography.

A. D. H. MAYES

COOTE, R. B., and WHITELAM, K. W.: *The Emergence of Early Israel in Historical Perspective* (The Social World of Biblical Antiquity Series, 5). 1987. Pp. 212. (Almond, Sheffield. Price: £25.00 ($37.50); ISBN 1 85075 073 4. Paperback price: £10.50 ($16.50); ISBN 1 85075 072 6)

This study argues that our understanding of the emergence of Israel has been obscured by the Pentateuchal and Deuteronomistic presentations (designed 'to legitimise the present reality of David and Josiah' and their kingdoms) and by recent historiographical emphases. Better guides are to be found in archaeological data and socio-economic theory. Chapter 2 presents a picture of settlement patterns and social relations throughout Palestinian history to set Israel's emergence in the context of Braudel's *la longue durée*, pointing to a cyclical pattern of expansion, decline and regeneration: thus Israel's Early Iron Age emergence is no longer seen as an isolated or unique episode. Particularly important to this cycle are factors of trade and external suzerainty. Chapter 3 examines local geography and social relations, noting particularly the constant role of the urban elite, bandits, nomads and peasants. The major themes appear in chapters 4 and 5. The new subsistence hill-country agriculture of Early Iron Age I arose as an *internal* response to the economic collapse of the Late Bronze Age, and not from external invasion. 'Israel' developed as peasants, nomads and bandits combined in loose federation in the hill country, expanded their territory, increased their food production and their population. The monarchy developed naturally from this situation (it was not 'some alien cancer in the Israelite body politic' (p. 148)).

Much here is persuasive, but we are left asking why the Late Bronze world collapsed, why this emergent confederation took the name 'Israel', and above all why the Old Testament so heavily emphasises the theme of exodus and the wilderness travel. Is it enough to say (p. 171f.), 'The Davidic scribe' [Davidic?] 'makes the Egyptian state the foil of Israel's national identity, and through the "exodus" portrays the emergence of *landed* Israel in terms of a crisis in the perennial tension between Egypt and the loyal bedouin of south-western Palestine'? It is the combination of archaeological data and socio-economic theory that gives this book its importance.

J. R. Bartlett

Danieli, P. G. (ed): *La Storiografia nella Bibbia: Atti della XXVIII Settimana Biblica*. 1986. Pp. 169. (Edizioni Dehoniane, Bologna. Price: Lire 18,000. ISBN 88 10 30251 6)

These papers on Biblical Historiography (hereafter HG) are all in Italian. Their subjects are: Biblical HG in relation to that of ancient Greece and the Near East, with reference especially to A. Momigliano, H. Cancik and J. Van Seters (G. L. Prato); The oldest Israelite HG (J. A. Soggin); HG and ideology in 1 Kgs 3–10 (R. Gelio); The idea of 'remnant' as moral justification in face of a conquering power (O. Carena); 'Abraham among the Chaldaeans of Nabonidus' (G. Garbini); HG in the Book of Daniel (A. Bonora); 2 Maccabees and Josephus' *Bell. Jud.* as Hellenistic Jewish HG (G. Jossa). This useful symposium is rounded off by two papers on Luke-Acts (G. Betori and V. Fusco) and one on the model of the 'Righteous sufferer' in the Passion.

R. P. R. Murray

Garbini, G.: *History and ideology in ancient Israel*. 1988. Pp. xvi, 222. (SCM Press, London. Price: £10.50. ISBN 0 334 00621 X)

Garbini's target is the wishful thinking of much recent historiography. Ancient Israel's last true historian was Wellhausen; Noth, Herrmann, and Fohrer are dismissed as '*Alttestamentler*, professors from German theological faculties', while Albright, Bright, Hayes and Miller represent an archaeologically-based apologetic strand. The Old Testament offers theological reflection upon history, not history, as Garbini proceeds to demonstrate. Some interesting theses emerge. Solomon's achievements have been magnified by legend, and by the transfer to him of material which rightly belonged to Azariah (whose apparent lack of achievement was then explained by leprosy). Israelite religion was virtually Canaanite before the seventh century B.C. Yahwistic revolution (the evidence of Kuntillet ʿAjrud — 'largely unpublished (and perhaps largely destined to remain so)' — comes in handy here), and the Old Testament picture of Israel arriving into Canaan with a new God, Yahweh, is a retrojection of the exiles' return from Babylon. The patriarchal narratives (compared with the *logoi* of Herodotus) similarly reflect the concerns of exilic Jews. The intolerance of Moses (Exod. 32) reflects late priestly attitudes, for early Israel was tolerant in religious matters. The twelve-tribe system is likewise an idealistic post-exilic construct. The books *Joshua, Judges*, written in the spirit of the Chronicler, are not trustworthy evidence for pre-monarchic history. The Alexandrian Hellenistic Jewish literature presents Jewish history from an Egyptian-Jewish tradition which is just as valid (or invalid) as the canonical presentation, which reflects the Jerusalem hierarchy's philo-Babylonian, anti-Egyptian attitude. The LXX was translated to present the authentic Jewish law to Egyptian Jews. The final *tour-de-force* (owing much to Torrey) denies the existence of Ezra and the associated Persian period reforms, linking 'Ezra' with Alcimus and the origins of Qumran (to un-riddle this, see chapter 13).

This is an original and stimulating book. The point that the Old Testament writers have theological axes to grind is hardly new, but some of the axes are. The suggestion that the naming of Ur and Harran in Genesis might remind Nabonidus of places dear to him prompts obvious questions. It is not clear why Isa. 49–55 are the work of Deutero-Isaiah's 'continuator', or why Isa. 14 has to refer to Xerxes, or why the royal psalms can generally be dated to the Hasmonaean period. Garbini affirms that the Old Testament cannot be trusted as historical evidence without external attestation; but should not this principle be extended to the equally tendentious Herodotus, the Assyrian records, the Moabite stone, or the Merneptah stele (on which Garbini puts great weight)? Are Israel's records intrinsically less reliable than Moab's or Egypt's, or totally different in kind?

Garbini acknowledges a debt to Rowley, G. R. Driver, and Barr, and to 'the healthily empirical attitude' of the British biblical school; he might equally have acknowledged Wellhausen, Robertson Smith, Torrey and Kennett, for we seem to be back in their world. But we are in Garbini's debt, as he compels us to evaluate more carefully the nature of our historical sources before we write our histories.

J. R. BARTLETT

GONEN, R.: *Biblical Holy Places: an illustrated guide*. 1987. Pp. 288. (A. & C. Black, London. Price: £11.95. ISBN 0 7136 2872 3)

Like Noort's guide (p. 39) this is a book for the general visitor — or armchair traveller — but in this case the author is an Israeli archaeologist. There are other differences. There are no introductory chapters, the whole book being given over to descriptions of individual places. The scope is geographically wider, covering not only Israel and the West Bank (which are, regrettably, both treated as 'Israel'), but also sites in Cyprus, Egypt (i.e. Sinai), Greece, Italy, Jordan, Malta, Syria and Turkey. Topically the scope is narrower, as the title implies, so that important archaeological sites such as Hazor and (even more surprisingly) Qumran are omitted in favour of places with greater religious interest, some of them quite obscure. The text appears to be generally reliable, and the excellent colour illustrations (many of them of churches) are a reason in themselves for acquiring the book.

G. I. DAVIES

KALLAI, Z.: *Historical Geography of the Bible. The Tribal Territories of Israel*. Pp. xii, 543, 4 maps. (Brill, Leiden, and Magnes Press, Jerusalem. Price: Fl. 125.00. ISBN 965 223 631 4)

Since publishing *The Tribes of Israel* (Hebrew) in 1967 (not noted in *B.L.*), Z. Kallai has pursued his studies of territories and boundaries in numerous articles and now has distilled his views in this enlarged translation of the 1967 volume. The five parts cover 'The Historical Framework', geographical and historical analyses of the tribal boundary system, 'The Town-Lists in Joshua', and 'The List of Levitic Cities'. A 'General Summary' is followed by a 'Table of the Sources and their Territorial Testimony' which is a synopsis of Kallai's conclusions, setting the biblical references in chronological order, with a note of the circumstances accompanying each (pp. 482–95). Finally there is a 'Table of Settlement Names' setting the occurrences in parallel columns by passage. Kallai's theory is that the biblical lists are based on reality, a reality which belongs to the latest stage where there has been a process of literary growth. He seeks, therefore, moments in Israelite history when the various towns and territories were under Israelite control, and finds most fit the later part of David's reign and the early part of Solomon's, including the Levitic lists. The lists represent the situation at the end of the consolidation of the settlement process. Some lists are later, the Benjamite list in Joshua 18:21–28 belongs to the time after Abijah's victory, the Judahite list (Jos. 15:21–62) to the days of Hezekiah or Josiah. Kallai would treat each list or section as an individual unit for analysis and only afterwards combine the information from various lists. In this and other attitudes he disagrees with A. Alt, M. Noth and Y. Aharoni. He does not hesitate to point to weaknesses in the arguments of these and other scholars. For him, the boundaries were formed where territories of towns met, so a town was not necessarily itself at a border, and there were no shared or mixed settlements. Throughout there are valuable discussions on the identities of sites, with references to other studies and to archaeological evidence. In the nature of the case, much remains hypothetical, and the author realizes that; nevertheless, his work is a major contribution to the understanding of the biblical boundary descriptions, whether one agrees with it or not, and should stimulate a fresh look at many of the problems.

A. R. MILLARD

NOORT, E.: *Israel und das westliche Jordanufer: Eine Reiseführer* (translated from the Dutch by W. Bunte). 1987. Pp. viii, with 4 maps and 107 plans, drawings, and photographs. (Neukirchener, Neukirchen-Vluyn. Price: DM 39.80. ISBN 3 7887 0791 7)

This is an unusual tourist guide, in that it is written by a professional Old Testament scholar and archaeologist, but it is designed for the general educated visitor, not for Noort's fellow professionals. There are introductory chapters on the use of archaeology, attitudes to the holy places, the present day religious and political situation, and the history of the country. Over half the book is devoted to an alphabetical description of places of interest (not only archaeological sites). In general the author is a well-informed and judicious guide, but his plan of Megiddo is misleading, and the tour of Ophel in Jerusalem is a muddle which seems to be due to the conflation of two alternative itineraries! However such blemishes appear to be rare, and the book can be recommended as a useful companion, with plenty of practical good advice.

G. I. DAVIES

PETERS, F. E.: *Jerusalem: The Holy City in the Eyes of Chroniclers, Visitors, Pilgrims, and Prophets from the Days of Abraham to the Beginnings of Modern Times*. 1985. Pp. xiv, 656, and 40 pp. of illustrations (Princeton University Press, New Jersey. Price: £22.00 ($35.00.) ISBN 0 691 07300 7)

Those who love Jerusalem will readily add this fine volume to their shelves. Others may run the risk of joining their number as they browse in it. The author of *Children of Abraham: Judaism, Christianity, Islam*, 1982 has assembled a large selection of words about Jerusalem, and has presented them more extensively than often. These begin with the Abraham traditions in Genesis and conclude with Edward Robinson's account of Easter in the Holy City during his first visit in 1838 for a 'professed excursion into biblical archaeology'. Mostly they are allowed to speak for themselves, set in a modest, well-informed, and fully documented connecting text, with some fine reproductions and recent photographs. Only the first three of the thirteen chapters, 'Holy Land, Holy City', 'Jews and Greeks in Jerusalem', and 'Not a Stone Upon a Stone: The Destruction of the Holy City', are of immediate concern to the *Book List*.

A. G. AULD

PITARD, W. T.: *Ancient Damascus: A Historical Study of the Syrian City-State from Earliest Times until its Fall to the Assyrians in 732 B.C.E.* 1987. Pp. ix, 230. (Eisenbrauns, Winona Lake, Indiana. Price: $20.00. ISBN 0 931464 29 3)

The early early history of Damascus is most obscure. After examining the sources, Pitard concludes it was probably *ipwm* of the Execration Texts, but not Apum of the Mari archive. As Upi it had a minor place in surviving texts from the Late Bronze Age. Only with the rise of the Arameans did it gain importance. For this, as for all historical references, only non-Damascene records survive. Pitard's work, therefore, is to evaluate biblical, cuneiform and other sources. He is not afraid to take sides on disputed points, refuting B. Mazar's concept of Hazael's empire, dating Adad-nirari III's defeat of Marʾī in 796 B.C. He has been beguiled into offering a new reading for the Melqart Stele (pp. 138–44), the fifth in fifteen years, and this is equally uncertain. For the history of the ninth and eight centuries B.C. Kings is the most extensive source, and Pitard examines current theories about the reigns of Ahab and his successors, showing weaknesses in them. Regrettably, his own, placing 1 Kings 20–2 Kings 8 after Hazael's reign, also assumes alterations to the text without clear evidence, a step in the process which allows each historian to reconstruct history as he wishes. From the ancient near eastern side, more can be drawn out of the *Cambridge Ancient History* III. 1, published in 1982, the year the thesis was completed, than Pitard has realized. Within these limits, this is now the best book to consult for the history of early Damascus, and has the merits of clarity in language and thought.

A. R. MILLARD

PRITCHARD, J. B. (ed.): *The Times Atlas of the Bible*. 1987. Pp. 254. (Times Books, London. Price: £25.00. ISBN 0 7230 0295 9)

The text of this ambitious atlas is meticulously written, with great attention to details. It serves a number of distinct purposes. At appropriate junctures there are sections on general cultural and economic conditions in various parts of the ancient Near East. The historical coverage ranges from the earliest times down to the second Jewish revolt, and every aspect of Near Eastern history which impinged on ancient Israel, early Judaism and nascent Christianity is covered, with reference to its significance. Palestinian history is also treated in considerable detail.

The maps and illustrations are more difficult to evaluate. There is a tendency to cram into one double page spread not only a map or maps covering details of a military campaign or the growth of an empire, but several illustrations of reliefs, statues, a town plan, or an inscription, often superimposed on one another, which gives a rather confused impression. A typical layout is almost talmudic in its complex arrangement of a brief introductory paragraph, a main exposition, often a biblical text, captions to all the pictures and legend to the map(s). The maps are a new departure in biblical atlases, being commonly based on a 'satellite' projection, as though viewed obliquely from space (inspired by the Landsat volumes?). This is usually fairly successful, except where at times the curvature of the earth is excessive (as on p. 142 where the eastern Mediterranean would seems to cover about a sixth of the planet's surface!). One extraordinary result of this projection is that the only maps in the entire volume with a distance scale are those of Palestine appearing in the endpapers. A varying scale based upon the grid system appearing on all maps of whatever projection would have been feasible, and its absence makes some of the historical scenarios less helpful than they might have been.

The problem with any atlas of the Bible is that juxtaposition of narrative account and maps lends a historical gloss to events the historical reality of which is scarcely agreed. This becomes critical with issues like the patriarchal narratives and the exodus account. While doubts about Abraham's historicity are acknowledged, a detailed map of his possible and probable routes from Mesopotamia to Palestine on pp. 30–31 gives a very clear indication of the editorial view. The same goes for the military campaigns of Genesis 14 (p. 33) and the exodus route (pp. 56–57), which with all the trade routes incorporated, looks more like a plan of the Paris Metro. This raises the further point that the additional detail on maps is generally more than is relevant to or necessary for a clear understanding of the text. The use of contemporary place names, particularly with regard to Palestine, sometimes means that the general reader would find it hard to recognize that Shechem, for instance, is to all intents the same location as Neapolis/Nablus/Sychar/Tell Balatah. Even the extensive cross-referencing in the place-name index does not link them. It also requires a visit to the index to recognize that Gath in the map on page 64 is to be identified with Tell es-Safi in that on page 67.

In such a richly illustrated book, the lack of aerial photographs is amazing. So far as the pre-Christian world is concerned we have only Persepolis (pp. 136–37), Qumran (p. 161) and Tell Beer Sheva (p. 189). The first of these seems an unnecessary luxury in the absence of more relevant examples. Indeed, the relative scarcity of landscape photographs seems to be a case of a missed opportunity in so prestigious a volume.

In spite of detailed criticisms of this kind, the atlas will no doubt remain a basic reference work for some time, and students at all levels will find it useful in providing a wider context for biblical studies.

N. Wyatt

Saulnier, C., with the collaboration of Perrot, C.: *Histoire d'Israël*, iii: *De la Conquête d'Alexandre à la Destruction du Temple*. 1985. Pp. 567. (Editions du Cerf, Paris. Price: Fr. 230.00. ISBN 2 204 02360 4)

Saulnier has written the third of a three-volume history of Israel (though his is in fact the first to appear). The book begins with a good survey of sources and secondary bibliography; each chapter also starts off with a synopsis of the original sources for the period as well as the main secondary studies. After the history proper, the third section contains a selection of texts in translation; a variety of studies on individual sources, institutions, and problems; and a number of tables and maps.

Saulnier has given us a good, up-to-date, middle-level text. The nearest equivalent in English is H. Jagersma, *A History of Israel from Alexander the Great to Bar Kochba* (1985). A comparison of the two is instructive. Although Jagersma is only half the number of pages, he is more concise (and the words per page is slightly denser). Thus, the two are roughly equivalent in the amount of detail covered. Saulnier gives more historical background and more detail from Josephus, but Jagersma may be broader in its compass of

Jewish institutions and culture; however, Jagersma does not have the same selection of quotations from original texts. But otherwise the two works are very comparable, and English-speaking students would be as well served by Jagersma. The many typographical errors in non-French bibliography will probably not cause problems, but I also found mistakes in some of the cross references which is more serious.

L. L. GRABBE

SMEND, R.: *Zur ältesten Geschichte Israels: Gesammelte Studien* Bd. 2. (Beiträge zur evangelischen Theologie, Band 100). 1987. Pp. 258. (Chr. Kaiser Verlag, München. Price: DM 48.00. ISBN 3 459 01704 X)

This is the second collection of Professor Smend's previously published works. Whereas the first collection contained his contributions to the field of Old Testament theology (see *B.L.* 1987, p. 91), Smend has in this volume collected works concerned with the important and alas difficult area of Israel's early history. Two monographs constitute the core of the collection: the method of Mosaic studies (published first in 1959 under the title *Das Mosebild von Heinrich Ewald bis Martin Noth*) and 'Yahweh War and Tribal Confederacy' (published in 1966 and translated into English in 1970). Both are important studies, the first because it described and analysed the methodology of previous works and the second because it challenged the view that the amphictyony was the original element in Israelite religion. The idea of the amphictyony was reviewed again by Smend in 1971, and that too has been included in the present volume. The other essays included are: tradition and history (1978), the Exodus from Egypt (1967), the tribe of Judah and early Isreal (1967), the land not conquered (1983) and the paper on the biblical and historical Elijah read to the Edinburgh Congress (1975). This collection will prove as useful as its companion and the bringing together of these studies is welcomed.

G. H. JONES

SMITH, M.: *Palestinian Parties and Politics that Shaped the Old Testament*. 2nd edition, 1987. Pp. x, 277. (SCM, London. Price: £12.50. ISBN 0 334 02238 X)

This is essentially a reprint of the 1971 edition (reviewed in *B.L.* 1973, p. 44), with a number of minor changes from the 1984 Italian edition. It is however the first British printing of the book and it is to be hoped that it will enjoy a better circulation than did the Columbia University Press edition of 1971. Morton Smith is too well known as a polemicist for anything from his pen to be uncontentious, but if biblical scholars will insist on ignoring the partisan nature of the biblical books then we must expect caustic critics like Smith to be less than kind to us! Most of what Smith writes is like manna from heaven in comparison to the usual pieties of biblical scholarship; it is a fresh breath of rational wind blowing through the dusty cells of biblical scholasticism and SCM are to be congratulated on making available this fine volume to a wider readership. It is a short 150 page book, with massive notes, which argues for the existence of a Yahweh-alone party as the ideological force behind much of the production of the Hebrew Bible. But the syncretistic cult of Yahweh also survived in many ways as may be seen in amulets and magical papyri and contributed to creating an environment which the Yahweh-alone party were able to expand in at a later period. In discussing Ezra and Nehemiah Smith argues for the prior arrival in Jerusalem of Ezra and provides a brilliant treatment of Nehemiah on the model of the Greek local tyrant. He takes his argument about the partisan nature of Jewish religion and society down to the Maccabaean period and provides an appendix savaging Alt's theories about the origins of the Samaritans. Smith's polemical tone will offend many biblical scholars, but speaking personally I prefer his caustic approach which discusses the views of opponents than the more traditional method of marginalizing scholars by ignoring them or dismissing their views in a couple of lines. So two cheers for Smith!

R. P. CARROLL

WEISS, H. (ed.): *The Origins of Cities in Dry-Farming Syria and Mesopotamia in the Third Millennium B.C.* 1986. Pp. 167, incl. figures. (Four Quarter Publishing Co., Guilford, Connecticut. Price: $18.95 plus $4.00 postage and handling. ISBN 0 931500 08 7)

The essays in this volume grew out of a symposium held in Chicago by the American Schools of Oriental Research in 1984 and are concerned with the urbanization of northern Mesopotamia and Iraq, the dry-farming zone which, unlike the irrigated south of Mesopotamia, relied on rainfall. A principal concern is the spread of urbanization from the south to the north and the northern impact of the Uruk culture. After Weiss' introduction come the following papers: D. Sürenhagen, 'The Dry Farming Belt: The Uruk Period and Subsequent Developments' (pp. 7–43); G. M. Schwartz, 'Mortuary Evidence and Social Stratification in the Ninevite V Period' (pp. 45–60); W. Orthmann, 'The Origin of Tell Chuera' (pp. 61–70); H. Weiss, 'The Origins of Tell Leilan and the Conquest of Space in Third Millennium Mesopotamia' (pp. 71–108); B. R. Foster, 'Agriculture and Accountability in Ancient Mesopotamia' (pp. 109–28); P. Michalowski, 'Mental Maps and Ideology: Reflections on Subartu' (pp. 129–56); I. J. Gelb, 'Ebla and Lagash: Environmental Contrast' (pp. 157–67).

J. F. HEALEY

WOOD, L. J.: *A Survey of Israel's History*. Revised and Enlarged Edition by D. O'Brien (Academie Books). 1986. Pp. xv, 416 and 16 pp. of maps. (Zondervan, Grand Rapids, Michigan. Price: $19.95. ISBN 0 310 34770 X)

This is a revised edition of a book first published in 1970 but not noted in the *Book List*. It is primarily intended for conservative evangelical students. The greater part of the text consists of a summary of the narrative books of the Old Testament together with selected archaeological data and historical information about the ancient Near East in as far as these can be made to support the fundamental assumption that the Bible cannot err. All other approaches to the study of the history of Israel are rejected out of hand.

R. N. WHYBRAY

4. TEXT AND VERSIONS

AUFRECHT, W. E.: *A Bibliography of the Job Targumim* (Newsletter for Targumic and Cognate Studies: Supplement 3). 1987. Pp. 13. (Department of Near Eastern Studies, University of Toronto)

Over a hundred items, plus reviews of a number of books specifically dealing with the Job Targums, cover the period 1863–1986. The gap between 1895 and 1944 contrasts sharply with the sustained activity from 1962 on. In the period since then all but ten of the items listed have appeared.

R. P. GORDON

DE AZCARRAGA SERVERT, M. J. (ed.): *Minḥat Šay de Y. S. de Norzi: Profetas Menores (Traducción y anotación crítica)* (Textos y Estudios 'Cardenal Cisneros', 40). 1987. Pp. lxvi, 259. (Instituto 'Arias Montano', Consejo Superior de Investigaciones Cientificas, Madrid. N.p. ISBN 84 00 06474 7; ISSN 0561 3481)

Shelomo Yedidyah Norzi's work *Goder Pereṣ* was completed in 1626 and published, without the Introduction and other matters, in Mantua in 1742–44, under the title *Minḥat Šay* (i.e. 'The offering of Shelomo Yedidyah'). The important *Introduction* was not published until 1819 by Samuel Vita della Volta. The object of Norzi's study was the whole of the Hebrew Bible, its consonantal text and vowel and accent signs as attested in manuscripts and printed editions, and he made use of the Aramaic targums, the Talmud and the midrashim, as well as the philological and exegetical works of medieval Jewish scholars. As the basic Bible text he used the Toledo Codex written in 1277. His concern was above all with the Masorah, and the purpose of his studies (to which he devoted a major part of his life) was to establish the true text of the Bible. His contribution to the study of the biblical text has been described as the most important until the present day (Yeivin). The languages of *Minḥat Šay* are Hebrew and Aramaic, and biblical, talmudic and midrashic quotations and allusions combine with Norzi's own brand of Hebrew to form a kind of mosaic in which the component parts can be difficult to separate out. The book under review is basically an annotated translation of Norzi's notes on the Minor Prophets, as published in Vienna in 1813–15, with some introductory chapters on Norzi's language, sources, style, and personality. Passages from Norzi's *Introduction* are incorporated in full in Spanish translation as appropriate, as are also the parts of *Minḥat Šay* outside the 'twelve' to which Norzi himself refers. Scriptural, talmudic and midrashic quotations and allusions are identified. The origin of masoretic material is traced as far as possible, discrepancies are identified, differences between Ben Asher and Ben Naphtali are collated. The work concludes with a bibliography and three indexes of sources, Hebrew words, and biblical passages. M. J. de Azcarraga Servert's book is an important contribution to the study of Norzi's work, and of the text of the Minor Prophets.

P. WERNBERG-MØLLER

BARTHÉLEMY, D., GOODING, D. W., LUST, J., and TOV, E.: *The Story of David and Goliath: Textual and Literary Criticism* — Papers of a Joint Research Venture (Orbis Biblicus et Orientalis 73). 1986. Pp. vii, 157. (Éditions Universitaires, Fribourg, Vandenhoeck & Ruprecht, Göttingen. Price: Sw.Fr. 39.00 ISBN 3 7278 0372 X, 3 525 53702 6)

Here is textual criticism made exciting! The several parts of this volume are themselves all fine studies, and some quite outstanding; however, the whole is much more than their sum. Two scholars generally more disposed to the Masoretic Text (Barthélemy and Gooding) and two to the Septuagint (Lust and Tov) agreed to prepare independent papers on 1 Sam. 17–18, where the Greek is some 45% shorter than the Hebrew. The papers were circulated, and each prepared responses to which two of the contributors again responded. After a Swiss mountain seminar, each prepared a concluding paper. The initial sympathies are still apparent at the end, despite considerable movement. But the standard of 'play' improves as the 'contest' proceeds. David and Goliath provide the subject matter — but not images of the contributors. Barthélemy writes in French, and the others in English. This little book is a classic statement of respectful but irreconcilable differences over a fascinating problem. The style of project too deserves to be copied in several areas of Biblical studies, where a scholar's peer group is small and internationally scattered. (For another expert treatment of the same passage, see A. Rofé's contribution to *Judaic Perspectives*, reviewed above on p. 22.)

A. G. AULD

BORBONE, P. G., and MANDRACCI, F.: *Concordanze del Testo Siriaco di Osea* (Memorie dell'Accademia delle Scienze di Torino, Classe di Scienze Morali, Storiche e Filologiche, Series v, Volume 11, Fasc. 1–4). 1987. Pp. 191. (Accademia delle Scienze, Torino; available through Dr Borbone: Instituto di Orientalistica, Via S. Ottavio, 20, 10124 Torino, Italy)

This concordance to the Peshitta of Hosea differs in its principles from that by W. Strothmann, K. Johannes and M. Zumpe for the Prophetical Books (reviewed in *B.L.* 1987, p. 40) in several respects: it is based on Gelston's edition in *Vetus Testamentum Syriace* III. 4 (1980), rather than on the London Polyglot and the Urmia editions; it is strictly alphabetical, rather than by root; the entries under each heading are not broken up according to different forms; the number of occurrences is given; variants are included; and the lemmas are considerably longer. The concordance was produced on a Personal Computer (IBM), and in the introduction Borbone gives details of how this was achieved. He has already produced a concordance to Peshitta Obadiah in *Henoch* 9 (1987), pp. 55–96. The design of the estrangelo letters could be improved here and there (especially for *nun*), and the absence of *seyame* is tiresome. But this will be a useful tool.

S. P. BROCK

CHILTON, B. D.: *The Isaiah Targum: Introduction, Translation, Apparatus and Notes* (The Aramaic Bible, vol. 11). 1987. Pp. lvii, 130 (T. and T. Clark, Edinburgh. Price: £22.50. ISBN 0 567 09468 5 (Isaiah); 0 567 09477 4 (series))

The aim of *The Aramaic Bible* project is to put into the hands of the interested reader a book by book translation into English of the ancient Aramaic version known familiarly as the Targum. The increasing interest among scholars and a larger public in the origin and development of early Jewish thought, not least as a backcloth to New Testament writings, has made the translation of the traditionally known Targum into modern English idiom a desideratum. The translation of the Isaiah Targum in this volume adheres to the format of the overall project in presenting the innovative wording of the meturgeman (the scribe who translated the original Hebrew text into Aramaic) in italics while the more straightforward rendering of the Hebrew text is presented in roman types. The Aramaic base text of this translation (B.M. 2211) is that used in the editions of Stenning (1949) and Sperber (1962).Those beginning Targum study will have recourse not only to the translation but also to the explanatory notes which are primarily concerned with the 'theology of the Targum'. The separate apparatus provides more technical information on the Targum and its relation to the Hebrew text. The editor is interested in the leading theological ideas and different levels of meaning contained in the Isaiah Targum and he devotes the first section of his introduction to a discussion of them. Other sections deal with various aspects of Targum studies: formation and historical circumstances, importance for the study of early Judaism and of the New Testament, early citations and manuscripts, editions and translations. To judge by this volume the series promises to be a useful and handsome one.

P. W. COXON

Clark, E. G. (ed.): *Newsletter for Targumic and Cognate Studies*. 14/1. 1987. Pp. 11. (Department of Near Eastern Studies, University of Toronto. ISSN 0704 59005)

Just over fifty items, including five books, are listed in the section dealing with Targum. A somewhat longer list of 'cognate studies', principally dealing with Aramaic, and information on reviews and dissertations are also provided. The editor would doubtless appreciate more information about dissertations completed or in the process of completion. R. P. Gordon

Cox, C. E. (ed.): *VI Congress of the International Organization for Septuagint and Cognate Studies, Jerusalem 1986* (Septuagint and Cognate Studies, 23). 1987. Pp. xxiii, 464. (Scholars Press, Atlanta, Georgia. Price: $22.95 (members' price: $14.95); ISBN 1 55540 171 6. Paperback price: $14.95 (members' price: $9.95); ISBN 1 55540 174 0)

This contains nineteen papers, the majority of which are on either exegesis in the LXX, or translation technique. There is also an introductory essay, surveying the contents, by the editor. The quality of the contributions is generally good, and this is a volume in which anyone with a concern for LXX studies will find much of interest. There are good indices (including biblical passages). S. P. Brock

Cox, C. E.: *Hexaplaric Materials Preserved in the Armenian Version* (Septuagint and Cognate Studies, 21). 1986. Pp. xv, 236. (Scholars Press, Atlanta, Georgia. Price: $12.95 (members price: $9.95); ISBN 1 55540 028 0. Paperback price: $9.95 (members price: $7.95); ISBN 1 55540 029 9)

It has long been recognized that many manuscripts of the Armenian version of the LXX preserve hexaplaric signs. Some indication of these is already to be found in Zohrabian's edition, but hitherto no collection of this important evidence has existed. Cox has thus earned the gratitude of all who work on the LXX for having now made these materials available in an eminently convenient form. Armenian witnesses preserve the hexaplaric signs in a total of 1,462 passages, and in 161 of these they are alone in doing so; the Armenian evidence is especially important for Genesis, Exodus, and I–II Samuel. The information is gathered from 35 manuscripts and is arranged by biblical book. S. P. Brock

Gelston, A.: *The Peshitta of the Twelve Prophets*. 1987. Pp. xxiv, 208. (Clarendon, Oxford. Price: £25.00. ISBN 0 19 826179 9)

This book is the third in a series of monographs produced as a by-product of the work of the Peshitta Project, based at Leiden University, which aims to provide scholars with a critical edition of the Syriac version of the Old Testament. But it goes beyond those produced by Dirksen on the Peshitta of Judges (1972) and Koster on Exodus (1977). Not only does it deal with the transmission of the Peshitta text, but in Part II Gelston goes on to consider the Peshitta of the Twelve as a version of the Hebrew. He provides a detailed, careful comparison with the Masoretic Text, with the Septuagint and with the Targum, and concludes with some remarks on the origins of the Peshitta. The book is a companion volume to Gelston's edition of the Peshitta of the Twelve Minor Prophets (Vol. iii; 4 of *The Old Testament in Syriac*, Leiden, 1980). In fact, to make proper use of the latter, it will be necessary for scholars to have both books side by side. As Gelston explains in his introduction, he has designed the monograph 'as an aid to the critical use of the EDITION of the Dodekapropheton in *Vetus Testamentum Syriace*' (p. xxi). Scholars will be especially interested in the list, provided on page 93, of the thirty places where Gelston thinks that a reading found in the Apparatus is to be preferred to that printed in the basic text of his edition.

For his final remarks on the origins of the Peshitta, Gelston relies heavily on the views of Paul Kahle that it was translated in the first century C.E. for the use of the Jewish community in Adiabene. I have yet to be convinced either that the Peshitta is a Jewish translation or that it can be dated any earlier than the end of the second century C.E. However, Gelston states his conclusions very tentatively and wisely remarks that overall statements on the origin of the Peshitta will be more firmly grounded when the whole of the *Old Testament in Syriac* has been published and made available for scholarly scrutiny.

A. P. HAYMAN

HARRINGTON, D. J., and SALDARINI, A. J.: *Targum Jonathan of the Former Prophets: Introduction, Translation and Notes*. (The Aramaic Bible, vol. 10). 1987. Pp. x, 320. (T. & T. Clark, Edinburgh. Price: £34.95. ISBN 0 567 09467 7)

This first English rendering of the Targum of the Former Prophets (Joshua–2 Kings) is based on Ms. Or. 2210 of the British Museum as edited by A. Sperber. Neither Sperber's apparatus criticus, nor any other Targum manuscript, has been taken into account, Harrington and Saldarini preferring (wisely, in the opinion of this reviewer) to translate the text of a single source because 'the individual manuscripts of what we call *Targum Jonathan* tend almost to constitute separate works'. (Textual criticism in the Judaica field is passing through a revolutionary upheaval, and the ground rules require complete reformulation.) Saldarini has provided a useful summary introduction to the translation technique and religious ideas of the targumists. Harrington, in turn, argues on the basis of the language and of the historical conditions reflected in the exegesis for a second-century C.E. date and Palestinian provenance of the substance of this Targum, although he admits subsequent reworkings which may have continued, partly in Babylonia, until as late as the seventh century.

G. VERMES

HAYWARD, C. T. R.: *The Targum of Jeremiah*. (The Aramaic Bible, vol. 12). 1987. Pp. xviii, 206 (T. & T. Clark, Edinburgh. Price: £29.95. ISBN 0 567 09469 3 (Jeremiah); 0 567 09477 4 (series))

The author translates Sperber's critical text into English, indicating with italics where the text of the Targum is longer than the Masoretic text. The apparatus which is provided consists of variant readings derived from Sperber's apparatus and translated into English. The notes engage with the Masoretic text, other ancient versions, Qumran fragments and a wide range of relevant Jewish literature. Thus the book has no independent text-critical value, but the English translation will be an aid to those who cannot read Sperber's critical Aramaic text or decipher his second apparatus.

The main scholarly value of the book then lies in its concern to set the Targum of Jeremiah in the context of Jewish use and Jewish literature and this is achieved through the notes and the introduction. In the latter Hayward picks out the nine uses of the book of Jeremiah in the synagogue lectionary and looks for evidence that the renderings of the Targum in these *Haftaroth* have been influenced by the corresponding *Torah* lections. He examines early citations from the Targum of Jeremiah in the Babylonian Talmud, in *midrashim*, in the Targum Neofiti and the Fragment Targum, and from this he draws the conclusion that in its Babylonian format the Targum of Jeremiah originated prior to 300 C.E.

Elsewhere, however, he explores the Palestinian origins of the Targum of Jeremiah which he sets 'during, or slightly before, the first century A.D.' (p. 38). The question of Palestinian provenance is also touched on in an inconclusvie section on the language of the Targum of Jeremiah to which is attached a list of Greek loan-words.

Other sections of the introduction consider the periphrastic characteristics of the Targum of Jeremiah, its setting in the wider field of Jewish exegesis and the nature of the theology which it projects. Those whose interests are not so much the text-critical use of the Targum in relation to the Masoretic text or its contribution to the history of exegesis of the Hebrew Bible, but who have a more specialized interest in extra-biblical Jewish studies will welcome the detailed work in this book.

W. McKane

Horn, J.: *Studien zu den Märtyrern des nördlichen Oberägypten I: Märtyreverehrung und Märtyrerlegende im Werke des Schenute — Beiträge zur ältesten ägyptischen Märtyrerüberlieferung* (Göttinger Orientforschungen, IV. Reihe: Ägypten, Band 15). 1986. Pp. xiii, 130. (Otto Harrassowitz, Wiesbaden. Price: DM 40.00. ISBN 3 447 02576 X; ISSN 0340 6342)

Strictly, this work is outside, or at most, marginal to, the interests of the *Book List*. Its main concern is to begin the study of Coptic martyrology through the writings of Shenoute (the outstanding literary figure of the early Coptic church), in confrontation with the 'cults' of two bishops of northern Middle Egypt. However, Horn does devote an excursus to the terms *diatagma* and *prostagma* in the Coptic Bible, with special reference to the LXX (pp. 83–88). Therefore, notice of this latter feature is made here for the convenience of Old Testament scholars who might be interested in these terms in the Greek and Coptic Old Testament.

K. A. Kitchen

Levey, S. H.: *The Targum of Ezekiel Translated with a Critical Introduction, Apparatus, and Notes* (The Aramaic Bible, 13). 1987. Pp. xiii, 145. (T. &. T. Clark, Edinburgh. Price: £22.50. ISBN 0 567 09470 7; 0 567 09477 4 (series))

The purpose of the series is to provide scholars as well as the public with a modern English translation of all the targums transmitted by rabbinic Judaism. The canonical book of Ezekiel, textually difficult, linguistically peculiar, and theologically in some ways out of line and even dangerous in the eyes of orthodox Jewry, has its official targum which in part cannot have originated in response to a need within the main stream of Jewish worship. This targum, apart from having much in common with the rest of Targum Jonathan (such as the general pattern of exegetical techniques and avoidance of anthropomorphisms), has some distinctive features of its own (such as a preoccupation with Merkabah mysticism and absence of any reference to the Messiah). Samson H. Levey, in this annotated translation with a critical apparatus (basically Sperber's) has produced a work which is both interesting in itself, as well as a useful tool in the hands of students of Late Judaism and Early Christianity, and of the literary remains from these periods including, of course, the Qumran documents, especially the Temple Scroll. The translation is preceded by an introduction and followed by a bibliography and ten indexes.

P. Wernberg-Møller

McGregor, L. J.: *The Greek Text of Ezekiel. An Examination of its Homogeneity* (Septuagint and Cognate Studies, 18). 1985. Pp. xv, 296. (Scholars Press, Atlanta, Georgia. Price: $18.25 (members' price $13.95); ISBN 0 89130 902 0. Paperback price: $13.95 (members' price $9.25); ISBN 0 89130 903 9)

It is argued that a good case can be made out for the theory of three translators (chs 1–25, 26–39, 40–48; McGregor places the break between the first and second translator two chapters earlier than did Thackeray), and that the first and third may be identical. There is a good chapter on methodology, and two chapters are devoted to the problem of the *nomina sacra* (for which a new solution is proposed). This is a valuable contribution to the study of Ezekiel LXX.

S. P. Brock

Paramelle, J. with Lucchesi, E.: *Philon d'Alexandrie, Questions sur la Genèse II 1–7; texte grec, version arménienne, parallèles latins* (Cahiers d'Orientalisme, iii). 1984. Pp. 269 and viii plates (Paul Cramer, Geneva)

In a fourteenth-century Greek manuscript (*Vatopedinus* 659), containing a very loosely arranged assortment of much earlier material ('into which the compiler seemed to have tipped his card-index, and indeed his wastepaper basket with all his drafts'), Fr Paramelle had the good fortune to discover several pages excerpted from the lost Greek text of Philo's *Questions on Genesis*, known otherwise from a very literal Armenian translation. The fragments are concerned with Noah's ark. Rather than simply publish them, he opted for a more ambitious project: a critical edition of these chapters of Philo, as closely as one can approach them through the Armenian, the new fragments, and various other remains, notably extensive citations in Ambrose's Latin. But there is far more as well in this magnificently printed and produced volume: a preliminary study of the manuscript, careful studies of the Armenian and Latin texts in question, a number of valuable appendices, and three excellent indices.

N. R. M. de Lange

Perez Castro, F. (ed.): *El Codice de Profetas de El Cairo*, v: *Jeremias* (Textos y Estudios 'Cardenal Cisneros', 37). P. 274. (Instituto 'Arias Montano', Consejo Superior de Investigaciones Cientificas, Madrid. No Price. ISBN 84 00 06474 9; ISSN 0561 3841)

This latest volume in the series of publications containing a critical edition of the Cairo Codex has been prepared by the same team responsible for vol. iv (see *B.L.* 1987, p. 39). For notices of the earlier volumes, see *B.L.* 1983, pp. 42f. and *B.L.* 1985, p. 46.

P. Wernberg-Møller

(*Peshitta*): *The Old Testament in Syriac According to the Peshitta Version*, edited on behalf of the International Organization for the Study of the Old Testament by the Peshitta Institute, Leiden. Part III, fasc. 1: *Isaiah*, prepared by S. P. Brock. 1987. Pp. xxxix, 121. (Brill, Leiden. Price: Fl. 92.00 (*c.* $41.75). ISBN 90 04 07766 9)

The Peshitta of Isaiah is a text for which invaluable groundwork had already been done by G. Diettrich (1905) and L. G. Running (1964), as is acknowledged by the editor in his Introduction. Following the revised rules limiting the manuscripts to be used for the edition (see *B.L.* 1977, p. 38 and 1978, p. 44), eleven, with two families, have been fully used, and are fully described in the Introduction. They are grouped for convenience as follows: (A) the three earliest complete (or nearly complete) MSS, including the Ambrosian which serves as the basic text for the edition (though it is emended when necessary); (B) seven early fragmentary MSS, including 5phl, the London palimpsest, B.L. Add. MS 14,512, the oldest dated biblical manuscript (459/60), of which Dr Brock gives a very full description; (C) a ninth-century family which occasionally shares with 5phl readings that may represent the original Peshiṭta text; (D) a twelfth-century manuscript mostly but not totally of the standard medieval text-type; (E) seven manuscripts representing the latter type, and (F) Lectionary manuscripts. The edition is all one expects of its editor and of the Peshiṭta Institute, among whose staff Mr K. D. Jenner is thanked for much careful help.

R. P. R. MURRAY

PETERS, M. K. H. (ed.): *Bulletin of the International Organization for Septuagint and Cognate Studies*, vol. 19. 1986. Pp. 34. (Copies available through Dr W. Bodine, IOSCS, Treasurer, Dallas Theological Seminary, 3909 Swiss Avenue, Dallas, Texas 75204. Price: $5.00)

The annual Bulletin of the IOSCS (constituted in 1968) contains news of meetings, colloquia, etc., select recent bibliography in LXX, and articles. The present number has a study by S. L. McKenzie of the Hebrew texts of 1 Kings 8 used by the Chronicler and underlying the Old Greek.

S. P. BROCK

PIETERSMA, A.: *The Acts of Phileas Bishop of Thmuis (Including Fragments of the Greek Psalter). P. Chester Beatty* XV *(With a New Edition of P. Bodmer* XX*, and Halkin's Latin Acta). Edited with Introduction, Translation and Commentary*. (Cahiers d'Orientalisme, VII). 1984. Pp. 117, 34 plates. (Patrick Cramer, Genève. Price: not stated)

The Acts of Phileas are preserved fragmentarily in P. Bodmer XX and P. Chester Beatty XV, and complete in a Latin translation. This book provides the first edition of the Chester Beatty fragments (whose text proves to be closer to the Latin than to P. Bodmer), together with a re-edition of the other two texts. The only connection of the two fragmentary Greek manuscripts with biblical studies lies in the fact that they both also contain some LXX Psalms (Rahlfs nos 2113 and 2151; the latter is edited here on pp. 80–83: parts of Pss 1–4).

S. P. BROCK

SOISALON-SOININEN, I.: *Studien zur Septuaginta-Syntax*. Zu seinem 70. Geburtstag am 4. Juni 1987 herausgegeben von Anneli Aejmelaeus und Raija Sollamo (Annales Academiae Scientiarum Fennicae, Ser. B, Tom. 237). 1987. Pp. 224. (Suomalainen Tiedeakatemia, Helsinki. Price: F.Mk. 100.00. ISBN 951 41 0551 6)

To celebrate the seventieth birthday of a distinguished Septuagint scholar two of his former pupils have edited this collection of seventeen of his articles that deal, with only one exception, with the syntax of Septuagint Greek. The four articles in the first section are concerned with methodological issues, twelve articles in the second section are devoted to individual problems ('The Renderings of the Hebrew Relative Clause in the Greek Pentatuech', 'Die Wiedergabe einiger hebräischer Zeitangaben mit der Präposition *b* in der Septuaginta', 'Der Gebrauch des *genetivus absolutus* in der Septuaginta', etc.), while the final article deals with 'Der *infinitivus constructus* mit *l* im Hebräischen'. The author himself has checked over the articles, and the two editors have harmonised their external form, but otherwise the articles appear to have been reprinted without change. The editors have also provided an index of biblical references. In his discussion of methodological issues the author comments on the need to study the syntax of the Septuagint in relation both to the underlying language and to the translation technique of the translators, and he demonstrates the importance of this in his treatment of individual aspects of Septuagint-syntax. All who are concerned with the Septuagint will be grateful to have this collection of Professor Soisalon-Soininen's articles available in this convenient form.

M. A. Knibb

Strothmann, W., assisted by Johannes, K., and Zumpe, M.: *Konkordanz zur syrischen Bibel: Der Pentateuch* (Göttinger Orientforschungen, Series 1, vol. 26). 1986. Pp. xi, 2556 (4 vols). (Otto Harrassowitz, Wiesbaden. Price: DM 340.00. ISBN 3 447 02669 3)

The publication of the Göttingen concordance to the Peshiṭta continues apace, with the listing and typesetting achieved by computer. This section on the Pentateuch follows the same principles and arrangement as that on the Prophets (*B.L.* 1987, p. 40). The great usefulness of this work is impaired by the continued decision to ignore the Leiden critical edition and instead use the Walton and Urmia prints. Thus the list of occurrences of *sēmā* gives no warning that the most ancient manuscript 5bl, available in Genesis and Exodus, nearly everywhere has instead *kespā*, which is probably original (cf MT *kesep*).

M. P. Weitzman

Stulman, L.: *The Other Text of Jeremiah: A reconstruction of the Hebrew Text Underlying the Greek Version of the Prose Sections of Jeremiah with English Translation.* 1986. Pp. v, 171. (University Press of America, Lanham, Maryland. Price: $12.75. ISBN 0 8191 4989 6)

After a brief Introduction and Bibliography (pp. 1–14), Stulman offers in paired lines his Hebrew retroversion of LXX of each passage treated, together with MT; and then in parallel columns an English translation of each with pluses underlined. After 7:1–8:3; 11:1–14; 16:1–15; 18:1–12; 21:1–10; 25:1–14; he deals extensively with chaps 26–29 (MT) and 32–45. Not all the reconstructions will command respect. But this teacher has already discovered that students will find it very useful to have this volume on the desk as they seek to evaluate the often laconic discussion in commentaries and handbooks of the relevance of the shorter Septuagint of Jeremiah.

A. G. Auld

Vermes, G.: *The Dead Sea Scrolls Forty Years On* (The Fourteenth Sacks Lecture, delivered on 20 May 1987). 1987. Pp. 19. (Oxford Centre for Postgraduate Hebrew Studies. Price: £2.00.)

After a short review of the sorts of scrolls found, and progress(?) made in publishing them, Vermes devotes most of his attention to 'the relationship and interaction between textual plurality and unity in the genesis of literary compositions in ancient Judaism'. Examples from Scripture and the War Rule show the same 'elasticity as the overall rule in textual transmission', as is found in subsequent rabbinic literature.

A. G. Auld

Vetus Latina. Die Reste der altlateinischen Bibel, nach Petrus Sabatier neu gesammelt und in Verbindung mit der Heidelberger Akademie der Wissenschaften herausgegeben von der Erzabtei Beuron. 11/2: *Sirach (Ecclesiasticus)*. Herausgegeben von Walter Thiele. 1. Lieferung: Einleitung. 1987. Pp. 1–80. (Verlag Herder, Freiburg im Breisgau. ISBN 3 451 04424 0)

The edition of the Book of Wisdom in the Old Latin has just been completed (see *B.L.* 1987, p. 41), and it is highly appropriate that the same editor should couple with it the edition of Sirach. This first fascicle contains only the first portion of the introduction, devoted to the manuscripts. The sequel will be warmly welcomed by all serious students of the Latin Bible.

J. BARR

Vetus Latina. Die Reste der altlateinischen Bibel nach Petrus Sabatier neu gesammelt und in Verbindung mit der Heidelberger Akademie der Wissenschaften herausgegeben von der Erzabtei Beuron. 12: *Esaias*. Edidit R. Gryson. 1. Lieferung: Introduction and Is. 1, 1–22. 1987. Pp. 80. (Verlag Herder, Freiburg im Breisgau. ISBN 3 451 00439 9).

With the commencement of the Isaiah volume this great edition enters upon the first major book of the Hebrew canon since Genesis was done some decades ago. Of interest to Hebraists will be the fact that for this book it has been possible to utilize the text of the Hebrew University Bible Project, and in addition to refer to variant readings from Qumran, although examples within this first fascicle are few and minor, yet nonetheless striking (cf. 'and' at 1, 16). This volume has been prepared at Louvain, with collaboration with the Vetus Latina Institute. It continues the meticulous and extremely detailed style of scholarship that attaches to the entire series.

J. BARR

WEITZMANN K., and KESSLER, H. L.: *The Cotton Genesis: British Library Codex Cotton Otho B.VI* (The Illustrations in the Manuscripts of the Septuagint, 1: Genesis). 1986. Pp. xiii, 250; VIII (colour) and 539 plates. (Princeton University Press, New Jersey. Price: £94.20. ISBN 0 691 04031 1)

This famous illuminated manuscript ('D' in the Göttingen Septuagint), probably of the late fifth century, suffered irreparable damage by fire in 1731. In this meticulous study, begun by Weitzmann in 1947 but interrupted by his work at St Catherine's Monastery, Mount Sinai, and then taken up again in 1979 in conjunction with Kessler, the authors discuss the early history and original structure of the codex, and then go on to attempt to reconstruct the contents of the illustrations (now either very damaged or lost) with the help of other witnesses to the same 'picture recension'. The authors are only interested in the LXX text in so far as considerations of space in its reconstructed form can indicate the number of illustrations missing on lost folios. Thus, in a series of drawings the LXX text is also reconstructed, with the help of Grabe's collation (made before the fire). I have noticed a few minor inaccuracies in the reconstructed text and so it should not (nor was it meant to) be used for text-critical purposes.

S. P. BROCK

WEVERS, J. W., with the assistance of QUAST, U. (eds): *Septuaginta. Vetus Testamentum Graece Auctoritate Academiae Scientiarum Gottingensis editum.* Vol. II, 2: *Leviticus*. 1986. Pp. 328. (Vandenhoeck & Ruprecht, Göttingen. Price: DM 179.00 (sub. price: DM 156.00); ISBN 3 525 53444 2)

This follows on Professor Wevers' editions of Genesis, Numbers and Deuteronomy LXX (see *B.L.* 1975, pp. 39–40; 1978, pp. 45–46; 1983, p. 44).

The introduction enumerates the textual materials and lists the manuscript groupings; detailed discussion of the textual history is reserved for a separate volume, MSU XIX, 1986 (see below). Text and apparatus are set out with the succinctness and clarity for which the Göttingen edition is justly renowned. There are two appendices, of which the first deals with Orthographica and Grammatica, while the second lists passages where the collations in Brooke-McLean are incorrect.

S. P. BROCK

WEVERS, J. W.: *Text History of the Greek Leviticus* (Mitteilungen des Septuaginta-Unternehmens (MSU), XIX: Abhandlungen der Akademie der Wissenschaften in Göttingen, Phil.-Hist. Klasse, III, 155). 1986. Pp. 136. (Vandenhoeck & Ruprecht, Göttingen. Price: DM 80.00. ISBN 3 525 82440 8)

This detailed monograph follows the pattern of previous volumes in the series (see *B.L.* 1976, p. 33; 1979, p. 50; 1984, pp. 47–8). There are four chapters, dealing with: The Hexaplaric Recension, The Byzantine Text, The Texts of A and B, and The Critical Text. The last chapter (which is the longest) is especially instructive. The materials are set out with clarity and ample use is made of lists. There is an index of passages cited.

S. P. BROCK

5. EXEGESIS AND MODERN TRANSLATIONS

ACHTEMEIER, E. R.: *Jeremiah* (Knox Preaching Guides). 1987. Pp. 114. (John Knox Press, Atlanta. Price: $7.95. ISBN 0 8042 3222 9)

This volume in a popular series of commentaries designed for preachers rests on the best contemporary scholarship, but selects material according to its theological and homiletical interest. It covers the entire book of Jeremiah in outline, but deals in more detail with only some sections of it. The Foreign Nation prophecies of chapters 46–51, for example, are treated only in a very brief way. Overall the book is excellently done, contrasting with the very large commentaries on Jeremiah that have recently appeared, and contains some interesting illustrative material to assist the preacher. It manages to avoid being simply a compressed version of the larger commentaries and should encourage preachers and teachers to turn to the less familiar biblical books in their work.

R. E. CLEMENTS

ACHTEMEIER, E.: *Nahum — Malachi* (Intepretation. A Bible Commentary for Teaching and Preaching). 1986. Pp. x, 201. (John Knox Press, Atlanta. Price: $17.95. ISBN 0 8042 3129 X)

The editors state that the series is aimed at the 'teacher' and the 'preacher' and for such the method is to bring 'an understanding of what the text says into dialogue with the critical questions and problems of contemporary life and faith'. It takes seriously 'the hermeneutical responsibility for the contemporary meaning and significance of the biblical text'. If this need not put the critical faculties on red alert, it is enough to set the amber hazard lights flashing. For, paradoxically, it is the zealous and scholarly exploration of the text in its historical context (including the whole history of its emergence into its final form) which most surely releases its contemporary relevance. Attempts to short-circuit this process in the name of 'devotion' or 'relevance' tend to usher in the subjective. The biblical text is called on to support the tradition of the expositor rather than standing over against that tradition in judgement.

However, if anyone can reduce the risks while achieving the aims of the editors it is Elizabeth Achtemeier. This commentary is a fine blend of scholarship and pertinent, thought-provoking reflection on the text. For good measure the author writes in clear and elegant English style, an achievement rare enough among biblical scholars to warrant appreciative comment. There should be some interesting, provocative and well-informed lessons and sermons on these books by those wise enough to read this commentary.

Achtemeier does the best anyone can with Nahum. Will any of us ever have the courage to admit in a popular commentary that the book really is rather a disgrace to the two religious communities of whose canonical Scriptures it forms so unwelcome a part?

R. A. MASON

AULD, A. G.: *Yoshua-ki, Shishi-ki, Rutsu-ki*. Translated by K. Ono. 1987. Pp. 464. (Shinkyō Shuppan-sha, Tokyo. Price: ¥2,800)

This is a Japanese translation of *Joshua, Judges and Ruth* (The Daily Study Bible: Old Testament, 1984). (See *B.L.* 1985, p. 48)

K. K. SACON

BALDWIN, J. G.: *The Message of Genesis 12–50: From Abraham to Joseph* (The Bible Speaks Today). 1986. Pp. 224. (Inter-Varsity Press, Leicester. Price £4.50. ISBN 0 85110 759 1)

This is a devotional commentary of a conservative cast which sees the patriarchal stories as an epitome of the Christian gospel. There is some polemic directed at upholding the historicity of the narratives and the experience of the patriarchs tends to be fitted into the pattern of evangelical piety. But the exegesis is carefully and sensitively done and the sheer humanness of the biblical characters is vividly brought out, though one would have welcomed a keener eye for the ironies, theological as well as situational, in which the Genesis story-teller from time to time indulges. The grace of God in action does not always make a pretty sight when we are confronted (as in chapter 33) with a forgiving Esau being left out; and a dash of irony is needed to make it bearable.

J. C. L. GIBSON

BARKER, K. L. (ed.): *The Making of a Contemporary Translation: The purpose and method of the New International Version*. 1987. Pp. 222. (Hodder and Stoughton, London, for the International Bible Society. Price: £7.95. ISBN 0 340 40263 6)

This book contains fourteen essays on the problems faced by the translators of the NIV, the new knowledge and materials available to them, and some specific *cruces*. The titles indicate the scope of the essays: 'The Importance of literary style in Bible Translation Today' (C. D. Linton); 'The Footnoting System' (B. L. Goddard); 'How the Hebrew and Aramaic Old Testament Text was Established' (E. S. Kallard); 'The Rationale for an Eclectic New Testament Text' (R. Earle); 'Why Hebrew *She'ol* was translated "Grave"' (R. L. Harris); 'When the Spirit was Poetic' (J. H. Stek); 'Translation Problems in Psalms 2 and 4' (B. K. Waltke); 'How the NIV made Use of New Light on the Hebrew Text' (L. L. Walker); '*YHWH SABAOTH*: "The Lord Almighty"' (K. L. Barker); 'Old Testament Quotations in the New Testament' (R. F. Youngblood); 'The One and Only Son' (R. N. Longenecker); 'When "Literal" is not "Accurate"' (H. M. Wolf); 'Anglicising the NIV' (D. J. Wiseman); 'Isn't the King James Version Good Enough?

(The KJV and the NIV Compared)' (E. H. Palmer). N. D. Hill contributes a brief 'In memoriam' tribute to E. H. Palmer to whom the book is dedicated. The essays provide not only a useful companion to the NIV, but much valuable information about the problems of Bible translation today.

G. W. ANDERSON

BARSOTTI, D.: *Meditazione sul Libro di Giuditta* (Collana Bibbia e Liturgia, 29). 1985. Pp. 142. (Queriniana, Brescia. Price: Lire 10,000)

The format of these *Meditazione* — as of the series, to which this is the author's twentieth contribution — comprises a ten-page introduction to contents, authorship, meaning, etc., followed by the text divided into twenty-six sections, accompanied by comments which may be literary, historical or aesthetic, but always end on a homiletic note. In short, it is a bible-reading aid. Judith is presented as a book of apocalyptic character which anticipates the messianic era, and God's victory over enemies. It is thus presented, sympathetically, as a parable of Israel's history and hopes, though even so somewhat in contrast, both generally and in particular, to an essentially non-apocalyptic Christianity.

P. R. DAVIES

BECKER, J.: *1 Chronik* (Die Neue Echter Bibel: Kommentar zum Alten Testament mit der Einheitsübersetzung, Lfg. 18). 1986. Pp. 120. (Echter Verlag, Würzburg. Price: DM 28.00; sub. price: DM 24.00. ISBN 3 429 01038 1)

The firmly established format, purpose and level of this series (cf. *B.L.* 1982, p. 51) mean that Becker can do little more than state his opinion on major issues in the brief introduction and the sparse running commentary. He is undecided about the relationship of Chronicles to Ezra and Nehemiah, but believes that Ezra 1–6, at least, belongs with the former. He doubts whether the Chronicler had access to any extra-Biblical sources (the source citations are 'fictitious') and is drawn towards T. Willi's understanding of *Die Chronik als Auslegung*. Strangely, however, he then rejects any literary-critical division of the text whatever (hardly compatible with Willi's view) and in the commentary he defends the unity of 1 Chronicles throughout chapters 1–9, and even 15–16 and 23–27. He suggests that the Chronicler's primary concern was with a proper understanding of Israel's identity and strongly approves of R. Mosis's interpretation of the narrative in terms of paradigmatic periods. By and large, readers will find here a fair cross-section of current scholarly opinions.

H. G. M. WILLIAMSON

BORRET, M. (ed.): *ORIGENE: Homélies sur l'Exode — Texte latin. introduction, traduction et notes* (Sources Chrétiennes, 321). 1985. Pp. 485. [Cerf, Paris. Price: Fr. 267.00. ISBN 2 204 02456 6, ISSN 0750 1978)

Thirteen homilies by Origen on Exodus have come down to us, together with his other homilies on the Hexateuch, translated into Latin by Rufinus at the beginning of the fifth century. The Latin text was definitively edited by W. A. Baehrens in the so-called Berlin Corpus of the Greek fathers in 1920. The homilies were translated from Latin into French by Joseph Fortier in 1947 as vol. 16 of the Sources Chrétiennes, when it was a more popular series presenting French translations without the original text. More recently, they were translated into English, together with the homilies on genesis, by Ronald E. Heine in 1982 for the series The Fathers of the Church. Now they have been reissued in the Sources Chrétiennes in a new French translation and accompanied by Baehrens's text and by brief notes, aimed as often at heightening the reader's appreciation of the biblical text as at clarifying Origen's work as an expositor. The readership envisaged is apparently more pious than academic, and the works referred to are virtually all in French, and rather elderly. Three useful indexes complete the volume.

N. R. M. DE LANGE

BRAUN, R. L.: *1 Chronicles* (Word Biblical Commentary). 1986. Pp. xlvi, 312. (Word Books, Waco, Texas. Price: $22.95. ISBN 0 8499 0213 4)

Braun follows the by-now well established pattern of this commentary series: an extended introduction and bibliography, followed by the commentary itself, here divided into forty-four sections, each with translation, textual notes (fuller and more helpful than in some volumes), 'form, structure and setting', verse by verse comment and an overall explanation. The view of Williamson and others, that Chronicles should be seen somewhat apart from Ezra-Nehemiah, is followed, with a first edition probably dating from the fifth century and the final form from the fourth. Various theological themes are identified, with particular emphasis on the Chronicler's view of Solomon. (This is slightly unexpected, as the main presentation of Solomon comes in 2 Chronicles, which is to be handled by a different author.) In the commentary itself particularly helpful insights are provided into the structure and function of the genealogies. This volume can certainly be recommended as a helpful addition to the steadily growing literature on this once neglected biblical book.

R. J. COGGINS

BUBER, M. with ROSENZWEIG, F: *Die Schriftwerke* (Die Schrift verdeutscht, 4), 6. Auflage der neubearbeiteten Ausgabe von 1962. With a supplement: *Zur Verdeutschung des letzten Bandes der Schrift*. 1986. Pp. 701, 26. (Verlag Lambert Schneider, Heidelberg. Price: DM 48.00. ISBN 3 7953 0183 1)

The main work is a further reprint of Buber's translation of the Writings, final section of the Hebrew Scriptures. For other volumes in more recent years see *B.L.* 1979, pp. 51–52; 1983, p. 46; and 1986, p. 50. The Psalms (*Preisungen*) were separately published in 1982, with an inserted supplement on their translation; both are now repeated in this new publication. The new supplement is in four sections: Psalms, Proverbs, Job, and Final Remarks.

A. G. AULD

DAVIDSON, R.: *Eremiya-sho, Aika*. Translated by S. Arai and A. Katoh. 1987. Pp. 582. (Shinyō Shuppan-sha, Tokyo. Price: ¥3,800)

This is a Japanese translation of *Jeremiah*, Volume 1, volume 2 and *Lamentations* (The Daily Study Bible: Old Testament, 1983 and 1986). (See *B.L.* 1984, p. 51 and 1987, p. 46.)

K. K. SACON

FOX, E.: *Now These Are The Names: A New English Rendition of the Book of Exodus*. 1986. Pp. xxxvii, 230. (Schocken Books, New York. Price: $16.95. ISBN 0 8052 4020 9)

Employing the 'Rhetorical' translation method developed by Buber and Rosenzweig, the author seeks to reproduce as faithfully as possible such features of the Hebrew text as repetition, allusion, plays on words, alliteration. Hence his description of his task as 'rendition' rather than simply 'translation'. The approach and method are explained in a Preface, which is followed by brief treatments of such matters as the name of God and its translation, the pronunciation of Hebrew names, and a longer introduction to the structure of the book of Exodus. The text of Exodus is subdivided into six subsections each of which is prefaced with a brief introduction. The notes which accompany the 'rendition' are largely concerned with literary features of the text. Comment on matters such as documentary sources and history are largely avoided or kept to a minimum. This is a very helpful work, and will prove especially useful for introducing students to the Hebrew text of Exodus.

E. W. NICHOLSON

GAEBELEIN, F. E. (gen. ed.): *The Expositor's Bible Commentary*. Vol. VI: *Isaiah–Ezekiel*. 1986. Pp. xvi, 996. (Zondervan, Grand Rapids, Michigan. Price: $29.95. ISBN 0 310 36480 9)

This work is appearing in twelve volumes: Vol. I (Introductory Articles) was published in 1979; six volumes cover the Old Testament and five the New Testament. The basic text is the New International Version, which is reproduced in full. In this volume Isaiah is expounded by G. W. Grogan, Jeremiah by C. L. Feinberg, Lamentations by the late H. L. Ellison, Ezekiel by R. H. Alexander. The viewpoint is conservative; due account is taken of other perspectives. The composition of all Isaiah is dated in the late eighth century B.C., but chapters 40–66 are expounded against the background of the sixth century: a 'prophecy may be given in one historical era and fulfilled in another' (p. 100). Ezekiel is interpreted with the aid of a millenarian hermeneutic which requires the visionary temple and its services of chapters 40–48 to be viewed as an order to be actualized on earth at a time yet future to us. The commentator on Isaiah goes a long way with this hermeneutic, but cannot accept 'the setting up of a temple and a sacrificial system again after Christ has made the final sacrifice' (p. 14). The short treatment of Lamentations, as one might expect, is good; so is the section on Jeremiah.

F. F. BRUCE

GOSLINGA, C. J.: *Joshua, Judges, Ruth* (Bible Student's Commentary). Translated by R. Togtman. 1986. Pp. 558. (Zondervan, Grand Rapids, Michigan. Price: $24.95. ISBN 0 310 45280 5)

This is another volume in the series of commentaries originally in Dutch: *Korte Verklarung der Heilige Schrift*. The Dutch commentaries, originally published in 1927 (Joshua) and 1933–38 (Judges and Ruth), both ran to third (revised) editions in 1955 and 1966: the English translation is based on these. The English biblical text printed is the New International Version with some, not many, footnotes on the original Hebrew. The commentary is explicitly aimed at lay readers — especially conservatives, for the conservative stance is often fiercely polemical: Goslinga accepts that forty years is sometimes 'only approximately accurate', although one should not 'rashly underestimate the chronological value of numbers in Scripture'. Indeed it is determinedly conservative: the Lord punishes Jephthah's 'thoughtless boast' by 'causing his daughter to be the first person . . . to meet him'. Sometimes commentary is only paraphrase of the biblical text. But much useful material is collected: it should prove useful, especially for conservatives.

J. G. SNAITH

Gross, G.: *Tobit; Judit* (Die Neue Echter Bibel: Kommentar zum Alten Testament mit der Einheitsübersetzung). 1987. Pp. 124. (Echter Verlag, Würzburg. Price: DM 28.00; subscription price: DM 24.00. ISBN 3 429 01096 9)

The latest addition to this series provides a helpful semi-popular commentary on the *Einheitsübersetzung* of the books of Tobit and Judith. The issues raised by these books are sensibly handled in the brief introductions. Gross favours the view that Tobit was composed in Alexandria and was specifically directed at the Diaspora. The rebellion against Artaxerxes III Ochus may provide the background to Judith, but the work is to be dated about 150 B.C. There is useful discussion of the literary character of both works and of their theological significance, while the bibliographies offer more than might be expected in comparable English publications.

M. A. Knibb

Gutierrez, G.: *Job: Parler de Dieu a partir de la souffrance de L'innocent.* 1987. Pp. 174. Cerf, Paris. Price: Fr. 98.00. ISBN 2 204 02680 8)

This is a French translation of a Spanish original, published in Lima in 1986, where the emphasis of the title was on innocent suffering with 'a reflection on the book of Job' forming the sub-title. Professor Gutierrez is best known as the pioneer in the area of Liberation Theology and he is naturally very much aware of his Peruvian scene. Job fits into that scene, first appearing passive, but then militantly rebellious, shaking his fist, as it were, at God and man alike. The work does not tackle any critical questions relating to the Book of Job. Instead, it tends to paraphrase the text and examine the emotions and the theology expressed. The author sees both in Job and in the contemporary situation the positing of an 'either . . . or'. One can have a predetermined concept of a God who operates almost mechanically in accord with inexorable rules or one can emphasize the free initiative of his love. The one approach leads to desperation or cynicism, whilst the other opens the way to a prophetic view of human life and the possibility of a deepening religious consciousness.

R. J. Hammer

Hermisson, H.-J.: *Deuterojesaja 45, 8–25* (Biblischer Kommentar, Altes Testament, xi,7). 1987. Pp. 80. (Neukirchener, Neukirchen–Vluyn. Price: DM 26.80; sub. price: DM 19.80. ISBN 3 7887 1258 9)

The necessarily abrupt conclusion of K. Elliger's commentary on Second Isaiah at 45:7 was noted in *B.L.* 1979, p. 52. Hermisson, in this first fascicle of the renewed commentary, handles vv. 8, 9–13, 14–17, 18–25 in customary format and detail. His text-critical independence of his predecessor is clear from the different handling of vv. 11 and 13, on which Elliger had left anticipatory notes (xi,6, pp. 526, 528).

A. G. Auld

Hiebert, T.: *God of my Victory. The Ancient Hymn in Habakkuk 3* (Harvard Semitic Monographs 38). 1986. Pp. xii, 205. (Scholars Press, Atlanta, Georgia. Price: $16.95. ISBN 1 55540 077 9)

A study of Hab. 3 using a reconstructed text based, in part, on the versions and owing much to the school of F. M. Cross and D. N. Freedman. Against common opinion, Hiebert argues strongly that this chapter is a victory hymn which eventually was attached to Hab. 1–2. Hiebert has solved some but by no means all of the textual and philological difficulties.

W. G. E. Watson

HOLMGREN, F. C.: *Israel Alive Again. A Commentary on the Books of Ezra and Nehemiah* (International Theological Commentary). 1987. Pp. xviii, 162. (Eerdmans, Grand Rapids; Handsel Press, Edinburgh. Price: £4.95. ISBN 0 8028 0259 1 [Eerdmans]; 0 905312 67 8 [Handsel])

Given the aims of this series, expressed by the editors as 'the Old Testament alive in the Church', this commentary must be counted quite a success. Its scholarship is precise and up-to-date, it addresses non-specialist readers agreeably in an accessible style, and it draws out theological elements of the text in an intelligent if somewhat conventional fashion. If it has a fault, it is that the author tends to accept the narrator's point of view at its face value — which is asking a lot of a modern reader, especially when it comes to the memoirs of the remarkable but eccentric character Nehemiah, or over the mixed marriages question ('The ideal of openness to others may not always be an option' (p. 85)). Nevertheless, there is sensitivity here to the theological dialectic set up by the narrative, as when the comment made on Ezra 2 is that 'a community that gives no attention to the preservation of its traditions may lose its character . . . But a community that focuses too much on its particularity may also suffer loss by becoming . . . exclusivistic' (p. 15).

D. J. A. CLINES

JACOB, E.: *Esaïe 1–12* (Commentaire de l'Ancien Testament, VIIIa). 1987. Pp. 175. (Labor et Fides, Geneva. Price: SwFr 37.00. ISBN 2 8309 0083 9)

This well-known series extends now over many years, and it is also to E. Jacob that we owe the section on Hosea in the volume (1965) devoted to the first six of the minor prophets (cf. *B.L.* 1967, p. 22; *Bible Bibliog.*, p. 22). Like other volumes in the series, this is a concise and readable work, and it would appear, though this is not stated precisely, that the whole book of Isaiah is to be treated by Jacob. As might be expected, the commentary shows wide knowledge of the literature, and is rich in theological comment; while textual discussion is kept short, there is evident awareness of the many problems which the text of Isaiah raises. Yet there is some haphazardness in the bibliographical references. In such a commentary, we might well expect that foreign language works would only occasionally be mentioned; that is not the case, though some of those included are either very slight or somewhat remote. On the other hand, for example, while R. P. Carroll's somewhat inaccessible article on dissonance theory of 1977 is included, I can find no reference to *When Prophecy Failed* (1979); and the detailed reading list to chapter 3 contains no mention of K. Nielsen's monograph *Yahweh as Prosecutor and Judge* (1978). It may be hoped that the further volumes of the commentary will not be too long delayed.

P. R. ACKROYD

Jeremjas Bog. Det gamle testamente i ny oversættelse. 1987. Pp. 172. (Det danske Bibelselskab, Copenhagen. Price: D.Kr. 95.00. ISBN 87 7523 229 4)

This year, the Danish Bible Society has released one volume in the series of trial translations of the Old Testament (see *B.L.* 1987, pp. 54–55), the Book of Jeremiah. It is translated by scholars connected with the department of Old Testament Studies at the University of Aarhus, and edited by S. Holm-Nielsen, B. Ejrnæs, and K. Jeppesen. On pp. 165–72 the deviations from the massoretic consonantal text are listed.

K. JEPPESEN

KEIL, C. F.: *Leviticus, Numeri und Deuteronomium* (Theologische Verlagsgemeinschaft). 1987. Pp. 610. (Brunnen Verlag, Giessen and Basel. Price: DM 98.00. ISBN 3 7655 9206 4)

This is a further volume in a series of reprints of older commentaries of which two (Delitzsch on Proverbs and Keil on the Minor Prophets) have already been noted in *B.L.* 1987, pp. 46 and 51. This volume, a reprint of the second edition of 1870, is a good example of German conservative scholarship of that period, and reflects Keil's view of the unity of the Pentateuch.

R. N. WHYBRAY

KILIAN, R.: *Jesaja 1–12* (Die Neue Echter Bibel: Kommentar zum Alten Testament mit der Einheitsübersetzung, Lfg. 17). 1986. Pp. 93. (Echter Verlag, Wüzburg. Price: DM 24.00; subscription price: DM 19.80. ISBN 3 429 01041 1)

The earlier commentary series, of which the present one is a replacement, is well-known. Of this new series, three issues were reviewed in *B.L.* 1987 (see pp. 43, 48). The companion New Testament series, also in progress, is noted at the back of this fascicle. No indication appears of the number of parts designed to cover the whole book of Isaiah which R. Kilian has undertaken. It offers the text of the Einheitsübersetzung, printed continuously, with comments, section by section — not sufficiently clearly printed so that the start of a new section is immediately observable — and with an occasional excursus (here on Immanuel). The commentary is preceded by a short introduction, mainly on message and structure, and a two-page bibliography. If, as we might expect in a series intended for the general reader, much of what is said is more or less traditional, there is in fact some very careful and critical consideration of accepted conclusions, and useful and positive assessment of the relationship between earlier and later elements in the text. There is a helpful stress on the actuality of the biblical text for its later readers.

P. R. ACKROYD

KOCH, K.: *Daniel (1,1–21)* (Biblisches Kommentar: Altes Testament, Band XXII, 1). 1986. Pp. 80. (Neukirchener, Neukirchen-Vluyn. Price: DM 26.80; subscription price: DM 19.80. ISBN 3 7887 0788 7)

Koch deserves a reputation for wide interests and novel approaches, both admirably suited to the exegesis of Daniel. The quality of discussion is a little uneven. For example, on the *Form* of Dan. 1:1–21, he utilizes 'signified', 'signifier' and 'macrosyntax' to reveal that the chapter on one level is a narrative which has two actants and three scenes, while another, non-narrative, level introduces a different actant, God; on *Gattung* he suggests that chapter 1 is neither wholly court-tale nor midrash, but *Ergänzungstext* on certain prophetic passages, e.g. Jer. 39:1, Isa. 39:7. The first conclusion adds nothing new, the second is simply confusing. Again, on the chronology of 1:1, that the authors of Daniel did not regard the books of Kings as canonical, though it seems they did Chronicles, is an unnecessary, even frivolous, inference from a sound analysis of the source-data. On the other hand, Koch's argument that chapter 1 was translated from Aramaic but at the same time expanded as an introduction to chapters 2–6 is entirely cogent (although his ingenuity can offer no reason why the translator desisted at 2:4!). Background details is copious; we get over five pages on √*mlk* and its connotations (rather unnecessary), and a good deal of information on Chaldean and Magian manticism (necessary and very useful). On this evidence, it is going to be a valuable commentary, but even more, an interesting one. And very long.

P. R. DAVIES

LARCHER, C.: *Le Livre de la Sagesse ou La Sagesse de Salomon*, volume 3 (Études Bibliques, Nouvelle Série 5). 1985. Pp. 459. (Gabalda, Paris. Price: Fr. 456.00. ISBN 2 85021 016 1)

This third volume brings to an end Larcher's monumental and magisterial commentary on Wisdom, and forms a fitting and brilliant completion to the life's work of this great scholar. The book covers the latter part of Wisdom, chapters 11:1 to 19:22, and offers us the author's own translation of the Greek text divided into appropriate units, followed by a detailed analysis of each verse. Problems of text, language, exegesis, and history are clearly explained in detail, and there is a wealth of references to relevant illustrative material in Hellenistic and Rabbinic sources. The author's intimate and profound knowledge of the text and his penetrating exposition of its meaning make this commentary in many respects a model of its kind, and essential reading for all students of post-biblical Judaism in general and of Wisdom in particular.

C. T. R. HAYWARD

MAARSINGH, B.: *Numbers: A Practical Commentary* (Text and Interpretation, translated by J. Vriend). 1987. Pp. vi, 122. (Eerdmans, Grand Rapids, Michigan. Price: $6.95. ISBN 0 8028 0104 8)

For earlier volumes in this series of popular commentaries translated from the Dutch see *B.L.* 1987, pp. 52 and 55. Here the meaning of the text is summarized and explained carefully, but with scarcely a hint of the historical problems which exist or the motives of the writers. The numerous references to the Targum of Pseudo-Jonathan will, however, provide some insight into Jewish biblical interpretation.

G. I. DAVIES

MOREL, C. (ed.): *GRÉGOIRE LE GRAND: Homélies sur Ézéchiel. Tome I — Texte latin, introduction, traduction et notes* (Sources Chrétiennes, 327). 1986. Pp. 541. (Cerf, Paris. Price: Fr. 216.00. ISBN 2 204 02584 4, ISSN 0750 1978)

Delivered in swift succession under the threat of the Lombard march on Rome in 593, Gregory's homilies on Ezekiel are a masterpiece of imaginative interpretation. There are twelve in this first volume, and they cover Ezekiel 1:1–4:3. The Latin text, apart from one or two minor points, is that of Marcus Adriaen in his CCL edition of 1971; the introduction and translation are brisk and vivid. Book II (ten homilies on the vision of the temple in Ezekiel 40) is in preparation.

N. R. M. DE LANGE

NAUTIN, P., and M.-T.: *ORIGÈNE: Homélies sur Samuel — Edition critique, introduction, traduction et notes* (Sources Chrétiennes, 328). 1986. Pp. 485. Cerf, Paris. Price: Fr. 156.00. ISBN 2 204 02587 9, ISSN 0750 1978)

Apart from a substantial series of homilies on Jeremiah, only one of Origen's once numerous homilies has come down to us in Greek. It concerns the story of the Witch of Endor in 1 Samuel 28, and it is of considerable interest both as a specimen of early Christian preaching and as an attempt to grapple with a famous biblical problem. Pierre Nautin had already given us a revised Greek text in his new edition of Erich Klostermann's 1901 Berlin Corpus text, published in 1983, and incorporating the evidence of a Toura papyrus discovered in 1942. Now he has added a French translation with a clear and useful introduction and brief annotations, as well as the other remains of Origen's preaching on 1 Samuel, namely a Latin translation of a homily on the story of Hannah that opens the book (Marie-Thérèse Nautin argues strenuously that the translator is Rufinus) and Greek crumbs from four more homilies, one of them a second homily on the Witch. The whole is a worthy supplement to Pierre Nautin's two S.C. volumes of the homilies on Jeremiah (to which it also offers several pages of addenda and corrigenda).

N. R. M. de Lange

Neri, U.: *Biblia. I libri della Bibbia interpretati dalla grande Tradizione.* AT 1: *Genesi.* 1986. Pp. cxlvi, 662. (Gribaudi, Torino. Price: Lire 90,000)

This modern version of the venerable genre of the catena brings together excerpts from representatives of a wide spectrum of christian tradition: from the Greek Fathers, Origen, Cyril of Alexandria and Procopius; from the Syriac, Ephrem, Narsai and Isho'dad of Merv; from the Latin, Ambrose, Augustine and Bede; from the Medieval west, Rupert of Deutz and Hugh of St Cher; from the Reformers, Luther and Calvin; and from modern commentators, Clamer, von Rad and Zimmerli. For the lemmata the Italian version produced under the auspices of the Conferenza Episcopale Italiana (1971) is used, and the main variants of the ancient versions and of the targumim are also provided. Further volumes are in preparation. The series is intended for a wide readership, and the present volume succeeds in bringing together a variety of materials, most of which are not of easy access to the non-specialist.

S. P. Brock

Nielsen, E.: *Første Mosebog fortolket.* 1987. Pp. 368. (Det danske Bibelselskab, Copenhagen. Price: D.Kr. 245.00. ISBN 87 7523 213 8)

In the Danish Bible Society's series of commentaries on the Old Testament (see *B.L.* 1985, p. 63, 1987, p. 50) E. Nielsen has published a well written and informative commentary on the Book of Genesis. Though it is a popular commentary, it provides a short, but adequate introduction to the documentary hypothesis, the redactional problems, as well as the theological aspects of the book; the chapters about 'The Books of Moses and Moses' and 'The real authors of Genesis' are especially to be emphasized. The commentary is divided into four parts: The creation of the world and the earliest history of mankind (1:1–11:26), the story of Abraham (11:27–25:18), the story of Jacob (25:19–36:43), and the story about Joseph and his brothers (37:1–50:26).

K. Jeppesen

Ogden, G. S., Deutsch, R. R.: *A Promise of Hope, A Call to Obedience: A Commentary on the Books of Joel and Malachi* (International Theological Commentary). 1987. Pp. x, 120. (Handsel, Edinburgh; Eerdmans, Grand Rapids, Michigan. Price: £4.95. ISBN 0 905312 70 8; 0 8028 0093 9)

Both prophetic books are placed in the post-exilic period; both illuminate in some measure the diversity of that period's thought. If at times the analysis of Joel may be thought too literary, particularly in its view of passages found in other prophetic books as being 'quotations' by Joel, there is nevertheless much sensible comment and a useful understanding of the use by these books of old forms in new ways. Surprisingly, the discussion of *'ur* in Joel (p. 43) fails to note its important appearances in 2 Chron. 36.22/Ezra 1.1 (and 5), and in Isa. 45.13. (Granted the limited space, both studies make useful contributions.

P. R. Ackroyd

OLOFSSON, S.: *Guds Ord och människors språk: En bok om bibelöversättning*. 1986. Pp. 199. (EFS förlaget, Uppsala. ISBN 91 7080 721 3)

It is already evident both from the new Swedish translation of the New Testament and from those portions of the Old Testament which have appeared that the task has been and is being carried out with exemplary thoroughness and literary sensitivity. In this book Staffan Olofssón, who has been one of the Swedish translators, discusses, with carefully selected examples, the factors of which account must be taken in the making of an idiomatic translation. The contrast between a more literal and an idiomatic rendering is brought out by comparisons between the 1917 Swedish bible and the new translation, notably in Ruth 2:1–13; but reference is also made to some of the ancient versions, Luther's Bible, and the like. One interesting example is based on the assumption that (God being an Englishman) the NEB is the original text. Ruth 2:1–3 (NEB) is then translated into Swedish literally, less literally, and idiomatically. There are discussions of the varying styles in biblical texts, the character of New Testament Greek, the rendering of idiomatic expressions and of special biblical terms. An abundance of data and of illustrative material is supplied. The conclusion of most of the arguments is that a strictly literal translation is an impossibility. The book contains a good bibliography and a subject and Scripture index. Clarity and common sense, as well as learning, characterize the entire work.

G. W. ANDERSON

RENAUD, B.: *Michée, Sophonie, Nahum* (Sources Bibliques). 1987. Pp. 329 (Gabalda, Paris. Price: Fr. 375.00. ISBN 2 85021 026 9)

The bulk of this volume — rather more than half — is devoted to the book of Micah. This is not surprising, for not only is Micah the biggest of the three but it is the book which has most interested Renaud. In 1964 he published a study of Micah 4–5 (*B.L.* 1965, p. 39) and in 1977, a major work, *La Formation du Livre de Michée* (*B.L.* 1979, p. 88). It is, therefore, good to see the distillation of his thoughts in the shape of a commentary. The commentary on all three books is stimulating, reflecting Renaud's interest in the composition of the prophetic literature and the theology of redaction. The strong interest in Micah has, perhaps, led the author to assume such familiarity with his earlier work that little need be said by way of introduction; hence, although there are introductions to Zephaniah and Nahum, the introduction to Micah is considerably shorter, amounting to little more than the division of the book into six sections.

This series offers a good layout, and is attractively produced, though the latter must have taken some time as the commentary by Hillers on Micah (1984) is nowhere referred to! Fuller bibliographies would have been helpful, and indexes would have been useful.

R. B. SALTERS

SARNA, N. M.: *Exploring Exodus: The Heritage of Biblical Israel*. 1986. Pp. xii, 277. (Schocken Books, New York. Price: $17.95. ISBN 0 8052 3982 0)

This succinct volume, intended for students, teachers, and educated laymen, complements the author's *Understanding Genesis*, 1970. The Introduction opens with a reminder that 'Biblical religion revolves around two themes, Creation and the Exodus'; outlines seven theological and didactic uses of the Exodus theme in the Bible; and locates in the 13th century B.C.E. the events described. While not a verse-by-verse commentary, most of the main issues and key expressions in Exodus are discussed in nine chapters that follow the book's own order: 'The Oppression' (1); 'The Birth and Youth of Moses' (2); 'The Commissioning of Moses' (3–4); 'The Ten Plagues' (5–11);

'The Passover and the Exodus' (12:1–13:16); 'From Egypt to Sinai' (13:17–18:27); 'The Ten Commandments; Moses and Monotheism' (19–20); 'The Laws' (21–24); and, in relative brevity, 'The Tabernacle and the Golden Calf' (25–40).

A. G. AULD

SCHARBERT, J.: *Genesis 12–50* (Die Neue Echter Bibel). 1986. Pp. 121–307. (Echter, Würzburg. Price: DM 34.00; subscription price DM 29.00. ISBN 3 429 01035 7)

The first part of this commentary, with which the pagination of this volume is continuous, was noticed in *B.L.* 1984, p. 58. As then noted, most of the conventional introductory material was included in that volume, so that here the commentary is prefaced only by a three-page note setting out the diversity of current views on literary, historical and sociological issues relating to the patriarchal accounts. The commentary itself accepts the four-document hypothesis in what has by now come to seem a slightly old-fashioned form, but despite the lack of specific reference to the work of other scholars, the author shows himself well aware of contemporary issues in the study of Genesis. The series continues the convention of numbering volumes in the order of their appearance; this is no. 16.

R. J. COGGINS

SEISHO: *Shin Kyōdō-yaku* (The New Common Bible). 1987. (Nihon Seisho Kyōkai, Tokyo. Price: ¥3,600 and ¥2,900)

Eighteen years of co-operative efforts and painstaking work by both Catholic and Protestant church people have culminated to produce two formats of the Common Bible, one with 'the Sequel Portion' (deutero-canonical/apocryphal books) and one without it, both of which include a forty-seven-page general introduction, glossaries, lists, other information and maps.

K. K. SACON

SEKINE, M.: *Sekine Masao Chosaku-shū. Dai 8 Kan: Izaya Sho Chūkai* (M. Sekine Works, Vol. 8: A Commentary on Isaiah). 1986. Pp. 400. (Shinchi Shobō, Tokyo. Price: ¥4,000)

This is a compact and condensed commentary on Isaiah, chapters 1–39. Though he follows the usual style of introduction, translation and exegesis, his main concentration is directed on the clarification of the logic of the Prophet Isaiah, which is seen in the metastatic view of history, i.e. abrupt change caused by God in history. He is positive in asserting the formation of eschatology in Isaiah and of the transition of eschatology into apocalypse in certain original passages.

K. K. SACON

SOGGIN, J. A.: *Judges* (2nd edition) (Old Testament Library). 1987. Pp. xx, 309. (SCM, London. Price: £12.50. ISBN 0 334 02108 1)

The first edition of this lively commentary was noted in *B.L.* 1982, p. 51. This new edition, again translated by J. Bowden, incorporates modifications made as the author prepared the first French edition (see below). Besides the correction of several misprints, four pages of bibliography have been added, and some modifications made to the commentary itself — notably on p. 88, where a changed stance is taken on the difficult *bʿmlq* in 5:14. Unhappily, some three lines of the new French text are not represented following the last word on the new p. 88. Following its final *šoršam*, we should read: '*baʿamaleq*, but without convincing reasons. H. J. Zobel, 1965, proposes a translation of the text, which favours the involvement of Ephraim, with a reference to the district of "Mount Amalek". "The captains": this reading follows the correction made by Craigie, 1972,' — much of this text formed the conclusion of p. 88 in the first edition. There is a similar loss at the end of p. 133.

A. G. AULD

SOGGIN, J. A.: *Le Livre des Juges* (Commentaire de l'Ancien Testament, Vb). 1987. Pp. 268. (Labor et Fides, Genève. Price: Fr. 195.00. ISBN 2 8309 0057 X)

In the case of Joshua, the French edition of Soggin's commentary appeared (1970 — see *B.L.* 1971, p. 32; *Bible Bibliog.*, p. 308) before an English one. French readers have waited many years for the companion volume, now translated by Mlle C. Lanoir. The revised text (see above) was completed in 1985 — a significant anniversary, noted by the editorial secretary, of the publication, thanks to a grant from the Waldensians in Piedmont, of the first Reformed commentary on the Bible in French, The author's change of mind on 'Amaleq' has led to difficulties here too (p. 82) — a fine if unfortunate illustration of the long entail of problems of text and versions!

A. G. AULD

SOGGIN, J. A.: *The Prophet Amos: A Translation and Commentary*. Translated by John Bowden (Old Testament Library). 1987. Pp. xix, 150. (SCM, London. Price: £9.50. ISBN 0 334 00053 X)

This is the English version of the Italian original reviewed in *B.L.* 1984, p. 60, and is a very welcome and important addition to the range of shorter commentaries on Amos in English; in particular it supplements Mays' 1969 commentary in the same OTL series. The Introduction (p. 1–23) deals fairly conventionally with questions of background and composition. As might be expected, there is a certain amount of emphasis on the historical aspects (much is made of the dateability of references supposedly contained in 1:3 ff. and 6:13–14; and the narrative of 7:10–17 is thought to be basically reliable). Wolff is broadly followed on matters of redaction and genre. The Commentary itself is organized in several major sections: after the Superscription and the Oracles against the Nations, chapters 3–6 are grouped as 'The Words of Amos of Tekoa I'; the Visions of 7:1–8:3; 9:1–6 are then all treated together; 7:10–17 is treated separately as an 'Interlude'; 8:4–14; 9:7–10 constitute 'The Words . . . II'; and 9:11–15 follows as an 'Epilogue'. These 'chapters' are subdivided into sections, each with its own specialized bibliography (there is a select general bibliography for the book as a whole). The translation, which is often refreshing and illuminating, is followed by detailed textual and philological notes and discussion, and then by a broader exegetical section which does not presuppose knowledge of Hebrew and Greek. Both these sections are invariably packed with a wealth of information, bringing into a brief compass a mass of relevant and up-to-date material from a wide range of scholars. On controversial issues, all sides of an argument are fairly set out, new hypotheses are judiciously aired, and there is a minimum of evaluation, so that readers are left to make up their own minds. This is undoubtedly one of the book's greatest strengths. When a case is argued to a conclusion, the touch is generally light, and the debate moved at least potentially forward (though the treatment of 7:7–9 is disappointingly fixated on the traditional 'plumb-line'). In the philological sections, abundant use is made of the LXX and other early versions, and at the other end of the time scale, of Ugaritic and Akkadian parallels. Alas, despite the work done to correct the original version (p. ix–x), there are still a number of printing errors and mistakes, some of them substantial (and n.b. the correct title of Barré's article, referred to on p. 31, is 'The Meaning of *l'* *'sybnw* in Amos 1:3–2:6'. It appears in *JBL* 105 (1986), 611–31). It is not the practice of the OTL Series to provide indices. But with the method of inserting bibliographies piecemeal throughout the text, which is now prevalent, an author index, at least, would be a helpful addition.

J. M. DINES

SZELES, M. E.: *Wrath and Mercy: A Commentary on the Books of Habakkuk and Zephaniah* (International Theological Commentary); translated by G. A. F. Knight. 1987. Pp. x, 118. (Handsel, Edinburgh; Eerdmans, Grand Rapids, Michigan. Price: £4.95. ISBN 0 905312 72 4; 0 8028 0242 7)

If we have ever wondered how the Books of Habakkuk and Zephaniah strike a reader in Cluj-Napoca, now we have the answer. The author of this little commentary from Rumania teaches in a Protestant seminary. In line with the series, she has given priority to the theological value of the books, while outlining historical and literary issues carefully. There are occasional references to various scholarly opinions. Her own preference is to date Habakkuk towards 597 and Zephaniah (apart from post-exilic additions) from 630 B.C. The exposition of the condemnation of corrupt officials (Zeph. 3:1–8) is an example of the strength of her writing. Altogether this is an effective commentary.

J. H. EATON

TESCAROLI, L.: *I salmi nella tradizione ebraica; nuova traduzione dal testo masoretico.* 1985. Pp. 327. (Città Nuova, Roma. Price: Lire 20,000. ISBN 88 311 4907 5)

This translation of the psalms is so close to the Massoretic Text that on occasion it is really over literal (e.g., 'mountain of your holiness', Ps. 15:1). Variations and conjectures, chiefly with reference to the ancient versions are relegated to footnotes but there is no mention of the Dead Sea Scrolls. Much of the brief introduction is wasted on the Hebrew alphabet, Massoretic accents, etc., leaving little space for more relevant items such as the literary forms of the psalms or problems of text and translation. The result is certainly accurate and solid but cannot be described as stimulating.

W. G. E. WATSON

VERHOEF, P. A.: *The Books of Haggai and Malachi* (The New International Commentary on the Old Testament). 1987. Pp. xxv, 364. (Eerdmans, Grand Rapids, Michigan. Price: $21.95. ISBN 0 8028 2376 9)

The books of Haggai and Malachi may seem strange bedfellows to be found in a commentary series. Presumably questions of length dictated the choice. Nevertheless, the arrangement does draw attention to a number of similarities of style and theme between the two books. Verhoef, writing from the conservative theological stance favoured by the NICOT, deals in the introductions to each book with issues of historical background, authorship, style, structure and unity. The work is marked by considerable erudition and the positive evaluation of these two prophetic books is a welcome contrast to so much earlier treatment which caricatured them as merely legalistic and ritualistic. The author is also anxious to show their relevance for the Christian Church and certainly directs our attention to theological issues.

Critical positions are occasionally flirted with. An apparently objective and balanced treatment of the authorship of the editorial framework of the Book of Haggai is to be found (pp. 9–13) although those who suggest Haggai's own hand (e.g. Eissfeldt, Weiser) are favoured. Yet the author soon leaves flirtation for the safety of home, and later on Van Der Woude's opinion that 1:12–14 is the work of a redactor is dismissed as hypothetical and irrelevant' (p. 80). Indeed, any critical scholarly view usually ends up with a label tied round its neck such as 'subjective' or 'arbitrary'. This commentary, in the end, for all its scholarship and value, illustrates the empty bank balance of so much 'conservative' biblical scholarship, too often reactive, too seldom itself creative.

R. A. MASON

WATTS, J. D. W.: *Isaiah 1–33* (Word Biblical Commentary, 24). 1985. Pp. lviii, 449. *Isaiah 34–66* (Word Biblical Commentary, 25). 1987. Pp. xxxiii, 386. (Word Books, Waco, Texas. Price: approx. $25.00 each volume. ISBN 0 8499 0223 1 and 0 8499 0224 X)

This commentary is the apotheosis, or if you prefer the reductio ad absurdum, of the 'final form' approach. Isaiah is a drama in twelve acts, dating from the fifth century, though employing some earlier material. Each act concerns the political relations of Judah (or Israel and Judah) in one of twelve successive 'generations' from that of Uzziah (1-6) to that of Ezra and Nehemiah (62–66). The subject of the drama as a whole is the execution of Yahweh's decision that his purpose for his people is no longer to be served by their political independence. They are to be a servant people with a religious calling, under the political sway of the great empires. There are clear advantages in this approach. The varied material of the book can be seen as parts of a unified work simply by assigning contradictory material to opposing speakers. But the division into chronologically successive 'acts' is a tour de force: thus chapters 36–39 can be dramatically fitted into Zedekiah's reign only by making them an ironically intended historical reading. Again and again theory triumphs over common sense: chapters 5 and 6, part of the Uzziah 'act', must be separated from chapters 7 ff. despite the presence of common material; chapter 8 must be directed solely against Israel and its sympathisers, since Judah has at the time the 'right' policy. Proper literary reading demands that one's view of the whole should be developed out of careful unbiased reading of the parts. Precisely the opposite happens here.

The commentary takes the form now familiar in this series, with a separate bibliography, translation, notes and commentary on each section. The bibliographies are useful, collecting much little-known material, and the textual notes also are copious. But Watts has poor exegetical judgement, frequently contradicts himself, and makes many strange errors (Anshan is on one page a king, and on another a city!). Although it is valuable to have a comprehensive interpretation of the book of Isaiah to wrestle with, and many of Watts' points are worthy of reflection, the commentary as such cannot be recommended without reservation.

W. J. HOUSTON

WEISER, A.: *Geremia 1–25, 14* (Antico Testamento). 1987. Pp. 404. (Paideia, Brescia. Price: Lire 38,000. ISBN 88 394 0396 5)

This has been translated from the eighth German edition (1981), which, like previous editions, represents only a slight revision over its predecessor. (Previous editions have been noted in *B.L.* 1953, p. 41) 1955, p. 40; 1967, p. 28 and 1970, p. 37.) English, of course, currently provides a far better range of modern Jeremiah commentaries than German; it is a pity for Italians that this commentary was commissioned before any of them appeared.

P. R. DAVIES

WEISER, A.: *Shihen Ge, 90–150 Pen*. Translated by Y. Ohtomo. 1987. Pp. 421. (ATD-NTD Seisho Chukai Kankō–kai, Tokyo. Price: ¥4,200)

This is a Japanese translation of Pss. 90–150 of *Die Psalmen* from its ninth edition (1979).

K. K. SACON

WESTERMANN, C.: *Genesis 37–50. A Commentary*. Translated by J. J. Scullion S.J. 1986. Pp. 269. (SPCK, London. Price: £30.00. ISBN 0 281 04277 2. Augsburg, Minneapolis. ISBN 0 8066 2197 4)

This third volume completes the translation of Westermann's Genesis commentary. The previous volume of the translation was noticed in *B.L.* 1987, p. 56, and the relevant fascicules of the originals were reviewed in *B.L.* 1983, pp. 55–56. This is not the place to assess the magisterial work of Westermann, but it is a matter of interest that we find here two introductions to the Joseph story, the first (pp. 15–30) on the standard matters of the origin and growth of the text and its relation to other Old Testament literature), the second (pp. 245–53) on the more literary topic of narrative art and on the theological issue, 'What does the Joseph Narrative say about God? It remains something of a curiosity that the commentary on the Blessings of Jacob (49:1–28a) is placed after that on chapter 50; an unconvincing justification is offered on p. 221. As with previous volumes the gratitude of scholars and students alike is due the translator for his fluent and faithful — and, indeed, self-sacrificial — work.

D. J. A. CLINES

ZENGER, E.: *Das Buch Ruth* (Zürcher Bibelkommentare — AT: 8). 1986. Pp. 128. (Theologischer Verlag, Zurich. Price: Sw.Fr. 22.00. ISBN 3 290 14740 1)

In line with the approach of the Zurich Bible Commentaries series Zenger's commentary on Ruth deals more with literary and theological exposition than detailed linguistic exegesis. It is marked by clarity of style and the detailed commentary is prefaced by some excellent sections on the literary and historical problems familiar to students of Ruth. In the discussion of the original extent of the book he supports the view that 4:18–22, the concluding genealogy, is secondary together with verse 17 which provides the link for the intrusive Davidic ancestry. The story ended at verse 16, the original 'name' of Naomi's child being transmitted in verse 14a, i.e. Goel — Redeemer. The original book of Ruth is the story of the birth of a redeemer to a family threatened with extinction. At the same time ordinary human affairs are shown to be the subject of divine guidance. The narrative is endowed with programmatic historical significance only in the final edition of the book when the Boaz of the original story is identified with the Boaz of the Davidic genealogy (attested in 1 Chron. 2) and the name Obed is attributed to the functional 'name' of 4:14a. It is argued that this was effected at the earliest among post-exilic circles in the second century B.C. when (a) the hope of a messianic kingdom was founded not on might but on the spirit of the community, and (b) it was felt that the new kingdom must be modelled not on the Jerusalem dynasty but on the pattern of the Bethlehemite shepherds (cp. Mi. 5:1–3). Other sections deal with the literary form of the book, the narrative technique of recurrent theme words (e.g. return, redeem), literary genre and origin (early exilic or post-exilic period). The volume has a select bibliography but lacks index of authors, subjects and biblical references.

PETER W. COXON

6. LITERARY CRITICISM AND INTRODUCTION

AEJMELAEUS, A.: *The Traditional Prayer in the Psalms*, and SCHMIDT, L.: *Literarische Studien zur Josephgeschichte* (BZAW, 167). 1986. Pp. 117 and 189. (De Gruyter, Berlin. Price: DM 140.00. ISBN 3 11 010480 6)

The first of the two studies in this volume concerns the psalms of individual complaint or lament, or, as the author prefers to call them, 'the prayer psalms of the individual'. She gives little or no consideration to the problems of the setting and the relation to royal prayers, but the opinion is expressed that the prayer psalms were largely oral and fluid in the pre-exilic period and, as Gerstenberger has suggested, belonged to the 'smaller forms of cultic life' practised by members of a primary group with the help of a cultic expert. What the study does offer is a thorough analysis of the phraseology of the petition and its immediately connected clauses in such psalms. This helps to display the direct and forceful characteristics of Israelite prayer.

The second study in the volume is a source analysis of the Joseph story. After a lucid survey of the great diversity of views on this question, the author undertakes a fresh examination of the materials to test the possibilities of distinguishing the sources and reaches definite conclusions. The Yahwist was responsible for making the received Joseph story bridge the traditions of the Fathers and the Exodus, and the Elohist used the J version as his basis. J and E were combined by a redactor who preferred whichever source gave most detail. P used the resultant JE as its basis. The final redactor of all these sources preserved all he could and also, where necessary, preferred the most detailed account. The relevance of these conclusions to the rest of the Pentateuch is pointed out. This well-informed and cogent study will reward close attention.

J. H. EATON

ALTER, R.: *The Art of Biblical Poetry*. 1987. Pp. xii, 228. (Basic Books, New York. Price: $8.95; ISBN 0 465 00431 8)

The first three chapters of the complementary volume to *The Art of Biblical Narrative*, 1981 (see *B.L.* 1983, p. 59) provide a foundation for what follows. Chapter 1 explains that 'synonymous' parallelism is really progressive in character; here, as Alter admits, he is in agreement with J. Kugel though J. G. Herder anticipated them both. Next, 'From Line to Study' shows how narrative can be a significant if neglected factor in Hebrew verse. Chapter three describes patterns of 'intensification' within poems.

Each of the following five chapters concentrates on different types of poetry within a particular genre: in the Book of Job (which 'looms above all other biblical poetry in virtuosity and sheer expressive power'), in the Psalms (originality within conventional language), in prophecy (largely direct address), in Proverbs ('the poetry of wit') and in the Song of Songs (metaphor). This approach is new and instructive. A final chapter sketches the post-biblical continuity of Hebrew verse tradition.

Alter is over-dismissive of certain scholars and, with a few exceptions, makes only generic acknowledgement of his debt to others since in his view he is breaking new ground. Certainly, the focus on narrative, on the poem as a whole and on parallelism as dynamic is largely new. Recognition of micro-structural patterns (e.g. chiasmus), though, is equally important in Alter's holistic approach.

W. G. E. WATSON

BAL, M.: *Lethal Love. Feminist Literary Readings of Biblical Love Stories*. 1987. Pp. vii, 141. (Indiana University Press, Bloomington and Indianapolis. Price: $25.00; ISBN 0 253 33327 7. Paperback price: $8.95; ISBN 0 253 20434 8)

This extraordinarily vital book, by turns engaging and daunting, offers different kinds of literary reading of the narratives of David and Bathsheba, Samson and Delilah, Ruth and Boaz, Judah and Tamar, Adam and Eve. In each chapter, the author, a narratologist by profession, but also an acute reader of the Hebrew Bible, deploys a different hermeneutical framework, whether plot-oriented, narratological or psychoanalytic (the psychoanalytic reading of Samson is particularly brilliant). And in each chapter she views the text from the perspective of a different type of reader, from the scholarly exegete to the writer of children's Bibles to the poet (especially striking is the reading of Ruth from the perspective of Victor Hugo's poem 'Booz endormi'). The argument is that a feminist consciousness, especially as informed by contemporary literary theory, suggests alternative readings of these tales of how lethal the love of women once proved. Her purpose is not to make out that the Bible is less misogynistic than it seems, but to expose how flimsy a support for male dominance these tales provide once their complexity is discerned. However tedious the theoretical discussions may be to many readers, Biblical scholars must note this book as a sample of the kinds of intellectual enquiry Biblical studies have become now that they are freed from the constraints of 'the original meaning of the text'.

D. J. A. CLINES

BEAUCAMP, E.: *Les prophètes d'Israël, ou le drame d'une alliance* (Lire la Bible, 75). 1987. Pp. 364 (Cerf, Paris. Price: Fr. 99.00. ISBN 2 204 02640 9; ISSN 0588 2257)

Intended for the general public, this work first saw the light of day in 1956 when it appeared with the title *Sous la main de Dieu — Le prophétisme et l'élection d'Israël*, then again, in 1968 with the present title. This should be its last appearance!

Apart from a short introduction on the election of Israel and its fundamental principles, and a concluding piece dealing with the Christian relationship to Israel, Beaucamp takes the prophets one by one and extracts the gist of the message of each prophet, ending with a brief analysis of the book's structure. When quoting from the biblical text, the author uses the Jerusalem Bible (first edition), though he is not tied to this (cf. Isaiah 40:9 where Zion is vocative). There are two maps and a small chronological table.

R. B. SALTERS

BLENKINSOPP, J.: *Kyūyaku no Chie to Hō*. Translated by K. K. Sacon and M. Shishido. 1987. Pp. 269 + 16 p. indices. (Yorudan-sha, Tokyo. Price: ¥2,600)

This is a Japanese translation of *Wisdom and Law in the Old Testament* (1983) (see *B.L.* 1984, pp. 87–88). Appended is an essay written by K. K. Sacon with an introduction to the author and his works, and an appraisal of the book.

K. K. SACON

BODENMANN, R.: *Naissance d'une Exégèse: Daniel dans l'Eglise ancienne des trois premiers siècles* (Beiträge zur Geschichte der biblischen Exegese, 28). 1986. Pp. 422. (Mohr, Tübingen. Price: DM 98.00. ISBN 3 16 14513 0)

As one might expect, this book does not deal with the whole of Daniel, but only with those sections that were of particular interest to early Christian writers up to Cyprian and Hippolytus. The key passages are 2:34f., 44f.; 7:9, 13f.; 9:24–27. An introductory chapter discusses text types, especially that attributed to Theodotion. The author is uncertain about this attribution, but opts for an early date — contemporary with or earlier than Aquila. The nature of the citations in the early Christian authors points, he argues, to a mixed text, a 'proto-Theodotion', which could date from as early as the second century B.C. The popularity of this version may be due to its having been mistaken for the Septuagint.

The bulk of the book treats of the early christological interpretation of the key passages — the stone not cut by human hand, the son of man, the anointed prince. The author shows how a predominantly eschatological reading yields gradually to a desire to place the book of Daniel in the history of salvation.

There are no obvious misprints, but the French style is generally clumsy and occasionally obscure, e.g. 'Déjà chez *Daniel*, le "fils d'homme" ne semble pas avoir été associé à la figure du messie'. This looks like a German idiom: it is certainly not French.

J. Ashton

Coggins, R. J.: *Haggai, Zechariah, Malachi* (Old Testament Guides). 1987. Pp. 89. (JSOT Press, Sheffield. Price: £3.50 ($4.95). ISBN 1 85075 025 4)

The author introduces the reader to the historical setting of these prophets (disclaiming precise knowledge in the case of Malachi), the 'role' of the prophets in the social and political context of the Persian Empire, the contents of the books, the main critical questions and issues of interpretation raised by the text, various scholarly approaches in the history of their study, and their larger 'canonical' setting in the 'Book of the Twelve'.

Among the interesting views supported by the author are the exaggeration in much scholarly writing of the effect of a 'return from exile' under the influence of Ezra 1–3 and the editorial framework of the book of Haggai; the similarity of the editorial framework' provided for both prophets who were yet strikingly different in a number of ways (Haggai a 'speaker', Zechariah a 'see-er', Zechariah paying less attention to Zerubbabel and the political nature of the restored community), and Zechariah 9–14 better seen as 'exegesis' of earlier 'scripture' than a quarry for supposed historical allusions. Especially valuable is the author's insistence that we must allow for the difference between the words and activities of the 'historical' prophet and the picture of him presented in the tradition of the final form of the book, and the effect of the canonical setting of these books in 'The Book of the Twelve', a task strangely neglected by Childs.

The author himself complains that many large issues have had to be ignored in so small a compass. The miracle is that so much has been accomplished here with such clarity. It is invaluable as an introduction to the study of the Restoration prophets.

R. A. Mason

Croft, S. J. L.: *The Identity of the Individual in the Psalms* (JSOT Supplement Series 44). 1987. Pp. 218. (Sheffield Academic Press. Price: £22.50 ($34.00); ISBN 1 85075 021 1. Paperback price: £10.50 ($15.95); ISBN 1 85075 020 3)

This very competent study is a revised and shortened version of Dr Croft's doctoral dissertation presented in 1984 to the University of Durham. The first two chapters approach the central issue via the associated problems of the identity of the psalmists' 'enemies' and the psalmists' description of themselves as 'poor'. The next three chapters examine all the 95 psalms in which an 'I' speaks, and the book closes with a short conclusion. In 41 of these 95 psalms, the 'I' is, according to Dr Croft, the king, in 33 the 'I' is a cultic minister (prophet or wisdom teacher or temple singer), and in 18 the 'I' is a private person; the other three are exilic or post-exilic prayers by non-royal spokesmen. In three of the cultic minister psalms and in four others where no 'I' appears he notes that the king is spoken of in the second or third person; and this gives him a total of 48 royal psalms against Gunkel's minimal 9–11 and J. H. Eaton's (in his *Kingship and the Psalms*, 1974) maximal 64. These statisics are revealing. They show that Dr Croft belongs essentially in Eaton's camp and with him wishes to extend as much as possible the presence of royal rites in the Psalter, including pre-eminently (in 21 psalms) the role the king played in the annual New Year festival. But though, like Eaton, he is patently enamoured of that putative ceremony, he resists Eaton's attachment to the theory that the king underwent a ritual humiliation during it; and he is clearly disappointed that he was not able to find more than 18 psalms composed for individual use. I feel that if he had trusted more his desire in chapter 2 to take the vocabulary of poverty at its concrete face-value, he could have increased that category considerably. But that is, like my use above of the adjective 'putative', to intrude my own views. I commend this monograph for its honest probing, its exegetical skill, and its refusal to solve complex problems by unitary means.

J. C. L. Gibson

Diamond, A. R.: *The Confessions of Jeremiah in Context: Scenes of a Prophetic Drama* (JSOT Supplements 45). 1987. Pp. 308. (JSOT Press, Sheffield. Price: £19.50; ISBN 1 85075 032 7. Paperback price: £9.95; ISBN 1 85075 033 5)

This is a published version of Diamond's Cambridge Ph.D. thesis on Jer. 11:18–12:6; 15:10–21; 17:14–18; 18:18–23; 20:7–18 which surveys current research on the subject of the 'confessions' of Jeremiah and argues for a particular proper interpretive context for their understanding. His argument is that the deuteronomistic editors have incorporated the 'confessions' into a double-axis pattern which serves the apologetic purpose of constructing a theodicy of Yahweh's destruction of Judah. He also favours the traditional ascription of the 'confessions' to Jeremiah, though allows that the authenticity question does not affect his overall thesis. The thesis is well argued and nicely presented in this Sheffield production — how rapidly the Sheffield Biblical Studies Department is becoming the Athens of biblical scholarship in Britain today! There is an excellent grasp and coverage of the secondary literature and a valuable section of discursive notes (pp. 193–281) which will make this a very useful volume for all future Jeremiah studies. Reading the poems as dramatic dialogues between Jeremiah and Yahweh reflecting subthemes of prophetic conflict, prophetic iconoclasm, and Jeremiah as a prophetic paradigm, Diamond makes the theodicy motif the undergirding principle of the editing of chapters 11–20. The 'confessions' contribution to this principle is its further explication in terms of the nation's apostasy manifested in its refusal to heed Yahweh's messenger (cf. the narratives which parallel this theme in 26–29; 36; 37–45). I was impressed by the lucidity and quality of this excellent study and, though not persuaded at all by its thesis, would thoroughly recommend it to those who wish to find their way through the thickets of this very vexed issue in Jeremiah studies.

R. P. Carroll

DIETRICH, W.: *David, Saul und die Propheten: Das Verhältnis von Religion und Politik nach den prophetischen Überlieferungen vom frühesten Königtum in Israel* (Beiträge zur Wissenschaft vom Alten und Neuen Testament, 122). 1987. Pp. 168. (Kohlhammer, Stuttgart. Price: DM 49.80. ISBN 3 17 009608 7)

After opening remarks about how Samuel, Nathan, and Gad all present contrasting faces to the kings with whom they deal, Dietrich in his first main chapter discusses 1 Sam. 15 and 28, and 2 Sam. 12 and 24, and proposes as their source a Book of Prophet Stories known to both the Chronicler and before him DtrP, the prophetic strand of Deuteronomistic redaction he first argued for in *Prophetie und Geschichte*, 1972. This Book of Prophet Stories had also supplied the later historians with such material as 1 Kgs 13; 22 and the traditions about Ahijah in 1 Kgs 14. Dietrich's second chapter concerns Samuel in the Book of David's Rise: David's anointing (1 Sam. 16:1–13); his rescue (19:18–24); and Saul's choice and rejection (9:1–10:16; 13:8–15). The third examines Samuel in the Book of Saul's Rise: Samuel's call by God (1 Sam. 1–3; 7); and Saul's call by Samuel (1 Sam. 8–11). There is much to learn from many of Dietrich's observations; but this reader is worried by so much literary–historical theorising accompanied by so little attention to text-critical problems and their implications, especially in the books of Samuel.

A. G. AULD

FESTORAZZI, F., with BONORA, A., and SISTI, A.: *Corso Completo di Studi Biblici: Il Messaggio della Salvezza, 5: Gli 'Scritti' dell'Antico Testamento*. 1985. Pp. 396. (Elle Di Ci, Torino. Price: Lire 25,000. ISBN 88 01 13829 6)

The present volume, the fifth in a projected series of nine forming an introduction to the Old Testament and the New Testment, is concerned with the 'Writings'. Part one, the wisdom books, covers Proverbs, Job, Qoheleth, Wisdom and Ben Sira. Part two presents the Psalms and part three the midrashic books: Tobit, Judith, Esther, Ruth and Song of Songs. 1 and 2 Maccabees form the subject of part four. For each book there is an introduction (authenticity, text and versions, overall structure, etc.) and full exegesis of selected passages. In these examples the problems that arise, whether philological, structural or theological are set out, documented and tackled. There is, besides, a short section on versification in Hebrew placed, unfortunately, in part three, the Psalms, as if only these were poetry. The bibliographies provided are certainly good, there is reference to ancient near Eastern literature and in general the presentation is sober and well-informed.

W. G. E. WATSON

FOLLIS, E. R. (ed.): *Directions in Biblical Hebrew Poetry* (JSOT Supplement Series 40). 1987. Pp. 312. (Sheffield Academic Press. Price: £25.00 ($37.50); ISBN 1 85075 013 0. Paperback price: £10.50 ($15.95); ISBN 1 85075 012 2)

Literary criticism in our discipline is broadening all the time and taking on board investigations of a kind that in the old days of source and tradition analysis would have been given short shrift by all but a few scholars. The present collection of studies, based on papers delivered in recent years at meetings of the Biblical Hebrew Poetry section of the Society of Biblical Literature, gives a good idea of the variety of such investigations and of the many ways in which they can illumine the interpretation of Old Testament texts. It begins with D. N. Freeedman's latest views (still involving syllable counting) on how Hebrew poetry is to be distinguished from Hebrew prose.

D. L. Christensen is interested in the same problem, and argues that the Book of Jonah is really a poem. Two studies devoted to parallelism follow: J. T. Willis on alternating parallelism and D. J. A. Clines on the parallelism of 'greater precision'. Thereafter come two papers on the Prophets (J. T. Willis tries his hand at identifying one of the larger literary units in Second Isaiah; and T. Hiebert writes on the use of 'inclusion' in Habakkuk 3), and two on the Psalms (Adele Berlin examines the device of the 'word chain' in Psalm 133; and H. Lenowitz argues that Psalm 137 is a mock 'song of joy'). The next two studies are wider ranging (M. O'Connor on the type of paradox called 'pseudosorites', and Elaine R. Follis on the poetic expression 'daughter of Zion'), after which we have two on Job (Sylvia Hubermann Scholnik discusses the use made of creation poetry in the courtroom setting of the Speeches of Yahweh; and Carole Fontaine employs Proppian folktale analysis to explicate not only the Prologue and Epilogue but the structure of the book as a whole). At this point W. J. Urbrock gives us his own imaginative and highly entertaining composition, 'Samson: A Play for Voices', an earlier version of which was entered in a radio competition; I would like to see this in Hebrew. The collection closes with two contributions on the ancient poems in Exodus 15 and Judges 5 (by A. J. Hauser) and on the song of Miriam (by B. W. Anderson), the last being supplemented with a short response by W. Brueggemann.

J. C. L. Gibson

Fox, M. V.: *The Song of Songs and the Ancient Egyptian Love Songs.* 1985. Pp. xxvii, 454. (University of Wisconsin Press, Madison. Price: $32.50. ISBN 0 299 10090 1)

The general affinity between the Song of Songs in the Old Testament and the love-poetry from Ramesside Egypt has long been recognized. But while the Song of Songs has suffered a surfeit of would-be commentators and commentators, the last edition of the Egyptian poems is ninety years old and does not contain any of the more recently discovered poems (e.g. the Chester Beatty series). In this book, Michael Fox presents a full translation of all the Egyptian poems now known and readable (plus related texts in an appendix) and includes also their full hieroglyphic text. He also translates and compactly annotates the Song of Songs in similar fashion. In both cases, the renderings overall are attractive (not needfully definitive, especially considering the textual problems in the Egyptian texts), and the discussions are refreshingly sensible. There is ample (but not verbose) discussion of the date, purpose, composition, of these two bodies of lyric text, and also of the principal themes and comparisons. Fox argues ably not only for the unity of the Song of Songs, but also in their own terms for various of the Egyptian collections. He would date the Song to perhaps fourth/third centuries B.C., which (even without invoking Solomon) seems improbably late, given the rather antiquated reasons offered. Ample indexes enhance the book's usability. Occasional crass errors occur: Nefertari at Luxor (pp. 270, 345) is in original *nineteenth* Dynasty texts and reliefs of Ramesses II, not of twentieth Dynasty, and use is not made of the recent *Ramesside Inscriptions* edition.

Overall, this handsomely produced volume does great credit to author and publisher; for the comparative study of lyric literature in the Bible and its Near-Eastern Context (the rare Mesopotamian material is also considered), this book will be an indispensable work of ready reference.

K. A. Kitchen

Friedman, R. E.: *Who Wrote the Bible?* 1987. Pp. 299. (Summit Books, New York. Price: $18.95. ISBN 0 67163161 6)

This is a curiously absurd book! Just when biblical scholars have begun to dismantle permanently the Wellhausen Documentary Hypothesis and to understand the nature of biblical literature as anonymously produced writing along comes a popular book written in a racy style to assert, with minor adjustments, the Wellhausen thesis and to name the author of some of the biblical books! It is, of course, an American book and is written in that brash, self-confident style so typical of American scholarship. Friedman reasserts the classical account of JEDP, follows the Israeli/Kaufman thesis of the priority of P, and identities D as Jeremiah or his editor Baruch. So now we know the identifies of the authors of the Bible from Genesis to Kings (i.e. J, E, P and Jeremiah/Baruch)! 'So what!' the sceptic may say. What follows from that? What do we know about P? Friedman has a very clear picture of Jeremiah: his history 'appears to be a sincere attempt, by a sensitive and skillful man, to tell his people's history — and to understand it. As a historian, he painted his people's heritage. As a prophet, he conceived of their destiny' (p. 149). Jeremiah as the Deuteronomist is a concept to savour and appears to want to turn the clock of scholarship back to the 1920s. It runs so counter to current Jeremiah studies that I find the book jaw-sagging in its naivety and bushy-tailedness. It is very much another product of the Albright–Bright–Cross school of American biblical scholarship and taken as such may be viewed as a fine example of that school's kind of writing. Always an easy read it is clearly intended for the non-professional reader of the Bible and perhaps should be judged at that level. It will entertain whoever reads it and will undoubtedly make the *Alttestamentler* reflect on the nature of this kind of book and the status of its arguments. What Rendtorff's BZAW 147 is doing listed in the Bibliography baffled this reader of Friedman!

R. P. Carroll

Frieling, R.: *Psalmen: Welten-Schau, Der Weg des Lebens, Das neue Lied* (Gesammelte Schriften zum Alten und Neuen Testament, II). 1985. Pp. 379. (Urachhaus, Stuttgart. Price: DM 46.00. ISBN 3 87838 344 4)

This is an enlarged and revised edition of a volume on selected Psalms which first appeared in 1958 (not noticed in *B.L.*). The additions are Psalms 31; 63; 91; 118; 119; 121, and the Song of the Three Holy Children, all of which have been published elsewhere. The author confesses that his choice of 28 out of the 150 in the Psalter is subjective. They are in three groups, as indicated by the subtitle. Sometimes exception might be taken to the inclusion of particular Psalms in a group (e.g., 84 and 121 in *Welten-Schau* and 24 and 46 in *Das neue Lied*, though the author might argue that his defence resides in his expositions). The rationale of the groups is a progress of thought from man as part of the cosmos to man in his need, reaching out to his Lord, Shepherd, and Saviour, and finally, in *Das neue Lied*, to the coming of the messiah and the vision of a new earth. This view of the relation of the groups indicates the character of the expositions. In an appendix there are (1) a brief enumeration of Psalm passages which played a part in the life of Christ, (2) a note on the Psalms in Christian usage, and (3) an account of the point of view presupposed by the expositions, with an acknowledgement of indebtedness to Rudolf Steiner's anthroposophy.

G. W. Anderson

GABEL, J. B., and WHEELER, C. B.: *The Bible as Literature: An Introduction.* 1986. Pp. 278. (Oxford University Press, New York. Price: £17.50. ISBN 0 19 503993 9)

By the Bible as literature the authors mean simply the Bible as a human document and not a source of religious faith. They are both professors in a department of English Literature in an American university which offers a course in Bible as one of its options, and this book is designed as an introduction for undergraduates enrolling in such a course. It is a book marked by a high degree both of tolerance and of common sense. It takes the whole Bible as its field and does not restrict itself to those portions which are considered to have literary value, as so many books with similar titles do. Nor is it inimical to the historical type of criticism which is dominant in introductions written for professional students of theology; J, E, D and P and the Gospel sources are given their due place alongside matters of literary appreciation, and there is a chapter on the formation of the Canon as well as one on the merits of the various English translations. An early chapter deals helpfully with problems of historicity and the final chapter eirenically with the difference between a literary and a religious reading of scripture. There is no chapter on the Psalms, a most surprising omission. An interesting note at the beginning states that the book was printed on acid-free paper.

J. C. L. GIBSON

GIBERT, P.: *Bible, Mythes et Récits de Commencement* (Parole de Dieu). 1986. Pp. 287. (Éditions du Seuil, Paris. Price: Fr. 95.00. ISBN 2 02 009379 0)

The programme of Gibert's book is: 1. Every 'beginning' is beyond our reach or grasp; 2. the Bible speaks of the (absolute) beginnings of the universe and of humanity and yet *in much the same way* of the (relative) beginnings of Israel or of Christianity; 3. what is the meaning and value of such speech? He argues, from historiography and psychology, that 'relative' beginnings are decided upon after the event, and from an account of the 'big bang' that 'absolute' beginnings are deduced from the world as it is. Neither is 'known' in the usual sense. The biblical story of Eden is distinguishable from its ancient Near Eastern relatives because it is not archetypal but inaugural, the opening scene of a larger history, an argument reinforced by a detailed comparison with the Amnon-Tamar story (2 Sam. 13). Gen. 1 is seen as a deliberate and unique fusion of prose and poetic forms to convey the ultimate ineffability of its subject matter, logical and orderly though its classification of the cosmic constituents is. Gibert then traces the manner in which other Old Testament and New Testament origin stories are penetrated by the absolute origin stories of Genesis. At the end of what he calls his 'meta-exegetical' analysis, he offers us a genre, 'origin story', which is to be understood not as 'bad science' or even as 'myth' but as a legitimate response of faith in what cannot be known for certain. Written for popular, Roman Catholic Francophone readership, this is an intriguing, generally subtle, and thought-provoking discussion worthy of a wider audience.

P. R. DAVIES

GRIMM, W.: *Fürchte dich nicht: Ein exegetischer Zugang zum Seelsorgepotential einer deuterojesajanischer Gattung* (Europäische Hochschulschriften 23; Theologie; Band 298). 1986. Pp. 238. (Lang, Frankfurt am Main, Bern, New York. Price: $23.75. ISBN 3 8204 9470 7; ISSN 0721 3409)

In this volume the author, whose earlier work shows a keen interest in constructing a biblical theology — *Die Verkündigung Jesu und Deuterojesaja* (1981), and *Die Heimkehr der Jakobskinder* (1985) (see *B.L.* 1986, p. 87) —

continues in the same vein to some extent but develops a further interest in applying some words of Deutero-Isaiah to present-day conditions of anxiety and depression. It is the 'Fear not . . .' passages which Grimm is interested in here, and he takes five passages: Isaiah 41:14–16; 41:8–13; 43:1–7; 44:1–5; and 54 which he investigates separately. Beginning with his translation and various textual notes, he proceeds to interpret each passage strophe by strophe. This is followed by the allusions to the *genre* in the New Testament, and by a section on its timeless meaning and application.

R. B. SALTERS

VAN GROL, H. W. M.: *De versbouw in het Klassieke Hebreeuws,* I: *Metriek*. 1986. Pp. 266. (Katholieke Theologische Hogeschool, Amsterdam. Price: Fl. 45.00)

It is well known that the metre of most Hebrew verse is not regular over long sections of text and Van Grol uses generative grammar to explain such an apparent anomaly. According to him every strophe, defined as a set of three to nine cola, has a basic metrical scheme. Each scheme, comprising 2+2, 3+2, 3+3 or 4+4 stressed words, can have different surface realizations derivable from the basic themes by very simple rules. The metre of classical Hebrew verse, then, is stress-based and regular.

To avoid circular reasoning Van Grol first analyses five passages, for which he formulates preliminary 'reading rules'. He then applies these rules to a second set of passages and refines his first formulation. In essense the author, who adopts P. van der Lugt's procedure for strophic analysis (see P. van der Lugt, *Strofische Structuren in de Bijbels-Hebreeuwse Poëzie*, 1980; *B.L.* 1981, p. 74) is in the tradition of R. Lowth, J. Ley, E. Sievers and G. B. Gray. In addition, he has used, in part, the approach B. Margalit, who also belongs in the same tradition, applied to metrical analysis of Ugaritic verse.

The author's analysis is to be taken seriously though it needs to be tested on a wider selection of texts. In spite of some rather technical paragraphs his thesis is quite readable. A six-page summary in English is provided, A second volume will deal with parallelism.

W. G. E. WATSON

GUNKEL, H.: *Das Märchen im Alten Testament.* 1987. Pp. 252. (Athenäum, Frankfurt am Main. Price: DM 58.00. ISBN 3 610 09110 X)

This is a reprint of Gunkel's 1921 essay on the *Märchen* in the Old Testament. The term *Märchen* is as imprecise in German as 'fairy-tale' is in English ('fairy-tale' would in any case be an inappropriate word to use in Old Testament *Gattungsgeschichte*, since fairies do not feature in the Old Testament). In the present work *Märchen* covers tales about nature (like Jotham's parable), about tools, about spirits, demons and ghosts, about magic, about giants, about children (a wonder-child like Samson or a heroine like Jephthah's daughter), about men and women. They all have some element of the fabulous about them. But the *Märchen*, he insists, is not a vehicle of revelation. In an appendix to this reprint, H.-J. Hermisson reviews Gunkel's essay and agrees with his conclusion that the *Märchen* is never a form for expressing faith in the Old Testament, but adds that it may serve as a demonstration or illustration of faith. But Gunkel, he says, can teach us to perceive the poetic narratives of the Old Testament in such a way as to recognize poetry, if not the *Märchen*, as a proper vehicle for the language of faith.

F. F. BRUCE

HERRMANN, W.: *Ester im Streit der Meinungen* (Beiträge zur Erforschung des Alten Testaments und des antiken Judentums, 4). 1986. Pp. 93. (Peter Lang, Frankfurt am Main. Price: Sw.Fr. 24.00 ($15.00), ISBN 3 8204 8947 9; ISSN 0722 0790)

The purpose of this short study in reception history is to survey the ways the book of Esther has been evaluated theologically since the eighteenth century, theological worth being for this confessedly Christian author the only justification for the book's inclusion in the Hebrew canon. In his opening chapter he interestingly tracks the changing estimation of the book in the present century by means of the reference made to it in the four collective SOTS volumes (ed. Peake, Robinson, Rowley, and Anderson). In further chapters, the catalogue of anti-Semitic sentiments that have been voiced under the guise of interpretation of Esther makes depressing reading. But appreciation of the religious values of the book has never been entirely lacking, and the author argues finally that Christian readers are obliged to come to terms with the kind of piety of which Esther is an example. The book would have benefited from chapter titles, bibliography, and indexes.

D. J. A. CLINES

HYERS, C.: *And God Created Laughter: The Bible as Divine Comedy*. 1987. Pp. ix, 130. (John Knox Press, Atlanta, Georgia. Price: $9.95. ISBN 0 8042 1653 3)

'It is not difficult', remarks Professor Hyers towards the beginning of this book, 'to imagine Jesus' hearers laughing heartily over the picture of a man with a log in his eye trying to take a speck of dust out of his brother's eye — and getting the point unforgettably.' Those who *do* have difficulty in stretching their imagination thus far might be advised to give this book a miss. In discussing certain biblical passages where irony is clearly intended, as in the Book of Jonah, it has some perceptive points to make, even if the title of the chapter in question ('The Day Jonah Swallowed the Whale') may not appeal to all tastes. The author is fully aware, unlike the congregation he remembers addressing on the topic, that Jonah is a story, not history. He is not a critical scholar, however, and his work is paraclesis rather than exegesis. 'The creation of Eve,' we are told, was the creation of laughter. 'Into Adam's loneliness and incompleteness came life and love and laughter.' One wonders how long he continued to see the joke. But whatever the defects of this book (among which I would include the title of chapter 4, 'Mary had a little lamb'), it cannot be accused of failing to take laughter seriously.

J. ASHTON

JEPPESEN, K.: *Graeder ikke saa saare: Studier i Mikabogens* sigte I–II. 1987. Pp. 605. (Aarhus Universitetsforlag. Price: D.Kr. 288.00. ISBN 87 7288 078 3)

The title of this substantial doctoral thesis, 'Weep not so sore' (Mic. 1:10) is taken by the author to be one of the indications that the book in its present form is a rearrangement in a coherent structure of the prophecies of a pre-exilic prophet. This rearrangement and editing took place during the Exile and was presented in such a way as to offer an explanation of the calamity of the Exile and to bring a message of hope. Critical study has in the past often left Micah with only about a third of the book to his name. Dr Jeppesen (who admits quite properly that he uses the methods of Scandinavian traditio-historical research) argues that virtually all of the contents of the book come from the prophet but are now directed at the exiles. Examples are given of other interpretations of pre-exilic material during the exilic period, e.g., in

Jeremiah, Ezekiel, and (Deutero–)Isaiah; and something similar is argued concerning Psalm 22. On the basis of this view Dr Jeppesen proceeds to expound the book in considerable detail, dividing it into seven sections: 1:2–16 (doom on the land and its cities); 2:1–3:8 (Israel's sin); 3:9–4:5 (prophecies on war and peace); 4:6–5:5 (overcoming Jerusalem's trouble); 4:6–5:5 (a link between hope in 4–5 and doom in 6); 6:1–7:6 (concerning the condemnation of the people); 7:7–20 (the restoration of the people). The analysis and the argument concerning the exilic use of the oracles are worked out thoroughly and with great learning. Dr Jeppesen has made a notable contribution to Micah studies. We may hope for more of this high quality from his pen.

G. W. ANDERSON

JEREMIAS, J.: *Das Königtum Gottes in den Psalmen: Israels Begegnung mit dem kanaanäischen Mythos in den Jahwe-König-Psalmen* (Forschungen zur Religion und Literatur des Alten und Neuen Testaments, 141). 1987. Pp. 189. (Vandenhoeck & Ruprecht, Göttingen. Price: DM 70.00. ISBN 3 525 53819 7)

This study centres on the 'Enthronement Psalms', which are then distinguished in two types: 93, 97, 99; and 47, 95, 96, 98. The first group are said to originate in an adaptation of Canaanite myth, whereby the repetition of primeval story is transformed into statements of present and enduring reality (*Yahweh malak* = 'it is Yahweh who rules as king'). The second group develops from the imperative hymnic form and bases God's universal reign on historical experience, and accordingly was used in dramatic actualizations. All these psalms are found to belong to the celebration of God's reign in the context of Jerusalem's autumn festival, and in this setting are fruitfully connected by Jeremias with other psalms such as 29, 68 and the Songs of Zion. While generally respecting the text and integrity of his psalms, Jeremias is at pains to distribute them through the broad phases of the religious history. In the early period he traces developments involving especially 29, 93, and 104 (which all illustrate myth becoming statement of the external and present) and the Deut. 33 framework, Pss. 68, 47, and Ex. 15 (which show myth adapted to the historical). In the later period he makes 95 and 99 depend on the Deuteronomic circle, 96 and 98 on Deutero–Isaiah, and 97 on the future hope of the Hellenistic age. The debt to Northern Israel is recognized in the early psalms and in the Ark tradition (to which an appendix is devoted).

This is a valuable contribution to a central subject, and is notable for its sensitivity to the different aspects of the tradition, even if some of the distinctions (e.g. his static interpretation of 93 and 29) are questionable and there may need to be more recognition of the dependence of Deuteronomists and Deutero–Isaiah on liturgical tradition.

J. H. EATON

JOÜON, P., S.J.: *Ruth. Commentaire philologique et exégétique*. Second, corrected, edition, 1986. Pp. xi, 100. (Pontifical Biblical Institute, Rome. Price: Lire 10,200. ISBN 88 7653 586 1)

It is a pleasure to welcome the re-edition of this little handbook, first published in 1953, well known to many generations of teachers of the Hebrew Bible. This second edition differs from the first only in the provision of short list corrigenda as p. 100. After a compact introduction of twenty-three pages, dealing with the usual matters, the book contains a translation at the head of each page, and detailed grammatical and exegetical notes by an acknowledged master. Though rather dated now exegetically, and nowhere near so thorough as Sasson's work (for example), this work continues to meet a need for those preparing to teach Ruth especially to classes of beginners in

Hebrew. Does not the inspired book of Ruth merit, asks the author, the same meticulous care that one gives to the explication of an eclogue of Virgil, for example?

D. J. A. Clines

Kaiser, W. C., Jr: *Toward Rediscovering The Old Testament* (Academie Books). 1987. Pp. 219, (Zondervan, Grand Rapids, Michigan. ISBN 0 310 37120 1)

This is a vigorous attempt by a very conservative Evangelical scholar to give the Old Testament the integral place in the church's life that Calvin (unlike Luther) thought it should have. Scholars such as himself, says Kaiser, believe that the Bible is the infallible Word of God, but that does not mean that they have closed minds. It is just that they believe that the events narrated in the Old Testament and their interpretation are one and the same thing, so that if the evidence adduced ever sufficed to disprove any one historical assertion the whole edifice of their faith would collapse. Nor is the historical critical method wrong in itself; it is, though, normally much abused by its practitioners. The Canon of the Old Testament is, for Kaiser, validated from within Scripture, for did not Jesus, in speaking of the righteous men slain from Abel (in Gen.) to Zechariah (in 2 Chron.), implicitly endorse a Canon running from Gen–2 Chron.? The Canon probably came about through each new book that was written being immediately placed in the sanctuary and given canonical status. Nothing in the Old Testament is untrue or is in conflict with the New Testament. What, you ask, about some Old Testament texts about the afterlife? A positive, if imperfectly developed, doctrine is evidenced by the Enoch story, by Abraham's words in Gen. 22:5 (interpreted in the light of Heb. 11:17–19), and by Eccles 3:21, rightly understood. Nothing in the Old Testament is obsolete, unless specifically stated to be so in the New Testament. The continuity of the Old and New covenants is, in Kaiser's view, sadly underrated: the New is 'new' only in the sense that the New Moon is new. Even the 'ceremonial' parts of the Torah embody permanently valid moral principles (if the Old Testament were more heeded, Christians would not give the ambiguous testimony that they do about abortion). Ingenious as much of this book is, the general argumentation is not likely to convince anyone who does not share the author's commitment to literal inerrancy.

B. P. Robinson

Kappler, C., *et al.*: *Apocalypses et Voyages dans l'Au delà*. 1987. Pp. 530. (Cerf, Paris. Price: Fr. 250.00. ISBN 2 204 02701 4; ISSN 0768 2980)

Kappler's general introduction to this collection of essays offers a clear and at times penetrating analysis of some of the problems which beset the student of apocalyptic. He is rightly concerned with the proper and reasonable definition of terms; and his survey of some recent attempts to define 'apocalyptic', 'apocalypse', 'eschatological', etc., is both helpful and positive. But the essays which follow deal with material deriving from widely separated times, places, and cultural milieux. We begin in Ancient Mesopotamia in the second millennium B.C. or earlier, and end in present-day Western Europe. From the stories of Ereshkigal and Gilgamesh, we travel via the Ugaritic myth of Baʿal and Mot, the surviving fragments of Philo of Byblos, and the Eleusinian Mysteries, to Jewish, Christian, and Islamic apocalyptic literature; we find ourselves briefly in the Middle Ages, and conclude with an essay on Apocalyptic and the nuclear threat. Of special interest to readers of the *Book List* will be the essays on Ereshkigal and Gilamesh (J. Bottéro); the myth of Ba'al and Mot (P. Xella); Philo of Byblos (S. Ribichini); Ideas of Inspiration in Jewish and Christian Apocalyptic (A. Piñero-Sáenz); Qumran

Apocalyptic (F. García-Martínez); the Latin Apocalypse of Paul (C. Kappler); the Nag-Hammadi library (M. Scopello); and the Mazdaean Apocalypses (P. Gignoux). While individual essays are well-written and informative, the lack of a concluding essay, which attempts to draw some general conclusions from the wealth of material presented, is unfortunate: the overall purpose of the collection is not as clearly enunciated as perhaps it might be.

C. T. R. HAYWARD

KNAPP, D.: *Deuteronomium 4: Literarische Analyse und theologische Interpretation* (Göttinger Theologische Arbeiten, 35). 1987. Pp. viii, 226. (Vandenhoeck & Ruprecht, Göttingen. Price: DM 48.00. ISBN 3 525 87386 3)

This 1986 Göttingen dissertation is a product of what the author calls the DtrGö school. Its main detailed discussion concerns the 'successive' development of the three main sections of Deut. 4:1–40 (1–14, 15–28, 29–40), which as a chapter assumes both the three that precede and the many that follow. Not only has the core of each part been built on the one before, but each has been subsequently expanded. The basis was provided by 4:1–4, 9–14 on obedience to the law; the addition of vv. 15–16a, 19–28 on idolatry marked the next main stage; and that of vv. 29–35 concerning 'return' the third. The expansions to each section followed in reverse order: vv. 35–40, 16b–18, and finally 5–8. Each of these six sections is an example of how the late Deuteronomistic period witnessed intensive development of the themes, motifs, and formulae of existing Deuteronom(ist)ic texts. Two appendices handle vv. 41–43, 44–49. On the 'introductory' vv. 44–49, Knapp concludes that vv. 45–46a represented the original transition from Deut. 1–3 to 5 ff., and were themselves successively supplemented. The little section on the Transjordanian refuge cities depends on both Deut. 19 and Josh. 20. A concluding section argues more briefly that Deut. 29:1–14, 15–27, and 30:1–10 reflect a parallel exegetical development of the three themes handled in 4:1–40; and notes links between this double 3-fold supplementation of 'Deuteronomy' and elements of the Deuteronomistic expansion of Jeremiah. Within its own terms, the details of Knapp's argumentation are attractive; yet this reader is worried by the deafening silence maintained over R. Polzin's equally 'literarische Analyse' of this and related material. Balancing panels like those Knapp has detected in Deut. 4 and 29–30 may demand a more aesthetic account.

A. G. AULD

LEENEX, G.: *De vroegere en de nieuwe dingen bij Deuterojesja.* 1987. Pp. 331. (VU Boekhandel/Uitgeverij b.v. De Boelelaan 1105, 1081 HV Amsterdam. ISBN 90 6256 340 6)

This doctoral dissertation appears as presented for examination at the Free University in Amsterdam in early December 1987. It was prepared under the supervision of Professor W. A. M. Beuken, whose own commentary on the latter part of the book of Isaiah has already covered chapters 40–55 (see *B.L.* 1985, p. 48) in the series De Predeking van het Oude Testament. The dissertation is based largely on a detailed discussion of the terms 'former', 'later', 'coming' and 'new' in Isa. 41–44, with comparative use of selected passages in the remainder of 40–48. The careful analysis of the terms leads to closer distinctions, especially in relation to chapter 48. Clearly, such analytical discussion is of great value in clarifying the issues, and the latter part in particular helps the author to avoid generalization on the basis of a limited text. There are wider issues to consider in connection with the context, both literary and historical, of the chapters studied. An English summary is provided on pages 323–31.

P. R. ACKROYD

LIWAK, R.: *Der Prophet und die Geschichte: Ein literar-historische Untersuchung zum Jeremiabuch.* (BWANT 121.) 1987. Pp. ix, 402. (Kohlhammer, Stuttgart. Price: DM 89.00. ISBN 3 17 009442 4)

Whether because it is profound or because it is unnecessarily obscure this *Habilitationsschrift* is extraordinarily difficult to read. It would take very many hours to get to the bottom of it and to be confident that one knew what was there.

It consists of a detailed study of Jer. 2–6 which is divided into 5 units (2; 3:1–4:4; 4:5–31; 5; 6), together with chapters which deal with historical, archaeological and topographical background and others which supply the theoretical parts of the book. The treatment of Jer. 1:1–3 falls into the background section, since these verses are regarded as a kind of historical framework for the book of Jeremiah. As the sub-title indicates the book has literary as well as historical concerns and these interact in various ways and with a high degree of complication.

Both on the historical and literary sides there are parts of the work which give expression to easily recognizable scholarly concerns. Attention is given to text, lexicography and grammar, although the author perhaps does not have a deep interest in these matters. The outcome of the long discussion on *dabar* (surely an exhausted subject!) is disappointing: 'history' is rightly rejected for *dib^{e}re* at Jer. 1:1, but instead of 'words' a fudge is proposed (*was Jeremia betrifft*) (p. 97). An interest is historical-critical exegesis is evident in the discussion of 'the enemy from the north' (pp. 218–23) and the Scythian hypothesis (pp. 136–47). Liwak rightly identifies the first with the Babylonians and suggests that the absence of an explicit equation in poetic passages is perhaps explicable as a reticence which was designed to enhance the rhetorical effectiveness of Jeremiah's utterance. Nevertheless, he finds references to the Scythians at 4:29 (p. 235) and 5:16 (p. 262). There is a recognition in his treatment of chapter 2 that the historical background of some passages of the book may be difficult to discover (pp. 185 f.).

The author distinguishes between words of Jeremiah in 2–6 and the exegesis which is appropriate to them, and the exegetical tendencies of 2–6 as a collection or complex. We should be agnostic as to whether or not Jeremiah regarded the fall of Jerusalem as a final disaster, whereas views of the future emerge in the collection 2–6: there is an explicit future perspective in chapters 2; 4:5 ff.; 5; 6 which belongs to the early exilic period and the hope of salvation appears later in 3:1–4:4 (p. 326).

It is the 'rhetorical' interest which particularly draws together the literary investigation and the theorizing about historiography. The description of 2–6, and especially chapter 2, as structures swarming with rhetorical devices implies that they are ordered in such a way as to maximize their power of persuasion. They aim to exercise pressure on the wills of those who hear or read and to persuade them that the attitudes which are struck should be adopted and acted on. Historiography in the context of prophetic literature acquires a special character in the first place because the past is made to serve the present and the future. Hence there is a convergence of recollection, experience and expectation. This does not invalidate the kind of interest in history which is expressed in the literature: an absolute distinction between fact and fiction has to be surrendered for all historiography which, because of its partial recovery of the past and its selectivity, has fictional aspects. A prophet like Jeremiah does not write political history nor does he ascribe to historical events an ultimate causative force. Israel's destiny is rather dependent on the quality of her trust in Yahweh and her degree of willingnes to be guided by him — this is the chorus of the rhetoric. History has an illustrative or 'concretizing' function in relation to these theological convictions. I am not sure how new this is. It is expressed in a manner which I would not choose.

W. McKane

Loretz, O. and Kottsieper, I.: *Colometry in Ugaritic and Biblical Poetry: Introduction, Illustrations and Topical Bibliography*. 1987. Pp. 166. (CIS-Verlag, Altenberge. Price: DM 49.80. ISBN 3 88733 074 9)

As is well known, the key to understanding the Ugaritic texts in verse is determination of correct stichometry. After an outline of their method for achieving this, which involves consonant counting but ignores vowels and stress, the authors show how it works in establishing the line-divisions of an extract in Ugaritic. In part 2 the method is illustrated with a selection of Hebrew texts which include short passages (Isa. 30:1–5; Ps. 19:5–6a; etc.) and complete poems (Ps. 114; Prov. 5).

The method certainly works for Ugaritic, though in the example given recognition of anacrusis and of thematic unity within a tricolon were as important as counting consonants in establishing the verse-lines. Transferred to Hebrew, the results of colometric analysis seem quite drastic even though the authors stress that the segments they bracket off are not simply to be deleted. Whereas the poetic texts in Ugaritic were virtually unaltered by later editing, biblical Hebrew verse, which belongs to the same tradition, is multi-layered. The authors argue that their approach will show us the various editorial changes to be found, particularly in the form of later accretions (glosses, expansions, etc.). Used judiciously, in fact, their method will certainly show where division into verse-lines is faulty but as they themselves are aware, length of line is only one of many significant factors in the analysis of verse.

The thirty-four-page 'topical bibliography' includes works on Akkadian and Egyptian (but none on Aramaic) though there is scant reference to these languages in the text. Occasionally, the underlying German shines through the English translation (by F. Renfroe) and there are a few misprints. There are useful indices.

W. G. E. Watson

Lurker, M.: *Wörterbuch biblischer Bilder und Symbole*. 3rd, expanded edition. 1987. Pp. 506. (Kösel, Munich. Price: DM 48.00. ISBN 3 466 20158 6)

The first edition of this work appeared in 1973 and its general character was described in *B.L.* 1974, p. 12. This third edition has been enlarged by over 170 pages, with 32 new articles and considerable enrichment of the bibliography. There is a useful register of 'things meant', correlated with the various symbols which point to them. The approach remains, perhaps, most suitable for preachers and teachers who want simple answers rather than enticement to pursue deeper mysteries, though the bibliography can serve the latter desire.

R. P. R. Murray

Meynet, R.: *Initiation à la rhétorique biblique: 'Qui donc est le plus grand?'* Tome 1: Texte; Tome 2: Planches ('Initiations'). 1982. Pp. 198 and 30 tables. Cerf, Paris. Price: Fr. 125.00 (set). ISBN 2 204 01868 6)

This is mainly a New Testament study but it contains some sections on Old Testament passages, notably from Kings (e.g. pp. 113–18). The author is convinced of the importance of the order of words, parallelism, chiasmus and that sort of thing. The second volume is a package of loose tables or diagrams which display these relations. All sorts of peculiarities in texts can be explained by their need to conform to the laws of balance, chiasmus, concentric composition and the like. The author is wrathful with modern translations for failing to represent precisely these patterns of word order (e.g. p. 29 n.): but is he not thereby demanding the impossible? J. BARR

MICHAUD, R.: *Qohélet et l'hellénisme: La littérature de Sagesse — Histoire et théologie,* II (Lire la Bible, 77). 1987. Pp. 221 (Cerf, Paris. Price: Fr. 90.00. ISBN 2 204 02692 1; ISSN 0588 2257)

This volume is in the series 'Lire la Bible' where Steinmann has already written on Qoheleth and where Michaud has *inter alia* published a more general introduction to wisdom (no. 65).

The book is in two parts of similar length. In the first part, entitled 'History', Michaud sets the scene, as it were, for the appearance of the book of Qoheleth by examining the history of the period. It may be usual to claim that hellenization of the east began in earnest with the conquest of Alexander the Great in 333 B.C., but the process had already begun a long time before the Conquest; and when Qoheleth was writing, the most ardent hellenists would have been of the Jewish community. In this connection Michaud cites the prominent Tobiad family in particular, and discusses its great influence over the centuries, before Alexander, during Alexander's rule, under the Diadochi and under the Ptolemies.

Part two, entitled 'Theology' then takes the book of Qoheleth and places it in a Jewish community, many of whose members were in favour of Greek culture. The fact that the book was originally written in Hebrew (or Aramaic, as it is sometimes argued) and not Greek, and that the first Greek translation of it seems to be as late as the second century A.D., is not considered.

What follows is not a commentary, but brief notes on the test of Qoheleth. Michaud discovers the author's position vis à vis cosmology (1:4–11) anthropology (1:12–3:15), sociology (3:15–4:16; 5:7–6:10), religion (4:17–5:6), ideology (6:11–9:6) and ethics (9:7–12:7), and finds the hellenistic hand everywhere.

While it is refreshing to have Qoheleth interpreted in the light of Greek culture, Michaud comes short of his apparent objective, and perhaps because of the format he has chosen for himself. The 'History' is useful and enlightening, but the 'Theology' lacks the depth needed to balance the scholarship of the first part. There is room only for the briefest comments; there is no room for hard facts and detailed argument which such a subject demands. R. B. SALTERS

DE MOOR, J. C.: *An Anthology of Religious Texts from Ugarit* (Nisaba 16). 1987. Pp. xiv, 309. (Brill, Leiden. Price: Fl. 78.00 ($39.00). ISSN 0169 930X; ISBN 90 04 08330 8)

DE MOOR, J. C., and SPRONK, K.: *A Cuneiform Anthology of Religious Texts from Ugarit* (Semitic Study Series 6). 1987. Pp. viii, 192. Brill, Leiden. Price: Fl. 68.00 ($34.00). ISSN 0169 9911; ISBN 90 04 08331 6)

The basic tools for anyone wishing to learn Ugaritic are now available: S. Segert's *Basic Grammar of the Ugaritic Language*, 1984 in spite of its shortcomings (see *B.L.* 1986, p. 142) and the two works under review. The second, by de Moor and Spronk, is essentially a chrestomathy and since the texts are given only in cuneiform the student is encouraged to read them in the original, not in transliteration. A simple glossary (with no cognates or discussion) and an experimental semantic glossary are also provided but there is no table of signs.

The companion volume, by de Moor alone, gives a translation set out in verse lines of the thirty-four selected passages. These comprise the standard mythological texts (Baal Cycle, Stories of Keret and Aqhat, etc.) plus four incantations as many rituals and six 'myth and rituals'. Ample footnotes explain difficulties with extensive reference to the Old Testament and for these alone the book can be recommended, even to specialists. The overall positive line of interpretation is particularly welcome. De Moor still considers the Baal Cycle to reflect the pattern of the seasons and a table (pp. 101–08) matches each episode of the story with what he suggests is its appropriate cultic event and date. There is an index of scriptural references and a subject index.

W. G. E. Watson

Neef, H.-D.: *Die Heilstraditionen Israels in der Verkündigung des Propheten Hosea* (BZAW 169). 1987. Pp. xiv, 299. (De Gruyter, Berlin. Price: DM 98.00. ISBN 3 11 01093 1)

This lightly revised Tübingen dissertation of 1984/85 deduces that Hosea exhibits continuity to inherited tradition as he develops in his preaching a series of themes basic to the story of Israel's faith. Most of the argument is presented in an exegesis of passages scattered through the book that deals with six topics: (1) Jacob as an example to sinful Israel, in 12:1–15 (here siding with those who have read the Jacob-traditions positively); (2) Moses as the prophet acting on behalf of Yahweh, in 12:14; (3) the choosing of Israel in the desert as a reinterpretation of the Sinai tradition, in 9:10–17; 10:1–2, 11–13a; 11:1–7; 13:4–8; 2:16–17; 12:10; (4) covenant as election, in 2:18–25; 6:7–11a; 8:1–3; 10:3–4; 11:2; (5) the anticipations of the decalogue tradition, in 12:10; 13:1–4; 8:4–6; 4:1–3; and (6) Mizpah, Tabor, and Šittim and the guilt of Israel's leaders, in 5:1–7. Neef's thesis is closely argued, with detailed attention to the complex text-critical situation in the book of Hosea (he has also published an article on MT/LXX in the book in *Biblica* 67, 1986); and it will repay equally close scrutiny.

A. G. Auld

Noth, M.: *The Chronicler's History*. Translated by H. G. M. Williamson, with an Introduction (JSOT Supplement Series, 50). 1987. Pp. 200. (Sheffield Academic Press. Price: £15.00 ($22.50); ISBN 1 85075 043 2. Paperback price: £5.50 ($9.50); ISBN 1 85075 044 0)

It is a pleasure to welcome the translation of the second section and appendix from Noth's classic *Überlieferungsgeschichtliche Studien* I, 1943, by a scholar who himself writes well — and not least because the translator is expert in Chronicles, Ezra, and Nehemiah, and has provided his own assessment of Noth's studies of the Chronicler (pp. 11–26). The volume complements the rendering of *The Deuteronomistic History*, published in 1981 as JSOT Suppl. 15 (see *B.L.* 1982, p. 69). The appendix, on 'The "Priestly Writing" and the Redaction of the Pentateuch', might have deserved mention in the title page and even in the Introduction; for it supplements Noth's conclusions about the Deuteronomist, rather than the work presently in hand, and is a vital anticipation of his *A History of Pentateuchal Traditions*.

A. G. Auld

VAN OORSCHOT, J.: *Gott als Grenze: Eine literar- und redaktionsgeshichtliche Studie zu den Gottesreden des Hiobbuches* (Beiheft zur Zeitschrift für die alttestamentliche Wissenschaft, 170). 1987. Pp. x, 259. (De Gruyter, Berlin. Price: DM 82.00. ISBN 3 11 011163 2)

Job 38:1–42:6 presents God's first speech and Job's response, then God's second speech and Job's response. Some critics have considered the first speech irrelevant, and many have found greater fault with the second, with its peculiar descriptions of Behemoth and Leviathan. Van Oorschot sets out the five main approaches to the problem: to exclude all this material from the original; to defend it as it stands; to posit a complex growth in several stages; to keep the first speech only, with no response; to reconstruct one speech (without Behemoth and Leviathan) and one response. His own proposal is of this last kind. His work will be valued as an orderly survey and evaluation of previous research, made all the clearer by an appendix systematically laying out the proposals and arguments of twenty-one scholars. J. H. EATON

PETERSEN, D. L. (ed.): *Prophecy in Israel: Search for an Identity* (Issues in Religion and Theology 10). 1987. Pp. xi, 178. (SPCK, London; Fortress Press, Philadelphia. Price: £3.95. ISBN 0 281 04275 6; 0 8006 1773 8)

This is a collection of seven articles and extracts from books on the subject of the identity of biblical prophets. The pieces are set in context by a useful introductory essay 'Ways of Thinking about Israel's Prophets' by the editor. Petersen isolates some six positions in the modern critical discussion of prophecy and then fits various writers into these six categories. The three extracts are from major figures in the field: Gunkel's 'The Prophets as Writers and Poets' from his *Die Propheten* (1923); Mowinckel's 'Cult and Prophecy' from his *Psalmenstudien* III (1922); Weber's 'The Prophet' from his *The Sociology of Religion* (German original 1922). Then follow four American articles: Ross, 'The Prophet as Yahweh's Messenger' from the Muilenburg *Festschrift*, *Israel's Prophetic Heritage* (1962); J. S. Holladay Jr's 'Assyrian Statecraft and the Prophets of Israel' from *HTR* 63 (1970); Mays's 'Justice: Perspectives from the Prophetic Tradition' from *Interpretation* 37 (1983); and Tucker's 'The Role of the Prophets and the Role of the Church' from *Quarterly Review: A Scholarly Journal for Reflection on Ministry* 1 (1981). A short select Bibliography concludes the book. It is an interesting volume, though the selection is a curious one. The combination of 1920s European masters and modern American journal articles is unusual in the extreme, though Petersen does orchestrate the disparate voices quite well. Every reader will be able to think of a different selection of extracts and articles, but I doubt if much improvement could be made on Petersen's strange miscellany of classical and modern viewpoints. An excellent book for introducing the vexed question of the identity of the biblical prophets. R. P. CARROLL

PREUSS, H. D.: *Einführung in die alttestamentliche Weisheitsliteratur* (Urban-Taschenbücher 383) 1987. Pp. 241. (Kohlhammer, Stuttgart. Price: DM 24.00. ISBN 3 17 009590 0)

It is more important, Preuss claims, to read the biblical text itself with understanding than to swot up modern literature on the Bible: thus he leads readers to recognize deeper signicance in what they read. First he sets the wisdom literature firmly within its environment: several pages each on comparable literature in Egypt, Mesopotamia, Ebla and Ugarit. Different collections and *Gattungen* of *Proverbs* are described, with ten vital pages on the place of Yahweh (rarely mentioned!). *Job* and *Ecclesiastes* are given special attention as 'turning-points' in the movement leading to works in later Judaism more closely related to contemporary thought: *Wisdom of Solomon*, *Ben Sira* and *Pirqê Aboth*. Discussion of the theological significance of wisdom in Old Testament and Christian belief (ancient and modern) conclude a book which should stimulate thought for all readers, specialist and non-specialist alike. This book should lead readers into the subject as a true introduction should.

JOHN G. SNAITH

PRICKETT, S.: *Words and The Word: Language, poetics and biblical interpetation*. 1986. Pp. xii,. 305. (Cambridge University Press, Cambridge. Price: £27.50. ISBN 0 521 32248 0)

The growth of interest in the literary interpretation of the Bible among biblical scholars and the increasing influence of literary criticism in current biblical studies will be further facilitated by this dense book from the Professor of English in the Australian National University (Canberra). Prickett takes as his central text 1 Kings 19:8–12 and, in particular, the phrase 'a still small voice' in order to scrutinize modern translations of the Bible and to discuss his long-standing interest in the study of religious language in nineteenth-century England. In five substantial chapters he conducts a very wide ranging analysis of the Bible in English literary theory and also the nature of the Bible as poetry. The first chapter deals with the problem of transparent and opaque texts, with special reference to recent translations of the Bible. His second chapter discusses the relation of the religious and the poetic in language and the effects of linguistic change on the notion of primal consciousness (Owen Barfield territory here). The third chapter looks at poetry and prophecy, in particular the language of the Great Code (Blake's famous phrase for the Bible) and the book of Nature. A fourth chapter considers Elijah and Dante (see *Purgatorio* Canto XXXII) and the problems of convention and realism. The final chapter in a complex discussion of metaphor and reality. In the course of these five chapters Prickett covers an immense area of writing on the Bible, religious language and the nature of the poetic: all the great names are here from Aristotle and Augustine to Coleridge and Hopkins, with a wealth of detailed discussion of Herder, Lowth, and many minor writers on the Bible and translation.

This book occupies a parallel universe of discourse to that of biblical studies, so some degree of translation and cultural pluralism must be allowed for by biblical scholars reading it. It is, however, well worth the concentration required to follow its arguments and the intricacies of its detailed expositions. It is not at all clear to me that Prickett does usefully clarify the significance of 1 Kings 19:12 and it does seem to me that he puts more weight on that text than it will bear. But full marks to him for raising such an interesting and far-reaching discussion around that particular story of Elijah on Mount Horeb. Many a biblical scholar has failed to do anything like the justice Prickett does to such complex matters of desynonymy and transparent texts. My one serious criticism of him is his misprision of Kenneth Grayston's attitude to the NEB and consequentially his unfair references to him on pp. 9–11. Otherwise this is a book which I hope will be taken up by many biblical scholars and used to enrich their understanding of the Bible.

R. P. CARROLL

DE PURY, A.: *Le Chant de la Création: L'homme et l'univers selon le récit de Génèse 1* (Cahiers Bibliques, 1). 1986. Pp. 30. (Editions du Moulin, Aubonne)

A contribution to the forum of 'Christians for the Year 2000' held at Geneva in 1986 has been issued as a booklet containing a full exegesis of the P account of creation. Though brief it contains many shrewd comments both on the frequent misinterpretations of Genesis 1 and by way of proposals for a better understanding. Most characteristic, as might be expected from this author, is its acute literary sensitivity.

R. J. COGGINS

RENDTORFF, R.: *Mōse-gosho no Denshō–shi-teki Mondai.* Translated by T. Yamaga. 1987. Pp. 337 + Index (pp. 10). (Kyōbunkwan, Tokyo. Price: ¥2,500)

This is a Japanese translation of *Das Überlieferungsgeschichtliche Problem des Pentateuch* 1976) (see *B.L.* 1978, p. 76). The translator appended an article, 'Some Trends in Recent Studies in the Pentateuch'.

K. K. SACON

RIESEN, R. A.: *Criticism and Faith in Late Victorian Scotland: A. B. Davidson, William Robertson Smith and George Adam Smith.* 1985. Pp. xxiv, 466. (University Press of America, Lanham, Maryland. Price: $18.75. ISBN 0 8191 4656 0)

This is a study of three distinguished Old Testament scholars who came out of the ranks of the star-studded, post-disruption Free Church of Scotland. It originated as a thesis in the Department of Ecclesiastical History in the University of Edinburgh, and so although it necessarily deals with Old Testament scholarship, it also undertakes to trace the complicated course of Higher Criticism in a particular ecclesiastical context, the conflicts which it awakened and the stances which are attributable to George Adam Smith, Andrew Bruce Davidson, and William Robertson Smith.

Those who are interested as Old Testament scholars may find the ecclesiastical entanglements difficult for an outsider to penetrate and perhaps too tortuous for their taste. George Adam Smith was a notable preacher, a gifted exegete and a traveller in the Holy Land who encapsulated his journeys in stylish prose. At one period a Professor of Old Testament in the Free Church College at Glasgow, his career reached its climax when he was appointed Principal and Vice Chancellor of the University of Aberdeen. A. B. Davidson was a very influential Professor of Old Testament at New College, Edinburgh, a man of wide learning and impressive spirituality. The range of learning which an educated man was expected to master in nineteenth-century Scotland is nowhere better illustrated than in his *Biblical and Literary Essays*. One cannot read him or Robertson Smith — in their work on the prophets, for example — without being aware that they have a philosophical education and that Locke and Hume are a background to what they have to say about prophetic dreams and visions.

To what extent Davidson had appreciated all the implications of higher criticism is difficult to judge in view of the posthumous publication of books whose material may reach back to earlier years, but his *Theology of the Old Testament* has a pre-critical appearance. Of the wholeness of Robertson Smith's critical scholarship there is no doubt: to the finger-tips he was a practitioner of biblical science and it was on his head that the wrath of the Church fell. He was surely the greatest Semitist to come out of Scotland, a Professor of Old Testament in the Free Church College at Aberdeen when he was twenty-four and Professor of Arabic at Cambridge when he died at the age of forty-eight. Those who have read the inscription on his headstone in the kirkyard at Keig will know that there is nothing on it about the earlier Scottish chapters of his life. It can hardly be accidental that they have been left unrecorded and that only his destination at Cambridge has been chronicled.

The author has a good subject and he has dealt with it very fully.

W. McKane

Sawyer, J. F. A.: *Prophecy and the Prophets of the Old Testament* (Oxford Bible Series). 1987. Pp. xii, 163. (Oxford University Press. Price: £19.50; ISBN 0 19 213249 0. Paperback price: £6.95; ISBN 0 19 213250 4)

Three thematic chapters open this handy and lucidly presented overview of Old Testament prophecy. 'The Phenomenon of Prophecy' locates the 'Writing Prophets' within the religious, political, and educational heart of ancient Israelite society. 'The Prophetic Literature' notes the strengths and weaknesses of form criticism, mentions the main types of speech and composition, and sketches editorial principles. Then their message is handled in terms of reform, divine intervention, the city of David, and the day of the Lord. The next three chapters review the prophets themselves: first the narratives from Moses to Huldah; then the books of Isaiah, Jeremiah, and Ezekiel; and finally Daniel to Malachi — with the Twelve presented in apt thumbnail sketches. The concluding chapter, on 'Prophecy and Interpretation', notes Islam's appropriation of the prophets but not of the Bible; and moves to consider the prophets separately in Christian and in Jewish tradition, and also the theme of prophecy and fulfilment — both within the Old Testament and in its daughter traditions together. Well chosen bibliographies conclude an able volume. Yet students will need to look elsewhere for an introduction to those issues which currently make academic study of these prophets exciting.

A. G. Auld

Schmithals, W.: *Mokushi-bungaku Nyūmon*. Translated by K. Toki, S. Eguchi and K. Takaoka. 1986. Pp. 296. (Kyōbunkwan, Tokyo. Price: ¥2,200)

This is a Japanese translation of *Die Apokalyptik: Einführung und Deutung* (1973). (See *B.L.* 1974, p. 90–91).

K. K. Sacon

Schmitt, J. J.: *Isaiah and his Interpreters*. 1986. Pp. vi, 137. (Paulist Press, Mahwah, New York. Price: $8.95. ISBN 0 8091 2826 8)

This book offers a useful and fairly comprehensive survey of the book of Isaiah, looking at the variety of scholarly contributions to its interpretation, showing the centrality of the prophet and of his message to the understanding of the complex book as a whole. If the selection in so short a compass is in some degree limiting, there is nevertheless helpful discussion of many issues of interpretation and a positive assessment of the value of the book.

P. R. Ackroyd

Schroer, S.: *In Israel gab es Bilder: Nachrichten von darstellender Kunst im alten Testament* (Orbis Biblicus et Orientalis 74). 1987. Pp. xiv, 553. (Universitätsverlag, Freiburg [CH]; Vandenhoeck & Ruprecht, Göttingen. Price Sw.Fr. 130.00. ISBN 3 7278 0526 9; 3 525 53704 4)

The author, working under Professors O. Keel and D. Barthélemy, presented this thesis in Fribourg in 1986. She claims (it seems with justification) that it is the first systematic attempt since F. de Saulcy

(1858, [2]1864) to establish what is affirmed in the short title, as against the theologically-determined thesis 'In Israel images were forbidden, therefore they did not exist'. The Introduction states the work's scope, to correlate the evidence of the biblical texts themselves with that of religious images actually found in Israel, and reviews the probable case for the prohibition of images having developed with monolatry, but only having reached its final form in exilic times. In the following chapters the data are discussed exhaustively, with full references to publications and with the help of 146 illustrations in the form of clear line drawings.

The chapters review in turn (1) Tree, plant and fruit images, including the meaning and probable illustrations of *'asherah* and other images connected with that cult; (2) Animal and *Mischwesen* images, the latter including 'cherubs' and *teraphim*, with the problem of the ephod; (3) Biblical data about anthropomorphic images in and around Israel; (4) Images of astral divinities in Israel and Judah; (5) The semantic field 'Image/Idol' in the Old Testament; (6) The main image-bearing materials mentioned in the Old testament, and (7) Old Testament information about Israelite craftsmanship and works of art.

The thesis is soberly argued, in a tone free from polemical animus as regards the book's main theme (though feminist animus finds expression here and there). Due weight is given to various theories for the interpretation of monuments, and relevant texts, both biblical and epigraphic, are competently discussed in a way which seems reliable as well as richly informative. This work gathers systematically the fruits of much work by scholars such as O. Keel, and both its treatments of details in the text and its full indices and bibliography should make it of lasting value.

R. P. R. MURRAY

SICRE, J. L.: *Los Profetas de Israel y su Mensaje: Antologia de textos* (Academia Christiana 35). 1986. Pp. 253. (Ediciones Cristiandad, Madrid. ISBN 84 7057 394 2)

In this volume the author distils, for a general audience, the fruit of his specialist studies on the Israelite prophets (see *B.L.* 1981, pp. 50–51; *B.L.* 1986, pp. 95–96). It takes the form of a thematic anthology of prophetic texts in two main sections deriving from Jeremiah's commission 'to pluck up and to break down' and 'to build and to plant', which for Sicre expresses the two poles of the entire message of the prophets. The first section has five parts dealing respectively with a history of sin, as seen in Jer. 2:2–19 and Ezek. 23:1–27 and 16; the action of God through the Exodus, the Covenant, the Temple and 'the Day of the Lord'; social injustice in Israel; and finally the military and economic imperialism of foreign powers. The two divisions in the second section are concerned with the future hope and the ideal king, followed by an epilogue on the Servant Songs. The aim is to bring the reader into contact with the prophets' own words, particularly so that they may be appreciated as poetry. Hence Sicre's comments are confined to the minimum necessary for understanding the text's contemporary purpose and original setting. An introductory chapter discusses the characteristics of prophecy in Israel and the formation of the prophetic corpus, paying special attention, in line with the general object of the work, to the literary genres. This is a lively and attractive book, easy to read and based on sound scholarship, which admirably fulfils the aim it sets itself. An English translation could have a wide appeal.

J. R. PORTER

SKA, J.-L.: *Le Passage de la Mer: Étude de la construction, du style et de la symbolique d'Ex 14.1–31* (Analecta Biblica, 109). 1986. Pp. 198. (Biblical Institute Press, Rome. Price: Lire 40,000. ISBN 88 7653 109 2)

Although from the point of view of source analysis Exodus 14 is composite, it is argued that the chapter has a unitary structure and coherent purpose rich in imagery and symbolism. Exodus 13:17–22 sets the scene by describing how Israel is now passing to a new life. Chapter 14 may be subdivided into three parts: 1–14 ('Confronted by the Sea'), 15–25 ('The Entry into the Sea'), and 26–31 ('The other side of the Sea'). The progress of the narrative as well as its style and symbolism thus mark the theme from slavery to freedom, from darkness to light, from death to life and in this way centres upon the birth of Israel as the people of Yahweh. Dr Ska also brings out the significance of the narrative and its symbolism for the 'Easter faith' of the Christian church. This is a stimulating and rewarding monograph.

E. W. NICHOLSON

SOGGIN, J. A.: *Introduzione all'Antico Testamento* (4th ed.) (Biblioteca di Cultura Religiosa, 14). 1987. Pp. 615. (Paideia, Brescia. Price: Lire 45,000. ISBN 88 394 03999 X)

The third edition of this book (1979) provided the basis of the revised English edition (1980), both reviewed in *B.L.* 1981, pp. 78–79. (For the first English edition, see *B.L.* 1977, p. 74. This edition, from which the third English edition is being translated, substitutes 'Yhwh' for 'Yahweh' and 'Hebrew Bible' for 'Old Testament'; but the text has been more substantially rewritten than previous editions were. It remains fairly conservative in its treatment nevertheless, and the structure, a compromise between chronological and canonical ordering, is unaltered. For those desiring a detailed, readable introduction in traditional style and format, this is surely the best available.

P. R. DAVIES

TÅNGBERG, K. A.: *Die prophetische Mahnrede. Form- und traditiongeschichtliche Studien zum prophetishen Umkehrruf.* (FRLANT, 143). 1987. Pp. 215. (Vandenhoeck & Ruprecht, Göttingen. Price: DM 54.00. ISBN 3 525 53822 7)

It has long been a problem, resolved in various ways, to discover the relationship between what appear to be absolute condemnations in the prophets of their contemporaries and words of exhortation and warning. This study sets out to provide a better basis for the discussion. After introductory matter, the author surveys the history of discussion, with some reference to prophetic material in the ancient near east. After a short consideration of terminology, the main part of the study is devoted to a survey of the actual material in the prophetic books and an attempt at defining the 'Gattung'. In short concluding chapters, the relationship to wisdom writings (and to prayers), to deuteronomic exhortations and an examination of traditio-historical considerations and again of some extra-biblical parallels are set out. The conclusions at the end are modestly and usefully handled, with a number of pointers to further areas of investigation. This is a helpful study, initiated under Professor Magne Sæbø, and continued in part in Munich especially with the help of Professor Jörg Jeremias. It shows the thoroughness and care which are characteristic of the best Scandinavian scholarship.

P. R. ACKROYD

THOMPSON, T. L.: *The Origin Tradition of Ancient Israel,* I: *The Literary Formation of Genesis and Exodus 1–23* (JSOT Supplement Series 55). 1987. Pp. 221. (Sheffield Academic Press, Sheffield. Price: £25.00 ($42.50); sub. price: £18.75 ($31.35). ISBN 1 85075 034 X)

More than a decade after the publication of his study of *The Historicity of the Pentateuchal Narratives* (1974; *B.L.* 1975, p. 76) and in due recognition of the subsequent revolution in Pentateuchal studies, Thompson has now turned his attention to the literary aspect of these books. In this study he presents a theory of the composition of Gen. 1–Exod. 23. Like Blum, to whose *Die Komposition der Vätergeschichte* (1984; *B.L.* 1986, p. 63) he unfortunately makes no allusion, although some more recent publications receive mention, he acknowledges dependence on Rendtorff's *Die überlieferungsgeschichtliche Problem des Pentateuch* (1977; *B.L.* 1978, p. 76) and attempts to build on its conclusions with an analysis of the material to define in detail each stage of composition, from 'smaller units and tales' to 'larger, compound tales' and on to 'the traditional complex-chain narrative', the 'toledoth structure' and finally the 'past [*sic!*] toledoth redaction', i.e. the final redaction. Like Rendtorff and other recent writers he finds no continuity which would justify a documentary hypothesis, and also rejects attempts to reconstruct earlier oral traditions: the process of composition was a purely literary one of which the final stage was probably reached in the late seventh or early sixth century B.C. The Pentateuch is not a history but a 'story' whose concern was the identity and place of Israel in the world. This is a valuable contribution to the current debate which at the same time illustrates the need for a really adequate methodology to replace the now widely discredited arguments of the source-critics.

R. N. WHYBRAY

THRONTVEIT, M. A.: *When Kings Speak: Royal Speech and Royal Prayer in Chronicles* (SBL Dissertation Series 93). 1987. Pp. xii, 150. (Scholars Press, Atlanta, Georgia. Price: £17.95 (member price: $11.95); ISBN 0 89130 998 5. Paperback price: $11.95 (member price: $8.95); ISBN 0 89130 999 3)

Researchers have often attempted to determine the particular theology of Chronicles by looking at the sections paralleled in 2 Samuel and 1–2 Kings (the synoptic passages). By an investigation of the royal speeches and prayers (mainly non-synoptic), T. seeks to bypass certain methodological problems with the former approach. After a form-critical study which allows him to eliminate the redactional insertions. he then applies the resultant data to several aspects of Chronicles study. T.'s conclusions are (1) that the speeches and prayers occur at important junctures in the Chronicler's history (*contra* Noth), and (2) that the speeches and prayers display the same *Tendenz* overall as that found in the synoptic sections (notably theology of theocracy, pan-Israel, and retribution). They also display two further interests: theology of 'rest' and help from Yahweh alone.

T. also makes suggestions about the dating of Chronicles, but his conclusions here are likely to be more controversial: original composition in the time of Zerubbabel with a later redaction around 400 B.C. Although he takes account of much recent work, no bibliographical item is later than 1982 (though the preface is dated February 1987). This means he is unaware of the commentaries of H. G. M. Williamson on Chronicles and D. L. Petersen on Haggai/Zechariah 1–8.

L. L. GRABBE

TURGMAN, V.: *De L'Autorité de Moïse: Ex 15,22–27.* 1987. Pp. 72. (KO'AMAR, Eilsbrunn. Price: DM 13.80)

It is argued that the main concern of this pericope is the imposition of Moses's rule over Israel and that this also is the main concern of the larger context to which the pericope belongs (Exod. 13:17–17:16). The imagery employed, however, suggests that behind the story is the issue of royal power in Israel. Other narratives are considered as further evidence of the debate about this issue (e.g. Exod. 17; Num. 11; 16; 20; Josh. 24). The discussion is rather tight packed and as a result deprives the findings of the lucidity they merit.

E. W. NICHOLSON

UNTERMAN, J.: *From Repentance to Redemption: Jeremiah's Thought in Transition* (JSOT Supplements 54). 1987. Pp. 223. (JSOT Press, Sheffield. Price: £27.50 (subscription price: £20.50). ISBN 1 85075 110 2; 1 85075 109 9 (pbk))

The published version of Jeremiah Unterman's doctoral disseration, written under the guidance of Jacob Milgrom and heavily influenced by Moshe Greenberg and Meir Weiss, is a good example of modern Jewish–Israeli scholarship on the prophets of the Hebrew Bible. Unterman's book is designed to correct a deficiency in Jeremiah scholarship which lacks a systematic and in-depth study of the relationship of repentance to redemption in Jeremiah. If the book of Jeremiah often resembles a complex maze to the reader Unterman transforms that maze into 'a multi-level house with clearly delinated stairs, rooms, and floors' (p. 21). This radical transformation of a metaphor is achieved by an intense scrutiny of the Hebrew text and the secondary literature on Jeremiah which trenchantly criticizes every scholar trespassing outside the bounds of Jewish scholarship. Virtually everything in the book of Jeremiah comes from the prophet Jeremiah, with only minimal redaction recognized by Unterman, and Jeremiah is credited with a coherent and near- systematic ideology of repentance giving way to redemption with the progress of time. The stages in Jeremiah's thinking on these subjects are defined by Unterman as: 1. 3:6–13, 19–4:2; 31:2–9, 15–22 which belong to the time of Josiah and stress the possibility of repentance; 2. 3:14–18; 24:4–7; 29:10–14; 50:4–7 which are assigned to 597–587 and reflect the motif of divine mercy outweighing that of human repentance; 3. 31:27–37; 32:37–41; 33:1–26; 50:17–20 (and probably 23:1–8; 42:9–12) set around 587 which abandon the principle of free will and the attendant demand for repentance in favour of redemption as solely the work of God. While there is much of interest in this book its arguments are vitiated by the number of question-begging assumptions made and, unfortunately, by a set of somewhat antiquated and specious non-arguments directed at scholars who differ in their interpretation of the book of Jeremiah.

R. P. CARROLL

VERMEYLEN, J.: *Job, Ses Amis et Son Dieu: La légende de Job et ses relectures postexiliques* (Studia Biblica II). 1986. Pp. 100. (Brill, Leiden. Price: Fl. 32.00. ISBN 90 04 07649 2)

In clear and concise fashion the author argues for three *relectures* of the Job story. He finds the original tale in only a few verses of the present framework. The first post-exilic development, seeing the nation's sufferings as remedial chastisement, added the friends' visit, most of the present discussion and the first speech of God with Job's reply. The next stage altered this view by introducing the idea of Satan's test and, through various additions, idealizing Job and condemning the friends. Finally there came a sharp reaction, perhaps linked with opposition to hellenization, and finding expression in the addition of Elihu, the second speech of God with Job's reply, and a few other verses. This is a significant attempt at tracing the growth of the Book of Job, even if the conclusions seem somewhat forced.

J. H. EATON

VIEWEGER, D.: *Die Spezifik der Berufungsberichte Jeremias und Ezechiels im Umfeld ähnlicher Einheiten des Alten Testaments* (Beiträge zur Erforschung des Alten Testaments und des Antiken Judentums 6). 1986. Pp. 180. (Verlag Peter Lang, Frankfurt am Main; Bern; New York. Price: Sw.Fr. 40.00. ISBN 3 8204 8948 7; ISSN 0722 0790)

This published version is the complete draft of Vieweger's dissertation undertaken for promotion in the Theology Section of Karl-Marx–University in Leipzig. It is a conventional analysis of the call accounts in the books of Jeremiah and Ezekiel along with similar reports elsewhere in the Hebrew Bible. (Moses, Gideon, Saul, and, to some extent, Isaiah). As is to be expected of such work it is more workmanlike than inspiring and has some useful tables analysing the different accounts. There is a competent, though by no means comprehensive, bibliography. On the positive side one notes the analytical thoroughness of Vieweger's dissection of each element in Jer. 1 and Ezek. 1–3 and the connections made between them and the other accounts in the Bible. This makes for useful treatment of what all the stories have in common and allows for some assessment of a pattern to the reports. Both pericopes in their respective books show a strong editorial interest in making connections betweeen the accounts and the main themes of the books and this reflects the needs of the exilic period to explain the obvious discrepancies between their beliefs and the disaster of 587. Each book takes a different approach to this problem, but the call accounts help to construct the responses of the editors to the crisis by incorporating it into stories in which prophets are called and so the crisis becomes controllable. A similar pattern may be detected in the other stories which use the call report form. I think this is a useful piece of analysis to have in published form, though I wish somebody would write a book in English on these texts!

R. P. CARROLL

VOGT, E.: *Der Aufstand Hiskias und die Belagerung Jerusalems 701 v.Chr.* (Analecta Biblica 106). 1986. Pp. viii, 105 (Biblical Institute Press, Rome. Price: Lire 23,000. ISBN 88 7653 106 X)

The death of Fr E. Vogt in February 1984 prevented his completing for publication this study of the confrontation between Hezekiah and Sennacherib in 701 B.C. which has received much attention in recent years. The work, however, was complete so far as its essential conclusions relating to the reconstruction of the events of 701 B.C. are concerned.

The study is set out with admirable clarity, marshalling the evidence for the separate problems with great care and seeking to build up a pattern of argument stage by stage. Beginning with the Assyrian records, Vogt sets out the details of Sennacherib's Annals and the Azekah and Lachish inscriptions. The study than moves on to examine the Old Testament records, paying most attention to the long account in 2 Kings 18:17–19:37. Vogt follows the majority of scholars in seeing here two separate narratives (usually labelled A and B), which have been combined into one. The author of the first narrative clearly drew upon authentic memories of the events of 701 B.C., but sought to fulfil a polemical and ideological purpose in the way he handled them. The second narrative carried this polemical purpose much further and must undoubtedly be regarded as of later origin.

Vogt follows these assessments with some valuable reflections on the implications they have for the date of composition of the books of 1 and 2 Kings. He places the first edition shortly after the death of Josiah in 609 B.C. Vogt remains convinced, rightly in the reviewer's opinion, that all the Old Testament accounts of a confrontage between Sennacherib and Hezekiah refer to what happened in 701 B.C.

In setting out a reconstruction of the events in Jerusalem of 703–701 B.C., it is gratifying to the reviewer to see Vogt's drawing fresh attention to the incongruity of the assertion of 2 Kings 19:35 regarding the slaughter of Sennacherib's army, when the information of the other accounts is fully considered. The study concludes with an examination of Ps. 44 and of the Isaianic prophecies of Isa. 1:4–9 and 22:1–4, 12–14 for their relevance to the interpretation of the events of 701 B.C. This is a further valuable contribution to an issue that has considerable bearing on Isaiah studies in general. Although it does not present much that is wholly new, it gives a clear lead concerning where the difficulties lie and shows where misinterpretations have arisen in the past.

R. E. CLEMENTS

WEBB, B. G.: *The Book of Judges: An Integrated Reading* (JSOT Supplement Series 46). 1987. Pp. 280. (Sheffield Academic Press. Price: £21.00 ($31.50); ISBN 1 85075 034 1. Paperback price: £8.95 ($14.95); ISBN 1 85075 035 1)

While not attempting 'to demonstrate unity of authorship', this revision of a Sheffield dissertation presented in 1985 argues successfully that Judges 'in its final form is a more meaningful narrative work than has generally been recognized'. Part I offers a Rationale, including a select review of scholarship; and a Sounding, in which the importance of 10:6–16 is argued as introduction to the entire Jephthah story (10:6–12:7). Part II analyses the three main sections of the Book: the Overture (1:1–3–6) in greatest detail (pp. 81–122); the Variations (3:7–16:31) relatively more briefly (pp. 123–79); and the Coda (17–21) in rather summary fashion (pp. 181–203). In tantalizing brevity the four-page Part III agrees with Polzin that Deuteronomic theology is less mechanistic than often portrayed, blames Alter for unnecessary concessions over the lack of characterization in Judges, and seeks to reopen discussion of 'the Deuteronomic History in its finished form'. Having offered in the Daily Study Bible (see *B.L.* 1985, p. 48) a brief reading of Judges tending in many similar directions, this reader welcomes Webb's more detailed observations. But he misses any mention of textual criticism (must the absence of 6:7–10 from a Qumran text not be admitted before these verses are asked to bear an important structural role?); and remains to be persuaded that it is sensible to call the canonical books around Judges the finished form of the Deuteronomic History.

A. G. AULD

WEBER-MÖCKL, A.: *'Das Recht des Königs, der über euch herrschen soll': Studien zu 1 Sam 8,11 ff. in der Literatur der frühen Neuzeit* (Historische Forschungen 27). 1986. Pp. 214. (Duncker & Humblot, Berlin. Price: Dm 88.00. ISBN 3 428 05963 8)

'Church history is the history of the exegesis of Holy Scripture': this principle (asserted by Gerhard Ebeling in 1947) is the background to Weber-Möckl's analysis of the understanding of 1 Sam. 8 in the sixteenth and seventeenth century. That period saw much radical rethinking about the role of monarchs in European society and always the biblical text was part of the political theorizing of the time. The first part of her study is a very useful consideration of the literary manifestations of typological thought in the period, their topoi, the typology of kingship, and the dissolution of typological thought after the reformation under the impact of the belief in progress. This section covers a wide range of complex ideas and important thinkers. A short second part looks at kingship in the Old Testament in terms of government and state in the book and of biblical kingship as a prototype (*Vorbild*) of the rational state and authority. The third and longest part of the book looks at the interpretation of 1 Sam. 8 in the period in all the complexities of that highly disputatious time. Much of this is taken up with Luther, Calvin and discussions among Protestant thinkers of the right to oppose political authority and the subsequent thinking of Calvinist theologians and jurists (much given to imposing authority themselves!). The development of such political thinking in England and Scotland is also discussed, including the work of Milton and Hobbes (138–49). Many of the names treated are now only dim echoes in the history of political thought, but Weber-Möckl's book usefully disinters them for her analysis. This book will have little interest for the average Old Testament scholar, but it is highly recommendable for those who wish to contemplate the history of biblical interpretation in the realm of practical politics.

R. P. CARROLL

WEHRLE, J.: *Prophetie und Textanalyse. Die Komposition Obadja 1–21 interpretiert auf der Basis textlinguistischer und semiotischer Konzeptionen* (Münchener Universitätsschriften — Arbeiten zu Text und Sprache im Alten Testament, 28). 1987. Pp xiii, 408. (Eos Verlag, St Ottilien. Price: DM 48.00. ISBN 3 88096 528 5)

Unlike most volumes in the series, this study does not follow the patterns of investigation established and developed by W. Richter, although it makes some use of his work. Its theoretical basis lies in the 'text linguistics' of E. Coserieu, W. Dressler and H. Weinrich, and particularly in procedures which define the 'macrostructure' of a text by attention to the formal markers of the beginning and end of (synchronic) layers within it and establish its coherence from syntactical or semantic cross-references (*Textphorik*). The author argues that this offers a better entry into the study of a poetic text than literary criticism or analysis of the normal kinds. He provides detailed analyses of the syntax, style and semantic fields of Obadiah, and each section is introduced by a discussion of the theoretical issues involved. Although their limits are recognized, the techniques employed here are a useful addition to the tools of research and the exposition of them is comparatively lucid. Wehrle concludes with brief reviews of the historical background of Obadiah, the composition of the book and its relation to later post-exilic prophecy; apart from the last these add little to previous investigations, and no account is taken of J. R. Bartlett's important article in *PEQ* 114 (1982), 13–24.

G. I. DAVIES

WESTERMANN, C.: *Prophetische Heilsworte im Alten Testament* (FRLANT 145). 1987. Pp. 219. (Vandenhoeck & Ruprecht, Göttingen. Price: DM 48.00. ISBN 3 525 53825 1)

This important book is essentially a supplement to the author's well-known *Grundformen prophetischer Rede*, of which the original was not noted in the *B.L.* but the English translation *Basic Forms of Prophetic Speech* was reviewed in *B.L.* 1968, p. 45; *Bible Bibliog.*, p. 99. Whereas that book concentrated on prophetic judgement sayings the present work supplements it with a detailed analysis of the form and content of salvation oracles. The main group, reflecting a common tradition, consists of announcements of deliverance and restoration. A second group announces destruction for Israel's enemies and salvation for Israel. These two groups reflect a tension like that between pre-exilic judgement and salvation prophets. Distinct from both are two further groups connected with non-prophetic forms: conditional announcements of salvation on Deuteronomic lines, and sayings contrasting the fate of the devout and the sinner on Wisdom lines. It is to be hoped that an English translation will soon be made.

A. GELSTON

WHYBRAY, R. N.: *The Making of the Pentateuch: A Methodological Study* (JSOT Supplement Series 53). 1987. Pp. 263. (Sheffield Academic Press. Price: £22.50 ($34.00); ISBN 1 85075 064 5. Paperback price: £10.50 ($14.95); ISBN 1 85075 063 7)

Professor Whybray has marshalled an impressive critique of Pentateuchal criticism as practised for over a century. To say that the results are largely negative is only to agree with the opening of the author's preface. Literary hypotheses are the concern of Part I (pp. 17–131); form-critical and traditio-critical hypotheses of Part II (pp. 133–219); and his alternative approach is much too briefly sketched in Part III (pp. 221–42). With deftness and clarity he unpicks the arguments and assumptions which led to the framing of the documentary, supplementary and fragmentary hypotheses, and their subsequent modifications. He draws attention in particular to the quite inconsistent use repeatedly made of canons of consistency, and to how, say, repetition is one scholar's evidence for literary-historical complexity and another's for aesthetic subtlety. Gunkel's move behind the written evidence is also well monitored, with careful scrutiny of the pioneering work on sagas by Olrik and Jolles which so influenced discussion of form and tradition in the Pentateuchal materials. Indeed this may be quite the most useful element in Whybray's study. Having concluded that to probe far behind the text of the Pentateuch is to attempt brick-making without straw, he proposes that the narrative is by a single historian, probably of the sixth century, who drew on available folklore (though of no proven antiquity) and his own literary imagination. Rather as with M. Noth, the 'Pentateuch' means for Whybray more or less the *narrative* of the 'Pentateuch' without Deuteronomy or much attention to the end of Numbers. Two issues are, therefore, left unexplored: how far portions of Numbers or Deuteronomy may have been available to the author of the rest as source-material; and whether it is sufficient simply to *state* that 'extensive bodies of law . . . have been embedded in the narrative text'.

A. G. AULD

WILCOCK, M.: *The Message of Chronicles* (The Bible Speaks Today). 1987. Pp. 288. (Inter-Varsity Press, Leicester. Price: £5.95. ISBN 0 85110 769 9)

'The Bible Speaks Today' is a series with a threefold aim: 'to expound the biblical text with accuracy, to relate it to contemporary life, and to be readable.' Chronicles is not, perhaps, a book that many would choose to write on for such a series, but perhaps for that very reason the need for such a work is all the greater. The theological stance of the series is conservative evangelical, and this may prejudice some readers against it from the outset. However, apart from occasional (ritual?) assertions of the historical reliability of the Chronicler throughout, Wilcock has succeeded splendidly in breathing life into what appear to many to be dry bones. He has taken careful note of recent English-language scholarship, so that as one who has contributed to this field I found it enormously instructive to observe how this can be put at the service of the lay Christian reading public in the most readable of styles. He is at his strongest when drawing out lessons from the kings of Judah on the nature of the pastoral ministry, but even in the case of such forbidding sections as the opening genealogies he manages to say something worthwhile without resorting to allegory or other-spiritualization. If the exposition occasionally appears to flag, this should not detract from what is overall a most successful example of its *genre*.

H. G. M. WILLIAMSON

WILLIAMSON, H. G. M.: *Ezra and Nehemiah* (Old Testament Guides). 1987. Pp. 104. (Sheffield Academic Press. Price: £3.50 ($4.95). ISBN 1 85075 065 3)

The ideal student guide should both give a clear and even-handed survey of current scholarship and also lead the student into the text itself. Nor is it always easy for one who has written a major contribution to a subject then to give a fair treatment of the opinions of others. Nevertheless, Williamson has managed to fulfil all the requirements and has produced an excellent introduction to Ezra and Nehemiah. He divides the work into four parts: sources, composition and date, history, and theology. Under each heading the text of Ezra/Nehemiah is examined along with a discussion of the major current views and scholarship. Williamson usually gives a fair hearing even to views with which he disagrees (e.g. the dating of Ezra's mission), and to suggest a different emphasis in any particular case would probably only reveal the prejudices of the reviewer! Undoubtedly one of the better volumes in a good series.

L. L. GRABBE

WINTHER-NIELSEN, N. (ed.): *'Davids hus'. Tekstkritiske, litterære, historiske og eksegetiske studier i 1. Samuel 17 og 2. Samuel 6, 7 og 9–20.* Haggamal 1. 1987. Pp. 242. (Dansk Bibel-Institut, Copenhagen. Price: D.Kr. 75.00. ISSN 0108 3023.)

'The House of David' is the first supplementary volume to a periodical, *Nemalah*, edited by members of a conservative school, the Danish Bible Institute. There are five articles dealing with topics from the books of Samuel, and it is stressed that they are all written from a 'believers'' point of view. Three of them are students' essays submitted to the faculty of theology in Copenhagen and deal with text criticism on the basis of 2 Sam. 6:1–19, with 2 Sam. 7 and the covenant of David, and with the historical aspects of Absalom's revolt. The first mentioned, written by A. L. Saxe, is the one of most interest to the learned world. One article is in German, 'Der Krieger wird Harfenspieler' by H. Möller (DDR). He suggests that the 'reduplications' in 1 Sam. 16–17 are a matter of style rather than a result of quotations from different sources. The leading article is by the editor; it is an analysis of 2 Sam. 11:1–12:25 inspired by the works of R. E. Langacre.

K. JEPPESEN

YEE, G. A.: *Composition and Tradition in the Book of Hosea. A Redaction Critical Investigation* (SBL Dissertation Series 102). 1987. Pp. xii, 428. (Scholars Press, Atlanta, Georgia. Price: £18.95 (member price: $13.95); ISBN 1 55540 090 6. Paperback price: $13.95 (member price: $10.95); ISBN 1 55540 091 4)

The author's main interest is the literary structure and theological orientation of the text's final form. From this standpoint she attempts to elucidate earlier stages of the tradition, relying on textual difficulties and unresolved tensions for clues to the process of compilation. She posits four such stages in chapters 1–3, allowing to the prophet himself little more than a few fragments in chapter 2. She envisages a collector of oracles (C), probably a disciple of Hosea, contemporary with Hezekiah's reform, and responsible for chapter 1 and insertions in chapter 2, a pre-exilic Judean redactor (R1) steeped in Deuteronomistic ideology, whose contribution is found in chapter 2, and an exilic Deuteronomistic redactor (R1), an author in his own right, whose contributions are notable for the abundant use of paronomasia. From him come chapters 3, 11, and 14 *in toto*, where oracles of hope reverse the received tradition and mark the tripartite division of the book. Chapters 4–11 are attributed to Hosea, R1 and R2; chapters 12–14 to Hosea and R2. On this basis the author is led to conclude that the adulterous mother of chapter 2 and, as reconstructed, of chapter 4 was Rachel originally, being interpreted only later as Gomer by the addition of chapter 1 (C). Whereas for Hosea 'harlotry' described political alliances with foreign nations, in R1 it has been applied to cultic apostasy. The chief concern of R2 is repentance of the exiles and restoration to the land.

G. I. Emmerson

Zurro, E.: *Procedimientos iterativos en la poesía ugarítica y hebrea* (Biblica et Orientalia 43). 1987. Pp. xv + 396. (Biblical Institute Press, Rome. ISBN 88 7653 344 3)

By listing different types of repetition patterns common to Ugaritic and Hebrew, Zurro — for whom these verse traditions virtually merge — has drawn our attention to an important stylistic device. In eight chapters he sets out various forms of strophic repetition using categories which are grammatical (repetition of nouns in the construct state, of nouns with adjectives, of identical verbs in different conjugations, etc.) or structural (anadiplosis, chiasmus, alternating parallelism). Two appendices list other types of repetition (anaphoric, epiphoric, pairing of identical words, etc.) and there are ample indices. Reference is made throughout the book to comparative lexical material from Ebla. This catalogue is particularly valuable for its juxtaposition of similar constructions involving repetition from which the interested reader can then formulate his or her own conclusions (since the author provides none) though some sifting of the data is required.

W. G. E. Watson

7. LAW, RELIGION, AND THEOLOGY

Ackroyd, P. R.: *Studies in the Religious Tradition of the Old Testament.* 1987. Pp. xiv, 305. (SCM, London. Price: £12.50. ISBN 0 334 01560 X)

No one could ever suggest that Professor Ackroyd, noted for his wide-ranging contributions to Old Testament studies, has had only one string to his bow. But this selection of his essays, ranging from his inaugural lecture at King's College, London (1961) through twenty-five years to a lecture at Princeton in 1986 (the one previously unpublished piece in this volume) shows the remarkable vitality and richness of a theme he has found himself returning to repeatedly: the theme of continuity. The word conjures up the problematics of unity and diversity within the Old Testament, of coherence, of innovation, of canon-formation. 'The problem . . . is how in the end it is proper and possible to describe the tradition as forming a whole' (p. vii). It would be a fruitful subject of research to trace how the scholar's own classroom exegesis of a text year by year, to which the author refers (p. viii), sets up exactly parallel questions of continuity and discontinuity, canon, identity, and the rest. Always in this volume the larger questions are investigated on the basis of an intricate examination of individual texts (the middle six chapters are for example concerned with the Isaiah tradition), the daunting generality of the topics at issue being rooted in a blessed specificity. The reissue of these essays, originally published in nine different countries and not always easily accessible, is an important and welcome event.

D. J. A. CLINES

ALONSO SCHÖKEL, L.: *Hermeneutica de la Palabra I: Hermeneutica biblica.* (Academia Christiana, 37). 1986. Pp. 267. (Ediciones Cristiandad, Madrid. Price: Ptas 1,000. ISBN 84 7057 401 5)

This is the first of three volumes — all in Spanish — on the hermeneutics of the Word. It deals with Biblical Hermeneutics; the other two are to follow shortly. The original places of publication of these essays, and their original languages, are noted at the end (pp. 247–49): 6 Spanish, 4 English, 2 each in Italian and French, 1 German, their original dates running from 1957–85. Some have also appeared in other languages, whether in full or in summary. While these essays are concerned with the wider issues of biblical exegesis and theology, they raise many questions of importance to Old Testament study, linguistics and liturgy. Most of the essays range widely, but some, e.g. no. 14 on David and the woman of Tekoa in 2 Sam. 14, discuss the wider issues in relation to specific problems. Indices of biblical quotations, of authors' names and subjects are usefully supplied. This is the beginning of what promises to be a rich collection from one who always handles the biblical text with sensitivity and poetic feeling.

P. R. ACKROYD

AUGUSTIN, M. and KEGLER, J.: *Bibelkunde des Alten Testaments: ein Arbeitsbuch.* 1987. Pp. 404. (Gerd Mohn, Gütersloh. Price: DM 48.00. ISBN 3 579 00079 9)

This is a study guide to the contents of the canonical Old Testament. General and detailed outlines of each of the books, with simple question and answer, mostly avoid any critical questions, although short booklists are included at various points, and a list of commentaries in thirty-six series is added at the end.

C. S. RODD

BARKER, M.: *The Older Testament: The Survival of Themes from the Ancient Royal Cult in Sectarian Judaism and Early Christianity.* 1987. Pp. x, 314. (SPCK, London. Price: £40.00. ISBN 0 281 04273 X)

The main thesis of this work will not be unfamiliar. It has been widely recognized that there was a rich mythology and ritual in pre-exilic Jerusalem, with the king at its centre and finding expression in the Temple worship, which has largely been suppressed in our existing Old Testament, so that only traces of its pattern remain. Again, the thought and imagery of the pseudepigraphical apocalypses have often been seen as a recrudesence of this ancient mythology, while in turn the apocalyptic movement has been considered the matrix of early Christianity.

Where this book breaks new ground is particularly in two directions. First, the author argues that the old pattern is seen most fully and clearly in 1 Enoch and similar works. The long first chapter seeks to demonstrate that the book of Enoch is not just a collection of materials of diverse background nor is it the product of non-Israelite ideas. Nor is it simply a literary revival of older imagery. Rather, all its parts reflect the old Jerusalem religious tradition and in this the distinctive angel mythology of 1 Enoch was also central. What has happened is that the pattern of the old royal cult has been attached to the Enoch figure.

Secondly, in the main part of her book, Margaret Barker examines in a series of separate studies what happened to the old religion in post-exilic Judaism, with the demise of the institutions which enshrined it. In successive chapters, she argues that Deuteronomy, Second Isaiah and Job all presuppose the ancient pattern: Deuteronomy de-mythologizes it, transferring the royal attributes to Moses, Second Isaiah, in identifying Yahweh and El for the first time, brings about the demise of its old deities, Job rejects the ancient wisdom which was at its heart and which the author discusses in an earlier chapter, with some cogent criticism of the deficient understandings of Israelite wisdom in recent studies. The Menorah is re-interpreted in the post-exilic era, as is the concept of the origin of evil by the Eden Stories. On the other hand, the tensions in the post-exilic community, the object of so much interest in current scholarship, reveal that the older religion remained very much alive among groups like the opponents of the returning exiles at the time of the restoration, whose outlook is to be found in Third Isaiah, in the circles which produced the apocalypses and at Qumran where the solar calendar, characteristic of the pre-exilic cult, was retained.

All this is argued in great and subtle detail to which a brief review cannot do justice. Probably nobody will fully agree with all the author's contentions and one may feel that sometimes she pushes her case too hard, especially in her numerous emendations of admittedly obscure texts. But the very range of the questions it raises indicates the stimulating and original nature of this work. Beyond doubt it is a most important study and any future examination of apocalyptic or of post-exilic Judaism will need to take account of it. In spite of Margaret Barker's statement that 'the whole must be read in the light of the New Testament', the relevance of her thesis for New Testament studies is only briefly sketched in the Introduction and tantalizingly hinted at in incidental comments. Do we have here a happy presage of a further book to come?

J. R. Porter

Breuning, W., Fuhs, H. F., Gross, W., Hossfeld, F.-L., Lohfink, N., Seidl, T., edited by Schreiner, J.: *Unterwegs zur Kirche, Alttestamentliche Konzeptionen*. 1987. Pp. 200. (Herder, Freiburg. n.p. ISBN 3 451 02110 2)

This volume belongs to a long-established series of books published since Vatican II, in which Catholic theologians tackle questions under dispute. It seeks to investigate the Old Testament roots of the Church' self-understanding of its own nature, but, whilst presenting a balanced assessment of the Biblical data, the study always has an eye to the contemporary situation. The essays are extremely well-documented and particularly valuable are the contributions of Professor Lohfink on 'the Kingdom of God' and of Professor Seidl on the People of God in Daniel. As one would expect, the emphasis on 'the People of God' raises questions of Church-State relations, for the Old Testament material will not allow of a dichotomy between the sacred and the secular.

R. J. Hammer

Brueggemann, W.: *Hope Within History*. 1987. Pp. 128. (John Knox Press, Atlanta. Price: $8.95. ISBN 0 8042 0918 9)

Set out here are five lectures of considerable interest to Old Testament theology and focused around the theme of hope which, as the title indicates, is directed towards a realization within the historical process. The first of them deals with the exodus narrative, finding in it certain fundamental features relating to the development of faith within the individual and in the community. The second essay is devoted to an examination of the meaning of righteousness as expression of power for living. It is concerned with a number of specific passages in Isaiah which highlight the biblical setting of the term 'righteousness'. The third essay, which carries the title 'Blessed are the History-makers', centres its attention upon the experience of the prophet Jeremiah and relates the prophet's experience of hostility to his prophesying with that of several contemporary rebel figures. The fourth essay explores the role of a visionary element in the nurturing of hope and the fifth developes some of its features further. It is concerned with the biblical testimony to the incorporation of sensations of shock and pain in the human encounter with God. It explores these in connection with certain dominant tendencies in the contemporary expression of faith. British readers may well feel that the volume has rather an American flavour to it, but it well repays study and is full of perceptive comments on the contemporary religious scene, criticized in the light of the biblical adventure of faith.

R. E. CLEMENTS

COHN-SHERBOK, D.: *On Earth as it is in Heaven: Jews, Christians, and Liberation Theology*. 1987. Pp. viii, 136. (Orbis, Maryknoll, New York. Price: $7.95. ISBN 0 88344 410 0)

After a Foreword by the Dean of Canterbury, Rabbi Cohn-Sherbok develops a very readable argument in 6 chapters: 'Judaism and Christianity: Their Differences'; 'Jesus as Prophet'; 'Ethics and the Kingdom of God'; 'Exodus and Freedom from Oppression'; 'Theology and Praxis'; and 'Common Ground and Shared Concerns'. It is especially in chapters 3 and 4 that material of special concern to *B.L.* readers is to be found.

A. G. AULD

DUCHROW, U., LIEDKE, G.: *Schalom. Der Schöpfung Befreiung, den Menschen Gerechtigkeit, den Völkern Frieden*. 1987. Pp. 251. (Kreuz Verlag, Stuttgart. Price: DM 16.80. ISBN 3 7831 0887 X)

This is not a work of Old Testament study in any narrowly technical sense. It is intended as a contribution to discussion among the churches called for at the Vancouver meeting of the WCC in 1983. This process of discussion was to be concerned with the establishment of justice, international harmony and the conservation of the earth's resources. A first section examines some aspects of the situation in which the Church finds itself where the imbalance of the earth's resources and misdirection of these resources in building up armaments are graphically illustrated. The main section of the book examines the biblical teaching on each of the main issues, all of which, it is claimed, are included in the concept *shālôm*. It is here that good use is made of the Old Testament material as a foundation for the continuation of the study into the New Testament in the attempt to present a *biblical* panorama. A final section looks at various patterns of church life and surveys a number of contemporary movements working towards *shālôm*.

This would be an invaluable stimulus to informed and well-directed group discussion and it is much to be hoped that it may be available to non-German-speaking church groups as well.

R. A. MASON

EBACH, J.: *Kassandra und Jona: Gegen die Macht des Schicksals*. 1987. Pp. 164. (Athenäum, Frankfurt am Main. Price: DM 48.00. ISBN 3 610 09150 3)

Cassandra predicted the fall of Troy: she was not believed, and the city fell. Jonah predicted the fall of Nineveh: he was believed, and the city was spared. But while both prophets were divinely inspired, there was this difference: Troy would have fallen whether Cassandra had been believed or not, for its destruction was decreed by inexorable fate; Nineveh's fall would have been a moral judgement pronounced by the ruler of the nations, but because the prediction of its fall was believed and led to the citizen's repentance, the judgement was averted, because it was a *moral* judgement. The difference between the impersonal 'counsel of Zeus', as Homer calls it, and the personal will of Yahweh is thus illustrated. Some observations are added on Michelangelo's portayal of Jonah on the ceiling of the Sistine Chapel.

F. F. BRUCE

EBERLEIN, K.: *Gott der Schöpfer — Israels Gott. Eine exegetisch-hermeneutische Studie zur theologischen Funktion alttestamentlicher Schöpfungsaussagen* (Beiträge zur Erforschung des Alten Testaments und des antiken Judentums, 5). 1986. Pp. 471. (Peter Lang, Frankfurt am Main. Price: Sw.Fr. 76.00. ISBN 3 8204 8921 5)

This revision of an Erlangen dissertation supervised by E. Kutsch is a fairly conventional treatment of a familiar topic. The issue is the relation between the concepts of God as universal creator and of God as the God of Israel's history. The author first sketches the positions of G. von Rad (salvation history is primary, creation theology secondary to that), C. Westermann (creation and salvation are alike the work of the blessing and saving God), and H. H. Schmid (creation theology is fundamental and pervasive). Reviewing statements about creation in Second Isaiah, in Psalms both pre-exilic and post-exilic, and in Genesis 1, as well as — more briefly — in other pre-exilic texts (e.g. the Amos doxologies) he concludes that the Old Testament tends to consider Yahweh's actions in history within a universal horizon, and to regard his activity in creation and history as a unity. The evidence of the texts does not support the claim that one or other theme, creation or history, is logically or historically prior.

D. J. A. CLINES

FERGUSON, D. S.: *Biblical Hermeneutics: An Introduction*. 1987. Pp. 220. (SCM Press, London. Price: £7.95. ISBN 0 334 01906 0)

The author, Professor of Religious Studies in Alaska Pacific University, undertakes to introduce the student to the modern hermeneutical debate. A precise definition of the term is difficult because its meaning is constantly shifting. As used by Gadamer and Ricoeur it means 'more than the interpretation of an ancient text; it involves the probing of the mysteries of ultimate reality through language'. The important role of preunderstanding is emphasized; the nature of the faith which is implied by preunderstanding when the Bible is the object of study is explored, and its relation to history is discussed. 'Revelation, history and faith are the crucial issues of hermeneutics.' The history of biblical hermeneutics is summarized, up to and including Bultmann and his successors. For the practice of the discipline today 'ten commandments' are recommended. The reviewer applauds the third of these: 'The Bible should be interpreted on a sound grammatical and historical basis. The best tools of language study and all of the resources of modern day historiography should be employed. As far as possible, all interpretations should be based on a study of the original languages.' These words should be set in italics or capitals.

F. F. BRUCE

FONTELA, C. A.: *La Esclavitud a travès de la Biblia*. 1986. Pp. 98. (Consejo Superior de Investigaciones Cientificas, Madrid. Price: Ptas 800. ISBN 84 00 06266 3)

This book, volume 9 in a collection of Spanish Biblical Studies, seeks to explore the developments in the institution of slavery, as depicted in the Bible. As a supervised research project, it begins by examining the vocabulary used, but here has little to say that is not to be found in better dictionary articles. It covers, however, a wide field and incorporates references to extra-Biblical Jewish materials, Graeco-Roman law and ancient Babylonian law.

It is useful to have so much within the compass of a comparatively small volume.

R. J. HAMMER

GARCÍA MARTÍNEZ, F., DE GEUS, C. H. J. and KLIJN, A. F. J. (eds.): *Profeten en profetische gestalten* (Essays in Honour of A. S. van der Woude). 1985. Pp. 180. (Kok; Kampen; Callenbach, Nijkerk. Price: Fl. 37.50. ISBN 90 242 4036 0)

A short foreword and a biographical sketch of Professor A. S. van der Woude's academic career introduce twelve essays on prophecy, and are followed at the end by a bibliography of his writings and a list of those associating themselves with a scholar whom this Society is glad to have among its Honorary Members.

The essays include a re-examination of the references to prophet in the Lachish letters (J. H. Hospers); three more general studies dealing with who the prophets were (C. H. J. de Geus), the prophetic consciousness (J. P. M. van der Ploeg), and the classification of the prophets as major and minor (A. Hilhorst). More detailed studies deal with the name change of Joshua in Num. 13:16 and its place in the Joshua traditions (E. Noort); Trito-Isaiah, discussing prophecy and its relation to learned writing (W. A. M. Beuken); the *mōre liṣdāqā* in Joel 2:23 (C. van Leeuwen); compositional techniques in Micah (C. J. Labuschagne); and a brief note on Zeph. 3:3b (B. Jongeling). García Martínez examines prophets and prophecy in the Qumran writings; H. G. Kippenberg the Davidic charismatic concept in Jewish, early Christian and gnostic liturgical material from Palestine; and M. de Jonge the concept of Jesus as prophetic son of David. A rich and varied collection.

P. R. ACKROYD

DE GENARO, G. (ed.): *L'Antico Testamento interpretato dal Nuovo: Il Messia*. 1985. Pp. 517. Dehoniane, Napoli. Price: Lire 40,000)

This is a collection of sixteen lectures given at the Studio Biblico Teologico Aquilano during 1982–83, mainly by Roman Catholic scholars but including Protestant and Jewish contributions: each lecture is followed by the questions and answers raised in a subsequent discussion period. The whole is concerned with Christology, the significance of applying to Jesus the Old Testament term Messiah or Christ. In spite of the overall title, some of the papers are not directly concerned with the Old Testament. The majority that are fall into two main groups. There are those that deal with messianic concepts in the Old Testament generally: Riccardo di Segni writes on Hebrew messianic ideas, a thoughtful essay by Gian Luigi Prato discusses the value and limitations of Biblical messianism, Giovanni Garbini reviews the concept of the annointed one in relation to Christ and Horacio Simian-Yofre surveys the Messiah in Isaiah and in prophecy as a whole. Then there are exegetical studies of particular passages or chapters. Two contributions are concerned with the Servant, Franco Festorazzi on Jesus and the Suffering Servant of Yahweh and Marco Adinolfi on the Servant of Yahweh in the consciousness of Jesus. Nicolo Loss makes proposals for a Christological reading of Gen. 1 and Maurice Gilbert provides an interesting and well-researched discussion of the possibility of seeing the righteous sufferer in Wisdom 2:12–20 as a messianic figure. A final essay by Ugo Vanni presents John's Apocalypse as a Christian Messianic re-interpretation of the Old Testament. Not all the contributions are of the same quality and perhaps none of them say much that is very new. But they all contain interesting comments and all are worth reading by those concerned with the question of the relevance of the Old Testament for Christology.

J. R. Porter

Goldingay, J.: *Theological Diversity and the Authority of the Old Testament.* 1987. Pp. ix, 308. (Eerdmans, Grand Rapids, Michigan. Price: $14.95. ISBN 0 8028 0229 X)

John Goldingay undertakes in this volume a detailed examination of a number of contemporary approaches to the problems of Old Testament theology and sets out to offer a restatement of the viability, aims and methods of such a theology. The starting-point is the awareness that the subject has become the target for quite a barrage of criticisms and objections during the past two decades and has failed to elicit any widely accepted agreement as to how the subject should be dealt with. Goldingay starts with the recognition that these criticisms and objections are neither wholly misplaced, or easily dismissed. There appears therefore to be little likelihood that a new consensus will soon emerge.

Goldingay's book is a revised version of a dissertation presented at Nottingham University (1983) and it should command deserved attention as an excellent analysis of a number of major problems with some helpful guidelines as to how the subject can be further developed. It is divided into three parts, the first of which is devoted to examining the impact of a historical contextual approach to the literature of the Old Testament. The effect of this has been to break up, almost completely, any attempt to build up a synthesis of biblical concepts and ideas on the assumption that some underlying framework holds them all together. The demands of exegesis compel attention to the proper historical context of each saying and formulation.

Part two of the book profers an alternative to this by outlining how a purely evaluative approach to the subject might proceed. It then tests this out with regard to the book of Deuteronomy.

The third part surveys the various attempts to present a unifying approach to the subject in which suggestions regarding a specific 'centre' are explored. Goldingay himself clearly favours proceeding in this manner, without ignoring the difficulties that others have run into when doing so. By taking the combined themes of Creation and Salvation, and by claiming that they are more integrally related to each other than has usually been recognized, Goldingay works out a basic outline for such a theology. A very full bibliography adds considerably to the value of the study.

This is a serious and well researched attempt to present some new lines for Old Testament theology to pursue, and, like most other recent works on the subject, is heavily burdened with an awareness of the problems that the subject has encountered in the past two decades. It too is forced to move in the direction of constructing very broad generalized themes to hold the diverse material together. Nevertheless it is constructive in its approach and provides an excellent review of what the subject aims to achieve and how current thinking on the subject has developed.

R. E. CLEMENTS

GOLDSWORTHY, G.: *Gospel and Wisdom: Israel's Wisdom Literature in the Christian Life*. 1987. Pp. 202. (Lancer, Homebush West, NSW, Australia; Paternoster, Exeter. Price: £4.95. ISBN 0 85892 326 6; ISBN 0 85364 459 4)

The author is especially concerned to understand the Old Testament Wisdom Literature as Christian Scripture. Not only is Christ taken to be the fulfilment of wisdom; we have to read wisdom always as functioning within the framework of salvation history. The firm lines of the author's thought are sometimes represented in diagrams with circles, arrows and boxes. 'The overview of wisdom in the Bible provides us with a base for our decision-making. Guidance is primarily directed at the responsibility of Christians to make decisions which conform to reality as it is revealed in the gospel.' This theological study in the evangelical tradition could help church people to embrace the Wisdom Literature more confidently within their scriptural resources.

J. H. EATON

HAAG, E., and HOSSFELD, F.-L. (ed.): *Freude an der Weisung des Herrn: Beiträge zur Theologie der Psalmen — Festgabe zum 70. Geburtstag von Heinrich Gross* (Stuttgarter Biblische Beiträge 13). 1986. Pp. xii, 533. (Verlag Katholisches Bibelwerk, Stuttgart. Price: DM 39.00. ISBN 3 460 00131 3)

This collection of twenty-seven contributions, in honour of a long-serving professor of Trier and Regensburg, contains some pieces devoted to a particular psalm (1; 2; 4; 18; 22; 23; 82; 88; 114–15; 119; 149), some to a psalm passage (8:7b; 39:6f; 95:11; 107:23–32; 110:7; 149), and some to a more general topic. The topics include the Qumran psalms scroll in relation to the canonicity of the Psalter, a sermon of Newman on the Christian understanding of the Psalms, the Individual in the Psalms, the function of psalm citations in the Epistle to the Hebrews, the logic of the psalm quotations in Romans 9–11, the domain of God's lordship, the oriental background of the 'we' in the Psalms, the death of the righteous in Wisdom 4:7–19 in relation to the Psalms, and the development of monotheism in the Psalms. The collection gives a good sample of the perspectives and approaches current in German Catholic scholarship.

J. H. EATON

HAUSMANN, J.: *Israels Rest: Studien zum Selbstverständnis der nachexilischen Gemeinde* (BWANT, 7. Folge, Heft 4). 1987. Pp. ix, 301. (Kohlhammer, Stuttgart. Price: DM 69.00. ISBN 3 17 009843 8)

Although recent monographs by G. Hasel (*The Remnant*, 1974) and W. Müller/H. Preuss (*Die Vorstellung vom Rest im Alten Testament*) have treated the 'remnant tradition' in pre-exilic Israel, its place in post-exilic theology has been given only sketchy notice. H.'s monograph closes this gap, showing that 'remnant' was one of the ways the post-exilic community defined itself. H. looks not only at the 'undoubted' post-exilic writings but also re-examines the earlier writings for redactional passages which seem to reflect the post-exilic situation. A special concern is the particular terminology used in different writings or literary strata.

H. concludes that the basic concept of remnant was forward-looking (the germ cell of a new future entity) and even eschatological; however, within the post-exilic writings there are varied views of who is the remnant (the cultic community; the political state; both those of Judah and of the northern kingdom; etc.). Finally, he considers his results in the light of broader issues and concludes that a complex situation is reflected in the post-exilic remnant passages while the older bald oppositions (e.g. O. Plöger's 'theocracy' versus 'eschatology') are simplistic. H. shows himself current with the latest scholarship on the post-exilic period and demonstrates that it is possible for German dissertations to be readable monographs rather than always exhaustive — and exhausting — tomes.

L. L. GRABBE

HAYTER, M.: *The New Eve in Christ: The Use and Abuse of the Bible in the Debate about Women in the Church.* 1987. Pp. x, 190. (SPCK, London. Price: £6.95. ISBN 0281 04262 4)

It is the author's contention that those — whether radical feminists or ardent anti-feminists — who allege that the God of the Bible is male and that he insists on a male priesthood to lead the worship of his people are guilty of perverse exegesis. She castigates arguments based on biblical imagery: God is no more a father or a husband in any substantive sense than he is a shepherd or an artisan; and there are, especially in the 'patriarchal' Old Testament, a surprisingly large number of quite specific female metaphors used to describe him. The subordination of women in ecclesiastical matters reflects their subordination in the Society of the times and, far from being something of eternal validity, belongs (like the institution of slavery) to those things which are doomed to pass away in the reversal of human values that is the mark of God's Kingdom, here already but still to arrive in fuller measure. Misogyny is found in quite a few texts but is no more to be emulated than the racism and the triumphalism to be found in quite a few other texts. The abiding principles are clearly and unambiguously present in Genesis 1:27 and Galatians 3:28 and only await a Church that really listens to scripture to put them into effect. There are risks attached to this open-ended kind of exegesis or eisegesis taking over, and the author does not entirely avoid them; but she writes with sensitivity and magnanimity, and that cannot always be said of those whose crabbed exegesis — be it in the interests of revolution or of reaction — she so rightly deplores.

J. C. L. GIBSON

JANOWSKI, B., and WELKER, M. (eds.): *Jahrbuch für Biblische Theologie*, Band 1: *Einheit und Vielfalt Biblischer Theologie.* 1986. Pp. 252. (Neukirchener, Neukirchen–Vluyn. Price: DM 46.00. ISBN 3 7887 1229 5)

This new annual for Biblical Theology deserves the *Book List*'s welcome. An editorial foreword introduces papers grouped in three sections. 'Perspectives and Problems' are provided by C. Westermann on the question of a Biblical Theology; R. Schnackenburg on New Testament Theology in the framework of an all-Biblical Theology; M. Oeming sketching the problem 'Unitas Scripturae?'; and U. Mauser on *Eis Theos* and *Monos Theos* in Biblical Theology. There are seven contributions to 'interdisciplinary discussion': P. Stuhlmacher discusses Biblical Theology as a way to knowledge of God — reviewing H. Seebass's book, *Der Gott der ganzen Bibel*; Seebass takes up the dialogue with Stuhlmacher with a paper on the righteousness of God; D. Ritschl puts some questions to the more recent discussion of the topic under the heading, '"True", "pure", or "new" Biblical Theology'; F. Mildenberger contributes 'Biblical Theology as ecclesiastical exposition of scripture', R. Bohren, 'Biblical Theology against latent deism', and I. Baldermann. 'Biblical Theology as a way of learning — didactic structures in the theology of Luther, Bonhoeffer and the self-understanding of the

"Kirchenbund"'. A final bibliographical section is made up of a review by H. Graf Reventlow of the book by M. Oeming reviewed in *B.L.* 1986, p. 93, and a very useful bibliography covering the years 1982–85 under more than thirty headings. Reventlow and Seebass had covered the period to 1981 in earlier publications. A further listing is promised in *JBTh* 4, 1989. Despite the naming of P. D. Hanson (Harvard), U. Mauser (Pittsburgh), and M. Sæbø (Oslo) as associates of the editorial board, and Mauser's reminder of his launch of *Horizons in Biblical Theology. An International Dialogue* in 1979, the discussion reflects the (German) language of all the contributions. For balancing Jewish measure, the closing essays in the composite volumes reviewed on pp. 22 and 110, should also be consulted.

A. G. Auld

Kugel, J. L., and Greer, R. A.: *Early Biblical Interpretation* (Library of Early Christianity, 3). 1986. Pp. 214. (Westminster Press, Philadelphia. Price: $18.95. ISBN 0 664 21907 1)

In the first part of this useful work, Kugel outlines the beginnings of Jewish biblical exegesis, from 'innerbiblical' interpretation to the methods employed in the Mishnah and early midrashim. The final chapter, 'A Look at Some Texts', discusses selected examples. The second part, by Greer, deals wih the formation and interpretation of the Christian Bible in the first four centuries A.D., with valuable suggestions about the theological context of Christian exegesis and a balanced account of the relation between Scripture and the 'rule of faith'. The material on Irenaeus is specially useful. Both authors have pertinent comments to make about the use of the Bible today, in both Christianity and Judaism.

J. Barton

Lohfink, N. F.: *Option for the Poor: The basic principle of Liberation Theology in the light of the Bible.* 1987. Pp. vii, 78. (BIBAL Press, Berkeley, California. Price: $6.95, plus postage. ISBN 0 941937 00 2)

In these Bailey Lectures at the American Baptist Seminary of the West, Lohfink sketches, without footnotes or bibliography, his understanding of the biblical teaching on the poor, concentrating on the Old Testament. After emphasizing that much of this teaching is common to other cultures in the ancient Near East, he finds the distinctive biblical message in the Exodus. His interpretation has marked differences from the usual Liberation Theology approach, however, since he argues that Yahweh's intervention does not aim at easing the suffering of the oppressed while leaving the system intact but removes them from the situation in which they are. God then brings them into a 'contrast society' in which there are no poor. This saving of the poor is then traced through Zephaniah and Deutero-Isaiah, with a final, brief, look at the New Testament. The Bible does not spiritualize the poor, but equally it makes it clear that God does not intend poverty and misery for his creation but rather wealth and plenty.

It is a valuable outline study, which Lohfink and his brother are planning to develop into a full-scale book.

C. S. Rodd

McAlpine, T. H.: *Sleep, Divine and Human in the Old Testament* (JSOT Supplements, 38). 1987. Pp. 264. (JSOT Press, Sheffield. Price: £25.00 ($37.50); ISBN 0 905774 98 1. Paperback price: £10.95 ($16.95); ISBN 0 905774 99 X)

The theme of this detailed study is an unusual one and one that has received very little attention in the past. There is, in fact, much material to work on and the author exploits this to the full, bringing the subject to life and producing a coherent picture. A chapter on lexical aspects sets the principal Hebrew words connected with sleep into a wider pattern of associated lexica. Traditional translations are sometimes confirmed, sometimes shown to be inadequate. A chapter on 'Cultural Patterns' is, by contrast, concerned principally with the *realia* of the practicalities of sleep — everything from beds and bedding to privacy and the hours of sleep. Much of the evidence is archaeological and from outside Israel. It is a fascinating collection of material, including much detail on dimensions of beds! Some of the evidence, especially for Israel, is secondary, being derived from tomb arrangements. A further chapter deals with Israelite understandings of sleep, the psychology of sleep, and the relationship between sleep and death. Again ancient Near Eastern evidence, principally from Egypt and Mesopotamia play a prominent part, along with Rabbinic and Classical sources: 'Sleep and the Divine' deals with such matters as incubation rituals, which are only incompletely attested in ancient Israel, though this is taken to be an aspect of Israelite practice which has been played down by the orthodox tradition. The last main chapter is concerned with divine sleep (Ps. 121, etc.), a theologically important notion based on the ideas of the guard neglecting his job and of the authority-figure who makes himself unavailable. It is a mistake, the author suggests, to think of mere anthropomorphism. McAlpine has brought together a mass of material, lexical, archaeological and theological. The coherence of his book is proof of the usefulness of the exercise.

J. F. HEALEY

McCARTHY, DENNIS J., S.J.: *Institution and Narrative. Collected Essays* (Analecta Biblica 108). 1985. Pp. xi, 438. (Biblical Institute Press, Rome. Price: Lire 40,800. ISBN 88 7653 108 4)

The sudden death during the IOSOT Congress at Salamanca in 1983 of Fr. Dennis McCarthy was a very sad loss to Old Testament scholarship. His range of studies, particularly in the fields of covenant in which he published his major dissertation, and of the Deuteronomistic History, have an exceptional value and interest. Where others appeared all too prone to press for one-sided, and heavily polemical, conclusions, Fr. McCarthy showed exemplary clarity, restraint and eminent good sense. The richness of his researches is well brought out in this volume of collected writings from his pen, which will serve as a lasting memorial and an effective prolongation of his life's work.

All but two of the essays included in the volume appear in the form in which they were originally published, and several of them have already become well known and familiar points of reference on specific questions. The collection is divided into three parts, the first of which contains eight studies dealing with ideas of covenant. In view of the importance of this to Professor McCarthy's studies, and of the value of his criticisms and modified support for the drawing of close comparisons between divine covenants in the Old Testament and ancient Near Eastern vassal-treaties, this section alone merits special attention.

The second part consists of thirteen exegetical studies dealing with a range of issues from Creation to Holy War, and largely devoted to passages from the historical books of the Old Testament (Exodus, Joshua, 1 and 2 Samuel). Part three is devoted to issues of biblical theology, but ranges beyond the more narrowly defined compass of the discipline to touch upon matters of literary, social and ethical interest. There is a characteristic freshness and enthusiasm which permeates all of them. The individual studies are too numerous to mention, but they can be relied upon to bring to the reader a range of fresh insights and perceptive suggestions which deserve to be followed up more fully. This is a quite exceptional collection of writings from a quite exceptional scholar.

R. E. CLEMENTS

McCOMISKEY, T. E.: *The Covenants of Promise: A Theology of the Old Testament Covenants*. 1985. Pp. 259. (Inter-Varsity Press, Nottingham. Price: £7.50. ISBN 0 85110 773 7)

The American publication of this book was noted in *B.L.* 1986, p. 92. There are no changes in this English edition.

E. W. NICHOLSON

MARTIN-ACHARD, R.: *La Loi, Don de Dieu: Aux Sources de l'Ancien Testament*. 1987. Pp. 82. (Editions du Moulin, Aubonne (CH). Price: Sw.Fr. 11.80)

In extremely simple and brief form the content, formation and development of the various law codes of the Old Testament are presented. The writer's purpose is to emphasize their function in ancient Israel as the gracious gift of a liberating God, not the rigorous imposition of tyrannical authority.

G. I. EMMERSON

MBITI, J. S.: *Bibel und Theologie im afrikanischen Christentum*. Translated by B. Ferrazzini. 1987. Pp. 212. (Vandenhoeck & Ruprecht, Göttingen. Price: DM 36.00. ISBN 3 525 56326 4)

The English language original was published as *Bible and Theology in African Christianity* by OUP in Nairobi in 1986, and itself developed out of lectures given in New York by the author in 1982. Of most interest to *B.L.* readers may be the second chapter, on the translation of the Bible and its use in the church. Old Testament is used extensively as well as New; and considerable affinity is felt in much of Africa with the Biblical thought-world.

A. G. AULD

MILLER, P. D., JR, HANSON, P. D., and McBRIDE, S. D. (eds.): *Ancient Israelite Religion: Essays in Honor of Frank Moore Cross*. 1987. Pp. xxv, 672. (Fortress, Philadelphia. Price: $44.95. ISBN 0 8006 0831 3)

It is always noteworthy when a *Festschrift* is devoted to a single field of research. The editors see these thirty-three essays in honour of Frank Moor Cross as continuing his own work on the religion of Israel, and in particular his essays published in 1973 as *Canaanite Myth and Hebrew Epic*, 'in the(ir) desire to address the subject with a broad range of data, models, and expertise'. The majority of the contributors are North American, and are either long-standing colleagues or one-time students of the dedicatee; yet the cast includes eight colleagues from Jerusalem, two from Germany, and one from Sweden. Many of the papers are very fresh, but some rather predictable.

The first fourteen essays are grouped in a section headed 'Sources and Contexts', and relate more especially to extrabiblical and archaeological material: W. W. Hallo, 'The Origins of the Sacrificial Cult: New Evidence from Mesopotamia and Israel'; T. Jacobsen, 'The Graven Image';

A. Malamat, 'A Forerunner of Biblical Prophecy: The Mari Documents'; P. D. Miller, Jr, 'Aspects of the Religion of Ugarit'; J. C. Greenfield, 'Aspects of Aramean Religion'; B. Peckham, 'Phoenicia and the Religion of Israel: The Epigraphic Evidence'; J. Naveh, 'Proto-Canaanite, Archaic Greek, and the Script of the Aramaic Text on the Tell Fakhariyah Statue'; M. D. Coogan, 'Canaanite Origins and Lineage: Reflections on the Religion of Ancient Israel'; J. A. Hackett, 'Religious Traditions in Israelite Transjordan'; P. K. McCarter, Jr, 'Aspects of the Religion of the Israelite Monarchy: Biblical and Epigraphic Data'; J. H. Tigay, 'Israelite Religion: The Onomastic and Epigraphic Evidence'; N. Avigad, 'The Contribution of Hebrew Seals to an Understanding of Israelite Religion and Society'; W. G. Dever, 'The Contribution of Archaeology to the Study of Canaanite and Early Israelite Religion; and J. S. Holladay, Jr, 'Religion in Israel and Judah Under the Monarchy: An Explicitly Archaeological Approach'.

The remaining nineteen, headed 'History and Character', have the biblical literature as their primary focus: M. Weinfeld, 'The Tribal League at Sinai'; D. N. Freedman, '"Who Is Like Thee Among the Gods?" The Religion of Early Israel'; G. E. Mendenhall, 'The Nature and Purpose of the Abraham Narratives'; C. Meyers, 'David as Empire Builder'; J. J. M. Roberts, 'In Defense of the Monarchy: The Contribution of Israelite Kingship to Biblical Theology'; P. Bird, 'The Place of Women in the Israelite Cultus'; H. Ringgren, 'The Marriage Motif in Israelite Religion'; R. A. Oden, Jr, 'The Place of Covenant in the Religion of Israel'; R. E. Murphy, 'Religious Dimensions of Israelite Wisdom'; N. Lohfink, 'The Cult Reform of Josiah of Judah: 2 Kings 22–23 as a Source for the History of Israelite Religion'; K. Baltzer, 'Liberation from Debt Slavery After the Exile in Second Isaiah and Nehemiah'; P. D. Hanson, 'Israelite Religion in the Early Postexilic Period'; E. M. Meyers, 'The Persian Period and the Judean Restoration: From Zerubbabel to Nehemiah'; J. G. Janzen, 'The Place of the Book of Job in the History of Israel's Religion'; J. J. Collins, 'The Place of Apocalypticism in the Religion of Israel'; J. D. Levenson, 'The Sources of Torah: Psalm 119 and the Modes of Revelation in Second Temple Judaism'; M. E. Stone, 'Ideal Figures and Social Context: Priest and Sage in the Early Second Temple Age'; Sh. Talmon, 'The Emergence of Jewish Sectarianism in the Early Second Temple Period'; and M. H. Goshen-Gottstein, 'Tanakh Theology: The Religion of the Old Testament and the Place of Jewish Biblical Theology'.

In many cases, quite properly, the distinction between sections proves arbitrary. The editorial Introduction draws attention to some of the discussions and variations of emphasis within the contributions as it anticipates their prime perspectives: origins and historical development; Josianic, exilic, and early post-exilic periods; comparative questions; the relation between public and popular, official and unofficial, normative and aberrant; the use of sociological and anthropological data and models; and the articulation of primary features. The volume concludes with a 203-item bibliography of Cross's publications, which began in *BA* 10 and *BASOR* 108 (both of 1947), and an index of biblical passages.

In a volume which is bound to become a standard resource, it is invidious to mention only one of many strong contributions. Yet I do draw attention to Goshen-Gottstein arguing the need for 'a hitherto nonexisting area of academic study in the field of biblical religion' — a topic which may have had 'to wait for the first half-century of Jewish academic Bible study to pass until we could allow ourselves the luxury of facing the bias on each side and put the question afresh: "What is Tanakh all about?"' (J. D. Levenson's different approach in *Judaic Perspectives* has been noted above on p. 22, and M. Tsevat's 1985 discussion on p. 24.)

A. G. Auld

NIELSEN, K.: *Incense in Ancient Israel* (Vetus Testamentum, Supplement 38). 1986. Pp. xi, 147, with one map. (Brill, Leiden. Price: Fl. 38.00. ISBN 90 04 07702 2)

An up-to-date treatment of incense and its associated equipment in Israelite and neighbouring cultures is badly needed. This dissertation prepared under M. Tsevat's supervision is a step towards filling that need, and all future studies will have to use it. After brief surveys of incense in Egypt, Arabia, and Syria–Palestine, Nielsen devotes himself to Israel, studying utensils, then lexical terms, cultic texts and secular uses. Within the Old Testament Nielsen makes a significant contribution in contesting Wellhausen's view that incense entered Israel's cult at the end of the Monarchy. Using 1 Sam. 2:27–36, passages in Kings, and Isaiah 6, he argues for its use as early as David, which is more reasonable in view of its common use elsewhere. Identifying the terms for specific plants and resins is difficult. Nielsen states his conclusions firmly, but treats cognates and the help they may give unsystematically, failing to use modern lexical resources fully (notably the *Chicago Assyrian Dictionary*). His summary of ancient utensils is also unsatisfactory in its brevity, omitting helpful examples (e.g. Ashurbanipal's banquet scene), and some discussion of the recipes for making incense in Hebrew and Akkadian sources could be expected. While not the definitive work, Nielsen has assembled much material and discussed a century of opinions, and so carried the study forward.

A. R. MILLARD

OEMING, M. and GRAUPNER, A. (eds.): *Altes Testament und christliche Verkündigung. Festschrift für Antonius H. J. Gunneweg zum 65. Geburtstag.* Pp. 422. (Kohlhammer, Stuttgart. Price: DM 89.00. ISBN 3 17 009607 9)

The title is appropriate to the work of Professor Gunneweg as pastor, longstanding teacher of homiletics, and since 1968 *Ordinarius* for Old Testament in Bonn. The contributions, all in German, are grouped in four sections and cover the following topics (titles mostly abbreviated and simplified: Section 1, *Biblical Theology*: Observations on the theme of Biblical Theology (P. Hoffken); 'Fate, suffering and God', on Qohelet (O. Kaiser); The question of human suffering (H. D. Preuß); The relationship of Mt. 21 to the Old Testament as a question of method in Biblical Theology (G. Sauer); God's work and human activity: Distinction of 'Law' and 'Gospel' in the Old Testament? (W. H. Schmidt); The first commandment as an axiom of Biblical Theology (H. Schroer). Section 2, *Hermeneutics, Systematic Theology and Wissenschaftsgeschichte*, contains: The question of the return of Christ (H. Graß); Christology and Ethics, with reference to D. Bonhoeffer (M. Honecker); 'One can only understand what one loves': faith and understanding in Old Testament hermeneutics (M. Oeming); Five letters of de Wette from Weimar, 1819–22 (E. Plumacher); Pesaḥ-haggadah and Easter sermon (G. Sauter); Human evil yet freedom for responsibility under God (E. Vellmer).

Section 3, *Exegesis*, contains: The inner contradiction in the Deuteronomistic judgement on kingship (U. Becker); The question of the historical Jesus (E. Graßer); Jeremiah 45 as '*Schußwort*' of the Book of Jeremiah (A. Graupner); the dispute of Yahweh and Jeremiah (H.-J. Hermisson); On Jer. 1:18 and 15:20 (S. Herrmann); Ps. 1 in ancient Jewish witnesses (J. Maier); The conflict of Church and Synagogue in N.T. times (W. Schmithals); 'Imago Dei', new reflexions on Gen. 1:26f. (J. A. Soggin); Ps. 127 (H. Strauß); Prophetic word and history in Kings (E. Würthwein). Section 4 contains two sermons, On Qoh 9:11f (H. H. Schmid) and on Isa. 38:9–20 (K. Wollenweber). The book closes with a bibliography of A. H. J. Gunneweg.

R. P. R. MURRAY

OHLER, A.: *Frauengestalten der Bibel.* 1987. Pp. 228. (Echter Verlag, Würzburg. Price: DM 24.80. ISBN 3 429 01056 X)

Nine studies of the role of women in the Bible are here presented, with special emphasis on the way in which they are often shown to be witnesses to the unpredictable character of God's work. Their position is seen as being especially important at times when the ordinary course of events is challenged in a way beyond human expectation. Those whose situation is presented in this way are Rachel and Leah, Tamar, Miriam, Deborah, and the beloved in the Song of Songs, together with Mary the mother of Jesus, Martha and Mary, Mary Magdalen and Prisca (with Aquila) from the New Testament. These attractively written studies, which are accompanied by imaginatively-chosen in-text illustrations, take full account of modern scholarly presuppositions; they also succeed in challenging some long-held male assumptions.

R. J. COGGINS

OLLENBURGER, B. C.: *Zion The City of the Great King: A Theological Symbol of the Jerusalem Cult* (JSOT Supplement Series 41). 1987. Pp. 271. (JSOT Press, Sheffield. Price: £22.50 ($33.50); ISBN 1 85075 015 7. Paperback price: £8.95 ($14.95); ISBN 1 85075 014 9)

The aim of this detailed study — there are seventy-five pages of notes and twenty-one of bibliography — is to examine the significance of Zion as the central symbol of the Jerusalem cult. In fact, it concentrates solely on what the author sees as that symbol's primary denotation, the kingship of Yahweh: the whole religious character of Zion is determined by the fact that this is the place where Yahweh rules as king. After an introduction, in the second chapter, it is argued that there was a celebration of Yahweh's kingship at the Autumn festival, which was the setting for the Enthronement Psalms, and, in the course of the discussion, it is suggested that the origin of Yahweh's kingship in Zion lies not in a hypothetical Jebusite background but is derived from the cult at Shiloh, which was influenced by Canaanite ideas. Yahweh could have been viewed as king at Shiloh but Ollenburger does not sufficiently consider the possibility that new elements characteristic of Jerusalem may have fundamentally transformed the concept there.

The third chapter discusses the exercise of the divine kingship. As king, Yahweh is also creator and it is by his victory over chaos that Zion is defended, has complete security and is a place of refuge for the 'poor', who are not so much a social class as those who have utter trust in Yahweh's protection. The author claims that Zion and Davidic traditions are to be clearly distinguished. Their traditio-historical background may perhaps be different but Ollenburger's concern is with Zion in the developed Jerusalem cult and here the case for an intimate fusion of these two elements is much stronger than he allows. His evidence is drawn from too narrow a base: for example, he says that neither David nor the monarchy is even mentioned in the Songs of Zion. But for him these Songs appear to comprise only Pss. 46, 48, 76 and thus he ignores v. 10 of Ps. 84 which is just as much a Song of Zion.

Chapter 4, the most novel and controversial, develops the distinctive Zion tradition as asserting that Zion's impregnability rests only on Yahweh's actions. It has no place for human synergism; all that man needs is faith and trust in Yahweh's promise. Isaiah's criticism of Ahaz and Hezekiah rests on this position and amounts to a radical rejection of all royal pretensions and even perhaps of the Davidic line entirely. Similarly, Hosea's denunciation of monarchy has the same base, for both he and Isaiah depend on the identical concept of Yahweh's 'exclusive prerogative' originally developed at Shiloh Again, the evidence for all this is slight and the whole case really depends on the over-clear differentiation of Zion and Davidic traditions.

A final chapter sets the Zion symbol over against the Exodus symbol, which figures so prominently in contemporary Liberation theology, and deplores its devaluation in many Biblical theologies. The point is well worth making but the author's discussion of it is disappointing. He concludes that 'the possibilities open to humankind are determined not by history or by nature, but by creation', yet he does not tell us what this means or what implications it might have for actual human behaviour and action. There are many interesting suggestions made in this book and its care and thoroughness are commendable, but one must conclude that its main thesis still fails to carry conviction.

J. R. Porter

Oost, R.: *Omstreden Bijbeluitleg. Aspecten en achtergronden van de hermeneutische discussie rondom de exegese van het Oude Testament in Nederland. Een bijdrage tot gesprek.* 1986. Pp. 122. Kok, Kampen. Price: Fl. 19.50. ISBN 90 242 5486 8)

The 'Amsterdam school' or 'Amsterdam tradition' in Old Testament exegesis is still not well known in the English-speaking world, although it probably antedates and anticipates aspects of the American 'canonical criticism' which has attracted more attention. This work is a short discussion of the movement by a scholar who is positively interested but also critical and also fair. Contrary views of Ps. 23 are taken as an illustration (pp. 108–11). A diagrammatic display of typical thoughts of the Amsterdam school is usefully given on pp. 96 f. The clear opposition of the school to customary 'historical' exegesis, its alliance with modern literary trends, and its dependence especially on Buber, Barth and Miskotte are rightly made clear. The book is useful and clear and one can only complain that it is perhaps too short. There is a five-page summary in English.

J. Barr

Sanders, J. A.: *From Sacred Story to Sacred Text: Canon as Paradigm.* 1987. Pp. xx, 200. (Fortress Press, Philadelphia. Price: $18.95. ISBN 0 8006 0805 4)

Students of 'canonical criticism' will be glad to have this collection of Sanders' articles and papers, arranged in chronological order of publication. It contains the following: 'Adaptable for Life: The Nature and Function of Canon'; 'Torah and Christ'; 'Canonical Hermeneutics'; 'Biblical Criticism and the Bible as Canon'; 'Canonial Hermeneutics: True and False Prophecy'; 'Torah and Paul'; 'Text and Canon: Concepts and Method'; 'Canonical Context and Canonical Criticism'; and 'From Sacred Story to Sacred Text' (the only chapter not previously published). There is a great consistency in Sanders' approach over the ten years or so covered by the collection, and it makes it easier to compare his position with that of B. S. Childs. His much greater interest in the canonical process, rather than in the text as a fixed entity, makes for a more flexible and (in the judgement of this reviewer) a more convincing theory about the function of the Bible in the Christian faith. But Sanders largely shares Child's assessment of the shortcomings of the biblical criticism for which canonical criticism is intended as a replacement — especially that it 'locked the Bible into the past'. Sanders and Childs propose slightly different cures for this disease: but is the diagnosis correct? This and a host of other questions are raised by this stimulating volume.

J. Barton

Smith, J. Z.: *To Take Place: Toward Theory in Ritual* (Chicago Studies in the History of Judaism). 1987. Pp. xvii, 183. (Chicago University Press, Chicago and London. Price: £21.95. ISBN 0 226 76359 5)

This is a specialist work of comparative religion written from the perspective of social anthropology. The author concentrates his attention on 'mental maps' reflected in rituals and texts. These maps elaborate fundamental structures of religious systems. The author takes three examples: the myth of the broken pole of the Tjilpa (an example apparently much loved by anthropologists), the temple visions of Ezekiel, and the Church of the Holy Sepulchre. There are four ideological maps in Ezekiel (40:1–44:3; 44:4–31; 45:1–8 and 47:13–48–35; 46). The first shows a hierarchy of power based on the sacred/profane dichotomy; the second is based on pure/impure; the third is civic and territorial; the fourth orientational. According to Smith the first two maps are classic hierarchies. The first displays the cartography of power, with Yahweh at the apex, while the second displays the cartography of status, with the Zadokite priests at the summit. It would need a social anthropologist to pass judgement on many aspects of this work — the theoretical framework is complex. However, the third (Ezekiel) chapter will be of direct value to Old Testament studies, while the ideas presented in the book as a whole are refreshing and stimulating. And despite his wider interests the author seems to be conversant with the technicalities of Old Testament studies in general and of the Book of Ezekiel in particular.

J. F. Healey

Soete, A.: *Ethos der Rettung — Ethos der Gerechtigkeit: Studien zur Struktur von Normbegründung und Urteilsfindung im Alten Testament und ihrer Relevanz für die ethische Diskussion der Gegenwart.* 1987. Pp. 359. (Echter, Würzburg. Price: DM 48.00. ISBN 3 429 01104 3)

The author suggests that this dissertation presented to the Catholic Faculty at the University of Bonn be regarded as a beginning for an interdisciplinary discussion arising from Old Testament ethics. It is consequently preferred to think of it as a work on moral theology rather than a piece of Old Testament exegesis. Nevertheless, seven of its nine chapters concentrate entirely on the Old Testament and engage in a wide-ranging discussion of its theology and teaching. In examining the basis of its ethics in *Heilsgeschichte* the topics discussed are: myth and revelation in history, the idea of God in history, the covenant community as a saved community and finally law and ethics. Again in the next section the way of judgement is examined in three parts: a study of the root *ṣdq*, exegesis of individual texts (the Tamar incident in Gen. 38, Jacob and Laban in Gen. 30:35–43, the pericope in Gen. 15, the flood narrative in Gen. 7:1–5) and the contribution of the Wise. It is in the final chapter that an attempt is made to relate the Old Testament to current discussion of ethics.

The main thrust of Annette Soete's argument is that in order to make the Old Testament relevant to interdisciplinary discussion there must be a concentration on its specific ethical orientation. A distinction is drawn between assembling material on the ethics of the Old Testament and concern with ethics in the Old Testament; the latter approach searches for its basic norm and the standard accepted for its judgements.

Undoubtedly those concerned with Old Testament studies cannot escape the quest for relevance. But, as proved by Soete's study, there are important questions of methodology to be discussed. On the one hand, there is need for complete mastery of Old Testament material, and on the other there must be some selection of what is relevant for current discussion. It is difficult to find a course that does both adequately without elaborating the one at the expense of the other.

G. H. Jones

SPANNER, D. C.: *Biblical Creation and the Theory of Evolution.* 1987. Pp. 191. Paternoster, Exeter. Price: £6.95. ISBN 0 85364 315 6)

The author of this fascinating study is a professional biologist who on his retirement from an academic Chair was ordained to the non-stipendiary ministry of the Church of England. He adheres to a conservative evangelical position; but it is not his purpose to set the biblical account of creation over against the theory of evolution; and indeed he can quite sharply castigate both 'creationists' and secular scientists who insist on conducting the debate about the beginning of things in adversarial terms. On the other hand, he does not wish simply to deny that there is a clash between the Genesis story and the findings or (as he would prefer to put it) the theories of modern science. Genesis is not under the judgement of modern science; for it is revelation, and it points the people of this or any age beyond the knowledge, be it little or much, that they have discovered of the world of nature or of human beings to the God who gave it and them existence in the first place. This is an important insight, and it is backed up by some skilful and imaginative exegesis of the opening chapters of Genesis. But does the truth of revelation, which Professor Spanner handles so sensitively, need to be undergirded by a conservative view of the authority of Scripture? I do not think so; and I regret that his eirenic treatment of Darwinism is not matched by a fairer treatment of those whose attachment to the doctine of creation is as solid as his but who cannot share his confident belief in the historicity of the Genesis narrative.

J. C. L. GIBSON

THOMA, C., and WYSCHOGRAD, M. (eds.): *Understanding Scripture: Explorations of Jewish and Christian Traditions of Interpretation* (Studies in Judaism and Christianity). 1987. Pp. viii, 168. (A Stimulus Book. Paulist Press, New York, Mahwah. Price: $7.95. ISBN 0 8091 2873 X)

The papers which comprise this book were first delivered at a symposium of Jewish and Catholic biblical scholars held at Lucern in 1984. Their present form represents revision in the light of the discussion there. The book is doubly welcome, first because such a meeting took place and second for the quality of the papers it provoked. The first three contributions (by N. Sarna, J. Mejia and W. Kirchschläger) pursue understanding of the place of Tradition and Inspiration in Scripture and are remarkable for the common ground between their authors. Much of this is due to the high place 'tradition' holds in both communities as illuminative of the Scriptures and to the growing recognition of the concept of 'inner-biblical exegesis' by which it is seen that their traditions have roots in the same (biblical) soil. Following essays (by D. Berger, M. Gilbert, F. Talmage, E. Synan and M. Wyschograd) illustrate exegetical traditions in both communities. A section on Medieval Hermeneutics has valuable contributions from both Jewish and Catholic scholars on Christian attitudes to Old Testament Law, where Wyschograd's critique of Aquinas raises the interesting question as to whether Paul's arguments in *Galatians* do really imply that the Law no longer has any relevance for *Jewish* Christians. The papers in the final section (by C. Thoma and S. Lauer) recognize the claims of Scripture on both traditions because of its rich *literary* heritage.

No one in this book claims to have arrived at definitive answers. The real tribute to them will be paid by the continuation of debate on the issues which they have here raised. It is to be hoped that the circles of the discussion will widen to include Protestant scholars, both to show the increasing place given to tradition in addition to that of *sola scriptura* by Protestants and to see whether any distinctive insights from them may help the debates along.

R. A. MASON

WAGNER, S., and Breit, H.: *Die Menschen-freundlichkeit Gottes: Alttestamentliche Predigten mit hermeneutischen Überlegungen*. 1986. Pp. 224. Lang, Frankfurt am Main. Price: SwFr 29.00. ISBN 3 8204 8997 5)

This volume is more a guide to preaching in the Evangelische Kirche in Germany than to Old Testament exegesis. Old Testament scholars would, however, find the introductory section on principles to be followed in preaching from the Old Testament of interest. There is emphasis on the value of historico-critical study, but the basis of preaching is unashamedly Christocentric and, whilst there is a brief exegetical study on the text utilised to accompany each sermon, it is not always clear that the sermon has come from the text. Rather, theological presuppositions have determined the application of the text. The sermons are all related to the Christian Calendar — with four based on Genesis, one on 2 Kings, two on the Psalms, and nine from the prophets, no fewer than five being based on Deutero-Isaiah.

R. J. HAMMER

WALSH, J. P. M.: *The Mighty from their Thrones: Power in the Biblical Tradition* (Overtures to Biblical Theology, 21). 1987. Pp. xvi, 206. (Fortress Press, Philadelphia. Price: $12.95. ISBN 0 8006 1546 8)

An introduction for the general reader, which concentrates much more heavily on the Old Testament than on the New. There is a broadly historical treatment of the realities of power in ancient Israel, which are thought to have co-existed with a theological commitment to ideals of powerlessness derived from the covenant, the origins of Israel as *ᶜapiru*, and the prophetic demand for justice. The influence of N. K. Gottwald and D. N. Freedman is strong and acknowledged, and in some ways the book represents a new kind of 'biblical theology' taking Gottwald's model of early Israel as its reference-point. As in the older biblical theology, keywords play an important role, and there are interesting suggestions about the meaning of *mišpāṭ*, *ṣedeḳ*, *nāqām*, and other central terms. The case for a distinctively Israelite world-view, opposed to the ideologies of the Canaanite city-states, is strongly advocated. An interesting example of how some recent sociological theories in Old Testament studies can be presented to a wider public.

J. BARTON

WILDAVSKY, A.: *The Nursing Father: Moses as a Political Leader*. 1984. Pp. xi, 262. (University of Alabama Press, distributed by Eurospan, London. Price: £10.30. ISBN 0 8173 0169 0)

Written by a political scientist, this book is about leadership. W. uses the Moses story as a paradigm, reading the text synchronically. After an introduction which is often very personal about his own quest for understanding, he presents four models of rulership or regime and then proceeds to interpret the life of Moses as a progression from one regime to the next: slavery, anarchy, equity, hierarchy.

Once W. has presented his models, his relating of them to Moses is very ingenious, but it is never clear how he derived them in the first place. Therefore, one cannot help feeling that he is simply reading his concerns into the text rather than from it; for those acquainted with the biblical interpretation of Philo of Alexandria a great deal will strike them as familiar. Whether W. has anything original to say about leadership is for political scientists to judge, but to the biblical scholar his effort appears to be using the biblical text as a vehicle rather than a source. Even though referring to structuralism, he appears simply to be deriving from the text whatever is helpful for his models rather than carrying out a true structural exegesis. Indeed, his whole enterprise smacks of more of the homiletic than the hermeneutic, bu preachers may find something of interest.

L. L. GRABBE

WILMS, F.-E.: *Das Tier: Mitgeschöpf, Gott oder Dämon* (Europäische Hochschulschriften XXIII; Theologie, Bd 306). 1987. Pp. 127. (Lang, Frankfurt am Main, Bern, New York. Price $18.65. ISBN 3 8204 9920 2; ISSN 0721 3409)

Partly in response to the modern concern for the environment, Wilms examines the position of animals in the ancient world and the Bible. He deals first with animals as man's fellow creatures, concentrating on the creation stories, the relation of animals and humans to God, the sacrifice of animals in place of humans, the significance of blood, and the enmity between animals and humans, with the future hope of peaceful coexistence. Shorter chapters consider animals as gods and demons, with reference to such creatures as Behemoth and Rahab, and the animal symbolism of apocalyptic. Finally biblical references to some twenty animals are collected, with short notes on the attitude of peoples in the ancient Near East and the classical world to these animals. It is a useful compendium of material without any deep analysis or discussion.

C. S. RODD

WONNEBERGER, R., and HECHT, P. H.: *Verheissung und Versprechung: eine theologische und sprachanalytische Klärung*. 1986. Pp. xiv, 273. (Vandenhoeck & Ruprecht, Göttingen. Price: DM 39.80. ISBN 3 525 60637 3)

Not a work of exegesis in the traditional sense, but an approach which applies 'speech act theory' to the concept of promise. The most original element is the use of daily ordinary language to work out the meanings and nuances: the reader will find utterances from *The Prime of Miss Jean Brodie*, from Mickey Mouse, and from Ronald Reagan here to enliven his studies. The approach is intended to build a kind of bridge between exegesis and ethics and homiletics. Biblical passages are brought into contact with the linguistic perceptions discovered. Some Hebrew citations (pp. 150 f.) unfortunately have many misprints. The whole approach seems interesting and promising.

J. BARR

WRIGHT, D. P.: *The Disposal of Impurity: Elimination Rites in the Bible and in Hittite and Mesopotamian Literature* (SBL Dissertation Series, 101). 1987. Pp. xxi, 380. (Scholars Press, Atlanta, Georgia. Price: $17.95 (member price: $12.95); ISBN 1 55540 056 6. Paperback price: $12.95 (member price: $9.95; ISBN 1 55540 057 4)

This is a fascinating and most careful account of impurities and their treatment in the Priestly tradition. In citing parallels from Mesopotamia and Anatolia the author limits himself to 'contrastive comparison', in which the differences between the phenomena being compared are given as much prominence as the similarities. This method is preferred to that of deducing historical connections between cultures and the ancient Near Eastern material is studied for its own sake rather than as a quarry from which to extract Old Testament parallels. Wright hardly even touches upon the anthropological aspect of this subject. As he notes himself, his work will be a sound basis for further work of this kind. Meanwhile, he is concerned with working out how the Priestly writers may have conceptualized the different categories of pollution which are of so much concern to them.

The body of the work is a mass of detail, though it is easy enough to read and follow. Major sections are devoted to non-human bearers of impurity, including, of course, the scapegoat, and the restrictions attached to human impurities. The extra-biblical parallels, especially the Hittite rituals (which include a ritual involving a scapemouse!), have not previously been used to the full in this context. Priestly concern with purity is seen to be focused on the danger of pollution in the sanctuary, as rites connected with the readmission of previously impure persons show. Although Wright shows different levels of development in the Priestly material, it is noteworthy that the Old Testament rituals show much less sign of the demonic and magical aspect of impurity which is prominent in the extra-biblical sources. The clearest remnant of such conceptions in the Priestly corpus seems to be the scapegoat designated for Azazel.

J.F. HEALEY

8. THE LIFE AND THOUGHT OF THE SURROUNDING PEOPLES

ABITZ, F.: *Ramses III. in den Gräbern seiner Söhne* (Orbis Biblicus et Orientalis, 72). 1986. Pp. 148. (Universitätsverlag Freiburg; Vandenhoeck & Ruprecht, Göttingen. Price: Sw.Fr. 38.00; DM 54.00. ISBN 3 7278 0369 X (Freiburg), ISBN 3 525 53701 8 (Göttingen))

This work is a detailed study of the decoration to be found in six royal tombs of princes of the reign of Ramesses III (early twelfth century B.C.) in the Valley of the Queens in Western Thebes. The brilliant colouring of the decoration apart, the most striking feature of all these tombs is the predominant role of the king, not the tomb-owner. It would appear that the king acts as intermediary between his sons and the gods of the netherworld—and also enhanced his own fortunes in the afterlife (especially if his own tomb-decoration were to be destroyed). A book primarily for Egyptologists.

K. A. KITCHEN

ALBERTI, A., and POMPONIO, F.: *Pre-Sargonic and Sargonic Texts from Ur edited in UET 2, Supplement.* 1986. Pp. xv, 134, 4 plates. (Biblical Institute Press, Rome. Price: Lire 24,000. ISBN 88 7653 585 3)

This is a competent edition of Sumerian economic documents from the third quarter of the third millennium. It is for Sumerologists and cuneiform scholars, though its results will be helpful for the study of documents from Ebla, and Semitic personal names with religious interest do occur.

W. G. LAMBERT

BARGUET, P.: *Les textes des sarcophages égyptiens du moyen empire: introduction et traduction.* (Littératures anciennes du Proche Orient, 12). 1986. Pp. 725. (Cerf, Paris. Price: Fr. 270.00. ISBN 2 204 02332 9; ISSN 0459 5831)

From Ancient Egypt, we have three massive collections of funerary compositions: the Pyramid Texts (third millennium B.C.), the Coffin Texts (early second millennium B.C.) and the so-called Book of the Dead (later second and the first millennia B.C.). All are spells, hymns and the like for the benefit of the deceased in the afterlife; it should be added that the range of concepts in this literature is considerable and not without usefulness in broader Old Testament background.

A monumental edition of the middle corpus, the Coffin Texts, was produced by De Buck in seven volumes. The first reliable complete translation is that by R. O. Faulkner, *The Ancient Egyptian Coffin Texts*, I–III, 1973–78. Now, in just one thick but compact volume, we here have an elegant and excellent French translation by Barguet. The footnotes offer minimally brief explanations (as Faulkner did); the work includes a useful bibliography and index. A major departure is that the spells are grouped by general theme — not (as in Faulkner) in the numerical order of the hieroglyphic edition. However, a concordance (pp. 687–94) enables any spell to be located quickly. For readers of French, an invaluable compact translation of a considerable body of religious texts.

K. A. KITCHEN

BLANQUART, F. (ed.): *Le Création dans l'Orient Ancien* (Congrès de l'ACFEB, Lille (1985)) (Lectio Divina 127). 1987. Pp. 533. (Cerf, Paris. Price: Fr. 250.00. ISBN 2 204 02595 X; ISSN 0750 1919)

Selected papers given at the biblical congress on the theme of creation held at Lille in 1985 are provided in this paperback. Also included are five 'workshops'. After the foreword, which outlines philosophical approaches to the topic of Creation (J. Ladrière), comes the first section, dealing with Creation in texts from Mesopotamia (M.-J. Seux), Ugarit (J.-L. Cunchillos) and Egypt (B. Menu). Section II covers the Old Testament. Creation of the first couple (J. Briend), Creation and the Law (P. Beauchamp), Creation in Deutero-Isaiah (J. Vermeylen), in Jeremiah (L. Wisser), in Job (J. Lévêque) and in the Psalms (C. Westermann). Also, Gen. 1–3 as interpreted by the Book of Wisdom (M. Gilbert), Creation according to Philo (J. Cazeaux) and Creation according to 'The Paraphrase of Shem', a Gnostic tract from Nag Hammadi (M. Tardieu). The workshops dealt with the following topics: the paradise in the desert motif (G. Bienaimé); 2 Macc. 7:28 within the biblical 'mythos' of creation (P. Gibert), the literary form for describing origins (also Gibert) and 'Towards a semiotic analysis of Gen. 1–3' (J. Calloud). With no explanation for its inclusion here, the second workshop (J. Cazeaux) sets out to show how 1 Sam. 26 is an inversion of chapter 24 through the pivotal chapter 25. It is quite evident that with certain exceptions, notably Gen. 1–3, the principal theme of the congress was by no means dominant in ancient Near Eastern literature. It remains for the reader to compare and contrast the different traditions documented here on the topic of Creation. The book is indexed.

W. G. E. WATSON

CURTO, S., and MONTEVECCHI, O.: *Egitto e Società Antica* (Atti del Convegno Torino 8/9 VI–23/24 XI 1984). 1985. Pp. xii, 288. (Vita e Pensiero, Milano. Price: Lire 40,000. ISBN 88 343 3003 X)

Here are the proceedings of a convention held at Turin in two sessions in 1984 under the sponsorship of the Giuseppe Toniolo Centre for Culture and Studies. The convention concentrated on two areas of Egyptology — aspects of Pharaonic Egypt and problems of Graeco-Roman Egypt (especially papyrology). Of the seventeen readers of papers all are Italian scholars but one (P. W. Pestman of Leiden). The paper which approaches most closely to SOTS interests is that by E. Bresciani on Semites in Egypt in the Saitic and Persian period. The Pentateuchal narratives with an Egyptian setting are more *à l'Égyptienne* than authentically Egyptian in their colouring: they reflect the knowledge of Egypt acquired by Semitic visitors or immigrants from 600 B.C. on, not least by the Elephantine colony.

F. F. BRUCE

Dietrich, M., Loretz, O., and Desman, W. C.: *Ugarit-Bibliographie 1967–1971. Titel, Nachträge, Register* (AOAT 20/5). 1986. Pp. vii, 814. (Neukirchener Verlag, Neukirchen-Vluyn; Butzon & Bercker, Kevelaer. Price: DM 308.00 (subscription price: DM 280.00); ISBN 3 7887 1243 0; 3 7666 9459 6)

The first four parts of this extensive bibliography, covering 1928–66, appeared in 1973 (see *B.L.* 1975, p. 90). The present volume is concerned chiefly with 1967–71. The numerous references to secondary literature and the indexes make this work quite useful to Old Testament scholars.

W. G. E. Watson

Durand, J.-M., and Kupper, J.-R. (eds.): *Miscellanea Babylonica: Mélanges offerts à Maurice Birot*. 1985. Pp. 320. (Éditions Recherche sur les Civilisations, ADPF, Paris. Price: Fr. 270.00. ISBN 2 86538 147 3)

This collection of thirty-two papers in honour of one whose own publications have been mostly in the Old Babylonian and Mari fields is mainly concerned with the same areas. A number will be of particular interest to Old Testament scholars. H. Cazelles writes on the dedication of women and children to deities and the provision of particular garments for them. J.-M. Durand presents important new textual evidence for monoliths at places of worship in Syria. They were called *sikkannum*. A. Finet adds extra details on the cults of the dead at Mari. A. Lemaire offers an improved interpretation of § twelve of the Aramaic Ahiqar proverbs, and J. M. Sasson re-edits with commentary the letter in which Yarim-Lim of Aleppo declares war on another ruler.

W. G. Lambert

The Epigraphic Survey: *The Battle Reliefs of King Sety I* (Oriental Institute Publications, 107; Reliefs and Inscriptions at Karnak, 4). Pp. xiv, 166 (4to) and 50 plates (folio). (Oriental Institute of the University of Chicago, Chicago, 1986. Price: $90.00. ISBN 0 918986 42 7; ISSN 069 3367)

This magnificent work provides the definitive publication (mainly in superb line-drawn plates) of the famous battle-scenes of Sethos I (*c.* 1290 B.C.) showing his transit of the north-Sinai route (the biblical 'Way of the Philistines') and invasion of Canaan. In the accompanying quarto volume (enclosed within the plates–folio) full descriptions of the scenes are given, and excellent fresh translations of the accompanying texts that will replace those by Breasted (in his *Ancient Records*) which have served hitherto. This work is, therefore, of considerable importance (for consultation) for anyone utilising this body of Egyptian evidence in studying Canaanite toponymy, and the route from Egypt to Canaan.

K. A. Kitchen

Farber, W., Kümmel, H. M., and Römer, W. H. Ph.: *Rituale und Beschwörungen* I (Texte aus der Umwelt des Alten Testaments, II/2). 1987. Pp. v, 160–292. (Gerd Mohn, Gütersloh. Price: DM 98.00 (sub. price: DM 84.00); ISBN 3 579 00067 5)

For earlier parts of this work see last *B.L.* 1987, p. 95. Of the rituals and incantations given here, most are Babylonian (translated and introduced by Farber), somewhat fewer Sumerian (Römer), and a smaller number Hittite (Kümmel). Most were first put in writing in the second millennium, a few in the third, but some of the ritual practices and some of the words of the incantations go back much further. The relevance of such rituals for Old Testament study is well understood, but incantations less so because, being magic, they were not as much absorbed in orthodox Yahwism. In contrast they held an important place in Sumero-Babylonian religion and influenced neighbouring lands, as shown at Ebla, Boghaz-köy and Ras Shamra. They played a significant role in the development of an international ancient Near Eastern literary phraseology. Old Testament passages are sometimes described as 'incantational' by commentators, but not always from first-hand knowledge of such texts. The selection of both rituals and incantations given here is representative, not concentrating on those most relevant to the Old Testament, and is much limited by available space. The Babylonian New Year ritual is given from the Late Babylonian series only, not even supplemented by the few pieces on Late Assyrian tablets.

W. G. LAMBERT

GIDDY, L. L.: *Egyptian Oases. Bahariya, Dakhla, Farafra and Kharga During Pharaonic Times*. 1987. Pp. xix, 305, including maps, plans and figures. (Aris & Phillips Ltd, Warminster. Price: £25.00. ISBN 0 85668 367 1)

This book (originating in a doctoral thesis) tackles a subject that has enjoyed only pioneering treatment in old books of decades ago, or limited indepth explorations in more recent years to the present: the Oases to the west of the Nile Valley in Pharaonic times — in this case, for the first two-thirds of that span (*c.* 3000–945 B.C.), leaving aside later periods when the oases ceased to be clearly an 'outer frontier' region in Egyptian history (p. xviii). Nevertheless, evidence from later epochs than the twenty-first Dynasty cannot be wholly excluded, and is judiciously used when it is indispensable.

Ms Giddy divides her work into three parts. In the first, she gives a succinct but clear survey of the physical nature and extent of the four oases (water, climate, cultivation, etc.), and — with especial care — of the actual practicable routes between the oases and the Nile Valley, and linking the oases. In the second, she reviews critically (and almost too defensively) the possible ancient Egyptian nomenclature for the oases as a group and individually. Thirdly, she then surveys the actual remains — and the future archaeological potential — for the pharaonic (and sometimes other) period(s) so far discernible in these oases. It is very clear that they contain much that very urgently needs record and investigation, being also under threat from modern development, vandalism and cupidity. Although the content and bibliography do not go beyond 1983/84 (as Ms Giddy herself scrupulously points out), yet this study furnishes us with an invaluable balance-sheet of what is realistically to be known about the oases from ancient Egyptian sources, and from most of the known field-explorations prior to the last five years. Armed with this book and the readily-accessible reports of these last few years, any study of the antiquity of the oases is thus considerably facilitated. As for exclusions, Siwa has no known pharaonic remains, and the Qattara depression is totally barren; so they do not feature here except marginally. A useful contribution.

K. A. KITCHEN

GIVEON, R., and KERTESZ, T.: *Egyptian Scarabs and Seals from Acco from the Collection of the Israel Department of Antiquities and Museums*. 1986. Pp. 48 and 20 unnumbered plates. (Universitätsverlag, Freiburg (CH). Price: Sw.Fr. 19.00. ISBN 3 7278 0371 1)

This pleasingly-produced brochure publishes 176 scarabs, seals and seal-impressions in line-drawing and photographs, with succinct descriptions of each item. Almost all these pieces were found in and around Acco over the years, coming to light casually, not by regular excavations. Most are from the Lefkovitz collection (now in the Israel Museum); some forty items are in the Beter and Goldmann collections at Haifa.

These pieces range in date from the Middle Kingdom and Hyksos periods (*c.* 1800–1550 B.C.; nos. 1–34) to roman times (no. 122). Some fifty items date to the New Kingdom (*c.* 1550–1070 B.C.), and another seventy to subsequent periods. None are outstanding; many find parallels from other collections and excavations. Some add new details, forms or motifs to the known repertoire. Number 71 should be read 'Thoth, Lord (*nb*) of Hesre(t)'. On no. 76, the 'king' may be reading from a scroll. Numbers 99, 100 show men riding horses; no. 141 is a battle-scene. It is always useful to have such material fully published.

K. A. KITCHEN

GORDON, C. H., RENDSBURG, G. A., and WINTER, N. H. (eds.): *Eblaitica: Essays on the Ebla Archives and the Eblaite Language*, vol. 1. 1987. Pp. x, 145. (Eisenbrauns, Winona Lake, Indiana. Price: $22.50. ISBN 0 931464 34 X)

The tendency to publish in journal form is on the increase, and this volume, despite its cloth binding and glossy dust-jacket, is the first volume of such from the Center for Ebla Research set up by Cyrus Gordon at New York University. It contains three contributions by Gordon himself, four from students or former students, and five from A. Archi, currently epigrapher of the Ebla expedition, who normally appears in Italian. For Old Testament scholars his survey 'Ebla and Eblaite' (pp. 7–17) is well worth reading as the views of one who has been working intensively on the whole archive for some years (but not, of course, necessarily final truth). Three articles, by Gordon, C. Wallace and Rendsburg, deal with *wm* 'and also' in the Old Testament, reviewing the examples proposed by F. I. Andersen and adding Neh. 5:11, though the Eblaite *ūma* is not certainly related. Not all the etymological material from Sumerian, Akkadian, Hebrew and Eblaite advanced by Gordon in 'Eblaitica' (pp. 19–28), such as the equation of Sumerian *eden* 'steppe' with '(Garden of) Eden', is generally accepted.

W. G. LAMBERT

GREEN, M.: *The Coptic* share *Pattern and its Ancient Egyptian Ancestors. A Reassessment of the Aorist Pattern in the Egyptian Language*. 1987. Pp. vi, 92. (Aris & Phillips Ltd, Warminster. Price: £12.00. ISBN 0 85668 380 9)

In Coptic — the last form of the Ancient Egyptian language, as written in a modified Greek alphabet and used principally in Christian Egypt — there is a variety of tense-forms, most of which can be traced back to their etymological ancestors in the language of the pharaonic epoch. Dr Green treats the tense with prefix *share*, often called 'Habitude' or 'Praesens Consuetudinis' in standard Cotic grammars. As these names might suggest, it is there often defined as a tense of general habit or custom, not a time-bound form. The Greek term 'aorist' has sometimes (and very improperly) been applied to this tense-form.

Here, Dr Green has very usefully and forcefully surveyed all available contexts of the ancestral Egyptian forms *sdm.hr.f* and *hr(.f) sdm.f* and a mass of examples in original Coptic (i.e. not Coptic translations from Greek particularly Scripture), leading to the result that both the Egyptian and proper Coptic constructions are in essence a 'consequential' tense-form. If such-and-such is the case, *then* such-and-such will follow [this tense], to put it in a nutshell. The vast majority of the examples seem to bear this, either explicitly or implicitly; some are not so evident, but do not contradict the findings. Pp. 38–39, PT 696, the treatment is not satisfactory; rather render (still in line with his findings) '. . . (thus) you are not to bring the scent of your *hdn*-plant to T'. Also, when returning to Biblical Coptic (and other text translations from Greek) — not the subject of this work — a generalizing or 'habit' usage is undeniable; but, in the light of this study, it may be a secondary feature.

K. A. KITCHEN

HART, G.: *A Dictionary of Egyptian Gods and Goddesses.* 1986. Pp. xvi + 229, with 2 maps and numerous line-drawings in the text. (Routledge and Kegan Paul, London, Boston and Henley. Price: £5.95. ISBN 0 7102 0965 7 (cloth), 0 7102 0167 2 (paperback))

To the casual enquirer, Ancient Egypt appears to have been inhabited by almost as many deities as ordinary people. This delightfully-produced volume in handy, compact format, presents an A-to-Z series of articles (from fourteen pages (Amun) to just two lines (Fetket) in length) on all the major deities of ancient Egypt, besides many lesser figures. Many appear also in impeccably clean, accurate line-drawings in the side-columns of each page — even more of these would be welcome. Welcome is the list of provinces ('nomes') with resident deities of each; the maps of these would be enhanced if the nome-numbers could be included on them also. Likewise welcome is the list of 'Alternative renderings of divine names' — again, addition of most modern spelling-variants would perhaps enhance its usefulness. Amid such a wealth of data, very clearly and succintly presented, small points for query inevitably arise. E.g., pp. 91, 174, 210, the text on the 'Shabaka stone' may belong to the thirteenth century B.C. rather than the Pyramid Age (Schlögl); p. 117, viziers were often entitled 'priest of Maat'. The book has no bibliography (to be found in standard works, or in Helck/Westendorf, *Lexikon der Ägyptologie*, I–VI); it is aimed at a very wide non-specialist audience, and should render excellent service to the interested general public.

K. A. KITCHEN

HECKER, K., and SOMMERFELD, W. (eds.): *Keilschriftliche Literaturen: Ausgewählte Vorträge der XXXII. Rencontre Assyriologique Internationale* (Berliner Beiträge zum Vorderen Orient, Bd. 6). 1986. Pp. xviii, 164 and 1 plate. (Dietrich Reimer Verlag, Berlin. Price: DM 38.00. ISBN 3 496 00879 2)

Of these seventeen papers read to Assyriologists some are highly technical and specialized, others of more general interest and so relevant to the Old Testament. H. Vanstiphout writes on genre in Mesopotamian literature; A. Finet on allusions as sources of knowledge for the spread of literature; W. G. Lambert on sources compiled in the Babylonian Epic of Creation; H. D. Galter on historical writing with a 'Wisdom' purpose; W. Röllig on popular literature; A. Ünal on the exposing of infants in Anatolian literature; E. Lipinski on 'The King's Arbitration'; and G. Del Olmo Lete on an Ugaritic ritual text.

W. G. LAMBERT

KITCHEN, K. A.: *The Third Intermediate Period in Egypt (1100–650 B.C.)*, 2nd edition, with supplement. 1986. Pp. xvii, 608. (Aris & Phillips, Warminster, Wiltshire. Price: £24.00. ISBN 0 85668 298 5)

The original (1973) edition of this fundamental work on the chronology, leading families and political history of the Late Period in Egypt was noticed in *B.L.* 1974, p. 79. Its renewed availability is welcome and particularly so in view of the author's energetic efforts, in a Supplement of over eighty pages, to maintain its value as an up-to-date account of a subject where new publications and fresh interpretations demand expert evaluation. In some cases (e.g. the chronology of the twenty-third Dynasty) this leads him to revise his earlier views; elsewhere he provides a characteristically thorough rebuttal of newer suggestions, as in the case of the events of 701 B.C. (though he allows the possibility of a co-regency between Shabako and Shebitku). Presumably W. H. Shea's fresh defence of a second campaign of Sennacherib in Palestine (*JBL* 104 (1985) 401–18) reached him too late for consideration here, and we must await his response to it elsewhere!

G. I. Davies

Macqueen, J. G.: *The Hittites and their Contemporaries in Asia Minor* (Ancient Peoples and Places, 83). 1986. Pp. 176. (Thames and Hudson, London. Price: £12.50. ISBN 0 500 02108 2)

This is a revised and enlarged edition of a volume which first appeared in 1975. It is a superb volume, matching others in the same series, and containing a comprehensive introduction to ancient Anatolia. The earlier history, as far as it can be understood, and the post-Hittite period down to the Persian period are outlined, but the main focus is the Hittites and the second millennium B.C. Covered in detail are the identification of the Hittites, the history of the Hittite empire, warfare, society and administration, daily life, religion, art and literature. 149 illustrations, maps and plans complement the finely-judged text. There is, of course, virtually nothing connected with Old Testament studies, but the book is useful even in this context in so far as it gives an account of the 'real' Hittites. In the wider context of ancient Near Eastern studies it is a most useful work which belongs alongside O. R. Gurney's Pelican, *The Hittites*, 1952 (and subsequent editions), and K. Bittel's *Hattusha, Capital of the Hittites*, 1970. It should also have a more popular readership and may be recommended to the more serious tourist visiting central Turkey and especially Bogazköy.

J. F. Healey

Moran, W. L. (with the collaboration of V. Haas and G. Wilhelm): *Les Lettres d'El Amarna: correspondance diplomatique du pharaon* (Littératures anciennes du Proche-Orient, 13). 1987. Pp. 630. (Cerf, Paris. Price: Fr. 290. ISBN 2 204 02645 X; ISSN 0459 5831)

One hundred years after the discovery of the archive, eighty years after J. A. Knudtzon's standard edition was made, and forty since his studies began to appear, W. L. Moran has made a major contribution to the understanding of the Amarna Letters and their significance. His renderings are accurate, though easy to read, and well convey the often petulent tone of the originals. Each translation has appropriate notes on problematic readings — Moran collated these — and linguistic obscurities which offer many improvements and incorporate the most recent as well as older solutions, carefully weighed. The Introduction outlines the history of the discovery, content and nature of the archive, and the political events of its time. G. Wilhelm translated the Hurrian letter (no. 24, from Tushratta), and V. Hass the Hittite (nos. 31, 32, Arzawa). As in other volumes in the series, there are helpful indices of proper names and words discussed. It is hard to praise this book too highly; it will be the standard translation for years to come, and historians, linguists, and Old Testament scholars will all use it with gratitude to W. L. Moran, his collaborators, and the translators of the French edition, D. Collon and H. Cazelles.

A. R. Millard

PETTINATO, G.: *Ebla: Nuovi orizzonti della storia*. 1986. Pp. 455. (Rusconi, Milano. Price: Lire 35,000. ISBN 88 18 12036 0)

Just over ten years after the important discoveries at tell Mardikh by the *Missione Archaeologica Italiana in Siria*, Pettinato, the epigrapher of the excavation team, has written another book about Ebla. Though not intended to replace his previous work, *Ebla. Un impero inciso nell'argilla* (Milan 1979; reviewed in *B.L.* 1981, pp. 108–09; E.T.: *The Archives of Ebla. An Empire Inscribed in Clay*, Garden City, New York, 1981) it does update and correct some of his earlier conclusions. The book under review is really a sequel and describes the history of Ebla and the surrounding countries in the light of the cuneiform tablets from that city. As in the first book texts with accompanying translation are provided, here relegated to an appendix.

There are three sections: Ebla as an empire founded on trade; Ebla within the Fertile Crescent; the cultural legacy of Ebla. This last section, especially the discussions of language (Eblaite is a new North (west) Semitic language) and religion (politics and religion were distinct), is of direct interest for the Old Testament.

Several photographs, colour plates, drawings, maps and tables illustrate the book. Five appendices provide chronological and dynastic tables, lists of towns, villages, kings and kingdoms documented at Ebla and a selection of texts. There is a bibliography plus indices. In spite of the occasional polemics Pettinato has made a significant contribution to the history of Syria in the second half of the third millennium B.C.

W. G. E. WATSON

PETTINATO, G.: *Semiramide*. 1985. Pp. 438. (Rusconi, Milano. Price: Lire 39,000. ISBN 88 18 18003 7)

In 812 B.C. Shamshi-Adad V, ruler of Assyria, died on a punitive expedition against Babylon. His son, the future Adad-Narari III, was then only ten years old and so his wife, the legendary Sammuramat — better known as Semiramis — took control until 806 B.C. In very great detail Pettinato describes the background to this unique event, comparing later accounts, especially that by Ctesia, with the historical records of Babylonia, Assyria, Syria and Anatolia. As expected there are numerous refererences to the history of Israel. In fact, Pettinato draws explicit parallels between Semiramis and the office of queen mother (*g*[e]*ḇîrâ*) in Israel and Judah, tracing its origin to Ugarit and Anatolia. The appendix provides a list of Assyrian kings, a chronological table and a bibliography. The book is indexed. In addition, there are sixteen full-page plates, some in colour, twenty drawings, maps and plans as well as several tables.

W. G. E. WATSON

REINER, E.: *Your thwarts in pieces, Your mooring rope cut. Poetry from Babylonia and Assyria.* (Michigan Studies in the Humanities, 5). 1985. Pp. xiv + 120. (Horace H. Rackham School of Graduate Studies at the University of Michigan. Price: $10.00. ISBN 0 936534 04 4)

Although the poetic texts from Babylonia and Assyria are not unknown to Old Testament scholars they have been appreciated more for their mythological and religious content than for their literary merit. A move towards a better understanding of how these ancient poems are constructed has been made by no less a scholar than the editor-in-charge of the *Chicago Assyrian Dictionary*. Her close reading of nine passages including the whole of the Hymn to the Sun-god and an Assyrian elegy (from which the book draws its title) is illuminating. She pays particular attention to strophic structure, shown to be marked principally by verb forms, but takes into account other poetic devices.

W. G. E. WATSON

ROWLANDS, M., LARSEN, M. and KRISTIANSEN, K. (eds.): *Centre and Periphery in the Ancient World* (New Directions in Archaeology). 1987. Pp. viii, 159. (Cambridge University Press. Price: £25.00. ISBN 0 521 25103 6)

The title of this volume, and several of the papers in it, arise out of an interest in the possibility of applying aspects of I. Wallerstein's theory of capitalist expansion in the modern world to the study of ancient economic history. The specific idea that a 'centre' flourishes at the expense of 'peripheral' areas proves to be too simple to describe the overlapping networks of trade in the ancient Near East, to which six of the eleven essays are devoted; but the search for regional perspectives in economic development emerges as a fruitful one. Students of Near Eastern history will find it useful to have conveniently available these essays which reflect current approaches to the subject, especially those by C. Zaccagnini and M. Liverani, much of whose work is in Italian. The comprehensive bibliography of over twelve large pages is a valuable resource in itself. Only Liverani's essay on the Late Bronze/Iron Age transition bears directly on biblical history, but anyone seeking to understand the wider aspects of Solomon's or the Omride dynasty's international contacts and trade or the growing corpus of administrative texts in Hebrew would find much stimulating reading here.

G. I. DAVIES

SADER, H. S.: *Les états araméens de Syrie depuis leur fondation jusqu'à leur transformation en provinces assyriens.* (Beiruter Texte und Studien, 36.) 1987. Pp. xiii, 306. (In Kommission bei Franz Steiner Verlag, Wiesbaden. Price: DM 74.00. ISBN 3 515 04925 8; ISSN 0067 4921)

A major part of this dissertation written under the guidance of W. Röllig at Tübingen presents the Assyrian and Aramaic texts concerning six states: Guzan, Bīt-Adini, Bīt-Agusi, Sam̉al, Hamath, and Damascus. The texts are transliterated and translated, with a few supportive notes. They include the Sefire treaties, the treaty of Assur-nirari V with Mati-el, and the Tell Fekheriyeh Statue *in toto*. The hieroglyphic Hittite texts are only summarized. On the basis of these documents, some Old Testament references, and archaeological discoveries, H. Sader reconstructs the history of each state. The scope of her work precludes such detail as W. Pitard has given for Damascus (see above, p. 40), but an up-to-date account for the others is useful, and the texts collected for each one make this a helpful handbook. Various points attract attention, among them discussions of the meaning of the Assyrian term for the Damascene, 'donkey-land', the date of the Tell Fekheriyeh Statue (the eighth century is preferred to the ninth, and the reign of Zakkur of Hamath. The author announces an as yet unpublished inscription from Arslan Tash made by Hadad-ezer king of Sobah in the time of Shalmaneser III (p. 263). This book is a stepping-stone on the way to an improved understanding of the affairs of Israel's northern neighbours.

A. R. MILLARD

VEENHOF, K. R. (ed.): *Cuneiform Archives and Libraries. Papers read at the 30ᵉ Recontre Assyriologique Internationale, Leiden, 4–8 July, 1983.* 1986. Pp. x, 307. (Nederlands Instituut voor het Nabije Oosten, Leiden. Price: Fl. 100. ISBN 90 6258057 2)

Twenty-nine papers read on the subject published here cover collections of texts from the mid-third millennium B.C. to Persian times. What sorts of documents were kept in archives, how long they were kept and in what order are among questions discussed pertinent to the history or prehistory of biblical books. W. H. van Soldt, for example, describes one part of the palace archives at Ugarit, reconstructing their original organization. Three studies deal with the Nineveh tablet collections: J. E. Reade gives information about provenances and groups of texts, S. Parpola outlines the royal documents by king, and T. Kwasman the legal ones. Parpola notes the storage of single prophecies written from dictation and larger tablets on which several oracles were collected. J. C. Greenfield surveys remnants of archives from Persian times, noting variants of the Behistun inscription in Persian, Babylonian and Aramaic texts, and points to evidence that royal edicts were preserved in provincial centres, observations relevant for post-exilic works. P. Garelli tells of the Brussels tablets in Assyrian and Aramaic, and A. M. Bisi of bullae from Phoenician and Punic sites (comparable to Hebrew ones, but rarely inscribed). The editor's 'Cuneiform Archives, an Introduction' (pp. 1–36) is an excellent overview, pointing out the range of private family archives which could include property ownership deeds two centuries or more old. Collections from Ebla, Babylon, Mari, Hattusha, Assur and other sites are also analysed. The whole volume is a reminder of the great amount of writing that scribes of cuneiform were doing throughout the Old Testament period.

A. R. MILLARD

WACHSMANN, S.: *Aegeans in the Theban Tombs* (Orientalia Lovaniensia Analecta, 20). 1987. Pp. xx, 146, and 70 plates. (Uitgeverij Peeters, Louvain. ISBN 90 6831 066 6)

This elegant volume provides a thorough and detailed re-examination of the representations of Aegean peoples in the Theban tomb-chapels of the fifteenth century B.C., such as the Keftiu, biblical Caphtor, ancient Cretans. Not all the scenes are good evidence; some show only imaginative figures with hybrid figures made up of Levantine and Aegean elements. This book will be of importance for anyone studying this Mediterranean aspect of the Old Testament world. One flaw is its author's use of the impossibly-high Egyptian chronology by Wente and Van Siclen; this key datum of 1450 B.C. (death of Tuthmosis III; virtual end of proper Aegean representations) must be lowered to 1425 B.C. on the total data now available.

K. A. KITCHEN

WALKER, C. B. F.: *Cuneiform. Reading the Past.* 1987. Pp. 64, 39 photos, and diagrams. (The British Museum, London. Price: £4.95. ISBN 0 7141 8059 9)

For a long time there has been a need for a convenient authoritative introduction to cuneiform writing in English. Now Walker, of the Department of Western Asiatic Antiquities at the British Museum has met it admirably. In seven succinct chapters he describes the history of the script, the types of document written and found, and gives information about scribes and libraries, the spread of cuneiform writing, and its decipherment. He presents a few sample texts with transliteration and translation, starting with notes on a Jemdet Nasr tablet. The book closes with a warning about casts and fakes, and a list of museums where cuneiform inscriptions are displayed (the list ranges all over the world but omits the Israel Museum). This book is a description, not a primer of cuneiform, and should be read by all who plan to learn the script as well as by everyone who has any interest in the writing system which dominated the Old Testament world for many centuries. The happy chance that led the Babylonians to write upon clay has resulted in our being able to read about every aspect of their life in a way denied in Palestine. This book begins to show the wealth of the cuneiform sources, and allows us to imagine, by analogy, what was written in Israel on papyrus which has perished.

A. R. MILLARD

XELLA, P. (ed.): *Archaeologia dell'Inferno: L'Aldilà nel mondo antico vicino-orientale e classico*. 1987. Pp. 307. (Essedue Edizioni, Verona. Price: Lire 34,000. ISBN 88 85697 15 1)

The netherworld is described here as it appears from the ancient texts and monuments of Egypt (G. Scandone Matthiae), Mesopotamia (J. Bottéro), Anatolia (G. F. Del Monte), Syria (P. Xella), Iran (H.-J. Klimkeit) and the Phoenician and Punic world (S. Ribichini). Against this background T. Podella portrays the *she'ol* of the Old Testament and C. Grottanelli the episode of the female necromancer of Endor. Additional contributions are by F. Saracino on the New Testament, and B. Zannini Quirini on the classical world.

Ugarit was very much oriented towards death, as was Egypt; its ancestor worship can be traced to the period of Ebla but its personification of Death was original (Xella). The official Old Testament conception of the afterlife, instead, was largely a reaction to Canaanite and Mesopotamian beliefs and to popular religious practices (Podella), these last exemplified by 1 Sam. 18, shown to be an 'inversion' of 1 Kings 22 (Grottanelli).

Here then is a succinct, balanced and well documented survey of ideas on life after death current at various times in this part of the world which, as the editor notes (Foreword) are equally valid as reflections on life before death.

W. G. E. WATSON

XELLA, P.: *Gli antenati di Dio: Divinità e miti della tradizione di Canaan*. 1982. Pp. 237 (Essedue Edizioni, Verona. Price: Lire 12,000. ISBN 88 85697 06 2)

Thanks to Paolo Xella a faithful translation of the principal poetic texts in Ugaritic is now available (in paperback) to readers of Italian. These texts comprise the Baal Cycle (Baal and Yam; The Palace of Baal; Baal and Mot; i.e. CTA 1–2; 3–4 and 5–6 respectively), the Keret Story (CTA 14–16) and the Myth of Danilu and Aqhat (CTA 17–19). There is an introduction to each text, with summaries and brief explanatory footnotes. The opening chapters show how discovery of the Ras Shamra tablets has contributed to our knowledge of Canaanite mythology, particularly in connection with the Old Testament; and at the close there is some reference to other texts in Ugaritic, especially the rituals. It is also made quite evident that there was a general preoccupation with death. A map, table of the Ugaritic alphabet and bibliography complete the volume which complements his significant edition of the ritual texts (reviewed in *B.L.* 1983, p. 102).

W. G. E. WATSON

XELLA, P.: *La Terra di Baal (Ugarit e la sua civilità)* (Biblioteca di Archaeologia). 1984. Pp. 175, including many plans and coloured illustrations. (Armando Curcio, Rome. Price: Lire 35,000. ISBN 88 7555 011 5)

The discovery of Ugarit, the decipherment of its language and a summary of its history are set out in the first three chapters. The next two are concerned with the art and architecture of the ancient city. Four chapters then describe its society, its religion and its myths. Throughout there are drawings, maps, plans, diagrams and black and white photographs, as well as coloured plates, several full-page. The illustrations alone make this volume worth acquiring. Though intended for the general reader interested in archaeology, this survey is valuable because in addition to the familiar mythological texts (which are quoted at length) the author draws on non-literary texts, many of which are illustrated and explained. There is a short, annotated bibliography.

W. G. E. WATSON

9. APOCRYPHA AND POST-BIBLICAL STUDIES

BAR-ILAN, M.: *The Mysteries of Jewish Prayer and Hekhalot* (Hebrew). 1987. Pp. 186. (Bar-Ilan University Press, Ramat Gan. ISBN 965 276 072 X)

Proceeding from the assumption that insufficient attention has been paid to the *hekhaloth* literature in reconstructing the history of standard Jewish prayer and liturgical poetry, Bar-Ilan sets about the task of rectifying this state of affairs. He cites the familiar versions of the relevant texts in some detail, pointing to the obvious parallels and challenging the reputable theories offered to explain them. His own view is that mystical texts usually dated in the post-talmudic period are of greater antiquity and therefore shed light on the development of rabbinic liturgy such as the *ʿamidah* in the tannaitic period. As the author himself virtually admits in his preface, his outlook is based on the personal impressions of a scholar well-versed in the prayers rather than on the disciplines of philology or the phenomenology of religion. As a result, there is insufficient discrimination between texts and ideas, between prayer and fixed liturgy, and between argument and apologetic, for the conclusions to be treated as more than speculative.

S. C. REIF

BURGMANN, H.: *Vorgeschichte und Frühgeschichte der essenischen Gemeinde von Qumran und Damaskus* (Arbeiten zum Neuen Testament und Judentum, 7), 1987, Pp. 530. (Lang, Frankfurt am Main, Bern, New York. Price: SwFr 78.00 ($52.00). ISBN 3 8204 9503 7)

Burgmann builds his history of the 'Qumran Essenes' around three 'catastrophes'. The first was the desertion of the 'Man of the Lie' Simon from the 'Pious' who supported the cause of the legitimate Zadokite high priest, the 'Teacher of Righteousness'; the second was a schism which sent many of the followers of the 'Teacher' to Syria; and the third was the overthrow of the 'Teacher of Righteousness' by the 'Wicked Priest' Jonathan who had usurped the High Priesthood from the Zadokites. Some elements in this reconstruction are novel, although the historical background conforms substantially to the 'consensus' which reigned from the mid-1950s until quite recently. Equally familiar to those who have read widely in Qumran studies are the confident assertions coupled with lack of method and bereft of critical argumentation, and the frequent use of a second hypothesis to explain problems caused by a first. Individual texts and passages are selected without regard to documentary context or genre, to acquire detailed history out of poetry and biblical commentaries. From just this 'method' innumerable contradictory 'histories' of Qumran could be fabricated (and many have). This book is an unwelcome diversion from the pursuit of Qumran history.

P. R. DAVIES

CHESTER, A.: *Divine Revelation and Divine Titles in the Pentateuchal Targumim* (Texte und Studien zum Antiken Judentum 14). 1986. Pp. xv, 432. (Mohr, Tübingen. Price: DM 128.00. ISBN 3 16 145113 9)

This completely revised doctoral dissertation provides a lucid and thorough analysis of a great deal of primary material. Two-thirds of the book is devoted to a complete survey of the use of *ʾitgly* in the various Targums to the Torah. A more general chapter on the Targums and Anthropomorphism presents a judicious critique of previous scholarship in this area. Attention is then given to the terms Memra, Shekinah and Yeqara, to the renderings of the divine name and to the use of divine titles and epithets. Throughout oversimplification is eschewed and the complexity of the issues is recognized.

There is a constant awareness of the difficulty of tracing the interrelationships of the several Targums and of the primary purpose of Targum: 'the practical exercise of explaining the biblical text to the ordinary person' in the synagogue. This is an important contribution to Targum studies.

A. Gelston

Delling, G.: *Die Bewältingung der Diasporasituation durch das hellenistische Judentum.* 1987. Pp. 96. (Vandenhoeck & Ruprecht, Göttingen. Price: DM 18.80. ISBN 3 525 53576 7)

This short paperback describes what happened when orthodox Jews met the liberal trends in the hellenistic world: how far did they take their policy of separatism? Delling assumes readers' knowledge of political and religious history, organizing his material under subject headings rather than under historical events or authors. He covers, among other things, forms of religious life in the community, special privileges and the significance of the Jerusalem temple for Jews of foreign lands, also problems of sabbath observance and food laws. Much seems to overlap with Hengel's work, but the chief value of this book lies in its direct dependence on primary sources: the letter of Aristeas and the works of Philo and Josephus continually appear, together with references to corpora of papyri and inscriptions. However, there is no index! So students and researchers must search the footnotes for themselves — where they will certainly find a wealth of useful material.

J. G. Snaith

Egger, R.: *Josephus Flavius und die Samaritaner: Eine terminologische Untersuchung zur Identitätsklärung der Samaritaner* (Novum Testamentum et Orbis Antiquus, 4). 1986. Pp. 412. (Universitätsverlag, Freiburg; Vandenhoeck & Ruprecht, Göttingen. Price: Sw.Fr. 98.00; DM 142.00. ISBN 3 7278 0373 8; ISBN 3 525 53903 7)

The basic issue addressed by this Freiburg dissertation is the significance of the varied descriptions employed by Josephus to refer to the inhabitants of Samaria. A brief introduction assesses the relevant sources, and the contemporary state of research is analysed; then the main body of the book offers a full discussion of each relevant text in both the Antiquities and the Jewish War. Six excursuses discuss other significant passages such as Ecclus. 50. The conclusion shows how the term 'Samaritan' is often inappropriate as a translation of Josephus's usage; often he is speaking of other inhabitants of the area or of distinct groups. Various other characteristics of religious usage and history are considered. An appendix sets out the Greek texts which have been discussed and there are full bibliography and indexes. All told this is a most valuable addition to the literature on both Josephus and the Samaritans.

R. J. Coggins

Endres, J. C.: *Biblical Interpretation in the Book of Jubilees* (C.B.Q. Monograph Series 18). 1987. Pp. x, 284. (Catholic Biblical Association of America. Catholic University of America, Washington DC. Price: $8.50. ISBN 0 915170 17 5)

This volume sets out to study Jubilees as a text in its own right, and not as one tangential to others. The first chapter describes the book and gives an excellent summary of earlier work on Jubilees before outlining the author's intention to study Jubilees as an example of Rewritten Bible. He devotes the rest of the volume to a thorough investigation of exegetical methods and hermeneutical principles in order to discover what motivated the author of

Jubilees. The greater part of this volume is concerned with the Jacob traditions (Jub. 19–30) which are treated as a representative sample. From them Fr. Endres identifies four major concerns: the covenant, retributive justice, sacred persons and places, and sacred time. He suggests that the author was 'within a priestly group which held a nascent apocalyptic stance' (p. 245). He was alarmed at the hellenistic assimilation of the mid second century, especially among the Zadokite priests, and wrote Jubilees as a work of exhortation. For his inspiration he used an early Palestinian biblical text, but he used it so freely that perhaps he 'located the sacredness of the text somewhere else than in its precise words' (p. 249). Jubilees comes from a time before the standardization and sacralization of the biblical texts; sacred story was his basis, and thus he set out to show 'the antiquity of Jewish election as a priestly people' (p. 250).

This is an interesting and well written book raising issues as relevant to contemporary methods of interpretation as to those in the second century.

M. Barker

Feltes, H.: *Die Gattung des Habakukkommentars von Qumran (1QpHab): Eine Studie zum frühen Jüdischen Midrasch* (Forschung zur Bibel, 58). 1986. Pp. 355. (Echter Verlag, Würzburg. Price: DM 48.00. ISBN 3 429 01051 9)

This 1984 Bochum dissertation is concerned with the question of the literary *Gattung* of the Habakkuk Commentary. After an introduction and a survey of previous work on the problem, Feltes discusses the occurrence of inner-biblical exegesis within the Old Testament, and then the emergence and the character of Jewish exegetical literature, particularly the rabbinic writings. Two chapters are devoted to biblical exegesis at Qumran, with particular attention being paid to the pesher-form and the methods of interpretation employed in the Habakkuk Commentary. There follows a comparison with other exegetical writings that have been held to have some kind of relationship with the literary form of the Habakkuk Commentary (Pistis Sophia, the Demotic Chronicle, other Qumran writings, the Targum, Jewish-apocalyptic literature (primarily Daniel), rabbinic midrash), while in the final chapter the author presents his results. His main conclusion is that the Habakkuk Commentary is a pre-classical haggadic-exegetical midrash, which is characterized by the combination of the use of pre-classical exegetical methods and a concern for actualization which has a marked apolalyptic orientation. There is nothing particularly novel about this conclusion, which — although one might wish to express it differently — is surely on the right lines. But it has to be said that while some interesting comments are made, the author goes over some fairly familiar ground in his treatment of the subject, and that his case is argued overmuch in relation to the secondary literature — sometimes in relation to studies that now seem outdated. There is no index.

M. A. Knibb

Fuss, A. M. (ed.): *Jewish Law Association Studies* Vol. iii: *The Oxford Conference Volume*. 1987. Pp. vii, 209. (Scholars Press, Decatur Ga. Price: $29.95; paperback price: $21.95. SP Series Code: 15 00 03)

Four articles in this collection will be of particular interest to readers of the *Book List:* J. Bazak, 'Judicial Ethics in Jewish Law' (mainly concerned with biblical sources); B. S. Jackson, 'Some Semiotic Questions for Biblical Law' (including the relationship between drafting forms and narrative structures); B. Meislin, 'The Role of The Ten Commandments in American

Judicial Decisions'; and D. Piatelli, 'The Fugitive Slave in the Legislation of the Ancient Near East and as elaborated in Rabbinic Jurisprudence' (including substantial consideration of the *apeleutheros* in the Pauline texts). The other articles are: J. D. Bleich, 'Artificial Heart Implantation'; D. Cohn-Sherbok, 'Euthanasia and Reform Judaism'; D. Novak, 'The Legal Question of the Investigation of Converts'; S. M. Passamaneck, 'Notes on Violence and Combative Behavior in Jewish Law'; and N. Rakover, 'Ethical Standards for Public Servants in Jewish Law'.

B. S. JACKSON

GOODMAN, M.: *The Ruling Class of Judea: The Origins of the Jewish Revolt against Rome* A.D. *66–70*. 1987. Pp. xiv, 263. (Cambridge University Press. Price: £25.00. ISBN 0 521 33401 2)

Goodman begins by listing the standard causes of the Jewish revolt with the accompanying arguments; however, he immediately points out why they are insufficient — whether separately or collectively — to explain the rebellion. Many others under Roman rule had equal grievances, while conversely the Jews were given certain special privileges allowed to no others. So why did the Jews revolt? Goodman suggests there is another cause: the struggle for power within the Jewish upper class. On the one hand, the Roman policy was for the local ruling class to carry out the normal provincial administration; on the other hand, for a variety of reasons the upper class did not have general popular support or even recognition. The revolt seemed an opportunity to gain the popular backing and the real power base which they lacked before.

Although Josephus attempts to imply that most of the rebels and rebel leaders were men of low status, and thus to deflect responsibility from those of his own class, his own data show that the leaders were primarily from the upper class. As a Roman historian Goodman is thoroughly at home in general Roman history and culture as well as in the Jewish sources. As usual, his documentation is thorough and his argumentation careful and convincing. Definitely a major contribution to the history of Roman Judaea.

L. L. GRABBE

GRADWOHL, R.: *Bibelauslegungen aus jüdischen Quellen*. Band 2: *Die alttestamentlichen Predigttexte des 4. Jahrgangs*. 1987. Pp. 331. (Calwer Verlag, Stuttgart. Price: DM 34.00. ISBN 3 7668 0812 5)

The first volume of this work was reviewed in *B.L.* 1987, p. 64. This volume follows the same pattern, covering twenty-one Old Testament passages appointed for preaching in the fourth year of the German Evangelical cycle. Four of these passages are from the Torah, three from the former prophets, thirteen from the latter prophets and one from Job. This volume also contains a chronological table of important Jewish exegetes from Saadia Gaon to the twentieth century to supplement the historical sketch given in the first volume.

A. GELSTON

HAASE, W., and TEMPORINI, G. (eds.): *Aufsteig und Niedergang der römischen Welt: Geschichte und Kultur Roms im Spiegel der neueren Forschung*. Teil II: *Principat*. Band 20/1 Religion (*Hellenistisches Judentum in römischer Zeit, ausgenommen Philon und Josephus*). 1987. Pp. x, 667. (De Gruyter, Berlin. Price: DM 410.00. ISBN 3 11 010367 2)

Under the rubric 'Religion' in the second part ('Principat') of the series *Aufstieg und Niedergang der römischen Welt* a total of six volumes is to be devoted to Judaism. Four of these have already appeared, two primarily concerned with Palestinian Judaism (II, 19, 1, and 2), and one each with Philo (II, 21, 1) and Josephus (II, 21, 2); see *B.L.* 1981, pp. 129–30 (where there is also a brief description of the series as a whole) and 1985, p. 146. The present volume (II, 20, 1, edited by Haase) forms the first of two that are to deal with Hellenistic Judaism apart from Philo and Josephus and contains thirteen articles. Two of these articles stand a little apart from the rest: the late G. Delling wrote, by way of an introduction to the volume, on 'Die Begegnung zwischen Hellenismus und Judentum', and C. Aziza discusses the use of the exodus tradition in anti-Jewish polemic (L'utilisation polémique du récit de l'Exode chez les écrivains alexandrins (IVème siècle av. J.-C — Ier siècle ap. J.-C.)). Apart from these two contributions the volume consists essentially of an introduction to Hellenistic-Jewish literature of the intertestamental period.

N. Walter provides an overview of the entire corpus of this literature down to the time of Philo apart from the writings of the Hellenistic-Jewish historians; the latter are treated by R. Doran. Three articles are devoted to the Septuagint: E. Tov provides a survey of all aspects of Septuagint studies in an updated version of an article on 'Die griechischen Bibelübersetzungen' originally published in Hebrew in vol. 8 of *Encyclopaedia Miqra'it* (1982); O. Munnich writes on the relationship between the translation of the Psalms and the *kaige*-recension; and A. Paul discusses the ideological background of the recension of Aquila. Paul also contributes an article on 3 Maccabees that amounts almost to a commentary. A. Barzanò writes (in Italian) on Justus of Tiberias and M. de Jonge on 'The Testaments of the Twelve Patriarchs: Central Problems and Essential Viewpoints'. There are two articles on the Sibylline Oracles, a general introduction to the corpus by J. J. Collins, and a detailed treatment by the late V. Nikiprowetzky of the question whether Book 3 contains fragments deriving from a Babylonian or Erythrean Sibyl ('La Sibylle juive et la "Troisième Livre" des "Pseudo-Oracles Sibyllins" depuis Charles Alexandre'). The volume ends with a monograph-length article by C. Burchard on 'Der jüdische Asenethroman und seine Nachwirkung. Von Egeria zu Anna Katharina Emmerick oder von Moses aus Aggel zu Karl Kerényi', which includes, as its final section, a survey of current research on Joseph and Aseneth.

With the exception noted, the articles are written in German, French, or English. It is again a matter of regret that there is no index, but the articles are of a high standard, and there is much of value and interest in this important volume.

M. A. KNIBB

HALL, B. W.: *Samaritan Religion from John Hyrcanus to Baba Rabba: A critical examination of the relevant material in contemporary Christian literature, the writings of Josephus, and the Mishnah* (Studies in Judaica, 3). 1987. Pp. viii, 352. (Mandelbaum Trust, University of Sydney. Price: A$37.50, plus A$5.00 postage and packing. ISBN 0 949269 06 9; ISSN 0818 8696)

The sub-title gives much the more accurate indication of the contents of this work; it is not a history of Samaritan religion, but an assessment of three types of evidence relevant to such a history. After an introductory discussion of the chronological problems, which reaches the tentative conclusion that Baba Rabba should probably be placed in the third century, successive chapters discuss Christian references from the New Testament to Origen; Josephus; and the Mishnah. On Josephus it is regrettable that Egger's detailed study (noted above, p. 131) was not available. For the most part Hall's conclusions are fairly conventional; he is doubtful how much can be known about the Dositheans or Samaritan messianism, and is sceptical of the alleged influence of Simon Magus on Samaritan traditions. This will be a useful handbook; it is marred only by a tedious repetitive style.

R. J. Coggins

Hedrick C. W., Hodgson, R., Jr. (eds.): *Nag Hammadi, Gnosticism and Early Christianity*. 1986. Pp. xliv, 332. (Hendrickson, Peabody, Massachusetts. Price $14.95. ISBN 0 913573 16 7)

This volume comprises thirteen papers presented at the 1983 Working Seminar on Gnosticism and Early Christianity held in Springfield, Missouri. The papers represent a spread of interests in the disciplines of gnosticism, New Testament Studies and early church history. The common thread that runs through them all is the investigation of the Nag Hammadi texts with their fifty-one tractates and their importance for early Christian origins. The papers are gathered under three headings. I Non-Christian Gnosticism: 'The Problem of "Jewish Gnostic" Literature' (B. A. Pearson), 'The Riddle of the Thunder (NHC VI,2): The Function of Paradox in a Gnostic Texts from Nag Hammadi' (B. Layton), 'Sethian Gnosticism: A Literary History' (J. D. Turner). II Gnosticism, New Testament, and Early Christian Literature: 'Gnosticism and the Church of John's Gospel' (G. W. MacRae†), 'Gnostic Sayings and Controversy Traditions in John 8:12–59' (H. Koester), 'The Function and Background of the Beloved Disciple in the Gospel of John' (H.-M. Schenke), 'On Bridging the Gulf from Q to the Gospel of Thomas (or Vice-Versa)' (J. M. Robinson), 'The Use of Early Christian Literature as Evidence for Inner Diversity and Conflict' (F. Wisse). III Gnosticism and the Early Church: 'Gnostic and Orthodox Disciples in the Second and Third Centuries' (D. M. Parrott), 'Ordering the Cosmos: Irenaeus and the Gnostics' (P. Perkins) 'The Gospel of Truth as an Exoteric Text' (H. W. Attridge), 'Exegesis and Exposition of the Genesis Creation Accounts in Selected Texts from Nag Hammadi' (E. H. Pagels), 'With Walter Bauer on the Tigris; Encratite Orthodoxy and Libertine Heresy in Syro-Mesopotamian Christianity' (S. Gero).

P. W. Coxon

Jackson, B. S. (ed.): *Jewish Law Association Studies* Vol. ii: *The Jerusalem Conference Volume*. 1986. Pp. viii, 156. (Scholars Press, Decatur, Ga. Price: $26.95. ISBN 0 89130 950 0; paperback price: $19.95. ISBN 0 89130 951 9)

Five articles in this collection will be of particualr interest to readers of the *Book List*: A. I. Baumgarten, 'R. Yohanan and Resh Lakish on Anonymous *Mishnayot*' (this dispute taken to reflect conflicts over authority structures within early Judaism); L. E. Goodman, 'The Biblical Laws of Diet and Sex' (a major study of the underlying rationales of the ritual laws, relating the categories of dietary and sexual restriction); A. Rofé, 'Methodological Aspects of the Study of Biblical Law' (including important observations on the relationship between the priestly and Deuteronomic strata); H. Schiffman, 'Reproof as a Requisite for Punishment in the Law of the Dead Sea Scrolls'; and E. J. Wiesenberg, 'Exogamy and Moloch Worship' (presented as an abstract, but really a mini-article). Also included are: D. I. Frimer, 'Israel, The Noahide Laws and Maimonides: Jewish–Gentile Relations in Maimonidean Thought'; Y. Kahana, N. Munk, M. Slae, 'Estimating Bodily Damages according to Jewish Law: A Comparative Legal Study'; Y. Meron, 'The Contemporary Encounter between Jewish and Moslem Law'; and D. B. Sinclair, 'Law and Morality in Halakhic Bioethics'; Abstracts of articles by S. M. Passamaneck and M. Drori.

B. S. Jackson

JAFFEE, M. S.: *The Talmud of Babylonia: An American Translation*, XXVI. *Tractate Horayot* (Brown Judaic Studies, 90). 1987. Pp. 221. (Scholars Press, Atlanta, Georgia. Price: $27.95. ISBN 1 55540 119 8)

The principles underlying this new translation of the Bavli are set out by its general editor, Jacob Neusner, in the earlier volumes (see *B.L.* 1985, p. 136). Two differences from the Soncino edition are immediately noticeable: (1) the new translation is in a more modern (not to say, American) idiom, and makes more copious use of explanatory additions in square brackets; and (2) the text is laid out exhaustively analysed into its structural components. This latter feature, which is characteristic of Neusner's translations, is undoubtedly of great help in reading classic Rabbinic literature. It is a pity that the volumes are made up from camera-ready typescript which gives a rather confused appearance to the page and lessens the visual impact of the analytical presentation. Jaffee's volume differs from the earlier ones by Neusner in a number of small ways. It has a fuller introduction to the tractate in hand. As well as a running commentary summarizing the argument and structure of the *sugyot*, it also contains notes on philological and textual matters (the translation itself is based on the Vilna text). And its indices are rather fuller. In general the translation is competent and conscientious. Students are bound to welcome any aid which helps them to chart a course across the 'sea of the talmud'.

P. S. ALEXANDER

KNIBB, M. A.: *The Qumran Community* (Cambridge Commentaries on Writings of the Jewish and Christian World 200 B.C. to A.D. 200, 2). 1987. Pp. xi, 275. (Cambridge University Press. Price: £32.50 ($49.50); ISBN 0 521 24247 9. Paperback price: £12.95 ($16.95); ISBN 0 521 28552 6)

The series to which this volume belongs is a welcome supplement to the Cambridge Bible Commentary series (for other volumes see *B.L.* 1985, pp. 134, 149; 1986, pp. 111, 124–25). The volume supplies in the well-known Cambridge format introductory information concerning, a translation of, and quite detailed notes to selected excerpts from the Qumran sectarian literature. Considering the student constituency for which it is intended, Professor Knibb was probably right to concentrate on the Damascus Document, the Community Rule, the Hymns and the Habakkuk Commentary which are given respectively 64, 68, 26, and 26 pages out of a total of just over 250 pages devoted to texts. Also included are smaller sections dealing with the Rule of the Congregation, the Commentaries on Nahum and Psalms, Florilegium, Testimonia and (non-sectarian but important for the history of exegesis) the Genesis Apocryphon and the Prayer of Nabonidus. Room might have been made for a page or two on the Job Targum and for one of the apocryphal psalms from the Psalms Scroll, but adequate reasons (see p. 2) are given for omitting the complicated War and Temple Scrolls. The translations do not read so smoothly as Vermes's, but they are accurate and crisp and avoid paraphrase; and the commentary is quite excellent: clear, concise and illuminating. Professor Knibb has given us an admirable guide through very difficult territory. Its usefulness would, however, have been greatly increased had the Cambridge format been departed from and he had been allowed to add an index of scriptural and other references and had he, alongside his many allusions to Jewish apocryphal and pseudepigraphical writings, supplied rather more to the New Testament. Is it worth a comment that the review copy was of the paperback edition and that a couple of pages have already prised themselves loose?

J. C. L. GIBSON

LACHS, S. T.: *A Rabbinic Commentary on the New Testament: The Gospels of Matthew, Mark and Luke.* 1987. Pp. xxix, 468. (Ktav, New York. Price: $29.50; paperback price: $16.95. ISBN 0 88125 089 9)

Samuel Tobias Lachs of Bryn Mawr College presents 'to the open-minded reader' a superb 'limited commentary to the Synoptic Gospels' giving 'insights into the text' that arise from 'an examination of rabbinic traditions from the close of the Bible through the Mishnah, Targum, Talmud, and classical midrashim'. He deliberately makes no judgemental comments about the Synoptics. He accepts that rabbinic literature may be too late to be of use, but reminds us that even late material can be instructive. 'There has always been an unbroken transmission of rabbinic traditions.'

The cited material — some familiar, much unfamiliar — is endlessly fascinating. Lachs, not content with merely offering parallels, also makes some interesting conjectural emendations based on turning the Greek back into Hebrew and/or Aramaic. In Matt. 7:6 'do not throw pearls' misunderstands *toru*, 'teach' as well as 'throw': 'do not teach "pearls", i.e. biblical passages or any nuggets of "wisdom", before swine'. *Epiousios* was originally *dē mahsarenu*, 'sufficient for our needs', confused with *dē maḥarenu*, 'sufficient for our tomorrow'. T. W. Manson is far and away the modern commentator most often cited. Essential for students of the Gospels and Judaism.

J.C. O'NEILL

LOHFINK, N.: *Das Jüdische am Christentum: Die verlorene Dimension.* 1987. Pp. 268. (Herder, Freiburg, Basel, Wien. Price: DM 29.80. ISBN 3 451 20994 2)

This book is a collection of addresses delivered at different times and to different audiences, all prompted, however, by a single overriding concern. Until very recently, the author feels, the church has focused too exclusively upon what he terms 'Innigkeit und Jenseitshoffnung' at the expense of all social and political involvement. As an exegete, he believes that one way of redressing the balance is to re-introduce into Christian teaching the lessons and concerns of the Old Testament. It is the social or worldly interests of the Old Testament writers that Lohfink calls, somewhat tendentiously, 'das Jüdische'. He disowns any immediate purpose of furthering Jewish–Christian dialogue, but hopes even so that his book may make some incidental contribution towards this.

The first chapter is a meditative reflection upon the recent writings of Peter Handke on the topic of the 'Langsame Heimkehr'. The themes of the remaining addresses emerge most clearly, with one exception, from their sub-titles: 'Ein Gespräch mit Verfechtern der Volkskirche', 'Wider die Entscheidung der Christen zur Weltlosigkeit', 'Zur Funktion der Rede vom Gottesreich bis zu Jesus von Nazaret', 'Das Gottesreich und die Wirtschaft', 'Zur Option für die Armen im Alten Orient und in der Bibel', 'Das Gottesvolk der Bibel als Lerngemeinschaft', 'Das Alte Testament und Der Begriff der Erbsünde', 'Von wann ab ist eine Friedensbewegung christlich?', 'Die Einheit der Bibel und die neuere deutsche Übersetzungen'. Interesting as these themes are, I think that the book should have been given a less misleading title.

J. ASHTON

MAYER, G.: *Die jüdische Frau in der hellenistisch-römischen Antike.* 1987. Pp. 142. (Kohlhammer, Stuttgart. Price: DM 44.00. ISBN 3 17 009391 6)

Mayer gives a useful summary of the data about Jewish women of Greco-Roman times as found in the various sources, including not only the 'intertestamental' and rabbinic literature but also inscriptions and papyri. The book begins with a brief overview of the history of the Jews in various places and a chart situating the different literary sources according to language and approximate chronology. Although the chart is useful (despite an inevitable dogmatism about certain works whose dating is uncertain or disputed), the historical and cultural survey is probably too sketchy to be of great help to those without any prior knowledge. More helpful would have been a closer look at the major sources and a discussion of their limitations and the methodological problems in their use.

The bulk of the book is a study under the rubrics one would expect (such as marriage and divorce), but of special interest are the detailed studies on names. There is a tendency in any such survey to stereotype the information (e.g. 'the marriage celebration') as if there were not differences according to time and place, and to ignore the fact that our sources do not necessarily give a complete picture. But all in all, the book represents a useful survey in a hundred pages even if a more nuanced examination would have been desirable.

L. L. GRABBE

MENDELS, D.: *The Land of Israel as a Political Concept in Hasmonean Literature* (Texte und Studien zum Antiken Judentum, 15). 1987. Pp. x, 181. Mohr [Paul Siebeck], Tübingen. Price: DM 78.00. ISBN 3 16 145147 3)

Scholarship does not exist in a vacuum, and it was perhaps inevitable that the rise of Zionism and the establishment of the State of Israel should lead (after a lapse of time) to a reassessment of the 'territorial dimension' of Judaism. W. D. Davies' *Gospel and the Land* (1974) and *Territorial Dimension in Judaism* (1982) are indicative of the new academic interest in the subject. Mendels surveys systematically the political concept of the Land of Israel in the Hasmonaean era (*c.* 190–63 B.C.E.) — a period which saw the emergence of an independent Jewish state, its expansion to cover most of the Promised Land, its contraction and final absorption into the Roman province of Syria. As Mendels shows the concept of the Land of Israel (its borders, its purity, the status of aliens) was a burning issue of the day, which is amply reflected in the contemporary literature. It is, perhaps, regretable that he has chosen to force the copious material into a rigid, procrustean chronological schema, divided into decades. On the basis of a controversial dating of Jubilees to 125 B.C.E. which is never fully justified, he takes this work as representing Jewish attitudes in 'the twenties' of the second century B.C.E. (pp. 56 ff.). His dating of Genesis Apocryphon to 'some point during the last half of the first century B.C. and the first century A.D.' (p. 124) will also raise a few eyebrows: palaeographically the scroll is usually dated to the first half of the first century B.C.E., the work itself having been composed a little earlier. Mendels tosses out his date of Genesis Apocryphon *en passant*, and it is probably in the light of it that he rather glosses over 1QGenAp XXI — a text highly relevant to his theme which should have been discussed at length, whether or not it falls within his narrowly defined chronological limits. Mendels can also be faulted for not making more of some of the texts which he does analyse in depth. His discussion of Jubilees on the Table of the Nations (pp. 64 ff.) does not emphasize enough the sharply polemical nature of Jubilees' account. Surely Jubilees whole point here is to establish Israel's right to the Land. Canaan, whose true patrimony lay in North Africa (around Carthage), usurped the Land and so broke the solemn agreement entered into by the sons of Noah in the presence of their father. His violent usurpation, which contrasts with Madai's peaceful reallocation, is echoed in Rabbinic literature in the 'Joshua the Robber' traditions, some of which may go back to Hasmonaean times (see *JJS* 33 [1982], p. 200). Despite these caveats,

Mendels has produced a valuable survey, a serious contribution to an ancient and on-going debate.

P. S. ALEXANDER

Mishuna. Pesahim. Translated by K. Ishikawa. 1987. Pp. 171. (Erusarem Shūkyō Bunka Kenyūjo, Tokyo. Price: ¥1,200)

This is the fourth book of the *Mishnah* translated from the Hebrew. So far published are *Aroth Horayoth* (1985), *Berakoth* (1985), *Taanith*, *Megillah*, *Moed Katan* and *Chagigah* (1986). The translator appended an exposition and reference books at the end of each volume. The project is planned to be completed in thirty-two volumes.

K. K. SACON

NEUSNER, J.: *The Bavli and its Sources: The Question of Tradition in the Case of Tractate Sukkah* (Brown Judaic Studies, 85). 1987. Pp. xvi, 209. (Scholars Press, Atlanta, Georgia. Price: $27.95. ISBN 1 55540 117 1)

The Bavli, asserts Neusner, is everywhere represented as a traditional document. Its (ultimate) authorship is portrayed as mainly taking up materials from prior sources and reworking them into a systematic and canonical statement for generations to come. It is portrayed as essentially a document that heavily draws upon sources, and enjoys standing and authority because of its representation of what is in those sources. What in particular makes the Bavli traditional is its relationship to the prior writings of the system of which it constitutes the authoritative statement (see p. 10). Neusner tests this hypothesis by analysing how a representative section of Talmud (Bavli Sukkah) uses its sources (Mishnah, Tosefta, Yerushalmi, and the Midrashim). He concludes that far from being simply the 'seal' of the preceding tradition, the Bavli offers a fresh and original statement of its own, cogent and defined within the requirements of an inner logic, proportion and structure that imposes an essentially autonomous vision upon whatever materials its authorship received from the past. To use a geological metaphor: the Bavli is not like sedimentary rock, built up by slow increments over a long period of time; rather it is igneous in character — the product of a volcanic eruption which coalesced and solidified more or less at once. This monograph carries forward Neusner's grand design to describe and analyse one by one the documents that make up the canon of classical Judaism. Its general conclusions with regard to the Bavli will be familiar to those who have read a number of Neusner's earlier studies (e.g. *The Integrity of Leviticus Rabbah* [1985], and *Comparative Midrash* [1986]): the Bavli, like the other documents of the classical canon, is found to be an autonomous, authored work, with a distinctive plan and programme of its own. The issues raised are profoundly important, affecting as they do the way in which we should read the classic Rabbinic texts. Neusner's insistence that the integrity of the classic texts should be respected, and that they should be investigated for any distinctive message which they might convey is a necessary counterweight to the harmonizing approach of both religious and academic orthodoxy. However, he has a tendency to state his position so uncompromisingly as to leave it open to misconstruction. Take, e.g. the claim that 'the system — the final and complete statement — does not recapitulate the extant texts. The antecedent texts — when used at all — are so read as to recapitulate the system. The system comes before the texts and defines the canon' (p. 193). This might apply *simpliciter* to Gnostic use of Scripture, but as a description of Bavli's use of its sources it raises obvious questions. Where did this autonomous system spring from? If it emerged within Rabbinic society then it emerged among people who devoted a great deal of their time to meditating on the traditional texts. Did those texts provide nothing except material to be manipulated in the interests of a system which arrived from elsewhere, like a bolt from the blue? It is also, perhaps, a little unfair to see Susan Handelman's idea of 'intertextuality' as simply an attempt to make the traditionalist harmonizing approach academically respectable. The original sense of a text can only be determined by comparing and contrasting it with other texts of its time and place (as Neusner himself acknowledges *en passant*). The autonomy of the document should not be pushed to the extent of implying that it will yield up its meaning only if analysed in its own terms, without reference to genre and setting. One should not confuse religiously motivated harmonization with the valid academic tool of heuristic comparison.

P. S. ALEXANDER

NEUSNER, J.: *From Tradition to Imitation: The Plan and Program of Pesiqta Rabbati and Pesiqta deRab Kahana* (Brown Judaic Studies 80). 1987. Pp. xv, 230. (Scholars Press, Atlanta, Georgia. Price: $24.95; member price: $18.95. ISBN 1 55540 113 9)

In this book Neusner performs a parallel exercise to that in his *Comparative Midrash* (1986) where he compared the 'Plan and Program of Genesis Rabbah and Leviticus Rabbah'. Here, having completed his translation of *Pesiqta deRab Kahana* (Brown Judaic Studies, vols 122–23, 1987), he sets out to compare *PRK* and *Pesiqta Rabbati*. For this purpose, in Part One he translates *PR*, *Pesiqtaot* 1–5 and 15 (= *PRK* 15). There then follows, in Part Two, a discussion of the 'Literary Structures of *PR* and *PRK*, the material for the latter being taken from the introduction to his translation of *PRK*.

Neusner argues his by now familiar case that these midrashim are carefully structured literary texts and not just 'scrapbooks' containing loose collections of unrelated exegeses of biblical texts. He establishes a sequence from *Leviticus Rabbah* > *PRK* > *PR*, both in historical succession and in the development of literary structures. But the line from *PRK* to *PR* runs downhill: 'the authorship of Pesiqta Rabbati has merely imitated, without real understanding, the remarkable mode of cogent discourse fully worked out by the authorship of Pesiqta deRab Kahana — hence *from tradition . . . to* (uncomprehending) *imitation*' (p. 3).

Neusner's description of the literary structures of *LevR*, *PRK* and *PR*, is particularly useful in detecting the primary document to which the shared material between these three midrashim belongs. His chapter 10 presents an interesting comparison of *PRK*, *PR* and *Sifre Numbers* on Numbers 7:1. The exercise serves to confirm his oft-stated conclusion that comparing exegeses of biblical verses without considering the overall programme of the midrash in which the exegesis occurs will not tell us anything very interesting or important. On pp. 207 ff., contrary to what is indicated, Neusner does not translate *PRK* 27 but gives us his translation of *LevR* taken from his *Judaism and Scripture* (1986), pp. 505 ff. It is only episodically revised in line with the text of *PRK*.

A. P. HAYMAN

NEUSNER, J.: *Israel and Iran in Talmudic Times: A Political History* (Studies in Judaism). 1986. Pp. xiii, 250. (University Press of America, Lanham, New York; London. Price: $14.75. ISBN 0 8191 5730 9)

NEUSNER, J.: *Israel's Politics in Sasanian Iran: Jewish Self-Government in Talmudic Times* (Studies in Judaism). 1986. Pp. xii, 190. (University Press of America, Lanham, New York; London. Price: $12.25. ISBN 0 8191 5726 0)

These two volumes contain exerpts from volumes II–V of Neusner's standard *History of the Jews in Babylonia* (overlooked by the *Book List* when they first appeared between 1965 and 1970). *Israel and Iran* is concerned with the external relations of the Jews of Babylonia to their Sasanian overlords, *Israel's Politics* with the internal organization and self-government of the Jewish communities. The period covered (third–seventh centuries C.E.) was of immense significance in the history of religions: it witnessed not only the triumph of Rabbanism in Babylonian Jewry, but also the resurgence of Mazdaism, the emergence of Manichaeism, the eastward expansion of Christianity from Edessa, and the westward expansion of Mithraism into the Roman empire. The region described, lying between the eastern and western power-blocs, was a cosmopolitan kaleidoscope of cultural, political and religious influences. In his early historical writing Neusner still relied on the essential accuracy of attributions to date Rabbinic traditions. From the standpoint of his later, more sophisticated methodology, these works must be seen as standing 'only at the beginning of a critical inquiry' (*Israel and Iran*, p. ix). However, the value of the great *History* endures, and it is unlikely ever to be totally superseded. For full documentation and bibliographies the reader is referred to the larger work. Vol. I of the *History* (2nd ed., 1969), covering the Parthian period, was re-issued in paperback in 1984 (see *B.L.* 1985, p. 138). Other thematic collections of excerpts are: *Judaism, Christianity, and Zoroastrianism in Talmudic Babylonia* (Lanham, 1986); *The Wonder-Working Lawyers of Talmudic Babylonia: The Theory and Practice of Judaism in its Formative Age* (Lanham, 1987); and *School, Court, Public Administration: Judaism and its Institutions in Talmudic Babylonia* (Atlanta, 1987). Neusner has performed a service in making the substance of the *History* more accessible to undergraduates.

P. S. ALEXANDER

NEUSNER, J.: *The Mishnah Before 70* (Brown Judaic Studies 51). 1987. Pp. xiv, 290. (Scholars Press, Atlanta, Georgia. Price: $39.95; member price: $26.95. ISBN 1 55540 106 6)

In this book Neusner abstracts and reprints from his *History of the Mishnaic Law of Purities* (1974–77) 'a statement of those elements of the Mishnah tractates in the Division of Purities that', in his judgement, 'derive from the period before 70' (p. ix). He feels the need to do this because, in his view, scholars are not bothering to read his 43-volume *History of the Mishnaic Law*, and hence the position that 'nothing in the Mishnah antedates the Mishnah' is being falsely attributed to him. For those without the time or the inclination to read the larger work, this will certainly be an easier way to get the flavour of Neusner's novel approach to the Mishnah.

A. P. HAYMAN

NEUSNER, J.: *Understanding Seeking Faith: Essays on the Case of Judaism*. Vol. 2: *Literature, Religion and the Social Study of Judaism* (Brown Judaic Studies 73). 1987. Pp. xi, 234. (Scholars Press, Atlanta, Georgia. Price: $29.95 (member price: $22.95). ISBN 1 55540 053 1)

This is a collection of papers going over the various fields of study in which Neusner is interested. The introduction, entitled 'What is at stake in the Religious Study of Judaism' goes over, yet again, the familiar ground of Neusner's dispute with the 'ethnic approach' to the study of Judaism. He rails, with some justification, against what he calls 'the policy of *Todschweigen*' being pursued by some scholars who refuse to take his work seriously or even acknowledge that it exists. In this volume James Kugel, in particular, is attacked for ignoring Neusner's work on Midrash. The overlapping chapters 1 and 10 successfully expose the shallowness of Kugel's definition of midrash. Whatever reservations one might have over some aspects of Neusner's work, scholars cannot safely research in the same areas and ignore it.

Chapter 2 (The Literary Structure of Pesiqta Rabbati) is identical with the material to be found in *From Tradition to Imitation*, chapters 1 and 7. Chapter 3 (Oral Tradition in Judaism: The Issue of Mnemonics) takes up again an issue discussed many times before by Neusner, as does chapter 8 (Art and the Study of Judaism) — on the debate over Goodenough's *Symbols*.

Chapter 4 (From Corpus to Canon) outlines Neusner's future research programme which is going to involve doing for the rabbinic canon (especially the Babylonian Talmud) what Brevard Childs has done for the Old Testament canon. The argument of this chapter is rather confusing, perhaps even muddled, as are Neusner's comments in *From Tradition to Imitation* on the canonical status of Pesiqta deRab Kahana and Pesiqta Rabbati. Because the Bavli later *became* canonical does not mean that it was framed *in order to be* canonical. So how it treats earlier texts need tell us nothing useful about how texts *become* canonical. About the actual historical process by which the Bavli became canonical Neusner tells us nothing here, and, judging by his outlined research programme, proposes to tell us nothing in the future.

Chapter 5 (Constantine, Shapur II and the Jewish–Christian Confrontation in Fourth Century Iran) updates Neusner interest in the context in which Aphrahat wrote his anti-Jewish disputations. Chapter 6 (The Sage and the Emperor) was clearly written for some other book than this one (a *Festschrift*?) since it refers on pages 143 and 149 to an 'honoree' for whom it was written. Who this is, we are not told. The content reflects his recent work on the *Fathers According to Rabbi Nathan* and updates his earlier work on the context in which the legends surrounding Yohanan ben Zakkai emerged. Neusner's interest in the study of American Judaism is represented by chapter 7 (Sociology and the Study of Judaism: Nathan Glazer's *American Judaism* after Thirty Years).

Although some of the doubts which Neusner expresses about recent appropriation of rabbinic modes of interpretation by literary critics seem well-founded, his argument in chapter 9 (Literature and the Study of Judaism: Intertextuality and the Text) is quite confusing. In fact, this chapter seems to be only a draft; in the first paragraph it refers to 'quotations above' where no such quotations are provided! (In chapter 5, p. 127, a whole page is repeated by mistake and throughout the book printing errors are endless). Does Scholars Press never proof-read Neusner's books? Despite these irritating problems of presentation, the book is an important work of scholarship and well worth persevering with.

A. P. HAYMAN

NEUSNER, J.: *Vanquished Nation, Broken Spirit: The Virtues of the Heart in Formative Judaism*. 1987. Pp. xiv, 184. (Cambridge University Press, Cambridge, New York. Price: £20.00 ($24.95). ISBN 0 521 32832 2)

This book goes over in more detail some of the ground covered in Neusner's *Judaism in the Matrix of Christianity* (see *Booklist* 1987, p. 113). It surveys the whole range of rabbinic literature in order to discover what particular emotions and affections were inculcated by the rabbis in the wide variety of types of literature which they composed. Neusner finds everywhere a uniform doctrine of the emotions. His thesis is simple: 'the emotions encouraged by Judaism in its formative age, such as humility, forbearance, accommodation, and a spirit of conciliation, exactly correspond to the political and social requirements of the Jews' condition in that time' (p. 3). That rabbinic Judaism worked so well because it was finely adapted to the circumstances of life in exile is not a new thesis, but Neusner restates it here in an interesting and informative manner. Whether the rabbis were conscious of what they were doing is an issue that Neusner does not directly tackle. From his few isolated remarks (see, e.g. p. 102) he seems to assume that the rabbis simply thought that they were uncovering what was already there in Scripture. In which case, he is presupposing a sort of evolutionary model of Judaism: the religion almost automatically reacts to new circumstances (loss of the Temple and the triumph of Christianity) by growing new limbs — 'the virtues of the heart in formative Judaism'. The problem then becomes: why did this form of Judaism alone have this innate capacity to adapt whereas others did not, and why in the modern era does it seem to have lost this capacity? This important book provokes serious reflection on the whole nature of Rabbinic Judaism.

A. P. HAYMAN

RUSSELL, D. S.: *The Old Testament Pseudepigrapha: Patriarchs and Prophets in Early Judaism.* 1987. Pp. xv, 144. (SCM, London. Price: £5.50. ISBN 0 334 02229 0)

This is an introductory volume for the non-specialist. It is clearly written and assumes no prior knowledge of the subject. The author deals with the extra-biblical material associated with the biblical figures: Adam, Enoch, Daniel, Job, the Patriarchs, Moses, and Ezra. The first chapter deals with the non pseudepigraphic sources (Philo, Josephus, rabbinic material), and there is an interesting section on pseudonymity. He then recounts material in each of the pseudepigrapha and gives an indication of how this fits into the general picture of second temple Judaism. This is an introductory volume for the non-specialist. It is clearly written, assumes no prior knowledge of the subject, and would form an excellent introduction to this still largely unknown area.

M. BARKER

SCHÜRER, E.: *The History of the Jewish People in the Age of Jesus Christ (175 B.C.–A.D. 135).* A New English Version revised and edited by G. Vermes, F. Millar and M. Goodman. Volume III, 2. 1987. Pp. xx, 705–1015. (T. & T. Clark, Edinburgh. Price: £20.00. ISBN 0 567 09373 5)

Earlier volumes of the new Schürer were noticed in *B.L.* 1974, p. 91; 1980, pp. 125–26; 1987, pp. 118–19. This final volume completes the introduction to Jewish literature of the intertestamental period, the first part of which was contained in volume III, 1. Section 33B provides an introduction to writings whose original language of composition is uncertain, and section 34 an introduction to the work of Philo; the former was prepared jointly by Geza Vermes and Martin Goodman, the latter by Jenny Morris. This volume also contains the long-awaited indexes to the entire work, which were prepared by Léonie Archer: a Main (i.e. name and subject) Index of over a hundred pages, and two short Lists of Greek and of Hebrew and Aramaic words that receive significant discussion., Much has already been written about the new Schürer, and this is not the place to attempt a detailed evaluation. Here it must suffice to say that for the wealth of information it contains, and for its overall balanced judgement (whatever disagreement over points of detail one might have), there can be no question that this work will continue to be used and valued by scholars for many years.

M. A. KNIBB

SIRAT, C., CAUDERLIER, P., DUKAN, M., and FRIEDMAN, M. A.: *Le Ketouba de Cologne: un contrat de mariage juif à Antinoopolis* (Abhanglungen der Rheinisch-Westfälischen Akademie der Wissenschaften: Papyrologica Coloniensia, XII). 1986. Pp. 72 and 20 plates. (Westdeutscher Verlag, Wiesbaden. Price: DM 52.00. ISBN 3 531 09921 3; ISSN 0078 9410)

Some of the most important research in medieval Hebrew palaeography has been done in recent years by Colette Sirat of Paris and this monograph makes a further contribution to that field of study. It also provides new evidence for the use of Greek and Aramaic in the Jewish diaspora, the development of the Jewish marriage contract, and the social history of the Jews in the Byzantine period. Papyrus Inv. 5853 in the Institute of Archaeology at the University of Cologne, which contains the *Kethubbah* of Metra who married Samuel in A.D. 417 in the city of Antinoopolis, about 150 miles south of Cairo on the east bank of the Nile, is the only dated document in Hebrew characters that has survived from the period between Bar Kokhba and the ninth Christian century, The languages of the document are transcribed Greek and Aramaic, there is a trousseau list, and the formula has affinities with the Palestinian Genizah texts already published by Friedman (*Jewish Marriage in Palestine*, Tel-Aviv and New York, 1980). The monograph comprises introduction, transcription, translation, notes, Greek index and plates.

S. C. REIF

Übersetzung des Talmud Yerushalmi, herausgegeben von M. Hengel, H.P. Rüger, P. Schäfer. Band I/2; *Pea-Ackerecke*, übersetzt von G.A. Wewers. 1986. Pp. xviii, 231. (Mohr, Tübingen. Price: DM 122.00. ISBN 3 16 745068 1)

Gerd Wewers died in December 1985 at the tragically early age of forty-one, and this volume marks his final contribution to the German version of the Yerushalmi edited by Schäfer, Rüger and Hengel. In a remarkably short space of time Wewers produced fine translations of eleven tractates, and it is largely due to his industry and erudition that the German Yerushalmi has established so secure an international reputation. Always careful and workmanlike, Wewers's touch became more assured with each successive tractate. In this volume, as in the earlier ones, the translation is presented broken down into its main structural units. Copious footnotes cover variant readings, parallels, archaeological and philological matters, as well as (occasionally) halakhic problems. The whole is rounded off with indices of citations (Bible, Mishnah and Tosefta) and of names (Rabbis and places). In a preface Schäfer and Hengel offer an appreciation of Wewers's achievement. Standards of printing and general production are of a high order. This volume is a fine memorial which leaves one regretting what might have been.

P. S. ALEXANDER

VERMES, G.: *The Dead Sea Scrolls in English*. 3rd edition. 1987. Pp. xvi, 320. (JSOT Press, Sheffield. Price: £25.00 ($42.50). ISBN 1 85075 151 X)

Geza Vermes's translation of the Qumran scrolls has established itself as perhaps the most authoritative of those available in English and has been very widely used. It was originally published in 1962 (*B.L.* 1963, p. 64 (Decade, p. 458)), and a second edition, in which a number of supplementary documents were included at the end, was issued in 1975. For this third edition the text has been completely reset, and several substantial changes have been made. The original introduction has been replaced by an abridged version of chapters 4, 6, and 7 of *The Dead Sea Scrolls: Qumran in Perspective*. The

Temple Scroll has been included, the documents placed at the end in the second edition have been incorporated in appropriate places in the body of the book, and account has been taken of the material published in *DJD* 7 (e.g. in the treatment of the War Scroll) and in other recent publications of Qumran documents. Finally, the proper system of abbreviations for the scrolls has been used, and the bibliography at the end has been somewhat enlarged. It remains a matter of regret that line-numbers have still not been included, but this aside, there is no doubt that in its new form this excellent translation is assured of continued success. (A paperback edition is published by Penguin Books.)

M. A. KNIBB

VILLALBA I VARNEDA, P.: *The Historical Method of Flavius Josephus* (Arbeiten zur Literatur und Geschichte des hellenistischen Judentums XIX). 1986. Pp. xxiv, 296. (Brill, Leiden. Price: Fl. 96.00. ISBN 90 04 07616 6)

Villalba's subject is how Josephus goes about writing his history in the light of Greco-Roman ideas about historiography. The first part of her study looks at Josephus's statements about historical causation and takes mainly the form of a terminological study of words such as *aitia* and fate. The second is a detailed examination of the more rhetorical side of Josephus's historical writing: the technique of constructing his narrative by the use of such historiographical elements as speeches, focus on a personality, and geographical description, and such structural devices as anticipation and novelistic colouring. Villalba's third chapter is a quite long and detailed conclusion which summarizes some of what was covered in the first two chapters but concentrates more on extending the discussion to other areas.

Much of her study seems well done and useful, but Villalba does not really draw her results together adequately (despite the detailed concluding chapter). One would especially have liked more on the implications of her work for using Josephus for historical purposes. The translation was evidently done by one who is not a Josephus scholar and seems to employ the wrong terminology at times, which sometimes leads to the suspicion that the argument was clearer in the original.

L. L. GRABBE

WEINFELD, M.: *The Organizational Pattern and the Penal Code of the Qumran Sect* (Novum Testamentum et Orbis Antiquus, 2). 1986. Pp. 100. (Universitätsverlag, Freiburg; Vandenhoeck & Ruprecht, Göttingen. Price: Sw.Fr. 26.00. ISBN 3 7278 0363 0; ISBN 3 525 53901 0)

Weinfeld compares 1QS and CD, but 1QS V–VII in particular (which he regards as the Qumran legal constitution), with some seventeen codes of guilds and religious associations of third century B.C.E. to second century C.E., mostly from Egypt. Equations are made between *serekh*, *yaḥad*, *rabbîm* and *taxis-speira*, *koinon-koinōnia/ekklēsia, plēthos* respectively. The 'council of the community' and various offices (*paqîd*, *m^{e}baqqer* and priest) are also compared, entrance procedures, laws and penalties, and a number of other minor details. Appendices provide the Statutes of the Iobacchi, the inscription from the Ein-Gedi synagogue, the Epistle of Peter to James from the Pseudo-Clementines and passages from Hippolytus, *Constitutiones Apostolorum*. In what is essentially a long article with copious appendices and indices, one finds adequate ground for an argument rather than a conclusive case. The distinction between organization and the ideology which Weinfeld urges (the former typical, the latter unique) is important for research even if perhaps ultimately over-simple. Like Schiffmann's work, which is reviewed in a final appendix, contradictions within 1QS are ignored (e.g. the notoriously problematic 'council of the community'); and while (unlike Schiffmann) a footnote recognizes the 'Damascus sect' (represented by CD) as distinct from that of Qumran, this is not carried through in his text. Hence Weinfeld must be seen as having assembled important materials for the unfulfilled task of identifying and scientifically describing the nature, function and evolution of the 'Qumran community'.

P. R. DAVIES

10. PHILOLOGY AND GRAMMAR

ANDERSEN, F. I., and FORBES, A. D.: *Spelling in the Hebrew Bible. Dahood Memorial Lectures* (Biblica et Orientalia, 41). 1986. Pp. xxii, 379. (Biblical Institute Press, Rome. Price: Lire 30,000. ISBN 88 7653 342 7)

This book, with a preface by D. N. Freedman, is based on the Dahood Memorial Lectures given in the University of Michigan in February 1983. It is concerned with *matres lectionis* in the Hebrew Bible, the history of their use (especially the evidence of ancient inscriptions), the reasons for spelling particular words in particular ways, and the differences in different parts of the Old Testament. Vowel letters were first used at the ends of words: they were later used sparingly for some long vowels within words in pre-exilic times, and more extensively after the exile. Numerous questions are discussed, such as the following. Why is the feminine plural ending *-ōt* written sometimes with, and sometimes without, a *waw*? Does the stress make any difference to the spelling? Can the spelling of a particular word be influenced by that of a nearby word? The discussion is illustrated by many tables and figures. The details of the book are difficult to summarize in a short review, because so much evidence is examined, and use is made of statistics and mathematical theory. Despite the 'attempt . . . to explain matters in an elementary way, so as to reveal the power of the concepts involved without inducing dread in non-mathematical readers' (p. xv), some readers (like the present reviewer) are likely to find them intimidating. Throughout the book, arguments are advanced cautiously, and attention is paid to alternative ways of understanding the evidence. Among the conclusions are: 'The spelling in the *textus receptus* still reflects a stage in the transmission of the text that is later than pre-exilic times but not as late as Greek times' (p. 312); and 'the tradition of spelling in masoretic texts comes from the period during which the Hebrew Bible was taking final shape', which 'may be narrowed to 550–350' B.C. (p. 319). It is possible that the occasion for fixing the spelling was 'the change-over to the Aramaic "square" character' (p. 321). The book ends with a bibliography, and indexes of biblical references, scholars' names, and subjects. The authors deserve praise for this pioneering work.

J. A. EMERTON

BARR, J.: *Comparative Philology and the Text of the Old Testament* (with additions and corrections). 1987. Pp. ix, 436. (Eisenbrauns, Winona Lake, Indiana. Price: $20.00. ISBN 0 931464 33 1)

The original edition of Barr's *Comparative Philology* was published by OUP in 1968, and reviewed in *B.L.* 1969, p. 63–4; *Bible Bibliog.*, pp. 189–90. What has been made available now, and at very modest cost, is a reprint of the original of this standard work but for the correction of typographical slips, to which have been added (in 82 pages) a Postscript which briefly reviews reaction to the volume and its contribution, and three related articles published since 1968: 'Philology and Exegesis: Some General Remarks with Illustrations from Job', 1974; 'Ugaritic and Hebrew "ŠBM"?', 1973; and

'Limitations of Etymology as a Lexicographical Instrument in Biblical Hebrew', 1983. The continued discussion is essentially with Fr. Dahood.

A. G. AULD

BEALL, T. S., and BANKS, W. A.: *Old Testament Parsing Guide: Genesis — Esther*. 1986. Pp. viii, 391. (Moody Press, Chicago. Price: $25.95. ISBN 0 8024 6315 0)

What a labour! Verse by verse, every occurrence of every verb, over 42,000 in all, is listed, fully parsed and supplied with a page reference to BDB and a meaning. This volume proceeds in this way through all the Hebrew books in the order of the English bible from Genesis to Esther; a second volume is promised to treat the remaining books. The information is tabulated with great skill and clarity. The work has been done with commendable thoroughness and care. Happy they who need it not! And happy they who, needing it, obtain it!

J. H. EATON

COHEN, D.: *La Phrase nominale et l'évolution du système verbal en sémitique. Études de syntaxe historique* (Collection Linguistique publiée par la Société de Linguistique de Paris, LXXII). 1984. Pp. vii, 629. (Éditions Peeters, Leuven and Paris. Price: B.Fr. 2,520.00. ISBN 2 8017 0000 0)

The main theme of this large, learned and complicated work is the way in which forms which originally belonged to the nominal sentence came to be part of the verb system, a process that altered the function of the 'older' elements of that system and thus brought about a 'renewal' of the relations within it. Such a process can be traced in ancient sources but continues down to the present day, as is well seen in modern Aramaic. After a general chapter on noun, verb and predication, there is a long review of the Hamito-Semitic conjugations, followed by chapters on Ethiopic, on Akkadian, on the participle in Arabic and Hebrew, and (longest of all) on Aramaic, plus a conclusion. The section on Hebrew concerns particularly the participial phrase, and valuable statistics and precisions are furnished, along with a short piece on the transition to Mishnaic usage. The material is important also for any discussion of the verb 'be', of the definite article, of aspect, of word order, and of emphasis. The learning of the author shows itself as truly formidable.

J. BARR

COOK, E. M.: *Word Order in the Aramaic of Daniel* (Afroasiatic Linguistics, Vol. 9, Issue 3). 1986. Pp. 16. (Undena Publications, Malibu; distributed by Eisenbrauns, Winona Lake, Indiana. ISBN 0 890003 156 8; ISSN 0362 3637)

This is a brief, but interesting study, of some aspects of the syntax of the Aramaic of Daniel. Particularly interesting is the suggestion that when the author of Daniel 'wishes to describe a sequence of events, whether in narrative or otherwise, the VO [= verb + object] construction is preferred. If the writer departs from the sequential time-line to describe a previous action (perfect/pluperfect), contemporaneous action (circumstantial), or future action, the OV [= object + verb] construction is preferred' (p. 12). This VO construction is regarded as analogous to the *waw*-consecutive construction in Biblical Hebrew. Anything that throws light on the use of the tenses in Biblical Aramaic is to be welcomed and this little booklet certainly does.

A. P. HAYMAN

ECKHARDT, W.: *Computergestützte Analyse althebräischer Texte: Algorithmische Erkennung der Morphologie* (Münchener Universitätsschriften — Arbeiten zu Text und Sprache im Alten Testament, 29). 1987. Pp. xi, 135. (Eos Verlag, St Ottilien. Price: DM 24.00. ISBN 3 88096 529 3)

The use of a computer for all but the simplest kinds of study of a Hebrew text requires that every word of the text should first be supplied with a morphological analysis in some kind of coded form. To do this 'by hand' for every word of the Old Testament is an enormous task and computer programs have been devised which can analyse at least a proportion of the words automatically. This book is a description of the algorithm or logical structure of one such program, known as SALOMO, which is probably the first to be properly published. At last two others are in use, in Holland and the United States. The treatment presupposes a thorough knowledge of computer programming, and the book's readership is likely to be further diminished by the fact that the program described presupposes that the biblical text has already been transcribed according to the idiosyncratic system devised by W. Richter. Nevertheless its publication is another indication of the efforts that are being made, in several countries, to harness new technology for the use of biblical scholars.

G. I. DAVIES

FALES, F. M.: *Aramaic Epigraphs on Clay Tablets of the Neo-Assyrian Period* (Studi Semitici N.S. 2). 1986. Pp. xx, 287, 17 plates. (Università degli studi 'La Sapienza', Rome; available from Harrassowitz, Wiesbaden. Price: DM 62.00)

Since L. Delaporte published all Aramaic epigraphs on clay tablets known to him in 1912, continuing discoveries and increasing comprehension make this new, thorough edition of those from Assyrian times very welcome. Sixty-one texts are edited in full, with hand-copies or photographs of many, and a table of letter forms. Most of these texts are annotations of a few words summarizing the content of the cuneiform lines, a few are more complete documents, probably written on clay when papyrus was not available. These relatively minor inscriptions give precisely dated examples of Aramaic handwriting from the eastern region, and show the interaction of Assyrian and Aramaic in the seventh century B.C., a matter which the author examines in detail. He prefers to speak of an Assyrian–Aramaic symbiosis rather than a Mesopotamian dialect of Aramaic, taking account of the Tell Fekheriyeh bilingual. The examples of Assyrian words transcribed into Aramaic letters which these epigraphs supply are a valuable guide to the spoken Assyrian of the time, also shedding light on the biblical forms of Assyrian names and words. While a few readings may be open to doubt, Dr Fales has provided a sober evaluation of this peculiar material which future discoveries will expand but are unlikely to contradict. All concerned with the early history of Aramaic will have to take account of it.

A. R. MILLARD

LOPRIENO, A.: *Das Verbalsystem im Ägyptischen und im Semitischen: zur Grundlegung einer Aspekttheorie* (Göttinger Orientforschungen: IV. Reihe, Ägypten; Band 17). 1986. Pp. xv, 213. (Otto Harrassowitz, Wiesbaden. Price: DM 88.00. ISBN 3 447 02583 2; ISSN 0340 6342)

This is an important book, powerfully thought out, well expressed, and showing a fine command of modern linguistic concepts. The basis lies in Egyptian but as the title implies the work belongs to the comparative study of Egyptian and Semitic and is specially concerned with the study of aspect, the importance of which for Hebrew study is well known. In addition, the book is interested in the nature of the common substance found in Afro-asiatic

(Hamito-Semitic in older terminology) and discusses this illuminatingly, especially in the first and last chapters. Old Testament scholars who lack the technical equipment to read through the core of the book would do well to read these two chapters. There is no section devoted to Hebrew as such, but the text and notes include a number of remarks on it. A very impressive achievement.

J. Barr

Muraoka, T.: *Classical Syriac for Hebraists*. 1987. Pp. xv, 131. (Harrassowitz, Wiesbaden. Price: DM 58.00. ISBN 3 447 02585 9)

The design of this new Syriac grammar, as the title makes clear, is to facilitate an approach to the language especially for students already acquainted with Hebrew or Arabic, or perhaps both. Generations of students accustomed to T. H. Robinson's grammar (first published in 1915, revised by L. H. Brockington in 1962) might agree that the exercises in it are less than stimulating. The principal aim of the new grammar is to help the student acquire a measure of competence in reading Syriac texts with or without vowel points. With this in mind the author has assembled an interesting Chrestomathy of Syriac texts which are used in close collusion with his up-to-date grammar. The first three or four texts are analysed in detail in the ample footnotes which contain references to the appropriate explanatory paragraphs in the body of the grammar. The main sections of the grammar (Orthography and Phonology, Morphology and Morphosyntax, Syntax) are based primarily on the standard Work by T. Nöldeke. Muraoka uses the Estrangela script in the grammar and in the texts (p. 101 has Psalm 1:1–3 in the three Syriac scripts) and all the illustrative examples are taken from Syriac documents. New insights and improvements on his predecessors' description of the language have contributed in making this a readable and lucid piece of work. It comprises the best introduction to classical Syriac available in English.

P. W. Coxon

Murtonen, A.: *Hebrew in its West Semitic Setting: A Comparative Survey of Non-Masoretic Hebrew Dialects and Traditions*. Part One: A Comparative Lexicon. Section A: *Proper Names*. (Studies in Semitic Languages and Linguistics, xiii). 1986. (Brill, Leiden. Price: Fl. 192.00. ISBN 90 04 07245 4)

Those who are familiar with the author's previous investigations into the history of the Hebrew language will be pleased to learn that he is revising these and issuing them in a more definitive form. Part One of his project, entitled rather misleadingly *Comparative Lexicon*, will treat the basic uninflected material on which the other parts will be based, viz. personal names (in the present volume), the root system (in two further volumes) and numerals, pronouns and particles (in a fourth volume). We are given no indication of the size of the other parts, but there will be three of them (entitled respectively Phonetics and Phonology; Morphosyntactics; and Historical Synopsis). Part One, Volume 1 lists all the extant Hebrew personal names in the Bible and selected non-Biblical sources for the Pronunciation of which we have external evidence in non-Tiberian sources (Akkadian, Greek and Latin transcriptions; the orthography of the inscriptions and the Scrolls; Palestinian and Babylonian vocalizations; recordings of Samaritan speakers). This evidence is given in full after every name. In the long introduction there is exhaustive discussion of the problems of assessing such evidence (including the use of statistical methods, a section I found very difficult to follow) and a commentary on the list. The most important element in the list is Professor

Murtonen's own transliteration which comes immediately after each name and reconstructs the prototype to which, in his estimation, the evidence, taken as a whole, points. The ultimate purpose of the project is to present a comprehensive survey of Hebrew from the earliest traceable beginnings to the period of activity of the principal Tiberian Masoretes about the turn of the tenth century A.D. It is this vast material that he calls non-Masoretic, though pre-Masoretic would give a clearer indication to the uninitiated of what he is about. If the first volume is anything to go by, everything that is of possible relevance will be ferreted out, recorded and annotated in the utmost detail. The mind boggles at what is in store for us, but there can be no doubt that this massive undertaking will, when it is finally finished, be a major contribution to Hebrew historical linguistics. We can only admire Professor Murtonen's erudition, his ambition and his energy.

J. C. L. GIBSON

NIEHR, H.: *Herrschen und Richten: Die Wurzel* špt *im Alten Orient und im Alten Testament* (Forschung zur Bibel 54). 1986. Pp. xii, 458. (Echter Verlag, Würzburg. Price: DM 56.00. ISBN 3 429 01012 8)

This exhaustive and fruitful study is concerned with the semantic development of the root *špt* and its derivitives in the ancient near east, including the Old Testament and the Qumran texts. A review of previous studies leads to the formulation of guidelines for the present investigation, including particularly the shifting of emphasis from etymology to usage. Having then briefly determined the basic significance of the word to be a verb of speaking, with the senses of 'judge' and 'rule' being differentiations based on a semantic development of the root determined by its use in different contexts, the author devotes the substance of his study to the use of *špt* first in pre-biblical near eastern texts, then the Old Testament and finally in Qumran. The biblical usage is examined in four periods: the monarchic period to the fall of the northern kingdom, 721–586 B.C., the exilic and the post-exilic periods. Within a general framework which sees a development from a mainly administrative and political sense to a predominantly forensic sense, with neither being totally lost at any stage, the author traces the various new meanings which accrued to the word in its different forms in different linguistic and social contexts. In the Old Testament the verbal form is argued to have had the sense of rule in the earliest examples of the first period (as with reference to the 'minor judges'), a forensic sense in other examples from the first period and in the second period, while both usages appear in the exilic and post-exilic periods. A shorter concluding section examines major contexts within which the root appears: the so-called *mešarum* institution, the idea of order, the theological context with Yahweh as subject, and as an element in proper names. This is a rich and rewarding study.

A. D. H. MAYES

POMPONIO, F., RIBICHINI, A. and XELLA, P.: *Studi Epigrafici e Linguistici sul Vicino Oriente antico*. Vol. 3. 1986. Pp. 136. (Essedue Edizioni, Verona. Price: Lire 32,000)

Volume 4 (1987) of this periodical has already appeared and volume 5, a *Festschrift* for Professor O. Loretz, is in preparation. Accordingly, *SEL*, an annual for 'epigraphical, linguistic and historical studies on texts from preclassical Near Eastern cultures' is now well established and deservedly so. The present issue has twelve contributions, only five in Italian, the others in French, Spanish, German and English.

Using excavation reports A. Lemaire shows that the two portions of the Deir ʿAlla plaster 'Balaam' inscriptions are totally unrelated. R. M. Good explains the water festival of Carthage, possibly reflected in Num. 25:1 ff. and elsewhere. G. del Olmo Lete gives a translation and interpretation of a Ugaritic text which he shows to be the liturgy for a king's funeral. Part of the sacrificial rites were to be carried out in a 'garden', evidently a royal cemetery as in Ebla, Ugarit and Israel (cf. 'garden of the king', 2 Kings 25:4, etc.). There are also contributions on Sumerian, Hittite, Ugaritic, Palmyrene, Punic and Indo-European.

W. G. E. WATSON

POSTGATE, J. N., and POWELL, M. A. (eds.): *Bulletin on Sumerian Agriculture*, Volume III. 1987. Pp. vi + 162. (Aris and Phillips, Warminster. ISSN 0267 0658)

Identification of ancient names for fruit, vegetables, trees, shrubs and herbs is notoriously difficult. In an attempt to resolve some of the problems involved the Sumerian Agriculture Group has been holding meetings over the past few years and publishing its findings. The present volume was prepared from the 1985 meeting and deals with the onion family, cucurbitaceous plants, the date palm, various types of fruit, etc., as documented in the clay tablets of Mesopotamia. Though principally of importance for Sumerian, the material collected here, set as it is against a solid botanical background, is relevant for other languages including Hebrew. For example, Jonah's 'gourd' is discussed (add now B. P. Robinson, *ZAW* 97 (1985). pp. 390–403) as well as Hebrew, Aramaic and Syriac terms for 'juniper', 'water melon' (Num. 11:5) and 'cucumber'. This is a valuable contribution to lexicography and palaeobotany. There are several tables, some illustrations, select bibliographies but no index.

W. G. E. WATSON

ULLENDORFF, E.: *Studia Aethiopica et Semitica* (Äthiopistische Forschungen, 24). 1987. Pp. xiv, 325. (Franz Steiner, Wiesbaden. Price: DM 78.00. ISBN 3 515 04889 8)

An earlier volume of articles and reviews was issued by Edward Ullendorff in 1977 under the title *Is Biblical Hebrew a Language? Studies in Semitic Languages and Civilizations*; see *B.L.* 1978, p. 22. The present, somewhat smaller, collection contains eighteen articles and is divided into the two sections indicated by the title; the articles have been reproduced photographically without change, but some additions and a few minor corrections have been included in a four-page introduction, and there is a comprehensive index. In addition to a series of important articles that deal with Amharic documents and letters, the first section contains three articles of direct relevance to readers of this *Book List*: 'Hebraic–Jewish Elements in Abyssinian (Monophysite) Christianity' (1956); 'Hebrew. Aramaic, and Greek: The Versions underlying Ethiopic Translations of Bible and intertestamental Literature' (1980); and 'The Challenge of Amharic' (1965), the author's Inaugural Lecture as Professor of Ethiopian Studies in the University of London (see *B.L.* 1966, p. 67 (*Decade,* p. 687)). The second section contains three articles of direct importance for Old Testament and Semitic studies: 'Comparative Semitics' (1970); 'Ugaritic Marginalia IV' (1978); and 'The Bawdy Bible' (1979; see *B.L.* 1981, p. 135). In addition there are reprints of reviews of D. Biale's *Gershom Scholem* and of the volume edited by W. Haas, *Writing without Letters*. Finally, there are reprints of an article on 'D. H. Baneth and Philological Precociousness' (1979) and of the obituary notice of Stefan Strelcyn that was published in the Proceedings of the British Academy. The reviewer of the earlier volume referred to 'the impressive wide range and the profundity of Professor Ullendorff's scholarship', and these qualities are again more than amply illustrated by the present collection.

M. A. KNIBB

Books Received too Late for Notice in 1988

The books in the following list will be reviewed in the *Book List* for 1989.

ALBA CECILIA, A.: *Biblia Babilonica: Jeremias* (Textos y Estudios 'Cardenal Cisneros' de la Biblia Poliglota Matritense, 41). 1987. (CSIC, Madrid. ISBN 84 00 06681 2)

ALONSO SCHÖKEL, L. (ed.): *Materiales para un Diccionario Biblico Hebreo + Español* I: *Parte Lexicografica (alef, bet-ḥmt)*. 1988. (Biblical Institute Press, Rome)

BÄCHLI, O.: *Das Alte Testament in der Kirchlichen Dogmatik von Karl Barth*. 1987. (Neukirchener, Neukirchen-Vluyn. ISBN 3 7887 0792 5)

BAL, M.: *Murder and Difference: Gender, Genre, and Scholarship on Sisera's Death* (Indiana Studies in Biblical Literature). 1988. (Indiana University Press, Bloomington & Indianapolis. ISBN 0 253 33905 7)

BARAG, D., FOERSTER, G., NEGEV, A. (eds): *Eretz-Israel*, Vol. 19 (Michael Avi-Yonah Memorial Volume). 1987. (Israel Exploration Society, Jerusalem)

BARUCQ, A., CAQUOT, A., DURAND, J. M., LEMAIRE, A., MASSON, E.: *Ecrits de l'Orient ancien et sources bibliques* (Petite Bibliothèque des Sciences Bibliques: Ancien Testament 2). 1986. (Desclée, Paris. ISBN 2 7189 0308 2)

BOLING, R. G.: *The Early Biblical Community in Transjordan* (The Social World of Biblical Antiquity Series, 6). 1988. (Sheffield Academic Press. ISBN 1 85075 094 7)

BONORA, A.: *Qohelet. La gioia e la fatica di vivere* (Leggere oggi la Bibbia 1/15). 1987. (Queriniana, Brescia)

BONORA, A. (ed.): *La Spiritualità dell'Antico Testamento* (Storia della spiritualità I). 1987. (EDB, Bologna. ISBN 88 10 30411 X)

BOTTERWECK, G. J., RINGGREN, H., FABRY, H.-J. (eds): *Theologisches Wörterbuch zum Alten Testament*. Band VI, Lfg 3/5 (cols. 225–608). 1987. (Kohlhammer, Stuttgart. ISBN 3 17 009817 9)

CAQUOT, A., HADAS-LEBEL, M., RIAUD, J. (eds): *Hellenica et Judaica* (Hommage à V. Nikiprowetzky). 1986. (Peeters, Leuven–Paris. ISBN 90 6831 054 2)

CASALIS, G., ROUSSEL, B. (eds): *Olivétan, traducteur de la Bible* (Actes du colloque Olivétan, Noyon, mai 1985). 1987. (Cerf, Paris. ISBN 2 204 02637 9)

CASTEL, F.: *"Dio disse . . .". I primi undici capitoli della Genesi*. Translated from French by L. Zardi. 1987. (Paoline, Cinisello Balsamo (MI). ISBN 88 215 1218 5)

CATE, R. L.: *An Introduction to the Old Testament and its Study*. 1987. (Broadman, Nashville, Tennessee. ISBN 0 8054 1233 6)

CHAMPDOR, A.: *Les Civilisations du Jourdain* (50 illustrations; documents de l'Institut Pontifical de Rome). 1987. (Albert Guillot, Lyon. ISBN 2 850960016)

COATS, G. W.: *Moses: Heroic Man, Man of God* (JSOT Supplement Series 57). 1988. (Sheffield Academic Press. ISBN 1 85075 096 3; 1 85075 095 5(pbk))

CORNELIUS, J. B.: *La Genèse et la Préhistoire*. 1986. (Lanore, Paris. ISBN 2 85157 022 6)

CROCETTI, G.: *1–2 Samuele. 1–2 Re* (Leggere oggi la Bibbia 1/8). 1987. (Queriniana, Brescia)

DELCOR, M.: *Studi sull'Apocalittica* (translated from French by Antonio Zani) (Studi Biblici 77). 1987. (Paideia, Brescia. ISBN 88 394 0385 X)

Die Fünf Bücher der Weisung: verdeutscht von Martin Buber gemeinsam mit Franz Rosenzweig — mit einer Beilage: *Martin Buber: Zu einer neuen*

Verdeutschung der Schrift. 1987. (Verlag Lambert Schneider, Heidelberg. ISBN 3 7953 0180 7)

DIEZ MACHO, A. with the collaboration of A. NAVARRO PEIRO: *Biblia Babilonica: Fragmentos de Salmos, Job y Proverbios* (Ms. 508 A del Seminario Teologico Judio de Nueva York) (Textos y Estudios 'Cardenal Cisneros' de la Biblia Poliglota Matritense, 42). 1987. (CSIC, Madrid. ISBN 84 00 06680 4)

DIEZ MARINO, L.: *Targum de Qohelet. Edicion Principe del Ms. Villa-Amil No. 5 de Alfonso de Zamora* (Bibliotheca Hispana Biblica, 13). 1987. (CSIC, Madrid. ISBN 84 00 06661 8)

DILLARD, R. B.: *2 Chronicles* (Word Biblical Commentary 15). 1987. (Word Books, Waco, Texas. ISBN 0 8499 0214 2)

DRÖGE, C.: *Gianozzo Manetti als Denker und Hebraist* (Judentum und Umwelt 20). 1987. (Lang, Frankfurt am Main, Bern, New York. ISBN 3 8204 9127 9)

ENERMALM-OGAWA, A.: *Un langage de prière juif en grec: Le témoinage des deux premiers livres des Maccabées* (Coniectanea Biblica, NT 17). 1987. (Almquist & Wiksell, Stockholm. ISBN 91 22 00927 2)

ESLINGER, L. M.: *Kingship of God in Crisis: A Close Reading of 1 Samuel 1–12* (Bible and Literature Series 10). 1985. (Almond, Sheffield. ISBN 0 907459 40 4; 0 907459 41 2 (pbk))

FANULI, A. (ed.): *Sapienza e Torah; Associazione Biblica Italiana—Atti della XXIX Settimana Biblica*. 1987. (EDB, Bologna. ISBN 88 10 30252 4)

FARROW, D.: *The Word of Truth and Disputes about Words* (Carpenter Books). 1987. (Eisenbrauns, Winona Lake, Indiana. ISBN 0 931464 36 6)

FINKELSTEIN, I.: *The Archaeology of the Israelite Settlement*. Translated from Hebrew by D. Saltz. 1988. (Israel Exploration Society, Jerusalem. ISBN 965 221 007 2)

FREDE, H. J.: *Kirchenschriftsteller* (Vetus Latina. Die Reste der altlateinischen Bibel, nach Petrus Sabatier neu gesammelt und herausgegeben von der Erzabtei Beuron. 1/1B: Aktualisierungsheft 1988). 1988. (Herder, Freiburg im Breisgau. ISBN 3 451 00479 8)

FRIELING, R.: *Old Testament Studies* (translated from German by M. and R. Koehler). 1987. (Floris Books, Edinburgh. ISBN 0 86315 057 8)

GARSIEL, M.: *Midrashic Name Derivations in the Bible* (in Hebrew). 1987. (Revivim, Ramat-Gan; distributed by Beit Alim, 3 Karel Neter St., Tel Aviv)

GERATY, L. T., HERR, L. G. (eds): *The Archaeology of Jordan and other studies presented to Siegfried H. Horn*. 1986. (Andrews University Press, Berrien Springs, Michigan; distributed by Eisenbrauns, Winona Lake, Indiana. ISBN 0 943872 27 8)

GLAZIER-MCDONALD, B.: *Malachi: The Divine Messenger* (SBL Dissertation Series 98). 1987. (Scholars Press, Atlanta, Georgia. ISBN 1 55540 093 0; 1 55540 094 9 (pbk))

GREENSPOON, L.: *Max Leopold Margolis: A Scholar's Scholar* (Society of Biblical Literature Centennial Publications). 1987. (Scholars Press, Atlanta GA. ISBN 1 55540 146 5; 1 55540 147 3 (pbk))

GREENWOOD, D. C.: *Structuralism and the Biblical Text* (Religion and Reason 32). 1985. (De Gruyter, Berlin. ISBN 3 11 010336 2)

HAAG, E. (ed.): *Gott, der einzige. Zur Entstehung des Monotheismus in Israel* (Quaestiones Disputatae, 104). 1985. (Herder, Freiburg, Basel, Wien. ISBN 3 451 02104 8)

HAHN, J.: *Das "Goldene Kalb": Die Jahweh-Verehrung bei Stierbildern in der Geschichte Israels*, 2. erg. Auflage (Europäische Hochschulschriften: Reihe 23, Theologie, Bd. 154). 1987. (Lang, Frankfurt am Main, Bern, New York. ISBN 3 8204 8657 7)

HALIVNI, D. W.: *Midrash, Mishnah, and Gemara: The Jewish Predilection for Justified Law*. 1986. (Harvard University Press, Cambridge, Mass. and London. ISBN 0 674 57370 6)

HARRIS, R. L., SCHONFIELD, J., GIBSON, S. (eds): *Bulletin of the Anglo-Israel Archaeological Society*, Vol. 6 (1986–7). 1987. (The Anglo-Israel Archaeological Society, London. ISBN 0266 2442)

HILTON, M., MARSHALL, G.: *The Gospels and Rabbinic Judaism: A Study Guide*. 1988. (SCM, London. ISBN 0 334 02021 2)

JERVELL, J. and KAPELRUD, A. S.: *Studia Theologica: Scandinavian Journal of Theology*. Vol. 41, no. 2. 1987. (Norwegian University Press, Oslo. ISSN 0039 338X)

KIRISYTOKYO GAKU (Christian Studies). New Series, 26, 29 (Japanese). 1984, 1987. (The Association of Christian Studies, St. Paul's (Rikkyo) University, Tokyo. ISBN 0387 6810)

KIUCHI, N.: *The Purification Offering in the Priestly Literature: Its Meaning and Function* (JSOT Supplement Series 56). 1987. (Sheffield Academic Press. ISBN 1 85075 103 X; 1 85075 102 1 (pbk))

KLOPFENSTEIN, M.: *Mitte der Schrift? Ein jüdisch-christliches Gespräch* (Texte des Berner Symposions vom 6.–12. Januar 1985) (Judaica et Christiana, Bd. 11). 1987. (Lang, Frankfurt am Main, Bern, New York. ISBN 3 261 04077 7)

KOCH, K.: *Studien zur alttestamentlichen und altorientalischen Religionsgeschichte* (Zum 60. Geburtstag von Klaus Koch herausgegeben von Eckart Otto). 1988. (Vandenhoeck & Ruprecht, Göttingen. ISBN 3 525 53579 1)

KÖCKERT, M.: *Vätergott und Väterverheissungen: Eine Auseinandersetzung mit Albrecht Alt und seinen Erben* (FRLANT 142). 1987. (Vandenhoeck & Ruprecht, Göttingen. ISBN 3 525 53821 9)

KRASOVEČ, J.: *La justice* (ṢDQ) *de Dieu dans la Bible hébraïque et l'interprétration juive et chrétienne* (Orbis Biblicus et Orientalis 76). 1988. (Universitätsverlag, Freiburg (CH); Vandenhoeck & Ruprecht, Göttingen. ISBN 3 7278 0549 8; 3 525 53705 0)

KROLL, W. M.: *Psalms: The Poetry of Palestine*. 1987. (University Press of America, London. ISBN 0 8191 5750 3; 0 8191 5751 1 (pbk))

KÜCHLER, M., UEHLINGER, CH.: *Jerusalem: Texte — Bilder — Steine* (Novum Testamentum et Orbis Antiquus 6). 1988. (Universitätsverlag, Freiburg (CH); Vandenhoeck & Ruprecht, Göttingen. ISBN 3 7278 0552 8; 3 525 53905 3)

La Vie de la Parole: De l'Ancien au Nouveau Testament (Etudes d'exégèse et d'herméneutique bibliques offertes à Pierre Grelot professeur à l'institut Catholique de Paris). 1987. (Desclée, Paris. ISBN 2 7189 0329 5)

LAATO, A.: *Who is Immanuel? The Rise and the Foundering of Isaiah's Messianic Expectations*. 1988. (Åbo Academy Press; distributed by Tidningsbokhandeln, PB 33, SF-21601 Pargas. ISBN 951 9498 22 2)

LABUSCHANGE, C. J.: *Deuteronomium*, deel I A/B (De Prediking van het Oude Testament). 1987. (Callenbach, Nijkerk. ISBN 90 266 0727 X; 90 266 0743 1)

Le Origini di Israele: Convegno sul Tema — Roma, 10–11 Febbraio 1986. 1987. (Accademia Nazionale dei Lincei, Roma. ISSN 0391 8130)

LIMET, H.: *Archives Royales de Mari* XXV: *Textes administratifs relatifs aux metaux*. 1986. (Éditions Recherche sur les Civilisations, Paris. ISBN 2 86538 155 2)

MAGEN, U.: *Assyrische Königsdarstellungen — Aspekte der Herrschaft: eine Typologie* (Baghdader Forschungen 9). 1986. (Von Zabern, Mainz. ISBN 3 8053 0835 3)

MANNS, F.: *Leggere la Misnah* (translated from French by Giulio Busi) (Studi Biblici 78). 1987. (Paideia, Brescia. ISBN 88 394 0394 9)

MARTINEZ BOROBIO, E. (ed.): *Targum Jonatan de los Profetas Primeros en tradicion babilonica*. Vol. II: *I–II Samuel* (Textos y Estudios 'Cardenal Cisneros' de la Biblia Poliglota Matritense, 38). 1987. (CSIC, Madrid. ISBN 84 00 06437 2)

MAYS, J. L., ACHTEMEIER, P. J. (eds): *Interpreting the Prophets*. 1987. (Fortress, Philadelphia. ISBN 0 8006 1932 3)

MCCREESH, T. P. (ed.): *Old Testament Abstracts*. Vol. 10, No. 3. 1987. (The Catholic University of America, Washington D.C. ISSN 0364 8591)

MEYERS, E. and C.: *Haggai, Zechariah 1–8* (Anchor Bible 25B). 1987. (Doubleday, New York. ISBN 0 385 14482 2)

MILLER, J. W.: *Meet the Prophets: A Beginner's Guide to the Books of the Biblical Prophets*. 1987. (Paulist Press, Mahwah, New Jersey. ISBN 0 8091 2899 3)

MILNE, P. J.: *Vladimir Propp and the Study of Structure in Hebrew Biblical Narrative* (Bible and Literature Series, 13). 1988. (Sheffield Academic Press. ISBN 1 85075 087 4; 1 85075 086 6 (pbk))

MONTES-PERAL, L. A.: *Akataleptos Theos: Der unfassbare Gott* (Arbeiten zur Literatur and Geschichte des hellenistischen Judentums, 16). 1987. (Brill, Leiden. ISBN 90 04 06928 3; ISSN 0169 7390)

MORALDI, L.: *I Manoscritti di Qumran* (2nd ed) (Classici delle Religioni: La Religione ebraica). 1986. (UTET, Torino. ISBN 88 02 03926 7)

MÜLLER, H.-P. (ed.): *Zeitschrift für Althebraistik*, Bd. 1. 1988. (Kohlhammer, Stuttgart. ISSN 0932 4461)

MUÑOZ LEON, D.: *Deras. Los caminos y sentidos de la Palabra Divina en la Escritura*. Primera Serie: Deras Targumico y Deras Neotestamentario (Bibliotheca Hispana Biblica, 12). 1987. (CSIC, Madrid. ISBN 84 00 06139 X)

NEUSNER, J.: *What is Midrash?* (Guides to Biblical Scholarship, New Testament Series). 1987. (Fortress, Philadelphia. ISBN 0 8006 0472 5)

NEUSNER, J.: *Christian Faith and the Bible of Judaism: The Judaic Encounter with Scripture*. 1987. (Eerdmans, Grand Rapids, Michigan; Paternoster, Exeter. ISBN 0 8028 0278 8)

O'CONNOR, M. P.: FREEDMAN, D. N. (eds): *Backgrounds for the Bible*. 1987. (Eisenbrauns, Winona Lake, Indiana. ISBN 0 931464 30 7)

ODISHO, E. Y.: *The Sound System of Modern Assyrian (Neo-Aramaic)* (Semitica Viva 2). 1988. (Harrassowitz, Wiesbaden. ISBN 3 447 02744 4; ISSN 0931 2811)

OGDEN, G.: *Qoheleth* (Readings. A New Biblical Commentary). 1987. (Sheffield Academic Press. ISBN 1 85075 071 8; 1 85075 070 X (pbk))

PAUL, A.: *Le Judaïsme ancien et la Bible* (Relais-études 3). 1987. (Desclée, Paris. ISBN 2 7189 0341 4)

PRIOTTO, M.: *La prima Pasqua in Sap 18,5–25. Rilettura e attualizzazione* (Associazione Biblica Italiana: Supplementi alla Rivista Biblica 15). 1987. (EDB, Bologna. ISBN 88 10 30203 6)

RAINEY, A. F.: *Egypt, Israel, Sinai: Archaeological and Historical Relationships in the Biblical Period* (The Kaplan Project on the History of Israel and Egypt). 1987. (Tel Aviv University Press, Tel Aviv. ISBN 965 224 008 7)

RAVASI, G.: *La terra promessa. Guida storica, archeologica e biblica della Palestina*. 1987. (EDB, Bologna. ISBN 88 10 80668 9)

Revista Biblica Brasileira. Ano 4,3–4; 5,1. 1987; 1988. (Nova Jerusalém, Fortaleza CE. Brazil)

ROBBINS, G. L.: *"And in the Seventh Day"* (American University Studies: Series 7, Theology and Religion. Vol. 36). 1987. (Lang, Frankfurt am Main, Bern, New York. ISBN 3 8204 0504 3)

RUIZ GONZALEZ, G.: *Comentarios Hebreos Medievales al Libro de Amos* (Traduccion y notas a los Comentarios de Rasi, E. de Beaugency, A. 'ibn

'Ezra, D. Qimhi, J. 'ibn Caspi) (Publicaciones de la Universidad Pontificia Comillas, Madrid; Serie I: Estudios, 31; Theologia I, 20). 1987. (UPCM, Madrid. ISBN 84 85281 67 5)

SCHÄFER, P., together with REEG, G. (eds): *Konkordanz zur Hekhalot-Literatur*, I: *'-k* (Texte und Studien zum Antiken Judentum 12). 1986. (Mohr. Tübingen. ISBN 3 16 145030 2; ISSN 0721 8753)

SCHMIDT, W. H.: *Alttestamentlicher Glaube in seiner Geschichte*. 6. überarbeitete und erweiterte Auflage (Neukirchener Studienbücher 6). 1987. (Neukirchener, Neukirchen-Vluyn. ISBN 3 7887 1263 5)

SCHREINER, J.: *Die Zehn Gebote im Leben des Gottesvolkes*. 1988. (Kösel, München. ISBN 3 466 20297 3)

SCHULMAN, A. R.: *Ceremonial Execution and Public Rewards: Some Historical Scenes on New Kingdom Private Stelae* (Orbis Biblicus et Orientalis 75). 1988. (Universitätsverlag, Freiburg (CH); Vandenhoeck & Ruprecht, Göttingen. ISBN 3 7278 0548 X; 3 525 53704 2)

SCHULZ, H.: *Leviten im vorstaatlichen Israel und im Mittleren Osten*. 1987. (Chr. Kaiser, München. ISBN 3 459 01713 9)

SCHWARZ, G.: *Jesus und Judas; Aramaistische Untersuchungen zur Jesus-Judas Überlieferung der Evangelien und der Apostelgeschichte* (BWANT 123). 1987. (Kohlhammer, Stuttgart. ISBN 3 17 009663 X)

SEYERSTED, P.: *Gilgames.j. Han som så alt*. Norsk utgave ved Per Seyersted. Innledning av professor Arvid S. Kapelrud. 1987. (J. W. Cappelsens Forlag, Oslo. ISBN 82 02 04301 8)

SKEHAN, P. W., DI LELLA, A. A.: *The Wisdom of Ben Sira* (Anchor Bible 39). 1987. (Doubleday, New York. ISBN 0 385 13517 3)

SMITH, M. S.: *Psalms: The Divine Journey*. 1987. (Paulist Press, Mahwah, New Jersey. ISBN 0 8091 2897 7)

STÄHLI, H.-P.: *Antike Synagogenkunst*. 1988. (Calwer, Stuttgart. ISBN 3 7668 0823 0)

STEINSLAND, G. (ed.): *Words and Objects: Towards a Dialogue between Archaeology and History of Religion* (Institute for Comparative Research in Human Culture, Oslo. Series B: Skrifter, Vol. 71). 1986. (Universitetsforlaget, Oslo. ISBN 82 00 07751 9)

STRUPPE, U.: *Die Herrlichkeit Jahwes in der Priesterschrift* (Österreichische Biblische Studien 9). 1988. (Österreichisches Katholisches Bibelwerk, Klosterneuburg. ISBN 3 85396 077 4)

TARDIEU, M. (ed.): *Les règles de l'interprétation* (Centre d'Etudes des Religions du Livre). 1987. (Cerf, Paris. ISBN 2 204 02523 2)

TOV, E.: *A Computerized Data Base for Septuagint Studies: The Parallel Aligned Text of the Greek and Hebrew Bible* (Computer Assisted Tools for Septuagint Studies (CATSS) Volume 2) (Journal of Northwest Semitic Languages, Supplementary Series 1). 1986. (JNSL, Stellenbosch)

TREVES, M.: *The Dates of the Psalms: History and Poetry in Ancient Israel*. 1988. (Giardini, Pisa)

Vetus Latina. Die Reste der altlateinischen Bibel, nach Petrus Sabatier neu gesammelt und herausgegeben von der Erzabtei Beuron. 12: *Esaias*. Herausgegeben von R. Gryson. 2. Lieferung: *Is.1,22–5,7*. 1987. (Herder, Freiburg im Breisgau. ISBN 3 451 00441 0)

WENHAM, G. J.: *Genesis 1–15* (Word Biblical Commentary 1). 1987. (Word Books, Waco, Texas. ISBN 0 8499 0200 2)

WIESER, F. E.: *Die Abrahamvorstellungen im Neuen Testament* (Europäische Hochschulschriften: Reihe 23, Theologie. Bd. 317). 1987. (Lang, Bern, Frankfurt am Main, New York, Paris. ISBN 3 261 03732 6)

WILLIAMS, T.: *Form and Vitality in the World and God: A Christian Perspective* (paperback edition). 1988. (Clarendon, Oxford. ISBN 0 19 826698 7)

Wright, G. R. H.: *As on the First Day: Essays in Religious Constants*. 1987. (Brill, Leiden. ISBN 90 04 08172 0)

Yassine, Kh.: *Archaeology of Jordan: Essays and Reports*. 1988. (Available from the author: Kh.N. Yassine, P.O. Box 410403, Amman, Jordan)

Index of Authors

(N.B. — Names occurring more than once in the same review or on the same page are listed on their first occurrence only.)

The Society for Old Testament Study is a British Society for Old Testament scholars. Candidates for membership, which is not confined to British subjects, must be nominated by two members of the Society. Residents of the British Isles are normally admitted to ordinary membership and non-residents to associate membership. All correspondence concerning domestic affairs of the Society should be sent to:

Dr A. H. W. Curtis
Faculty of Theology
University of Manchester
Manchester M13 9PL
England

ISBN 0 905495 07 1

THE SOCIETY FOR
OLD TESTAMENT
STUDY

BOOK LIST

1989

Printed for the Society

The Society for Old Testament Study

BOOK LIST 1989

Printed for the Society

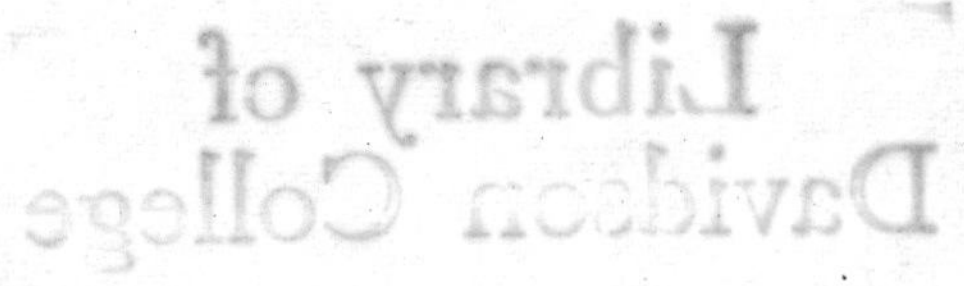

ISBN 0 905495 08 X

PRINTED BY W. S. MANEY AND SON LTD HUDSON ROAD LEEDS LS9 7DL

Contents

One copy of the *Book List* is supplied free to all members of the Society.

Copies of the *Book List* for 1989 may also be obtained from M. E. J. Richardson, Esq., Department of Middle Eastern Studies, University of Manchester, Manchester M13 9PL, England. Back numbers of the *Book List* are also available from Mr Richardson. Orders should not be accompanied by payment; an invoice will be sent. The price of these is £6.00 plus postage or $16.00, for a single copy. Payment should be made by cheque in sterling or U.S. dollars payable to the Society for Old Testament Study, or direct to Post Office Giro Account No. 50 450 4002.

Review copies of books for the *Book List* should be sent to the Editor:

Dr A. Graeme Auld
New College, Mound Place
Edinburgh EH1 2LX,
Scotland

PREFACE

Some aspects of an editorial task may be tedious. But it is a pleasure to thank annually and publicly the many colleagues who make this editor's job both easier and more pleasant: the publishers who offer, and readily respond to requests for books; those both nearer home and far overseas who review and recommend volumes; and our printers, Messrs W. S. Maney and Son, who turn script processed in many different ways into clear and accurate published type.

Some other names must also be named. Dr H. Barstad of Oslo is this year part of an international support group along with, as before, Professor B. Albrektson, Professor H. Cazelles, Dr F. García Martínez, Dr K. Jeppesen, Professor G. L. Prato, Dr K. K. Sacon, and Professor A. S. van der Woude. Then, within these islands, books have been drawn to my attention or reviews offered from personal copies by Professor G. W. Anderson, Dr R. P. Carroll, Mr R. J. Coggins, Professor K. A. Kitchen, Professor M. A. Knibb, Mr A. R. Millard, Dr S. C. Reif, Dr W. G. E. Watson, Professor R. N. Whybray, and Dr N. Wyatt. And it is a particular pleasure to include this year a review commissioned from Professor N. W. Porteous, whose recent 90th birthday gave pleasure to the Society.

An error in *B.L.* 1988, for which the reviewer was not responsible, was particularly unfortunate as it was itself part of an attempt to correct the volume under review: on the second line of p. 66 the Hebrew should have read *l' 'šybnw*.

The following abbreviations and symbols are employed as in earlier issues:

B.L.	=	*Book List*
Eleven Years	=	*Eleven Years of Bible Bibliography* (1957)
Decade	=	*A Decade of Bible Bibliography* (1967)
Bible Bibliog.	=	*Bible Bibliography 1967–1973: Old Testament* (1974)

NEW COLLEGE EDINBURGH — A. GRAEME AULD

1. GENERAL

BARAG, D., FOERSTER, G., and NEGEV, A. (eds): *Eretz-Israel*, Vol. 19 (Michael Avi-Yonah Memorial Volume). 1987. Pp. xii, 333 (Hebrew); xii, 83 (English/French). (Israel Exploration Society, Jerusalem. Price: $50.00)

Friends and former pupils commemorate Michael Avi-Yonah, who died, in 1974, by contributing essays that mostly concern his principal areas of interest, the Hellenistic to Byzantine periods of Palestinian history and culture. Among them, C. Vermeule publishes examples of art from Egypt and explores Palestinian connections, and S. S. Weinberg presents a Seleucid bronze weight. Several scholars report their excavations at synagogue, church, village, and burial sites (mostly in Hebrew), other discuss various pieces of sculpture and glassware. C. Dauphin considers the limits of demographic study through her survey of Byzantine occupation, and E. Meyers pleads for increased co-operation between Judaic studies and archaeology. There are also essays on the history of Jerusalem and its water-supplies. Relevant to Old Testament studies are N. Avigad's identifications of owners of Hebrew seals known from bullae with Old Testament characters, and the owner of the seal of *'lyhw bn mšlm* with the man of 2 Kings 22:3, and the late Y. Shiloh's publication of three South Arabian graffiti from his excavations in Jerusalem, signs, he argued, of trade links in the late Monarchy period. A posthumous note by R. D. Barnett draws attention to an Elamite precursor of the serpent support of Plataea, and L. Mildenberg identifies coins inscribed *bʿnʾ* as issues of a Sidonian king late in the fifth century B. C.

A. R. MILLARD

BENWARE, P. N.: *Survey of the Old Testament* (Everyman's Bible Commentary). 1988. Pp. 267. (Moody, Chicago. Price: $8.95. ISBN 0 8024 2091 5)

This offers a basic introduction to the books of the Hebrew Canon from an uncompromisingly conservative evangelical standpoint. The Pentateuch is 'an inspired, inerrant, authoritative document written by the man Moses'. Proverbs, Ecclesiastes, and the Canticle are Solomonic. Lamentations was written by Jeremiah. Daniel is a product of the sixth century (the Dead Sea Scrolls disproving the liberal theory of a second-century date!).

B. P. ROBINSON

BERGERHOF, K., DIETRICH, M., LORETZ, O. (eds): *Ugarit-Forschungen: Internationales Jahrbuch für die Altertumskunde Syrien-Palästinas*. Vol. 19 (1987). 1988. Pp. vi, 498. (Neukirchener, Neukirchen-Vluyn; Butzon & Bercker, Kevelaer. Price: DM 124.00. ISBN 3 7887 1281 3; 3 7666 9552 5; ISSN 0342 2356)

The following articles are those most directly relevant to the Old Testament. M. Dietrich and O. Loretz maintain that Ugaritis *tʿ* means 'Herr' and *tʿy* 'Minister, Wesir', and compare the words with Hebrew *šwʿ*. W. Herrmann sees the reference to El in Ps. 19:2 as an exilic application to Yahweh of old mythological ideas. L. B. Kutler analyses the elements in the challenge before battle in the Old Testament and notes Accadian and Ugaritic parallels. O. Loretz discusses the composition of Isaiah 19, noting the motif of the 'rider on the clouds' in verse 1, and suggesting that 'the language of Canaan' in verse 18 may be Aramaic. S. M. Olyan discusses the identity of the Queen of Heaven in Jer. 7:17–18 and 44:15–28 and Hermopolis Letter 4:1, and argues that 'the best case can be made for West Semitic Aštart'. E. Otto compares the presentation of the laws in the Book of the Covenant with that of the Laws of Eshnunna. H. Rouillard and J. Tropper discuss the meaning and history of interpretation of *'wb* and *yd'ny* in the Old Testament, which originally denoted deceased ancestors and were associated with the ancestor cult. M. Smith discusses Jer. 9:20. J. Tropper examines the phrase *tmym 'm yhwh*, which he translates 'vollkommem vor dem Herrn'. D. T. Tsumura compares Hebrew *tōhû wābōhû* with an Accadian phrase. M. Vervenne argues that Hebrew *šālîš* is best rendered 'knight', and that Ugaritic *tlt* may have had a similar meaning except where it is a numeral. N. Wyatt investigates the connotations of 'sea' and 'desert' in the Old Testament and other West Semitic texts, and also seeks to detect an Egyptian motif in the accounts of the birth of Solomon and of his elder brother, who died soon after being born. S. Segert discusses the meaning of Ugaritic *nqd* which, of course, has a bearing on Hebrew *nōqēd*. The book reviews include some works on the Old Testament.

J. A. Emerton

Blank, S. H. (ed.): *Hebrew Union College Annual*, Vol. lviii (1987). 1988. Pp. vii, 276 and 48 (Hebrew). (Hebrew Union College, Cincinnati. Price: $20.00. ISSN 0360 9049)

Four of the articles in an issue that maintains the journal's high standards are particularly relevant to Bible study. Eleanor K. Vogel adds about four hundred entries in the third part of her bibliography of research on Holy Land sites to those that appeared in volumes XLII and LII. A detailed literary-critical analysis of the sabbath and festival laws in Leviticus 23 by Israel Knohl leads to the identification of an earlier source centred on the cult and a later editor more interested in agriculture and history. The views of L. Perlitt and J. van Seters on Joshua 24 are challenged by S. David Sperling whose own verse-by-verse examination leads him to a single author in the early eighth century. In Michael V. Fox's essay, Qohelet's ideas about knowledge are philosophically defined as primitively empirical and consequently unique in Near Eastern Wisdom literature. Also covered are the Mesopotamian antecedents of hermeneutical principles in rabbinic 'aggadah (Stephen J. Lieberman); tannaitic, amoraic, and post-amoraic layers in the talmudic *sugya* (Judith Hauptman); the defence of legality in the talmudic and other systems of law (Haim H. Cohn); and a homily about the ten trials of Abraham edited from MSS Cambridge Add. 1497 and Oxford Opp. 4° 79 (Lewis M. Barth, in Hebrew).

S. C. Reif

Botterweck, G. J., Ringgren, H., and Fabry, H.-J. (eds): *Theologisches Wörterbuch zum Alten Testament*. Band vi, Lfg. 3/5 (cols. 225–608). 1987. (Kohlhammer, Stuttgart. Price: DM 118.00. ISBN 3 17 009817 9)

This triple fascicle begins with the final columns of *'ēmeq* (with *'āmaq*, *'āmōq*, K.-M. Beyse) and ends with the first two columns of *pll* (E. Gerstenberger). It contains fifty-seven complete articles. The words and roots most fully treated are *'ānāh* (two articles: i by F. J. Stendebach and ii by Gerstenberger); *'āṣam* (N. Lohfink), with *'eṣem* (Beyse) treated separately; *'rb* i (E. Lipiński) and *'rb* ii/iii (Fabry and H. Lamberty-Zielinski) followed by *'ereb* (H. Niehr) and *'ōrēb* (A. Angerstorfer); *'ēt* with *'attāh* (T. Kronholm); *'āśāh* (Ringgren). Other important words treated include *'ēṣ* (Ringgren and K. Nielsen), *'aštrt* (H.-P. Müller), *pādāh* (H. Cazelles), *peh* (F. García López), *pl'* (J. Conrad), and *plṭ* (G. F. Hasel). No words of theological or religious importance appear to have been omitted, but some of only minor relevance have been included, e.g. *'ēnāb*, *'eres* and *pē'āh* (all by Angerstorfer) and *'tq* (H. Schmoldt). Several roots are covered in this fascicle which offered the opportunity for discussion of long-standing problems. In particular only two roots *'nh* are recognized, *'ānāh* i covering all derivatives except those related to the meaning 'be afflicted' (*'ānāh* ii with *'anāwāh*, *'ānī*, *'ānāw* etc.).

Under *ʿrb* at least six different roots appear to be recognized; *ʿarābāh* has been dealt with in an earlier volume under *midbār*.

R. N. WHYBRAY

BOTTERWECK, G. J., RINGGREN, H., and FABRY, H.-J. (eds): *Theologisches Wörterbuch zum Alten Testament*. Band VI, Lfg. 6/7 (cols. 609–864). 1988. (Kohlhammer, Stuttgart. Price: DM 78.00. ISBN 3 17 009919 1)

This double fascicle begins with the final part of the article on *pll* and ends with the first part of that on *ṣōʾn*. It contains thirty-three complete articles, of which the longest are those on *pānīm* (H. Simian-Yofre, thirty columns), *pāsaḥ* with *pesaḥ* (E. Otto, twenty-three), *pātaḥ* and cognates (R. Bartelmus, twenty-one) and *pāšaʿ* with *pešaʿ* (H. Seebass, eighteen), followed by *pqd* (G. André, fourteen), *pārāh* with *perī* (B. Kedar-Kopfstein, twelve), *pth* (R. Mosis, eleven), and *pll* (E. Gerstenberger, ten). Some words, e.g. *pereʾ* (H.-J. Zobel) and *pered* (P. Maiberger), are somewhat lacking in theological content. In accordance with the policy on proper names there is no article on *pelištī*, though there is one on *parʿōh* (H. Cazelles), presumably because this is a title and not a personal name. No words of theological or religious significance seem to have been omitted.

R. N. WHYBRAY

BRIEND, J. and COTHENET, E. (eds): *Supplément au Dictionnaire de la Bible*. Vol. XI. Fasc. 62 (Salut): 1988. Cols 513–740: (Letouzey & Ané, Paris. Price: Fr. 200.00 (subscr). ISBN 2 7063 0161 9 (series); 2 7063 0116 3 (vol. XI))

The whole of this fascicle is devoted to the long article on salvation (*salut*, 254 columns), which was begun in the previous fascicle. It will be completed in fasc. 63; but so that subscribers will not have to wait for the completed article, the remaining four columns have been printed here by anticipation. The article begins with a substantial treatment (29 columns) of Egyptian (D. Meeks), Mesopotamian (A. Bouchard), and Hittite (E. Laroche) ideas supposedly comparable with the biblical concept of salvation. There follow sections on the Old Testament (E. Beaucamp, 37 columns), Qumran (P.-H. Poirier), the Old Testament Pseudepigrapha (P.-H. Poirier), Philo (J. Laporte), Josephus (P.-H. Poirier), and the New Testament: Synoptic Gospels and Acts (J. Delorme), Paul (M. Carrez), the Catholic Epistles (Cothenet), and the Johannine literature (M. Morgan). The section entitled 'Salvation according to the Bible in the Old Testament' was previously announced at the beginning of the art in fasc. 61 as 'The evolution of the Hebrew notion of *yšʿ* in the course of the composition of the Bible before, during and after the prophetic movement'. It is in fact mainly a study of *ysʿ* in the Old Testament, and makes a substantial and in some respects original contribution to the subject. On the questions of the etymology of *yšʿ* and its socio-political background the contribution of J. F. A. Sawyer is recognized and his views followed up. Although the meaning of the term 'salvation' has been widely stretched in this article to bring under a single heading so many widely differing notions (from ancient Egypt to the New Testament!), it is valuable to have so much potentially comparative information brought together in this way.

R. N. WHYBRAY

BROMILEY, G. W. (gen. ed.): *The International Standard Bible Encyclopedia*, Vol. IV: Q–Z. 1988. Pp. xix, 1211. (Eerdmans, Grand Rapids MI; distributed by Paternoster, Exeter. Price: $39.95; £28.95. ISBN 0 8028 8164 5; 0 8028 8160 2 (set))

The present volume completes the publication of the revised edition of *The International Standard Bible Encyclopedia*. The character of this new edition was described in the review of volume 1 (*B. L.* 1981, pp. 10–11), and subsequent volumes were noticed in *B. L.* 1983, p. 9, and *B. L.* 1987, p. 10. G. H. Wilson has replaced L. T. Geraty as Consulting Editor for Old Testament, but the other members of the editorial team remain the same (Bromiley, E. F. Harrison, R. K. Harrison, W. S. LaSor, and E. W. Smith, Jr). As in previous volumes, the contributors come from a wide range of scholarly backgrounds, and this is reflected in the articles, which vary considerably in quality and approach. But the *Encyclopedia* continues to provide much useful factual information, and the present volume in particular contains a number of very helpful articles, with up-to-date bibliographies.

M. A. Knibb

Caquot, A., Hadas-Lebel, M., and Riaud, J. (eds): *Hellenica et Judaica* (Hommage à V. Nikiprowetzky). 1986. Pp. 519. (Peeters, Leuven — Paris. Price: B.Fr. 2,880. ISBN 90 6831 054 2)

This massive volume is dedicated to the memory of Valentin Nikiprowetzky whose specialist interests in the field of Hellenistic Judaism are reflected in the separate sections on Philo, Josephus, Qumran, late Biblical and Pseudepigraphical Writings, Ancient Judaism, Mediaeval and Modern Judaism, Christianity, and Miscellaneous. i. Philo. M. Alexandre, 'Rhetorical Argumentation as an Exegetical Technique in Philo of Alexandria' (pp. 13–28); C. Lévy, 'Le "scepticisme" de Philon d'Alexandrie: une influence de la Nouvelle Académie?' (pp. 29–42); O. Munnich, 'Note sur la Bible de Philon: *κλοποφορεῖν*/* *κλοποφρονεῖν* en *Gen.* 31, 26 et en *Leg. 11.* iii, 20' (pp. 43–52); J. Neusner, 'Philo and the Mishnah. The Matter of the Soul after Death' (pp. 53–60); M. Philonenko, 'Philon d'Alexandrie et l'"Instruction sur les Deux Esprits"' (pp. 61–68); R. Radice, 'Ipotesi per una Interpretazione della struttura della Kosmopoiia nel *De Opificio Mundi* di Filone di Alessandria' (pp. 69–78); D. T. Runia, 'Redrawing the map of Early Middle Platonism: Some Comments on the Philonic Evidence' (pp. 85–104); D. Winston, 'Theodicy and Creation of Man in Philo of Alexandria' (pp. 105–11). ii. Josephus: L. Feldman, 'Josephus' Portrait of Deborah' (pp. 115–28); A. Paul, 'Le récit de la Creation dans les *Antiquités juives* de Flavius Josèphe: traduction et commentaire' (pp. 129–38); B. Thérond, 'Discours au style indirect et discours au style direct dans *La guerre des Juifs* de Flavius Josèphe' (pp. 139–52). iii. Qumran. M. Delcor, 'Réflexions sur l'investiture sacerdotale sans onction à la fête du nouvel An d'après *le Rouleau du Temple* de Qumran (xiv, 15–17)' (pp. 155–64); D. Dimant, '*4 Florigelium* and the Idea of the Community as Temple' (pp. 165–90); A. Lemaire, 'L'enseignement essénien et l'école de Qumran' (pp. 191–203). iv. Late Biblical Documents and Pseudepigrapha: P. M. Bogaert, 'La chronologie dans la dernière vision de Daniel (*Dn* 10.4 et 12. 11–12)' (pp. 207–12); A. Caquot, 'Les Hasmonéens, les Romains et Hérode : Observations sur *Ps Sal* 17' (pp. 213–18); J. H. Charlesworth, 'Greek, Persian, Roman, Syrian and Egyptian Influences in Early Jewish Theology: A Study of the History of the Rechabites' (pp. 219–44); E. Hilbert, '"By the Sea of Jamnia". *TNaph* 6:1' (pp. 245–56); J. Riaud, '"Le Puissant t'emportera dans ta tente". La destinée ultime du Juste selon les *Paralipomena Jeremiae Prophetae*' (pp. 257–66); J. Schwartz, 'Récits bibliques et moeurs perses' (pp. 267–77). V. Ancient Judaism. M. Cohen, 'La maxime des hommes de la Grande Assemblée. Une reconsidération (pp. 281–96); M. Hadas-Lebel, 'Rome "Quatrième Empire" et le symbole du porc' (pp. 297–312); R. Neher-Barnheim, 'L'assimilation linguistique des Juifs d'Alexandrie: une des sources de L'antijudaïsme antique' (pp. 313–20); C. Orrieux, 'Les papyrus de Zénon et la préhistoire du movement maccabéen' (pp. 321–34); M. Petit, 'Le contenu de l'Arche d'alliance: génération et addition de thèmes' (pp. 335–46). vi. Mediaeval and Modern Judaism:

B. Blumenkranz, '*Synagoga*: mutations d'un motif de l'iconographie médiévale (Allemagne, 12–15 siècles)' (pp. 349–56); D. R. Blumenthal, 'Maimonides on Angel Names' (pp. 357–70); R. Goetschel, 'Philon et le judaïsme hellénistique au miroir de Nachman Krochmal' (pp. 371–84); A. Neher, 'Les références à Philon d'Alexandrie dans l'oeuvre du Rav Hanazir, disciple du Rav Kook *(Qol HaNevoua*, 1970)' (pp. 385–90); E. Starobinski-Safran, 'La confrontation du judaïsme et de l'hellénisme dans Maïmonide, *Guide des Égarés* III, 54' (pp. 391–400). VII. Christianity; M. Alexandre, 'L'épée de flamme (*Gen*. 3, 24): textes chrétiens et traditions juives' (pp. 403–42); J. M. Dillon, Aisthêsis Noêtê: A Doctrine of Spiritual Senses in Origin and in Plotinus' (pp. 443–56); M. Harl, 'La "ligature" d'Isaac (*Gen*. 22:9) dans la Septante et chez les Pères grecs' (pp. 457–72); R. Joly, 'Parallèles païens pour Justin, *Apologie* I, XIX' (pp. 473–81). VIII. Miscellaneous: G. Salanitro, 'Ennio nella critica testuale di Giuseppe Scaligero' (p. 485–90); M. Smith, 'P. Leid J. 395 (*PGM* XIII) and its Creation Legend' (pp. 491–98); E. Will, '"Influence": note sur un pseudo-concept' (pp. 499–506); A. Derczanski, 'Odessa, Berceau de la renaissance hébraïque (pp. 507–10). Appended is a bibliography of Nikiprowetsky compiled by B. Delavault and J. Riaud.

P. W. COXON

CARSON, D. A. and WILLIAMSON, H. G. M. (eds): *It is Written: Scripture Citing Scripture: Essays in Honour of Barnabas Lindars*. 1988. Pp. xx, 381. (Cambridge University Press. Price: £37.50. ISBN 0 521 32347 9)

The essays in this *Festschrift* are divided into three sections, each of which reflects the wide scholarly interests of Professor Lindars in Old Testament, Inter-Testamental Literature, and New Testament. An introductory essay by I. H. Marshall sets out the book's programme and objectives: these are, by and large, well realized. Readers of the *Book List* will be particularly interested in the first two sections. There we find essays by H. G. M. Williamson on Old Testament History; J. Day on Prophecy; A. A. Anderson on Psalms, and R. E. Clements on Wisdom. The period between the Testaments is represented by S. P. Brock, 'Translating the Old Testament'; P. S. Alexander, 'Retelling the Old Testament'; B. D. Chilton, 'Commenting on the Old Testament'; A. N. Chester, 'Citing the Old Testament'; and C. Rowland, 'Apocalyptic Literature'.

It is clear that the editors have been necessarily strict in applying word limits to the contributions. One consequence of this policy is the highly concentrated and condensed material in some of the essays. But the high quality of the papers, many of which make important new contributions to their subjects, is evident despite this restriction on space. This is an impressive collection of essays, and the editors deserve congratulation.

C. T. R. HAYWARD

CLAASSEN, W. (ed.): *Text and Context: Old Testament and Semitic Studies for F. C. Fensham* (JSOT Supplement Series 48). 1988. Pp. 321. (Sheffield Academic Press. Price: £25.00 ($42.50). ISBN 1 85075 040 8)

In addition to a select bibliography of Professor Fensham (most academic publications) and a tribute to him, this has twenty-two studies: the Aramaic orthography of the Tell Fekherye bilingual (F. I. Andersen and D. N. Freedman), recent advances in Old Testament textual criticism (J. Cook), parallels and reinterpretation in Joel (F. E. Deist), Psalm 122 (H. Donner), the location of Bethso (J. A. Emerton), 'hem' in 1 Sam. 15:27 (P. A. Kruger), Judah between Egypt and Babylon (A. Malamat), *qṣwṣy p'h* in Jer. 9:25, etc., and Ugaritic *pat mdbr* (W. McKane), Ugaritic text KTU 1.119 and its significance for prayer and sacrifice in Israel (P. D. Miller), second thoughts on Ebla and the Old Testament (L. M. Muntingh), *paʿam* as a unit of a length (M. J. Mulder), Psalm 132 and covenant theology (P. Nel), the question of 3rd m. s. *taqtul* in Hebrew (A. Schoors), social and economic analysis of data for ancient Israel (J. A. Soggin), structural linguistics and textual criticism (J. B. van Zijl), Job and Mesopotamian parallels (M. Weinfeld), Mesopotamian *mēšarum* and the Israelite sabbatical year (H. Olivier), Zion as the 'stone' in Zech. 3 and 4 (A. S. van der Woude), the *pendens* sentence construction in Hebrew (W. Groß), dates in Haggai (P. A. Verhoef), the unity of of Zech. 8:1–8 (S. Mittmann), and computer-assisted methods in studying the text and language of the Old Testament (W. T. Claassen).

L. L. GRABBE

DANKER, F. W.: *A Century of Greco-Roman Philology: Featuring the American Philological Association and the Society of Biblical Literature* (SBL Centennial Publications: Biblical Scholarship in North America, 12). 1988. Pp. xvii, 299. (Scholars Press, Atlanta, Georgia. Price: $26.95 (member price: $19.95); ISBN 0 89130 985 3. Paperback price: $19.95 (member price: $13.95); ISBN 0 89130 986 1))

This is an informative and frequently entertaining account of the progress of classical and biblical studies in America from the closing years of the nineteenth century to the present day, and of the interaction between the two disciplines. There is little pertaining to the specific interests of the S.O.T.S., apart from a section on Hellenistic Judaism and some passages on LXX lexicography, with a disparaging reference (by Harry Orlinsky) to the citation of LXX evidence in the apparatus of BH^3 and another (by Morton Smith) on attempts 'to square the facts of the Old Testament as far as possible with the traditional teachings of the institutions, and even more, to make them serviceable for homiletical presentation'. But we can all profit by a chapter on 'philological voodoo or pseudorthodoxy' and by another on 'arts and hazards of reviewing'. The author is himself a classical scholar and continuing editor of the Bauer-Arndt-Gingrich *Greek–English Lexicon of the New Testament and Other Early Christian Literature*. When he cites the inscription on the 'Praenestine fibula', allegedly from *c.* 600 B.C., *Manios med fhefhaked Numasioi* (*CIL* 14.4123), he would do well to add that an increasing number of scholars today consider that *fhefhaked* is best translated 'faked'.

F. F. BRUCE

DÍAZ ESTEBAN, F. and SAENZ-BADILLOS, A.: *Volumen en Homenaje al Prof. Pérez Castro* (Sefarad 46). 1986. Pp. 506. (CSIC, Madrid.)

This volume in honour of the great masoretic scholar F. Pérez Castro contains, besides a *curriculum vitae* and personal bibliography, forty-six articles (mostly in Spanish) of which more than half concern Jewish (especially Sephardic) history and literature. Here will be noted only those falling within the scope of this *Book List*. Two articles comment on Ugaritic texts: the letter KTU 2.38 from the king of Tyre to that of Ugarit (J. L. Cunchillos) and the processional ritual KTU 1.43 (G. del Olmo Lete). Z. Ben-Ḥayyim gives an English version of his 'Reflections on the Vowel System in Hebrew', and A. Tal 'The Dialect of Jewish Palestinian Aramaic and the Palestinian Targum to the Pentateuch'. The other mainly linguistic articles are by M. Rubato Díaz on the word **'Aggān* (e.g. Ex. 24:6), L. F. Girón on Greek and Latin words in *Exodus Rabbah* and S. Morag on '"Latent Masorah" in Oral Language Traditions'.

On the text of the Hebrew Bible and its versions, A. Dotan and E. Fernández Tejero have articles on the Cairo codex of Prophets; H. M.

Orlinsky and M. Weinberg contribute 'Notes on some *Masora Parva* of Amos', L. Vegas Montaner studies the *metheg* in the Complutensian Polyglot, and I. Yeivin (in Hebrew) the *dageš mafrid* in MS Vat. Urbinati 2. On targums we have C. Alonso Fontela on Tg Šir ha-Širim in the Polyglot of Amberes, and E. Martínez Borobio on Spanish texts of Onqelos; on the LXX, N. Fernández Marcos on the Hexaplaric text of 1 Kings 14:1–20 as given in the Moscow MS Bibl. Syn. 31 (with photographs). Only a few articles are in the fields of exegesis or hermeneutics: 'Prov 31:21 in four Castilian Bibles' (M. J. de Azcárraga), '*Bwr'yk* (Qoh 12:1) reconsidered' (J. R. Busto Saiz), a discussion of the idiom in Ps. 119:99 (F. Díaz Esteban), 'Reflections of Hebrew Parallelism in the *Vetus Latina*' (J. Trebolle Barrera), 'Hermeneutics of the Tannaim: exegesis introduced by *lmmh n'mr*' (M. Pérez Fernandez) and 'Reflections on the methods of Moshe ibn 'Ezra' (M. Abumalham). The whole volume is beautifully produced, with a number of facsimiles, though there are misprints, especially in R. Loewe's contribution 'A trilingual diatribe against Pilate'.

R. P. R. Murray

Dröge, G.: *Gianozzo Manetti als Denker und Hebraist* (Judentum und Umwelt 20). 1987. Pp. x, 234. (Lang, Frankfurt am Main, Bern, New York. Price : Sw.Fr. 52.00. ISBN 3 8204 9127 9)

Manetti (1396–1459) is one of the principal figures associated with the beginnings of the revival of Hebrew learning among Christians. This book, an abbreviated version of a dissertation submitted at Bonn in 1983, gives a general account of his thought and work, but focuses particularly on his Hebrew study and his attitudes to Judaism. Readers of this *Book List* will be most interested in the discussion of Manetti's Latin translation of the Psalter, of which some specimens are given, together with other versions for purposes of comparison, in an appendix. The standard of the work is competent, if superficial in places. As a book, however, this is not a satisfactory production. It is directly reproduced from a typescript of variable quality, showing no signs of editing, not justified, and with cramped margins. The notes are added at the end, numbered by chapter but with no running heads; there is a bibliography but no index. It is surprising that authors continue to entrust their work to publishers who apparently take so little interest in their books, when better alternatives are available.

N. R. M. de Lange

Emerton, J. A. (ed.): *Congress Volume. Jerusalem 1986* (Supplements to *Vetus Testamentum* XL). 1988. Pp. vii, 303. (Brill, Leiden. Price: fl. 120.00 (ca. $60.00); sub. price: fl. 104.00 (ca. $52.00). ISBN 90 04 08499 1; ISSN 0083 5889)

This volume contains most of the papers read at the first of the three-yearly congresses of the International Organization for the Study of the Old Testament to be held outside the continent of Europe. It opens with the presidential address by Benjamin Mazar, on 'Jerusalem: from Isaiah to Jeremiah'; and closes with articles on recent developments in Old Testament studies: L. Alonso Schökel on 'Trends: plurality of methods, priority of issues'; C. H. Gordon on 'Ebla as background for the Old Testament'; and R. Rendtorff, 'Between historical criticism and holistic interpretation: new trends in Old Testament exegesis'.

The other contributors and their papers are: N. Avigad, 'Hebrew seals and sealings and their significance for biblical research'; F. M. Cross, 'A report on the Samaria papyri'; F. Crüsemann, 'Das Bundesbuch — historische Ort und institutioneller Hintergrund'; M. H. Goshen-Gottstein, 'The Hebrew Bible in the light of the Qumran Scrolls and the Hebrew University

Bible'; W. W. Hallo, 'Texts, statues and the cult of the divine king'; R. Hanhart, 'Die Bedeutung der Septuaginta für die Definition des "hellenistischen Judentums"'; M. Haran, 'On the diffusion of literacy and schools in ancient Israel'; T. Ishida, 'Royal succession in the kingdoms of Israel and Judah with special reference to the people under arms as a determining factor in the struggles for the throne'; K. A. Kitchen, 'Egypt and Israel during the first millennium B.C.'; W. G. Lambert, 'Old Testament mythology in its ancient Near Eastern context'; B. Lang, 'Life after death in the prophetic promise'; E. Lipiński, 'Royal and state scribes in ancient Jerusalem'; A. Malamat, 'Pre-monarchical social institutions in Israel in the light of Mari'; M. Ottosson, 'Eden and the land of promise'; E. Puech, 'Les écoles dans l'Israël préexilique: données épigraphiques'; H. Ringgren, 'Israelite prophecy: fact or fiction?'; J. J. M. Roberts, 'Does God lie? Divine deceit as a theological problem in Israelite prophetic literature'; L. E. Stager, 'Archaeology, ecology, and social history: background themes to the Song of Deborah'; H. Stegemann, 'The Origins of the Temple Scroll'; B. Uffenheimer, 'Prophecy, ecstasy, and sympathy'; and M. Weinfeld, 'The pattern of the Israelite settlement in Canaan'.

This is a finely presented record of a memorable occasion; but also a useful introduction to a wide range of topics.

A. G. AULD

ESLINGER, L. M. and TAYLOR, G. (eds): *Ascribe to the Lord: Biblical and other studies in memory of Peter C. Craigie* (JSOT Supplement Series 67). 1988. Pp. xv, 633. (Sheffield Academic Press. Price: £30.00 ($50.00). ISBN 1 85075 189 7; ISSN 0309 0787)

Peter Craigie's untimely death in 1985 at the age of forty-seven was a severe loss to Old Testament scholarship. In this memorial volume, thirty-seven of his friends and colleagues have combined to produce a handsome tribute to him both as a scholar and a man. Their contributions fall into three sections. The first is devoted to Ancient Near Eastern Studies. J.-L. Cunchillos, writing in French, gives a translation of, and commentary on, *KTU* 2.16, R. K. Harrison re-assesses Philistine origins, K. A. Kitchen discusses 'Bedspreads and Hibernation from Rio de Janeiro to the Middle Euphrates', T. Kleven considers Ugaritic kingship, D. Pardee the divine name Milkashtart and an article in French by G. Saade surveys the intellectual life of Ugarit.

The second part is concerned with Ugarit and the Bible, an area with which Craigie has a special concern. It comprises a discussion of *mizzĕbul lô* in Ps. 49:15 by P. Bordreuil (in French), J. C. de Moor on 'O death, where is thy sting?', M. Dietrich and O. Loretz on *ʿm/lpny* in Ps. 72:5 (in German), H. H. P. Dressler on Prov. 26:23, C. H. Gordon on 'Ugaritic *RBT/RABĪTU*', J. G. Taylor on *KTU* I.161 and parallels, and W. G. E. Watson on 'Some Additional Wordpairs'.

The third and longest section is 'Biblical and Theological Studies'. Several deal with various psalms: A. Caquot ('Cinq observations sur le Psaume 45'), R. C. Culley ('Psalm 88 Among the Complaints'), C. M. Foley ('A Literary Analysis of Psalm 23') and F. Renfrae ('Persiflage in Psalm 137'). R. W. E. Forrest writes on the Prologue to Job and J. C. L. Gibson on evil in that book. Two contributions are concerned with Genesis, E. Combs 'Has Yhwh cursed the ground?' and M. P. Deroche, 'The *rûaḥ ʾĕlōhîm* in Gen. I:2c.', and three with passages in I Samuel, L. Eslinger on I Sam. 16, S. Walters on the same chapter and R. Polzin on I Sam. 11:1–15. G. Auld writes on 'Word of God and Word of Man: Prophets and Canon' and P. E. Dion on the first Servant Song and Appointment Ceremonies. A number of essays deal with aspects of Israelite history and archaeology: W. E. Aufrecht ('Genealogy and History in Ancient Israel'), J. Gray ('Israel in the Song of Deborah'),

T. R. Hobbs ('An Experiment in Militarism'), A. R. Millard ('King Og's Bed') and J. G. Taylor ('The Two Earliest Known Representations of Yahweh'). More general articles, raising hermeneutical issues, are J. Rogerson ('Can a Doctrine of Providence be based on the Old Testament?') and J. Sandys-Wunsch ('A Tale of Two Cities: A Hermeneutical Story with a moral for those born since 1802'). The appendix contains H. G. Coward's academic biography of Craigie and N. Wagner's moving address given at his memorial service. The book concludes with the bibliography of Craigie and indices of authors and textual citations.

J. R. PORTER

FERGUSON, S. B. and WRIGHT, D. F. (eds.): *New Dictionary of Theology*. 1988. Pp. xix, 738. (IVP, Nottingham. Price: £18.95. ISBN 0 85110 636 6)

Very few entries will be of interest to Old Testament scholars. Apart from 'Old Testament Theology' (W. C. Kaiser), most references to the Old Testament are found within articles on general theological issues such as 'Apocalyptic' (R. J. Bauckham), 'Biblical Criticism' (F. F. Bruce), 'Biblical Theology' (D. L. Baker), 'Infallibility and Inerrancy of the Bible' and 'Scripture' (J. I. Packer), 'Hermeneutics' (A. C. Thiselton), 'Myth' (I. H. Marshall), and 'Prophecy, Theology of' (E. E. Ellis), not all of which are as rigidly conservative as that on 'Adam' in which R. B. Gaffin Jr. asserts that 'the biblical understanding of creation, of man, of the person and work of Christ, and of salvation is rooted in the historicity of Adam' (contrast 'Creation' by O. R. Barclay).

C. S. RODD

FLORES D'ARCAIS, F. (ed.): *Noè, il diluvio universale e la preistoria dell'alleanza. Atti del Seminario invernale (Paestum, 22–25 gennaio 1987)*. 1987. Pp. 243. (BIBLIA: Associazione laica di cultura biblical, Settimello (FI)

The seminar at which these papers were read brought together 'professionals' and amateurs, coordinated by the journalist F. Flores d'Arcais, who opens with 'The navigator of the Flood: the human theology of Mario Brelich', discussing that writer's reflections on the story. A. Fanuli follows with two pieces, 'Genealogies and history from Adam to Abraham' and 'The Noah cycle: sources and exegesis'. The lay writer G. Limentani contributes 'Jewish interpretations of the Flood cycle', an attractive display of some of the delights of midrash (which she rightly views as an ongoing game essentially involving humour), free from all constraint of scholarly documentation or dating. A. di Nola rapidly sketches 'The mythology of the Flood' in its various forms all over the world. The Waldensian pastor E. Campi surveys 'Christian interpretations of the Flood cycle', summarizing patristic interpretation and then concentrating on Luther's exposition of the theme. V. Marcozzi in 'The Origin of peoples' briefly sums up current paleontological opinion, and F. R. de Gasperis closes with 'Lettura attualizzata del ciclo del diluvio', an attempt at a reading which will 'get across' today; it is interesting to compare this modern Christian reading with those by the lay participants, who may perhaps be better skilled in *attualizzazione*.

R. P. R. MURRAY

FRERICHS, E. S. (ed.): *The Bible and Bibles in America* (The Bible in American Culture). 1988. Pp. ix, 224. (Scholars Press, Atlanta, Georgia. Price: $18.95 (member price: $12.95). ISBN 1 55540 096 5)

The editors' introduction and eight essays in this impressive volume give an informative survey of the translation, dissemination, and use of the Bible in America and of the problems involved in the work of translation. John

Alden's 'The Bible as Printed Word' describes the part played by the Bible in the great migration to the west. Keith Crim writes on Bible translation by committees and Harold Scanlin on the formidable number of translations by American individuals from 1808 till 1984. J. D. and N. M. Šarna contribute an illuminating account of Jewish Bible scholarship and translations in the United States; and G. P. Fogarty writes on Roman Catholic translations since 1790. Three contributions deal with publications which diverge from the main traditions: F. F. Church on Thomas Jefferson's Bible, *The Life and Morals of Jesus of Nazareth*; K. P. Jackson on 'The Sacred Literature of the Latter Day Saints'; and R. Peel on Mary Baker Eddy's *Science and Health with Key to the Scriptures*. The value of this admirable volume is enhanced by the ample bibliographies and documentation provided.

G. W. Anderson

Giltner, J. H.: *Moses Stuart: The Father of Biblical Science in America* (SBL Centennial Publications: Biblical Scholarship in North America, 14). 1988. Pp. viii, 158. (Scholars Press, Atlanta, Georgia. Price: $19.95 (member price: $14.95); ISBN 1 55540 104 X. Paperback price : $14.95 (member price: $9.95); ISBN 1 55540 105 8)

This book deserves attention as a detailed historical account of the impact of European biblical criticism in America in the early nineteenth century. Richard Simon and Jean Astruc in France and Robert Lowth in England had already given warning of what was to come; but it was the German scholar Eichhorn who attracted the attention of the orthodox Calvinist Moses Stuart, professor in Andover, protagonist in the conflict with the liberal views of the Unitarians. Stuart, orthodox though he was, felt compelled to recognize the cogency of many of Eichhorn's critical views, and in his teaching and innumerable commentaries we can trace the development of biblical science in the USA. This preceded the similar movements in England and Scotland. Stuart was also a pioneer in America in the study and teaching of the biblical languages, in which he was largely self-taught; and in his recognition of the indispensability of a knowledge of German for biblical study. It is curious that he failed to realize the importance of Old Testament books like Amos, Hosea, and Jonah. It took him some time to come to terms with Hebrew vocalization and the debate about the point system. The author is pardonably naive in his references to Stuart's speed in 'mastering' difficult languages. Stuart is important for enabling many of his students eventually to proceed beyond himself in assimilating the new critical and linguistic knowledge.

N. W. Porteous

Graham, W. A.: *Beyond the Written Word: Oral Aspects of Scripture in the History of Religion*. 1987. Pp. xiv, 306. (Cambridge University Press, Cambridge and New York. Price: £25.00; $32.50. ISBN 0 521 33176 5)

William A. Graham is Professor of the History of Religion and of Islamic Studies at Harvard University. In this book he looks at the ways holy writ has functioned among Jewish, Christian, and Muslim communities, with a chapter on Hindu scriptures. His focus is on the fundamental orality of scripture and so is somewhat disjunctive with our contemporary society where the printed word bombards us on every side. It is therefore an important book on this central aspect of scripture which is often forgotten, ignored or poorly treated in the productions of the biblical scholarship guild.

To study the oral dimension of scripture (and thereby play down the usual excessive emphasis on the documentary text) is to undertake a consideration of the dynamic and personal aspect of scripture in relation to those communities which possess and process sacred writings. In four short parts — it is quite a short book (perhaps 150 pages of text plus introduction and conclusion, lengthy notes and a 40-page bibliography) — Graham examines written and spoken words in relation to literacy in the premodern West, written and spoken scripture in Jewish, Christian, Muslim, and Hindu perspectives, the Qur'ān as a spoken book, and the Bible as a spoken book (with particular emphasis on the rhetoric of Martin Luther). There is here a wealth of detail and observation, as well as technical discussion, which must make this a welcome book for biblical scholarship. It will help to overcome the dichotomization between oral-written in favour of an approach to scripture as the interpenetration of the written and spoken word. An interactionist account is required which will give due weight to the holding communities which use scripture for their own purpose, though the oral-written distinction does allow for a dialectical account of the tensions between the written text and what communities have made of it. Graham's book reminds us that the dominance of oral/aural interaction with sacred texts has been the rule rather than the exception for the majority of communities throughout history. As a contribution to the study of what Graham calls 'the persistent presence, the peculiar staying power, of scripture in verbal, and especially oral, discourse' (p. 171) this is a fine book which should stimulate the further study of an immense subject often overlooked in our obsessive study of a written text.

R. P. Carroll

Greenspoon, L.: *Max Leopold Margolis: A Scholar's Scholar* (Society of Biblical Literature Centennial Publications). 1987. Pp. xi, 190. (Scholars Press, Atlanta, Georgia. Price: $19.95 (member price: $15.95). ISBN 1 55540 146 5. Paperback price: $15.95 (member price: $12.95). ISBN 1 55540 147 3)

Although much information on Margolis is to be found in a volume of essays entitled *Max Leopold Margolis: Scholar and Teacher*, which appeared in 1952, twenty years after Margolis's death, the present academic biography will be welcomed by all admirers of Margolis's scholarship. The first two chapters are biographical, while the remaining three assess Margolis's work in three main areas, biblical translation, textual criticism (notably his work on the LXX), and exegesis and theology. As an appendix, Reider's bibliography of Margolis's works has usefully been reproduced from the volume of 1952. It is good to learn that Margolis's unpublished work on Masius and the last fascicle of his edition of LXX Joshua, both presumed lost, have now been located, and are to be published — a testimony to their lasting value. The interest of the book is enhanced by the fact that the author has also worked on LXX Joshua (see *B. L.*, 1985, p. 45).

S. P. Brock

Hartman, L. (ed.): *Svensk exegetisk årsbok*, 53 (1988). Pp. 149. Uppsala, 1988. (Wallin & Dahlholm Boktryckeri, Lund. ISBN 91 40 05115 3)

This issue begins with three short Old Testament studies: H. Gossai (in English) on '*Ṣaddîq* in Theological and Economic Perspectives'; A. Laato on the place and significance in Ecclesiastes of Solomon; and a study of Dan. 5:5ff. by A. Wiig, who argues that the reason why the wise men could not understand or even read the inscription was that it consisted not of words but of symbols for weights with which Daniel was familiar. B. Gerhardsson presents a comparative study of the narrative parables in the Gospels with their Old Testament counterparts (Jdg. 9:9–15 (7–21); 2 Sam. 12:1–4 (1–15); 2 Kings 14:9 (8–14); Isa. 5:1–6 (1–15); Ezek. 17:3–10 (1–24)), emphasizing important differences. In a study of Mark 11:15–19, J. Neusner offers a new interpretation of the overturning of the moneychangers' tables. Under the title 'Marginalia sino-theologica' C. Harbsemeier discusses (in English) some of the problems encountered in translating Christian terms and texts into Chinese. The work of A. Fridrichsen (the centenary of whose birth fell in 1988) in the Theological Faculty at Uppsala is described in an illuminating article by E. Beijer, who also indicates something of the impact which Fridrichsen had on Church life. H. Riesenfeld contributes a brief memoir of B. Reicke, who was one of Fridrichsen's most distinguished disciples. Except where otherwise indicated, the articles are in Swedish. There are thirty-eight pages of reviews.

G. W. Anderson

JEPPESEN, K. and LEMCHE, N. P. (eds): *Scandinavian Journal of the Old Testament*, Vols 1, 2. 1988. Pp. vii, 203. (Aarhus University Press. ISBN 87 7288 085 6; 87 7288 086 4; ISSN 0901 8328)

The first editor's rule that the *Book List* reviews annuals but not periodicals is not lightly breached; but the contents of the fourth number of *SJOT* require that our welcome to a newcomer be extended for a second year. The earlier of the numbers being noted contains five articles: M. R. Hauge considers 'Some Aspects of the Motif "The City facing Death" of Ps. 68,21'; in 'The Covenant as Agreement', A. S. Kapelrud argues that *berîth* in the Israelite-Canaanite world was what we call a non-aggression pact; N. P. Lemche contributes the second part of his treatment of 'Rachel and Lea' begun in 2,1987; D. V. Edelman writes on 'The Authenticity of 2 Sam. 1:26 in the Lament over Saul and Jonathan'; and S. Norin develops an element of his 1986 monograph *(B. L.* 1987, p. 124) in 'Die Wiedergabe JHWH-haltiger Personennamen in der Septuaginta'. With the exception of an important study at the end by S. Olofsson on 'The Translation of Jer. 2:18 in the Septuagint. Methodological, Linguistical and Theological Aspects', the second number (pp. 1–168) is devoted to a series of essays edited by H. M. Barstad and M. Ottosson on 'The Life and Work of Sigmund Mowinckel'. J. B. Hygen writes on the man and the teacher; N. A. Dahl on the Historian of religion and theologian; M. Sæbø on Mowinckel's relation to the literary critical school and H. Ringgren on his relation to the Uppsala school of Old Testament study; K. Jeppesen reviews his conception of the Day of Yahweh; M. R. Hauge writes on Mowinckel and the Psalms, with 'A Query into his Concern'; A. S. Kapelrud discusses his study of the prophets; and H. M. Barstad considers 'Some Aspects of Sigmund Mowinckel as historian'. Most of these papers had been read in 1984, the centenary of his birth, either at the Mowinckel session during the SBL meeting in Strasbourg or at the Mowinckel symposium in Oslo. They are completed by a comprehensive and annotated bibliography of Mowinckel prepared by D. Kvale and D. Rian. The whole volume will prove a vital basis for further evaluation of a great scholarly contribution.

A. G. Auld

JERVELL, J. and KAPELRUD, A. S.: *Studia Theologica: Scandinavian Journal of Theology*. Vol. 41, no. 2. 1987. Pp. 85–156. Vol. 42, no. 1. 1988. Pp. 1–68. (Norwegian University Press, Oslo. Price: $30.00; N.Kr. 180.00 (per vol.); $33.00; N.Kr. 200.00 (per vol.). ISSN 0039 338 X)

These two issues contain only one Old Testament discussion: James Barr, 'Mowinckel, the Old Testament, and the Question of Natural Theology'. (Vol. 42, pp. 21–38), being the text of the second Mowinckel Lecture, delivered in Oslo on 27 November 1987. It contains a careful exposition of natural theology as an essential element in biblical theological discussion, and thus provides a useful critique of some contemporary (and particularly Barthian) discussions. Other essays have marginal importance for the Old

Testament. They are C. Olson on Eliade and van der Leeuw, H. W. Boers on Pauline thought, and A. Hassing on the church in occupied Norway (all in Vol. 42, no. 1); K. Alfsvåg on Luther and S. Pedersen on Jesus (in Vol. 41, no. 2).

P. R. ACKROYD

KATUNARICH, S. M.: *Breve storia dell'ebraismo e dei suoi rapporti on la cristianità*. 1987. Pp. 300. (PIEMME, Casale Monferrato. Price: Lire 25,000. ISBN 88 384 1199 9)

A breathless and inevitably superficial romp through two and a half millennia of Jewish history, from the Babylonian Exile (when the characteristic features of contemporary Judaism were allegedly fixed) to the present day. The author is a Jesuit who has founded a 'Christian-Jewish ecumenical group' in Milan, and this book, based on lectures he has given, is addressed primarily to Italian catholics. Hence (presumably) an emphasis on Italy (refreshing in the light it casts on the Jewish experience in Europe) and on catholicism; both Byzantine and reformed Christianity are mentioned only in passing, and with a somewhat negative focus. It would be easy to point to shortcomings in the presentation and in the scholarship; what is impressive is the author's sincerity and enthusiasm, and his commitment to improving the image of Judaism among Christians. The final chapter, on Christian-Jewish dialogue, which is the longest in the book and the only one to be equipped with an apparatus of footnotes, is a serious and interesting contribution to the subject.

N. R. M. DE LANGE

Kirisutokyo Gaku (Christian Studies). New Series, 26–29 (Japanese). 1984–87. Pp. 206, 160, 121, 159. (The Association of Christian Studies, St Paul's (Rikkyo) University, Tokyo. ISSN 0387 6810)

In no. 26, K. Okawa discusses 'The Bible in the Interpretations of Recent Oxford Scholars' (W. Abraham, J. Barr, and J. Muddiman). In no. 28, S. Kobayashi reconsiders the fifth vision of Amos (9:1–4, 5–6). In no. 29, K. Kida, in 'What is a Prophet?', considers recent views of prophecy in the light of the political and cultural circumstances of the ancient Near East in various periods in the history of Israel, and S. Kobayashi postulates a literary connection between Amos and Jeremiah with special reference to Amos 1:14–15 and Jer. 49:2–3.

R. N. WHYBRAY

KOHLENBERGER, J. R. III: *The NIV Interlinear Hebrew-English Old Testament. Four Volumes in One: Genesis-Malachi* (Regency Reference Library). 1987. Pp. xxxvi, 586, 512, 601, 591. (Zondervan, Grand Rapids, MI; distributed by Hodder & Stoughton, London, Price: £49.00. ISBN 0 310 44220 6; 0 340 42588 1)

As the subtitle makes clear, this now rather bulky volume combines the four volumes given a welcome, at the same time warm and cautious, in *B. L.* 1982, p. 36; 1983, p. 42; and 1987, p. 38. It is necessarily a very expensive tool for students; but it ought to be available in the libraries to which they have regular recourse.

A. G. AULD

Der Königsweg: 9000 Jahre Kunst und Kultur in Jordanien und Palästina. 1987. Pp. 372, with 144 colour and 345 black and white illustrations. (Von Zabern, Mainz. Price: DM 59.80. ISBN 3 8053 0960 0)

An earlier and very similar French version of this finely illustrated and presented catalogue was reviewed in *B. L.* 1988, p. 35. The exhibition it introduces moved from Paris to three locations in Germany and Austria. This translated volume includes an essay on German research in Jordan in the nineteenth and twentieth centuries by Dr Ute Wagner-Lux, one-time director first of the Jerusalem, then of the Amman German Institute.

A. G. AULD

KÜCHLER, M. and UEHLINGER, CH.: *Jerusalem: Texte — Bilder — Steine* (Novum Testamentum et Orbis Antiquus 6). 1988. Pp. 233. (Universitätsverlag, Freiburg (CH); Vandenhoeck & Ruprecht, Göttingen. Price: Sw.Fr. 58.00; DM 84.00. ISBN 3 7278 0552 8; 3 525 53905 3)

This is no usual official Festschrift, but is offered by friends in the Fribourg University Biblical Institute to celebrate the joint attainment of a century by a Professor Othmar Keel and his wife Hildi. Most of the six contributions reflect his influence in the interplay of iconography and exegesis. The first section focuses on the topography of Jerusalem — indeed, mainly on the Mount of Olives. M. Küchler, on the tradition of Jesus's footprints, argues that the Lukan account of the ascension is coloured by the Mount's associations as a cult place (cf. 2 Sam 15:32) where, fittingly, both Ezekiel saw the divine chariot-throne rest (11:23) and Zechariah located his version of judgement (14:4–5); all this was understood by Eusebius (Dem. Ev. 6,18). Three scholars have collaborated in the *editio princeps* of a tenth-century Judaeo-Arabic fragment from the Cambridge Genizah collection. This is part of a Jewish pilgrims' guide to Jerusalem, which (among much else of interest) relates the steps up the Mount of Olives to the old solar calendar. The text seems to be from before the crusades. Next comes the publication, by F. G. Nuvolone, of a sixteenth-century fresco of the Mount of Olives in a church in Lugano, which is reproduced in colour and discussed.

The second section, 'Old Testament and ancient eastern iconography', contains the major contribution to exegesis in this volume: a study by C. Uehlinger on Ezekiel's significant and dramatic actions in Ezek 4: first the sketch or model of the besieged city and then the representations of the fate of those caught within it. Iconographical material is skilfully used to argue that the sketch was more probably in elevation than in plan, or was perhaps a model, while for the nature of the whole action B. Lang's category of political 'street theatre' is preferred to other explanations. Next Ms S. Schroer studies the female figures found in Palestine and Cyprus which are either associated with, or even represented as, a tree or branch. Relevant biblical passages are briefly referred to, and it is suggested that such a concept may underlie the theme of Wisdom as 'tree of life' in Prov 3:18 and even still in Sir 14:26–15:3 and 24:19–21. The final paper in the volume, by A. Laufer, identifies three sarcophagus-like objects in the Fribourg Biblical Institute as Syrian Christian reliquaries.

R. P. R. MURRAY

LANG, B. (ed.): *Internationale Zeitschriftenschau für Bibelwissenschaft und Grenzgebiete*, Bd XXXIV 1986/87. 1988. Pp. xiv, 488. (Patmos, Düsseldorf. Price: DM 158.00. ISSN 0074 9745)

Bernhard Lang with some three dozen colleagues, of whom a third are from outside the German-speaking countries, have assembled 3056 entries reporting on articles and reviews from over 450 periodicals, and also on many books. The entries are grouped in helpful categories; and the editor and his associates are to be congratulated over the speed with which they make available each year such wide coverage of biblical and related studies.

A. G. AULD

McCreesh, T. P. (ed.): *Old Testament Abstracts*. Vol. 10, nos. 2–3 (June, October, 1987); Vol. 11, nos. 1–2 (February, June, 1988). Pp. 99–206, 207–343; 1–96, 97–210. (The Catholic University of America, Washington D.C. Price: $14.00 per volume. ISSN 0364 8591)

Under its new editor this valuable bibliographical tool continues to provide both abstracts of articles in a wide range of periodicals that are relevant to Old Testament study and reviews of a number of books.

M. A. Knibb

Männchen, J.: *Gustaf Dalmans Leben und Wirken in der Brüdergemeine, für die Judenmission und an der Universität Leipzig 1855–1902* (Abhandlungen des Deutschen Palästinavereins). 1987. Pp. vii, 158 with frontispiece. (Harrassowitz, Wiesbaden. Price: DM 68.00. ISBN 3 447 02750 9; ISSN 0173 1904)

Gustav Dalman is justly renowned for his reference works on the Aramaic language and his comprehensive accounts of Palestinian village life at the beginning of this century. It is not so well known that he was also the first director of the German Archaeological Institute in Jerusalem where Albrecht Alt and Martin Noth later achieved so much. Even before he went to Jerusalem in 1902 Dalman had distinguished himself as a scholar, and it is this fascinating and formative part of his life that is described in detail for the first time here — his upbringing and early career among the *Brüdergemeine* communities, from whom he broke away in 1887–88, his direction of the *Institutum Judaicum* at Leipzig in succession to his mentor Franz Delitzsch, and his many-sided teaching in the university there. The biographical narrative is followed by an assessment of his early academic work and his involvement in missionary work among the Jews. It is a worthy memorial to a great scholar.

G. I. Davies

Mayes, A. D. H. (ed.): *Proceedings of the Irish Biblical Association*. Vol. 11. 1988. Pp. v, 96. (Irish Biblical Association Publications, Dublin. Price: IR£7.00 ($7.00) plus 80p (80c) postage)

This issue has six contributions: a valuable piece by S. Giversen on 'The Manichaean Papyri of the Chester Beattie Library'; F. Ó Fearghail on 'Israel in Luke-Acts'; A. D. H. Mayes on the sociology of ancient Israel: 'Idealism and Materialism in Weber and Gottwald'; J. Murphy O'Connor on 'Pneumatikoi in 2 Corinthians'; and two pieces by M. McNamara: 'Midrash, Culture Medium and Development of Doctrine. Some Facts in Quest of a Terminology'; and 'Hiberno-Latin Bulletin', an account of the progress to date on the project to publish in the Corpus Christianorum series Hiberno-Latin material dealing with the Bible, the great part of which lies 'unedited in different libraries'.

M. Barker

Muraoka, T. (ed.): *Abr-Nahrain* xxvi (1988). 1988. Pp. vii, 129 and 7pp. of plates. (Brill, Leiden. ISBN 90 04 08887 3)

This issue contains five articles and a number of book reviews. J. Bowman continues his interesting series on Old Testament figures in the New Testament background (see his contributions to volumes xxiii and xxv of this journal on Solomon and Jonah) with 'Elijah and the Pauline Jesus Christ' (pp. 1–18). He raises the question of the influence of popular thought and *midraš* about Elijah as angelic messenger, mediator, and assistant in the resurrection of the dead upon Paul's heavenly Christ. Bowman produces a mass of detail. The article would have benefited from better editing. G. W.

Clarke writes about some short Greek texts: 'Funerary Inscriptions near Joussef Pasha, North Syria' (pp. 19–29). These date to the fourth/fifth centuries A.D. and contain Semitic names (e.g. *ouabaious*, *baroiarou*). B. E. Colless, 'Recent Discoveries Illuminating the Origin of the Alphabet' (pp. 30–67), presents the case for the view that the Proto-Sinaitic/Proto-Canaanite alphabet had only 23 letters originally. In fact this is hard to prove, though it may be that *some* texts *were* written in a short alphabet (as were some cuneiform alphabetic texts). J. Mansour presents in 'Texts in the Judaeo-Arabic Dilect of Baghdad' (pp. 68–79) some short accounts of marriage and family customs and two anecdotes in transcription and translation. The informants were residents of Israel and both had been over twenty years in Israel when the texts were produced. No linguistic conclusions are drawn. Finally T. Muraoka and Z. Shavitsky complete in 'Abraham Ibn Ezra's Biblical Hebrew Lexicon. The Five Megilloth: II' (pp. 80–111) a work begun in *Abr-Nahrain* xxv (1987), pp. 68–91. Of the book reviews note J. Blau on A. Murtonen's *Hebrew in its West Semitic Setting* (pp. 122–26).

J. F. HEALEY

NORTH, R. (ed.): *Elenchus of Biblical Bibliography*, 1: *Elenchus of Biblica 1985*. 1988. Pp. 1048. (Biblical Institute Press, Rome. ISBN 88 7653 568 3)

The *Elenchus* has a new title, with fresh volume number to match (and an ISBN in place of an ISSN). But essentially the structure of this massive bibliographic contribution is unchanged, with its separate sections for the studies produced in 1985 on everything from beatitudes to population statistics and from numismatics to god-talk. Readers unfamiliar with its predecessor may be surprised at the wide range of its concerns — from Indian Buddhism, through feminist theology, to Qabbala. Many readers are grateful for its compendious cross-referencing, and will look forward to the realisation of the editorial hopes expressed in the final volume of the previous series about earlier on-line computerized access to similarly prepared material.

A. G. AULD

PATRICK, G. A.: *F. J. A. Hort: Eminent Victorian* (Historic Texts and Interpreters in Biblical Scholarship). 1988. Pp. 127. (Almond, Sheffield. Price: £21.50 ($36.50). ISBN 1 85075 098 X; 1 85075 197 1 (pbk))

A useful biography of an elusive subject which is marred by a repetitious style and by an evaluation of Hort's text-critical work which suffers from a lack of adequate historical perspective (e.g. Griesbach, Lachmann, and Tischendorf go unmentioned, while E. C. Colwell's classic essay 'Hort Redivivus: A Plea and a Program' is not picked up).

D. G. DEBOYS

SUCUPIRA, L. (ed.): *Revista Bíblica Brasileira*. Ano, 4, 3–4; 5. 1–4. 1987; 1988. Pp. 81–184; 1–200. (Nova Jerusalém, Fortaleza CE. Brazil. Price: $20.00 p.a.)

In the two concluding issues of Year 4, P. Minette de Tillesse continues with his introduction to the Old Testament. 4, 3 contains a lively account of the development of Pentateuchal studies from the eighteenth century onwards, and of the rise of Form and Redaction Criticism. 4, 4 deals with (1) M. Noth's thesis on the Deuteronomistic History, (2) the composition of Deuteronomy (including P. Minette de Tillesse's own contribution to the debate, cf. *VT* 12 (1962), 29–87) and (3) the sources — especially the annalistic ones — used by Dtr. Extensive book reviews underline the importance of sound method in the study of Old Testament texts, and reinforce the *RBB*'s pedagogical aims. Year 5 is devoted to New Testament topics (the

Synoptic Problem, Form Criticism and the Authorship of the Fourth Gospel), and contains further reviews of recent books on Old Testament topics. 5, 4 ends with indices for the year.

J. M. DINES

TALMON, SH.: *Gesellschaft und Literatur in der Hebräischen Bibel*. Gesammelte Aufsätze, Bd 1 (Information Judentum, Bd 8). 1988. Pp. 234. (Neukirchener, Neukirchen-Vluyn. Price: DM 62.00. ISBN 3 7887 0794 1; ISSN 0344 4767)

This is not a German translation of *King, Cult and Calendar in Ancient Israel* (*B. L.* 1987, p. 19) but an independent selection. The following articles are shared in common with *King, Cult and Calendar*: kingship and ideology in ancient Israel, Judges 18–21, the cult and calendar reform of Jeroboam I, the Judean *ʿam hā'āreṣ*, the emergence of Jewish sectarianism in the early Second Temple period, and types of messianic expectation at the turn of the common era. The German edition has the following articles which do *not* appear in *King, Cult and Calendar*: the biblical traditions regarding the early history of the Samaritans (Hebrew original), the calendar of Qumran (English original in *Scripta Hierosolymitana* 4), the development of prayer as an institution in Israel in the light of Qumran (English original in M. Delcor, ed., *Qumran — Sa piété, sa théologie et son milieu*). Several articles in the English collection are not found in this volume. In some cases the text of articles which have appeared in English has been slightly revised in the translation here.

L. L. GRABBE

TÖKEI, F.: *Acta Orientalia Academiae Scientiarum Hungaricae*. Tom. XLI, Fasc. 1. 1987. Pp. 172. (Akadémiai Kiadó, Budapest. HU ISSN 0001 6446)

There is one article relevant to Old Testament study : E. den Blaauwen discusses object suffixes in Biblical Hebrew.

J. A. EMERTON

ULLENDORFF, E.: *The Two Zions: Reminiscences of Jerusalem and Ethiopia*. 1988. Pp. x, 249. (Oxford University Press. Price: £19.50. ISBN 0 19 212275 4)

This beautifully-written book provides a fascinating account of the author's experiences as a student in the late thirties at the then recently-established Hebrew University of Jerusalem and of his wartime service in Eritrea and Ethiopia. The author also refers briefly to his period in Jerusalem immediately after the war and gives some impressions of many return visits to Ethiopia in the period up to 1974. The title of the book reflects the fact that in Ethiopian tradition Ethiopia is referred to as 'the Second Zion'. From one point of view this book is not directly relevant to the concerns of the *Book List*, but from another it is highly relevant. This derives both from the fact that the author provides valuable portraits of a number of scholars who are important for Old Testament, Jewish, and Semitic studies, including particularly Buber, Scholem, and Polotsky, and from the author's observations on many matters of scholarly concern, including the revival of Hebrew in the modern period.

M. A. KNIBB

La Vie de la Parole: De l'Ancien au Nouveau Testament (Etudes d'exégèse et d'herméneutique bibliques offertes à Pierre Grelot professeur à l'institut Catholique de Paris). 1987. Pp. xlv, 486. (Desclée, Paris. Price: Fr. 580.00. ISBN 2 7189 0329 5)

This volume in honour of Pierre Grelot is divided into four sections and contains thirty-six essays. *L'Ancien Orient et la Bible* has pieces by J. C.

Greenfield, E. Puech, B. Porten, A. Caquot, M. Delcor, R. le Déaut, D. Muñoz Leon, and J. Margain. *Études de Textes de l'Ancien Testament* has pieces by H. Cazelles, P. Beauchamp, G. Couturier, L. Neveu, P.-M. Bogaert, C. Wiéner, B. Renaud, P. Féghali. *Études de textes du Nouveau Testament* has pieces by J. Delorme, M. Gourges, M. Vellanickal, X. Léon-Defour, L. Legrand, C. Perrot, M. Trimaille, S. Légasse, R. Beauvery. *Théologie Biblique* has pieces by J. A. Díaz, D. Barthélemy, A. M. Dubarle, J. Guileet, P. Haudebert, E. Cothenet, A. Moreno, M. Carrez, M. Hubaut, J. Bernard, A. Paul.

M. Barker

Whitaker, R. E.: *The Eerdmans Analytical Concordance to the Revised Standard Version of the Bible*. 1988. Pp. xiv, 1548. (Eerdmans, Grand Rapids MI. Price: $49.95. ISBN 0 8028 2403 X)

This should prove to be a very useful volume to many readers, and at remarkably reasonable price. It provides finally for the Revised Standard Version what Young's *Analytical Concordance* has long offered for the Authorised Version of the Bible; and at first sight it is very similar. On closer scrutiny the format resembles more closely that of Hatch and Redpath's *Concordance to the Septuagint*, with all the terms in the original languages listed and numbered under each heading; and then a complete listing of the English word or phrase according to the order of books in the *Common Bible* (or *Revised Standard Version with Apocrypha*). At the end of each line of context is either a number corresponding to the original language word, or one of three signs showing that the word was supplied by the translator, or translated an idiom not easily shown in the concordance, or rendered a word from a language not included in the concordance. Names are listed separately at the end, as are numbers (at least fractions and numerals over twenty — numbers from one to twenty appear in the main concordance). And the volume concludes with Hebrew, Greek, and Latin indexes listing every original word or phrase and its RSV translation(s). Some of the entries in these indexes are very long, and handily supply the evidence which will facilitate appreciation and criticism of the translation itself. Compiler and publishers are to be warmly congratulated.

A. G. Auld

Wright, G. R. H.: *As on the First Day: Essays in Religious Constants*. 1987. Pp. viii, 174. (Brill, Leiden. Price: Fl. 64.00. ISBN 90 04 08172 0)

This volume contains twelve essays, ten of which are reprints of articles published between 1968 and 1985. A particular style of comparative religion is the common element in topics ranging from Simeon Stylites to 'The Upside Down Tree on the Vatican Hill'. Simeon's pillar is connected with phallic cult at Hierapolis, it being undeniable that pagan cults persisted in the area well into the Christian period. In another article a symbolic meaning of the Reed Sea (*yam sūf*) is identified. Again the impact of the Dumuzi and Inanna myths is found in the biblical account of David's court, while Joseph, originally a divine being, is tied in with Christ, Osiris, Dionysos, and the Omphalos at Shechem. The Book of Ruth is interpreted in the light of the Eleusis cult and the legends of Demeter and Persephone. Another paper treats of accounts of the birth of Christ in Christian and Islamic tradition (though the birth of Buddha is included too). Finally there are papers on death, on the dismemberment of Egyptian corpses at burial, and on parallels between African and Egyptian ideas about the dead.

J. F. Healey

2. ARCHAEOLOGY AND EPIGRAPHY

CURTIS, J. (ed.): *Bronze-working Centres of Western Asia c.1000–539 B.C.* 1988. Pp. 342 and 182 plates. (Kegan Paul in association with the British Museum, London and New York. Price: £30.00. ISBN 0 7103 0274 6)

The title of this collection of papers from a British Museum colloquium held in 1986 is self-explanatory. There are twenty-one papers by specialists over a wide geographical area from Iran and Oman to Phrygia. It deals with important general background to Old Testament studies, though it is inevitably those contributions directly concerned with Syria, Phoenicia, and Palestine/Jordan which are of most immediate interest in view of Old Testament information on the initial dependence of the Israelites on outsiders for some technical expertise in metallurgy. Syria and Phoenicia had important centres of metallurgical craftsmanship (contributions by I. J. Winter [pp. 193–225] and G. Falsone [pp. 227–50]). J. N. Tubb (pp. 251–70) gathers information on Palestine/Jordan, concluding that the Sea Peoples/Philistines dominated metallurgy of both bronze and iron in the area. T. C. Mitchell provides a most useful lexicographical study of 'The evidence of bronzeworking in the West Semitic texts' (pp. 271–84). Mitchell decides to take the biblical texts at their face value so far as dating is concerned. This is, perhaps, understandable, though it may be noted that even when a later author is accurately recording events long before his time he is unlikely to use any other technological vocabulary than that of his own day. There is thus no getting away from the fact that the Old Testament texts can only be relied on to tell us about technology at the time they were written. There is a plan to turn this colloquium into a series: this would be very welcome in view of the excellent start reflected in the present volume.

J. F. HEALEY

DEVER, W. G. (editor and principal author), with the assistance of LANCE, H. D. and several contributors: *Gezer IV: The 1969–71 Seasons in Field VI, the "Acropolis"*. Part 1, Text; Part 2, Plates, Plans (Annual of the Nelson Glueck School of Biblical Archaeology). 1986. Pp. x, 1–275; iii, 277, plus 62 plates of drawings with facing descriptions and 58 photographic plates and a pocket of 25 separately folded plans. (Nelson Glueck School of Biblical Archaeology, Jerusalem. ISBN 0 87820 304 4)

More than twelve years after the appearance of *Gezer II* (cf. *B. L.* 1976, p. 22), it seems that the publication of this important excavation (1964–74) is at last being resumed in earnest (volume III is said to be in the press; volume V was scheduled for 1986 and volume VI for 1988; and two further volumes are projected, thus revising the original publication plans). The present volumes provide a final report on Field VI, an area selected to provide a major exposure of domestic areas in one of the few parts of the mound left available for such an operation. 12 strata (by no means equally represented) from MB IIA to the Hellenistic period are each described in three main sections: general discussion of stratigraphy and architecture, pottery and objects, and summary, which includes some correlation with other areas of the site and occasional historical observations. It is stressed, however, that major interpretation is being held over for a final volume in the series, when the results from all fields can be co-ordinated. Appendix A, 'locus indices', then fills nearly half the text volume, and it is followed by further brief appendices on scarabs (B. Brandl), flint caches (S. A. Rosen), and a neutron activation analysis of selected pottery (M. J. Hughes and R. J. Smith). In the accompanying 'Plates and Plans' volume, in addition to the usual plates of pottery, small finds, and photographs, there are twenty-five detached plans and section drawings which can be taken from their pouch for ease of consultation in association with the text. The whole is a model of clarity and presentation (though not of proof-reading). Of particular interest to readers of the *Book List* will be the light shed by strata 7–5 on the arrival and material culture of the Philistines (there are two well preserved 'four-room' houses from the twelfth-eleventh centuries B.C.), but later periods are more poorly represented.

H. G. M. WILLIAMSON

DRINKARD, J. F., jr, MATTINGLY, G. L., and MILLER, J. M. (eds): *Benchmarks in Time and Culture: An Introduction to Palestinian Archaeology Dedicated to Joseph A. Callaway* (Archaeology and Biblical Studies 1). 1988. Pp. 487. (Scholars Press, Atlanta, Georgia. Price: $44.95 (member price: $29.95). ISBN 1 55540 172 4. Paperback price: $29.95 (member price: $19.95). ISBN 1 55540 173 2).

After an introductory essay, 'Antecedents to modern archaeology', by J. M. Miller, Part I contains five excellent surveys of the contribution of American (P. J. King), British (G. I. Davies), French (P. Benoit), German (M. and H. Weippert), and Israeli (A. Mazar) archaeologists to Palestinian archaeology. Part II describes modern archaeological techniques, including the newer techniques of palynology (A. Horowitz), remote sensing (T. L. Sever), and the use of computers (J. F. Strange). Part III synthesizes, with articles on the 'new archaeology' (W. G. Dever), historical geography (A. F. Rainey), socio-cultural anthropology (Ø. S. LaBianca), settlement patterns of Early Bronze Moab (G. Mattingly), epigraphy as a dating method (J. F. Drinkard: Drinkard uses his analysis to support Aharoni's dating of the Arad inscriptions from Strata VIII, VII, VI), and the future of 'biblical archaeology' (J. K. Eakins) (which 'can and should be regarded as a branch of archaeology. After all, in the name "biblical archaeology", it is the word "biblical" which functions as the adjective and it is the word "archaeology" which stands as the noun' (p. 444). On the whole, however, this book is descriptive rather than argumentative, and it is informative about the concerns and techniques of contemporary archaeology in the Palestinian field. The book ends with a biographical sketch of Joseph Calloway, and a bibliography of his writings. (A regrettable blemish is the discrepancy between several illustrations and their descriptive titles at pp. 116–18, 147, 422–23.) Sadly, Joseph Callaway died shortly after the publication of this well-deserved and useful *Festschrift*.

J. R. BARTLETT

FINKELSTEIN, I.: *The Archaeology of the Israelite Settlement*. Translated from Hebrew by D. Saltz. 1988. Pp. 380. (Israel Exploration Society, Jerusalem. Price: $36.00 (members price: $27.00), plus $3.00 postage. ISBN 965 221 007 2)

This work, a revision of a volume published in Hebrew in 1986, offers English readers the first substantial synthesis of excavations and detailed surveys in the West Bank of the Jordan carried out in the twenty years since 1968. Part I first attempts to plot the characteristics of Israelite settlement sites, then offers a region by region survey of the archaeological data from all of Israel and the Transjordanian plateau. Part II offers a regional study of the territory of Ephraim, with particular reference to excavations at Shiloh — both the older Danish ones and the recent ones by Bar-Ilan University. Part III concerns material culture: first early Israelite architecture, then Iron I pottery in the central hill country. And Part IV turns to the process of Israelite settlement: first the archaeological evidence is reviewed and the views of the conquest, infiltration, and sociology 'schools'; then chronological issues, the size of the settlement, the origin of the Israelites, and the manner of their settlement are treated in turn.

In the hill country between Jerusalem and Jezreel, 300 'Israelite' Iron I sites have been identified: 75 per cent of all those known in the Land of Israel. This suggests to the author that the territories of Manasseh first, in the later twelfth century B.C., followed by the more southerly Ephraim and Benjamin in the eleventh, were the original heartlands of Israelite settlement. These sites are almost completely without fortification; and many resemble stone-built camps. Finkelstein estimates their total population at 40,000–55,000.

A. G. AULD

GERATY, L. T. and HERR, L. G. (eds): *The Archaeology of Jordan and other studies presented to Siegfried H. Horn*. 1986. Pp. xv, 716. (Andrews University Press, Berrien Springs, Michigan; distributed by Eisenbrauns, Winona Lake, Indiana. Price: $40.00. ISBN 0 943872 27 8)

Out of the 28 studies under this title, only 11 concern Jordan, and only 6 Jordan in Old Testament times, of which one (Albright's 1953 'Notes on Ammonite history') is a reprint. L. T. Geraty and L. A. Willis, however, present a useful summary of archaeological research in Jordan up to 1980; H. O. Thompson describes the contents of an Iron Age tomb at Madeba (found 1967; the material has already been published elsewhere). There are some 'philological ears of grain' from the Moabite stone (M. Dahood), and an Ammonite ostracon from Hesbân listing personal names (F. M. Cross). Ø. S. LaBianca studies animal exploitation and social organisation at Tell Hesbân. F. Zayadine's reinterpretation of a Petra inscription, now seen to mention a symposiarch, will interest Nabataean scholars. Among other papers, A. E. Glock defends Albrightian biblical archaeology, and R. M. Little offers a portrait of G. A. Reisner. J. S. Holladay, Jr., firmly interprets Palestinian tripartite pillared buildings (including the Megiddo buildings) as stables. W. G. Dever studies 'Abel-Beth-Maʿacah (=T. ʿAbîl el-Qamh). R. S. Boraas and L. G. Herr present Iron Age pottery from T. Balâtah and Tekoaʿ respectively. G. Garbini identifies some seals as Philistine, while G. Mendenhall tackles the 'hopeless naivete of most scholars' in the matter of Philistine origins. J. Neuffer presents the importance of Ptolemy's Canon and Almagest for Old Testament chronology with great clarity, while E. R. Theiele discusses the bearing of two Assyrian steles on the dating of Jehoash and Menahem of Israel. G. F. Hasel argues that *'aḥarît* means 'remnant' in five or perhaps eight Old Testament passages, and S. D. Waterhouse explores the meaning of 'the river dragon' in scripture. The editor regrets that the book's contents were almost a decade old on publication; he and the honorand may be reassured that their contributors' work has stood the ten-year test well.

J. R. BARTLETT

GIVEON, R.: *Scarabs from Recent Excavations in Israel*, edited by D. Warburton and C. Uehlinger (OBO 83). 1988. Pp. vii, 114, and pp. 9 of plates. (Universitätsverlag, Freiburg (CH); Vandenhoeck & Ruprecht, Göttingen. Price: Sw.Fr. 36.00; DM 52.00. ISBN 3 7278 0581 1; ISBN 3 525 53712 3)

This compact volume, probably its author's last work on Egyptian scarabs and seals, has been skilfully composed and completed from surviving notes. It opens with a short memorial biography of Giveon by Othmar Keel, and a handy bibliography of Giveon's publications. The works presents 122 items derived mainly from scientific excavations on known sites in Israel — which lends greater value to this collection of data than is usually true of such easily-displaced minor objects. The interpretations offered are generally sound; but perhaps note the following. P. 22f., No. 4: the signs may be not

Egyptian but early alphabetic proto-Canaanite: *1–yšt*, 'belonging to Yashīt'? P. 24f., No. 6, with p. 32, No. 17: almost certainly read just *R' ity Iwnw*, 'Re, sovereign of Heliopolis', thus eliminating needless 'cryptographic' speculation. P. 30, end: read 'solar', not 'scholar'. P. 46, No. 40: undoubtedly read: *R'mss m3'ty*, i.e. Ramesses IV (Not I or II); the resulting date, *c.* 1150 B.C., agrees neatly with its archaeological context (*c.* 1150–1100 B.C.). The work ends helpfully with indexes and admirably clear plates. A sketch-map of the sites quoted would have been useful.

K. A. KITCHEN

HACHLILI, R.: *Ancient Jewish Art and Archaeology in the Land of Israel* (Handbuch der Orientalistik). 1988. Pp. xxiv, 427 and 109 plates. (Brill, Leiden. Price: fl 220.00 (sub. price: fl 192.00); ca. $110.00 (sub. price: ca. $96.00). ISBN 90 04 08115 1)

In this splendidly produced volume Hachlili makes a convincing case for the view that a specifically Jewish form of art existed from Hellenistic to Byzantine times. Although always assimilating elements from outside, that form remained essentially true to the religious ideas of Judaism and was created by Jewish craftsmen for Jewish communities. The two parts of the volume cover, respectively, the Second Temple period and Late Antiquity and are illustrated with over three hundred figures and plates. Although the book constitutes a detailed catalogue of sites, buildings, decorations and tombs, and their changing usage, there is also discussion of their historical context and communal function, with particular attention being paid to the latest scholarly views on such institutions as temple, synagogue, and *miqweh*. A major theme is the slow transformation of the synagogue from a communal assembly-hall in the first pre-Christian century into a functionally planned house of worship with lavish decoration some four or five centuries later.

S. C. REIF

HARRIS, R. L., SCHONFIELD, J. and GIBSON, S. (eds): *Bulletin of the Anglo-Israel Archaeological Society*, Vol. 6 (1986–87). 1987. Pp. 66. (The Anglo-Israel Archaeological Society, London. Price: £8.00 ($24.00). ISSN 0266 2442)

With this issue, the Bulletin aims to become a journal by publishing original articles as well as reports of the Society's activities. It starts with an essay by the late R. D. Barnett on representations of people with six fingers or toes, ranging from Neolithic Jericho to the Renaissance, including 2 Sam. 21:18ff. Y. Hirschfeld offers a survey of traditional Arab stone houses in the Hebron region, with a note on the high density of occupation (approximately 2 sq. m. per head). The first century 'Galilee boat' is described by S. Wachsmann, and its salvage by O. Cohen. R. Chapman re-assesses a Middle Bronze Age tomb at Jericho (p. 19), arguing that the three male skeletons minus their right hands were slaughtered by soldiers who took hands as trophies; he also reviews critically the report of Y. Yadin's small excavation at Beth-Shean produced by S. Geva. The lecture summaries cover A. Flinder on Locating Ezion-geber at Jeziret Fira'un, A. R. Millard on archaeological discoveries wrongly reckoned religious, and R. Gonen on explorations in the Negev revealing, among much else, extensive Early Iron Age farming there. Betar, Emmaus' bath-house, Herodium, and recent occupation at Petra were the topics of lectures by D. Ussishkin, M. Gichon, E. Netzer, and P. Bienkowski. The Bulletin now deserves regular consultation by all concerned with ancient Israel.

A. R. MILLARD

HUTTER, M.: *Behexung, Entsühnung und Heilung: Das Ritual der Tunnawiya für ein Königspaar aus mittelhethitischer Zeit (KBo XXI 1 — KUB IX 34 — KBo XXI 6)* (Orbis Biblicus et Orientalis, 82). 1988. Pp. 180. (Universitätsverlag, Freiburg (CH) and Vandenhoeck & Ruprecht, Göttingen. Price: DM 52.00. ISBN 3 7278 0580 3; 3 525 53712 3)

Hutter edits and translates (with extensive philological notes) a series of tablets which constitute a Hittite ritual designed to relieve the king and his queen from the evil influences threatening them. It is possible that the king is under threat from within his own household, though this may be manifested in his illness. The ritual is the work of Tunnawiya, a wise woman (originally 'midwife'), who is connected with several Hittite rituals. There are elaborate preparations and apparently a ritual act involving the raising up of the royal couple from the ground, symbolically from death. The sun-goddess is invoked and is expected to restore the king's fortunes. The text may belong to the Luwian stratum of Hittite religion and comes, perhaps, from the beginning of the fourteenth century B.C.

J. F. HEALEY

LAPERROUSAZ, E.-M. (ed.): *Archéologie, art et histoire de la Palestine: Colloque du Centénaire de la Section des Sciences réligieuses, École Pratique des hautes Études (Sept. 1986)*. 1988. Pp. 262. (Cerf, Paris. Price: Fr. 125.00. ISBN 2 204 02785 5; ISSN 0768 2980)

This volume publishes the fifteen papers delivered at a French-Israeli colloquium in September 1986 held to celebrate the centenary of the 'Sciences réligieuses' section of Paris's École Practique des Hautes Études. B. Vandermeersch treated Palestine's first burials; A. Malamat, the kingdom of Judah between Egypt and Babylon: a small state wedged in the confrontation of the great powers; J. C. Greenfield, recent epigraphic discoveries at the service of history, from the return from the exile till Bar-Kochba; and A. Biran, a tale of two cities (in fact Laish and Dan). J.-B. Humbert reported on Tell Keisan between sea and mountain, archaeology between text and context; R. Cohen on the excavations of Qadesh-Barnea and the fortresses of the Negev; and A. Lemaire, on Lachish: archaeology, epigraphy, and history. There were three papers on older Jerusalem: by the late Y. Shiloh, on ancient Jerusalem, a Canaanite city and an Israelite capitol; by N. Avigad, on the topography of Jerusalem in the Israelite and Hasmonean periods; and one on the excavations directed by B. Mazar next to the enclosure of the Haram esh-Sherif, by Laperrousaz, the editor of the volume, who also contributed a paper on three high places of Judah: the herodian palace-fortresses of Herodium and Masada, and the Essene convent of Qumran and its 'Dead Sea Scrolls'. The remaining contributions are by Gabrielle Sed-Rajna, on the paintings of the Dura-Europos synagogue in the light of current research; by C. Lepage, on the restitution of a Palestinian cycle on the basis of the illustrations in two Ethiopic manuscripts of the fourteenth century; by D. Bahat, on new discoveries concerning the Crusaders in Jerusalem; and by Miriam Rosen-Ayalon, on recent discoveries in Islamic archaeology.

A. G. AULD

LIMET, H.: *Archives Royales de Mari* XXV: *Textes administratifs relatifs aux métaux*. 1986. Pp. viii, 289 with 4 plates of texts. (Éditions Recherche sur les Civilisations, Paris. Price: Fr. 198.00. ISBN 2 86538 155 2)

This is a further volume, dedicated to metalwork, in the Mari text publication series, for which a new computerised method of publication is now being used. The gathering together of all texts of a particular type has the advantage of preparing the way for more coherent secondary studies on particular themes. The texts are ordered according to keywords (e.g.

šubultum texts recording gifts to foreign kings), with some sections dealing with particular types of metalwork (e.g. bronze). 819 texts are thus presented in transliteration, with translations as appropriate. There is little in the way of comment (gathered at the end of the volume, pp. 271–89) and cuneiform copies are not provided (though there are four plates of selected cuneiform readings to help the cuneiformist). Many of the texts are dated (principally to the reign of Zimri-Lim). Indexes list geographical, personal, and divine names. This is an important volume which will push forward research on the technology and administration of metalworking in the early second millennium B.C.

J. F. Healey

Mare, W. H.: *The Archaeology of the Jerusalem Area*. 1987. Pp. 323. (Baker Book House, Grand Rapids MI. Price: $19.95. ISBN 0 8010 6126 1)

Several opportunities seem to have been missed in this rather unexciting account of a fascinating topic. The introductory chapter offers an overview, while chapters 2–11 treat in turn Jerusalem before David, under David, under Solomon, during the kingdom of Judah, after the exile, in the Herodian era, in the Roman period, in the Byzantine period, in the early Islamic period, and finally under Crusaders, Mameluks, and Turks. Harold Mare's New Testament interests readily explain why almost half the text is devoted to Herodian, Roman, and Byzantine periods. But even here the presentation is spoiled by the very poor reproduction of the photographs, which gives the volume a very dated feel. While it is claimed that the stress is on archaeological evidence, and that the picture is filled in with details from the Bible and elsewhere, the earlier chapters appear to work the other way round, with a very uncritical reading of the biblical record providing the framework.

A. G. Auld

del Olmo Lete, G. and Aubet Semmler, M. E.: *Los Fenicios en la Peninsula Ibérica*. Vol. I: *Arqueologia, Ceramica y Plastica*; Vol. II: *Epigrafia y Lengua. Gliptica y Numismatica. Expansion e Interaccion Cultural*. 1986. Pp. 323 + 391. (Editorial AUSA, Barcelona. Price: $120.00. ISBN 84 86329 06 X)

The two volumes of this work provide a comprehensive treatment of the present state of our knowledge of Phoenician penetration of and Punic expansion in the Iberian peninsula. The 40 articles are divided into six categories: archaeology; ceramics, terracottas, and metalwork (vol. I); epigraphy and language; glyptic art and numismatics; expansion and cultural interconnections; and an appendix on Phoenician influence on Balearic culture (Vol. II). The main sites are dealt with extensively, and some are treated in several articles from different angles. The discussions likely to be of most direct interest to *Book List* readers are the following: in Vol. I a survey of the current state of knowledge in the field (M. E. Aubet Semmler); in Vol. II on the relation of Ugaritic and Phoenician (G. del Olmo Lete), a possible inscription from Ekron found at Málaga (E. Lipiński), the smiting scene on the gem MAI 3650 from Ibiza (E. Gubel), a Moabite seal from Palma (P. Bordreuil), and the reference of Tarshish in the Bible, with particular reference to Isaiah 23 (Ju. B. Tsirkin).

The work is extensively illustrated with monochrome and colour photographs of sites and artefacts, drawing of pottery types, maps, and site plans. In view of the rich coverage and considerable value of the discussions in the context of the history of the western Mediterranean world in the first millennium B.C.E., it is to be regretted that no indices are included. There is a good annotated and classified bibliography by C. J. Perez. While most of the articles are in Spanish, all are prefaced by an abstract in English (occasionally with delightful misspellings!).

N. Wyatt

SMELIK, K. A. D.: *Historische Dokumente aus dem alten Israel*. Translated from Dutch by H. Weippert (Kleine Vandenhoeck-Reihe, 1528). 1987. Pp. 167. (Vandenhoeck & Ruprecht, Göttingen. Price: DM 21.80. ISBN 3 525 33536 9)

With this German translation, Helga Weippert has made Smelik's very readable translation of and historial introduction to some seventy inscriptions available to a wider readership. The original Dutch edition was reviewed in *B. L.* 1986, pp. 33f.

A. G. AULD

STEINSLAND, G. (ed.): *Words and Objects: Towards a Dialogue between Archaeology and History of Religion* (Institute for Comparative Research in Human Culture, Oslo. Series B: Skrifter, Vol. 71). 1986. Pp. 283. (Universitetsforlaget, Oslo. ISBN 82 00 07751 9)

The eighteen papers in this volume were read at an interdisciplinary conference held at Fredrikstad in Norway in 1984, and most of them have a specific reference to Nordic religion and archaeology. But more general theoretical issues in the interpretation of mythology and archaeological evidence are also touched on and two interesting essays are entirely of this type: 'Religion and Archaeology: Revelation or Empirical Research?' (O. Johansen), and 'The "Meaning" of the Rock Carvings and the Scope for Religio-Historical Interpretation: Some Thoughts on the Limits of the Pheomenology of Religion' (J. P. Schjødt). Several essays have to do with the interpretation of a prehistoric rock-carvings and might, with due care, have something to offer to studies of similar phenomena in Palestine, such as those from the Chalcolithic period at Megiddo. What at first sight seems an unpromising volume on a distant topic in fact contains much to stimulate and refine the thinking of Old Testament scholars.

G. I. DAVIES

SUSSMAN, A. and GREENBERG, R. (eds.): *Excavations and Surveys in Israel 1987/88*, Vol. 6 (English Edition of *Hadashot Arkheologiyot*, nos 90–91, edited by I. Pommerantz). 1988. Pp. vii, 120. (Israel Department of Antiquities and Museums, Jerusalem. ISSN 0334 1607)

The latest issue of this valuable collection of reports (cf. *B. L.* 1988, p. 34) follows the same pattern as its predecessor. The reports, which relate mainly to work done in 1986 and 1987, include a long one (39 pages) on an exciting new project which envisages large-scale excavation of the Roman and Byzantine remains at Bet-shean and the site's development at a tourist attraction, and a shorter one on new work in 'the land of Geshur' east of the Sea of Galilee. There are also accounts of the continuing excavations at, for example, Tel Dan (rooms of the ninth-eighth-century cult place, metal industry of Iron Age I), Tel Dor (Iron Age fortifications), Mount Ebal (Iron Age I buildings and pottery), Hebron (where a cuneiform tablet was found in 1986) and Yoqneam, and news of a survey of an area north-east of Jerusalem, where several identifications of biblical sites, including Nob, are proposed.

G. I. DAVIES

WEIPPERT, H.: *Palästina in Vorhellenistischer Zeit* (Handbuch der Archäologie: Vorderasien II, 1). 1988. Pp. xxix, 744, with 201 illustrations within the text, and 71 illustrations on 23 plates. (C. H. Beck, München. Price: DM 338.00. ISBN 3 406 32198 4)

This is a beautifully produced publication of an almost encyclopedic account by a single author of what has been learned through archaeology about Palestine (west and east of the Jordan) from around 700,000 B.C. down to the year 333 B.C. By a well-known biblical scholar, it stands in the best tradition of informed lay archaeological reportage: seeking out first and foremost what the other discipline is able to say, and only remarking on the problems or contributions provided thereby to one's own.

Almost equal space is given to the Introduction (1–68) on the task in hand, the geography of the area, relative and absolute chronologies, and methods of surface survey and excavation; and to the chapter on the Stone Age (69–139), which alone is printed in smaller but still perfectly readable type. The Bronze Age occupies the second quarter of the text (140–343), with the largest space given to the Late period (1550–1150 B.C.). Architectural and material culture are carefully discussed; gods identified and their relationships classified; the few inscriptions mentioned; and international relationships plotted.

Almost all of the remaining half of the volume (344–681) is devoted to a five-part discussion of the Iron Age (1250–586 B.C.). First, its general characteristics are briefly sketched. Then, on Iron I (1250–1000), the subheadings are chronology, deurbanization in the interior, the discussion about the Philistines, the village culture inland, pottery, burials, and evaluation. Iron IIA (1000–900) is reviewed in terms of historical and chronological framework, town-plans of the period, elements of town architecture, an excursus on Jerusalem, villages and farms, fortifications outside towns, burials, manufacture, and trade. After the general characteristics and chronology of Iron IIB (925/900–800) are mentioned, it is discussed in terms of the north-south-divide in urban consolidation, elements of urban architecture, and fortifications outside towns. Then a longer section on Iron IIC (850–586) sketches its general characteristics and chronological delimitation; evidence from writing and inscriptions; developments in urban architecture; other fortifications; cultic buildings and customs; graves and burial places; and farming, craft, and trade.

The volume is concluded by a much briefer account (628–718) of the Babylonian-Persian period (586–333 B.C.), capped by an appendix by Leo Mildenberg (719–728) on coinage in the Persian province of Judah.

Helga Weippert is to be warmly congratulated for a remarkable and fair-minded synthesis. The bibliographies which open each main chapter-section appear comprehensive down to the completion of the text at the beginning of 1986. And the illustrations are a model of clarity. A similarly generous volume in English would be very useful; but a translation would require no mean effort — not least the updating of both text and bibliographies before publication.

A. G. AULD

YASSINE, KH.: *Archaeology of Jordan: Essays and Reports*. 1988. Pp. 273. (Available from the author: Kh.N. Yassine, P. O. Box 410403, Amman, Jordan. Price: $30.00 (plus $3.00 postage))

This useful volume reprints thirteen of Yassine's published essays and archaeological reports (from *ADAJ*, *BASOR ZDPV*, and elsewhere; regrettably, references to the original publications are not given). The first six discuss Ammonite fortresses, anthropoid coffins, dolmens, Iron Age burial practices, the el-Mabrak building, and archaeological features that may or may not be related to the Hyksos, Hurrians, and Philistines. Part Two reprints excavation reports of Tell el Mazar (Field I; the Iron Age sanctuary; Ammonite and Aramaic inscriptions (with J. Teixidor); Ammonite seals). Part Three reprints reports from the East Jordan Valley survey (with M. Ibrahim and J. Sauer) and from three reservoir areas in northern Jordan (with K. M. Kerestes, B. G. Wood, and J. M. Lundquist). In these articles Yassine has made some original and important contributions to the archaeology of

Jordan. The book concludes with an excellent brief survey article by Yassine and J. Sauer, 'History and archaeology of Jordan in perspective'.

J. R. BARTLETT

ZINK, J.: *Tief ist der Brunnen der Vergangenheit: Eine Reise durch die Ursprungsländer der Bibel*. 1988. Pp. 400. (Kreuz, Stuttgart, Price: DM 78.00. ISBN 3 7831 9037 X)

Magnificently illustrated with many fine photographs in black and white and in colour and several maps, and plans, this volume also offers an imaginative and well-informed text. A short introduction, Europe — daughter of the east, precedes twelve main chapters, of which the first four occupy as much space as the remainder: Look with me into the spring treats the original culture of Mesopotamia; Wanderer Abraham, nomadic ways in Syria; A break-out into freedom, Egypt and the Sinai wilderness; A dream becomes reality, David, Solomon, and the Phoenicians; The queen of Sheba and the incense route, Yemen, and southern Arabia; A thousand years of Israel, Assyria, Babylon, and the Persians; Traces of a childhood, Nazareth and Bethlehem; Blessed land, Jesus in Galilee; The mystery of death and life, Jesus in Jerusalem; Driven by the spirit, the first church in Syria; A troublesome journey, Asia Minor — Greece — Rome; and Write to the angel of the congregation, the localities of the apocalypse of John.

Striking as much of the photography is (not least of the less familiar Yemenite scenery), it is not in the volume for its own sake, but is well integrated with the text. Jörg Zink and the Kreuz Verlag deserve congratulation. An English translation printed to the same standard would be welcome.

A. G. AULD

ZUCKERMAN, B.: *Puzzling out the Past: Making Sense of Ancient Inscriptions from Biblical Times*. 1987. Pp. 48. (Obtainable from Maarav, 6055 Montemalaga, Rancho Palos Verdes, California 90274. Price: $ 10.00)

This exhibition catalogue is a convenient introduction to the problems facing epigraphists. Several scholars have contributed short essays on the reading of various texts, including the 'cook a kid in its mother's milk' tablet from Ugarit (showing why that reading is to be discarded), the 'Melkart Stele' (W. Pitard argues for the reading 'Bir-Hadad, son of Attarhamek, king of Aram'), six West Semitic seals, including the seal of a 'servant of YHWH' (studied by F. M. Cross), Elephantine papyrus fragments of the story of Hor bar Punesh (B. Porten and others), and a Samaria Papyrus (F. M. Cross). Each study is accompanied by fine photographs in colour or black and white, often enlarged, and appropriate diagrams. While every interpretation may not be acceptable, the way the reader is led step by step through the problems is instructive, and has not been set out in other works.

A. R. MILLARD

3. HISTORY AND GEOGRAPHY

AHARONI, Y. and AVI-YONAH, M.: *Makumiran Seisho-Rekishi-Chizu*. Translated by Y. Ikeda. 1988. Pp. 198. (Hara-shobō, Tokyo. Price: ¥15,000)

This is a translation of the second revised edition of *The Macmillan Bible Atlas* (1977). The translator writes a 4-page comment on the books, editors, corrections, and so forth.

K. K. SACON

BILDE, P.: *Flavius Josephus between Jerusalem and Rome: His Life, his Works, and their Importance* (Journal for the Study of the Pseudepigrapha Supplement Series 2). 1988. Pp. 272. (Sheffield Academic Press. Price: £30.00 ($45.00). ISBN 1 85075 060 2)

The author of this book has built upon his earlier work, particularly his dissertation *Josefus som historieskriver* (*B.L.* 1984, p. 121), to provide a comprehensive introduction to the study of Josephus. The core of the book consists of three closely-interrelated chapters in which Bilde discusses the life of Josephus, his writings, and the main trends in modern Josephus research. The conclusions that he draws from his discussion of these topics are then presented systematically, while in the final chapter Bilde considers the significance of Josephus by examining the uses that have been, and can be, made of his writings. There is an excellent bibliography as well as reference, author and subject indexes.

Bilde's method of presentation has led to a certain degree of repetition, perhaps unavoidable, but there can be little question that he has produced an interesting and important study. In common with a number of recent authors (e.g. Rajak) he offers a much more positive evaluation of the career and writings of Josephus than was often the case in the past. Thus, for example, he argues that Josephus maintained throughout his life and writings a consistent attitude towards the question of the relationship between the Jewish people and Rome, and that although there are differences between the accounts in the War and the Life of Josephus's activity in Galilee, these accounts are not contradictory. The Life is not to be interpreted primarily as Josephus's response to personal accusations made against him by Justus, but rather more broadly as a defence of Josephus's qualifications to write the War and the Antiquities. His writings represent an attempt to come to terms with the tragedy of the fall of Jerusalem and in their different ways can be seen to have had an apologetic aim. Thus they offer a defence of Judaism and of the Jewish people addressed to the Graeco-Roman world, although the War was also directed at Jewish readers. Bilde also argues that, despite his personal involvement, Josephus has in general not given a distorted picture of contemporary events, and that his reliability as a historian is surprisingly high. Josephus's Hellenization is somewhat superficial, and he remains 'closer to Old Testament and Jewish tradition than to Hellenistic literature and historiography.'

M. A. KNIBB

BOARDMAN, J., HAMMOND, N. G. L., LEWIS, D. M., and OSTWALD, M. (eds): *The Cambridge Ancient History*, 2nd edn Vol. IV: *Persia, Greece and the Western Mediterranean c. 525 to 479 B.C.* 1988. Pp. xxi, 928. (Cambridge University Press. Price: £60.00 ($100). ISBN 0 521 22804 2).

BOARDMAN, J. (ed.): *The Cambridge Ancient History. Plates to Vol. IV: Persia, Greece and the Western Mediterranean c. 525 to 479 B.C.* 1988. Pp. xi, 248. (Cambridge University Press. Price: £37.50 ($65.00). ISBN 0 521 30580 2)

These two splendid volumes are each divided into three parts, covering the Persian empire, the Greek world, and the west (Italy, Sicily, Carthage). *Book List* readers may focus on I. Eph'al's 'Syria-Palestine under Achaemenid rule', which uses Persian, Greek, biblical and epigraphic souces to give an up-to-date, detailed and balanced account. However, equally important are T. Cuyler Young's section on the Persian empire under Darius and Xerxes (with clear assessments of Cambyses in Egypt, the Gautama/Bardiya rebellion, Persian administration and religion: the tolerance of Persian provincial administration is asserted), and J. D. Ray's section 'Egypt, 525–404 B.C.' (but did Darius visit Egypt early in his reign or not? compare pp. 64, 262). This enormous volume underlines for us the importance of seeing the tiny area of Judah in the wider context of the interacting Persian and Greek worlds, and a reading of the essays on 'Religion and the state' (J. K. Davies) and 'The development of ideas, 750–500 B.C., (G. S. Kirk) prompts speculation on the contents of similarly entitled essays referring to Israelite society. The reading of classical history and its historians is a salutary experience for the biblical scholar. In the accompanying volume of plates, the Persian empire is well illustrated and annotated by P. R. S. Moorey, the Greek world by Sir John Boardman, and the West by R. J. A. Wilson. There is much fine scholarship in these volumes, supported by a bibliography of almost 100 pages.

J. R. BARTLETT

BOLING, R. G.: *The Early Biblical Community in Transjordan* (The Social World of Biblical Antiquity Series, 6). 1988. Pp. 80. (Sheffield Academic Press. Price: £15.95 ($25.00). ISBN 1 85075 094 7)

Boling's summary of recent archaeological evidence, mainly from surveys, for the nature of settlement in Transjordan from Middle Bronze II – Iron Age I (chapter 1) appears to suggest that in Late Bronze the number of settlements in the Jordan valley decreased (due to political turbulence?), while the number in northern Transjordan remained much the same (though re-located), and the number of Moab more than doubled. In the early Iron Age, the number of settlements in the Jordan valley and northern Transjordan increased again; we have as yet no statistical evidence for Moab, but the few early Iron settlements in northern Edom are seen as 'a spillover from a burgeoning population on the plateau to the north'. Meanwhile, however, the northern Hejaz had a flourishing settled population.

Chapter 2 tries to relate these findings of a densely settle Late Bronze Moabite plateau to the biblical traditions of Sihon and Og (Num. 21: 27b–29 is taken to describe Sihon's conquest of Moabilte-held cities north of the Arnon, though Boling is forced to admit that Tell Hesban cannot be Sihon's Heshbon) and of Moab (Boling struggles uncertainly with Judges 11). In the light of this, the essay ends with an attempt (following Freedman) to use the supposedly twelfth–eleventh century B.C. poems in Gen. 49, Exod. 15, Num. 23–24, Deut. 33, and Judges 5 as evidence for thirteenth–twelfth century B.C. Israelite tribal settlement of Transjordan. The risk of circular argument here is apparent. Boling appears to connect the early Yahwist settlers of Transjordan with Midian (p. 62; cf. pp. 26–28), but his reasons ('Midianite' pottery in the Negeb and W. ʿArabah?) are not clear. There is much work yet to be done before we can present a coherent picture of Late Bronze – Iron I Transjordan.

J. R. BARTLETT

CALLAWAY, P. R.: *The History of the Qumran Community: An Investigation* (Journal for the Study of the Pseudepigrapha Supplement Series 3). 1988. Pp. 270 (Sheffield Academic Press. Price: £30.00 ($45.00). ISBN 1 85075 107 2)

The purpose of this volume is 'to re-examine all the documentary and non-documentary data that is [*sic*! cf. also p. 12] usually adduced as evidence for Qumran history' (p. 7). In order to determine the real strength of the 'current consensus', the author proceeds to survey the arguments in the form of a 'dialogue' with four (five) representatives of the Maccabaean thesis, G. Jeremias, H. Stegemann, J. Murphy-O'Connor (P. R. Davies), and F. M. Cross. In so doing, he produces a valuable conspectus and analysis of the evidence used by his chosen scholars. The conclusions are far from adventurous: the main chronological framework of Qumran history is sound, but beyond this, it is impossible to be definite regarding the actors and events of the sect's history. No doubt, most serious scholars would agree with this assessment at least as far as the difference in degrees of probability between the main outline and the individual details of the jigsaw puzzle is concerned. Finally, the reviewer is in two minds whether to feel flattered or ill-done-by, for while he is presented as the originator of the 'consensus' theory, his own views, which do not always coincide with those of Professors Jeremias, Stegemann *et al.*, are not discussed because his 1953 book on the subject 'was not available for examination' (pp. 212 f.). He fares better, however, than Yigael Yadin, whose name figures only in the bibliography but not in the body of this monograph.

G. VERMES

CHAMPDOR, A.: *Les Civilisations du Jourdain* (50 illustrations; documents de l'Institut Pontificial de Rome). 1987. Pp. 145. (Albert Guillot, Lyon, Price Fr. 150.00. ISBN 2 850960016)

This is a work of *vulgarisation*. The title is misleading: the author describes with effusive rhetoric the Jordan valley and its major sites: Nebo, Teleilat Ghassual, Qumran, Jericho, Bethshan, Megiddo, Tiberias, Capernaum, Hittin, and Hazor. The contents are out of date and not always accurate, and the illustrations, by modern standards, are poor.

J. R. BARTLETT

GIARDINA, A., LIVERANI, M., and SCARCIA, B.: *La Palestina* (Libri di base 116). 1987. Pp. 205. (Editori Riuniti, Roma. Price: Lire 8,500. ISBN 88 359 3088 X)

This little textbook, based on *Annales* principles of historiography, traces the history of Palestine from the prehistoric period to the present day— necessarily a sketchy account, but one which gives prominence to all three major religions which have claim to it. If the Old Testament is given a little too much credence, and Judah is somewhat privileged in the Iron II and Persian periods, these minor derivations from the principle deface the conception of the volume as a whole very little. The temptation of such a volume, to give a potted recital of 'political' history has been resisted; geography, society, and economy have their place here. There are several, but not too many, maps and tables, a subject index, chronological chart and short (but polyglot) reading list. This is well-conceived and well-written popular book.

P. R. DAVIES

HAYES, J. H., and HOOKER, P. K.: *A New Chronology for the Kings of Israel and Judah and Its Implications for Biblical History and Literature*. 1988. Pp. 112. (John Knox, Atlanta. ISBN 0 8042 0152 8)

Fifteen basic assumptions are accepted by the authors in their attempt to solve a most difficult conundrum in Old Testament history, viz. the chronology of the kings of Israel and Judah. Among the more significant points are: a rejection of the concept of co-regencies, placing a calendar change in the reign of Josiah, and accpeting the principle of counting a king's reign from the first autumn festival of his reign until his death, drawing a distinction between Israel's Marheshvan calendar and Judah's Tishri calendar. The authors' detailed studies of the ten periods between Jeroboam I and Gedaliah are accompanied in each case by a full chronological table and a short bibliography. At the end of the volume the implications of the study are noted and a full chronological chart is provided.

In many instances the authors accept the reckoning of the Old Testament in preference to the revised figures of later chronologists. For instance a reign of 29 years for Hezekiah is preferred to the shorter one of 18/19 years accepted in many schemes; similarly a reign of 16 years is proposed for Jotham, whilst several schematists have accepted a reduced figure of 6. On the other hand, there are many cases in which the scheme diverges wideley from biblical chronology: Amaziah's reign of 29 years is reduced to 14 years, or 17 at the most; Azariah's 52-year reign is cut by half; and Pekah's 20 years have diminished to 4. Although such treatment of biblical data at first appears arbitrary, a full discussion of biblical and extra-biblical evidence gives the authors support in what they propose. Indeed one of the main strengths of their study is the use made of ancient near eastern sources.

All the evidence is expertly sifted and a coherent chronological scheme is presented. Nevertheless, it is not likely to be the last word on the subject; as past experience has demonstrated, rival schemes will no doubt be presented, preferred, and supported.

G. H. Jones

Kuhrt, A. and Sherwin-White, S.: *Hellenism in the East: The interaction of Greek and non-Greek civilisations from Syria to Central Asia after Alexander*. 1987. Pp. xv, 192. (Duckworth, London. Price: £28.00. ISBN 0 7156 2125 4)

These days there are few scholars with expertise in both classical and cuneiform sources; thus, not many works like the present one have appeared in recent years, and it is most welcome. S. Sherwin-White shows that Greek rule in Babylonia did not mean the cessation of the traditional culture. Not only did it continue to thrive but did so with Seleucid encouragement. A. Kuhrt examines Berossus's writing in the context of early Seleucid rule. R. J. van der Speck concludes that the coming of Hellenization did not change the basic character of the Seleucid city, despite some adoption of Greek styles as time went on. J.-F. Salles finds that the main interest in 'The Arab-Persian Gulf under the Seleucids' was one of economic control, not conquest; there is little sign of Greek settlement or major Greek influence. F. Miller continues his investigation of the process of Hellenization, this time looking at Syria. One of his main points is how difficult it is to assess the question because of the sparseness of the sources. M. Colledge studies a question often neglected, that of 'Greek and non-Greek Interaction in the Art and Architecture of the Hellenistic East'. Greek influence began before Alexander, and native art flourished long after his conquest. The two thrived side by side, but 'hybrid' types developed early and became more and more dominant as time passed.

L. L. Grabbe

Lemche, N. P.: *Ancient Israel: A New History of Israelite Society* (The Biblical Seminar). 1988. Pp. 276. (Sheffield Academic Press. Price: £22.50 ($35.00); ISBN 1 85075 187 0. Paperback price: £8.95 ($14.95); ISBN 1 85075 017 3

This book, hailed as a 'provocative text' which 'presents a new model of how we should understand Israelite society, its history and its religion', is an attempt to synthesize recent work which Lemche and others have been pursuing especially in the sociological and anthropological fields. Following a general discussion of climate and agriculture, and the forms of life to which they give rise, the author moves on to a discussion of the Old Testament as a source for historical reconstruction. His negative conclusions in this connection lead into a general account of the origins and nature of Israel which, departing radically from the biblical presentation, is based mainly on extra-biblical sources and general anthropological considerations. So, the continuity of Late Bronze Age and Iron Age culture is noted, and it is argued that the social and historical changes presupposed in the emergence of Israel took place within the population already present in the land rather than as a result of the immigration of a new ethnic group. Having continued the story of Israel down to the post-exilic period, the author turns to Israelite religion. His approach here is to describe first, on the basis of the Ugaritic texts, the religion of Canaan, then 'Israelite legalistic religion of the post-exilic period', before turning to pre-exilic Israelite religion. The latter is argued to have been 'basically Canaanite', and its transformation the work of the classical prophets and the deuteronomists.

The book is a refreshing attempt to provide a new approach. It is surprising, however, in view of the author's presentation of Israelite origins, that he gives so little prominence to internal factors in the emergence of the Israelite monarchy. This could have led to a fruitful consideration of the social tensions at play within Israel during the monarchic period, which could perhaps have formed an effective context for a better integration of the treatment of Israelite religion into the study of her social structure and her historical experience.

A. D. H. MAYES

MARGALITH, O.: *The Sea Peoples in the Bible* (in Hebrew). 1988. Pp. 260. (Dvir, Tel Aviv. ISBN 965 01 0233 7)

In the two main chapters of this book, Margalith looks first at the Philistines and the other peoples who may have been absorbed by them, such as the *b*[e]*nê* [a]*nāq*, the Carians and the 'Pelethites', and then at other groups whom he identifies as Sea Peoples, such as the Girgashites, the Hivites (see his English articles in *ZAW* 100 [1988] 60–70), and the Danites (largely repeating material published in English in four articles in *VT* 35–37 [1985–87]). Despite the opening sentence of his foreword, it is clear that he does have something of a case to press, namely the recognition of the influence of Aegean language, literature, religion, and culture on the Hebrew speaking peoples, and it is at this point that some of his suggestions seem at first sight rather far-fetched. But there is much well documented material here that deserves careful consideration. It would have been interesting, moreover, had Margalith conducted his survey within the context of the most recent views of the origins of Israel itself.

H. G. M. WILLIAMSON

MERRILL, E. H.: *Kingdom of Priests: A History of Old Testament Israel*. 1987. Pp. 546. (Baker Book House, Grand Rapids, Michigan. Price: $24.95. ISBN 0 8010 6220 9)

What has another History of Israel to offer in comparison with those already available? The publishers are in no doubt: 'after decades of doing without a comprehensive history of Israel, evangelicals now have one that should be a satisfying standard for many years'. In his Introduction, the author sets out with admirable clarity the assumptions that govern his method of working — the Old Testament texts are of divine origin and hence the Old Testament is an inerrant witness to the history of Israel. Nevertheless, a present day history of Israel, he says, cannot be just a re-telling of the biblical story but must be a reconstruction 'along the lines of normal historiography'. What this seems to mean is accepting all the events narrated in the Bible as historical facts, as against the view that the record may contain contradictions or reflect the divergent views of various authors, fitting them into a coherent narrative and using the literary and archaeological evidence of the ancient Near East to buttress their veracity. Hence, also, as its title makes clear, this is a History of *Old Testament* Israel: it does not go beyond the Hebrew canon and the latest period with which it deals is that of Ezra and Nehemiah. From his own standpoint, Merrill has done his work well. He writes clearly, his footnotes show acquaintance with a wide range of scholarship and he is not afraid to confront opinions differing from his own, giving reasons for his own position and on occasion scoring some good points. Those who share the author's theological outlook will find here a useful textbook — others will continue to look elsewhere.

J. R. PORTER

MERRILLEES, R. S.: *Alashia Revisited* (Cahiers de la Revue biblique 22). 1987. Pp. 87. (Gabalda, Paris. Price: Fr. 153.00. ISBN 2 85021 027 7)

Everyone who deals with written or material remains from the past should read this book! The topic may not hold universal interest, but Dr Merrillees' portrayal of the way it has been studied lays open the type of scholarship which is too common in every field. For a century the location of Alashia has been a puzzle, the dominant view identifying it with Cyprus or part of the island. The author has always dissented, seeking a site near Ugarit on the mainland. In his first chapter, 'The Medium' (pp. 13–59), he shows how one writer's assumptions were accepted by his sucessors, how evidence was mishandled or ignored, and how alternatives were overlooked. His incisive criticisms spare no one, not even himself. To identify Alashia is a goal yet to be reached; the author sets out a route which can be taken (Ch. II, 'The Message', pp. 61–74), challenging epigraphists and archaeologists to work together and analyse their evidence impartially. He remains agnostic over the possible equation with biblical Elishah.

A. R. MILLARD

Le Origini di Israele: Convegno sul Tema — Roma, 10–11 Febbraio 1986. 1987. Pp. 121. (Accademia Nazionale dei Lincei, Roma. Price: Lire 25,000 ISSN 0391 8130)

In this volume, containing papers given at a Congress in February 1986, J. A. Soggin discusses the origins of Israel as problem for the historian, stressing that the Old Testament gives us postexilic Judah's view of the history of Israel. H. Tadmor draws attention to the fact that in explicitly post-exilic biblical literature (Ezekiel, Chronicles, Ezra-Nehemiah) differing opinions about the origins of Israel are present, all of which focus on claims to the land. G. Garbini also addresses myths of origin in Hebrew ideology, comparing Abraham, Moses, and Joshua as alternative 'founders' of the nation. L. Moraldi compares, via the figures of Adam and Seth, varying Jewish perspectives on the identity of Israel, namely exclusivity/sin/election (Adam-Shem-Abraham) and identification with the primordial righteous man (Seth). H. Donner's paper considers Gen. 49:14–15 (the 'blessing of Issachar') as evidence of early tribal *Landnahme*, P. Sacchi credits the Deuteronomistic historian with creating national identity through a chronologically based history. A. G. Auld's examination of the term *mṭh* and *šbṭ* points him in the direction of a post-exilic development of the (real or theoretical) tribal system. The paper by G. Tamani deals with the people and the land of Israel in the thought of Yehudah Halevi. The contributors have provided, within a fairly brief scope, very appetizing fare on a topic which will provide a rich banquet over the next few years.

P. R. DAVIES

PRAG, K.: *Jerusalem* (Blue Guide). 1989. Pp. 331, including many plans and illustrations, and pp. 12 of maps. (A. & C. Black, London; W. W. Norton, New York. Price: £11.95; $19.95. ISBN 0 7136 2944 4; 0 393 30480 9)

This is an excellent introduction to the 'archaeology' of Jerusalem in the widest and most old-fashioned sense of that word, written by a professional

archaeologist (in the best modern sense!) who dug in the city with Kenyon and now shares responsibility for the publication of the Kenyon excavations of the 1960's. Readers of the *Book List* will want to have this guide along with Murphy O'Connor's *The Holy Land* when next they visit Jerusalem.

A general introduction precedes a crisply presented history (pp. 16–42) and much useful general information for the visitor, including bibliographic. The main body of the text describes seventeen 'routes', of which the final two take us as far as Bethany (and the Good Samaritan Inn), and Bethlehem (and east to Mar Saba). Within Jerusalem proper, the second 'route', on the *Haram al-Sharif*, treated in seven sections, has pride of place. Those Old Testament scholars not immediately planning a visit to the Holy City will still want to consult Kay Prag for a very open account of the eighth–sixth-century expansion of Jerusalem towards the western hill, and to read those of her routes' which traverse the southern quarters of the 'Old City', and the ancient city and associated valleys to its south.

A. G. AULD

RAINEY, A. F.: *Egypt, Israel, Sinai: Archaeological and Historical Relationships in the Biblical Period* (The Kaplan Project on the History of Israel and Egypt). 1987. Pp. 171. (Tel Aviv University Press, Tel Aviv. Price: $12.00. ISBN 965 224 008 7)

This attractive little volume originated in a symposium at Tel Aviv University (April 1982). From that occasion, this book presents the following eight papers: R. Gophna, 'Egyptian Trading Posts in Southern Canaan at the Dawn of the Archaic Period' (seven sites, Early Bronze IB period, show an Egyptian presence at start of the First Dynasty); R. Giveon, 'The Impact of Egypt on Canaan in the Middle Bronze Age' (compiled from earlier works of the deceased; concerns Egyptian seals and scarabs found in MB Canaan); M. Bietak, 'Canaanites in the Eastern Nile Delta' (carefully works out East-Delta links first with Phoenicia, then with Canaan (early second millennium B.C.), from his excavations at Tell el-Dabʿa); I. Beit-Arieh, 'Canaanites and Egyptians at Serabit el-Khadim' (reports on excavations in Mine 'L', to obtain archaeological dating-evidence for the Proto-Sinaitic texts, finding one naming 'El; his results indicate a New-Kingdom date (from 1550 B.C.), not earlier); E. D. Oren, 'The "Ways of Horus" in North Sinai' (invaluable preliminary report on three sites on the North-Sinai route from Egypt to Canaan: transit-settlement, Egyptian fort, and administrative centre, mainly fourteenth–twelfth centuries B.C.); T. Dothan, 'The Impact of Egypt on Canaan during the 18th and 19th Dynasties in the Light of the Excavations at Deir el-Balah' (report on a south-Canaanite Egyptian fort and settlement, fourteenth–eleventh centuries B.C.); D. B. Redford, 'An Egyptological Perspective on the Exodus Narrative' (R.'s idiosyncratic personal views; repeats the erroneous identification of Tell el-Maskhuta as 'Pithom'); M. Bietak, 'Comments on the "Exodus" (refreshingly modest, a needed corrective to Redford in method, data, and results). There is no index; but the value of the volume well surpasses its modest size.

K. A. KITCHEN

SANCISI-WEERDENBURG, H. (ed.): *Achaemenid History*, I: *Sources, Structures and Synthesis* (Proceedings of the Groningen 1983 Achaemenid History Workshop). 1987. Pp. xiv, 196. (Nederlands Instituut voor het nabije Oosten, Leiden. Price: fl. 85.00; sub. price: fl. 75.00. ISBN 90 6258 401 2)

SANCISI-WEERDENBURG, H. and KUHRT, A. (eds): *Achaemenid History*, II: *The Greek Sources* (Proceedings of the Groningen 1984 Achaemenid History Workshop). 1987. Pp. xiii, 175. (Nederlands Instituut voor het nabije Oosten, Leiden. Price: fl. 80.00; sub. price: fl. 70.00. ISBN 90 6258 402 0)

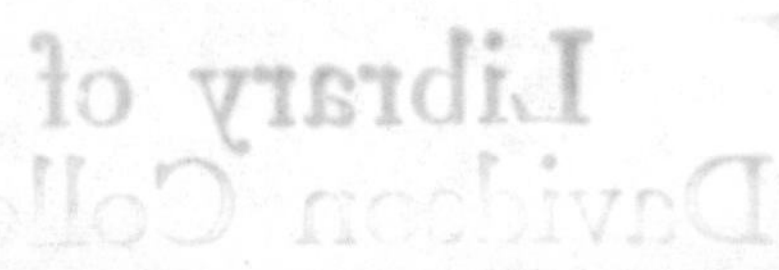

KUHRT, A., and SANCISI-WEERDENBURG, H. (eds): *Achaemenid History*, III: *Method and Theory* (Proceedings of the London 1985 Achaemenid History Workshop). 1988. Pp. xv, 228. (Nederlands Instituut voor het nabije Oosten, Leiden. Price: fl. 95.00; sub. price: fl. 85.00. ISBN 90 6258 403 9)

The three volumes in this series on an often neglected area of study are identical in format; each is devoted to a specified theme, which some contributors have interpreted in a wide-ranging way. Two essays are directly devoted to Old Testament topics. In I, J. C. H. Lebram questions the historicity of the biblical portrait of Ezra, and, by what will be regarded by some as rather speculative methods, reaches the conclusion that his presentation emerged from a second-century proto-Pharisaic group whose 'patron saint' he was. In III, P. R. Ackroyd discusses 'Problems in the handling of biblical and related Sources in the Achaemenid Period'. He discusses chronology, personalities, and narrative function, with special reference to Ezra and Nehemiah; he is sceptical of Lebram's reconstruction.

Each volume contains other essays of less direct Old Testament interest. In I, where the overall theme is the alleged decadence of the fourth-century Achaemenid empire, G. van der Kooij writes on Tell Deir Alla, and G. van Driel's discussion of 'Continuity and Decay' includes an assessment of the Murashu archive (see also p. 127 below). In II, O. Murray's essay on 'Herodotus and Oral Tradition' has interesting insights on the nature of oral tradition, and H. Sancisi-Weerdenburg ('The Fifth Oriental Monarchy and Hellenocentrism') has some provoking thoughts on 'orientalism' as seen through western eyes. In III M. Boyce argues that Cyrus was a Zoroastrian, and finds support for her views in Isa. 40–55, and a wide-ranging survey of Egyptian history by P. Briant places the Elephantine material in context. It is to be hoped that there will be a continuing exchange of ideas between Old Testament scholars and those who work in the field of Achaemenid history.

R. J. COGGINS

SCHARBERT, J.: *Zwangsumsiedlungen in Vorderasien zwischen dem 10. und dem 6. Jahrhundert V. Chr. nach altorientalischen und biblischen Quellen* (Sitzungsberichte der Sudetendeutschen Akademie der Wissenschaften und Künste (Geisteswissenschaftliche Klasse), Jahrgang 1988, Heft 1). 1988. Pp. 39. (Verlagshaus Sudetenland, München. ISBN 3 922423 30 2)

This examination of the forced resettlement of conquered peoples in pre-Christian times has been undertaken by the author because of his interest in the fate of the Jews in the twentieth century A.D., and especially in the so-called 'fourth Bayern tribe'. However, a detailed documentation illustrating the practice of deportation in the time of the Neo-Assyrian and the Neo-Babylonian empires has been assembled from a variety of sources, including cuneiform and Accadian inscriptions, the annals and chronicles of Assyrian and Babylonian kings, the text of the Old Testament, and to a lesser extent letters, transactions, and pictures.

It is only in his conclusion to this full rehearsal of the evidence that the author suggests that the material provides a paradigm for the Jews of all centuries, can be a source of comfort and encouragement to them and can bring light and understanding to those subjected to a similar fate.

G. H. JONES

SCHULZ, H.: *Leviten im vorstaatlichen Israel und im Mittleren Osten*. 1987. Pp. 203. (Chr. Kaiser, München. Price: DM 45.00. ISBN 3 459 01713 9)

This new study of the Levites in early Israel begins with a brief review of previous research and an analysis of a selection of biblical texts, but its approach has little in common with earlier monographs on the priesthood.

Among its distinctive features are a sociological orientation, the determination to see priestly functions as only one aspect of the Levites' role in village and tribal society and a long comparative chapter which shows how in similar societies elsewhere (not only in the Middle East, but also in Africa) 'priestly' figures have had a number of other responsibilities as well. At times assumptions are made which others would question and some of the suggestions are far-fetched (e.g. that the blesssings at Kuntillet Ajrud were pronounced by Levites). But the cultural parallels are worthy of further study, and a more nuanced picture of the early Levites may well emerge from Schulz's fresh approach.

G. I. Davies

Strange, J.: *Bibelatlas*. 1988. Pp. 64. (Det danske Bibelselskab, Copenhagen. Price: D.Kr. 150. ISBN 87 7523 215 4.

Fifty years ago, Aa. Bentzen prepared a Bible atlas for the Danish Bible Society; it has long been outdated and out of print and has now been replaced by a modern one. Dr Strange's atlas is divided into sections with geographical, historical, and biblical historical maps, and finally city maps, each characterized by a special ground colour. The separation between historical and biblical historical is useful, but not always totally consistent. Still, it is a beautiful and thorough work, indispensable for all Danish students of the Bible.

K. Jeppesen

Thompson, T. L., Goncalves, F. J., and Van Cangh J. M.: *Toponymie Palestinienne: Plaine de St Jean d'Acre et Corridor de Jérusalem* (Publications de l'Institut Orientaliste de Louvain 37). 1988. Pp. 132. (Université Catholique de Louvain; distributed by Peeters, Leuven. Price: BFr. 750.00. ISSN 0076 1265)

A short Introduction explains first that this volume is a preliminary and very partial point of departure for much vaster researches on Palestinian Toponymy which will treat the country in eleven northern and twenty southern regions. The initial research is concentrated on two internally varied and mutually contrasting regions: the Plain of Acre (from immediately south of Akko northwards to the Lebanese frontier, and some 12–8 km. inland); and the Jerusalem corridor (the rectangle 20 km. westwards from the western exit from Jerusalem, and some 7–8 km. both north and south of that line). In each area, particular attention is paid to changes in agriculture and industry, in communications, demography, and hydrology, that have occurred in stages since 1800. Names of watercourses, springs, and wells are probed; and a provisional annotated list provided of settlements both contemporary, and of the nearer and further past. All this is reinforced by the concluding maps which detail the known and named wadis and inhabited localities of the two regions in each of three periods: Turkish, British Mandate, and State of Israel. The authors, who properly claim that their research is purely technical and objective, insist that the preservation of the memory of Arab toponyms is an urgent task for all those interested in the history of the country in its different periods. They remark that in some exceptional cases the current desire to suppress Palestinian Arab traces is even stronger than the desire to preserve Israel's own biblical patrimony. We look forward to the next stages in this large project.

A. G. Auld

Van Seters, J.: *Der Jahwist als Historiker* (Theologische Studien 134). 1987. Pp. 95. (Theologischer Verlag, Zürich. Price: Sw.Fr. 14.00. ISBN 3 290 17134 5)

Those two proponents of the late dating of the historical Jahwist H. H. Schmid (editor) and J. Van Seters (author), have colluded in bringing out this 'preliminary report' of the American *enfant terrible* in the German language — not inappropriate for the subject matter. (However, a succinct version of the contents will be found in the 1986 *SBL Seminar Papers*, pp. 37–55). The first of the book's three sections, 'Das formgeschichtliche Problem des Jahwisten' is an *Unheilsgeschichte*, charting what Van Seters regards as a virtually complete lack of progress in Pentateuchal scholarship since Wellhausen. The second section, 'Der Jahwist und antike Historiographie' follows the lines which any reader of his 'In Search of History' can reconstruct — ancient Near Eastern and Greek historiographical parallels are adduced to point to a date for the Jahwist as an historian. Finally, 'Mythos und Geschichte: Die Frage nach den Anfängen' again draws on comparative materials to illustrate the use of myth — including the important genre of genealogy — in constructing historiographies. The conclusion is that J is an historian writing in the exile, and that much of what was hitherto taken as evidence of the earliest stages of Israelite oral narrative is in fact the invention of this historian. At the same time, of course, the Yahwist — like the P writer later — mythologized history by tracing its origins to the very beginnings of the world, in the age of the gods. Although his arguments are by no means as straightforward as he undoubtedly believes, Van Seters chooses the right views to attack. One awaits with interest the appearance of his book (in English!) on the Yahwist, if only to see whether he has anything to add to what he has already said.

P. R. DAVIES

4. TEXT AND VERSIONS

ALBA CECILIA, A.: *Biblia Babilonica: Jeremias* (Textos y Estudios 'Cardenal Cisneros' de la Biblia Poliglota Matritense, 41). 1987. Pp. xxi, 164. (CSIC, Madrid. Price: Ptas 1,400. ISBN 84 00 06681 2)

This volume, the fifth in the series planned to contain all the books of the Hebrew Bible according to the babylonian tradition, and Alba Cecilia's third, follows the lay-out of her two previous volumes (Ezekiel and Isaiah, see *B.L.* 1982, p. 34). The material for the book of Jeremiah is incomplete, and the text published here has been put together from a number of fragments selected from MSS. listed, described and published by Díez Macho, Merino, Kahle, Yeivin, and others. The critical apparatus contains variant readings gleaned from the available babylonian MSS. and lists all deviations from the text published in the third edition of Biblia Hebraica. A short bibliography concludes the work.

P. WERNBERG-MØLLER

AMMASSARI, A. (ed.): *Il Salterio latino di Pietro* (3 vols). 1987. Pp. 905 (I), 150 (III), and a volume of plates (II). (Città Nuova, Roma. Price: Lire 130,000. ISBN 88 311 7230 1)

The Monte Cassino Latin Codex 557 contains Jerome's version '*iuxta Hebraeos*', his version '*iuxta Septuaginta*' (the Gallican or Vulgate Psalter), the old version from the LXX (the Roman Psalter), and a unique version, 'Anonyma Cassiensis' (hereafter Cas). A critical text and examination was published by A. M. Amelli (Rome, 1912), followed by only a handful of significant studies (Burkitt, Capelle, Allgeier) till Ammassari began his own exhaustive examination. After exploratory articles in 1976–78, he has now presented the fruit of his labours: critical text (Vol. III), full photographs (Vol. II) and introduction, and commentary (Vol. I). Most predecessors had agreed that there is dependence between Cas and Jerome's *Iuxta Heb.*, but disputed which way. Ammassari makes a conclusive case for Cas being the earlier. It is clearly independent of the Roman Psalter, and full of original ways of representing the Hebrew (sometimes by crude calques, sometimes by transliteration, even of the accusative marker *'et*). It omits all the psalm-titles but keeps the fivefold division. Ammassari judges many of its turns of translation to have a 'midrashic' character. Detailed examination has led him to construct a theory that Cas is a Judaeo-Christian production, reflecting the earliest Christian preaching and theology in Italy. He believes that it was designed for continuous use (daily but always omitting Sunday and Thursday) for six-monthly periods, beginning in the spring, and that hints in the translation would correlate with seasons and feasts in a solar calendar of the kind found in the Qumran Temple Scroll. On the basis of many other hints and touches, which he compares with expressions in 5 Ezra and other early western Christian writings, he argues that Cas reveals traces of a Judaeo-Christian theology, which he expounds at length. Unfortunately, like most of the Franciscan School in Jerusalem (where he has worked), he does not get to grips with the fundamental problems of identity and definition involved in such speculation. He is, however, modestly tentative in his hypothesis that the author wrote 'in persona Petri'.

This is an extraordinary study, and it would be a pity if its sheer weight discouraged students from exploring the peculiarities of Cas as they are examined at length in Ammassari's fascinating commentary, and from responding to his most original and stimulating thesis.

R. P. R. Murray

Clarke, E. G. (ed.): *Newsletter for Targumic and Cognate Studies*, Vol. 14.2 (1987); 15.1 (1988). 1988. Pp. 8; 8. (Department of Near Eastern Studies, University of Toronto. Price: $5.00. ISSN 0704 59005)

The number of items on Targum remains small enough, though that is certainly not the fault of the *Newsletter*. The tally of *volumes* on Targum in No. 15.1 is swollen by the welcome appearance of several volumes in the Aramaic Bible series, published by Michael Glazier, Inc., Wilimington (see *B.L.* 1988, pp. 45, 47f and below p. 46f. Coverage of cognate studies remains especially valuable, and there is a good listing of reviews of volumes in the Targumic and cognate fields.

R. P. Gordon

Diez Macho, A. with the collaboration of A. Navarro Peiro: *Biblia Babilonica: Fragmentos de Salmos, Job y Proverbios* (MS. 508 A del Seminario Teologico Judio de Nueva York) (Textos y Estudios 'Cardenal Cisneros' de la Biblia Poliglota Matritense, 42). 1987, Pp. lxxiv, 106. (CSIC, Madrid. Price: Ptas 1,400. ISBN 84 00 06680 4)

The MS edited here (=Kahle's EC 22), one of the collection of Yemenite MSS in the Jewish Theological Seminary, New York, although only containing a small part of the Hebrew Bible (50-odd psalms, 3 chapters of Job and 6 of Proverbs), is of the greatest interest to the student of the biblical text, and it is good to see this work published (albeit 3 years after Diez Macho's death). The article which Diez Macho published in 1959 (*Estudios Biblicos* 18, pp. 325–56) on this MS, its place within the palestinian and babylonian textual tradition, and the problems it presents e.g. in its use of pataḥ, Šewa, and qameṣ, serves as an introduction to the work. The MS (provided with babylonian, supralinear punctuation) differs frequently from the *textus receptus* in its orthography and vocalization. In the critical apparatus the editors have not aimed at a systematic collation with all other known babylonian MSS and have concentrated on comparison with EC 1, MT and the ancient versions; particularly valuable features are the comments and observations (in Spanish) concerning the often problematic additions and corrections introduced into the MS by a later scribe, and the linguistic material contained in the variations from tiberian masora in nominal and verbal patterns.

P. Wernberg-Møller

Diez Merino, L.: *Targum de Qohelet. Edición Príncipe del MS. Villa-Amil no. 5 de Alfonso de Zamora* (Bibliotheca Hispana Biblica 13). 1987. Pp. 405. (Consejo Superior de Investigaciones Científicas, Madrid. Price: Ptas 3,500. ISBN 84 00 06661 8)

In this series in which the author intends to publish the Aramaic version and the Latin translation of the Prophets and Hagiographa (prepared by Alfonso de Zamora for the Complutensian Polyglot but never printed), there has already appeared a volume on Psalms (*B.L.* 1985, p. 45), a volume on Job, and another on Proverbs (*B.L.* 1986, p. 43). The present work, like these predecesors, not only includes the Aramaic text and Alfonso's Latin translation of Qohelet (MS. Villa-Amil No. 5, fols. 154b–175a) but also a number of important surveys of the textual transmission, theological contents, liturgical settings, sources, and language of the TgQoh that amount to a complete monograph and cover the first 200 pp. of the book. A series of comparisons with the Antwerp, Paris, and London Polyglots and, specially, detailed indexes of themes, Aramaic words, persons, and geographical terms in the text enhance the value of this fine work.

F. García Martínez

Dirksen, P. B. and Mulder, M. J. (eds.): *The Peshiṭta, Its Early Text and History: Papers read at the Peshiṭta Symposium held at Leiden 30–31 August 1985* (Monographs of the Peshiṭta Institute Leiden IV). 1988. Pp. x, 310. (Brill, Leiden. Price: fl. 110.00 (ca.$55.00). ISBN 90 04 08769 1; ISSN 0169 9008)

R. J. Owens, 'Aphrahat as a Witness to the Early Syriac Text of Leviticus' (pp. 1–48) examines the thirty Leviticus citations in Aphrahat's Demonstrations. The citations in question are inexact, though Aphrahat's text was generally close to the main P(eshiṭta) tradition. S. P. Brock, 'Text History and Text Division in Peshiṭta Isaiah' (pp. 49–80) outlines the development of the P Isaiah by analogy with M. D. Koster's analysis of Exodus. The divisions of the text in its earliest form are consistent and frequently coincide with Qumran Isaiah spacings and later Masoretic breaks. A. Gelston, 'Some Readings in the Peshiṭta of the Dodekapropheton' (pp. 81–98), concludes that the Hebrew *Vorlage* only rarely diverges from the consonantal M(asoretic) T(ext) and that the P was produced shortly before the MT was fixed. M. D. Koster, 'Which Came First: the Chicken or the Egg? The Development of the Text of the Peshiṭta of Genesis and Exodus in the Light of Recent Studies' (pp. 99–126) in fact mainly discusses a 1952 Manchester M.A. thesis by H. Gordon on P Exodus and argues that the early P text was not targumic. P. B. Dirksen writes on 'The Ancient Peshiṭta MSS of Judges and their Variant Readings' (pp. 127–46) and J. Cook on 'The Composition of the Peshiṭta Version of the Old Testament (Pentateuch)' (pp. 147–88). In the latter the view is again reiterated that P did not originate as a targumic text, a theme in several contributions to the Symposium. M. J. Mulder writes on the P of Ezekiel (pp. 169–82) and other contributions are on particular MSS — A. van der Kooij on 5b1 (pp. 183–99), K. D. Jenner on 8a1 (pp. 200–24) and M. P. Weitzman on 9a1 (pp. 225–58). To the Symposium papers is appended information on variant readings in new MSS for those books of the Leiden Peshiṭta which have already been published.

J. F. Healey

DORIVAL, G., HARL, M., and MUNNICH, O.: *La Bible grecque des Septante. Du judaïsme hellénistique au christianisme ancien* (Initiations au christianisme ancien). 1988. Pp. 368. (Éditions du Cerf/Éditions du C.N.R.S., Paris. Price: Fr. 194.00. ISBN 2 204 02821 5 (Cerf), ISBN 2 222 04155 4 (C.N.R.S.))

Part of the spin-off from the French Septuagint Project (*La Bible d'Alexandrie*), this is the first handbook to the Septuagint in French, and the most up-to-date and useful in any language. It is clearly set out, with concise but limpid explanations of the most complex problems, and excellent bibliographies. The material is divided into bite-sized pieces, which are easy to find one's way around, and short specialized bibliographies accompany each section. The main divisions are as follows (the abbreviations indicate the author of each section): The history of the translation and its setting in ancient Judaism (GD); the text and its history (OM), relationship between LXX and MT, and the Greek language of the LXX (MH); the LXX in the New Testament and the Greek Fathers (MH), the Christian canon and translations derived from the LXX (GD). The emphasis, in each section, is on presenting the problems, distinguishing clearly between established fact and scholarly conjecture, and in the case of disputes setting out the rival views and the arguments supporting them. In other words, this is a book that can be safely entrusted to beginners, yet in which even experienced scholars will find answers to their questions. It should be in every biblical library, and should ideally be translated into English as soon as possible, while the discussion and bibliographies are still fresh and up to date.

N. R. M. DE LANGE

FREDE, H. J.: *Kirchenschriftsteller* (Vetus Latina. Die Reste der altlateinischen Bibel, nach Petrus Sabatier neu gesammelt und herausgegeben von der Erzabtei Beuron. 1/1B: Aktualisierungsheft 1988). 1988. Pp. 100. (Herder, Freiburg im Breisgau. Price: DM 74.00; sub. price: DM 64.00. ISBN 3 451 00479 8)

This is a sort of updating, following a similar *Aktualisierungsheft 1984*, of the patristic information used in the *Vetus Latina* project. It lists new editions, improvement in the knowledge of dating and sources, and corrections and additions in general.

J. BARR

GROSSFELD, B.: *The Targum Onqelos to Genesis* (The Aramaic Bible, vol. 6). 1988. Pp. xiv, 193. (T. & T. Clark, Edinburgh. Price: £34.95. ISBN 0 567 09463 4 (Genesis); ISBN 0 567 09477 4 (series))

GROSSFELD, B.: *The Targum Onqelos to Exodus* (The Aramaic Bible, vol. 7). 1988. Pp. xv, 120. (T. & T. Clark, Edinburgh. Price: £29.95. ISBN 0 567 09464 2 (Exodus); ISBN 0 567 09477 4 (series))

GROSSFELD, B.: *The Targum Onqelos to Leviticus and Numbers* (The Aramaic Bible, vol. 8). 1988. Pp. xv, 171. (T. & T. Clark, Edinburgh. Price: £29.95. ISBN 0 567 09465 0 (Leviticus and Numbers); ISBN 0 567 09477 4 (series))

GROSSFELD, B.: *The Targum Onqelos to Deuteronomy* (The Aramaic Bible, vol. 9). 1988. Pp. 126. (T. & T. Clark, Edinburgh. Price: £29.95. ISBN 0 567 09466 9 (Deuteronomy); ISBN 0 567 09477 4 (series))

The Aramaic Bible series, which aims to translate into English all the extant Targums, has already received attention in *B.L.* 1988, pp. 45, 47f, with notices of the first four volumes. The first volume of the Pentateuch provided B. Grossfeld with the opportunity to revise, expand, and update his earlier work *Targum Onkelos to Genesis* which he co-edited with M. Aberbach (reviewed in *B.L.* 1983, p. 39), but more significantly enabled him to present a study of Targum Onqelos (TO) to the entire Pentateuch. The volumes are special in that they comprise the first critical edition in English of this official Targum and draw on the vast resources of Rabbinic literature and the versions (Sept., Vulg., Pesh., Sam. Pent., Aramaic Bibles, and the other extant Targumim) in the illuminating chapter comments. The editor bases his translation on Sperber's critical text, indicating in italics where the meturgeman (the scribe who translated the original Hebrew text into Aramaic) expands or alters the Masoretic Text. A critical introduction to all the books of TO heads the Genesis volume, the sixth in the series, and is particularly informative on matters of date and provenance, relationship to the Hebrew text, and to Jewish exegesis. Also useful is the lengthy section on theological concepts in the Targum; a variety of topics is discussed including the long history of the interpretation of the *memra* ('word') in the context of Targumic anthropomorphism and anthropopathism.

The first volume contains the bibliography and detailed biblical Targumic, rabbinical, and post-biblical indices.

P. W. Coxon

Gryson, R. and Bogaert, P. M.: *Recherches sur l'histoire de la Bible latine* (Cahiers de la Revue Théologique de Louvain, 19). 1987. Pp. 153. (Publications de la Faculté de Théologie, Louvain-la-Neuve; distributed by Peeters, Leuven. ISSN 0771 6019)

A collection of papers presented at a colloquium to celebrate the award of an honorary doctorate to Professor H. J. Frede. Two are particularly concerned with the Old Testament, namely that of P. Petitmengin on citations of Isaiah in Tertullian, and that of W. Thiele on the title of the Book of Sirach in the Latin tradition.

J. Barr

Harlé, P. and Pralon, D.: *Le Lévitique. Traduction du texte grec de la Septante, introduction et notes* (La Bible d'Alexandrie, 3). 1988. Pp. 224. Cerf, Paris. Price: Fr 125.00. ISBN 2 204 02972 6)

This annotated French translation of the Greek Leviticus follows the Model of M. Harl's Genesis (see *B.L.* 1987, p. 37), indeed Mme Harl had a hand in editing it. The text translated is basically that of Rahlfs, with some improvements due to Wevers. The introduction discusses, among other topics, the structure of the book, its vocabulary, and its style. The notes make frequent reference to the Hebrew, to the other, fragmentary, Greek versions, and to the Greek Jewish and Christian interpretations. The next volume, Exodus, is promised for Spring 1989.

N. R. M. de Lange

Jeansonne, S. P.: *The Old Greek Translation of Daniel 7–12* (CBQ Monograph Series 19). 1988. Pp. 147. (Catholic Biblical Association of America, Catholic University of America, Washington DC. Price: $5.00 ($4.00 for CBA members). ISBN 0 915170 18 3)

After an introductory chapter outlining earlier work on the Old Greek of Daniel the author studies in turn the general character of the translation (taking Dan. 8:1–10 as a sample), errors in reading made by the translator, and subsequent corruptions in the transmission of the Old Greek. These studies provide the background for the main chapter of the book which discusses passages where some theological or historical *Tendenz* on the part of the translator has been alleged. The author concludes that there is little basis for such claims. The methodology is generally sound and the case is on the whole well, if a little rigidly, argued (though it is occasionally marred by some weakness on the Greek side).

S. P. Brock

KOCH, K.: *Deuterokanonische Zusätze zum Danielbuch: Entstehung und Textgeschichte*. Bd I: *Forschungsstand, Programm, Polyglottensynopse*; Bd II: *Exegetische Erläuterungen* (AOAT 38). 1987. Pp. 216; 214. (Butzon & Bercker, Kevelaer; Neukirchener, Neukirchen-Vluyn. Price: DM 160.00 ISBN 3 7666 9525 8; ISBN 3 7887 1267 8; ISSN 0931 4296)

The surprising linchpin of this edition of the Deuterocanonical Additions to the book of Daniel is the advocacy of the claim made by Moses Gaster in 1894 that he had located the original Aramaic composition of Dan. 3:25–90; 14:23 ff (Song of Azariah, Song of the Three Holy Children, and Bel and the Dragon; Susanna was not included) in the mediaeval Chronicle of Jerahmeel. The possibility that a Semitic original lay behind the Greek versions of the Additions had often been recognised and in 1930 led to Kuhl's famous reconstruction of an alleged Hebrew original, but only in these two comprehensive volumes has Gaster's claim been given serious consideration. Dalman's assertion in 1898 that the author of the Chronicle had stated that he had simply translated the texts from Theodotion, accepted as conclusive by all his successors, is questioned by Koch, and the vital notice 'I am copying the missing praises and songs of the three young men . . . which Theodotion found' is taken to mean that Jerahmeel has produced the (Aramaic) text which Theodotion found and used as the basis for his own (Greek) translation. In a thorough verse by verse comparison with the ancient versions Koch attempts to demonstrate that the Aramaic text (Am*) does not derive from Theodotion, LXX or Peshiṭta but represents the *Vorlage* on the basis of which deviations, verse transpositions, and distortion of meaning in the versions can be accounted for. In vol. I the major texts are displayed systematically in Columns (Am*, Peshiṭta, Theodotion, LXX, Vulgate), accompanied by a detailed critical apparatus. A lengthy introduction deals with textual problems, the versions, the Chronicle of Jerahmeel and Gaster's thesis, and Kuhl's reconstruction. Vol. II contains exegesis and comment based on the synoptic presentation of the columns. The position of the Peshiṭta in the second column is justified on the grounds that it occupies an intermediate position between Am* and Theodotion. The few points of contact between the Peshiṭta and Theodotion which deviate from Am* perhaps derive from a later recension which has been contaminated by the Greek text. Koch admits that a major difficulty with Am* is that its Aramaic does not correspond to Biblical Aramaic (*pace* Gaster) but Middle Aramaic as it is represented at Qumran but more especially in the Targums of Onkelos and Jonathan. He suggests that Am* stems originally from a circle other than that of the protocanonical book of Daniel and need not be later in origin. A corollary of his linguistic analysis is Koch's view that the status of the Deuterocanonical Additions, which played such a significant role in the liturgy of the Eastern and Western churches as part of the traditional Catholic canon of scripture, has been diminished by their exclusion from the Jewish-Protestant Canon and that insufficient attention has been devoted to their content. A pertinent example is the Song of Azariah in which the martyrs' death is viewed as an expiatory sacrifice. If Am* is an authentic representation of the original text of the Additions and descends from the ancient cycle of traditions which eventually crystallized in the book of Daniel then there is reason to believe that Dan. 3:40f is the oldest evidence we possess for the idea of vicarious sacrifice by individuals sentenced to death on account of their allegiance to God.

P. W. COXON

NERI, U. (ed.): *Il Cantico dei cantici. Targum e antiche interpretazioni ebraiche* (Tradizione d'Israele, 1). 1987. Pp. 212. (Città Nuova, Roma. Price: Lire 18,000. ISBN 88 311 4908 3)

The paraphrastic Targum to Canticles has already been translated into Latin (by Walton), English (by Gill, Gollancz, and Pope), German (by

Riedel), Dutch (by Mulder), French (by Vulliaud), Spanish (by Díez Merino), and Italian (by Piattelli). Neri's version, based on Sperber's text in *The Aramaic Bible* IV/a (which transcribes BM Or. 2375), marks an advance on earlier efforts, partly because Neri has had the good sense to take over what was useful in his predecessors (though he seems unaware of Pope, Mulder, and Merino). However, the real strength of his work lies in his extensive footnotes which concentrate largely on the parallels to the Targum in classic rabbinic literature. The introduction, aimed at the general reader, puts the Targum into its historical and literary setting. This attractive little volume should serve to open up to Biblical scholars an enigmatic Jewish interpretation of Canticles from the early Middle Ages.

P. S. ALEXANDER

PEREZ CASTRO, F. (ed.): *El Codice de Profetas de El Cairo*.VI: *Ezequiel* (Textos y Estudios 'Cardenal Cisneros', 44). 1988. Pp. 235. (Instituto 'Arias Montano', Consejo Superior de Investigaciones Cientificas, Madrid. ISBN 84 00 06758 4, ISSN 0561 3841)

This part of the Cairo Codex, containing the book of Ezekiel, has been prepared for publication by the team of scholars responsible for the immediately preceding volumes. For notices of the volumes which have appeared so far, see *B.L.* 1988, p. 49 and the further references given there.

P. WERNBERG-MØLLER

SCOTT, W. R.: *A simplified Guide to BHS: Critical Apparatus, Masora, Accents, Unusual Letters & Other Markings*. 1987. Pp. iii, 88. (BIBAL, Berkeley, California. Price: $5.95 plus $1 for postage and handling. ISBN 0 941037 04 5)

This useful volume provides basic guidelines for understanding the critical apparatus, Masora, accents and symbols contained in the *Biblica Hebraica Stuttgartensia* (BHS). When the BHS edition is used initially the array of marginal comments in abbreviated Hebrew and Aramaic, together with the Latin critical apparatus, can be a daunting prospect to the Hebrew beginner. In addition to providing a key to utilize BHS more effectively, Scott has produced a ready reference to the principal elements of the Masoretic textual tradition. Especially helpful are the index of symbols and abbreviations, accompanied by an English translation, of the small Masora (ch. VI) and for the non-Latinist H. P. Rüger's English key to the Latin words, abbreviations, and symbols of the critical apparatus. For more advanced students ch. V describes and explains the two accentual systems of the Hebrew text. In the small section which transliterates names and terms (in ch V) *šin* has been consistently misprinted as *śin* in the Hebrew and Aramaic column.

P. W. COXON

Targum Jonatán de los Profetas Primeros en tradición babilónica. Vol. II: I–II Samuel. Editado por E. MARTINEZ BOROBIO (Textos y Estudios 'Cardenal Cisneros' de la Biblia Políglota Matritense, 38). 1987. Pp. 387. (Instituto de Filología, Departamento de Filología Bíblica y de Oriente Antiguo, C.S.I.C., Madrid. Price: Ptas 3,500. ISBN 84 00 06437 2)

The aim of this work is to offer a complete edition of all the extant MSS of the TgJon of I–II Sam. which preserve a true Babylonian Aramaic text and a true Babylonian vocalization. The only MSS left out because of the bad state of preservation are the small fragments Y. L. Nahum 122 and 222–23, and fols. 7–11 of Firkowitsch I. 133. A detailed Introduction describes the MSS edited in the book and characterizes the vocalization system used by every one of them. The arrangement of the text is basically the same throughout: the author uses the MS 229 of the Jewish Theological Seminary of New York as his basic text and prints in parallel all the other preserved witnesses, so that his edition is more of a synopsis than of a traditional critical edition. When JTS 229 is missing the author has supplemented it with JTS 230, and when both MSS are lacking he uses Qafih 2 in order to provide a continuous text of the Targum, although these two late MSS are of inferior quality and they are heavily contaminated by the Tiberian phonetical traditions. Although the critical notes are kept to a minimum, the author has provided a useful and reliable tool for targumic research.

F. García Martínez

Tov, E.: *A Computerized Data Base for Septuagint Studies: The Parallel Aligned Text of the Greek and Hebrew Bible* (Computer Assisted Tools for Septuagint Studies (CATSS) Volume 2) (Journal of Northwest Semitic Languages, Supplementary Series 1). 1986. Pp. xiv, iv, 144. (JNSL, Stellenbosch)

This monograph is an extended introduction to the parallel aligned text of the Greek and Hebrew Bible. As such it is an essential tool in the hands of anyone wishing to use this text. But the complexities of the transliteration/ system of equivalence markers must be seen as significant deterrents to a wider readership (despite the editors' claim that the volume is 'aimed at all scholars who . . . turn to the textual criticism of the Bible' [ii]).

D. G. Deboys

Vetus Latina. Die Reste der Altlateinische Bibel nach Petrus Sabatier neu Gesammelt und in Verbindung mit der Heidelberger Akademie der Wissenschaften herausgegeben von der Erzabtei Beuron. 11/2 *Sirach (Ecclesiasticus)*, herausgegeben von Walter Thiele: 2. Lfg: *Einleitung* (Schluss). 1988. Pp. 81–160. (Herder, Freiburg im Breisgau. Price: DM 81.50; sub. price: DM 72.00. ISBN 3 451 00425 9)

This fascicle brings to a conclusion the introduction to this extremely detailed edition. Much in these pages concerns divisions of the texts, *Kapitelsreihen*, 'internal titles', the mode of division of the Laus patrum, and discussion of the theories of Theilmann and de Bruyne.

J. Barr

Vetus Latina. Die Reste der altlateinischen Bibel, nach Petrus Sabatier neu gesammelt und herausgegeben von der Erzabtei Beuron. 12: *Esaias*. Herausgegeben von R. Gryson. 2. Lieferung: *Is. 1, 22–5, 7*. 1987. Pp. 81–160. (Herder, Freiburg im Breisgau. Price: DM 81.50; sub. price: DM 72.00. ISBN 3 451 00441 0)

This second fascicle follows swiftly upon the appearance of the first, and gives hopes that the entire book will be rapidly published. The highly detailed presentation continues to be remarkable: one single verse, Isa. 5:6, takes up almost six pages, mainly of notes in double columns. The patristic quotations collected provide a rich display for the connoisseur of the older exegesis.

J. Barr

Vetus Latina. Die Reste der altlateinischen Bibel, nach Petrus Sabatier neu gesammelt und herausgegeben von der Erzabtei Beuron. 12: *Esaias*. Herausgegeben von R. Gryson. 3. Lieferung: *Is. 5, 8–7, 14*. 1988. Pp. 161–240. (Herder, Freiburg im Breisgau. Price: DM 81.50; sub. price: DM 72.00. ISBN 3 451 00442 9).

The third fascicle of the edition of Isaiah in the Old Latin continues the high standard of the series (see *B.L.* 1988, p. 52). The present portion comes to an end, tantalizingly, at one of the most important places in the book, namely, the beginning of the Emmanuel prophecy.

J. Barr

5. EXEGESIS AND MODERN TRANSLATIONS

BECKER, J.: *2 Chronik* (Die Neue Echter Bibel: Kommentar zum Alten Testament mit der Einheitsübersetzung, Lfg.20). 1988. Pp. 133. (Echter Verlag, Würzburg. Price: DM 28.00 (sub. price: DM 24.00). ISBN 3 429 01135 3)

Being the direct continuation of Becker's commentary on 1 Chronicles in the same series (cf. *B. L.* 1988, p. 55), this volume has no separate introduction, but the exegesis naturally demonstrates the same interpretation as was set out there. Once again, the comments are terse and economical, though reflecting the fruit of study of (mainly German) secondary literature. Scholars will regret that Becker does not have the luxury of space to engage with the views of those with whom he disagrees, but general readers will no doubt find this a helpful introduction to the world of the Chronicler, with theology dominating over historical concerns.

H. G. M. WILLIAMSON

BOICE, J. M.: *Genesis: An expositional commentary*, vol. 3: *Genesis 37:1–50:26* (Ministry Resources Library). 1987. Pp. 366. (Zondervan, Grand Rapids, Michigan. Price: $20.95. ISBN 0 310 21590 0)

This volume, dealing with the Joseph story, is the third in Dr Boice's homiletic commentary on Genesis (the first two appeared in 1982 and 1985 and were not reviewed in the *Book List*). It is divided into studies of roughly sermon length. Joseph is now an example to believers facing the temptations of a secular society, now a type of Christ in his submission to and overcoming of suffering. The studies are both scholarly and topical. They will appeal to readers who share the author's evangelical and very conservative approach to scripture, but others may find them stiff and restricted in range.

J. C. L. GIBSON

BRANDSCHEIDT, R.: *Das Buch der Klagelieder* (Geistliche Schriftlesung, Altes Testament, Bd 10). 1988. Pp. 168. (Patmos, Düsseldorf. Price: DM 29.80; sub. price: DM 26.00. ISBN 3 491 77166 8)

The author accepts that the book of Lamentations belongs to the period of the destruction of Jerusalem and its temple (586 B.C.) and reflects the grief of the people who experienced such a catastrophe, and finds its main thought to be concerned with the question of the justice of God's wrath and with the related question of the attitude of the faithful to the obscurity of God. These are themes of perpetual and of current interest.

Dr Brandscheidt has examined these themes and the book of Lamentations in her previous work on 'forensic lament' (see *B. L.* 1985, p. 73), but this time the treatment is presented in a more popular form. The greater part of her commentary is devoted to the text and content of the five laments, but there are sections on the book as an exposition of Israel's forensic songs and on the concern with these themes as a preparation for the suffering of Christ.

An attempt is made throughout the discussion to bring out the spiritual relevance of the book to present-day problems.

G. H. JONES

CASALIS, G. and ROUSSEL, B. (eds): *Olivétan, traducteur de la Bible* (Actes du colloque Olivétan, Noyon, mai 1985). 1987. Pp. 198. (Cerf, Paris. Price: Fr. 90.00. ISBN 2 204 02637 9)

The four hundred and fiftieth anniversary of the first publication of Pierre Robert Olivétan's French translation of the Bible was marked by a colloquium held in Noyon, the translator's birthplace, in May 1985. This volume contains twelve papers contributed to the colloquium; several of them deal with the life, times, and environment of Olivétan. His native province of Picardy was visited and influenced by Erasmus, it was the native province of Jacques Lefèvre d'Étaples, Olivétan's predecessor as a Bibler translator, and Olivétan himself was John Calvin's cousin. For our present purpose the most relevant parts of the volume are those which deal with Olivétan as a translator of the Old Testament. He could read Hebrew, but sought help where he could find it — notably in Zwingli's annotations and in the Latin versions of Oecolampadius and Pagnini. One sample of his translation is given from the book of Isaiah — the catalogue of female finery in Isa. 3:16–24 — with an analysis of his renderings; and S. Amsler uses chapter 53 of the same book to illustrate the qualities of his Old Testament version, its strengths and its weaknesses, and the translator's personal engagement with the text on which he works.

F. F. BRUCE

CRENSHAW, J. L.: *Ecclesiastes* (Old Testament Library). 1988. Pp. 192. (SCM, London. Price: £10.50. ISBN 0 334 00361 X)

As we would expect from a scholar who has devoted so much of his life's work to the study of Israel's wisdom literature, this is an excellent commentary on Qohelet. A very comprehensive bibliography and a fifty-page introduction provide us with a fairly complete survey of present day attitudes to the book. Crenshaw has no new solutions to offer to the notorious problems of understanding this text. He expounds it as basically the work of one author, though, along with a perhaps less fashionable older tradition of scholarship, he does see the hand of a glossator in a few passages. But mostly he accepts that the contradictions in the book 'express the ambiguities of daily existence and the absurdity of human efforts to understand it' (p. 49). Along with the consensus of scholars he adheres to a date for the work somewhere between 250 and 225 B.C.E. Unlike most volumes in the Old Testament Library the commentary is based on the Hebrew text, though non-Hebrew readers should still find much of benefit in it, especially in the introduction. The translation Crenshaw offers is most attractive, combining accuracy with real literary qualities. All in all, I would expect this commentary to supersede that of Gordis as the standard work on the text in the English-speaking world.

A. P. HAYMAN

DEISSLER, A.: *Zwölfpropheten III: Zefanja, Haggai, Sacharja, Maleachi* (Die Neue Echter Bibel: Kommentar zum Alten Testament mid der Einheitsübersetzung, Lfg. 21). 1988. Pp. 235–342. (Echter Verlag, Würzburg. Price: DM 28.00 (sub. price: DM 24.00). ISBN 3 429 01138 8)

The earlier parts of this commentary were reviewed in *B. L.* 1983, p. 47 and *B. L.* 1985, p. 55. The present volume completes Deissler's commentary on the Twelve Prophets, and maintains the high standard of the earlier parts. A general characterization of this series may be found in *B. L.* 1982, p. 51.

Zephaniah's prophecy is dated to the earlier part of Josiah's reign, and about two thirds of the book is attributed to the prophet, the last seven verses being post-exilic in origin. The basic redaction of Haggai's prophecies was completed before the dedication of the Temple in 515. 2:11–14 does not refer to the Samaritans. Zechariah 1–8 essentially derives from the prophet, but 3 is a secondary insertion into the cycle of night-visions. 6:9–15 originally referred to Zerubbabel. 9–14 stems from several sources, but all from the late fourth or third century. Malachi reflects a background similar to that of Nehemiah. Only 3:1b–4 and 3:22–24 are later.

A. GELSTON.

DILLARD, R. B.: *2 Chronicles* (Word Bible Commentary 15) 1987. Pp. xxiv, 323. (Word Books, Waco, Texas. Price: $24.95. ISBN 0 8499 0214 2)

The overall format of this commentary follows the by-now well-established pattern of the series. The introduction is very brief, since most of the usual introductory matters have already been dealt with by R. L. Braun in his contribution on 1 Chronicles in this series (see *B. L.*, 1987, p. 56). The commentary itself is clear and well-structured, with perhaps more concern to salvage the Chronicler's reputation as a historian than has been shown by most recent scholars. There are useful excursuses on the presentation of Solomon (which owes much to the work of Williamson), on the theme of retribution, on Jehoshaphat, and on Hezekiah, so that overall a valuable contribution is here made to the understanding of this neglected book. Helpful also is the extensive bibliographical information, both in the main bibliography and in those which accompany each chapter.

R. J. COGGINS

DURHAM, J. I.: *Exodus* (Word Biblical Commentary, 3). 1987. Pp. xxxiv, 516. (Word Books, Waco, Texas. Price: $24.95. ISBN 0 8499 0202 9)

In many ways this is an excellent commentary. Its central concerns are with the translation of the text and the elucidation of its theological affirmations. Although matters such as source-criticism are not so highly regarded, the commentary is informative about them. Durham sees the book of Exodus as dominated by 'the theology of Yahweh present with and in the midst of his people Israel', alternately revealed and proved: an insight which he acknowledges that he owes to his teacher G. Henton Davies (but his name is surprisingly misspelt on p. xxvii). All this, and much else, is well done. But there is a certain tendency to overstate a good point. It is strange, for example, that the introduction to a commentary which makes much of the importance of the canon begins, quite deliberately, with the statement: 'The Book of Exodus is the first book of the Bible'. This is surely a theological as well as a numerical error!

G. I. DAVIES

Femte Mosebog, Josva & Dommerbogen. (Det gamle Testamente i ny oversættelse). 1988. Pp. 258. (Det danske Bibelselskab, Copenhagen. Price: D.Kr.80.00. ISBN 87 7523 205 7)

In the series of trial translations of the Old Testament, the books of Deuteronomy, Joshua, and Judges have now been published. By this edition more than sixty per cent of the Old Testament has appeared in a new Danish translation, and the discussion for and against making it into a new authorized version goes on vividly in the Danish press. The present translations are made by E. Nielsen and B. Ejrnæs, and edited by B. Ejrnæs, S. Holm-Nielsen, and K. Jeppesen.

K. JEPPESEN

FUHS, H. F.: *Ezechiel II 25–48* (Die Neue Echter Bibel: Kommentar zum Alten Testament mit der Einheitsübersetzung, Lfg. 22). 1988. Pp. 135–275. (Echter Verlag, Würzburg. Price: DM 28.00 (sub. price: DM 24.00). ISBN 3 429 01137 X)

This second volume of the Ezekiel commentary for the New Echter Bible follows on directly from the first (see *B. L.* 1985, p. 55), and completes the coverage of the book. It offers a fresh translation and a detailed exposition of the book, with almost all the critical and theological comment contained in this. Accordingly the introduction to the separate units is kept to a minimum, and the overall effect is of remarkable compactness. The commentary itself is very clear and readable and, on critical issues regarding the book, follows quite closely the main lines advocated by Zimmerli. An original prophetic nucleus has been expanded in a lengthy developmental process by an Ezekiel 'School' so that the final stratum has a distinctly apocalyptic character. The primary message of hope for the future given by Ezekiel is contained in Ezek. 33–37, which was given a conclusion in the vision of the restored temple. The basis of this vision is to be found in 40:1–2; 43:4–7; 47:1–12, which has then undergone extensive elaboration. Later still the Gog-pericope of 38–39, which was originally quite separate and self-contained, was inserted before this great temple vision.

Altogether this is an excellent commentary, well abreast of contemporary scholarship and thoroughly readable in presentation.

R. E. Clements

Die Fünf Bücher der Weisung: verdeutscht von Martin Buber gemeisam mit Franz Rosenzweig — mit einer Beilage: *Martin Buber: Zu einer neuen Verdeutschung der Schrift*. 1987. Pp. 582, 44. (Verlag Lambert Schneider, Heidelberg. Price: DM 54.00. ISBN 3 7953 0180 7)

The main work, the eleventh edition of Buber's translation of the *Torah*, is described as an improved edition of the tenth, noted in *B. L.* 1983, p. 46. That edition already contained the inserted supplement with Buber's comments on his new translations of the Scriptures. The latest edition of the Writings in this series was noted in *B. L.* 1988, p. 56.

A. G. Auld

Gerstenberger, E. S.: *Psalms*. Part 1, with an *Introduction to Cultic Poetry* (The Forms of the Old Testament Literature, xiv). 1988. Pp. xv, 260. (Eerdmans, Grand Rapids MI; distributed by Paternoster, Exeter. Price: £15.95. ISBN 8 8028 0255 9)

Of the twenty-four volumes projected for the series this is the fifth to appear. The introduction (17pp.) sketches the types of Hebrew poetry and shows the author's interest in small-group rituals and social needs. This outline is reinforced by a glossary of terms commonly used for genres and formulas. After a few further pages on the growth and structure of the Psalter, each psalm is treated in turn under the headings of Text (only a brief characterization), Structure, Genre, Setting, Intention, Bibliography. If this regimented presentation, in accordance with the series, makes for rather indigestible reading, the author has succeeded in providing a useful tool for research. Amidst all the references to conflicting views, his own are stated clearly and often favour post-exilic, even synagogal, origin. This volume reaches Ps.60; a further volume will complete the Psalter and include Lamentations.

J. H. Eaton

Hartley, J. E.: *The Book of Job* (The New International Commentary on the Old Testament). 1988. Pp. xiv, 591. (Eerdmans, Grand Rapids, Michigan; distributed by Paternoster, Exeter. Price: £19.50. ISBN 0 8028 2362 7)

After a comprehensive introduction (60pp.), the author presents the text in his own close translation, each portion being followed by exegesis undergirded with numerous footnotes and concluded by a discussion of 'aim' (i.e. relation to the overall theme). It is a substantial and economical commentary which should be much used. Cautious and conservative, it frankly states and faces difficulties of text and structure and achieves a balanced treatment. It provides much linguistic and bibliographical information in the ample footnotes, leaving the main commentary quite accessible to the general reader.

J. H. EATON

HERRMANN, S.: *Jeremiah (1.1–19)* (Biblischer Kommentar: Altes Testament XII/1). 1986. Pp. 1–80. (Neukirchener, Neukirchen-Vluyn. Price: DM 26.80 (sub. price: DM 19.80). ISBN 3 7887 0787 9)

1986 not only saw the appearance of commentaries on Jeremiah by Carroll, Holladay, and McKane, it also was the year when Herrmann's major BKAT made its initial contribution to Jeremiah commentaries in the form of fascicle 1 on Jer.1.1–19 (or at least the first eighty pages of commentary on Jer.1!). Should Herrmann live long enough to complete his undertaking this will be the longest of the current Jeremiah commentaries — indeed, if this fascicle is anything to go by the completed work will run to over two thousand pages (the law of diminishing returns may set in after ch.25 and reduce the final number of pages, but we shall have to wait and see).

The BKAT format of bibliography, text, form, location, exegesis, and purpose is followed and Herrmann provides an exhaustive discussion of everybody's viewpoint on various issues in the text. If Herrmann continues this pace and style, then this will be the definitively informative commentary on Jeremiah. It is too early to assess where Herrmann will appear on the spectrum of recent Jeremiah commentaries — to the left of Holladay, and to the right of McKane, and Carroll, I expect — because the 'Einleitung' section always appears at the end of BKAT productions; but Herrmann's position on Jeremiah is well-known from other writings of his and this commentary gives some evidence of no major change on Herrmann's part. He recognizes elements of deuteronomistic editing in ch.1 (e.g. in v.16), but the larger issues of the composition of the book are not addressed here. Impressively comprehensive in its treatment of the secondary literature on Jer.1 it will be interesting to see if the English-speaking guilds of biblical scholarship will require this BKAT to be translated into English whenever it is completed. In the meantime I wish Professor Herrmann long life, good health, and extraordinary good luck.

R. P. CARROLL

JAGERSMA, H.: *Numeri*. Deel II (De predeking van het Oude Testament). 1988. Pp. 198. (Callenbach, Nijkerk. Price: fl 69.50 (sub. price: fl 62.50). ISBN 90 266 0733 4)

Volume 1, covering Numbers 1–15 was reviewed in *B. L.* 1984, p. 54. Volume 2 takes the commentary to the end of the Balaam cycle (24:25). One small variation between the volumes is that the author now places the beginning of the Balaam cycle at 21:21 as against 22:2 in the introduction to Volume 1. An exilic or post-exilic date is proposed for much of the material in 16–24. References to Moab and Edom are exilic, Numbers 19 (the red heifer) is a free composition from the post-exilic period, while the reference to Kittim in 24:24 indicates a date shortly before the death of Alexander the Great (323) for this section. On the other hand, earlier material that has been utilized includes the story of the brazen serpent (21:4–9) which was originally a justification for the Jerusalem serpent cult abolished by Hezekiah. The theological expositions highlight the theme of 'liberation', especially in chapters 16–18, dealing with priestly matters. Priestly office must not be seen as an opportunity for power, but for service of the God of Israel who sets his people free.

J. W. ROGERSON

KEIL, C. F.: *Die Bücher der Könige* (TVG Kommentare). 1988. Pp. x, 430. (Brunnen Verlag, Giessen. Price: DM 68.00. ISBN 3 7655 9207 2)

To mark the centenary of the death of Carl Friedrich Keil in May 1888 the second edition of his commentary on the books of Kings (1876) has been republished; a biography, assessing his work and contribution is also promised for 1989. However, Keil's work on Kings is set in its proper context in a useful introduction by Peter Siemens.

Although C. F. Keil and F. Delitzsch differed in many respects, notably in their handling of Pentateuchal Criticism and in their attitude towards eschatology, they worked together to produce the great 'Keil-Delitzsch' commentary on the whole of the Old Testament. Keil's contribution on the books of Kings appeared as part of that project in 1865, but it had already made its appearance as a book in 1846, and even before, as early as 1835, the author was engaged on the work. Therefore, the appearance of an improved and enlarged second edition in 1876 concluded a project on which Keil had been engaged for some forty years.

The commentary is characterized by a careful philological and textual analysis of the Hebrew text, an expert handling of historical and geographical information on various localities, an exact archaeological description of Israelite and non-Israelite institutions and a subtle symbolic understanding of Israel's cult. Added to these characteristics are his concern for relating the material to other books, especially those of the New Testament, and, as benefits a pupil of E. W. Hengstenberg, his search for its spiritual and theological meaning.

G. H. JONES

KIDNER, D.: *The Message of Jeremiah* (The Bible Speaks Today). 1987. Pp. 176. (Inter-Varsity Press, Nottingham. Price: £4.50. ISBN 0 85110 779 6; ISBN 0 8308 1225 3(USA))

This volume is one of a series of expository commentaries, whose editors claim that they are meant 'to expound the biblical text with accuracy, to relate it to contemporary life, and to be readable'.

If one adjudges this commentary by these criteria, one may say that the first passes the test. While it is a *tour de force* to attempt an exposition of Jeremiah is so small a volume, the commentary, though very conservative (e.g. the part played by Baruch in the preservation and editing of the material seems somewhat exaggerated), does set the writings into their historical context. The second requirement is not so satisfactorily fulfilled, as modern issues are introduced somewhat obtrusively into the exposition and the two worlds (of yesterday and today) are not really integrated. So far as readability is concerned, one must enquire about the expected readership. The book could hardly be put into the hands of the general reader, as the allusions pre-suppose a readership already immersed in the biblical materials. The vocabulary also presupposes readers who share the theological and experiential background of the writer.

Rather than attempting to work systematically through Jeremiah's fifty two chapters, the writer might perhaps have found a thematic approach more palatable.

R. HAMMER

KING, P. J.: *Amos, Hosea, Micah — An Archaelogical Commentary*. 1988. Pp. 176. (Westminster, Philadelphia. Price: $20.95. ISBN 0 664 21876 8. Paperback price: $15.95. ISBN 0 664 24077 1)

This is more of an archaeological 'companion' to the books in question than a commentary in the strict sense, as it does not work through the text section by section and inevitably many verses are left without any specific comment. But the intention, to supply in a convenient form the archaeological material that helps to clarify the meaning of the text, is an admirable one and excellently carried out. King (whose close involvement in American archaeological enterprises fits him well for the task) begins with general chapters on archaeology and the eighth-century prophets, and their historical and geographical setting. Then follow 'Architecture, Fortifications, and Warfare', 'Cult in Israel and Judah', 'Agriculture, Plants, and Animals' and (with specific reference to Amos 6) 'The *Marzeaḥ*: Banquets and High Living'. As well as adding to the understanding and enjoyment of some much-studied books, the volume provides a useful summary of recent discoveries about the religion of ancient Israel and is in general a splendid introduction to biblical archaeology in the best sense of the term.

G. I. DAVIES

KNIGHT, G. A. F. and GOLKA, F. W.: *Revelation of God: A Commentary on the Books of The Song of Songs and Jonah* (International Theological Commentary). 1988. Pp. ix, 136. (Handsel, Edinburgh; Eerdmans, Grand Rapids, Michigan. Price: £4.95. ISBN 0 905312 74 0; ISBN 0 8028 0336 9)

The *International Theological Commentary* goal is: The Old Testament alive in the Church, and is addressed to ministers and Christian educators. It does not claim to deal with critical problems but 'offers a theological interpretation of the Hebrew text'.

The trouble writing such a commentary on the Song of Songs is that one is forced into a very tight corner, for the book was probably 'admitted' to the Jewish canon (and only, incidentally, by the skin of its teeth) on the basis of an allegorical interpretation of the text — God was the lover and Israel the beloved — and taken over by the Christian Church where Christ was the lover and the Church or individual was the beloved. If, as is likely, the book is a collection of love poems, then this interpretation is forced, to say the least. In fact this interpretation belongs to a period in Judaism and early Christianity when allegory was considered by some, a respectable exegetical method of interpretation. Otherwise the book would have remained outside the canon.

Knight seems, however, to reject the allegorical approach (p. 8), but his position, which is difficult to share, owes much to it. The sacred editor 'has placed his poems, by divine inspiration, in such an order that he is able, step by step, to show the meaning of true love. He thus reveals not just the love of a young human couple for each other, but actually the love of the living God'.

By contrast the Jonah commentator has an easier task; but whereas Knight writes for the ministers and laymen, Golka seems to feel that Old Testament scholars are breathing down his neck, as it were, and is not, therefore, so digestible. He divides the text into eleven passages and offers a brief but interesting interpretation of these in turn. In addition he offers two 'Digressions' — on the authorship of the Jonah Psalm, and the meaning of *raʿah* in Jonah and the Old Testament, and a brief chapter on 'the Message of the Book of Jonah'. Finally, because of his constituency, he feels obliged to add an Epilogue on 'The Sign of Jonah'.

R. B. SALTERS

LABUSCHAGNE, C. J.: *Deuteronomium*, deel I A/B (De Prediking van het Oude Testament). 1987. Pp. 305, 36; 299, 45. (Callenbach, Nijkerk. Price: fl 87.50 (each volume); (sub. price: fl 78.75). ISBN 90 266 0727 X; ISBN 90 266 0743 1)

Volume I of Professor Labuschagne's commentary devotes nearly 700 pages to chapters 1–11. Future volumes will deal respectively with chapters 12–26 and 27–34. Any commentary on this scale promises to be a major work. This commentary certainly qualifies for such a description, but it is also a highly unusual and original work. Anyone who has studied the author's articles on logo-technical analysis will not be surprised to learn that such analyses play an important part in the commentary. Professor Labuschagne argues that the composition of Deuteronomy was based upon the employment of various models in which the numbers of words in a literary unit played a significant part. In order to assist the reader, the two parts of volume 1 are accompanied by booklets which print a complete transliterated Hebrew text together with the logo-technical analysis. The analysis helps to determine the exact limits of larger and small units, and indicates formal structures within units, such as structures based upon the numerical values of the name Yhwh. The analysis also suggests that there are few, if any, later additions to the book.

Professor Labuschagne takes the time of composition to be the late exile, and the function of the book to be instructions to returning exiles in the form of a farewell address attributed to Moses. He does not deny the older, northern origin of the material, nor that an earlier version was concealed in the temple and discovered. However, his exposition eschews attempts to reconstruct earlier, hypothetical versions, and concentrates upon the final form in its late-exilic setting.

Many readers may find the approach strange and the underlying theory unlikely. Is it possible that ancient writers composed texts in the quasi-artificial way implied here? Yet there seems to be evidence from the middle ages that such techniques were employed, and a hundred years ago it would have been difficult to believe that a time would come when music was composed on the basis of a serial of twelve notes. Although this commentary, and its subsequent volumes will make great demands upon its readers, it deserves careful and sympathetic attention. Only thus will scholarship be able to judge the significance or otherwise of logo-technical analysis.

J. W. ROGERSON

MAARSINGH, B.: *Ezechiel*. Deel II (De Prediking van het Oude Testament). 1988. Pp. 303. (Callenbach, Nijkerk. Price: fl 82.50; sub. price: fl 74.50. ISBN 90 266 0742 3)

Deel I of this commentary was noted in *B. L.* 1986, pp. 55f. This volume has the advantage of reaching a convenient ending, with the completion of the foreign nation oracles at ch. 32, and leaves the remainder of the book to Deel III. The normal pattern of the series is here followed.

The first section of the commentary, ending at ch. 24, is completed with some useful discussions, including a fairly full section on ch. 18 (pp. 47–64). The text is divided into chapter units, which do not (e.g. at 21:1–37, commentary on 20:45–21:32) always coincide with the Hebrew, but clearly it is a mistake to assume that text-divisions in the ancient texts and in modern translations always coincide. In the foreign nation chapters, a division is made by the objects of the various oracles — 25, near neighbours; 26–28, Tyre; 29–32, Egypt.

There are extensive end-notes and a selective bibliography, but, regrettably, no index. Recent Ezekiel commentaries are listed, though it might be useful to some readers to see a note of the English translation of Zimmerli.

P. R. ACKROYD

MEYERS, E. and C.: *Haggai, Zechariah 1–8* (Anchor Bible 25B). 1987. Pp. xcvi, 478 (Doubleday, Garden City, New York. Price: $20.00. ISBN 0 385 14482 2)

The features of this long-established commentary series are here followed, both in outline structure, and in the tendency for successive volumes to increase in length. (The original series plan envisaged six minor prophets in one volume; here nearly 600 pages are devoted to 1½ of the collections.) More graciously, one can readily recognize the value of the Meyers' work: careful and detailed commentary, with full notes on each phrase supplemented by overall comments, is preceded by an introduction which attempts a precise historical reconstruction of the period of the prophets' ministry. The work of Haggai and Zechariah is assessed in very positive terms. Haggai and Zech.1–8 are held to form a composite work, put together not later than 515 and perhaps edited by Zechariah himself. The authors recognise that in this reconstruction they are often going against the trends of recent scholarship, and so they offer a brief and fair survey of current scholarly work, and a full bibliography. Much here is of interest; one can still wish that it had been expressed more concisely.

R. J. COGGINS

MULDER, M. J.: *Koningen*. Deel I: *1 Koningen 1–7* (Commentar op het Oude Testament). 1987. Pp. 306. (Kok, Kampen. Price: fl 67.50. ISBN 90 242 0784 3)

This series of commentaries on Old Testament books was launched shortly after the end of the Second World War. The earlier volumes were uncompromisingly conservative but, as N. H. Snaith wrote of one of them in 1954, 'the discussions are full and detailed, the translations are scholarly and accurate, and the linguistic scholarship leaves nothing to be desired' (*Eleven Years*, p. 572). Today, under a new generation of editors (J. L. Koole, J. C. de Moor, M. J. Mulder, and E. Noort), this positive testimony remains valid, but in critical matters one notes a more open interaction with contemporary scholarship.

In this volume on 1 Kings 1–7, for example, due account is taken of the significance of the first two chapters as the concluding portion of the 'succession narrative' and of the light thrown by the Abiathar section on the two rival orders of priesthood. The LXX variants in ch. 2, as studied by D. W. Gooding and G. Krautwurst, receive attention. The details of the temple construction are carefully discussed in the light of linguistic and archaeological research; in addition, there is a section on the cosmic significance attached to them in later days. It would be a pity if the helpfulness of this work were restricted to students able to read Dutch.

F. F. BRUCE

NELSON, R. D.: *First and Second Kings* (Interpretation). 1987. Pp. ix, 273. (John Knox, Atlanta, Georgia. ISBN 0 8042 3109 5)

This new series of commentaries is aimed at those who use the Bible in the church and seeks to meet the needs of teachers and preachers. Consequently Professor Richard Nelson from Gettysburg, in writing on the two books of Kings, has concentrated on the work as theological literature rather than as a historical document. By focusing on it as a canonical whole rather than taking it as a collection of earlier materials or as part of the Deuteronomistic History he tries to draw the reader into an engagement with the text itself and with the 'meaning effect' it has on its modern readers. Difficulties are not ignored, and in concluding his treatment of each section the commentator gives an indication of the problems that arise when the text is used as Scripture today, and he also suggests directions for using the text in preaching and teaching.

The task has been skilfully executed and Nelson has avoided the temptation of spiritualizing the text superficially and has escaped from any hint of shallowness. His analysis reflects a sound knowledge of the literary, textual and historical issues that arise in dealing wtih the text; although he does not allow such considerations to dominate his approach, it is from this base that he has moved on to a theological interpretation of each section. It is a most interesting attempt to produce a commentary that is different in emphasis, and the result is a very readable and useful volume.

G. H. Jones

Odgen, G.: *Qoheleth* (Readings. A New Biblical Commentary). 1987. Pp. 236. (Sheffield Academic Press. Price: £25.00 ($45.00). ISBN 1 85075 071 8; ISBN 1 85075 070 X (paperback))

Qoheleth is a difficult work, and any serious attempt towards elucidating its problems is on the whole, to be welcomed. It is clear from the Preface of this book, that the author feels he has written 'a commentary which makes more sense of the book than I was able to find in so much of the secondary materials'. While it may not be for him to say this, he has set about his task in a workmanlike manner.

Before tackling the commentary proper Ogden sets the scene with an introduction dealing with the Unity, Structure and Purpose of the book and in which he offers two Appendices on 'The meaning of the term *hebel*' and 'The term *yitron*'. Since an understanding of these two terms is vital to the interpreting of Qoheleth it is helpful and appropriate to have them dealt with at this point.

Ogden is right to examine the ways in which Qoheleth uses the term *hebel* rather than accepting its meaning from other Old Testament passages, and he arrives at the conclusion that its meaning for Qoheleth is 'enigma'. While it may be difficult to find a good English translation for this term Old Testament students may not be convinced with this rendering. Again, in the second Appendix the author goes too far in his treatment of *yitron* when he says 'it seems also to incorporate the possibility of some experience beyond death'.

This commentary is well structured and nicely laid out; but it is uneven in quality and depth. While the author saves space by not including a translation there are times when one requires to have one, and in some cases. e.g. at 3:15, he advances arguments without a thorough examination of the text.

At the end of the work Ogden has an Excursus entitled 'Chinese Wisdom and Biblical Revelation' — reflecting the experience of the author in East Asia and echoing some of his earlier publications — in which he draws attention to similarity of themes and style in Chinese and Old Testament literature, and asks about the implications for Theology.

R. B. Salters

Ringgren, H.: *Psaltaren 1–41* (Kommentar till Gamla Testamentet). 1987. Pp. 248. (EFS-förlaget, Uppsala. ISBN 91 7080 771 X)

This is the first of a series of commentaries on Old Testament books, following the pattern of the New Testament series, Kommentar till Nya Testamentet. The Swedish Bible Commission's draft translation of Pss. 1–41 (of which 1–7; 22–25; 33; 36 have already been published) is used as a basis for the commentary. Each psalm is followed by notes on the language, so far as that is necessary to explain the meaning. A knowledge of Hebrew is not presupposed and Hebrew words are transliterated. Then come sections on literary type, structure, and related matters, and finally exposition. There is no general introduction; but at various points detached notes are supplied on the problems involved in translating the Psalms, Messianic psalms, psalm types, superscriptions, the penitential psalms, parallelism, the Hebrew text, the Servant psalms, Psalm 22 and the New Testament, and the problem of tenses in the Psalms. Within the text there are some 17 illustrations (most taken from ancient monuments) and maps. The volume is a model of clear and concise presentation.

G. W. Anderson

RUIZ GONZALEZ, G.: *Comentarios hebreos medievales al libro de Amós*. (Publicaciones de la Universidad Pontificia de Comillas, Madrid, Estudios, 31). 1987. Pp. liii, 300. (UPCM, Madrid. ISBN 84 85281 67 5)

In this posthumous work the late Old Testament Professor of the Pontificial University of Comillas (Madrid) offers an annotated Spanish translation of the Commentaries to the Book of Amos of Raši, E. de Beaugency, A. 'ibn 'Ezra', D. Qimḥi, and I.'ibn Caspî. The book is quite straightforwardly organized: the biblical lemmata (in the fifteenth century Spanish translation of the *Biblia de Alba*) are followed, verse by verse, by the various commentaries, each with the corresponding annotations. The translations are faithful and the annotations not only make explicit the biblical, targumic or talmudic references, illuminate grammatical problems, or show the relationships between the various commentaries, but dig abundantly in the inexhaustible mine of the Jewish Medieval grammatical and exegetical writings, opening wide the rich but practically unexploited field of Medieval Jewish Exegesis. The work has been revised by Dr M. T. Ortega Monasterio who has also written the Introduction providing short sketches of the life and works of the Commentators and placing them in the context of Medieval Jewish Exegesis.

F. GARCÍA MARTÍNEZ

SAWYER, J. F. A.: *Izaya-sho I*. Translated by S. Higuchi. 1988. Pp. 519. (Shinkyō Shuppan-sha, Tokyo, Price: ¥3,800)

This is a Japanese translation of Isaiah. Volume 1 (The Daily Study Bible: Old Testament, 1984) (See *B. L.* 1985, p. 65) and chs. 33–39 of Isaiah. Volume 2 1986) (See *B. L.* 1987, p. 55)

K. K. SACON

SCHMIDT, W. H.: *Exodus (5, 1–6, 30)* (Biblischer Kommentar: Altes Testament II/4). 1988. Pp. 241–312, with vii pages of Introduction to the complete volume. (Neukirchener, Neukirchen-Vluyn. Price: DM 26.80 (sub. price: DM 19.80). ISBN 3 7887 0421 7)

After a long interval, of which the author is very conscious and seeks to excuse, the commentary has resumed progress, bringing to a conclusion the first volume of the projected three volumes of Exodus (for reviews of previous fascicles see *B. L.* 1975, p. 50; 1979, p. 61; 1984, p. 59). The schedule for the series now indicates a different author for the third volume covering Ex. 25–40. The delay has, however, enabled the author to engage thoroughly with most recent work on Pentateuchal criticism which has fundamentally questioned the traditional critical approach. In the present fascicile this is most relevant to 6:2–12 in relation to which the author dismisses the view that P was a stage in redaction, in favour of the earlier generally accepted view that it represents an originally independent narrative source, only secondarily combined with JE. Ex.6:2–12 forms, with Ex.1:13f.; 2:23*ab*–25, a narrative connection, making a formal unit in that 6:2ff. is the divine response to the need and complaint described there. Though parallel with Ex.3, Ex.6 is remarkably independent of the intertwined JE story of the call of Moses, which in turn indicates that the redactor who connected J and E is not identical with the redactor who added Ex.6. Additional points of particular interest in this fascicle concern Ex.5. Against Noth, the author argues that it is impossible to use this story to argue that Moses does not belong originally to the exodus tradition; there is no stage of the story in which the elders alone represent Israel before Pharaoh. In relation to the title 'God of the Hebrews' (5:3), the author holds that *ʿpr/ ḫap/biru* is best understood as a sociological term which may, however, have undergone a change in significance, but that 'Hebrew' is best taken as an ethnic term, one belonging to Israel, and so the 'God of the Hebrews' can scarcely mean anything older than 'Yahweh, the God of Israel'.

A. D. H. MAYES

SKEHAN, P. W. and DI LELLA, A. A.: *The Wisdom of Ben Sira* (Anchor Bible 39). 1987. Pp. 648. (Doubleday, New York. Price $22.00. ISBN 0 385 13517 3).

At long last we have a large, definitive commentary on Ecclesiasticus which seems to cover all aspects of the book. Textually the authors consider the latest evidence for the original Hebrew from Qumran and Masada, and in the translation, which is based on the New American Bible, make judgements that seem 'most reasonable for the particular text under consideration'. Textual discussions and commentary seem thorough, and the 35-page bibliography shows wide scholarly coverage. A useful introduction discusses canonicity, literary genres, links with the Hebrew Old Testament, and ancient foreign literature, a summary of the teaching, and coverage of the book's poetry (assonance, chiastic patterns, inclusion, etc.). There follows a survey of Ben Sira's teaching.

This book will be excellent for all students of Ecclesiasticus: the language is not too technical to confuse beginners. Skehan completed most of the translation before his death, and we owe a large debt to Di Lella for completing Skehan's work with introduction and commentary.

J. G. SNAITH

STUART, D.: *Hosea-Jonah* (Word Biblical Commentary 31). 1987. Pp. xlv, 537. (Word Books, Waco, Texas. Price: $24.95. ISBN 0 8499 0235 5)

In accordance with the general pattern of the series each section of the text is here provided with bibliography, translation, textual notes, comment, and explanation, with an introduction to each prophetic book treated. A brief general introduction (betraying, incidentally, a rather limited view of modern scholarly approaches to the prophets) lists and classifies pentateuchal curses and blessings as the basis for understanding the prophetic formulations. Regrettably the volume is a disappointment and needs to be used with caution. The textual notes in particular are unreliable and lack discrimination as is immediately apparent in the first such section, and sporadically throughout (a particularly careless example occurs in the exegetical comment on Hosea 3:5), and there are not a few surprising statements. The treatment as a whole lacks balanced judgement. Important exegetical questions are in some instances ignored; in others discussion is replaced by too ready resort to sometimes highly suspect emendation. The treatment of Jonah is particularly disappointing. Its artistry and wealth of meaning are obscured by a thoroughly simplistic approach altogether inadequate for so dramatically structured a work. It is hardly a balanced treatment which devotes more space to the expression 'king of Nineveh' than to discussing message and purpose! Undoubtedly one of the most useful features of this work is its extensive bibliographies.

G. I. EMMERSON

STUHLMUELLER, C.: *Rebuilding with Hope: A Commentary on the Books of Haggai and Zachariah* (International Theological Commentary). 1988. Pp. xv, 165. (Handsel, Edinburgh; Eerdmans, Grand Rapids, Michigan. Price: £4.95. ISBN 0 905312 75 9; ISBN 0 8028 2374 2)

For Stuhlmueller, as for Hanson, Second Isaiah and Ezekiel represent two very different traditions, and the prophets Haggai and Zechariah belong firmly to the Ezekiel tradition, a tradition rooted in the temple and the Zadokite priesthood. Haggai sees the rebuilt temple as a sign of the new age (unlike the Chronicler who sees temple and liturgy as ends in themselves), and in Zerubbabel a renaissance of the Davidic tradition. Only the returned exiles form the true remnant. The present book stems from Haggai and his editor who, however, faithfully follows the prophet's emphases. Zechariah gradually eliminates hope in Zerubbabel in favour of the high priest. For him the sanctuary is even more clearly the centre of messianic fulfilment, while for Second Zechariah it has become a 'messianic sanctuary' without any presence of a Davidic Messiah. Zechariah 'slows down' Haggai's immediate eschatological expectations, seeing a greater need in the interim time for purity and social justice. Second Zechariah is probably to be dated (with R. L. Smith) about the end of the sixth or the beginning of the fifth century B.C.E., since its 'apocalyptic' expectations are less developed than those of Isa. 24–27 or Dan. 7–12, compared with which 'Second Zechariah remains less certain and final' in his hopes. There is full recognition of the role of tradents throughout the whole book of Zechariah: 'We are speaking. . .of an inspired tradition of. . .Zechariah rather than of a single inspired author' (p. 47).

Stuhlmueller compresses an immense amount of material into 160 pages, writing with pungency, scholarship, and spiritual perceptiveness. This book will be of great service to a wide range of readers.

R. A. Mason

Wenham, G. J.: *Genesis 1–15* (Word Biblical Commentary 1). 1987. Pp. liii, 353. (Word Books, Waco, Texas. Price: $24.95. ISBN 0 8499 0200 2)

This volume, to be succeeded by the author dealing with chapters 16–50, follows the established format of the Word Biblical series, a format which with its clearly defined procedures is particularly suitable for students studying the text in Hebrew. For each portion of the text Wenham gives his own translation, accompanied by quite detailed grammatical and textual notes. There then follow in succession a section on form, structure and setting; a full verse by verse analysis; and a section entitled 'explanation' which sums up his findings on the portion and sketches briefly its central meaning and its theological thrust. The Introduction of some fifty pages is a crisp, if at times slightly evasive, account of the Documentary hypothesis as it applies to Genesis and of the recent critcisms of it by Van Seters, Rendtorff, Whybray and others. Like them Wenham is straining after a single 'author' or editor who was responsible for the present literary shape of the Pentateuch, but unlike them he places the final composition in the 10th century or even earlier. In this conclusion Wenham betrays his conservative background; but his book will also perturb many stricter conservatives, for it fully accepts the necessity for source analysis and marks a clean break with any lingering attachment to Mosaic authorship. Even a cursory comparison of this volume with Kidner's commentary on Genesis in the Tyndale series is enough to make it abundantly clear that things have been moving in conservative academic circles in the last decade or so. Wenham's comments on the futility of what he calls the Bible-versus-science debate are also much sharper than Kidner's. I wish this commentary well; it not only makes a brave attempt to bring conservative discussions of the most sensitive book in the Old Testament into the mainstream of Old Testament scholarship, but is itself a very good commentary. It combines meticulous exegesis with keen theological insight, and it does not neglect either the new 'Eng. Lit.' approach associated with names like Alter and Fokkelman. If it has a substantial fault, it is that it is rather too discreet; it is not really a tentative commentary, though it sometimes pretends to be one.

J. C. L. Gibson

Westermann, C.: *Genesis: A Practical Commentary* (Text and Interpretation). 1987. Pp. xiii, 338. (Eerdmans, Grand Rapids, Michigan; distributed by Paternoster, Exeter. Price: $16.95; £12.95. ISBN 0 8028 0106 4)

This commentary is on a much grander scale than others in the popular series of Dutch origin to which it belongs. It is based on Westermann's magisterial three-volume commentary in the *Biblischer Kommentar* series, and readers are referred to this for philological support for the translation and for detailed treatment of the historical and literary problems, as well as for further bibliography. I doubt whether many of them will take advantage of this invitation and I suspect, therefore, that they will find some of the dense exegesis rather difficult. The great man might have been better advised to have started afresh for the constitutency of busy clergy and interested laypersons for whom this series is designed. I hope nevertheless that those who pick up his volume will persevere with it. It may not always be easily digestible, but it will introduce them to the mature reflection of a master and the distilled wisdom of decades of hard research. The practical lessons, drawn often in a couple of sentences, are theological rather than topical — and none the worse for that.

J. C. L. Gibson

Westermann, C.: *Genesis*. Translated by D. E. Green. 1988. Pp. xiii, 338. (T. & T. Clark, Edingburgh. Price: £9.95. ISBN 0 567 29160 1)

The American edition of this translation, noted above, has been followed by a welcome British one, independent of any series — and now without the Dutch sub-title 'A Practical Commentary'.

A. G. Auld

6. LITERARY CRITICISM AND INTRODUCTION

Alonso Schökel, L.: *A Manual of Hebrew Poetics* (Subsidia Biblica 11). 1988. Pp. xi, 228. (Biblical Institute Press, Rome. Price: Lire 24,500. ISBN 88 7653 567 5)

For various reasons Alonso Schökel's *Estudios de poetica hebrea* (Barcelona 1963) was not so widely read as it deserved to be. We now have a pruned, revised and translated edition of that pioneering work, and the result is warmly recommended. Although the author simply numbers his chapters consecutively, I prefer to describe the contents in more structured form. The introductory section comprises chapters on the history of research into Hebrew poetry, a brief account of poetic genres, and discussion of sound and rhythm in poetry. The main part of the book describes parallelism, and then synonymy, repetition, merismus, and antithesis. The last two topics are imagery and figures of speech. Closing chapters deal with structure: dialogue versus monologue in a poem, and development of a theme versus composition from a variety of units.

By example the book will encourage readers to study Hebrew poetry not in atomistic detail but as a series of individual compositions, each with its own unique character and flavour. It should prepare the student for more technical works and could, in fact, be described as a more advanced version of R. Alter's *The Art of Biblical Poetry* (see *B. L.* 1988, p. 69). Hebrew quotations are transliterated. As well as the introductory bibliography there are references for most of the chapters and useful indices.

W. G. E. Watson

Aurelius, E.: *Der Fürbitter Israels: Eine Studie zum Mosebild im Alten Testament* (Coniectanea Biblica; OT Series 27). 1988. Pp. 224. (Almqvist & Wiksell, Stockholm. Price: Sw.Kr. 167.00. ISBN 91 22 00940 X)

This dissertation deals with the element of the Moses tradition of the Old Testament which focuses upon his role as intercessor. In it Aurelius is primarily concerned with the long admonitory speech of Moses in Deut.9:6–29 which recalls the intercessions of Moses at the time of the rebellious actions of Israel in the wilderness. This speech is therefore not in itself an intercessory prayer but marks a primary aspect of the Deuteronomistic treatment of the rebellion in the wilderness theme. It is at the same time a very carefully constructed reflection on the theology of intercession, the role of prophetic mediation in Israel's faith, and the unique authority of Moses as leader. As a distinctive feature of the Deuteronomistic theology, the speech stands in a position of great prominence and indicates a very fresh and highly theological development of the 'Moses as Leader' theme.

R. E. CLEMENTS

BAL, M.: *Murder and Difference: Gender, Genre, and Scholarship on Sisera's Death* (Indiana Studies in Biblical Literature). 1988. Pp. x, 150. (Indiana University Press, Bloomington & Indianapolis. Price: $35.00. ISBN 0 253 33905 7)

This short and brilliant book (translated by Matthew Gumpert) is another intensely dense work from Mieke Bal, whose previous book *Lethal Love* (1987: Indiana University Press) scintillated and obfuscated in about equal parts. It is a close reading of Judges 4–5 using a number of disciplinary (historical, theological, anthropological, literary) and transdisciplinary (thematic, gender) codes in the service of the *critical* enterprise of reading texts. For Bal criticism is a differentiating process which in practice also seeks to denounce ideologies considered dangerous. Her book is therefore an important contribution to current literary concerns with the ideologies of texts and can be read in terms of the code *Ideologiekritik*. As a study in intersemiotic readings of texts this is, in no sense, a conventional close reading of a biblical text. The key to her approach is that of *code*: the conventions governing it, its plurality, materiality, constraints and the institutions where it has its natural setting. Apart from her treatment of the text which is very sophisticated and illuminating, she carries on a highly critical argument with the secondary literature on Judges 4–5 which makes her book a valuable contribution to Judges studies. Her emphasis on and explication of the ambiguities inherent in the text give her work a sophistication often lacking in other (male!) analyses of the story of Deborah and Barak, Sisera and Jael. At the same time she indicates the immense richness of the text, especially when trawled by different coded readings. Much of the virtue of her approaches to the text arises from her own placement outside the guild of conventional biblical scholars (she is professor of Comparative Literature at the University of Rochester) and is undoubtedly due to her resolutely feminist ideological code (she is also Susan B. Anthony, Professor of Women's Studies at Rochester). In themselves these factors provide the exegete with a vantage point from which to do an excellent piece of work on the ethics of reading. Characteristic of Bal's sophisticated readings of biblical texts is her ability to do readings of paintings which bear on the text: in *Lethal Love* she examined the 'Samson and Delilah' of Rembrandt and Rubens, here she considers Artemisia Gentileschi's 'Giudetta e Oloferne'.

If criticism be permitted of Bal's work it must be about the excessively formalist nature of this book. Also at times she appears to practise the very vices she accuses other scholars of — a fault perhaps inevitable in this kind of passionately committed ideological writing. Her feminist code tends to dominate the analysis without benefit of a corresponding *Ideologiekritik* of this currently fashionable mode of reading the Bible. Her book is a hard read: indeed, there is about it a stubborn impenetrability which renders it unreadable at times (or at least requires a number of readings in order to grasp its meaning). Some of this unreadability may be due to the book's origins in a language other than English; though the density of its ideological and semiotic analyses cannot be ruled out as culpable here. Summarizing what she has to say about Judges 4–5 is impossible and that is the fault of her style. But these criticisms about the formal aspects of her work should not be allowed to mask the excellence of her analysis nor undermine the brilliance of her demonstration of the semiotic uncertainty of the text. I think every biblical scholar should be made to read this book as a salutary instruction in how to read biblical texts. Another very interesting volume in the Indiana Studies in Biblical Literature.

R. P. CARROLL

BALDERMANN, I.: *Einführung in die Bibel*. 3rd revised edition of *Die Bibel — Buch des Lernens* (Uni-Taschenbücher 1486). 1988. Pp. 291. (Vandenhoeck & Ruprecht, Göttingen. Price: DM 27.80. ISBN 3 525 03268 4)

Starting from the surprising way the Bible has come alive in today's world, Baldermann aims at showing how it leads its readers to an experience of learning (note the earlier title of the book). He finds the key to understanding the Bible in speech (*Sprache*) rather than story or narrative, and points to ways in which the experiences found in the Bible relate closely to our twentieth-century experiences, social and personal. Although all the technical methods of biblical criticism and exegesis are adopted and often explained, this is expressly *Einführung* not *Einleitung*, and the chapters have such headings as 'Basic concepts', 'Characteristics of biblical speech', and 'Nodal points', the last being creation, 'suffering — for us', and resurrection. The only individual 'authors' discussed at length are the Priestly writers, Paul, and John, since they alone stand out from the long process of anonymous tradition. Baldermann does not hesitate to express opinions that differ from currently received wisdom, as when he questions whether 'Scheltwort' is a correct term to apply to the words of the prophets since it implies that their hearers are aware of their wrongdoing. From time to time the message of the Bible is related to modern situations and the writings of significant theologians such as Bonhoeffer are quoted. Altogether this is a rich and fascinating study in which the Old Testament has a very large place.

C. S. RODD

BALL, I. J., Jr.: *Zephaniah: A Rhetorical Study*. 1988. Pp. iv, 308. (Bibal, Berkeley, California. Price: $16.95 plus $1.00 for postage and handling. ISBN 0 941037 02 9)

The preface by D. L. Christensen states that this work was written fifteen years before as a dissertation, and that is has not been brought up to date. Ball describes his aim as 'to examine the literary structure and meaning of the Book of Zephaniah by means of rhetorical analysis' (p. 1), and the introduction describes in a thorough way the details of the analytical method to be used. The main body of the book consists of three chapters, each devoted to a chapter of Zephaniah. First, there is a study of the Hebrew text of the chapter discussed, and then a rhetorical and exegetical discussion of its contents. The concluding chapter examines 'the structure of the book of Zephaniah as a whole', and also suggests a possible historical background for different parts in the late seventh century B.C. There follows a translation, together with the unpointed Hebrew text, and a bibliography. This book is to be commended for its attempt to hold together textual and philological study on the one hand, and rhetorical criticism on the other. While there are places where the discussion is open to criticism (e.g. although the evidence of the LXX, Vulgate and Targum is regularly cited, that of the Peshiṭta is not, and yet some textual evidence could have been presented even before the publication of A. Gelston's edition), and the evidence is sometimes open to a different evaluation, this is a substantial contribution to the study of Zephaniah and will help all who work on the prophet in the future.

J. A. EMERTON

BARRÉ, L. M.: *The Rhetoric of Political Persuasion: The Narrative Artistry and Political Intentions of 2 Kings 9–11* (CBQ Monograph Series 20). 1988. Pp. ix, 161. (Catholic Biblical Association of America, Catholic University of America, Washington DC. Price: $5.00 ($4.00 for CBA members). ISBN 0 915170 19 1)

In this extremely well presented and well argued doctoral dissertation Barré applies source, form-critical, and literary analyses to 2 Kings 9–11 in order to determine its nature and intention. He finds an independent account, which he designates a 'political novella', written by royal scribes soon after Jehoiada's coup to justify his actions to the elders of Judah whose support for the new regime was vital. The method adopted by these scribes was to contrast Jehu's bloody revolt with the non-violent transition of power to Joash and to stress the purity of Jehoiada's motives. The additions made by the Deuteronomistic redactor and post-Dtr editors modify the story in line with their own interests, and further modifications of the text can be seen in the account by the Chronicler. The narrative is similiar to other politically motivated texts such as the Succession Narrative and the History of David's Rise. A feature of the study is the examination of the characterization of the actors in the two dramas.

C. S. RODD

BARSOTTI, D.: *Le Prophète Malachie*. Translated from Italian by E. de Solms. 1988. Pp. 75. (Tequi, Paris. Price: Fr 33.00. ISBN 2 85244 866 1)

The aim of this small book 'is not to express our opinions, but to listen to God who speaks to us through the inspired books'. It is thus more a devotional meditation than a scholarly commentary, but it engages honestly and intelligently with the text. An introduction sets the historical context for 'Malachi' (a functionary title, not a proper name) dating him about 480 B.C.E. or a little later. The main divisions of the book deal with (i) the covenant relation between God and Israel; (ii) the relation between men and women in the family; (iii) the relation between individuals and the nation, a relation which calls for social justice. Marriage is a sacramental expression of the covenant between God and his people. It can be recognised that in such a passage as 2:17 — 3:6 two independent motifs have been later joined, but we have to listen to the final form of the text because that is the form inspired by God and given by the Church (p. 53). Those who argue for the primacy of the 'final form of the text' are not always as open about their motives.

This little study is full of wisdom and searching insights. Many more groups and individuals would benefit from its translation into English.

R. A. MASON

BAUMGARTNER, W.: *Jeremiah's Poems of Lament*. Translated by D. E. Orton (Historic Texts and Interpreters in Biblical Scholarship). 1987[?1988]. Pp. 115. (Almond, Sheffield. Price: £17.50 ($29.95). ISBN 1 85075 116 1. Paperback price: $6.95 ($10.95). ISBN 1 85075 115 3)

It is good to have this excellent English translation (with not a German technical term in sight!) of Baumgartner's seminal work, *Die Klagegedichte des Jeremia* (1917), which examines the relationship between Jeremiah's poems of lament and the individual songs of lament in the Psalter, illustrating in passing the impact of Gunkel's form critical work. After a brief historical survey of the question, and an examination of the various elements which constitute the individual songs of lament type, Baumgartner considers Jeremiah's poems of lament, of which he identifies six (11:18–20, 21–23; 15:15–21; 17:12–18; 18:18–23; 20:10–13), assigning to an appendix the four related poems (12:1–6; 15:10–12; 20:7–9; 20:14–18) which conform less strictly to the songs of lament style. The final chapter addresses the question of the authenticity of Jeremiah's poems of lament, using as a criterion prophetic elements discernible in them but absent from the Psalter. Baumgartner concludes that Jeremiah adopted a literary form already in existence, though not to the detriment of his poetic creativity. Reference to the German original is facilitated by the inclusion in square brackets of page numbers of that edition. A note indicator on p. 39 is incorrect.

G. I. EMMERSON

BEYERLIN, W.: *Bleilot, Brecheisen oder was sonst? Revision einer Amos-Vision* (OBO 81). 1988. Pp. 61. (Universitätsverlag, Freiburg (CH); Vandenhoeck & Ruprecht, Göttingen. Price: SwFr. 19.00; DM 28.00. ISBN 3 7278 0579 X; ISBN 3 525 53710 7)

This patient and masterly unpacking of the meaning of Amos's third vision (7:7–8) is prefaced with the surprised confession that the author had been teaching as recently as summer 1987 the now rejected *opinio plurium*. The negative starting point hinted at in his title is that *'nk* does not mean 'lead'. Surprisingly, the bibliography does not note H. Gese (in *Vienna Congress Volume*, VT Suppl. 32, 1981) among his predecessors in this respect. The main elements of his own account are that the proper meaning is 'tin' (and shining brightness is a frequent visionary component); that the wall (of tin) is to be understood in its normal sense of defensive city wall, and not more generally as a reference to a large mass of the metal; that the tin in Yahweh's hands implies the potential for weapons; and, importantly, that it is divine speech which introduces the surprise threat that such weaponry will be aimed at Israel's heart. Pharaonic parallels are noted, as is the wider context in Amos of pictures of apparent safety transposed into total destruction. Certainly a fresh seeing of the original seeing!

A. G. AULD

BONORA, A.: *Qohelet. La gioia e la fatica di vivere* (Leggere oggi la Bibbia 1/15). 1987. Pp. 158. (Queriniana, Brescia. Price: Lire 15,000)

The author, who is one of the editors of the series *Leggere Oggi La Bibbia*, and in which he is also the author of three other volumes, tackles the book of Qoheleth in the style of *Einleitung*, albeit on rather more popular lines. The target constituency is the intelligent layman in the Church today.

While Bonora writes clearly, it is not always easy to find one's way around in the book, which is divided into ten chapters dealing with such themes as 'The God of Qoheleth', 'Qoheleth and Women', 'Death and Human Morality', with the final chapter tackling the Christian understanding of the book. There is a biblical index and a number of very brief bibliographical notes.

R. B. SALTERS

BONORA, A. (ed.): *La Spiritualità dell'Antico Testamento* (Storia della spiritualità I). 1987. Pp. 559. (EDB, Bologna. Price: Lire 38,000. ISBN 88 10 34011 X)

Louis Bouyer's great French study *A History of Christian Spirituality* has long been recognized as a classic. But Bouyer only began with the New Testament and, as part of a new Italian translation of his work, it was felt desirable to produce an opening volume dealing with Old Testament spirituality. Hence the present book is entirely new, the result of collaboration between a number of Italian scholars. As a prelude to the whole undertaking, the opening section consists of two essays, one on the problem of writing a history of Christian spirituality by P. L. Boracco, the other on the Old Testament as a literature of hope by the editor. The next section is made up of six studies of the epochs and types of spirituality in the Old Testament, covering the *Tōrāh* and the Deuteronomic tradition (A. Fanuli), the Prophets (A. Spreafico), Wisdom (F. Festorazzi), Apocalyptic (U. Vanni), and the Psalter (G. Ravasi). Then follows a section on some typical representatives of Old Testament spirituality, in which various scholars discuss not only such figures as Abraham, Moses, and David but also such topics as priestly spirituality, the theme of martyrdom, and the figure of the Servant. Finally, since this volume is to form part of a history of *Christian* spirituality, a closing chapter by M. Cimosa looks at the significance of the Old Testament for the faith of the Church. Old Testament spirituality has been somewhat neglected recently, but there are signs of a revival of interest in it, to which this book makes an important contribution. Throughout it displays sound scholarship based on extensive and up-to-date reading, though a slight cavil might be that older English scholarship is rather neglected, e. g. there is no mention of Wheeler Robinson. There is a three-volume English translation of Bouyer's *History*: to accompany it, a similar translation of this new work would be very desirable.

J. R. Porter

Braulik, G.: *Studien zur Theologie des Deuteronomiums* (Stuttgarter Biblische Aufsatzbände, 2). 1988. Pp. 342. (Verlag Katholisches Bibelwerk, Stuttgart. Price: DM 39.00. ISBN 3 460 06021 2)

The general editors (Gerhard Dautzenberg and Norbert Lohfink) envisage the new series to which this book belongs as contributing to Catholic German biblical scholarship by providing reprints (though occasionally original publications) of papers on a particular theme by one or more authors, or of the collected works of an author on particular areas of study. Reference to the original place of publication is facilitated by the indication in each paper of its original pagination.

The present collection of studies on Deuteronomy is intended to make a selection of Braulik's work more easily and generally accessible, especially to those who wish to follow up the background and more detailed justification for the exegesis of Deuteronomy given by the author in the recently published first part of his commentary on Deuteronomy (*Die Neue Echter Bibel*). None of these ten studies is unimportant, but particular attention may still be drawn to the earliest of them, Braulik's analysis of deuteronomic legal terminology, dating from 1970. Other articles are closely related to Braulik's other major work, on Deut. 4:1–40: *Die Mittel deuteronomischer Rhetorik*; others deal with cult and festival and Deuteronomy, with the relationship between the order of the laws in Deut. 12–26 and the decalogue, and with diverse theological themes in Deuteronomy and the deuteronomistic history. This is a varied and impressive collection which establishes both the centrality of deuteronomic study in Old Testament scholarship, and also Braulik's standing as a major contemporary contributor in that area.

A. D. H. Mayes

Buchholz, J.: *Die Ältesten Israels im Deuteronomium* (Göttinger Theologische Arbeiten 36). 1988. Pp. 140. (Vandenhoeck & Ruprecht, Göttingen. Price: DM 28.00. ISBN 3 525 87389 1)

The study begins with a discussion of the significance of the reference to the elders in the deuteronomistic Deut.31:9–11, where the original text presented them alone as those to whom Moses gave the law. Passages from the hand of a later deuteronomistic editor, however, no longer assign them this theological function but see them simply as part of a varied range of leadership types in Israel. This latter picture is to be found in those parts of

Joshua which represent additions to the work of the deuteronomistic historian. For the deuteronomistic historian the elders were protectors of the Yahwistic faith, political representatives of the people and the ones who accompany the ark of Yahweh.

This idealized picture of the elders is a reaction to the criticism of their cultic activities expressed by Ezekiel. To his prophecies, however, secondary material has been brought in order to rehabilitate them and to give them the task of communicating to the exiles the justice of Yahweh's judgment. The role of the elders in Ex.24:1a, 9–11 is also a late assertion of their cultic integrity.

The positive presentation of the elders takes up their demonstrable judicial and ritualistic role in the monarchic period, and is related to the exilic need to find a leadership body in Israel after 587 which could undertake the theological task of making known that the destruction of Judah was the result of apostasy. The changed presentation of the elders in the work of the later deuteronomist makes it doubtful that they ever fulfilled the function which the historian envisaged for them.

This is an excellent and detailed study, making use of latest developments in the literary criticism of the deuteronomistic history, and offering some support to recent questioning of the early dating of much Tetrateuchal material.

A. D. H. Mayes

Castel, F.: *'Dio disse...'. I primi undici capitoli della Genesi*. Translated from French by L. Zardi. 1987. Pp. 202. (Paoline, Cinisello Balsamo (MI). Price: Lire 10,000. ISBN 88 215 1218 5)

Originally published in French, this short book consists of a series of theological comments, designed for the general reader, on the text of the first eleven chapters of Genesis. It is not a scholarly work, although the author shows a sound acquaintance with the general critical understanding of these chapters. What gives his undertaking a degree of freshness and originality, as compared with similar productions, is his use of comparative material from three other areas. First, he regularly compares — and contrasts — Genesis with texts from ancient Egypt and Mesopotamia and, secondly, he extends this process, following the methodology of Eliade, to include evidence from many other civilizations. Thirdly, he finds illumination in the Jewish exegetical tradition, quoting frequently from the Targums and Midrash. This tradition, as the editor states, is probably little known to the general Christian public and those unacquainted with it will find considerable interest in the way Castel uses it.

J. R. Porter

Cate, R. L.: *An Introduction to the Old Testament and its Study*. 1987. Pp. 539. (Broadman, Nashville, Tennessee. Price: $19.95. ISBN 0 8054 1233 6)

The Professor of Old Testament at Golden Gate Theological Seminary has written this introduction for beginners in Old Testament study — for beginners, too, with very conservative presuppositions. He tries to make them familiar with the methods and findings of biblical criticism as painlessly as possible: they need not jettison what they have hitherto believed, but are invited to appreciate another approach to the literature. Daniel, for example, 'had its origin in the early Persian period but . . . was later revised and edited in the Maccabean era to speak with a new freshness to those troubled times'. On Isa. 7:14 he thinks it 'possible that God was trying to reveal the virgin birth [of Jesus] to Isaiah but that it was so unbelievable that he chose a word which would allow such but not require it'. But it was for Ahaz that the message was intended: what was *he* expected to make of it? One may hope that the author will succeed in his laudable enterprise without himself being suspected of heresy.

F. F. BRUCE

COATS, G. W.: *Moses: Heroic Man, Man of God* (JSOT Supplement Series 57). 1988. Pp. 250. (Sheffield Academic Press. Price: £22.50 ($35.00). ISBN 1 85075 096 3. Paperback price: £9.50 ($14.95). ISBN 1 85075 095 5)

In the introduction Coats describes his book as an exploration of the Moses traditions 'on the basis of a particular kind of literary analysis', distinct from but related to the historical and sociological points of departure preferred by other scholars. As a foundation for this analysis Coats argues that the narratives can be treated as 'heroic saga', which puts him closer to Gressmann than to Noth and von Rad, although he does not deny the importance of the 'credal' elements in the tradition emphasized by the latter. He seeks by an examination of the individual stories to recover a 'Moses image' which has impressed itself on the tradition in various ways, and he finds it to be, in the older material, a subtle combination of leadership and initiative ('heroic man') with witness of and to God's action in saving his people ('man of God'). In P the latter aspect is determinative. The groundwork for this outstanding book has been done over more than twenty years, and it is a pleasure to welcome, and commend, its author's carefully considered conclusions.

G. I. DAVIES

CORNELIUS, J. B.: *La Genèse et la Préhistoire*. 1986. Pp. 191. (Lanore, Paris, Price: Fr. 75.00. ISBN 2 85157 022 6)

The author of this work is neither a theologian nor a palaeontologist by profession; he has spent a good part of his life as a seaman. He is a man of wide reading, in the natural sciences as well as in biblical literature; he has mastered what he has read and thought deeply about its significance. In this book he endeavours to relate his study of prehistory to the study of Genesis: both sources of knowledge, he finds, bear witness to the existence of a divine will. The work is commended in a preface by the Dominican scholar R.-L. Bruckberger.

F. F. BRUCE

CRENSHAW, J. L.: *Chie no Maneki*. Translated by K. Nakamura. 1987. Pp. 350. (Shinkyō Shuppan-sha, Tokyo. Price: ¥2,800)

This is a Japanese translation of *Old Testament Wisdom: An Introduction* (1981) (See *B. L.* 1982, p. 59).

K. K. SACON

CROCETTI, G.: *1–2 Samuele. 1–2 Re* (Leggere oggi la Bibbia 1/8). 1987. Pp. 158. (Queriniana, Brescia. Price: Lire 15,000)

This volume is one of a series designed to help individuals or study groups wishing to 'read the Bible today' with understanding and profit. Its level is more or less that of the Daily Study Bible, though the exposition is less detailed. Crocetti, who has already produced a volume on Joshua, Judges, and Ruth for this series, divides the narrative of Samuel and Kings into fourteen sections, each with a dominant theme. He deals adequately for his purpose with literary and historical criticism. Between the basic material and the final deuteronomic redaction he discerns a prophetic recension, and illustrates the tensions set up in the process by the fact that Elijah offers a highly approved sacrifice on a 'schismatic' altar. The historical evidence of Egyptian, Assyrian and Babylonian records is adduced to illustrate the biblical narrative. The critical approach strengthens the doctrinal and ethical lessons which are drawn from each section.

F. F. Bruce

Delcor, M.: *Studi sull'Apocalittica*. Translated from French by Antonio Zani (Studi Biblici 77). 1987. Pp. 281. (Paideia, Brescia. Price: Lire 26.000. ISBN 88 394 0385 X)

These essays are not intended as an introduction to the topic (which is actually Jewish apocalyptic), but nine essays on major topics: an outline of the history of research; of the origin of Jewish apocalyptic; the conception of God in apocalyptic writings; the myth of the fall of the angels and the giants; the sources of Daniel 7; mythology and apocalyptic; Is. 25:6–9 (the eschatological banquet) in the light of Ugarit; the transition from the prophetic to the apocalyptic era; and Daniel 2 and 7 in apocalyptic literature with particular reference to the Roman Empire. These essays bring to mind the impressive breadth of Delcor's scholarship, but they contain little that is new or recent, either in their agenda (as the titles of the essays reveals!) or in their bibliographical resource (as the footnotes testify!). For example, the names (and ideas) of Frost, Rowland, and Collins are nowhere apparent.

P. R. Davies

Eslinger, L. M.: *Kingship of God in Crisis: A Close Reading of 1 Samuel 1–12* (Bible and Literature Series 10). 1985. Pp. 115. (Almond, Sheffield. Price: £29.95 ($49.95). ISBN 0 907459 40 4. Paperback price: £13.50 ($22.25). ISBN 0 907459 41 2)

This is essentially a commentary on 1 Samuel 1–12, but of such a length that had Eslinger followed his central thesis through and written on the other nineteen chapters of 1 Samuel his book would have been well over a thousand pages long! It is a close reading of the text in which every verse is considered individually (occasionally two verses are treated together) and the secondary literature on 1 Samuel thoroughly discussed. There is a most useful 'state of the question' introductory chapter which prepares the way for Eslinger's own new approach to 1 Samuel 8–12 and a worthwhile discussion of the problems of defining the literary unit in Samuel. The close reading approach, very much derived from the 'new criticism' theoretical approach to English literature, 'seeks to uncover and describe the intricate reticular connections that unite the narrative (or poem), making it into a singular entity, however complex or devious its plot may be' (p. 40). Eslinger's focus on 1 Samuel 1–12 is determined by Buber's label 'biblical politeia. Where he differs from the usual historical-critical approach to the text is in paying close attention to the narrative's voice structure and so is able to dissolve most of the so-called irresolvable ideological conflicts detected in the text. Such a unitary reading of the text may call into question some of the more usual critical assumptions, especially as it depends upon a holistic literary approach. While this is an overlong book whose central thesis tends to undermine its author's performance — after all, if a close reading of the remainder of the deuteronomistic history is necessary to evaluate a close reading of 1 Samuel 1-12, then we cannot evaluate this mere scratching at the surface of a few chapters of that history! — there is a wealth of exegetical detail, lengthy notes, and many smart literary moves in this book which will make it necessary reading for all subsequent work on the books of Samuel and the deuteronomistic history.

R. P. Carroll

EXUM, J. C. and BOS, J. W. H. (eds): *Reasoning with the Foxes: Female Wit in a World of Male Power* (Semeia 42). 1988. Pp. vii, 156. (Scholars Press, Atlanta, Georgia Price: $14.95 (member price: $9.95); sub. price: (for 4 units) $35.00 (member price: $25.00). ISSN 0095 571X).

The five essays of this collection make fascinating and challenging, not to say controversial, reading. The contributors, all biblical scholars, explore the place of trickery and deception in biblical narrative, particularly in relation to women. Discussion is sharpened by the inclusion of three responses, two from scholars with academic positions outside the biblical field, Kathleen Ashley and Mieke Bal, the other from E. M. Good, the only male contributor. Insights from sociological and anthropological studies make this an interdisciplinary exercise. The role of trickster in the Hebrew Bible is discussed in the light of trickster tales in West African and Afro-American folklore (Naomi Steinberg), and the trickster paradigm applied to the female personifications in the book of Proverbs (Claudia Camp). Johanna Bos brings Tamar, Jael, and Ruth 'out of the shadows', asserting their significance in the biblical story as a challenge to patriarchy; Esther Fuchs compares the presentation of Rachel in Genesis 31 with that of Jacob and Laban, arguing that the former is slanted in such a way as to bolster patriarchal structures, and Carole Fontaine's interest focuses on the Sumerian Inanna and Hittite Inaraš as goddess counterparts to the deceptive female characters of the Hebrew Bible.

The volume is to be commended for the variety of its content and of the methodologies exemplified. There is no doubt that the work achieves its declared aim of demonstrating the 'powerful intellectual challenge posed by feminism to the established critical principles of academic discourse'.

G. I. EMMERSON

FANULI, A. (ed.): *Sapienza e Torah: Associazione Biblica Italiana — Atti della XXIX Settimana Biblica*. 1987. Pp. 266. (EDB, Bologna. Price: Lire 35,000. ISBN 88 10 30252 4)

This symposium was carefully planned, as is outlined in the Introduction by A. Fanuli and the opening paper by F. Festorazzi. The project was to discuss the relationship of Wisdom and Torah from Deuteronomy through early Jewish texts to the New Testament. The two key words are frequently referred to as a *binomio*, a noun without exact parallel in English, which makes one uneasy as to how much correlativity it assumes. *Torah* is subdivided into the broader-than-legal sense and the legal sense for which *nomos* is used, but not in other relevant ways; 'Wisdom' is taken as in the 'Wisdom books' without discussion of its wider connotations. The papers are entitled as follows: 'Deuteronomy: birth of Torah as offer of wisdom' (F. Foresti, who sadly died young before publication); 'The pair [*binomio*] Wisdom-Torah in hermeneutics and in the genesis of the Wisdom texts (Job 28, Prov 8, Sir 1 and 24, Wis. Sol. 9)' (A. Bonora); 'Torah as Wisdom, face to face with the Hellenistic cultural world' (A. Paul, in French); 'Wisdom and Torah in some Jewish texts (Jubilees, the Essenes, 4 Ezra, 2 Baruch)' (L. Moraldi); 'The prominence of Torah as Wisdom in 4 Maccabees and the writings of Josephus' (C. Marucci); 'Jesus as Wisdom and Law in the Gospel of Matthew: soundings in Mt 11–12' (E. Manicardi); 'Breach and recovery of the relationship between Law and Wisdom in Paul' (R. Penna); 'The "wisdom coming from on high" and the "law of freedom" in James' (R. Fabris), and 'The relationship between wisdom motifs and *Nomos* in the Christology of the Fourth Gospel' (V. Pasquetto). There follow four 'communications': 'Gen 2:17: commandment and wisdom-contest in Gen 2–3' (A. Fanuli); 'The motif of the rising waters in Ez 47:1–12 and Sir 24:30–31, and in their developments' (M. Nobile); 'The terminology of crimes in Ptolemaic amnesty decrees and in the LXX' (A. P. dell' Acqua) and 'Sacred order and Law in the Temple Scroll' (E. Jucci).

This is a learned collection, but the assumptions and exclusions in the basic plan leave the discussion too nearly circular, one more testimony to the success of the deuteronomic synthesis. There were those who did not buy its concepts of law and wisdom, and 1 Enoch proves. It would have much enriched this collection if the latter had been taken into account.

R. P. R. MURRAY

FISCH, H.: *Poetry with a Purpose: Biblical Poetics and Interpretation* (Indiana Studies in Biblical Literature). 1988. Pp. ix, 205. (Indiana University Press, Bloomington. Price: $37.50. ISBN 0 253 34557 X)

Harold Fisch is known (or ought to be known) among biblical scholars for his very fine, sensitive treatment of the Aqedah in relation to Auschwitz in his essay 'The Binding of Isaac' (*A Remembered Future: A Study in Literary Mythology*, Indiana University Press, 1984, 81–101). In this book, devoted entirely to essays on the Hebrew Bible, he offers to the thoughtful reader a series of literary appreciations of the 'significant and sinewy' (Robert Boyle's 1653 phrase) quality of the Bible. But this is not just another volume in the growing production of books on the Bible as literature; Fisch is too intelligent and sophisticated for such a banal approach. He wishes to focus on the tension, the dialectic of likeness and unlikeness which the Bible exhibits in relation to other literature. Ultimately the Bible 'commands', as sacred texts command, and this fact must have 'disturbing implications' for the whole enterprise of levelling the Bible with other kinds of literature. Such is the essence of Fisch's approach (pp. 1–7).

Nine chapters constitute the book: 'Esther: Two Tales of One City'; 'What is Beautiful?'; 'Job: Tragedy Is Not Enough'; 'Prophet and Audience: A Failed Contract' (on Ezekiel); 'The Song of Moses: Pastoral in Reverse'; 'Song of Solomon: The Allegorical Imperative'; 'Psalms: The Limits of Subjectivity'; 'Hosea: A Poetics of Violence'; 'Qohelet: A Hebrew Ironist'. There are Notes and Indexes. Fisch is Professor of English and Comparative Literature at Bar-Ilan University, Israel and brings to these studies of biblical books a wealth of Jewish and professional learning combined with a particularly sensitive response to the text. Nobody could fail to learn from any of these chapters or not to be taken further into the depths of sinewy Hebrew literature by Fisch's shrewd analysis. I was much impressed by his chapters on Job, Psalms, Song of Solomon, and especially Qoheleth, but found each chapter to be stimulating and well-worth study. His book scintillates at times and is to be recommended highly. It is also another very fine volume in the Indiana Studies in Biblical Literature series, which in a few years time will be a most impressive series.

R. P. CARROLL

FLANDERS, H. J. jr, CRAPPS, R. W., and SMITH, D. A.: *People of the Covenant: An Introduction to the Old Testament*. Third Edition. 1988. Pp. xiii, 498. (Oxford University Press, New York and Oxford. Price: £22.50. ISBN 0 19 504438 X)

For the second edition see *B. L.* 1974, p. 47. This new edition, with a different imprint, incorporates mostly minor changes to the text and illustrations. In the earlier chapters, however, the updating is a little more extensive and the text is expanded somewhat (e. g. to take more account of the role of 'story' in Genesis and Exodus). Points for reflection and discussion have been added to each chapter. Inclusive language has been adopted (thus 'persons of faith' replaces 'men of faith'). The appearance of the book has been enhanced, though there seem to be more printing errors.

B. P. ROBINSON

GABEL, J. B. and WHEELER, C. B.: *The Bible as Literature: An Introduction*. 1986. Pp. xiv, 278. (Oxford University Press, New York and Oxford. Price: £8.95. ISBN 0 19 503994 7 (paperback))

B. L. 1988 (p. 76) welcomed the original hardback edition of this volume by two American professors of English; and it is a pleasure to note the appearance in 1988, though with unchanged date, of a paperback edition at half the price.

A. G. AULD

GARSIEL, M.: *Midrashic Name Derivations in the Bible* (in Hebrew). 1987. Pp. 202. (Revivim, Ramat-Gan; distributed by Beit Alim, 3 Karel Neter St., Tel Aviv. Price: $19.00)

Although he alludes to scholarly etymologies and makes due reference to the specific explanations (sometimes characterized as aetiological) offered for names, it is with the less explicit and freer uses of names by the biblical writers that Garsiel is most concerned. Dissatisfied as he is with the degree of independent attention given to the topic by most modern scholars, he builds on the work of Y. Devir and Y. Zakovitch and expands its treatment to take account of a great variety of literary and linguistic devices. The hundreds of examples that he cites exemplify, sometimes strikingly, such devices as assonance, word-play, riddle and allusion, and he points to earlier Jewish identification and appreciation of the phenomenon. Garsiel's challenging conclusion is that what is being isolated here is a significant element that was blended into the textual, poetic, and rhetorical composition of the literary unit and that left its mark on later rabbinic exegesis.

S. C. REIF

GLAZIER-MCDONALD, B.: *Malachi: The Divine Messenger* (SBL Dissertation Series 98). 1987. Pp. vii, 288. (Scholars Press, Atlanta, Georgia. Price: $34.95 (member price: $23.95). ISBN 1 55540 093 0. Paperback price: $23.95 (member price: $15.95). ISBN 1 55540 094 9)

A short introduction (rightly) urges the importance of Malachi, whose central theme is 'the honour of Yahweh'. There follow brief surveys of the history of the Persian period, discussion of the date of the prophet (*c.* 460 B.C.E.), and of the form of the prophecy. The six main sections of the book are then dealt with, each under the three headings 'Content and Structure', 'Text and Commentary' (there is a detailed and scholarly engagement with the Hebrew text), and 'Discussion'.

Among the interesting arguments are a defence of the term '*Disputationsworte*' (in spite of recent questionings) for the form of the oracles; that 'Malachi' can be regarded as a legitimate shortened form of a proper name; that a distinction is made between 'priests and Levites' in 1:6—2:9 that 2:17—3:5 is a unity, with the 'messengers of the covenant' being Malachi himself and that it is the Sinaitic covenant of which he is a messenger, a conclusion based on the dependence of 3:1 on Exod. 23:20f.

The author favours conservative positions, sometimes simplistically so. So 4:4–6 (Heb. 3:22–23) is counted as Malachi's own because it echoes his vocabulary and style. That closes no arguments, however, since a glossator may consciously imitate. The marked change of form and the function of the verses as closing, not only the book, nor even The Book of the Twelve, but the whole prophetic canon, show the words to belong to a late stage of transmission. Again, the alleged 'sources' cited to show that 1:2–5 relates to some contemporary destruction of Edom are far too remote to make the argument other than speculative, and in any case one which rather misses the symbolic function of 'Edom' in that passage.

Such heavy-handed literalism occasionally mars a book which generally contains much careful attention to detail and is a useful addition to the limited material on Malachi.

R. A. Mason

Gosse, B.: *Isaíe 13, 1–14, 23 dans la tradition littéraire du livre d' Isaíe et dans la tradition des oracles contre les nations* (Orbis Biblicus et Orientalis 78). 1988. Pp. 300. (Universitätsverlag, Freiburg (CH); Vandenhoeck & Ruprecht, Göttingen. Price: SwFr 88.00; DM 128.00. ISBN 3 7278 0559 5; ISBN 3 525 53707 7)

Gosse has written an important study of the prophetic unit Isa. 13:1 — 14:23 and has set this within the overall context supplied by the other prophetic collections of oracles against foreign nations. He succeeds very well in placing a number of familiar problems in a new light and in recognizing the importance of this type of prophecy within the prophetic writings. More extensively than other sections of this literature, they offer the major key towards understanding the changing patterns of interpretation which led to the transition from prophecy to apocalyptic.

Gosse regards the primary text unit of Isa. 13:2–14:23 as composed of two separate, but related, prophecies, viz. 13:2–22, addressed to Babylon and the second, a *mashal*, addressed to an unidentified tyrant in 14:4b–21. These have been combined to establish a prophetic message concerning the fate of Babylon which has literary connections with other parts of the book of Isaiah, notably 21:1–10 and chapters 60–62. as well as the prophecies of Ezek. 32 and Jer. 50–51. On the basis of its content and these literary affiliations, the combined unit is dated by Gosse after the fall of Babylon in 538 and after the accession to power of Darius.

What is fresh in this approach is the concern to interpret the prophecies of Isa. 13–14 against this larger literary setting and to see these chapters as more important to the formation of the Book of Isaiah than has usually been the case. In questioning the overall thesis some of the literary connections adduced appear at times to be a little strained and the essential literary unity of Isa. 13:2–22 needs further examination. Nevertheless this is a valuable step forward towards unravelling some of the outstanding questions relating to the structure of the book of Isaiah's prophecies.

R. E. Clements

Greenwood, D. C.: *Structuralism and the Biblical Text* (Religion and Reason 32). 1985. Pp. 155 (De Gruyter, Berlin. Price: DM 64.00. ISBN 3 11 010336 2)

David Greenwood of the University of Maryland held doctorates in English Literature from Dublin, and in Theology from the Catholic University of Maryland. He was a sympthetic but not wholly enthusiastic student of structuralism. At his death in 1984 he left the completed text of this book, a lucid, concise survey of literary structuralism in general, and its application to Biblical studies in particular. Its principal chapters concern Lévi-Strauss, Barthes, Greimas, and Güttgemanns, there is a brief and somewhat negative assessment of the value of structuralism, and the book concludes with a short analysis of the individual *lexies* of Genesis 22 and of the Prodigal Son story. The book makes no breakthrough in structuralist method, but it will prove educational to any who are not already expert in the field. The author's reservations, however, are strangely grounded: e.g. structuralism does not 'take into account the inspired nature of the biblical text', and, structuralism cannot provide an interpretative method since 'no Biblical author had a structuralist perspective' and 'a text cannot validly be interpreted from a perspective different from the original author's' (p. 118).

D. J. A. Clines

GUNNEWEG, A. H. J.: *Esra* (Kommentar zum Alten Testament 19/1). 1986. Pp. 217. (Gütersloher (Gerd Mohn), Gütersloh. Price: DM 68.00. ISBN 3 579 04280 7)

In his introduction to this commentary on Ezra, Professor Gunneweg discusses the name and position of the work in the Canon, its text and versions, its relation to 3 Esdras and Chronicles, and the unity of Ezra-Nehemiah. The commentary itself takes the book to consist of two main sections, chapters 1–6 and 7–10, each being sub-divided into three smaller parts. Brief textual notes are provided with a translation of the text at the beginning of each unit, and then follows a detailed exposition of the text, its significance and meaning. A fuller discussion of three topics is found in three excursuses: the origin of the list in 2:1–67 and its relation to Nehemiah 7; the historical background of the edict of Artaxerxes; the theology of the chronistic circle behind Ezra. The volume is concluded with the inclusion of A. Jepsen's chronological table.

This is a traditional commentary, as befits a work belonging to the series founded by Sellin; its interest is obviously in textual and historical research, particularly the latter.

G. H. JONES

GUNNEWEG, A. H. J.: *Nehemia* (Kommentar zum Alten Testament 19/2). 1988. Pp. 216. (Gütersloher (Gerd Mohn), Gütersloh. Price: DM 68.00 (sub. price: DM 60.00). ISBN 3 579 04281 5)

Gunneweg's introduction to his commentary on Ezra is published again as an introduction to this volume on Nehemiah, as is Jepsen's chronological table at the end. As would be expected this companion volume is of the same style and approach as the previous one. The two books are taken to be one continuous work, and to the two main sections of Ezra are added a third and a fourth in Nehemiah, viz. chapters 1–10 and 11–15. The two excursuses found in this volume give attention to the characteristics of the Nehemiah memoir and to the topography and archaeology of Jerusalem, the latter being contributed by Manfred Oeming.

G. H. JONES.

HAGSTROM, D. G.: *The Coherence of the Book of Micaah: A Literary Analysis* (SBL Dissertation Series 89). 1988. Pp. ix, 152. (Scholars Press, Atlanta, Georgia. Price $16.95 (member price: $10.95). ISBN 0 89130 972 1. Paperback price: $10.95 (member price: $7.95). ISBN 0 89130 973 X).

Scholars have long been of the opinion that the book of Micah is a collection of passages, and that while some of these passages are related to one another the book is not a unity. The purpose of this work by Hagstrom is to show that 'the book of Micah in its final form is so shaped as to render the book a unified, coherent whole; that is, the individual units of Micah are so shaped, structured and linked together as to make it possible to read the book as a unit'.

This book is essentially a Ph.D. thesis of Union Theological Seminary in Virginia, and it is clear that a lot of energy and effort has gone into it. The problem seems to be that the author has started with an assumption which he has attempted to prove, willy-nilly, and has not given due regard to the nature of his material. Other prophetic books of the Old Testament are collections of passages which occasionally relate to one another but which often are unrelated. Micah is no exception; and this thesis would have been more convincing if the author had allowed for the *possibility* that some material in the book of Micah may be, at the very least, out of context. The attempt to fit 2:12–13 into its present context is a case in point. Students of the Old Testament may not, therefore, be convinced of the conclusions offered here.

R. B. SALTERS

HANSON, P. D.: *Old Testament Apocalyptic* (Interpreting Biblical Texts). 1987. Pp. 144. (Abingdon, Nashville Tennessee. Price: $9.95. ISBN 0 687 28750 2)

This splendid little volume ably fulfils the intention of the series as a whole in identifying and illustrating what is involved in relating the meaning of biblical texts in their own times to the meaning in ours. Part I discusses the meaning of apocalyptic texts within their original and historical settings, and the applicability of apocalyptic texts to contemporary realities. Outrageous misuses of biblical 'Apocalyptic' in certain publications in the United States are pin-pointed and analysed. The message of 'Apocalyptic' is not timeless, written for anyone in any setting but is written for those suffering under specific conditions. Designating apocalyptic literature as crisis literature, in Part II Professor Hanson traces the primary themes of the genre in specific texts selected from the books of Isaiah, Zechariah, and Daniel.

P. W. COXON

HAYES, J. H. and IRVINE, S. A.: *Isaiah the Eighth-century prophet: His Times and his Preaching* (Bible and Bible Study). 1987. Pp. 416. (Abingdon, Nashville Tennessee. Price: $15.95. ISBN 0 687 19705 8)

This work, written from a critical perspective but opposed to much current form and redaction criticism, is based on two major assumptions. Apart from chapters 34–35 and a few minor editorial additions the prophetic speech material in Isaiah 1–39 derives from the prophet himself. Apart from chapters 28–33 and 38–39 this material is arranged in chronological order. Chapter 6 narrates not an initial call-vision but how Isaiah moved into a new phase of his prophetic ministry. The success of this challenge to current orthodoxy must await the judgement of specialists.

Most of the book consists of a commentary on each of the 36 sections into which the text is divided with only selective discussion of details. Bibliographies are provided for each section, and occasionally a new translation of the text is offered. The emphasis is historical, and a substantial introductory historical survey of the second half of the eighth century is provided.

A. GELSTON

HENDEL, R. S.: *The Epic of the Patriarch: The Jacob Cycle and the Narrative Traditions of Canaan and Israel* (Harvard Semitic Monographs 42). 1987. Pp. xiv, 194. (Scholars Press, Atlanta Georgia. Price: $13.95 (member price: $8.95). ISBN 1 55540 184 8)

This study continues the analysis of the patriarchal narratives, with particular reference to those concerning Jacob or thematicaly relating to them. The author surveys briefly the main landmarks in the story so far (Herder, Gunkel, Alt, Noth, Albright, Thompson, Van Seters, and Cross). Then using the more adequate conceptual framework made possible by the work of Parry and Lord, he leads us through the main themes of the Jacob cycle, arguing the case for an oral substrate with appropriate comparisons with neighbouring traditions. Thus the birth narrative is dealt with in conjunction with the Keret and Aqhat episodes (but without reference to the equally relevant *KTU* 1. 23). The passage traditions — Bethel, Penuel — are examined in the context of liminality. Cultic overtones and common themes are found in a comparison of Rachel and Pughat, with the parallels perhaps subject to slight exaggeration, while Jacob at Penuel is further compared with Giglamesh in his struggle with the Bull of Heaven. Jacob and Esau are treated along with Gilgamesh and Enkidu, Horus and Set, and Hypsouranios and Ousoos in accordance with Lévi-Strauss's raw and cooked dichotomy, and finally attention is drawn to parallels in the narrative presentation of Jacob and Moses. This is a suggestive and perceptive study which occasionally overstates the case.

N. WYATT

HOUSE, P. R.: *Zephaniah: A Prophetic Drama* (JSOT Supplement Series 69, Bible and Literature Series 16). 1988. Pp. 146. (Almond, Sheffield. Price: £22.00 ($37.50). ISBN 1 85075 075 0; ISSN 0260 4493; 0309 0787)

This is a revised form of a dissertation supervised by J. D. W. Watts. Chapter 1 surveys previous scholarly work on Zephaniah and points out what House regards as its weaknesses. Page 20 states his own presuppositions: 'the text itself is valuable aside from its historical background', and 'the text is a unity' (but should not the latter be a possible conclusion reached after study rather than a presupposition?); House attempts a 'wedding of genre criticism and formalism'. Chapter 2 describes genre criticism. Chapter 3 subjects Zephaniah to a close reading, and concludes that 'Zephaniah's structure is created by a series of alternating speeches ... its plot has a definite conflict and resolution' and 'is shaped by an overwhelming emphasis on the "day of Yahweh"', and 'an almost totally dramatic point of view pervades the book' (p. 89). Chapter 4 seeks to relate the findings of chapter 3 to chapter 2, and argues that the book of Zephaniah is not an epic or lyric, but is best described as a prophetic drama. Chapter 5 contains a translation of the book, divided as a prophetic drama, and textual notes based on *BHS* (but often expressing a different opinion). The book ends with a bibliography, and indexes of biblical references and authors. This work has two principal weaknesses. First, the bibliography fails to list some standard works on Zephaniah such as (among others) those of G. Gerleman, F. Horst, K. Marti, W. Nowack, W. Rudolph, E. Sellin, and J. Wellhausen — and one wonders whether this has any bearing on House's claim on p. 9 that 'Zephaniah has received minimal critical attention'. Second, there are shortcomings in the translation (e.g. *yhwh* is translated in three different ways; *ṣᵉbāʾ* in 1:5 is treated as a plural; *ûbᵉnê* in 2:9 is ignored), and the critical notes are too closely related to *BHS* and lack evidence of a wider study of the problems of the Hebrew on the basis of an independent study of the versions and the commentaries. There are also errors and misunderstandings: thus, the suggested pointing *ʾōsēp* (instead of *ʾāsēp*) in 1:2 is thought to be a participle (p. 126), an improbable form in the context, rather than the first person singular of the imperfect; the emended form *ûmᵉmahēr* in 1:14 is thought to be 'Qal' — and the list could be extended. Fortunately, such weaknesses do not detract from the main argument in chapters 3 and 4, where House's principal contribution to the study of Zephaniah lies, a contribution that must be taken seriously.

J. A. EMERTON

JOHNSON, D. G.: *From Chaos to Integration: An Integrative Reading of Isaiah 24–27* (JSOT Supplement Series 61). 1988. Pp. 150. (Sheffield Academic Press. Price: £25.00 ($46.50). ISBN 1 85075 112 9; ISBN 1 85075 061 0 (paperback)

This is a published version of the author's thesis which was done under the guidance of J. J. M. Roberts (with B. W. Anderson, B. Ollenburger, and K. Sakenfeld in the background). It is a study of the so-called Isaiah apocalypse (24–27) using the literary techniques of an integrative reading which treats the four chapters as a unity. Johnson offers a brief analysis of the history of the interpretation of the chapters and proposes to solve the interpretive problems by treating 24–27 as an ordered composition produced during the exilic period with its referent in the future. According to his treatment the composition comprises three major parts: section A (24:1–20) was written on the eve of the fall of Jerusalem in 587 B.C.E.; section B (24:21–27:1) is an announcement of the imminent victory of Yahweh and was added during the exile when the author looked forward to the destruction of Babylon; section C (27:2–13) Yahweh's triumph is brought to its logical conclusion with the theme of the reunification of Israel. Problems of identifying the city are resolved in favour of Babylon as the target of Yahweh's wrath and Jerusalem's destruction in 24 as the object of the languge of chaos used there. The overriding theme which ties the composition together is the *Chaoskampf*. In the poems the royal traditions are universalized and eschatologized so that Yahweh's victory *in the future* is anticipated. The author Isa.24–27 was positive in his view of Yahweh's activity in the world, so Johnson disagrees with Hanson's view of 24–27 and denies the legitimacy of his describing the chapters as early-apocalyptic. Disagreement with Hanson is a step in the right direction, but I doubt if Johnson's dating of the text to the exilic period can be sustained on the grounds he offers. The whole notion of an exilic age needs to be rethought radically and Hanson's 'apocalyptic' schema reassessed critically and in the light of Rowland's *The Open Heaven*. At the moment it is being used far too uncritically in biblical studies and far too often it is systematically misleading the interpretation of specific texts in the 'prophets'. But that criticism apart, this is a fine, short book which clearly argues its case and offers a viewpoint worth arguing with and learning from.

R. P. CARROLL

JÓNSSON, G. A.: *The Image of God: Genesis 1:26–28 in a Century of Old Testament Research* (Coniectanea Biblica, Old Testament Series 26). 1988. Pp. xvi, 253. (Almqvist & Wiksell, Stockholm. Price: SEK 188.00. ISBN 91 22 01215 X)

This history of the various interpretations of the image of God in Genesis 1:26–28 in Old Testament studies over the past century clearly demonstrates the way in which exegesis is always 'situational exegesis', whether the dominant situational influence is dialectical theology, ecological concerns, feminist theology, or liberation theology. The dominance of a relational interpretation based on dialectical theology is traced through the period from 1919 to 1960. This has largely been replaced, with significant dissentient voices, e.g. Barr and Westermann, by a functional interpretation which lays emphasis upon man's sharing in God's dominion over the rest of creation. The book deserves a warm welcome as a contribution to the history of exegesis, providing comprehensive coverage of the relevant literature in Scandinavian, German, French, and English sources from Jewish as well as Christian authors. It should prove to be an indispensible work of reference.

R. DAVIDSON

JOSIPOVICI, G.: *The Book of God: A Response to the Bible*. 1988. Pp. xvi, 350. (Yale University Press, New Haven and London. Price: £18.95 ($29.95). ISBN 0 300 04320 1)

Josipivici is an accomplished literary critic who has learned the biblical languages and mastered an impressive amount of its secondary literature; he is to be pigeonholed neither as a biblical scholar nor a layman, but as a highly competent reader. His 'response to the Bible' opens with the image of Moses receiving the tables of the law, and closes with that of the Bible as a person to be encountered rather than an object to be known. Between these points is stretched an argument that the Bible is not to be interpreted, but responded to. We are shown at first the reader confronted with a book handed down, by

God or man, as authoritative. Given the post-modernist collapse of the idea of artistic authority, Josipovici likens our own attitude to the Bible to that of the adult towards stories learned in childhood: they have constituted the self, they have been accepted without question. Next, the Bible itself comes up for definition in a way which makes much canonical criticism seem leaden. Is it a book? Books? Certainly there is no one Bible. Then: how is this not-one but also not-many Bible to be read? The question is broached from a number of angles in the central part of the book, in each case illustrated by biblical episodes touched lightly or in depth and occasionally accompanied by Proust or Dante, Mann or Joyce. We are invited to gauge first the rhythm of the Bible (a composite of linguistic, stylistic, theological, and narrative beats) in the stories of creation, of Joseph, building of the tabernacle and the book of Judges; then its speech (repetitive or quasi-repetitive devices such as retold stories and genealogies; the compulsion of speech but also the distance in much of its dialogue), then character (characterized — David by tears, Jesus by incarnation, Paul by subjectivity). The thesis draws to its climax as interpretation itself is treated through the instance of Hebrews; like the New Testament as a whole, this proclaims the one and only meaning of history; by contrast, the Old Testament declares that there *is* meaning, but a meaning disclosed in memory and repetition, not in kerygma. By now one ought to grasp that Josipovici is on the side of the Old Testament. To make sure, he takes a final (and justified) snipe at over-interpreters, who will not allow narrative to withhold meaning — as with the 'man in the field' of Genesis 37 or the young man clothed in white of Mark 14.

This book succeeds in neither containing the Bible, nor smothering it in detail nor drowning it in theory. It is well-informed, subtle, lucid, and illuminating and, like the Bible itself, is better encountered than interpreted.

P. R. Davies

Kirkpatrick, P. G.: *The Old Testament and Folklore Study* (JSOTS 62). 1988. Pp. 152. (Sheffield Academic Press. Price: £25.00 ($42.00). ISBN 1 85075 114 5)

The title of this book may lead one to expect rather more than it in fact provides. It is primarily concerned with the question of how far it is justifiable to postulate oral sources behind parts of the Old Testament and it concentrates mainly on the patriarchal narratives in Genesis. As the author suggests, Old Testament scholars dealing with this area are still often governed by pre-suppositions which modern folklorists have long abandoned and so the first chapter is a survey of the influence of earlier folklore studies on past Old Testament studies, as exemplified by Wellhausen, Gunkel, Alt, von Rad, Noth, and the Scandinavian school. Here Gunkel is the pivotal figure and Kirkpatrick perhaps does not always represent his views quite accurately or sufficiently appreciate the caution with which he expresses them. The following chapter looks at modern folkore research into oral narrative composition and transmission: its material will be familiar to folklorists but its value for Old Testament studies is in showing how complicated the situation is and how difficult it is to arrive at assured results with regard to the possibility of oral sources underlying Genesis. The final section discusses the genre classification of the patriarchal narratives. Again, the author's overriding concern with the issue of 'orality' tends to miss the real significance of genre study for folklore. Thus, she states that because the criteria for such classification are culturally bound, 'the discipline of folklore genre research can be of little use to Old Testament studies,' but the folklorist would rather subscribe to some words from the volume edited by G. W. Coats (*B.L.* 1986, p. 65) 'genre studies are ... particularly valuable in understanding cultures other than one's own'. Nevertheless, Kirkpatrick's work is always lively and provocative; and if its conclusions are finally negative, showing the difficulties in marrying folklore study with the Old Testament, they are none the worse for that.

J. R. PORTER

KIUCHI, N.: *The Purification Offering in the Priestly Literature: Its Meaning and Function* (JSOT Supplement Series 56). 1987. Pp. 204. (Sheffield Academic Press. Price: £25.00 ($42.50). ISBN 1 85075 103 X. Paperback price: £12.95 ($19.95). ISBN 1 85075 102 1.

This study concentrates on Leviticus chapters 4–17 and on the *ḥaṭṭā't* offering. This term should be translated as purification or purgation offering rather than sin offering, because it deals with both uncleanness and *ḥēṭ'* (sin). The author sees thematic unity in the material he examines, and assigns a vital role to Leviticus 10:16–20. He argues that *ḥaṭṭā't* blood is effective being substitutionary, that is, by symbolising a substitutionary death. The same conclusion is proposed with regard to the priest who makes the offering and to Aaron on the Day of Atonement. Both bear the guilt associated with uncleanness and sin. This enables a new interpretation of the ceremony of the Day of Atonement to be offered, in which the Azazel goat is seen as a special form of the *ḥaṭṭā't* offering.

This is an important contribution to the understanding of Old Testament sacrifice which requires close study. It is a pity that the author presumably completed his work before the publication of D. P. Wright's *The Disposal of Impurity*, to which reference is made only in footnotes, and that no anthropological studies have been consulted. However, this study will be a stimulus to further research.

J. W. ROGERSON

KLEIN, L. R.: *The Triumph of Irony in the Book of Judges* (JSOT Supplement Series 68; Bible and Literature Series 14). 1988. Pp. 260. (Almond, Sheffield. Price: £25.00 ($42.50). ISBN 1 85075 100 5)

Here is a further fine 'literary' reading of the book of Judges, too hot on the heels of Barry Webbs' (see *B. L.* 1988, p. 95) to know more than its name. Its main point is well taken: that we can hardly be over subtle in reading Judges, or attending to every possible nuance in its wording. Lillian Klein is also right to have made her translations word for word, and not in the phrase translation of much contemporary theory. In her broadly convincing account of Judges 'as a *tour de force* of irony', she portrays the exposition (1:1–3:11) as devoid of irony although it supplies images later used for ironic purposes. Irony is gradually intensified in the central chapters, and from Gideon onwards in the very person of the judge. The resolution of the book, in its closing five chapters, is found to be thick with multi-layered irony.

It is a pity that her welcome invitation to pay close attention to words is spoiled by transliteration of Hebrew that is inconsistent, has gone badly awry on pp. 54 and 70, and is very confused over 'and'. And 'literary' readers ought to learn not to ignore totally issues of textual criticism and literary history. To 'regard the work as an entity and credit the work of perhaps many hands to a single author' (p. 11) may lead to the missing of nuances; and there is no point in making capital out of Gideon apparently not having heard the message of the prophet (p. 50), if that prophet was only intruded relatively late in the text's transmission. Yet her reading is often rich in insight, and captures much of the book's (serious) fun.

A. G. AULD

KÖCKERT, M.: *Vätergott und Väterverheissungen: Eine Auseinandersetzung mit Albrecht Alt und seinen Erben* (FRLANT 142). 1987. Pp. 387. (Vandenhoeck & Ruprecht, Göttingen. Price: DM 98.00. ISBN 3 525 53821 9)

This is an exhaustive and comprehensively documented exercise in clearing the ground for the eventual development of a new understanding of the patriarchal traditions. Except in the last few pages, where the bare outline of an alternative approach is sketched, the work is devoted to a critical examination of Alt's theory of the nature of patriarchal religion, and modifications of that theory in the work of those who still remain within its general framework. The author begins by placing Alt in context, especially against the background of Wellhausen's argument that from the traditions we attain to no historical knowledge of the patriarchs but only of the time when the stories about them arose in Israel. Building on the work of Gunkel, Alt separated significant elements of these traditions from the Yahwistic faith of Israel, and, on the basis of sociological considerations, religio-historical analogies and traditio-historical conjectures, penetrated to a pre-Mosaic patriarchal situation. His work found wide agreement, particularly with von Rad, Noth, Jepsen, Maag, Cross, and others, all of whom, despite differences among themselves and with Alt, are fundamentally dependent on his reconstruction of a pre-Yahwistic religion. Recent study is described in terms of the alternatives presented by Westermann, who attempted to give a new foundation to Alt, and Hoftijzer, whose work here wins approval at least insofar as it redirects attention to the literary forms and functions of the promises to the patriarchs in their present context.

The major part of the book is devoted to a critical examination of the two mutually supporting aspects of Alt's theory: the religion of the patriarchs as a pre-Yahwistic religious form, and the promises to the patriarchs which give concrete content to this religion. The first provides the context to which the latter is traced; the latter saves the religion from being simply a schematic abstraction. Alt's reliance on the designations used for the patriarchal gods, the contrast which he and others developed with the worship of the El deities in the land, the use of extra-biblical material, the socio-cultural model which was presupposed, and the nature of patriarchal religion in the supposed nomadic social context which he and his followers described, are all shown to provide a very unreliable foundation for the theory of patriarchal religion as a pre-Yahwistic religious form. The presumed content of this form, the promises to the patriarchs, is discussed with respect to covenant, election, and promise. The first two are shown to be late ideas; the third, extensively treated with particular reference to Gen. 15 and Gen. 12:1–4a, is also an exilic theme. Further development of an alternative to Alt will attend both to this late date and also in particular to the question of the literary function of the promises within the overall composition of the story of Israel's origins. Literary function will also be the basis of an explanation of the titles of the patriarchal gods, on which Alt relied so heavily, while patriarchal religion as a type should be understood, following Albertz, as a family religion, which may have existed alongside official Yahwistic religion with no necessary link to nomadism.

A. D. H. MAYES

KROLL, W. M.: *Psalms: The Poetry of Palestine*. 1987. Pp. ix, 453. (University Press of America, London. Price: £31.50 ($37.50); paperback price: £20.50 ($24.75). ISBN 0 8191 5750 3; ISBN 0 8191 5751 1 (paperback))

This is a devotional commentary from the pen of the President of the Practical Bible Training School. It cites always the King James Version and its sympathies and insights are rooted in the 'pre-critical' period. It will be valued as a thorough and useful work within these horizons.

J. H. EATON

LAATO, A.: *Who is Immanuel? The Rise and the Foundering of Isaiah's Messianic Expectations*. 1988. Pp. 394. (Åbo Academy press; distributed by Tidningsbokhandeln, PB 33, SF-21601 Pargas. ISBN 951 9498 22 2)

This detailed redactional and exegetical study is concerned primarily with Isa.7:14–17; 8:5–10; 8:23b–9:6; 11:1–9; and 32:1–8. This is well-worked ground; Laato's originality lies in linking the Messianic theme with that of the Assyrian invasion in Isaiah. His thesis is that Isaiah expected the Assyrians to be the divine agents of destruction on the royal house and all the wicked in Judah, after which they would themselves be destroyed by direct divine intervention without having been able to conquer Zion; then the royal scion whose birth Isaiah announces, but whose identity he did not know, would take over the kingdom and reign in peace and righteousness over the whole of David's former realm. This tripartite scheme Laato finds repeated in three major sections of the book: 6:1–9:6, 10:5–11:9 and 28–33. Isaiah, he believes, continued to preach this message in the crisis of 705–01, but most have been disappointed by the outcome, with Hezekiah retaining his throne and Immanuel failing to emerge. However, in the redaction, including 36–39, Immanuel tends to be identified with Hezekiah, the pious king in whose reign the Assyrians were supposed to have been miraculously destroyed before the gates of Jerusalem; and thus the dissonance is resolved. Laato includes historical discussion of the events of 701.

This thesis clearly implies the Isaienic authorship of much that has frequently or generally been seen as redactional. Much of the book consists of detailed redactional discussion with other scholars, and not all of Laato's arguments will be found plausible by everyone. (Can Isaiah really have believed both in the inviolability of Zion and in the impending fall of the royal house?) The book does not make easy reading, particularly as the English text seems to have been written by someone with an imperfect grasp of the language. Nevertheless, there are insights which make it worth persisting, and some of the points made against other scholars are well taken.

W. J. HOUSTON

LOHFINK, G.: *Enfin Je Comprends la Bible* (Essais Bibliques 14). 1987. Pp. 148. (Labor et Fides, Geneva. Price: SwFr 25.00. ISBN 2 8309 109 6)

This is a translation by Bernadette Neipp of *Jetzt verstehe ich die Bibel*, published in 1973 by Katholisches Bibelwerk, and rightly commended in *B. L.* 1975, p. 64. It explains for the general reader the importance of recognizing *genre* for understanding what we read, and the fact that in dealing with most modern *genres* we operate the rules instinctively, needing help only for more distant texts.

A. G. AULD

LONGMAN, T., III: *Literary Approaches to Biblical Interpretation* (Foundations of Contemporary Interpretation, 3). 1987. Pp. xi, 164. (Zondervan, Grand Rapids, Michigan. Price: $12.95. ISBN 0 310 40941 1)

Two-thirds of this book is a survey and exposition of contemporary literary theories, mainly grouped as author-centred, text-centred and reader-centred theories. There are brief and generally well-illustrated accounts of new criticism, structuralism, deconstruction, and so on. In the second part of the book, the author applies some of the approaches represented by these theories to five Old Testament and two New Testament passages. The author is obviously very concerned to persuade his conservative audience that 'the literary approach', as he sometimes calls it, need not derogate from the historical validity of the Bible. His own preference is markedly for homegrown formalist literary criticism, concentrating on plot, characterization and point of view. Literary theories that demote the role of the author or that deny a referential function to literature are suspect. Though the book would not claim to make an original contribution, it may be welcomed as a moderate introduction for those of the author's circle. It is not so clear, however, that contemporary literary theory — materialist, feminist and deconstructionist, for example — can be applied to the Bible with no more subversive results than the author would wish.

D. J. A. CLINES

LORETZ, O.: *Die Königspsalmen: Die altorientalisch-kanaanäische Königstradition in jüdischer Sicht*, I — *Ps. 20, 21, 72, 101, 144* (Ugaritisch-Biblische Literatur 6). 1988. Pp. vii, 261. (Ugarit-Verlag, Münster; distributed by Cornelsen Verlagsgesellschaft, Postfach 8729, D–4800 Bielefeld. Price: DM 78.00 (sub.price: DM 70.00). ISBN 3 917120 01 4)

Loretz begins with a survey of work on the so-called royal psalms since the latter part of the nineteenth century and the problem of the speaker in the first person singular. He believes that light can be shed on the problem by the use of colometric analysis, i.e. a method whereby the text is studied after it has been divided into parallel cola and the number of consonants in each has been counted. He also believes that light is shed on Ps. 20 by a comparison with the related Aramaic psalm in demotic script in 12:11–12 of Papyrus Amherst 63, and I. Kottsieper contributes a reconstruction of this Aramaic psalm, which he dates in the fourth century B.C. and regards as derived from an original composed in Lebanon. Loretz examines Ps. 20 on the basis of the questionable hypotheses that the Hebrew text is a translation and adaptation of an Aramaic psalm closely related to the one in the papyrus, and that the words 'his anointed' in verse 7 and 'the king' in verse 10 (which he believes to be secondary) refer, not to an individual Israelite monarch, but to the post-exilic Jewish people. The following chapters examine the other psalms listed in the title of the book, and distinguish between pre-exilic parts referring to a king and post-exilic additions in which the older material is reprinted and applied to the nation. There are bibliographies in the chapters on particular psalms, and a general bibliography at the end of the book, as well as indexes of the biblical passages discussed, and of Aramaic and Ugaritic texts. While the arguments presented are not always convincing, Loretz raises some interesting questions and his discussion deserves careful attention.

J. A. EMERTON

LYS, D.: *Treize Énigmes de l'Ancient Testament* (Initiations). 1988. Pp. 261. (Cerf, Paris. Price: Fr. 138.00. ISBN 2 204 02891 6)

This book offers not original scholarship but reflection upon some of the implications of other scholars' work. The thirteen enigmas of the title are in the nature of paradoxes created by two antithetical notions (e.g. particularism and universalism). Each chapter is designed to stand on its own, though the book is so arranged as to bring out an implicit continuity: we move from questions of historical and geographical setting to consideration of the Book, the People and the Message. Each chapter follows a set pattern: the reader is directed to read a specific book or article; he is asked to undertake an 'exercise' (either looking something up in the Old Testament or pondering a question; the enigma is then propounded, firstly in summary form then at length; and the chapter ends with suggestions for further reading (of items in French). Some of the chapters make rather greater demands on the reader than others, but all who find it interesting to ask, for example, to what extent the meaning of texts is fixed or fluid; or whether for a Christian the Old

Testament is revelation in itself or only in the context of Scripture as a whole; or whether God-talk should have its own language or should take the risk of recycling secular language, will find matter to ponder here (though I doubt if many will prepare themselves for working through each chapter by doing the prescribed 'reading' and 'exercises'). No definitive answers are given, but some light is shed.

B. P. ROBINSON

MAYS, J. L. and ACHTEMEIER, P. J. (eds.): *Interpreting the Prophets*. 1987. Pp. xii, 287. (Fortress, Philadelphia. Price: $14.95. ISBN 0 8006 1932 3)

The chapters constituting this book first appeared as five issues of *Interpretation: A Journal of Bible and Theology* during the years 1978–85. To them have been added a brief foreword by James L. Mays and a three page 'Resources for Studying the Prophets' by James Limburg. Four introductory chapters deal with 'Early Israelite Prophecy' (R. R. Wilson), 'Prophecy from the Eighth Through the Fifth Century' (H. W. Wolff), 'Prophetic Speech' (G. M. Tucker), and 'The Canonical Shape of the Prophetic Literature'. The books of Isaiah and Jeremiah each receive four chapters: 'The Unity of the Book of Isaiah' (R. E. Clements), 'Isaiah in Old Testament Theology' (J. J. M. Roberts), 'Isaiah in Luke' (J. A. Sanders), 'John Calvin on Isaiah 6: A Problem in the History of Exegesis' (D. C. Steinmetz), 'A Living Tradition: The Book of Jeremiah in Current Research' (J. L. Crenshaw), 'The Book of Jeremiah: Portrait of the Prophet' (W. Brueggemann), 'The Years of Jeremiah's Preaching' (W. L. Holladay), and 'Jeremiah in the Lectionary' (T. M. Raitt). *Five* chapters are devoted to Ezekiel: 'Prophecy in Crisis: The Call of Ezekiel' (R. R. Wilson), 'Sin and Judgment in the Prophecies of Ezekiel' (M. Fishbane), 'A Maker of Metaphors: Ezekiel's Oracles Against Tyre' (C. A. Newsom), 'Life in the Present and Hope for the Future' (W. E. Lemke), and 'The Design and Themes of Ezekiel's Program of Restoration' (M. Greenberg). Then, to the surprise of this reader, there follow four chapters on *Daniel* (a switch from the Hebrew to the Greek canon!) which are intended to show the way in which prophecy makes a transition into apocalyptic: 'Is Daniel Also Among the Prophets?' (K. Koch), 'Daniel and His Social World' (J. J. Collins), 'A Journey Through Danielic Spaces: The Book of Daniel in the Theology and Piety of the Christian Community' (J. G. Gammie), and 'The Preacher in the Lions' Den' (W. S. Towner).

These are all excellent essays of their kind and typify the concerns of the journal *Interpretation* which encourage those aspects of biblical scholarship compatible with Jewish and Christian piety. the slight imbalance in favour of Ezekiel is not as fault-worthy as the remarkable paucity of consideration given to Amos, Hosea, Micah, and other volumes in the Book of the Twelve. While the inclusion of Daniel among the prophets has good Christian precedents it has no good scholarly grounds and it really is time that the influence of Hanson's thesis about apocalyptic having its roots in prophecy was modified in the light of Rowland's *The Open Heaven* (SPCK 1982). Otherwise this is a very useful American (with a few European guests) collection of essays on the currents state of prophetic studies.

R. P. CARROLL

MILGROM, J.: *The Binding of Isaac: The* Akedah, *a Primary Symbol of Jewish Thought and Art*. 1988. Pp. xii + 322. (BIBAL, Berkeley California. Price: $16.95, plus $1.00 for postage and handling. ISBN 0 941037 05 3)

The title of this 1978 Ph. D. thesis (essentially unrevised) is a good statement of its contents. It attempts to investigate the place of the 'binding of Isaac' as a powerful symbol or myth in Judaism, with mystical, sociological, and psychological functions. Chapter I gives a 'literary analysis' which has a great deal in common with rabbinic midrash. Chapter II on the concept of testing also owes much to midrashic techniques. Chapters III–IV look at the interpretation of the Akedah in various extra-biblical writings up to about 600 C. E. (the important article by P. R. Davies and B. D. Chilton [*Catholic Biblical Quarterly* 1978, pp. 514–46] is omitted). Chapter V takes up close to half the text and deals with the Akedah in a selection of about forty works of Jewish and Christian art from antiquity to the present day. L. L. GRABBE

MILLER, J. W.: *Meet the Prophets: A Beginner's Guide to the Books of the Biblical Prophets*. 1987. Pp. ix, 250. (Paulist Press, Mahwah, New Jersey. Price: $11.95. ISBN 0 8091 2899 3)

This introduction to the prophet literature of the Old Testament follows what has become by now a well established pattern. It falls into three sections, the first of which deals with the general character of the prophetic literature of the Old Testament. It explains the importance of the historical setting of each of the prophets and the character of the Deuteronomistic history. A brief chapter deals with the divinatory character of prophecy. The main part of the book then consists of two long sections, the first dealing with the prophets of the Assyrian period and the second those of the Babylonian, and Persian periods. The approach throughout is that of providing a readable presentation, without too much technical detail and with a broad summary of the main features of each prophet's message.

In overall perspective the book well fulfils its purpose of providing the newcomer to serious biblical study with a good general guide and with helpful notes on other literature that is available. Perhaps the time has come, however for re-examining so strongly historical and biographical an approach to each prophet. The separate treatments, for instance, of Second and Third Isaiah in isolation from the original of Jerusalem certainly begs many questions which are increasingly being posed about the unity and structure of the book. It would also be helpful to have had a little more guidance on the way in which earlier prophecy was being reinterpreted in the late post-exilic age. This is simply to note, however, that there is much to be said about the nature of Old Testament prophecy. Professor Miller's guide is a very well written, if by now rather conventional, introduction to the subject.

R. E. CLEMENTS

MILNE, P. J.: *Vladimir Propp and the Study of Structure in Hebrew Biblical Narrative* (Bible and Literature Series, 13). 1988. Pp. 325. (Sheffield Academic Press. Price: £25.00 ($42.40). ISBN 1 85075 087 4. Paperback price: £9.95 ($16.50). ISBN 1 85075 086 6)

Almond Press has done biblical scholarship a great service by publishing this book because it is about time the discipline had an accessible introduction to Vladimir Propp's *Morphology of the Folktale* (original Russian edition appeared in 1928, with an English translation appearing in 1958). Of course the sensible scholar will read Propp but the busy scholar may need some guidance in the first place as to whether Propp is relevant before embarking on a considerable intellectual journey. Pamela Milne's monograph provides two boons: a detailed introduction to the morphology of the folktale and an analysis of it in relation to the court tales of Daniel 1–6. Whatever the judgment of the experts in folktale or Daniel on this book, it is in my opinion a very valuable volume to have on the shelf.

The book itself contains a comprehensive treatment of all the significant studies on Propp's morphology, as well as a consideration of structural analysis of narrative in the Hebrew Bible. The structuralist analysis associated with Lévi-Strauss is also analyzed, so that the book is a useful introduction to the perspective known as 'structuralism'. After more than 165 pages of discussion of the folktale, Milne offers nearly hundred pages of analysis of the court tales in Daniel 1–6 as a programme of Proppian application. Here she examines every important study of the stories which scholars have produced recently and regularly shows how Propp's morphology elucidates or, more often, fails to elucidate the Daniel material. The stories in Daniel are (surprisingly?) resistant to such analysis but Milne's judgment that they form a particularly appropriate text for testing the usefulness of Propp's work is sound. In her treatment of the tales Propp's morphology functions as a heuristic device and that seems to be the correct level for a Proppian analysis of biblical stories. The immensely detailed analyses of the stories, especially in relation to the secondary literature on them, make this part of the book a most useful contribution to biblical studies in general and Daniel studies in particular. Tabulated appendices set out the functions of the Heroic Fairly Tale, the roles of the Heroic Fairy Tale, and the Combination of Moves in such tales. Notes and Bibliography complete a most useful monograph.

R. P. CARROLL

MORGAN, R. with BARTON, J.: *Biblical Interpretation* (The Oxford Bible Series). 1988. Pp. ix, 342. (Oxford University Press. Price: £29.50. ISBN 0 19 213256 3. Paperback price: £8.95. ISBN 0 19 213257 1)

This is a book which should be made compulsory reading for all theological students. It tackles head on, and in a helpfully selective way, the major problems surrounding the use of the Bible today. While recognising the legitimacy of non-religious as well as religious uses of the Bible, and drawing illustrations from non-Biblical, including classical sources, it is concerned to plot a way through the faith — reason tension, by suggesting that the biblical material should be regarded as 'religion, and thus capable of being interpreted from several different perspectives. Through an analysis of the impact of creative figures in each discipline, the influence is assessed of historical criticism, tradition history, sociological, including liberation and feminist, approaches, and literary studies with an insightful section on the limitations of structuralism. In every case the attempt is made to expose the problems raised for, and to explore the interplay with, theology. Each section includes a useful bibliography, and there is an 'Annotated Index of Names' providing brief, but helpful, information about the main figures whose work is highlighted in the book or whose influence lies behind its analysis. Should there be any carping about the selectivity or the analysis, the authors may rightly shelter behind their own wise words, 'The risk of getting it wrong is a condition of all interpretation and all communication' (p. 296).

R. DAVIDSON

NASUTI, H. P.: *Tradition History and the Psalms of Asaph* (SBL Dissertation Series 88). 1988. Pp. vii, 204. (Scholars Press, Atlanta, Georgia. Price: $20.95 (member price: $13.95). ISBN 0 89130 970 5. Paperback price: $13.95 (member price: $9.95). ISBN 0 89130 971 3)

Dr Nasuti takes to task a previous study of the Asaphite psalms (by Illman – see *B.L.* 1978, p. 68) for concluding that they do not have enough in common to enable us either to identify a distinctive tradition behind them or to posit firm links between them and the Asaphite guild mentioned in Chronicles. He sensibly rejects so negative a conclusion about a tradition complex which, unlike many others which have been discovered, is sharply delineated for us in the biblical text; and he rightly suspects that the traditio-historical methods which Illman uses have something to do with it. By bringing in form critical and lexical considerations which tradition criticism does not normally think relevant, he succeeds in building up a not unconvincing picture of the special interests of the Asaphites, of their Ephraimite origin and of their subsequent activity in Judah. Whether what Nasuti gives us will be adjudged proper tradition criticism I am not sure; but it seems to work, and that surely is the most meaningful test of a method. The bibliography stops around 1980, which suggests that the work was rather a long time languishing in the press.

J. C. L. Gibson

Noth, M.: *Kyūyaku-seisho no Rekishi-bungaku*, Denshōshi-teki Kenkyū. Translated by T. Yamaga. Pp. 494. (Nihon kirisuto Kyōdan Shuppankyoku, Tokyo. Price: ¥6,500)

This is a Japanese translation of *Überlieferungsgeschichtliche Studien*, 3rd ed. (1967). The translator appended a detailed history of study and developments on the deuteronomistic history (pp. 439–82).

K. K. Sacon

O'Connor, K. M.: *The Confessions of Jeremiah: Their Interpretation and Role in Chapters 1–25* (SBL Dissertation Series 95). 1988. Pp. xv, 183. (Scholars Press, Atlanta, Goergia. Price: $14.95 (member price: $10.95). ISBN 1 55540 000 0. Paperback price: $10.95 (member price: $7.95). ISBN 1 55540 001 9)

We are working in a period rich in Jeremiah studies. Kathleen O'Connor has submitted a careful account, not just of the 'confessions', but of the first half of Jeremiah as a whole. A short introduction anticipates her conclusions: that the confessions, far from providing 'evidence of a petulant and disturbed personality', in fact 'served a public prophetic function in the original life-setting of the prophet'. Jeremiah is disclosed as a 'prophet of Yahweh's praises'. It is purposeful editing, for literary and theological reasons, which has placed the poems exclusively in chapters 11–20.

The opening five chapters provide fresh translations and full textual and literary discussions of the five poems: 11:18–20+12:1–5; 15:10–12, 15–21; 17:14–18; 18:19–23; and 20:7–13 (the associated 11:21–23; 12:6; 16:1–13; 18:18; and 20:1–6 have a 'midrashic' relationship with the parent poems).

In her discussion of the confessions as a collection of poems, O'Connor moves beyond von Rad's judgment that they 'played both a private and a public role during Jeremiah's lifetime': they were preserved because they claimed that Jeremiah's prophecy was true, and they appealed to God's authority for that truth. Their argument is expressed most fully in the final one. Chapter 7 notes that they are regularly placed near 'narratives which decry Israel's failure to heed God's word': they provide evidence of the people's crimes. After sketching a plausible structure for Jer. 1–25 as a whole (ch. 8), the author recapitulates her results in a concluding chapter, which argues that 'the question of the justice of God receives an enlarged response in the confessions' new literary context of cc 1–25. Their original theme of theodicy is used by the redactor in a reverse manner to illustrate why the curse against the nation had to be enacted. The people rejected the prophetic word' (p. 160).

A. G. Auld

O'Connor, M. P. and Freedman, D. N. (eds.): *Backgrounds for the Bible*. 1987. Pp. xii, 369. (Eisenbrauns, Winona Lake, Indiana. Price: $17.50. ISBN 0 931464 30 7)

The reviewer was startled to find a quotation from his review on the sleeve of this collection of essays before he had opened it! The explanation is that there is a considerable overlap with an earlier volume by the same editors: *The Bible and its Traditions* (Michigan Quarterly Review XXII/3), which he reviewed in *B. L.* 1984, p. 22. Nineteen of the articles in the present volume appeared in the earlier one, including those specified in the *B. L.* notice. Of the five new articles three are of direct interest to students of the Old Testament: On Reading Genesis 1–3 (F. I. Andersen), Biblical Cosmology (T. Frymer-Kensky), and The Language of Holiness (B. A. Levine). The other two concern the relation between the Bible and modern literature. A number of contributions, mostly of a literary nature, are not reproduced from the earlier volume. In its new form this collection will continue to stimulate and inform the general reader.

A. GELSTON.

PRICKETT, S.: *Words and the Word: Language, poetics and biblical interpretation*. 1988. Pp. xii, 305. (Cambridge University Press. Price: £11.95 ($17.95). ISBN 0 521 36838 3)

Full and glowing tribute has already been paid in *B. L.* 1988, p. 87 to the original 1986 edition of this study by the Professor of English in the Australian National University. That hardback is now priced at £30.00 ($44.50).

A. G. AULD

PROVAN, I. W.: *Hezekiah and the Books of Kings* (BZAW 172). 1988. Pp. xiii, 218. (De Gruyter, Berlin. Price: DM 90.00. ISBN 3 11 011557 3)

This revision of Iain Provan's Cambridge thesis of 1986 is an important study, based on careful research. It opens with a crisp account of research on Kings and the Deuteronomists since Noth's work of 1943, drawing renewed attention to both older and more recent views that a first (Dtr) edition of Kings ended with Hezekiah. Chapter 2 reviews the treatment of the Judgement formulae in Kings by H. Weippert, R. Nelson, A. F. Campbell, and A. Lemaire, as well as responses to their studies. The concluding critique demonstrates the need for a fresh scrutiny: this is very persuasively offered in the following two main chapters.

The third chapter, on the *bamot* in Kings, concludes that 'a primary theme may be found in 1 Kings 3 — 2 Kings 18. The *bamot* are viewed as Yahwistic shrines, and Hezekiah as the good king who removed them, centralizing Yahweh-worship in Jerusalem'. It is in redactional additions within these chapters and in material towards the end of Kings, that they are viewed as idolatrous places of worship. Chapter 4 then argues that the David found as a promissory figure in 1 Kings 15 — 2 Kings 15 is also the original Davidic element in 1 Kings 1–14, though that has been overlaid there by conditional elements. Full discussion of 2 Kings 22:2 and of the 'B2' account of Jerusalem's deliverance in 2 Kings 18–20 confirm that changes were made in the exile to the Davidic theme as to the *bamot* one.

The fifth chapter first offers three further illustrations of formulae (this time regnal) changing usage after Hezekiah; then argues that 2 Kings 21–25 as a whole is exilic; and finally suggests the reign of Josiah as the historical setting for this first draft of Kings down to the period of Hezekiah. Chapter 6 proposes in modest summary first that something like the present books of Samuel are a necessary precursor of the original Kings; then that Deuteronomic Judges stems from the exilic redactor of Samuel–Kings rather than from its late monarchic author. Since Judges effects a link with Deuteronomy-Joshua, these books too had been added to Samuel-Kings after the exile. A final chapter briefly restates the case.

There is much to be learned from many an illuminating discussion of individual passages and issues. There is surely also much more to be made of the evidence than Provan has begun to. The first draft of Kings he argues for is much closer than the familiar text to some of the leading ideas of Chronicles, not least those linked with David. Kings' Josiah is a much more Mosaic figure. In fact this reader wonders just how Deuteronomistic, or even proto-Deuteronomistic, Provan's 'original' Samuel-Kings was.

A. G. AULD

VON RAD, G.: *Insuraeru no Chie*. Translated by H. Katsumura. 1988. Pp. 537. (Nihon Kirisuto Kyōdan Shuppan-kyoku, Tokyo. Price: ¥7,800)

This is a translation of *Weisheit im Israel* (1970) (See *B. L.* 1972, p. 45f.).

K. K. SACON

RAST, W. E.: *Kyūyaku-seisho to Denshō-shi*. Translated by S. Higuchi. (Kyōbunkwan, Tokyo. Price: ¥1,500)

This is a Japanese translation of *Tradition History and the Old Testament* (1972) (See *B. L.* 1974, p. 57).

K. K. SACON

ROFÉ, A.: *The Prophetical Stories: The narratives about the Prophets in the Hebrew Bible — Their Literary Types and History* (Publications of the Perry Foundation for Biblical Research in the Hebrew University of Jerusalem). 1988. Pp. 218. (Magnes, Jerusalem. Price: $22.00. ISBN 965 223 685 3)

This volume represents a very welcome translation of the revised Hebrew edition (of 1986) of Rofé's 'attempt to describe the whole prophetical narrative in the Hebrew Bible' whose first Hebrew appearance (in 1982) was described and commended in *B. L.* 1984, pp. 80f. It is to be hoped that a much wider readership will now engage with these studies, at the same time modest and of far-reaching implications.

A. G. AULD

RÜTERSWÖRDEN, U.: *Von der politischen Gemeinschaft zur Gemeinde. Studien zu Dt 16, 18–18, 22* (Bonner Biblische Beiträge 65). 1987. Pp. 167. (Athenäum, Frankfurt. Price: DM 48.00. ISBN 3 610 09101 0)

This book significantly contributes to three questions: the distinction between the original deuteronomic law and the deuteronomistic editing of that law; the setting and purpose of the deuteronomic law; the intention of the deuteronomistic editing of that law. Literary critical methods are used to distinguish deuteronomistic editing (considered to be not nearly so pervasive as sometimes proposed) from the original deuteronomic law concerning officials in 16:18–18:22. In its deuteronomic form this is seen to be not a closed unit, but a thematic unit forming part of a continuous layer to which it is linked by the transitional passage in 16:18–17:1. The unit uses a standard scheme for treating judge, king, priest and prophet, and this, together with the deliberate arrangement in which human participation in setting up the officials recedes more and more in favour of Yahweh, is taken to indicate that there is an overall theoretical conception behind the presentation. This conception, which emphasizes the role of the full citizen and his right to act as local judge, and which limits the authority of the king, finds an analogy in the constitution of the Greek *polis*, while the nearest Old Testament analogy is the Israelite city of the period of the judges. The deuteronomic law, presupposing an independent judiciary, kingship and cult, and so pre-exilic, proposes the outline of a constitutional theory for a political community. Deuteronomistic editing, on the other hand, has introduced generalized references to the law and the levitical priests as its guardians, along with reference to the tribal affiliation of Israelites. It is marked also by an emphasis on the role of the prophet whose standing is no lower than that of the Mosaic legislator. This reflects an exilic background in which the law was determinative, the prophet being the legislator and the levitical priests the executive. The Israel envisaged here is no longer an independent political community but a congregation.

A. D. H. MAYES

SAVASTA, C.: *Forme e strutture in Gen. 1–11* (Collana Ricerche e Proposte 3). 1988. Pp. 160. (Edizioni Dr Antonio Sfamemi, Messina. Price: Lire 15,000. ISBN 88 7820 018 2)

The author is a mathematics teacher with no expertise in the Old Testament; consequently, he is dependent on secondary sources. Also, his presentation is unnecessarily repetitive. He examines the text of Gen. 1–11 in its final form, concentrating on chapters 5–8. He stresses that the text should provide its own key to analysis and comes to the conclusion that the present arrangement of Gen. 1–11 is clearly artificial and ultimately chiastic. It is structure that counts, not content. He has, besides, some novel suggestions concerning such topics as the reason for the flood (fratricide), the identity of the *nephilim* or giants (they are equated with the patriarchs), and so on. An article in a journal would have been adequate for the substance of this interesting book.

W. G. E. WATSON

SCHARBERT, J.: *Ich bin Josef, euer Bruder: Die Erzählung von Josef und seinen Brüdern, wie sie nicht in der Bible steht*. 1988. Pp. 114. (EOS, St. Ottilien. Price: DM 14.80. ISBN 3 88096 703 2)

This book is not, as one might expect from the sub-title, a treatment of the Joseph story as found in extra-biblical sources. In fact it deals with the biblical text in a work designed to introduce non-specialists to the traditional source-criticism of Genesis 37–50. A section on the recent history of scholarship leads to the printing of the biblical text of the Joseph story in, successively, the Yahwistic, Elohistic, and Priestly versions. Each separate story is accompanied by a commentary. Professor Scharbert's view is that there existed a pre-monarchic story of Joseph preserved by the Joseph tribes. This contained the main outlines of the story as we know it in the Bible. The Yahwist learned this story at Solomon's court, and incorporated it into his work. The E version was written down in the north around 722, whence it was brought south and later combined with the J version. The author leaves open the question whether Joseph was an historical figure.

The book is beautifully produced and includes a map, and five photographs from Egyptian sources.

J. W. ROGERSON

SCHMIDT, E. R., KORENHOF, M., and JOST, R. (eds.): *Feministisch gelesen: 32 ausgewählte Bibeltexte für Gruppen, Gemeinden und Gottesdienste*, Bd 1. 1988. Pp. 296. (Kreuz, Stuttgart. Price: DM 29.80. ISBN 3 7831 0909 4)

Feminist theology is often associated with the U. S. A., but this volume is one of many indications of its wider impact in the western world. This book introduces thirty two Biblical passages, in which feminist interests would seem to be relevant. Sixteen are from the Old Testament and one from the Apocrypha. The sections are meant to be basic raw material for group and congregational study or for preaching at public worship. As one would expect from a book of this character published in Germany, there is no lack of solid biblical exegesis, to which the notes and bibliographies bear witness; but it cannot be claimed that the feminist interests and customary exegesis have been skilfully integrated. As times, the feminist material seems to be tacked on; and, occasionally, bibliographies portray sociological rather than theological concern.

The influence of writers like Elizabeth Schüssler-Fiorenza is very evident. Whilst most of the studies are by German women theologians, there are some contributions translated from English. Of the women characters in the Bible considered, studies in Hagar, Samson's choice of women, Rizpah, Huldah, Esther, and Susanna are of particular interest.

R. HAMMER

SCHREINER, J.: *Die Zehn Gebote im Leben des Gottesvolkes*. 1988. Pp. 152. (Kösel, München. Price: DM 29.80. ISBN 3 466 20297 3)

This thoroughly revised edition of a study first published in 1966, and praised in *Bible Bibliog.*, p. 42, handles the Ten Commandments in seven clearly presented chapters: covenant and decalogue; many precepts, yet only 'ten words'; the basic divine demand (first and second commandments); basis of human society (third and fourth); life's great possessions (fifth to tenth); decalogue and preaching; instruction pregnant with future. Professor Schreiner, now of Würzburg, accepts the arguments for the greater originality of the Deuteronomy text, especially at the end, over coveting the neighbour's wife (distinct from adultery) and desiring the house, and follows the enumeration which that decision implies.

A. G. AULD

SMITH, M. S.: *Psalms: The Divine Journey*. 1987. Pp. 85. (Paulist Press, Mahwah, New Jersey. Price: $4.95. ISBN 0 8091 2897 7)

This brief discussion of the Psalms has developed from three lectures at St Paul Seminary. It is organized around the image of a journey: first to meet the language and forms of the psalms, then their world of thought; then we accompany the Psalmists as they encounter God in Jerusalem and temple, whither God also makes the journey of his 'coming'. Finally the journey to the present is the history of the use of the Psalms in communities and in the stages of an individual's life. The book concentrates on a few generously quoted examples and succeeds fairly well in introducing the psalmists' language, world-view and religious experience. The substantial notes are strong on archaeology.

J. J. EATON

STRUPPE, U.: *Die Herrlichkeit Jahwes in der priesterschrift* (Österreichische Biblische Studien 9). 1988. Pp. v, 258. (Österreichisches Katholisches Bibelwerk, Klosterneuburg. Price: ÖS 268.00; DM 40.00; SwFr. 32.60. ISBN 3 85396 077 4)

Building on recent study of the priestly writing, and accepting it as an originally independent source in the Pentateuch, the author aims for a comprehensive treatment of the idea of the glory of Yahweh, which is seen as a leitmotif of the priestly account of the history of Israel. Within the section. Ex. 16–Num. 20, the glory of Yahweh is shown to be central to those stories which are marked out as text units by a system of notes on Israel's wanderings. There are two groups of *kabod* notices: one in the Sinai pericope and the other in the wilderness narrative. In the Sinai group, Ex.24:15b–18 is an 'overture' incorporating elements and motifs which are later further developed. Particularly significant is that the glory of Yahweh appears not only before Moses but before all the congregation of Israel. The community is of fundamental importance for P. The final reference to the glory of Yahweh in this group, in Lev. 9, marks the occasion of the first sacrifice; in between come the directions for the building of the tent and the story of that being carried out. Ex.29:43–46 is central, and of major importance for P, containing the divine promise and expressing the purpose of the revelation of the glory of Yahweh: the presence of God with Israel. The theme of the glory of Yahweh as his effective presence with Israel in her history, in the role of both deliverer and judge, is central also to the wilderness narrative group of priestly passages.

This is a clearly presented and fruitful study, with a strong emphasis on detailed linguistic and semantic analysis of the relevant texts. It has made a solid contribution to the study of the priestly writing. A. D. H. MAYES

SUZUKI, Y.: *Shinmeiki no Bunken-gaku-teki Kenkyū* (A Science-of-Literature Study in Deuteronomy). 1987. Pp. 698. (Nihon Kirisutokyō Shuppan-kyoku, Tokyo. Price: ¥7.400)

Based upon the results of his Ph.D. dissertation 'The 'Numeruswechsel' in Deuteronomy, Claremont Graduate School, U. S. A.), Suzuki discusses the long process of the literary formation of Deuteronomy with full use of form-critical, tradition-historical, and redaction-historical methodologies. The result is reinforced with his scrutinized analysis of each pericope with special attention to the change of the grammatical number in Deuteronomy. The formation process starts from the basic strata consisting of the casuistic laws in the third person and of the admonitions in the second person singular in the early monarchical period. Then follow two editorial stages of admonition in the second person singular in the early and late period of Josiah, and two editorial stages in the second person plural of the early deuteronomistic between Josiah's death and the end of Judah. An early exilic deuteronomistic edition in the first person plural and a late exilic post-deuteronomistic edition in the second person singular are detected. The process ends with the book presented as the testament of Moses in the third person in the Second Temple period. The work is worthy of being carefully considered. K. K. SACON

SWEENEY, M. A.: *Isaiah 1–4 and the Post-Exilic Understanding of the Isaianic Tradition* (BZAW 171). 1988. Pp. X, 211. (De Gruyter, Berlin. Price: DM 98.00. ISBN 3 11 011034 2; ISBN 0 89925 403 9 (US))

This interesting monograph originated in a Ph.D. thesis of 1983, supervised by R. P. Knierim. It offers an excellent introduction to, and also a fine contribution to the contemporary discussion of the Book of Isaiah. A short introductory chapter recapitulates the main emphases of H. Barth, O. Kaiser, J. Verymeylen, H. Wildberger, P. R. Ackroyd, B. S. Childs, R. E. Clements, and R. Rendtorff. Then a further preliminary chapter examines the evidence within Isaiah for viewing that book as a redactional unity: the role of Babylon in chs 1–39; the rather different depiction of Hezekiah in Isaiah 36–39 from 2 Kings 18–20; ch. 35 deliberately drafted as an introduction to chs 40ff; the theme of Israel's deafness and blindness that both halves of Isaiah share; the relationship between ch. 1 and the rest of the book, especially Isa. 65–66; and the way in which the presentation of material in Isa. 1–39 reflects the concerns of post-exilic Judaism. The first of the two larger chapters (pp. 27–99) reviews the structure of the whole of Isaiah: first Isa. 1 and 36–39; then Isa. 2–35; then Isa. 40–66; and a final overview. The 'exhortation', that comprises the whole variety of literary types in the book, would best have served the needs of the late, fifth century Jewish community in Jerusalem. As an illustration of the detailed analysis required to justify his broader account, Sweeney offers in the second main chapter (pp. 101–184) analyses first of Isa. 1, then of Isa. 2–4. It was especially here that this reader was not always persuaded by the argumentation. However, the whole discussion is impressively clear, eminently fair and well-informed, and appears to be asking the right questions.

A. G. AULD

TERINO, A.: *L'origine del Pentateuco* (Prospective Evangeliche). 1986. Pp. 355. (UCEB, Fondi (LT). Price: Lire 19,500)

The author writes for members of protestant denominations in Italy finding themselves unsettled by the results of Pentateuchal criticism as communicated, for example, in the notes to the Jerusalem Bible. To this readership Terino offers a short but well-documented account of the origins and history of traditio-history criticism of the Pentateuch, followed by a full-scale critique which includes extensive exposition of its presuppositions. He then states and defends his claim for Mosaic authorship. He has drawn on a wide range of conservative scholarship, from which he quotes extensively. The tone is only partly polemic: Terino takes his readers seriously, and as a presentation of the pre-critical position this is in its own way a scholarly performance.

C. J. A. HICKLING

TOURNAY, R. J.: *Voir et Entendre Dieu avec les Psaumes,* ou *La liturgie prophétique du second temple à Jérusalem* (Cahiers de la Revue Biblique 24). 1988. Pp. ix, 221. (Gabalda, Paris. Price: Fr. 302.00. ISBN 2 85021 031 5)

Father Tournay of the Ecole Biblique, Jerusalem, has contributed some thirty articles in the field of psalmody over the past forty years, and it is good to have his views gathered up and presented in one study with admirable clarity and conciseness. He represents a characteristic French view in preferring the post-exilic centuries, and especially the world of the Chronicler *c.*300 B.C., as the main setting for the Psalms. Along with elements of early psalmody, the legacy of the great prophets has passed into the use of the liturgical prophet-psalmists, such as are depicted in Chronicles, and from these we have a Psalter full of divine utterance, revelation, and messianic hope. Most of the psalms are referred to this context, including the royal psalms, which are taken messianically. This prophetic and messianic reading of the Psalms is finally shown to fit well with Christian interpretation and usage. This comprehensive study is well documented and will be used with profit and respect by scholars of various persuasions.

J. H. EATON

TREVES, M.: *The Dates of the Psalms: History and Poetry in Ancient Israel*. 1988. Pp. 109 (Giardini, Pisa)

In this work it is maintained that with only two or three exceptions (e.g. Ps. 45, which is held to be wedding song for Ahab and Jezebel) all the Psalms should be dated between 170 and 103 B.C. and their authorship attributed to outstanding characters of that period (e.g. Onias, Judas, Jonathan, Simon, John Hyrcanus). Among the criteria for dating are (a) that expressions like 'Holy Hill' indicate a date later than Josiah, (b) that references to wars fought by Jews cannot be from the period 585–167, (c) that parallels to prophetic images and ideas usually indicate a date later than the prophets, (d) that some terms such as 'Rock' and 'Most High' for God and 'Jeshurun' for Israel are very late, (e) that parallels to Greek literature, of which many are suggested, indicate a date in the Hellenistic period. On this basis conjectural chronological and historical notes are provided on all the Psalms, e.g. 24 was composed for the first Hanukkah; 68 celebrates the victory over Nicanor; 72 is a panegyric of Ptolemy II Philadelphus; 'Return, O LORD' in 90:13 'suits the year 164, before the return of the LORD to his abode'; the 'brethren' in 133 are probably Aristobulus and Antigonus. The ingenuity displayed fascinates even when it fails to convince.

G. W. ANDERSON

TUCKER, G. M.: *Kyūyaku-seisho to Yōshiki-shi*. Translated by K. Ii. 1988. Pp. 179. (Kyōbunkwan, Tokyo. Price: ¥1,800)

This is a Japanese translation of *Form Criticism of the Old Testament* (1971). (See *B. L.* 1972, p. 49).

K. K. SACON

UTZSCHNEIDER, H.: *Das Heiligtum und das Gesetz: Studien zur Bedeutung der sinaitischen Heiligtumstexte (Ex 25–40; Lev 8–9)* (Orbis Biblicus et Orientalis 77). 1988. Pp. vi, 320. (Universitätsverlag, Freiburg (CH); Vandenhoeck & Ruprecht, Göttingen. Price: Sw.Fr. 90.00; DM 130.00. ISBN 3 7278 0558 7; ISBN 3 525 53706 9)

A dense and detailed structural study of the Pentateuchal sanctuary and tent-of-meeting texts to establish their significance. Utzschneider initially offers methodological reflections, then surveys previous work before examining 'Die sinaitischen Heiligtumstexte und ihre Kontexte', 'Makrostruktur und Konzepte der sinaitischen Heiligtumstexte' and 'Der Oberflächentext der sinaitischen Heiligtumstexte' in chapters three to five. Chapter six focuses on three ideas which have emerged in the course of the study — 'die Lade-Wohnungs-Konzeption', 'die Volk-Heiligtums-Konzeption' and 'die Ohel-Moed-Konzeption'. Chapter seven relates the material to historical (second temple, the Persians), social ('die "Burger-Tempel-Gemeinde"') and literary (Jer. 3, 23, 31; 1 Kings 6–8) referents. Utzschneider proposes an alternative methodology to either the historico-critical or literary approaches. He suggests that the biblical texts considered are best explained on a model of successive superstructures — each succeeding structure the result of inner biblical interpretation which is described as 'die triebende Kraft biblischer Textbildung'. Utzschneider dates the projection of the sanctuary texts to the period of Persian domination. In this context the 'Volk-Heiligtums-Text' pointed out a way to maintain Israel's identity and assert 'dass über allen Loyalitäten (also auch über den "Gesetzen der Meder und Perser") das Gesetz des Gottes vom Sinai steht' while 'Die Lade-Wohnungs-Text folgert daraus: Ein Heiligtum kann nur als "Ort des Gesetzes" einen legitimen Platz im Leben Israels beanspruchen'. Interaction with English language works is a trifle patchy: J. Milgrom's 1977 *ZAW* article is cited as is G. J. Wenham's 1981 *ZAW* article, but neither the latter's major commentary on Leviticus nor anything else by the former is cited. J. Gray's commentary on Kings is known only in its second edition, while no mention is made of M. Fishbane, *Biblical Interpretation in Ancient Israel*.

D. G. DEBOYS

VAN LEEUWEN, R. C.: *Context and Meaning in Proverbs 25–27* (SBL Dissertation Series 96). 1988. Pp. xi, 171. (Scholars Press, Atlanta, Georgia. Price: $14.95 (member price: $10.95). ISBN 0 55540 004 3. Paperback price: $10.95 (member price : $7.95). ISBN 0 55540 005 1)

In rejecting the view that the wisdom sentence is a small literary creation encapsulating a single thought in a memorable form, Van Leeuwen is also departing from an editorial explanation of the adjacency of sentences with similar subject-matter. 'Themes' which are editorial arrangements of originally independent sentences do not satisfy the kind of over-arching structure which he perceives in the sentence literature. Nevertheless, within the narrow limits of chapters 25–27 his hypothesis meets an impediment and in 27:1–22 ('a proverb miscellany') he falls back on a view of how sentences relate to each other not far removed from the general hypothesis which he attempts to demolish.

Van Leeuwen works with the concept of a 'proverb poem' and he defines four of these poems (25:2–27; 26:1–12, 13–16, 17–28). These are separate artistic entities, but it is not clear whether we are to suppose that one poet is responsible for all of them or whether they are the work of four different poets. When Van Leeuwen says that *kbd* is a stitch which links 25:2–27 with 26:1–12 (25:2, 27/26:1) and that *ḥkm b'ynyw* similarly links 26:1–12 with 26:13–16 (26:12/26:16), is he indicating a secondary editorial association or is he producing evidence that the same poet composed the first three poems?

Van Leeuwen specifies three different methods which he is employing: (a) a two-fold structural approach; (b) a poetic or rhetorical criticism; (c) a semantic analysis. In connection with the first he uses language which is at home in phonological and syntactical contexts in general linguistic theory, but he appears to dissolve the distinction which is maintained there between a paradigmatic opposition and a syntagmatic relationship. He urges that a 'proverb poem' has an architecture which does not answer to a 'narrative syntagmatic' continuity and he states that paradigmatic options are organized to create syntagmatic patterns.

What Van Leeuwen calls 'poetics' is said by him to be akin to rhetorical criticism. It is an interesting question how the relation of his first two methods to his final category of 'semantics' is to be envisaged: his analyses do not exist in separate compartments and neither of the first two can be disengaged from 'semantics'.

There is one striking example of bad exegesis in the book: the treatment of 27:23–27 is close to a kind of allegorical interpretation. There is no doubt that this is a poem about good husbandry in the rearing of livestock (sheep and goats). To refuse this level of exegesis and to insist that that the passage is a parable which encapsulates a theory of kingship is indefensible.

This is a book which is the fruit of diligent research, but I am not persuaded by it. It is a singular irony that books which set out to enhance the architectural grandeur of Old Testament literature are themselves so devoid of literary attractiveness.

W. McKane

Van Der Wal, A.: *Nahum, Habakkuk: A Classified Bibliography* (with a special paragraph concerning literature on the Qumran Commentaries on Nahum and Habakkuk). 1988. Pp. xiii, 208. (Free University Press, Amsterdam. Price: fl 70.00. ISBN 90 6256 662 6)

This work is similar to *Amos: A Classified Bibliography* reviewed in *B. L.* 1984, p. 26. It lists about 1250 books and articles from 1800 till 1987. After separate sections on Nahum and Habakkuk, of which the greater part in each case consists of literature referring to particular verses or sections of the text, there is a further section, comprising about a fifth of the whole, on the Qumran Peshers of Nahum and Habakkuk. There is an index of authors. Although it is almost impossible to guarantee comprehensiveness in a bibliography of this kind, and some items are listed in several places, this bibliography will clearly be indispensable to students of these texts.

A. Gelston

White, H. C. (ed.): *Speech Act Theory and Biblical Criticism* (Semeia 41). 1988. Pp. vii, 178. (Scholars Press, Atlanta, Georgia. Price: $14.95 (member price: $9.95); sub. price (for 4 units): $35.00 (member price: $25.00). ISSN 0095 571X)

This volume of *Semeia* is devoted to a discussion of the philosophical theory of language use developed by J. L. Austin and systematized by J. R.

Searle and its application to the Bible. While it has taken biblical scholars rather a long time to get around to considering the work of Austin (and Searle) in relation to reading biblical language this book must be welcomed as an analytical introduction to the subject (individual scholars have written on the Bible using Austinian language analysis long before now).

The editor contributes two useful pieces: an introduction to the subject which includes a brief summary of each article in the issue and a valuable survey article on the value of speech act theory for Old Testament hermeneutics. M. Hanchers' 'Performative Utterance, the Word of God, and the Death of the Author' discusses performative language in relation to Barthes, Beneviste, and Derrida using various biblical phrases and notes the inaccuracies of their appropriation of speech act theory. In the application of the theory to problems of biblical exegesis there are three pieces: S. S. Lanser's '(Feminist) Criticism in the Garden: Inferring Genesis 2–3'; D. Patte's 'Speech Act Theory and Biblical Exegesis'; and R. L. Grimes's 'Infelicitous Performances and Ritual Criticism'. Responses to these articles are by M. J. Buss ('The Contribution of Speech Act Theory to Biblical Studies'), R. Detweiler ('Speaking of Believing in Gen.2–3'), and C. E. Jarrett ('Philosophy of Language in the Service of Religious Studies'). Two valuable bibliographies conclude the volume.

R. P. Carroll

Winquist, C. E. (ed.): *Text and Textuality* (Semeia 40). 1987. Pp. vi, 168. (Scholars Press, Atlanta, Georgia. Price: $14.95 (member price: $9.95); sub. price (for 4 units): $35.00 (member price: $25.00). ISSN 0095 571X)

'In theological text production, instantiation and ideation mark a text that is not a text at all' (Winquist, 1f.): with these words the editor sets the key of this issue of Semeia. R. P. Scharlemann's opening paper 'Theological Text' includes the statements '. . .the apophantic thought is that the Text of God *is* itself *as* what it is not. Adonai makes of Jahweh a nontext; but as this nontext Jahweh is the text it is. "The Writing of God" writes, similarly, a "not" across any text; but then the text, which is a text but not the Text of God ("God is God", written by God), can be the text *as* which the Text of God is what it is'. (p. 18). Biblical scholars who follow the argument here can now read on. . . M. C. Taylor's 'Shades of Difference' discusses Hegel's *Phenomenology of Spirit* with a good deal of assistance from Derrida, Nietzsche, and Peirce. C. A. Raschke's 'From Textuality to Scripture: The End of Theology as Writing' looks at theology from the privileged position of post-structural criticism and Barth's indictment of religion. D. L. Miller's 'The Question of the Book: Religion as Texture' reflects on text as that which is woven and as a penal colony (cf. Kafka's story). S. E. Shapiro's 'Failing Speech: Post-Holocaust Writing and the Discourse of Postmodernism' considers the limits of representational discourse with reference to the Shoah and uses the writings of Paul Celan, Nelly Sachs, and Edmond Jabès. C. P. Christ's 'Finitude, Death, and Reverence for Life' is a feminist analysis of the threat of nuclear extinction and apocalypticism which sees such denial of the finitude of life on earth as a male madness to be resolved by feminist visions of nature. J. D. Crossan's 'Living Earth and Living Christ: Thoughts on Carol P. Christ's Finitude, Death, and Reverence for Life' responds to Christ's article critically, accusing her of romanticism and a failure to recognize the terror of nature as well as its beauty. K. H. Richards's 'From Scripture to Textuality' is a brief response to Raschke's paper. R. C. Martin's 'Text and Contextuality in Reference to Islam' takes issue with deconstructive theology as a type of fideism and argues for a more sophisticated treatment of the role of the Qur'an in Islamic society. W. S. Green's 'Romancing the Tome: Rabbinic Hermeneutics and the Theory of Literature' argues for the kaleidoscopic nature of rabbinic use of scripture and against the current tendency to depic rabbinic hermeneutics as a harbinger of contemporary dissenting theories of literature.

While there is much of interest in some of these articles there is also a good deal of 'nonsense on stilts' in the first half of the volume, redeemed by the critical edge of the responses. For the lowly biblical scholar who is tempted to bemoan the lack of theory in the discipline, some of these theory-laden pieces of obscurantist writing may illustrate the impoverishment which theory also can bring to a subject if it is inappropriate theory. The pieces by Crossan, Martin, and Green are most useful.

R. P. CARROLL

7. LAW, RELIGION, AND, THEOLOGY

ANDERSON, G. A.: *Sacrifices and Offerings in Ancient Israel: Studies in their Social and Political Importance* (Harvard Semitic Monographs 41). 1987. Pp. xiii, 160. (Scholars Press, Atlanta, Georgia. Price: $14.95 (member price: $9.95). ISBN 1 55540 169 4)

A suggestive monograph which examines a number of terms for 'offering' in their Israelite and Canaanite social contexts. Anderson suggests that where *šay* In Hebrew 'never developed the technical cultic usage it acquired in other Canaanite circles' (53) the use of both *minḥâ* and *šlmm* exhibits strong parallels 'among the cultic centres of Israel, Phoenicia and Ugarit' (54). *Minḥâ* was used both for political tribute and gift offering, a contention which is illustrated by a close reading of the Ehud narrative in chapter three. *Šlmm* had a covenantal context and in the DH 'plays a strong role in the national . . . festivals of Israel' (49). '*The distinctiveness of the Israelite cult*' (author's italics) is asserted to be '*nothing other than the limitation of cultic activity to one particular patron deity*' (3). The fourth chapter seeks to explicate two texts — Gen. 14: 18–20, 1 Sam. 8: 10–17 — argued to come from the period of the united monarchy, which evince radically different evaluations of the tithe. The largest, fifth chapter explores the significance of the close connection between temple-building and the fertility of the land in the post-exilic prophets. ANE evidence is surveyed which suggests that the relationship between king and temple on the one hand and economic wellbeing (including the ability to bring offerings) on the other could be portrayed in 'mythic' terms — maintenance of the cult brings prosperity — or, in royal inscriptions, in a more realistic manner — the land is prospering because the king has exercised strong rule, irrigated the land, built storehouses, etc. Consequently Anderson, inviting his readers to discard the legacy of Frazerian interpretation, argues that 'A renewed Temple cultus and offering system accompanied by a strong leader could inaugurate an era of prosperity . . . not simply because these were magical or supernatural institutions, but because the social realities they represented had historical referents (124). 'The temple was both an economic and a spiritual centre' (125). The book concludes with appendices examining briefly the terms *mas'ēt, *matni'u, tĕnûpâ, tĕrûmâ*.

D. G. DEBOYS

BÄCHLI, O.: *Das Alte Testament in der Kirchlichen Dogmatik von Karl Barth*. 1987. Pp. xii, 368. (Neukirchener, Neukirchen-Vluyn. Price: DM 68.00. ISBN 3 7887 0792 5)

The task of writing an Old Testament theology is in disarray at the present time and one reason for this lies in the awareness that the subject has tended to remain too aloof from what major theologians have actually made of the Old Testament. The present volume therefore, which examines the way in which the distinguished Swiss theologian Karl Barth uses the Old Testament, is especially welcome. All the more so because Bächli is both an established biblical scholar and is thoroughly well versed in the many writings of Barth, as well as the voluminous secondary literature relating to them.

The volume is divided into three sections: Dialogue — Exegesis — Hermeneutical, with the central, and longest, section on exegesis being further subdivided. These examine the nature of exegesis as a theological task, the use of major themes and exegesis as a form of theological commentary. Two features particularly stand out: the first is that Barth began his early theological work with little interest in the Old Testament but came increasingly to explore its contents more and more fully in his writings. The second feature is that this use of the Old Testament is integrated into the *Dogmatik* in a very complex way so that it is scarcely possible to abstract it, or a few selected passages where it occurs, as representing a kind of separate — Old Testament — treatment. The subject therefore demands a very full and detailed knowledge of Barth's writing and preaching, together with an appreciation of his way of handling biblical texts. All of this is well taken care of in Bächli's excellent coverage.

This turning towards the Old Testament by Barth is explained partly as a consequence of his going back to the Church Fathers of the early centuries, partly as a response to his interest in the Christian perception of Judaism, and partly as a reflection of a broadening concern with ethical and political issues.

The initial appearance from what is presented here is that Barth was himself singularly unsystematic in his use of the Old Testament, but so often strikingly perceptive and stimulating in his comments upon it. This sense of freshness is enhanced by the great variety of passages and themes that come into his purview. So much is concrete and precise in relation to specific texts, with an eschewing of abstractions and broad generalizations, that the reader knows clearly what biblical passage is in mind.

This study ought certainly to encourage the awareness that interpreting the biblical text is a many-sided discipline which cannot ignore the dimension that we customarily ascribe to theology. I hope therefore that it will encourage students of theology to maintain a strong interest in the Old Testament. At the same time, it must be noted that what Bächli strives to do is to point to the many passages, sermons and articles where Barth deals with the Old Testament, rather than to systematize what is found there. Access to at least some of Barth's writings is therefore necessary if the book is to be properly used. The book is thoroughly to be recommended and one can hope that an English translation may be forthcoming. It is full of interest and stimulus for further research and reflection.

R. E. Clements

Barton, J.: *People of the Book? The authority of the Bible in Christianity* (The Bampton Lectures 1988). 1988. Pp. xi, 96. (SPCK, London. Price: £4.95. ISBN 0 281 04387 6)

In these exemplary Bampton lectures, Barton seeks to free the Bible from its current enthralment to Christian fundamentalism. Using their own arguments, he demolishes the biblicists' case both in relation to early Christian understanding of scriptural authority, the Old Testament, and the canon, as well as their attitudes to historical, theological, literary, and liturgical issues posed by Biblical study.In my view contemporary fundamentalism encourages the thought that the Bible should carry a Government health warning. Barton's approach renders this unnecessary by starting with the Gospel of the love of God which pre-dates any Bible, but to which both testaments challenge response. As he argues, here lies the authority of the Bible — not in a hankering after a perfection of necessity denied to anything human.

A. Phillips

Beaucamp, E.: *Les grands thèmes de l'Alliance* (Lire la Bible 81). 1988. Pp. 265. (Cerf, Paris. Price: Fr. 88.00. ISBN 2 204 02926 2; ISSN 0588 2257)

One and a half years' residence in a Moslem country turned E. Beaucamp's thoughts to the Biblical concept of the covenant, a concept which he had found largely ignored in Islam. It had also, he came to think, been seriously underrated in Christianity. He takes the divine initiative embodied in the covenant as the basic fact from which springs the whole of Old Testament religion. The creation of the world, the gift of the land, the ransoming from Egyptian servitude, salvation, justice, final victory over evil, and the coming of God's kingdom — all these are to be construed as theological themes deriving from the fact of the covenant. (Oddly, Beaucamp has no chapter analysing and explaining the covenant itself.) The sense that things did not have to be as they are but are so by virtue of a divine act of choice, this imparted to Israel a dynamic vitality missing from other religions and coloured her perception of the laws of morality as the Covenant-God's personal demands for a personal response. Life is a progress from darkness to light, from death to life, from present fear to an unknown future that can, nevertheless, be confidently embraced; it is 'a unique and irreversible adventure'. Beaucamp's (Christian) synthesis of Old Testament theology is expounded clearly and attractively. Expounded, not argued, for the author does not engage with the views of those who see things differently, nor does he very often even direct the reader to books and articles from writers sympathetic to his own viewpoint.

B. P. Robinson

Bovati, P.: *Ristabilire la Giustizia: Procedure, vocabolario, orientamenti* (Analecta Biblica 110). 1986. Pp. 446. (Biblical Institute Press, Rome. Price: Lire 45,000 ($35.00). ISBN 88 7653 110 6)

This study, presented as a doctoral thesis to the Pontifical Biblical Institute, consists of a detailed examination of the terminology and procedure of justice throughout the Bible, and especially in the Old Testament. Every stage of the judicial process, from initial accusation or plea to ultimate discharge or sentence and execution, is subjected to careful analysis; several cases of different kinds are reviewed. The study is not confined to the judicial incidents in the narrative books: the free use of juridical language in psalmists and prophets is also considered. There are, for example, some interesting comments on the use in prayer of the roots *qrb* and *rḥq* in the light of their legal usage: God draws near to help (e.g. Lam. 3:37), whereas ,the absence of help implies that he is far away (e.g. Ps. 22:2 MT; cf. vv. 12, 20). But *qrb* may be used of the adversary and not only of the advocate or witness for the defence (e.g. Ps. 27:2); similarly an accuser as well as a defender may stand at one's right hand (contrast vv. 6 and 31 of Ps. 109). Not only the student of Israel's institutions but the expositor of the Old Testament in general will find much illumination in this work.

F. F. Bruce

Boyce, R. N.: *The Cry to God in the Old Testament* (SBL Dissertation Series 103). 1988. Pp. ix, 93. (Scholars Press, Atlanta, Georgia. Price: $16.95 (member price: $10.95). ISBN 1 55540 229 1. Paperback price: $10.95 (member price: $7.95). ISBN 1 55540 230 5)

This study traces the widespread occurrence of the 'cry' motif in diverse Old Testament contexts. Good use is made of modern linguistic techniques to plot the semantic fields of the key Hebrew words *zʿq* and *ṣʿq*, both in terms of interpersonal relationships and the God-people relationship. Studies in the 'Setting in Life' and the 'Setting in Lierature' of these verbs seek to demonstrate how the basic Exodus cry to God is appropriated by later editors and compilers, royal, prophetic, and priestly, with the royal and prophetic, though not the priestly, strands broadening the category of the cry to embrace the future action of god. This is not only a detailed and scholarly word study, but it has real value for anyone interested in exploring the Old Testament contribution to petitionary prayer.

R. Davidson

CHRISTENSEN, D. L. (ed.): *Experiencing the Exodus from Egypt*. n.d. Pp. v, 95. (Bibal, Berkeley, California. Price: $7.95, plus $1.00 for postage and handling. ISBN 0 941037 03 7)

This volume is the result of cooperative Bible study among Jews and Christians in California and is difficult to be absorbed existentially by those who were not part of the joint experience. Biblical history is seen as contemporary history and the exegesis we now associate with Liberation Theology is abundantly present.

Most fascinating is the use made of ancient midrashic material, and, in particular, its emphasis on basic images, to provide a pattern for the union of the actual text with modern and/or psychological experience. The writers claim that an existential self-identification with the text can provide a way forward for Jewish-Christian dialogue and mutual understanding.

R. HAMMER

CLEMENTS, R.: *When God's Patience Runs Out: The truth of Amos for today* (Living Word Series). 1988. Pp. 192. (Inter-Varsity Press, Nottingham. Price: £3.95. ISBN 0 85110 496 7)

Dr Clements, a Baptist minister in Cambridge, has preserved *verbatim* a series of expository sermons on the Book of Amos. One is not surprised, therefore, to find the style homiletic and somewhat anecdotal.

For a congregation that had not sat under Dr Clements for a considerable time, much more would be needed to put Amos into its own historical and cultural background, although, to do him justice, this aspect is far from neglected. Because Dr Clements is concerned for contemporary relevance and application, there is less of the solid exposition to be found in preachers of a past age, such as (e.g.) George Adam Smith.

The final epilogue on 'Amos, Hell, and Jesus' may raise questioning in the mind of readers who are less ready to transfer the judgement theme in Amos, seen in temporal or historical terms, to the realm of the ultimate or eternal.

R. HAMMER

COSTACURTA, B.: *La Vita Minacciata: Il tema della paura nella Bibbia Ebraica* (Analecta Biblica 119). 1988. Pp. 360. (Biblical Institute Press, Rome. Price: Lire 48,000. ISBN 88 7653 119 X)

This appears to be the first comprehensive treatment of the theme of fear, in all its aspects, in the Old Testament. The first part consists of a detailed lexicographical study of the Hebrew roots which express the concept of fear. A second section analyses a number of Biblical passages describing various situations which provoke fear, such as war, a personal enemy, the presence of God or the numinous, physical sickness and child-birth. The final part is a broad study of the phenomenon of fear in the Old Testament, discussing such topics as the ways in which it arises, how it affects the body and human faculties and emotions and the means by which it may be combated and overcome. There is a twenty-two page bibliography, indices of Biblical citations, Hebrew words, grammatical terms and modern authors, and a subject index. What gives the work its particular value is its thorough and comprehensive character and its careful discussion of the relevant Hebrew terminology. It will provide a useful quarry for all future students of Biblical anthropology.

J. R. PORTER

COWARD, H.: *Sacred Word and Sacred Text: Scripture in World Religions*. 1988. Pp. x, 222. (Orbis, Maryknoll (New York); distributed by Gill & Macmillan, Dublin. Price: £7.95. ISBN 0 88344 6054 9 (paperback))

A clearly written and well-presented, and documented, analysis of the idea of 'Scripture' (both written and oral tradition) as maintained in the chief 'scriptural religions' — Judaism, Christianity, Islam, Hinduism, Sikhism, and Buddhism. The inclusion of the last three (or at any Hinduism and Buddhism) may surprise readers familiar with the notion of the first three as 'religions of the book', as though this was a distinctive feature. This book should be on the reading lists of all theology courses aiming at a culturally contextual treatment of the Bible (thus it is salutary to have the Hebrew Bible treated as Jewish rather than Christian Scripture); it will also be an extremely valuable addition to those of teachers and students in the broader area of Religious Studies, allowing valuable comparative treatments and underlining the universal and fundamental role of language in all human or divine communication.

N. WYATT

DEARMAN, J. A.: *Property Rights in the Eighth-Century Prophets* (SBL Dissertation Series 106). 1988. Pp. x, 171. (Scholars Press, Atlanta, Georgia. Price: $16.95 (member price: $10.95). ISBN 1 55540 192 9. Paperback price: $10.95 (member price: $7.95). ISBN 1 55540 195 3.

Dearman's dissertation, which was submitted at Emory University, focuses upon an aspect of the eighth-century prophets which has been much publicized and discussed, but seldom examined in detail. It begins by looking at a number of broad characterisations of prophecy which have lent to the prophets a special sense of contemporary relevance. Their sense of moral order, of a divine law, and of a traditional sense of social justice and order have variously been claimed as unique in the ancient world, and based on a theological sense of world order.

Dearman notes how readily scholars have fallen into purely apologetic explanations, branding certain systems of unlimited land-tenure as 'Canaanite', and seeing the roots of economic oppression as by-products of an ancient 'Capitalist' economic order. He opposes both assumptions, showing that they have little real evidence in support of them and they fail to look in detail at the strictures of the prophets themselves.

He follows Alt, who was himself much indebted to some of the analyses of Max Weber over this specific issue, in regarding the introduction of the monarchy as the primary cause of injustice in respect of conventions of land tenure and property law. Time and again it is the members of local bureaucracy who owed their position to the royal court and the crown-appointed judicial system, who receive the heaviest criticisms of the prophets. The non-accountability of royal appointees to local control, and the pressure for political reasons for the royal court to seek to maintain control over land-exchange and judicial appointments, meant that many in Judah and Israel found themselves sorely improverished and totally unable to obtain redress aginst injustice through the court.

Dearman supports his thesis with comparative evidence drawn from Neo-Assyrian administrative documents, and argues that, in general, it is almost impossible to obtain any clear picture of the social effect of Assyrian imperial influence over Judah during the eighth century. This is certainly a good dissertation which aims to put an end to some over-hasty generalisations. In finding one convincing line of explanation, however, it is nevertheless inclined to regard this as sufficient for all the main passages. It would still appear that other factors also were not unimportant.

R. E. CLEMENTS

DULIN, R. Z.: *A Crown of Glory: A Biblical View of Aging*. 1988. Pp. viii, 145. (Paulist Press, Mahwah, New Jersey. Price: $8.95. ISBN 0 8091 2940 X)

This book sets out to discuss what the Hebrew Bible has to say about aging and old age, with a view to its relevance for the problems faced by the increasing number of the elderly in modern Western societies. Successive chapters consider the expression 'length of days', the physical and psychological characteristics of old age, the old and the community, and old age as seen in the Wisdom literature and Chronicles. Some useful material is collected together here, including indices of Biblical references and Hebrew terms for aging. But the discussion is in general rather superficial and repetitive, making no use of sociology or anthropology, and there are too many digressions which stray away from the main point. More importantly, the author's interpretation of the sources is often suspect; e.g. does the statement 'he advocated that joy in youth should not become despair in old age' accurately reflect the views of Qoheleth? There are too many wrong references and Dulin too frequently misrepresents or misunderstands the views of other scholars. It is a pity also that the material surveyed is limited to the Hebrew canon, so that a very relevant book like Ben Sirach is excluded.

J. R. PORTER

DUMBRELL, W. J.: *The Faith of Israel: Its Expression in the Books of the Old Testament*. 1988. Pp. 286. (Baker Book House, Grand Rapids, Michigan. Price: $12.95. ISBN 0 8010 2976 7)

The blurb on the rear cover promises that 'Evangelicals looking for a first-rate introduction to the theology of each Old Testament book will find it at last in *The Faith of Israel*'. Within the stated constraints this volume is irenic, reasonably informative, and in touch with much critical discussion. Though influenced by Childs' canonical criticism, Dumbrell treats the Bible's books in the 'Hebrew canonical sequence'; and by probing the individuality of each allows their various themes to emerge, over against the 'illusory' quest for a central Old Testament theme. Yet a book which is in several respects attractive is marred by an approach which knows too much in advance about the biblical books: not least that these texts had authors working with defined objectives in mind.

A. G. AULD

FARROW, D.: *The Word of Truth and Disputes about Words* (Carpenter Books). 1987. P. xiv, 234. (Eisenbrauns, Winona Lake, Indiana. Price: $11.95. ISBN 0 931464 36 6)

The debate concerning the inerrancy of scripture has aroused far greater division and furore in the USA than in Great Britain, but the reverberations have certainly been felt on this side of the Atlantic and may yet be so more extensively. Dr Farrow's book is an excellent guide to the debate and offers some sensible and constructive comments towards resolving the difficulties. The first part looks at the way in which the debate has taken shape and its theological roots. Part two examines the way in which scripture is understood from within the biblical tradition and the third part raises wider theological issues. It is here that the author is at his best, pointing to the complex nature of language itself, and especially to the difficulty in using human language to express truth about a transcendent deity.

The book is written with a strong sense of personal involvement in the issues and out of a desire to probe beyond using words as mere slogans and symbols to defend entrenched positions. Its essential thesis is that Fundamentalist notions of inerrancy have imposed a far stricter notion of truth than language about God permits or the Bible itself demands. At the same time it is warmly sympathetic regarding the centrality of the Bible in the life and devotion of the Protestant tradition.

To those outside the battle lines the debate must frequently appear to be futile and pointless; to those caught up in the discussion, however, its seriousness will be readily apparent. For anyone interested in the issues this is an excellent introduction, being balanced, eirenic, and sharply focused on the main issues.

R. E. Clements

Frieling, R.: *Old Testament Studies*. Translated from German by M. and R. Koehler. 1987. Pp. 159. (Floris Books, Edinburgh. Price: £10.95. ISBN 0 86315 057 8)

The author of these studies was leader of The Christian Community from 1960 to his death in 1986; it is not surprising, therefore, that they are evidently indebted to the philosophy of Rudolf Steiner. They are thus imaginative rather than critical, but many readers will appreciate the author's insights. For example, 'like the creation of the world the building of the tabernacle is *a work of seven parts*' (the same sevenfold pattern is recognized in the making of the priestly vestments). Various Old Testament texts and themes are expounded, including the binding of Isaac, the Balaam saga, the dragon myth, and the part played by trees, wells, and sacred stones in the patriarchal narratives.

F. F. Bruce

Gerstenberger, E. S.: *Jahwe — ein patriarchaler Gott? Traditionelles Gottesbild und feministische Theologie* (Urban-Taschenbücher 391). 1988. Pp. 160. (Kohlhammer, Stuttgart. Price: DM 20.00. ISBN 3 17 009947 7)

Starting from the question of the four-year-old daughter of a minister, 'Daddy, does God have a penis?', Gerstenberger examines the position of women in the Old Testament from the perspective of women's roles in modern industrial society and the feminist movement. He argues that before the exile women had a significant place in the social and religious life of Israel despite the patriarchal form of the society, and that it was only after the return that their position worsened and they became severely subordinated to men. The well known archaeological discoveries of references to Yahweh and his Asherah are brought forward as evidence that monotheism developed only after the exile, and the question is then raised whether it is monotheism with a masculine God which led to the later subordination of women (Gerstenberger suggests that monotheism and the structure of society interacted). In the latter part of the book Gerstenberger turns specifically to the church of today, arguing that the emphases upon women's spirituality and a female deity are no way forward in the quest for equality between men and women. An appendix deals with exegesis and biblical theology in the light of feminist criticisms.

C. S. Rodd

Grollenberg, L.: *Unexpected Messiah, or How the Bible can be misleading*. Translated from Dutch by J. Bowden. 1988. Pp. viii, 199. (SCM, London. Price: £6.95. ISBN 0 334 02402 1)

This able and interesting essay in *haute vulgarisation* is a brave attempt to answer the question how the Christian message of a crucified Messiah was seen from the outset as the fulfilment of Old Testament prophecy. The author, a Dutch Dominican, certainly explains the anxiety of the first Christians to present their faith as the fulfilment of prophecy but offers no new insights into the logic of their beliefs. Instead he gives us a survey of the post-exilic history of Israel, a rapid run-through of certain writing of both Testaments, especially the Gospels, and finally a more detailed study of certain key texts such as Ps. 22 and Wisdom 1–2. All this is competently done, and despite many lacunae, especially in the intertestamental literature, the book can be confidently recommended as a painless way of introducing A-level students, and even first-year undergraduates, to the study of the New Testament.

J. F. Ashton

Groves, J. W.: *Actualization and Interpretation in the Old Testament* (SBL Dissertation Series 86). 1987. Pp. vii, 223. (Scholars Press, Atlanta, Georgia. Price: $17.95 (member price: $12.95). ISBN 0 89130 966 7. Paperback price: $12.95 (member price: $8.95). ISBN 0 89130 967 5))

The concept of *Vergegenwärtigung* or chronological actualisation as proposed by von Rad and developed in a variety of ways as a hermeneutical tool is here subjected to a detailed analysis and critique. Attention is drawn to a threefold defect in this approach; its failure to demonstrate (a) the uniqueness of Biblical contemporisation (b) the unity of Scripture which the method presupposes, and (c) the centrality of the concept in the Biblical material. Once stripped of inflated claims which have been made for it, however, it remains a useful tool in analyzing some aspects of the tradition process within the Bible, once greater stress is laid upon the literary function and linguistic level of words in a pericope — a thesis illustrated by discussion of Deut. 5:1–3, Amos 9:11–15, and Isaiah 36–39. All in all a careful and thought provoking study which goes far to clarifying a concept which has played a prominent role in recent study in the field of Old Testament theology.

R. Davidson

Haag, E. (ed.): *Gott, der einzige. Zur Entstehung des Monotheismus in Israel* (Quaestiones Disputatae 104). 1985. Pp. 192. (Herder, Freiburg. Price: DM 44.00. ISBN 3 451 02104 8)

Six essays by Catholic scholars are an important contribution to the discussion of the origin of monotheism in ancient Israel. In particular, the writers are concerned to examine B. Lang's thesis that Israel's religion was polytheistic until the rise of a 'Yahweh-alone movement' in the eighth century began to move it towards monotheism. N. Lohfink sketches the history of the discussion, particularly in the past 100 years, concluding that the pre-monarchic Israelite tribal association worshipped Yahweh in a form of religion, which, if not yet monotheistic, was no longer polytheistic. E. Zenger analyses the relation between Yahweh and other divinities in the J work in order to show that the work presupposes a 'Jahwesierung' of pre-monarchic Israel. G. Hentschel argues that Elijah was familiar with the commandment prohibiting the worship of other gods than Yahweh. H.-W. Jüngling examines the authentic oracles of Isaiah of Jerusalem in the light of the discovery of the 'Venus of Jerusalem' and of inscriptions suggesting polytheism. He concludes from Isaiah 6:1–5 that the prophet worshipped Yahweh alone, and from Isaiah 6:1–5 and 31:1–3 that Yahweh and El were identical for the prophets. The ground of Isaiah's condemnation of the rulers is his faith in Yahweh. G. Braulik traces in Deuteronomy a progression from the affirmation in 6:4 that Yahweh is unique to the statement in 4:35 (dating from the exile) that there is no God but Yahweh. This doctrine is compared with Deutero-Isaiah's monotheism. J. Scharbert discusses Exodus 34 and what J. Halbe designates as the oldest collection in Exodus 20–23 in order to show that pre-monarchic Israel possessed Yahwistic cultic and legal ordinances. There is an extensive bibliography compiled by Scharbert.

J. W. Rogerson

HAHN, J.: *Das 'Goldene Kalb': Die Jahweh-Verehrung bei Stierbildern in der Geschichte Israels*, 2.erg.Auflage (Europäische Hochschulschriften: Reihe 23, Theologie, Bd. 154). 1987. Pp. 395. (Lang, Frankfurt am Main, Bern, New York. Price: SwFr. 73.00. ISBN 3 8204 8657 7)

This is essentially a reprint of the work first published in 1981 and reviewed in *B. L.* 1983, pp. 66–67. The only changes appear to be the addition of a new foreword, which includes a further bibliographical item, and an extra sentence in the author's *curriculum vitae*.

G. I. DAVIES

HØGENHAVEN, J.: *Problems and Prospects of Old Testament Theology* (The Biblical Seminar, 6). 1987. Pp. 136. (Sheffield Academic Press. Price: £7.95 ($12:95). ISBN 1 85075 180 7)

This is a useful, if somewhat compressed, study of some of the major themes and problems in contemporary studies in the field of Old Testament theology. A brief historical survey of the discipline is followed by a critical analysis of major issues, particular attention being paid to von Rad and the radical critique of his position represented by Baumgärtel. A general discussion of the relationship between theology and the Bible leads into a suggested outline of an Old Testament theology based on common accepted literary categories. The suggested order, (a) Wisdom, (b) Psalmic literature, (c) Narrative literature, (d) Law, and (e) the Prophets, recognizes the recent significance attached to the influence of wisdom thought throughout the Old Testament. Whether this suggested outline solves any of the problems thrown up by other approaches is open to question, but at least there is a healthy recognition that any Old Testament theology must be heavily dependent upon the current state of historical and exegetical research.

R. DAVIDSON

JERGER, G.: *'Evangelium des Alten Testaments': Die Grundbotschaft des Propheten Deuterojesaja in ihrer Bedeutung für den Religionsunterricht* (Stuttgarter Biblische Beiträge 14). 1986. Pp. vii, 469. (Katholisches Bibelwerk Verlag, Stuttgart. Price: DM 39.00. ISBN 3 460 00141 0)

The primary interest of this doctoral dissertation is in the use of Second Isaiah in Catholic religious education in the archdiocese of Freiburg since the beginning of the last century, and more than two-thirds of the book are devoted to the educational aspect. The first of the three parts offers a summary account of the current exegesis of Isaiah 40–55 and the basic message of Second Isaiah from a biblical theological perspective. This begins with the historical context and form-critical analysis of these chapters, and continues with an outline of the prophet's leading themes, culminating in the self-revelation of Yahweh to all men in the Servant. Old Testament scholars will not look here for new developments in the exegesis of Second Isaiah or in the evaluation of his message, but they will welcome the plea for religious education to be informed by a sound study of the text.

A. GELSTON

KAUFMANN, Y.: *Christianity and Judaism: Two Covenants*. Translated from the Hebrew by C. W. Efroymson. 1988. Pp. xi, 230 (Magnes, Jerusalem. Price: $20.00. ISBN 965 223 694 2)

This work is a translation of chapters 7, 8, and 9 of the first volume of Kaufmann's *Golah ve-Nekhar* published in 2 volumes in 1929–30. It is, therefore, somewhat dated. The chapter headings are: The Religion of Israel Among the Gentiles; Origins of the Christian Church; Israel's Religious-Racial Identity.

Students of the Old Testament are acquainted with Kaufmann's work: 'The History of the Religion of Israel', and may only have a fleeting knowledge of his interest in the socio-political problems of Zionism and, earlier, his analysis of the problem of Jewry's existence and fate as a diaspora nation-community. It is his interest in the latter which led him on to his more familiar work on the history of Israel's region.

Kaufmann argues that the natural tendency and destiny of ethnic communities which have been disrupted and scattered amongs other alien societies is to be absorbed into those foreign contexts. He observes that the dispersed Jewish communities from the Babylonian exile onwards, even to the present century, tended, on almost every level, to assimilate, intellectually and linguistically, with the foreign community; on every level, that is, except religion. The Jewish religion prevented and prevents complete assimilation, in the earlier pagan cultures, and the later Christian and Moslem societies.

These chapters describe the defeat of paganism by Christianity and Islam. At the time of the emergence of Christianity, Judasim, which is inherently universalist in content as well as aspiration, was about to transcend the boundaries of the land and people; but now, with the triumphant progress of the Christian and, later, Islamic covenants, Judaism was confined to the Jewish people — a 'tribal' religion of universal content.

R. B. SALTERS

KLOPFENSTEIN, M., LUZ, U., TALMON, S., and TOV, E. (eds): *Mitte der Schrift? Ein jüdisch-christliches Gespräch* (Texte des Berner Symposions vom 6.–12. Januar 1985) ((Judaica et Christiana, Bd. 11). 1987. Pp. 389. (Lang, Frankfurt am Main, Bern, New York. Price: SwFr. 98.00. ISBN 3 261 04077 7)

The participants in this symposium of Jews and Christians on the search for the centre of scripture are all well-known biblical scholars and theologians. H. Graf Reventlow contributes a critical balance-sheet on the view of the Old Testament in recent Christian sketches of biblical theology; M. Weiss addresses the question of a Jewish hermeneutic in Tanak research; S. Talmon writes on holy scripture and canonical books from a Jewish viewpoint, with reflections on the formation of the scriptures in Judaism; P. Stuhlmacher offers a piece on Jesus of Nazareth and New Testament christology in the light of holy scripture; J. Fraenkel considers 'the centre of Tanak' from the viewpoint of rabbinic Judaism; U. Luz writes on Pauline theology as biblical theology; H. Stegemann discusses 'the centre of scripture' as seen by the Qumran community; K. Koch outlines the meaning of apocalyptic for the interpretation of scripture; Y. Amir looks at 'the centre of scripture' as seen by the Qumran community; K. Koch outlines the meaning of apocalyptic for the interpretation of scripture; Y. Amir looks at 'the centre of scripture' from the viewpoint of hellenistic Judaism; E. Tov contributes a lengthy piece on the LXX in its theological and tradition-historical relation to the Hebrew Bible; B. Childs's contribution on the meaning of the Jewish canon in Old Testament theology has been translated into German; M. Klopfenstein provides a study of Hebrew words relating to law in the prophets; H. Gese analyzes the Old Testament theology; M. Greenberg contributes a consideration of the use of the Bible in contemporary Israel, with critique and recommendation included; N. Lohfink offers a common perspective on the two testaments in terms of the theme of God's care in relation to the right society; two of the editors, Klopfenstein and Luz, provide a brief concluding essay attempting to say what on balance the Symposium has achieved in terms of the basic questions posed to it about 'the centre of scripture' (a quite normative Christian notion, but at best a *Reibungspunkt* for Jews). All the contributions are in German.

This is a very interesting collection of pieces on a complex but important topic relating to the uses of scripture among different religious and scholarly communities. There is also some very good but technical material to be found in some of the articles (esp. Talmon and Tov); with a variety of fascinating theological reflections from the Christian contributors. The volume will repay scrutiny from all biblical scholars and is a useful contribution to that important practice of Jews and Christians talking to each other about the things they have in common which are so entirely different in themselves!

R. P. CARROLL

KOCH, K.: *Studien zur alttestamentlichen und altorientalischen Religionsgeschichte* (Zum 60. Geburtstag von Klaus Koch herausgegeben von Eckart Otto). 1988. Pp. 254. (Vandenhoeck & Ruprecht, Göttingen. Price: DM 68.00. ISBN 3 525 53579 1)

The ten essays in this volume all provide links in the interpretation of Old Testament religion and the understanding of the ancient oriental world. Except for the first essay, they have all appeared in print previously. This first essay: 'The gods whom your fathers served' (pp. 9–31), offers a critique of Alt's work on Israel's early period, and then a comparative study, which has the advantage that much material is adduced from the same period as is being considered. One of the great weaknesses of Alt's work (and, for example, that of Noth) is the tendency to use much later evidence for the evaluation of ancient Israel (cf. p. 83 above). This essay ends with a summary statement of the light shed on Christianity and on religion in general by the examination of the Old Testament in the light of comparative evidence.

The remaining essays have all appeared elsewhere. 'The death of the religious founder' (pp. 32–60), cf. *Kerygma und Dogma* 8 (1962), concludes with a survey (pp. 55–60) of recent developments and changes. 'Word and unity of the creator god in Memphis and Jerusalem' (pp. 61–105, cf. *ZThK* 62 (1965))has a similar survey on pp. 103–5. The third 'The promise of a son to the Ugaritic Daniel' (pp. 106–16, cf. *ZfAssyr.*, N.F.24 (1967), additions on pp. 116): here some elements in the original discussion of the paper in 1965 have been incorporated in the text. 'Shaddai' (pp. 118–52, cf. *VT* 26 (1976), additions on p. 152); 'The letters containing prophetic material from Mari' (pp. 153–88, cf. *UgF.* 4 (1972))and 'The origin of the worship of Ba'al' (pp. 189–205, cf. *UgF.* 11 (1979)), both have supplements, at pp. 185–88 and 204, the latter with a bibliographical statement on pp. 204f. 'păḥăd yiṣḥaq — a divine title' (pp. 206–14, cf. *FS* Westermann 1980) and 'Reflections on the concepts of souls and spirits in the Pyramid texts', (pp. 215–42, cf. *FS* Helck 1984) have supplements at pp. 214 and 242. The original page numbers are printed at the top for articles 2–10. A rich and careful collection, made and introduced by E. Otto for Professor Koch's sixtieth birthday in 1986.

P. R. ACKROYD

KRAŠOVEC, J.: *La justice* (ṢDQ) *de Dieu dans la Bible hébraique et l'interprétation juive et chrétienne* (Orbis Biblicus et Orientalis 76). 1988. Pp. 452.)Universitätsverlag, Freiburg (CH); Vandenhoeck & Ruprecht, Göttingen. Price: SwFr. 110.00. ISBN 3 7278 0549 8; ISBN 3 525 53705 0)

One may wonder about the need for a large volume on the root *ṣdq*, especially when it deals with only 140 of the 523 occurrences, those referring to the justice of God, and the author promises a further study of the remaining instances which are concerned with human justice. Krašovec, however, justifies his enterprise on two grounds. First, he claims that previous studies have not been sufficiently detailed and, in particular, have overlooked the crucial distinction between texts where God is the subject of *ṣdq* and those where man is the subject. Secondly, his own investigation is determined by the insights of modern linguistics and semantics, an area with which he has previously been concerned (see e.g. *B.L.* 1986, p. 73). The present work is in three sections. The first briefly surveys earlier work on the subject, explains the author's own approach, and discusses the significance of *ṣdq* in other Semitic languages. The second analyses in turn all the Old Testament texts concerned with the justice of God, followed in each case by a review of the interpretations of the passage by Jewish and Christian commentators up to Luther and Calvin. This leads on to a final section which discusses the Old Testament semantic field of the concept of divine justice, divine justice in the ancient translations of the Old Testament and in the New Testament, the notion of justice in the European languages and the relationship between hebraic and European ideas of the justice of God. Krašovec concludes that the Old Testament concept of God's justice essentially indicates a personal salvific relationship with His people, and thus has a wide range of meanings, but it does not constitute a 'norm' or represent strict or impartial justice or really correspond to 'natural law'. As he is aware, this is to take issue with the views of many other scholars and we shall have to wait for his further study of *ṣdq* in the human sphere before his conclusions can be properly evaluated. Probably this book tries to do too much and it is not always easy to see the wood for the trees. But its thorough and comprehensive character makes it an important and valuable source of reference for any future investigations into the notion of *ṣdq*.

J. R. Porter

Maillot, A.: *Gros Plan sur l'Ancien Testament: ses thèmes et ses défis*. 1987. Pp. 106. (Du Moulin, Aubonne (CH). Price: SwFr. 12.80.)

Israel's desacralization of both space and time, and then Old Testament thought about the cult, man, and God, occupy most of this short, attractively written, and reliable popular presentation of Old Testament theology. The distinctivenss of Israel's faith is located in its critical stance towards religion — its own as well as its neighbours' — and morality.

C. J. A. Hickling

Martin-Achard, M.: *La Mort en Face selon la Bible Hébraïque* (Essais Bibliques). 1988. Pp. 136. (Labor et Fides, Genève. Price: SwFr. 24.00. ISBN 2 8309 0128 2)

This short study begins with discussion of the life-affirming nature of Israelite religion. Following surveys of Egyptian and Mesopotamian conceptions of death and its aftermath, we have a treatment of the relevant biblical passages, from the earliest, reflecting 'Canaanite views' (it is a pity that the contribution of Ugarit here is not more extensively dealt with — the *rpum* appear briefly in their Hebrew guise, pp. 76f.), to later ones asserting Yahweh's power beyond the grave, and the apocalyptic development of a doctrine of resurrection. A useful survey of the biblical allusions to the theme, countering the rather strange views of Dahood and Spronk (though they, like Ugarit, deserve a fuller assessment).

N. Wyatt

Mettinger, T. N. D.: *Namnet och Närvaron: Gudsnamn och Gudsbild i Böckernas Bok*. 1987. Pp. 222. (Bokförlaget Libris, Örebro. Price: Sw.Kr. 260.00. ISBN 91 7194 497 4)

The Swedish title of this book means 'The Name and the Presence: Names of God and Ideas of God in the Book of Books'. It is an admirable example of popularisation, based throughout on scholarly research, both the author's own works and those of his colleagues all over the world. The reader gets a lively impression of Old Testament exegesis as an international phenomenon. Thanks to the author's pedagogic gifts and his enthusiastic style it is always easy to follow his argument. As the title indicates, the main subject of the book is the different names and designations of God in the Old Testament. They are each assigned a chapter: one on the name Yahweh, one on 'The God of the Fathers', one on Sabaoth, etc. Together they give a full and varied picture of Israelite ideas of God.

It is salutary that the author is so matter-of-fact and honest about the origin and date of biblical books and about foreign influences on Israel's religious ideas, especially in a work intended for the general public, including priests, pastors, and students. In the end, however, it is difficult to escape the impression that this is at bottom an apologetic work: the less agreeable traits in the Israelite image of God are tactfully passed over. In this respect the book resembles too much a well-informed and admiring biography of a king, written by a courtier while his sovereign was still alive.

B. ALBREKSTON

MONTES-PERAL, L. A.: *Akataleptos Theos: Der unfassbare Gott* (Arbeiten zur Literatur und Geschichte des hellenistischen Judentums, 16). 1987. Pp. viii, 235. (Brill, Leiden. Price: fl. 60.00. ISBN 90 04 06928 3; ISSN 0169 7390)

This study of Philo's understanding of God, originally a doctoral thesis submitted to the Ludwig-Maximilian University, Munich, in 1978/79, is in three parts, dealing respectively with transcendence, immanence, and the contemporary significance of Philo. It is not of direct relevance to this *Book List*, except in so far as it presents Philo's interpretation of biblical theology.

N. R. M. DE LANGE

MONTORSI, G.: *I Salmi. Preghiera di ogni giorno*. 1987. Pp. 350. (Messaggero, Padova. Price: Lire 19,500. ISBN 88 7026 669 9)

This is a pocket companion to the psalms and canticles as arranged in the Roman Catholic liturgy of the hours. For each psalm or other poetic passage there are brief hints on four contexts of prayer to bear in mind: that of the first authors or users, that of Jesus, that of the Church and that of the persons actually using a text in prayer. Only the notes on the first context are relevant to this *Book List*; but, though it is praiseworthy that this reminder always stands first, the hints are so brief and generalized that they rarely throw light on a particular text.

R. P. R. MURRAY

MULDER, M. J.: *Sodom en Gomorra. Een verhaal van dode steden*. (Series Exegetische Studies 4). 1988. Pp. 93. (Kok, Kampen. ISBN 90 242 3083 7)

This valuable little book traces traditions about Sodom and Gomorrah from the Old Testament through the Apocrypha and Pseudepigrapha to Qumran, Josephus and Philo, the Rabbinic literature, and the New Testament. It also mentions Christian literature (I Clement to the fifteenth century) and texts from Ugarit and Ebla (where no mention of the cities can be found) ending with Nag Hammadi and the Qur'an. More important than the attempt to locate the geographical whereabouts of these cities is the way their names function in the tradition. They are object lessons that speak of the justice and mercy of God.

J. W. ROGERSON

NICHOLSON, E. W.: *God and His People: Covenant and Theology in the Old Testament*, paperback ed. 1988. Pp. xii, 244. (Clarendon, Oxford. Price: £8.95. ISBN 0 19 826727 4)

This serviceable review of the discussion of 'covenant' in the last hundred years of Old Testament scholarship, and of a handful of key texts in Exodus, Joshua, and Hosea was described with warm approval in *B.L.* 1987, pp. 88f. It is a welcome addition to the company of affordable books which can be confidently recommended to students.

A. G. AULD

NIEHR, H.: *Rechtsprechung in Israel: Untersuchungen zur Geschichte der Gerichtsorganisation im Alten Testament* (Stuttgarter Bibelstudien, 130). 1987. Pp. 144. (Verlag Katholisches Bibelwerk, Stuttgart. Price: DM 29.80. ISBN 3 460 043016)

This clear, informative, and well organized account studies Israelite legal procedure against the background of forms known from Mesopotamia and Syria-Palestine. Outside Israel there is a common distinction between the administration of justice by the king and his officers on the one hand, and that by the elders and popular assembly on the other, with temple justice sometimes appearing as a third form. In the segmentary society of Israel justice was administered by the family father, by elders and, in certain cases, by priests, but there was no central court or professional judicial office. The rise of the monarchy deprived the elders of their political power, but they consolidated their position by taking over judicial functions formerly exercised by the family father. The legal authority of the king was not that of a court of appeal; it was a separate organ of administration of justice, in which the law was used to further the king's political aims, or, in the case of his officials, for self-enrichment. The reform of Josiah affected the law in that now for the first time professional judges appeared, taking over the judicial tasks formerly exercised by the priests at the local sanctuaries. As Deuteronomy makes clear, however, these judges also tended to take over the judicial tasks formerly exercised by the priests at the local sanctuaries. As Deuteronomy makes clear, however, these judges also tended to take over the judicial functions of the elders. In post-exilic time the law was administered through two chief organs: the local judicial authority of clan and community, and the central authority of the state appointed governor. Eventually, both local and central powers were united in the person of the high priest, but by Hasmonean times the latter's functions came to be limited to the temple and its service.

A. D. H. MAYES

OEMING, M.: *Gesamtbiblische Theologien der Gegenwart: Das Verhältnis von AT und NT in der hermeneutischen Diskussion seit Gerhard von Rad* (2nd ed.). 1987. Pp. 272. (Kohlhammer, Stuttgart. Price: DM 69.00. ISBN 3 17 009712 1).

This is a second edition of a dissertation that was first published in 1985 (*B.L.* 1986, p. 93). A brief, four-page postscript has been added together with a supplement to the bibliography. The volume has clearly proved very useful and reviews critically attempts to present a distinctive biblical theology since the contribution of Gerhard von Rad. Particular attention is paid to the suggestions of H. Gese and B. S. Childs, but the whole field is well covered.

R. E. CLEMENTS

OTTO, E.: *Wandel der Rechtsbegründungen in der Gesellschaftsgeschichte des Antiken Israel: Eine Rechtsgeschichte des 'Bundesbuches' Ex XX 22 — XXIII 13* (Studia Biblica III). 1988. Pp. viii, 107. (Brill, Leiden. Price: fl. 40.00; ca.$20.00. ISBN 90 04 08346 4; ISSN 0169 9954)

This densely written but richly rewarding study is a detailed investigation of the history of development of the Book of the Covenant, which relates the history of law in Israel to developments in Israelite society. The conclusion, against the currently prevalent idea that in general legal history is a process of secularization, is that the law increasingly came to be grounded in the will of Yahweh.

In the first part of the Book of the Covenant, Ex. 21:2–22:26, the casuistic laws show a development from concern with regulating conflict to a concern with punishment, reflecting a social shift from a trial society comprising equal families to a state in which the class structure of society had to be maintained. The concern of casuistic law with punishment also reflects the transfer of apodictic law, with its sanctions, from its original family context to the context of the administration of law in the local court. The beginning of a further development of casuistic law is found in Ex. 21:2–11, where older law relating to slavery has been loosed from its original context in the administration of law and has become theological law protecting the weak in society. This theologizing of existing law is continued in Ex. 22:20–26, where the lack of any sanction for disobedience implies a transition from the legal context to that of ethical preaching. The theology behind this development is that of Yahweh as king who hears the complaints of his subjects; the social context of this theology is that of increasing disparity between rich and poor, so that the unity of society in itself could no longer function to motivate and legitimate laws protecting the weak and poor. This development belongs to the Jerusalem temple cult of the monarchic period.

The second part of the Book of the Covenant, Ex. 22:27–23:12, which combines profane law on legal procedures with sacral law concerning Yahweh's dues, also reflects the theologizing of older secular law: all law is now led back to Yahweh as source, and obedience to Yahweh involves the performance of secular law. The two parts of the Book of the Covenant are held together by an outer framework (Ex. 21:2–11; 23:10–12) and in inner (22:20–26; 22:28f.), which combine social law protecting the weak and poor with sacral law, and it is this which constitutes the overall theological outlook of the whole collection. The deuteronomistic redactor, who incorporated the Book of the Covenant into the Sinai pericope, continued the development by presenting the collection as covenant law for a restored community, in which cult and daily life are brought together in a new Israel.

A. D. H. Mayes

Plum, K. Friis, and Hallbäck, G. (ed.): *Det gamle Testamente og den kristne fortolkning* (Forum for bibelsk eksegese 1). 1988. Pp. 137. (Museum Tusculanums Forlag, Copenhagen. ISBN 87 7289 034 7)

Five members of the department of biblical studies at the University of Copenhagen and an author have in this volume published an essay each illuminating points of view on the Old Testament in Christian interpretation. J. Høgenhaven introduces the post-war discussion about biblical theology with emphasis on Germany and the United States; K. Friis Plum demonstrates convincingly, using the book of Jonah as her example, that there is no necessary conflict between exegesis and biblical theology; while J. Strange regrets that the Church has not taken the full consequence of the historical critical research when dealing with the Song of Songs. T. Engberg-Pedersen examines steadily the metaphor, the heart as a tablet, from Deuteronomy through Jeremiah and Ezekiel to Paul, and M. Müller explores thoroughly the defence of the Septuagint in the early Church. The author, E. Kløvedal Reich, known as a writer of historical novels and as a consultant for the Danish Old Testament translation board, has written a very remarkable prophecy and policy, free speech, and apocalyptic.

K. Jeppesen

POYTHRESS, V. S.: *Science and Hermeneutics* (Foundations of Contemporary Interpretation, 6). 1988. Pp. 184. (Zondervan, Grand Rapids, Michigan. ISBN 0 310 40971 3)

Poythress attempts to apply the insights of T. S. Kuhn, *The Structure of Scientific Revolutions*, to the question of biblical hermeneutics. Unfortunately, even though science is invoked, evoked, and provoked, the book has little to do with science but much to do with 'Evangelical' (i.e. fundamentalist) views about the Bible. This does not mean that the author's presuppositions are disguised; indeed, at times he can be quite candid about them. But he makes no attempt to justify them, and he completely misapprehends critical scholarship. (Whenever he talks about the 'historical-critical method', other than with the vaguest reference, he seems to identify it with source analysis.)

More importantly, he uses a false analogy, comparing it with certain scientific theories. The proper analogy is, of course, with the scientific method itself, not a particular theory. Historical criticism is a *method of research* which includes public debate and the recognition of no dogmas and no questions as off-limits (however much the temporary dominance of fads and particular schools may complicate the process). Poythress's fundamentalist approach skews all forms of inquiry by an unargued presupposition about the nature of the Bible itself. It is not scientific in any sense of the word. No doubt some readers, with time and patience, will derive something of value from this book, but most will do better to expend the effort elsewhere, such as on a book genuinely about science and religion (e.g. D. Stanesby, *Science, Reason and Religion*).

L. L. GRABBE

ROBBINS, G. L.: *'And in the Seventh Day'* (American University Studies: Series 7, Theology and Religion. Vol. 36). 1987. Pp. xvi, 242. (Lang, Frankfurt am Main, Bern, New York. Price: SwFr. 53.40. ISBN 3 8204 0504 3)

This study of the fourth commandment of the Decalogue is divided into seventeen short chapters and endeavours to emphasize the great importance of it. It does this by drawing upon allusions to the sabbath and its themes from throughout the entire Bible and it displays at many points a heavily homiletical character. At times the treatment is so discursive and wide-ranging that it is difficult to perceive the connection with the central theme.

The author's thesis is that the observance of the sabbath was, from the outset, indissolubly linked in ancient Israel to the affirmation concerning God's 'resting' on the seventh day after creation. The sabbath is therefore a sign of God's blessing of the world and a symbol of hope for humanity. Special attention is drawn to Exod. 31:16–17 as a definition of the covenant status of the sabbath rule and its eternal validity. One looks in vain for any detailed use of comparative data from among Israel's neighbours regarding cult-days and taboo days, or even the structuring and measurement of time, to offer much help with the Old Testament material. At times the homiletical stance becomes rather oppressive.

R. E. CLEMENTS

ROBINSON, R. B.: *Roman Catholic Exegesis Since 'Divino Afflante Spiritu': Hermeneutical Implications* (Society of Biblical Literature Dissertation Series, 111). 1988. Pp. vii, 183. (Scholars Press, Atlanta, Georgia. Price: $17.95 (member price: $11.95). ISBN 1 55540 240 2. Paperback price: $11.95 (member price: $8.95). ISBN 1 55540 241 0)

In this 1982 Yale thesis, Robinson discusses the work of three scholars in the period since Pius XII's1943 encyclical authorised Catholics to practise critical methods: R. E. Brown, L. Alonso-Schökel, and N. Lohfink. The author welcomes their move away from the idea of texts as primarily bearers of historical information, and away also from the explication of meaning with reference to historical causes. In following Protestants down the historical critical path, Catholics had previously opted for an approach which made exegesis hypothetical and tentative, and had postponed *sine die* the important task of theological reflection. Robinson applauds the current move toward 'intrinsic' criticism, which sees meaning as a function of the pattern of literary relations within a text, a move which is explicit in Alonso-Schökel and Lohfink and implicit in Brown's *sensus plenior* theory (inasmuch as it down plays the human authors and looks to a unitary meaning of the Bible). Intrinsic criticism is less hypothetical than historical criticism because 'the givens of the text . . . are always directly before the reader'. Alonso-Schökel and Lohfink are criticised, however, for reintroducing historical criticism by the backdoor. What is needed, Robinson believes, is a more thoroughgoing intrinsic approach, which respects the fluidity of meaning. Help in the intrinsic enterprise can be derived from structuralism, and more especially from reception theory. Meaning is generated in the contact between text and reader. The hermeneutical issues that Robinson confronts are of the first importance and his discussion is illuminating. Some readers, however, will conclude that an exclusively 'intrinsic' approach can only be purchased at too high a price. The scholars studied by Robinson may have been only partly successful in marrying historical criticism with intrinsic criticism, but they may have been quite right in their unwillingness to jettison historical criticism.

B. P. Robinson

Schmid, J. H.: *Biblische Theologie in der Sicht heutiger Alttestamentler* (2nd edition). 1988. Pp. vi, 250. (Brunnen, Giessen. Price: DM 38.00. ISBN 3 7655 9326 5)

The author is very much concerned with the achievement of a biblical theology which is built on the *whole* Christian Canon. Thus the Old Testament plays a vital, but not an exclusive part in this task. The interests of both historical biblical study and systematic theology find expression in such an approach. The work of four contemporary Old Testament scholars is examined to see how each has made his contribution to constructing a truly biblical theology. H. Gese's understanding of the role of tradition, C. Westermann's emphasis on the Old Testament as the record of God's dealing with his people and the world, W. Zimmerli's concern with its witness to God's self-revelation, and A. Gunneweg's existentialist theology, have all witnessed in their various ways to a properly 'Christian' significance of the Old Testament.

For all the recognition that historical and confessional elements must inter-act in a proper study of the Old Testament and for all the valuable insights this study provides, marginal anxieties must remain about this programmatic determination to force the Old Testament into a doctrinal framework of which its writers knew nothing.

R. A. Mason

Schmidt, W. H.: *Alttestamentlicher Glaube in seiner Geschichte*. 6, überarbeitete und erweiterte Auflage (Neukirchener Studienbücher 6). 1987. Pp. 392. (Neukirchener, Neukirchen-Vluyn. Price: DM 39.80. ISBN 3 7887 1263 5)

The popularity and usefulness of Professor Werner Schmidt's introduction to the faith of the Old Testament is well demonstrated by the call for a sixth edition. Reviews of the earlier German editions appeared in *B.L.* 1969, p. 51 (*Bibl. Bibliog.*, p. 177) and 1976, p. 77. A review of the English translation from the fourth edition appeared in *B.L.* 1984, pp. 102–03. The work is essentially a faith history of ancient Israel, combining many of the features of an Old Testament theology with a history of the religion. Accordingly it endeavours to set the main religious ideas against their historical background, and particularly with a view to the nature and character of Canaanite religion.

The major changes introduced for this edition are the introduction of a new excursus on 'Old Testament Ethics' and a further one on 'The Old Testament as Law'. An additional chapter on 'Hope for the Nations' has also been included in the treatment of the late period. Besides these, however, the bibliographies have been brought up to date and other alterations made to set the book in the mainstream of contemporary scholarship. The author notes how, when first conceived, a much greater consensus existed over many major issues of a literary and historical nature (M. Noth, G. von Rad), than exists among Old Testament scholars of the present. In many respects this book admirably fills some of the gaps left and is thoroughly recommended.

R. E. CLEMENTS

SITARZ, E. (ed.): *Höre, Israel! Jahwe ist einzig. Bausteine für eine Theologie des Alten Testaments* (Biblische Basis Bücher, 5). 1987. Pp. 350. (Verlag Katholisches Bibelwerk, Stuttgart; Butzon & Bercker, Kevelaer. Price: DM 34.00. ISBN 3 460 27051 9; ISBN 3 7666 9231 3)

The sub-title of this book reveals its purpose. It is to provide blocks (Bausteine) with which to construct a Theology of the Old Testament. Various contributors deal with different parts of the Canon in such a way as to introduce laypeople to contemporary methods of biblical investigation while giving special attention to the theology of each. F.-L. Hossfeld deals with the Pentateuch, beginning with a summary of its theology as a whole, then dealing with the Yahwistic narrative, the Elohistic 'fragments', the work of Jerusalem 'Yahwists' who brought J and E together, Deuteronomy, and the Priestly Writing. D. Kellermann deals with the books of Joshua and Judges, O. Wahl with Samuel and Kings, S. Wypych with the work of the Chronicler (including Ezra and Nehemiah) and E. Beck with the four 'Novellen', Ruth, Tobit, Judith, and Esther. D. Kellermann covers the books of Maccabees, H. Reinelt treats the theology of the Psalms, B. Lang the theology of the Wisdom literature. E. Beck the Song of Songs. F. J. Stendebach the theology of the prophets and D. Bauer the book of Daniel.

There is an immense amount of good and informative material here from which by no means only Catholic laypeople will benefit. Perhaps the aim of the book would have been even better served if there had been just a little more noticeably a guiding editorial hand, one which could have offered even a brief summary and synthesis at the end.

R. A. MASON

STUHLHOFER, F.: *Der Gebrauch der Bibel von Jesus bis Euseb: Eine statistische Untersuchung zur Kanonsgeschichte*. 1988. Pp. 160 (TVG; Brockhaus, Wuppertal. Price: DM 28.00. ISBN 3 417 29335 9)

Franz Stuhlhofer is a polymath, who has written on the history of science and philosophy as well as on theological subjects. Here he applies statistical methods to questions relating to the biblical canon. With the help of the *Biblia Patristica* he has analyzed the use of biblical books in the first four Christian centuries. Instead of asking which books writers regarded as 'canonical', he established which books they cite, and whether they cite them more or less often than one would expect if one were attending simply to their size; thus it becomes possible to establish which books were in practice, rather than simply in theory, authoritiative. The results are presented with elegance and simplicity: this is the sort of book that gives statistics a very good name. The author shows that until formal decisions about the extent of the canon (hardly taken before Athanasius) the two-way distinction canonical/non-canonical is far less illuminating than a threefold division: (a) books about whose authority there had never been any doubt, and which were used frequently by almost all writers; (b) books which were little used, but which *later* were declared either canonical or uncanonical by various churches; (c) books which were not used at all or were regarded as positively bad. 'Canonization' was the act of drawing a line through the second category. Many disputed questions about the history of the canon are here illuminated, while others are shown to be largely disputes about terminology. The author stresses, surely rightly, that for much more than half of the present canon of Scripture there has never been any question of its authority in the Church, so that most of the process we call canonization was a passive acceptance of what had been received from the past. Even as early as the 'Apostolic Fathers' this is true of nearly all the books in what would later be called the canon. But to avoid anachronism we must not fall into speaking as though the question of which books were 'in' and which 'out' was already being asked in this early period. Stuhlhofer prefers to speak of the history of the canon, and to say that books were authoritative or (still more neutrally) much used, rather than 'canonical'. This is an extremely important book, whose statistical tables should prove invaluable for countless further studies of the use of the Bible in the patristic period, and whose moderation, intelligence, clarity, and learning make it one of the most significant contributions to the question of the canon in recent years.

J. BARTON

TARDIEU, M. (ed.): *Les règles de l'interprétation* (Centre d'Etudes des Religions du Livre). 1987. Pp. 232. (Cerf, Paris. Price: Fr. 149.00. ISBN 2 204 02523 2)

This is a valuable collection of papers published under the auspices of the Centre d'études des religions du livre associated with the Centre National de la Recherche Scientifique. A number of scholars consider the relation of philosophical and theological systems to the classic or canonical texts associated with them, and show how in each case various hermeneutical techniques and rules have been developed to force the texts to accord with the presuppositions of the interpreter. The systems of thought studied here include Neoplatonism, Christianity (in the patristic age), Judaism (both ancient and medieval), Gnosticism, Manichaeism, and Islam; there are also studies of sixteenth and nineteenth-century philosophical and religious thought in Europe. The papers are as follows: P. Hadot, 'Théologie, exégèse, révélation, écriture, dans la philosophie grecque'; H. Cazelles, 'Le Pentateuque comme Torah'; B. Barc, 'Le texte de la Torah a-t-il été récrit?'; J.-D. Dubois, 'L'éxégèse des gnostiques et l'histoire du canon des Écritures'; I. Hadot, 'Les introductions aux commentaires exégétiques chez les auteurs néoplatoniciens et les auteurs chrétiens'; M. Tardieu, 'Principes de l'exégèse manichéenne du Nouveau Testament'; G. Monnot, 'La démarche classique de l'exégèse musulmane'; R. Goetschel, 'Exégèse littéraliste, philosophe et mystique dans la pensée juive médiévale'; B. Roussel, 'L'épître aux Éphésiens, de Laurent Valla à Sixte de Sienne et Théodore de Bèze: quelques aspects de l'histoire des écrits bibliques au XVIe siècle'; P. Marsauche, 'La masique guérit les mélancolies: étude sur le commentaire de Dom Calmet'; and M.-D. Richard, 'La méthode exégétique de Schleiermacher dans son application au platonisme'. As is commonly the case with collections such as this, some articles are more closely related than others to the stated theme; those by the two Hadots, Cazelles, Barc, and Dubois will be of special interest to readers of the *Book List*.

J. BARTON

Trembath, K. R.: *Evangelical Theories of Biblical Inspiration: A Review and Proposal*. 1987. Pp. x, 154. (Oxford University Press, New York and Oxford. Price: £22.50. ISBN 0 19 504911 X)

Trembath bases his study on the evangelical principle of salvation in Christ. After examining the theories of biblical inspiration proposed by seven past and present evangelical writers, he develops suggestions made by William J. Abraham, and discusses in turn the recipient of the inspiration, the Bible as the medium of divine inspiration, and God, 'the initiator of salvation and inspiration'. Along the way he considers three traditional evangelical assertions about the inspiration of the Bible, verbal and plenary inspiration, and inerrancy, modifying the first two and rejecting the third because it confuses the doctrine of God and the doctrine of scripture, invests scripture with attributes which only God can possess, and tends to place the written mediator of the Christian's relationship to God above that relationship. He summarizes his theory in this way: 'the phrase "biblical inspiration" refers to the enhancement of one's understanding of God brought about instrumentally through the Bible, rather than to the mysterious and nonrepeatable process by which "God got written what He wanted" in the Bible'. Of special interest is the way Trembath draws from Roman Catholic theologians, and emphasizes the importance of the believer's Christian community; the ultimate criterion for determining the 'Christianness' of anything is 'compatibility with salvation as understood by their community'. This is an important contribution to the subject from the evangelical camp.

C. S. Rodd

Tucker, G. M., Petersen, D. L., and Wilson, R. R. (eds): *Canon, Theology, and Old Testament Interpretation: Essays in Honor of Brevard S. Childs*. 1988. Pp. xix, 347. (Fortress, Philadelphia. Price: $39.95. ISBN 0 8006 0854 2)

This Festschrift for Brevard S. Childs bears eloquent witness to the breadth of his interests and the varying responses which his work has elicited, particularly his canonical approach to the Old Testament. The essays come from German and British scholars as well as from Child's colleagues and former students in the U.S.A. The essays are grouped into four sections: (1) Canon and Theology: with a typically shrewd contribution by James Barr, 'The Theological Case against Biblical Theology'; E. S. Gerstenberger on 'Canon Criticism and the Meaning of *Sitz im Leben*'; P. D. Hanson on 'Biblical Interpretation: Meeting Place for Jews and Christians'; R. F. Melugin on 'Canon and Exegetical Method'; R. R. Wilson on 'Approaches to Old Testament Ethics'; B. C. Birch on 'Old Testament Narrative and Moral Address'; and D. L. Petersen on 'Israel and Monotheism: The Unfinished Agenda'. (2) The Interpretation of the Torah and the Former Prophets: with discussion of the Sinai pericope by J. Van Seters; Healing and the Mosaic traditions by G. W. Coats; the Tragedy of the House of David by J. W. Whedbee; and Elisha and the Shunnamite by B. O. Long. (3) The Interpretation of Prophetic Texts includes essays on general prophetic themes: R. E. Clements on 'Patterns in the Prophetic Canon: Healing the Blind and the Lame'; G. M. Tucker on 'The Law in the Eighth-Century Prophets', G. T. Sheppard on 'True and False Prophecy within Scripture'; as well as discussion of more specific texts: J. Jeremias on Amos 3–6, B. W. Anderson on Isaiah 5–10(11), and A. Rofé on Isaiah 55:6–11. (4) The Interpretation of the Writings; with studies on Daniel 1 by W. Sibley Towner, Psalm 118 by J. L. Mays, and the Song of Songs by M. H. Pope. The volume is rounded off by a bibliography of Childs' contributions to Old Testament study: books, articles, and reviews.

R. Davidson

Uffenheimer, B. and Reventlow, H. Graf (eds): *Creative Biblical Exegesis: Christian and Jewish Hermeneutics through the Centuries* (JSOT Supplement Series 59). 1988. Pp. 225. (Sheffield Academic Press. Price: £27.50 ($46.50). ISBN 1 85075 082 3; ISSN 0309 0787)

This is a collection of papers read at a conference in Israel in 1985 on Creative Biblical Exegesis, under the joint auspices of the Rosenberg School for Jewish Studies, Tel-Aviv University, the Evangelisch-Theologische and the Katholisch-Theologische Fakultät, Bochum. The aims of the organisers were (a) to make a contribution to research into various Jewish and Christian readings of the Bible throughout the ages, (b) to contribute to Jewish-Christian relations, and (c) to take another step toward the rebuilding of bridges between the Jewish and the German people.

The papers, all but one of which are in English, are M. Banitt, 'Exegesis or Metaphrasis'; P. Carny, 'Philo's Uniqueness and Particularity'; M. Dubois, 'Mystical and Realistic Elements in the Exegesis and Hermeneutics of Thomas Aquinas'; D. Flusser, '"Today if You Will Listen to this Voice" Creative Exegesis in Hebrews 3–4'; C. Frey, 'The Function of the Bible in Recent Protestant Ethics'; Y. Hoffman, 'The Technique of Quotation and Citation as an Interpretive Device'; J. Levinger, 'Maimonides' Exegesis of the Book of Job'; R. Liwak, 'Literary Individuality as a Problem of Hermeneutics in the Hebrew Bible'; K. Raiser, 'A New Reading of the Bible? Ecumenical Perspectives from Latin America and Asia'; H. Smolinsky, 'The Bible and its Exegesis in the Controversies about Reform and Reformation'; E. Touitou, 'Courants et Contre-Courants dans L'Exégèsis Biblique Juive en France au Moyen-Âge'; J. Wallmann, 'Luther on Jews and Islam'; B. Uffenheimer, 'Some Reflections on Modern Jewish Biblical Research'; H. Graf Reventlow, 'Humanistic Exegesis: The Famous Hugo Grotius'. Finally, there is a 'Panel Discussion' — three short papers introduced by B. Uffenheimer. Z. W. Falk, 'Jewish and Christian Understanding of the Bible'; M. Dubois, 'Roman Catholic Understanding of the Bible'; and H. Graf Reventlow, 'Protestant Understanding of the Bible'.

R. B. Salters

Van Der Plas, D. (ed.): *Effigies Dei: Essays on the History of Religions* (Supplements to *Numen* 51). 1987. Pp. vii, 170. (Brill, Leiden. Price: fl. 75.00 (ca. $37.50). ISBN 90 04 08655 2; ISSN 0169 8834)

Of the twelve essays in this book, four are likely to be of direct interest to *Book List* readers. D. van der Plas (following on from M. Doresse) analyzes the theology of the veiled images of Amun (Wainwright's so-called 'aniconic form') in the cult of Amenapet; P. H. J. Houwink Ten Cate examines the relation between the Sun god of heaven and the king in Hittite society, as mediators between the divine and human worlds; H. S. Versnel's essay on Graeco-Roman epiphanies raises some of the issues applying to the problem of biblical epiphanies, while P. W. van der Horst gives a first English translation of BM 10675, the oldest *Shiur Qomah* manuscript, which describes the measurements and qualities of the divine body. A fifth paper, J. G. Hahn's study of the portrayal of Jesus in films, is an interesting exercise in celluloid iconology!

N. Wyatt

Walzer, M.: *Shutsu-Ejiputo to Kaihō no Seiji-gaku*. Translated by S. Arai. 1987. Pp. 234. (Shinkyō Shuppan-sha, Tokyo. Price: ¥2,200)

This is a Japanese translation of *Exodus and Revolution* (1985).

K. K. Sacon

WERNER, W.: *Studien zur alttestamentlichen Vorstellung vom Plan Jahwes* (BZAW 173). 1988. Pp. xi, 334. (De Gruyter, Berlin. Price: DM 140.00. ISBN 3 11 011255 8)

Werner examines not only all passages in the Latter Prophets (not in the Psalms or wisdom) where the verb or the noun *y*[c]*ṣ* or the noun [c]*ṣh* is used with reference to God, but also Amos 3:7, 2 Chron. 25:1–8, and the theological passages in the Succession Narrative. The former group includes many passages in Isaiah, especially in 1–39, as well as a few in Jeremiah and Micah. Werner's discussion is dominated by redaction criticism, and he has taken for his mentors some of the most radical scholars in that field. On this basis he is able to dismiss the influential view of Isaiah as the originator of a theology of Yahweh's 'plan' on the grounds that all the passages where it appears are redactional and post-exilic (except Isa. 46:9–11 — Deutero-Isaiah). Nor do they in reality, according to Werner, exhibit a single conception, but rather a variety of reflections on personal life and national and international history by which faith is enabled to see, with hindsight, Yahweh at work with deliberate purpose in history. The present form of Isa. 5:11–19 in particular is seen as a response to a sceptical attitude to life traceable in Old Testament sources to the fourth or third century.

W. J. HOUSTON

WILLIAMS, T.: *Form and Vitality in the World and God: A Christian Perspective* (paperback edition). 1988. Pp. xi, 356. (Clarendon, Oxford. Price: £10.95. ISBN 0 19 826698 7)

This is a welcome paperback re-edition of the 1985 study of 'the story of Israel, Judaism, and the phenomenon of Jesus' which was widely hailed, as in the review in *B.L.* 1986, p. 98.

A. G. AULD

8. THE SURROUNDING PEOPLES

ARCHI, A. (ed.): *Eblaite Personal Names and Semitic Name-Giving* (Archivi Reali di Ebla, Studi I). 1988. Pp. xiii, 306, 1 pl. (Missione Archeologica Italiana in Siria, Università degli Studi di Roma 'La Sapienza'. Price: Lire 70,000.)

The fourteen papers will interest linguists foremost, but several make points of importance to a wider readership. D. Pardee's 'Personal Names from Ebla from a West Semitic Perspective: Pantheon Distribution according to Genre' (pp. 119–51) discusses Hebrew names with possibly polytheistic elements, with kinship terms perhaps reflecting the name-giver's relation to a personal deity, then examines the distribution of names in texts from Phoenicia, Ugarit, and Ebla, showing different patterns of occurrence in different types of text. Semitic names of the Pre-Sargonic period from Babylonia reveal, according to A. Westenholz, Ilum, and Ishtar as almost exclusively the gods revered, a surprising situation not shared at Mari or Ebla, or in Sumerian names (chance recovery of text may affect the picture). Name-forms occupy P. Fronzaroli, H. Limet, D. O. Edzard, J. Krecher (survival of toponyms), H.-P. Müller, and notably M. Krebernik whose careful analysis of Prefixed Verbal Forms (pp. 45–69) concludes this is the dominant type at Ebla, corresponding to Akkadian preterites, with no trace of anything related to later West Semitic 'perfect' forms (see below p. 125). R. D. Biggs compares names at Ebla and at Abu Salabikh in Babylonia, O. Roualt describes a process for computerized study, J. Renger concludes that *mlk* in the El-Amarna Letters has a West Semitic meaning, C. H. Gordon compares various names from Ebla with some from the Old Testament and elsewhere, while A. R. Millard notes how rare words and archaic forms appear in names, and points to analogies between names at Ebla and in the Old Testament. A. Archi, M. Biga, L. Milano provide important 'Studies in Eblaite Prosopography' (pp. 205–306) clarifying names of kings, their families and their retainers, with noteworthy consequences for reconstructing the history of Ebla.

A. R. MILLARD

BARUCQ, A., CAQUOT, A., DURAND, J. M., LEMAIRE, A., and MASSON, E.: *Écrits de l'Orient ancien et sources bibliques* (Petite Bibliothèque des Sciences Bibliques: Ancien Testament 2). 1986. Pp. 318. (Desclée, Paris. Price: Fr. 135.00. ISBN 2 7189 0308 2)

Our French-speaking colleagues seem to have a genius for *haute vulgarisation* and this outstanding volume is a typically thorough and encyclopaedic example of the genre. It is one of a series of eleven volumes aimed modestly at members of Bible study groups and students, though some of the contributions are so authoritative and well documented that they will also be of use to researchers and teachers. A. Lemaire contributes sections on writing and languages, Phoenician texts and Aramaic texts. Each is a masterly survey with excellent documentation. The section on writing includes discussion of scribes, schools, and archives, as well as an analysis of the development of literary works which would be usefully read by scholars working on similar matters in the Old Testament context. Not quite so well documented, but equally authoritative, is the section by A. Caquot on Canaanite texts (mainly concerned with Ugaritic). Egypt is dealt with by A. Barucq, Mesopotamia by J. M. Durand, and Hittite texts by E. Masson. The authors are not over-concerned with making comparisons with the Old Testament. The civilizations of the ancient Near East are allowed to stand on their own feet, the only wise basis for comparison. J. Auneau provides an index and a chronological table.

J. F. HEALEY

BRUNNER, H.: *Das hörende Herz: Kleine Schriften zur Religions- und Geistesgeschichte Ägyptens* (OBO 80). 1988. Pp. x, 433. (Universitätsverlag, Freiburg (CH); Vandenhoeck & Ruprecht, Göttingen. Price: SwFr. 98.00; DM 145.00. ISBN 3 7278 0567 6; 3 525 53709 3)

This substantial volume offers a collection of forty-five papers by the well-known Egyptologist Hellmut Brunner, grouped under eight headings. Papers are reproduced directly from the original publications except when unsuitable formats have required resetting. The eight sections are: 'The understanding heart' (3 papers); Egyptian wisdom-literature and education (6 papers); Egyptian religion (17 papers, the heart of the book); Egyptian kingship (4 papers); Egyptian funerary beliefs (4 papers); Egyptian concepts of space and time (3 papers); on Egyptian literature and art (2 papers); and finally the impact of Ancient Egypt on the Bible and Christianity (6 papers). While it is the first and last sections that have the most direct relevance to Old Testament scholars, much useful background information on the history of concepts and attitudes in Old Testament times is tucked away in most of the others also. A compact index completes this useful compilation.

K. A. KITCHEN.

BUTTERWECK, C., CONRAD, D., DELSMAN, W. C., DIETRICH, M., HECKER, K., STERNBERG-EL-HOTABI, H., KAMMERZELL, F., LORETZ, O., MÜLLER, H.-P., MÜLLER, W. W., OCKINGA, B., RÖMER, W. H. PH., and ROSCHINSKI, H. P.: *Grab-, Sarg-, Votiv- und Bauinschriften* (Texte aus der Umwelt des Alten Testaments, Bd II, Lfg 4). 1988. Pp. 453–640. (Gerd Mohn, Gütersloh. Price: DM 138.00; sub. price: DM 118.00. ISBN 3 579 00069 1)

In this continuation of *TUAT* (see *B. L.* 1988, p. 121 for the last fascicle) Römer translates the Sumerian; Hecker the Akkadian; Dietrich and Loretz a

Mari inscription and two in Ugaritic; Sternberg, Kammerzell and Ockinga the Egyptian; Conrad the Hebrew; Delsman the Aramaic; Butterweck, H. -P. Müller and Roschinski the Phoenician and Punic; W. W. Müller the South and North Arabic. There is no change in the style or character of this new part. The renderings are fully competent, and the introductions, notes, and bibliographies are well informed and up to date. The problem of selection remains, however. The choice of twenty-five out of the thousands of Mesopotamian texts of the types being drawn upon cannot but appear whimsical. They are meant as representative of their types, not being selected as relevant to the Old Testament. The same applies to the sixteen Egyptian texts. Hebrew is more fully represented due to the paucity of the material. Such an old favourite as the Siloam inscription appears of course, but more recent finds such as those from Kuntillet 'Ajrud are also presented, also a big group of seal inscriptions. The Hebrew and Phoenician are given more technical treatment: only the original language is missing, but even that is sometimes quoted in the notes. While offering the older, well-known Phoenician and Aramaic inscriptions, less well known and important more recent discoveries such as the Givat ha-Mivṭar funerary inscription and Punic *MLK*-offering material are also given. There is much here not in *ANET* and other similar works.

W. G. Lambert

Cananea selecta. Festschrift für Oswald Loretz zum 60. Geburtstag (Studi Epigrafici e Linguistici sul Vicino Oriente antico, vol. 5). 1988. Pp. x, 229 with one photograph. (Essedue edizioni, Verona. Price: Lire 45,000)

Of the seventeen contributions to this birthday issue of *SEL* only two are directly concerned with the Old Testament. They are G. del Olmo Lete's study of Bashan as the Canaanite Netherworld (pp. 51–60) and D. Pardee's 'The Poetic Structure of Psalm 93' (pp. 163–70). Other studies will be of interest, too, including several on Ugaritic texts (by M. C. Astour, A. Caquot, J.-L. Cunchillos, J. C. de Moor, J. F. Healey, J. M. Sasson, W. G. E. Watson, and P. Xella) and philology (by P. Bordreuil, E. Lipiński, and J. Sanmartin). The long bibliography of works by Professor Loretz (compiled by P. Xella) includes a substantial number of items which are significant for Old Testament studies.

W. G. E. Watson

Dietrich, M. and Loretz, O.: *Die Keilalphabete: Die phönizisch-kanaanäischen und altarabischen Alphabete in Ugarit* (Abhandlungen zur Literatur Alt-Syrien-Palestinas (ALASP) 1). 1988. Pp. xiv, 357 and 1 map. (Ugarit-Verlag, Münster; distributed by Cornelsen Verlagsgesellschaft, Postfach 8729, D–4800 Bielefeld. Price: DM 89.00 (sub. price: DM 80.00). ISBN 3 917120 00 6)

The discovery by A. G. Lundin that the cuneiform tablet from Beth-Shemesh presents the signs in the order of the South Semitic alphabet (Le Muséon, 100 (1987), 243–50) enabled the authors to develop their view of the arrival at Ugarit of a dominant class of 'Arab' people who imposed their 'long' alphabet on the existing 'short' one. These people already knew cuneiform and had transferred their inherited linear alphabet to it. A chart attempts to show relations between the Ugaritic cuneiform signs, the linear alphabet and the South Semitic alphabets, but the similarities are less than convincing. Much of Dietrich and Loretz's argument rests on their minute analysis of texts in the 'shorter' alphabet from Ugarit and the examples of 'Ugaritic' texts found elsewhere (ch.4, pp. 145–276). The following chapter treats the Beth-Shemesh tablet in detail. The authors' thesis is based on relatively few documents and may demand too much of them. With its comprehensive bibliographies and histories of research it should stimulate further discussion and facilitate the evaluation of future discoveries. It is also a reminder of the variety of dialects and scripts in the Levant on the eve of Israel's emergence.

A. R. MILLARD

La Dona en l'antiquitat (Orientalia Barcinonensia 1). 1987. Pp. 141. (Editorial AUSA, Barcelona. Price: $12.00. ISBN 84 86329 11 6)

It is an interesting reflection on the scholarly coverage of the ancient world in a European university that this symposium on Woman in Antiquity held in Barcelona should result in a book with seven chapters devoted mainly to the classical world (itself limited to Greece), while the author of the remaining paper is almost apologetic in his explanation that the expression 'the ancient Orient' is in effect restricted to 'the Mesopotamian-Anatolian-Syrian ambit'!

This paper, by G. del Olmo Lete, considers women's roles in ancient Near Eastern societies as being dictated above all by their sexual function, though this could involve considerable power in dynastic contexts. On the literary plane he notes three significant types of female representation: mythology/goddess, epic/heroine, and liturgy/officiant. A goddess's role is generally connected with the status of her consort, who may be a primordial father figure or a usurper figure of a later generation. ᶜAnat is noted as a goddess who collaborates actively in her husband's roles, while Ishtar is a similarly paradoxical combination of erotic and martial traits. In epic, Enkidu's harlot and Rahab of Jericho symbolize the link between sex and culture, Hurriya and Helen trigger off wars, while Pughat in avenging her brother anticipates various biblical heroines. In the cult, the priestess-goddess is at the centre of the sacred marriage rite, epitome of cosmic fertility. The king's role appropriates her symbolism to the political realm.

N. WYATT

EGGEBRECHT, A. (ed.): *Ägyptens Aufstieg zur Weltmacht (1550–1400 v.Chr.): Zeugnisse einer glanzvollen Epoche*. 1987. Pp. 384. (Von Zabern, Mainz. Price: DM 49.80. ISBN 3 8053 0964 3)

This really magnificent volume is the permanent catalogue and record of a splendid exhibition staged at the Roemer- und Pelizaeus-Museum in late 1988. The subject was the period of the first half of the Egyptian eighteenth Dynasty (*c.* 1550–1400 B.C.), before the days of the notorious Akhenaten or the gold of Tutankhamun. This first half of that Dynasty saw Egypt's rise to superpower status in that epoch, ruling from North Syria into the depths of the Sudan at its acme. The first half of the volume is divided between introductory essays on the rise of Egypt to such power, the kings and officialdom, the role of Egypt's ample gold-supplies in imperial use and politics and religion of the time, and a presentation of a full-scale model of the vividly-coloured tomb-chamber of Sennufer, Mayor of Thebes, created in collaborated with Kodak, using new photographic techniques. The second half of the book shows a wealth of objects: statuary, everyday furnishings, writing-kits, and typical documents, tools, weapons, the inevitable funerary effects, all in profusion and in the finest colour-reproductions. It gives a window on to life in Egypt during the time of the reputed sojourn of the Hebrews in Egypt up to a century and more before the exodus. The book also has abundant bibliographical notes. The initial essays are good, if occasionally idiosyncratic and unduly dogmatic on a few doubtful details — but not so as to detract from the book's undoubted worth.

K. A. KITCHEN

FARKAS, A. E., HARPER, P. O., and HARRISON, E. B. (eds): *Monsters and Demons in the Ancient and Mediaeval Worlds: Papers Presented in Honor of Edith Porada*. 1987. Pp. xv, 114, and 54 plates with 66 drawings and 101 photographs. (Von Zabern, Mainz. Price: DM 98.00. ISBN 3 8053 0912 0)

A beautifully produced volume worthy of the aesthetic interests of its dedicatee. She herself offers a useful introduction, which is followed by nine articles: H. G. Fischer on Egyptian monstrosities; E. Reiner on figurines, amulets, and talismans in Mesopotamia; W. G. Lambert on the development of the Gilgamesh tradition in literature and art; D. P. Hansen on seals from Lagash; M. J. Mellinck on links between Anatolian and Minoan libation pourers; J. Boardman on classical marine monsters; P. H. von Blanckenhagen on 'Easy monsters' — reduced from supernature to genre figures in fashionable Graeco-Roman art; D. Bishop on the demonization of gods in the Iranian tradition; and W. M. Voelkle on the seven deadly sins illustrated in Morgan MS M 1001 (*c*. 1475). Biblical scholars may look with envy on the rich iconographic repertoire illustated here which the Jews were so often assumed to have rejected (but see Goodenough!). In the final paper they will be gratified to discover a mediaeval iconographic tradition including (Baal/El) Berit and Ashtarot of Judges, and Asmodeus of Tobit. These papers while thoroughly scholarly have evidently been written with relish and enjoyment, traits all too often lacking in academic publications.

N. WYATT

FAZZINI, R. A.: *Egypt: Dynasty XXII–XXV* (Iconography of Religions, Section XVI: Egypt, Fasc. 10). 1988. Pp. xii, 36 and XLVIII plates. (Brill, Leiden. Price: fl.42.00; ca.$21.00. ISBN 90 04 07931 9)

Part of an ongoing series, this fascicle covers the religious concepts of Ancient Egypt and their expression in the visual arts (scenes on temple and tomb walls; stelae; statuary; funerary effects) during the period *c*.1000–650 B. C. i.e. most of what is habitually termed the 'Third Intermediate Period' in Egypt — not because it was (or should be) deemed unimportant, as the author complains (p. 1), but because it was a period of disunity between periods of unity and power. Prefaced by an excellent and relatively up-to-date bibliography, the author gives special abbreviations, list of dates, and a deft historical outline. Then he surveys a rich variety of religious concepts and artistic formulations. These include scenes of pharaoh's triumph (that of Shishak/Shoshenq I being the classic one here), the very popular theme of the divine youth upon a lotus (cf. the Samaria ivories and many others), various themes that directly reflect the immense growth in the cult of Osiris, Isis, and Horus; the style of stelae commemorating land-donations, the jubilee-ceremonies (Osorkon II, ally of Ahab), statuary, not least of the high priestesses, 'God's Wives of Amun', and the funerary fashions and beliefs of the period. The whole compact and clear account is illustrated by forty-eight well-chosen and well-produced plates, bringing together a variety of subjects not otherwise available within one pair of covers. Useful background in dealing with Egyptian connections on the religious plane, for the period of the Hebrew 'divided monarchy'.

K. A. KITCHEN

GOLOMB, D. M. (ed.): *"Working with No Data": Semitic and Egyptian Studies Presented to Thomas O. Lambdin*. 1987. Pp. xiv, 264. (Eisenbrauns, Winona Lake IN. Price: $28.50. ISBN 0 931464 35 8)

Seventeen essays, almost all on aspects of Semitic languages, honour the Harvard grammarian. W. R. Bodine summarizes uses of Graphemics, Translation Theory, and Discourse Analysis in biblical and related studies. C. T. Hodge argues for the Egyptian suffix conjugation as part of a prehistoric

Afroasiatic-Indo-European language, and J. Huehnergard uses analogy to explain three items of Akkadian morphology. In the El-Amarna Letters the phrase 'to become an ʿApiru' means just that, affirms W. L. Moran, not 'to join the ʿApiru' as M. Liverani has maintained. L. R. Shehadeh analyses the writing of voiceless consonants in 'Proto-Canaanite' (a very tentative exercise) and especially in West Semitic names at Ugarit. Citing Lambdin's scepticism that Ugaritic can be read with any certainty, R. J. Clifford proceeds to study Mot's invitation to Baal (CTA 5 i), noting parallel expressions in Hebrew and finding the order CTA 4, 5 probably wrong. The Nora fragment in Phoenician (CIS I.149) belongs to the eleventh century B.C. according to F. M. Cross who offers a new interpretation and comments on trade and colonization (but it is unlikely that the stone can be treated so certainly). B. Halpern concludes that the language of the Deir Alla Balaam text is a local Canaanite dialect of elevated style with a southern Aramaic flavour, warning that Judean Hebrew was not monolithic. (The possibility that the text was old when copied is not considered.) For Targumic studies, D. M. Golomb shows systematic differences of rendering *l*ᵉ*hištaḥ*ᵃ*wôt* between the Targumim, and argues that the Targumim are sophisticated products of rabbinic scholarship, not popular paraphrases; and D. J. Harrington explores the Targum Jonathan on Hannah's Song, discovering allusive apocalyptic elements distinguishing it from the rest of the Targum, marking it as a post-A.D. 70 composition to encourage the depressed. S. E. Fassberg identifies two Palestinian supralinear signs as equivalents of Tiberian *dagesh* and *raphe*. Ethiopic Enoch was translated from Greek, not Aramaic, according to J. C. Vanderkam, *contra* E. Ullendorff and M. Knibb, while E. Isaac claims that one Ethiopic MS (K9) militates against the Aramaic exemplar theory while being closer to the Qumran fragments in some points. U. L. Perking tries to demonstrate that the *yeqattel* imperfective G was integral to Proto-Ethiopic. With two other essays, this volume offers many things worthy of attention by a variety of scholars.

A. R. Millard

Krebernik, M.: *Die Personennamen der Ebla-Texte: Eine Zwischenbilanz* (Berliner Beiträge zum Vorderen Orient 7). 1988. Pp. xvii, 353. (Dietrich Reimer, Berlin. Price: DM 68.00. ISBN 3 496 00906 3)

As they edit the 8,000 or so tablets of the Ebla archive, the scholars responsible list all the personal names in them. Now Manfred Krebernik has combined all the names from those lists and from texts given in other publications to make a preliminary analysis of the Ebla onomasticon. The inventory of personal names and name elements occupies pages 115–318 of this clearly typed book. Earlier chapters set out details of publication, deal with questions of sign values and readings, orthography, types of name, phonology and morphology, listing identifiable roots and the elements of compound names. In these earliest Semitic names recorded from Syria the strongest flavour is Akkadian, and the majority of explanations that can be offered with assurance are based on Akkadian or Akkadian and Common Semitic. The explanations in West Semitic terms proposed by G. Pettinato and M. Dahood are noted, but often discounted on technical grounds. No West Semitic *qatal*-perfective forms are found, but the type seen in *iš-ra-il* (probaby the same as Israel) is common. Other words found in Biblical Hebrew are noted, some certain (e.g. *gōy*, p. 84) others doubtful (e.g. *ʾadam*, pp. 71, 75). The list of roots gives succinct discussions of the various possibilities the writing system allows. This book is an interim presentation, but it is a masterly survey, set on reliable foundations; an important contribution to comparative Semitic lingustics and eventually to knowledge of the early population of Syria.

A. R. Millard

MAGEN, U.: *Assyrische Königsdarstellungen — Aspekte der Herrschaft: eine Typologie* (Baghdader Forschungen 9). 1986. Pp. xv, 176, and 31 plates. (Von Zabern, Mainz. Price: DM 180.00. ISBN 3 8053 0835 3)

Despite the lavish format and matching price this is an archaeological Ph.D. thesis written under Th. Beran in Frankfurt, with help in Akkadian from K. Deller and Ph. Hibbert of Heidelberg. It aims to study and explain the representations of the Assyrian king in Assyrian art, most examples of which are first-millennium. On occasion he is ambiguously represented as hunter or builder, but what is the king doing when, e.g. he holds up his right hand with index finger extended? The art is systematically collected, and presented, with a fair selection reproduced in the plates. The explanations attempt to draw in all directly relevant material from both representations and from written sources, not only from the period dealt with, but also from the second and later half of the third millennium B.C. This is largely pioneering work, and comprehensive in its attempt to reconcile monuments and texts. As a thesis it deserves commendation, though it relies too much on the ubiquitous charts and not enough on profound knowledge of the wider context of each category of material. Fuller study of these will undoubtedly bring improvements. There is comparable linguistic material in Hebrew, but pathetically little art to compare.

W. G. LAMBERT

PALEY, S. M. and SOBOLEWSKI, R. P.: *The Reconstruction of the Relief-Representations and Their Positions in the Northwest-Palace at Kalhu (Nimrud)* II (Baghdader Forschungen, 10). 1987. Pp. xvii, 93, with 6 plates and 6 plans. (Von Zabern, Mainz. Price: DM 135.00. ISBN 3 8053 0888 4)

Excavation of this ninth century B.C. Assyrian royal palace has continued now for almost 150 years since Layard. Recent work has uncovered the ruined west wing. Here a range of rooms (S,T,Z) with reliefs of large sized human and divine winged figures, with but a single royal figure and escort, shows that, as in another room(I), they were meant to impress the visitor with such religious connotations. Another smaller room (WI) is lined with a lion-hunt and Nisroch figure. These are art forms already known. The frontage of this wing to an inner courtyard bears fragmentary scenes of a siege, chariot warfare, and official procession.

This is a well produced but very technical catalogue primarily concerned to marshal the evidence to reconstruct these few rooms. It can be fully interpreted only by reference to the previous works of the late Janusz Meuszyński and related articles for no detailed illustrations of these sculptures are included here. This book is a step towards the final reconstruction of the palace which, when the other results from all excavations are brought together, will enable the Old Testament reader to see better the centre of Assyrian military might which was directed against Palestine.

D. J. WISEMAN

SCHULMAN, A. R.: *Ceremonial Execution and Public Rewards: Some Historical Scenes on New Kingdom Private Stelæ* (Orbis Biblicus et Orientalis 75). 1988. Pp. xxix, 223 and 35 figures and 6 plates. (Universitätsverlag, Freiburg (CH). Price: SwFr. 74.00. ISBN 3 7278 0548 X. Vandenhoeck & Ruprecht, Göttingen. ISBN 3 525 53704 2)

This ingenious work falls into two very distinct parts. In the first, the author surveys the known stelæ set up by private individuals in the Egyptian New Kingdom (*c.* 1550–1070 B.C.) that have an initial scene at the top, showing the pharaoh triumphantly striking down a foreign foe, normally before a deity. This pose is a highly-traditional one (going back to Narmer, before 3000 B.C.), often found on the grand scale on temple-entrances, symbolizing the pharaoh's role as protector of Egypt and champion of the gods. On these private monuments, Schulman advocates the very dramatic view that such scenes reflect in each case a specific ceremonial occasion when Pharaoh did so slay a foe ritually, and at which the dedicator of the stela was present. Unfortunately, there is no particle of positive evidence in favour of so daring a hypothesis; and the circumstances of several stelæ (e.g. of the Viceroy Setau) speak volumes against it. Rather, it is simply a 'loyalist' motif, without historical reference.

In the second part, on the contrary, Schulman is fully justified in emphasizing the historical reality of scenes of reward and/or promotion on private stelæ (in tomb-chapels — occasionally in temples, so the high priest Amenhotep by Ramesses IX); the texts in various cases explicitly support him here. So, this book contains within itself a vivid contrast in use of data and in its results, part invalid, part valid.

K. A. KITCHEN

SCHUMACHER, I. W.: *Der Gott Šopdu — der Herr der Fremdländer* (OBO 79). 1988. Pp. xiv, 352. (Universitätsverlag, Freiburg (CH); Vandenhoeck & Ruprecht, Göttingen. Price: SwFr. 94.00; DM 135.00. ISBN 3 7278 0566 8; 3 525 53708 5)

Originally a thesis, this work is the first full-scale study of the Egyptian god Šopdu, 'Lord of the East'. The authoress is able to demonstrate that Šopdu was not of Semitic origin (as sometimes suggested), but purely Egyptian. His cult is seemingly first located in the region of Memphis; only from the Middle Kingdom onwards is he found in the East Delta lands bounding the deserts out towards Sinai, the 'East' of which he was 'Lord', and then onwards shared with Hathor and Thoth the patronage of Egyptian expeditions to Sinai. Šopdu was essentially a deity of second rank; this book will be the essential reference for him.

K. A. KITCHEN

SEYERSTED, P.: *Gilgamesj. Han som så alt.* Norsk utgave ved Per Seyersted. Innledning av professor Arvid S. Kapelrud. 1987. Pp. 83. (J. W. Cappelsens Forlag, Oslo. ISBN 82 02 04301 8)

This Norwegian rendering of the Gilgamesh epic first appeared in 1967 (not noticed in *B.L.*), having been commissioned for Teaterverkstedet in Oslo, where it was staged. It is a free rendering into idiomatic Norwegian of the Assyrian text, to which Sumerian, Babylonian, Hittite, and Hurrian fragments have been added, the whole being arranged and edited by the translator to form a unified whole, to which his foreword provides a literary preface. Professor A. S. Kapelrud contributes a historical and archaeological introduction.

G. W. ANDERSON

STOLPER, M. W.: *Entrepreneurs and Empire: the Murašu archive, the Murašu Firm, and Persian Rule in Babylonia* (Uitgaven van het Nederlands Historisch-Archaeologisch Instituut te Istanbul, LIV). 1985. Pp. XXI, 324. (Nederlands Instituut voor het Nabije Oosten, Leiden. ISBN 90 6258 054 8)

What was originally a doctoral dissertation presented to the University of Michigan in 1974 has now been thoroughly revised for publication some eleven years later. By concentrating on a very specific area, namely the Murašû archive from Babylon belonging to the middle of the Achaemenian Empire, Dr Stolper's study aims to elucidate two areas in particular, provincial social and economic history and also imperial, political history. After setting the stage for describing Achaemenid Babylon, the author gives a survey of the Murašû archive and a brief description of the Murašû firm. The first main section of the work concentrates on the personnel concerned with the management and administration of various categories of property, and by doing so provides valuable information about social and economic conditions. The second main section turns to the political and economic context of the archive and devotes particular attention to mortgages. In addition to his analysis the author presents previously unpublished texts from the archive housed in the University Museum and the British Museum, and he also provides transliterations. This is a valuable study that will be of interest to biblical scholars concerned with the history of this particular period.

G. H. JONES

WATANABE, K.: *Die* adê–*Vereidigung anlässlich der Thronfolgeregelung Asarhaddons* (Baghdader Mitteilungen, Beiheft 3). 1987. Pp. vii, 248, and 16 black and white plates. (Mann, Berlin. Price: DM 69.00. ISBN 3 7861 1446 3)

Esarhaddon as king of Assyria made an unusual arrangement for his succession. His son Ashurbanipal was made crown prince of Assyria, while an elder son Shamash-shumu-ukin was designated to become king of Babylon.. To ensure that this unprecedented arrangement was respected, Esarhaddon required all the high officials of his realm to take an oath that they would actively support his decision. This oath was carefully drawn up in writing and still survives in broken multiple copies, from which a text of 663 lines has been reconstructed. It was first published in 1958 by D. J. Wiseman as *The Vassal Treaties of Esarhaddon* and as a treaty has attracted much attention in Old Testament circles. The language is mainly Neo-Assyrian, which is still a little known dialect of Akkadian. Also the curses contain a wealth of imagery (and words for it) previously unattested. Hence study since 1958 has made a new edition a desideratum, and this Heidelberg thesis written under K. Deller supplies the need. It is a reliable work with much new in it, supplying text, translation, linguistic notes, and a systematic introduction with material relevant to Old Testament studies. Knowledge of Akkadian is presumed, but the matter relevant to other fields can be obtained without it.

W. G. LAMBERT

9. APOCRYPHA AND POST-BIBICAL STUDIES

ANGELES NAVARRO, M., DE LA FUENTE A., and PIÑERO, A. (eds): *Testamentos o Discursos de Adios* (Apocrifos del Antiguo Testamento, V). 1987. Pp. 527. (Ediciones Cristiandad, Madrid. ISBN 84 7057 421 3; 84 7057 324 1 (complete work))

For the previous volumes of this series, planned and inaugurated by the late A. Díez Macho, see *B. L.* 1986, p. 118 (Vol. 1) and 1985, pp. 129–30 (Vols. 2–4). The contents of this volume form a clear unit, containing the same eight Testaments as Charlesworth. The introductions and translations are respectively by A. Piñero (Testaments of the XII Patriarchs, of Job and of Solomon), by L. Vegas Montaner (Testaments of Abraham and Moses), by G. Aranda Pérez (Testaments of Isaac and Jacob) and by F.-J. Martínez Fernández (Testament of Adam). Any general introduction to testaments or farewell discourses as a genre must be sought in Vol. 1; in Vol. 5 each work is described and discussed purely in itself. The introductions are mostly longer than in either Charlesworth or Sparks, and are both informative and generally well argued. The bibliographies usually (though not always) refer to the corresponding items in Charlesworth, but never to those in Sparks (a pity, since in some cases these are the most authoritative currently available in

English). The Spanish text is accompanied by explanatory notes comparable in quantity and character to those in Charles — a most desirable feature, in which this publication surpasses Sparks and all but a few items in Charlesworth. The Spanish text itself appears to maintain the high standard of previous volumes in this series and others from this publishing house. It would be a tragedy for biblical studies in the Spanish-speaking world if, following the sad death last year of its proprietor, Ediciones Cristiandad were unable to continue.

R. P. R. MURRAY

BARKER, M.: *The Lost Prophet: The Book of Enoch and its influence on Christianity*. 1988. Pp. xi, 116. (SPCK, London, Price: £4.95. ISBN 0 281 04381 7)

This is a popularized version of the author's *The Older Testament (B. L.* 1988, pp. 100–01) but looking more particularly at the application of its thesis to Christianity. Like its larger predecessor, it is a challenging and stimulating book and provides a useful dimension to biblical studies not often found in the responsible popular religious press. It also shares the major weakness of the scholarly study, viz. the speculative nature of much of the reconstruction. Perhaps more problematic, though, is the reductionist way in which the argument is pressed. One gains the clear impression that the Enochic tradition is *the* way to understand much of early Christianity — *the* key to all sorts of passages normally given another explanation in New Testament study — which sometimes leads to sweeping statements in which a great deal of scholarship is dismissed without proper argument or qualification (e.g. 'almost everything in the New Testament can be seen to stem from Palestine' — p. 53). An annoying habit of the author is to express opinions on a variety of issues which seem to have little to do with the subject at hand (e.g. 'medicine and religion have been separated to their mutual improverishment' — p. 37; women and the priesthood — p. 39). But despite the weaknesses the book is a refreshing change from the pabulum in many works for the laity. The important thing is not whether it is right but the challenge it presents to widespread assumptions and ways of perceiving the Christian tradition. Greater bibliographical guidance would have been helpful.

L. L. GRABBE

BEALL, T. S.: *Josephus' Description of the Essenes illustrated by the Dead Sea Scrolls* (SNTS Monograph Series 58). 1988. Pp. vii, 200. (Cambridge University Press. Price: £22.50 ($37.50). ISBN 0 521 34524 3)

The passages in Josephus which refer to the Essenes are here set out in the original and in translation, and the major part of the book is then devoted to a commentary on them in the light of the Dead Sea Scrolls, in particular the Manual of Discipline and the Damascus Document. A concluding chapter suggests that more than forty parallels can be identified, with only a small number of apparent discrepancies, and this is held to justify the 'working hypothesis' that the sectaries were indeed Essenes. There is a full bibliography, three indexes, and few misprints (though p. 132 did produce one nonsense). Many detailed points of value are made, and the hypothesis remains perhaps the most probable one, but there must be doubts whether precise comparisons of this type between writings of different literary genres are entirely convincing.

R. J. COGGINS

BENJAMIN VON TUDELA: *Buch der Reisen (Sefär ha-Massa'ot)*, translated into German by R. P. Schmitz, I: *Text* (Judentum und Umwelt, 22). 1988. Pp. 82. (Lang, Frankfurt am Main, Bern, New York, Paris. Price: SwFr. 24.00; $18.45. ISBN 3 8204 1442 8; ISSN 0721 3131)

A major source for the twelfth-century history of the Mediterranean and Near Eastern Jewish communities, and their general environment, is the itinerary of the Jewish traveller, Benjamin of Tudela. Having spent years journeying from Spain via the north Mediterranean to the Persian Gulf and returning through Egypt, he could report not only on the religious customs of the communities but also on their size, structure, and socio-economic activity. Of particular interest to Bible students are his travels in Crusader Palestine, his description of synagogal lectionaries in Cairo, and his comments on the reading of a reputedly ancient scroll of Ezekiel in central Iraq. In this reliable series for the general German reader, the translator, basing himself on the Hebrew edition of M. N. Adler (London, 1906), offers a clear translation, bibliographical preface, and indexes of subjects, personalities and places, and promises a second volume of commentary.

S. C. Reif

Borgen, P.: *Philo, John and Paul: New Perspectives on Judaism and Early Christianity* (Brown Judaic Studies 131). 1987. Pp. 324. (Scholars Press, Atlanta, Georgia. Price: $41.95 (member price: $27.95). ISBN 1 55540 183 0)

On the very last page of this collection, after the index, is found the information that 'the studies are either reproductions, elaborations or modifications of essays which have been previously published'. In fact the majority have been published twice before and at least one of them ('God's Agent in the Fourth Gospel') has already appeared three times! They are divided here into three groups: Philo, John, and Paul. They range in date from 1963 to 1984, so the term 'new perspectives' in the title is slightly misleading. What is true is that these are all original contributions by a scholar who has done more than any other contemporary exegete to demonstrate the relevance and importance of the works of Philo Judaeus to the study of the New Testament. Though the book is not printed in the ordinary sense, the publisher has taken the trouble to justify the margins of the photographed typescript.

J. F. Ashton

Buchholz, D. D.: *Your Eyes Will Be Opened: A Study of the Greek (Ethiopic) Apocalypse of Peter* (SBL Dissertation Series 97). 1988. Pp. ix, 482. (Scholars Press, Atlanta, Georgia. Price: $19.95 (member price: $12.95). ISBN 1 55540 024 8). Paperback price: $12.95 (member price: $8.95). ISBN 1 55540 025 6

This volume provides an edition and translation of the Ethiopic text of the early Christian Apocalypse of Peter, with an introduction and notes on the Ethiopic text. The edition is based on two manuscripts: Paris, Abbadianus 51, which was also used for the edition and translation published by S. Grébaut earlier this century, and Ṭānāsee 35. The edition raises a number of questions, but here it must suffice to note that the volume is not directly relevant to the concerns of the *Book List*.

M. A. Knibb

Bunte, W.: *Die Mischna: Text, Übersetzung und ausführliche Erklärung* VI. *Seder Toharot 2. Traktat Ohalot*. Pp. ix, 471. 1988. (De Gruyter, Berlin, New York. Price: DM 298.00. ISBN 3 11 009808 3)

This further instalment of the long-running Beer-Holtzmann edition of the Mishnah follows the pattern of the earlier volumes: pointed Hebrew text with facing German translation; notes largely of a philological nature at the foot of the page; introduction covering such topics as the name of the tractate and its place in the Mishnah, its composition and relationship to the Tosefta, the idea of corpse-impurity in the Near East and in Judaism; text-critical appendix with variants from major mss, Genizah fragments and editions; and finally a series of indices (including one of Greek and Latin loanwords). Bunte has done his work carefully and his valuable notes will undoubtedly help to initiate scholars and students into a closer reading of this difficult Mishnaic tractate.

P. S. ALEXANDER

BURKHARDT, H.: *Die Inspiration heiliger Schriften bei Philo von Alexandrien*. 1988. Pp. xi, 265. (Brunnen Verlag, Giessen. Price: DM 39.00. ISBN 3 7655 9340 0)

In this dissertation (presented in Göttingen) an exhaustive survey is undertaken of Philo's theories about the inspiration of 'scriptural' texts. The author notes that previous studies have relied on a small number of passages which have come to form a little 'canon' of Philonic references to inspiration, and that few of these are in fact about the inspiration *of Scripture*: most of them are about the ecstatic inspiration of prophets or other religious figures, and have simply been assumed to provide evidence for what Philo must have thought about the inspiration that produced scriptural writings.

After a survey of every reference to 'holy writings' in Philo, Burkhardt examines those places where he explicitly discusses the nature of the inspiration that led the scriptural authors (more often than not, in practice, Moses) to write their works. He concludes that this is seldom of an ecstatic kind, and usually does not imply the suspension of normal intellectual processes; in particular, Philo seldom speaks of a verbal inspiration. His model is commonly inspired *wisdom*, in which the author is inspired to express his ideas in the highest form of which he is capable, and his natural powers are heightened rather than replaced by divine wisdom. Thus Philo anticipates the theory of 'personal inspiration' (cf. Schleiermacher) rather than having much in common with the dictation theories of Protestant orthodoxy. This is an important study of Philo, which has much to say also about the origins of the Old Testament canon and touches on the inspiration theories of Josephus, early rabbinic Judaism, and the later works of the Old Testament itself. It should establish itself as the standard work in its field.

J. BARTON

COHN-SHERBOK, D.: *The Jewish Heritage*. 1988. Pp. xiii, 204. (Basil Blackwell, Oxford. Price: £25.00 ISBN 0 631 15413 2. Paperback price: £7.95. ISBN 0 631 15414 0.

This book has a curiously dated feel to it. It reminds this reviewer of the sort of books which moulded his initial introduction to Old Testament Studies in the early sixties. From reading it one would gain the impression that not much has happened in Old Testament and Jewish Studies since then. It is, like so many of the older and depressingly many of the newer text books, theology in the guise of history. In that sense it is, of course, in smooth continuity with a lot of its source material.

It purports to give 'a full history of the Jewish religion and tradition'. Its scope extends from the beginnings of Mesopotamian civilization right down to the present day. But in its presentation of the material it is a prime example of the type of pseudo-history so able exposed by Giovanni Garbini in his *History and Ideology in Ancient Israel* (see *B. L.* 1987, p. 32; 1988, p. 37). For the most part Cohn-Sherbok simply paraphrases his sources without asking whether the material can in any way be utilised for historical purposes. Particularly in his treatment of biblical and rabbinic material he is simply unaware of contemporary scholarly debate. How else could he begin his second chapter with the statement that 'scholars generally consider that the Jews (*sic*!) emerged as a separate people between the nineteenth and sixteenth centuries B.C.'? This chapter shows no knowledge of contemporary work on the patriarchal narratives and the almost universal scepticism over the possibility of utilising them for historical reconstruction. When the book does mention scholarly doubts about the historicity of parts of the biblical story it usually marginalises them by a concluding statement like the following: 'nevertheless, the fact that parts of Canaan were destroyed during this period provides some corroboration for the accuracy of the Joshua account' (p. 21). The apologetic thrust is evident as much in what it omits as in what it states. For example, in its treatment of biblical law while stating that 'biblical legislation treated all equally' (p. 9) it omits to mention the highly discriminatory treatment of women or the fact that the Old Testament legalizes rape (Deut. 22:28f).

Its treatment of the rabbinic period shows no awareness of the revolution which has overtaken study of this period in recent years. Cohn-Sherbok's lack of awareness is not surprising since the bibliography for the chapter on Rabbinic Judaism cites no work written after 1949! Not a single Neusner! The absence of any influence from the latter's work can be seen in the uncritical way in which the attribution of sayings in the rabbinic texts is taken at face value, without any regard for the fact that in most cases several centuries separate the time of the alleged sayings and the sources in which they are first cited. The same naive attitude towards the sources leads the author to completely overestimate the influence of the rabbis in their society (p. 57).

The tendency towards apologetics, amidst the torrent of dryly recorded facts, reappears in the treatment of the modern period. For example, we are told that during the Israeli War of Independence 'more than 650,000 Arab inhabitants of Palestine escaped (*sic*) from Israeli held territory' (p. 166). Opposition to Israeli behaviour is put down to anti-semitism (p. 170).

The final chapter (Inconclusion: the Future) is much the best part of the book as it succinctly lays out the dilemmas and challenges which threaten the survival of the Jewish heritage the book sets out to describe. But it still manages to completely avoid mentioning the problem of the Palestinians and the challenge that poses, not only to Israel, but also to the image of the Jewish community world-wide. As an introduction to Judaism for students (which is how the publisher describes this book) it should in no way be allowed to displace the much superior *Judaism* by Nicholas de Lange (Oxford, 1986).

A. P. Hayman

Davies, P. R.: *Behind the Essenes. History and Ideology in the Dead Sea Scrolls* (Brown Judaic Studies, 94). 1987. Pp. 150. (Scholars Press, Atlanta, Georgia. Price: $24.95. ISBN 1 55540 140 6)

At first sight, the seven essays gathered in this volume might appear to lack unity. They include 'Qumran Beginnings'; 'CD and the History of the Essenes'; 'History and Hagiography'; and 'A Comparison of Three Essene Texts'. But in the Introduction, Philip Davies demonstrates how these papers constitute elements in a coherent programme. He is concerned to subject the Qumran literature to historical-critical analysis, employing methods familiar to biblical scholarship but so far little used in research on the Scrolls. His approach succeeds in raising fundamental questions about the documents, often in acute terms; and he challenges, sometimes quite trenchantly, received wisdom on the Essenes and the scholarly methods which that wisdom assumes. Davies wishes to stimulate discussion and debate, and his wish will no doubt be fulfilled; indeed, a number of his arguments have already been questioned, and in some of these essays he is engaged in a defence of his position. Davies's work is significant and potentially fruitful. It is therefore a pity that the book suffers from several typographical errors, inconsistencies in transliteration of Hebrew words, and editorial carelessness which includes the omission of footnote 28 in chapter seven.

C. T. R. Hayward

ENERMALM-OGAWA, A.: *Un langage de prière juif en grec: Le témoinage des deux premiers livres des Maccabées* (Coniectanea Biblica, NT 17). 1987. Pp. x, 157. (Almquist & Wiksell, Stockholm. ISBN 91 22 00927 2)

This Uppsala dissertation provides a very detailed study of the prayers that occur in 1 and 2 Maccabees with the intention both of considering the significance of these prayers in their context and of examining their characteristics as representatives of a language of Jewish prayer in Greek. The study is structuralist in character, and the prayers are treated under the rubrics of context, vocabulary, style and organisation. Comparisons are drawn, particularly in regard to vocabulary, with a group of more-or-less contemporary Jewish and Christian prayers from works that range from Tobit to Book 7 of the Apostolic Constitutions. The prayers in 1 Maccabees, like other non-narrative passages ('textes intermédiaires') in the book, provide the opportunity for comment or reflection on the course of events and are related to the theme of holy war that provides the book's conceptual framework. The prayers in the main body of 2 Maccabees are closely woven into the narrative and, apart from 14:35–46 and 15:22–24, are only summarized, not quoted verbatim; they reflect the theme of 2 Maccabees, the victory of God.

M. A. KNIBB

GEORGI, D.: *The Opponents of Paul in Second Corinthians*. 1986. Pp. xv, 463. (Fortress, Philadelphia. T. & T. Clark, Edinburgh (1987). Price: £19.95. ISBN 0 567 09356 5)

The author's seminal thesis of 1964 (in German) included a widely-documented reconstruction of the beliefs of Hellenistic Judaism as a proselytizing movement. This translation updates all parts of the argument of the original book, and students of Second Temple Judaism will find here erudite if sometimes provocative discussions of, for example, the design of synagogues in the Diaspora and the nature of the liturgy carried out in them (pp. 371–77). Pages 394ff. study the 'divine man' motif in Sirach. There are comprehensive bibliographies.

C. J. A. HICKLING

HAASE, W., and TEMPORINI, H. (eds.): *Aufstieg und Niedergang der Römischen Welt: Geschichte und Kultur Roms im Spiegel der neueren Forschung*. Teil II. *Principat*. Band 20/2: *Religion (Hellenistisches Judentum in Römischer Zeit, Ausgenommen Philon und Josephus)*. 1987. Pp. vii, 669–1304. (De Gruyter, Berlin, New York. Price: DM 390.00. ISBN 3 11 011231 0; 0 89925 316 4 (US))

The publication of this volume completes the set of six devoted to Judaism in the series *Aufstieg und Niedergang der Römischen Welt*; a brief description of the series was given in *B. L.* 1981, pp. 129–30, while for other volumes see most recently *B. L.* 1988, pp. 133–34. The present volume forms one of two concerned with Hellenistic Judaism apart from Philo and Josephus, but whereas the earlier one (II, 20, 1) dealt primarily with Hellenistic-Jewish literature, this volume is meant to dealt with some themes that are relevant to the history of Jewish religion. In fact, the articles assembled in this volume form something of a mixed bag.

L. H. Kant gives a useful brief account of Jewish inscriptions in Greek and Latin and discusses their significance, while M. Hadas-Lebel writes interestingly on the evolution of Jewish attitudes towards Rome in the period from the Maccabees to the aftermath of the fall of Jerusalem in A.D. 70. G. Lease discusses 'Jewish Mystery Cults since Goodenough', and D. M. Hay examines 'The Psychology of Faith in Hellenistic Judaism', by which he means 'considerations of the subjective elements and dynamic processes involved in religious belief'. Both articles are concerned to a great extent with the interpretation of evidence in Philo, and Philo — specifically his De Vita Contemplativa — is also the concern of J. Riaud, who gives what is primarily a critical survey of research on the problem of the identity of the Therapeutae ('Les Thérapeutes d'Alexandrie dans la tradition et dans la recherche critique jusqu'aux découvertes de Qumran'). His conclusion is that Essenes and Therapeutae ought to be completely separated. The remaining three articles are all concerned with astrology. A. Strobel ('Weltenjahr, grosse Konjunktion und Messiasstern. Ein themageschichtlicher Überblick') discusses an enormous range of material, including a variety of Jewish texts that in his view bear on astrological matters. There are two articles by J. H. Charlesworth. The first ('Jewish Interest in Astrology during the Hellenistic and Roman Period') is an expanded version of an article published in *Harvard Theological Review* 70 (1977), 183–200. The second ('Die "Schrift des Sem": Einführung, Text und Übersetzung') is largely a German version of his contribution on the Treatise of Shem in volume 1 of *The Old Testament Pseudepigrapha*; the chief difference from the English version is the inclusion of an edition of the Syriac text. Charlesworth dates the Treatise of Shem to shortly after 31 B.C., but as had been pointed out, this is very unlikely (see *B.L.* 1979, pp. 125–26; 1984, p. 123). The inclusion of the two articles by Charlesworth seems more than a little surprising.

Three of the articles (those by Hadas-Lebel, Strobel, and Riaud) are of monograph length. Apart from the main articles, there is a short 'postscript' by L. H. Feldman to his massive work, *Josephus and Modern Scholars* (*B. L.* 1985, p. 130). There is again no index, and the lack of indexes in thse volumes seriously diminishes their usefulness.

M. A. Knibb

Halivni, D. W. *Midrash, Mishnah, and Gemara: The Jewish Predilection for Justified Law*. 1986. Pp. 164 (Harvard University Press, Cambridge, Mass. and London. Price: £19.50. ISBN 0 674 57370 6)

The great value of this monograph lies in a happy combination of matchless traditional Jewish learning with a fresh and creative modern approach to the literature of the Sages. David Weiss Halivni, author of a monumental Hebrew commentary on the Talmud (*Sources and Traditions*), sets out to investigate the redactional and transmissional development of legal traditions in Judaism from the Bible to the medieval commentators. He cogently argues for the basic priority of the Midrash form against the Mishnah on the grounds that in post-biblical thought, justified law is as it were naturally preferred to the apodictic variety. The Mishnah, which *qua* genre is an abridgment of the Halakhic Midrash, enjoyed a brief period of triumph, its main advantage being that it was fairly easy to learn by heart. To summarize in the author's own words, 'In the Bible, God is His own justification. In the post-biblical period, the Midrash served as the link to the Bible . . . After the interruption of the apodictic Mishnah, . . . the Amoraim gradually . . . reverted back to the vindicatory style, providing the Mishnah with either biblical . . . or logical justification . . .' (p. 69). The anonymous final redactors of the Talmud laid particular emphasis on the discursive element, leading to the medieval phenomenon of exegesis practised for its own sake as Torah study, quite independently from practical halakhah. Odd neologisms apart (Patriarchate family, apodicity, de-apodictation), this is an exciting book to read.

G. Vermes

Halperin, D. J.: *The Faces of the Chariot: Early Jewish Responses to Ezekiel's Vision* (Texte und Studien zum Antiken Judentum 16). 1988. Pp. xxi, 610. (Mohr, Tübingen. Price: DM 178.00. ISBN 3 16 145115 5; ISSN 0721 8753)

This massive scholarly tome deserves to be carefully read by all who have an interest in rabbinic Judaism. There is much also to interest the biblical scholar. After Schäfer's *Synopsis of the Hekhalot Texts* it is the most important recent contribution to the study of the impact on Judaism of Ezekiel's vision of the chariot. Starting from the interpretation of the vision discernible in the text of the Book of Ezekiel itself Halperin carefully traces out, and attempts to account for, the mixture of fascination and horror with which Jews studied this text. He handles an enormous range of texts with considerable skill and dexterity, though from time to time he does tend to 'hang a mountain' of speculations on a thin 'thread' of midrashim.

His principle theses are that the earliest level of exegesis connects Ezekiel 1 together with the Sinai pericope (Exodus 19–20) through the use of Ps. 68:18–19; that the latter text gives rise to the whole idea of the ascension of Moses, and that this is the prototype for the ascensions to the *merkabah* attested in the Babylonian Talmud version of the 'Four who entered the Garden' and in the *Hekhalot* texts. This represents an expansion, in some cases a modification, but overall very strong additional support for the case he argued in his earlier book *The Merkabah in Rabbinic Literature* (1980).

One of the most interesting parts of the book is Halperin's identification of the *ḥayyot* as part of the 'dark and inimical forces of the cosmos' (p. 113). It is the vision at the Red Sea of the *Merkabah* — with its 'beasts' whose feet 'were like the sole of a calf's foot' (Ezek. 1:7) and one of which 'had the face of an ox' — which led the Israelites to make the Golden Calf. This is the real reason why some of the rabbis sought to ban the reading of Ezekiel 1 in the Synagogue and carefully control its exegesis, not any attempt to prevent the supposed mystical ecstasies of the 'riders on the chariot'. Halperin argues that what really worried the rabbis was that 'the golden calf, the object of the first and most hateful of Israel's apostasies, the emblem of what God most hates, came from God himself. The Israelites worshipped it because of what they had seen when God exposed himself to them as he was' (p. 190). So 'certain rabbis' had 'caught glimpses of frightening ambiguities in the divine, amidst the fantastic swirl of Ezerkiel's images' (p. 450).

Halperin finds the locus of the *Hekhalot* traditions, not in esoteric circles of mystics, but in the synagogue tradition of the exegesis of Ezekiel 1 as the *haftarah* for Exodus 19–20 at the festival of *Shabu'ot*. He also argues that the *Sar Torah* element in the *Hekhalot* texts is central to their interest, and is to be located sociologically amongst the *'am ha'aretz* seeking a short cut by magical means to get hold of the *Torah* learning which was the source of the social prestige and power of the rabbinic elite. *He* throws a lot of new light on the problem of the origin and function of the figure of *Metatron* arguing that 'in his role as an exalted and near divinized human being' he 'is more than a little reminiscent of the Moses of the Sinai-ascension *haggadot*' (p. 422). As for Metaron's title *na'ar* (youth, servant?), this Halperin explains with the help of Freud: 'the youth stands for a faith that a human being can gain divinity, and become master of those godlike beings who once lorded it over him' (p. 427).

The book crackles with ideas like these which may be unconvincing to some but which certainly cannot be lightly dismissed. Overall, it is one of the most interesting books this reviewer has read in a long time.

A. P. HAYMAN

HILTON, M., MARSHALL, G.: *The Gospels and Rabbinic Judaism: A Study Guide*. 1988. Pp. viii, 167. (SCM, London. Price: £6.95. ISBN 0 334 02021 2)

One author is a rabbi and the other a Dominican priest. In each unit passages printed from both rabbinic sources and the Synoptic Gospels are expounded, discussed and provided with 'points for discussion and dialogue'. The units are on the Great Commandment, the Synagogue, the Parable and the *Mashal*, the Ox in the Pit, *Shabbat*, Divorce, and Who can forgive? There is a glossary and a bibliography. The book was designed for study groups containing both Christians and Jews, but it would prove interesting and valuable to other groups and to students working by themselves.

J. C. O'NEILL

IDEL, M.: *Kabbalah: New Perspectives*. 1988. Pp. xx, 419. (Yale University Press, New Haven and London. Price: £30.00 ($49.00). ISBN 0 300 03860 7)

This is a comprehensive and impressive study of Jewish mysticism mainly in its medieval, kabbalistic phase, and is, therefore, likely to be outwith the area of interest of most members of the Society. It is not an easy book to read. Much is taken for granted, and the language is often opaque. It presupposes considerable knowledge of the Kabbalah and takes us immediately into the heart of scholarly debate over its nature. It is emphatically not a book for beginners. On the other hand, it makes a major contribution to our knowledge of the subject, particularly in those areas neglected by Scholem, for example, the mystical techniques utilised by the Kabbalists. Above all, it rightly corrects Scholem's over-emphasis on the speculative, theosophical elements in Jewish mysticism in favour of a much fairer treatment of the mystical, experiential elements. In particular, Idel argues that the *unio mystica* plays a central role in Jewish mysticism as it does in other religions. He says that 'far from being absent, unitive descriptions recur in Kabbalistic literature no less frequently than in non-Jewish mystical writings, and the images used by the Kabbalists do not fall short of the most extreme of other types of mysticism' (p. 60). Idel also re-evaluates Scholem's views on the origin of the Kabbalah in favour of the more traditional view that it is an organic development from an ancient Jewish esoteric tradition. Idel's methodology in making these claims leaves a lot to be desired. Too often we get a mountain of speculation constructed on a molehill of texts! Nevertheless, this is an important study which merits the attention of all scholars who are interested in Jewish mysticism.

A. P. HAYMAN

KADDUSHIN, M.: *A Conceptual Commentary on Midrash Leviticus Rabbah: Value Concepts in Jewish Thought* (Brown Judaic Studies 126). 1987. Pp. xiii, 252. (Scholars Press, Atlanta, Georgia. Price: $36.95 (members price: $24.95). ISBN 1 55540 175 9)

Max Kadushin (1895–1980) taught at the Jewish Theological Seminary of America and wrote a number of works, *The Rabbinic Mind* (New York, 1952) perhaps the most famous of them, in which he sought to explain the unique character of rabbinic thought. In the brief introduction to this volume he summarises his ideas about the 'value-concepts' that underlie such thought and how they expand the notions contained in the Hebrew Bible. Such abstract concepts as *torah, miṣwah, ṣedaqah* and *qedushah* are organically, not logically integrated and are given concrete expression through *halakhah* and *haggadah*. Since *haggadah* by no means requires unqualified belief, multiple interpretations are stimulated by the text of the Hebrew Bible. Consistent with the introduction, the brief annotations to the text of the M. Margulies edition (Jerusalem, 1953–60) are primarily concerned not with contemporary scholarship but with the provision of particular examples of his general thesis. The volume (part of his literary remains?) will further enlighten those familiar with the earlier expressions of his ideas and occasionally illuminate the midrashic text.

S. C. REIF

MANNS, F.: *Leggere la Mišnah* (translated from French by Giulio Busi) (Studi Biblici 78). 1987. Pp. 242. (Paideia, Brescia. Price: Lire 22,000. ISBN 88 394 0394 9)

This is a fluent and readable translation of an introduction to the Mishnah addressed to students of the New Testament, which was originally published in French in Jerusalem in 1984. There are four main sections; the first gives the historical background from Alexander to Judah the Nasi; the second is devoted to the twin topics of Halakhah and Aggadah; the third is about the Mishnah itself; and the fourth is an annotated translation of the tractate *Abot* (based in part in part on an earlier Italian translation by Y. Colombo). The book is well produced, but the review copy had eight blank pages. Among the stronger points of the presentation, the author takes account of the discoveries in the Judaean Desert and of Israeli scholarship, some of it available only in Hebrew. On the other hand, the use made of Talmudic sources is not very critical. Moreover, even within the genre of Christian works of this kind the book has a dated and somewhat slanted look. In a random sample of 60 titles from the large bibliography, more than half were dated before 1940 and the latest appeared in 1967 (13 appeared in the last century). *Torah* is translated *legge* throughout, and the wider meanings of the term are not explained. The section on early relations between Jews and Christians (notably on the thorny question of the *Birkat ham-minim*) turns its back on modern discussions, and the book ends with an appendix arguing that crucifixion, not mentioned in the Mishnah, is accepted as a punishment by some ancient Jewish sources.

N. R. M. DE LANGE

MEADE, D. G.: *Pseudonymity and Canon. An Investigation into the Relationship of Authorship and Authority in Jewish and Earliest Christian Tradition*. 1987. Pp. 257. (Wm. B. Eerdmans Publishing Co., Grand Rapids, Michigan, by special arrangement with J. C. B. Mohr, Tübingen. Price: £28.70. ISBN 0 8028 3645 3)

A slightly revised version of a doctoral thesis supervised by J. D. G. Dunn and defended in 1984, this book seeks to discover how Canon, with its overtones of truth and authority, can include pseudepigraphic material, which conjures up notions of forgery and falsehood. Meade rejects both the conservative view, that Canon and pseudepigraphy are mutually exclusive, and the liberal contention, that canonicity is essentially irrelevant. He argues that pseudonymity was used in both Old and New Testaments not primarily as a statement of literary origins, but as a means of claiming that particular writings represent an authoritative tradition.

The author is concerned primarily with the New Testament; but the Old Testament furnishes him with a 'pattern' which he sees repeated in the New. Taking as examples the developed literary traditions of the Prophets (particularly the Isaiah corpus), Wisdom (especially as regards its attribution to Solomon), and Apocalyptic (where he focusses on the Daniel and Enoch writings), Meade notes how original divinely inspired utterances are regarded as having continuing significance for the future, as being autonomous and representing a coherent divine plan, and thus as being open to re-interpretation in the light of changed circumstances and conditions. The later unfolding and *Vergegenwärtigung* of original words of particular prophets, wise men, and seers may therefore legitimately be ascribed to those very individuals, for they are part of a genuine and authoritative tradition associated with and deriving ultimately from them.

Meade's use of Old Testament material, though largely dependent on the work of others, seems well-judged and reasonable. However, discussion of pseudonymity in Rabbinic Literature, and Jacob Neusner's work on Rabbinic theories of authority and attribution in the case of Oral Law, is strangely lacking. This omission sadly limits the value of an otherwise informative book, which is also marred by numbers of typographical mistakes.

C. T. R. HAYWARD

MORALDI, L.: *Le apocalissi gnostiche. Apocalissi di Adamo, Pietro, Giacomo, Paolo* (Biblioteca Adelphi 181). 1987. Pp. 254. (Adelphi, Milano. Price: Lire 22,000)

The five Apocalypses from among the fifty two Nag Hammadi tractates are here translated from the Coptic into Italian, with a liberal and helpful sprinkling of Greek equivalents for significant terms. Four of the texts are from Codex 5, and the Peter Apocalypse comes from Codex 7. Each text is introduced, summarized and annotated, with adequate attention to problems of text and meaning. A brief general introduction puts the Apocalyptic genre in its context within Christian literature. The rather full discussions of concepts central to Gnosticism, and especially the provision of parallels, will be appreciated beyond the Italian readership for whom the volume must primarily be intended. There is some awareness of the traditions of Jewish mysticism, on the one hand, and of neo-Platonic speculation, on the other; divorced from these contexts, the texts cannot be understood. However, the opening up of larger questions is on the whole eschewed. Thus, it is assumed that the two James Apocalypses have a 'Jewish-Christian' background, but no clear construction is ever put upon the designation 'Judaeo-Christian'; nor, in fact, is that particular claim substantiated in the commentary.

T. RAJAK

MORALDI, L.: *I Manoscritti di Qumran* (2nd ed.) (Classici delle Religioni: La Religione ebraica). 1986. Pp. 906. (UTET, Torino. Price: Lire 68,000. ISBN 88 02 03926 7)

The first edition of this collection of (lightly) annotated translations appeared in 1971 (not noted in the *Book List*). As expected, major new texts have been added — the Job Targum and Temple Scroll — and the bibliography tolerably updated. The introduction remains commendably (and almost uniquely in its genre) free of speculation and the indexes of biblical references, authors and subjects are especially useful. Almost inevitably, revision and updating does not extend to the interpretation of the individual books — and in any case what kind of coherent comments on the text can a volume of this kind offer? They are bound to be mostly desultory. Less excusable is the quantity of typographical errors (noteworthy is 'Tree Tempels' for 'Three Temples', p. 741). Nevertheless, measured against its rivals (including those in other languages) this volume comes out very well.

P. R. DAVIES

MUÑOZ LEON, D.: *Derás. Los caminos y sentidos de la Palabra Divina en la Escritura*. Primera Serie: Derás Targúmico y Derás Neotestamentario. (Bibliotheca Hispana Biblica, 12). 1987. Pp. 718. (Consejo Superior de Investigaciones Científicas, Madrid. Price: Ptas 5,000. ISBN 84 00 06139 X)

The author, well known for his work in the field of targumic studies (*B.L.* 1977, pp. 37–38; *B.L.* 1985, p. 110), tries in this book to compare the interpretation of the Old Testament done in the New Testament with the interpretation reflected in the targumim. After an introductory section (pp. 17–61), in which the author defines his understanding of the Derash and of the different sorts of Derash as well as the basic principles underlying the Derash, its methods, literary forms and contents, the book offers an analysis of all these elements in the targumim (especially in the TgNeofiti) ((p. 67–200) and in the New Testament (pp. 203–540). Each one of the two leaves of this diptych is considered in his own right, but the main thrust of the author is to use the light provided by the study of the targumic derash to understand better the New Testament. The main difference between the two forms of interpretation of the Old Testament, rests in the concept of fulfilment, peculiar to the New Testament. The book comprises also an excursus in which the author studies the way in which the words of Jesus and the traditional narrative and discursive materials are treated inside the New Testament and that he designates as 'Derás intraneotestamentario' (pp. 543–608). More than 50 pp. of Bibliography, an index of authors and of references, and a very detailed (27 pp.!) Table of contents complete the work.

The reader who can not wait until the publication of the forthcoming second volume of the series: 'Derás Apocalíptico neotestamentario e intertestamentario', or who is deterred by the voluminous appearance of the present book, can easily find the essentials of the author's thought in his contribution to *Salvación en la Palabra. Targum. Derash. Berith. En memoria del professor Alejandro Díez Macho*. Madrid 1986, pp. 657–76: 'Deras Neotestamentario y Deras Intertestamentario (Avance de un proyecto)'.

F. García Martínez

Neusner, J.: *Christian Faith and the Bible of Judaism: The Judaic Encounter with Scripture*. 1987. Pp. xviii, 205. (Eerdmans, Grand Rapids, Michigan; Paternoster, Exeter. Price: $12.95; £10.60. ISBN 0 8028 0278 8)

Professor Neusner is well-known in the field of Jewish studies, but here he enters an area not customarily associated with him. His concern in this volume is to examine the methodology of Jewish exegesis of the Hebrew Bible and to introduce it to Christian readers in the hope that it might stimulate joint Jewish-Christian study of the scriptures.

He believes that Jews and Christians alike are concerned to find in the scriptures a word from God for contemporary life. He draws upon the exegesis of the Torah — and the Genesis Rabbah, the Leviticus Rabbah and the Sifre to Numbers in particular — to illustrate that traditional commentary has been less concerned with historicist references and more concerned with the application of the text to life in general. 'Every part of the Biblical narrative', we are told, 'forms in microcosm the entirety of scriptural reality.' The commentators are seen as 'addressing issues of history and salvation, taking up critical concerns of the public life of the nation vis-à-vis history and the world beyond'. Professor Neusner also illustrates how Jewish interpretation of the text has sought to make sense of seeming contradictions.

R. Hammer

Neusner, J.: *From Tradition to Imitation: The Plan and Program of Pesiqta deRab Kahana* (Brown Judaic Studies 80). 1987. Pp. xv, 230. (Scholars Press, Atlanta, Georgia. Price: $24.95. ISBN 1 55540 113 9

Following lines of inquiry laid down in earlier studies of the classic rabbinic midrashim, Neusner argues that Pesiqta Rabbati's units of discourse may be classified into four types: (1) the legal colloquy, (2) the intersecting-verse/base-verse construction, (3) the exegetical form, and (4) the propositional list. Within any given *pisqa* the legal colloquy naturally comes first, but thereafter the document shows no preference for the order in which it uses the other forms. The rhetorical plan of the Pesiqta, defined by these basic facts, may be compared with that of the earlier Pesiqta deRav Kahana which consistently uses only types 2 and 3 and which always puts the intersecting-verse/base-verse construction before the exegetical form. These differences, though interesting, are not fundamental, and both Pesiqtas fall redactionally and formally into the same literary genus. In terms of their topical programmes they are also very much the same: both follow the synagogue lections from early spring to late autumn. Where they do diverge radically is in the fact that whereas in Pesiqta deRav Kahana each *pisqa* presents a tightly constructed argument in which a single important proposition is worked out syllogistically through the literary forms, in Pesiqta Rabbati the *pisqaot* are made up of diverse propositions and statements on a single theme. The cogency of Pesiqta deRav Kahana's discourse is, consequently, greater than that of Pesiqta Rabbati. The *pisqaot* of the latter are little more than collages or even scrapbooks of sayings on a single topic. The authorship of Pesiqta DeRav Kahana 'has a very specific message which it wishes to register with great force and urgency'; the authorship of pesiqta Rabbati 'plans only to collect and arrange important materials'. Thus we face a contrast between the creative thinker and the heir or successor, between the formative mind and the traditional one. This study presents further important evidence for Neusner's distinctive view that the midrashim are authored works and that analysis should, in consequence, begin at the level of documentary discourse and work inwards.

P. S. ALEXANDER

NEUSNER, J., GREEN, W. S., and FRERICHS, E. S. (eds): *Judaisms and their Messiahs at the Turn of the Christian Era*. 1987. Pp. xvi, 299. (Cambridge University Press. Price: £27.50 ($39.50). ISBN 0 521 34146 9. Paperback price: £9.95 ($12.95). ISBN 0 521 34940 0.

The purpose of this symposium was to assume that there existed many Judaisms, and then to use the many views of the Messiah — including views which had no place for the Messiah — to differentiate those Judaisms. Jacob Neusner, who set the agenda, knows the dangers inherent in the method ('what we treat here are books, and no religion was ever born in a book or lived in a book or even died by a book'), but he perseveres with the enterprise on the ground that 'a book does form a detail of a system, and, in the study of a religion, God lives in the details' (p. x).

Green argues that the primacy of 'the messiah' as a subject of academic study derives not from ancient Jewish preoccupation bu from early Christian theology. B. L. Mack thinks the authors of Sirach, Wisdom of Solomon and Psalms of Solomon idealized three sorts of wise men to solve their problems of social order. G. W. E. Nickelsburg argues that 1 Enoch shows there were Jews who had no messianic expectation. J. Goldstein argues that the silence of 1 and 2 Maccabees about the messianic prophecies is deliberate: 'They did not believe in the coming of a Davidic Messiah.' J. J. Collins finds no strong and developed interest in messianism except in Qumran and the Psalms of Solomon. Sh. Talmon argues that the balance of Davidic Messiah and Aaronic Messiah in Qumran shows that the community looked for a new Return from exile unmarred by the blemishes of the first Return. R. D. Hecht seeks to show that Philo's messianism might be understood as at best a 'realized eschatology'.

G. MacRae argues the further one gets from the earliest preaching the more the issue of Jesus as Messiah gains prominence. H. C. Kee says that Mark's Jesus does not fit the categories of Jewish piety. M. E. Stone shows that in 4 Ezra the Messiah is pre-existent, whose kingdom will come to an end (cf. 1 Cor. 15:28). J. H. Charlesworth thinks it was impossible that Jesus' earliest followers saw him as the Messiah. Neusner argues that although earlier Jewish systems before the Mishnah and the later systems in the Talmuds both invoked the Messiah as saviour and redeemer of Israel, the Mishnah itself constructed a system of Judaism with scarcely a hint of a need to invoke the person or functions of a Messianic figure of any kind.

The scholars writing here tend to think the authors of the documents they study were 'authors' like themselves, independent solvers of social problems, rather than members of various religious communities that all sang the Psalms together every day. The most intelligent of the contributions is from Jacob Neusner, who knows what I mean. His own characterization of the Mishnah, however, seems to me misleading. The very sparseness of explicit reference to the Messiah shows how crucial the Messiah was. The Mishnah's single-minded concern with sanctification is to prepare Israel for the Messiah and so for our Father in heaven.

J. C. O'NEILL

NEUSNER, J.: *Judentum in frühchristlicher Zeit* (translated by W. Hudel). 1988. Pp. 120. (Calwer, Stuttgart. Price: DM 24.80. ISBN 3 7668 0775 7)

This is a translation of the author's *Judaism in the Beginning of Christianity* (see *B. L.* 1985, pp. 139f), amplified only by an index of places and by the division of the subject-index into slightly expanded indications of names and subjects.

C. J. A. HICKLING

NEUSNER, J.: *The Mishnah: A New Translation*. 1988. Pp. xlv, 1162. (Yale University Press, New Haven and London. Price: £45.00 ($65.00). ISBN 0 300 03065 7)

In this weighty volume Neusner has collected together all the translations of the Mishnah tractates to be found in his monumental *History of the Mishnaic Law* (1974–82), and the translations (of *Seder Zeraim*) prepared by his pupils. The result is a new Danby. But the translation is very different in style from that presented by Danby fifty-five years ago. 'A literal translation, closely following the syntactic and formal traits of the Hebrew, highlighting the stichs of the Mishnah's completed thoughts, showing the ways in which the Mishnah repeats a given form and then, when the subject changes, chooses to switch into some other formal pattern — this is what lies before the reader' (Preface, p.x.). Readers of Neusner's books will be well acquainted by now with this style which has often been commented on in this publication (see, e.g., *B.L.*, 1982, p. 113). Neusner admits that the reader of Danby's more literary translation will get a clearer notion of the gist of the Mishnah, but rightly claims that his translation gives a much better idea of '*how* the Mishnah says what it says' (*ibid*). The text Neusner chooses to translate is that provided by H. Albeck, and the translation choices he makes will often be explained if one glances down the page in Albeck's edition to the short commentary he provides.

Neusner has done us all a service by putting his translations together in one volume. In future we shall have to study the Mishnah with both Danby and Neusner open alongside our copies of Albeck's edition. The two translations are indeed complementary. Of the two, Neusner's translation will be of more help to students struggling to read the Hebrew text. The thirty page introduction is a concise summary of Neusner's voluminous writings on the Mishnah. The contrast with the introduction of Danby's translation is stark in the extreme.

A. P. HAYMAN

NEUSNER, J.: *What is Midrash?* (Guides to Biblical Scholarship, New Testament Series). 1987. Pp. xii, 114. (Fortress, Philadelphia. Price: $5.95. ISBN 0 8006 0472 5)

Neusner gives a thorough analysis of the meanings of the term 'midrash' illustrated with numerous examples, In Part One ('What is Midrash?') it is argued that there are three types of Midrash-process: paraphrase, prophecy, and parable; then that there are three dimensions of midrash: process of exegesis, compilations of exegeses (i.e. documents), and particular exegeses of a scriptural verse Neusner maintains that the second of these is primary in the task of comparison, providing the only concrete context for each exegesis or exegetical process. Parts Two and Three illustrate midrash as paraphrase (Septuagint, Targumim), prophecy (*pesharim*) and parable or allegory (rabbinic literature) — the most extensive part of the book. The argument throughout is characteristically powerful and the working of the logic clear. In the interests of pedagogy, to which this series is devoted, a little more space might have been taken either in the text (and certainly in the bibliography) to familiarise the student with other theories of midrash or treatments based in other principles — many of which Neusner has, of course, dissected in print elsewhere.

P. R. DAVIES

PAUL, A.: *Le Judaïsme ancien et la Bible* (Relais-études 3). 1987. Pp. 316. (Desclée, Paris. Price: Fr. 195.00. ISBN 2 7189 0341 4)

In what is fundamentally a work of Christian apologetics, aimed at spelling out the differences between Christianity and Judaism, the author offers some erudite and often challenging approaches to well-worn questions, punctuated by some original insights. The book is in four parts, each consisting of three chapters. Part One, on 'Scripture and Torah in early Judaism', looks in turn at Rabbinism, Qumran (or what Paul calls 'le Quoumrânisme'), and Karaism. Part Two is devoted to Judaism and Hellenism, and looks particularly at the Letter of Aristeas and III Maccabees. Part Three is on Josephus, with a special focus on the way that he retells biblical history. Part Four, loosely entitled 'La constitution des systèmes et des mythes, des concepts et des corpus', addresses itself successively to Aquila, to the myth of Massada, and to the origins of apocalypticism. The whole, although it lacks coherence (several of the chapters have appeared as articles elsewhere), can be read with profit by anyone who is interested in early Judaism and its development.

N. R. M. DE LANGE

PRIOTTO, M.: *La prima Pasqua in Sap 18, 5–25. Rilettura e attualizzazione* (Associazione Biblica Italiana: Supplementi alla Rivista Biblica 15). 1987. Pp. 279. (EDB, Bologna. Price: Lire 35,000. ISBN 88 10 30203 6)

This work is the fruit of doctoral studies at the Rome Biblical Institute, where the author had the benefit of the learning and help of both M. Gilbert and R. le Déaut. This is a magisterial literary study, too rich to summarize. After sketching the structure of Wis. 11–19, as a series of 'diptychs' in the form of *syncrisis*, of which 18:5–25 is the sixth (ch. 1), the pericope is subjected to detailed literary and theological exegesis in five chapters, full of illumination and good critical judgement, of which perhaps the fourth, ch. 5, 'The punitive action of the Logos (vv. 14–19)' is the most excitingly rich. Priotto brings out throughout the features which reveal the author as preaching to his own Alexandrian community, and in the concluding chapter sums up the essential theological values of the Wisdom of Solomon.

R. P. R. MURRAY

RUBINKIEWICZ, R.: *L'Apocalypse d'Abraham en vieux slave: Introduction, texte critique, traduction et commentaire* (Towarzystwo Naukowe Katolickiego Uniwersytetu Lubelskiego, Źrodła i monografie, 129). 1987. Pp. 288. (Société des Lettres et des Sciences de l'Université Catholique de Lublin. Price: Zl. 400)

This is the revised version of a 1978 Rome dissertation that was supervised by R. Le Déaut and J. Olšr. The preface dates from February 1982, and the volume was evidently in the press for some time. The main part of the work provides, on facing pages, an edition of the Slavonic text of the Apocalypse of Abraham with a textual apparatus, and a French translation with a helpful textual and exegetical commentary. This is preceded by an introduction in which Rubinkiewicz discusses both the textual evidence for the Apocalypse and such matters as its unity, literary structure, and genre; the language and milieu in which it was composed; its relationship to other Jewish traditions about Abraham; the biblical and pseudepigraphical works that influenced the author; and the theology of the Apocalypse. The volume also contains a photographic reproduction of the manuscript used as a base text, a bibliography, and indexes.

Rubinkiewicz argues that, apart from a few interpolations, the work is a unity. The author, who came from priestly circles and may have been an Essene, probably wrote the Apocalypse in Hebrew for Jews in Palestine between 79 and 81. The translation into Old Salvonic was apparently made in the eleventh or twelfth century from a Greek version, but Rubinkiewicz leaves open the possibility of direct translations from the original Hebrew. Once translated into Slavonic, the Apocalypse suffered a limited degree of revision at the hands of Bogomils. Not all these points are equally convincing, and there are places in the introduction where greater precision of discussion would have been desirable. But it is good to have available this much fuller presentation of Rubinkiewicz's work on the Apocalypse of Abraham than is given in his contribution on this same writing in Volume 1 of J. H. Charlesworth (ed.), *The Old Testament Pseudepigrapha*.

M. A. KNIBB

The Rylands Haggadah. A Medieval Sephardi Masterpiece in Facsimile. Introduction, notes on the illuminations, transcription, and English translation by Raphael Loewe. 1988. Pp. 76 + 114 of full colour facsimile. (Thames and Hudson, London. Price: £48.00. ISBN 0 500 23519 8)

Rylands Hebrew MS 6 is a splendid illuminated Passover Haggadah of fourteenth-century date and of Catalan type (like the better-known Sarajevo Haggadah, or the 'Golden Haggadah' in London). The text is very complex, involving not only the usual ritual for the Passover meal and the grace after food (in an exceptional form), but a large number (more than eighty) of poetic compositions; a marginal appendix consisting of a summary of the rules for Passover in Hebrew verse, a commentary on the Haggadah attributed to Rashi, and the text of the various pentateuchal lections for Passover; and micrographic decorations containing a halakhic digest based on the Talmud. A beautiful facsimile of the entire manuscript is here accompanied by translations of all the texts except the micrography, which is summarised. The Hebrew poems are rendered into appropriate English verse, and equipped with notes which help the reader to pick up the biblical allusions. The introduction addresses both the newcomer and the more experienced reader. The whole is a monument of erudition, good taste and technical excellence.

N. R. M. DE LANGE

SAFRAI, S. (ed.): *The Literature of the Sages. First Part: Oral Tora, Halakha, Mishna, Tosefta, Talmud, External Tractates* (Compendia Rerum Iudaicarum ad Novum Testamentum. Section Two: The Literature of the Jewish People in the Period of the Second Temple and the Talmud 3). 1987. Pp. xxi, 464. (Van Gorcum/Fortress Press, Assen/Philadelphia. Price: fl. 95.00. ISBN 90 232 2282 2/ 0 8006 0605 1).

This first half of Section II, Part 3 of the slowly proceeding *Compendia* series deals with the legal contents of rabbinic literature; the forthcoming second half is reserved to Midrash, Targum and Prayer. Safrai (Oral Tora, Halakha) and Abraham Goldberg (Mishna, Tosefta, Palestinian and Bablonian Talmuds) are responsible for the bulk of the present volume with I. M. Gafni sketching the historical background, M. B. Lerner supplying chapters on Avot and the External tractates of the Talmud, and M. Krupp presenting a brief survey of Mishnah, Tosefta and Talmud manuscripts. In his introduction, the editor complains that outstanding Talmudic studies, mostly written in Hebrew, are often neglected in research works appearing in European languages. Since all the contributors to *The Literature of the Sages* are fully versed in traditional rabbinic learning, they can be accepted as trustworthy *meturgemanim* of truly traditional teaching. But old yearnings still transpire: 'If . . . we embrace a maximalist approach equating rabbinic tradition with ('Oral Tora'), . . . our *terminus a quo* for the history of rabbinic tradition may find us not far removed from Mt. Sinai itself', but 'by necessity . . . we find ourselves forced to embrace . . . a more limited task' (Gafni, p. 1). Nevertheless, efforts are being made, not always successfully, to marry modern scholarship with the best of traditional approach. Note that Danby's by now semi-classic *Mishnah* is described by Abraham Goldberg as 'a monumental work' in which 'mistranslations and inaccuracies of interpretation abound because 'while in Jerusalem, [Danby] did not consult with really knowledgeable scholars' (pp. 248f). Part 2 is awaited with curiosity.

G. VERMES

SCHÄFER, P., together with REEG, G. (eds.): *Konkordanz zur Hekhalot-Literatur*, I: *'–k*; II: *l–t* (Texte und Studien zum Antiken Judentum 12, 13). 1986. 1988. Pp. xiii, 1–364; vi, 366–732. (Mohr, Tübingen. Price: DM 235.00; 225.00. ISBN 3 16 145030 2; 3 16 145179 1; ISSN 0721 8753)

These two large volumes bring to completion Peter Schäfer's great project to present the basic manuscript texts of the *Hekhalot* literature before the scholarly world. The *Konkordanz* is based on the text of his *Synopse zur Hekhalot-Literatur* (1981), and also includes all the texts published in his *Geniza-Fragmente zur Hekhalot-Literatur* (1984). In addition he has fed into the *Synopse* the text published by Jellinek as *Masekhet Hekhalot*, that published by Wertheimer as *Ma'aseh Merkavah* (but in each case using the best available manuscript), and *Re'uyyot Yeḥezqel* as edited by Ithamar Gruenwald. He also includes in its variants from three manuscripts that were not used in the *Synopse*.

The *Konkordanz* is based on the text of the New York manuscript (N8128). It contains the complete text of this manuscript and the variants from it in the other manuscripts, plus the complete text of the Geniza fragments. But naturally other manuscripts had to be used as base texts for material not contained in N8128. Not all manuscript variations could be noted (e.g. variations in verbal themes or *plene* and defective spelling are not recorded), but given the importance of proper names (often magical) in this literature, all their variant spellings are included. Verbal forms are listed under their roots, though there is no attempt to assign nouns to their putative root forms.

The length of the context in which the key word is cited is variable. In contrast to the way in which the bulk of the material was processed, this crucial aspect of the work was done by hand. So the context given for each lemma may vary from a few words to a couple of lines, depending on the need for intelligibility. This is a great improvement on other computer-prepared concordances which often give a fixed number of words either side of the lemma regardless of the sense. The references given are to the relevant paragraph in the *Synopse* and to the folio and line number of the manuscripts. An attempt is made to single out corrupt readings, and sometimes a suggested emendation is offered.

This concordance is a very useful tool for research on the *Hekhalot Texts* and anybody working in this field will need to have access to it. But the cost is prohibitive. To purchase all four of the volumes mentioned in this review would cost around £400. Surely the days of this kind of expensive (tree-consuming!) publication are numbered. All this material could be made available, at a fraction of this cost, on floppy disk. Using machine-readable texts with suitable text-searching software is a far more efficient way for scholars to study large corpuses of texts like these. One day publishers will wake up to the fact that academics can afford floppy disks but not books that come with a price tag of £150!

A. P. HAYMAN

SEGAL, A. F.: *The Other Judaisms of Late Antiquity* (Brown Judaic Studies 127). 1987. Pp. xvii, 213. (Scholars Press, Atlanta, Georgia.) Price: $35.95 (member price: $23.95). ISBN 1 55540 178 3)

There is no strong central theme in this collection of Segal's articles although each of them partly focuses on non-rabbinical Judaism of the first few centuries, and it is the author's purpose to portray Judaism and Christianity over that period as deeply related Jewish movements. In 'Dualism and Judaism, Christianity and Gnosticism: A Definitive Issue', (pp. 1–40) the author tries to show that behind the variant traditions of 'two powers in heaven' was a halakhic, exegetical, sociological and theological issue about the status of angelic powers in first century Judaism. In 'The Ruler of This World' (pp. 41–77) the development of the tradition of the 'Ruler' or 'Lord of the World' in Christianity (negative portrayal) and Judaism (positive portrayal) is set in the context of communities in conflict. Conflict sharpened each group's central definition. The structural theory of mythology and anthropology of religion is applied to the problems of defining Hellenistic magic in 'Hellenistic Magic: Some Questions of Definition' (pp. 79–108). In 'The Sacrifice of Isaac in Early Judaism and Christianity' (pp. 109–30) the author argues that a literary appreciation of midrashic style contributes to a clearer understanding of the Akedah traditions. In the remaining essays 'Torah and *Nomos* in Recent Scholarly Discussion' (pp. 131–46), 'Covenant in Rabbinic Writings' (pp. 47–94) the major issues of law, covenant and dietary laws are discussed from the viewpoint of social psychology and sociology.

P. W. COXON

SIEGERT, F.: *Philon von Alexandrien. Über die Gottesbezeichnung 'wohltätig verzehrendes Feuer'* (De Deo) (Wissenschaftliche Untersuchungen zum Neuen Testament 46). 1988. Pp. viii, 190. Mohr (Paul Siebeck), Tübingen Price: DM 89.00. ISBN 3 16 145234 8; ISBN 0512 1604)

Philo's fragmentary work known as *De Deo* is preserved only in Armenian and has as a result been unduly neglected. Siegert, who had earlier included a German translation in his *Drei hellenistisch-jüdische Predigten* (1980; see *B. L.* 1981, p. 128), here devotes to the brief work a much more detailed study. After a short introduction he provides the Armenian original (reproduced from Aucher's edition), an annotated retroversion into Greek (a feasible exercise, seeing that the Armenian is a mirror version of the lost original), a new German translation based on the retroversion, and a valuable extended commentary. There are excellent indexes.

S. P. BROCK

STÄHLI, H.-P.: *Antike Synagogenkunst*. 1988. Pp. 112. (Calwer, Stuttgart. Price: DM. 29.80. ISBN 3 7668 0823 0)

The English reader, spoilt with books on Jewish art in general and synagogue art in particular, might be forgiven for finding the publication of this modest but attractively-produced little book in 1988 somewhat mystifying. Beginning from a rhetorical exclamation of surprise at the existence of a synagogue art (can there really be readers who still think that ancient Judaism was aniconic?), the author presents in successive chapters the often-discussed literary and archaeological evidence, ending with separate studies of Beth Alpha and Dura-Europos. There is a profusion of illustrations, many of them in colour, and a short bibliography (but, frustratingly, no index). The whole constitutes a useful first introduction to the subject; this reader's only serious complaint is that the author is content to tread in well-worn paths, and does not either subject his material to critical interrogation, or explore its wider implications. English readers will continue to be grateful for richer and more challenging books such as H. Shanks, *Judaism in Stone*, and L. I. Levine (ed.), *Ancient Synagogues Revealed* (see *B. L.* 1982, pp. 28 and 24 respectively).

N. R. M. de Lange

Wieser, F. E.: *Die Abrahamvorstellungen im Neuen Testament* (Europäische Hochschulschriften: Reihe 23, Theologie. Bd. 317). 1987. Pp. 209. (Lang, Bern, Frankfurt am Main, New York, Paris. Price: SwFr. 46.20. ISBN 3 261 03732 6)

In this thesis all the *direct* reference to Abraham in the New Testament are collated and compared. Wieser concludes that the relevant texts fall into two main categories: in the first the patriarch is seen as an exemplar of faith under fire (the *Bewährungsmodell*) and in the second as the object of God's free elective choice (the *erwählungsgeschichtliches Modell*). This model is subjected to a critical review, which leads to an important distinction between Abraham's natural progeny (*Sperma*) and his 'true' children (*Tekna*). Occasionally, as in Gal. 4, the two models are combined, and Paul avails himself freely of both. Other texts examined include Matthew, Luke-Acts, John, and Hebrews. Less significant passages, e.g. James 2:14–16, are given more cursory treatment. The book concludes with a useful survey of a large number of relevant passages in the Jewish literature.

J. F. Ashton

Will, E., Orrieux, C.: *Ioudaïsmos-Hellénismos: Essai sur le judaïsme judéen à l'époque hellénistique*. 1986. Pp. 230. (Presses Universitaires, Nancy. Price: Fr. 160.00. ISBN 2 86480 249 X)

Despite its title, this study devotes only one chapter to specifically cultural interaction, with little new to say apart from some stress on 'colonial' features of hellenization. The authors' overall view is that the collision of Judaism with Hellenism had less to do with exclusive claims made for the God of the Jews than with the problem of the law and 'its extension . . . of ethnic Judean culture' (p. 225). The rest of the book is essentially a narrative of the political history of Judea during the last three centuries B.C.E. Writing as ancient historians (one of them being also a biblical specialist), the authors give due weight to economic and broadly political factors in their interpretation of the various kinds of evidence they collate and compare. The focus is sharpest in the pages discussing the actions and motives of Antiochus IV during the crisis in Jerusalem; but elsewhere, too, some suggestive observations and questions are put forward on, for example, the nature of the early growth of the Diaspora in Egypt (p. 69), the possibility that the Diaspora in general supplied soldiers for the Maccabees' evidently well-equipped army (p. 160), and the light cast by the Temple Scroll on the political balance of the Hasmonean state (pp. 207ff). Apart from such points as these, a fairly familiar story is retold at too great length, with several wordy and fruitless excursuses on historiographical principle. Footnotes allude a little sparingly to some recent work, but there is no bibliography. Hengel's name occurs only twice, and there is no reference to his *Judaism and Hellenism*. There are no indices.

C. J. A. HICKLING

WILLIAMS, J. A.: *Biblical Interpretation in the Gnostic Gospel of Truth from Nag Hammadi.* (SBL Dissertation Series 79). 1988. Pp. 220 (Scholars Press, Atlanta, Georgia. Price: $15.95. ISBN 0 89130 876 8. Paperback price: $11.95. ISBN 0 89130 877 6)

The presumption of this book is that the Coptic *Gospel of Truth* (GTr), one of the major finds of the gnostic corpus from Nag Hammadi in Upper Egypt, derived from the hand of the second century gnostic theologian Valentinus and is in fact more a meditation on the gospel than a pristine 'gospel' *per se*. The study attempts to demonstrate that Valentinus used many of the writings that would form the New Testament. Seventy-three passages of the Coptic text are produced, the English translation of the original in parallel columns with the proposed New Testament literary sources, and the context of GTr and the New Testament passages are then discussed in detail with a comparison of common elements. Finally Valentinus' interpretation of the proposed source is discussed. Aside from Genesis, which is usually interpreted typologically, the texts that are used in GTr fall into three distinct groups: Matthew, the Johannine literature, and the Pauline literature. This study of GTr will interest not only specialists in the gnostic field but also will inform the biblical student of the depth of insight that Christians in the second century could bring to their interpretation of Christian texts.

P. W. COXON

ZAHAVY, TZ.: *The Mishnaic Law of Blessings and Prayers: Tractate Berakhot* (Brown Judaic Studies 88). 1987. Pp. xi, 159. (Scholars Press, Atlanta, Georgia. Price: $29.95. ISBN 1 55540 120 1)

This is a further instalment of the Brown project to describe and analyse the Mishnah tractate by tractate. Since the forms and general traits of Berakhot are similar to those of the other Mishnaic tractates, Zahavy sensibly does not repeat what Neusner and others have already adequately described in earlier studies, but concentrates on what is distinctive to his chosen material. He presents his analysis in the form of a running commentary which embodes a complete English version not only of Mishnah but also of Tosefta. The nature of this commentary differs radically from that of the usual academic commentary represented by Bunte's *Ohalot* (see above). Bunte's work is dominated by the traditional disciplines of philology and text-criticism, and treats the text atomistically, offering discrete glosses on individual *mishnayot*. Zahavy's approach is holistic and is concerned with the structure of thought and with discovering the unifying 'philosophy' behind the tractate. Under his skilful analysis, order emerges out of the surface confusion: chaps 1–3 of Berakhot are shown to deal with the *Shema'*, chaps 4–5 with the *Shemoneh 'Esreh*, chaps 6–9 with blessings relating to food. For Zahavy these three topics suffice to articulate a comprehensive and innovative phenomenology of prayer which deals with (1) the types of prayer (independent primary prayers which constitute the main elements of a ritual v. dependent secondary prayers which serve as adjuncts to other rituals); (2) the function of prayer as framing certain acts or rituals and marking them off as holy, or as framed by rituals and so set apart from ordinary activity; (3) the elements of prayer, notably its verbal and mental components (i.e. the act of recitation and the state of concentration). Berakhot has long been a popular tractate for study on Hebrew and Jewish Studies courses in universities and college. This book exemplifies a fruitful way of reading the Mishnah and teachers will undoubtedly find it a useful work to put in the hands of their students.

P. S. Alexander

10. PHILOLOGY AND GRAMMAR

Alonso Schökel, L. (ed.): *Materiales para un Diccionario Biblico Hebreo + Español*, I: *Parte Lexicografica (alef. bet-hmt)*. 1988. Pp. 364 (in 2 vols). (Biblical Institute Press, Rome. Price: Lire 6,000; 13,000)

These unpretentious volumes, reproduced from typescript and using only transliteration of the Hebrew, represent a significant attempt to come to terms with Hebrew semantics. They are refreshingly independent of the German–English lexicographical tradition, at many points compelling the user to rethink conventional categories. Each word is first glossed by a series of Spanish terms which can serve as translations in various contexts. Thereafter, the body of each article contains a semantic analysis with chapter and verse reference to illustrative examples, a certain amount of syntagmatic data, especially of the objects of verbs, and in some cases a collection of idioms, and a notation of synonyms and antonyms. There is no evidence of dialogue with contemporary linguistic theory, nor is there any introduction to the principles of the editor and his twelve named collaborators; but in many respects, both in what these volumes omit and in what they contain, the desiderata of a modern dictionary are implicitly supplied.

D. J. A. Clines

Amadasi Guzzo, M. G.: *Scritture alfabetiche* (Metodi). 1987. Pp. 248, and 16 tables. (Valerio Levi Editore, Roma. Price: Lire 28,000).

This survey describes the early history of several alphabetic scripts. Pride of place, of course, is given to the Ugaritic and Phoenician alphabets. In the author's opinion the Ugaritic writing system is an adaptation of an earlier alphabet to Mesopotamian cuneiform and was really syllabic in character. Also included in the survey are Hebrew, Phoenician, and Aramaic as well as the South Semitic scripts, the Greek alphabet and its derivatives, and the alphabets of ancient Italy. Early Indian writing systems are also mentioned, briefly.

The book is profusely illustrated, with 22 black and white photographs, 59 line drawings (tables of scripts and inscriptions) and four maps. There is a classified bibliography of 31 pages and a short index. In all, a handy introduction to a fascinating topic.

W. G. E. Watson

Beit-Arié, M., with E. Engel and A. Yardeni: *Specimens of Mediaeval Hebrew Scripts*, Vol. I: *Oriental and Yemenite Scripts* (in Hebrew, with an English Foreword) (The Hebrew Palaeography Project). 1987. Pp. vii, 14, and 154 plates. (Israel Academy of Sciences and Humanities, Jerusalem. ISBN 965 208 081 0)

The study of Hebrew palaeography has yet to reach maturity but if it has in recent years progressed from infancy to adolescence much of the credit is due to the co-operative efforts of Malachi Beit-Arié of Jerusalem and Colette Sirat of Paris in such projects as this. Here, plates and alphabet charts are superbly reproduced from 154 varied manuscripts (mainly from Oxford, Cambridge, Jerusalem, London, and New York) together with details of date, provenance, scribe, class-mark and size, as well as definition of handwriting. In the English preface and its slightly longer Hebrew equivalent the editor explains why he has been careful to use only two divisions for characterizing oriental handwriting, setting semi-cursive (*bēnōnī* or Rabbinic or Mashait) alongside the more cursive rather than defining it as an independent form, and that his future plans include a fuller and more systematic utilization of Genizah documents.

S. C. Reif

Fowler, J. D.: *Theophoric Personal Names in Ancient Hebrew: A Comparative Study* (JSOT Supplement Series 49). 1988. Pp. 321. (Sheffield Academic Press. Price: £20.50 ($34.95). ISBN 1 85075 038 6; 1 85075 039 4 (paperback))

In the two main parts of this work, Biblical and extra-Biblical theophoric names are classified and discussed with particular attention to what they reveal about conceptions of the deity; and then the results are compared with surveys of the Ugaritic, Phoenician, Amorite, Aramaic, Akkadian, and Palmyrene onomastica. A concluding chapter attends to the similarities and differences between these two bodies of material, and maintains that there are some distinctive characteristics in the Hebrew onomastica which accord well with our knowledge of Israelite religion. A series of appendixes provides lists of names of Jews in Babylonia, at Elephantine and of all ancient Hebrew theophoric personal names, which are then tabulated according to form and date. Fowler wrestles with some of the problems raised by the uneven distribution of names in the Old Testament, and though she manages to demonstrate weaknesses in Gray's treatment of the Chronicler, for instance (though these are not as great as she makes them appear, because she has misunderstood the basis on which Gray compiled his statistics; cf. his Appendix III), she nevertheless is unable to suggest a more convincing alternative explanation for the unusual features which remain even after her careful screening. In view of this and the uncertainties over whether the names included in our texts are fully representative of any given period, she wisely refrains from attempting any discussion of the history of Israelite religion. The chief value of this work is its painstaking collection and thoughtful classification of a mass of onomastic data which should serve as a resource for years to come.

H. G. M. Williamson

Fronzaroli, P. (ed.): *Miscellanea Eblaitica* I (Quaderni di Semitistica 15). 1988. Pp. ix, 279. (Dipartimento di Linguistica, Università di Firenze)

Six articles make up this volume, all written in Italian, and all but one substantial in size and content. They are studies based mainly on the published texts from Ebla, and all are technical and require knowledge of cuneiform and Sumerian to be handled critically. However, they are well informed, sober, and as reliable as the present state of knowledge permits. Four of them have interest for Old Testament studies and can be followed without Sumerian or cuneiform for the most part. The editor himself (pp. 1–33) reconstructs and edits with translation and comments part of a ritual attesting further the cult of dead kings at Ebla. M. V. Tonietti (pp. 79–119) collects the fascinating evidence for professional 'singers' (written in Sumerian *nar*, Semitic equivalent so far unknown). M. Bonechi (pp. 121–72) studies the verbal conjugational prefix *ti-* in various branches of Akkadian and in the tablets found at Ebla. A. Catagnoti (pp. 183–277) collects and studies personal names in Ebla tablets which employ kinship terms, *abu, aḫu, ʿammu*, etc.

W. G. Lambert

HUEHNERGARD, J.: *Ugaritic Vocabulary in Syllabic Transcription* (Harvard Semitic Studies 32). 1987. Pp. xviii, 371 and a 2-page addendum. (Scholars Press, Atlanta, Georgia. Price: $22.95 (member price: $14.95). ISBN 1 55540 201 1)

Yet another study of syllabically written Ugaritic words might seem superfluous. D. Sivan's *Grammatical Analysis and Glossary of the Northwest Semitic Vocables in Akkadian Texts of the 15th–13th C.B.C. from Canaan and Syria* (Neukirchen-Vluyn, 1984) has already been reviewed (*B.L.* 1985, p. 156) and there is also the unpublished dissertation on a similar topic by J. L. Body III (Chicago, 1975). Unlike these, however, Huehnergard's book draws 'its data from a linguistically uniform corpus of texts, those written by the scribes at Ugarit' (p. 16). Also, several new readings have led to the identification of many additional Ugaritic forms.

The book has three parts. After an introduction the polyglot vocabularies are set out, followed by a detailed commentary. There are some 235 entries, with equivalents in Sumerian, Akkadian, and Hurrian, though the spelling for only about 114 Ugaritic words can be determined. Part II is the glossary with words listed by root; most entries include a discussion section which is often quite lengthy. The final part is a description of the orthography and grammar used in the syllabic transcription. Bibliography and indices complete the volume; Hebrew words are listed but not the occasional Old Testament references in the body of the text. This is a reliable reference work which contributes to the understanding of Ugaritic vocabulary in terms of meaning and of pronunciation.

W. G. E. WATSON

KÖHN, R.: *Hebraisk grammatikk*, 3, utgave. 1988. Pp. 196. (Universitetsforlaget, Oslo. Price: N.Kr. 190.00. ISBN 82 00 02540 3)

This attractive little book is meant to be an introduction to Biblical Hebrew for students of theology in Norway. Whereas the two previous editions of this introductory grammar (1971) and 1972) were written as a companion to the somewhat larger *Lærebok i hebraisk grammatikk* by Harris Birkeland (Oslo 1949 and 1967), the present edition has been revised and expanded and can now be regarded as a satisfactory tool for beginners. Many pages of Köhn's book are nevertheless still heavily indebted to Birkeland's approach. Similar to not a few recent authors of introductions to Biblical Hebrew, Köhn has wanted to avoid the often rather inaccessible methods and terminology of traditional grammars. To quite some extent she has been successful in this. Against this background it is somewhat disappointing to find that the presentation of the verbal system occasionally appears to be more confusing than necessary.

There are thirty-five pages of paradigms, a rich subject index, and an index of biblical passages. The very short list of literature appears to be somewhat advanced in years and does not contain recent Anglo-American items at all. For a book of this kind the printers have done a satisfactory job, and all the Hebrew has come out very nicely. Altogether this is a book to be recommended.

H. M. BARSTAD

MEYER, R. and DONNER, H. (eds): *Wilhelm Gesenius Hebräisches und Aramäisches Handwörterbuch über das Alte Testament*. Eighteenth completely revised and enlarged edition. Fasc. 1: *Alef bis Gimel*. 1987. Pp. xxx, 233. (Springer Verlag, Berlin. Price: DM 248.00. ISBN 3 540 18206 3)

The publication of a new Hebrew dictionary, even its first volume, is a notable event, especially when the appearance of the volume is so attractive and clear. The editors stress how firmly this eighteenth edition stands in the tradition of Wilhelm Gesenius, but many readers will notice rather how many improvements the present volume introduces. Notable are the many Hebrew examples, phrases and clauses, each accompanied by German translation, illustrating 'constructions'. Equally welcome are the excisions of the older wordy explanations and the use of a taut precise syntax for the entries. Most articles have been thoroughly reworked, always with greater precision, more detail, or better organization.

This dictionary remains a dictionary of Biblical Hebrew (and Aramaic). The evidence of non-Biblical Hebrew, from Ben Sira, Qumran, and the inscriptions, has indeed been drawn upon to illustrate the Biblical vocabulary, and all the vocabulary of Ben Sira has been included, but there is no intention here to produce a dictionary of the classical Hebrew language. Such a privileging of the Biblical texts, however traditional, becomes increasingly hard to justify. One might also wonder whether the detailed listing of all attested Semitic cognates, constituting as much as 25 per cent of some pages, is not a somewhat baroque elaboration of a traditional feature of Hebrew lexicography that now needs reconsideration.

D. J. A. CLINES

MITCHELL, C. W.: *The Meaning of* BRK *'To Bless' in the Old Testament* (SBL Dissertation Series 95). 1987. Pp. xiii, 207. (Scholars Press, Atlanta, Georgia. Price: $21.95. ISBN 0 55540 002 7. Paperback price: $15.95. ISBN 0 55540 003 5)

In this very thorough study, Mitchell examines all 402 occurrences of the verb *bārak* and the noun *b^erākāh* in the Hebrew Bible, and discusses them under three heads, 'God blessing man', 'Man blessing man', and 'Man blessing God', each divided into subsections according to the type of blessing. He rejects all 'magical' ideas (that blessing can be obtained from sources other than God), and therefore the view of Pedersen and others that blessing derives from the strength of the 'soul' of the one who imparts the blessing. With Thiselton he also dismisses the idea that the Israelites believed that the spoken word possessed power in itself once it was uttered, interpreting the blessing of Isaac as a death-bed testament, partly on linguistic grounds, partly on the basis of archaeological evidence from Nuzi. Social custom, he suggests, plays a major part in the practice of blessing. The main effect of this is to move the cultural ideas of ancient Israel much closer to our own than has been common since the work of Pedersen and Mowinckel. There is a short summary of relevant linguistic theory at the beginning, and indexes of synonyms and antonyms of *brk* and the biblical verses containing the word.

C. S. RODD

MORAG, SH.: *Vocalised Talmudic Manuscripts in the Cambridge Genizah Collections*, Vol. I: *Taylor-Schechter Old Series* (Cambridge University Library Genizah Series 4). 1988. Pp. xii, 56 and 8 pages of plates. (Cambridge University Press. Price: £30.00 ($49.50). ISBN 0 521 26863 X)

The purpose of this monograph is 'to present and analyse the vocalised words that appear in the Talmud MSS of the Old Series of the Taylor-Schechter Genizah Collection'. The 168 MSS comprise mainly fragments of the Bavli, but the Yerushalmi, Alfasi, Halakhot Gedolot, and Vayyiqra Rabba are also represented. The texts, in both Hebrew and Aramaic, display different systems of vocalization — Tiberian, Babylonian, Palestinian, and Palestino-Tiberian. Though interested primarily in the vocalized *words*, Professor Morag provides extensive or complete transcriptions of some of the fragments. No. 95a, T–S F2(1).204 (= b.Hag. 13a–20a) is noteworthy for its striking divergences from the printed editions. This is a work of painstaking scholarship which makes a significant contribution to the study of *niqqud*.

P. S. Alexander

Müller, H.-P. (ed.): *Zeitschrift für Althebraistik*, Bd. 1/1. 1988. Pp. 145. (Kohlhammer, Stuttgart. Price: DM 89.00. ISSN 0932 4461)

This new periodical deserves a warm welcome. It fills a long existing gap in the range of studies with which the Society for Old Testament Study is — or ought to be — concerned. Its purpose is two-fold: to help consolidate what it calls 'Old Hebrew' studies within the Oriental disciplines, and to offer Biblical commentators a reliable philological basis for their researches. By *Althebraistik* is meant the language of the Old Testament along with the epigraphic remains of Ancient Israel and the Hebrew of the Samaritans, insofar as the evidence for the latter pertains to the pre-Christian era; but the Hebrew of the Qumran scrolls and Mishnaic Hebrew are excluded. This seems to me unnecessarily restrictive. If we are seriously intent on recovering the pronunciation and shape of Old Hebrew, the history of the language up to Massoretic times has to be taken very seriously indeed; and one of the most challenging problems in Hebrew studies at the moment is the relation of Scrolls Hebrew to Biblical Hebrew on the one hand and to Mishnaic on the other. I hope that it is not the intention of the editors to ignore these fascinating and vital problems.

In this initial number J. B. Curtis writes on the Hiphil Infinitive Absolute of *hālak*, J. H. Hospers on 'polarity', E. Jenni on the phrases *lšlwm* and *bšlwm*, B. Kedar-Kopfstein on 'synaesthesia', and E. Lipiński on traces of Sumero-Akkadian in Biblical Hebrew. There follows a long and important article by the editor, to be continued, on the linguistic background of Old Hebrew with special reference to the varied meanings of the 'perfect' conjugation. Two smaller studies complete the articles, one by St. Segert on geographical names and one by W. von Soden on the nominal form *ma/iqtāl*. At the end come two sections of documentation, one on recent bibliographical references to Old Testament words and constructions, and one on newly discovered epigraphic texts; these two sections will be regular features of the periodical.

The *ZAH*, as it asks to be called, promises to be a very valuable aid to Old Testament scholars, not least in challenging them to adopt a more professional approach to linguistic matter.

J. C. L. Gibson

Odisho, E. Y.: *The Sound System of Modern Assyrian* (Neo-Aramaic) (Semitica Viva 2). 1988. Pp. xvii, 146. (Harrassowitz, Wiesbaden. Price: DM 64.00. ISBN 3 447 02744 4; ISSN 0931 2811)

The phonetics of the Modern Aramiac of the Assyrian community will be somewhat remote for most Old Testament scholars, but the appearance of the new series Semitica Viva should be recognized. There is a brief study of the 'ethnolinguistic history' of the people and one also of relations between local speech-forms and the 'Koine'. Hebraists will recognize many of the words quoted, even if in rather unfamiliar forms. And surely someone will get an idea from the fact the same word appears to be used for both 'yesterday' and 'tomorrow' (p. 31)?

J. Barr

Revell, E. J.: *Nesiga (Retraction of Word Stress) in Tiberian Hebrew* (Textos y Estudios 'Cardenal Cisneros', 39). 1987. Pp. 155. (Instituto 'Arias Montano', Consejo Superior de Investigaciones Cientificas, Madrid. Price: Ptas 3,500) ISBN 84 00 06476 3; ISSN 0561 3481)

A highly technical subject from most people's point of view, and one little discussed in recent times; but handled by Dr Revell with precision, objectivity, and illuminativeness. The full index is particularly to be commended. A very substantial contribution to Hebrew linguistics. J. BARR

SAGARIN, J. L.: *Hebrew Noun Patterns* (Mishqalim): *Morphology, Semantics, and Lexicon* (Scholars Press handbook series). 1987. Pp. xiv, 149. (Scholars Press, Atlanta, Georgia. Price: $26.95 (member price: $19.95). ISBN 1 55540 030 2. Paperback price: $19.95 (member price: $13.95). ISBN 1 55540 031 0

Curiously enough, this is the first book in English to be devoted to the well-known feature of Hebrew grammar, the formation of nouns according to a limited number of patterns (*mishqalim*). The term has been used since the tenth century by Hebrew grammarians, and the phenomenon was treated by Y. Avineri in Hebrew (1976), and analysed briefly by A. Even-Shoshan in his Dictionary (1966–70) and by S. Barkai in his *Luah Hashemot* (1969), but Sagarin's handbook is the first listing of all words belonging to each *mishqal*. Sagarin recognizes 199 *mishqalim*, some with many variations, such as the four principal segholate types comprising seventeen different sub-types. For each type, the morphological peculiarities are displayed, followed by a list of nouns of the given type, in Hebrew with a simple English gloss. Biblical words are marked with an asterisk. The work is more interesting than useful; but the author may be right in supposing that advanced learners of the language will profit from it. The work is innocent of linguistic theory, historical linguistics and comparative Semitics, which do not fall within its purview.

D. J. A. CLINES

SCHWARZ, G.: *Jesus und Judas: Aramaistische Untersuchungen zur Jesus-Judas Überlieferung der Evangelien und der Apostelgeschichte* (BWANT 123). 1987. Pp. 308. (Kohlhammer, Stuttgart. Price: DM 69.00. ISBN 3 17 009663 X)

This book belongs more to New than to Old Testament studies but will be of special interest to SOTS members because of the rich use it makes of Aramaic in its attempt to solve the riddles surrounding the figure of Judas Iscariot. Judas was a 'man of the city', i.e. Jerusalem and, though the only Judaean among the twelve, enjoyed as close a relationship with Jesus as any of the others. In particular, he did not 'betray' Jesus, but 'handed him over' on Jesus's own instructions. The positive role he played has been overlaid by an anti-Judas tradition which, along with more widespread anti-Jewish traditions, has fatally obscured the course of events leading up to Jesus's death. This thesis is supported by detailed reconstructions of the original Aramaic behind the relevant Gospel passages, not a few of which seemed to me to carry conviction. A long and valuable Appendix investigates the nature of the sources which have to be manipulated and the methodology involved in such reconstructions. J. C. L. GIBSON

Books Received too Late for Notice in 1989

The books in the following list will be reviewed in the *Book List* for 1990.

AMSLER, S., LACOCQUE, A., VUILLEUMIER, R.: *Aggée—Zacharie—Malachie.* 2nd ed. (Commentaire de l'Ancien Testament XIc). 1988. (Labor et Fides, Genève. ISBN 2 8309 0131 2)

AUFRECHT, W. E., HAMILTON, G. J.: *The Tell Fakhariye Bilingual Inscription: A Bibliography* (Newsletter for Targumic and Cognate Studies, Supplement 4). 1988. (Department of Near Eastern Studies, University of Toronto. ISSN 0704 59005)

AXELSSON, L. E.: *The Lord Rose Up From Seir: Studies in the History and Traditions of the Negev and Southern Judah.* Translated by F. H. Cryer (Coniectanea Biblica, OT Series 25). 1987. (Almqvist & Wiksell, Stockholm. ISBN 91 22 00876 4)

BAR-EFRAT, SH.: *Narrative Art in the Bible.* Translated by D. Shefer-Vanson (JSOT Supplement Series 70; Bible and Literature Series 17). 1989. (Almond, Sheffield. ISBN 1 85075 138 2)

BAUCKHAM, R.: *The Bible in Politics: How to read the Bible politically* (A Third Way Book). 1989. (SPCK, London. ISBN 0 281 04402 3)

BLENKINSOPP, J.: *Ezra-Nehemiah* (Old Testament Library). 1989. (SCM, London. ISBN 0 334 00444 6)

BLOCK, P., BLOMQUIST, J., SUNDSTRÖM, G.-B., ÅSBERG, C.: *"God och nyttig läsning": Om Gamla Testamentets Apokryfer.* 1988. (Proprius förlag, Stockholm. ISBN 91 7118 624 7)

BOTTERWECK, G. J., RINGGREN, H., FABRY, H.-J. (eds): *Theologisches Wörterbuch zum Alten Testament.* Band VI, Lfg 8/10 (cols 865–1248). 1989. (Kohlhammer, Stuttgart. ISBN 3 17 010230 3)

BRUEGGEMANN, W.: *To Pluck Up, To Tear Down: A Commentary on the Book of Jeremiah 1–25* (International Theological Commentary). 1988. (Handsel, Edinburgh; Eerdmans, Grand Rapids, Michigan. ISBN 0 905312 87 2; ISBN 0 8028 0367 9)

CASSIRER, H. W.: *Grace and Law: St. Paul, Kant, and the Hebrew Prophets.* 1988. (Eerdmans, Grand Rapids, Michigan; Handsel, Edinburgh. ISBN 0 8028 0317 2; ISBN 0 905312 78 3)

CHARLESWORTH, J. H.: *Jesus within Judaism: New Light from Exciting Archaeological Discoveries.* 1989. (SPCK, London. ISBN 0 281 04406 6)

CLARKE, E. G. (ed.): *Newsletter for Targumic and Cognate Studies,* Vol. 15.2(1989). 1989. (Department of Near Eastern Studies, University of Toronto. ISSN 0704 59005)

COTTERELL, P., TURNER, M.: *Linguistics and Biblical Interpretation.* 1989. (SPCK, London. ISBN 0 281 04358 2)

DENIS, A.-M.: *Concordance grecque des pseudépigraphes d'Ancien Testament: Concordance, Corpus des Textes, Indices.* 1987. (Université Catholique de Louvain, Institut Orientaliste, Louvain-la-Neuve; distributed by Brill, Leiden. ISBN 90 04 09021 5)

ESKENAZI, T. C.: *In An Age of Prose: A Literary Approach to Ezra-Nehemiah* (SBL Monograph Series 36). 1988. (Scholars Press, Atlanta GA. ISBN 1 55540 260 7; ISBN 1 55540 261 5 (paperback)

FEWELL, D. N.: *Circle of Sovereignty: A Story of Stories in Daniel 1–6* (JSOT Supplement Series 72; Bible and Literature Series 20). 1988. (Almond, Sheffield. ISBN 1 85075 158 7)

FLANAGAN, J. W.: *David's Social Drama: A Hologram of Israel's Early Iron Age* (JSOT Supplement Series, 73; The Social World of Biblical Antiquity Series, 7). 1988. (Almond, Sheffield. ISBN 1 85075 201 X; ISBN 1 85075 202 8 (paperback))

García Martínez, F., Puech, E. (eds): *Mémorial Jean Carmignac: Etudes Qumrâniennes* (Revue du Qumran, Num. 49–52, Tome 13). 1988. (Gabalda, Paris. ISSN 0035 1725)

Gibson, S., Harris, R. L., Schonfield, J. (eds): *Bulletin of the Anglo-Israel Archaeological Society*, Vol. 7 (1987–8). 1988. (The Anglo-Israel Archaeological Society, London. ISSN 0266 2442)

Gowan, D. E.: *From Eden to Babel: A Commentary on the Book of Genesis 1–11* (International Theological Commentary). 1988. (Handsel, Edinburgh; Eerdmans, Grand Rapids, Michigan. ISBN 0 905312 85 6; ISBN 0 8028 0337 7)

Hartmann, G. H., Budick, S. (eds): *Midrash and Literature*. 1986, 1988. (Yale University Press, New Haven and London. ISBN 0 300 04198 5)

Jaeckel, T.: *Anything But a Quiet Life: Ideas of God in the Bible*. Translated from German by J. Bowden. 1989. (SCM, London. ISBN 0 334 01874 9)

Jastrow, O.: *Der neuaramäische Dialekt von Hertevin (Provinz Siirt)* (Semitica Viva, 3). 1988. (Harrassowitz, Wiesbaden. ISBN 3 447 02767 3)

Jervell, J. and Kapelrud, A. S.: *Studia Theologica: Scandinavian Journal of Theology*. Vol. 42, no. 2. 1988. (Norwegian University Press, Oslo. ISSN 0039 338 X)

Johnson, M. D.: *The Purpose of the Biblical Genealogies, with special reference to the setting of the genealogies of Jesus*. 2nd ed. (Society for New Testament Studies Monograph Series, 8). 1988. (Cambridge University Press. ISBN 0 521 35644 X)

Kampen, J.: *The Hasideans and the Origin of Pharisaism: A study in 1 and 2 Maccabees* (Septuagint and Cognate Studies 24). 1988. (Scholars Press, Atlanta GA. ISBN 1 55540 284 4; ISBN 55540 285 2 (paperback))

Khan, G.: *Studies in Semitic Syntax* (London Oriental Series 38). 1988. (Oxford University Press. ISBN 0 19 713607 9)

Kiraz, G. A.; *The Syriac Primer: Reading, Writing, Vocabulary & Grammar*. With a cassette recording by S. Adam and G. Kiraz (JSOT Manuals, 5). 1985, 1988. (Sheffield Academic Press. ISBN 1 85075 199 4; ISSN 0262 1754)

Kreuzer, S.: *Die Frühgeschichte Israels in Bekenntnis und Verkündigung des Alten Testaments* (BZAW 178). 1989. (De Gruyter, Berlin. ISBN 3 11 011736 3)

Krieg, M.: *Todesbilder im Alten Testament, oder "Wie die Alten den Tod gebildet"* (AThANT 73). 1988. (Theologischer Verlag, Zürich. ISBN 3 290 10006 5)

Krüger, T.: *Geschichtskonzepte im Ezechielbuch* (BZAW 180). 1989. (De Gruyter, Berlin. ISBN 3 11 011473 9)

Levine, E.: *The Aramaic Version of the Bible: Contents and Context* (BZAW 174). 1988. (De Gruyter, Berlin. ISBN 3 11 011474 7)

Levison, J. R.: *Portraits of Adam in Early Judaism, from Sirach to 2 Baruch* (Journal for the Study of the Pseudepigrapha Supplement Series 1). 1988. (Sheffield Academic Press. ISBN 1 85075 062 9)

Lewis, I. M.: *Ecstatic Religion: A study of shamanism and spirit possession*. 2nd edition. 1989. (Routledge, London and New York. ISBN 0 415 00799 2)

Lichtheim, M.: *Ancient Egyptian Autobiographies chiefly of the Middle Kingdom: A Study and An Anthology* (OBO 84). 1988. (Universitätsverlag, Freiburg (CH); Vandenhoeck & Ruprecht, Göttingen. ISBN 3 7278 0594 3; ISBN 3 525 53713 1)

Lindars, B., SSF: *Law and Religion: Essays on the Place of Law in Israel and Early Christianity*, by members of the Ehrhardt Seminar of Manchester University. 1988. (James Clarke, Cambridge. ISBN 0 227 67907 3)

Lipshitz, A. (ed.): *The Commentary of Rabbi Abraham Ibn Ezra on Hosea*, Edited from Six Manuscripts and Translated with an Introduction and Notes. 1988. (Sepher-Hermon, New York. ISBN 0 87203 127 6)

LOHFINK, N.: *Unsere neuen Fragen und das Alte Testament: Wiederentdeckte Lebensweisung* (Herder Taschenbuch 1594). 1989. (Herder, Freiburg. ISBN 3 451 08594 1)

MACCOBY, H.: *Judaism in the First Century* (Issues in Religious Studies). 1989. (Sheldon, London. ISBN 0 85969 550 6)

MANNS, F., O.F.M.: *John and Jamnia: How the break occurred between Jews and Christians c. 80–100 A.D.* Translated by M. Duel and M. Riadi. 1988. (Franciscan Printing Press, Jerusalem)

MCCREESH, T. P. (ed.): *Old Testament Abstracts.* Vol. 11, No. 3. 1988. (The Catholic University of America, Washington, D.C. ISSN 0364 8591)

VAN DER MEER, W. DE MOOR, J. C. (eds): *The Structural Analysis of Biblical and Canaanite Poetry* (JSOT Supplement Series 74). 1988. (Sheffield Academic Press. ISBN 1 85075 194 3)

MEYERS, C.: *Discovering Eve: Ancient Israelite Women in Context.* 1988. (Oxford University Press, New York and Oxford. ISBN 0 19 504934 9)

MINOKAMI, Y.: *Die Revolution des Jehu* (Göttinger Theologische Arbeiten 38). 1989. (Vandenhoeck & Ruprecht, Göttingen. ISBN 3 525 87391 3)

MÜLLER, G. (ed.): *Theologische Realenzyklopädie* (TRE), Bd.17: *Jesus Christ V — Katechismuspredigt.* 1988. (De Gruyter, Berlin. ISBN 3 11 011506 9)

NELSON, M. D.: *The Syriac Version of the Wisdom of Ben Sira compared to the Greek and Hebrew Materials* (SBL Dissertation Series 107). 1988. (Scholars Press, Atlanta GA. ISBN 1 55540 193 7; ISBN 1 55540 194 5 (paperback))

NIELSEN, K.: *There is Hope for a Tree: The Tree as Metaphor in Isaiah.* Translated from Danish by C. and F. Crowley (JSOT Supplement Series 65). 1989. (Sheffield Academic Press. ISBN 1 85075 182 X)

ODASHIMA, T.: *Heilsworte im Jeremiabuch: Untersuchungen zu ihrer vordeuteronomistischen Bearbeitung* (BWANT 125). 1989. (Kohlhammer, Stuttgart. ISBN 3 17 009842 X)

OLYAN, S. M.: *Asherah and the Cult of Yahweh in Israel* (SBL Monograph Series 34). 1988. (Scholars Press, Atlanta GA. ISBN 1 55540 253 4; ISBN 1 55540 254 2 (paperback)

POHLMANN, K.-F.: *Die Ferne Gottes — Studien zum Jeremiabuch* (BZAW 179). 1989. (De Gruyter, Berlin. ISBN 3 11 011828 9)

RAVASI, G.: *La terra promessa. Guida storica, archeologica e biblica della Palestina.* 1987. (EDB, Bologna. ISBN 88 10 80668 9)

ROGERSON, J. W., DAVIES, P. R.: *The Old Testament World.* 1989. (Cambridge University Press. ISBN 0 521 34006 3)

SAGGS, H. W. F.: *Civilisation before Greece and Rome.* 1989. (Batsford, London. ISBN 0 7134 5277 3)

SCHMIDT, W. H., THIEL, W., HANHART, R.: *Altes Testament* (Grundkurs Theologie, 1) (Urban-Taschenbücher, 421). 1989. (Kohlhammer, Stuttgart. ISBN 3 17 010267 4)

SCHREINER, J. (ed.): *Beiträge zur Psalmenforschung: Psalm 2 und 22* (Forschung zur Bibel 60). 1988. (Echter, Würzburg. ISBN 3 429 01174 4)

SCHWARZ, H.: *Die biblische Urgeschichte: Gottes Traum von Mensch und Welt* (Herder Taschenbuch 1608). 1989. (Herder, Freiburg. ISBN 3 451 08603 5)

SHANKS, H. (ed.): *Ancient Israel: A Short History from Abraham to the Roman Destruction of the Temple.* 1989. (SPCK, London. ISBN 0 281 04404 X)

STANSELL, G.: *Micah and Isaiah: A Form and Tradition Historical Comparison* (SBL Dissertation Series 85). 1988. (Scholars Press, Atlanta GA. ISBN 0 89130 962 4; ISBN 0 89130 963 2 (paperback))

STRECKER, G., MAIER, J.: *Neues Testament — Antikes Judentum* (Grundkurs Theologie, 2) (Urban-Taschenbücher, 422). 1989. (Kohlhammer, Stuttgart. ISBN 3 17 010266 4)

STROTHMANN, W. (ed.): *Wörterverzeichnis der apokryphen-deuterokanonischen Schriften des Alten Testaments in der Peshitta* (Göttinger Orientforschungen, I. Reihe: Syriaca, Bd.27). 1988. (Harrassowitz, Wiesbaden. ISBN 3 447 02683 9)

SUCUPIRA, L. (ed.): *Revista Biblica Brasileira.* Ano 6, 1–2. 1989. (Nova Jerusalém, Fortaleza CE. Brazil)

TÖKEI, F.: *Acta Orientalia Academiae Scientiarum Hungaricae.* Tom. XLI, Fasc. 2. 1987. (Akadémiai Kiado, Budapest. HU ISSN 0001 6446)

VERMES, G., GOODMAN, M.D. (eds): *The Essenes According to the Classical Sources* (An Oxford Centre Textbook). 1989. (Almond, Sheffield. ISBN 1 85075 139 0)

WÉNIN, A.: *Samuel et l'instauration de la monarchie (1 S 1–12)* (Europäische Hochschulschriften, Reihe XXIII, Bd. 342). 1988. (Lang, Frankfurt. ISBN 3 631 40384 4; ISSN 0721 3409)

WILLIAMSON, H. G. M.: *Annotated Key to Lambdings Introduction to Biblical Hebrew* (JSOT Manuals, 3). 1987, 1989. (Sheffield Academic Press. ISBN 1 85075 065 3; ISSN 0262 1754)

WRIGHT. T. R.: *Theology and Literature* (Signposts in Theology). 1988. (Basil Blackwell, Oxford. ISBN 0 631 14848 5; ISBN 0 631 14849 3 (paperback))

ZELLER. D. (ed.): *Menschwerdung Gottes — Vergöttlichung von Menschen* (Novum Testamentum et Orbis Antiquus 7). 1988. (Universitätsverlag, Freiburg (CH); Vandenhoeck & Ruprecht, Göttingen. ISBN 3 7278 0604 4; ISBN 3 525 53906 1)

VAN ZIJL, A.H.: *1 Samuel.* Deel I (De Prediking van het Oude Testament). 1988. (Callenbach, Nijkerk. ISBN 90 266 0739 3)

Index of Authors

(N.B. — Names occurring more than once in the same review or on the same page are listed on their first occurrence only.)

The Society for Old Testament Study is a British Society for Old Testament scholars. Candidates for membership, which is not confined to British subjects, must be nominated by two members of the Society. Residents of the British Isles are normally admitted to ordinary membership and non-residents to associate membership. All correspondence concerning domestic affairs of the Society should be sent to:

Dr P. M. Joyce
Ripon College
Cuddesdon
Oxford OX9 9EX
England

THE SOCIETY FOR

OLD TESTAMENT

STUDY

BOOK LIST

1990

Printed for the Society

ISBN 0 905495 08 X

The Society for Old Testament Study

BOOK LIST
1990

Printed for the Society

ISSN 0309 0892

ISBN 0 905495 09 8

PRINTED BY W. S. MANEY AND SON LTD HUDSON ROAD LEEDS LS9 7DL

Contents

One copy of the *Book List* is supplied free to all members of the Society.

Copies of the *Book List* for 1990 may also be obtained from M. E. J. Richardson, Esq., Department of Middle Eastern Studies, University of Manchester, Manchester M13 9PL, England. Back numbers of the *Book List* are also available from Mr Richardson. Orders should not be accompanied by payment; an invoice will be sent. The price of these is £12.50 including postage or $25.00, for a single copy. Payment should be made by cheque in sterling or U.S. dollars payable to the Society for Old Testament Study, or direct to Post Office Giro Account No. 50 450 4002.

Review copies of books for the *Book List* should be sent to the Editor:

Dr A. Graeme Auld
New College, Mound Place
Edinburgh EH1 2LX,
Scotland

PREFACE

It is a pleasure again this year to express my thanks to many colleagues abroad and at home who have drawn many titles to my attention, and in several cases have supplied reviews from personal copies of books. The *Book List* never achieves the sort of completeness to which it aspires. But its coverage would this year have been very much less adequate had it not been for the friendly cooperation of Professor B. Albrektson, Professor H. Cazelles, Dr F. García Martínez, Dr K. Jeppesen, Dr K. Nielsen, Professor G. L. Prato, Dr K. K. Sacon, and Professor A. S. van der Woude; and, within these islands, of Professor G. W. Anderson, Dr R. P. Carroll, Mr R. J. Coggins, Professor K. A. Kitchen, Professor M. A. Knibb, Mr A. R. Millard, Dr S. C. Reif, Professor J. W. Rogerson, Dr W. G. E. Watson, Professor R. N. Whybray, and Dr N. Wyatt. Of course a very much larger number of members of the Society have answered as ever my invitations to review. I also gladly draw attention to the publishers who offer, and readily respond to requests for books; and our printers, Messrs W. S. Maney and Son, who turn script processed in many different ways into clear and accurate publishable type.

The sixth and seventh Newsletters charting the steady progress of the Comprehensive Aramaic Lexicon were received in Spring and Autumn 1989. The editors of CAL, based in the Department of Near Eastern Studies, The Johns Hopkins University, Baltimore MD 21218, USA welcome offprints or notification of publication of all Aramaic studies. The fourth trimestrial number of *Interface* was received at the end of 1989 from CIB-Maredsous, B-5198 Denée, Belgique, with news from the world of the merging worlds of computing and biblical studies — and details of varied subscription methods. And the *Revista Bíblica Brasileira* (which remains one of our warmest supporters) sent us not only the fascicles of year 6, but a set of two bound volumes containing years 1–3 and 4–6, and costing together $100.

The following abbreviations and symbols are employed as in earlier issues:

B.L. = *Book List*
Eleven Years = *Eleven Years of Bible Bibliography* (1957)
Decade = *A Decade of Bible Bibliography* (1967)
Bible Bibliog. = *Bible Bibliography 1967–1973: Old Testament* (1974)

NEW COLLEGE EDINBURGH — A. GRAEME AULD

1. GENERAL

Abramo, padre di una moltitudine di uomini. Atti del Seminario invernale (Rocca di Papa, 28–31 gennaio 1988). 1989, Pp. 277. (BIBLIA: Associazione laica di cultura biblica, Settimello (FI). Price: Lire 10,000)

This volume contains, without introduction or conclusion, ten papers presented to this Seminar on the theme of Abraham. Alberto Soggin begins with a consideration of the historical basis of the biblical traditions, which stem from a later age, and Giuseppe Laras ends with a survey of Abraham in Jewish tradition. Four of the remaining contributions, two of them by L. Alonso Schökel, deal with particular narratives concerning Abraham, one consists of five classical comments on the *ʿaqedah*, one considers its place in anthropology and the history of religion, one considers the women in Abraham's circle, and one surveys Abraham and Ishmael in Islamic tradition. All these non-specialist studies are concerned with the significance of Abraham in Jewish, Christian, and Islamic tradition. The diffusion of scholarship in the context of interconfessional dialogue is to be welcomed, and the publication of the essays will enrich the understanding of a wider public.

A. GELSTON

ALBERTZ, R., GOLKA, F. W., and KEGLER, J. (eds): *Schöpfung und Befreiung. Für Claus Westermann zum 80. Geburtstag*. 1989. Pp. 284. (Calwer, Stuttgart. Price: DM 48.00. ISBN 3 7668 3034 1)

This celebration of a further decade in the life of a great Old Testament scholar has among its joint editors one of the editors (Albertz) of the previous *Festschrift* (see *B. L.* 1981, pp. 7f) and one of its contributors (Golka). Nineteen articles are grouped in four sections: Torah and Narrative, Prophecy, Psalms and Wisdom, and Judaism and Christianity as Inheritors of the Old Testament. G. Liedke writes on the contribution of Gen. 1 to the ecological crisis; J. J. Scullion on original sin in Gen. 1–11 and Romans 5:12; Albertz on the intentions of the Deuteronomistic historical work and its representatives; and Kegler on the diminished significance of the exodus tradition in the books of Chronicles. J. R. Porter contributes a study of the supposed Deuteronomic redaction of the prophets; E. Rupprecht, of the call of Jeremiah 'in his youth' and his 'early preaching'; H. Weippert, of creation and salvation in Jer. 45; M. Weippert, of the 'confessions' of Deutero–Isaiah; M. Saebø, of some inner-biblical interpretations — from the individual to the collective; and W. Brueggemann, of a poem of summons (Isa. 55:1–3) and a narrative of resistance (Dan. 1:1–21). Then F. Crüsemann, in a study entitled 'In the Net', seeks to answer Gunkel's question about the specific emergency that gives rise to the complaint of the individual; Golka compares Biblical and African wisdom expressed in proverbial sayings; M. Augustin discusses the Marxist interpretation of Job by M. Machovec; and H.-P. Müller writes on new aspects of the questions tabled by Job. Finally, R. Rendtorff discusses W. Vischer and G. von Rad under the heading 'Christological exegesis as "deliverance" of the Old Testament'; H. E. Tödt writes on the Protestant Church and the Jewish pogrom in November 1938; D. Vetter discusses learning and teaching in Old Testament, Judaism, and New Testament; R. Landau urges the contemporary relevance for Christian congregations of aspects of F. Rosenzweig's Free Jewish Study-House in Frankfurt of the 1920's; and U. Bergmann poses the question of Melanesian Christians to theology and church praxis in Europe, America, and Australia: 'Has the Bible a message for the whole of humanity?'

A. G. AULD

Anis al-Assiouty, S.: *Origines Égyptiennes du Christianisme et de l'Islâm* (Recherches comparées sur le Christianisme Primitif et l'Islâm Premier III). 1989. Pp. 296. (Letouzey et Ané, Paris. Price: Fr 118.00. ISBN 2 7063 0175 9)

This is the third volume of a series devoted to Christian and Islamic origins. At the end of the second volume the author has concluded that Jesus' family was non-Jewish: his mother was an Egyptian woman resident in Galilee.

The present volume, sub-titled 'Résultat d'un siècle et demi d'archéologie', sets out to explore the 'historical realities' about Jesus and the 'dialectical evolution' of Muhammad. The author has amassed a vast collection of data from ancient Egyptian, Jewish, Islamic, and early Christian sources but shows little critical ability in evaluating and comparing them. The *Gospel of Peter* is treated as a serious historical source and from the remark in b*Shabbath* 104b that Ben Stada brought spells from Egypt in a cut in his flesh it is argued that Jesus was educated in Egypt and studied medicine in a school attached to some Egyptian temple. The description of Jesus' 'triumphal' entry into Jerusalem is explained by the consideration that Passover was a festival of Egyptian origin, commemorating the passion of Osiris. As for Islam, 'Egypto-Christian thought forms the general framework of Koranic concepts' (p. 225). The work is copiously documented from the author's wide reading, and a study of the footnotes could supply the basis, to anyone so minded, for a more scientific assessment of the historical and literary data.

F. F. Bruce

Arai, S., Ishida, T. et alii (eds): *Kyūyaku Shinyaku Seisho Dai-jiten*. 1989. Pp. 1454 with numerous illustrations, maps, and indexes. Three large maps are also appended. (Kyobunkwan, Tokyo. Price ¥46,350. ISBN 4 7642 4006 8 C 3516)

With the consent of Vandenhoeck & Ruprecht, this one volume Japanese edition of *Biblisch-historisches Handwörterbuch*, 1966–1979, was updated with translation, supplements or entirely new articles replacing the original. A 43-page chronological chart from B.C. 10,000 to A.D. 200 is freshly attached to this volume. About 70 collaborators, including six capable editors working ten years, accomplished the dictionary to a high standard.

K. K. Sacon

Baarda, T., Hilhorst, A., Luttikhuizen, G. P. and van der Woude, A. S. (eds): *Text and Testimony. Essays on New Testament and Apocryphal Literature in Honour of A. F. J. Klijn*. 1988, Pp. 286. (Kok, Kampen. Price: fl 75.75. ISBN 90 242 3404 2)

The majority of the 25 contributions are concerned with New Testament topics. Those of more direct interest to readers of the *Book List* are J. H. Charlesworth, 'Biblical interpretation: the crucible of the Pseudepigrapha'; F. García Martínez, 'Les limites de la communauté: pureté et impureté à Qumrân et dans le NT'; A. Hilhorst, 'Biblical metaphors taken literally'; M. de Jonge, 'Jesus' death for others and the death of the Maccabean martyrs'; G. P. Luttikhuizen, 'The Jewish factor in the development of the Gnostic myth of origins'; J. Reiling, 'Wisdom and the Spirit' (on I Cor. 2:6-16); J. Roldanus, 'L'héritage d'Abraham d'après Irenée'; and K. Treu, '"Apocryphe relatif à Jacob et Joseph" (Van Haelst no. 571) und der Sitz im Leben von Apocrypha Papyri'. The volume concludes with a bibliography of Klijn's writings.

S. P. Brock

BARBLAN, G. (ed.): *Dante e la Bibbia. Atti del Convegno Internazionale promosso da "Biblia" (Firenze, 26–27–28 settembre 1986)* (Biblioteca dell' "Archivum Romanicum", Serie I, Vol. 210). 1988. Pp. 370. (Olschki Editore, Firenze. Price: Lire 58,000. ISBN 88 222 3580 0)

This volume contains the papers of a conference on 'Dante and the Bible', organized in Florence in 1986 by the association 'Biblia', founded two years earlier to foster knowledge of and interest in the Bible on the part of the widest possible public. Dante scholars from many countries were invited and the conference was attended by more than 800 participants. This was clearly a most imaginative interdisciplinary initiative and of great value for the history of culture, but the biblical focus of these twenty papers is more on Dante's relationship to the methods of mediaeval exegesis (perhaps half the papers) than on the Old Testament in itself. In fact only one is precisely thus focused, namely that by Rachel Jacoff on 'Dante, Jeremiah and the problem of the prophet's role'. She argues convincingly that a number of images and phrases in Dante, expressing the poet's anger and agony that his moral message will not be heard, can be traced to his reading of Jeremiah. The other paper which comes closest to Old Testament texts is by Menachem E. Artom, 'Biblical and Talmudic precedents on retribution' [i.e. Dante's understanding of it], showing that talion is too narrow a term to do justice to any of the three. For the rest, more articles are focused on New Testament themes, especially in the Book of Revelation.

R. P. R. MURRAY

BECKING, B., VAN DORP, J., and VAN DER KOOIJ, A. (eds), *Door het oog van de profeten. Exegetische studies aangeboden aan prof. dr. C. van Leeuwen* (Utrechtse Theologische Reeks, 8). 1989. Pp. 171 (Faculteit der Godgeleerdheid. Rijksuniversiteit te Utrecht. ISBN 90 72235 08 8)

This volume, presented to Professor van Leeuwen on the occasion of the 12½th anniversary of his professorship at the State University of Utrecht, contains, besides a preface and a bibliography, thirteen articles (mostly in Dutch) of which the majority is concerned with Old Testament prophetism. B. Becking compares Jer. 31:15–17 with Matth. 2:18; P. Beentjes deals with prophecy in the Wisdom of Ben Sira; and Fokkelien van Dijk-Hommes treats Jer. 31:22b. J. van Dorp provides annotations to 1 Kings 22:2b and A. van der Kooij studies the Greek text of Amos 9:11–12. B. Maarsingh comments on Ezech. 43:8ab. Ophira Shapiro surveys medieval Jewish commentaries on Joel 2:1–11. K. Smelik deals with Jeremiah 26 from a literary point of view, and J. van Soest examines the structure of Judges 3 and 4. N. Tromp treats Psalm 122 and K. Vriezen investigates the vocabulary of roads and road-construction in the Prophets and the Writings. Helga and Manfred Weippert offer an interesting study on Solomon's judicial decision (1 Kings 3) by comparing the text of the story with the petition of Mezad Hashavjahu. Finally, T. Wever wants to translate *tamîd* in Hab. 1:17 by 'O Eternal' and finds an *inclusio* with 1:12. There is much to be learnt from the variegated contributions to this *Festschrift*.

A. S. VAN DER WOUDE

BERGERHOF, K., DIETRICH, M., LORETZ, O. (eds): *Ugarit-Forschungen: Internationales Jahrbuch für die Altertumskunde Syrien-Palästinas*. Vol. 20 (1988). 1989. Pp. vi, 418. (Neukirchener, Neukirchen-Vluyn; Butzon & Bercker, Kevelaer. Price: DM. 104.00. ISBN 3 7887 1310 0; 3 7666 9640 8; ISSN 0342 2356)

This volume is dedicated to Loretz on the occasion of his sixtieth birthday, and a photograph of him appears as a frontispiece. In addition to other articles on Near Eastern subjects, the following essays of direct interest to Old Testament scholars may be noted. G. del Olmo Lete's discussion of *ṯ‘*, *ṯ‘y* and *ṯ‘t* in Ugaritic detects a root **ṯw‘* cognate with Hebrew *šôa‘*. J. F. Healey considers the lexicography of Ugaritic in relation to Hebrew, Aramaic, and other Semitic languages. K. Koch examines the evidence for the worship of Asherah as the queen of heaven in Judah, and traces it to Assyrian influence in the period before Josiah. W. T. Koopmans analyses the structure of Ps. 78:40–55. W. G. Lambert defends his interpretation of an Accadian text and refutes the attempt of D. T. Tsumura to relate the text to *tōhû wābōhû* in Gen. 1:2. J. C. de Moor argues that the Moabite Stone and the Zakkur and Kilamuwa inscriptions were written as narrative poetry and suggests that vestiges of such poetry may be found in the Old Testament. An article by de Moor and H. F. de Vries maintains that Hebrew *hêdād* means 'thunderstorm'. M. H. Pope argues that vocative *lamedh* is to be found in Ps. 119:126 and also 3:9 (emended), and that 'Hosanna in the highest' in the New Testament arose from a misunderstanding of a Semitic original that meant 'Save, now, O Most High.' F. Renfroe's discussion of several words includes the view that the meaning 'sich drehen, winden' is most likely for the root *brḥ* in Isa. 27:1 and its Ugaritic parallel. U. Rüterswörden discusses the symbolism of the bow in Gen. 9. A. Schoors refutes M. J. Dahood's theory that Ecclesiastes was originally written in Phoenician orthography. W. von Soden examines Hebrew *'etnān* in the light of its cognates. D. T. Tsumura advances the hypothesis that *lammabbûl* in Ps. 29:10 means 'since before the Deluge'.

J. A. Emerton

Bigger, S. (ed.): *Creating the Old Testament: The Emergence of the Hebrew Bible*. 1989. Pp. xx, 364. (Basil Blackwell, Oxford and Cambridge MA. Price: £37.50; paperback price: £9.95. ISBN 0 631 16249 6)

We are told that the idea of this book grew out of discussion in the Society for Old Testament Study, fertile soil for the germination of fruitful thought. A need was felt for an introductory book for 'students, teachers, churches and synagogue study groups, and general readers'. There is always a problem about 'Introductions'. Are they to introduce the text and contents of the bible itself or the work and methods of scholars? The editor mentions D. J. A. Clines' distinction between 'first-order' and 'second-order' methods and claims that this book seeks to strike a balance between 'literary and historical methods'. Adrian Curtis opens with a chapter on 'The Hebrew World' and this is followed by a treatment of 'The Authority and Use of the Hebrew Bible' from Jewish, Christian, Muslim, and Humanistic perspectives. The editor provides a useful chapter on 'Symbolism and Metaphor in the Hebrew Bible' and then come the main sections on 'Torah', 'Prophets' (K. Whitelam on the 'Former Prophets, P. R. Davies on 'Jerusalem', M. W. Thompson and the editor on prophetic narrative, and A. Graeme Auld on 'Prophecy and the Prophets'). R. J. Coggins, R. Tomes, D. J. Clines, S. Sheridan, and M. Barker contribute to the final section on 'The Writings'. The editor and contributors are to be congratulated on both and the conception and production of this book, made all the more useful by its judicious lists of items headed 'Further Reading'. Let is hope for the fruits of many more such discussions at the bar in meetings of the Society.

R. A. Mason

Botterweck, G. J., Ringgren, H., Fabry, H.-J. (eds): *Theologisches Wörterbuch zum Alten Testament*. Band VI, Lfg 8/10 (cols 865–1248). 1989. (Kohlhammer, Stuttgart. Price: DM. 124.00. ISBN 3 17 010230 3)

This triple fascicle begins with the final part of the article on *ṣō'n* (E.-J. Waschke) and ends with the first part of that on *qōl* (B. Kedar-Kopfstein). It contains fifty-two complete articles. A single forthcoming fascicle will complete the volume. The principal articles in terms of length are those on Zion (*ṣiyyōn*, thirty-three columns, E. Otto), *ṣādaq* (with *ṣedeq*, *ṣedāqāh* and *ṣaddīq*, twenty-six columns, Ringgren and B. Johnson), *ṣwh* (twenty-three columns, F. García López — but *miṣwāh* has already been treated in an earlier volume), *qdš* and cognates (twenty-three columns, W. Kornfeld and Ringgren), *qāhāl* (and cognates, and including a brief discussion of *qōhelet*, eighteen columns, F. L. Hossfeld, Kindl and Fabry), and *ṣebā'ōt* (seventeen columns, H.-J. Zobel). Other terms of particular religious or theological importance include those on *ṣābā'* (Ringgren), *ṣūm* (with *ṣōm*, H. D. Preuss), *ṣelem* (F. J. Stendebach), *ṣāpōn* (E. Lipiński) and *qeber* with cognates (K. Koch). As usual some words discussed -e.g. *ṣe'eṣā'īm* (D. Kellermann), *ṣoh°rayim* (H. Niehr), *ṣī* (H.-P. Müller), *ṣemer* (U. Rüterswörden) — are of only minor relevance. Since it is hardly possible or desirable to include *every* term which is used metaphorically in the Old Testament in a religious context, it is not clear on what basis some of these words have been chosen for inclusion.

There are a number of cross-references to words which have been or will be dealt with elsewhere: *ṣūq* II (under *yṣq*), *ṣāḥaq* (*śāḥaq*), *ṣinnāh* (*māgēn*), *ṣā'aq* (*zā'aq*).

The article on Zion is remarkable for the immense bibliography of more than 380 items. *ṣar* I and II with their cognates are dealt with in separate articles (by Fabry and Ringgren respectively), but the distinction between the two is held to be uncertain. *qādīm*, *qedem* and cognates and *qādam* (all by T. Kronholm) have each a separate article, comprising fourteen columns in all.

R. N. Whybray

Botterweck, G. J., Ringgren, H., Fabry, H.-J. (eds): *Theologisches Wörterbuch zum Alten Testament*. Band VI, Lfg 11 (cols 1249–1274, index and title pages). 1989. (Kohlhammer, Stuttgart. ISBN 3 17 010230 3)

This final fascicle of Band VI, which is supplied with a binding cover for the volume, consists mainly of the usual concluding matter: a list of subjects and themes in German, a select index of biblical references (references to the literature of Qumran, though regularly covered in the articles, are not included) and corrigenda. The last of these items includes not only corrigenda to this volume but also additional corrigenda to volumes IV and V. Only two articles appear here: *qōl*, by B. Kedar-Kopfstein, continued from Band V, and *qūm*, by J. Gamberoni. The fascicle concludes with the preliminary matter to be placed at the beginning of the volume when bound: title page, list of contributors to the volume, and table of contents — the last of these surely unnecessary in an alphabetically arranged dictionary.

R. N. Whybray

Brekelmans, C. (ed.): *Continuing Questions in Old Testament Method and Theology*. Revised and expanded edition edited by M. Vervenne (Bibliotheca Ephemeridum Theologicarum Lovaniensium XXXIII). 1989. Pp. 244. (University Press, Leuven; distributed by Peeters, Leuven. Price: BFr. 1,200. ISBN 90 6186 332 5)

The first edition of these essays, presented first at the 23rd session of the *Colloquium Biblicum Lovaniense* in 1972, was published in 1974 (see *B. L.* 1975, pp. 8–9) under the French title *Questions disputées d'Ancien Testament: Méthode et Théologie*, a title maintained on the title-page although the front cover of this new edition uses only the English sub-title. The eleven papers are reproduced unchanged; but supplementary discussion and bibliography for each has been provided on pp. 205–222, mostly by the original authors but by

M. Vervenne for P. A. H. de Boer, M. Dahood, and D. J. McCarthy. The questions addressed, biblical semantics, covenant, and biblical theology, continue to be as open now as when they were addressed in the early seventies at Leuven.

A. G. AULD

BUSI, G. (ed.): *ʿOvadyah Yare da Bertinoro e la presenza ebraica in Romagna nel Quattrocento*. Atti del Convegno di Bertinoro 17–18 maggio 1988. Supplemento a "Henoch" Anno XI, 1 (Quaderni di Henoch 1). 1989. Pp. xvi, 3 plates, pp. 111. (Silvio Zamorani, Torino. Price: Lire 25,000. ISBN 88 7158 001 X)

Obadiah of Bertinoro is best remembered today for his commentary on the Mishnah, which usually accompanies the traditional printed texts. His supercommentary on Rashi on the Pentateuch, however, is virtually forgotten, although it is an important work that deserves to be better known, as Bruno Chiesa explains in a valuable short description. The other contributions to this volume are mainly concerned with aspects of the history of the Jews in the Romagna.

N. R. M. DE LANGE

CATHCART, K. J. and HEALEY, J. F. (eds): *Back to the Sources: Biblical and Near Eastern Studies in honour of Dermot Ryan*. 1989. Pp. 191. (Glendale, Dublin. Price: £19.50. ISBN 0 907606 61 X)

This collection was planned as a 65th birthday *Festschrift* but, sadly, it had to become a memorial volume for this scholar who was Professor of Semitic Languages at University College, Dublin and then became Archbishop of that city. Seven of the eight pieces are by former students of Dr Ryan's, while the eighth is by his successor in his chair, K. J. Cathcart. The papers relevant to this *Book List* are: 'Biblical Theology and the History of Israelite Religion' (J. J. Collins: the post-Childs dilemma still allows real possibilities); 'The Last of the Rephaim' (J. F. Healey: Ryan's unpublished thesis of 1954 is appreciated and the present state of the *rpʾum/rephaʾim* question surveyed); 'The Treatment of Biblical Anthropomorphisms in Pentateuchal Targums' (C. McCarthy, RSM: a useful analysis which brings some needed precision to several points); 'Some Observations on the Dating of Targum Job' (C. Mangan, OP: on the rabbinic Targum, not 11QTgJob, though they are compared); 'Psalms as Prayers of the Poor' (J. McPolin, SJ: a careful summary of the textual data but also on using this aspect of the Psalms today), and 'The Biblical and Other Early Christian Manuscripts of the Chester Beatty Library (K. J. Cathcart: a valuable description with 15 plates). The subjects of the other two pieces lie respectively in the Synoptic Gospels and in the Arabic literature of appreciation of calligraphy.

R. P. R. MURRAY

CHARLESWORTH, J. H.: *Jesus within Judaism: New Light from Exciting Archaeological Discoveries*. 1989. Pp. xvi, 265. (SPCK, London. Price: £9.95. ISBN 0 281 04406 6)

In this unabashedly confident, popularising book, Charlesworth enthuses about the contribution of the Pseudepigrapha, the Dead Sea Scrolls, the Nag Hammadi documents (to be precise, the Gospel of Thomas), and various recent archaeological discoveries to what must now be called 'Jesus research' (to distinguish it from the more theologically motivated old and new quests for the historical Jesus). Pseudepigraphical studies show Jesus was influenced by apocalyptic ideas (especially the Son of Man in Dan. 7 and 1 Enoch 37–51), by eschatology, and by ideas of sin and forgiveness common in early Judaism. The Qumran literature shows that though Jesus was hardly an Essene he shared the same milieu. The Gospel of Thomas is an important witness to the Jesus tradition, but this derives from Syrian Christianity and is heavily dependent on Judaism. All this shows that Jesus belonged within Judaism, and that enables us to reconstruct something of Jesus' concept of God and even of his own self-understanding as son of God. Here Charlesworth relies too much on 'Abba' (shades of Jeremias; Barr is not yet in sight) and on the parable of the wicked tenant farmers (Mk 12, Gospel of Thomas 65).

Charlesworth is conducting several crusades — against negative criticism which would deny that we can ever know much about Jesus, and against confident conservatism which would assert that we can read the *ipsissima verba Jesu* (Charlesworth is concerned 'not with the sound of his own voice [*ipsissima vox*], but with the meaning he poured forth', p. 166; but if we cannot hear the *ipsissima vox*. . . .?). Charlesworth is also concerned to discount Perrin's 'principle of discontinuity', for that, taken to its logical end, would take Jesus outside Judaism. Charlesworth's somewhat sensationalist approach may irritate *Book List* readers, but they will find useful the survey of 'son of God' texts from early Judaism (pp. 149–52), the guide to major books on Jesus from 1980–1984 (pp. 187–207), and the selected and annotated bibliography on the Jesus of history (pp. 223–243).

J. R. Bartlett

Clements, R. E. (ed.): *The World of Ancient Israel: Sociological, anthropological and political perspectives*. Essays by Members of the Society for Old Testament Study. 1989. Pp. xi, 436. (Cambridge University Press. Price: £45.00 ($65.00). ISBN 0 521 34243 0)

The Society for Old Testament Study continues its long tradition of useful summaries of Old Testament scholarship. As the subtitle suggests, the focus is generally sociological and anthropological even when the essays have a fairly traditional title. The editor introduces the subject, followed by general essays on anthropology (J. W. Rogerson) and sociology (A. D. H. Mayes). Most of the essays after that focus on individual institutions or topics of current interest: the ecology and settlement patterns in the Late Bronze-Iron I (F. S. Frick); Israel as a tribal society (J. D. Martin); kingship (K. W. Whitelam); the changing significance of the term 'Israel' in the transition to the post-exilic period (H. G. M. Williamson); origins of the Diaspora (R. J. Coggins); law (B. S. Jackson); prophecy (R. P. Carroll); wisdom (R. N. Whybray); apocalypticism (P. R. Davies); holiness and the cult (P. J. Budd); holy war (G. H. Jones), covenant (R. Davidson); the land (E. W. Davies); women (G. I. Emmerson); and life and death (M. A. Knibb).

This is a very informative work, not the least of whose merits is its being quite up to date (bibliographical entries even for 1988 in some cases). There is little formal overlap between it and the recent Society of Biblical Literature volume, *The Old Testament and its Modern Interpreters* (*B. L.* 1986, p. 18), and the two complement each other well. One area deserves criticism, however: the use of chapter endnotes, so that one has to flip first to the notes then to the bibliography to follow up a reference. Surely CUP is still capable of producing footnotes.

L. L. Grabbe

Elayi, J., Sapin, J. (eds): *Transeuphratène* I: Études sur la Syrie-Palestine et Chypre à l'Époque perse. 1989. Pp. 199 and v pp. of plates. (Gabalda, Paris. Price: Fr 235.00. ISBN 2 85021 036 6)

All the articles in the first issue of this new periodical are relevant to Old Testament studies inasmuch as Judah was part of the Persian Empire, but some are more pertinent than others. E.-M. Laperrousaz argues that Nehemiah's Jerusalem embraced the Western Hill, then, observing the cessation of Jewish governors with the fall of Persia, asks if the theocratic state which followed is reflected in Chronicles. A. Lemaire usefully lists and describes Semitic inscriptions of Persian times from Palestine and Transjordan, including seals and seal impressions, revealing a great mixture of personal names from the whole of the Fertile Crescent, and the common use of Aramaic script. Among the seal impressions are those thought to name governors of Judah. E. Lipiński re-interprets the crucial *pḥw'* as 'steward', not 'governor', by derivation from an Accadian verb once found as 'to stop a jar'; he stresses the problems of the translation 'governor', but his own is no more convincing. Gaza in the Persian Period is the topic of H. J. Katzenstein's detailed essay. M. Heltzer analyzes the personal names in Ostracon 7 from Tell Mazar (Jordan) as Ammonite, Hebrew, and Persian, which illustrates Neh. 4:6; he also argues for a Persian date for Judith on the ground of the Ammonite name of Achior and his role. Other essays discuss the coinage of Byblos (J. Elayi), the topography and history of the Homs gap in the light of archaeological surveys (J. Sapin, a model study), local power in Hellenistic and Roman Syria (M. Sartre). A feature of the periodical is to be a Bulletin including annotated Bibliographies and surveys of current work in Archaeology, Numismatics, and Old Testament. In the last P. Abbadie summarizes studies on the Chronicler by S. Japhet, R. L. Braun, H. G. M. Williamson. There are also book reviews. The quality of contributions promises well.

A. R. MILLARD

GILEADI, A.: *Israel's Apostasy and Restoration: Essays in Honor of Roland K. Harrison* (Biblical Studies). 1988. Pp. xiii, 325. (Baker Book House, Grand Rapids MI. Price: $24.95. ISBN 0 8010 3830 8)

The volume opens with a brief, but warm and moving tribute to R. K. Harrison by Peter C. Craigie who, unhappily, died soon after he had written it. Twenty-four essays follow, the variety of contributors paying its own tribute to Harrison. Very broadly they follow an historical progression from Israel's exodus from Egypt to the late post-exile literature, the final contribution being H. M. Wolf's study on the prophetic hope of future reversal of the covenant curses. It will not escape notice that the title suggests a view of Israel's history of which the Deuteronomists would have approved. This is no coincidence. Too often the method adopted, at least in some of the articles, is to follow the biblical narrative, calling in the findings of archaeology and knowledge of the ancient world where they seem to support the essential historicity of that narrative. There is much here that is thoughtful, provocative and scholarly, and to this extent there is much which is fitting tribute to the one being honoured by this book. But there is also sad reminder that it has not generally been 'conservative' biblical scholarship which has enriched the church by throwing new light and opening exciting new perspectives on the Bible.

R. A. MASON

GLEBE-MØLLER, J. (ed.): *Studia Theologica: An International Journal or Nordic Theology*. Vol. 43, no. 1. 1989. Pp. 1–163. (Copenhagen University Press. Price: D.Kr. 220.00 (per vol.). ISSN 0039 338X)

With this issue (see also p. 18 below), the journal moves to a new sub-title — though the old title is preserved inside the cover — and a new editor — Jens Glebe-Møller, with a move to Copenhagen. This issue is entirely devoted to a series of articles concerned with feminist approaches to the New Testament and early Christian history.

P. R. ACKROYD

Greenstein, E. L.: *Essays on Biblical Method and Translation* (Brown Judaic Studies, 92). 1989. Pp. xvi, 147. (Scholars Press, Atlanta, GA. Price: $44.95. ISBN 1 55540 122 8)

In this very readable collection of papers mostly published previously in diverse places, Greenstein treats questions of the relation of theory and practice in Biblical criticism. He is a practical critic first and a theorist second, so his remarks on theory have a refreshing down-to-earth quality about them. For example, to a teacher who reproved him for spending too much time on theory instead of concentrating on primary sources he replied that 'our work as scholars . . . is shaped by our manner of thinking, organizing and analyzing material no less than by the amount of material we study and the depth in which we study it. If I am classifying trees, and my criteria are flawed, it does not help to have greater discipline in collecting trees and more trees at my disposal' (p. x). His essays are thoughtful, well-read, wide ranging, and richly annotated, with a special emphasis on Jewish contributions that is not easily paralleled elsewhere. This is a book to which I will often be returning.

D. J. A. Clines

Hanson, R. P. C. and A. T.: *The Bible without Illusions*. 1989. Pp. ix, 150. (SCM, London; Trinity Press International, Philadelphia. Price: £6.95. ISBN 0 334 00101 3)

The intended readership for this book is perhaps roughly the same as for James Barr's *Escaping from Fundamentalism* (see *B. L.* 1985, p. 103): intelligent Christian lay people who need to be talked out of fundamentalist or near fundamentalist attitudes to the Bible. Whereas that book attempts gentle persuasion, the Hansons proceed by frontal assault. For example, the attempt to use biblical prophecy for calculating the date of future events is described as 'an abuse of scripture [which] must be left to fanatics, fools, and semi-literates'. (The intellectual attitude which lumps semi-literates with the other two groups is rather shocking in two Christian theologians.) The book certainly explains the non-fundamentalist character of mainstream biblical scholarship, and in the process gives the reader a fair picture of the main contents of the Bible as assessed in such scholarship, as well as much valuable information about patristic exegesis. The great learning of the Hanson brothers is thus attractively packaged for the general reader. But the tone is crusty, and there are many sideswipes at the feeble-mindedness of parish clergy and ordinary believers which may well alienate most of the intended readers. The reviewer shares the authors' belief that fundamentalists are wrong, but is equally sure, on the other hand, that they are usually neither stupid nor ill-intentioned. This book is a great opportunity wasted through bad temper.

J. Barton

Harrison, R. K. (ed.): *The New Unger's Bible Dictionary*. Revised and updated edition. 1988. Pp. xv, 1400 and 15 pp. of maps. (Moody Press, Chicago IL. Price: $29.95. ISBN 0 8024 9037 9)

This updated and expanded version of a dictionary first published in 1957 will be valued by fundamentalists. Those students of the Old Testament, however, who find it difficult to stomach the Solomonic authorship of Ecclesiastes and the Song of Songs, the historicity of the Book of Jonah and the unity of the Book of Isaiah, will, despite the wealth of factual information on such subjects as fauna and flora here available, be well advised to look elsewhere.

B. P. Robinson

HARTMAN, L. (ed.): *Svensk exegetisk årsbok*, 54 (1989). Pp. 244, portrait. (Wallin and Dahlholm Boktryckeri, Lund. ISSN 1100 2298)

An impressively representative range of Scandinavian scholars have contributed to this *Festschrift* for Magnus Ottoson on his sixtieth birthday. G. Ahlström writes on King So and the downfall of Israel. B. Albrektson provides an illuminating commentary on the new Swedish draft translation of Psalm 8. G. André offers a comparison of Deutero-Isaiah and Job. H. Barstad contributes an onomastic note on *rāḥāḇ*. R. A. Carlson discusses the relation between dream and temple. S. Erlandsson writes on 'The struggle for the throne of Babylon — the Assyrian world ruler as king of Babylon'. Hartman comments on John 2:13–22. S. Holm-Nielsen reconsiders the archaeological evidence relating to Shiloh. K.-J. Illman discusses 'friend' and 'enemy' in the individual laments. In 'Everlasting life was not given to him', A. S. Kapelrud reconsiders the consequences of the 'Fall' in Genesis 3 in the light of the relevant texts from Assyria and Babylonia. T. Kronholm examines the messianic interpretation (Matthew 1:18–25) of Isaiah 7:14 in the light of rabbinic texts. N. P. Lemche reconsiders Jeremiah 7:12–14 and the mystery of the vanished temple at Shiloh, concluding that the former is of Deuteronomistic authorship. I. Ljung examines the parallel between Jezebel, the prophetess in Thytira (Revelation 2:20–22), and the Merovingian queens Brynhilda and Bathilda. T. D. Mettinger considers some problems relating to the *Gottesbild* in ancient Israel. E. Nielsen discusses references to fish in the Old Testament. B. Otzen investigates the form and function of the inscriptions from Kuntillet ʿAjrud. H. Ringgren comments on a problem of translation in Psalm 54:8 (cf. 52:11). M. Saebø writes on the relationship between Sheshbazzar and Zerubbabel. R. Sollamo investigates the text and meaning of Psalm 74:5 and its context. S. O. Steingrimsson examines the syntax and structure of Hosea 10:1–2. J. Strange writes on architecture and theology. S. Tengström discusses exegetical method and the problem of dating the Pentateuch. T. Thordarson contributes notes on the semiotic context of *niḥam* in Jonah. T. Veijola reconsiders the date and message of Genesis 22:1–9. The Festschrift is a fitting pan-Scandinavian tribute to a distinguished scholar.

G. W. ANDERSON

HERBERT, M. and MCNAMARA, M.: *Irish Biblical Apocrypha. Selected texts in translation*. 1989. Pp. xxxiii, 196. (T. & T. Clark, Edinburgh. Price: £19.95. ISBN 0 567 09524 X)

The growing interest in the Apocrypha of both the Old and New Testaments has encouraged the Irish Biblical Association to support an important research project for the study and publication of Irish apocryphal material. Some of the writings are in Latin, but most have been handed down in Irish Gaelic. Dr Maire Herbert, a distinguished scholar in the department of Early and Medieval Irish at University College, Cork, has produced a valuable translation of selected texts which vary in age from the eighth to the fourteenth centuries. Martin McNamara, well known to biblical scholars for his work on the Targums, is also an Irish Gaelic scholar, and has written the introduction to this volume. He stresses that much work remains to be done. For example, only future research will test the validity of the view that 'in Ireland we have very early Apocrypha of Eastern or even Syrian origin, which in the view of some came to Ireland through Visigothic Spain.' Only one sixth of the texts presented here is 'Old Testament Apocryphal material', most of it dealing with Adam. These translations and notes will be a work of invaluable resource and the editors deserve our warm thanks.

K. J. CATHCART

HUPPER, W. G.: *Index to English Periodical Literature on the Old Testament and Ancient Near Eastern Studies*. Vol. II (The American Theological Library Association Bibliography Series, No. 21). 1988. Pp. xxxviii, 502. (Scarecrow Press, Metuchen NJ and London. Price: $45.00. ISBN 0 8108 2126 5)

Although from the same bibliographical family as the volume on Jerusalem reviewed below (p. 22), this second volume by Hupper is something of a curiosity. It accumulates over 7,000 references from more than six hundred periodicals published in the two centuries between 1769 and 1969. The ordering within each section is chronological. After some general studies on Ancient Near Eastern history, this volume quickly moves to the business of its first major sub-section with some general biographical studies. Then we find an alphabetical listing of persons (pp. 6–110) and then of peoples (pp. 111–71) — from Abyssinians to Zuzim. Then following some general studies on chronology (date formulae, and regnal years), are references to biblical, Assyrian, Babylonian, Egyptian, Greek, Ptolemaic, Sumerian, and unclassified chronology — and a final subsection on various ANE dynasties apart from those of Israel and Judah. The second major section in this volume is headed 'Modern Scientific Studies on the Ancient Near East and Old Testament'. It has shorter sections on scientific thought in the ancient near east and Old Testament; astrology and astronomy; ecological and meteorological studies; geological studies. Then geographical studies are themselves subdivided, and have as their concluding section (pp. 312–502) a listing of articles on places from Abel-Mehola to Zoheleth. The section on Jerusalem (pp. 400–21) contains a number of references not in the Purvis Bibliography noted below, but that aimed to be representative of scholarship rather than complete. The restriction of this selection to works in English (though some of their titles are entirely in hieroglyphs) gives a very unbalanced picture of scholarship; for most of those who wrote them were reading in several languages.

A. G. AULD

"In Principio . . .". Atti del Seminario invernale (Prato, 23–26 gennaio 1986). 1986. Pp. 308. (BIBLIA: Associazione laica di cultura biblica, Settimello (FI). Price: Lire 15,000)

'Biblia' is an Italian lay association which aims, by means of periodic conferences, to bring out the abiding significance of the Bible for Western society and culture. This volume is made up of eleven papers delivered at such a conference in January, 1986. On the basis of the first three chapters of Genesis, the contributions concern themselves with the origin of the world, of man, and of evil. Not all the participants are Biblical scholars or theologians: they also include an astrophysicist, a geneticist, and an anthropologist. Under the first heading, Pelio Fronzaroli, a Semitic philologist, reviews parallel ancient Near Eastern accounts of creation, Marco Adinolfi discusses the origin of the universe as seen in Gen. 1–2:4a, while Paolo de Benedetti deals with rabbinic interpretations of the Biblical account of creation, concentrating on Rashi and *Bereshith Rabba*, and Elena Giannarelli with early Christian understandings of the theme: the essay by Giannina Poletto on modern cosmology has no direct bearing on the Old Testament. Under the second heading, Daniele Garrone writes on the origin of humanity in Gen. 2 and Ida Zatelli on the lexicography of creation in the Bible: again, the long essay by Marcello Buiatti on evolutionary models of human development and that by Paolo Chiozzi on myths of human origins in primitive cultures only marginally touch on the Bible. Thirdly, Paolo Sacchi examines Gen. 3 and the problem of evil and Armido Rizzi discusses the role of this chapter in the development of the concept of evil in Christian thought. Most of the contributions are accompanied by brief bibliographies for further reading. This is not a book for the specialist *Alttestamentler* but is succeeds well in its aim of making Biblical scholarship available to a wider public.

J. R. Porter

Jeppesen, K. and Strange, J. (eds): *Skriv synet tydeligt på tavler. Om problemerne ved en ny bibeloversettelse*. 1989. Pp. 168. (G. E. C. Gads Forlag, Copenhagen. ISBN 87 12 01895 3)

This collection of essays, the main title of which is a quotation from Hab.2:2, 'Write the vision clearly on tablets', is a *Festschrift* for Professor Svend Holm-Nielsen on the occasion of his seventieth birthday. He is a leading member of the team which has been working on a new Danish version of the Old Testament, and to honour him sixteen contributors, all in different capacities engaged in the new translation, have elucidated various aspects of the task, usually on the basis of a particular passage. In this way most of the fundamental problems which confront Bible translators are treated in the volume, and all essays are written so as to be intelligible to the general public, not just to specialists. The articles, all in Danish, cannot be enumerated here; suffice it to say that among the authors are a number of biblical scholars well known to readers of *B. L.*: besides the editors, names like N. P. Lemche, E. Nielsen, B. Noack, and B. Otzen may be mentioned. It is to be hoped that the discussion in Denmark about the modern translation, a discussion that has to a certain extent been distorted by theological prejudice, will profit by the many scholarly, sober, and sensible contributions in this volume.

B. Albrektson

Jervell, J. and Kapelrud, A. S.: *Studia Theologica: Scandinavian Journal of Theology*. Vol. 42, no. 2. 1988. Pp. 69–167. (Norwegian University Press, Oslo. Price: $33.00; N.Kr. 200.00 (per vol.). ISSN 0039 338X)

Vol. 42/2 contains no Old Testament articles. One is on John's Gospel; and one on Paul. There is an article of modern American Theology, dealing with J. M. Gustafson's Ethics. One is on Constantine and Arius.

P. R. Ackroyd

Johanning, K.: *Der Bibel-Babel-Streit: Eine forschungsgeschichtliche Studie* (Europäische Hochschulschriften, Reihe XXIII, Bd.343). 1989. Pp. 471. (Lang, Frankfurt. Price: Sw.Fr. 76.00. ISBN 3 8204 1455 X; ISSN 0721 3409)

This thesis examines the currents and cross-currents set up by the publications of Friedrich Delitzsch between 1902 and 1920. By his time cuneiform had been deciphered for a century, but it was his towering scholarship and interpretation of the ancient Mesopotamian literature which set the 'Bible-Babel' controversy in motion. It is instructive to see that not only the findings of the nineteenth-century literary critics such as Wellhausen gave impetus to the debate, but 'liberal' ideas of progression in religion and a latent anti-semitism played their part, for the Old Testament could now be seen as only relative to the other literature of the ancient near east and Judaism only one religion of many, waiting indeed to be superseded by Christianity. It is strange that Friedrich should be the son of that pillar of the theologically conservative establishment, Franz Delitzsch; and Johanning traces conservative reaction to the controversy in the persons of König, Rudolph Kittel, Köberle, and Oettli. It turns out to be their arguments which have supplied the armoury of much conservative writing since. Catholic and Jewish reactions are charted and the movement of the 'pan-Babylonian' school, Stucken, the forerunner, Hugo Winckler, and Alfred Jeremias.

Strangely, their work was welcomed by conservative scholars since they demonstrated the genuine antiquity of the world and cultures described in the biblical patriarchal and Mosaic narratives.

A conclusion shows how the controversy has gained new relevance today with the demise of the post-second world war 'Biblical Theology' movement which tried to stress again too one-sidedly the uniqueness of Israel. Johanning believes that we are having to take seriously again the 'earthing' of ancient Israel in the world and religious of its time and to offer only those theories of 'revelation' which take historical reality seriously.

This is an informative, discerning and highly entertaining work. If only all academic theses were as readable.

R. A. MASON

MCCREESH, T. P. (ed.): *Old Testament Abstracts*. Vol. 11, No. 3; Vol. 12, No. 1,2. 1988; 1989. Pp. 211–369; 1–128; 129–234. (The Catholic University of America, Washington D.C. Price: $14.00 per volume. ISSN 0364 8591)

The character of this invaluable aid to research is unchanged from previous years.

M. A. KNIBB

MCKANE, W.: *Selected Christian Hebraists*. 1989. Pp. x, 268. (Cambridge University Press. Price: £30.00 ($49.50). ISBN 0 521 35507 9)

With the origins of much of its scripture in the Jewish world, and its own linguistic background shared between Hebrew, Aramaic, and Greek, the Christian Church has always faced a dilemma in measuring the significance of the Hebrew Bible and its literal interpretation against its own theological commitments. In McKane's own words (p. 4), 'Christological exegesis . . . is difficult to reconcile with the fact that the Hebrew Bible belonged to Israel and to the Jews before it belonged to the Church' and a substantial part of his book deals with the 'fear of Judaizing tendencies awakened in the Church by the Hebrew Bible and the Jewish scholarship associated with it' (p. 192). The author offers a thoroughly researched and clearly written history of the dilemma as demonstrated in the basic work of Origen and Jerome and in the differing approaches to ancient versions, Jewish tradition, Church authority, vernacular translation, historical and textual scholarship, and rational thought evinced by Andrew of St Victor (12th century France), William Fulke and Gregory Martin (16th century England), Richard Simon (Paris, 1638–1712), and the Scot, Alexander Geddes (1737–1802), all but one of them, the Anglican Fulke, from the Catholic Church.

S. C. REIF

MOMIGLIANO, A.: *Pagine ebraiche*. Edited by S. Berti. 1987. Pp. xxviii, 254. (Einaudi, Torino. Price: Lire 26,000. ISBN 88 06 59927 5)

This volume of 'Jewish Pages' by Arnaldo Momigliano (1908–1987) presents in Italian twenty-three essays (including some memorial tributes) written between 1931 and 1986 by this great historian of antiquity who, after his exile in 1938, brought honour to chairs in Oxford, Bristol, and University College, London. About ten of these essays fall within the range of interest of this *Book List*: some were originally in English, at least one in German, and the rest in Italian. The select titles which follow were almost all originally published in Italian, so that the English titles here are by the reviewer except the one with an asterisk: 'Biblical studies and classical studies'; 'Jews and Greeks'; 'Daniel and the Greek theory of the succession of empires'; 'The Second book of Maccabees'; 'Problems of method in interpreting Jewish-Hellenistic symbols' (naturally, on E. R. Goodenough); 'An Apologia for

Judaism: the *Contra Apionem* of Flavius Josephus'; 'What Flavius Josephus did not see'; 'Flavius Josephus and Alexander's visit to Jerusalem'*; 'Preliminary hints on Apocalypse [i.e. apocalypticism] and Exodus in tradition', and 'Prophecy and historiography' (original in German). (The pieces not mentioned here are also valuable and often fascinating.)

R. P. R. MURRAY

MULDER, M. J. (ed.): *Mikra. Text, Translation, Reading and Interpretation of the Hebrew Bible in Ancient Judaism and Early Christianity* (Compendia Rerum Iudaicarum ad Novum Testamentum. Section 2,1). 1988. Pp. XXVI, 929. (Van Gorcum, Assen; Fortress, Philadelphia. Price: $79.95. ISBN 90 232 2363 5; 0 8006 0604 3)

'The emphasis of this volume . . . is on the biblical text and its translations, especially in the period of the Second Temple and the talmudic era' (p. XXIII). After the introduction by the editor, A. Demsky writes on systems of writing, literacy, and the book in the biblical period, and M. Bar-Ilan on scribes and books in the late Second Commonwealth and rabbinic times. R. T. Beckwith discusses the formation of the Hebrew Bible and the canon. M. J. Mulder surveys the transmission of the text, and C. Perrot the reading of the Bible in the ancient synagogue. The versions are discussed by E. Tov (the LXX), A. Tal (the Samaritan Targum to the Pentateuch). P. S. Alexander (Jewish Aramaic translations), P. B. Dirksen (the Peshiṭta), and B. Kedar (Latin versions). The remaining chapters deal with biblical interpretation: M. Fishbane on the Qumran texts (this essay is not well written, but the persistent reader can learn much from it), D. Dimant on the Apocrypha and Pseudepigrapha, Y. Amir on Philo, L. H. Feldman on Josephus, P. W. van der Horst on minor Hellenistic Jewish writers, S. Kasher on the rabbis, R. Boid (M. N. Sarif) on Samaritan tradition, B. A. Pearson on Gnostic literature, E. E. Ellis on the Old Testament canon in the early church and Old Testament interpretation in the New Testament church, and W. Horbury on the Church Fathers. There are a cumulative bibliography and an index of sources. This massive book is useful work of reference, and writers give up-to-date information (though Ellis still writes confidently about 'corporate personality' and 'God himself as a corporate being', and 'an indefinable extension of' Yahweh's 'personality' in his agents on p. 718). It is a pity that the whole work was not vetted by a native speaker of English with a feeling for style, that 'Mikra' is used by some writers as if it were an English word, and that a more satisfactory system of transliterating Hebrew was not adopted; the very title of the book might give the misleading impression that it is concerned wtih little things. But such defects are minor irritants in a valuable work. One misprint deserves to be recorded: 'in civil cases the murder [read 'number'] of witnesses required is two' (p. 516).

J. A. EMERTON

MÜLLER, G. (ed.): *Theologische Realenzyklopädie* (TRE), Bd.17: *Jesus Christ V — Katechismuspredigt*. 1988. Pp. 814. (De Gruyter, Berlin. Price: DM 360.00. ISBN 3 11 011506 9)

This volume contains an unusually large number of articles of particular interest to readers of the *Book List*. There are three articles on Old Testament books — Joel (by J. Jeremias), Jonah and Joshua (the last two by H. J. Zobel); and one on the 'Josephnovelle' (Gen. 37–50) by L. Schmidt. Jehoiachin and Jehoiakim (G. Wanke), Jehoshaphat (P. Welten), and Josiah (H. Spieckermann) have each a short article. There are articles on Kadesh and Carmel, both by K.-H. Bernhardt. (Judea will be covered in a forthcoming article on Palestine.) A substantial article on Canaan (F. Stolz) deals with the name Canaan, its geography, history and social, economic and cultural life, but not its religion: this will be covered in due course in an article on west semitic religions. On post-biblical literature there are articles on the Book of Jubilees (G. Schelbert) and on Judith (E. Zenger), and on Joseph and Aseneth (C. Burchard) and Josippon (A. Vivian). A comprehensive article on Judaism (forty-six pages) by F. Dexinger devotes fifteen pages to the period between 538 B.C. and A.D. 70 (there is a further article on Chasidism by K. E. Grözinger). L. M. Barth writes on Johanan ben Zakkai, G. Mayer on Josephus, G. Stemberger on 'Judaistik' (the history of Jewish studies), R. Goetschel on the Kabbala, and A. Schenker on the Karaites. The article on Canon (W. Künneth) deals with the concept of canon, its historical development, the problem of inspiration, and implications for ecumenism. There is a short section on the canonical place of the Old Testament in the Christian canon, but the problems of the Old Testament canon in itself are not specifically discussed. There are two short bibliographical articles on modern scholars: Benjamin Jowett (B. M. G. Reardon) and Paul Kahle (Bernhardt). Several New Testament articles have some relevance to Old Testament studies, and aspects of the relationship between Judaism and Christianity are discussed in the articles on Judenchristentum (G. Strecker) and Judentum und Christentum (J. T. Pawlikowski). The fullness of the bibliographies continues to be a notable feature of the work.

R. N. Whybray

Müller, G. (ed.): *Theologische Realenzyklopädie* (TRE), Bd.18: *Katechumenat/Katechumenen — Kirchenrecht*. 1989. Pp. 778. (De Gruyter, Berlin. Price: DM 360.00. ISBN 3 11 011613 8)

No article in this volume is entirely devoted to the Old Testament. The article on the Catenae (E. Mühlenberg) however, is of interest for textual and philological study and for the history of interpretation. The article on the University of Kiel (H.-J. Birkner) refers to the many notable Old Testament scholars who have held, or now hold, posts there. In several articles, notably those on the Church (K. Berger), Church and State (R. M. Grant and H. D. Betz), the ecclesiastical year (K.-P. Jörns and K.-H. Bieritz) and ecclesiastical law (J. Gaudemet) the Old Testament, and early Jewish background is discussed. The final article — placed here presumably because it was overlooked in the compilation of Band XV, though there is a cross-reference to it in its proper place in that volume — is on the Hermetic literature (K.-W. Tröger). The Kenites and the 'Kenite hypothesis' will be dealt with in forthcoming articles on nomadism (*Nomadentum im Alten Testament*) and on the history of the religion of Israel (*Religionsgeschichte Israels*).

R. N. Whybray

Neu, E. and Rüster, C. (eds): *Documentum Asiae Minoris Antiquae. Festschrift für Heinrich Otten zum 75. Geburtstag*. 1988. Pp. x, 420. (Harrassowitz, Wiesbaden. Price: DM 212.00. ISBN 3 447 02866 1)

Not many of the learned contributions to this Festschrift for a senior German Hettitologist are of interest to Old Testament scholars. A reading of 'Herding and Herdsmen in Hittite Culture' (G. Beckman) will at least raise questions which need investigation in the Israelite context. 'Magie in hethitischen Gärten' (V. Haas) deals with worship and ritual in gardens, and 'The Song of Silver — A Member of the Kumarbi Cycle of "Songs"' (H. A. Hoffner) gives the most complete and reliable edition of this myth so far. A damaged letter from Boğazköy naming Urhi-Teshub mentions Megiddo (I. Singer).

W. G. Lambert

North, R. (ed.): *Elenchus of Biblica 1986* (Elenchus of Biblical Bibliography, 2). 1989. Pp. 969. (Biblical Institute Press, Rome. ISBN 88 7653 569 1)

This latest bibliographical compendium is a little shorter, in fact by 79 pages, than the 'bumper number' which inaugurated the new series in 1988. However, close on 13,500 items are noted: testimony to the vitality of the discipline as well as the energy of Father North.

A. G. Auld

La posizione del debole nella Bibbia. Atti del Convegno nazionale (Casale Monferrato, 16–17 maggio 1987). 1988. Pp. 139. (BIBLIA: Associazione laica di cultura biblica, Settimello (FI). Price: Lire 8,000)

This work has the same format as the book reviewed above (p. 17), consisting of six papers delivered at the national congress of 'Biblia' in May 1987. Compared with the former collection, however, it is somewhat disappointing. The topic of the 'weak' in the Bible is widely discussed today but for its satisfactory treatment it demands a thorough investigation of law and society in Israel and there is comparatively little of this here. Hence the best essay is that by Silvio Ortona on peasant poverty under the monarchy. The remaining contributions review various categories of the disadvantaged in the Bible. Rabbi Emanuele Artom discusses those suffering oppression, Enzio Bianchi considers the position of both lepers and other diseased persons and also the widow and orphan, referring to the New Testament and rabbinic sources, while a rather rambling essay by Vivetta Pagella deals with God and the stranger. Domenico Maselli on woman is mainly concerned with the New Testament. The whole begins with a general introduction to the subject by Giuseppe Ghiberti and concludes with a record of a discussion by the participants on the question 'who are the poor today?' As a general presentation, this collection has some merit but it does not go very deep.

J. R. Porter

Purvis, J. D.: *Jerusalem, the Holy City: A Bibliography* (The American Theological Library Association Bibliography Series, No. 20). 1988. Pp. xii, 499. (Scarecrow Press, Metuchen NJ and London. Price: $42.50. ISBN 0 8108 1999 6)

The compiler of this Bibliography, himself an Old Testament specialist and author of a work on Samaritan origins (*B. L.* 1969, p. 63; *Bible Bibliog.*, p. 189), will have put specialists in many fields deeply in his debt. He has organized almost 6,000 bibliographical items in forty chapters within eight major divisions: general studies; Jerusalem during the biblical period to 587; Jerusalem during the second temple period; Roman Jerusalem; Jerusalem in Judaism; Christian Jerusalem; Jerusalem as a Muslim city; and Jerusalem in modern times (the final chapter collects items on the city from 1967 to 'the present'). Many more readers will be complimentary about the scale and thoroughness of the enterprise than will cavil at the inevitable arbitrariness of some of the classification. And all will be daunted when they ponder the size the volume would have been had it not excluded titles in European languages with non-Latin script, in Arabic, and much modern Hebrew material judged not readily accessible in North American libraries.

A. G. Auld

Reif, S. C. (ed.): *Published Material from the Cambridge Genizah Collections. A Bibliography: 1896–1980* (Cambridge University Library Genizah Series 6). 1988. Pp. xiv, 608. (Cambridge University Press. Price: £75.00 ($125.00). ISBN 0 521 33336 9)

Under the overall direction of Dr Reif, the energetic and successful leader of the Cambridge Genizah Research Unit, a comprehensive catalogue of publications up to 1980 has been compiled by three principal collaborators, Simon Hopkins (1975–78), Paul Fenton (1978–82), and Geoffrey Khan (1983–). The computerization of the data was started by Deborah Patterson and brought to completion by Shulamit Reif. This substantial volume includes a list of documents arranged in order of classwork and followed by references to scholarly works dealing with them (pp. 1–432); an alphabetical register of modern authors accompanied by the list of publications relative to Genizah documents identified by classmark (pp. 435–587); and finally a catalogue of works cited in an abridged form (pp. 591–608). Here is a most valuable bibliographical aid for students of texts originating from the Cairo Genizah.

G. VERMES

REVENTLOW, H. Graf, SPARN, W., and WOODBRIDGE, J. (eds): *Historische Kritik und biblischer Kanon in der deutschen Aufklärung* (Wolfenbütteler Forschungen, Bd 41). 1988. Pp. vii, 293. (Herzog August Bibliothek; distributed by Harrassowitz, Wiesbaden. Price: DM 98.00. ISBN 3 447 02884 X)

At the Wolfenbüttel symposium in December 1985, of which this volume contains the papers, two of the contributions were given as public lectures. Reventlow's lecture on Johannes Clericus, as well as his paper at the symposium, argued that biblical criticism was a legacy of humanism. He thus rejected the view of those who argue for the importance of the Lutheran reformation for the emergence of biblical criticism, a view defended by Hornig at the symposium in his paper on Semler. Woodbridge's essay on German responses to Richard Simon indicated that Simon's influence on eighteenth-century Protestant German criticism needs also to be considered in the discussion. Other contributions pertinent to the Old Testament are those of D. Bourel on Oriental Studies in eighteenth-century Germany, and R. Smend on J. G. Carpzov's *Critica sacra Veteris Testamenti* (1728). Of the contributions outside the area of Old Testament study, that of O. Bayer on the dispute between Hamann and Kant on reason and the authority of the Bible is outstanding, while S.-A. Jørgensen's study of Hamann's use of the Bible during his London crisis draws additional attention to this fascinating and thought-provoking figure.

J. W. ROGERSON

RODD, C. S. (ed.): *The Expository Times* 101,1. 1989, Pp. 32. (T. & T. Clark, Edinburgh. Price: £1.50 (annual subscription: £15.95, including postage and packing))

This number marks the beginning of the second century of this well known periodical. Its purpose remains the bridging of the gap between theological study and the church, and it will continue to combine an interest in pastoralia with biblical and theological scholarship. This issue contains information about new books, ranging from advertisement or brief mention to review article, including a thorough and perceptive review article by the Editor on the *Revised English Bible* (see also below, p. 60). He also offers a detailed account and critique of two recent books on the atonement in his editorial. There is a selection of sermon outlines for varied situations. New features envisaged in future numbers include a correspondence page and a series of articles on the spirituality of major figures from Augustine to Thomas Merton. We salute an old friend which is showing evidence of much vitality, and wish it well as it starts a new century.

A. GELSTON

Rogerson, J. W. and Davies, P. R.: *The Old Testament World*. 1989. Pp. 384. (Cambridge University Press. Price: £19.50. ISBN 0 521 34006 3)

The aim of these two scholars from the University of Sheffield is to reflect the way the Old Testament is being explored by present-day scholarship, in particular by utilizing the methods of archaeology and the social sciences and by approaching the books as literature. The former methods predominate in the chapters on the geography and ecology of the land and the social organization of the peoples in the area, and inform the account of the history of Israel. The books are approached by way of genre, and the closing chapters move to early Judaism and the development of the canon. Inevitably there is considerable compression, and sometimes controversial issues are settled too quickly; but this is a useful introduction both to modern study of the Old Testament and to the history and religion of Israel, critical in stance and aware of the limitations of modern knowledge. Were it not so expensive it would provide a useful textbook for first year undergraduates.

C. S. Rodd

Rossano, P., Ravasi, G., and Girlanda, A. (eds): *Nuovo Dizionario di Teologia Biblica*. 1988. Pp. xxii, 1739. (Paoline, Cinisello Balsamo (Milano). Price Lire 70,000. ISBN 88 215 1579 6)

This octavo volume of two columns to a page is a *multum in parvo*. The contributors are mostly Catholic scholars, but there are a few others, including Bruno Corsani of the Waldensian Faculty in Rome, author of the entry on 'Word' (*Parola*). The entries that one would normally expect to find in a Bible dictionary are all here, but special attention is paid to their theological significance (especially in the entries on biblical authors and books). The leading themes of biblical theology have entries to themselves, and there is a special entry of nearly 20 pages on 'Biblical Theology'. In this entry the section on Old Testament theology is contributed by A. Bonora; it includes a survey of the works on this subject by E. Jacob, M. G. Cordero, G. von Rad, and W. Eichrodt, chosen as representing respectively the descriptive, dogmatic-didactic, diachronic, and thematic methods. A subject not often treated in biblical or theological dictionaries, 'Bible and culture', receives a long entry of nearly 70 pages, comprising sections on art, literature, and music. There is a related, but shorter, entry on 'Culture and acculturation'. The entries conclude with select bibliographies. For Italian (and Italian-reading) students of the Bible and theology this promises to be a very useful handbook.

F. F. Bruce

Saggs, H. W. F.: *Civilization before Greece and Rome*. 1989. Pp. 322. (Batsford, London. Price: £19.95. ISBN 0 7134 5277 3)

This work ranges far and wide, from the Mediterranean to the Indus Valley, and from Anatolia to South Arabia, providing a fascinating description of the achievements of the peoples who were the precursors of the Greeks and the Romans. A brief introduction to the various groups is followed by a more detailed consideration of aspects of life and culture. There is a tendency to concentrate on Egypt and Mesopotamia, but the contributions of peoples from elsewhere in the ancient Near East are noted. References to the Israelites (included among the 'minor centres of civilization') are limited, so the work's main value for students of the Old Testament will be in providing information about the wider context within which those who produced the Hebrew Bible emerged. Topics discussed include the development of city-states and kingdoms, law, international relations, trade, the construction of pyramids and ziggurats and features of the building of cities such as water supply and sewage disposal, and natural resources. Consideration of intellectual achievements includes a detailed treatment of the development of writing and scribal education, mathematics, astronomy, and medicine. The final chapter on ancient religion makes a number of claims which will not go unchallenged, not least the use of the adjective 'indisputable' in describing the burning-bush incident as a 'case of a numen associated with a tree' (p. 282) and the idea of creation by the thought and word of Ptah as a 'foreshadowing of the Logos doctrine of Neo-Platonic Christianity' (p. 291).

A. H. W. CURTIS

SCHMIDT, W. H., THIEL, W., and HANHART, R.: *Altes Testament* (Grundkurs Theologie, 1) (Urban–Taschenbücher, 421). 1989. Pp. 216. (Kohlhammer, Stuttgart. Price: DM 22.00. ISBN 3 17 010267 2)

This is the first volume in a series presenting a general overview of academic theology today. Later volumes will deal with church history, history of doctrine, systematic theology, ethics, practical theology, church related issues, and ecumenics and mission. The level is for the well-informed general reader and theological student.

Schmidt offers a fairly traditional 'Introduction' with considerable emphasis on the history of interpretation and discusses current issues in the presenting of Old Testament theology. Von Rad's *Theologie* is seen as marking the watershed. Thiel sets out the history of Israel from its origins in Palestine (conquest, infiltration, revolution, evolution models are considered) to the Graeco-Roman period. He also contributes the third section of the book, a discussion of the archaeology of Palestine in the Old Testament period, dealing in turn with its history and methods, and then outlining the finds under the main ages. The final section by Hanhart, 'Septuagint' covers a wide range of issues, including origins, history (with reference to questions of canon and the relation between Jewish and Christian forms of the Greek translations, and the history of the text. There are twenty-nine pictures and line drawings at the end. The bibliographies will be of special value to British and American readers.

C. S. RODD

SCHUNCK, K.-D.: *Altes Testament und Heiliges Land: Gesammelte Studien zum Alten Testament und zur biblischen Landeskunde*. Band I (Beiträge zur Erforschung des Alten Testaments und des Antiken Judentums, 17). 1989. Pp. 276. (Lang, Bern — Frankfurt-am-Main. Price: Sw.Fr. 60.00. ISBN 3 8204 1187 9; ISSN 0722 0790)

This first volume of collected essays gathers twenty-four studies from a thirty-year period (1957–87). Seven reflect Schunck's historico-geographical interests. Others deal with prophetic themes, especially the day of Yahweh and topics in Isaiah; with the decalogue; and with wider theological issues such as the Old Testament concept of *torah* (the only essay not previously published), the spirit in the Old Testament, and the Old Testament view of nature. Two early contributions of his to classical studies round off a volume which, even without them, would have displayed a wide range of expertise and a good mix.

A. G. AULD

SMEND, R.: *Deutsche Alttestamentler in drei Jahrhunderten*. 1989. Pp. 336, including 18 illustrations. (Vandenhoeck & Ruprecht, Göttingen. Price: DM 78.00. ISBN 3 525 53584 8)

Of the eighteen studies contained in this volume most have been published previously in various contexts but now appear in revised and expanded form. The scholars dealt with (Michaelis, Eichhorn, de Wette, Gesenius, Bleek, Kamphausen, Wellhausen, Duhm, Stade, Marti, Meinhold, Gunkel, Gressmann, Alt, Rudolph, von Rad, Noth, Zimmerli) exemplify the development and achievements of German Old Testament scholarship during the past three centuries. Professor Smend's accounts of the scholarly work of each of his subjects would of themselves make his book of outstanding value. It is further enriched, however, by the descriptions of personal traits and the comments (favourable and hostile) of academic contemporaries and of those who as students had sat at the feet of the scholars described (e.g. Wellhausen on de Wette: 'Ein gescheiter Kerl! Was ich im alten Testamente gemacht habe, steht ja schon alles bei ihm'; and the young Karl Barth on Marti's teaching: 'eine arg trockene Weisheit'.). These features not only add liveliness and human interest to the volume (to which the portraits also contribute), but give a more rounded presentation of the scholars and their achievement. It is impossible within the limits of a short notice to do justice to the contents and quality of this volume; but we may venture to offer to our distinguished Honorary Member our congratulations and gratitude for a work of absorbing interest and fine scholarship.

G. W. Anderson

Il sogno nella Bibbia. Atti del Convegno nazionale (Ravenna, 7–8 maggio 1988). 1989. Pp. 125. (BIBLIA: Associazione laica di cultura biblica, Settimello (FI). Price: Lire 8,000)

This volume contains the five papers delivered at a conference devoted to the theme of biblical dreams. Two are by the same author, Gaetano Benedetti, and represent the viewpoint of a modern psychiatrist. Antonio Bonora presents a comprehensive survey of dreams and their interpretation in the Old Testament. Detailed studies are devoted to the two dreams of Nebuchadnezzar in Daniel 2 and 4 (Antonio Alberto Semi) and those of Joseph in Matthew 1 and 2 (Piero Stefani), the latter considered against the background of the Old Testament and rabbinic tradition. There is a short account of a verbal comment made by Kristina Berggren on the paper on Nebuchadnezzar's dreams. The lack of any introduction or conclusion gives the work a somewhat disjointed appearance, but it is a useful collection of material, and the conference no doubt stimulated a dialogue between students of the Bible and of psychiatry which is to be welcomed.

A. Gelston

Strecker, G. and Maier, J.: *Neues Testament — Antikes Judentum* (Grundkurs Theologie, 2) (Urban-Taschenbücher, 422). 1989. Pp. 192. (Kohlhammer, Stuttgart. Price: DM 22.00. ISBN 3 17 010266 4)

In this volume, which will mainly be of interest to students of the New Testament, George Strecker provides a widely ranging introduction to the New Testament, chiefly by way of a historical and critical discussion of the secondary literature, and Johann Maier considers the Judaism of the intertestamental period as a background to early Christianity — outline history, literature, religious groups, Greek and Persian influences, the diaspora, and rabbinic judaism. There are full bibliographies. It should prove a very useful reference work for the German undergraduates for whom it is intended.

C. S. Rodd

Sucupira, L. (ed.): *Revista Biblica Brasileira*. Ano 6, 1–2, 3. 1989. Pp. 1–80, 81–156. (Nova Jerusalém, Fortaleza CE. Brazil. Price: $20.00 p.a.)

Each of the first three issues for 1989 contains a major article by P. Minette de Tillesse. In the first, he argues that the so-called 'Succession

Narrative' of 2Sam.9 — 1 Kgs 2 (NB accidental references to *2* Kgs 2 on p. 5) should more appropriately be regarded as 'The History of Solomon's Accession' and should extend to 1 Kgs 8 or even 9. In the second, he suggests that the account of the finding of the lawbook in 2 Kgs 22–23 is a theological construct triggered by 2 Kgs 12 and Jer. 36. In the third, he defends the existence of the 'Yahwist' as an author with a purpose (the defence of David's and Solomon's conquests) and extracts the entire 'J' text from the Tetrateuch, in preparation for further discussion. Each article is followed by a résumé in French, a new feature which will make the *RBB* more accessible to non-Portuguese-reading scholars. The fourth issue is devoted entirely to book reviews and indices. Among the reviews in Issue 2, the *Book List* is once again promoted as a tool for study, and a request is made for the provision of a list of names and addresses of SOTS members, to facilitate contact between scholars in the international outreach of Biblical Studies (p. 62).

J. M. Dines

Tökei, F.: *Acta Orientalia Academiae Scientiarum Hungaricae*. Tom. XLI, Fasc. 2, 3. Tom. XLII, Fasc. 1. 1987; 1988. Pp. 173–340, 341–497; 1–160. (Akadémiai Kiadó, Budapest. HU ISSN 0001 6446)

There is nothing in these issues concerned with the Old Testament.

J. A. Emerton

Urban, L.: *A Short History of Christian Thought*. 1986. Pp. xv, 319. (Oxford University Press. Price: £8.95. ISBN 0 19 503717 0)

The study of Religion is popular in American Universities, but Christian Studies tend to lose out because of the great variety of denominational and sectarian interpretations. As a result students often have a better grasp of other world religions. This book is designed as a text book for undergraduates to provide a more comprehensive introduction to Christian thought from a non-sectarian viewpoint. The aim is to provide the background to the history of major Christian doctrines, but, at the same time, to assess the changes in interpretation in the light of scientific and critical study. There is stress particularly on modern approaches — with questions about inter-religious dialogue, Liberation, and Feminist Theologies all included!

It is doubtful whether the extensive bibliography, whilst an indication of the author's reading and interests, will be of much use to the intended readers, as there is no indication of the level at which they are written.

For readers of this *Book List*, the first chapter is the only one immediately relevant, dealing, as it does, with scriptural sources. The Old Testament is relevant as the background to the understanding of the teaching of Jesus and the way in which his message was likely to be understood. Hence there is most emphasis on the understanding of God and the development of apocalyptic and messianic expectations. Like most writers prior to the discovery of the Aramaic version of the Book of Enoch among the Dead Sea Scrolls, Professor Urban appears to assume the pre-Christian origin of the Similitudes, as he discusses the interpretation of the 'Son of Man' sayings in the gospels.

This reviewer would have expected a more stringent examination of the scriptural basis for Christian thought and more material on the history of interpretation.

R. Hammer

VAN BEEK, G. W. (ed.): *The Scholarship of William Foxwell Albright: An Appraisal.* Papers delivered to the Symposium 'Homage to William Foxwell Albright'. The American Friends of the Israel Exploration Society. Rickville, Maryland, 1984 (Harvard Semitic Studies, 33). 1989. Pp. 73. (Scholars Press, Atlanta GA. Price: $16.95 (member price: $10.95). ISBN 1 55540 314 X)

This symposium is the fourth volume devoted to Albright since his death in 1971. The symposium coincided with the announcement of a newly established William Foxwell Albright Chair of Biblical and Near Eastern Studies at Johns Hopkins University. Some of his distinguished former students reflect on his influence on Epigraphy, Philology and Palaeography (F. M. Cross), and Archaeology (Gus W. Van Beek who also gives a short biography). Regrettably the paper by S. Iwry on Albright and Biblical Studies is not included for that was his major interest as a furtherer of 'Biblical Archaeology'. Albright as an Orientalist was a 'generalist' as were many of his day, versed in the whole range of languages, literatures, history, and religion. He was among the first to use his detailed typological methods to date the Dead Sea Scrolls, Proto-Sinaitic script, the Gezer Calendar, and some ceramic sequences; and many of his conclusions stand today.

Two of the contributors, D. N. Freedman on Albright as a historian and D. R. Hillers on him as a philogist, seem unecessarily critical both of his 'imaginative' and 'conservative' tendencies. It is always easy to forget the precise state of studies at the time of his many writings. Yet all teachers must note that a man who supervised 57 published Ph.D. theses (twice the number of the honorary doctorates he himself was awarded) is still influential. Those who knew him personally will never forget his energy, enthusiasm, example, and encouragement.

D. J. WISEMAN

WALTER, K. and BARTOLOMEI, M. C. (eds): *Donne alla riscoperta della Bibbia.* Translated from German by P. G. Oxenius. 1988. Pp. 207. (Queriniana, Brescia. Price: Lire 17,000. ISBN 88 399 1749 7)

Of the 26 women — Protestant, Catholic, and Orthodox — who have contributed to this collection of short reflective essays on biblical subjects and themes related to the role of women, only ten have theological qualifications and only one (Dorothee Sölle, who has written on Mary and Martha under the subtitle 'the unity of action and vision') is likely to be known to most readers of the *Book List.* In various ways, most of these offerings are essays in 'feminist reading' of the texts selected — though no strident overtones are to be detected. Subjects taken from the Old Testament are the creation of Eve, motherhood in the Old Testament, Wisdom's creative power, Elijah's journey, the daughter of Jephtha, Ruth, and the widow of Zarephath.

C. J. A. HICKLING

VAN DER WOUDE, A. S. (ed.): *New Avenues in the Study of the Old Testament.* A Collection of Old Testament Studies Published on the Occasion of the Fiftieth Anniversary of the Oudtestamentisch Werkgezelschap and the Retirement of Prof. Dr M. J. Mulder (*Oudtestamentische Studiën* XXV). 1989. Pp. ix, 166. (Leiden, E. J. Brill. Price: fl.110.00 ($55.00). ISBN 90 04 09125 4)

This volume was published on 30 October 1989 to mark the 50th anniversary of the Oudtestamentisch Werkgezelschap, and it contains English versions of the lectures that were delivered in Dutch on that occasion. It also contains essays in honour of Professor Martin Mulder on the occasion of his retirement in January 1989. It says much for Dutch-speaking scholarship and publishing that those attending the Jubileum had before them the English texts of the lectures that were delivered.

A brief note by van der Woude on the history of the Dutch society is followed by W. A. M. Beuken on 1 Kings 3:16–28 (the good whore may be added to the typology of the wise women), K. A. Deurloo on the narrative structure and function of 1 Kings 3, P. B. Dirksen on the *Vorlage* of the four early Nestorian MSS of the Peshitta, J. Hoftijzer's philological-grammatical note on 1 Kings 11:14, van der Woude on the history of the border between Judah and Israel, Mulder on the Solomonic temple in the light of the syncretistic Yahwism of the monarchy, B. E. H. J. Becking on Jeremiah 30:4–11, P. C. Beentjes on the treatment of Hezekiah and Isaiah in Ben Sirah 48:15–25, C. Brekelmans on Joshua 5:10–12 (there is no direct connection between vv. 11–12 and the passover feast of v. 10), J. P. Fokkelman on the relation between time (including the ages of the patriarchs at various times) and structure in the Abraham cycle, C. Houtman on Exodus 17: 15b–16a, C. J. Labuschagne on the numerical significance of the life-spans of the patriarchs, K. A. D. Smelik on the ark narrative of 1 Samuel (it is best understood as a commentary on the situation after the destruction of Jerusalem), N. J. Tromp on Psalm 80 (using the literary method of J. Geninasca), and N. A. van Uchelen on Psalm 23 (the nominal phrases *yhwh rʿy* and *ky ʾth ʿmdy* in 1b and 4c are decisive for interpretation).

This volume is an impressive tribute to the depth and creativity of the scholarship of our Dutch-speaking colleagues.

J. W. Rogerson

van der Woude, A. S. (ed.): *The World of the Old Testament* (Bible Handbook, II). 1989. Pp. xi, 300. (Eerdmans, Grand Rapids MI; distributed by Paternoster, Exeter. Price: $34.95; paperback price: £19.50. ISBN 0 8028 2406 4; 0 8028 0443 8 (pbk))

This is the second volume of the *Bible Handbook* whose first volume was reviewed in *B. L.* 1987, p. 21. It follows the same format and maintains the same high standards. The translation by S. Woudstra is clear and reads well. The first major section covers the history of Israel, from the beginnings to the Babylonian captivity (M. J. Mulder), and thence to Alexander the Great (A. S. van der Woude). (The Hellenistic period and its literature are not treated in this book.) The second section (H. H. Brongers) provides an excellent description of the varied genres of Israelite literature (with occasional over-emphasis on the 'Solomonic renaissance'). The third section turns to the individual books of the Old Testament. C. Houtman writes an outstanding and up-to-date study of Pentateuchal criticism, a valuable introduction for any student. The comprehension of the more recent 'literary-functional approach' shown in this essay is less evidenced in the following essays on the historical books (H. H. Grosheide), the prophetic books (B. J. Oosterhoff), and the writings (J. P. M. van der Ploeg), which stay with the more usual literary-historical problems. Each section ends with a useful bibliography. The book is half-heartedly illustrated with black and white and a set of line-drawn maps. The index is for this volume only. Altogether, however, this volume is an excellent introduction to the history and literature of the Old Testament, and should find its way to the shelves of many students, both junior and senior.

J. R. Bartlett

Zeller, D. (ed.): *Menschwerdung Gottes — Vergöttlichung von Menschen* (Novum Testamentum et Orbis Antiquus 7). 1988. Pp. 223. (Universitätsverlag, Freiburg (CH); Vandenhoeck & Ruprecht, Göttingen. Price: SwFr. 58.00. ISBN 3 7278 0604 4; 3 525 53906 1)

Most of the seven papers in this volume were originally presented to a seminar in the Johannes Gutenberg University of Mainz. B. Lang's study of 'the deified king in polytheistic Israel' is the exception: it was written specially for the published collection, and is one of the two contributions directly relevant to Old Testament study. Lang rejects the view of H. Frankfort and others that the Hebrews maintained a sharp distinction between the transcendence of God and the humanity of the king; he argues that the royal ideology of early Israel was of the same character as obtained throughout the ancient Near East, and that allowance must be made for a thoroughgoing monotheistic redaction of pre-exilic Old Testament texts. The other paper in the Old Testament field is D. Michel's study of the fall narrative of Genesis 3, which (he holds) is, as it stands now, the Yahwistic adaptation of a Canaanite myth in which the promise, 'Ye shall be as God', meant exactly what it says—likeness to God being achieved through the experience of sexuality and the overcoming of death.

Other papers deal with the divine ruler in Egypt, Iran and imperial Rome, with the New Testament incarnation in the light of the history of religions, and with the humanization of the concept of God in modern culture.

F. F. Bruce

2. ARCHAEOLOGY AND EPIGRAPHY

Bartlett, J. R.: *Edom and the Edomites* (JSOT Supplement 84; PEF Monograph Series 1). 1989. Pp. 281. (Sheffield Academic Press. Price: £14.50; $20.95. ISBN 1 85075 205 2; ISSN 0309 0787)

It is a pleasure to welcome this first volume of the new *Palestine Exploration Fund Monograph Series* (even if, unaccountably, practically all trace of its sponsorship is missing from the book itself). Bartlett's researches on ancient Edom have extended over more than twenty-five years and have displayed an admirable command both of biblical and other written material and of the growing evidence from surveys and excavations. *Edom and the Edomites* represents the logical culmination of this work in a synthesis which can claim to be the first major published work on the subject (M. Weippert's renowned *Habilitationschrift* never having been formally published) since that of F. Buhl in 1893. The heart of the book consists of a series of chapters treating the evidence for successive periods of the history (and prehistory) of Edom. They are preceded by accounts of modern exploration in the area and the geography of Edom, and followed by studies of 'Edom and Judah' and 'Religion in Edom' and an annotated *corpus* of the epigraphic evidence from Edom, which is more substantial than might have been expected. Two maps, an extensive bibliography and three indexes complete the work. Ancient historians, archaeologists, and biblical scholars alike will be grateful to the author for his authoritative, comprehensive, and up-to-date treatment of the subject. Only the lack of any pictures is a justifiable cause for regret; but perhaps he can be persuaded to put together a companion volume of the 'coffee-table' genre!

G. I. Davies

Dearman, A. (ed.): *Studies in the Mesha Inscription and Moab* (Archaeology and Biblical Studies, 2). 1989. Pp. xii, 324. (Scholars Press, Atlanta GA. Price: $19.95 (member price: $12.95); paperback price: $12.95 (member price $8.95). ISBN 1 55540 356 5; 1 55540 357 3 (pbk))

This collection of studies centres on the Mesha inscription, but framing it we have at the beginning an informative survey by J. M. Maxwell of what is at the present time known about Moab and the Moabites, and at the end two shorter essays, one by the late W. H. Morton (to whom the volume is dedicated) on the three excavations at Dhiban which he directed in the '50s and the '60s, and one by Mary L. Mussell on a hitherto unpublished seal impression found in these excavations which contains a picture of the Moabite deity Chemosh. In between there are six essays devoted solely or mainly to the famous inscription. M. P. Graham gives an absorbing account of the discovery and, after it was broken, of the reconstruction of the inscription; K. P. Jackson and J. A. Dearman (the editor) print out what they consider to be the most trustworthy transcription; Jackson translates this text, with copious notes and a valuable section on the linguistic affinities of Moabite; J. F. Drinkard discusses the literary genre, drawing on the whole field of Northwest Semitic epigraphy; Dearman re-investigates its historical importance compared with the information in the Bible; and G. L. Mattingley writes on what can be recovered from the inscription and other sources, including the Bible, about Moabite religion. There is not a great deal that is new in the collection, but it is an excellent guide to a long and still intriguing story of skullduggery, argument, and scholarship. We need these 'state of the art' evaluations from time to time, and this is a good one of its kind.

J. C. L. Gibson

Gibson, S., Harris, R. L., and Schonfield, J. (eds): *Bulletin of the Anglo-Israel Archaeological Society*, Vol. 7 (1987–88). 1988. Pp. 76. (The Anglo-Israel Archaeological Society, London. Price: £8.00 ($24.00). ISSN 0266 2442)

This Bulletin has now become a journal, publishing papers, reviews, summaries of lectures, and reports on research. Its range is wider than Old Testament studies, including 'Plans for the Settlement of Palestine in the Nineteenth Century' (R. Kark). Relevant to the Old Testament are M. Broshi's comparison of Troy and Jericho, each the subject of oral traditions celebrating largely fictitious accounts of events set about 1200 B.C., and A.D. Crown's 'The Biblical Samaritans in the Present Day' which observes a number of variations and changes within a closed religious community. There are summaries of lectures on the Dead Sea Scrolls after Forty Years by G. Vermes, 'Plants and the Bible' by F. N. Hepper (a concise catalogue with biblical references, noting that 'land of milk and honey' seems to indicate an abandoned agricultural land), and S. Gibson who described his work on the ancient landscape at Sataf near Jerusalem. O. Borowski reported on his excavations at Tell Halif, perhaps Rimmon, which was unfortified at the start of the Iron Age, then walled, destroyed, probably by Sennacherib, and deserted soon after. In different vein, J. Zias spoke about head-lice recovered from first century combs, Middle Bronze Age dental treatment, and Chalcolithic trephination. Grants by the Society aided S. Shalev in archaeometallurgical research to discover the origins and working processes of bronzes from Lachish and other sites, while F. Vitto was enabled to attend a congress on ancient synagogues on which she reports at length. The Society's supporters deserve gratitude for enabling a wider circle to share the products of its activities.

A. R. Millard

Gubel, E.: *Phoenician Furniture: A Typology based on Iron Age Representations with Reference to the Iconographical Context* (Studia Phoenicia VII). 1987. Pp. viii, 329 and xlix plates. (Peeters, Leuven. Price: B.Fr. 3,360. ISBN 90 6831 110 7)

This doctoral thesis from the Free University of Brussels is a catalogue of 174 pieces representing articles of furniture which can be deemed Phoenician. The furniture itself does not survive; it is known only from sculptures, seals, and designs on metalwork. Seats, rigid and folding, footstools, tables, and pot-stands are the main types, with boxes and beds in minor place. Egypt exercised a strong influence in most furniture fashions, although two out of the twenty classes of seat follow Syrian types. Phoenician fashions in turn had an impact on Greek and Roman cabinet-makers, the low table, with three S-shaped legs descending through Greece and Rome to the present day. An introductory chapter discusses the sort of evidence available and the material used, their sources and means of working them. The *kiôr* of 2 Chron. 6:13 is identified with the socle on which gods and worshippers are depicted, in the light of one Phoenician relief. Certain shapes of throne are associated with particular deities, the lion-throne being linked with a Cybele-like figure (contrast Solomon, 1 Kings 10:19ff). Wealthy Israelites enjoyed fine furniture (Amos 6:4), and this valuable collection illustrates the choice they would have had in the emporia of Tyre or Sidon. A photograph or drawing is given for each piece catalogued, and other drawings supplement them in the text. The book is carefully indexed. There is no comparable work on this subject.

A. R. MILLARD

HOMÈS-FREDERICQ, D. and HENNESSY, J. B. (eds): *Archaeology of Jordan*. II *Field Reports*. 1. *Surveys and Sites A-K*, 2. *Sites L-Z* (Akkadica, Supplementum VII–VIII). 1989. Pp. 650. (Peeters, Leuven. Price: B.Fr. 3,400. ISBN 90 6831 180 8)

This most useful resource (covering all archaeological periods) reveals just how much effort has been put over the last two decades into archaeological survey and excavation in Jordan. The first section reports on Regional surveys (of interest to biblical scholars are the ʿAqaba-Maʿan, Baqʿah, Wadi Hasa, Irbid-Beit Ras, Kerak, NW Ard el-Kerak, S. Ghor, and Wadi Yabis surveys), and the second on individual sites. Each report, written by the appropriate expedition director, follows the same plan: site name and map reference; geography and environment; history of exploration; periods represented; history of the sites; significant archaeological material; the environment as known from the excavation or survey; prospects for future work; and bibliography. The position of each site is illustrated by a small map. Plans and illustrations abound. In addition to the well-known sites such as ʿAmman airport, Deir ʿAlla, Dhiban, Hesban, ʿIraq el-Amir, and Tell Saʿidiyeh, there are important entries on lesser known or more recently excavated sites such as Baʿja, Tadun (whose location is wrongly described, p. 19), Feinan, Gharandal (the warning not to confuse this place, near Buseirah, with Arindela in the ʿAraba is ignored by the accompanying map, p. 228), Ghrareh, T. Iktanu, Irbid, Lehun, T.el-Mazar, and others. The editors are to be congratulated on the comprehensiveness and value of this timely book. Two further volumes are projected: Vol. III on comparative Stratigraphy, and Vol. IV on specialized reports on environmental and other studies. Meanwhile, serious students must equip themselves with the K737 series of maps, from which most map references are given, and with Volumes I and I.1, which contain the general bibliography and its up-dating.

J. R. BARTLETT

KNAPP, A. B. (ed.): *Journal of Mediterranean Archaeology*, Vol. 1, No. 2. 1988. Pp. 118. (Sheffield Academic Press. Price: £15.00 ($25.00) p.a. for individuals; £45.00 ($75.00) p.a. for institutions. ISSN 0952 7648)

The sample sent to the *Book List* of this new journal is the second of the two numbers constituting its first subscription unit. It contains three substantial articles: 'Ceramic Production and Social Differentiation: The Dalmatian Neolithic and the Western Mediterranean' (pp. 3–25), by J. C. Chapman; 'Pottery Production in Prehistoric Bronze-Age Cyprus: Assessing the Problem' (pp. 27–55), by D. Frankel; and 'Ceramic Production and Social Change: Archeometric Analysis of Bronze Age Pottery from Jordan' (pp. 57–113), by the editor with P. Duerden, R. V. S. Wright, and P. Grave, who have all been associated with the Australian excavations at Pella. Dr Knapp belongs to the Faculty of Classics in the University of Cambridge.

A. G. AULD

LIVINGSTONE, A.: *Court Poetry and Literary Miscellanea* (State Archives of Assyria, Vol. III. 1989. Pp. xxxvii, 183, XVI plates and 1 microfiche. (Helsinki University Press, Price: Sw.Kr. 157. ISBN 951 570 043 4)

This excellent series gives reliable translations into English with the texts of Assyrian state archives of the first millennium B.C. It will be a reliable reference to many documents not otherwise readily available and some of this corpus of 52 (some fragmentary) texts covering a wide variety of type and content will repay comparison with similar literary examples preserved in the Old Testament. No commentary is given but the extensive introduction partly serves as that.

About half are poetic texts — hymns to gods, temples, cities and kings, and one for the coronation of Ashurbanipal (*c.* 627 B.C.). Epical poems praise royal exploits in war and elegies include a righteous sufferer's prayer, a dialogue between a king and his god, a memorial for a woman, and mourning for the death of a god (Tammuz?). Literary letters and royal propaganda have among them the underworld vision of a prince and details of the sin of King Sargon. Letters from gods, some in response to royal letters (an important category linked with Akkadian prophecy but not included here) merit study.

Overall these confirm that the Assyrians adapted many Babylonian literary forms in a royal ideology based on a centralized state which differed from the pluralized city-state system of Babylonia. Mystical, cultic explanatory works, commentaries, and incantations (Nos 34–40, 48–52) are a category of texts virtually absent from the Old Testament. The inclusion of illustrations, other than texts, must be questioned as adding unnecessarily to the cost of this well-produced volume.

D. J. WISEMAN

MALAMAT, A.: *Mari and the Early Israelite Experience* (The Schweich Lectures 1984). 1989. Pp. xiii, 161 and VIII plates. (Oxford University Press, for the British Academy. Price: £22.50. ISBN 0 19 726072 1)

The Professor of Jewish History at the Hebrew University, Jerusalem, here presents a summation of much of his work over the last few decades on Mari and the Old Testament, with recent additions. After introducing the site and the Old Babylonian palace, from which the main archives come, the Patriarchal period is dealt with. The chronological spread from Mari to Moses is solved by arguing that the Biblical three generations result from telescoping a much longer period, and the relevance of the Mari archives is that they contain a whole range of Amorite loan-words attesting institutions also found under the Hebrew cognates in the older parts of the Old Testament or as archaisms in Hebrew poetry. A serious case is presented, though here and there a point is strained. 'Intuitive' prophecy, i.e. not resulting from special techniques, is treated at some length. There is indeed a similarity between the men and women who gave their messages as reported from Mari and the Old Testament prophets (true and false). The lack of similar phenomena elsewhere, e.g. in Babylonia, gives the strength to the case. Worship of dead kings and tribal ancestors as an Amorite institution is considered to be reflected in certain Old Testament institutions and passages. Finally, it is argued that significant similarities exist between the achievements of certain kings of Mari, and other Amorite rulers, as described in their royal inscriptions and passages in the Old Testament, especially Psalm 29.

Literature up to 1987 is incorporated in the published form of these lectures, but publication continues. *ARM* 26 (1988) consists so far of two massive volumes with much new material from Mari on divination, prophecy, and dreams (see below pp. 120f). Also some finds from Ebla, such as the evidence for the cult of dead kings (*B. L.* 1989, p. 149), appeared too late to be used. Thus the subject is far from being closed, but it is useful to have this systematic presentation from one who has especially exploited this material.

W. G. Lambert

Mitchell, T. C.: *The Bible in the British Museum: Interpreting the Evidence*. 1988. Pp. 112. (British Museum, London. Price: £5.95. ISBN 0 7141 1698 x)

The title of this attractive and useful guide may mislead some, though not those who are aware that the author is Keeper of Western Asiatic Antiquities in the British Museum. It is not primarily about biblical manuscripts in the Museum (though two such are illustrated), but about a variety of texts and other antiquities (most of which can be seen in the Museum), which are related in some way to biblical history or religion. Sixty 'documents' are illustrated and discussed, and the author takes particular care to explain the process of their interpretation (or even, in certain cases, their misinterpretation). Full translations of the texts are not generally given, but a special feature is that in several cases the original cuneiform or palaeo-Hebrew text of part of an inscription is set out with a transliteration and translation in adjacent columns, so that the nature of the ancient writing-systems can be better understood. There is a brief introduction, and also a map, chronological tables, bibliographical notes, and indexes. The volume will be particularly helpful to school groups and others who are able to visit the Museum for themselves.

G. I. Davies

Murphy O'Connor, J.: *The Holy Land: An archaeological guide from earliest times to 1700*. 2nd revised and expanded edition. 1986. Pp. xviii, 381. (Oxford University Press. Price: £6.95. ISBN 0 19 285158 6)

Many reviewers were less cautious than our own (*B. L.* 1982, p. 27) in commending the first edition (1980) of Father Murphy O'Connor's now very widely used guide. The extended edition of 1986, already reprinted in 1988, has expanded the coverage of Jerusalem by some twenty per cent, taking account of new researches and the recent publication of older ones; and there are now descriptions of 103 sites and areas in the rest of the country, rather than ninety-four. It remains excellent value for money.

A. G. Auld

Neu, E.: *Das Hurritische: Eine altorientalische Sprache in neuem Licht* (Abhandlungen der Geistes- und Sozialwissenschaftlichen Klasse, 3). 1988. Pp. 48. (Akademie der Wissenschaften und der Literatur, Mainz — Franz Steiner, Wiesbaden — Stuttgart). Price: DM 24.00. ISBN 3 315 05179 1)

In 1983, during excavations by the Deutsches Archäologische Institut (Berlin) at Boğazkale (previously named Boğazköy) a fragment of a Hurrian-Hittite bilingual tablet was found. Two years later, another bilingual fragment was unearthed there. Neu's booklet (the text of a talk given in 1986) gives us a foretaste of these fragments which should be published quite soon. Given the scarcity of documents in Hurrian they are of particular interest to specialists in that language. Also, the texts are sapiential in character and are, in fact, the first examples of wisdom literature in Hittite. As far as can be ascertained, they were to be recited on an occasion corresponding to the

Israelite jubilee year when debtors and slaves were emancipated. In addition, one of the allegorical tales relates how copper, formed into a cup, curses its maker which, as the author points out, is reminiscent of Isa. 29:16. Our appetite has been whetted for full publication of these texts by H. Otten and C. Rüster in KBo XXXII.

W. G. E. WATSON

PARDEE, D.: *Les Textes Para-mythologiques de la 24e Campagne (1961)* (Ras Shamra-Ougarit IV). 1988. Pp. 333. (Éditions Recherche sur les Civilisations, Paris. Price: Fr 198.00. ISBN 2 86538 185 4; ISSN 0291 1655)

This is an exhaustive study of nine Ugaritic para-mythological texts, eight previously published in *Ugaritica V* (1968) and one in *Ugaritica VII* (1978). They came from a building which may have been a priest's house or small, specialized school. Unusually and most laudably there is a preliminary note by J.-C. Courtois on the archaeological context of the finds (pp. 4–12). The main body of the work consists of a detailed study of each text. Apart from the extensive bibliographies, new copies of each text are provided, based on direct examination of the tablets — Professor Pardee is the doyen of this aspect of Ugaritic studies. The new copies are superior to those published earlier and will now replace them. Translations have the benefit of the many insights into these texts that have come from specialists since they were first published. Note may also be made of the provision of vocalised texts, which are particularly valuable. As to the content of the texts, the chapter-headings assigned to them indicate their importance beyond Ugaritology: 'Ilu gets drunk, the blessing of Rapi'u, Baʿlu in the form of a mountain, the hunger of Mîtu, the feast of the Manes, the visit to Dutanu, Ḥôrānu and the serpents, Šapšu and the serpent, the request for a palace. Pardee's work will be the *point de départ* for all further study on these texts.

J. F. HEALEY

SASS, B.: *The Genesis of the Alphabet and its Development in the Second Millennium B.C.* (Ägypten und Altes Testament 13). 1988. Pp. xi, 221, 294 figures. (In Kommission bei O. Harrassowitz, Wiesbaden. Price: DM 148.00. ISBN 3 447 02860 2)

By collecting photographs and drawings of the Proto-Sinaitic inscriptions and the Late Bronze Age alphabet documents from the Levant, Sass has made firm foundations for the future study of the alphabet's birth and infancy. Many of the pictures are new, the author having examined the texts themselves wherever possible, and made his own drawings. Consequently, he offers new readings, giving good reasons for rejecting some earlier ones. His treatment of these obscure yet important texts is cautious, leading to far less optimistic results than the work of W. F. Albright and others since his time. Sass accepts only five words in the Proto-Sinaitic texts as 'more or less certain' in their reading. From his collations, he proceeds to discuss the forms of the characters, the date of the texts, and the origins of the alphabet. He offers arguments for either a 12th or an 18th Dynasty date for the Proto-Sinaitic, preferring the earlier (i.e. *c.* 1800 B.C.), with Sinai the place of the script's origin. Egyptian hieroglyphic monuments there include signs which could serve as prototypes for all the Proto-Sinaitic characters when Semites met and wanted to imitate the Egyptian. These first letters spread to Southern Palestine where they developed more cursive forms, evident in the Late Bronze Age and culminating in the Phoenician alphabet. The cuneiform alphabet, the Old Arabian and the Greek receive brief attention, Sass choosing the ninth century B.C. for the Greek borrowing. With its comprehensive facsimiles and its sober attitude, this book marks a major stage in knowledge of the beginning of the script which was becoming widespread and stable by 1000 B.C. and so ready for Israel's authors to use.

A. R. MILLARD

VON WEIHER, E.: *Spätbabylonische Texte aus Uruk*. Teil III (Ausgrabungen der deutschen Forschungsgemeinschaft in Uruk-Warka, 12). 1988. Pp. IX, 341 incl. 77 plates. (Mann, Berlin. Price: DM 120.00. ISBN 3 7861 1508 7)

The publication of the finds from the S.E. mound at Uruk (biblical Erech, Babylonia) continues with 62 tablets from the 1970–77 seasons. Presented in an exemplary manner with copies of the cuneiform texts, transliterations, translations, and notes, they are of primary interest to those studying the range of cuneiform texts commonly found in the libraries of incantation priests. Here we have spells against demons, rituals for averting evil, hymns, and prayers to gods (Ayya, Ishtar, and Ea-Marduk). The reference books for medical and exorcist priests include omens from malformed births, astrology, the calendar, and plants. A revised edition of a previously published part of the Gilgamesh-Humbaba myth is included. Colophons on fifteen texts show that the whole 'classical' range of texts was still being copied here as late as the sixth year of Philip Arrhidaeus (318 B.C.).

D. J. WISEMAN

WIGHTMAN, G. J.: *The Damascus Gate, Jerusalem: Excavations by C.-M. Bennett and J. B. Hennessy at the Damascus Gate, Jerusalem, 1964–66* (BAR International Series 519). 1989. Pp. ii, 366. (British Archaeological Reports, Oxford. Price: £23.00. ISBN 0 86054 660 8)

Readers of this *List* will glean some useful comments from Wightman's sifting and comprehensive publication of the excavations carried out for the Jordanian Department of Antiquities by two former Directors of the British School of Archaeology in Jerusalem. The absence of any evidence of quarrying in the immediate vicinity of the gate suggests to him that the central (or Tyropean) valley had from ancient times provided a major approach route to the city. Then he dashes the hopes of those who had looked to this dig for an end to the controversy about Josephus' Third Wall. While Wightman shares Hennessy's and Kenyon's view that that wall was in the vicinity of the north wall of the present 'old city' of Jerusalem, and not on the maximalist line of the Mayer-Sukenik hypothesis, he insists that the Roman gate now visible under the present one could not have been part of it. For under it is an Herodian tower-like structure; and the Third Wall was built to enclose a previously unfortified northern quarter.

A. G. AULD

3. HISTORY AND GEOGRAPHY

BALY, D.: *Basic Bible Geography*. 1987. Pp. 80. (Fortress, Philadelphia. Price: $4.95. ISBN 0 8006 1922 6)

Here is a first-class compact introduction to the geography of Palestine. Baly shows how the land lies in the Fertile Crescent, in geological and climatic terms, describing regional variations of climate season by season. He sets out briefly the main patterns of farming, of herding, and mentions the wild animals and untamed regions. Ch. 4, 'The Regions of Palestine', is particularly helpful, its clear characterizations emphasizing the differences, and notes of distance underlining the small area of the land. Balancing this chapter is one on the Transjordanian region, which is equally clear. The final chapter concerns New Testament Palestine, drawing attention to the changes Hellenism brought. Throughout there are illuminating quotations from the biblical text, and the Scripture Index should be consulted also. Basic bible geography this is, very successfully presented. (The rather grey photographs and absence of several places from the maps are the only faults.)

A. R. MILLARD

BAR-KOCHVA, B.: *Judas Maccabaeus: The Jewish Struggle Against the Seleucids*, 1989. Pp. xvi, 672. (Cambridge University Press. Price: £70.00. ISBN 0 521 32352 5)

This continues B.-K.'s well-known work as a military historian of antiquity by being a study primarily of the battles of Judas Maccabaeus (contrary to the implications of the title, it is not intended as a biography of the Jewish revolutionary). Part I is a 'Historical Evaluation' which considers general matters about the Jewish army of Judas in the light of what is known about Seleucid military craft. Part II consists primarily of an introduction to and detailed commentary on 1 Maccabees 3:10–4:36; 6:18–63; 7:26–32, 39–50; 9:1–22. One useful chapter surveys the primary sources. Appendixes discuss diverse topics relevant to the study (e.g., the location of the Acra). There are also ample indexes and bibliography.

One of the main conclusions is that, contrary to popular opinion, the Jewish military successes were not extraordinary. The early sources are misleading about the relative size of the Jewish and Seleucid armies. Judas' genius lay not in defeating overwhelming odds but in developing a regular army which might lose some battles but was able to win in the long run. Although specialists will disagree about individual interpretations, B.-K.'s study is masterful and should be welcomed not only by students of Jewish history but by classical military historians as well. But could not *something* be done about the awful price?

L. L. GRABBE

CARENA, O.: *History of the Near Eastern Historiography and its Problems: 1852–1985*. Part I: 1852–1945 (AOAT 218). 1989. Pp. xviii, 143. (Neukirchener, Neukirchen-Vluyn; Butzon & Bercker, Kevelaer. Price: DM 67.00. ISBN 3 7887 1293 7; 3 7666 9637 8)

The interest of this work will be somewhat marginal for most users of the *Book List* as for its author 'The Near East' includes only Mesopotamia and the Hittites. He begins with an account of the malaise of much contemporary study of Mesopotamia as this is perceived, for example, by M. Liverani (domination by philologists has held back historical interpretation) and then provides an annotated bibliography of works published between 1852 and 1945 and a review of the tendencies apparent at different stages of this period. The English is not always very good, but there are occasional cameos of wider interest which will reward the persevering reader, such as the comments on S. A. Cook's characterization of ancient Semites in the *Cambridge Ancient History* and on the political reasons (so it is suggested) for much of the interest in the Hurrians in the 1930s. A comparative table helpfully correlates discoveries and publications in different fields, but the dates given here for two publications by Wellhausen and Graf are unfortunately wrong. The second part of this study is intended to conclude the history of research and discuss various proposals for improving historical methodology in Mesopotamian studies.

G. I. DAVIES

CATE, R. L.: *A History of the Bible Lands in the Interbiblical Period*. 1989. Pp. 176. (Broadman, Nashville TN. Price: $10.95. ISBN 0 8064 1154 2)

This book takes up where Cate's *History of Israel* (*B. L.* 1986, p. 36) leaves off, namely, the arrival on the scene of Alexander the Great. It ends with the Bar Kochva Revolt. The author's stance is openly evangelical and conservative, and this controls his approach to the history of the period and his sources. When an author lists the following among his presuppositions: 'I believe that the other ancient documents from which we get our information about the inter-biblical period, while sometimes written by pious and devoted people, are of a different nature from the biblical materials written in a similar time and by similar people', one cannot expect history-writing as most other historians would conceive it. However, since most of the sources for this period are non-biblical, the author is not, in principle, opposed to handling these critically. His intended audience is 'the beginning student', 'the busy pastor' and 'the interested layperson'. It is too elementary for first-year students at British universities and colleges, but could be useful for the rest of his intended audience. However, since most of it consists of yet another potted summary of I and II Maccabees and Josephus, one cannot help feeling that the audience would find the original sources more interesting. Less constant recital of 'facts', and more analysis of the sources, would have made this a better book.

A. P. HAYMAN

FLANAGAN, J. W.: *David's Social Drama: A Hologram of Israel's Early Iron Age* (JSOT Supplement Series, 73; The Social World of Biblical Antiquity Series, 7). 1988. Pp. 373. (Almond, Sheffield. Price: £24.00 ($45.00); paperback price: £14.95 ($22.00). ISBN 1 85075 201 X; 1 85075 202 8 (pbk))

This detailed and densely written study aims to fill the gap created by the demise of traditional accounts of the history of David based on the literary sources. The 'social drama' of the title is a metaphor for social transformation; the 'hologram' of the subtitle is a three dimensional image constructed by the use of comparative sociology to create a fresh pattern out of the information derived from the analysis of literary and archaeological sources. These provide independent images which only at the second level of interdisciplinary study are integrated by comparative sociology.

The archaeological images of the early Iron Age are derived from, on the one hand, the study of geomorphology, geography, soil, climate and vegetation, and, on the other, the settlement patterns reflected in surface surveys and site excavations. The possibility for microenvironments with the potential for different economies, residence strategies, and life styles, which the first suggests, is confirmed and illustrated by the second. Impressions of material cultural unity do not emerge, if at all, until the latter half of the tenth century. A complex matrix of material and social development must be envisaged in which there are no sharp contrasts between urban and rural, pastoral and cultivating, sedentary and nomadic: the pattern reflected is one of the synchronic interaction of the different units of a segmentary society at different stages of evolution.

The literary images are those of Psalms, Chronicles, Deuteronomistic History, and the books of Samuel. David stands at the juncture of several worlds, at a point of transition. From the earliest expressions in Samuel through to Chronicles, he is consistently a mediator standing betwixt and between, between north and south, between Benjaminites and Judahites, between Saul's and his own dynasties, between egalitarianism and monopolized force, between human and divine realms.

The hologram which emerges is of a segmentary society becoming a chieftainship. David was an astute leader who could use the mechanisms of a segmentary society to create a web of alliances that drew people towards fuller centralization.

A. D. H. MAYES

GUNNEWEG, A. H. J.: *Geschichte Israels: Von den Anfängen bis Bar Kochva und von Theodor Herzl bis zur Gegenwart*. 6th revised and expanded edition (Theologische Wissenschaft 2). 1989. Pp. 253 and 2 pp. of maps. (Kohlhammer, Stuttgart. Price: DM 26.00. ISBN 3 17 010511 6)

For the fifth edition see *B. L.* 1985. The sixth edition has incorporated a few relatively minor modifications to the historical presentation of earlier editions; otherwise the most significant change is the addition of a new forty page concluding chapter on the history of the modern state of Israel up to the 1988 elections. The topics covered include the rise of Zionism, Theodor Herzl, the Zionist organization and settlement in Palestine up to the First World War, the British mandate, the foundation of the state and the first Arab-Israeli war, consolidation of the state, and the six-day war. The history of the new state of Israel is held to be a late continuation of the history of ancient Israel, after the centuries of the diaspora, and even if it is not to be seen as the fulfilment of the messianic hope, this later history is not without theological relevance and may contribute indirectly to a deeper understanding of the Old Testament.

A. D. H. MAYES

KNAUF, E. A.: *Midian. Untersuchungen zur Geschichte Palästinas und Nordarabiens am Ende des 2. Jahrtausends v. Chr.* (Abhandlungen des Deutschen Palästinavereins). 1988. Pp. xii, 194. (Harrassowitz, Wiesbaden. Price: DM 78.00. ISBN 3 447 02862 9)

Knauf begins with a study of the limited evidence for Midian, seen as located along the east coast of the Gulf of ʿAqaba and its hinterland. The Midianites, at least at the end of the second millennium B.C., were not 'bedouin' (i.e. camel-mounted warriors) but cattle rearers, farmers, camel breeders, traders, and miners. Their speech was a form of proto-Arabic; they originated as early Israel's contemporaries in the Late Bronze–Iron Age transition period. Midian was the original home of Yahweh, and Knauf's major aim is to show how this Midianite deity became Israel's God.

Knauf's thesis, based on detailed and highly selective source analysis of Exodus 1–15, is that Moses is to be identified with the Asiatic *by/ʾrśw*, who after a short rule was ejected from Egypt in 1187–86 B.C. Moses headed *ʿapirū* groups who had entered Egypt from Palestine, either as prisoners of war or by self-enslavement; on leaving Egypt they naturally headed for Palestine. Among Moses' followers, however, were also some Midianite *shōsu*, who had their own tradition, preserved in the victory song of the Midianitess Miriam, of Yahweh's destruction of some Egyptian chariots in the *yam sūp*, i.e. the Gulf of ʿAqaba, while on an expedition against Midian. This Midianite experience of salvation from Egyptian power was adopted by the larger group entering Palestine; thus Yahweh became Israel's God. The final section explores the development of Israelite tradition about Midian in the Old Testament.

Knauf is emphatic that the exodus story is Israel's interpretation of events now totally lost to us, and that 'history' is really myth which must not be mistaken for political reality. We can reconstruct historical events out of narrative only when we have the external controls of material, archaeological and epigraphic evidence. Knauf therefore limits severely what may be used, yet in spite of his strictures against over-readiness to accept the evidence of 'oral tradition' readily isolates his own core of reliable early tradition. This is a valuable and original study which puts new life into the Midianite hypothesis.

J. R. BARTLETT

Minokami, Y.: *Die Revolution des Jehu* (Göttinger Theologische Arbeiten 38). 1988. Pp. 220. (Vandenhoeck & Ruprecht, Göttingen. Price: DM 44.00. ISBN 3 525 87391 3)

This admirably clear study progressively divests 2 Kings 9–10 of a series of supplements in order finally to lay bare the first biblical telling of the story of Jehu. It is heavily indebted to the work of R. Smend, and also of Ch. Levin his fellow student, to whom also this publication is dedicated. For a review of Levin's similar study of 2 Kings 11 see *B. L.* 1984, pp. 38f. It is unfortunate, however, that Minokami's discussion partners write almost exclusively in German. He does pay attention throughout to differences between MT and LXX; but makes no mention of an important study published between Levin's of 1982 and his own: J. C. Trebolle-Barrera's 1984 work on text and literary composition in 2 Kings 9–11, *Jehú y Joás* (*B. L.* 1985, p. 96). Trebolle points us in rather different directions from Minokami, and deserves an answer.

A. G. Auld

Rogerson, J.: *Shin Seisho-chizu*. Translated by K. Onodera under the supervision of the Prince Mikasa. 1988. Pp. 237 with numerous illustrations and maps. (Asakura-shoten, Tokyo, ¥22,000. ISBN 4 254 16598 6 C 3325)

This is a Japanese translation of *The New Atlas of the Bible*, 1985 (See *B. L.* 1986, pp. 41–42).

K. K. Sacon

Roth, M. T.: *Babylonian Marriage Agreements, 7th–3rd Centuries B.C.* (AOAT 222). 1989. Pp. xviii, 154. (Neukirchener, Neukirchen-Vluyn; Butzon & Bercker, Kevelaer. Price: DM 93.00. ISBN 3 7887 1311 9; 3 7666 9636 X).

The author here provides transliteration, translation and notes on forty-four neo-Babylonian marriage agreements, eighteen of which are previously unpublished. An introduction provides a summary outline of the forms and terminology of the agreements and concludes with a discussion of their purpose. The author promises wider-ranging studies of the material elsewhere. No attempt is made here to relate the terms of these documents to biblical institutions, but the book will undoubtedly interest serious students of the early history of Jewish marriage law, not least because of the availability of some comparable Jewish marriage agreements from the intertestamental period.

B. S. Jackson

Schley, D. G.: *Shiloh: A Biblical City in Tradition and History* (JSOT Supplement Series 63). 1989. Pp. 256. (Sheffield Academic Press. Price: £25.00 ($42.50). ISBN 1 85075 161 7)

This work began as a dissertation presented to Emory University in 1986, and is curious both as a dissertation and as a monograph. It is at its best when reviewing Shiloh in nineteenth-century criticism, and 'the Wellhausian revolution and its critics'. The third chapter, 'Discussion of Shiloh in the Twentieth Century', reviews the Danish excavations and the recent results of Finkelstein (*B. L.* 1989, pp. 26f); then the literary/historical studies of Kaufmann, de Vaux, Haran, Eissfeldt, Cody, and Cross. There follow chapters on Shiloh in Joshua, in Judges, in Samuel, and in Kings, Psalms, and Jeremiah. And the study concludes with a review of first the traditions and then the history of Biblical Shiloh. Here and there the argument may be fresh, but is largely superficial. The reviewer's several relevant studies could easily have been overlooked. However, when the only post-war commentaries in the bibliography are those by Noth on Joshua, McCarter on Samuel, and Kraus on the Psalms, the professed '*forschungsgeschichtlich* perspective', and the claim 'that the present discussion has not really moved beyond the place it was 130 years ago' are themselves put in perspective.

A. G. AULD

SCHUR, N.: *History of the Samaritans* (Beiträge zur Erforschung des Alten Testamentes und des antiken Judentums, 18). 1989. Pp. 305. (Lang, Frankfurt am Main, Bern, New York, Paris. Price: Sw.Fr. 65.00. ISBN 3 631 40340 2; ISSN 0722 0790)

In the plethora of recent studies of different aspects of Samaritanism no-one has so far ventured on the daunting task of compiling an overall history, and so Schur deserves our gratitude for undertaking this. It is also helpful that he has written in English rather than Hebrew, so that his work will be the more widely available. The limitations inherent in these two aspects of his work are, first, that a great deal of the book consists of a somewhat uncritical presentation of secondary sources of very disparate quality; and secondly, that mistakes of grammar, syntax, and spelling abound. In fairness it must also be said that he is aware of the first of these limitations, and warns of the partial nature of our knowledge of many aspects of Samaritan history, as well as offering his own evaluations of the sources from time to time. For the period likely to be of most interest to readers of this *Book List* Schur's view is that the Samaritans must be regarded as inheritors of the Old Northern traditions of Israel, so that later rivalry between Samaritans and Jews is a continuation of age-old tension.

R. J. COGGINS

SHANKS, H. (ed.): *Ancient Israel: A Short History from Abraham to the Roman Destruction of the Temple*. 1989. Pp. xix, 267. (SPCK, London. Price: £12.95. ISBN 0 281 04404 X)

This is an attractively produced, well illustrated and moderately priced collection of essays by P. Kyle McCarter, Nahum Sarna, Joseph Callaway, André Lemaire, Siegfried Horn, James Purvis, Lee Levine, and Shaye Cohen on successive periods of Israelite history. As with all such joint efforts there are problems of consistency. The writers seem to have had a very general brief which laid particular emphasis on the inclusion of reference to non-biblical sources and archaeology, for in this respect they seem to be thorough and up-to-date. In other respects, however, there is considerable variation. In their treatment of literary problems and their use of recent work on anthropological and sociological aspects of Israelite history, some essays, particularly that on the patriarchal age, are excellent, while others betray little awareness of recent work. Despite this unevenness, however, the book may still serve a useful function for its intended student and general readership.

A. D. H. MAYES

SIGRIST, C. and NEU, R. (eds): *Ethnologische Texte zum Alten Testament*. Bd 1: *Vor- und Frühgeschichte Israels*, 1989. Pp. 230. (Neukirchener, Neukirchen-Vluyn. Price: DM 48.00. ISBN 3 7887 1289 9)

This collection has its origins in a perceived need to strengthen German Old Testament scholarship by making it more aware of the type of ethnological study that has been developed mainly in English speaking scholarship. The volume contains studies of social, political, economic and religious conditions in segmentary societies which allow conclusions to be drawn on social institutions, and developments in pre-monarchic Israel. Divided into five major sections, each with its own brief introduction, it contains articles or sections of books, translated where necessary into German, on the economy, social organization, political organization, religion, and law of segmentary societies, the contributors including some whose names are by now certainly familiar to Old Testament scholars: M. D. Sahlins, M. Fortes, C. Sigrist, E. E. Evans-Pritchard, M. Weber, and E. Durkheim. The introduction by Sigrist draws attention to the paradigm shift in Old Testament study from treating the pre-monarchic period simply as preparatory for the state to an understanding of it as a social and religious form and time in its own right, a shift of view made possible especially by the analytic presuppositions provided by British social anthropology. A useful introductory essay by Neu discusses the significance of ethnology for Old Testament study by showing how cultural comparisons of the type followed by Nyström, de Vaux, Soggin, Buccellati, Klengel, Mendenhall, Gottwald, and Thiel have been weakened either by a lack of independent information on contemporary non-Israelite societies or by an inability to relate such information as does exist to the Israelite situation; the studies of Malamat, Crüsemann, and Schäfer-Lichtenberger, on the other hand, have opened up new possibilities by developing a theoretical framework which, though based on cultures temporally and spatially far removed from Israel, may also be useful for illuminating Israelite social evolution.

A. D. H. Mayes

Vardiman, E. E.: *La grande svolta. La Giudea tra ellenismo e primo cristianesimo*. 1987. Pp. 379. (Garzanti, Milano. Price: Lire 18,000. ISBN 88 11 54897 7)

This is the Italian translation of a German work, *Die grosse Zeitwende — Zwischen Hellenismus und Urchristentum*, published in Vienna and Düsseldorf in 1978. It is a popular work (written for readers who need to be told, in a footnote to the first page of the Introduction, that the Diadochi were Alexander's successors), describing the everyday culture and life of Palestine from Alexander's conquest to the establishment of the Roman peace under Hadrian. Among the matters treated are agriculture, animal life, maritime and urban occupations, commerce, language and writing, death and burial, religion, relations with the imperial power. Readers with no previous knowledge of these subjects will find the book informative, and will be helped by the illustrations.

F. F. Bruce

de Vaux, R.: *Zoku Isuraeru-Kodai-shi. Shishijidai*. Translated by T. Nishimura. 1989. Pp. 240. (Nihon Kirisuto-Kyōdan Shuppan-kyoku, Tokyo. Price: ¥3,400. ISBN 4 8184 0014 9 C 3016)

This is a Japanese translation of *Histoire ancienne d'Israël: La période des Juges* (Etudes Bibliques), 1973 (See *B. L.* 1975, p. 33).

K. K. Sacon

Vermes, G. and Goodman, M. D. (eds): *The Essenes According to the Classical Sources* (An Oxford Centre Textbook). 1989. Pp. xi, 103. (Almond, Sheffield. Price: £16.50 ($28.00). ISBN 1 85075 139 0)

This is the first of a new series of textbooks intended 'to facilitate the historical and linguistic study of inter-Testamental and rabbinic literature from the original sources'. The intended market is university and college students. This volume contains a comprehensive collection of Greek and Latin sources dealing with the Essenes (and, in an appendix, the Therapeutae). The texts are accompanied with a translation on the facing page and brief notes, mainly indicating parallel references. Martin Goodman has contributed the translations or revised existing ones. Geza Vermes is responsible for the seventeen page introduction which simplifies and condenses his account of the Essenes in §30 of the revised edition of Schürer's *History of the Jews in the age of Jesus Christ*, vol. II. For the intended market, this is an excellent textbook. Let us hope that it helps to keep alive the honourable tradition of placing students in first-hand contact with the original sources. But scholars also will find it helpful to have such a convenient collection of the original sources close to hand.

A. P. HAYMAN

4. TEXT AND VERSIONS

ALEXANDRE, M.: *Le commencement du livre Genèse I–V: La version grecque de la Septante et sa réception* (Christianisme Antique 3). 1988. Pp. 408 and 23 plates. (Beauchesne, Paris. Price: Fr 372.00. ISBN 2 7010 1151 5)

This book is a fruit of the French Septuagint project (*La Bible d'Alexandrie*). The annotated translation of the whole of Genesis, by Marguerite Harl, appeared in 1986 (see *B. L.* 1987, p. 37). Madame Harl was able to make use of Monique Alexandre's translation and detailed notes for the first five chapters, which are here published in full, but her scope was severely limited. (The chapters in question take up only forty pages of the earlier book.) Madame Alexandre is able to go into greater detail, and she is also able to range more widely, not only investigating the history of the Greek words and the reception of the LXX in the Greek Patristic tradition, but also glancing at the Latin and Hebrew traditions of biblical interpretation, and even at the iconography of the creation. This a very rich commentary indeed, and a work of considerable erudition. No doubt it will be appreciated mainly as a work of reference; but it is possible, if not to read it from cover to cover, at least to browse in it with great profit.

N. R. M. DE LANGE

AUFRECHT, W. E. and HAMILTON, G. J.: *The Tell Fakhariyah Bilingual Inscription: A Bibliography* (Newsletter for Targumic and Cognate Studies, Supplement 4). 1988. Pp. 7. (Department of Near Eastern Studies, University of Toronto. Price: $5.00. ISSN 0704 59005)

About seventy-five articles and books featuring the Tell Fekherye bilingual are listed for the period 1981–88 (though only two are given for 1988). Single page, or even footnote, references in studies dealing with other topics are included in this total. There is also information on reviews of the 1982 publication of the texts by A. Abou-Assaf, P. Bordreuil and A. R. Millard. The only omission noticed by the reviewer (with the help of *Newsletter for Targumic and Cognate Studies*) is F. Leemhuis, 'An Early Witness for a Fronted /g/ in Aramaic? The Case of the Tell Fekherye Inscription', in H. L. J. Vanstiphout (ed.), *Scripta signa vocis; Studies about Scripts, Scriptures, Scribes and Languages in the Near East, Presented to J. H. Hospers* (Groningen, 1986), pp. 133–42.

R. P. GORDON

CLARKE, E. G. (ed.): *Newsletter for Targumic and Cognate Studies*, Vol. 15.2 (1989); 16.1 (1989). 1989. Pp. 7; 10. (Department of Near Eastern Studies, University of Toronto. Price: $5.00. ISSN 0704 59005)

Between them these two issues record the publication of six volumes and fifty-five articles on Targum and a considerably larger number of items (almost all articles) on cognate studies.

R. P. GORDON

DIRKSEN, P. B.: *An Annotated Bibliography of the Peshiṭta of the Old Testament* (Monographs of the Peshiṭta Institute 5). 1989. Pp. xiv, 119. (Brill, Leiden. Price: fl 64.00; ca. $32.00. ISBN 90 04 09017 7; ISSN 0169 9008)

With the completion (hopefully!) of the Peshiṭta Project in sight, P. B. Dirksen has drawn up this comprehensive bibliography of an important biblical version, most of which is now at last available in a proper critical edition. Dirksen edited Judges (along with a monograph on the text) for the Project and has, in recent years, been one of the key figures in the Peshiṭta Institute. He is, therefore, excellently qualified to perform this onerous task. 532 books, articles, and significant reviews, are listed. The material is divided up into nine sections making it easy to find a bibliography, for example, on the general problems of the Peshiṭta, on an individual book, on the relationship with the MT, or even on a particular manuscript. Inevitably, there is a considerable degree of overlap but the internal reference system (with each item separately numbered) is easy to follow and there is a comprehensive author index at the end. Occasionally, there is a summary of the academic debate on a particular issue (for example, the relationship between P and MT on pp. 88ff), while the information on the origin of Lee's edition (1823) for the British and Foreign Bible Society represents original research. I was particularly intrigued to learn that the apocryphal Psalm 151 had to be cut out of the remaining stock of Lee's edition after the General Committee of the BFBS took an ideological decision (in 1826) not to take any part in publishing apocryphal texts!

A. P. HAYMAN

FERNÁNDEZ MARCOS, N. and BUSTO SAIZ, J. R.: *El Texto Antioqueno de la Biblia Griega*, I. *1–2 Samuel* (Textos y Estudios "Cardenal Cisneros" de la Biblia Políglota Matritense, 50). 1989. Pp. lxxxix, 173. (CSIC, Madrid. ISBN 84 00 06971 4)

This critical edition of 1 and 2 Kingdoms is meant as a first step towards a complete edition of the Antiochian Greek Bible, as it might have existed in the fourth century. The edition is based on the five manuscripts recognized as Lucianic (for Kingdoms) by Rahlfs, which have been entirely re-collated, and on the quotations in Theodoret, whose *Quaestiones in Reges et Paralipomena* appeared in a critical edition by the same editors in this series in 1984. The scarcity of textual variants of the edited text of Theodoret against the biblical manuscripts appears to be a striking vindication of this procedure. A second textual apparatus provides readings from the Hebrew fragments found at Qumran, Josephus (collated by M. V. Spottorno), the Antiochian Greek Fathers, the *Vetus Latina*, and Latin Fathers who used it, and also the Armenian version, collated by S. P. Cowe (editor of the Armenian texts of these books which is due to be published in the same series). Dr Cowe has also written a section on the Armenian version (in English) for the very clear and comprehensive introduction.

This is a valuable contribution to the study of the biblical text. I have only two cavils of a general nature; one is the inappropriate use of the Hebraic book title 'Samuel'; the other is the lack of running heads over the Greek text, which makes it difficult to find one's way around.

N. R. M. DE LANGE

LE BOULLUEC, A. and SANDEVOIR, P.: *L'Exode. Traduction du texte grec de la Septante, Introduction et Notes* (La Bible d'Alexandrie, 2). 1989. Pp. 394. (Cerf, Paris. Price: Fr. 185.00. ISBN 2 204 03066 X)

The fruit of a happy collaboration between a Hellenist and a Hebraist, this volume of the French Septuagint series offers a careful translation of Rahlfs's Greek text, accompanied by a rich commentary which includes comments on the Greek language and a comparison with the Masoretic Text, brief discussions of the (mainly Greek Patristic) tradition of interpretation, and useful references to the modern literature. The introduction considers, among other subjects, certain general aspects of the Greek vocabulary and its influence on the subsequent Greek tradition, as well as the classic problem of the major discrepancies between LXX and MT in chapters 35–40. Volume 3 (Leviticus) has already appeared (see *B. L.* 1989, p. 47).

N. R. M. DE LANGE

LEVINE, E.: *The Aramaic Version of the Bible: Contents and Context* (BZAW 174). 1988. Pp. xiv, 258. (De Gruyter, Berlin. Price: DM 118.00. ISBN 3 11 011474 7)

Levine does for the various Targums what L. Smolar and M. Aberbach have done for Targum Prophets in their 1983 volume (*Studies in Targum Jonathan to the Prophets* — see *B. L.* 1985, p. 47), viz. highlight in fairly short sections a number of leading themes and characteristics, though with less discussion of historical and geographical matters. A reasonable attempt has been made to meet the competing claims of ancient rabbinic references and modern academic discussion of a wide variety of Targumic issues. Chapters on topics whose presence could not be taken for granted in a volume like this include 'The Angelic, the Demonic, the Occult', 'Israel of the Flesh; Apologetic Biography', 'The Legitimation of Pharisaic Authority', 'Anti-Christian/ Anti-Moslem Polemic'. The volume will be of greatest usefulness to the non-Targumist wishing to learn about the theology (ideology?) of the Targums, but it is a book that specialists should not overlook. What is needed now is a series of studies of the indivdual topics which will both probe more deeply into the rabbinic and other comparative material and also integrate into the discussion the very considerable insights and refinements that have been achieved in recent decades. It is a pity that Levine's very knowledgeable contribution is so besprinkled with typographical and other minor errors.

R. P. GORDON

MORANO RODRIGUEZ, C.: *Glossas Marginales de* Vetus Latina *en las Biblias Vulgatas Españolas: 1–2 Samuel* (Textos y Estudios "Cardenal Cisneros" de la Biblia Poliglota Matritense, 48). 1989. Pp. lxxxiii, 61. (CSIC, Madrid. ISBN 84 00 06993 5)

At last, after a long period of false starts and failed promises by other scholars, the marginal glosses to the *Vetus Latina* of 1–2 Samuel have been published in a critical edition complete with photographs of the manuscript pages. The previous edition of these two books by C. Vercellone (Rome, 1860 and 1864) was flawed for various reasons. The present edition is based on meticulous collation of all the MSS containing the glosses in question

In the introductory sections the editor describes the codices, provides a potted history of previous research and then gives an outline of the language used in the glosses. The text of the glosses takes up some fifty pages and the usual indices follow. Textual critics stand to gain from this scholarly edition which will be of particular interest to those working on the books of Samuel.

W. G. E. WATSON

NELSON, M. D.: *The Syriac Version of the Wisdom of Ben Sira compared to the Greek and Hebrew Materials* (SBL Dissertation Series 107). 1988. Pp. viii, 142. (Scholars Press, Atlanta GA. Price: $17.95 (member price: $11.95); paperback price: $11.95 (member price: $7.95). ISBN 1 55540 193 7; 1 55540 194 5 (pbk))

After a succinct description of discoveries of texts of Ben Sira written in Hebrew and Syriac and an account of the Greek versions, Nelson outlines the history of work on Ben Sira during this century. Syriac versions of the Old Testament, both manuscripts and editions, are given special attention: a lengthy chart compares presence and absence of verses in different versions throughout the section 39:27–44:17, and a comparative translation is given. Interesting differences are detected in the Syriac version covering various subjects: doubt on life after death, women's status, famous men, and poverty and wealth. Two Syriac versions are detected: one composed for Syriac-speaking Jews near Edessa in the third or fourth century C.E., and a revision for Christian readership before the middle of the fifth century.

J. G. SNAITH

REHKOPF, F.: *Septuaginta-Vokabular*. 1989. Pp. ix, 318. (Vandenhoeck & Ruprecht, Göttingen. Price: DM 38.00. ISBN 3 525 50172 2)

This handy volume provides at a glance a clear overview of the complete vocabulary of the Septuagint. The alphabetical listing is derived from Hatch and Redpath's *Concordance*. Each item receives two lines of text set out in three columns. The upper line of the left column provides the Greek citation-form, with in the central column a German rendering and the Hebrew or Aramaic original if the Greek is a transliteration. The lower line in the central column provides or sketches the frequency of usage: up to four instances are separately listed, five to twenty are counted, while for more frequent terms we are told how many columns or half-columns of Hatch and Redpath are required for the entry in question. The lower line of the right-hand column is used to list or summarize the New Testament usage of the word, or to direct us to W. Bauer's *Wörterbuch* (1988 edition) if the word in question is found only in other early Christian literature. A few marginal notations economically enhance the coverage. This is the sort of information that suitably programmed computer data bases can readily provide. But for several years to come a digest like this will be even more serviceable to many scholars and students.

A. G. AULD

STROTHMANN, W. (ed.): *Kohelet-Kommentar des Dionysius bar Salibi: Auslegung des Septuaginta-Textes* (Göttinger Orientforschungen, I. Reihe: Syriaca, Bd. 31). 1988. Pp. xi, 116. (Harrassowitz, Wiesbaden. Price: DM 30.00. ISBN 3 447 02855 6)

Having edited Dionysius' 'factual' commentary on Ecclesiastes in GOF.S 29, Strothmann here edits the accompanying 'spiritual' commentary, which is based on the Syrohexapla, rather than the Peshiṭta. Once again no translation is given, but there is a word index.

S. BROCK

STROTHMANN, W. (ed.): *Kohelet-Kommentar des Johannes von Apamea: Syrischer Text mit vollständigem Wörterverzeichnis* (Göttinger Orientforschungen, I. Reihe: Syriaca, Bd. 30). 1988. Pp. xliv, 283. (Harrassowitz, Wiesbaden. Price: DM 56.00. ISBN 3 447 02854 8)

The commentary by the early fifth-century Syriac monastic writer John of Apamea (John the Solitary) is preserved complete in a single manuscript

(Sinai syr. 16), and Strothmann here provides the editio princeps of the text (no translation is provided). John's running commentary, after quoting the Peshiṭta text, takes the form of paraphrase and moralizing comments; his introduction (addressed to Theogenes) has some interesting remarks on differing Greek and Hebrew attitudes to literary structure, and the Peshiṭta text he quotes offers a number of intriguing agreements with 7g2 in the Leiden edition (*B. L.* 1981, p. 47).

S. Brock

Strothmann, W. (ed.): *Das syrische Fragment des Ecclesiastes-Kommentars von Theodor von Mopsuestia: Syrischer Text mit vollständigem Wörterverzeichnis* (Göttinger Orientforschungen, I. Reihe: Syriaca, Bd. 28). 1988. Pp. xxviii, 146.(Harrassowitz, Wiesbaden. Price: DM 36.00. ISBN 3 447 02852 1)

At the beginning of this century a fragment of the Syriac translation of Theodore of Mopsuestia's lost Commentary on Ecclessiastes was discovered in Damascus; although the original manuscript cannot now be located, a photographic copy survives and it is this which serves as the basis for Strothmann's edition. The fragment breaks off at 7:24. Footnotes draw attention to borrowings in the later Syriac commentaries. A word index is provided, but no translation.

S. Brock

Strothmann, W. (ed.): *Syrische Katenen aus dem Ecclesiastes-Kommentar des Theodor von Mopusuestia: Syrischer Text mit vollständigem Wörterverzeichnis* (Göttinger Orientforschungen, I. Reihe: Syriaca, Bd. 29). 1988. Pp. xxxiii, 133. (Harrassowitz, Wiesbaden. Price: DM 34.00. ISBN 3 447 02853 X)

This is an edition of the 'literal' or 'factual' commentary on Ecclesiastes taken from the commentary on the whole Bible by the West Syriac scholar Dionysius bar Ṣalibi (d. 1171). Since Strothmann believes (for rather slender reasons) that Dionysius cannot be the author of this part of the commentary, he simply entitles it 'Syrische Katenen'. In common with the East Syriac commentator Ishoʿdad of Merv (and others) the work proves to be quite heavily based on Theodore of Mopsuestia's commentary, and so is particularly valuable where the fragment of the latter (edited by Strothmann in GOF.S 28) breaks off at 7:24. Although no translation is provided, the parallels to the extant parts of Theodore's commentary, to Ishoʿdad of Merv (for whom a French translation is available) and other Syriac sources. are given at the foot of each page, and there is a word list at the end. (Dionysius' 'spiritual' commentary is edited by Strothmann in GOF.S 31).

S. Brock

Strothmann, W. (ed.): *Wörtverzeichnis der apokryphen-deuterokanonischen Schriften des Alten Testaments in der Peshiṭta* (Göttinger Orientforschungen, I. Reihe: Syriaca, Bd. 27). 1988. Pp. xii, 492. (Harrassowitz, Wiesbaden. Price: DM 86.00. ISBN 3 447 02683 9)

For the Peshiṭta, Strothmann has already supplied concordances to the Pentateuch and Prophets (*B. L.* 1988, p. 51; 1987, p. 40), and N. Sprenger a concordance to Psalms (*B. L.* 1979, p. 49). Strothmann now presents a list of occurrences (without context) of each Syriac vocabulary item in the Apocrypha (plus 3–4 Maccabees and the poetry in part IV.6 of the Leiden edition). Two of these translations have recently been viewed as early monuments of Christianity (see M. M. Winter, 'The Origins of Ben Sira in Syriac', *V.T.* 1977, pp. 237–253, 494–507; H. J. W. Drijvers, 'The Peshitta of *Sapientia*

Salomonis', Festschr. J. H. Hospers [*B. L.* 1988, p. 25], pp. 15–30). For the text of Wisdom, Lagarde is surprisingly followed rather than the Leiden edition. The LXX additions to Daniel 3, apparently an original component of the Peshitta text, attested in the manuscripts, are covered neither here nor among the Prophets; the literal version of 1 Mac 1–14 in 7a1, with its archaic pronoun *menda'mta* (8:14), is also excluded; and spot checks showed the omission of 'I prayed' at Wisdom 7:7. The word-list is still a valuable tool for biblical and patristic studies.

M. P. WEITZMAN

TREBOLLE BARRERA, J.: *Centena in Libros Samuelis et Regum: Variantes Textuales y composición literaria en los libros de Samuel y Reyes* (Textos y Estudios "Cardenal Cisneros" de la Biblia Políglota Matritense, 47). 1989. Pp. 235. (CSIC, Madrid. ISBN 84 00 06964 1)

As readers of this *Book List* will be aware, Trebolle has been an industrious student of the text and history of the Books of Kings for a good decade (see especially *Bl. L.* 1985, pp. 95f). In this book he presents a careful study of a hundred passages containing major textual problems in Samuel and Kings, with a view to penetrating behind the existing texts and versions to an understanding of how the original Hebrew text came into being. An example from a medieval Spanish chronicle illustrates the author's contentions about the ways in which the process of redaction of a text can leave certain tell-tale clues, such as doublets. This meticulous study advances a bold challenge to some current attitudes in textual criticism of the Bible.

N. R. M. DE LANGE

WRIGHT, B. G.: *No Small Difference: Sirach's Relationship to its Parent Hebrew Text* (Septuagint and Cognate Studies, 26). 1989. Pp. xx, 354. (Scholars Press, Atlanta GA. Price: $19.95 (member price: $12.95); sub. price: $12.95 (member price $8.95). ISBN 1 55540 374 3; 1 55540 375 1 (pbk))

This doctoral dissertation seeks, by analysis of the parts of Ben Sira's work extant in both Hebrew and Greek, to assess how far we may reconstruct the original Hebrew from the Greek where the Hebrew text is missing. The grandson's translation technique is examined: adherence to Hebrew word order, segmentation of Hebrew words, consistency of lexical representation are all discussed. Wright traces the influence of Jewish-Greek translations of other works, and investigates specific cases where the Greek Pentateuch was used. Skehan's work is seen to provide examples of the complications involved. An appendix discusses use in this kind of study of computers: electronic data, hardware, software. There is a massive bibliography and indexes of biblical passages, and authors quoted. The publication of so much detailed information is welcome: this book will be most valuable to students of both textual tradition of Ben Sira and early Greek translations generally.

J. G. SNAITH

WÜRTHWEIN, E.: *Der Text des Alten Testaments: Eine Einführung in die Biblia Hebraica*. 5th edition. 1988. Pp. 263, (Deutsche Bibelgesellschaft, Stuttgart. Price: DM 42.00. ISBN 3 438 06006 x)

This latest edition of W's useful introduction to the two standard editions of *Biblia Hebraica* has been thoroughly revised, partucularly where dealing with the history of the Hebrew text and its translation into Greek and Syriac, and the significance of this increase in knowledge for textual criticism. For earlier notices and bibliographical references, see *B. L.* 1974, p. 28 and 1981, p. 49.

P. WERNBERG-MØLLER

5. EXEGESIS AND MODERN TRANSLATIONS

AMSLER. S., LACOCQUE, A., and VUILLEUMIER, R.: *Aggée — Zacharie — Malachie*. 2nd ed. (commentaire de l'Ancien Testament XIc). 1988. Pp. 262. (Labor et Fides, Genève. ISBN 2 8309 0131 2)

The first edition of this book was reviewed in *B. L.* 1983, p. 45. One needs good eyesight and a fine toothcomb to find many differences in the text but the editors' claim that it has been 'corrigée et mise à jour' is justified by a number of additional bibliographies which extend the life and usefulness of an established and authoritative commentary.

R. A. MASON

Anden Mosebog 16 til Fjerde Mosebog 36, Ruts Bog, Højsangen, Prædikerens Bog, Klagesangene, Esters Bog, Jobs Bog, Ordsprogenes Bog, Daniels Bog. Det gamle Testamente i ny oversættelse. 1989. Pp. 270, 103, and 187 (Det danske Bibelselskab, Copenhagen. Price: D.Kr. 80, 120 and 120. ISBN 87 7523 211 1, 87 7523 241 3, 87 7523 237 5)

During this year the three last volumes of the trial translation to a new Danish authorized Bible have been published. Exod. 16–Num. 36, the five Megilloth, and the Books of Job, Proverbs, and Daniel. The translations to the books of Chronicles, Ezra, and Nehemiah will not be published, but were ready in manuscript in November, at the same time as a trial translation of the New Testament was released. The translations are made by scholars related to the faculties of theology in Copenhagen and Aarhus, and the present volumes of the Old Testament translations are edited by B. Ejrnæs, S. Holm-Nielsen, and K. Jeppesen. The trial translations, of which the first part was published in 1977, are now to be revised and the plan is to have the new translation authorized within a couple of years.

K. JEPPESEN

ANDERSEN, F. I. and FREEDMAN, D. N.: *Amos: A New Translation with Introduction and Commentary* (Anchor Bible 24A). 1989. Pp. xlii, 979. (Doubleday, New York. Price: $30.00. ISBN 0 385 00773 6)

The authors have outdone even the scale of their earlier collaborative commentary on Hosea (AB 24, 1980 — a gap in the *Book List*). It is a measure of the success of the Anchor Bible project that the publishers can make available over one thousand pages at less than 3c per page. And of course we are offered many opportunities of learning afresh from a familiar and well-loved biblical text. The fresh translation (xxv–xlii) is supplied with many headings and sub-headings, anticipating the general approach of the commentary. The full Introduction (1–178) again adumbrates the main lines to be followed in its largest section (23–73) on the Contents of the Book. The authors propose a three-fold major division of Amos: The Book of Doom (1:1–4:13); The Book of Woes (5:1–6:14); The Book of Visions (7:1–9:15). Their own style is eminently readable and clear, if also leisurely to the point of repetitious. We are in the hands of two experienced teachers who often pause to explore at length how their reading of Amos fits with their reading of many other portions of the Bible. At length — but far from exhaustively; for it is a major disappointment that in a commentary that spends more than a hundred pages on each page of Hebrew text there is so little explicit interaction with other scholarship. The bibliography is tolerably complete (to 1986). Yet comparison between the authors listed there and the index recording where these are mentioned or debated within the main text is instructive. Such discussion as is offered is mostly on textual and lexical questions. I suspect that it will be for their fresh and thoughtful translation that the authors will most be thanked. It is good to see a defence of the oft-emended *hrbwt* in 4:9;

and the spacious type-setting helps their frequently quite literal adherence to Hebrew idiom to work. Yet their conventional English 'brand plucked' of 4:11 has eluded correction to the more literal 'brand rescued' that would have allowed the English reader to spot the Hebrew connection with the remains of the sheep 'rescued' in 3:12. However, on matters of interpretation the approach is different. It is lamentably typical of much of the commentary that, while two articles by Ackroyd relevant to Amos 7:10–17 appear in the Bibliography, only the earlier note on the rendering of vv. 14f is cited in the discussion of these verses; there is no engagement with his later discussion of how to read that whole passage in a wider biblical context. When they do anticipate criticism it is often too briefly, in a treatment that minimizes the force of counter-positions, despite the lavish space available. Too often, our authors seem simply to take their own route. Will they, even if they offer more pages, persuade readers that Judah and Israel, introduced separately in 2:4–5 and 2:6–8, are linked together in 'oracles against the whole of Israel' in Amos 2:9–3:8?

A. G. Auld

Anderson, A. A.: *2 Samuel* (Word Biblical Commentary 11). 1989. Pp. xl, 302. (Word Books, Dallas TX. Price: $24.99. ISBN 0 8499 0210 X)

The introduction to this eleventh volume in the World Biblical Commentary series contains three sections. The first discusses the text of 2 Samuel; the second the literary history of the book; and the third its use elsewhere in the Bible. The commentary adopts the structure found in other contributions to the series, a short bibliography being followed successively by a translation of the text with textual notes; discussion of its form/structure/setting; comment upon it; and a general explanation.

This is a solid enough volume of its type, and will no doubt be read with profit by those for whom it is intended. However, within the context of present scholarly debate about biblical texts, and particularly biblical narrative, it is a book noticeably out of step with the times. For example, more than half the introduction is given over to a discussion of the precise limits of the History of David's Rise and the Succession Narrative; but the more important questions, which are not addressed, are whether the older distinction between these two hypothetical entities should any longer be maintained, particularly in view of the difficulties which scholars (including the author) have had in plausibly reconstructing them, and if it should, what difference this should make to the exegete. The commentary often appears to have been written as if the hermeneutical debate of the recent past had never taken place; and nowhere is this more apparent than in the way literary, theological, and historical concerns merge in the treatment of the text. One example will suffice. In his treatment of 2 Sam. 1:1–16, the author first argues (p. 5), after noting that 1 Sam. 31:4 and 2 Sam. 1:1(cannot both be historically 'true', and that scholars have differed on which is correct, that the *literary* setting of 2 Sam. 1 after 1 Sam. 31 invites us to regard the Amalekite as a liar. This he assumes, without argument, to have also been the *historical* reality; and he goes on to explain how it was that David was (historically) faultless in executing the Amalekite (though innocent) and the editor faultless in including the Amalekite's story (though fictitious) in the book. David's innocence in particular seems important. Of his presence among the Philistines prior to the battle of Gilboa we read: 'It is quite likely that David had no option, and we do not know what he might have done had he taken part in the decisive fight'. It is questionable whether such a confusing mixture of literary analysis, apology, and historical speculation is really what we require in modern commentary. The author seems never to have made up his mind whether he is trying to write a history of David's reign, a commentary on the supposed redactional blocks within the text, or a commentary on 2 Samuel.

I. W. Provan

BLENKINSOPP, J.: *Ezra-Nehemiah* (Old Testament Library). 1989. Pp. 366. (SCM, London. Price: £15.00. ISBN 0 334 00444 6)

Professor Blenkinsopp's full commentary on Ezra-Nehemiah follows the same format as the other volumes in the Old Testament Library series. After an introduction, which discusses, among other topics, the composition of the work and also its political and social context, there follows a detailed commentary on the text. A bibliography at the head of each section precedes the printed text, which is the author's own translation, with the necessary minimum of textual notes; then follows an introduction to the section and a verse by verse commentary.

The author has thoroughly re-assessed all the major issues arising in connection with these two books, and in presenting his own conclusions presents evidence in support and where appropriate criticism of other views that have been rejected. For instance, Ezra's arrival in Jerusalem is dated in the seventh year (458) and Nehemiah's in the twentieth year (445) of Artaxerxes I, and the case for reversing their chronological order is found unacceptable. Again the recently favoured view that Chronicles and Ezra-Nehemiah were distinct books and had a completely separate origin is not found convincing; Professor Blenkinsopp finds the shared religious interests and ideology of the two volumes, together with the evidence of progression from the one to the other, as an indication of a unity of concept which binds the two works into a single history with its own distinctive point of view and purpose. Finally, the argument that Ezra 1–6 was composed after the combination of the Ezra and Nehemiah records, and thus represents the final stage in the formation of the books, is found to lack supporting evidence and is again rejected.

The clarity with which these issues are explored, and with which the text itself is expounded, makes this commentary well worth reading. It certainly illuminates the religious history of the Second Temple, and this is the author's main interest.

G. H. JONES

BONORA, A.: *Isaia 40–60. Israele: servo di Dio, popolo liberato* (Leggere oggi la bibbia 1.19). 1988. Pp. 157. (Queriniana, Brescia. Price: Lire 15,000. ISBN 88 399 1569 9)

For another contribution of this author to this series see *B. L.* 1989, p. 68. The intelligent layman for whom the book is intended is directed to articles in the learned journals and to works in English, French, and German, as well as Italian! The book will probably prove more useful to non-specialist teachers, students, and clergy. After an introductory survey of the three main divisions of Isaiah and of the historical background to the later chapters a whole chapter is devoted to the prologue (40:1–11) and epilogue (55:6–13), whose keynote is taken to be the Word of God. Some interesting observations on the question of unfulfilled prophecies are to be found on pp. 42–44. The rest of the presentation is thematic, with more detailed discussion of selected passages. The analysis of the structure of 40–55 is dominated by the doxologies and will not convince all readers. A final chapter is devoted to 56–66.

A. GELSTON

BORRET, M. (ed.): *ORIGENE: Homélies sur Ézéchiel – Texte Latin, Introduction, Traduction et Notes* (Sources Chrétiennes 352). 1989. Pp. 526. (Cerf, Paris. Price: Fr. 292.00. ISBN 2 204 04000 2, ISSN 0750 1978)

The text of Jerome's Latin translation of these fourteen homilies (of which the Greek originals are lost) is reproduced from Baehrens' Berlin Corpus edition of 1925. It is accompanied by a brief introduction, a French translation, and discreet notes. The question whether the homilies are more properly to be attributed to Origen or to Jerome is touched on obliquely in the introduction; by way of compromise or by oversight no author's name is printed on the spine — an inconvenience in a series which includes homilies on Ezekiel.

N. R. M. de Lange

Brownlee, W. H.: *Ezekiel 1–19* (Word Biblical Commentary 28). 1989, Pp. xlii, 321. (Word Books, Dallas TX. Price: $22.99. ISBN 0 8499 02 10 X)

Professor Brownlee's untimely death in 1983 prevented his finishing the commentary on Ezekiel which had occupied so much of his attention for the preceding years. He had completed work as far as chapter 19, and so the present work represents his own researches, save that some updating of bibliographical material and the expanding of text notes has been added. The introduction to the book, which is of considerable significance in view of the distinctiveness of Professor Brownlee's approach, is taken from an entry written by him for the revision of the *International Standard Bible Encyclopedia* and published in 1982. It explains well the major premises upon which the commentary is based.

Brownlee, in company with many recent commentators, recognizes that an extensive process of editing has served to shape the present book. Unlike the majority since the work of G. Fohrer, W. Eichrodt, and W. Zimmerli, however, Brownlee argues that the original prophet, called to his ministry in 593 B.C., was primarily active in Judah. His location of activity was Gilgal, a city which figures prominently in the prophet's preaching. Quite distinctively Brownlee sees in the formula 'set your face against . . .' a formula of dispatch, indicating that the prophet was sometimes commissioned to undertake special journeys to convey his messages.

The general format of the Word commentary series is adhered to, with a fresh translation and substantial text notes, together with comments on matters of form and style. In the detailed exegesis Brownlee ascribes some of the editorial work to the prophet himself and some to a disciple. The more extensive midrashic-type editing, however, which recast Ezekiel as a prophet of exile ministering in Babylon, is seen as a later post-exilic literary activity. This is undoubtedly an important commentary, the incompleteness of which will probably lessen the scale of the challenge that it presents to more established views. Nevertheless, with an introduction which covers the whole book, its positions are generally clear and will certainly command attention.

R. E. Clements

Brueggemann, W.: *To Pluck Up, To Tear Down: A Commentary on the Book of Jeremiah 1–25* (International Theological Commentary). 1988. Pp. x, 222. (Handsel, Edinburgh; Eerdmans, Grand Rapids, Michigan. Price: £6.75. ISBN 0 905312 87 2; 0 8028 0367 9)

The prolific Walter Brueggemann here offers us the first volume of a two volume commentary on the book of Jeremiah and thus adds to the growing production of commentaries in English on Jeremiah. Size and price put this series in the middle-order of commentaries: not to be compared with the major commentary series such as *OTL*, *ICC*, or *Hermeneia*, but to be considered with such series as *Interpretation: A Bible Commentary for Preaching and Teaching* (see below, p. 53). Whatever mode of comparison is used it has to be said that Brueggemann has produced a very mature and superior piece of commentary writing on Jeremiah. As an expository commentary this book will serve well the theological concerns of the series in which it appears. A brief introduction considers such matters as historical context and theological tradition of the book of Jeremiah, the literary composition of Jeremiah, the person of Jeremiah; and provides an account of Brueggemann's own interpretive perspective. Sociological and literary analyses form that perspective and yield 'a critique of ideology' and a 'practice of liberated imagination' (p. 17). These in turn cause us to rediscern our own situation and rethink our values and structures. But the text does not need to be applied to or interpreted from our own experience and circumstance; we need to submit to the text for fresh discernment. The target of Brueggemann's characteristically dynamic reading of Jeremiah is (of course) the military-industrial complex of the contemporary American establishment-empire. Thus Jeremiah becomes a voice on the left of current American politics or a spokesman of a quasi-liberation theology confronting establishment or bourgeois ideology in modern America.

Brueggemann is generally a responsible and intelligent expositor of the text. Often stimulating and never less than interesting, one seldom fails to find a thought-provoking analysis in his work. But occasionally his religio-ideological holdings overdetermine his reading of Jeremiah. A good example of this failing is his treatment of the temple sermon of 7:1–15 (pp. 74–78) which he reads as a critique of the dominant class and the ideological underpinning of the establishment. This approach might work better for 22:1–5 or the treatment of the sermon in ch. 26, but the text of 7:1–15 is addressed to 'all Judah' rather than to the ruling class (i.e. those who go to the temple to worship there). Thus the critique of ideology so characteristic of the book of Jeremiah is more radical than even Brueggemann allows for and is directed against *all* the people just as much as it is against the ruling classes. Such a critique will serve no contemporary interests, least of all an ideology of the divine option for the poor. That observation apart, this is a superior example of middle-order commentary writing and I look forward to seeing Brueggemann's treatment of Jer. 26–52.

R. P. CARROLL

CIMOSA, M.: *Isaia, l'evangelista dell'Emmanuele (Is 1–39)*. 2nd edition (Piccola biblioteca di teologia 2). 1988. Pp. 235. (Dehoniane, Roma. Price: Lire 16,000. ISBN 88 396 0234 8)

Writing as he has done for a non-specialist Christian readership, the author devotes a good deal of space to the passages traditionally regarded as messianic prophecies, and proportionately less to, for example, the oracles on the nations. He provides his own, sometimes somewhat paraphrastic, translation, with occasional brief comment on individual Hebrew words. The historical background is sketched in for each main section, and where material is generally regarded as later than the time of Isaiah of Jerusalem, Cimosa says so. A short summary, under convenient headings, of the teaching of these chapters forms a concluding section; in the pages on 'Emmanuel and the Messiah' literal, typical, and 'integral Christian' levels of interpretation are briefly distinguished. Given the very limited space available to him, Cimosa has provided a reliable introductory commentary to Isaiah 1–39.

C. J. A. HICKLING

CLEMENTS, R. E.: *Jeremiah* (Interpretation). 1989. Pp. xii, 276. (John Knox Press, Atlanta. Price: $17.95. ISBN 0 8042 3127 3)

Seven Old Testament volumes in the *Interpretation* series have now been published (not all of them noticed in the *Book List*), and the distinctive characteristics of the series are now well established. Aimed at preachers and teachers, these commentaries expound their text section by section rather than verse by verse, have a minimum of footnotes, and only small scale bibliographies. In one sense the task of Professor Clements (the only British Old Testament scholar listed as a contributor) was made more difficult by the spate of recent commentaries on Jeremiah, but he has turned this to advantage by leaving aside the detailed consideration of technical matters and concentrating here on the book, regarded as substantially complete by *c.* 550 B.C., as the product of editing in circles closely related to the Deuteronomistic school; the role of Baruch is more highly regarded here than by some commentators. Clements is also more willing than has recently become customary to make affirmations about the personality of the individual prophetic figure. Overall, the present-day importance of the book of Jeremiah is well brought out, without any attempt to wrest 'relevance' from every element in it.

R. J. Coggins

Cogan, M. and Tadmor, H.: *II Kings*. A New Translation with Introduction and Commentary (Anchor Bible 11). 1988. Pp. xxxv, 371. (Doubleday, New York. Price: $20.00. ISBN 0 385 02388 X)

The formal introduction to the books of Kings in the Anchor Bible series is to be contained in the forthcoming volume on 1 Kings by the same authors; and the introduction to the volume under consideration here is therefore shorter than one might otherwise expect. It contains brief sections on the content of 2 Kings; on the usefulness of extra-biblical documentation in elucidating the history of the period in which the narrative is set; on the utility of Akkadian and Aramaic for explicating its language; on texts and versions; and on translation and commentary. A final section provides a synchronous outline of the historical events described in 2 Kings. It is immediately clear to the reader that history is the dominating interest of the authors; and as one reads through the commentary, one does indeed find a wealth of historical comment and reconstruction, together with helpful photographs, plans, and maps. The first appendix, which brings together in one place a selection of relevant extra-biblical texts, is particularly useful. Both historians and those interested in interpretation or theology will, however, find reason to be dissatisfied with this commentary. On the one hand, although the authors accept in the introduction that both books of Kings are ideological pieces of work, and indeed, are the work of pre-exilic and exilic Deuteronomists, this does not for the most part seem to make a significant difference to the way in which they read history from the text. On the other hand, the concern about history is so dominant in the commentary that one often feels the text is not actually being read as text at all. Interpretation of the story is not among the book's strengths; and there is some evidence that the authors are not always fully aware of the secondary literature in this area. Responsibility for weaknesses such as these cannot be laid at any door other than the authors'. It is presumably the editors and the publishers, however, who must share the blame for allowing the publication of the commentary before something had been done about the poor quality of the print, the missing punctuation, and the rather poor English to be found on certain of its pages.

I. W. Provan

Goldingay, J. E.: *Daniel* (Word Biblical Commentary 30). 1989. Pp. liii, 351. (Word Books, Dallas TX. Price: $24.00. ISBN 0 8499 0210 X)

The book of Daniel has never lacked an audience and a consequence of this has been the availability of a shelf-full of substantial commentaries. Room must now be made for vol. 30 of the Word Biblical Commentary by J. Goldingay. The format of this series is one of its major assets and is based on the *Biblischer Kommentar*. Each chapter has a title heading followed by an extensive bibliography related to it with the author's name printed in heavy type. A translation of the text follows with brief textual and linguistic notes. The ensuing discussion has the Form/Structure/Setting pattern of the German series and is followed by extended Comment and Explanation sections.

The commentary has a useful Introduction and Conclusion where recent views on the book's form, the stream of tradition behind it, the book's structure, origin, and significance are fully aired. Little that has been written on the book in recent years has escaped the author's careful scrutiny. The same cannot be said of the book's proof reader who has allowed a rash of misprints to mar the book's otherwise splendid layout.

P. W. Coxon

Gowan, D. E.: *From Eden to Babel: A Commentary on the Book of Genesis 1–11* (International Theological Commentary). 1988. Pp. ix, 125. (Handsel, Edinburgh; Eerdmans, Grand Rapids, Michigan. Price: £4.95. ISBN 0 905312 85 6; 0 8028 0337 7)

The series to which this commentary belongs aims at a theological interpretation of the Hebrew text and wants to get beyond 'the usual critical-historical approach to the Bible'. I am not sure that the General Editor will have entirely welcomed Professor Gowan's contribution on Genesis 1–11. He discusses terms like myths and saga; he tells his readers about J and P; he takes them assiduously, if crisply, through the exegetical problems of the chapters; he carefully points out the many places where Christian theology has manipulated the text and got it wrong; and only then does he turn to the text's own theological position, which is sketched incisively but rather lightly. I would have liked to have seen more little sections like the excellent two pages (100–01) of 'Reflections on the Theology of the Flood'. What Professor Gowan gives us is not so much a theological commentary on Genesis 1–11 as a prolegomenon to such. But what he gives us is rather well done.

J. C. L. Gibson

Holladay, W. L.: *Jeremiah II: A Commentary on the Book of the Prophet Jeremiah Chapters 26–52* (Hermeneia). 1989. Pp. xxxi, 543. (Fortress Philadelphia; SCM, London. Price: £34.50. ISBN 0 8006 6022 6)

This volume completes Holladay's *magnum opus* on Jeremiah (see *B.L.* 1987, p. 49 for his first volume). Taken together the volumes run to more than twelve hundred pages and constitute a formidable contribution to contemporary Jeremiah studies. They are a magnificent achievement and biblical scholarship should salute Holladay's sustained performance as commentator. The second volume is shorter than the first and consists of ninety-five pages of general introduction to Jeremiah, three hundred and forty-five pages of commentary on Jer. 26–52, additional bibliographical material, and indices for both volumes. The volume is dedicated to the memories of Saint Jerome and James Muilenburg. Holladay has not changed his mind substantially from the first volume so the commentary on 26–52 continues the lines of exploration and exegesis developed for 1–25. He does not however add any further argumentation for the hypothesis, advanced in the first volume, of the septennial readings of Deuteronomy and Jeremiah's prose sermons as counter-proclamations to them, but he does set out most clearly what he regards as the contents of the two scrolls underlying the production of the book of Jeremiah. Apart from its rather repetitive nature, the commentary is clear and poses very few problems of comprehension for the reader. Holladay does tend to regard the book of Jeremiah as one might view a Rubik's Cube: i.e. as something to be rearranged into a pattern and he rearranges the text from time to time to suit his own arguments. Also at times his argument takes the form of 'there is no way to be sure . . . but it is virtually certain' (e.g. p. 140b) and always prefers the historicist reading of the text. But these are minor faults in the overall work, which must be regarded as the last word in the reading of Jeremiah from a historical viewpoint.

R. P. CARROLL

HOUTMAN, C.: *Exodus* II (7:14–19:25) (Commentar op het Oude Testament). 1989. Pp. 413. (Kok, Kampen. Price: fl. 85.00. ISBN 90 242 0925 0)

Volume 1 of this commentary was reviewed in *B. L.* 1987, p. 50. Volume 2 deals with Exodus 7:14 to 19:25 and is a mine of information on text-critical, philological, literary-critical, and history of interpretation matters. Although the exegesis deals with the final form of a work held to be part of an exilic Genesis to 2 Kings, the author deals fully with the standard critical questions. The source-division of the plagues narrative is discussed, as are the origins of passover and unleavened bread, and their relationship to the tenth plague and to the dedication of first-born animals. Indeed, this section on the passover and connected matters amounts to a major study in its own right. On selected issues the author holds that the account of the plague is a literary composition with no specific knowledge of Egypt. It is a dramatic composition in the service of preaching. Passover and unleavened bread were originally separate, but it is to facile to say that the passover is an historicized pre-Israelite ceremony. Israel was well able to make creative use of elements of various existing ceremonies to express its faith. On Exodus 15, Houtman takes the presence of archaisms in the poem more as evidence of its poetic nature than of its antiquity. This is an immensely informative and illuminating commentary which no one working on Exodus can afford to overlook.

J. W. ROGERSON

HUBBARD, D. A.: *Hosea* (Tyndale Old Testament Commentaries). 1989. Pp. 234. (Inter-Varsity Press, Leicester. Price: £6.25. ISBN 0 85111 641 8; 0 85111 843 7 (pbk))

This is an excellent commentary for its size. The author succeeds in maintaining an appropriate balance between discussion of the many textual problems and a non-technical approach suited to the non-Hebraist. An occasional Additional Note supplements the discussion of major critical questions provided in the Introduction. The ample footnotes contribute greatly to the volume's usefulness. Literary forms, links with the love poetry of the Song of Songs, and themes of the book are discussed. Clearly not all points at issue can be treated in a commentary of this size, but the author is to be complimented on making accessible in so readable a form much of the contribution of modern scholarship to an understanding of this difficult text.

G. I. EMMERSON

HUBBARD, D. A.: *Joel and Amos* (Tyndale Old Testament Commentaries). 1989. Pp. 245. (Inter-Varsity Press, Leicester. Price: £6.25. ISBN 0 85111 642 6; 0 85111 844 5 (pbk))

Dr Hubbard will have put many readers of the Old Testament in his debt through his commentaries published in 1989. This one belongs to the same Tyndale series as the study on Hosea reviewed above. A surprising amount of well-briefed discussion with other scholars' views is achieved in the relatively short compass, though they are quoted more fully when they agree than when they disagree with the thrust of the commentary. The author's own predispositions are irenically conservative, towards unity of composition in both books. The many links between Joel and other parts of the Bible are probed, and that book is set tentatively around 500 B.C.

A. G. AULD

HUBBARD, R. L., Jr.: *The Book of Ruth* (NICOT). 1988. Pp. xiv, 317. (Eerdmans, Grand Rapids MI. Price: $26.95. Distributed by Paternoster, Exeter. Price: £20.95. ISBN 0 8028 2358 0)

It is good to find a single, substantial volume given entirely to the book of Ruth, allowing the author space adequately to address important exegetical problems and to provide detailed textual notes. The knotty problems of legal background are well handled. The commentary is sensitive throughout to the artistry of the story telling and the significance of audience reaction. Points at which the motive is literary rather than historical are indicated. A pre-exilic date is favoured, though other views are carefully noted, and the possibility is allowed that a woman was its author. The book's purpose is understood to be the countering of opposition to the Davidic monarchy, possibly during Solomon's reign. The hiddenness yet continuity of Yahweh's working in the world, and the intimate relation between divine and human action are among the key theological assumptions of the seemingly secular book of Ruth. The translation is Dr Hubbard's own. The biblical text is well served and the drama of the story illuminated by the balanced treatment and careful scholarship of this work. For clarity of discussion, thoroughness, and readability it is to be recommended.

G. I. EMMERSON

JEPPESEN, K.: *Jesajas bog fortolket* 1988. Pp. 315 (Det danske Bibelselskab, Copenhagen. Price: D.Kr. 245. ISBN 87 7523 238 3)

Knud Jeppesen's commentary on the Book of Isaiah belongs to a series of commentaries published by the Danish Bible Society. The commentary is written for the lay people who are familiar with the Bible and want to use the commentary for further Bible studies. The author knows his audience; he carefully explains the historical background of the book from the beginning of the preaching of Isaiah to the final redaction of the whole book, in two introductory chapters (pp. 17–42, 202–12). The commentary is not written verse by verse, but each section (form critically defined unit) is commented upon with due attention to the need of the reader. His approach is redaction-critical and his main point of view is concerned with the redaction of the Isaiah-disciples who faced the catastrophe of 587. He sees the redaction of Isa. 1–39 as a deliberate actualization of the prophet's oracles in a new situation. Isa. 1–39 has been formed in order to give a trustworthy background both for the fall of Jerusalem and for the following preaching in Isa. 40–66. To underline this point he divides his commentary in two parts: The Jerusalem Isaiah, and The Babylonian Isaiah (i.e. Isa. 40–55+56–66). For lay people (including young students) this commentary gives valuable information on the history of the period and the book that came out of this history. And for 'those who have ears to hear' Jeppesen's approach is a challenge to reinterpret the old words in a new context.

K. NIELSEN

LIPSHITZ, A. (ed.): *The Commentary of Rabbi Abraham Ibn Ezra on Hosea*, Edited from Six Manuscripts and Translated with an Introduction and Notes. 1988. Pp. 148, 3 plates, and pp. 38 (Hebrew). (Sepher-Hermon, New York. Price: $19.95. ISBN 0 87203 127 6)

The commentary on Hosea by Ibn Ezra was first published (with that on the other Minor Prophets) in Venice (1525–26) and has been, for the most part, neglected by scholars. The reason for this neglect may be the corrupt state of the text of the commentaries as they appear in the editions of the Rabbinic Bible; but it is a neglect which needs to be remedied. Critical editions (and translations) of these commentaries are needed for proper understanding of these writings, and we are surely indebted to Lipshitz for beginning the task for us. The text adopted here is based on six manuscripts: 1. BM 24,896; 2. Leeuwarden 4,2; 3. Michael 33; 4. Montefiore 34,2; 5. Roma Angelica 80,2; 6. Vatican 75. All manuscripts are complete apart from a short lacuna in Leeuwarden 4,2.

Lipshitz begins with a short but interesting introduction in which he gives a brief resumé of Ibn Ezra's life and work, shows how he influenced Maimonides and David Qimchi, demonstrates that he was a giant in the field of Biblical exegesis during his lifetime and later (some of his work was translated into French and Latin, and he was greatly praised by the seventeenth-century Christian exegete, Richard Simon), and, with the help of a glance at his commentary on the Pentateuch, draws attention to Ibn Ezra's strong views on Biblical exegesis. As an adherent of the *peshat* form of exegesis, Ibn Ezra rejects the approaches of those who, like Saadya Gaon, are inclined to introduce extraneous matter into their commentaries, and those, like the Qaraites, who reject tradition. He also disapproves of those who are inclined to mysticism and midrash. Where Ibn Ezra is, perhaps, unique is in his effort to establish a connection between the chapters or verses with a view to showing the text's coherence and continuity of thought.

The commentary on Hosea is not a long one — comprising a little over 30 pages in this book — but Lipshitz has produced an English translation with copious notes, and the result is a very satisfactory piece of work. With a bibliography and a useful index, Ibn Ezra's commentary on Hosea is made accessible to a wide readership.

R. B. SALTERS

MINISSALE, A.: *Siracide: Le radici nella tradizione* (Leggere oggi la bibbia 1.17). 1988. Pp. 102. (Queriniana, Brescia. Price: Lire 9,500. ISBN 88 399 1567 2)

This contribution to a series intended for lay Christian believers offers a straightforward introduction to the Wisdom of Ben Sira, covering its structure, historical background, major theological themes, moral teaching, and literary style, with a final chapter on 'Ben Sira between the Old and New Testaments', where its later use by Jewish and Christian traditions is also mentioned. The great message of Ben Sira for our times, concludes Minissale, is solidarity with one's society and its traditions, especially in a time of cultural change — and hence the book's title.

P. R. DAVIES

MONARI, L.: *Ezechiele: un sacerdote-profeta* (Leggere oggi la bibbia 1.21). 1988. Pp. 142. (Queriniana, Brescia. Price: Lire 13,000. ISBN 88 399 1571 0)

This series is designed to promote the intelligent reading of the Bible. The author of the present volume, who teaches Sacred Scripture in the Interdiocesan Theological School at Reggio Emilia, seeks to provide guidance for someone reading Ezekiel for the first time. He begins with an outline of the book's contents, a brief and simple account of the present state of critical opinion about the book, and a sketch of its historical setting. Then come five chapters dealing one by one with the main divisions of the book — the prophet's call, oracles against Jerusalem, oracles against the nations, oracles of salvation, the new Jerusalem — and a final chapter summing up the main characteristics of Ezekiel and his ministry and the main theological lessons to be learned from the book.

F. F. BRUCE

MOWVLEY, H.: *The Psalms, Introduced and Newly Translated for Today's Readers*. 1989. Pp. vii, 327. (Collins, London. Price: £6.95. ISBN 0 00 599172 2)

Many will find it good to have such a handy translation of the Psalms accompanied by substantial and pertinent introductions to each psalm. If the translation at times jars aesthetically, it will nevertheless succeed in giving the reader a fresh angle from which to view the thought.

J. H. EATON

NIELSEN, K.: *Ezekiels Bog fortolket*, med et bidrag af J. Strange. 1988. Pp. 273. (Det danske Bibelselskab, Copenhagen. Price: D.Kr. 245. ISBN 87 7523 235 9)

In The Danish Bible Society's series of commentaries for the lay reader K. Nielsen has published a very informative and readable commentary on Ez. 1–39. In the introduction the author takes her point of departure in the Babylonian captivity and the prophet Ezekiel and his preaching in this context; then she goes on traditionally to the redaction of the book, but in this part she utilizes her scholarly interest in imagery in a very fruitful way. Here and through the commentary she discusses where the traditions of the book come from and how they developed into later biblical tradition until the Book of Revelation. In the last section of the introduction she deals with the impact of the datings in the Book of Ezekiel. The interpretation follows the prophetical book section by section through the four main parts, chs. 1–3 the call of the prophet, chs. 4–24 doom over Judah and Jerusalem, chs. 25–32 prophecies against foreign people, and chs. 33–39 salvation.

The last part of the commentary (pp. 223–73) on chs. 40–48 is written by J. Strange. Applying his great knowledge of archaeology, history, and geography, he has provided a short introduction to and an interpretation in two parts, chs. 40–46 The New Temple, and chs. 47–48 The New Land, of these difficult chapters.

K. JEPPESEN

PATERSON, R. M.: *Kitab Yeremia*. 1: *Fasal 1–24* (Tafsiran Alkitab). Pp. 243. (BPK Gunung Mulia, Jakarta)

PATERSON, R. M.: *Kitab Yeremia*, 2: *Fasal 25–52* (Tafsiran Alkitab). 1985. Pp. 209. (BPK Gunung Mulia, Jakarta)

PATERSON, R. M.: *Kitab Nabi Maleakhi* (Tafsiran Alkitab). 1985. Pp. 60. (BPK Gunung Mulia, Jakarta)

These commentaries on Jeremiah and Malachi are original publications in Indonesian by a member of the Society for Old Testament Study.

A. G. AULD

RASHI DE TROYES: *Commento all'Esodo*, edited by S. J. Sierra ("Ascolta Israele" 5). 1988. Pp. xxxii, 368. (Marietti, Genova. Price: Lire 43,000. ISBN 88 211 8456 0)

This Italian translation of Exodus with Rashi's commentary follows essentially the format of the translation of Genesis in the same series (see *B. L.* 1986, p. 50).

N. R. M. DE LANGE

RAVASI, G.: *Qohelet* (La Parola di Dio I/I). 1988. Pp. 474. (Paoline, Cinisello Balsamo (Milano). Price: Lire 25,000. ISBN 88 215 1624 5)

This study of Ecclesiastes falls into three parts. The first is introductory, discussing such questions as date and authorship, the structure of the book, the problem of its message, and how it is to be interpreted: here Ravasi takes issue in particular with those scholars who, in his view, understand Ecclesiastes too optimistically or play down his radical originality. In the central second part, the work is divided into fourteen sections: for each of these a new translation of the Hebrew text is provided, followed by a detailed exegetical commentary. The final part traces parallels to, and influences of, Ecclesiastes in a wide range of literature from ancient Egypt and Mesopotamia, through Biblical, Jewish, and Christian sources down to contemporary writers in a variety of languages.

In many ways, this is a novel and lively undertaking. It has the same unusual characteristics that mark this prolific author's earlier publications, several of which have been noted in the *Book List*, e.g. *B. L.* 1987, p. 53. It will appeal especially to an educated non-specialist reader who wants to understand a book which has always exercised a great attraction. The author has a very well-stocked mind and he employs his extensive reading effectively, giving his comments a distinctive tone. At the same time, though he eschews detailed textual notes, he shows himself fully at home and up to date with scholarly work on Ecclesiastes, so that his work will also be of value to Old Testament specialists. In short, here is an enjoyable study and one to be commended.

J. R. Porter

The Revised English Bible with Apocrypha. 1989. Pp. xvii, 236. (Oxford University Press/Cambridge University Press. Price: £9.95. ISBN 0 19 101220 3, 0 521 50724 3)

The Old Testament and the Apocrypha of *The New English Bible* were published in 1970, but by 1974 the Joint Committee of the Churches decided to organize a major revision of the text. Under the chairmanship of W. D. McHardy, panels of scholars have prepared *The Revised English Bible*. It is important to bear in mind that this is a *revision* of *The New English Bible*. Frequently the two versions do not differ, but where they do, the *REB* is usually better. The 'you' form has replaced the 'thou' form (see especially the Psalms) but the policy to use 'inclusive' language is not quite successful. *'ādām* is translated by 'human beings' in Gen. 1:26, 27, which seems reasonable. However *'ādām* is 'human being' in 2:7 but 'man' in 2:8. Peculiar turns of phrase have been eliminated: 'anoint yourselves' is clearly better than 'lard yourselves' at Amos 6:6, and *NEB* 'the new wine is desperate' in Job 1:10 is replaced by 'the new wine has come to naught'. G. R. Driver's 'dhows of Arabia' have not made it into the *REB* at Isa. 2:16 where we now have 'stately vessels'. the conditional meaning of *kî* in Mic 5:4–5 has been correctly appreciated. But the *REB* still retains some dubious translations: e.g. 'spies . . . agents' in Nah. 3:16–17. The version offered at Hab. 2:2 is inferior to that in *NEB*, and the 'angelic powers' at Ps. 29:1 are something of a surprise. 'Temple girls' in Amos 2:7 reflects a precise exegetical stance, though it may not be the correct one.

This is a very good version of the Scriptures and the scholars who undertook it are to be congratulated.

K. J. Cathcart

Russell, D. S.: *Daniel: An Active Volcano*. 1989. Pp. 141. (Saint Andrew Press, Edinburgh. Price: £4.95. ISBN 0 7152 0632 X)

This book, in its own words, 'does not claim to be a commentary in either the "critical" or the "theological" sense of that word', but 'a series of reflections on the text of Daniel in the light of God's revelation in Jesus Christ and in the light also of the world in which we now live' (pp. 9f). Each of its chapters addresses the biblical book explicitly as part of Christian holy scripture, with abounding reference to New Testament texts.

P. R. Davies

Sasson, J. M.: *Ruth: A New Translation with a Philological Commentary and a Formalist-Folklorist Interpretation*. 2nd edition with corrections (The Biblical Seminar). 1989. Pp. xix, 292. (Sheffield Academic Press. Price: £13.95; $19.95. ISBN 1 85075 213 3; ISSN 0226 4984)

This valued translation and commentary, welcomed in *B. L.* 1980, p. 56, was first published in 1980 by The Johns Hopkins University Press, but was very quickly sold out. The JSOT Press is to be congratulated for making it available again. The author, in addition to correcting typographical errors, has added a short foreword to the new edition, regretting having featured the work of Propp on folk-tale even as modestly as he did, suggesting alternative renderings at some dozen points in the translation, and adding modestly to the bibliography.

A. G. Auld

Scharbert, J.: *Exodus* (Die Neue Echter Bibel: Kommentar zum Alten Testament mit der Einheitsübersetzung, Lfg. 24). 1989. Pp. 151. (Echter Verlag, Würzburg. Price: DM 34.00; sub. price: DM 29.00. ISBN 3 429 01245 7)

Scharbert has already contributed the two volumes on Genesis to this well-established series of popular commentaries (cf. *B. L.* 1984, p. 58; 1988, p. 64), and as one might expect he adopts a similar approach here on critical issues. Much of the limited space available is devoted to the identification of material from the different sources and a description of their varying presentations of the tradition. Scharbert finds little trace of a Deuteronomistic hand in the Sinai pericope, attributing much of the 'covenant' material to an earlier redactor who combined the J and E accounts and holding that both these sources included legal material (though not the Decalogue, which he regards as a very late addition in Exodus). On Ex. 16 he follows the recent view of P. Maiberger that the whole chapter (and all Old Testament references to manna) are from the priestly source or later. The commentary includes a number of references to specifically Christian interpretations of Exodus, among which are some judicious comments on its use in liberation theology (p. 10).

G. I. Davies

Schmitt, A.: *Weisheit* (Die Neue Echter Bibel: Kommentar zum Alten Testament mit der Einheitsübersetzung, Lfg. 23). 1989. Pp. 88. (Echter Verlag, Würzburg. Price: DM 24.00; sub. price: DM 19.80. ISBN 3 429 01212 0)

The series in which this brief commentary appears is based on the Einheitsübersetzung published by the Katholische Bibelanstalt in Stuttgart. Short notes indicate places where the author prefers a different Greek text or an alternative translation. As befits the general purpose of the series, the emphasis is on the informative and judicious rather than the innovative. In the Introduction reasons are given for single authorship and for the late second or early first century B.C. as the date of composition. The Book of Wisdom is addressed both to believing and to apostate Jews, and is intended to foster a sense of Jewish identity, glorifying the past and offering both encouragement in the present situation and a promise for the future of the members of the Jewish community in Alexandria which was passing through difficult times. The theology of the book is fully discussed, and its influence on

New Testament theology pointed out. The commentary is particularly concerned to show how contemporary Hellenistic ideas have been used in such a way as to bring out the distinctiveness and superiority of the Jewish faith.

R. N. Whybray

Stine, P. C. (ed.): *Issues in Bible Translation* (UBS Monograph Series 3). 1988. Pp. viii, 296. (United Bible Societies, London. Price: $4.50. ISBN 0 8267 0453 0)

This is a collection of fifteen papers read at a workshop for translation consultants of the Bible Societies, held in West Virginia in 1987. The sections comprise discourse studies (including an essay on the structural symmetry of the Book of Ruth), sociolinguistics, and sociological approaches to biblical studies. This last includes a discussion of canonical issues facing the translator and treatments of several Old Testament passages (Ex. 4:24–26; 23:20; Isa. 40:3; Mal. 2:10–16; 3:1,23).

J. H. Eaton

Studium Biblicum Franciscanum: *Shinmeiki* (Deuteronomy). 1989. Pp. vi, 224 with a map. (Chūō Shuppan-sha, Tokyo, Price: ¥2,800)

This volume follows the usual format: an introduction, a translation from the BHS text into Japanese as well as explanatory notes, and comments. A text-critical note is added at the end.

K. K. Sacon

Tournay, R. J., op.: *Word of God, Song of Love: A Commentary on the Song of Songs*. Translated from French by J. E. Crowley. 1988. Pp. vi, 194. (Paulist, Mahwah NJ. Price: $11.95. ISBN 0 8091 3007 6)

This study is an attractive modern version of the traditional presentation of the Song of Songs as a historical allegory or midrash. The most notable proponent of the allegorical interpretation in recent years has been the French scholar Andé Robert whose views have been supported and extended by his pupils André Feuillet and Raymond Tournay. The latter argues for the book's literary unity briefly on the basis of the great number of pointed repetitions and the subtle use of *mots crochets* throughout the whole text. In the Persian period an inspired poet selected old love songs of Egyptian origin and incorporated them, along with a lot of other material of varying background, into the original poetical work destined for Jewish believers of his time. Tournay argues that Solomon, the lover of the Song, is not (*pace* Robert) YHWH the King, but is the *new* Solomon to whom the daughter of Zion is engaged by virtue of the promises of the Covenenat. The central position provided for Solomon in the Song corresponds to the position he occupies in the book of Chronicles. The Chronicler assiduously eliminates the shadows over the reign of the historical Solomon of the book of Kings and idealizes him as the son of David, a prototype of the Messiah expected by Israel. Thus, e.g. the poetic image of the young man's sleep and of his eventual awakening after several 'quests' takes on a very special significance if it is seen in the light of the delay in the coming of the new Solomon, the Messiah so much awaited by the new daughter of Zion, the chastened survivors of the exile. Tournay's exposition is based on a study of themes and images in the Song. He also offers a new translation and an analysis of its structure and divisions.

The Song is often shunted into the sidelines of the Old Testament canon because of the alleged absence of a theological dimension. Tournay's insistence on a wider context of literary allusions and parallels from within the

Bible to illuminate its allegorical meaning represents a serious challenge to this almost universally held point of view.

P. W. Coxon

Vos, H. F.: *1, 2 Kings* (Bible Study Commentary). 1989. Pp. 231. (Zondervan, Grand Rapids MI. ISBN 0 310 33921 9)

In keeping with the aims of the Bible Study series of commentaries, the author gives a running commentary on the contents of the two books of Kings. The first two chapters, one on the biblical drama on the international stage and the other giving an introduction to the books of Kings, are followed by a section by section commentary on the books, which is divided into five main parts: the reign of Solomon, division of the monarchy and hostility of the kingdoms, peace and alliance between the two kingdoms, renewed hostilities, and the fall of Samaria, the surviving kingdom of Judah.

As would be expected, Dr Vos, a Professor of History and Archaeology, is particularly good at filling in the historical background. However, many other problems are passed over wwithout mention, and the commentary tends to be a mere re-presentation of the biblical narrative annotated with comments which are devout and devotional in tone. A number of topics for further study appear at the end of each chapter.

G. H. Jones

Wendland, E. R.: *The Cultural Factor in Bible Translation: A Study of Communicating the Word of God in a Central African Cultural Context* (UBS Monograph Series 2). 1987. Pp. xii, 221. (United Bible Societies, London)

Here are treated the cultural obstacles facing the Bible translator in East Africa (the Chichewa and Chitunga languages). There are abundant illustrations of how behaviour reported in the Hebrew might be misunderstood or give offence in translation. A chapter is devoted to Ruth, noting some sixty points sensitive to cultural shock. Even her falling on her face, it seems, might be misconstrued. The discussion contains practical suggestions and has aspects of general interest.

J. H. Eaton

Whybray, R. N.: *Ecclesiastes* (New Century Bible). 1989. Pp. xxiii, 179. (Eerdmans, Grand Rapids MI; Marshall, Morgan & Scott, London. Price: £8.99 ($13.95). ISBN 0 8028 0406 3; 0 551 01853 4)

The recent spate of commentaries on Ecclesiastes continues with this worthy addition to the corpus. It begins with a twelve-page bibliography which is followed by a thirty-one page introduction. The commentary, while it is based on the text of the RSV, would need a knowledge of Hebrew to be fully appreciated. It would, however, be much more comprehensible to the non-Hebrew reader than Crenshaw's commentary. On date, place of authorship, and similar issues, Whybray sticks close to the general consensus of scholars — Jerusalem in the mid-third century B.C.E. The book is regarded as almost entirely the work of Qohelet apart from 1:2–3 and 12:8–14, though a few glosses have probably crept in. On the contradictions in the book he takes an eclectic position. They may be due to Qohelet's use of quotations but mostly they 'represent hesitations or even inconsistencies within his own mind'. Whybray sees no clearly defined structure in the book and is less inclined than other recent commentators to see continuity of thought in the text. The commentary is, on the whole excellent, with the author taking strong positions (known previously from his articles) on some texts, often against the prevailing trend. Two features, however, make it a little less satisfying than Crenshaw's commentary — a lack of interest in the literary artifice of Qohelet, and an occasional tendency to 'pull his sting' (as, for example, in the treatment of 3:14, 7:16–18, and 11:8).

A. P. Hayman

6. LITERARY CRITICISM AND INTRODUCTION

Abela, A.: *The Themes of the Abraham Narrative: Thematic Coherence within the Abraham Literary Unit of Genesis 11, 27–25, 18*. 1989. Pp. x, 141. (Studia Editions, Malta)

In this study, a portion of the doctoral dissertation of the Maltese scholar Anthony Abela presented to the Pontifical Biblical Institute, the Abraham story of Genesis 11:27–25:18 is considered as a literary whole and its internal dynamics are explored. Abela identifies three themes, 'blessing', 'son', and 'land', which are interwoven throughout the narrative, in a manner so coherent that he can argue that the narrative has indeed been conceived as a unity. Promising though the approach is, and capable though the study of the individual pericopes is, the treatment could have been more tautly organized, and it would perhaps have been more illuminating to focus rather on the development of the plot, in purely narratological terms, than upon the occurrence of the crucial items of vocabulary. Can 'theme' really be established by considering all the relevant verbal references, such as those to 'blessing', or must not the framework for such a study be a reader-response appreciation of the plot as it unfolds?

D. J. A. Clines

Allen, L. C.: *Psalms* (Word Biblical Themes). 1989. Pp. 139. (Word Books, Dallas TX. Price: $9.99. ISBN 0 8499 0789 6)

A helpful introduction of a non-technical kind is here provided to some of the main theological characteristics of the Psalms. An introduction on 'function' spells out the likely cultic setting of many Psalms and some of the hermeneutical methods which have been applied in their interpretation; Allen himself makes creative use of Brueggemann's model of 'orientation/disorientation/re-orientation'. Succeeding chapters deal with praise, faith, blessing, salvation, and hope; and a final section explores the implication of the Psalms being part of the canon of Scripture, in both Old Testament and New Testament contexts. This is one of an intended series of such volumes (see below pp. 78, 93, and 95); and it certainly provides an admirable lay companion to the more technical Word Biblical Commentaries.

R. J. Coggins

Alt, A.: *Essays on Old Testament History and Religion*. Translated by R. A. Wilson (The Biblical Seminar). 1989. Pp. x, 274. (Sheffield Academic Press. Price: £10.95 ($17.95) pbk. ISBN 1 85075 204 4)

This is a new edition of a translation, first published in 1966 by Blackwell, of five of Alt's most important essays (cf. *B. L.* 1967, p. 3; and *Bible Bibliography*, p. 3).

I. W. Provan

Alter, R. and Kermode, F. (eds): *The Literary Guide to the Bible*. Paperback edition. 1989. Pp. 678. (Fontana, London. Price: £9.99. ISBN 0 00 686170 9)

The original hardback edition, published by Collins in 1987, was not reviewed in the *Book List*. The paperback edition, attractively priced, offers the general reader and student 22 chapters on Old Testament books, 8 on the New Testament, and 10 general articles. The authors include Biblical specialists and literary critics, their aim being to 'bring the approaches of modern literary analysis to this greatest of all works of literature'. Noteworthy among the Old Testament articles are those of D. Damrosch on Leviticus, L. Alonso Schökel on Isaiah, and F. Landy on Lamentations. The work is solid, respectable, and largely inoffensive. It also breathes the self-confident air of the literary criticism of the 1970s, and betrays no anxiety over the highly problematic concepts of 'literary' and 'interpretation'. The conflicts that make current literary criticism so exciting are programmatically excluded; here there is no feminist, materialist, deconstructionist, ideological, or psychoanalytic criticism, but a bland assumption that we all know what literary study is. The Biblical literary critic might also question the propriety of omitting the Apocrypha entirely, and of treating self-evidently unitary works like the Primary History (Genesis — 2 Kings) in eight separate articles written by seven different people.

D. J. A. Clines

Amihai, M., Coats, G. W. and Solomon, A. M. (eds): *Narrative Research on the Hebrew Bible* (Semeia 46). 1989. Pp. vii, 179. (Scholars Press, Atlanta GA. Price: $14.95 (member price: $9.95; member price for unit of 4 numbers: $25.00))

This volume consists of eleven papers delivered by members of the Narrative Research Group of the Society of Biblical Literature. Delay in publication has meant that three have appeared elsewhere, 'The Institutional Matrix of Treachery in 2 Samuel 11' by Joel Rosenberg, 'His Story Versus Her Story: Male Genealogy and Female Strategy in the Jacob Cycle' by Nelly Furman, and 'The Literary Characterization of Mothers and Sexual Politics in the Hebrew Bible' by Esther Fuchs. Mary Gerhard presents a highly theoretical study, 'The Restoration of Biblical Narrative'. Four articles deal with various aspects of the Pentateuch: 'Can Genesis Be Read as a Book?' by Everett Fox; 'The Genealogical Framework of the Family Stories in Genesis' by Naomi Steinberg; 'The Structure of The Chronicler's History: A Key to the Organization of the Pentateuch' by Anne M. Solomon; and 'Another Form-Critical Problem of the Hexateuch' by George W. Coats. Three are grouped under the heading 'Narrative Tricks': 'The Reported Story: Midway between Oral Performance and Literary Art' by Antony F. Campbell; 'Spatial Form in Exod. 19:1–8a and in the Larger Sinai Narrative' by Thomas B. Dozeman; and Rosenberg's paper. The Third feminist study beside those by Furman and Fuchs is the interesting 'The Harlot as Heroine: Narrative Art and Social Presupposition in Three Old Testament Texts' by Phyllis A. Bird. Anne M. Solomon provides an introduction, 'Story upon Story'; and James G. Williams a concluding 'Response'. Despite the attempts at grouping, there is little unity in the volume. Literary approaches to the Bible still lack coherence.

C. S. Rodd

Anderson, B. W.: *Fukaki Fuchiyori. Gendai-ni Katari-kakeru Shihen*. Translated by K. Nakamura. 1989. Pp. 310. (Shinkyō Shuppan-sha, Tokyo. Price: ¥2,400. ISBN 4 400 12378 2)

This is a Japanese translation of *Out of the Depths. The Psalms Speak for us Today*, 1983.

K. K. Sacon

AXELSSON, L. E.: *The Lord Rose Up From Seir: Studies in the History and Traditions of the Negev and Southern Judah*. Translated by F. H. Cryer (Coniectanea Biblica, Old Testament Series 25). 1987. Pp. xiii, 208. (Almqvist & Wiksell, Stockholm. Price: Sw.Kr. 140.00. ISBN 91 22 00876 4)

Axelsson's thesis is that Yahweh, associated in the ʿAmara W. text with the Shāsu and in the Old Testament with Seir, Edom, Teman, Paran, and Sinai, originally belonged to the regions south of Canaan, reaching Judah and Jerusalem via the Calebites and David, and Israel via Moses groups, and the Transjordan. The geographical link between Seir and Judah is the Negev, and Axelsson begins with the archaeological evidence for its history: largely uninhabited in Late Bronze, peacefully developed around Beersheba with unfortified villages in Iron I, fortified further south by Solomon at the end of the Iron IA, devastated towards the end of Iron IIA (Shishak), recovering in Iron IIC (seventh century), before its end in the early sixth century B.C. (Axelsson's dating and identification of Tell el-Kheleifeh may be questioned; and R. Cohen has revised his dating of some Negev fortresses.) From analysis of Old Testament settlement/conquest traditions, Axelsson argues for settlement from the south into Judah (the Calebites round Hebron, the Othnielites round Debir, the Simeonites at Hormah, and in the Beersheba region, etc.); this settlement is seen in the unfortified villages of Iron I. These groups were related to the Esau clans of Seir (located west of the W. ʿAraba) and reached Judah as immigrants from the south (contrast I. Finkelstein's recent thesis that Judah was settled from the central hill country), bringing with them their Yahwism from its home in Seir. David himself came from Judah, and skilfully united these groups by his choice of wives and supporters, ultimately bringing their Yahwism to Jerusalem.

With this analysis goes a thesis of the development of the Abraham and Isaac traditions. The Abraham tradition begins in Seir (on the evidence of the place name *p.hqr 3brm* in the Shishak list) and moves with the Calebites to Hebron/Mamre (the Chaldaean connections are much later). The Isaac tradition came with the Simeonites to the Beersheba region (and thence with some Simeonite emigrés to Israel, cf. Amos 7:9,16).

Axelsson tackles anew some well-worn themes of tradition history. His book begs all the questions of that art, but scores in relating the traditions carefully to his reconstruction of the archaeological evidence for the Negev. For example, he is clear that the tendency of some historians to make Kadesh the focus of Israel's wilderness period will not survive a critical examination of either the tradition or the archaeological evidence; the narratives regarding Kadesh as central derive from the late Judaean kingdom when Kadesh was important. Axelsson is also sensible on the dating and provenance of the traditions of Yahweh's southern origins (Deut. 33:2; Judg. 5:4 etc). rightly referring them to monarchic rather than early pre-monarchic times. This is an essential study for all students of the early history of Yahwism.

J. R. BARTLETT

BAL, M.: (ed.): *Anti-Covenant: Counter-Reading Women's Lives in the Hebrew Bible* (JSOT Supplement Series 81; Bible and Literature Series 22). 1989. Pp. 243. (Almond, Sheffield. Price: £25.00 ($42.50). ISBN 1 85075 207 9; ISSN 0260 4493; ISSN 0309 0787)

This is a fascinating collection of eleven essays, all of them, with one exception, contributed by women from a variety of disciplines and professions. The discussions are pentrating, provocative, and controversial. The general content and perspective are clear from the three section headings: two essays on the Akedah story are entitled 'The Legacy of Abraham: Male Dominance and Female Autonomy'; four on the Deborah episode are headed 'Until I Arose: The Effect of Effective Women' (stories in which, it is argued, 'subjugating readings' turn powerful women into 'wicked monsters or into subordinated, secondary leaders'), and five, which include among others the two Tamar stories and Jephthah's daughter, come under the heading 'Commemorating the Dead: Sacrificed Women and Readings of Revenge'.

It is expressly stated that the readings presented here make no positivistic claims to truth. The emphasis is on reader response, and they are an attempt to illuminate the repressed female perspective. Their approach is largely narratological. Of particular interest are the comparison between Delilah and Judith (Meredith), discussion of the disappearance of Deborah in the text of Judges 4.14b–15 (Rasmussen), a critique of two contemporary popular rewritings of Judges 4–5 illustrating the relativity of readings of the biblical text (Shaw), and Pseudo-Philo's account of Jephthah's daughter (Baker). The editor's concluding essay 'Toward a Feminist Philology' also addresses itself to the story of Jephthah's daughter, concluding that 'what is wrong with biblical scholarship is not that its readings are male-oriented, but that they are not recognized *as readings*, hence, that they are put forward as claims to objective truth, positive knowledge, exclusive insight.' Only with the recovery of a female perspective can the balance be restored.

Despite the challenge and stimulus of the presentations, for this reviewer there was in the end a surfeit, a predictability, not helped by a number of simplistic generalizations about biblical attitudes. G. I. EMMERSON

BAR-EFRAT, SH.: *Narrative Art in the Bible*. Translated by D. Shefer-Vanson (JSOT Supplement Series 70; Bible and Literature Series 17). 1989. Pp. 295. (Almond, Sheffield. Price: £26.50 ($45.00). ISBN 1 85075 138 2)

Among the many recent studies of the literary art of the Hebrew Bible, this work stands out for its simplicity of style, its wealth of illustrative material, and its convincing analyses of the effect that Hebrew narrative produces in a careful reader. The author is much influenced by M. Weiss, and provides an account accessible to the general reader as well as the biblical scholar of the insights of his school. Successive chapters examine 'The Narrator', 'The Characters', 'The Plot', 'Time and Space', and 'Style', with examples taken from all over the Hebrew Bible but especially from Genesis and Samuel; a concluding chapter illustrates the techniques identified in the rest of the book by presenting a close reading of the story of Amnon and Tamar (2 Samuel 13:1–22). The reader is invited to apply the book's insights to the Joseph Narrative and Ruth, to which end there are no examples from these two narratives. This is an attractive and readable book which admirably accomplishes its aim of initiating readers into the art of the narrative portions of the Bible, and it deserves to be widely used. The excellent translation (from the Hebrew original of 1979) is by Dorothea Shefer-Vanson. J. BARTON

BERGES, U.: *Die Verwerfung Sauls: Eine thematische Untersuchung* (Forschung zur Bibel 61). 1989. Pp. XVIII, 332. (Echter, Würzburg. Price: DM 48.00. ISBN 3 429 01224 4)

The story of Saul does not show the characteristic features of DtrG which are so prominent in Judges and Kings, but it has been made to serve the same ends. The aim of this study is to show how this is achieved in the final form of the text. This is shown to have a well integrated plan, continuing from the end of Judges through to the establishment of David's rule in 2 Samuel 5. The rejection of the Elides, the request for a king and his subsequent downfall, and the triumph of David, are all related to the Dtr interpretation of history and the laws in Deuteronomy. There are also telling comparisons with the prophecy of Jeremiah. At every point the traditions used are made to serve the needs of the exiled people. The king's duties are known through the protestations of a prophet, and Saul is rejected for disobedience. David, refusing to touch the Lord's anointed, sedulously upholds the law. Through the guiding hand of Yahweh his cause is advanced through the crimes of others, but his own hands remain clean. The accumulation of details which bear out the thesis in chapter after chapter of 1 Samuel is most impressive. There is also consideration of the reasons for the very short account of this history in 1 Chronicles, which omits the struggle between Saul and David altogether. It would be easy to jump to the conclusion that the Dtr rewriting of the story of Saul is so drastic that all attempts at historical reconstruction and traditio-historical analysis are doomed to failure. But this is not the intention of the author, as he makes clear at the beginning. His point is that a thorough understanding of the final text is an essential prerequisite for these other aspects of research, which are liable to reach false conclusions if this is not done first. This book thus prepares the ground for new research. It is a light revision of the author's doctoral thesis at the Gregorian University, and can be warmly recommended. It is a pity that no index has been added.

B. LINDARS

BRENNER, A.: *The Song of Songs* (Old Testament Guides). 1989. Pp. 106. (Sheffield Academic Press. Price: £4.95 ($7.95). ISBN 1 85075 242 7)

In less than a hundred pages this book provides an admirably clear and succinct synthesis of scholarly opinion on all aspects of the Song of Songs (SoS). Important sections deal with theories on the nature and composition of the work, the theory of comprehensive interpretation or unity of authorship being rejected in favour of the verbal or literary interpretation, that is, viewing it as an anthology of profane love lyrics loosely strung together. Brenner observes pertinently that chiastic structures, beloved by many recent literary interpreters do not necessarily exclude editorial activity. Chapters on 'Authorship', 'Daily Life: Settings, Contexts, the Environment', 'Intertextual Connections: the SoS within the Biblical Context' and 'Extra-biblical Parallels' all draw attention to important critical issues and have useful bibliographies appended. Some of these are informed by the agenda of feminist research; see chs, 2, 8, 9, and especially 10 which is entitled 'Feminist Readings of the SoS' — the interesting suggestion is made, for example, that the dreams of 3:1–4 and 5:2–7 are 'female dreams representing female inner psychological reality and fears within the social reality' (p. 89). Discussing authorship Brenner concludes that the predominance of female figures and the bold directness of female voices in the SoS do in fact suggest a *female* author/editor. Perhaps insufficient allowance is made here for the creative imagination of the original poet, be she/he female or male.

P. W. COXON

BROWN, R. E., FITZMYER, J. A., and MURPHY, R. E. (eds): *The New Jerome Biblical Commentary*. 1989. Pp. xlviii, 1484. (Geoffrey Chapman, London. Price: £60.00. ISBN 0 225 66588 3)

The Jerome Biblical Commentary was published in 1968 and reviewed fully in *B. L.* 1969 (p. 20; see also *Bible Bibliog.*, p. 146) by a former editor. The same troika has edited a new volume as similar to the first and as different from it as specialists in the field might properly expect after an interval of twenty-one years. In fact the editors estimate that two-thirds of the material is new. Certainly well over half the eighty-three chapters are by new authors; and in many further cases the 1968 author has been joined by another. And the price has risen from £10 10*s*. to £60!

The Introduction to the Pentateuch is shorter: it has much less to say about JEDP. After the article on Kings, there is no longer an excursus on

Israel and her neighbours. 'Post-Exilic Period: Spirit, Apocalyptic' has become 'Old Testament Apocalypticism and Eschatology'. 'Deutero-Isaiah' has become — this time perhaps against the trend of the times — 'Deutero-Isaiah and Trito-Isaiah'. And Ruth and Lamentations are now handled separately. Articles on modern Old and New Testament Criticism have been moved towards the end of the volume, as has the article on Paul (no longer the Life of) which has been joined by a new article on Jesus. John's Gospel is treated just before instead of just after the Johannine Epistles. Only here has the rather idiosyncratic order in which the biblical books were treated in the original edition been changed. There is a further new article called 'Early Church'. And the final two words have gone from the old title 'Inspiration and Inerrancy'.

The authors may all be catholics. However, what we read in this commentary is the fruit of the labours of an international, inter-confessional, academic community, made available by some seventy catholic scholars. If such a volume reassures catholic readers that territory once deemed dangerous is now safe, or non-catholic readers that catholic thinking does represent the mainstream of scholarship, then the outward trappings of its confessional presentation will have served well. Equally it is very much a North American product, with some assistance from Australia and Ireland. But that second accident of its birth will not make it any less serviceable in the homeland of this *Book List*. Old Testament specialists may take some wry pleasure that despite the fact that pagination is now continuous through the volume, the major two-fold distinction has been maintained between 'The Old Testament' (the real Bible?) and 'The New Testament and Topical Articles'.

A. G. AULD

BROYLES, C. C.: *The Conflict of Faith and Experience in the Psalms: A Form-Critical and Theological Study* (JSOT Supplement series 52). 1989. Pp. 272. (Sheffield Academic Press. Price: £25.00 ($42.50). ISBN 1 85075 052 1)

This study of the psalms of lament is a revised doctoral thesis supervised by D. J. A. Clines at Sheffield. The author looks into a number of questions in a reasonable and well-informed manner. He favours a distinction between psalms of plea (which affirm the praise of God) and psalms of complaint (where God appears not to live up to the praise), and shows how motifs have differing functions according to their context. Indeed, it is his conviction that many previous discussions overlook important distinctions and nuances and so give the false impression of a uniform category. Distinctions and variations are tabulated in detail. This is a substantial discussion from which the patient reader must derive benefit.

J. H. EATON

CARROLL, R. P.: *Jeremiah* (Old Testament Guides). 1989. Pp. 128. (Sheffield Academic Press. Price: £4.95 ($7.95). ISBN 1 85075 146 3)

This is not the book for anyone looking for an easy way in to the content and interpretation of the book of Jeremiah. On the contrary, it warns the student away from a simplistic approach which obscures 'its diversities, its contrary and conflicting voices'. On the author's own admission argument and ignorance are the twin emphases of his approach to 'this sprawling, angry biblical volume', and his book amply illustrates this. But it is honest about the subjectivity of the treatment, and the annotated bibliographies make generous reference to scholars whose different approaches will 'redress any danger of imbalance'. Dr Carroll raises questions rather than attempts answers: is the figure of Jeremiah historical or fictional, creator of the tradition or created by it? What is the relation of the shorter LXX edition to the MT with its numerous references to 'Jeremiah *the* prophet' (four in the former against twenty-six in the latter), a hint perhaps of the development of the tradition? Are the symbolic actions street theatre rather than magical practices? Are the commonly called 'confessions' of Jeremiah not rather laments by the community over the sufferings of the righteous at the hands of the wicked? The complex editing of Jeremiah is taken seriously. It is this, he argues, which must determine the way we read the material, rather than the constituent pieces.

Dr Carroll's book is provocative and stimulating. Whether it is, as the series intended, a useful first introduction to Jeremiah for students is a moot point. But if, as the author perhaps over optimistically hopes, the reader will already have read Jeremiah several times before approaching his volume, that may well be the case! The determined student will certainly not go away empty. Dr Carroll is courageous to have attempted this brief guide after his massive commentary in the Old Testament Library series in 1986.

G. I. EMMERSON

CLEMENTS, R. E.: *Deuteronomy* (Old Testament Guides). 1989. Pp. 104. (Sheffield Academic Press. Price: £4.95 ($7.95). ISBN 1 85075 214 1)

This short introduction wears its scholarship lightly. Within discussions of Deuteronomy's form and structure, the lawcode, the framework, the central theological themes, authorship and background, the relationship of the book to the social development of Israel, and its wider literary and theological context in the Old Testament, the author has brought out for a first inspection the major problem areas and topics of significance. Familiar ground is traversed from a fresh point of view and more recent perspectives are given a balanced appraisal. Among the latter, reference may be made especially to the author's discussion of the purpose of Deuteronomy in the context of the stage of social and economic development that Israel had reached: it is designed to strengthen her consciousness of being a nation state at a time when Israel was an economically advanced community with many of its citizens living in cities. This study admirably fulfils its purpose of introducing students both to tried and tested results of scholarship and the most recent developments in the field.

A. D. H. MAYES

CLOETE, W. T. W.: *Versification and Syntax in Jeremiah 2–25: Syntactical Constraints in Hebrew Colometry* (SBL Dissertation Series, 117). 1989. Pp. ix, 257. (Scholars Press, Atlanta GA. Price: $16.95 (member price: $10.95); paperback price: $10.95 (member price: $7.95). ISBN 1 55540 389 1; 1 55540 390 5 (pbk))

This study formed the writer's D.Litt. dissertation at the University of Stellenbosch in 1987. Its title and subtitle describe its contents perfectly. Cloete prefers to work with the terms 'verse' and 'versification' for what biblical scholars call (often loosely) 'poetry' and he engages with the work of Kugel and Watson on Hebrew poetry and, in particular, Collins on line-forms in Hebrew poetry and O'Connor on Hebrew verse structure. He sets out the Hebrew of Jeremiah 2–25 in forty pages of colometric analysis which allows the reader to see at a glance how the cola are presented (the prose passages are necessarily edited out of his presentation). This is very much a book for the technical expert, but it is also a useful contribution to the much discussed topic of the 'poetic' elements in the book of Jeremiah. His conclusions are that binarism has been overemphasized in studies of Hebrew verse, the term anacrusis should be avoided, enjambement very seldom occurs in Hebrew verse, and the Hebrew poet could possibly for purposes of gross structure have used two cola where one might expect one to be used. A salutary blow to our overuse of reference to parallelism in analyzing Hebrew verse.

R. P. Carroll

Coote, R. B. and Ord, D. R.: *The Bible's First Historian: From Eden to the court of David with the Yahwist*, 1989. Pp. x, 308. (Fortress, Philadelphia. Price: $24.95. ISBN 0 8006 0878 X)

The J document draws its inspiration from an anti-establishment milieu, as is evidenced by its pivotal narrative, that of the rebellion and escape of a band of corvée slave labourers. It was written in the time of David, and the animus that it displays against Egypt reflects the threat which that country posed to the house of David (a threat that was much reduced by the reign of Solomon, the more traditional period for the dating of J, as favoured, for example, by P. F. Ellis in *The Yahwist*, 1968, the only parallel study of J to this by Coote and Ord). If the Hebrews of J's story are predominantly bedouin rather than—with four fifths of Israelite society—peasants, that is because it was among bedouin that the young David moved, and it was with bedouin that he made the alliances which brought him to power and kept him there. The patriarchal stories all serve as propaganda for David. Like Abraham, David was associated with Hebron and owed much of his success to his close ties with bedouin groups. Like Jacob and Joseph, he was a younger son. Like Jacob, he shaped his own career yet was credited with divine approval. J is a prototypical liberationist: his very first narrative, his Eden story, is concerned to replace a traditional view of man as a slave labourer in the universe with a view of man as a free, royal, figure. Coote and Ord offer a complete translation of the passages that they assign to J, and they examine the text section by section—from Adam to Balaam, from the talking snake, and the set of curses in Gen. 3 to the talking ass in Num. 22–24 and the list of blessings which neatly reverse these curses — finding J to be a totally coherent and artistic whole, with a message calculated to challenge most of its present day readers, whose life-style is more 'Egyptian' than 'Israelite'. Those many scholars who believe that J is late, or doubt the very existence of J as a unified document, or hold that it is the canonical text that matters, will scarcely be made to stop in their tracks by the arguments here deployed against them (for Coote and Ord, I note, the Canon is a hierarchical, 'pro-imperial', even 'anti-biblical' construct). Some of the more incidental exegesis seems rather contrived, such as that of Gen. 18 in terms of the deity 'cuckolding' Abraham by impregnating Sarai, but the exegesis which is central to the argument is at least tenable. If there was a unified pre-exilic J, Coote and Ord have shown it to be at least as likely to have been Davidic as Solomonic. A minor quibble: the racy language of the chapter headings ('It's in the Bag', 'Who's in Charge Here?', &c) sits oddly with the rather turgid sociological diction found in some of the exposition.

B. P. Robinson

Davis, E. F.: *Swallowing the Scroll: Textuality and the Dynamics of Discourse in Ezekiel's Prophecy* (JSOT Supplement Series 78; Bible and Literature Series 21). 1989. Pp. 184. (Almond Press, Sheffield. Price: £21.50 ($36.50). ISBN 1 85075 206 0)

This dissertation devoted to the book of the prophet Ezekiel concentrates on questions relating to the tensions between orality and literacy in its formation. It begins with the recognition that prophecy was originally a spoken form of address and that most recent scholarship on the prophetic literature has concentrated upon examining the oral forms and units which are found in it. This has given rise to the emphasis upon the analysis of forms in the commentary by W. Zimmerli and the search for larger 'holistic' units by M. Greenberg. Davis contends that the transition to literality has exercised a creative, and not simply preservative, role in ancient Israel's intellectual growth. It brought about a restructuring of language and transformed the earlier oral forms of speech.

Starting with the claim that Ezekiel composed his prophecies in written form, Davis argues that this prophet marks the shift in the functioning of prophecy and remodelled its role in social interaction. Prophecy became text, rather than preaching, which necessitated the reshaping of its forms. Such prophetic texts then operated in the religious community very differently from the earlier prophetic discourses and gave to prophecy a new life and purpose. Not only do we find in Ezekiel the marks of this new literary form, but we also see that its very contents show prophecy to be in transition.

This is certainly a valuable dissertation. Probably it overstresses the uniqueness of the literary features of Ezekiel, since he cannot have been the first 'writing' prophet, if we take seriously the contention of an Isaianic memoir. Nevertheless Dr Davis brings out the importance of the social and functional shifts implicit in written, as distinct from preached, prophecy, and the work well repays careful study.

R. E. Clements

Dietrich, W.: *Die Josephserzählung als Novelle und Geschichtsschreibung. Zugleich ein Beitrag zur Pentateuchfrage* (Biblisch-Theologische Studien 14). 1989. Pp. 78. (Neukirchener, Neukirchen-Vluyn. Price: DM 19.80. ISBN 3 7887 1306 2; ISSN 0930 4800)

This brief monograph is an investigation of the character, function, and significance of the 'Joseph story' (Gen. 37–50). Redaction-critical, linguistic, historical, and theological methods are employed. The argument depends largely on the plausibility of the theory that an original *Novelle* has been expanded to more than twice its length by a later single redactor. The earlier version, which ended in ch. 45 with the 'revival of the spirit' of Jacob as its climax, presents a positive picture of Egypt and was composed at the time when Egypt gave support to Jeroboam in his rebellion against Solomon and Rehoboam; the expanded version, pro-Judaean and less favourable to Egypt, dates from the period immediately following the destruction of the northern kingdom. There are interesting insights into the religious dimensions and literary merits of both versions, especially the first, and these are the most valuable features of the work; but it is too brief to deal satisfactorily with the many problems involved. There is very little discussion of other views of the Joseph story, and insufficient justification of the proposed dating. The historical judgements are somewhat superficial, especially the claim that Shishak (Sheshonq)'s attack on Jerusalem (1 Kings 14:25–28) may have been carried out in order to provide support for the northern kingdom in its struggle with Judah. Despite the subtitle, the author does not really come to grips with the current debate on the composition of the Pentateuch.

R. N. Whybray

Dozeman, T. B.: *God on the Mountain: A Study of Redaction, Theology, and Canon in Exodus 19–24* (SBL Monograph Series, 37). 1989. Pp. xi, 224. (Scholars Press, Atlanta GA. Price: $26.95 (member price: $17.95); paperback price: $17.95 (member price: $11.95). ISBN 1 55540 358 1; 1 55540 359 X (pbk))

This new study of the almost intractable literary-critical problems of the Sinai pericope takes its departure from the now common view that the biblical redactors were creative theological writers, and in particular from the work of R. Rendtorff and L. Perlitt on the Pentateuch. Dozeman distinguishes a single original tradition of theophany and sacrifice, a Deuteronomistic redaction, and a Priestly redaction, each with its distinctive theology of the divine presence at the mountain: an initial 'immanentist' view, related to pre-exilic Zion theology, was in due course integrated with theologies which laid more stress on divine transcendence. There are some valuable insights here, and the critical position is not unlike that taken by W. Johnstone (*ZAW* 99 (1987) 16–37). But the reliance on Perlitt's work and on the questionable idea of the Priestly Writer as a redactor leave this reviewer unconvinced. The most valuable parts of the book in the long run may well be those chapters (5 and 6) which attempt to grapple with the canonical shape and shaping of the Sinai pericope, and its social context in the mission of Ezra.

G. I. Davies

Eskenazi, T. C.: *In An Age of Prose: A Literary Approach to Ezra-Nehemiah* (SBL Monograph Series 36), 1988. Pp. viii, 211. (Scholars Press, Atlanta GA. Price: $29.95 (member price: $19.95); paperback price: $19.95 (member price: $13.95). ISBN 1 55540 260 7; 1 55540 261 5 (pbk))

This engaging and fluent monograph is a superb example of the application of literature criticism to Old Testament texts. Taking Ezra-Nehemiah in its present form as a literary whole, Dr Eskenazi analyses its structure, themes, and characterization, concluding that its basic story-line is 'how the people of God build the house of God in accordance with authoritative documents' (p. 175). Following the schematization of story structure by Claude Bremond, she identifies Ezr. 1:1–4 as 'potentiality' or definition of the objective, Ezr. 1:5–Neh. 7:72 as 'process of actualization', and Neh. 8:1–13:31 as 'success' or realization of the objective, which she understands as the completion of the house of God. One major claim, however, is questionable: that the creation of the community — which is the subject-matter of most of the work — is in some sense the building of the 'house of God'. The study proceeds at every point in expert awareness of historical-critical research, and its integration of traditional scholarship with the newer literary criticism is highly successful.

D. J. A. Clines

Eslinger, L.: *Into the Hands of the Living God* (JSOTS 84; Bible and Literature Series 24). 1989. Pp. xii, 272. (Almond, Sheffield. Price: £20.00; $35.00. ISBN 1 85075 212 5; ISSN 0260 4493; 0309 0787)

The author's contention is that most existing historical-critical readings of biblical narrative are vitiated by the lack of sophistication which besets their literary analysis. His own reading of the Deuteronomistic History which is presented in this book makes use of the tools of a new discipline of biblical narratology. Chapters on Jos, Jgs 1–2, 1 Sam. 12, 1 Kgs 1–11 and 2 Kgs 17:1–23 are followed by a general description (perhaps best read first) of the role which computing software played in the analysis. There is nothing in the conventional literary ontology of the narratives in the DH, he maintains, which implies that more than one author is expressing himself. The DH does not present us with theodicy, but theology. Its message about the ways of God with man is much more complex than is usually thought.

There is much in this book which is of interest and value, in terms both of the general theoretical discussion and of the individual readings of passage which it contains. Historical critics must surely pay greater attention to the literary qualities of texts than they have generally done in the past. This reviewer's enjoyment of the book was marred, however, by its somewhat arrogant and polemical tone. Historical critics apparently never read the text with any great insight or care (cf., for example, p. 78, n. 22), and certainly lack the objectivity with regard to the text which is shared by Eslinger and (some) other literary critics (cf., for example, p. 23, n. 20). The *certainties* of literary criticism are frequently contrasted with the *hypotheses* of historical criticism; and this allows the author to insist that 'first-order' (i.e. literary) solutions of exegetical difficulties are always to be preferred to 'second-order' (historical) solutions. Those scholars who, while intent on careful reading and as much objectivity as possible, are not prepared to accept that the 'knowledge' possessed by literary critics is of a higher order than any other kind, will not always be convinced by this book. They will, I suspect, be suspicious of a style of argumentation which depends to such a great extent upon appeal to the subtlety of the biblical authors and the implicit meanings of their texts. Authorial subtlety must certainly be considered among the possible explanations of why any text is as it is. If the integrity of the text as a whole can only be defended, however, by comprising various of its individual parts through implausible exegesis (cf., for example, the reading of the accounts of complete conquest in Jos. as irony), one wonders why anyone who did not in the first place have a methodological of theological axe to grind would wish to do it.

This is a stimulating and useful book, then, but certainly not one without serious flaws. A number of minor and not-so-minor typographical errors and omissions are also to be found.

I. W. PROVAN

EXUM, J. C. (ed.): *Signs and Wonders: Biblical Texts in Literary Focus* (Semeia Studies). 1989. Pp. vii, 247. (Scholars Press, Atlanta GA. Price: $32.95 (member price: $21.95); paperback price: $21.95 (member price: $14.95). ISBN 1 55540 249 6; 1 55540 250 X (pbk))

The volume comprises six essays on a number of Old Testament topics, each with a response by another writer. The intention behind it is to show that only a pluralistic approach to the literary reading of biblical texts can do justice to the diverse material contained in them. F. Landy writes on narrative techniques and symbolic transactions in the Akedah (response by J. P. Fokkelman), J. Cheryl Exum on the story of Jephthah as 'tragedy' (response by W. L. Humphreys), Y. Amit on the form and message of the Ehud story (response by D. Jobling), D. M. Gunn on the David of the biblical narratives (response by P. D. Miscall), T. C. Eskenazi on texts in community in Ezra-Nehemiah (response by D. J. A. Clines), and E. F. Davis on Ezekiel the dumb prophet (response by K. P. Darr). The level of discourse is as good as the reputations of the contributors would lead one to expect. Sociologists of the modern literary criticism of the Hebrew Bible will note that the responses range from the complaisant-on-principle (or 'anything goes'?) to the (reassuring for this reader) 'I-beg-to-differ' approach.

R. P. GORDON

FEWELL, D. N.: *Circle of Sovereignty: A Story of Stories in Daniel 1–6* (JSOT Supplement Series 72; Bible and Literature Series 20). 1988. Pp. 207. (Almond, Sheffield. Price: £25.00 ($42.50). ISBN 1 85075 158 7)

This study offers a close reading of the stories in Daniel 1–6, and the bulk of the work consists of a fairly literal translation and a reading of each story. This is prefaced by a discussion of recent form-critical studies of Daniel 1–6 — the author opts for the classification 'short story' — and of the methodologies and ideas that influenced the reading, while in a short epilogue, by way of a look forward, two themes that run throughout Daniel 1–6 and also extend into the second half of the book are briefly considered. There are notes, a bibliography, and reference and author indexes.

The study raises some interesting questions about the interpretation of biblical literature in general and the meaning of the stories in Daniel 1–6 in particular, and on the latter it may be said that the author makes some good points as well as some that seem totally unconvincing. But a more significant weakness is that the author does not really consider whether it is appropriate to treat Daniel 1–6 as a unit, nor whether the methodology she uses is appropriate to the kind of materials contained in these chapters, and the consequence of this is that at times what she offers appears to be an overreading. As an incidental point, it is surprising to read with reference to 2:1: 'The apparatus to the Massoretic text suggests that the phrase be emended to "the tenth year", but there is no textual support for this change' (p. 173).

M. A. Knibb

Fischer, G.: *Jahwe unser Gott: Sprache, Aufbau und Erzähltechnik in der Berufung des Mose (Ex 3–4)*. (OBO 91). 1989. Pp. 262. (Universitätsverlag, Freiburg (CH); Vandenhoeck & Ruprecht, Göttingen. Price: Sw.Fr. 68.00. ISBN 3 7278 0646 X; 3 525 53721 2)

Dr Fischer's thesis presents a detailed literary study of Exod. 3–4 recounting the call and commissioning of Moses. What is new is its application of contemporary literary theory about the conventions, structure, and dynamics of narrative. It begins by noting the high prevalence among scholars of theories which have sought to explain repetitions, tensions, and unevennesses in the development of narrative by suppositions regarding the use by the author of sources. More recently still there has arisen a reaction against this by resort to literary, or theological, dogmatism which has determined to consider only the final form of the text.

Fischer wants to adhere to neither path in examining the themes, language, and unfolding movement of the story of Moses' call and commissioning. He offers a fresh translation of the text, backed up by ample notes on textual and grammatical issues. The heart of the thesis, however, is devoted to a study of the major themes of the story. He focuses these themes upon four main semantic fields: seeing, sending, believing, and speaking, all of which revolve around the experience of an encounter with God, recognition of a divine plan, and its reception by Moses.

On the basis of this initial survey Fischer proceeds to an examination of the manner in which the narrative account is developed. He discerns a positive planned unity in the entire sequence of events in Exod. 3:1–4:17, which accords with accepted patterns of narrative structure. This does not rule out that older elements have been used in its composition, but recognizes that the whole is a skilfully put together literary composition. Fischer relates this conclusion to other recent studies which have found within the Pentateuch as a whole evidence of a comprehensive redactional unity. Fischer's study is primarily concerned with the story elements of the exodus event, rather than with cultic, historical, or legal aspects of it. It raises major questions about what constitute adequate criteria for source analysis and shows how complex may be the structures which determine the unity of a narrative. Elements of tension and disjunction may serve a planned narrative purpose and form part of an overall coherence and unity.

R. E. Clements

Fox, M. V.: *Qohelet and his Contradictions* (JSOT Supplement Series 71; Bible and Literature Series 18). 1989. Pp. 384. (Almond, Sheffield. Price: £25.00 ($42.50). ISBN 1 85075 148 X)

Parts of this book have appeared in different forms in various journals, but the author, while adhering to his main conclusions there, acknowledges that his interpretations of specific passages have occasionally departed from the published work.

In his introduction, Fox compares Qohelet with Camus, places the book in the Hellenistic period, and surveys other attempts at dealing with the Qohelet contradictions. The early interpretations reveal that forced harmonization was the name of the game. He questions Loader's thesis that the anomalies are to be explained by polarity of thought, and is doubtful of Hertzberg's use of the *Zwar-Aber Tatsache* as an interpretative principle. The approach which identifies additions in the text is also questionable: first of all, the so-called additions are often linked syntactically to material usually thought to be original; secondly, they do not fulfil the purposes ascribed to their authors; thirdly, if removed, the sceptical character of the book remains; and fourthly, their removal does not result in consistency. He also finds unsatisfactory the approach which sees Qohelet as quoting other sources. There follow 5 chapters: *The Meaning of Hebel and Re'ut-ruaḥ in Qohelet*; *Toil and Pleasure*; *The Way of Wisdom: Qohelet's Epistemology*; *Justice and Theodicy*; and *Commentary*. The latter — by far the longest in the book (pp 151–348) — is not a complete commentary on Qohelet in that it does not tackle various exegetical problems. It deals with some key words in Qohelet, Qohelet's language, Literary structure, Greek and Syriac translations, and general exegesis, ending with a paraphrase of the text. There is a good bibliography and indexes (references, authors, subjects, Hebrew words).

This book is the fruit of many years study, and there is a lot of information and good argument here. There may be times when Fox is unconvincing, but always he is stimulating, and students of Qohelet will benefit from a study of this work.

R. B. Salters

Green, A. (ed.): *Jewish Spirituality from the Bible through the Middle Ages* (World Spirituality). 1989. Pp. xxv, 450. (SCM, London. Price: £17.50. ISBN 0 334 02427 7)

The first British hardback edition was published by Routledge & Kegan Paul in 1986 (the American original had appeared in 1985), and was noted critically in *B. L.* 1987, pp. 83–84. This first British paperback edition, now from SCM, is available at less than half the original price.

A. G. Auld

Grossberg, D.: *Centripetal and Centrifugal Structures in Biblical Poetry* (SBL Monograph Series, 39). 1989. Pp. ix, 111. (Scholars Press, Atlanta GA. Price: $19.95 (member price: $12.95); paperback price: $12.95 (member price: $8.95). ISBN 1 55540 360 3; 1 55540 361 1 (pbk))

Here, Grossberg applies the categories 'centripetal' and 'centrifugal', first coined by E. Stankiewicz for the structural analysis of poetry (in *Semiotica* 38 [1982], pp. 217–42), to three sets of Hebrew verse: the 'Songs of "Ascents"' (pss. 120–134), the Song of Songs, and Lamentations.

The terms 'centripetal' and 'centrifugal' refer to characteristics and devices which help or hinder the cohesion of a poem. The combination of both types contributes to a poem's dynamic tension. Accordingly, G. lists fifteen features for Hebrew (repetition, syntactic structures, lexis, etc.) which can be either centripetal or both centripetal and centrifugal.

In his search for the two categories in Hebrew the author is far from mechanical; instead he is sensitive to the individual character of each of the three compositions. In effect, he shows how the various features, wherever they might be placed on the continuum between centripetal and centrifugal. function within a poetic composition. Also, he has advanced beyond the analysis of the line and the couplet to discussion of complete poems and sets of poems. Grossberg's book marks a positive advance in our appreciation of Hebrew compositional techniques and will stimulate others to study the remaining books of the Old Testament in a similar way.

W. G. E. WATSON

HA, J.: *Genesis 15: A Theological Compendium of Pentateuchal History* (BZAW 181). 1989. Pp. xii, 244. (De Gruyter, Berlin. Price: DM 82.00. ISBN 3 11 011206 X)

In this slightly revised edition of his 1986 Rome doctoral dissertation, in which the influence of Rendtorff is particularly apparent, Ha attempts to sketch the relationship between Gen. 15 and other parts of the Pentateuch. Part one of the dissertation is devoted to a discussion of Gen. 15 itself. A reasonably convincing, if conservative, resolution of the textual difficulties in the chapter (pp. 15–26) is followed by a helpful description of the exegetical problems which confront the interpreter, and the various ways in which previous readers have attempted to address these (pp. 27–38). Ha prefers those readings which do not resort to theories about sources or redactors, and sets out to demonstrate that there are major arguments for the unity of the chapter which have not hitherto been treated (pp. 39–62). In the final section of part one (pp. 63–89), he further argues that Gen. 15 betrays prophetic influence, and in particular depends upon Isa. 7:1–17 and Jer. 34:18–20. Part two of the dissertation treats the chapter as 'a theological compendium of Pentateuchal History'. Ha defends the proposition that the author of Gen. 15 knew the Pentateuch in virtually its final form (pp. 93–103); and maintains (pp. 105–96) that the chapter is a recapitulation and 'theologization' of the Pentateuchal history, which highlights the two theologoumena central to that history (the divine oath to the patriarchs and their response of faith). The position of the chapter in Genesis is due to its appropriateness, along with the complementary chapters 12–13, as a 'preface' to the entire Pentateuch (pp. 197–212). Gen. 15 was composed during the exilic period by an author of uncertain affiliation.

Though parts of it inevitably already have a somewhat dated look, this will clearly be an important book for those interested in Genesis and in Pentateuchal criticism. It is not clear, however, that the author is entirely successful in his attempt to explain Gen. 15 as a unity (cf., for example, the rather tortuous exegesis of vv. 5 and 12 on pp. 51–52). It is consequently not clear, though several of the sections of the book which describe links between Gen. 15 and other parts of the Pentateuch are interesting and provocative, that his assessment of the significance of these links is correct. One scholar's 'literary influence' is, after all, another's 'common source' or 'common redactor'. Critics who remain open to, even if no longer totally convinced by, the older models of Pentateuchal criticism will not necessarily be convinced by this book, though they will certainly be stimulated by it.

I. W. PROVAN

HARTMAN, G. H. and BUDICK, S. (eds): *Midrash and Literature*. 1986, 1988. Pp. xvii, 412. (Yale University Press, New Haven and London. Price: £12.95 ($19.95). ISBN 0 300 04198 5)

This excellent collection of contemporary writing on midrash, especially in its modern applications and practice, contains some very fine work by an assortment of first-rate scholars and writers. The eighteen contributions are divided into five sections. 1. Bible and Midrash consists of two essays: Geoffrey H. Hartman's 'The Struggle for the Text' and Michael Fishbane's 'Inner Biblical Exegesis: Types and Strategies of Interpretation in Ancient

Israel'. 2. Midrash and Aggadah has four pieces: Joseph Heinemann's 'The Nature of the Aggadah', Judah Goldin's 'The Freedom and Restraint of Haggadah', James L. Kugel's 'Two Introductions to Midrash', and David Stern's 'Midrash and the Language of Exegesis: A Study of Vayikra Rabbah, Chapter 1'. 3. From Midrash to Kabbalah contains three contributions: Joseph Dan's 'Midrash and the Dawn of Kabalah', Moshe Idel's 'Infinities of Torah in Kabbalah', and Betty Roitman's 'Sacred Language and Open Text'. 4. Literature and Midrash is the longest section with seven chapters: Frank Kermode's 'The Plain Sense of Things', Sanford Budick's 'Milton and the Scene of Interpretation: From Typology toward Midrash', Harold Fisch's 'The Hermeneutic Quest in *Robinson Crusoe*', Joshua Wilner's 'Romanticism and the Internalization of Scripture', Myrna Solotorevsky's 'The Model of Midrash' and Borges's 'Interpretative Tales and Essays', Jill Robbins's 'Kafka's Parables', and Gershon Shaked's 'Midrash and Narrative: Agnon's "Agunit"'. 5. Contemporary Midrash consists of Jacques Derrida's 'Shibboleth' and Edmund Jabès's 'The Key'. The book represents the fruits of a collective research project carried out by The Centre for Literary Studies of The Hebrew University of Jerusalem from 1983–85.

To the purist for whom the term 'midrash' can only be applied to a limited period of ancient literary production this volume may seem at times to be perverse and no doubt there will be protests at the extension of the term to cover modern literary activity. However, words, where not moribund, move on as all living things tend to and we cannot be bound by ancient etymologies or outdated dictionary-determined attitudes as if language were static and not developmental. As a word, perspective, mode of activity, and category 'midrash' works well in this volume to describe many of the writing operations behind modern as well as ancient texts. Midrash embodies the capacity to bring about the rebirth of tradition and affirms the integrity and authority of texts while, at the same time, fragmenting them. As the editors say in their Introduction (pp. ix–xiii) 'midrash is the open word, the open door, through which we are always just passing' (p. xiii). This then is a very fine collection and well worth reading by every biblical scholar, whatever precise meaning they give to the word 'midrash'.

R. P. Carroll

Hobbs, T. R.: *1, 2 Kings* (Word Biblical Themes). 1989, Pp. xiii, 104. (Word Books, Dallas TX. Price: $9.99. ISBN 0 8499 0795 0)

Following the two volumes on the books of Kings in the Word Bible Commentary, one by S. de Vries and the other by the author of this book, an attempt is now made to stand back and 'to sketch in broad strokes some of the major themes that emerge'. Professor Hobbs concentrates on six: kings, prophets, the people of God, the covenanted land, sin and judgement, hope, and the anger of God.

This is a study that usefully strings together the texts from Kings that illustrate the author's chosen themes and provide a basis for his fuller exposition of them. The theme that is not substantially supported is that of the covenanted land; although the books of Kings show step by step how the land was lost with the carrying of the people into exile, the theme itself is mostly dormant and is not developed or expounded to an extent that deserves for it a listing among the major themes. Nevertheless, an attempt such as this to bring together the main theological themes in biblical books does provide a valuable companion and supplement to commentaries which usually concentrate on textual, historical, and literary matters.

G. H. Jones

HOSSFELD, F. L. (ed.): *Vom Sinai zum Horeb: Stationen alttestamentlicher Glaubensgeschichte*. Für Erich Zenger. 1989. Pp. 196. (Echter, Würzburg. Price: DM 29.00. ISBN 3 429 01248 1)

The six essays contained in this volume are presented in tribute to Dr E. Zenger on his fiftieth birthday for his major researches into the biblical Sinai narratives. They show an especial concern with the Decalogue, a subject to which the two major studies are devoted. The first, by C. Dohmen, surveys the entire question of what the biblical narrative intends to present as the contents of the original Mosaic tablets of law. Beginning with J. W. Goethe's observations of 1773, Dohmen notes that the biblical narrative is neither clear nor consistent on this point. Furthermore the emphasis upon the written form of the two law tablets has a distinct bearing upon the question of the origin of the Pentateuch as expressing the conditions of the Sinai covenant. From this the whole concept of a sacred 'Scripture' emerges.

Besides editing the volume F.-L. Hossfeld also offers an extended synoptic comparison of the two Decalogue formulations of Exod. 20 and Deut. 5. This effectively provides an excellent survey of recent studies of the subject. Law also provides the subject matter for L. Schwienhorst-Schonberger who devotes an essay to the subject of the structure of the Book of the Covenant, offering a valuable critique of the major studies by J. Halbe and E. Otto. H.-J. Fabry examines the historical implications of Gen. 27:1–45 and Georg Steins writes on the structure and origin of Exod. 24:12–31:18. The volume concludes with a brief survey by Robert Wenning of the excavations at Meṣad Ḥašavyahu, dating the occupation of the site to either 600–598 or 598–588 B.C.

R. E. CLEMENTS

JOHNSON, M. D.: *The Purpose of the Biblical Genealogies, with special reference to the setting of the genealogies of Jesus*. 2nd ed. (Society for New Testament Studies Monograph Series, 8). 1988. Pp. xxxiv, 310. (Cambridge University Press. Price: £30.00 ($49.50). ISBN 0 521 35644 X)

The first edition of this standard work (published in 1969 and noted in *B. L.* 1970, p. 76) is here reprinted unchanged, but the author has added a twenty-two page introduction in which he briefly surveys a number of studies which have appeared in the meantime. Nevertheless, he states that 'I have not found it necessary to abandon my basic approach nor radically to revise any foundational interpretative stance', a conclusion which testifies to the solid worth of the original publication. Unfortunately, the indexes have not been revised to include the material from this new introduction.

H. G. M. WILLIAMSON

JOYCE, P.: *Divine Initiative and Human Response in Ezekiel* (JSOT Supplement Series 51). 1989. Pp. 186. (Sheffield Academic Press. Price: £25.00 ($42.50). ISBN 1 85075 041 6)

In many ways the most recent discussion of the book of Ezekiel has focused heavily upon problems of literary structure and the relationship between the prophet's original preaching and the final form of the text. It is welcome therefore to have a detailed treatment of one of the major theological themes posed by the book, which takes full account of the literary tensions within it, but which looks behind them. This draws attention to the elements of paradox between Ezekiel's emphasis upon divine sovereignty and initiative and the concern with human accountability and response to the divine action. The former feature appears prominently in the use of the formula of divine self-disclosure 'I am the Lord' and the assertion that Yahweh acts 'for his name's sake'. Alongside this the prophet lays emphasis upon individual accountability, especially in the legal formulation of Ezek. 18, but also in chapters 9, 14 and in the promise of a spiritual outpouring and empowering in Ezek. 36.

Joyce argues that this tension is true to human experience and represents a prophetic sharpening of tensions which exist throughout Israel's spiritual history. The heavy stress on each citizen's accountability for Israel's misfortunes is placed over against the promise that God alone will exert his initiative to restore and rebuild Israel. That the period of crisis in which the prophet worked generated a measure of literary hyperbole is admitted, but Joyce claims that both aspects of the prophetic message belong to Ezekiel's theological inheritance. Altogether this is a most readable and stimulating study.

R. E. CLEMENTS

KANG, S.-M.: *Divine War in the Old Testament and in the Ancient Near East* (BZAW 177). 1989. Pp. xv, 251. (De Gruyter, Berlin. Price: DM 118.00. ISBN 3 11 011156 X)

This revised version of Dr Kang's dissertation, written under the supervision of Professors Haran and Weinfeld in Jerusalem, adds to the rather impressive list of books on the Divine War theme that have appeared in trhe last few decades — Fredriksson (1945), von Rad (1951), Smend (1963), Stolz (1972), Miller (1973), Lind (1980), and Craigie (1981).

However, the author has attempted to make an advance in this field of research by highlighting three main issues for discussion: the distinction between holy war and YHWH war, the distinction between the mythical and historical realities of YHWH war, and the possible connection between YHWH war in the Old Testament and divine war in the ancient Near East. In addressing himself to these issues, Dr Kang has in Part One of his study undertaken a survey of Divine War in the ancient East, giving particular attention to the context, the concept, divine warriors, and war conduct in Mesopotamia, Anatolia, Syro-Palestine, and Egypt. When he turns in Part Two to the Old Testament material, he concentrates on wars in three main traditions, firstly the Exodus-Conquest tradition, then the Judges and Saul complex, and finally the Davidic narratives.

Dr Kang's main conclusion is that it was in the rising period of the Davidic kingdom that the motifs of YHWH war appeared in historical battles; such motifs were not found in the historical realities of the Exodus-Conquest battles nor in the wars of the Judges and Saul, only in the later theological understanding of them in the light of YHWH war.

This study is a welcome addition to the volumes listed above, on account of both the comprehensiveness of its approach and the interesting analysis of Old Testament material which is presented in it.

G. H. JONES

KARTVEIT, M.: *Motive und Schichten der Landtheologie in I Chronik 1–9* (Coniectanea Biblica, Old Testament Series 29). 1989. Pp. 176. (Almqvist & Wiksell, Stockholm. Price: Sw.Kr. 157.00. ISBN 91 22 01277 X)

Ninety-pages of this dissertation comprise a detailed textual and literary-critical study of 1 Chr. 1–9. Kartveit concludes that a *Grundschicht* belongs to the original work of the Chronicler, but that significant additions to this (e.g. 3:1–9; 5:27–41; 6:39–66) were made in two main stages of editorial revision as well as some others which affect only the Judah-section. The *Grundschicht* made, according to the author, an important contribution to the Chronicler's theology of the land by its presentation of the geographical extent of Israel's inheritance. In the south, east, and west this involved claims to territory which had not traditionally been reckoned as Israelite and which was in post-exilic times occupied by Edomites and others, while all interest in Galilee seems to have been given up. This Kartveit takes to reflect the Chronicler's view of Judah's entitlement to territory in his own day (apart from the Transjordanian territories), or at least at some future date. The point is not developed as fully as it might be, and some attempt at a correlation with Obadiah 19–21 would be worthwhile, to see whether the Chronicler's view could be associated with this specific prophetic expectation.

G. I. DAVIES

KREUZER, S.: *Die Frühgeschichte Israels in Bekenntnis und Verkündigung des Alten Testaments* (BZAW 178). 1989. Pp. IX, 301. (De Gruyter, Berlin. Price: DM 120.00. ISBN 3 11 011736 3)

This is a study of Old Testament historical summaries or creeds which have had considerable significance for theories about the origins of the Pentateuch. The first third of the book provides a lucid account of the history of the study of the topic, from Jirku's pioneering work through Galling, who first emphasized the significance of Deut. 26:5ff and its early origin, to von Rad and Noth, reactions to whom have either questioned von Rad's particular cultic assumptions or argued for a late date for Deut. 26. The author then turns to the historical summaries to be found in Gen. 15:13–16; Ex. 3:7f, 9f, 16f; Nu. 20:15f; Deut. 6:20–25; 26:5–9 and Josh. 24. In almost all cases there is no old traditional credal form to be found, which could serve as a foundation for theories about the early history of Israel or the development of the Pentateuch/Hexateuch. Rather, they are generally literary creations which presuppose a conception of the history of Israel. Older elements are to be found only in Nu. 20:15f, and in the reference to the wandering Aramean in Deut. 26:5. Nu. 20:15f is a presentation of the exodus theme which has its roots in a cultic song of thanksgiving, and as such may be distinguished from its present R^{JE} context; Deut. 26 represents a relatively late combination of this with an old, pre-state thanksgiving for land referring to the precarious existence of the Aramean ancestor. The other historical summaries reflect an existing combination of patriarchal, exodus and conquest themes which, as Ex. 3 in particular shows, is to be found already in J, from the early monarchic period, and E. from the time of Jeroboam II. This is a useful contribution to an ongoing debate, incorporating many significant studies of individual texts.

A. D. H. MAYES

KRISPENZ, J.: *Spruchkompositionen im Buch Proverbia* (Europäische Hochschulschriften, Reihe XXIII, Bd. 349). 1989. Pp. 188. (Lang, Frankfurt. Price: Sw.Fr. 43.00. ISBN 3 631 40690 8; ISSN 0721 3409)

Krispenz argues that the book of Proverbs does not have a context in the sense of an external frame of reference, whether historical or sociological, in which its interpretation can be set. In particular, attempts to furnish a *Sitz im Leben* by postulating the 'school' as a setting in which the wisdom sentences functioned are criticized. It is held that a different kind of context exists in the book of Proverbs, one which is internal and literary in kind and which manifests itself compositionally. The literary devices which create these clusters of sentences are various, but *Paronomasie* is thought to be especially significant. The identification of such compositions enriches the exegesis of the individual sentences which comprise them. Hence the book of Proverbs possesses a linguistic and literary autonomy and in so far as it reaches out to the external world it does so by hinting at correspondences between its own linguistic and literary domain and domains which are beyond it.

These features are said to belong to 'poetic texts' or 'poetic sayings', but it is clear that 'poetic texts' or 'poetic sayings' has a special sense, since scholars who have sought historical or social frameworks for the interpretation of the book of Proverbs have not doubted that the wisdom sentences have a metrical form — that they are poetry not prose. But when Krispenz faces the task of producing a sharper definition of 'poetic texts', we are transported into a somewhat rarified atmosphere and invited to sit at the feet of Jean-Paul Sartre and others. One feels the need of oxygen in order to breathe. We are told that poetic texts are primarily language-related, whereas prose texts are fact-related. The free use of figures of speech is an indication that language has a primary creative role in the formation of 'poetic texts'. *Paronomasien* (puns or word-plays) receive special mention as devices used in Proverbs to transcend the boundaries of individual wisdom sentences.

Compositions of wisdom sentences allegedly so formed can be inspected in part 2 of the book and *Paronomasie* reappears in part 3, where a comparison between Proverbs and Egyptian wisdom literature is offered. Egyptian 'Instructions' are disengaged from the biblical book of Proverbs because they hardly at all feature *Paronomasien*, while Egyptian cultic texts with *Paronomasien* are enlisted in order to display a special kind of relationship of word and fact. This leads on to a type of observation with which Old Testament scholars are familiar in other connections, which exaggerates the conceptual distance between the present and Old Testament times. Is it true that the book of Proverbs is so inaccessible to us as Krispenz maintains? For the most part it does not seem to me that this is so. We are not alienated from its conceptuality by a barrier which its antiquity or its mental strangeness raises.

W. McKane

Krüger, T.: *Geschichtskonzepte im Ezechielbuch* (BZAW 180). 1989. Pp. xi, 524. (De Gruyter, Berlin. Price: DM 178.00. ISBN 3 11 011473 9)

Dr Krüger's study of Ezekiel uses the notion of concepts of history to undertake a comprehensive examination of the theological and political ideas of the prophet Ezekiel. This is therefore a valuable and perceptive study of many of the most central features of the prophetic book, and it concludes with a broad reappraisal of the redactional history which has shaped it. Its starting point lies in the recognition that a particular historical perspective on the past and future inevitably implies a very basic attitude towards the present. Krüger's detailed exegesis, accordingly, focuses upon the summary historical characterizations of Israel's past presented in Ezek. 5:5–17, the allegories of Ezek. 16:1–43 and 23:1–30, and the lengthy survey of Ezek. 20. The latter, in particular, points forward to a hope of restoration because it presupposes Israel's scattering among the nations, as again in chapters 36–37.

Overall a relatively conservative approach is adopted towards the authenticity of the text, at least in contrast with some recent studies, but Krüger discerns an ongoing process of redaction which extended well after the prophet's lifetime. A community, or 'school', of Ezekiel found it necessary to clarify and elaborate the original prophetic words in the light of the changing historical situation which the divided and exiled Judeans experienced.

Certainly this is an attractive interpretation of the prophet and his legacy which recognizes that later material has been added to the original prophetic words in order to shape them into a meaningful book, but takes considerable care to explore the reasons which have brought this about. The author contends that a concept of history which hinges on notions of divine punishment and hope lies at the centre of biblical theology. This is perceptively explored in examination of the specific reasons which the prophet adduces for divine action. The study lies close to the traditio-historical approaches of G. von Rad and W. Zimmerli, but carries the debate into a much more detailed analysis of the way in which the book of Ezekiel reflects the broken and changing structure of Israel as a community after 598 and 587 B.C. Altogether this is a most attractive piece of research.

R. E. CLEMENTS

LACOCQUE, A. and P.-E.: *Le Complexe de Jonas: une étude psycho-religieuse du prophète* (Initiations). 1989. Pp. 2320. (Cerf, Paris. Price: Fr. 180. ISBN 2 204 03075 9; ISSN 0298 5586)

This is a considerably reworked French edition of the original English version *The Jonah Complex* (John Knox Press, 1981). The main differences that I can see between the editions, apart from the extended bibliographical material and the more general sophistication of rewriting, are an extra chapter dealing with heroes, monsters, and initiation rites: a response to Carl Jung, a longer second chapter on Jonah as satire (the English version treats Jonah as symbolic narrative), and an appendix on Jonah as a stage on the way to apocalyptic. Mircea Éliade's foreword appears in both editions (and symbolizes the connection between the book and the Chicago Theological Seminary). In my opinion this book is a brilliant treatment of the biblical text of Jonah as well as a fine psychoanalytical reading of it. It is a psychotheological analysis of Jonah which demonstrates yet again how profoundly interesting and interrogating generations of readers have found that short story, satire, subversive parable of the 'prophet' Jonah. In a few columns of beautifully structured Hebrew the author has composed a tale of profound significance and undying literary interest. The epithet to the Lacocques' book is, needless to say, from Father Mapple's sermon in Melville's *Moby Dick* (at great length Melville's classic work rewrites the Jonah legend). The Lacocques mean by the phrase 'the Jonah complex' (influenced here by Abraham Maslow's existential psychology) the fear, or refusal, to actualize one's vocation (i.e. the rejection of the sublime, the Outer Voice, God) or, in more human terms, the refusal to grow up (i.e. Jonah as the permanently infantile figure). For their Jonah is not simply the protagonist of the biblical story: 'il est un être humain, il est chacun de nous' (p. 265). A fine book and well worth reading — in whichever version.

R. P. CARROLL

LANGER, B.: *Gott als "Licht" in Israel und Mesopotamien: Eine Studie zu Jes 60, 1–3. 19f.* (Österreichische Biblische Studien 7). 1989. Pp. viii, 255. (Österreichisches Katholisches Bibelwerk, Klosterneuburg. Price: ÖS 198.00; DM 29.40; Sw.Fr. 25.50. ISBN 3 85396 078 2)

Building upon the work of earlier scholars, Langer here argues that Old Testament light-symbolism is at many points to be understood as sun-symbolism, including places where it refers to Yahweh. Particular emphasis is laid on passages where light is associated with *ṣᵉdāqāh* and *mišpāṭ* and on the use of the verbs *zāraḥ* and *yaṣā'*, to suggest a connection with Shamash as the god of justice, and on the association between light and life, which appears both in Mesopotamia and in the Bible. Isaiah 60 forms a natural starting-point for this investigation. As a purely comparative study this dissertation is of unusual interest, but the additional point that some Old Testament poets may have used light-symbolism in ways derived ultimately from Mesopotamia is also carefully and convincingly made. Whether there was as much Assyrian influence as Langer thinks on pre-exilic Judaean religion may perhaps be doubted, and it may be preferable to see in the evidence to which she draws attention a revival and reuse of conceptions which had established themselves in Canaan at a much earlier date.

G. I. DAVIES

LANGER, G.: *Von Gott erwählt – Jerusalem* (Österreichische Biblische Studien 8). 1989. Pp. xiv, 352 and 22 pages of texts and tables. (Österreichisches Katholisches Bibelwerk, Klosterneuburg. Price: ÖS 328.00; DM 48.80. ISBN 3 85396 079 0)

This detailed study is concerned with the interpretation of Deut. 12 in early Jewish exegesis, with a view to any contribution that might make to modern exegesis. Following an overview of present study of Deut. 12, covering its redaction, formulaic language and themes, and including a detailed commentary, the author turns to the interpretation of the chapter in the intertestamental literature, with a particularly useful account of its exegesis in the Temple Scroll. Succeeding sections on the versions and the Samaritan literature are followed by the major concern of the study: Deut. 12 in rabbinic exegesis. Here reference is made especially to Sifre and the Tannaitic Midrash on Deuteronomy, but also to Midrash Rabbah and all references to Deut. 12 in the Mishnah, Tosefta, the Talmuds, and midrashim. Introductory issues relating to the nature and interrelationship of the rabbinic materials are left aside in favour of an emphasis on collecting the relevant rabbinic references in a verse by verse treatment of Deut. 12. A distinction is made between exegesis of material which was historically relevant and that which was of theoretical interest. Although the sacrificial laws, which had no immediate practical reference for the rabbis, may have been studied for a possible restoration of the sanctuary, the theoretical study of this law was itself reckoned as fulfilment of the sacrificial cult. In that rabbinic exegesis was based upon and presupposed the unity of scripture and the significance of all its parts, it has more in common with modern literary study than with historical critical enquiry.

A. D. H. MAYES

MCCONNELL, F. (ed.): *The Bible and the Narrative Tradition*. 1986. Pp. 152. (Oxford University Press, New York and Oxford. Price: £15.00. ISBN 0 19 503698 0)

Increasingly, Biblical scholars are finding their own professional terrain invaded by interlopers from the field of general literature. The Bible is being rediscovered, not simply as a 'great' or profound or influential work of literature, but as the kind of tantalizing, ambiguous, elliptical, and self-referential text that appeals to the modern literary sensibility. Biblical scholars will do well to accommodate within their conception of the boundaries of their subject the work of such major literary critics as those represented in this volume, Harold Bloom, Hans Frei, Frank Kermode, Herbert Schneidau, and others. It is, at the least, stimulating to read Bloom's evaluation of the Yahwist as 'a writer more inescapable than Shakespeare, and more pervasive in our consciousness than Freud' (p. 20), but even more valuable perhaps to encounter perceptions of our texts such as those of Schneidau, when he argues that it is quintessential to the Old Testament history that it 'has no *logos* to manifest' and that its narratives 'transcend, even evade, theology' (pp. 147, 133). I was grateful for this book which developed my understanding of why (for what purpose) I was an Old Testament scholar.

D. J. A. CLINES

VAN DER MEER, W.: *Oude Woorden worden Nieuw: De opbouw van het boek Joël*. 1989. Pp. x, 346. (Kok, Kampen. Price: fl 49.50. ISBN 90 242 4821 3)

This book, a Kampen dissertation (1989) supervised by E. Noort and J. C. de Moor, investigates the structure of the book of Joel. An introductory chapter considers the relevant questions and surveys scholarly discussion of them, and also sets out the methods to be used in this study. Chapter 2 analyses the book from the point of view of form into the following cantos: 1:2–12; 1:13–20; 2:1–14; 2:15–27; 3:1–4:8; 4:9–17, and a sub-canto: 4:18–21; and the relation of the cantos to one another is discussed. Chapter 3 analyses the cantos from the point of view of subject matter. Chapter 4 draws together the conclusions. The kernel of the book of Joel (perhaps from the 8th–7th century B.C.) is found in 1:5–12, 13–20; 2:18–19c, 21–4; 3:1, 3–5b. This was expanded in the late 7th-early 6th century by the addition of 1:2–4; 2:1–14;, 15–17, 19d–20, 25–7; 3:2, 5c; 4:1–3 (minus 4:1aγ), 9–17. Finally, the following verses were added: 4:1aγ, 4–8, 18–21. The book ends with a concordance of the Hebrew words in Joel, a list of abbreviations, and indexes of authors, biblical references, and Hebrew words (including the words used in parallel with them).

J. A. EMERTON

VAN DER MEER, W. and DE MOOR, J. C. (eds): *The Structural Analysis of Biblical and Canaanite Poetry* (JSOT Supplements 74). 1988. Pp. ix, 423. (Sheffield Academic Press. Price: £22.50 ($37.50). ISBN 1 85075 194 3)

Fifteen essays are gathered together in this volume, which seeks to promote a new method of structural analysis of West Semitic poetry according to principles developed over the last few years by P. van der Lugt and J. C. de Moor. Metre and syllable-count are rejected as sure guides to structure, which is isolated into sub-groups of diminishing size from Cantos, through Canticles (Watson's Stanzas), Strophes, Verses, Cola (predominantly Bicola), down to Feet. The Foot is a stressed sense-unit varying from one to eight syllables in length. In their introductory essay M. C. A. Korpel and J. C. de Moor explain these principles, not with entire clarity, and argue that the variability in extent of each prosodic unit is an important tool among West Semitic poets, who were thus enabled to explore a wide range of poetic experience through an infinitely adaptable traditional form. Chiasmus was also a fundamental element of structure (p. 61) though not so named, often determining the form of large-scale units. Psalm 78 is treated as a test-case.

K. Spronk applies these ideas to an analysis of the Keret story, a little optimistically, since so much of the text is missing, and argues that the structures he discerns in (imposes upon?) the text are clues to the overall interpretation. W. T. Koopmans makes a good case for Joshua 23 being a poetic narrative; M. C. A. Korpel convincingly argues that Isa. 5:1–7 is a clever allegorical interplay of love-song and lawsuit forms; while R. de Hoop shows that Jonah 1:1–16 is both poetic and chiastic in form. J. C. de Moor re-examines Micah 1, and H. W. M. van Grol Zephaniah 2–3, while W. van der Meer argues that Psalm 110 is pre-exilic, updated in the exile. P. van der Lugt surveys 150 years of Job scholarship, and in a further essay concentrates on ch. 28. J. Renkema then contributes four chapters on a thoroughgoing analysis of Lamentations, and the book concludes with a reconstruction of an Aramaic poetic original for the Lord's Prayer by de Moor. While individual points of discussion in these studies may fail to convince readers, it is encouraging to see a departure from the all too atomistic approach common in exegetical work, and a collection of essays with nine authors all testing the same theory is perhaps a first outside the physics laboratory!

N. WYATT

METTINGER, T. N. D.: *In Search of God: The Meaning and Message of the Everlasting Names*. Translated by F. H. Cryer. 1988. Pp. xiv, 251. (Fortress, Philadelphia. Price: $24.95. ISBN 0 8006 0892 5)

This engaging volume, rendered into lucid English by the experienced translator F. H. Cryer, is a translation from Swedish of *Namnet och*

Närvaron: Gudsmann och Godsbild i Böckernas Bok, 1987. A full review by B. Albrektson, both welcoming and with a sting in its tail, appeared in *B. L.* 1989, pp. 110–11.

A. G. AULD

MICHEL, D.: *Untersuchungen zur Eigenart des Buches Qohelet*, mit einem Anhang von R. G. Lehmann, 'Bibliographie zu Qohelet' (BZAW 183). 1989. Pp. vii, 329. (De Gruyter, Berlin. Price: DM 118.00. ISBN 3 11 012161 1)

This volume brings together a number of studies by Michel, two of which ('Vom Gott, der im Himmel ist' and 'Qoheletprobleme: Überlegungen zu Qoh 8:2–9 und 7:11–14') have appeared elsewhere. All are the fruit of many years research on the book of Qoheleth.

Qoheleth is often described as unique in the Old Testament, not only in regard to its philosophy, but also in its language. While the latter has been considered as approximating that of the Mishnah, detailed study has shown that the differences are considerable; and while there are obvious affinities with the older literature, Qoheleth is already at odds with it too.

Chapter 1 (pp. 1–83) is a careful study of Qoh 1:3–3:15 where Michel believes that the essence of Qoheleth's philosophy may be distilled. The second chapter, although already in print, is included because it is apropos of the subject matter, and is a study of Qoh 8:2–9 and 7:11–14. Chapters 3–6 are exegetical studies of Qoh 3:19–22; 7:1–10; 6:1–12; 9:1–10 respectively, and the *raison d'être* of the book, viz. passages in which Qoheleth is engaging in polemic with contemporary thinking. There follow three chapters which deal with Qoheleth's use of *yēš*, *kî*, and *'ašer*, while chapter 10 'Zur Eigenart des Buches Qohelet' is to some extent a drawing together of the factors involved in Qoheleth's individuality.

There are two appendixes: 'Vom Gott, der im Himmel ist' and 'Bibliographie zu Qohelet'. The latter, by Reinhard G. Lehmann, though not without its errors (e.g. Vox (twice) p. 319 should read Fox and appear on p. 299), is very comprehensive and will certainly serve Qoheleth studies for some time. Its usefulness is, however, diminished by the absence of an Abbreviations register; but there are good indexes (author, reference, Hebrew word, and subject).

R. B. SALTERS

NIELSEN, K.: *There is Hope for a Tree: The Tree as Metaphor in Isaiah*. Translated from Danish by C. and F. Crowley (JSOT Supplement Series 65). 1989. Pp. 301. (Sheffield Academic Press. Price: £25.00 ($42.50). ISBN 1 85075 182 X)

Translated from a Danish original this book is a perceptive and painstaking study of the central metaphor of the tree in Isa. 1–39. Part A contains a useful review of historical definitions of the metaphor and sets out the major topics dealt with in the study. These are: 1. The contents of the tree metaphors and their informative function in providing theological interpretations of the political situation; 2. The function of the tree metaphor which is to engage and affect the audience by means of its expressive power, and 3. The suitability or openness of figurative language in reinterpreting the original proclamation. The 'polyvalence' of imagery is thus identified as a vital feature in the origin and perpetuation of prophetic oracles. In Part B Nielsen applies her thesis in a close analysis of texts which she divides into three groups: vineyard metaphors (Isa. 5:1–7; 27:2–6), tree-felling metaphors (Isa. 10:33–11:9,10; 14:4b–20; 37:22b–32; 6:12–13; 2:12–17; 4:2–6; 32:15–20) and forest-fire metaphors (Isa. 9:7–20; 10:16–19; 1:29–31). On the basis of her analysis the author supports those scholars (von Rad, Wildberger) who find judgement statements and salvation statements in Isaiah's original message. She argues that the tension between judgement and salvation is maintained by means of the metaphor of the tree which is destroyed, yet puts out new shoots. A final section discusses the main themes of Isaiah's theology.

Apart from its own intrinsic value this volume draws attention to important discussions of figurative language in recent literary criticism which have appeared in German and Scandinavian books and articles not readily available to a wider English audience. The extensive footnotes are a mine of information in this respect.

P. W. Coxon

O'Brien, M. A.: *The Deuteronomistic History Hypothesis: A Reassessment* (OBO 92). 1989. Pp. xiii, 319. (Universitätsverlag, Freiburg (CH); Vandenhoeck & Ruprecht, Göttingen. Price: Sw.Fr. 86.00. ISBN 3 7278 0647 8; 3 525 53722 0)

This monograph, a revised version of a 1987 Melbourne thesis, represents an ambitious attempt to provide a comprehensive theory about the composition of Deuteronomy-Kings in the light of the enormous quantity of recent research on various parts of these books. O'Brien agrees with those who believe that the first edition of the Deuteronomistic History ended with Josiah, and was composed during his reign by an author who supported the Deuteronomic reform. This history was subsequently edited in three Deuteronomistic stages. It was first of all extended by the addition of most of the material in 2 Kings 23:28–25:21; then revised more substantially in order (*inter alia*) to make Manasseh a more central figure. A still later Deuteronomist extensively revised the history in a 'nomistic' manner; and this final Deuteronomistic edition was subsequently expanded by the addition of other material (e.g. Judges 1).

This is obviously a piece of work into which has gone an enormous amount of effort. It will be useful as a reference work for those working on Deuteronomy-Kings and interested in work on these books up to 1987 (no serious attempt is made to interact with work later than this, though some of it is cited in the footnotes). Whether the synthesis which is attempted in it is a convincing one, however, is another matter. Like all work on the composition of the Deuteronomistic History, it is in the end the plausibility of the treatment of the books of Kings which will determine the plausibility of the whole; and here, at least, O'Brien's theory has serious weaknesses. On the one hand, in joining Cross and Nelson with regard to the end-point of the history in 2 Kings 23, he has boarded what is fast becoming regarded by many scholars in the field as a sinking ship; and he does not have sufficient new material to effect the necessary repairs. He does not, for example, take note of criticisms which have been voiced with regard to Cross's view of the structure of Kings. Nor does he demonstrate anew why it is that we must believe in a pre-exilic Deuteronomistic version of 2 Kings 21–23. The distinction between his original author of Kings and his first two redactors must therefore be regarded as questionable. On the other hand, he is heavily dependent in his treatment of the remainder of Kings upon the work on the judgment formulae carried out by his supervisor, A. F. Campbell (in *Of Prophets and Kings*, reviewed in *B. L.* 1987, p. 60). Campbell's explanation of these formulae as deriving from two pre-Deuteronomistic sources, as well as from both pre-exilic and exilic Deuteronomists, is, however, unconvincing. There are insufficient grounds for denying that the majority of these formulae between 1 Kings 3 and 2 Kings 18 derive from one author. If they *are* from one author, however, then they point, not just to a 'Southern Document' ending with Hezekiah, as Campbell and O'Brien would have it, but to an original version of the whole of Kings which ended there. In short, O'Brien is attempting belatedly to occupy ground which has long since been abandoned by those who believe in an exilic Deuteronomistic History, and which is slowly being vacated by those who believe in a pre-exilic one. It will require further work on his part if scholars from either group are to be persuaded to repossess it.

I. W. PROVAN

ODASHIMA, T.: *Heilsworte im Jeremiabuch: Untersuchungen zu ihrer vordeuteronomistischen Bearbeitung* (BWANT 125). 1989. Pp. xiii, 353. (Kohlhammer, Stuttgart. Price: DM 79.00. ISBN 3 17 009842 X)

Taro Odashima's book is based on his 1984 dissertation at Bochum under the supervision of Siegfried Herrmann, the doyen of German Jeremiah scholarship. It also owes something to the influence of Henning Graf Reventlow, another distinguished Jeremiah scholar at Bochum. Apart from the obvious examination of Jer. 30–31, it analyzes the *Heilsworte* to be found in 2:2–4; 3:12–13, 21–25; 6:16–17, 22–26; 10:17–25. This is essentially a study of the pre-deuteronomistic elements in the book of Jeremiah which concentrates on developing the analysis already undertaken by Thiel on the deuteronomistic redaction of Jeremiah and by Böhmer's treatment of 30–31 in *Heimkehr und neuer Bund* (1976). Odashima argues for the land of Judah as the place where this pre-deuteronomistic edition (*Bearbeitung*) of salvation elements was produced and dates its production to the period between 587 and 550 (the fall of Jerusalem and Thiel's date for the deuteronomistic edition of Jeremiah), favouring the first third of the sixth century as the most probable time (cf. pp. 295–97).

This is an honest and workmanlike piece of work, with some very useful excursuses on a number of topics. His treatment of Giesebrecht's 1894 commentary on Jeremiah as the forerunner of Duhm's more famous methodological approach chimes in with what a number of Jeremiah scholars feel to be the case. His excursus on McKane's commentary (pp. 72–80) is an interesting early response to that major 1986 work and his excursus on 31:22b (pp. 129–38) gathers together a useful collection of insights. The absence of any consideration of Christoph Levin's *Der Verheissung des neuen Bundes* (1985) weakens Odashima's claims for an early dating of the *Heilsworte* factor (Levin's sophisticated arguments for the long, slow development of the Jeremiah tradition make his work very promising for current Jeremiah studies). I just notice the equal absence of any knowledge of Carroll's work on Jeremiah, but hope that is a corrigible omission in Odashima's thinking.

R. P. CARROLL

OHLER, A.: *Studying the Old Testament: From Tradition to Canon*. Translated by D. Cairns. Paperback edition. 1985. Pp. 388. (T. & T. Clark, Edinburgh. Price: £12.50. ISBN 0 567 29166 9)

This unaltered paperback edition, but for price and ISBN, appeared in 1989. R. P. Carroll's commendation in *B. L.* 1986, p. 78, has been corrupted on its back cover.

A. G. AULD

PARAN, M.: *Forms of the Priestly Style in the Pentateuch: Patterns, Linguistic Usages, Syntactic Structures*, with an Introduction by M. Haran. 1989. Pp. 400 and pp. xvi of English summary. (Magnes, Jerusalem. Price: $23.50. ISBN 965 223 692 6)

Meir Paran died in 1985 at the age of 41, and his 1984 PhD dissertation was prepared for publication by Menahem Haran. The work begins with a comparison of the styles of the Holiness Code and Deuteronomy (there are no suitable parallels between P and D) using the results to concentrate upon P.

Literary features identified include the 'circular inclusio' (repetition of the predicate of the sentence, a feature also found fairly frequently in Ezekiel), the use of poetry-like parallelism, including the expansion of one-clause prohibitions into double clauses with parallelism, and the use in pericopes of inclusio, chiasm, and digression. The author accepts the view of Haran that P was kept in priestly circles and disclosed only after the return from exile. This explains why, in the author's view, Deutero-Isaiah uses language peculiar to P, and D was dependent upon H. The volume is an important contribution to scholarship and a fitting memorial to its author.

J. W. ROGERSON

PARDEE, D.: *Ugaritic and Hebrew Poetic Parallelism. A Trial Cut (*ʿnt *I and Proverbs 2)* (VTS, 39). 1988. Pp. xvi, 202. 3 fold-out charts. (Brill, Leiden. Price: fl. 120.00 (ca. $60.00). ISBN 90 04 08368 5)

In an attempt to supply empirical data for determining the character of Ugaritic and Hebrew poetry, Pardee has provided an extremely detailed analysis of two passages: the first twenty-five lines of KTU 1.3 (the first tablet in the Baal Cycle) and chapter 2 of Proverbs. Both texts are described in terms of their 'parallelistic structure', which involves various types of parallelism (repetitive, semantic, positional, phonetic).

Before presenting his own findings he modestly applies the analytical methods of four scholars (T. Collins, M. O'Connor, S. Geller, and B. Kaiser) to these two passages and evaluates the results. There are two appendices, both previously unpublished lectures by the author on Ugaritic and Hebrew poetry, which are convenient summaries of his approach. Indices are provided.

The analytical model described by P. and so rigorously applied to the chosen texts reveals a wealth of previously unnoticed features and replaces impressionistic descriptions with concrete data, especially on alliteration in its widest sense. The differences and similarities between Ugaritic and Hebrew poetry are also highlighted. His method now needs to be tested on other poetic texts from both traditions.

W. G. E. WATSON

POHLMANN, K.-F.: *Die Ferne Gottes — Studien zum Jeremiabuch* (BZAW 179). 1989. Pp. x, 232. (De Gruyter, Berlin. Price: DM 88.00. ISBN 3 11 011828 9)

Karl-Friedrich Pohlmann's *Studien zum Jeremiabuch*: *Ein Beitrag zur Frage nach der Entstehung des Jeremiabuches* (FRLANT 118, 1978: reviewed in *B. L.* 1979, p. 88) was one of the better German monographs published on Jeremiah in the 1970s. In this more recent book, which has the lengthy subtitle *Beiträge zu den "Konfessionen" im Jeremiabuch und ein Versuch zur Frage nach den Anfängen der Jeremiatradition*, he returns to some of the same issues but with a different focus from that of the earlier book. The book includes some material from his 1985–87 seminars on the book of Jeremiah. Pohlmann is a careful exegete of the text and is sensitive to the nuances of disputed and difficult interpretive moves in the handling of the vexed question of the laments. His placement of the word '*Konfessionen*' in inverted commas is testimony to his awareness of the complexities of the issue and he considers a wide range of texts in Jeremiah in his discussion of the origins, future expectations, and the role of the opponents in the laments. He is also wise enough to place the word '*Jeremia*' in inverted commas at times in order to indicate his view that the Jeremiah of much of the laments is a contribution of the writer of the poems. Rightly, in my opinion, he sees parallels between the ascription of the laments to Jeremiah and the *lᵉdāwid* titles of some of the Psalms. In the shorter second part of the book Pohlmann analyzes the premonition of doom and laments of doom in Jer:2–9 in relation to the origins of the Jeremiah tradition. The book concludes with some considerations of and questions about the problematics of current research into biblical prophecy. Another very useful book on Jeremiah from a very fine Jeremiah scholar.

R. P. CARROLL

POLLEY, M. E.: *Amos and the Davidic Empire: A Socio-Historical Approach*. 1989. Pp. xii, 243. (Oxford University Press, New York and Oxford. Price: £24.00. ISBN 0 19 505478 4)

The author, who teaches Religion at Davidson College, North Carolina, disclaims novelty in his treatment of Amos, and credits G. Henton Davies (who happily is not as 'late' as Polley describes him) and J. Mauchline with the essentials of the views he presents, that the Judean prophet 'went north to condemn Israel's division of the Davidic kingdom'. After an Introduction, two main chapters review Kingship and state religion, first in Egypt, Mesopotamia, and Canaan, and then in Judah and Israel. Chapter four restates the argument that the peoples rebuked in Amos 1:3–2:3 are linked by former ties with David. Polley next assembles the arguments that Amos's cultic rebukes were directed against syncretistic forms of Yahwism practised at shrines other than Jerusalem. The sixth chapter suggests that the school where issues of social justice were sharpened for him was the royal 'court' in Tekoa recently established by Jehoshaphat — Israel's illegitimate monarchy could offer no guarantee of justice. And the final two chapters argue that only when it was clear to Amos that the north had spurned his call for a repentance that involved return to Judah did he proclaim destruction of guilty and innocent alike. The author has paid thorough attention to a wide-ranging bibliography. It may be that when so many studies of Amos are available, his own case may suffer from the cost of purchasing it.

A. G. AULD

DE PURY, A.: *Le Pentateuque en Question: Les origines et la composition des cinq premiers livres de la Bible à la lumière des recherches récentes* (Le Monde de la Bible). 1989. Pp. 421. (Labor et Fides, Genève. ISBN 2 8309 0148 7)

This volume comprises the texts of the papers read at a research seminar organized in 1987 by the French-speaking universities of Switzerland, together with brief accounts of the discussions which followed. Papers originally delivered in other languages have been translated into French. The list of contributors, all of whom have published notable studies elsewhere on Pentateuchal questions, is alone sufficient to indicate the importance of the work: S. Amsler, E. Blum, F. Crüsemann, A. de Pury, R. Rendtorff, T. Römer, M. Rose, H. H. Schmid, H. Seebass, J.-L. Ska, J. Vermeylen, and E. Zenger. The first part, a seventy-page 'introduction' by de Pury and Römer, brilliantly describes the course of Pentateuchal criticism from its beginnings, concluding with a presentation of the main problems at present under discussion. Parts 2 and 3, respectively entitled 'Les couches littéraires' and 'Thèmes et traditions', form a kaleidoscope of differing views on all these questions. The final papers, by Crüsemann and Schmid, hardly succeed as 'essais de synthèse', but this is not surprising: such a task would be as impossible now as it was three years ago. Almost all of the contributions are of a very high quality. Those who wish to follow the current debate on the Pentateuch in all its richness and diversity will find here the best account of it so far available. The lack of either an index of authors or a bibliography is, however, particularly unfortunate in a volume of this kind.

R. N. WHYBRAY

REID, S. B.: *Enoch and Daniel: A Form Critical and Sociological Study of Historical Apocalypses* (Bibal Monograph Series 2, Berkeley 1989. Pp. xiii, 147, (BIBAL, Berkeley, CA. Price: $12.95 plus $1.00 postage and handling. ISBN 0 941037 07 X)

This book claims that form criticism, anthropology, sociological models, and the study of mantic activity have been under utilized in the study of Apocalyptic. It comprises a good introductory piece 'History of Research and its Proper Utilisation' and then detailed studies of the historical Apocalypses of 1 Enoch and Daniel. The emphases are on apocalypticism as a mantic activity and on the fine use of sociological analysis; not all apocalypses had the same point of view or came from the same sector of society. It is good to see these elements being given serious consideration, especially as they will help to bring the apocalypses back to the centre of our picture of inter-testamental Judaism and thus correct a serious distortion. The book is very tightly written and there are good bibliographies.

M. BARKER

SCHREINER, J. (ed.): *Beiträge zur Psalmenforschung: Psalm 2 und 22* (Forschung zur Bibel 60). 1988. Pp. 384. (Echter, Würzburg. Price: DM 48.00. ISBN 3 429 01174 4)

This volume consists of papers read at a conference of Catholic Old Testament scholars in Salzburg, 1987. O. Loretz uses colometric analysis to argue that Ps. 2 is a post-exilic composition which also contains some pre-exilic material. F. Diedrich systematically discusses the main aspects of the final form of Ps. 2 to achieve a comprehensive view, also a post-exilic setting. A. Deissler considers the position of Ps. 2 in the Psalter; it is seen as composed by a scribe learned in scripture and wisdom, with Ps. 1 already before him as prelude to the Psalter. It expounds God's law for the nations, who are to submit to his Messiah, and all the following Davidic psalms are to be read in this messianic light. P. Maiberger treats the understanding of Ps. 2 in LXX, Targum, Qumran, early Judaism, and New Testament.

G. Vanoni analyses the great variety of literary-critical treatments of Ps. 22 in terms of 'models' and with much tabulation. It is difficult to say what he achieves. H. Irsigler seeks to uncover an exegetical process in the actual text of Ps. 22. He finds the primary text in vv. 2–27, which arose as a whole in post-exilic times as a prayer-formula kept at the temple for individuals in need. The expanded text reflects the eschatological outlook around 300 B.C. Structural observations are ingeniously presented in tables and charts. J. Schreiner writes on the implications of Ps. 22's position in the Psalter; consideration of the series constituted by Pss. 3–41 leads to recognition of the mid-way position of Ps. 22 as emphasizing the journey from the depths to the heights. H.-J. Fabry traces Ps. 22's way through the Versions, Qumran, rabbis, New Testament, and (in summary) the Fathers; it is a way which relativizes the question of the 'final text'.

Finally, N. Füglister gives a noteworthy treatment of the use of the Psalms at the turn of the era. It is a factual, well annotated study. It refutes the hallowed notion that the Psalter was the hymnbook of the Second Temple and the synagogue and disposes the lectionary cycles for this period. The purpose of the collection is set instead in the realm of private piety. These are all solid contributions and form a valuable collection.

J. H. EATON

SEITZ, C. R.: *Theology in Conflict: Reactions to the Exile in the Book of Jeremiah* (BZAW 176). 1989. Pp. 329. (De Gruyter, Berlin. Price: DM 138.00. ISBN 3 11 011223 X)

This study seeks to break through the literary impasse in the study of the book of Jeremiah by a detailed socio-historical investigation of events in

Judah, notably after the death of Josiah. It reveals increasing internal instability and conflicting views within the community on the significance of 597 and 587 B.C.E. and the relationship between them. 2 Kings 24, the work of one deported in 597, regards the events of 597 as the end of Judah, an attitude drawing on the harsher elements of judgement in earlier Jeremiah oracles. An exilic redaction, with close points of contact with Ezekiel tradition and the Dtr history climaxing in 2 Kings 25, questions the validity of continuing life in the land or kingship post 597 and places all hope for the future on the restoration of the deportees. A scribal chronicle, however, mainly in chs. 37–47, with introductory material in 27–29, and the continuing activity of the prophet post 597, views the possibility of legitimate existence for a remnant community, and kingship, in the land post 597 and post 587. The thesis of such divergent theological traditions is grounded in detailed textual analysis. An interesting excursus examines the role of the 'people of the land' in the period under review. Based on a Yale dissertation presented in 1986, this book is essential reading for anyone trying to crack the Jeremiah tradition code. It was completed too early to take account of more recent studies by Carroll, Holladay, and McKane.

R. DAVIDSON

SEKINE, S.: *Die Tritojesajanische Sammlung (Jes 56–66) Redaktionsgeschichtlich Untersucht* (BZAW 175). 1989. Pp. xi, 303. (De Gruyter, Berlin. Price: DM 138.00. ISBN 3 11 011633 2)

This revised dissertation continues the discussion of the perennial questions of the authorship and redactional history of Isaiah 56–66. The author starts from the supposition of a general agreement that 56:1–8 and 66:18–24 form a redactional framework to the whole, and that chapters 60–62 are central to the teaching of the 'Einzelperson' known as Trito-Isaiah. From these passages he reaches certain conclusions about the styles and theological viewpoints of both redactor and prophet, and then compares these with the rest of the work. He thus divides these chapters into their component 'strata'. Next he checks his results on the basis of the presence in or absence from each designated passage of a set of fundamental theological concepts. He concludes that these chapters consist of 1. the words of a 'liberal' prophet, floruit ca. 519–15 B.C.; 2. seven other strata expressing different points of view and dating from before 537 to the late post-exilic period; 3. additions made by the final redactor. A critique of Elliger's arguments in favour of unity of authorship forms a concluding excursus. This is a careful piece of work; the author is, however, perhaps more successful in demonstrating multiplicity of authorship than in explaining how and why this disparate material has been brought together and in this particular order.

R. N. WHYBRAY

SOGGIN, J. A.: *Introduction to the Old Testament. From its origins till the closing of the Alexandrian Canon*. 3rd edition. Translated by John Bowden. 1989. Pp. xxxii, 608. (SCM, London. Price: £17.50. ISBN 0 334 00702 X)

This third edition of Soggin's *Introduction*, a translation of the fourth Italian edition (see *B. L.* 1988, p. 91), has been thoroughly updated and recast from the editions noted in *B. L.* 1977, pp. 74–75; and 1981, pp. 78–79. As always with his work, a feature of this edition is the range of its annotated and up-to-date bibliographies, for which the author had the assistance of R. J. Coggins. Typically the Preface shows Soggin already foreshadowing the next edition with an apology that he has not begun this present one with Deuteronomy and the so-called 'Deuteronomistic' history, and has not treated the Book of Isaiah as a single redactional complex. Modestly, he notes the importance of 'exegesis more as literary criticism', but leaves that task to others who have the capacity for aesthetic criticism.

A. G. AULD

SPIECKERMANN, H.: *Heilsgegenwart: Eine Theologie der Psalmen* (FRLANT 148). 1989. Pp. 342. (Vandenhoeck & Ruprecht, Göttingen. Price: DM 118.00; paperback price: DM 80.00. ISBN 3 525 53829 4; 3 525 53830 8 (pbk))

This is not a comprehensive theology of the Psalms, but a tracing of their theological core. The focus is on the ideas of Yahweh present in his temple: sustainer and replenisher of the world, lord of all creatures. Exodus tradition is integrated into the temple themes descended from canaanite sources, but it is a temple theology, not salvation-history, which characterizes the Psalms and should not be undervalued. The greater part of the argument arises from the exposition of selected psalms, which are printed in Hebrew and in translation in a way that shows structure and supposed layers of additions. From these texts the themes unfold: God creator and sustainer (Pss. 104, 148, 19), God of his people (Ex. 15; Pss. 137, 74, 78, 114), Lord of his sanctuary (29, 93, 48, 24, 21), God of the human being (8, 22, 30, 23). The author has skilfully charted his course through the wealth of material and his sober expositions of the texts will be especially valued.

J. H. EATON

STANSELL, G.: *Micah and Isaiah: A Form and Tradition Historical Comparison* (SBL Dissertation Series 85). 1988. Pp. vii, 165. (Scholars Press, Atlanta GA. Price: $16.95 (member price: $10.95); paperback price: $10.95 (member price: $7.95). ISBN 0 891310 962 4; 0 89130 963 2 (pbk))

In this 1981 Heidelberg dissertation done under H. W. Wolff, Stansell investigates the similarities which have been noted for a century and more between the oracles of Isaiah of Jerusalem and those of Micah of Moresheth, seeking by a close analysis of the prophetic forms used and the ways in which the prophets had adapted traditional themes and motifs to discover whether Micah was directly influenced by Isaiah. (Because of problems of authenticity, only chapters 1–3 of Micah are considered.) An examination of the use made of the theophany tradition by the two prophets suggests that 'these two eighth-century prophets can reach back to the same ancient traditional material and yet adapt it in importantly contrasting ways' (p. 34) — in terms both of form and content: a judgement subsequently confirmed by an examination of the Jerusalem/Zion tradition (Micah 'is engaged in a sharp polemic against the Zion tradition'; Isaiah's attitude is 'more complex': 'Zion may be punished but she will not be destroyed'). Again both men clashed with groups of rival prophets, but the backgrounds of the opponents differed and the contentious issues were not identical. Both prophets denounced social oppression, but again differences of both form and content are evident. It is concluded that direct influence of Isaiah on Micah is unproved; close verbal similarities are to be put down to a common redaction, a topic which is adjudged to call for further research, as is the measure of kinship between the books of Micah and Jeremiah. A lucid monograph, despite the wealth of technical discussion of the relevant texts.

B. P. ROBINSON

STUART, D.: *Hosea–Jonah* (Word Biblical Themes). 1989. Pp. x, 121. (Word Books, Dallas TX. Price: $9.99. ISBN 0 8499 0789 6)

This is a companion volume to the author's Word Biblical Commentary published in 1987. It seeks to elucidate the main themes of these prophetic books and to draw out their theological implications, relating them also to the New Testament. As an introductory book, less technical than the commentary, it will be of some use to the general reader who shares its fundamentalist outlook, but the limitations of its size do not permit treatment in sufficient depth to serve adequately its professed purpose of assisting preaching and teaching. Occasionally, most obviously in the comment on forgiveness in Jonah, it becomes more of a general homily than elucidation of a particular text. It is a little surprising to read of Amos' intercession in 7:1–3 that 'God graciously accepted his prophet's plea, knowing full well, of course, that he had yet other options for punishing his people in mind', namely 9:1–4 which is regarded as a disaster of rather less significance. And can Hosea 14:8 be regarded as 'the very last verse of the book' (p. 19)?

G. I. EMMERSON

TSUMURA, D. T.: *The Earth and the Waters in Genesis 1 and 2: A Linguistic Investigation* (JSOT Supplement Series 83). 1989. Pp. 201. (Sheffield Academic Press. Price: £22.50 ($33.50). ISBN 1 85075 208 7; ISSN 0309 0787)

In this important monograph Dr Tsumura scrutinises the vocabulary of earth and waters in Gen. 1 and 2 and concludes that both chapters reflect essentially the same cosmology. There is no need to posit for the picture in ch. 1 a Babylonian origin linked with the battle between Tiamat and Marduk and for that in ch. 2 a local Palestinian origin in which the contrast is not between chaos and cosmos but between wilderness and oasis. Rather ch. 1 describes an earlier stage in the one creation process when the waters cover the earth, ch. 2 a later stage (as in 1:9–10) when the waters have separated and the dry land has appeared. Dr Tsumura's argument is thus far clear and convincing and ought in my view to be accepted by future commentators on Genesis. But do his findings, as he thinks they do, necessitate writing out all trace of menace in the early verses of Gen. 1? And if they do, where does that leave the *Chaoskampf* motif in the Psalms, Job, and other poetic books, a motif which is closely connected with the themes of creation and providence? Are there two creation theologies in the Old Testament, one in which there is no lurking Leviathan in his created world with which God has to deal, and one in which there is? And if there are, which of the two is more relevant for today's thinking on creation? Having whetted our appetites with this stimulating study, Dr Tsumura owes us another book.

J. C. L. GIBSON

VERMEYLEN, J. (ed.): *Le Livre d'Isaïe: Les oracles et leurs relectures. Unité et complexité de l'ouvrage* (Bibliotheca Ephemeridum Theologicarum Lovaniensium LXXXI). 1989. Pp. X, 475. (University Press, Leuven; distributed by Peeters, Leuven. Price: B.Fr. 2,700. ISBN 90 6186 304 X; 90 6831 164 6)

The 30 articles assembled in this year's *Journées Bibliques* (ed. J. Vermeylen) represent papers read at the 37th 'Colloquium Biblicum Lovaniense' held at Louvain in August 1987. Dedicated to Christiaan H. W. Brekelmans on the occasion of his 65th birthday they concentrate on the book of Isaiah 'in all its literary complexity and theological richness'. Special attention is focused on the problems of unity and inner diversity of the work, its literary and theological history, its use of older material, and its influence on post-biblical literature. The articles are concentrated in 3 major sections. 1. Isaiah as a whole: J. Vermeylen (Bruxelles), 'L'unité du livre d'Isaïe (11–53); O. Kaiser (Marburg), 'Literarkritik und Tendenzkritik. Überlegungen zur Methode des Jesajaexegese' (55–71); R. Rendtorff (Heidelberg), 'Jesaja 6 im Rahmen der Komposition des Jesajabuches' (73–82); E. Talstra (Amsterdam), 'Grammar and Prophetic Texts. Computer-Assisted Syntactical Research in Isaiah' (83–91); G. I. Davies (Cambridge), 'The Destiny of the Nations in the Book of Isaiah' (94–120); C. T. Begg (Washington), 'Babylon in the Book of Isaiah' (121–25); A. van der Kooij (Utrecht), 'The Septuagint of Isaiah: Translation and Interpretation' (127–33); J.-C.

Haelewyck (Louvain-la-Neuve), 'L'édition de la Vetus Latina d'Isaïe' (135–45); P.-M. Bogaert (Louvain-la-Neuve), 'L'organization des grands recueils prophétiques' (147–53); P. C. Beentjes (Utrecht), 'Relations between Ben Sira and the Book of Isaiah. Some Methodical Observations' (155–59); J. van Ruiten (Amsterdam), 'The Influence and Development of Is. 65,17 in 1 En. 91,16 (161–66). II. First Isaiah (Isa. 1–39): C. Brekelmans (Leuven), 'Deuteronomistic Influence in Isaiah 1–12' (167–76); P. Bovati (Rome), 'Le language juridique du prophète Isaïe' (177–96); N. J. Tromp (Utrecht), 'Un démasquage graduel. Lecture immanente d'Is 5,1–7' (197–202); A. L. H. M. van Wieringen (Eindhoven), 'Jesaja 6–12: Die Vegetationsbildsprache und die prophetische Struktur' (203–07); M. Nobile (Roma), 'Jes 6 und Ez 1,1 — 3,15: Vergleich und Funktion im jeweiligen redaktionellen Kontext' (209–16); Y. Gitay (Beer Sheva), 'Isaiah and the Syro-Ephraimite War' (217–30); J. Høgenhaven (Kopenhagen), 'Die symbolischen Namen in Jesaja 7 und 8 im Rahmen der sogenannten «Denkschrift» des Propheten' (231–35); A. K. Jenkins (Cardiff), 'The Development of the Isaiah Tradition in Is 13–23' (237–51); R. E. Clements (Cambridge), 'Isaiah 14,22–27: A Central Passage Reconsidered' (253–62); S. Amsler (Lausanne), 'Des visions de Zacharie à l'apocalypse d'Esaïe 24–27' (263–73); J. Lust (Leuven), 'Isaiah 34 and the *ḥerem*' (275–86). III. Second and Third Isaiah (Isa. 40–46): H.-J. Hermisson (Tübingen), 'Einheit und Komplexität Deuterojesajas. Probleme der Redaktionsgeschichte von Jes 40–45' (287–312); J. van Goudoever (Amstelveen), 'The Celebration of the Torah in the Second Isaiah' (313–17); J. F. A. Sawyer (Newcastle), 'Christian Interpretations of Isaiah 45:8' (319–23); P. Beauchamp (Paris), 'Lecture et relectures du quatrième chant du Serviteur. D'Isaïe à Jean' (325–55); H. C. Spykerboer (Brisbane), 'Isaiah 55:1–5: The Climax of Deutero-Isaiah. An invitation to Come to the New Jerusalem' (357–59); O. H. Steck (Zürich), 'Tritojesaja im Jesajabuch' (361–406); A. Rofé (Jerusalem), 'Isaiah 59:19 and Trito-Isaiah's Vision of Redemption' (407–10); W. A. M. Beuken (Nijmegen), 'Servant and Herald of Good Tidings. Isaiah 61 as an Interpretation of Isaiah 40–55' (411–42).

J. Lust pays a 4 page tribute to Brekelmans and this is followed by a bibliography of Brekelmans' publications.

P. W. COXON

WATTS, J. D. W.: *Isaiah* (Word Biblical Themes). 1989. Pp. xi, 120. (Word Books, Dallas TX. Price: $9.99. ISBN 0 8499 0669 5)

Word Biblical Themes is a companion series to the Word Biblical Commentary. According to the General Editor, David A. Hubbard, in his foreword, it 'seeks to distill the theological essence of the biblical books as interpreted in the more technical series and serve it up in ways that will enrich the preaching, teaching, worship, and discipleship of God's people.' In this volume the 'themes' of Isaiah are arranged under the two broad headings of 'Knowing God and His ways' and 'Serving God and His plan'; there are appendices on the New Testament's use of Isaiah and on Isaiah in Handel's Messiah, and a scriptural index. This treatment hardly does justice to the complexity of the book of Isaiah. Nor is it easy to see how this volume will enrich God's people in the ways suggested better than a commentary of similar size. At all events it would be hard to understand it without referring to Watt's commentary in the companion series (*B. L.* 1988, p. 67). It depends upon the highly individual view of the book presented there, and expounds the theological aspect of that view without explaining its literary foundation. Many of the commentary's exegetical perversities are repeated here. Watts urges that the book is Yahweh's call to Israel to take a new and humbler place in his purposes, abandoning the task of government to the great empires, Assyrian or Persian, and accepting the role of a non-political religious community with a witnessing and worshipping vocation. Watts correctly perceives the dialectic in Isaiah between the power of God and the frequently lacking human response. But he quite fails to perceive the ambivalent attitude of the book to imperial power: even its hostile attitude to Babylon he traces to Merodach-Baladan's revolt against Assyria rather than to its later oppression of the Jews. In his hands Isaiah becomes the prophet of the separation of church and state as in the U.S. Constitution, and the true complexity of the book's political thinking is unacceptably simplified. The uncompromisingly holistic approach also means that many great 'themes' of parts of the book are ignored. This book, like the commentary, is full of wrong references and careless mistakes (e.g. 'Camlyses' (thrice) for Cambyses).

W. J. Houston

Wénin, A.: *Samuel et l'instauration de la monarchie (1 S 1–12)* (Europäische Hochschulschriften, Reihe XXIII, Bd. 342). 1988. Pp. 490. (Lang, Frankfurt. Price: Sw.Fr. 76.00. ISBN 3 631 40384 4; ISSN 0721 3409)

This is one of the better examples of close-reading of a section of the Hebrew Bible. Wénin concentrates on the depiction of Samuel in 1 Samuel 1–12. The difference between his approach and the more traditional source-conscious brand is, predictably, most apparent in the discussion of the 'ark chapters' (chs. 4–6) in which Samuel is a non-participant. In Wénin's hands the issue between this section and what precedes is that of the mode by which Israel encounters, and responds to, the will of Yahweh. Imagination may exceed the bounds in such a situation, nevertheless Wénin shows the value, if not the necessity, of pressing beyond the (apparent) source divisions of the text. A great amount of attention is paid to structural (architectural) aspects of the text, partly in the hope that excessive subjectivity will be avoided in the process. There are very extensive end-notes (150 pp.) and an annotated translation of 1 Samuel 1–12.

R. P. Gordon

Westermann, C.: *The Living Psalms*, translated by J. R. Porter. 1988. Pp. 320. (T. & T. Clark, Edinburgh. Price: £9.95. ISBN 0 567 29156 1)

This translation of *Ausgewälte Psalmen. Übersetzt und erklärt* (Göttingen 1984: see *B. L.* 1985, p. 89) is the product of a lifetime of research into the history and meaning of the Psalms, begun, the author tells us, in a prison camp during the Second World War. After a brief discussion of the evolution, classification, and background of the Psalms, and other preliminaries, the Psalter is divided up into eleven chapters, according to *Gattung*. Each contains a few representative Psalms in a new translation with detailed commentary, and some general discussion of other Psalms of the same type. Most of the book is naturally taken up with Psalms of Lament, Psalms of Trust, and Psalms of Praise (Hymns), but a few pages are devoted to Royal Psalms, Liturgical Psalms, Songs of Zion, Psalms of Blessing, and 'Psalms and Wisdom'. A final chapter on 'The Psalms and Jesus Christ' explains the selection, partly by reference to the Magnificat (esp. Luke 1:46–55) and Mark 15:34, and partly by renouncing as un-Christian 'the petition against the enemies' (Pss. 82 and 137 are omitted altogether). At the end of the 1980s one might have expected some recognition of the fact that 'living Psalms' come close to the heart of Jews as well as Christians, and that for many people nowadays, Jews and Christians, the distinction between 'petitions against the enemies' and cries for justice and freedom is far from clear (cf. Luke 1:51f).

There is an index of biblical references to enable the reader to locate the psalms discussed, but no bibliography: the distinguished author's scholarship speaks for itself throughout.

J. F. A. Sawyer

WHYBRAY, R. N.: *Ecclesiastes* (Old Testament Guides). 1989. Pp. 88. (Sheffield Academic Press. Price: £4.95 ($7.95). ISBN 1 85075 211 7)

This series does not permit the authors to be expansive or to wax lyrical. Space restricts them in such a way that they often cannot do justice to the problems or topics which they may raise or discuss. Whybray is often conscious that he has more to say than he is able to say. Fortunately, for him, he has published — almost simultaneously — a commentary on Ecclesiastes where he has been able to expand somewhat, so that the present work serves not only to whet the appetite of the student but as an introduction to the fuller work.

After a short introduction, Whybray treats his subject under the following heads: 'The Author and his Times'; 'Language, Style and Structure'; 'Place in the History of Thought'; and 'Qoheleth's Characteristic Ideas'. Old Testament scholars will wrestle with the commentary, but this is a compact and very useful addition to the series.

R. B. SALTERS

7. LAW, RELIGION, AND THEOLOGY

BALDERMANN, I. and LOHFINK, N. (eds): *Der eine Gott der beiden Testamente* (*Jahrbuch fur Biblische Theologie*, Bd 2). 1987. Pp. 267. (Neukirchener, Neukirchen-Vluyn. Price: DM 48.00. ISBN 3 7887 1266 X)

The first volume of this *Jahbruch* was noted in *B. L.* 1988, pp. 107f (and for the third see p. 115 below). The second also concentrates on a single topic, this time 'The One God of Both Testaments' which is handled in three sections of very different length. 'The One God' is treated in three articles: by H. Merklein, on the uniqueness of God as the material basis of Jesus' proclamation; by W. H. Schmidt, on theological and religio-historical aspects of the question about the unity of the Old Testament; and Y. Amir, on the Jewish belief in one God as stumbling-block in the Hellenistic-Roman world. Seven articles follow under the heading 'The God of both Testaments'. O. Hofius writes on 'Justification of the Godless' as theme of biblical theology; Lohfink, on the violent God of the Old Testament and the search for a society free of violence; Baldermann, on the passionate God and dispassionate exegesis; R. Weth, on the one God of *diakonia* — practical theology as problem and task of biblical theology; B. Janowski, on the structure and genesis of the exilic *shekina*-theology, 'I will dwell in your midst'; M. Welker, on the angel of God — systematic-theological relections arising from Westermann and Gese; and finally K.-H. zur Mühlen, on doctrine and exegesis in Luther's *De servo arbitrio*. The third section offers a report by K. H. Neufeld on scripture in Karl Rahner's theology; and a review by U. Rüterswörden of René Girard's book on the end of violence.

A. G. AULD

BAUCKHAM, R.: *The Bible in Politics: How to read the Bible politically* (A Third Way Book). 1989, Pp. x, 166. (SPCK, London. Price: £6.95. ISBN 0 281 04402 3)

Dr Bauckham's aim is to help readers of the Bible to understand its relevance for modern politics by a more imaginative and disciplined approach than is common. His first chapter deals with general principles and methods, and the remaining nine chapters contain expositions of selected passages and themes, six from the Old Testament: Lev. 19, Prov. 31:1–9, Pss. 10 and 126, the Exodus, the Book of Esther (linked with the Jewish holocaust), and the Flood (related to a nuclear holocaust). The book ends with a reflection on 'The Political Christ'. Bauckham describes the idea that the Bible has nothing to do with politics as a 'modern Western Christian aberration', answers objections to applying the Bible to politics, and replies to those who stress the difference between the biblical world and modern industrial society and imply that it can have little of modern relevance. While acknowledging that the Christian's ethics will be grounded in Jesus so that the whole Bible needs to be read in the light of Christ, he denies that the Old Testament can be put aside as being pre-Christian. What is required in applying the Bible to current political issues is an awareness of its historical and canonical settings, linked with careful attention to the contemporary context. This will prevent the political use of the Bible being limited to texts that possess surface relevance, wrenched out of their contexts.

Dr Bauckham is Reader in the History of Christian Thought in the University of Manchester, an expert on Moltmann, and the author of a fine commentary on 2 Peter and Jude. His wide-ranging expertise makes this a book which Old Testament specialists will read with profit.

C. S. Rodd

Brettler, M. Z.: *God is King: Understanding an Israelite Metaphor* (JSOTS 76). 1989. Pp. 239. (Sheffield Academic Press. Price: £25.00 ($43.50). ISBN 1 85075 224 9; ISSN 0309 0787)

There have been many studies dealing with the kingship of God, but these have been concerned most with the history of the concept in Israel, its relationship to the institution of monarchy in the ancient world, or its cultic actualization. Brettler's interest is in the functioning of the metaphor as such — what 'God is king' meant to the Israelite community. He begins with theoretical consideration of metaphor and insists that a contextual understanding of human kingship in ancient Israel (the vehicle of the metaphor) is essential to understanding its implications for their ideas of the kingship of God (the tenor of the metaphor). Admitting that the headings are to some extent arbitrary and incomplete he examines the human aspects of kingship as reflected in i) royal appellations; ii) royal qualities; iii) royal trappings; iv) the king and domestic affairs, and v) becoming king (the actual duties and responsibilities of the king being a surprising ommission). In the last chapter, 'Becoming King', he disagrees with Mowinckel's understanding of the 'Enthronement Psalms' as a cultic re-enactment of enthronement. Instead they refer to the recognition by the Gentile nations of a divine kingship which is eternally true.

There is much erudition here and much that is of interest. Occasionally it all produces rather unsurprising results (e.g. '. . . his [i.e. God's] throne is larger and more luxurious than the human throne . . . and is associated with absolute justice', p. 85). There is some poor printing, with the first line of n. 1 of the Introduction being repeated in n. 1 of chapter 1, while something has gone wrong with lines 4ff. on p. 15. Brettler riddles his readers with split infinitives like buckshot. While, however, one may emerge from reading this book with literary sensitivities seared, one also emerges the richer for the study. Surely it points to the need for a greater engagement with biblical metaphor as such in biblical scholarship.

R. A. Mason

Cassirer, H. W.: *Grace and Law: St Paul, Kant, and the Hebrew Prophets*. 1988. Pp. xvi, 176. (Eerdmans, Grand Rapids, Michigan; Handsel, Edinburgh. Price: £7.50 ($12.95). ISBN 0 8028 0317 2; 0 905312 78 3)

The author, a university lecturer in philosophy, was engaged on a commentary on Kant's *Critique of Pure Reason* when, at the age of fifty, he took up the Greek New Testament for the first time and experienced a Pauline conversion while reading Romans 7:7–13. Paul sent him back to his own ancestral heritage in the Hebrew prophets — hitherto unexplored territory for him (his father, Ernst Cassirer, a Jewish philosopher, had been described as a man who had read every book but the Bible and knew every language but Hebrew). The chapter in this book on 'The Teaching of the Old Testament Prophets on Sin and Release from Sin' is the section most relevant to SOTS interests. The contrast is emphasized between the Kantian doctrine of absolute moral freedom and the prophets' insistence that human beings, in order to lead the good life, can never rely wholly on their own resources but stand in constant need of divine assistance. The prophets, he finds (sampling their moral teaching widely and almost haphazardly), provide 'a most penetrating analysis of man's alienation from God which makes him give himself up to a life of depravity and wickedness', and at the same time a moving picture of the mercy with which God heals his people's faithlessness and loves them freely. But when they tell how God in the last days will intervene and cleanse the human heart of depravity and sin, he has difficulty in gathering any clear idea of the means by which this inward change is brought about. What he thinks is lacking in the prophets here, he finds in Paul.

F. F. Bruce

Coppens, J.: *Le Messianisme et sa Relève Prophétique*. Revised Edition (Bibliotheca Ephemeridum Theologicarum Lovaniensium XXXVIII). 1989. Pp. xiii, 265. (University Press, Leuven; distributed by Peeters, Leuven. Price: B.Fr. 1,000. ISBN 90 6186 312 0; 90 6831 163 8)

For a notice of the first edition of this book see *B. L.* 1976, p. 69. In this reissue a few supplementary details have been added to the list of abbreviations, but no changes or additions appear to have been made to the text, footnotes, or index. Nevertheless, the new edition may be welcomed as a model of balanced critical judgement and a mine of bibliographical information up to 1974.

G. W. Anderson

Cotterell, P. and Turner, M.: *Linguistics and Biblical Interpretation*. 1989. Pp. 348. (SPCK, London. Price: £9.95. ISBN 0281 04358 2)

The primary aim of this comprehensive and lucid introduction to modern linguistics is to define modern linguistic terms and concepts, in a style likely to win over a few doubters among students of the Bible and with examples and case-studies chosen mainly from the New Testament. After some very useful general introduction to 'the phenomenon of human language', 'pragmatics', 'universals', the synchronic/diachronic distinction, the nature of 'meaning' and the like, the chapters on 'The use and abuse of word-studies in theology', 'Lexical Semantics' and 'Non-literal Language' go over ground already fairly familiar to biblical scholars. But those on 'sentence and sentence clusters' and 'discourse analysis' (including 'the special case of conversation') introduce and illustrate some less familiar insights and should help to bridge the gap between the commentaries and the grammar books, as well as that between biblical studies in general and the rest of human experience.

J. F. A. Sawyer

Day, P. L.: *An Adversary in Heaven*: śāṭān *in the Hebrew Bible* (Harvard Semitic Monographs, 43). 1988. Pp. xi, 177. (Scholars Press, Atlanta GA. Price: $17.95 (member price: $11.95). ISBN 1 55540 248 8)

This is a valuable re-examination of the four well known Old Testament passages in which the noun 'satan' describes a divine being. It argues convincingly that in none of these passages is the noun yet (as it later becomes) a proper name nor, indeed, does it over the four of them denote a single celestial office. The exegesis is detailed, taking in not only the immediate but the wider context of the four references and exploiting new critical insights brought about, e.g., by comparisons between the Balaam pericope and the Deir Alla text. I was not convinced by Ms Day's attempt to link the umpire, witness and redeemer passages in Job 9, 16, and 19 ironically with the 'satan' figure in the Prologue; this smacked too much of 'deconstruction' for my liking. But that criticism apart, I warmly commend her monograph. It deals quite devastatingly with older theories of the emergence of Satan, and it is crisply and attractively written. A helpful appendix investigates the links that later arose between Satan and Beelzebul or Beelzebub. An index of biblical references ought to have been supplied.

J. C. L. GIBSON

DESHAYES, H.: *Chercher Dieu dans la Bible*. 1989. Pp. xii, 195. (Letouzey et Ané, Paris. Price: Fr 120.00. ISBN 2 7063 0174 0)

This book, written by a French Roman Catholic layman who died in 1988, reflects the wide interest in Bible Study which has marked Roman Catholicism since Vatican 2 and which has been sponsored by such organizations as The World Catholic Federation for the Biblical Apostolate. The writer, whilst not unaware of modern tendencies in biblical studies and the results of historical study, operates on a 'de fide' stance and is more concerned with a meditative and devotional approach to the text than with an historico-critical approach. He is concerned to find 'the Word of God' in the scriptures, and, in his search for God within the Bible, he follows a linguistic and statistical path. What is the language used of God? What epithets are used of him? How is his kingdom to be understood? He stresses repeatedly the unity of the two covenants, but, accepting, as he does, the centrality of Jesus Christ, Christian pre-suppositions influence his examination of Old Testament materials. Whilst there are occasional sections on the transmission of the text, there is little suggesting an acceptance or appreciation of the value of a form-critical approach. We are primarily introduced to the contemporary reader confronting the text of scripture. This may be a corrective for a more arid and detached use of scripture, but one looks for an existential approach, in which scholarship and devotion are more integrated.

The book, however, is a tribute to the zeal of a man who was an economist and the fascination that the scriptures had for him.

R. HAMMER

EATON, J.: *The Contemplative Face of Old Testament Wisdom in the context of world religion*. 1989. Pp. ix, 150 (SCM, London; Trinity Press International, Philadelphia. Price: £7.50. ISBN 0 334 01913 3)

The theological rehabilitation of the wisdom tradition is here given a new focus by directing attention to themes and elements with Old Testament wisdom which link it with the contemplative and mystical tradition in the wider world of the ancient near east, in Buddhist, Sufi and Confucian tradition, and in modern contemplatives such as Thomas Merton and Bede Griffiths. Eaton traces such a contemplative tradition firstly in the Old Testament wisdom literature and then in the Psalms before seeking to evaluate its contribution for today. Any attempt to relate Old Testament material to a wider religious context, both past and present, deserves a warm welcome. Refreshingly catholic and comprehensive in its approach this study opens up lines of thought well worth further exploration.

R. DAVIDSON

FISHBANE, M.: *Biblical Interpretation in Ancient Israel* (Clarendon Paperbacks). 1985. 1988. Pp. xviii, 617. (Oxford University Press. Price: £14.95. ISBN 0 19 826699 5)

Fishbane's celebrated *magnum opus* (the *Book List*'s encomium appeared in 1986, pp. 68–69) will now be available at modest cost to a deservedly wider readership. Apart from 'reformulations of some infelicities and details', the edition is unchanged but for eighteen addenda gathered on pp. 545–48.

A. G. AULD

FOX, M. V. (ed.): *Temple in Society*. 1988. Pp. vi, 138. (Eisenbrauns, Winona Lake IN. Price: $15.00. ISBN 0 931464 38 2)

Of the seven chapters in this published symposium, four are likely to be of some interest to *Book List* readers: a survey of the character of temples in Girsu, Nippur, Erudu, and Erech by S. N. Kramer; a discussion of aspects of the Jerusalem temple, emphasizing the centrality of the sacrificial cult — 'worship is tantamount to sacrificing' (p. 23) — by M. Haran; a wide-ranging treatment of Greek temples, their cult and theoretical status by W. Burkert; and a synoptic essay by D. M. Knipe drawing together the broad conclusions of the symposium. A promised paper on Egyptian temples did not materialize.

Burkert's contribution is excellent, and Knipe's of considerable interest, though he fails to develop some of his more significant insights; Kramer and Haran are disappointing. The latter stresses the peculiar social status of the priesthood, and the place of prayer in the cult, which, perpetuated in the synagogue worship, enabled Judaism to survive the loss of the second temple.

N. WYATT

GAMMIE, J. G.: *Holiness in Israel.* (Overtures to Biblical Theology). 1989. Pp. xvi, 216. (Fortress Press, Minneapolis, Price: $12.95. ISBN 0 8006 1549 2

The importance of holiness as a basic theological concept in the Old Testament is readily apparent, although the distinct nuances that attach to the term are often far from clear. This must derive in large part from the fact that it was already deeply rooted in Semitic culture at a very early stage. Professor Gammie's study examines the main areas where the term is used in the Old Testament and groups them into four main sections. These cover the Priestly usage, to which is then added a group of passages from Ezekiel and the Chronicler, and the Prophetic, to which is added a separate chapter on Jeremiah and the Deuteronomic literature. The third section is that on the Wisdom literature, to which is attached a chapter of variations from this in Qoheleth, Ben Sira, and the Wisdom of Solomon, with the fourth section dealing with apocalyptic writings.

Overall the study is thoroughly exegetical in method, seeking to work outwards from the actual linguistic usage towards a broader picture of the intellectual development that is revealed. This shows an interesting series of shifts in which a concept that was originally concerned with quasi-physical notions of divine presence and power came to express ideals of human virtue and piety. The summons to cleanness and God-relatedness which the term implies took on progressively a more emphatically moral and spiritual character, although not in any evolutionary pattern. The basic trend of the development will appear familiar to most readers, but the detailed study of particular passages is most welcome and revealing. Altogether this is a valuable contribution to a central theme of Old Testament theology, which has often been cast in a rather negative light.

R. E. CLEMENTS

DE GENNARO, G. (ed.): *Lavoro e riposo nella bibbia* (Studio biblico teologico aquilano). 1987. Pp. 406. (Dehoniane, Napoli. Price: Lire 45,000)

This book consists of thirteen papers delivered at the Studio Biblico Teologico Aquilano during 1984–85 on the theme of work and rest in the Bible; the previous volume in the series was noticed in *B. L.* 1988, p. 104. Apart from Alberto Soggin, all the contributors are Roman Catholic scholars. Four of the essays are concerned exclusively with the New Testament. Of the rest, two deal with aspects of the topic in the Wisdom literature, Gian Luigi Prato on the social dichotomy of Ecclus. 38:24–39:11 and Nicolo Maria Loss's more general survey of aspects of work in the Wisdom writings, while these are also considered in Settimio Cipriani's contribution on work and rest in the Wisdom material and the Psalms. Antonio Fanuli discusses rest as the goal of work in the Bible, with particular reference to the Sabbath, and this also features largely in Alberto Soggin's suggestive essay on work as both a divine vocation and a judgment on humanity. Old Testament material forms a considerable part of Emanuele Testa's discussion of the theology and spirituality of work in the Bible and that of Salvatore Garofalo on work in the eschatological perspective. Two interesting and rather more unusual contributions in the Old Testament field are those by Cecilia Carniti on woman's work and by Maurice Gilbert on the Biblical condemnation of fabricating idols. As tends to happen with a series of essays, there is a certain amount of repetition but all the contributors are concerned to indicate the relevance of the Biblical material for the problems of society today and this gives a particular freshness and interest to the whole collection.

J. R. PORTER

GREIDANUS, S.: *The Modern Preacher and the Ancient Text: Interpreting and Preaching Biblical Literature*. 1988. Pp. xvi, 374. (Eerdmans, Grand Rapids MI; IVP, Leicester. Price: £9.95 ($19.95). ISBN 0 8028 0360 1; 0 85111 573 X)

Dr Greidanus describes the aim of his study as 'to bridge the gap between the department of biblical studies and that of homiletics', and thus bring 'together the results of recent biblical scholarship as they pertain to preaching'. Consequently his volume contains a mixed menu; on the one hand stand surveys of the methods and emphases of biblical scholarship and on the other discussions of preaching and of sermons. After an introduction to biblical preaching, the author devotes a chapter each to the historical-critical method, literary interpretation, historical interpretation, and theological interpretation. Turning to the sermon Dr Greidanus discusses textual-thematic preaching, the form of the sermon and the relevance of the sermon. Finally, the two sections are brought together by focusing on four biblical areas for preaching — Hebrew Narratives, Prophetic Literature, the Gospels, and the Epistles.

Although conservative in standpoint, as is seen from his appraisal of source criticism and from his comments on historical reliability, Dr Griedanus has made it his business to acquaint himself with all aspects of contemporary biblical scholarship; he is not negative in his approach, but is genuinely constructuve in his attempt to build bridges. His work will no doubt prove useful to seminary students, for whom it is intended.

G. H. JONES

HØGENHAVEN, J.: *Gott und Volk bei Jesaja: eine Untersuchung zur biblischen Theologie* (Acta Theologica Danica, xxiv). 1988. Pp. x, 271. (Brill, Leiden. Price: fl 86.00, ISBN 90 04 08863 6)

The 'Isaiah' of the title is 'Isaiah of Jerusalem', this is, the material in chs. 1–39 which can confidently be regarded as emanating from the prophet himself. There are three main sections: first, a study of the usage of 'Israel' and of *ʿam* and *goy* in those sections, together with an analysis of Isaiah's appeal to past traditions; secondly, an exploration of the political implications of Isaiah's preaching, in his understanding both of foreign relations and of the domestic situation; and thirdly, theological considerations relating both to the understanding of God and of his demands upon his people. Høgenhaven accepts more of the foreign nations material as genuinely Isaianic than have most scholars, but his most unusual argument is that the historical prophet was actually a supporter of Ahaz's policy and an opponent of Hezekiah's resistance to the Assyrians. Whether or not this interpretation is accepted, the whole is of interest as reflecting an approach very different from the contemporary tendency to concentrate on the whole Isaiah tradition in its final form.

R. J. COGGINS

JAECKEL, T.: *Anything But a Quiet Life: Ideas of God in the Bible*. Translated by J. Bowden. 1989. Pp. x, 100. (SCM, London. Price: £4.95. ISBN 0 334 01874 9)

Written out of long missionary experience in the Far East, this is an extended essay in the reinterpretation of biblical ideas in the modern world. The book begins with a brief, racy survey of the biblical material with heavy, and somewhat unbalanced emphasis being laid in the Old Testament section on the radical newness of the prophetic tradition from Amos onwards. Biblical belief is described not in terms of dogma but as a confident trust maturely prepared to meet life's demands. While the critical judgement brought to bear on the biblical material may at times be questionable, all who have attempted to communicate biblical faith to the contemporary scene will find here food for thought. A postscript contains a biblical creed for 'outsiders', challenging both in what it retains and in what it omits of classical Christian theology.

R. DAVIDSON

KITTEL, G.: *Der Name über alle Namen*. Biblische Theologie/AT. 1989. Pp. 227. (Vanderhoeck & Ruprecht, Göttingen. Price: DM 29.80. ISBN 3 525 61283 4)

Designed for a wide readership, this is the first of two volumes aimed at presenting a biblical theology in its wholeness. A strong emphasis is placed upon the unity of the Bible in its twofold canonical division. The continuity of the whole is seen to be established through the unfolding of certain key themes. Central among these is that contained in the volume's title — the revelation of God through his Name. Hence the self-revelation of God at the Burning Bush establishes the starting point and centre, showing God summoning his people in faith and obedience.

Four major themes are then dealt with, beginning with the call to freedom from slavery and the recognition that this God is unlike the gods of other nations. In turn this leads to a summoning of God's people to faith and to a recognition that ultimately this is a call to reach towards a new future which will embrace all peoples.

The volume is most readable and well grounded on the biblical text, with ample documentation of current scholarly debates and discussions. It draws together very attractively the major biblical themes without becoming enmeshed in too much detail. Altogether this represents a most constructive volume relating exegesis to major theological concerns.

R. E. CLEMENTS

KOESTER, C. R.: *The Dwelling of God: The Tabernacle in the Old Testament, Intertestamental Jewish Literature, and the New Testament* (CBQ Monograph Series 22). 1989. Pp. x, 228. (Catholic Biblical Association of America, Washington, DC. Price: $9.00 (member price: $7.20). ISBN 0 915170 21 3)

An important study whose focus is 'on the role of the tabernacle in the earliest Christian sources, those of the New Testament' (ix) with the author attempting to answer the question as to why the early Christians expressed themselves in 'the language of the tabernacle, which had been defunct for centuries' (4). A concise opening chapter surveys 'The Tabernacle in the Old Testament'; a substantial chapter then examines 'The Tabernacle in Jewish Sources 200 B.C.–A.D. 150' indicating how Jewish development of the Old Testament portraits of the tabernacle formed the basis for the Christian use of tabernacle imagery. The remaining chapters are devoted respectively to the New Testament Books of Acts, John, Revelation, and Hebrews.

Some brief comments on the Old Testament section: there are good theological summaries on pages 13–17 while the conclusion usefully brings together both the emphases in the present form of the text and its underlying sources. Because Koester is apparently unaware of the existence of analogous portable structures in the second millennium B.C. (documented already in *Tyndale House Bulletin* 5–6 [1960], 7–13; or now in ISBE vol. II, 230) and because of his dating of P, he arguably misreads the tabernacle in terms of the Solomonic temple, whereas both the external evidence and an earlier dating of P's material suggest the need to read the temple in terms of the tabernacle.

The volume is enhanced by a series of charts: e.g. chart 1 gives data synoptically concerning furnishings, dimensions, architecture, courts and structures for the Temple Scroll, the tabernacle in Exodus, Solomon's temple in Kings and Chronicles, Ezekiel, and the post-exilic temple. Somehow M. H. Woudstra, *The Ark of the Covenant from Conquest to Kingship* (Philadelphia 1965) has eluded the author.

D. G. DEBOYS

KRIEG, M.: *Todesbilder im Alten Testament, oder "Wie die Alten den Tod gebildet"* (AThANT 73). 1988. Pp. 792. (Theologischer Verlag, Zürich. Price: SwFr. 72.00. ISBN 3 290 10006 5)

In this large volume, Krieg offers a detailed study of the imagery employed to describe death and its effects in the Old Testament. His concern is two-fold: to examine the character of the images or metaphors in question and then to see how they depict death itself. Hence the first main section adopts a hermeneutical approach, dealing with literary and philosophical issues, and concluding with an attempted grammar of metaphor. The influence of modern linguistic studies is prominent here and anyone who has not some acquaintance with them will find this part hard going. Perhaps more accessible is the second main section, comprising the bulk of the book, where the author turns to exegetical questions. Noting that the relevant imagery is confined almost exclusively to poetical texts — does he not somewhat exaggerate here? — he discusses in turn the areas of Wisdom, cultic psalmody, and prophecy, presenting first the *Formgeschichte* of the imagery of death in each and then the *Traditionsgeschichte*: a useful supplementary booklet is provided, giving the unpointed Hebrew and a German translation of the passages dealt with. The final part gives a summarizing account of the theology of the Old Testament images of death. The whole work is marked by careful and thorough discussion of the various issues and textual questions involved, taking full account of the secondary literature: there is an eighteen page bibliography. A brief review can hardly do justice to this complex study, which makes considerable demands on the reader, but the originality of its approach and the wealth of information it provides will merit the attention of all future students both of the topic with which it deals and the texts it surveys.

J. R. PORTER

LEWIS, R. M.: *Ecstatic Religion: A study of shamanism and spirit possession*. 2nd edition. 1989. Pp. 200. (Routledge, London and New York. Price: £10.95. ISBN 0 415 00799 2)

The first edition of Ioan Lewis's *Ecstatic Religion* (Pelican 1971) proved itself to be a most important analysis of spirit possession and shamanism, indeed of all forms of the seizure of the human by the divinity, and even influenced a number of biblical scholars in their treatment of prophecy as intermediation (most notably Thomas Overholt, David Petersen and Robert Wilson). It thus has justified its appearance in a second edition. This revision of the older work is not simply the first edition with an update section appended; there are signs of rewriting throughout the chapters and the literature references have been updated. In fact, the bibliography is now very much larger than in the original work and Lewis has taken into account the work done on 'the politics of possession' since 1971. The one noticeable loss between the two editions is the deletion of the photographs and illustrations of possession which were a feature of the Pelican volume. Lewis has taken the opportunity to reflect on criticisms of his earlier work and to incorporate them into this more nuanced account of his position. But he remains firmly convinced of his initial analysis of shamanism as 'the religion *par excellence* of the spirit made flesh' (1971:204; 1989:183) and of peripheral cults as responses to oppressive conditions. The extent to which his very important book holds promise for the investigation of biblical prophecy in terms of spirit possession and central-peripheral status conflicts remains on the agenda of current biblical scholarship, though Lewis himself offers virtually no comment on such an application of his thesis (beyond noting that his approach has been enthusiastically applied to the Bible). But it is good to have this excellent book back in print.

R. P. CARROLL

LEWIS, T. J.: *Cults of the Dead in Ancient Israel and Ugarit* (Harvard Semitic Monographs, 39). 1989. Pp. xv, 230. (Scholars Press, Atlanta GA. Price: $20.95 (member price: $13.95). ISBN 1 55540 325 5)

This is an excellent survey, treatment, and assessment of recent discussion in both Ugaritic and Old Testament studies on the subject of death and its ritual observance, with particular reference to the 'cult' of the dead — that is, the provision of food and drink to them in return for favours, generally of an oracular kind. The important Ugaritic Text *KTU* 1. 161 is treated in the greatest detail, as evidence of the cult of the royal dead (supplemented by the evidence of *KTU* 1. 113). The *marzeaḥ* texts are discussed, with the conclusion that there is no compelling reason to set them in a funerary context.

The author then turns to the Old Testament, dealing in turn with deuteronomistic material (laws in Deuteronomy and historical narratives), prophetic passages (Isa. 56:9–57:13 is handled particularly well), Priestly texts, the Psalms, and wisdom literature. Some passages are perhaps dealt with too cursorily, but such argumentation as we are given makes a convincing case for a tradition of a cult of the dead, in refutation of the assertions of G. E. Wright, R. de Vaux, and Y. Kaufmann, with which the study begins.

N. WYATT

LIGHTSTONE, J. N.: *Society, the Sacred, and Scripture in Ancient Judaism: A Sociology of Knowledge* (Studies in Christianity and Judaism 3). 1988. Pp. xiv, 126. (Wilfrid Laurier University Press, Waterloo, Ontario. Price: Can $14.95 ($17.50). ISBN 0 88920 975 8)

This is a useful sociological study of how the Hebrew Bible functioned in early Judaism, with examples from (a) the Restoration in the early Persian period, (b) the Greco-Roman Diaspora, (c) the Mishnah, and (d) the post-Mishnaic rabbinic literature. L. well illustrates how the same entity (i.e., 'the Law of Moses') shows great diversity of social function in the different contexts. For example, the Mishnah shows a quite different conceptualization from the Talmuds, demonstrating that 'rabbinic Judaism' was far from homogeneous.

Much in the book will be familiar to those acquainted with the writings of Jacob Neusner, but L.'s intention is not primarily to be original. Rather, his is a contribution to a series of socio-religious introductions. On the whole, it serves its intended purpose, with most of the chapters clearly written. However, parts of the theoretical discussion in the first chapter may be rather opaque for those not already knowledgeable of the subject. Not only students of Judaica but also biblical scholars will find much stimulating material here, especially those who have thus far approached the subject of Scripture only from a theological perspective.

L. L. GRABBE

LINDARS, B., SSF (ed.): *Law and Religion: Essays on the Place of Law in Israel and Early Christianity*, by members of the Ehrhardt Seminar of Manchester University. 1988. Pp. xvi, 209. (James Clarke, Cambridge. Price: £25.00. ISBN 0 227 67907 3)

A collection of 13 essays studying the relationship between law and religion in the Old and New Testaments. Part I addresses 'the law in Israelite religion', with essays by Adrian Curtis, 'God as "judge" in Ugaritic and Hebrew thought', Arnold Anderson, 'Law in Old Israel: laws concerning adultery', Roger Tomes, 'A perpetual statute throughout your generations' (a formula of the priestly writers which, it is argued, is used to draw attention to long-established practices whose continuing relevance has been challenged, but which the priestly writers consider essential to the life of the Jewish community), George J. Brooke, 'The Temple Scroll: a law unto itself?' (concluding that the Temple Scroll is to be associated with the groups who were responsible for *Jubilees* and the earliest forms of the traditions in the *Damascus Document*, probably disaffected cultic personnel), and Philip S. Alexander, 'Jewish law in the time of Jesus: towards a clarification of the problem'. Part II groups four essays under the rubric 'The law in the Jesus tradition': Barnabas Lindars 'All foods clean: thoughts on Jesus and the law', Richard Bauckham, 'Jesus' demonstration in the temple', Christopher Tuckett, 'Q, the law and Judaism', and George J. Brooke, 'Christ and the law in John 7–10'. The final section considers 'The law in Paul and the apostolic tradition': F. F. Bruce, 'Paul and the law in recent research', Barnabas Lindars, 'Paul and the law in Romans 5–8: an actantial analysis' (using a structural method derived from Greimas and Patte), Martin Kitchen, 'The status of law in the Letter to the Ephesians', and F. Gerald Downing, 'Law and custom: Luke-Acts and Late Hellenism'. There is much of interest in this volume, which attests to the liveliness of the Ehrhardt Seminar at Manchester University.

B. S. JACKSON

LOHFINK, N.: *Der niemals gekündigte Bund: Exegetische Gedanken zum christlich-jüdischen Dialog*. 1989. Pp. 120. (Herder, Freiburg. Price: DM 15.80. ISBN 3 451 21597 7)

We are presented here with twelve exegetical studies, relating to central passages from the Old and New Testaments and all focused on the theme of the new covenant. They constitute an essay in Jewish-Christian dialogue and start from the premise that much traditional Christian understanding of a new covenant which abrogates, and even repudiates, the old Mosaic covenant contains an inevitable anti-Semitic assumption. Against this Lohfink finds it to be false both to the central basis of Jer. 31 and to the earliest Christian appeal to it. Essentially there is only one covenant in the overall biblical perspective.

However, since the very notion of covenant is not significantly present in Jewish thought, Lohfink argues that the notion of *torah* to which the Old Testament idea of covenant is inseparably bound offers a more fruitful basis for serious Jewish-Christian dialogue. Altogether this is a most stimulating a rewarding study which brings exegesis forward into a very positive field of contemporary religious concern. It suggests a constructive approach to a debate which has so often earlier proved sterile.

R. E. CLEMENTS

LOHFINK, N.: *Unsere neuen Fragen und das Alte Testament: Wiederentdeckte Lebensweisung* (Herder Taschenbuch 1594). 1989. Pp. 157. (Herder, Freiburg. Price: DM 12.90. ISBN 3 451 08594 1)

Norbert Lohfink has for many years combined his work as a penetrating literary-historical scholar with a sensitivity to the mission of the church and to contemporary issues. This volume of semi-popular essays dating from 1965 to 1983 covers the relationship between historical and Christian exegesis of the Old Testament, the Old Testament background to the teaching of Vatican II on the church as the people of God, the church as a hierarchial institution in the light of the Bible, the biblical view of the sabbath, work and recreation, the Old Testament and other religions, the ethics of the Old Testament compared with those of the New Testament, and the relationship between Christianity and peace movements. The essays are a model of balanced judgement and judicious exegesis, tempered throughout by Lohfink's commitment to a church which, freed from coercive power, is a serving community witnessing to God's liberating reality.

J. W. ROGERSON

LONG, T. G.: *Preaching and the Literary Forms of the Bible*. 1989. Pp. 144. (Fortress, Philadelphia. Price: $8.95. ISBN 0 8006 2313 4)

Here is a plea to take seriously for purposes of preaching not only traditional literary and historical criticism, but the literary and rhetorical form of the biblical material — the genre of the text, the rhetorical form the genre uses, the literary devices employed to achieve the rhetorical effect. This should all be grist to the mill of preachers as they seek to communicate in a new setting what the text says in its setting. The thesis is then applied to preaching from the Psalms, Proverbs, Narratives, the Parables of Jesus, and the epistles. Attractively presented and well illustrated, this may not solve all the preacher's problems, but it should make him/her think again about the uses of biblical material.

R. DAVIDSON

LONGMAN, T. III: *Literary Approaches to Biblical Interpretation* (Foundations of Contemporary Interpretation, 3). 1987. Pp. xi, 164. (Apollos, Leicester. Price: £6.95. ISBN 0 85111 502 0)

This is a British edition of the work reviewed in *B. L.* 1989, pp. 84f.

A. G. AULD

MAILLOT, A.: *Eve, Ma Mère: Étude sur la femme dans l'Ancien Testament*. 1989. Pp. 183. (Letouzey et Ané, Paris. Price: Fr. 120.00. ISBN 2 7063 0178 3)

This is a useful contribution to current discussion of the status of women in the Old Testament, providing balanced comment on a wide variety of material. After initial discussion of Genesis 1–3 ('textes fondateurs') the author proceeds to a brief study of individual women throughout the Old Testament period, including the Deutero-canonical literature. There are chapters on woman in Wisdom literature, and on marriage and laws relating to women in ancient Israel. The final chapters concern women in ancient Egypt, Mesopotamia, Greece, and Rome, with a brief section on the intertestamental period. The author concludes that, with the exception of Rome, the status of women in these cultures declined over the centuries. The ultimate in misogyny was reached, he suggests, in Athens, itself a probable influence on developments in Judaism. The author admits that the material has not yielded such clear results as he had originally envisaged. Attitudes to women in the Old Testament cannot be neatly categorized, nor can an Old Testament concept of femininity be readily formulated. 'Le fond du mystère est resté intact'!

G. I. EMMERSON

MEYERS, C.: *Discovering Eve: Ancient Israelite Women in Context*. 1988. Pp. xi, 238. (Oxford University Press, New York and Oxford. Price: £19.50. ISBN 0 19 504934 9)

Meyers sets out to reconstruct the life of ancient Israelite women with the help of three sources of information — the Bible (selected texts; most of the Old Testament knows little of the typical Israelite woman in her village); archaeology; and comparative social anthropology — concentrating on 'the most thoroughly investigated period to date . . . the period of Israelite origins' (p. 14). At this time, she finds, society accorded no dominance to the male sex. In economic matters men and women were complementary to each other. So it was too in education (Prov. 1:8 and 6:20 parallel the teaching of the mother with that of the father) and socialization; here, indeed, women may have had a greater role to play than men. Further, Israelite law vested authority over junior and dependent members of the family in both parents, not just the father. Women may also have had a substantial role in the religious life of the home; they certainly were responsible for one area of public religion, the composition and performance of Victory Songs. In certain areas, males were accorded a superior authority, notably in the marriage relationship, but there may have been functional reasons for this, associated with land-tenure. The overall picture is one of gender-mutuality and interdependence, or of 'male authority offset by female power' (p. 43).Useful comments are made on a number of parts of the Old Testament, notably the Song of Songs ('It preserves a glimpse of gender mutuality and female power that existed in family households' (p. 180); females and images of power are, Meyers notes, prominently linked in the Song) and Gen. 2–3, interpreted not in terms of a Fall ('none of the words that are part of the Hebrew vocabulary for sin and transgression are present': p. 87) but as an aetiology of the harsh conditions of life in the pre-monarchic hill-country. An epilogue considers the effects of the rise of the monarchy: the parity that had marked the formative period in Israel's history ended, and male control became the order of the day, at least in the new urban centres with their male élites of soldiers, politicians, and priests, but increasingly in rural areas too.

An illuminating and thoughtful study, persuasively argued. There is, however, some use of jargon and a measure of repetitiveness.

B. P. ROBINSON

NAVONE, J., SJ; *Teologia del Fallimento*. 1988. Pp. 245. (Editrice Pontificia Università Gregoriana, Roma. Price: Lire 17,000. ISBN 88 7652 587 4)

This rather diffuse study of failure — the concept itself being very broadly understood — includes several pages on death in the Old Testament and rather fewer on the apocalyptists' view of history and on 'remembering' in the Old Testament, but the treatment is very general and unlikely to be of interest to readers of this Booklist.

C. J. A. HICKLING

NEUSNER, J., FRERICHS, E. S., and LEVINE, A. J. (eds): *Religious Writings and Religious Systems: Systemic Analysis of Holy Books in Christianity, Islam, Buddhism, Greco-Roman Religions, Ancient Israel, and Judaism*. Vol. II: *Christianity* (Brown Studies in Religion, 2). 1989. Pp. xi, 201. (Scholars Press, Atlanta GA. Price: $47.95 (member price: $31.95). ISBN 1 55540 333 6)

Most of the ten papers in this volume cite Neusner's view that religious systems are composed of a world view, a way of life and a social entity, and acknowledge their indebtedness to his 'documentary method' for studying them. They are the product of two summer seminars for college teachers held at Brown University in 1988. Each attempts, by studying a religious text as an autonomous statement, to 'expose the religious system it reflects and to identify the urgent question to which the system supplies an answer'. The texts selected are Matthew, Romans, I Corintians 8, Colossians, Hebrews, the Didache, Clement of Alexandria's *Stromata*, Eusebius' *Praeparatio* and *Demonstratio*, Theodoret's *Commentary on Daniel* (Chapter 2), and the Free Methodists' *Discipline* (1860). Even although *B. L.* readers may find little of direct relevance to their research and teaching here, there is plenty to prove how productive such a methodology can be, moving as it does away from the perennial questions of date, authorship, source, historicity, etc. to literary structure, content, and social function.

J. F. A. SAWYER

NIEWIADOMSKI, J. (ed.): *Eindeutige Antworten? Fundamentalistische Versuchung in Religion und Gesellschaft*. 2., aktualisierte Auflage (Theologische Trends 1). 1988. Pp. 210. (Österreichischer Kulturverlag, Thaur. Price: ÖS 198.00; DM 28.00; Sw.Fr. 23.50. ISBN 3 85395 134 1)

Ten Roman Catholic scholars have here collaborated in a description and appraisal of contemporary fundamentalisms: in traditionalist Catholicism, in US Protestantism, in Islam, and in some parts of the 'green' movement. After the initial descriptive essays. three more studies, which are likely to be those of most direct interest to readers of this *Book List*, consider the phenomenon in the light of the Bible. J. M. Oesch deals with the way in which archaeological discoveries have been claimed to support a literal reading of the Bible; M. Hasitschka emphasizes the literary variety within the Bible as a warning against belief in inerrancy; and R. Oberforscher shows how fundamentalism lacks any satisfactory hermeneutical basis. The last three essays are of a more general kind, exploring the whole phenomenon of the rise of fundamentalist mentality in the modern world. First published in May 1988, a new foreword setting out fresh developments was already required for this second edition of December 1988.

R. J. Coggins

Niewiadomski, J. (ed.): *Verweigerte Mündigkeit: Politische Kultur und die Kirche* (Theologische Trends 2). 1989. Pp. 254. (Österreichischer Kulturverlag, Thaur. Price: ÖS 198.00; DM 28.00. ISBN 3 85395 131 7)

This collection of essays emanates from the same group of Austrian Roman Catholic scholars as the first volume in the series (noticed above). Here the theme is the frequent tendency of the church to deny the maturity of, especially, its lay members. Ruth Frick-Pöder uses 2 Sam. 13:20 ('Hold your peace, my sister') as the starting-point for a feminist reading of the Old Testament despite its male-structured world; and J. M. Oesch bases a discussion of authority in the contemporary world on an exegesis of the stories in Judges and 1 Samuel on the establishment of monarchy. The remaining essays in this (too?) wide-ranging collection are often thought-provoking but not directly related to this *Book List*.

R. J. Coggins

Olyan, S. M.: *Asherah and the Cult of Yahweh in Israel* (SBL Monograph Series 34). 1988. Pp. xiv, 100. (Scholars Press, Atlanta GA. Price: $19.95 (member price: $12.95); paperback price: $12.95 (member price: $8.95). ISBN 1 55540 253 4; 1 55540 254 2 (pbk))

The complex problem of the significance of the biblical term *hāʾăšērâ* has of late been given considerable airing since the publication of the inscriptions from Kuntillet Ajrud and Khirbet el-Qom. Olyan has provided a judicious updating of the discussion on all fronts, surveying all the biblical and extra-biblical data. He argues that Asherah was a goddess in Israel and Judah who was the consort of Yahweh, and whose cult was accepted as legitimate even in prophetic circles until the rise of the deuteronomi(sti)c school. Apparent understanding of her as the consort of Baal is propagandistic. This short study is a useful corrective to contemporary understanding of the Hebrew Bible which still too frequently accepts a deuteronomistic view as the norm, all variations to be seen as false religion. The historical reality was far more interesting.

N. Wyatt

Otto, E.: *Rechtsgeschichte der Redaktionen im Kodex Ešnunna und im 'Bundesbuch': Eine redaktionsgeschichtliche und rechtsvergleichende Studie zu altbabylonischen und altisraelitischen Rechtsüberlieferungen* (OBO 85). 1989. Pp. 209. (Universitätsverlag, Frieburg (CH); Vandenhoeck & Ruprecht, Göttingen. Price; Sw.Fr. 54.00. ISBN 3 7278 0602 8; 3 525 53715 8)

The author here follows up his study of the 'Covenant Code' (*Wandel der Rechtsbegründungen in der Gesellschaftsgeschichte des Antiken Israel — see B. L.* 1989, pp. 112f — which dealt relatively briefly with the editorial structure of the document) with a full analysis of the document's redactional history, in comparison with the Code of Eshnunna. He argues that the editorial techniques of the Covenant Code belong to the legal culture of the ancient Near East: parallels between the two documents show that some of the techniques of the Israelite lawgivers have their pre-history in Cuneiform law. But whereas earlier studies have tended towards a uni-directional comparison — applying the results of analysis of the ancient Near Eastern laws to the biblical *corpora* — Professor Otto works in both directions. In particular, he argues for the presence of 'literary' techniques of presentation, and particularly chiasmus, in the Laws of Eshnunna, based upon a model emerging principally from biblical reasearch. With Eshnunna §§15–35 he sees two parallels series, related by anthology. On this, he offers no specific biblical parallel, but his account is suggestive of Carmichael's identification of a 'double series' in the Covenant Code (*ZAW* 84 (1972), 19–25; cf. *The Laws of Deuteronomy*, 1975, 62–65). Otto, however, sees the whole of Exodus 21:2–22:26 as organized in a single chiasmus, and Exodus 22:28–23:12 as a second chiasmus. In the course of this study, the author provides text, translation and brief commentary on the whole of Eshnunna, with relevant comparison to the Covenant Code. Whether one agrees with all his conclusions or not, this is a significant contribution to the study of the legal rationality of the ancient codes, which poses basic questions about the relationship (and identification) of larger and smaller units, and the nature of the analogical thinking which governs the relationships between passages.

B. S. Jackson

Patrick, D. (ed.): *Thinking Biblical Law* (Semeia 45). 1989. Pp. iv, 109. (Scholars Press, Atlanta GA. Price: $14.95 (member price: $9.95; member price for unit of 4 numbers: $25.00))

This collection of papers on biblical law, by members of the SBL biblical law group, is united mainly by the quest for interdisciplinary approaches which will contribute to a humanistic understanding of the text. Ralph Knierim, 'The Problem of Ancient Israel's Prescriptive Legal Traditions', considers the *mot yumat* laws in the light of the difference between 'legislative' and adjudicative language as viewed by H. Schulz, G. Leidke, and V. Wagner; asks whether the casuistic laws are reports of decisions or prescriptions for decisions; and questions whether the prohibition (apodictic) form is necessarily non-legal. Dale Patrick, 'Studying Biblical Law as a Humanities' [*sic*!], seeks to develop the approach to biblical law of Greenberg and Finkelstein (but without considering objections, as is later done in the volume by Haas), in pursuit of the view that the law is a repository of a culture's reigning metaphysics, anthropology, and ethics. He reviews Finkelstein's treatment of the goring ox, and traces the concepts there identified in other provisions, under the headings of 'causation', 'the hierarchy of being', and 'the unquantifiable human'. Martin Buss, 'Logic and Israelite Law', uses some categories of deontic logic in order to examine the logical structure of Israelite law. Peter Haas, '"Die He Shall Surely Die", the Structure of Homicide in Biblical Law', argues through structuralist and anthropological analysis that the pentateuchal laws of homicide know of two-clear cut categories, premeditated murder (bad, resulting in blood-guilt) and socially mandated killings (good, no blood-guilt), together with an intermediate category of homicide which is bad but produces no blood-guilt (e.g. accidental manslaughter). This tripartite structure is confirmed by examination of the rules of killing animals for food or for the altar. Tikva Frimer-Kensky, 'Law and Philosophy: the Case of Sex in the Bible', notes that sexuality was largely excluded from theological thinking, and kept as far away from the cult as possible, while still calling for social control. The Bible indicates anxiety about the topic, but does not provide an adequate way to discuss and channel its anxieties. (One might contrast L. E. Goodman, 'The Biblical Laws of Diet and Sex', *Jewish Law Association Studies II*, Scholars Press, 1986, 17–57, not here considered.) Finally, Jacob Milgrom, 'Rationale for Cultic Law: the Case of Impurity', explores through the detail of the biblical law of impurity, allied to anthropological evidence, the associations between three pairs of binary opposites: life and death, holiness and impurity, good and bad.

B. S. Jackson

Podella, T.: *Ṣôm–Fasten. Kollektive Trauer um den verborgenen Gott im Alten Testament* (AOAT, 224). 1989. Pp. xi, 327. (Butzon & Bercker, Kevelaer; Neukirchener, Neukirchen-Vluyn. Price: DM 84.00; sub. price: DM 76.00. ISBN 3 7666 9638 6; 3 7887 1309 7)

Podella's densely written work is a sociological study of ritual fasting in the Old Testament against the background of ancient Near Eastern practice, particularly the rites associated with the disappearing god of Mesopotamia, Syria (Ugarit), and Anatolia. The topics of death and mourning, and of collective and individual fasting are examined and special attention is paid to the relevant Old Testament texts (Judg. 20; 1 Kings 21; Isa. 58; Jer. 14; 36; Joel 2; Jonah 3; etc.). In the final chapter an attempt is made at reconstructing the '*ṣôm* Ritual'. The same chapter is also a summary of the whole book where the author outlines the development of ritual fasting from its funereal origins to its final form. Altogether thorough and thought-provoking.

W. G. E. Watson

Propp, W. H.: *Water in the Wilderness: A Biblical Motif and Its Mythological Background* (Harvard Semitic Monographs, 40). 1987. Pp. xi, 144. (Scholars Press, Atlanta GA. Price: $14.95 (member price: $9.95). ISBN 1 55540 157 0)

As its sub-title indicates, the thesis of this monograph is that the Biblical descriptions of the divine provision of water in the desert are influenced by a mythology of creation and fertility, attested also in the ancient Near East and particularly in Canaan. In the first chapter, the author discusses various passages which tell how Yahweh satisfies an individual's thirst and relates these to creation texts and to the Zion tradition which portray Yahweh as the source of fertilizing water. In the second chapter, the locus of this water is defined more specifically as the sacred mountain. Chapter three deals with the Massah and Meribah traditions, which are ascribed to the Elohist and the final chapter is concerned with the theme of water in the desert in the prophecies of restoration in Jeremiah, Ezekiel, and Second Isaiah.

All this is carefully worked out, with many interesting suggestions, but sometimes the case is pushed too far and there are too many weak links in the chain of argument. This is particularly so with regard to the crucial third chapter. Certainly some passages in the psalms use mythical language to describe the provision of water during the wilderness wanderings and view it as the fertilization of nature. But they seem to reflect the traditions of Zion as the divine mountain from which fructifying waters flow: can we assume that the Elohist, if indeed it was he, had such traditions in view? The author argues that *ṣur* and *sela* mean 'mountain' and that the *ṣur* of Massah/Meribah is the divine mountain and to be identified with Horeb, which is also the site of the battle against Amalek which in turn represents the concept of the *Völkerkampf*. Much of this seems very doubtful. Again, the author closely links Exod. 17:1–7 and Exod. 32, largely on the ground that Exod. 32:20 refers to the springs of Horeb which are a 'symbol of fertility', but, whatever is the precise significance of the water in this verse, it hardly seems to have much to do with fertility, as indeed the author's full discussion on p. 87f. shows. So, although there is much of value in this book, its most original proposals are not wholly convincing.

J. R. Porter

Robinson, G.: *The Origin and Development of the Old Testament Sabbath* (Beiträge zur biblischen Exegese und Theologie, 21). 1988. Pp. 442. (Peter Lang, Frankfurt am Main — Bern. Price: $57.70. ISBN 3 8204 1373 1)

The dissertation the substance of which is here reproduced was submitted at Hamburg in 1975, under K. Koch. The delay in publication, though no doubt unavoidable (Robinson is an Indian scholar who is now the Principal of Tamil Nadu seminary in Mandurai), has meant that no reference can be made, either in the text or in the extensive bibliography, to work published in the last 15 years. Robinson's own thesis is that the Sabbath reached its characteristic form in the post-exilic period as a combination of two originally separate institutions: a moon-related observance with its focus in the royal rites of the Jerusalem temple, the exact nature of which is now irrecoverable; and a 'seventh-day rest' observance related to the agricultural festivals. There are obvious difficulties in such a reconsruction, e.g. in the various closely related Hebrew terms, and the assumptions made about Pentateuchal sources, but the case is presented clearly and in great detail. It is good to welcome a major piece of work from a Third World scholar, though much of it is in fact steeped in the solid German tradition of detailed exegesis.

R. J. Coggins

Rowland, C. and Corner, M.: *Liberating Exegesis: The Challenge of Liberation Theology to Biblical Studies* (Biblical Foundations in Theology). 1990. Pp. ix, 205. (SPCK, London. Price: £10.95. ISBN 0 281 04437 6)

Many readers of this *List* will share the reviewer's surprise, given the prominent place accorded the Old Testament by many liberation theologians, that a book with such a title and sub-title makes only four or five brief forays into the Old Testament and Old Testament studies. However, this comment intends no criticism of an interesting discussion that focuses principally on some of the parables of Jesus, the apocalypse, and on encouraging liberation theology in a first world context.

A. G. Auld

Schubert, M.: *Schöpfungstheologie bei Kohelet* (Beiträge zur Erforschung des Alten Testamentes und des antiken Judentums, 15). 1989. Pp. 212. (Lang, Frankfurt am Main, Bern, New York, Paris. Price: Sw.Fr. 54.00. ISBN 3 8204 1130 5; ISSN 0722 0790)

The argument of this 1986 Leipzig dissertation is that the key to the interpretation of Ecclesiastes is a theology of creation drawn principally from the Old Testament but radically reinterpreted. A tension is set up between the confession (*Bekenntnis*) that the world, including man, is wholly determined by the Creator and the human struggle to use God-given wisdom to understand the world (*Erkenntnis*), an aim which is never more than very fragmentarily achieved or achievable. This tension Qoheleth never resolves. Man is saved from despair, however, by the fact that sometimes, though always unpredictably, the Creator provides men and women with an opportunity for enjoyment which it is not within their power to obtain by their own efforts. The subsumption of the whole of Qoheleth's thought under the rubric of creation theology is a novel approach to Ecclesiastes which leads to some interesting detailed exegesis; but it may be questioned whether the density of argumentation which characterizes this study was necessary in order to reach its sound but not startling conclusions. This is emphatically not a book for the beginner.

R. N. Whybray

Schwarz, H.: *Die biblische Urgeschichte: Gottes Traum von Mensch und Welt* (Herder Taschenbuch 1608). 1989. Pp. 158. (Herder, Freiburg. Price: DM 12.90. ISBN 3 451 08608 5)

The main part of the book originated in a series of sermons. Gen. 1–3; 8:21b–9:7; 11:1–9; 12:1–4, 6–9 and 13:1–15 are expounded with reference to the New Testament and the present day, and a German translation of the inaugural address given by the author at the North American Conference on Christianity and Ecology 1987 has been added at the end.

C. S. Rodd

Seely, P. H.: *Inerrant Wisdom: Science & Inerrancy in Biblical Perspective*. 1989. Pp. 216. (Evangelical Reform, Portland OR. Price: $11.95. ISBN 0 9622295 0 4)

The author adhered for many years to the tenets of the International Council on Biblical Inerrancy (recently disbanded on the ground of 'mission accomplished'). In this sense 'inerrancy' is held to be stricter than 'infallibility', the latter traditionally being predicated of matters of faith and life, whereas the former extends to matters of science and history. He now undertakes to show that 'inerrancy' is untenable, arguing that neither Jesus nor Paul held it and that the proof-texts commonly adduced in support of it do not mean what inerrantists suppose them to mean. The case for which he argues is one that most readers of the *Book List* would take for granted, but his discussion of the issue may help some who hold the position which he formerly held.

F. F. Bruce

Segal, R. A.: *Religion and the Social Sciences: Essays on the Confrontation* (Brown Studies in Religion, 3). 1989. Pp. 184. (Scholars Press, Atlanta GA. Price: $43.95 (member price: $28.95). ISBN 1 55540 295 X)

This is a collection of thirteen essays and reviews published between 1978 and 1987. Although the subjects covered range from Lévy-Bruhl's theory of primitive mentality through Victor Turner's theory of ritual acts, Jung's view of evil and Fustel de Coulanges as the first social scientist of religion, to Eliade's defence of the irreducibility of the study of religion, the main concerns of the author recur again and again. These are to distinguish between the truth, the origin, the function, and the meaning of religion, and to establish the distinctive contribution of social science to the study of religion. Segal rightly maintains that to demonstrate the origin, function or meaning of religious beliefs or actions is not to prove their truth, and he is particularly concerned that these distinctions should not be blurred by the tendency of writers such as Geertz, Berger, Mary Douglas, and Turner to give priority to the understanding by participants of the significance of their religious beliefs or acts. These writers, Segal argues, for all their attractiveness to students of religion, are reductionists who account for religion in secular ways. Particular criticism is directed towards Eliade for his assumption that religious beliefs and acts arise from contact with the sacred. Not only is this contention often not provable from the accounts given by religious observers themselves, but it begs the question of whether there is such a thing as the sacred, and cannot be the basis for Eliade's assertion that religion cannot be adequately explained in terms of the methods of the social sciences.

The issues discussed here are important ones, which might have been more satisfactorily dealt with by use of the emic/etic distinction. The essays could be usefully employed as texts for seminar discussion of the issue of the truth or falsity of religious claims about the world, including those made in the Old Testament.

J. W. Rogerson

SILVA, M.: *Has The Church Misread The Bible? The history of interpretation in the light of current issues* (Foundations of Contemporary Interpretation, 1). 1987. Pp. viii, 136. (Academie Books, Grand Rapids MI; Apollos, Leicester. Price: £5.95. ISBN 0 85111 501 2)

This learned and intelligent book serves two purposes: to act as an introductory volume to the series *Foundations of Contemporary Interpretation*, and to present some considerations about the history of biblical interpretation. The series is an attempt to provide conservative evangelicals with a coherent and well-informed account of general hermeneutics, and to assess the impact of philosophy, literary criticism, linguistics, history, science, and theology on the study of the Bible. S. offers some very brief introductory comments on each in his opening chapter. The rest of the book sketches the history of biblical interpretation, criticizing what he sees as the consensus view of this among 'critical' scholars, and discussing such issues as allegorical interpretation, the perspicuity of Scripture, and cultural relativism. To a reviewer who by no means shares the conservative evangelical stance of the author. it seemed that the need to show that modern study posed no real challenge to conservatism had an unfortunately Procrustean effect on his wide learning and sensitivity to subtle lines of argument. The book fully confirms the intellectual sophistication of modern evangelical scholars, but also their continuing need to avoid any conclusions that might be judged 'unsound' by their (less sophisticated) public. Even with these caveats, the book can be recommended as a serious attempt to wrestle with the history of interpretation from a position of commitment. The brief format means that rather too much material has to be summarized, and the effect is rather breathless — e.g., four pages headed 'From Schleiermacher to Bultmann'! But not a book to be dismissed lightly.

J. BARTON

STEMBERGER, G. and BALDERMANN, I. (eds): *Zum Problem des biblischen Kanons* (*Jahrbuch fur Biblische Theologie*, Bd 3). 1988. Pp. 294. (Neukirchener, Neukirchen-Vluyn. Price: DM 49.80. ISBN 3 7887 1288 0)

The second volume of this annual is reviewed above, p. 97. This third volume is the first in any real sense to live up to the promise implied in the inclusion of non-German-speaking members among the editorial advisors of the *Jahrbuch*. As usual, the volume is structured in three sections. There are five essays on canonical exegesis: by B. S. Childs on biblical theology and Christian canon; by N. Lohfink asking, with Psalm 6 as an example, whether canonical exegesis makes a difference; by H.-J. Kraus offering biblical-theological meditations on the *Telos* of *torah*; by H.-G. Link on the canon in ecumenical perspective; and by Baldermann on the implications of the biblical canon for religious lessons in schools. These are followed by seven on the history of the emergence of the canon and of its subsequent results (stated more neatly in German as *Entstehungs- und Wirkungsgeschichte des Kanons*). M. Saebø writes on aspects of the traditio-historical final stages of the Old Testament under the title 'From "thinking-together" to Canon'; J. Maier, on the question of the biblical canon in early Judaism in the light of the Qumran finds; H. Hübner, on the question of the Old Testament canon in New Testament perspective; Stemberger, on Jamnia and the canon; H. P. Rüger, on the evolution of the Christian Old Testament; and R. Berndt, on whether the Church Fathers belong to Holy Scripture — the canon theory of Hugo of St Victor. The customary third section entitled 'Report and Review' has five contributions: P. D. Miller, Jr. reports on the canon in contemporary American discussion; M. Oeming reviews Childs' *Old Testament Theology in a Canonical Context* under the title 'Text — Context — Canon: A new route for Old Testament Theology'; M. Weinrich, under the title 'on the charisma of biblical provocations', celebrates H.-J. Kraus's seventieth birthday by discussing his view of systematic theology within the horizon of biblical theology; Stemberger reviews D. G. Meade's book *Pseudonymity and Canon*; while E. Dassmann discusses Bruce Metzger's latest book, *The Canon of the New Testament. Its Origin, Development, and Significance*. English readers will welcome the wider perspective of this number; however, it remains predominantly a German-language forum.

A. G. AULD

TRIBLE, N.: *Kami to Ningen-sei no Shūji-gaku. Feminizumu to Seisho-kaishaku* . Translated by N. Kawano. 1989. Pp. 331 and 6-pages index. (Yorudan-sha, Tokyo. Price: ¥3,300. ISBN 4 8428 0038 0)

This is a Japanese translation of *God and the Rhetoric of Sexuality*, 1978. The author's preface to Japanese readers is also translated.

K. K. SACON

WEILER, G.: *Das Matriarchat im Alten Israel.* 1989. Pp. 368. (Kohlhammer, Stuttgart. Price: DM 29.00. ISBN 3 17 010773 9)

This is a book for whose aims one can have sympathy, while entertaining severe reservations about the methods and conclusions. The author wishes to defend feminism against the charge of anti-Judaism, a charge which arises from the claim made by some feminists that patriarchal religion comes from the Old Testament. She accordingly offers an interpretation of ancient Israelite religion that emphasizes its matriarchal aspects. However, her scholarship is not in the class of Fiorenza or Myers, and will strike most specialists, including those sympathetic to her cause, as naive and superficial. The author's lack of familiarity with Old Testament scholarship is suggested by some strange references in the bibliography to e.g. Alfred Alt, Otto Kehl (for Otmar Keel), and Robert Ranke-Graves.

J. W. ROGERSON

WESTBROOK, R.: *Studies in Biblical and Cuneiform Law* (Cahiers de la Revue Biblique 26). 1988, Pp. x, 150. (Gabalda, Paris. Price: Fr 160.00. ISBN 2 85021 034 X)

Written as the first stage of a research project on the biblical law of obligations, this book comprises studies of (ch. 1) 'Abuse of Power', (ch. 2) 'Revenge, Ransom and Talio', (ch. 3) 'Maltreatment of Slaves', and (ch. 4) 'Theft and Receiving Stolen Goods'. The first rejects both Jackson's and Milgrom's accounts of the biblical verb *GZL* and argues for dual understanding of the verb, one part of which belongs to the concept of 'abuse of power', the remedy being petition directly to the King (who had discretionary powers to deal with such abuses, even by overturning legally established rights). The second rejects general historical schemes of the relationship between monetary and physical sanctions for death or injury, and argues that revenge and ransom were co-terminus institutions, the law codes sometimes regulating one, sometimes the other, but in either case with the unexpressed assumption that the other aspect still exists as an alternative. There is an excursus on the stoning of the goring ox. The third considers Exodus 21:20-21 (killing of one's own slave), wounding (Exodus 21:26), and sexual abuse (Leviticus 19:20–22). The final chapter studies Exodus 21:37–22:3, arguing that the three offences form a coherent whole, and follow a logical order. The passage reflects the same principle of the alternative of revenge or ransom studied in Chapter 2. The passage draws together the two traditional problems found in the ancient near eastern law codes: the three-cornered situation of owner, thief/seller and purchaser, and the case of attempted burglary. There is an excursus on the theft of Joseph's cup. A brief but suggestive conclusion sketches four concepts which biblical law shared with the ancient Near East, but which are foreign to modern law: the role of status, the correlated institutions of revenge and ransom, the special liabilities of public authorities, and the discretionary authority of the King to act outside the system. The differences between biblical and cuneiform law reside primarily in the nature of the literary sources, the Bible containing 'the voice of dissent as much, if not more, than that of the establishment'. One looks to the further elaboration of these theses. However, Westbrook has here presented a book which requires the serious attention of all students of biblical law.

B. S. JACKSON

WILSON, M. R.: *Our Father Abraham: Jewish Roots of the Christian Faith*. 1989. Pp. xxi, 374. (Eerdmans, Grand Rapids MI; distributed by Paternoster, Exeter. Price: £12.50. ISBN 0 8028 0423 3)

This is a well-informed and well-reasoned appeal to Christian readers not to forget their Jewish or Hebrew roots, but to remember that vital relationship and indebtedness to those who were trueborn children of Abraham long before they themselves became his children by adoption. The author, who is Professor of Biblical and Theological Studies in Gordon College, Wenham, Massachusetts, is a former pupil of C. H. Gordon and an appreciative student of the writings of A. J. Heschel.

There are some churches in which an Old Testament lesson is read at every regular service, but the author knows of many, especially in his own country, where congregations hear no reading from the Old Testament, let alone a sermon on an Old Testament text, from one year's end to another. (He deprecates the use of the term 'Old Testament' and the attitudes to which it gives rise.) This cutting of Christianity from its roots means the death of Christianity rightly so called. His survey ranges from Israelite beginnings (what he says about 'corporate personality' and other features of Hebrew thought calls for some modification in the light of more recent study), through the record of Jewish-Christian relations over the centuries (a record in which a Christian reader can take no pride), down to the issues raised in our own day by the Holocaust and the establishment of the State of Irael.

F. F. BRUCE

WRIGHT, T. R.: *Theology and Literature* (Signposts in Theology). 1988. Pp. viii, 243. (Basil Blackwell, Oxford. Price: £27.50; paperback price: £8.95. ISBN 0 631 14848 5; 0 631 14849 3 (pbk))

This stimulating book describes and explains recent interest in the connections between theology and the study of literature — it could almost be seen as providing a rationale for the journal *Literature and Theology* of which the author is associate editor. Readers of the *Book List* may turn naturally to chapter 2, 'On Reading the Bible as Literature', where they will find a balanced account both of traditional biblical criticism and of the work of Alter and Kermode, together with lively readings of Genesis and Mark. But they should also read chapter 3, 'Narrative Theology: The Stories of Faith , which illuminates biblical and ecclesiastical narrative by a comparison both with biography and autobiography in the Middle Ages and the seventeenth century (Margery Kempe, Bunyan) and with modern novels and the narratives of metafiction. There are also good chapters on poetry and drama. W. draws on a wide range of material; sometimes this becomes rather breathless, and exposition of plots and themes predominates too heavily over analysis. There is no conclusion, which is a pity, since the argument needs to be pulled together at the end. But the book remains an excellent account of a subject growing in appeal to both theologians and literary critics, and badly in need of this kind of lucid and readable exposition.

J. BARTON

8. THE SURROUNDING PEOPLES

ABITZ, F.: *Baugeschichte und Dekoration des Grabes Ramses' VI* (OBO 89). 1989. Pp. 196. (Universitätsverlag, Freiburg (CH); Vandenhoeck & Ruprecht, Göttingen. Price: Sw.Fr. 49.00. ISBN 3 7278 0637 0; 3 525 53719 0)

In this work, Abitz continues his studies of the form and decoration of the great royal tombs of New-Kingdom Egypt (*c*. 1550–1070 B.C.) in the Valley of the Kings at Luxor. Here, he presents the lavishly-decorated tomb of Rameses VI (*c*. 1140 B.C.), seen by so many modern visitors. In its arrangement of corridors and halls, this tomb follows tradition. Its original owner (Rameses V) began traditional decoration, but died early; so R. VI took it over and imposed a radically new programme of decoration on the tomb: essentially the entire *Book of Gates* and *Book of Caverns* on facing walls the length of the tomb. The theological implications are then set out. The whole is prefaced with an inquest into the history of the two royal mummies involved, and with some discussion of the family relationships of thes two kings (R. V and VI). A book of more interest to Egyptologists than to Old Testament scholars.

K. A. KITCHEN

BARUCQ, A., CHRISTMANN-FRANCK, L., DURAND, J. M., SEUX, M.-J., and DE TARRAGON, J.-M.: *Prières de l'Ancien Orient* (Documents autour de la Bible). 1989. Pp. 99. (Cerf, Paris. Price: Fr 53.00. ISBN 2 204 03085 6)

This brief anthology falls into four parts. The first cites three Sumerian and eighteen Akkadian texts; the second six Hittite texts; the third five Ugaritic ones, and the fourth nine Egyptian ones. The title is erroneous: judging from the contents and the headings of the sections it should be *Hymnes et Prières* . . . A short introduction is provided for each section and each text, and biblical passages similar in form, idiom for thought are plentifully cited. Suggestions for further reading are given as an appendix, followed by an index of biblical references, and a useful grid chart showing the incidence of biblical theological motifs and their analogues in the Near Eastern material. The hymn to the Aten (pp. 68–72) is *not* suggested as a source for biblical monotheism! This is an attractive presentation of some of the most typical expressions of popular and official piety from the ancient world.

N. WYATT

CAQUOT, A., DE TARRAGON, J.-M., and CUNCHILLOS, J.-L.: *Textes Ougaritiques*. Tome II: *Textes religieux, Rituels, Correspondance* (Litteratures Anciennes du Proche-Orient, 14). 1989. Pp. 478. (Cerf, Paris. ISBN 2 204 02916 5; ISSN 0459 5831)

The second volume of *Textes Ougaritiques* has appeared fifteen years after the publication of the first volume, *Mythes et Légendes* (reviewed in *B. L.* 1975, p. 89). Three different types of material are presented: (a) religious texts (by A. Caquot), (b) rituals (by J.-M. de Tarragon), and (c) correspondence (by J.-L. Cunchillos). As the title implies, the texts treated were written in the Ugaritic language (or, in the case of one of one or two rituals, Ugaritic and Hurrian); most were found at Ras Shamra, but a few were discovered at nearby Ras Ibn Hani. The introduction to each text includes such information as the size and state of preservation of the tablet, the location of its discovery, or comments on its contents. A bibliography is provided for each text, and the translations are very fully annotated. A commendable feature of the notes is the extent to which the translators acknowledge and present differing interpretations of other scholars. In common with other volumes of the *Littératures Anciennes du Proche-Orient* series, no transcription of the texts is provided. There are separate indices for the religious texts, rituals, and correspondence.

The religious texts comprise a number of mythological fragments, mythico-magical texts, and what Caquot describes as vestiges of a mythico-ritual complex about the Rephaim, who are regarded as divinised ancestors. An interesting feature of the rituals is the clues they provide to the nature of the king's participation in the cult. De Tarragon notes that a ritual text would have served as an *aide-mémoire* for the priest, so it is not surprising that the actual ritual is not described in detail. In presenting a selection of letters, Cunchillos suggests that Ugaritic would have been used only for domestic and internal correspondence; he is not convinced that any of the translation into Ugaritic, as has been suggested.

This volume is to be welcomed not only for its detailed treatment of the texts included, but for the fact that the translations will make available to a wider audience some little known material. An English equivalent would be welcome!

A. H. W. Curtis

Cunchillos-Ilarri, J. L.: *Estudios de epistolografía ugarítica* (Fuentes de la Ciencia bíblica, 3). 1989. (Institución San Jerónimo, Valencia. ISBN 84 86067 29 4)

Generally speaking, the eighty-five or so letters in Ugaritic now available to scholars have received scant attention. The present volume, the first and only book specifically on this topic (but note the book reviewed immediately above), is in fact a collection of articles by the author, some translated from French. He prefaces these studies with a summary account of the excavation and history of Ras Shamra followed by a bibliography of works on the Ugaritic letters. The next chapter examines seven of the letters and in the following three chapters the grammar, semantics, and religious elements of these letters are described. The last chapter discusses the syntagma *šmʿ l* in Gen. 17, 20 and in Ugaritic. The book is completed by 24 pages of line drawings, a general bibliography, and copious indices. The book reflects the author's changes of mind over the years and there is some unnecessary repetition. Even so, it will help and encourage students to read these interesting documents.

W. G. E. Watson

Dalley, S.: *Myths from Mesopotamia: Creation, The Flood, Gilgamesh, and others*. Translated with an Introduction and Notes. 1989. Pp. xxi, 337. (Oxford University Press. Price: £35.00. ISBN 0 19 814397 4)

Babylonian Myths and Legends would have described this book more accurately, since Sumerian texts are not included, and Gilgamesh is hardly myth. The texts rendered are: Atrahasis, Gilgamesh, the Descent of Ishtar, Nergal and Ereshkigal, Adapa, Etana, Anzu, the Epic of Creation, the Theology of Dunnu, and the Erra Epic (here called Erra and Ishum). This is thus all the major and adequately preserved Babylonian texts of the genres, and of the last it is the first more or less reliable translation in English. The work is scholarly in that it is based on the original texts and draws on the whole range of previous work, but it is not meant as a definitive edition. The original tablets were not collated, and in some cases important corrections would have resulted. Brief notes at the end of each translation explain the basis of the interpretations adopted, but otherwise the book is meant for readers who are not cuneiformists. Each text is introduced and a Glossary explains names. Also the translations are readable. This can then replace the translations of N.K. Sandars in the Penguin Classics, those of E. A. Speiser in *ANET*, and the Gilgamesh and Epic of Creation, those of A. Heidel. However, due to the state of the field these translations must not be relied upon as might good translations from Greek and Latin Classics. Also the author's wide reading is matched with a certain whimsicality, so that in the Introductions, which tend to give material for scholars rather than explanations of the texts, simple factual material is not always correct. To illustrate from two examples with Old Testament interest, the name Uta-napishtim in the Gilgamesh Epic is written Uta-naishtim on a single tablet, probably by scribal error. The author considers it just possible that by abbreviation: (Uta-)naish(tim) is the origin of the name Noah in Genesis. It is also stated that in Genesis the mountain on which the ark landed is named Ararat.

The price will no doubt discourage many.

W. G. LAMBERT

DOLCE, R. and ZACCAGNINI, C. (eds): *Il Pane del Re — accumulo e distribu-zione dei cereali nell'Oriente Antico* (Studi di Storia Antica 13). 1989. Pp. 135, (Editrice Cooperativa Libraria Universitaria Editrice Bologna, Bologna. Price: Lire 20,000)

This slim, elegant volume (based on a seminar of April 1985) reviews the storage and distribution of grain and its products in the ancient Near East. The five essays run in chronological sequence. R. Dolce briefly considers possible archaeological traces of food-storage, bakery-quarters, and the like in Mesopotamia (Abu Salabikh; Tells Brak, Asmar, Chagar Bazar; Ur) and Syria (Hama) in the 4th/3rd millennia B.C. M. Frangipane reconsiders the correlation between the 'bevelled rim bowls' of Mesopotamia and S.E. Anatolia and the three levels of grain-ration attested in third-millennium texts. Some 67% of recipients had only small portions, some 27% or so merited middle-sized portions, and only 2–6% rated big portions. L. Milano usefully outlines the rise, development, and decline of the state/temple ration-issuing systems in Mesopotamia and Syria for the 3rd to 2nd millennia B.C., noting changes that arose in successive periods and between these two areas. C. Zaccagnini in turn continues the theme for the 2nd and 1st millennia B.C. Besides Mesopotamia, he touches on Genesis 46–47 and on Egyptian data of the New Kingdom. Finally, C. Grottanelli considers grain-distribution and religious ideals in the Hebrew Bible, from its rather different vantage-point; he deals with David, Joseph, Boaz, Elisha, and Hezekiah, not always convincingly. Overall, this work is a convenient first reference enabling through its references those interested to go further.

K. A. KITCHEN

DURAND, J.-M.: *Archives épistolaires de Mari*, I/1 (Archives royales de Mari, 26). 1988. Pp. xi, 693, and 3 fiches. (Editions Recherche sur les Civilisations, A.D.P.F., Paris. Price: Fr 236.00. ISBN 2 86538 189 7)

CHARPIN, D., JOANNÈS, F., LACKENBACHER, S., and LAFONT, B.: *Archives épistolaires de Mari*, I/2 (Archives royales de Mari, 26). 1988. Pp. 589, and 3 fiches. (Editions Recherche sur les Civilisations, A.D.P.F., Paris. Price: Fr 229.00. ISBN 2 86538 190 0)

That Mari letters have been available for many years is not a reason to neglect these two volumes. The appointment of a new team of workers some few years ago has resulted in a much more systematic and thorough examination of the whole archive, accompanied by exhaustive studies of matters of content. Whereas the previous volumes have been mainly first attempts at decipherment and translation, these volumes (and a third of the series yet to appear) attempt a systematic gathering of related material with appropriate commentary. And many of the letters are published for the first time. The first of these two volumes deals with letters of mainly religious content, the second with those of more historical relevance. The main topics covered in the first volume, in descending order of quantity of material, are divination, prophecy, dreams, omens, the river ordeal, and sickness. There is much of Old

Testament interest here both in the letters and in the author's comments. Though each author is responsible for his own section, their work in a common physical environment means that mutual help and criticism result in higher standards than would otherwise be achieved. For the date of publication this is an authoritative work, and for the quantity of material remarkably inexpensive.

W. G. LAMBERT

GREENE, J. T.: *The Role of the Messenger and Message in the Ancient Near East* (Brown Judaic Studies, 169). 1989. Pp. xx, 346. (Scholars Press, Atlanta GA. Price: $65.95 (member price: $43.95). ISBN 1 55540 324 7)

In spite of its title this doctoral dissertation (completed in 1980) focuses mainly on the Hebrew scriptures. Unlike the semitic linguist Meier, whose more recent study *The Messenger in the Ancient Semitic World* is reviewed on p. 124, Greene is a biblical scholar and devotes less than one quarter of his book to the ANE evidence 'from ca. 3000 to ca. 30 BCE'. After a thorough 'taxonomic' study of biblical passages where *ml'k* and related terms (e.g. *'bd*, *rkb ssym*, *hmrglym*, *mazkir*) occur, Greene moves on in Part II to examine the evidence for what he terms the 'Great Individual Prophet as Messenger'. This involves a historical study of prophecy from the Mari texts to I Macc. 4:46, and a detailed literary analysis of the relevant formulae and *Gattungen* in the prophetic literature. There is then a final comparative study of ANE messengers, the messenger of the Hebrew scriptures, and the Great Individual Prophet. Greene has little difficulty in showing how rarely the text specifically uses Hebrew terms for 'messenger' and 'message' in relation to the prophets (only Haggai is actually described as a messenger), and how imprecise some of the conventional form-critical categories are. A function-comparative study of the biblical prophet and ANE messengers, however, proves to be far less negative, and on the last page the author wisely updates his original research by recommending N. K. Gottwald and R. R. Wilson for further reading.

J. F. A. SAWYER

HENNINGER, J., SVD: *Arabica Varia: Aufsätze zur Kulturgeschichte Arabiens und seiner Randgebiete* (OBO 90). 1989. Pp. 498. (Universitätsverlag, Freiburg (CH); Vandenhoeck & Ruprecht, Göttingen. Price: Sw.Fr. 120.00. ISBN 3 7278 0638 9; 3 525 53720 4)

This collection of twelve essays and seven reviews (all previously published between 1938 and 1976) by the veteran ethnologist and orientalist is uniform with his earlier collection, *Arabica Sacra*, OBO 40, 1981, noted in *B. L.* 1982, p. 14.

The articles cover a wide range: especially, ancient Bedouin society, Arab genealogy, property rights among the modern Bedouin, the rights of the first-born, Arabian 'pariah' tribes, polyandry in pre-Islamic Arabia, totemism, alleged circumcision practices in S.W. Arabia. The reviews discuss works on Bedouin laws and customs by E. Gräf, J. Chelhod, C, G. Feilberg and J. Sonnen, and three volumes on rock-art in central Arabia by E. Anati. While impeccably scholarly and phenomenological in approach, a major concern, as in earlier works of his, is to illuminate the biblical narrative (so, even in the shorter articles on leather garments, cf. Elijah, John the Baptist, and the song of the angels at the Nativity). The approach has been somewhat out of fashion since the great days of W. Robertson Smith: the volume does much to bridge the gap between then and now (the article on totemism, beginning with a critical appraisal of Smith's work, is particularly helpful in this regard). A welcome feature, so often irritatingly lacking in such collections, is that, though the original pagination is indicated, the author's views have been brought up-to-date by often substantial additions in square brackets both to the text and the copious notes. The work concludes with a bibliography of the author's works from 1976 to 1989.

W. JOHNSTONE

KEEL, O., KEEL-LEU, H., and SCHROER, S.: *Studien zu den Stempelsiegeln aus Palästina/Israel* (OBO 88). 1989, Pp. x, 349 including many illustrations. (Universitätsverlag, Freiburg (CH); Vandenhoeck & Ruprecht, Göttingen. Price: Sw.Fr. 88.00. ISBN 3 7278 0629 X; 3 525 53718 2)

Within the multiplicity of designs on stamp and cylinder seals found in Palestine there are numerous motifs which can be identified and followed over the centuries. Four of the essays in this volume deal with such topics. Othmar Keel discusses the omega-like shape appearing on scarabs and cylinder seals from the Middle Bronze Age onwards, believed to represent the womb, while Silvia Schroer collects examples of the naked goddess in various poses, and of the goddess' head alone, both being found especially with leaves or branches, blending Egyptian and Levantine motifs. Keel continues with a catalogue of scarabs which he argues share features with the Syrian 'Green Jasper Workshop' of the seventeenth century B.C. isolated by D. Collon, and have Egyptianising traits of worshipper and falcon denoting loyalty to the king, and contrasting with the omega type. He then examines the falcon-headed figure on Hyksos period seals and scarabs, identifying it with Horus and Canaanite Baal (later equated with Seth), and finally investigates designs displaying the god Ptah from *c.* 1600 B.C. All these engravings exhibit varying degrees of interplay and influence from Egypt, Babylonia, and Syria in Palestine. Their significance is considered in each case and personal relationships with the deities suggested, a matter which has to remain speculative. Nevertheless, these investigations underline the richness and variety of iconography in Canaan during the second millennium B.C. Hildi Keel-Leu's opening essay in a useful catalogue of the stamp-seals from Palestine from Neolithic times to *c.* 2000 B.C.

A. R. MILLARD

KESSLER, D.: *Die heiligen Tiere und der König.* Teil I: *Beiträge zu Organisation, Kult und Theologie der spätzeitlichen Tierfriedhöfe* (Ägypten und Altes Testament, 16). 1989. Pp. xi, 303 and 10 photographic tables. (Harrassowitz, Wiesbaden. Price: DM 78.00. ISBN 3 447 02863 7)

This closely-printed volume represents the most detailed consideration so far of the well-known 'animal cults' of Ancient Egypt; a second volume is to follow this one. In the latest periods of Egyptian history, from the 26th to 30th Dynasties (*c.* 664–340 B.C.) and especially during the Ptolemaic and Roman periods (323 B.C. to 3rd century A.D.), concern with sacred animals reached unprecedented proportions. In earlier times particular exemplars were chosen in single succession (e.g., the Apis Bull), as a 'living image' in the cult of a deity. But in these later periods, whole species of animals — involving thousands of cats, ibises, etc. — were reared, kept, and buried in vast cemeteries the length of Egypt. Previously, this development had been explained as a 'nationalist' reaction, to be different to Greeks and others, or as an upsurge of latent popular 'grass-roots' religion. Instead, Kessler would relate it to the reorganization of the state cult of the pharaoh, with the animals playing a specific role in the festivals of kingship (as did the Apis). However (unless in Volume II), he does not explain why such a reorganization should lead to the *en masse* rearing and ceremonial burial of so many of these creatures. This volume surveys the known centres of such cults from all sources, all the known types of animals involved, and the appropriate administrative and religious organizations attested; Volume II is to deal with the animals' function in the royal feasts.

K. A. KITCHEN

Lesko, B. S.: (ed.): *Women's Earliest Records. From Ancient Egypt and Western Asia*. Proceedings of the Conference on Women in the Ancient Near East held at Brown University in November 1987 (Brown Judaic Studies, 166). 1989. Pp. xl, 350. (Scholars Press, Atlanta GA. Price: $69.95 (member price: $49.95). ISBN 1 55540 319 0)

This volume contains the proceedings of a conference held in Brown University, Rhode Island in 1987 on the subject of Women in the Ancient Near East, in particular non-royal women. The papers read by the thirteen contributors are each followed by notes of the ensuing discussions sustained by seventeen official respondents chosen from a range of disciplines, together with an occasional interjection from the audience! The papers in the main concern the role and status of women in Egypt and Mesopotamia in the third, second, and first millennia. Only two papers deal directly with ancient Israel, the subjects being 'Women and the Domestic Economy of Early Israel' (Carol Meyers) and 'Women's Religion in Ancient Israel' (Phyllis Bird). There is some discussion of the particular problems associated with enquiry into the biblical past in the light of the long transmission of the traditions within the religious communities of Judaism and Christianity. Detailed footnotes and extensive bibliographies add to the volume's usefulness, and there are thirty-six illustrations.

G. I. Emmerson

Lichtheim, M.: *Ancient Egyptian Autobiographies chiefly of the Middle Kingdom: A Study and an Anthology* (OBO 84). 1988. Pp. 171, and 10 plates. (Universitätsverlag, Freiberg (CH); Vandenhoeck & Ruprecht, Göttingen. Price: SW.Fr. 85.00. ISBN 3 7278 0594 3; 3 525 53713 1)

This latest study by Miriam Lichtheim brings together a series of clear, modern translations of sixty ancient Egyptian texts of a particular type: the formal 'autobiography' of the kind that Egyptiam officials delighted to place in their tombs or on stelae. Here, the author presents a well-dated series covering almost a millennium, from about 2600 B.C. to the 13th Dynasty, about 1700 B.C. Hence, one may see step by step the clearly-documented growth of a literary tradition, based directly on tangible data, not on speculation. Earliest forms rapidly crystallized around essential features, with an ongoing history, varying some elements with time's passing.

Basic elements are the funerary formula, the official's full titles, biographical details of varying extent and originality, an appeal to the living for their prayers if not offerings, and a warning to visitors not to harm the monument or tomb. Two special topics receive excellent treatment. One is the 'Abydos formula', a phrase that covers good wishes for an afterlife with the god Osiris, which show a development. The other is the 'terrace of the great god' at Abydos, which the author would identify as 'the Osiris . . . temple complex or a particular part of it' (p. 131). One may rather suggest that it was the processional ascent from that temple to the necropolis, overlooked by the tombs, votive chapels, and stelae of the pious who looked for Osiris's blessing. The book ends with excellent plates, illustrating four notable stelae, and (in colour) relevant areas at Abydos.

K. A. Kitchen

Margalit, B.: *The Ugaritic Poem of Aqht. Text. Translation. Commentary* (BZAW, 182). 1989. Pp. xvii, 534. 4 photographic plates. 1 map. (De Gruyter, Berlin. Price: DM 198.00. ISBN 0 89925 472 1)

Up till now there has been no comprehensive study of the lengthy Ugaritic poetic text 'Aqht' (KTU 1.17, 18, and 19). Margalit's full-scale study is the first such commentary to appear and is certainly very welcome. A critical survey of previous work on 'Aqht' by twenty-seven scholars is followed immediately by a prosodic analysis of the Ugaritic text and some comments on textual criticism. The full text of the poem is then set out, followed by a translation, and detailed 'textual and epigraphic notes'. These preliminaries over, as it were, the next couple of hundred pages are devoted to a 'literary commentary' interspersed with a series of excursuses (22 in all) many on philological topics. The book closes with a few pages on 'Ugaritic Literature and the Hebrew Bible' and the principles of Ugaritic prosody are set out in the Appendix. There are indices and a bibliography.

The author follows a very strong line of interpretation which not all scholars accept. He is to be congratulated for providing a collated edition based on the original tablets and for giving such a comprehensive account of a difficult Ugaritic text. He is also correct in explaining the text on its own terms without depending too much on comparative material. The result is a scholarly, stimulating yet very readable account of an important document from Ras Shamra.

W. G. E. WATSON

MAZZA, F., RIBICHINI, S., and XELLA, P.: *Fonti classiche per la civiltà fenicia e punica*, I. *Fonti letterarie greche dalle origini alla fine dell'età classica* (Collezione du Studi Fenici, 27, Testimonia Phoenicia 1). 1988. Pp. 158, 4 plates (Consiglio Nazionale delle Richerche, Istituto per la Civiltà Fenicia e Punica, Rome)

Under the aegis of Sabatino Moscati Phoenician studies have blossomed in Italy, and one need revealed has been a collection of all references to Phoenicians, their country, culture, religion, and language from ancient foreign sources. This first volume of Greek texts provides all available references from Homer to Hanno, including fragments and scholia. The texts are clearly printed in Greek and arranged in chronological order, without comment. A list of editions used is given at the beginning of the book and an index of all authors quoted at the end. There are comprehensive indices of names and subjects (e.g. human sacrifice, navigation, textiles). Four black and white reproductions of medieval and renaissance manuscripts relieve the text. When the project is complete, it will provide easy access to both well-known and obscure Greek and Latin writers and allow a more balanced picture of classical knowledge of the Phoenician world than the often-cited major authors offer. It is interesting, too, to compare the features that evoked comment from Greek authors with those the Old Testament books highlight.

A. R. MILLARD

MEIER, S. A.: *The Messenger in the Ancient Semitic World* (Harvard Semitic Monographs, 45). 1988. Pp. xvii, 269. (Scholars Press, Atlanta GA. Price: $13.95 (member price: $9.95). ISBN 1 55540 289 5)

This is a very interesting study of an important, though largely neglected part of the ancient Semitic world. Although it is restricted to an analysis of passages where West Semitic *mal'āk* and Akkadian *mār šipri* happen to occur, it throws much light on the role of messenger and the procedures for delivering and receiving messages. The material is clearly and imaginatively arranged under the headings 'selecting the messenger', 'commissioning the messenger', 'the messenger on the road' (including 'Safety in numbers?'), 'the messenger's arrival' (including 'Who bows to whom?), 'translators', 'memorizing the message', 'deceptive messengers', 'interrogating the messenger', 'caring for the messenger', and so on. Because of its terms of reference it has little to say directly on many familiar examples from the Bible, and the approach is linguistic (Cross, Moran, Lambdin, et al.) rather than literary (Alonso Schökel, Westermann, Alter, et al.). It is for others to build on Meier's valuable research and apply it where it is needed.

J. F. A. Sawyer

Niwinski, A.: *Studies on the Illustrated Theban Funerary Papyri of the 11th and 10th Centuries B.C.* (OBO 86). 1989, Pp. xxxii, 402 with xvii tables and 49 black and white plates. (Universitätsverlag, Freiburg (CH); Vandenhoeck & Ruprecht, Göttingen. Price: Sw.Fr. 118.00. ISBN 3 7278 0613 3; 3 525 53716 6)

This very substantial study is devoted to Egyptian funerary papyri of specifically the 21st Dynasty (*c.* 1070–945 B.C.). At that period, after the palmy days of the Empire were over and gone, lavishly-decorated tomb-chapels ceased to be made and used; aspirants to a good burial now had buried with them instead a pair of (usually) illustrated papyri for their other worldly benefit. One by the shoulder or chest would be a Book of the Dead, a selected set of spells 'for appearing by day'; the other, placed down between the legs, was the solar-oriented Am-Duat, 'What is in the Netherworld', and derived from a work previously the exclusive privilege of royalty.

Using the evidence of 427 manuscripts in the world's more accessible collections (still others exist), the author establishes the use of the papyri outlined above, and of the sub-classes of such documents, when classified by contents. A trend towards illustrations over texts is discernible; also, the text of a spell need not be given in full — the principle of *pars pro toto* meant that a maximum range of (supposedly) beneficial spells could be included notionally in any given document. The author gives a full list of all documents used, their owners' names and titles, and finally a fine set of photographic plates of representative documents of each type and sub-type. A valuable tool for Egyptologists rather than Old Testament scholars.

K. A. Kitchen

Parker, S. B.: *The Pre-Biblical Narrative Tradition* (SBL Resources for Biblical study 24). 1989. Pp. 248. (Scholars, Atlanta GA. Price: $29.95 (member price: $19.95); paperback price: $19.95 (member price: $13.95). ISBN 1 55540 300 X; 1 55540 301 8 (pbk))

Two introductory chapters outline and analyse the main features of Ugaritic poetry, with particular reference to parallelism, formulaic language, and various other stereotyped forms of speech occurring in the narrative poems. Two further chapters look in more detail at the Aqhat and Keret stories. The same approach is taken with each: a block-by-block analysis is made of the narrative, with frequent comparison with materials of similar structure from the surrounding world, leading at times to suggested reconstructions of lacunae, and constant allusion to the literary function of the forms outlined previously. Final assessments are made of each: Aqhat is not a quarry for ideological studies or a fertility, or astral myth, it is a poem 'which may have been enjoyed as a satisfying portrayal of life in an idealized past era . . . a "classic" of ugaritic (*sic*) society' (p. 143). Keret, far from bolstering traditional royal ideological values, reveals the essential helplessness of the king in the face of tragedy: 'Superhuman status is not a feature of Keret's identity as king . . . He is, in fact, all too mortal' (p. 213). A final chapter argues that the traditional nature of the Ugaritic poetry, betraying very clearly its oral origins and bardic techniques, is useful both for an understanding of biblical literary forms, and for purposes of seeing theological development in West Semitic religion. The absence of indices is a matter for regret.

N. Wyatt

POWELL, M. A. (ed.): *Labor in the Ancient Near East* (American Oriental Society 68). 1987. Pp. xiv, 289. (Eisenbrauns, Winona Lake, Indiana. Price: $32.00. ISBN 0 940490 68 4)

These are the ancient Near East papers from an economic history congress held in Edinburgh in 1978, with some further contributions specially commissioned to fill gaps in the coverage. After a short introductory discussion of problems of definition by I. M. Diakonoff (pp. 1–3), there are twelve specialist papers on the theme of labour. Two major contributions are by C. J. Eyre on 'Work and the Organisation of Work' in Old and New Kingdom Egypt (pp. 5–47, 167–221). A paper by O. D. Berlev deals with Nubia under Sesostris I (pp. 143–57). Three contributions are concerned with aspects of the matter in pre-Sargonic and Ur III Mesopotamia (K. Maekawa [pp. 49–71], P. Steinkeller [pp. 73–115], H. Waetzoldt [pp. 117–411]). H. Klengel (pp. 159–66) surveys 'Non-Slave Labour in the Old Babylonian Period', while G. Dosch (pp. 223–35) covers the same subject for Nuzi. M. Heltzer (pp. 237–50) adds 'Labour in Ugarit' to the list of his important studies in Ugaritic economy and society. Forms of non-slave labour among the Hittites are studied briefly by G. G. Giorgadze (pp. 251–55). Finally the Neo-Assyrian Empire and very late Babylonia (to the 4th century B.C.) are the focuses of contributions by J. N. Postgate (pp. 257–70) and M. A. Dandamaev (pp. 271–79) respectively. Indices complete the volume, which is a useful contribution to the understanding of this important theme. Since it covers such a wide area, it should become a standard source of reference on the subject of labour. The background it provides is important for the study of Biblical society and law.

J. F. HEALEY

VON SCHULER, E. (ed.): *XXIII. Deutscher Orientalistentag (von 16. bis 20. September 1985 in Würzburg): Ausgewählte Vorträge* (Zeitschrift der Deutschen Morgenländischen Gesellschaft, Supplement VII). 1989. Pp. 717. (Franz Steiner, Stuttgart. Price: DM 298.00. ISBN 3 515 04961 4)

As might be expected, the papers of the 23rd *Orientalistentag* cover a wide range of topics. Very few are of Old Testament interest, others will be of interest to Semitists and Christian Orient, and ancient Near East specialists. K. Aartun writes on 'Ugaritisch *bnš(m)* ' (pp. 13–21), tackling the objections to the usual derivation from *bn+(')nš* as "son of man". He appeals to a supposed ancient Semitic *bū-* prefix (secondarily *'abū*), a determinative which indicates that the word that it is attached to denotes a particular species. This occurrence would be unique in Ugaritic. The author adduces examples from Mandaic and Arabic (though these latter are normally understood to be forms derived from *'abū*, 'father'). G. Wedel's paper on impediments to marriage among the Samaritans according to the eleventh-century Middle Arabic work of Abū l-Ḥasan of Tyre (pp. 28–37) involves detailed comparison with Lev. 18. Only H. Cazelles' paper on 'Die biblische Geschichtsschreibung im Licht der altorientalischen Geschichtsschreibung' (pp. 38–49) is directly biblical. On the biblical side, according to Cazelles, historical certainties are very few, especially in relation to the patriarchal texts, but in a wide-ranging discussion the author recommends study of ancient literary patterns as providing a firm starting-point. Christian Orient contributors deal with Mechitar of Sebaste (M. K. Arat, pp. 50–62), Cosmas Indicopleustes and Enoch (S. Uhlig, pp. 62–75) and Armenian sources for 5th-century (Armenian) church history (G. Winkler, pp. 76–94). To be noted are contributions on Hittite cultic cries and their relation to specific cultic acts (E. Badalì, pp. 282–92) and on Hurrian grammar (E. Neu, pp. 293–303). Finally there are a few papers of Semitic interest: R. Kontzi on Maltese (pp. 148–57). M. Woidich on verb-stems in Egyptian Arabic (pp. 200–10) and K. Petrácek on Saharan and Hamito-Semitic (pp. 543–60).

J. F. HEALEY

SEIDL, U. *Die babylonischen Kudurru-Reliefs: Symbole mesopotamischer Gottheiten* (OBO 87). 1989. Pp. 235 and 33 black and white plates. (Universitätsverlag, Freiburg (CH); Vanderhoeck & Ruprecht, Göttingen. Price: Sw.Fr. 64.00. ISBN 3 7278 0603 6; 3 525 53717 4)

Babylonian boundary stones (*kudurru*) date from *c.* 1400–600 B.C. and record assignments of land, mostly royal grants. Most end with a list of curses invoking gods against anyone who might seek to frustrate the transfer of land. In addition a majority have engraved on them pictorial symbols of the gods so invoked. In practice the names in the text on one stone never agree exactly with the carved symbols. Apparently one craftsman engraved the writing, another the art-work. These symbols are not limited to boundary stones but occur on many archaeological objects, some of great interest to Old Testament scholars. This work was a thesis written under the late A. Moortgat at the Free University of Berlin, first published as a long article in *Baghdader Mitteilungen* 4 (1968), and its reprinting is a testimony to its worth. It is a study strictly of the carved symbols. The whole corpus of stones is mustered in groups and each stone is described with pertinent details and full bibliography. Then the various symbols are studied one by one, with citation of literature for each. Examples from objects other than boundary stones are also collected so that the comments and attribution (where possible) to a named god have bearing on the symbols generally. There are two limitations: no first-hand use is made of ancient written sources, which indeed exist, and there is no discussion on the ideology and explanations of these symbols. Why was a spade the symbol of Marduk?

The new edition is reproduced from the original, but with smaller margins, and the plates are slightly reduced in size. Fifteen pages of *Nachträge* bring the book up to date, and include a most useful chart of drawings of the major symbols with the gods they indicated named.

W. G. LAMBERT

WILHELM, G.: *The Hurrians*. Translated by J. Barnes, and with a chapter by D. L. Stein (Ancient Near East Series). 1989. Pp. ix, 132. (Aris & Phillips, Warminster. Price: £16.00; paperback price: £8.75. ISBN 0 85668 442 2)

This is a translation and updating, with additional material, of the author's *Grundzüge der Geschichte und Kultur der Hurriter*, 1982 (see *Book List* 1984, p. 119). It is an excellent survey of history (to *c.* 1200 B.C.), society, religion, literature, and art (the last being covered by an additional chapter by Diana L. Stein). It is most useful to have this in English and at such a reasonable price. It has little direct relevance to the Old Testament, since the ancient Hurrians have little if anything to do with the Biblical *ḥōrīm* (see p. 1). There is, however, material of interest on religion, for example on cathartic rites, and some reference to discussions about Nuzi and Patriarchs. The book is well provided with bibliographies and illustrations (including a map).

J. F. HEALEY

9. APOCRYPHA AND POST-BIBLICAL STUDIES

BABCOCK, W. S.: *Tyconius: The Book of Rules*. Translated with an Introduction and Notes (SBL Texts and Translations 31; Early Christian Literature Series 7). 1989. Pp. xiii, 153. (Scholars Press, Atlanta GA. Price: $14.95 (member price: $9.95); paperback price: $9.95 (member price: $7.95). ISBN 1 55540 366 2; 1 55540 367 0 (pbk))

This is a welcome new edition of an important document in the history of biblical interpretation. Tyconius (died *c.* A.D. 400) was a member of the Donatist church whose theology was not Donatist but catholic; his rules for biblical interpretation were appreciated by Augustine, whose indebtedness to them is acknowledged especially in *De Doctrina Christiana*. The rules are grouped under seven headings: The Lord and his body, the Lord's bipartite body, the promises and the law, the particular and the general, times, recapitulation, the devil and his body. They present, over and above their stated subject, an exposition of the doctrine of the church. Tyconius understood the interplay of 'the one and the many' in biblical teaching; in one place he anticipates T. W. Manson's societary understanding of the Son of Man in the Gospels.

In this edition the Latin text is taken over with minor modifications from F. C. Burkitt's edition in Cambridge Texts and Studies (1894); it is exhibited on left hand pages with an English translation on the right, and the value of the work is enhanced by an introduction and notes.

F. F. BRUCE

BLANK, S. H. (ed.): *Hebrew Union College Annual*, Vol. LIX (1988). 1989. Pp. x, 288 and 11 (Hebrew). (Hebrew Union College, Cincinnati. Price: $30.00. ISSN 360 9049)

The current issue maintains the journal's high standards of stimulating content and technical production and offers four articles of special interest to students of the Old Testament. The prevalent interpretation of Exodus 23:5 is sharply challenged by A. Cooper in a historical and philological examination that concludes that it is *non*-intervention that is being enjoined. A detailed study of almost monograph length by B. Wacholder discusses the date, content, and liturgical significance of 11Q Psalms[a], speculatively relating it to an amalgam of David's historical and eschatological roles and to the history of Jewish liturgy, particularly at Qumran. The process of reconsidering Scholem's ideas about the continuation in hekhaloth literature of the apocalyptic tradition is taken further by M. Himmelfarb who demonstrates that while the liturgical aspects of the heavenly ascents support such a link, the details of the ascents themselves show greater parallels between the hekhaloth, gnostic literature, and magical papyri. The rare phenomenon of a dual competence in early Christian and rabbinic interpretations of scripture is exhibited by M. Hirshman in his comparative analysis of exegetical treatments of Ecclesiastes in the sixth and seventh centuries. Remaining contributions deal with the Balaamites of Deir ʿAlla (A. Wolters), Jewish Lydda in Roman times (A. Oppenheimer), quotation-forms in the Talmud (R. Kalmin), David Qimḥi's lexicography (N. Netzer, in Hebrew) and with themes in Jewish philosophy (H. Kreisel), Kabbalah (E. Wolfson), and Passover Haggadah illumination (J. C. Reeves and L. Waggoner).

S. C. REIF

BLOCK, P., BLOMQVIST, J., SUNDSTRÖM, G.-B. and ÅSBERG, C.: *'God och nyttig läsning'. Om Gamla Testamentets Apokrypher*. 1988. Pp. 234, many ills. in the text. (Proprius förlag, Stockholm. ISBN 91 7118 624 7)

The main title of this work, 'Good and useful reading', was Luther's characterization of the Old Testament Apocrypha. Its authors were the regular members of the panel which produced the new Swedish translation of the Apocrypha (see *B. L.* 1987, p. 43), to which this volume is an admirable companion. Two of the six essays in it are the work of J. Blomqvist. The first ('The Menace of Hellenization and the Jewish Resistance') is a sketch of the historical background from the death of Alexander till 63 B.C. The other ('Apocrypha and Pseudepigrapha') outlines the content and character of the apocryphal books and their relationship to the Old and New Testaments and the Pseudepigrapha, including the Qumran writings. In 'The Changing Religion' P. Block examines the modification of religious beliefs and moral standards under the pressure of events and changing circumstances and elucidates the position of the Apocrypha as a link between the Old and New Testaments. In 'Concerning Women' Gun-Britt Sundström writes about the attitude to women in the Apocrypha. She adopts a different approach to the same theme in 'Saint and Whore: the Judith Motif in Literature'. 'The Legacy of the Apocrypha', by C. Åsberg, is a survey of the influence of the Apocrypha on theological, devotional, and general literature, and a sketch of the steps taken towards the production of the new Swedish translation. The volume concludes with a brief bibliography and a series of educational exercises related to each of the essays. 'Good and useful reading' is an apt description of the entire work.

G. W. Anderson

Boid, I. R. M.: *Principles of Samaritan Halachah* (Studies in Judaism in Late Antiquity, 38). 1989. Pp. xiv, 362. (Brill, Leiden. Price: fl 155.00; ca. $77.50. ISBN 90 04 07479 1; ISSN 0169 961 x)

Boid's pioneering venture in the study of Samaritan halachah is a remarkable achievement. After a preliminary discussion of the present state of research, which is not flattering to his predecessors, his method is to study one topic in detail, so as to allow conclusions over a broader range of matters to be more specifically based. His chosen topic is the 'uncleanness' which is brought about through menstrual and other discharges. The relevant manuscripts are listed and discussed (with some pungent comments on the extent of misinformation in earlier catalogues and descriptions); five Arabic texts are set out in full, with translation and detailed notes, and two conclusions are reached which, if they can be sustained, will be of major significance for students of the divisions within Judaism and of the development of the Hebrew Bible. The first is that no distinctively *Samaritan* halachah can be traced; virtually every Samaritan opinion can be paralleled within either Rabbanite or Karaite Judaism (or, more rarely, among the Falashas). The second is that the text of the Torah itself is in its halachic sections deliberately worded in an ambiguous manner so as to allow for divergence of halachic opinions which was already current. There is great potential significance here for current debates on the formation of the canon, and it is to be hoped that the apparent technicality of Boid's treatment (and the unattractiveness of his subject-matter?) will not mean that his work is neglected.

R. J. Coggins

Brooke, G. J. (ed.): *Temple Scroll Studies: Papers presented at the International Symposium on the Temple Scroll, Manchester, December 1987* (Journal for the Study of the Pseudepigrapha, Supplement Series 7). 1989. Pp. 299. (Sheffield Academic Press. Price: £26.50 ($45.00). ISBN 1 85075 200 1)

This collection of papers aims to summarise the state of scholarly research on the Temple Scroll ten years after the appearance of Yadin's edition. It is divided into five parts. Part I (Architecture, Archaeology, and Date) contains papers by J. Maier, 'The Architectural History of the Temple in Jerusalem in the light of the Temple Scroll', M. Barker, 'The Temple Measurements and the Solar Calendar', M. Delcor, 'Is the Temple Scroll a Source of the Herodian Temple', E.-M. Laperrousaz, 'Does the Temple Scroll Date from the First or Second Century B.C.E.?', and B. Thiering, 'The Date of Composition of the Temple Scroll'. Part II (Composition and Status) has H. Stegemann on 'The Literary Composition of the Temple Scroll and its Status at Qumran', and P. R. Callaway on 'Extending Divine Revelation:

Micro-Compositional Strategies in the Temple Scroll'. Part III (Exegesis and Literary Affinities) has papers by J. Milgrom, 'The Qumran Cult: Its Exegetical Principles', G. J. Brooke, 'The Temple Scroll and the New Testament', P. R. Davies, 'The Temple Scroll and the Damascus Document', and J. C. Vanderkam, 'The Temple Scroll and the Book of Jubilee'. Part IV (The Law, the Levites, and the Sadducees) has L. H. Schiffman on 'The Temple Scroll and the Systems of Jewish Law of the Second Temple Period', H. Burgmann on '11QT: The Sadducean Torah', and M. R. Lehmann on 'The Beautiful War Bride and other *Halakhoth* in the Temple Scroll'. The volume concludes with a paper by Z. J. Kapera reviewing the state of East European Studies on the Temple Scroll.

The whole volume is an interesting example of the state of scholarly debate on the Dead Sea Scrolls. As an interested outsider to the debate I was left in a state of confusion after reading this collection of studies on the Temple Scroll. It seems as though paucity of data (when will the rest of the Scrolls be published, especially the so-called 'expanded Torah Scrolls' which all agree to be crucial to understanding 11QT?), confusion of methodologies, loose definitions of terms, etc., all lead to thoroughly contradictory conclusions. There seems to be no agreement amongst the experts on the date of the Scroll (estimates given range from the fifth century B.C.E. to the turn of the era), on whether it originated prior to the formation of the Qumran Community or within it, or on its purpose or role within the Community — from pivotal (Yadin, Wacholder) to of mere antiquarian interest (Stegemann). It is certainly useful to compare results in this way but the overall lesson is clear: what we need right now from Qumran scholars is editions and translations of the texts, not general studies that will inevitably sink into the dust of history when the as yet unedited texts finally emerge.

A. P. HAYMAN

BURGMANN, H.: *Die essenischen Gemeinden von Qumrân und Damaskus in der Zeit der Hasmonäer und Herodier (130 ante — 68 post)* (Arbeiten zum Neuen Testament und Judentum, Bd. 8)). 1988. Pp. 541. (Lang, Bern–Frankfurt–New York–Paris. Price: Sw.Fr. 82.00. ISBN 3 8204 9905 9; ISSN 0170 8856)

In a highly imaginative study, Dr Burgmann succeeds in weaving together the sparse historical data relating to the Essenes assembled from Qumran literature, archaeology, and Josephus with the more substantial information concerning Jewish history from John Hyrcanus I to the first Jewish rebellion against Rome. The author is an upholder of the Maccabaean hypothesis (Jonathan and Simon are the Wicked Priests) and, as the title reveals, is a firm believer in the Essene identification of the sect, but in the course of the argument he seeks to demonstrate the presence of Pharisaic, Sadducean, and even Christian connections. (The Gospel of Matthew is claimed to disclose a strong Essene influence and J. O'Callaghan's identification of a fragment of Mark in 7Q is thought to be 'überzeugend'.) Readers may find a number of interesting remarks in these 541 pages, but few, I fear, will be convinced by the thesis as a whole. Dedicated to J. T. Milik, the volume opens with a quotation from Mommsen: 'Ohne Beihilfe der Phantasie ist weder Poesie noch Geschichte möglich.'

G. VERMES

CORRENS, D.: *Die Mischna: Text, Übersetzung und ausführliche Erklärung*, II.9: *Taanijot, Fastentage*. 1989. Pp. vii, 154. (De Gruyter, Berlin. Price: DM 128.00. ISBN 3 11 002439 X)

This volume follows the established pattern of the series: Hebrew text (fully vocalized) and German translation on facing pages, accompanied by extensive footnotes; an introduction covering in this instance the name of the tractate and its place in the Mishnah, the history of fasting and fastdays (in the

Old Testament, in the New Testament Period, and in Rabbinic Literature); the relationship between Mishnah Ta'anit and Tosefta Ta'anit; and the significance of the tractate for the history of the liturgy. The work is rounded off with a textcritical appendix listing the variants from the MSS and early printed editions (particularly useful for its collection of the scattered Genizah fragments); and a series of indices (names of Rabbis mentioned in the tractate; Greek loanwords and so forth). The approach is functional throughout, the notes often elementary. The format seems to allow only superficial analysis of the questions raised. Little attempt is made to deal with form-critical problems. This whole edition of the Mishnah (which was begun under the editorship of Georg Beer and Oscar Holtzmann!) is still being cast in the mould of the earliest volumes. It now has a decidedly old-fashioned air. Correns bibliography of 'Wichtige Literatur' (p. 153) lists only three works dating from after the Second World War: one is Stemberger's revision of Strack, the other two are encyclopaedias. Schürer is cited from the 1901 German edition. However, despite the limitations, this work — like its companion volumes — will undoubtedly provide students with a helpful initiation into a tractate of the Mishnah.

P. S. Alexander

Crown, A. D. (ed.): *The Samaritans*. 1989. Pp. xxi, 865. (Mohr, Tübingen. Price: DM 398.00. ISBN 3 16 145237 2)

This encyclopaedic volume is a 'token and witness' to the current development of research in Samaritan studies, the first fruits of The Society of Samaritan Studies, and intended to become the 'new Montgomery'. This work, however, is composite. Menachem Mor, Bruce Hall, A. D. Crown, B. Z. Kedar, R. T. Anderson and N. Schur cover Samaritan history to present times; R. Pummer and G. D. Sixdenier between them cover archaeology, numismatics, and inscriptions; A. D. Crown explores the Samaritan diaspora. There follow chapters on the Samaritan Chronicles (P. Stenhouse), eschatology (F. Dexinger), sects and movements (J. Fossum), literature (R. T. Anderson, E. Tov, S. Noja, A. Tal, G. Wedel, H. Shehadeh), languages (Z. Ben-Ḥayyim, R. Macuch, P. Stenhouse), halachah (I. R. M. Bóid), rituals and customs (R. Pummer), Calendar and chronology (S. Powels), music (R. Katz), manuscripts (J.-P. Rothschild), bibliography (J. Margain); the book ends with a critical chapter on the last decade on Samaritan studies by S. Noja.

Much of the book is concerned with the history and literature of the Samaritans as a distinctive sect from the Byzantine age to the present. How far Byzantine and medieval evidence can be exploited to illuminate the origins and early beliefs of the Samaritans is a vexed question, but clearly the sect's own medieval presentation of its history in the Chronicles must be used with caution. A. D. Crown explains in the Introduction that the lack of published critical texts prevents discussion of the issues raised by J. Macdonald's *Theology of the Samaritans* (*B. L.* 1965, p. 48). (Dexinger, however, argues that Samaritan eschatology, especially in the case of the Taheb, exhibits traits which reach back to the 2nd century B.C. (p. 292), and points to the evidence of the variant readings of the Samaritan Pentateuch as confirmed by the LXX for the reconstruction of early Samaritan belief.) Particularly important for the Old Testament historian is the opening chapter by M. Mor, who argues that our knowledge of the Samaritans begins with Nehemiah's time but equally argues that the Samaritans began to legitimize their separate identity as a sect only after Hyrcanus' destruction of Gerizim and Shechem (when exactly, one wonders, did the Samaritans become the Samaritans, and why?). Hyrcanus acted from political as well as religious motives, and partly, it seems, from resentment of a rival priesthood that could claim Zadokite ancestry (as he could not) (though against this, see J. D. Purvis, 'The Samaritans and Judaism', in *Early Judaism and its modern interpreters*, ed.

R. A. Kraft and G. W. E. Nickelsburg, Atlanta, 1986, p. 88). Mor further argues that after A.D. 70, Jewish rivalry with the Samaritans disappeared; The Sages saw the Samaritans as part of Israel, and relationships deteriorated only after the Bar Kochba revolt. Presumably after A.D. 70 argument about the location of the proper centre for worship was irrelevant — but it seems unlikely that all animosity disappeared (cf. John 4:20). Pummer contributes a very useful chapter on archaeology, publicising the work of Y. Magen, which appears to show that there was 'no Hellenistic construction phase on the Tell' (so Bull's 'Building B' does not preserve the foundations of the Samaritan temple or altar), and that there is a complete walled city of some 30 hectares on the main peak of Mt. Gerizim (coins indicate dating from *c.* 200 B.C. to 128 B.C.) though without trace (so far) of either a temple or altar (see pp. 169–74). A. D. Crown collects much useful information on the Samaritan disapora in Egypt, Gaza, and elsewhere.

As Dexinger remarks, the decisive change in the scholarly outlook on Samaritan origins took place with the publication in 1968 of J. D. Purvis' *The Samaritan Pentateuch and the origins of the Samaritan sect*. This, and Purvis' subsequent essay quoted above, are important prolegomena for the present work. Crown's volume, however, contains much more than history, and textual scholars will be grateful for Emmanuel Tov's 'Proto-Samaritan texts and the Samaritan Pentateuch' and linguists for Z. Ben-Ḥayyim's 'Samaritan Hebrew — an evaluation', and R. Macuch's detailed analysis in 'Samaritan languages: Samaritan Hebrew, Samaritan Aramaic'.

This is altogether a most valuable scholarly resource, which university librarians should be persuaded to buy, for all its cost. The Society and its editor deserve our congratulations and thanks.

J. R. BARTLETT

DENIS, A.-M.: *Concordance grecque des pseudépigraphes d'Ancien Testament: Concordance, Corpus de Textes, Indices*. 1987. Pp. xxi, 925 and 9 microfiches. (Université Catholique de Louvain, Institut Orientaliste, Louvain-la-Neuve; distributed by Brill, Leiden. Price: fl 400.00 (ca. $200.00). ISBN 90 04 09021 5)

This concordance is a sophisticated and beautifully produced work which will greatly set forward and enhance future study of the Greek Old Testament Pseudepigrapha. The texts of fourteen complete and eighteen fragmentary items have been listed, and the compilers have used the best critical editions of the texts available. Understandably, textual variants are not included, but where doublets of texts are found, as, e.g., in the case of the *Testament of Abraham* and the *Lives of the Prophets*, the Concordance takes due note of them. The fine Introduction sets out clearly and unambiguously the procedures adopted by the compilers: within the body of the Concordance, a series of diacritical signs is used to indicate textual corrections, conjectural and doubtful readings, corruptions in the text, and editorial material supplied to aid understanding of difficult individual items. All this is done with commendable precision and brevity. The Concordance itself is in three parts: first, an alphabetical list of general vocabulary, listing the number of times each word occurs in individual texts and in the Pseudepigrapha as a whole. Asterisks are used to indicate *hapax legomenon* on the one hand, and on the other hand key-words which feature more than twenty times in the whole. Next comes the complete Concordance, the individual words set out in the centre of the page in their context. The work ends with the corpus of texts set out in its own section. Nine microfiches provide an alphabetical list of all word-forms in the texts complete with their *lemmata*; an index of *lemmata*; a list of words in all the texts and in individual texts arranged according to frequency of use; and a complete concordance of key-words occurring more than twenty times. These only further enrich the scholarly value of what the compilers have produced in this impressive enterprise.

C. T. R. HAYWARD

FELDMAN, L. H. and HATA, G. (eds): *Josephus, Judaism, and Christianity*. 1987. Pp. 448. (Wayne State University Press, Detroit; Brill, Leiden. Price: fl 80.00 (ca. $40.00). ISBN 90 04 08554 8)

Because of his prime importance as a source for the history of Second Temple Judaism, Josephus must continually be evaluated as a historian. This volume, while not an introduction like that of P. Bilde (*B. L.* 1989, p. 34), covers important areas of the subject. Although some of the titles may seem familiar, the essays are all new and relate to some aspect of Josephus or his writings: the Roman Empire as reflected in the *War* (M. Stern); Justus of Tiberias (T. Rajak); Masada (D. J. Ladouceur); Philo and Josephus compared for the same events (E. M. Smallwood); Abraham (L. H. Feldman); the matriarchs (J. L. Bailey); Moses in the context of anti-Semitism (G. Hata); *Ant.* 4.277, 288, and rabbinic law (D. M. Goldenberg); miracles (O. Betz); the occult (M. Smith); the Samaritans (R. J. Coggins); the Pharisees (J. Neusner); and conversion of the royal house of Adiabene (L. H. Schiffman).

Several essays look at how Josephus' writings were received in Christianity or later Judaism: the early church (H. Schreckenberg); Origen (W. Mizugaki); the *Testimonium Flavianum* and the martyrdom of James (Z. Baras); Pseudo-Hegesippus (A. A. Bell, Jr.); Byzantium (S. Bowman); Josippon (D. Flusser); illumination in the manuscripts (G. N. Deutsch); and Martin Luther (B. H. Amaru). The editor gives a long preface in which he summarizes and interacts with each essay. This may be useful to readers, though whether the essay authors will always be appreciative might be an interesting question to ask.

L. L. GRABBE

GARCÍA MARTÍNEZ, F. and PUECH, E. (eds): *Mémorial Jean Carmignac: Etudes Qumrâniennes* (Revue de Qumran, Num. 49–52, Tome 13). 1988. Pp. ix, 692. (Gabalda, Paris. Price: Fr. 950.00. ISSN 0035 1725)

What began as a 75th birthday celebration has become a memorial to the founder of *Revue de Qumran*. In addition to the bibliography of published works and a brief biography (drawing on C.'s own remarks in his 'Histoire de la Famille Carmignac'), there are 49 contributions on all aspects of Qumran study.

Section 1 publishes some new texts: 4Q370 (an admonition based on the Flood); 4Q Second Ezekiel (4Q385); a new restoration of 1QH 5.12–6.18 (= *editio princeps* 1QH 13–14), 1QH 23.13–16 (= 18.12–15), along with an unpublished fragment of 4QBeatitudes; and an unpublished fragment of 11QTemple. Section 2 consists of one or more studies each on 1QS, 1QM, 1QapGen, the Copper Scroll (3Q15), 4QEnoch, Songs of Sabbath Sacrifice (Shir-Shabb), 11QTemple, CD, Jubilees, and the Aramaic Levi. The thematic studies of Section 3 include pesher exegesis, vegetarianism, the date of the destruction of Qumran, pronunciation of the tetragrammatonn, the phrase 'service of the angels', the Torah of Ezekiel and the influence of Ezekiel at Qumran, internal criteria for dating the Scrolls, history of the interpretation of Psa. 37.1, 7, 8, and prayers at Qumran. Section 4 looks at linguistic matters: the vocalization of Aramaic *yat*, the genitive in 1QS, and the particle *bdyl* in 11QtgJob. Section 5 has studies on the text of the Old Testament in the light of various Qumran texts. Section 6 is on Qumran and the New Testament.

L. L. GRABBE

GRABBE, L. L.: *Etymology in Early Jewish Interpretation: The Hebrew Names in Philo* (Brown Judaic Studies 115). 1988. Pp. xvi, 268. (Scholars Press, Atlanta GA. Price: $49.95. ISBN 1 55540 080 9)

The 'engine-room' of this monograph comes in Part II, where all 166 of the Biblical names for which Philo provides an etymology are analysed and parallels in other ancient sources discussed. The theoretical discussion based upon these data comes in Part I. Philo's use of etymology in his allegorical exegesis is described, possible influences on him explored (Greek rather than Palestinian or Rabbinic), and the source of the etymologies investigated. Grabbe makes out a convincing case for the view that Philo had access to an onomastical list compiled by someone with a detailed knowledge of Hebrew and Aramaic (something which Philo himself is shown not to have had). This is a lucid and workmanlike presentation of a complex piece of detailed research and thus comprises a most auspicious beginning to the publications of the Claremont Philo Project, which aims at a full-scale analysis by a team of scholars of all aspects of the Philonic exegetical tradition.

H. G. M. WILLIAMSON

HELLHOLM, D. (ed.): *Apocalypticism in the Mediterranean World and the Near East. Proceedings of the International Colloquium on Apocalypticism, Uppsala, August 12–17, 1979*. 2nd edition, enlarged by Supplementary Bibliography. 1989. Pp. xi, 910. (Mohr, Tübingen. Price: DM 348.00. ISBN 3 16 145386 7)

This reprint of the work reviewed in *B. L.* 1984, pp. 128–29, differs from the original only by the addition of a comprehensive Supplementary Bibliography for the period 1979–88 compiled by Hellholm.

M. A. KNIBB

HENGEL, M.: *The Zealots: Investigation into the Jewish Freedom Movement in the Period from Herod I until 70 A.D.*, translated by D. Smith. 1989. Pp. xxiv, 487. (T. & T. Clark, Edinburgh. Price: £29.95. ISBN 0 567 09372 7; 0 567 29372 6 (pbk))

This is an English translation of the second edition of this book (1976) originally published in German in 1961. The first edition was reviewed in *B. L.* 1962 p. 71, *Decade* p. 381. The bibliographies have been revised for the English edition. In an appendix (pp. 388–404) and also in the Foreword (pp. xi–xvii) Hengel reviews the reception of his book and deals forthrightly with its critics, especially Morton Smith. He maintains his views essentially unchanged from 1961. This book remains the classic work on the subject.

A. P. HAYMAN

HOLLADAY, C. R.: *Fragments from Hellenistic Jewish Authors*. Vol. II: *Poets — The Epic Poets Theodotus and Philo and Ezekiel the Tragedian* (SBL Texts and Translations 30; Pseudepigrapha Series 12). 1989. Pp. x, 529. (Scholars Press, Atlanta GA. Price: $25.95 (member price: $16.95); paperback price: $16.95 (member price: $11.95). ISBN 1 55540 317 4; 1 55540 318 2 (pbk))

Volume I, covering the historians, was favourably reviewed in *B. L.* 1985, p. 132. The editor promises a final volume which will contain further texts, as well as indices covering the whole. The present work follows the same format as its predecessor, repeating, with some additions, it bibliographies but not the introduction dealing with the historical context and the transmission of the texts. The poetical excerpts reproduced here are preserved almost exclusively in the fourth century A.D. *Praeparatio Evangelica* of Eusebius of Caesarea, who took them from Polyhistor. The reviewer in *B. L.* 1985 noted that these fragmentary Jewish Hellenistic authors were not easily accessible in English; since then, the items contained in this volume have been translated and edited in volume two of J. H. Charlesworth's *The Old Testament Pseudepigrapha*, pp. 775–819 (see *B. L.* 1986, p. 144f.), and the problems of their interpretation can be appreciated by comparing the renderings there with those of Holladay. These writings are interesting in their own right as literature, especially the drama *The Exodus* of Ezekiel Tragicus, which represents the most extensive remains of any Hellenistic Jewish poet, but their particular importance is the light they throw on the reaction of educated Jews to Hellenism, the profound influence of Homer on Theodotus and Philo Epicus, and Ezekiel's adoption of the conventions of Greek tragedy to produce a play on a Biblical theme. Holladay's work, with its detailed textual notes, full discussions, and abundant bibliographical references, will be an indispensable tool for all students both of these texts themselves and the period from which they come.

J. R. PORTER

VAN DER HORST, P. W.: *De Onbekende God: Essays over de joodse en hellenistische achtergrond van het vroege christendom* (Utrechtse Theologische Reeks 2). 1988. Pp. 285. (Faculteit der Godgeleerdheid Rijksuniversiteit te Utrecht, Utrecht; distributed by T. Wever, Franeker. ISBN 90 72235 02 9)

This is a collection of eighteen essays of which nine deal with intertestamental and later Judaism. The topics covered are the biblical exegesis of the *Exagoge* of Ezekiel Poetica, a review of Schäfer, Maier, and Stemberger on early Judaism, a review of Gager's *The Origins of Anti-Semitism*, a sketch of early Jewish-Hellenistic epic, the view of women in the *Testament of Job* (with some reference also to the New Testament), the *birkat haminim* in recent research (Kimelman, Maier, Horbury and Schiffman), and an account of a Jewish inscription (an article first published in *JJS* 38 (1987)). As will be clear from the summary, many of the essays are reviews of ancient writings and recent scholarship. Of the essays that fall outside the scope of the *Book List* the most intriguing is a reconsideration of Norden's thesis in his famous *Agnostos Theos* in the light of new material.

J. W. ROGERSON

KAMPEN, J.: *The Hasideans and the Origin of Pharisaism: A Study in 1 and 2 Maccabees* (Septuagint and Cognate Studies 24). 1988. Pp. x, 241. (Scholars Press, Atlanta GA. Price: $17.95 (member price: $11.95); paperback price: $11.95 (member price: $7.95). ISBN 1 55540 284 4; 1 55540 285 2 (pbk))

The author examines the Hasideans in the light of the literary analysis of *1 and 2 Maccabees*, and comparison of the remarks of Josephus and references in early rabbinic texts (where he finds reason to doubt Safrai's theory that we find in the Hasideans a divergent halakhic tradition). *1 Maccabees* presents the Hasideans as leading citizens, scribes who were devoted to the Law, but tries to discount their value by portraying them as naive in seeking to negotiate with the Greeks. This is the perspective which the writer, a Hasmonean supporter, would have wanted to disseminate (also) of the Pharisees. The Author of *2 Maccabees* portrays the Hasideans as well-known influential people, renowned for their piety and purity during the time of Hellenisation — a picture similar to that found in Talmudic literature. The author of *1 Maccabees* seems to have believed that the Pharisees arose from the *Hasidim*. An analysis of the texts in *1 Maccabees* strongly suggests an identification of the Hasideans with the scribes. Persons involved in the Temple cult and in the scribal circles of third and second century Judaism found themselves in a situation where they identified with those persons who had been called *Hasidim* in the biblical Psalms. Regarding the Temple as central to Jewish life, they responded strongly to the decrees of Antiochus IV, but came to disagree with the Maccabees over tactics, resulting in their receiving a less favourable treatment in Hasmonean historiography. It may well be that within these scribal circles of the *Hasidim* we find the origin of Pharisaism.

B. S. JACKSON

KASHER, A.: *Jews, Idumaeans, and Ancient Arabs: Relation of the Jews in Eretz-Israel with the Nations of the Frontier and the Desert during the Hellenistic and Roman Era (332 BCE — 70 CE)* (Texte und Studien zum Antiken Judentum 18). 1988. Pp. xix, 264. (Mohr, Tübingen. Price: DM 118.00. ISBN 3 16 145240 2; ISSN 0721 8753)

Arieh Kasher, a Tel Aviv university historian, established himself in the non-Hebrew reading world with *The Jews in Hellenistic and Roman Egypt* (1985). His hallmark is the determination to push towards a resolution of seemingly insoluble problems through close and insistent textual reading together with vigorous argument. The new volume is one of a pair which examine the relationships between the Jews and the surrounding cultures in the Second Temple period. It is to be hoped that the companion volume on the Greek cities will soon be translated. The two are indispensable reading for anyone concerned with the political history of the Hasmoneans, the Herods, or the Great Revolt. The viewpoint is that of the Jewish state, perhaps inevitably, since nearly all our literature-based information comes from the Jewish historian, Josephus. The structure is that of traditional, strictly chronological narrative. Kasher takes a negative view of what archaeology can contribute to these matters, commenting on the paucity of surviving Idumaean material. But that cannot be said to be true of the Nabataeans (even if the great bulk of what has been found is of a somewhat later date); and it is only because K. is concerned to settle specific conundrums arising from the texts rather than to consider these interesting peoples in a broader cultural perspective, that he finds himself so limited, and this seems a pity. He is willing to fit a few of the more credible Talmudic traditions on the last days of Jerusalem into the picture, using here a rather more relaxed criterion of plausibility, but he himself has difficulty in extracting grains of 'truth' from them; he at one point refers aptly to 'faded traditions'. K's readings suggest that the Idumaeans converted to Judaism at the end of the second century voluntarily, not, as is commonly believed, under John Hyrcanus's compulsion, and (which is more uncertain) remained fully integrated with the Jews so as to be at one with them when they joined in the revolt against Rome; between Jews and Nabateans there was, by contrast, an inveterate hostility. On the Ituraeans, A. H. M. Jones's sketch of the urbanization of the area stands unrevised. Of all K's analysis, the most lasting insight is likely to be that of the presence of powerful threads of anti-Hasmonean propaganda in our surviving accounts; these need not, however, all go back to the Herodian Nicolaus of Damascus, as K. seems sometimes to imply.

T. RAJAK

KNIBB, M. A.: *Jubilees and the Origins of the Qumran Community*. An Inaugural Lecture. 1989. Pp. 20. (Available from the Department of Theology and Religious Studies, King's College, Strand, London)

In this inaugural lecture, Professor Knibb argues that the very close similarities which exist between the *Book of Jubilees* and certain of the Qumran texts, in particular the *Damascus Document*, are a probable indication that the Qumran sect, and the wider Essene movement of which the sect was most likely a part, originated in Palestine sometime in the second century B.C. He has elsewhere subjected to criticism the thesis, proposed by Jerome Murphy-O'Connor and Philip Davies, that the founders of the Qumran community came from Babylon. This lecture is much less a further negative criticism of that thesis: it is rather more concerned to draw out, discuss, and develop the many positive indications that Jubilees and the Qumran texts, especially *Damascus Document*, share a common theological, legal, and historical background. His approach is cautious, but constructive; and the lecture is not least valuable for pointing to areas as yet unexplored, where further research might yield answers to the many riddles of Essene-Qumran origins.

C. T. R. HAYWARD

KUHN, P.: *Offenbarungsstimmen im Antiken Judentum. Untersuchungen zur Bat Qol und Verwandten Phänomenen* (Texte und Studien zum Antiken Judentum 20). 1989. Pp. xii, 425. (Mohr, Tübingen. Price: DM 258.00. ISBN 3 16 145167 8)

This is a systematic survey of the references to heavenly voices in what is very loosely termed 'ancient Judaism'. The main emphasis is on the post-biblical literature, but there is a brief introductory chapter on the Hebrew Bible, and of course recurrent reference to biblical texts as they figure in the later writings. There is also a discussion of the evidence from Daniel in the section on Pseudepigrapha; and the Aramaic Targumim receive a section of their own. There is no analogous section, curiously, on the Greek versions. The other sections are devoted to 'rewritten Bible' (Jubilees and Pseudo-Philo), Hellenistic–Jewish authors, and (the longest section) the 'rabbinic literature', which seems to be treated as essentially a single, independent unit. It may be felt that the author has bitten off more than anyone can be reasonably expected to chew; he does however keep his fairly limited aims in view, and he is careful to present the material within the perspective of modern study. Despite some methodological uncertainties, this is a useful book, and a worthy addition to an excellent series.

N. R. M. DE LANGE

LAPERROUSAZ, E.-M.: *Gli Esseni secondo la loro testimonianza diretta*. Translated from French by T. Tosatti (Leggere oggi la bibbia 3.8). 1988. Pp. 115. (Queriniana, Brescia. Price: Lire 12,000. ISBN 88 399 1599 0)

Taking for granted the identification of the inhabitants of Qumran with the Essenes, Laperrousaz first assembles key passages from the reports of classical sources (Josephus, Philo, Pliny the Elder), followed immediately by an account of the site of Qumran/Feshkha and a survey of the (non-biblical) literature from the caves. The longest section reconstructs the history of the inhabitants at Qumran, recapitulating the views he has already argued at length in his *Qoûmran. L'établissement essénien au bord de la Mer Morte* (1976). Organization, and beliefs and rituals occupy the remaining two chapters. Recent scholarship on Qumran has moved beyond the approaches and attitudes of this book; 'the sect' and 'its organization and beliefs' no longer seem so readily defined and described; and even identification with Essenes is now adopted more cautiously than previously. Data and interpretation more than ever need to be distinguished — alas, a textbook is not the easiest format in which to effect that distinction!

P. R. DAVIES

LEVISON, J. R.: *Portraits of Adam in Early Judaism, from Sirach to 2 Baruch* (Journal for the Study of the Pseudepigrapha, Supplement Series 1). 1988. Pp. 255. (Sheffield Academic Press. Price: £30.00 ($45.00). ISBN 1 85075 062 9)

In one major respect, the purpose of this book is negative. Levison, deeply sceptical and highly critical of the supposed 'Adam-myth' espoused by certain students of the New Testament, is above all concerned to allow Jewish texts to speak for themselves. This he does by examining his chosen sources individually; by not presuming unproven underlying connections between them; and by setting the Adam material in the perspectives of the individual texts understood as complete works with specific programmes of their own. In the process, the positive aspects of his work come to the fore. He gives a new and illuminating analysis of the figure of Adam as he is presented by Jewish authors of the period 200 B.C. to 135 A.D. He discusses Sirach, Wisdom of Solomon, Philo, Jubilees, Josephus, 4 Ezra, 2 Baruch, and somewhat strangely, the Apocalypse of Moses and *Vita Adae et Evae*. His insights into and observations upon all these texts are always worthwhile, and often break new ground. Indeed, it becomes clear that each single text has its own over-arching dynamic which generally determines how Adam material is used: this, rather than any pre-existing 'Adam-myth', shapes the portraits of Adam in any given work. An unfortunate weakness in the book, however, is Levison's unwillingness to discuss texts which certainly fall within this period. Thus he offers no study of Adam material found in 1 Enoch and Pseudo-Philo's *Liber Antiquitatum Biblicarum*; and he is silent about those Qumran texts which refer to the *k^ebod 'Adam*. Such omissions are surprising, and, despite the important results gained in the study of the individual texts, they can only serve to cast a measure of doubt on the book's general conclusions.

C. T. R. HAYWARD

MACCOBY, H.: *Judaism in the First Century* (Issues in Religious Studies). 1989. Pp. viii, 136. (Sheldon, London. Price: £4.95. ISBN 0 85969 550 6)

As a concise introduction to Second Temple Judaism, which does not assume prior knowledge or background, this small book is welcome. It has a special interest because a good part of it is angled at the reader of the New Testament. Thus it has quite detailed discussions of the Sabbath laws in connection with healing and with reaping, of the use of parables in Jewish literature, of the Messiah figure in the parables of Enoch, and even of what could be unacceptable, in Jewish terms, in eating with tax-gatherers. This means that it has to be rather brief on other matters, including (perhaps surprisingly) on the Essenses. M. does give an idea of the whole spectrum of types of Judaism in the period, indicating 'their variety and richness'; but his central concern is, in fact, with the Pharisees, whom he is entirely willing to see through the later Rabbis's eyes, as precursors of themselves. The alternative view, that at this period Pharisaic activity existed mainly in those 'table-fellowships' which cultivated their own higher standards of ritual purity, is given short shrift, although the difficult concept of ritual purity itself is one of those which M. explains so well to the novice. The transference to this period of Rabbinic ideas and institutions, such as the *Am Ha-arets*, or reasoning by *Middot*, is rejected by the many historians; and on this problem teachers will need to offer guidance. In general, it has to be pointed out how much more uncertain the picture is than M.'s persuasive fluency makes it seem. With this *caveat*, the book is a stimulating introduction to important aspects of Judaism, and reveals M., not for the first ime, as especially in his element when he is presenting the Rabbis.

T. RAJAK

MANNS, F., OFM: *John and Jamnia: How the break occurred between Jews and Christians c. 80–100 A.D.* Translated by M. Duel and M. Riadi. 1988. Pp. 75. (Franciscan Printing Press, Jerusalem. Price: $5.00)

This pamphlet consists of a translation into English and then a republication of two articles originally published by Fr Manns in the LIBER ANNUUS of the Franciscan Biblical School in Jerusalem. The author's aim is to interpret the Gospel of John as a reaction to the decisions taken by the rabbis at Jamnia. In itself this is not an unreasonable hypothesis. Unfortunately the book is fatally flawed by a simplistic exegesis of the relevant texts and a pre-critical historical methodology. No attention whatsoever is paid to the late date of the sources quoted to illustrate Jewish reaction to the loss of the Temple and the reconstruction of Judaism at Yabneh. The texts are taken at face value as reliable historical sources. There is no attempt to assess their relative reliability or to study different versions of stories synoptically. The problem of utilizing much later rabbinic sources as background to John's Gospel is 'assumed to have been resolved' (p. 30). The author is aware of the problem (p. 54, n. 5) but chooses to bypass it. The one criterion that he offers for the antiquity of a rabbinic tradition is that it should show no traces of anti-Christian controversy. The formula appears to be: not anti-Christian, therefore pre-Christian. This is strange logic. A rather stronger argument than that is necessary, for instance, to prove that a tradition found in *Pesikta Rabbati* (a sixth-seventh century C.E. document) is prior to, or contemporary with John's Gospel (p. 56)!

A. P. HAYMAN

MENDELSON, A.: *Philo's Jewish Identity* (Brown Judaic Studies, 161). 1988. Pp. xiii, 158. (Scholars Press, Atlanta GA. Price: $28.95 (member price: $17.95). ISBN 1 55540 307 7)

This is one of three volumes on Jewish Self-Definition in the Greek-speaking Diaspora. The subject is an extremely important one because Philo was clearly at home in Hellenistic cultural, yet also a loyal Jew, and a leading figure in his own community. Far from being a marginal figure, Philo must be taken account of in any discussion of Jewish identity during this time. M. gives a lucid discussion of Philo's viewpoint on the subject.

He shows that Philo had a concept of orthodoxy which centred on monotheism and of orthopraxy which included such matters as circumcision, the food laws, the sabbath and Day of Atonement, and avoidance of intermarriage with Gentiles. Philo admired Greek culture and philosophy (absorbing a lot of it into his own theological system), and spent a good deal of effort countering the negative view of Judaism among some pagans. However, he ultimately drew a sharp boundary between Jew and Gentile in the religious sphere. He, as fiercely as the Maccabean and other martyrs, thought the points of orthodoxy and orthopraxy mentioned above were worth dying for. M. has made an important contribution both to Philonic studies and to the broader subject of Second-Temple Judaism.

L. L. GRABBE

NEUSNER, J.: *Judaism and its Social Metaphors: Israel in the History of Jewish Thought*. 1989. Pp. xiv, 258. (Cambridge University Press. Price: £25.00 ($34.50). ISBN 0 521 35471 4)

Neusner brings together a good deal of his recent research to address the question of how ancient Judaisms identify themselves. The response, Neusner argues, must be metaphorical, and the metaphor is 'Israel'. Only in the 'Judaism of the Dual Torah', however, does one find the 'astonishing' identification of the Israel of Scripture with all Jews in the here and now (p. 83). Even given this, the metaphor requires more detail: Israel as an entity *sui generis*, Israel as family, Israel as nation, or as caste, are all extracted from the sources, and expounded. Dividing the investigation into two periods ('statements'), 70–300 C.E. and 300–600 C.E. allows for the introduction of the problem of relating social structure to social metaphor and historical circumstance, for in the second phase, 'Israel' as the authors of the system conceived it was a palpable reality.

The way in which history and society 'inscribe' texts remains problematic in current debate; Neusner accepts (p. 247) that social entity logically precedes, and generates, systems (by which he means symbolic, religious, intellectual, systems: Judaisms, in this case). Groups frame systems: systems define canons and generate texts; exegesis enables the system to serve the society through time, until or unless the system becomes incompatible with social reality. (The system, of course, must be deduced by the scholar from the texts.) As this reviewer understands it, such 'systems' mediate between society and literature, yet have no history of their own; they are mortal but have an eternal character to them (p. 247f.) Is there, then, somewhere, a *Geist* in the machine?

P. R. DAVIES

NEUSNER, J.: *A Religion of Pots and Pans: Modes of Philosophical and Theological Discourse in Ancient Judaism* (Brown Judaic Studies, 156). 1988. Pp. xix, 200. (Scholars Press, Atlanta GA. Price: $39.95 (member price: $24.95). ISBN 1 55540 283 6)

The main issue confronted in this book concerns the religion of rabbinic Judaism as defined in the Mishnah. A 'religion of pots and pans' is how Neusner characterizes the way this religion is evaluated by, in particular, Maccoby and Sanders, both of whom, he believes, marginalize and misrepresent the Mishnah's concern with sanctification. Part One exemplifies how Neusner sees the Mishnah discoursing philosophically and theologically through its legal/ritual mode of thinking. In Part Two, Neusner explains his current agenda in the context of his entire *oeuvre*: moving from explication of the rational and systematic discourse of discrete documents, via the world-views which they express, to a sociological description of Judaism(s) — both ancient and modern. Neusner's academic work, of course, is inseparable from his concern with the redefinition of Judaism and the place of Jewish studies within academia, and one senses that for him this issue is becoming ever more central. It will therefore be interesting, and valuable, to see Neusner address the abolition, in post-modern hermeneutical theory, of 'objective meaning' and the consequent explicit privileging (as in some Christian circles already) of 'communities of faith' in the task of authoritative interpretation — perhaps a 're-ghettoising' tendency?

P. R. DAVIES

NEUSNER, J.: *The Formation of the Jewish Intellect: Making Connections and Drawing Conclusions in the Traditional System of Judaism* (Brown Judaic Studies 151). 1988. Pp. xiii, 178. (Scholars Press, Atlanta GA. Price: $46.95. ISBN 1 55540 255 0)

What marks out Jacob Neusner is not so much his prolixity (which is remarkable enough) but his propensity for relentlessly working back to the principles — first of text composition, then of the formation of religious systems, and finally (in the logical sense) of critical analysis itself. And unlike many gurus who finally abandon data for theory, Neusner continues to work with the primary sources.

The scope of this small book encompasses most of the above-mentioned principles. Part One analyses 'intellect' — in particular the kind of intellect at work in Judaism (wherein Neusner lays claim to his critical hermeneutic as more consonant with that of classical Judaism than the 'traditionalist', 'fundamentalist' hermeneutic (as he calls it) of the *yeshiva*. In Part Two, we find another characteristic Neusner enterprise, a comparative systemic analysis of Pentateuch, Qumran corpus, Mishnah, and the Talmud. Part Three resumes the engagement between 'system' and 'tradition', through a comparison between Jewish and Christian systems. The closing sentences extol the *hubris* of the Talmud, of the Jewish mind, and the Jewish system, represented in its claim to totality and autonomy. Neusner is claiming a place in that tradition.

P. R. DAVIES

RADICE, R. and RUNIA, D. T.: *Philo of Alexandria. An Annotated Bibliography 1937–1986* (Vigiliae Christianae Supplement 8). 1988. Pp. xli, 469. (Brill, Leiden. Price: fl 144.00; ca. $72.00. ISBN 90 04 08986 1; ISSN 0920 623x)

Roberto Radice's *Filone di Alessandria: bibliografia generale 1937–1982* (published in 1983, but not noticed in the *Book List*) is here translated into English. It has also been brought up to date to provide a record of Philonic studies during the fifty years from 1937, the last year covered by Goodhart and Goodenough in their *General Bibliography of Philo Judaeus* (1938). The chronological limits have not, however, been observed with absolute strictness, and the editors have included a few important works (mostly editions and translations) that were published prior to 1937 and have listed a number of Philonic studies that appeared in 1987 and 1988. The introduction gives an account of the origins of the work, its relation to other bibliographies of Philo, and the methods used in its compilation. In general these are the same as those used by Radice in his *Bibliografia generale*, but whereas Radice restricted his coverage to studies written in English, French, Italian, German, Spanish, and Latin, studies in Dutch and Modern Hebrew have now been included. The bibliography itself, which contains 1666 items, is divided into two parts: the first lists scholarly tools and instruments of research (bibliographies, editions, translations, etc.), the second critical studies. Within the second part, which is by far the larger, the items are organized by year of publication, and within each year alphabetically by author. For each item a brief objective summary has been provided; the majority of these were either taken over from Radice's *Bibliografia generale* or compiled by Radice or Runia, but the summaries of items in Dutch were prepared by R. A. Bitter, and those of items in Hebrew by a team consisting of D. Satran, N. G. Cohen, M. Mach, and D. R. Schwartz. Revues of books are listed, and there are comprehensive indexes, including a carefully-arranged Subject Index of some sixty pages. Although differently conceived and executed, this work in many ways forms a counterpart to L. H. Feldman's *Josephus and Modern Scholarship (1937–1980)* — see *B. L.* 1985, p. 130 — and is equally valuable. It is likely to remain indispensable to all those concerned, directly or indirectly, with the writings of Philo for many years to come.

M. A. KNIBB

ROTHSCHILD, J.-P. and SIXDENIER, G. D.: *Etudes Samaritaines: Pentateuque et Targum, exégèse et philologie, chroniques*. Actes de la table ronde: "Les manuscrits samaritains. Problèmes et méthodes" (Collection de la Revue des Études Juives 6). 1988. Pp. 315. (Peeters, Louvain-Paris. Price: B.Fr. 1,200. ISBN 90 6831 112 3)

The papers read at the 1985 Congress which gave rise to the Society for Samaritan Studies are here reproduced: 24 in all, mostly French, with those in Spanish or English being provided with a French summary. Following the introduction by A. Caquot there are four sections: (i) Palaeography and Codicology, in which P. de Robert outlines the birth of Samaritan studies in Europe and M. Delcor describes the correspondence between Europeans and Samaritans down to the nineteenth century. More closely related to the theme are C. Sirat's presentation of paleographical methods and problems, R. T. Anderson's tentative grouping of Samaritan manuscripts, and A. D. Crown's description of Samaritan bindings. (ii) Bible and Targum: A. Mikolasek discusses the enumeration of the decalogue; L. F. Giron-Blanc and Z. Ben-Ḥayyim reach different conclusions as to the significance of a vocalic marker in Samaritan Hebrew texts; R. le Deaut compares Jewish and Samaritan targum traditions; J. Margain notes the conservative characteristics of Samaritan targum ms J; G. D. Sixdenier describes the Samaritan Exodus targum; A. Tal advocates caution in describing the Samaritan targum tradition as literalist; and R. Macuch has interesting observations on the way in which philology and hermeneutics have influenced one another. (iii) Samaritan Hebrew Literature. Z. Ben-Ḥayyim has radical proposals for resolving the obscurities in Tibat (Memar) Marqe in advance of his new edition; J.-P. Rothschild discusses a Paris Samaritan ms; and H. Jamgotchian, from Armenia, describes the necessary preparations for setting up a dictionary of Samaritan mss. (iv) Samaritan Arabic Literature. H. Shehadeh outlines the characteristics of Arabic translations of the Samaritan Pentateuch; H. Zafrani writes on Jewish communities in Morocco, an essay which appears to have nothing to do with the remainder of the book; P. Stenhouse claims that Abul-Fath's chronology is less unreliable than has usually been claimed, and puts forward a third century date for Baba Rabba, the great Samaritan reformer; M. Baillet modifies his earlier comments on the features of Samaritan Arabic mss; H. Pohl entertainingly describes some of the ruses used by Samaritan copyists on unsuspecting buyers from the Western world; and S. Powels writes on Samaritan methods of astronomical calculation. In conclusion B. Tsedaka, himself a Samaritan, writes on the aspirations of the community; and Z. Ben-Ḥayyim, in a brief autobiographical sketch, sets out the importance of Palestinian Aramaic studies. A varied collection, but one which gives ample illustration of the current strength of Samaritan studies.

R. J. COGGINS

SAADIAH BEN JOSEPH AL-FAYYUMI: *The Book of Theodicy: Translation and Commentary on the Book of Job*. Translated from the Arabic by L. E. Goodman (Yale Judaica series 25). 1988. Pp. xvii, 481. (Yale University Press, New Haven and London. Price: £55.00. ISBN 0 300 03743 0)

While it remains a matter of controversy whether he wrote his Arabic biblical translations and commentaries in Hebrew or Arabic script, and much remains to be done on the preparation of critical editions of these works, there is little doubt that Saadiah (882–942) is, in our present state of knowledge, still the dominant figure of early medieval Jewish scholarship, including Hebrew Bible study. Convinced as Goodman is that the result of an exclusive concern with literary and linguistic matters in Job is 'not understanding but dissociation' (p. xi), he has set himself the task of setting Saadiah's philosophical exposition of that troublesome book before modern scholars interested in earlier treatments of the subject. To that end he has produced an impressive and lengthy introduction that sketches the Sura Gaon's turbulent life and his acquisition of the philosophical, philological, and rabbinic expertise of his day and explains his attempt at arriving at a comprehensive synthesis of Greek, Islamic, and Jewish ideas in the form of a 'Jewish counterpart to Muʿtazilism' (p. 33). Goodman's well-written essay, his readable translation, and the generous notes to the commentary make it unlikely that his efforts — and those of Saadiah — will remain unappreciated by contemporary students of the Hebrew Bible.

S. C. Reif

Safrai, S. and Stern, M. (eds) in co-operation with Flusser, D. and van Unnik, W. C.: *Sōsetsu Yudaya-jin no Rekishi Jō*. Translated by S. Nagakubo, S. Kawashima, K. Tsuchido and Y. Ikeda. 1989. Pp. L, 492 including 7 maps. (Shinchi-shobō, Tokyo. Price: ¥8,755. ISBN 4 88018 139 0 C 3016)

This is a Japanese translation of the first six chapters of *The Jewish People in the First Century. Historical Geography, Political History, Social, Cultural and Religious Life, and Institutions*, in two volumes, 1974 (see *B. L.* 1975, pp. 109–10)

K. K. Sacon

Segal, A. F.: *Rebecca's Children: Judaism and Christianity in the Roman World*. 1986. Pp. xii, 207. (Harvard University Press, Cambridge, Mass. and London. Price: £7.95. ISBN 0 674 75076 4 (pbk))

This study, described in *B. L.* 1987, p. 119, as 'middle of the road' and 'highly recommended for students', is now available in paperback at a price which most should be able to afford.

A. G. Auld

Sigal, P.: *Judaism: The Evolution of a Faith*. Revised and edited by L. Sigal. 1988. Pp. xxii, 326. (Eerdmans, Grand Rapids MI. Price: $21.95; paperback price: $14.95. ISBN 0 8028 3661 5; 0 8028 0345 8 (pbk))

Rabbi Sigal died in 1985. Of the projected five volumes of his large-scale work *The Emergence of Contemporary Judaism* only three were published, between 1977 and 1987. In 1986 a one-volume German abridgment appeared, and the present book is the English text on which the German translation was based, edited, and revised by the author's widow, who has added her own study entitled 'Images of women in Judaism' as an appendix. 'The audience for which this book is intended are lay and clergy people of all faiths or people of no particular faith who seek a cogent account of the evolution of Judaism from its origins to the present' (p. xv f.). Despite some weaknesses of conception, construction, and expression, this is actually quite a successful attempt at tackling an impossible task of compression, and the book can hold its own against rival one-volume treatments of Judaism. Its great strength is its bold originality, but critical spirits may feel that less informed readers might be led astray by the indiscriminate mixture of widely accepted and hlghly controversial views.

N. R. M. de Lange

Vanhoye, A.: *Structure and Message of the Epistle to the Hebrews* (Subsidia Biblica 12). 1989. Pp. ix, 120. (Biblical Institute Press, Rome. Price: Lire 16,000. ISBN 88 7653 571 3)

In 1980 Vanhoye published a substantial treatment of priesthood and sacrifice (*Prêtres anciens, prêtre nouveau selon le Nouveau Testament* [Paris]) which was translated six years later as *Old Testament Priests and the New Priest* (Massachussets). Neither was included in the relevant *Book List*. Vanhoye's earlier work majored on Hebrews because in that work alone of the New Testament writings priesthood is attributed to Christ. The focus of the present work is a structural analysis of Hebrews with a 'structured translation', uniting two previously published works *Le message de l'Épître aux Hébreux* (Paris, 1977) and *A Structured Translation of the Epistle to the Hebrews* (Rome, 1964).

Discussion of the Old Testament priesthood forms the backdrop for his elucidation of the author's portrayal of Christ's priestly ministry. He offers a highly condensed account of the essential function of the priest in Israel: 'the underlying theme of the Old Testament priesthood as an institution . . . consists of relations between persons' (p. 8). He notes the necessity of this separated (i.e. 'sacred') person acting in a set apart place, at a specified time to devote a victim to God (by immolation) on behalf of the people. Only after this 'ascending movement for successive separations' can one hope for 'a descending movement of divine favors' (p. 11). Sacrifice does not indicate 'a privation but a transformation' (p. 11). A lucid and incisive monograph, refreshingly bereft of footnotes or bibliography.

D. G. DEBOYS

WILLIAMSON, R.: *Jews in the Hellenistic World: Philo* (Cambridge Commentaries on writings of the Jewish & Christian World 200 B.C. to A.D. 200, 1.ii). 1989. Pp. xii, 314. (Cambridge University Press. Price: £35.00 ($54.50); paperback price: £12.95 ($19.95). ISBN 0 521 30511 X; 0 521 31548 4 (pbk))

Of all the volumes in this very useful series, Dr Williamson's volume on Philo will probably prove to be most indispensable. Where else can the Bible student go for a convenient and reliable introduction to Philo of Alexandria? E. R. Goodenough's *Introduction to Philo Judaeus* is half a century old (the changes in the 1962 edition are mainly stylistic) and his idiosyncratic approach to the subject excited controversy in its day. There is an excellent chapter in Philo in the last volume of the new Schürer, but it is scarcely designed for the beginner. Now, however, Dr Williamson has provided the book we need. He has been a student of Philo for many years and, knowing his own way about in Philo's writing so well, he is well qualified to be a guide to others. After an introduction on Philo's life and work he expounds successively his doctrine of God, his Logos doctrine, his allegorical exegesis and his ethical teaching, illustrating each topic with ample and well-chosen quotations from Philo's writings. He concludes that 'there is no better way for a student to begin his study of hellenistic Judaism than by reading Philo', and he shows such a student how Philo is to be read.

F. F. BRUCE

10. PHILOLOGY AND GRAMMAR

ANDERSEN, F. I. and FORBES, A. D.: *The Vocabulary of the Old Testament*. 1989. Pp. viii, 721. (Biblical Institute Press, Rome. Price: Lire 73,500. ISBN 88 7653 575 6)

This handsomely produced and easily used volume provides an analogous tool for Hebraists to that of R. Morgenthaler, *Statistik des neutestamentlichen Wortschatzes*, for New Testament scholars. It provides a wealth of statistical information about the Hebrew vocabulary, much of it unobtainable elsewhere or only with inordinate labour. Some examples of facts that can be learned from it are: cohortatives are six times commoner in poetry than prose (52 per 10,000 words), *ḥākām* and *ḥokmâh* are more frequent in Qohelet than Proverbs (in proportion to their length), *'am* is common in all the Pentateuchal sources except P, *waw*-consecutive is five times more common in the Former Prophets than in the poetical books. There are tables that show the distribution by book and groups of books of the occurrences of every word.

There are lists of all lemmata ('words') in the Old Testament (9980), all gentilics, proper names, deities' names, and an English-Hebrew index. Less obviously useful is the concordance, which lists only the references where words occur, and then only the first 40 occurrences; admittedly, this provides a full listing for 91% of the lemmata. You can manage most of the time without this book; but when you need it, you will need it badly.

D. J. A. Clines

Arnold, W.: *Lehrbuch des Neuwestaramäischen* (Semitica Viva. Series Didactica 1). 1989. Pp. xvii, 137. (Harrassowitz, Wiesbaden. Price: DM 39.80. ISBN 3 447 02910 2; ISSN 0935 7556)

This volume, the first in a series of teaching grammars, is a milestone in the study of the modern Aramaic from villages north of Damascus. It does not replace the reference grammer of A. Spitaler, *Grammatik des neuaramäischen Dialekts von Maʿlūla* (1938 reprint 1966), but breaks new ground in presenting this dialect (and the slightly different Aramaic of Baḫʿa and Jubbʿadīn) for the learner. The dialect of Christian Maʿlūla is the basis, with supplements on the other two villages (which are Muslim). The particular interest from the Biblical point of view is the fact that this form of Aramaic is among the modern dialects the one which is the most direct descendant of ancient Western Aramaic. Many readers of the *Book List* will be interested to see this work. All material is, of course, on phonetic script. The treatment is thorough and well organized with exercises, vocabularies, and sample texts. There are glossaries and keys to the exercises (necessary since virtually no user of this book will have access to an expert teacher of modern western Aramaic — unless he lives in Erlangen!). There is also a thirty-minute cassette, not yet available to the reviewer.

J. F. Healey

Barr, J.: *The Variable Spellings of the Hebrew Bible* (The Schweich Lectures 1986). 1989. Pp. xii, 239. (Oxford University Press, for the British Academy. Price: £27.50. ISBN 0 19 726068 3)

In this intriguing work, based on his Schweich Lectures, Professor Barr accepts that there is a detectable increase in the incidence of *plene* spellings as between the period of the Old Hebrew inscriptions and that of the Dead Sea Scrolls, and that the Massoretic Text occupies roughly a middle stage in this process. But he denies that this fact can at all be used for the purposes of dating any portion of the Hebrew Bible or that it supplies any real evidence for concluding that there was a large-scale official revision of the biblical orthography around the end of the Old Testament period. What emerges at this period is a recognizable form of the Hebrew consonantal text which later became the official Jewish text and later still was the one to which the Massoretes added their vowel and other 'points' – a very different thing. Barr is thus in sharp disagreement with the more positive conclusions reached by Cross and Freedman in 1952 and more recently by Andersen and Forbes in a book reviewed in *B. L.* 1988, p. 146. The bulk of his study is taken up with an investigation, with numerous examples, of the complex factors which have to be taken into account in explaining the many variant spellings that are encountered. I mention only a couple: the circumstance that the scriptures were so well known through constant recitation that there was no need for many centuries to supply them with a full vocalization, which strongly suggests that the earlier partial vocalizations through *matres lectionis* likewise cannot have been intended to increase intelligibility or remove ambiguities; and the possibility at every turn that what was decisive in such and such a spelling was simply the preference, conscious or unconscious, of a single scribe or scriptorium. Plainly this book is, in the way it unsettles received positions, on a par with several of Professor Barr's other books; and it is written in his typically limpid and elegant but deadly style. It will repay constant consultation by all of us who are involved with the close analysis of the biblical text and may, as Robert Burns puts it, 'from monie a blunder free us and foolish notion'. To help us there is a detailed index of words whose spelling is discussed in the body of the book and, as an appendix, a specimen profile of the spelling tendencies in the Book of Psalms.

J. C. L. Gibson

Isaksson, B.: *Studies in the Language of Qoheleth With Special Emphasis on the Verbal System* (Studia Semitica Uppsaliensia 10). 1987. Pp. 232. (Almqvist & Wiksell, Stockholm. Price: Sw.Kr. 150. ISBN 91 554 2109 1; ISSN 0585 5535)

This is a series of studies, mainly syntactical, in the language of Qoheleth. The author makes no claim to completeness and admits that 'most of the research in this field remains to be done'; but he presents his work in the hope that it will stimulate further linguistic research in the book, in the field of syntax and the structure of language, as well as in the area of words and etymologies.

After an introduction in which the author lays the foundations for his structuralist approach, based on the posthumous work of F. de Saussure, and in which he makes some observations on the Hebrew verbal system, there are 12 further studies which are concerned with the book of Qoheleth: 'The Autobiographical Thread'; 'Nifal of *ʿāsā*'; 'The SC as a Form for the Present'; 'The wSC Forms Outside the Thread'; 'Investigation of some Current Verbs in Qoheleth'; 'The Prefix Conjugation'; 'The Active Verbal Participle'; 'The Verbal System in Qoheleth'; 'The Pronouns in Qoheleth'; 'Adverbs of Existence and Negation'; 'The Word *ʿolam* in 3:11'; and 'Conclusions'.

Space forbids discussion of these issues here, but, while not everyone will share the author's approach or conclusions, his work is a significant contribution to the understanding of the place of Qoheleth in the history of the Hebrew language, and scholars will need to take him into account in the future study of the book.

The book, which has a good bibliography and an essential index of references, is accompanied by an *Errata* list which, unfortunately, is not comprehensive.

R. B. Salters

Jastrow, O.: *Der neuaramäische Dialekt von Hertevin (Provinz Siirt)* (Semitica Viva, 3). 1988. Pp. xxv, 234. (Harrassowitz, Wiesbaden. Price: DM 132.00. ISBN 3 447 02767 3)

This is a detailed linguistic description of the modern Aramaic dialect of Hertevin in eastern Turkey as it existed in 1970. The importance of the work is emphasized by the fact that this Chaldaean Christian village had been virtually abandoned and destroyed by 1982. Semitic studies owes much to the industry of Professor Jastrow of Erlangen in this and other publications in recording modern Aramaic dialects (notably his work of Ṭūryōyō of 1985 [3rd edition]: *Laut- und Formenlehre des neuaramäischen Dialekt von Mīdin im Ṭūr ʿAbdīn* and his article on the *Mlaḥṣo* dialect in *Journal of Semitic Studies* 1985). A number of researchers from the Erlangen school have published other important works in the field of modern Aramaic in recent times and there is now considerable activity in this field also in the USA. The dialect of Hertevin will be of interest particularly to those concerned with Syriac and Aramaic studies as well as Semitists in general. Apart from the usual sections on phonology, morphology, etc., there is at the heart of this work a large and important collection of transcribed texts (pp. 108–75) with translations. The book is completed by general and verbal glossaries (which are non-etymological in style).

J. F. Healey

Jobin, G.: *Concordance des Particules Cooccurrentes de la Bible Hébraïque* (Judentum und Umwelt, 25). 1988. Pp. xxv, 14. (Lang, Frankfurt am Main. Price: Sw.Fr. 43.00. ISBN 3 631 41818 3; ISSN 0721 3131)

This is an odd but none the less significant monograph, bringing the computer to the aid of modern students of the Massorah. It is concerned with those prepositions and other particles whose occurrence twice or more than twice in the same verse was noted in the margins of the Leningrad manuscript used by BHS. The particles are arranged alphabetically (beginning with *'ayin* and ending with *'al*), the total of double etc. occurrences is recorded, and the actual verse references are fully listed. Only a couple of pages of introduction precede the statistical lists, but these contain an implied invitation to others to get working on their computers and produce similar lists which can, of course, attain a level of detail that the classic concordances have never approached; and a few hints are dropped about how such information might be used in e.g. classifying manuscripts or investigating syntactical usages. The monograph itself could scarcely be called exciting, but it does open up exciting possibilities — though some of us may wish to ponder the irony that what the old Jewish Massoretes were only able to achieve after decades of arduous labour can now in this technological age be done almost at the press of a button.

J. C. L. Gibson

Khan, G.: *Studies in Semitic Syntax* (London Oriental Series 38). 1988. Pp. xxxix, 252. (Oxford University Press. Price: £37.50. ISBN 0 19 713607 9)

This study describes and analyses the structure and functions in a number of Semitic languages, including biblical Hebrew and Aramaic/Syriac, of two related grammatical features: extraposition (what used to be called *casus pendens*, e.g. Arabic 'Zayd — his father beat him', where 'Zayd' is in the nominative) and pronominal agreement (e.g. Syriac 'The queen — he slew her', which can be changed without making any difference to 'He slew her — the queen'). Both of these constructions have clause- or sentence-level functions, e.g. to emphasize a particular word, but Dr Khan shows that their most significant functions are macro-syntactic, to mark onset and closure, a change in topic, a shift from foregrounding to backgrounding, and so on. This is a very valuable discovery and owes much to Dr Khan's espousal of the methodology of discourse analysis, a methodology which concentrates on the larger units of a text and which, although modern and therefore burdened with a new terminology, is essentially pragmatic in its scope. One can get the hang of it without closing with a formidable body of theory, which is not the case with, e.g., structuralism or transformational grammar. So readers of the *Book List* need not be apprehensive! Semitists — and perhaps Hebraists in particular — have in the past been good at phonology and morphology but rather weak on syntax. This book should turn their thoughts to an area of language they have habitually neglected and is therefore important not only in itself but for the example it sets.

J. C. L. Gibson

Kiraz, G. A.: *The Syriac Primer: Reading, Writing, Vocabulary & Grammar*. With a cassette recording by S. Adam and G. Kiraz (JSOT Manuals, 5). 1985, 1988. Pp. 273. (Sheffield Academic Press. Price: £8.95 ($14.50). ISBN 1 85075 199 4; ISSN 0262 1754)

This primer is a revised edition of the author's previous work, *Syriac for Beginners with Exercises and Cassette activities*, published in 1986 by members of the St Ephraim Youth Organization (Syrian Orthodox) of Los Angeles. It is based on the Western Jacobite dialect (*Serṭa*) of Syriac and consequently emphasis throughout is put on training the student to read the living language clearly and accurately. Beginning with simple syllables the elements of grammar are taught in graded reading lessons, always with the aid of the cassette, and culminate in selections from the Peshiṭta and other classical Syriac works. Since the primer uses *Serṭa*, chapters 11 and 12 introduce Estrangela and Eastern Nestorian scripts respectively. The finer points of the *Quššāya* and *Rukkāka* are discussed in Ch. 13.

The primer will interest primarily students of Syrian Christianity but, given certain changes in the development of the language (e.g. *zqāfā* becomes *zqōfō* in *Serṭa*, admittance of modern vocabulary etc.) this approach will certainly enliven classes concerned only with the classical language. The English section of the book has a number of careless misprints and even in the Syriac section it is most unfortunate that in the introduction to the vowel signs, *rbāṣā* appears for *ʿṣāṣā*.

P. W. COXON

KITTEL, B. P., HOFFER, V., and WRIGHT, R. A.: *Biblical Hebrew: A Text and Workbook* (Yale Language series). 1989. Pp. xxiii, 429. (Yale University Press, New Haven and London. Price: £25.00. ISBN 0 300 04394 5)

Sumptuously produced, this workbook aims to teach Biblical Hebrew inductively, starting with the most common grammatical forms and vocabulary. From Lesson 13 on, additional extensively annotated readings accompany each Lesson. The strictly inductive approach is broken sometimes with sections of 'extra grammar', usually filling out paradigms which have been only partially introduced. Emphasis throughout is laid on recognition of forms from characteristic features. Evidently this course was used successfully by Kittel until her untimely death, but other teachers may find it less easy to use. As in many languages, 'most common' also means 'most irregular', so that constant modifications have to be made to what has previously been learned as the course proceeds. For many, it is less time-consuming simply to learn a paradigm than to go through all the possibilities of what a given element in a word may signify until, by a process of elimination, the correct diagnosis is achieved. A number of errors in the Hebrew will have to be corrected, including the 'howler' of *šānôt* (*sic*) as the principal example of feminine plural nouns! Some important grammatical forms are not fully explained (e.g. the pointing of the definite article) or need to be picked up by sharp-eyed students from the annotations to the readings. However, the authors bend over backwards to be 'user-friendly', so that teachers will be able to pick up some useful mnemonics, jokes, and other devices with which to spice their own classes.

H. G. M. WILLIAMSON

OGNIBENI, B.: *Tradizioni orali di lettura e testo ebraico della bibbia: Studio dei diciassette ketiv* L'/*qere* LW (Studia Friburgensia, Nouvelle Série 72). 1989. Pp. xvii, 274. (Éditions Universitaires, Fribourg (CH). Price: Sw.Fr. 38.00. ISBN 2 8271 0426 1)

This important study concentrates on seventeen passages in the Hebrew Bible where the *ketiv* and *qere* offer radically diverse meanings ('not'/'to him'). The relevant data for each passage are exhaustively researched: the Masoretic tradition, the exegesis of Talmud and Midrash, the textual evidence with special reference to Qumran readings and the most ancient versions, and the bearing of modern exegesis on the question of the most probable original reading. In all but five cases the textual and exegetical judgements concur. The main conclusions are that the *qere* readings are genuine ancient variants, and that (with varying degrees of probability) they are to be preferred to the *ketiv* in thirteen of the seventeen passages. There is inevitably room for differences of judgement over details and one may ask whether the rigorous separation of the textual and exegetical discussions is as practicable and desirable as suggested. But this is an indispensable tool for the study of these passages, and an important contribution to the textual criticism of the Hebrew Bible.

A. GELSTON

OWENS, J. J.: *Analytical Key to the Old Testament*. Vol. 4: *Isaiah–Malachi*. 1989. Pp. xi, 941. (Baker Book House, Grand Rapids MI. ISBN 0 8010 6713 8)

Of four projected volumes this is the first to appear. Following the English order, it includes Daniel. With generous and clear arrangement, every word of BHS is cited and parsed and given page reference to BDB, and a translation usually from RSV. Errors, alas, are not difficult to find, starting with the sample entry on p. x, where the feminine verb is said to be masculine; on p. 1 'Hithpalel' should be 'Hithpolel', *kebed* is not a noun, and so on. More puzzling will be the cases where the cited RSV actually translates an unmentioned emendation, and the addition in brackets of what is called the 'literal' translation (in fact the MT) does not clarify this; thus in Zeph. 1:3 we have after the parsed noun 'I will overthrow (and the stumbling blocks)'. The confusion increases with a really difficult verse such as Zeph. 3:18. This is a handsome work which many will be glad to have — a help, but no substitute for sound knowledge. For an earlier aid by this author, see *B. L.* 1979, p. 146.

J. H. EATON

WALTKE, B. K. and O'CONNOR, M.: *An Introduction to Biblical Hebrew Syntax*. 1990. Pp. xiii, 765. (Eisenbrauns, Winona Lake IN. Price: $37.50. ISBN 0 931464 31 5)

Old Testament studies have, as is well known and ought to be more widely regretted, paid much less attention to the language in which the Hebrew Bible was written than to the various textual, literary-critical, historical, and theological issues it has raised. There is a number, though it is not large, of specialist monographs; but in what other comparable discipline do the most frequently used language reference books (Gesenius-Kautzsch's *Grammar* and A. B. Davidson's *Syntax*) date from almost a century ago? It is difficult to know what can be done to fill this yawning gap, at any rate in the short term. The present reviewer is engaged on a revision of Davidson's handbook, hoping thereby to bring about a modest updating of the art of linguistic description among senior Old Testament students. Waltke and O'Connor in this excellent work, likewise aimed at students who have mastered a preliminary grammar, are much more ambitious. In their introduction of some 80 pages they survey the history of the study of the Hebrew language and helpfully sketch the rise of modern linguistics which is now deeply influencing the way in which language is treated in nearly every other field of literary endeavour, the Classics included. Thereafter they devote main sections to the noun (170 pages), to adjectives, numerals, and pronouns (85 pages), to verbal stems (110 pages) and to verbal conjugations and clauses (230 pages). I would like to have seen more space devoted to clauses which only begin to be discussed formally at p. 632, and less to the meanings of the various noun patterns and the verbal stems (Qal, Piel etc.), matters which seem to me to belong more to grammatical semantics than to syntax. Nor are we given much on the formation of sentences as distinct from clauses and, though recent linguistic tools like discourse analysis are approvingly mentioned in the introduction, macro-syntax is hardly more than very lightly touched upon. But we must be fair to the authors. Their chief purpose is to build on what students have got from an introductory Grammar, and that is probably the right stage at which to bring in the semantics of the various grammatical units. It is also understandable that, with such a purpose, they should concentrate on the role of these units within their immediate context, which is as often the phrase (or group) as the clause. Considering the restraints which they have imposed on themselves it is a moot point therefore whether what Waltke and O'Connor have given us might not more accurately have been described as a Grammar for advanced students than as a Syntax. But that is carping; there is no doubt in my mind that this book deserves the warmest of welcomes. I hope that it will be extensively used by the senior students at whom it is primarily aimed — and by their teachers as well! It is a valiant attempt to restore the years that the locust has eaten. Its publishers too deserve commendation for the most attractive way in which the book is laid out and for producing it at a cost that publishers on this side of the Atlantic could not have matched.

J. C. L. GIBSON

WILLIAMSON, H. G. M.: *Annotated Key to Lambdin's Introduction to Biblical Hebrew* (JSOT Manuals, 3). 1987, 1989. Pp. 208. (Sheffield Academic Press. Price: £6.50 ($10.95). ISBN 1 85075 065 3; ISSN 0262 1754)

This key is provided with comments which usefully supplement the instruction in Lambdin's grammar. The work is generously laid out with great clarity. For students working on their own or revising it will be a great boon.

J. H. EATON

Books Received too Late for Notice in 1990

The books in the following list will be reviewed in the *Book List* for 1991.

ARNOLD, P. M.: *Gibeah: The Search for a Biblical City* (JSOT Supplement Series 79). 1990. (Sheffield Academic Press. ISBN 1 85075 223 0)

ARNOLD, W.: *Das Neuwestaramäische*. I. *Texte aus Bax'a* (Semitica Viva, 4/I. 1989. (Harrassowitz, Wiesbaden. ISBN 3 447 02949 8)

BAILEY, R. C.: *David in Love and War: The Pursuit of Power in 2 Samuel 10–12* (JSOT Supplement series 75). 1990. (Sheffield Academic Press. ISBN 1 85075 209 5; ISSN 0309 0787)

BARR, J.: *The Bible in the Modern World*. 1973, 1990. (SCM, London; Trinity Press International, Philadelphia. ISBN 0 334 00113 7)

BEAULIEU, P.-A.: *The Reign of Nabonidus King of Babylon 556–539 B.C.* (Yale Near Eastern Researches, 10). 1989. (Yale University Press, New Haven and London. ISBN 0 300 04314 7)

BEN-TOR, A. (ed.): *Hazor III–IV. An Account of the Third and Fourth Seasons of Excavation, 1957–58*, by Y. Yadin and many others. 1989. (Israel Exploration Society, Jerusalem. ISBN 965 221 008 0)

BEN-TOR, A., GREENFIELD, J. C. and MALAMAT, A. (eds): *Eretz-Israel. Archaeological, Historical and Geographical Studies*. Vol. 20: *Yigael Yadin Memorial Volume*. 1989. (Israel Exploration Society, Jerusalem)

BEUKEN, W. A. M.: *Jesaja*. Deel III A; B (De Prediking van het Oude Testament). 1989. (Callenbach, Nijkerk. ISBN 90 266 0204 9; 90 266 0205 7)

BEYERLIN, W.: *Reflexe der Amosvisionen im Jeremiabuch* (OBO 93). 1989. (Universitätsverlag, Freiburg (CH); Vandenhoeck & Ruprecht, Göttingen. ISBN 3 7278 0658 3; 3 525 53723 9)

BIDDLE, M. E.: *A Redaction History of Jeremiah 2:1–4:2* (AThANT 77). 1990. (Theologischer Verlag, Zürich. ISBN 3 290 10078 2)

BLOOM, H.: *Ruin the Sacred Truths: Poetry and Belief from the Bible to the Present*. The Charles Eliot Norton Lectures 1987–88. 1987, 1989. (Harvard University Press, Cambridge MA and London. ISBN 0 674 78027 2)

BOCK, S.: *Kleine Geschichte des Volkes Israel — Von den Anfängen bis in die Zeit des Neuen Testamentes*. Mit einer Einleitung von N. Lohfink, SJ (HERDER TASCHENBUCH 1642). 1989. (HERDER, FREIBURG IM BREISGAU. ISBN 3 451 08642 5)

BOCKMUEHL, M. N. A.: *Revelation and Mystery in Ancient Judaism and Pauline Christianity* (Wissenschaftliche Untersuchungen zum Neuen Testament. 2. Reihe 36). 1990. (Mohr, Tübingen. ISBN 3 16 145339 5)

CHIESA, B.: *Creazione e caduta dell'uomo nell'esegesi giudeo-araba medievale* (Studi Biblici, 85). 1989. (Paideia, Brescia. ISBN 88 394 0418 X)

CLARK, D. J. and HATTON, H. A.: *A Translator's Handbook on the Books of Nahum, Habakkuk, and Zephaniah* (Helps for Translators). 1989. (United Bible Societies, New York and Stuttgart. ISBN 0 8267 0130 2)

CLARKE, E. G. (ed.): *Newsletter for Targumic and Cognate Studies*, Vol. 16.2 (1989). 1990. (Department of Near Eastern Studies, University of Toronto. ISSN 0704 59005)

CLINES, D. J. A.: *Job 1–20* (Word Biblical Commentary 17). 1989. (Word Books, Dallas TX. ISBN 0 8499 0216 9)

CLINES, D. J. A.: *What Does Eve Do to Help? and Other Readerly Questions to the Old Testament* (JSOT Supplement Series 94). 1990. (Sheffield Academic Press. ISBN 1 85075 248 6; ISSN 0309 0787)

CLINES, D. J. A., FOWL, S. E. and PORTER, S. E. (eds): *The Bible in Three Dimensions. Essays in celebration of forty years of Biblical Studies in the University of Sheffield* (JSOT Supplement Series 87). 1990. (Sheffield Academic Press. ISBN 1 85075 227 3; ISSN 0309 0787)

COGGINS, R.: *Introducing the Old Testament* (Oxford Bible Series). 1990. (Oxford University Press. ISBN 0 19 213254 7; 0 19 213255 5 (pbk))

COTTON, H. M. and GEIGER, J.: *Masada I. The Yigael Yadin Excavations 1963–1965: Final Reports*. The Latin and Greek Documents — with a contribution by J. D. Thomas. 1989. (Israel Exploration Society, Jerusalem. ISBN 965 221 011 0)

CROUZEL, H.: *Origen*. Translated by A. S. Worrall. 1989. (T. & T. Clark, Edinburgh. ISBN 0 567 09500 2)

DAVIDSON, H. E. (ed.): *The Seer in Celtic and Other Traditions*. 1989. (John Donald, Edinburgh. ISBN 0 85976 259 9)

DAVIES, W. D. and FINKELSTEIN, L. (eds): *The Cambridge History of Judaism*. Vol. II: *The Hellenistic Age*. 1989. (Cambridge University Press. ISBN 0 521 21929 9)

DAY, J.: *Molech: A God of Human Sacrifice in the Old Testament* (University of Cambridge Oriental Publications, 41). 1989. (Cambridge University Press. ISBN 0 521 36474 4)

DE VRIES, S. J.: *1 and 2 Chronicles* (The Forms of the Old Testament Literature, XI). 1989. (Eerdmans, Grand Rapids MI. ISBN 0 8028 0236 2)

DE VRIES, S. J.: *Bible and Theology in the Netherlands*. 2nd edition (American University Studies, Series VII, Vol. 22). 1989. (Lang, New York — Bern — Frankfurt-am-Main. ISBN 3 8204 1052 7; ISSN 0740 0446)

DERCHAIN-URTEL, M.-T.: *Priester im Tempel: Die Rezeption der Theologie der Tempel von Edfu und Dendera in den Privatdokumenten aus ptolemäischer Zeit* (Göttinger Orientforschungen. IV. Reihe: Ägypten, Bd. 19). 1989. (Harrassowitz, Wiesbaden. ISBN 3 447 02867 X)

DETIENNE, M. and VERNANT, J.-P. (eds): *The Cuisine of Sacrifice Among the Greeks*. Translated by P. Wissing. 1989. (University of Chicago Press, Chicago and London. ISBN 0 226 14353 8)

DION, P. E.: *The Jews During the Persian Period: A Bibliography* (Newsletter for Targumic and Cognate Studies, Supplement 5). 1990. (Department of Near Eastern Studies, University of Toronto. ISSN 0704 59005)

The Documents from the Bar Kokhba Period in the Cave of Letters. Greek Papyri, edited by N. Lewis. *Aramaic and Nabatean Signatures and Subscriptions*, edited by Y. Yadin and J. C. Greenfield. 1989. (Israel Exploration Society, Jerusalem. ISBN 965 221 009 9)

DOORLY, W. J.: *Prophet of Justice: Understanding the Book of Amos*. 1989. (Paulist, Mahwah NJ and New York. ISBN 0 8091 3089 0)

EFRON, J.: *Studies on the Hasmonean Period* (Studies in Judaism in Late Antiquity, 39). 1987. (Brill, Leiden. ISBN 90 04 07609 3; ISSN 0169 961 X)

ERIKSEN, E. O.: *Holy Land Explorers*. 1989. (Franciscan Printing Press, Jerusalem)

FELDMAN, L. H. and HATA, G. (eds): *Josephus, The Bible, and History*. 1989. (Brill, Leiden. ISBN 90 04 08931 4)

FLOSS, J. P.: *David und Jerusalem: Ziele und Folgen des Stadteroberungsberichts 2 Sam 5,6–9 literaturwissenschaftlich betrachtet* (Münchener Universitätsschriften. Arbeiten zu Text und Sprache im Alten Testament, 30). 1987. (Eos, St. Ottilien. ISBN 3 88096 530 7)

FORSYTH, N.: *The Old Enemy: Satan & the Combat Myth*. 1987. (Princeton University Press. ISBN 0 691 01474 4)

FRITZ, V., POHLMANN, K.-F., and SCHMITT, H.-C. (eds): *Prophet und Prophetenbuch: Festschrift für Otto Kaiser zum 65. Geburtstag* (BZAW 185). 1989. (De Gruyter, Berlin. ISBN 3 11 011339 2)

GELB, I. J. and KIENAST, B.: *Die altakkadischen Königsinschriften des dritten Jahrtausends v. Chr.* (Freiburger Altorientalischen Studien, 7). 1990. (Franz Steiner, Stuttgart. ISBN 3 515 04248 2)

GERATY, L. T. and RUNNING, L. G. (eds): *Hesban 3. Historical Foundations: Studies of Literary References to Hesban and Vicinity*. 1989. (Andrews University Press, Berrien Springs (MI). ISBN 0 943872 17 0)

Gibson, S., Harris, R. L., Schonfield, J. (eds): *Bulletin of the Anglo–Israel Archaeological Society*, Vol. 8 (1988–9). 1989. (The Anglo-Israel Archaeological Society, London. ISSN 0266 2442)

Gnuse, R.: *Heilsgeschichte as a Model for Biblical Theology: The Debate Concerning the Uniqueness and Significance of Israel's Worldview* (College Theology Society, Studies in Religion 4). 1989. (University Press of America, Lanham NY and London. ISBN 0 8191 7246 4)

Hals, R. M.: *Ezekiel* (The Forms of the Old Testament Literature, XIX). 1989. (Eerdmans, Grand Rapids MI. ISBN 0 8028 0340 7)

Hardmeier, C.: *Prophetie im Streit vor dem Untergang Judas: Erzählkommunikative Studien zur Entstehungssituation der Jesaja- und Jeremiaerzählungen in II Reg 18–20 und Jer 37–40* (BZAW 187). 1989. (De Gruyter, Berlin. ISBN 3 11 011735 5; ISSN 0934 2575)

Hayes, J. H.: *Amos The Eighth-Century Prophet: His Times and His Preaching*. 1988. (Abingdon, Nashville TN. ISBN 0 687 01040 3)

Hayes, J. H. and Miller, J. M. (eds): *Israelite and Judaean History*. 1977, 1990. (SCM, London; Trinity Press International, Philadelphia. ISBN 0 334 02435 8)

Hidal, S.: *Israel och Hellas. Studier kring Gamla testamentet och dess verkningshistoria* (Religio: Skrifter utgivna av Teologiska Institutionen i Lund, 27). 1988. (Teologiska Institutionen, Lund. ISSN 0280 5723)

Hiebert, R. J. V.: *The "Syrohexaplaric" Psalter* (Septuagint and Cognate Studies 27). 1989. (Scholars Press, Atlanta, Georgia. ISBN 1 55540 431 6; 1 55540 432 4 (pbk))

Hunter, A. V.: *Biblical Hebrew Workbook: An Inductive Study for Beginners*. 1988. (University Press of America, Lanham NY and London. ISBN 0 8191 5715 5)

Ibn Ezra's Commentary on the Pentateuch: Genesis (Bereshit). Translated and annotated by H. N. Strickman & A. M. Silver. 1988. (Menorah Publishing Company, New York. ISBN 0 932232 07 8)

Johnson, M. R.: *Genesis, Geology and Catastrophism: A Critique of Creationist Science and Biblical Literalism*. 1988. (Paternoster, Exeter. ISBN 0 85364 472 1)

Johnstone, W.: *Exodus* (Old Testament Guides). 1990. (Sheffield Academic Press. ISBN 1 85075 239 7; ISSN 0264 6498)

Jones, G. H.: *The Nathan Narratives* (JSOT Supplement Series 80). 1990. (Sheffield Academic Press. ISBN 1 85075 225 7; ISSN 0309 0787)

Keller, C.-A.: *Tu m'as fait Prophète: Le ministère prophétique dans l'Ancien Testament*. 1989. (Du Moulin, Aubonne (CH))

Knauf, E. A.: *Ismael: Untersuchungen zur Geschichte Palästinas und Nordarabiens im l. Jahrtausend v. Chr.* 2., erweiterte Auflage (Abhandlungen des Deutschen Palästinavereins). 1989. (Harrassowitz, Wiesbaden. ISBN 3 447 02892 0)

Knibb, M. A. and van der Horst, P. W. (eds): *Studies on the Testament of Job* (SNTS Monograph Series, 66). 1989. (Cambridge University Press. ISBN 0 521 37216 X)

Kutscher, R.: *Royal Inscriptions: The Brockman Tablets at the University of Haifa* (The Shay Series of the Zinman Institute of Archaeology). 1989. (Haifa University Press, Harrassowitz, Wiesbaden. ISBN 965 311 004 7; 3 447 02867 X)

Leslau, W.: *Concise Dictionary of Ge'ez* (Classical Ethiopic). 1989. (Harrassowitz, Wiesbaden. ISBN 3 447 02873 4)

Lindberg, C.: *The Middle English Bible. The Book of Judges*. 1989. (Norwegian University Press, Oslo; distributed by Clarendon, Oxford. ISBN 82 00 02811 9)

van der Lingen, A.: *Les Guerres de Yahwé. L'implication de YHWH dans les guerres d'Israël selon les livres historiques de l'Ancien Testament*

(Lectio Divina 139). 1990. (Cerf, Paris. ISBN 2 204 04069 X; ISSN 0750 1919)

LOZA, J.: *Las Palabras de Yahwe: Estudio del Decalogo* (Biblioteca Mexicana). 1989. (Universidad Pontificia de Mexico, México D.F.)

MCCREESH, T. P.: (ed.): *Old Testament Abstracts*. Vol. 12, No. 3. 1989. (The Catholic University of America, Washington D.C. ISSN 0364 8591)

MARTIN-ACHARD, R.: *L'homme de Teqoa. Message et commentaire du livre d'Amos*. 1990. (Du Moulin, Aubonne (CH))

MAYES, A. D. H.: *The Old Testament in Sociological Perspective*. 1989. (Marshall-Pickering, London. ISBN 0 551 01937 9)

MILLER, J. W.: *Biblical Faith and Fathering: Why we call God "Father"*. 1989. (Paulist, Mahwah NJ and New York. ISBN 0 8091 3107 2)

DE MOOR, J. C.: *The Rise of Yahwism: The Roots of Israelite Monotheism* (Bibliotheca Ephemeridum Theologicarum Lovaniensium XCI). 1990. (University Press, Leuven; distributed by Peeters, Leuven. ISBN 90 6186 358 9; 90 6831 203 0)

MORLA ASENSIO, V.: *El Fuego en el Antiguo Testamento: Estudio de semantica linguística* (Tesis y Monografias, 21). 1988. (Institucion San Jeronimo, Valencia. ISBN 84 86067 27 8)

MURAOKA, T. (ed.): *Abr-Nahrain* XXVII (1989). 1989. (Brill, Leiden. ISBN 90 04 09207)

NICCACCI, A., OFM: *Un profeta tra oppressori e oppressi. Analisi esegetica del capitolo 2 di Michea nel piano generale del libro* (Studium Biblicum Franciscanum, Analecta 27). 1989. (Franciscan Printing Press, Jerusalem.)

NORTH, R. (ed.): *Elenchus of Biblica 1987* (Elenchus of Biblical Bibliography, 3). 1990. (Biblical Institute Press, Rome. ISBN 88 7653 589 6)

OTZEN, B.: *Judaism in Antiquity. Political Development and Religious Currents from Alexander to Hadrian*. Translated by F. H. Cryer (The Biblical Seminar). 1990. (Sheffield Academic Press. ISBN 1 85075 197 8; 1 85075 090 4 (pbk))

PÉREZ FERNANDEZ, M.: *Midras Sifre Numeros. Version critica, introduccion y notas* (Biblioteca Midrasica, 9). 1989. (Institucion San Jeronimo, Valencia. ISBN 84 86067 34 0)

RIBERA FLORIT, J.: *El Targum de Isaias: Version critica, introduccion y notas* (Biblioteca Midrasica, 6). 1988. (Institucion San Jeronimo, Valencia. ISBN 84 86067 24 3)

RÖMHELD, D.: *Wege der Weisheit: Die Lehren Amenemopes und Proverbien 22, 17–24, 22* (BZAW 184). 1989. (De Gruyter, Berlin. ISBN 3 11 011958 7)

RUSSELL, D. S.: *Daniel: An Active Volcano*. 1989. (Westminster/John Knox Press, Louisville KY. ISBN 0 664 25090 4)

SCARPAT, G.: *Libro della Sapienza. Testo, traduzione, introduzione e commento*. Vol. I (Biblica. Testi e studi, 1). 1989. (Paideia, Brescia. ISBN 88 394 0429 5)

SCHIFFMAN, L. H.: *The Eschatological Community of the Dead Sea Scrolls* (SBL Monograph Series, 38). 1989. (Scholars Press, Atlanta, Georgia. ISBN 1 55540 329 8; 1 55540 330 1 (pbk))

SCHWANTES, M. (ed.): *Bibliografia Biblica Latino-Americana (1988)*, 1 (Programa Ecumênico de Pos-Graduaçao em Ciências da Religiao, Sao Paulo)

SEKKI, A. E.: *The Meaning of* RUAH *at Qumran* (SBL Dissertation Series, 110). 1989. (Scholars Press, Atlanta, Georgia. ISBN 1 55540 351 4; 1 55540 352 2 (pbk))

SMEND, R.: *Die Entstehung des Alten Testaments*. 4. durchgesene und durch einen Literaturnachtrag ergänzte Auflage (Theologische Wissenschaft, 1). 1989. (Kohlhammer, Stuttgart. ISBN 3 17 010811 5)

VON SODEN, W.: *Introduzione all'orientalistica antica*. Italian edition edited by C. Mora (Studi sul Vicino Oriente antico). 1989. (Paideia, Brescia. ISBN 88 394 0432 5)

STEMBERGER, G.: *Midrasch: Vom Umgang der Rabbinen mit der Bibel: Einführung — Texte — Erläuterungen*. 1989. (Beck, München. ISBN 3 406 33910 7)

STIEBING, W. H., Jr.: *Out of the Desert? Archaeology and the Exodus/Conquest Narratives*. 1989. (Prometheus Books, Buffalo NY. ISBN 0 87975 505 9)

SUCUPIRA, L. (ed.): *Revista Biblica Brasileira*. Ano 7, 1. 1990. (Nova Jerusalém, Fortaleza CE. Brazil)

TAGLIACARNE, P.: *"Keiner war wie er": Untersuchung zur Struktur von 2 Könige 22–23* (Münchener Universitätsschriften. Arbeiten zu Text und Sprache im Alten Testament, 31). 1989. (Eos, St. Ottilien. ISBN 3 88096 531 5)

THOMPSON, A.: *Who's Afraid of the Old Testament God?* 1988. (Paternoster, Exeter. ISBN 0 85364 433 0)

TOV, E., with the collaboration of R. A. KRAFT and a contribution by P. J. Parsons: *The Greek Minor Prophets Scroll from Nahal Hever (8HevXIIgr). The Seiyâl Collection 1* (Discoveries in the Judaean Desert, VIII). 1990. (Oxford University Press. ISBN 0 19 826327 9)

TOWNSEND, J. J.: *Midrash Tanhuma*. Translated into English with Introduction, Indices, and Brief Notes. (S. Buber Recension). Vol. I: *Genesis*. 1989. (Ktav, Hoboken NJ. ISBN 0 88125 087 2)

VERA CHAMAZA, G. W.: *Hizkijjahu Rey de Juda: Interpretacion y reconstruccion de las narraciones de Ezequias* (Tesis y Monografias, 20). 1988. (Institucion San Jeronimo, Valencia. ISBN 84 86067 19 7)

Vetus Latina. Die Reste der altlateinischen Bibel, nach Petrus Sabatier neu gesammelt und herausgegeben von der Erzabtei Beuron. 12: *Esaias*. Herausgegeben von R. Gryson. 4. Lieferung: *Is. 7,14–10,19*. 1989. (Herder, Freiburg im Breisgau. ISBN 3 451 00443 7)

WAGNER, R.: *Textexegese als Strukturanalyse: Sprachwissenschaftliche Methode zur Erschliessung althebräischer Texte am Beispiel des Visionsberichtes Jes 6, 1–11* (Münchener Universitätsschriften. Arbeiten zu Text und Sprache im Alten Testament, 32). 1989. (Eos, St. Ottilien. ISBN 3 88096 532 3)

VAN DER WAL, A.: *Micah: A Classified Bibliography* (Applicatio, 8). 1990. (Free University Press, Amsterdam. ISBN 90 6256 814 9)

WALTON, J. H.: *Ancient Israelite Literature in its Cultural Context: A Survey of Parallels between Biblical and Ancient Near Eastern Texts* (Library of Biblical Interpretation). 1989. (Zondervan, Grand Rapids MI. ISBN 0 310 36590 2)

WESTERMANN, C.: *Schöpfung — Wie Naturwissenschaft fragt — was die Bibel antwortet* (Herder Taschenbuch 1630). 1989. (Herder, Freiburg im Breisgau. ISBN 3 451 08630 1)

The Wisdom of the Zohar. An Anthology of Texts. Arranged by F. Lachower and I. Tishby, with extensive introductions and explanations by I. Tishby. Translated from the Hebrew by D. Goldstein. Vols. I–III (The Littman Library of Jewish Civilization). 1989. (Oxford University Press. ISBN 0 19 710043 0)

YADIN, Y., NAVEH, J. and MESHORER, Y.: *Masada I. The Yigael Yadin Excavations 1963–1965: Final Reports*. The Aramaic and Hebrew Ostraca and Jar Inscriptions. The Coins of Masada. 1989. (Israel Exploration Society, Jerusalem. ISBN 965 221 010 2)

ZAHAROPOULOS, D. Z.: *Theodore of Mopsuestia on the Bible* (Theological Enquiries). 1989. (Paulist, New York — Mahwah NJ. ISBN 0 8091 3091 2)

VAN ZIJL, A. H.: *1 Samuel*. Deel I (De Prediking van het Oude Testament). 1988. (Callenbach, Nijkerk. ISBN 90 266 0739 3)

VAN ZIJL, A. H.: *1 Samuel*. Deel II (De Prediking van het Oude Testament). 1989. (Callenbach, Nijkerk. ISBN 90 266 0192 1)

Index of Authors

(N.B. — Names occurring more than once in the same review or on the same page are listed on their first occurrence only.)

The Society for Old Testament Study is a British Society for Old Testament scholars. Candidates for membership, which is not confined to British subjects, must be nominated by two members of the Society. Residents of the British Isles are normally admitted to ordinary membership and non-residents to associate membership. All correspondence concerning domestic affairs of the Society should be sent to:

Dr P. M. Joyce
Department of Theology
University of Birmingham
P.O. Box 363
Birmingham B15 2TT
England